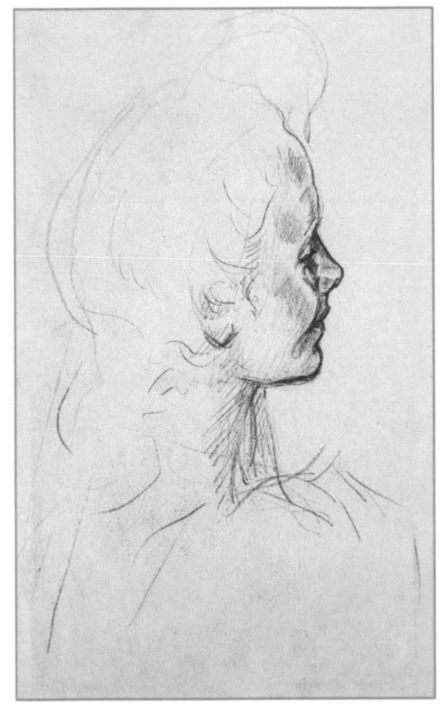
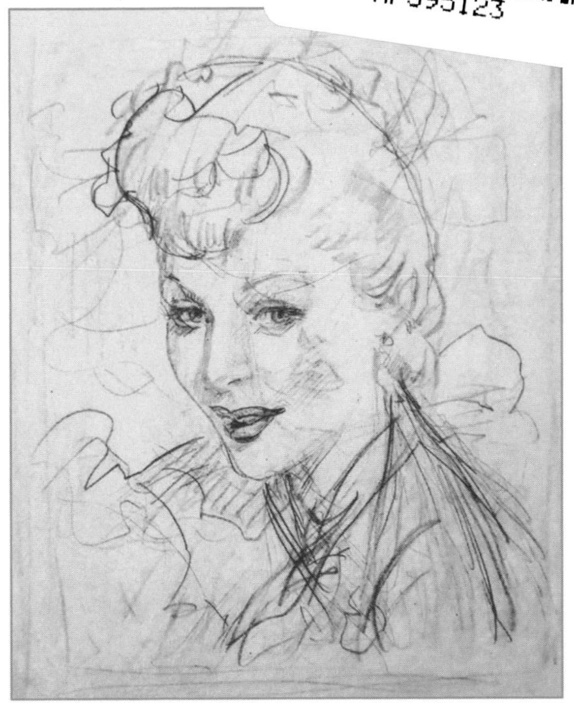
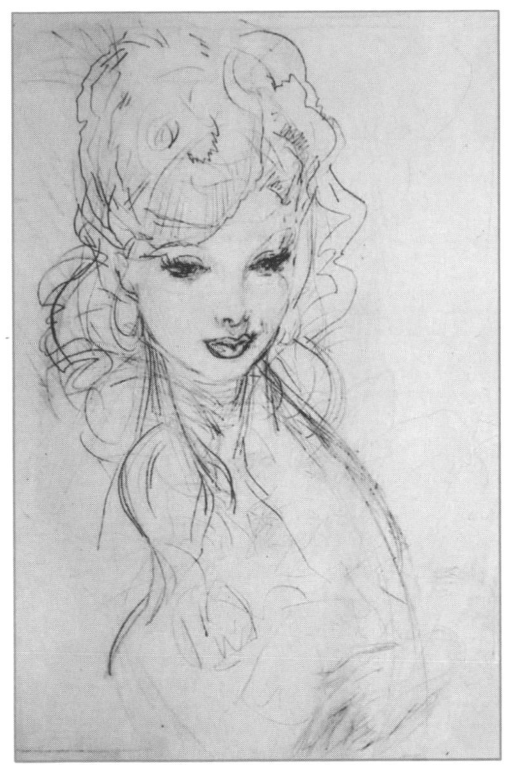
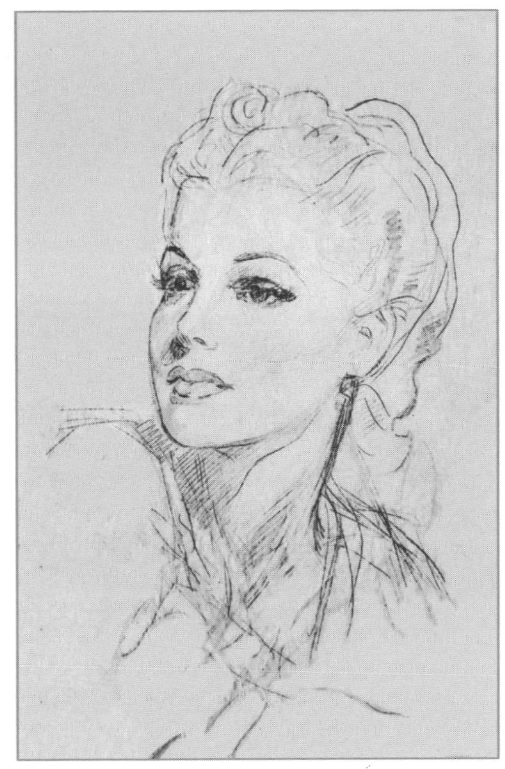

Four undated pencil roughs, probably drawn as preparatory sketches for oil portrait paintings.

The Art of Reginald Heade

Volume Two

The Art of Reginald Heade

Volume Two

Stephen James Walker

Steve Chibnall

First published in England by:
Telos Publishing Ltd
139 Whitstable Road, Canterbury, Kent CT2 8EQ, UK
www.telos.co.uk

Telos Publishing Ltd values feedback. Please e-mail any comments you might have about this book to: feedback@telos.co.uk.

ISBN: 978-1-84583-155-4

The Art of Reginald Heade – Volume Two
© 2020 Stephen James Walker and Steve Chibnall

The moral right of the authors has been asserted.

Design, typesetting and layout by Stephen James Walker.

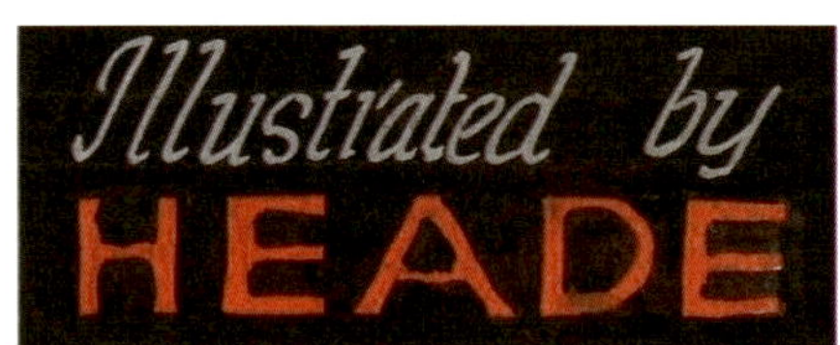

Printed in India by Imprint Press

The Hank Janson name, logo and silhouette device are registered trademarks of Telos Publishing Ltd.

British Library Cataloguing in Publication Data.
A catalogue record for this book is available from the British Library.

DEDICATION

This book is respectfully dedicated to Sally Ann Webb Heade.
We hope we have done full justice to your Dad's life and work.

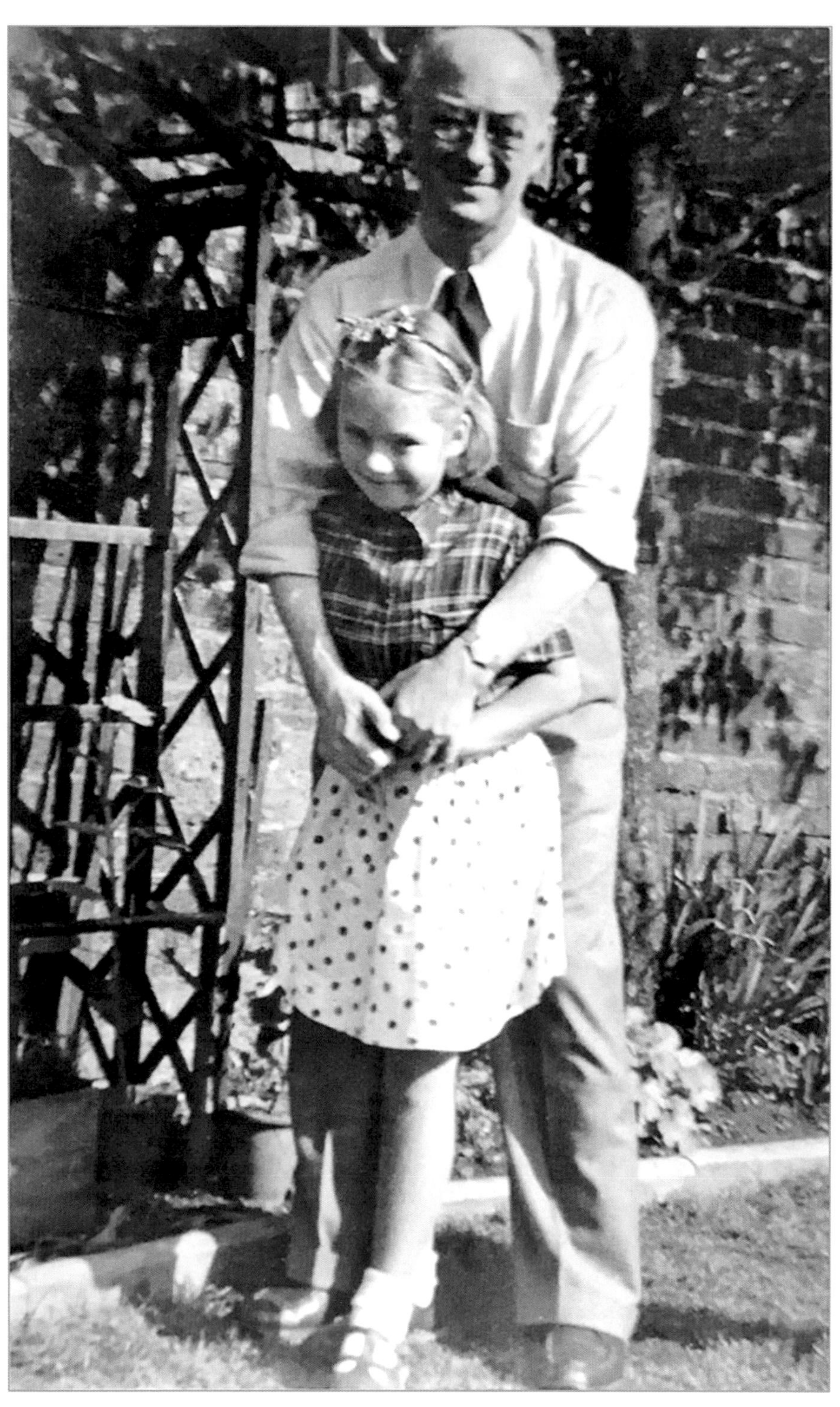

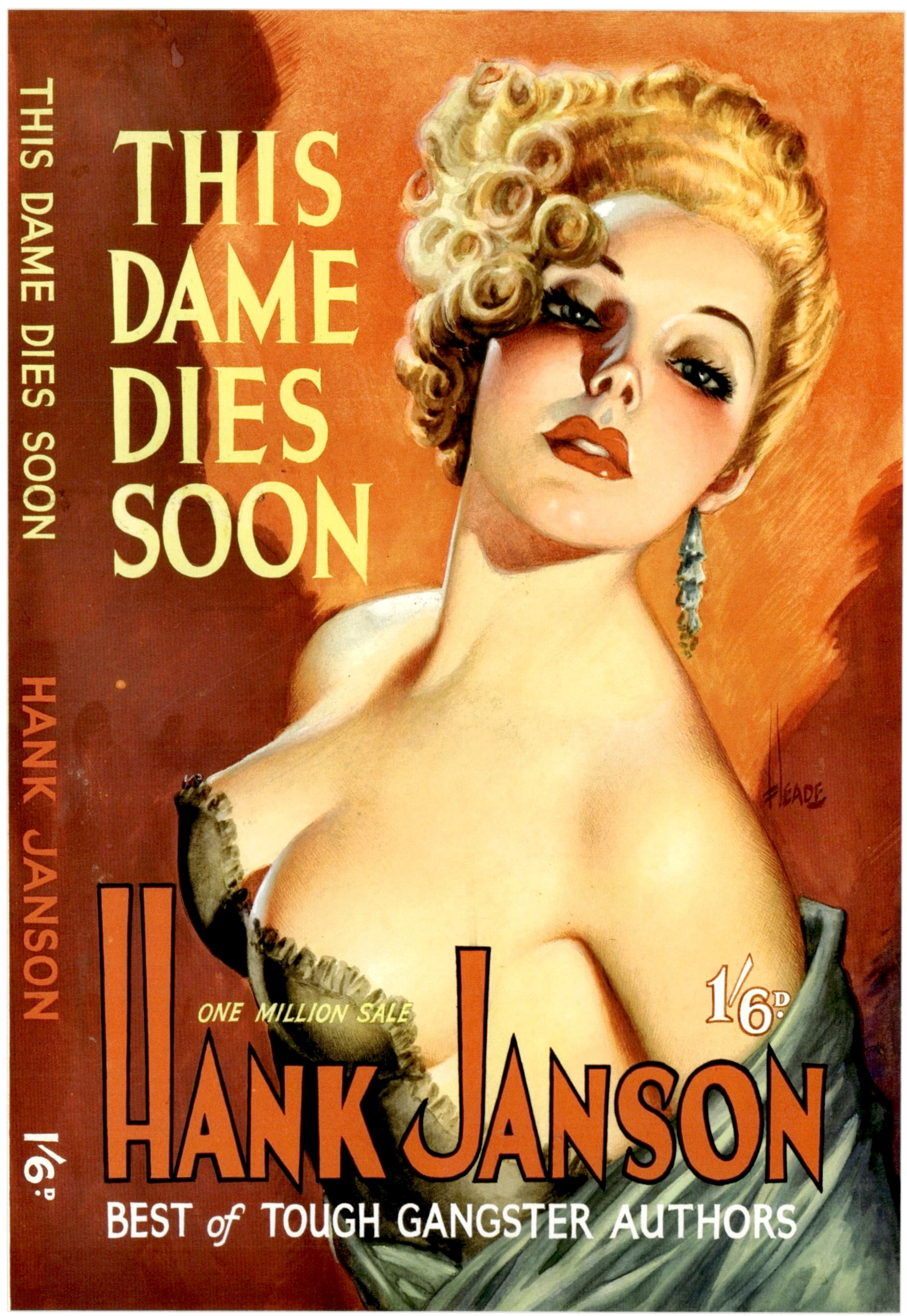

Heade's original painting for the cover of the Hank Janson novel *This Dame Dies Soon* (S D Frances, February 1951), showing much greater detail and subtlety of colour than on the printed paperback. (Image courtesy Rian Hughes.)

CONTENTS

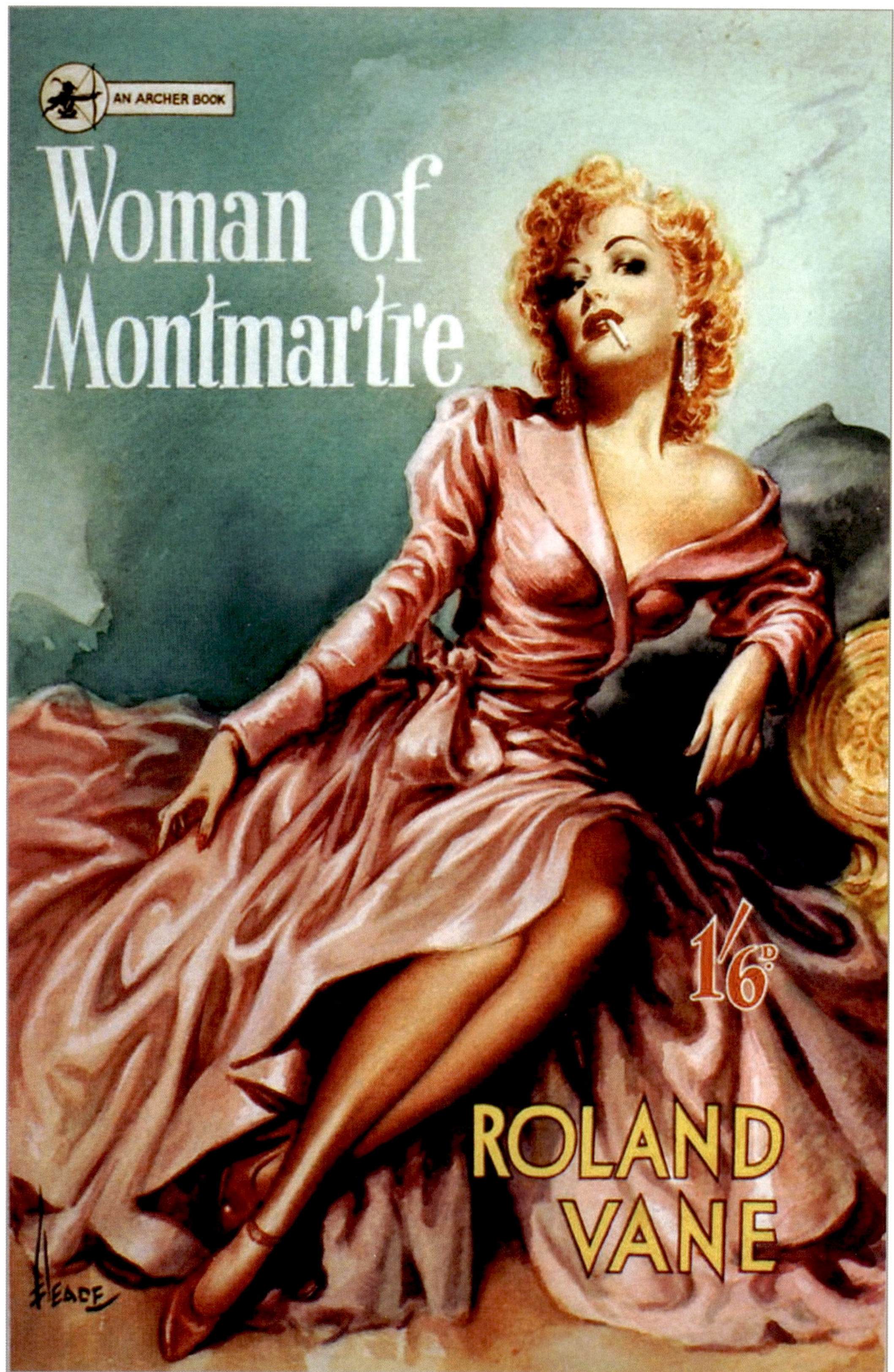

Heade's original painting for *Woman of Montmartre* by Roland Vane (Archer, 1952)

PREFACE

When I compiled the original edition of *The Art of Reginald Heade*, published at the very end of 2016, my aim was to showcase as much of Heade's celebrated pulp fiction paperback cover art as possible, along with a carefully-chosen selection of his other work. So well-received did the book prove to be, however, that I quickly began to assemble a revised and greatly expanded special edition, which I wanted to make as comprehensive as I realistically could. The result was *The Art of Reginald Heade – Special Edition*, published in August 2018. Even then, though, I felt it might not be my last word on the subject; and indeed, my ongoing research has since uncovered a wealth of previously-unseen Heade material – hence the second volume you now have in front of you, intended to serve as a follow-up and companion-piece to the first.

In preparing this book I have again had help from a number of other people and organisations. First, I would like to say a big thank you to Heade's daughter Sally and her husband Ray for their kind hospitality, and particularly to Sally for her unique personal insights into her father's life and work. I am also greatly indebted to Anna Murdoch and Claire Clough of the University of Reading Special

Collections team for enabling me to identify and photograph a large number of additional Heade dustjacket pieces for scarce Mills & Boon romance novels. Likewise, my thanks go to Princeton University in New Jersey, USA, for granting me access to their unique collection of early Hodder & Stoughton dustjackets. Other material has come from visits to the British Library, the London Metropolitan Archives, the Lambeth Archives and the Victoria and Albert Museum's National Art Library and Prints and Drawings Study Room, and I am grateful for all their help. Much appreciated assistance has come too from David Allsberry, Lorraine Courtenay, Wil Deurloo, Rian Hughes, Jim Kealy, Mike Lewis, Patrik Myrman, Tim Partridge, Tom Lesser and Susan Washinski, along with some private collectors who prefer to remain anonymous.

Lastly, I am delighted to have been joined this time by Steve Chibnall as my co-author. Steve was Heade's first biographer, back in the 1990s, and his input here, particularly the contribution of many images of original paintings from his own collection, has been invaluable in helping to make this volume the unparalleled celebration of the artist's life and work that we both hoped it would be. My sincere thanks go to him.

Stephen James Walker

Below: a small, unsigned and undated oil painting by Heade of a Scottie dog. This appears to have been over-painted on a magazine photograph or illustration, mounted onto a board.

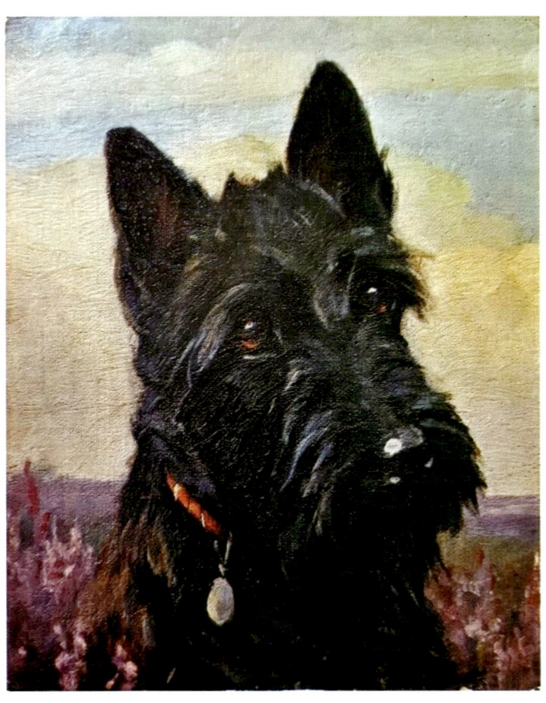

And my thanks go to Steve Walker for having me on board for the final stages of what has been a voyage of discovery of more than three decades since I first began researching Reginald Heade. I would like to acknowledge the help of some of the people and institutions already mentioned, but also Steve Holland, who first identified 'Cy Webb' as Heade, Richard Williams, Derek Thompson, Philip Harbottle, David Thacker, Allan Clewlow, Bob Adey, Peter Robbins and Ian Mason Hill; the artists Sam Peffer, Edward Mortelmans, James E McConnell, Pat Owen and John Vernon; and the art directors Peter Green, Colin Larkin and Stan Boswarva. I am grateful too to publishers Mills & Boon for allowing me to view their file copies. Finally, I am hugely pleased that Sally has made such a valuable contribution to this book, and excited to be publishing photographs of her father. In this age of mass photography, they are the first the world has seen.

Steve Chibnall

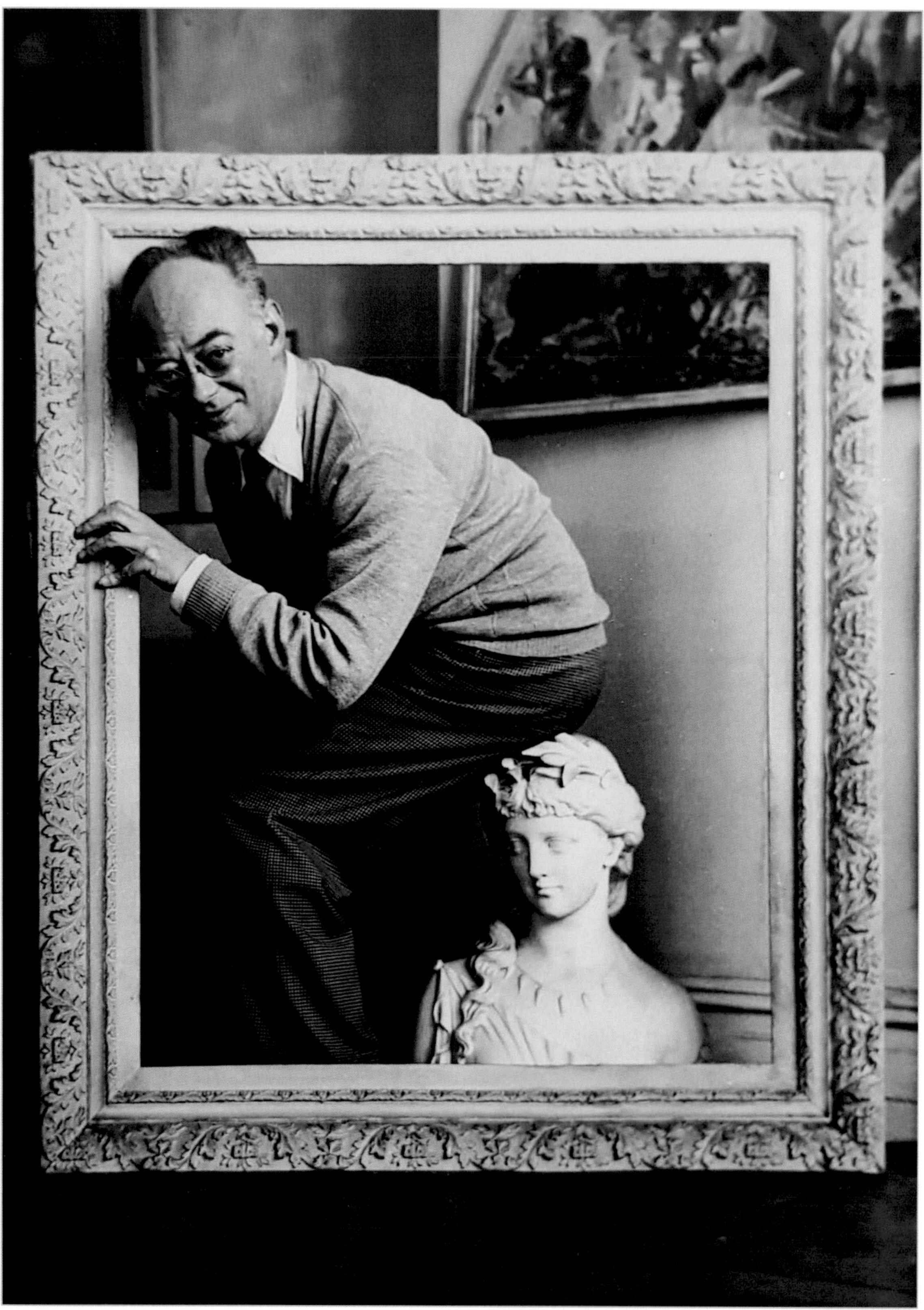

Reginald Cyril Webb Heade (1901-1957)

THE ARTIST'S LIFE

Greatly expanding upon, adding to and in certain respects revising the information provided in the first volume of this book, we now present by far the most detailed and comprehensive biography of Reginald Heade ever to be published.

Heade (pronounced 'Heed') was born Reginald Cyril Webb in Forest Gate, east London, very close to West Ham, to an unmarried 22-year-old barmaid named Annie Mary Webb (born 17 September 1879), who was part of a large family, with eight known siblings. The date was 21 September 1901, which means that Reginald was probably conceived around Christmas, just a month before the death of Queen Victoria. Although not identified on the birth certificate, the boy's father was James Heade, a gypsy traveller, probably of Irish descent, whose mother – Reginald's paternal grandmother – is said to have been one J J Heade.

There is no indication in the 1901 Census that Annie actually lived at 7 Clare Road, the address given on the birth certificate, so this could have been simply a place of convenience arranged by her parents, who lived just round the corner at 56 Leonard Road. Young Reginald was an Edwardian millennial, from a family that lived in close proximity to Whitechapel during Jack the Ripper's reign of terror. His grandfather, George Henry Webb (born c1844), worked as an East End postman, having previously been both a warehouse stock-keeper and a church verger, and would have felt the fear spreading. By the time Annie's son was walking, the streets were full of trams, hand-carts and horse-drawn vehicles. Boys on bicycles were common, motor cars still a novelty for the rich. A few buildings in the borough were being converted into picture houses as the cinema flickered into life.

Reginald's early years were spent with his mother at 56 Leonard Road. Annie worked just across the way from the house, as manageress of a commercial laundry on the corner of Bignold Road and Station Road (where a launderette still stands to this day). She had never married James Heade, but both she and Reginald were now using his surname. In the 1911 Census, she described herself as a widow, but this might have been simply to cover for the fact that the relationship with James had ended. She had since taken up instead with a butcher's assistant, William Wright (born 1873), who had recently moved in with her at the Leonard Road address. The small, end-of-terrace house must have

been a crowded one: also resident were Reginald's maternal grandmother Ann Webb, née Glasscock (born 1846), a former housemaid, who was now head of the family, grandfather George having succumbed to severe respiratory and heart problems in 1910 at the age of 66; Annie's sister Florence (born 1883), known as Florrie for short, who also worked at the laundry, as a 'starcher and preparer'; and a girl named Eliza Rumble (born 1897). Eliza, who was just a few years older than Reginald, had been living at the house for as long as he had, initially with her siblings Grace Rumble (born 1892) and Edward Rumble (born 1894); it appears that the three had been fostered by the Webbs.

With his mother hard at work in the laundry

Below: the modest Webb family home at 56 Leonard Road, London E7, as it is today.

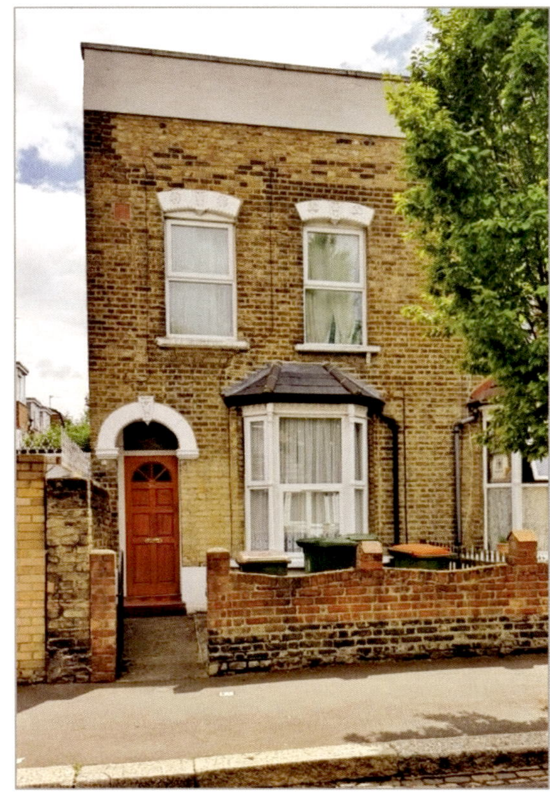

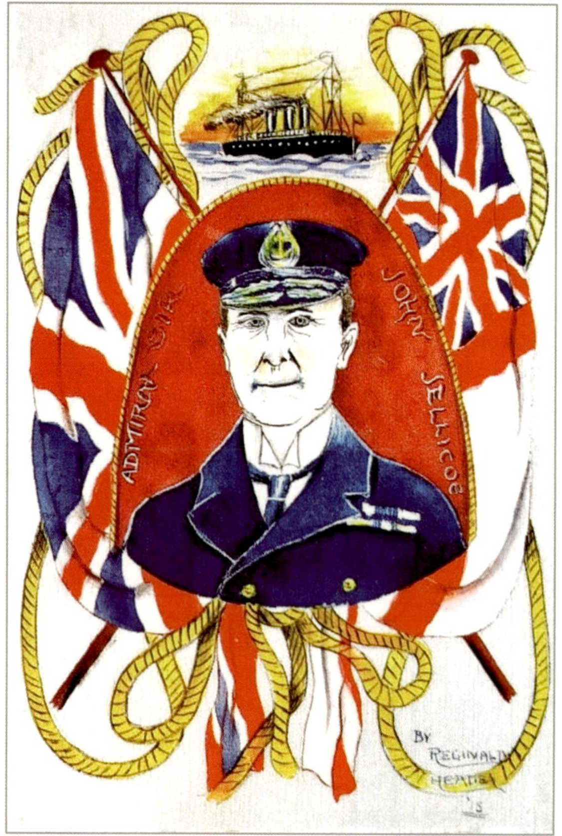

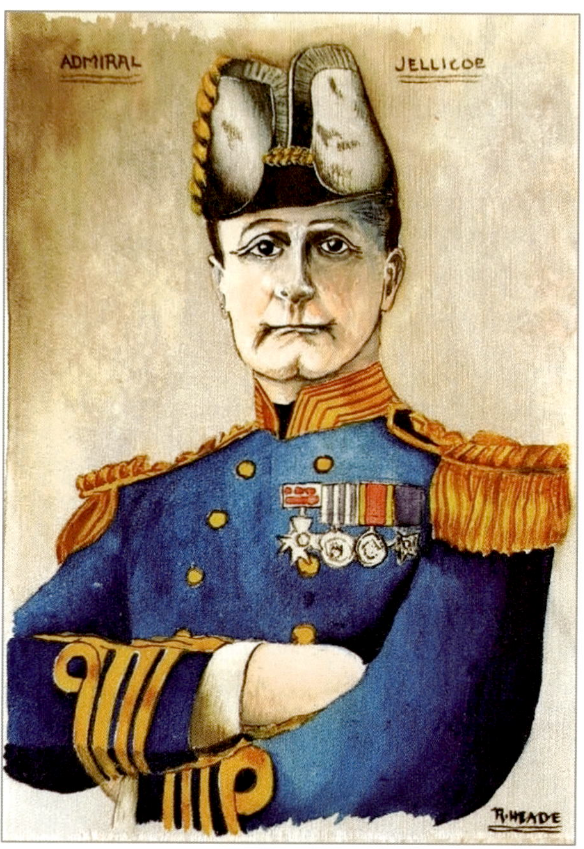

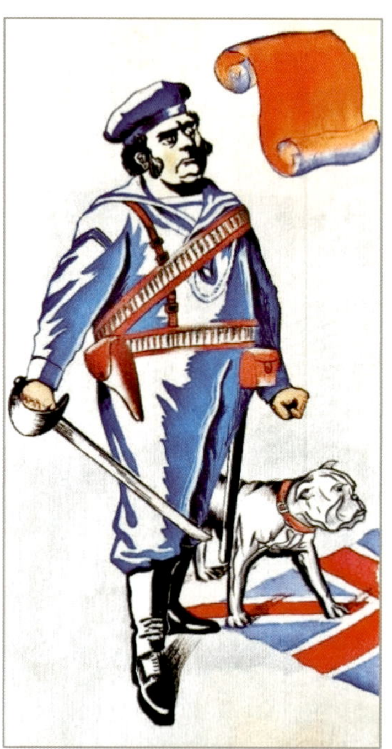

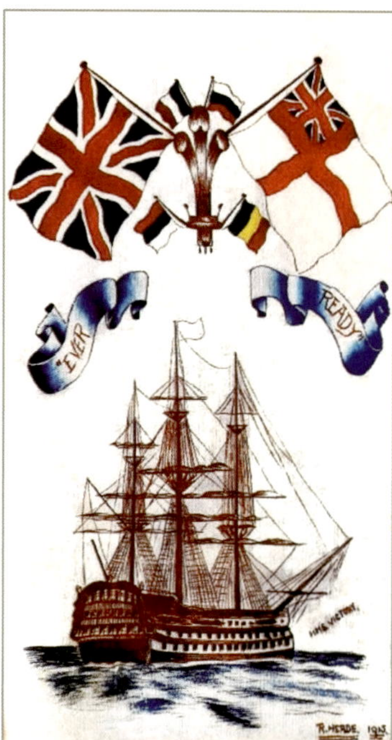

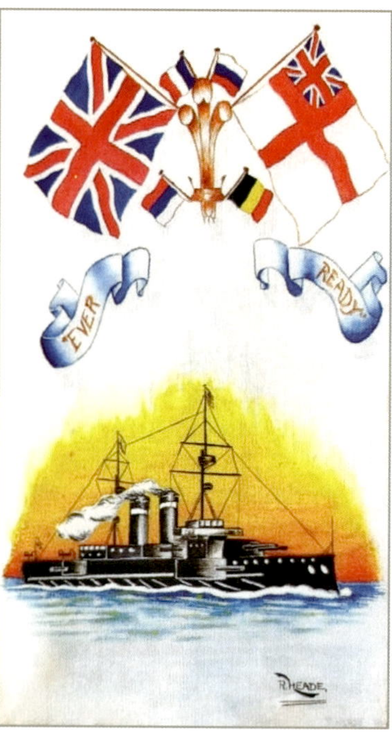

Five naval-themed pieces – including two portraits of distinguished officer Admiral Sir John Jellicoe – painted by Heade onto silk in 1915, when he was just 14 years old. These would no doubt have been inspired in part by his uncle Fred's service in the Royal Navy, but it seems that the artist retained an interest in nautical subjects throughout his life; and he was still painting naval vessels for Panther paperback covers not long before his death.

and his father out of the picture, Reginald found his upbringing entrusted mainly to his uncle Fred (born 1873), a naval man, and particularly to his youngest aunt, Nellie (born 1886). The two siblings initially resided close by; it seems that Nellie, who had worked as a domestic servant from age 14, acted effectively as a live-in housekeeper for her elder brother, who would have been away at sea for long periods. Some people may have mistakenly assumed that the pair were a married couple. Nellie, who was childless, treated Reginald as her own son, and quickly spotted and encouraged his artistic abilities, which were evident from an early age. When not attending the local school, he began to spend most of his time with his uncle and aunt, and while he adored the pair who effectively became his foster parents, he could not help resenting his mother's willingness to allow or encourage this informal adoption.

On 31 March 1917, at the relatively late age of 15, Reginald received a Church of England baptism at the local St Saviour Church. It seems, however, that when his uncle Fred was posted for a time to Falmouth on England's south-west coast during the First World War, the budding artist went with him. He painted various Falmouth scenes and might even have attended Falmouth College of Art, though this is currently unconfirmed.

Below: a Heade *Britannia and Eve* cover depicting his wife Lily.

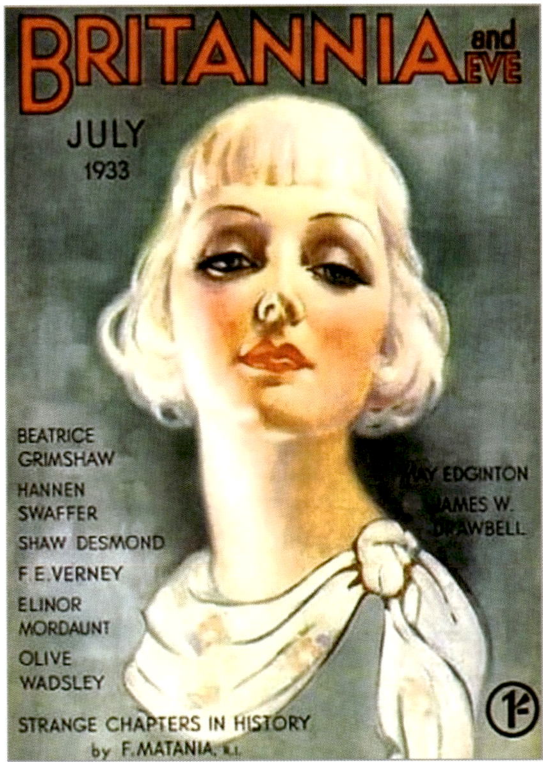

Meanwhile, Annie had moved to Romford, Essex, and on 16 December 1916 had married widowed father of two sons Robert Douglas (born 1866), a vaccination officer. On 24 October 1917 they had a daughter, Reginald's half-sister, Eileen Catherine Webb Douglas. Eileen was also baptised at St Saviour Church, on 6 June 1918; but sadly her father had already died, on 7 March that same year, of pneumonia. On 13 December 1920, though, Annie tied the knot again, this time with her previous partner William Wright, who became stepfather to Eileen; and on 20 February 1922 they had another child, Reginald's half-brother, Kenneth Arthur William Wright.

Surviving family photos give some interesting insights into Heade's life. The earliest shows him aged 18, wearing women's clothing and make-up for one of the fancy-dress parties that became fashionable in the inter-war years. Another reveals that by the age of 24 he was already wearing glasses. At this time, 1925, he was still living at 56 Leonard Road – where his grandmother, of whom he had painted an impressive oil portrait, would die from a brain haemorrhage a couple of years later – but his career had taken off sufficiently to justify him renting a studio in Chancery Lane in the City of London. For a short while, he joined forces with another artist in a company called Petterson & Heade. At some point it seems he also spent time in Switzerland, where he continued to produce art.

What exactly he was working on in the 1920s is a matter for speculation, but a photograph taken in his studio in 1932 may provide a substantial clue: he is seen painting an oil portrait of a woman. Had he been taking on regular commercial artwork for advertising and promotion, he would probably have occupied a drawing board in a communal agency, but a society portrait painter, working in oils, would have needed a private studio. It would have been no mean feat for a young working-class man from the East End of London to have been accepted by the class of person who commissioned portraits. Possibly presenting himself as the son of a naval officer might have helped. At any rate, by the start of the 1930s he had started taking on a rather different type of work: executing paintings for the publishing business.

It could have been the society connections he had made through portraiture that won him a regular commission to produce oil-painted covers for the high-class women's magazine *Britannia and Eve*. The contents page for the issues on which he worked carried the credit 'Cover by Heade'. Most of these paintings were thinly-disguised portraits of the same woman, a beautiful young model with brown hair and a centre parting. Named Lily Mildred Walker, née Christian (born 29 March 1911), she was affectionately referred to by Heade as 'Paddy'. By the mid-1930s, the two were living together as a couple; another photograph shows Heade sporting a stylish trilby and holding a lighted cigarette between gloved fingers, and the handwritten dedication is to 'my darling wife'.

Heade had previously rented a studio in a fashionable location at 433 The Strand, but the added responsibility of providing for Lily probably persuaded him to abandon the aspirations to be a 'fine' artist evidenced in his membership of the Artists' Society and Langham Sketching Club and his exhibition of works at both the Royal Institute of Painters in Watercolours and the Royal Academy. In 1934, he moved his studio to the first of a number of west London addresses, 2 Fosse Way, Ealing, a newly-built home next to Cleveland Park. The house was shared with a couple named William and Doris Hunt. By 1936, the artist had moved back to central London, renting accommodation in the Covent Garden area, first at 4-5 Adam Street WC2, and then at Drury Lane House, 69 Drury Lane WC2, not far from his agent, William Partridge, who at that time was based in Bloomsbury, close to the British Museum. But, as war approached, the Heades moved west again, to 21 Comeragh Road, Fulham; the street would be in the news two and a half decades later as a temporary abode of Christine Keeler and Mandy Rice-Davis, the young 'models' at the centre of the Profumo scandal. Eventually, Reg and Lily found a permanent home half a mile away on the top floor of Queen's Mansions, a fine Victorian block of apartments in Hammersmith, renowned as a lively entertainment centre.

Heade was just short of his thirty-eighth birthday when war was declared in 1939. He was still in regular contact with his aunt Nellie, who had returned to live at 56 Leonard Road with her brother Fred and sister Florrie. All three remained single. Fred had left the Navy, having attained the rank of Chief Petty Officer and been mentioned in dispatches by Churchill, and was now following in his father's footsteps by working as a postman; Florrie continued to earn a living as a laundry hand; and Nellie was undertaking domestic duties for the household. Annie was now living nearby, with her husband William, daughter Eileen and son Ken, and apparently there was no love lost between her and Nellie. The following year, Eileen married a man named Harold Kessock-Philip (born 1911), who was subsequently killed in wartime action in Sicily in 1943. William would die in 1948, Ken in 1999 and Eileen in 2002. Annie's fate is currently unknown.

NOTICE is hereby given that I, REGINALD CYRIL WEBB of 11, Queens Mansions, W.6, British subject do intend after the expiration of twenty-one days from the date of publication hereof to assume the surname of Heade in lieu of my present surname of Webb.—Dated this 21st day of April, 1945. (098)   REGINALD CYRIL WEBB.

Above: the official notification of the artist's formal change of surname, from *The London Gazette* of 24 April 1945.

During the war years, Heade himself was an in-demand cover artist for romantic fiction, with his own home studio and regular commissions from some of the country' leading publishers. His age, poor eyesight and other health issues probably accounted for him not being called up for the services. He had a goitre – an abnormal enlargement of his thyroid gland – which impeded his breathing, and his habit of chain-smoking while he worked was exacerbating a heart condition, angina, with which it seems he had been first diagnosed in his late teens. He and Lily had a daughter, Sally Ann Webb, on 8 February 1945, and it was then that the painter decided to change his name formally to Heade.

Sally was born while Hitler's V-2 rockets were

Below: Queen's Mansions, showing the position of Heade's apartment (top floor, left) and corner studio (top floor, right).

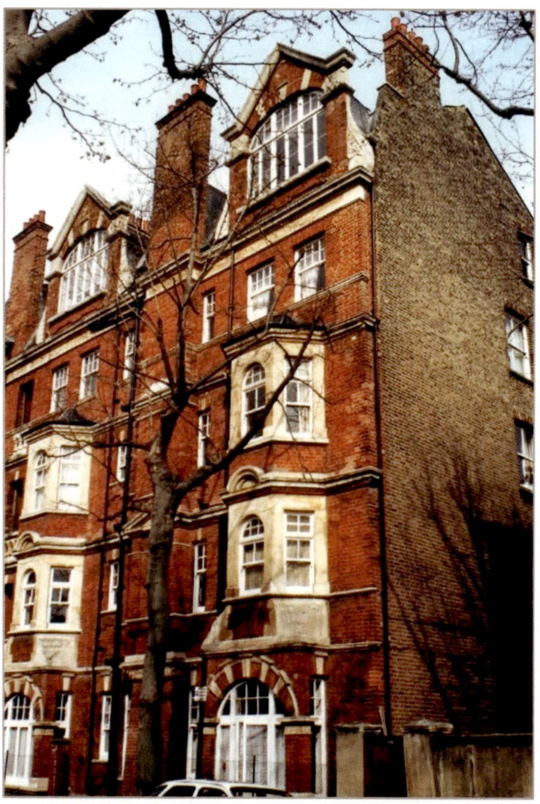

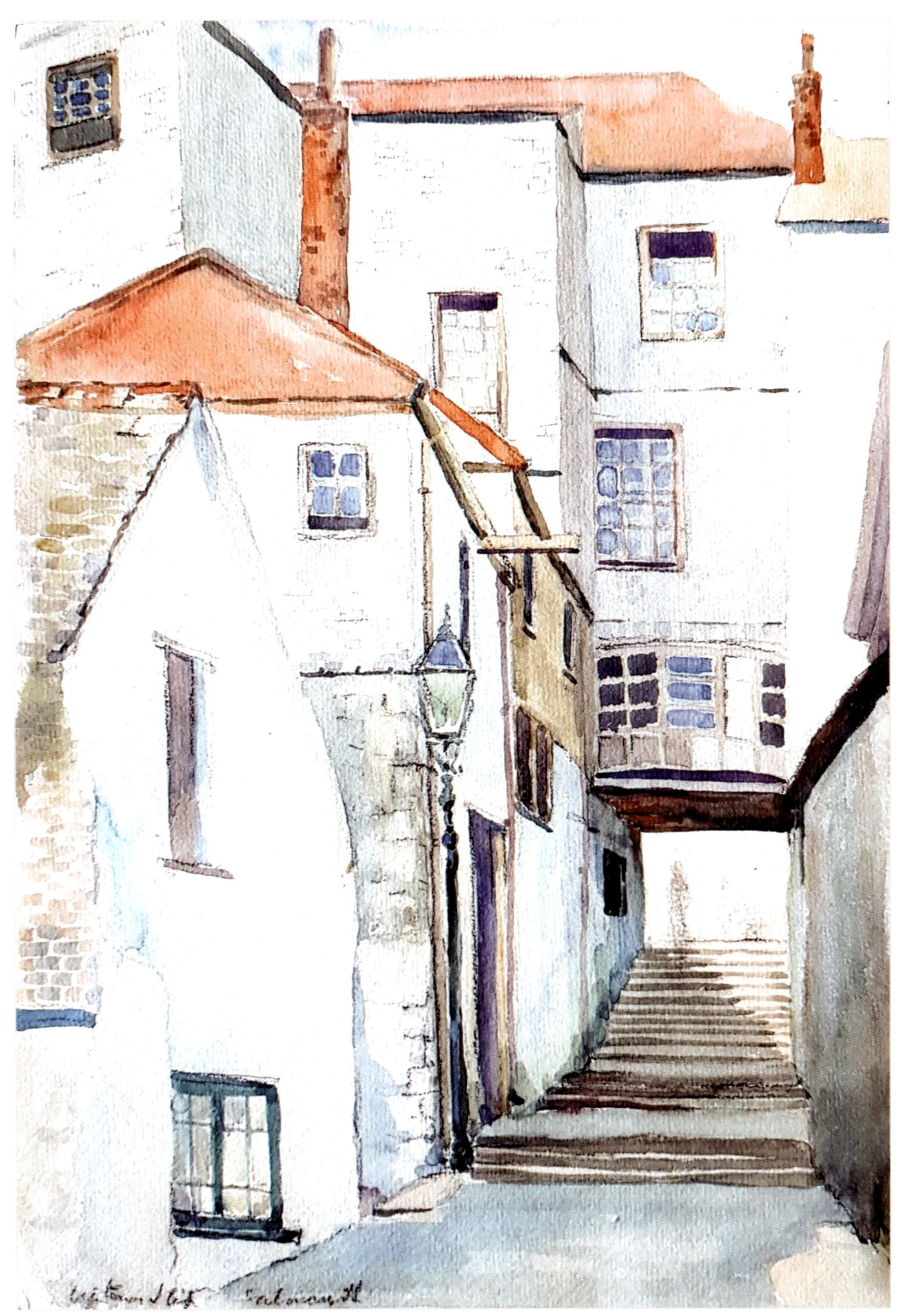

A street scene of Falmouth, Cornwall, painted by Heade when he was staying in the town at around the age of 18.

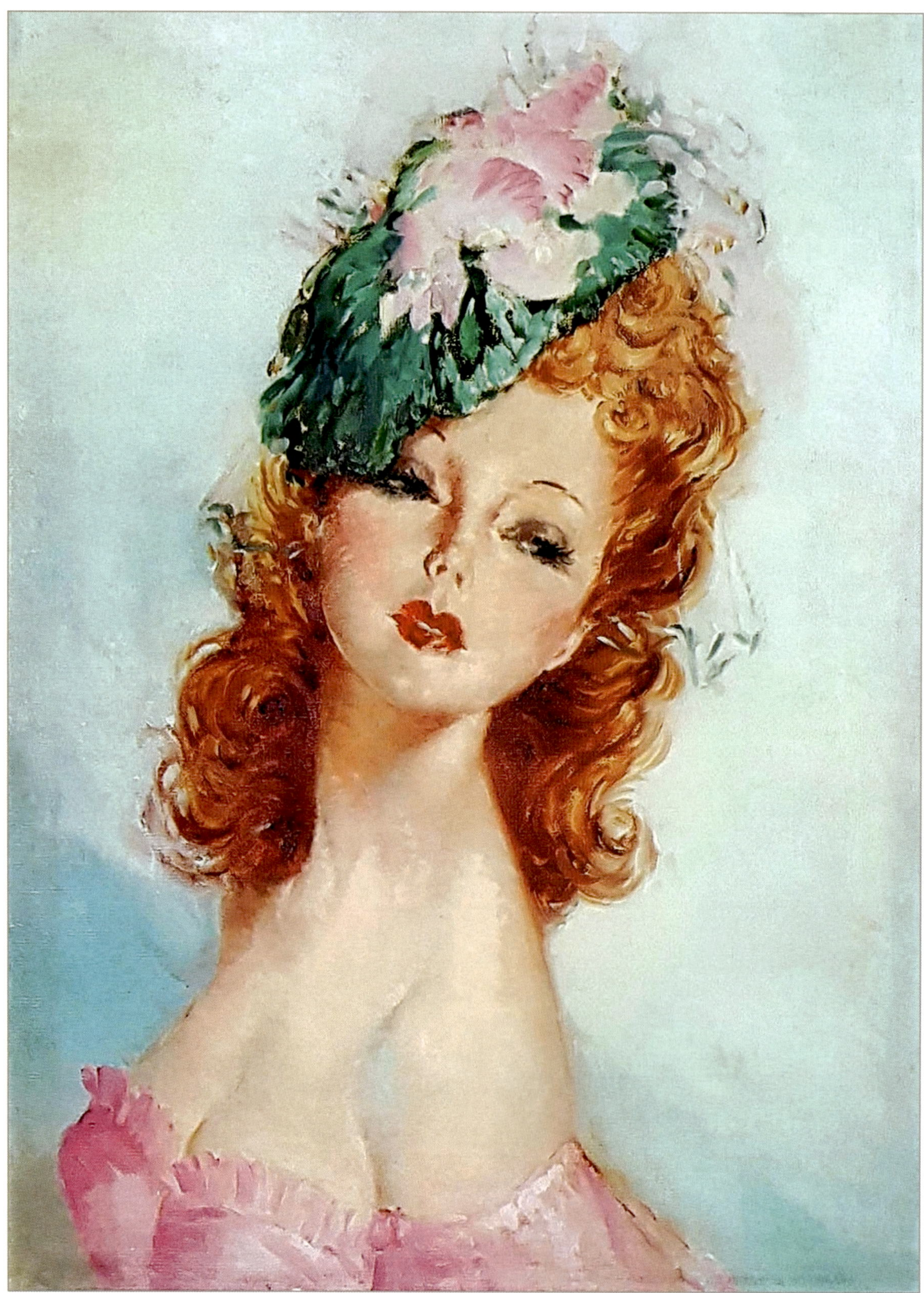

An unsigned and undated oil portrait by Heade. Again, the model was probably his wife, Lily.

still buzzing over London. Her pram was sometimes placed in a cupboard on the ground floor of the block for protection, and occasionally she was shielded from potential blasts by being put in one of the drawers of a wooden chest. It is not surprising that she developed claustrophobia. The apartment on the top floor of Queen's Mansions was, in fact, numbers 10 and 11, knocked through to provide both a family home and a studio space. The studio area was curtained off at one end, and Sally remembers seeing the puffs of cigarette smoke that rose from behind the curtain, signifying that her father was working and not to be disturbed. 'The immediate area where he worked at the end of the studio was a bit of a mess, as you'd expect for a busy artist,' she recalls. 'Tubes of paint adorned the floor everywhere. Dad needed peace, and I had to keep quiet and not fiddle around.'

To cover the top, half-moon-shaped area of the window at the front of the flat, which he felt let in too much light, the artist started painting an ambitious forest scene featuring nudes, horses and a wolfhound, on a large board in three sections (one side of which can be seen in the background of the photograph on page 10). Later, this was taken down and given to the Lewis family – Edwin, known as Eddie; his wife Joyce; their three young children, Linda, Mike and Susan; and Eddie's mother Doris, known as Granby – who lived in flat 2 on the ground floor of Queen's Mansions and with whom the Heades had become friendly. Eddie and Joyce would occasionally act as models for Heade, and Granby sometimes babysat for Sally, who called her 'Aunty Lulu'. The Lewises put the forest scene painting on their hall wall, where it remained when they moved to a different address in the early 1970s (as, although Sally would have liked to retrieve it, she found it too large and unwieldy to transport).

Heade's studio contained a library of reference books, including a series of volumes of *Shipping Wonders of the World*, with photographs and illustrations that he would often use when taking on nautical-themed commissions. Similarly, he owned a couple of volumes presenting pictures of costumes from different parts of the world, which he would use when called upon to paint figures in exotic attire. He supplemented these images with original photographs, posed for his compositions and taken at his direction by a young but well-regarded commercial photographer, Ken Simmonds, known as Simmy. The models were often professionals, including 'resting' actors, but Heade also used Paddy and friends and neighbours. While working, he wore an artist's smock or protective white coat, similar to a scientist's lab coat, over his regular

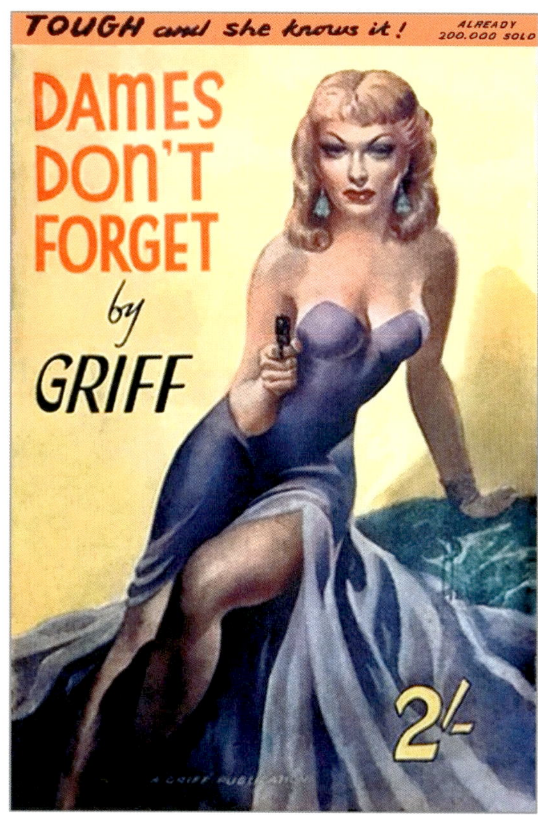

Above: *Dames Don't Forget* by Griff (Modern Fiction, c1949). An ultra-rare piece of Heade's celebrated pulp fiction cover art. (Image courtesy Tom Lesser.)

clothes. He used a classic handheld palette for oils, but most of his work was with water-based gouache paints for his book cover pieces, which were done on artist's boards and generally measured about 15 inches by 10 inches (roughly 38 cm by 25 cm). His roughs were generally sketched on paper, using an enlargement grid to plan out the composition. His deteriorating eyesight meant he needed powerful lenses in his round, wire-framed spectacles, and by the mid-1950s he was also using a magnifying monocle for the fine detail, which he painted with the thinnest of brushes – sometimes consisting of just a few strands. It was punishing work, necessitated both by the competition between the leading illustrators and by the gathering turn toward photographic covers. 'It was like a sweat shop,' his daughter recalls bitterly. 'He just didn't stop.'

In 1947, Heade had suddenly shifted direction in his art and commissions. He began using a second agent, wheeler-dealer Charles Montague Hall, aka Maurice Hall, based in his locality, and turned his hand to producing the dozens of superb cover paintings for mass-appeal pulp paperbacks on which his fame now largely rests. However, the increasingly salacious content of these books outraged Britain's self-appointed moral guardians and soon attracted the attention of the authorities. Stocks of various titles were seized and destroyed by the police, and some of those involved in their publication received prison sentences under the Obscene Publications Act. Heade luckily escaped prosecution, but had to watch his back.

Sally was enrolled in a convent school in nearby Barnes, suggesting that Lily was probably a Catholic. But the Heade family life was to take a tragic turn when Lily was diagnosed with breast cancer. She died on 7 July 1951 at just 40 years of age, leaving Heade to bring up his six-year-old daughter alone. This was made doubly difficult by his own health problems, which were to end his own life six years later. Unable to look after a young daughter and earn a living at the same time, he enlisted the aid of foster parents in Worthing on England's south coast. Sally would spend time with him in the school holidays, and he would make weekend visits to see her. She remembers:

'I gaily sailed on and tried to make light of the situation. My foster parents were very good. Dad

Below: Heade's fine charcoal drawing of his downstairs neighbour Edwin Lewis, known to family and friends as Eddie. This piece dates from circa 1947, and remains to this day a treasured possession of Lewis's family. (Image courtesy Susan Washinski.)

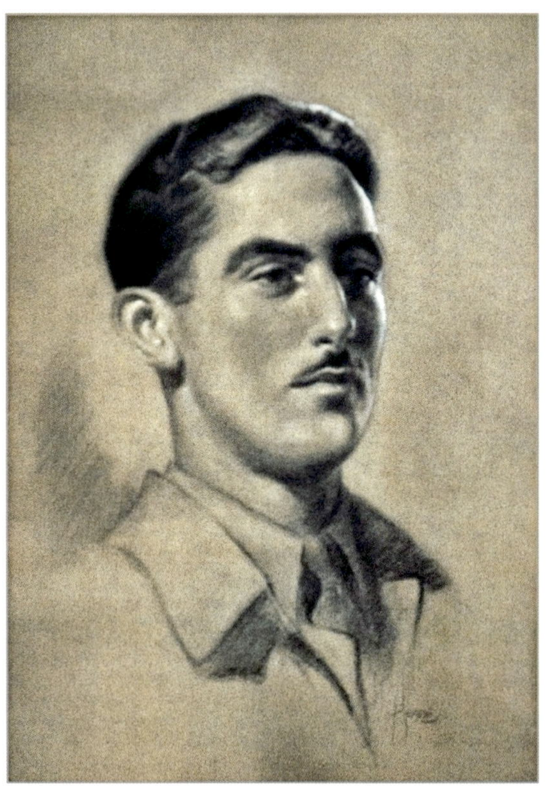

was ace. I get very angry sometimes when I think of how hard he had to work for so little reward. He was a poor man, with many debts, and he worked so hard to keep me.'

Sally also recalls how she tried to get her father to race her up the stairs – 84 in number – to their top-floor apartment, without appreciating what a challenge he found the climb. He would stop half way up and take a pill from the box he carried. But he would always by happy to race her *down* the stairs. Throughout the most celebrated decade of his career, he would get very tired, but was obliged to keep going to make ends meet. 'He was a shy and sensitive man, a very private man,' Sally confides, 'and toward the end, he became almost a recluse.'

Around the time of the Obscene Publications Act prosecutions – including of some of those involved with the Hank Janson books – Heade hosted the inaugural meeting of Artists Ltd, a new agency established by the agent Tony Bowen-Davies to address emerging issues. Also present were Harold Johns, James E McConnell, Bradford, an artist who specialised in historical subjects and worked for Blackie, Keay, Hodgeson, Dobson Broadhead of Greenwich Village, and Edward Mortelmans, who later said of his host: 'He was a very sick man when I met him. He was also a troubled man, no two ways about it. He didn't seem a very happy man at all. He seemed to have a bit of a chip on his shoulder, something that would make him prickly and touchy. He did have unspecified financial problems.'

After the Hank Janson prosecutions, Heade abandoned his agent Maurice Hall and his work for the pulp-fiction boys. With the help of new agent Tony Bowen-Davies he moved up-market, and stopped using the Heade signature. For a time in the mid-1950s, he left his work unsigned. Then, when the more lucrative commissions from Panther and then Pan began to flow, he became Cy Webb – a new identity for a new style of image-making. Bereft of a family life, he spent his days and nights at his drawing board, obsessively producing more and more detailed paintings that reached their apogee with his work for Pan.

He did, though, sometimes socialise with his downstairs neighbours, the Lewis family, and spent Christmas morning with them each year. He had previously done a fine charcoal portrait of Eddie Lewis, shortly after the latter had left the army, and the good neighbour would occasionally pose for photographs for Heade to use as reference. One example is the cover of *John L Sullivan* by Nat Fleischer (Panther, 1956), a paperback about the life of boxing's first heavyweight champion. Three of

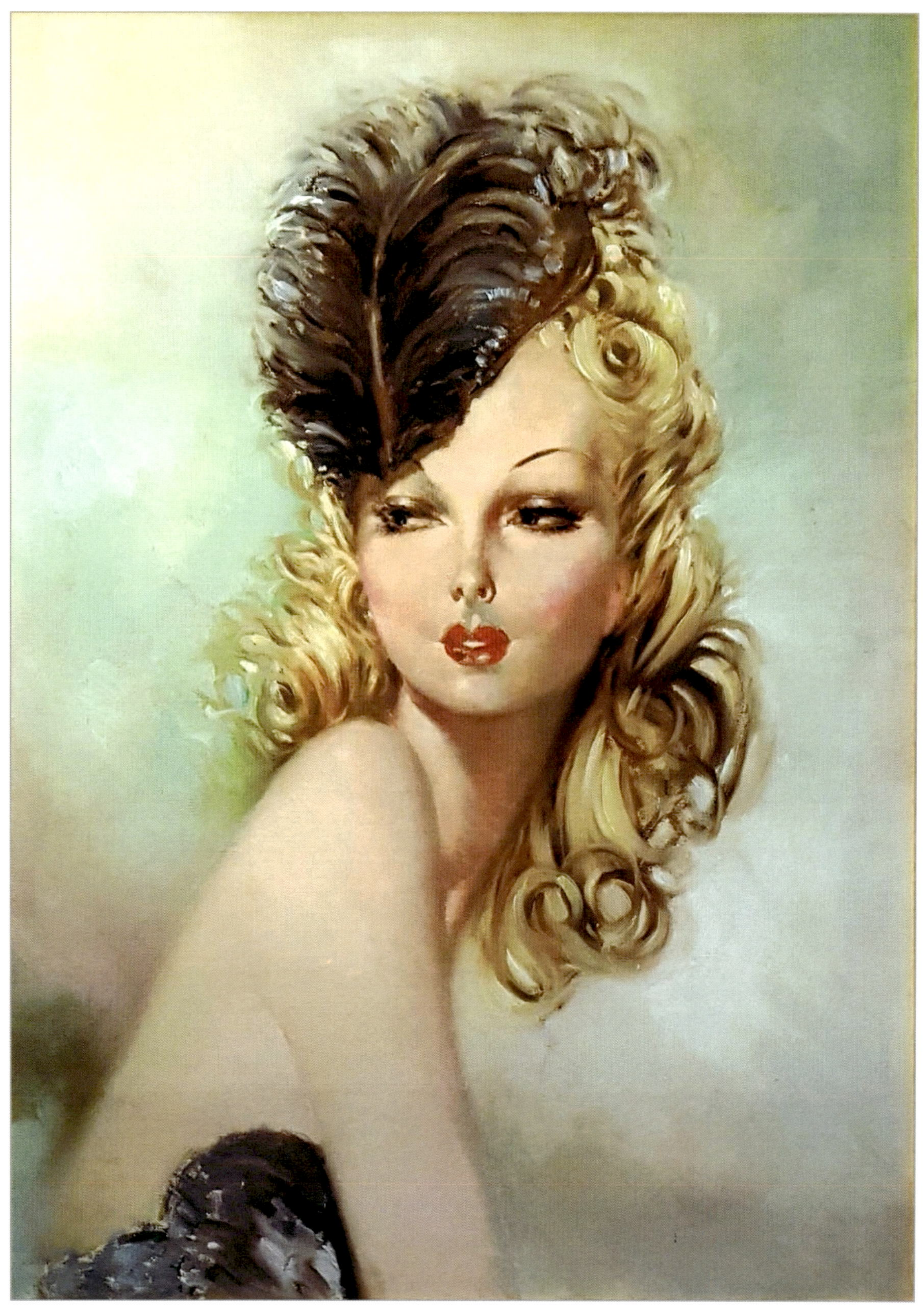

An unsigned and undated oil portrait by Heade. Once more, the model was probably his wife, Lily.

the figures in this painting, which Heade signed as Cy Webb, were based on stills of Eddie Lewis taken in Heade's studio: the boxer himself (although the face was naturally that of Sullivan, gleaned from vintage press shots); the coach holding the towel; and the man on the far right, with his arms folded on the canvas. When posing for the figure of Sullivan, Lewis was asked by Heade to extend his left arm along a cardboard tube, representing the rope around the boxing ring. The tube was in turn supported on top of some books in the *Shipping Wonders of the World* series.

At the time of his death of a heart attack, aged only 56 years old, on 14 October 1957, Heade left uncompleted a head-and-shoulders pencil rough of a young man dressed in Elizabethan-style clothes; presumably his latest cover commission from either Panther or, more likely, Pan. But, as Sally recalls, he was actually working on the cover painting for *The Diary of Anne Frank* (Great Pan, 1958) when he died. Pan would later publish the unfinished piece without any tribute to its painter. Heade's body is

Below: *The Diary of Anne Frank* (Great Pan, 1958)

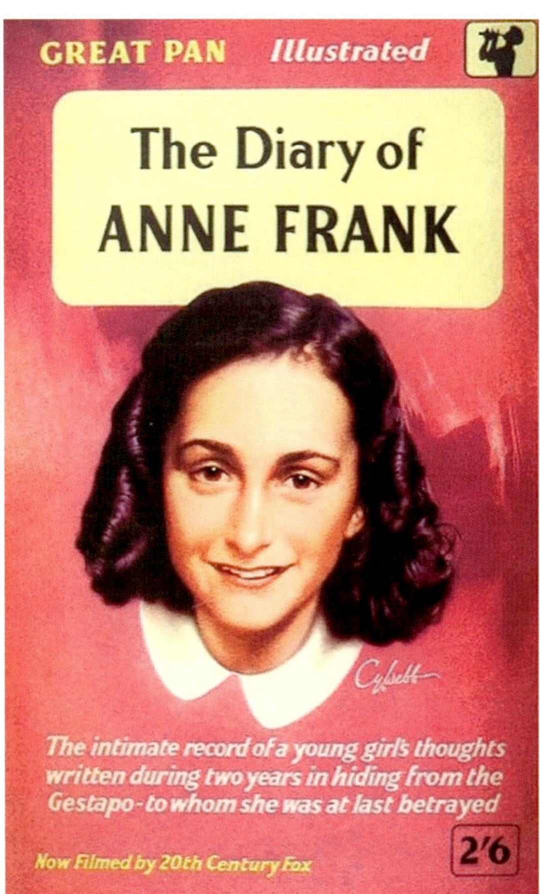

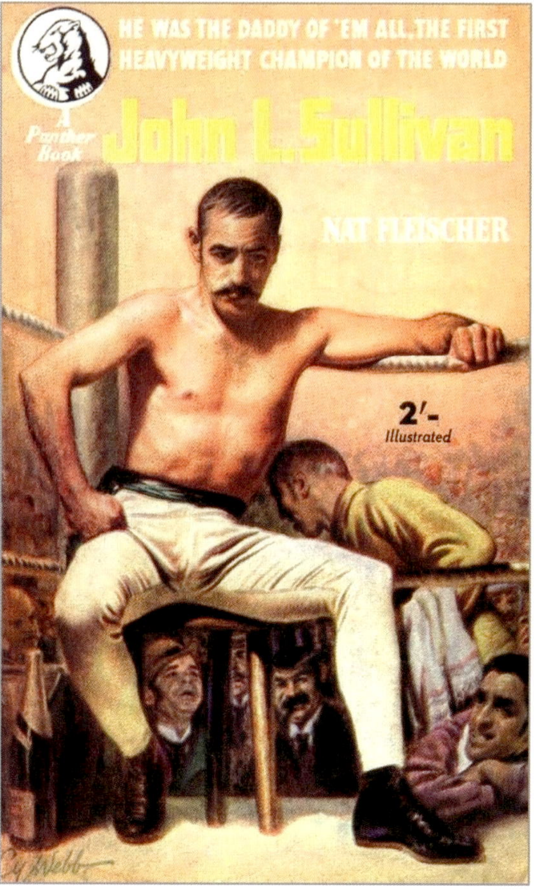

Above: *John L Sullivan* by Nat Fleischer (Panther, 1956)

said to have been found by the home help who came in daily to clean the flat, although Edward Mortelmans' account suggests that the police broke in after being informed that the artist was not answering his phone. His neighbours later took on the sad task of looking for a will amongst his papers, but did not find one; there were just piles of magazines and books used for reference, and some old letters, birthday cards and Christmas cards that were still in their envelopes, as Heade had not even bothered to open them. Aunt Nellie – reputedly a 'strict Victorian lady' who, although 14 years older than Heade, would long outlive him, eventually dying in 1991 at the extraordinary age of 104 – recovered what she could of his effects. But Heade had made provision for his daughter, leaving an estate totalling almost £700 (worth about £11,800 in today's money); when probate was finally settled on 25 March 1959, this was administered by Fred Williams, County Treasurer, and Margaret Ethel Cullen, Children's Officer.

It was a sad end to the life of one of the greatest commercial illustrators that Britain has produced.

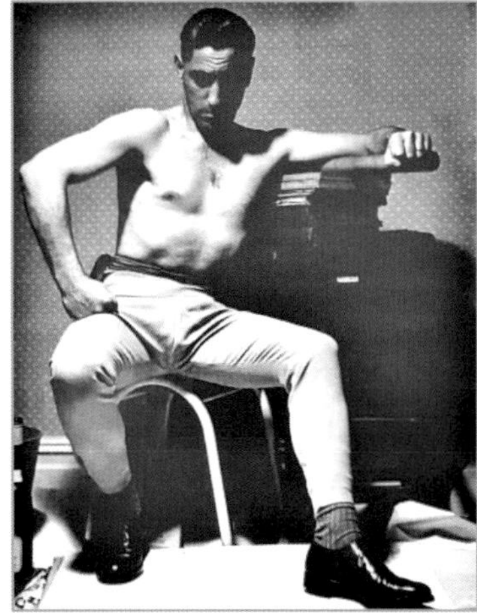 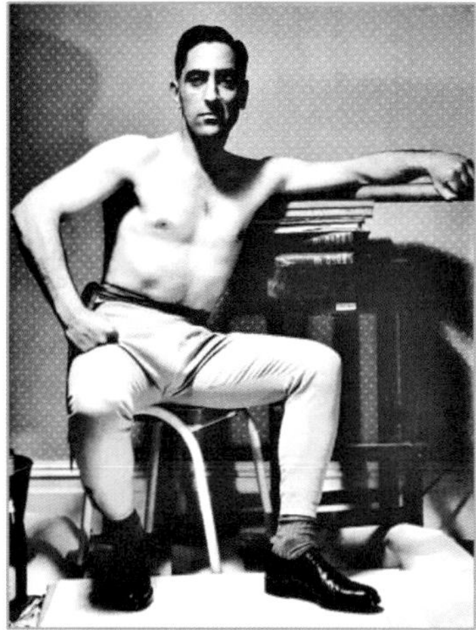 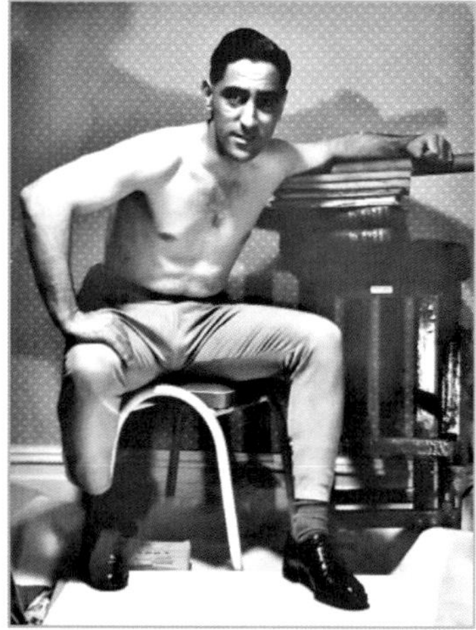

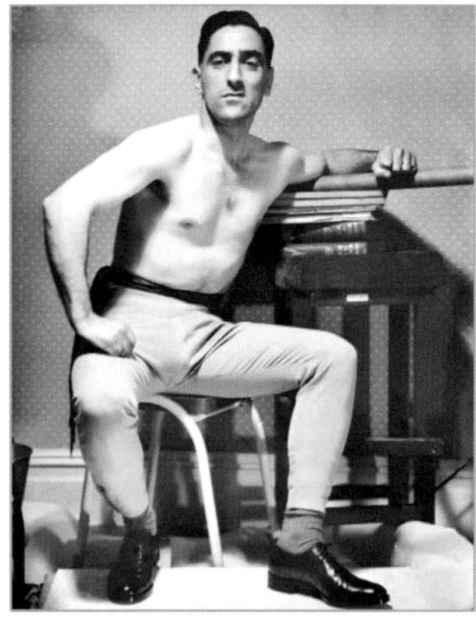 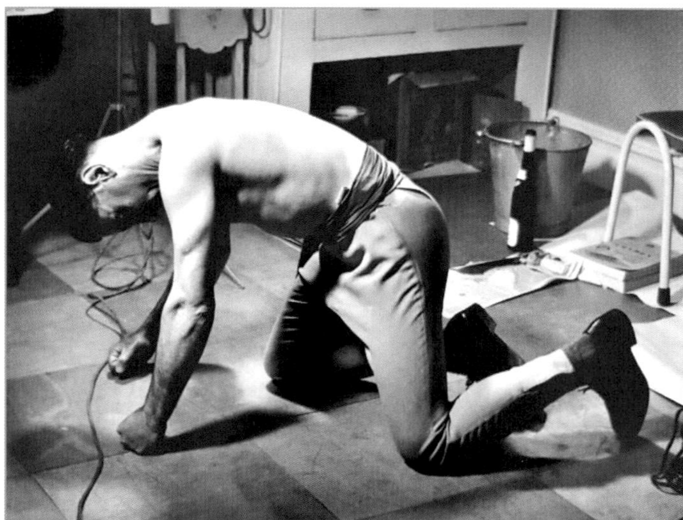

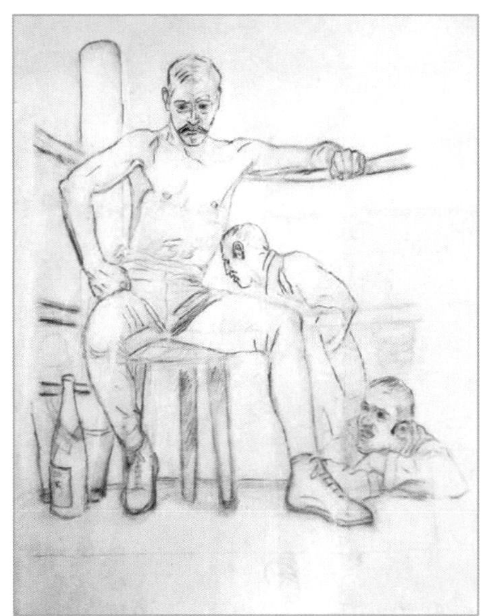 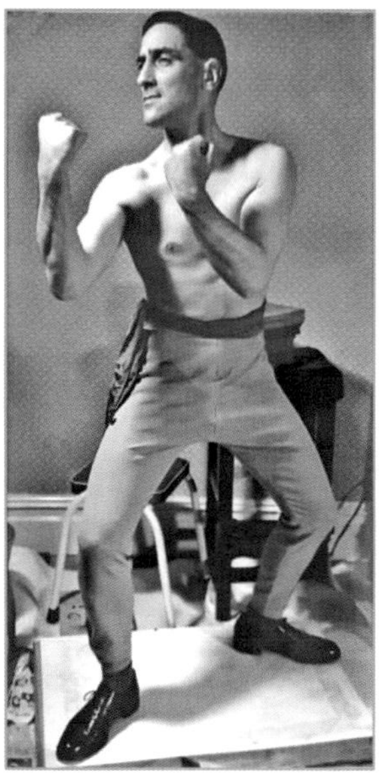 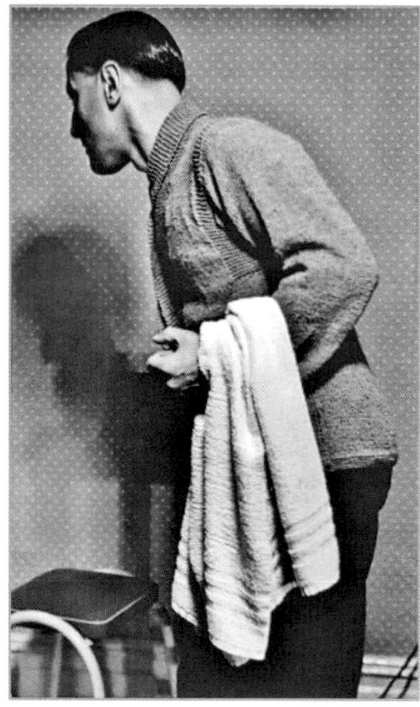

Photographs of Heade's downstairs neighbour Eddie Lewis, posing in the artist's studio for the cover of *John L Sullivan* by Nat Fleischer (Panther, 1956); and (bottom left) Heade's preparatory drawing traced from elements of these reference shots. The final composition omitted the pose from the one at middle row right, and only Lewis's head was taken from the one at bottom row centre. (With thanks to Mike Lewis.)

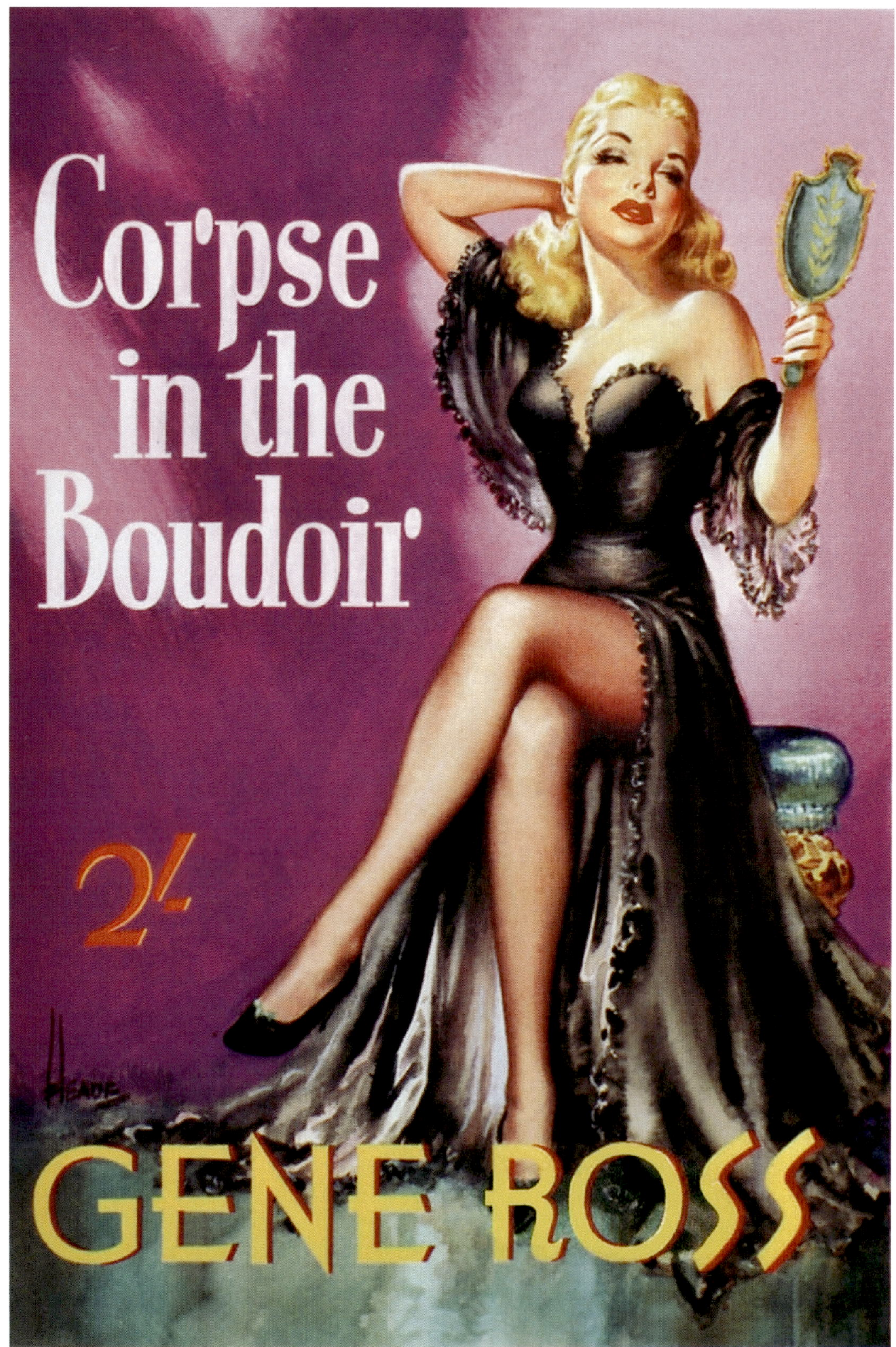

Heade's original painting for *Corpse in the Boudoir* by Gene Ross (Harborough, September 1953). (Image courtesy the Steve Chibnall Collection.)

But his legacy lives on, including in his daughter Sally, and in the grandson Russell (born 1968) and granddaughter Kerry (born 1971) he never lived to see – the latter of whom trained in graphic design at Falmouth College of Art, where Heade himself might once have studied. The material legacy of his art lives on too, in the original sketches, roughs and finished paintings that still survive as treasured possessions in private collections, and indeed in all the images of his published work that populate the pages of this volume and its predecessor. Those images, of course, speak to us of the age in which they were created, but they also transcend their time as icons – particularly of femininity. In the 1930s and '40s, Heade's work imagined romantic fiction in a way that now seems definitive: the look of love. And in a frenzy of gouache over the seven years preceding the Coronation of Queen Elizabeth, he visualised escapist desire in an age of austerity and repression. His shy ingénues suddenly became sexualised: brazen dames in flimsy lingerie and tattered gowns. He transformed monochromatic film noir iconography into vivid colour compositions that

genuinely unleashed (to quote the title of one of his steamiest covers) the 'Demon of Desire' so long bottled up by the reading public.

Some of his more eroticised scenarios might now be condemned as sexist, but however objectified as dangerous or endangered, the Heade woman somehow communicates her creator's philogyny rather than any misogyny; his fondness and admiration for the feminine, his empathy with the feelings of the woman in the situation in which he has placed her. Ultimately, the sensationalism of his depictions is balanced by an evident sensitivity that is conveyed subliminally through his brush strokes and colour palette – the pinks and lilacs, the mauves, the golden yellows and subtle greens that provide the continuity in his work. Above all, Heade was a romantic painter; but his idealised depictions were already becoming unfashionable at the time of his death, crushed between the jaws of realism and abstraction. It is only now, perhaps, in less doctrinaire times, that we can properly revisit his lush, sensuous body of work and fully appreciate its extraordinary quality.

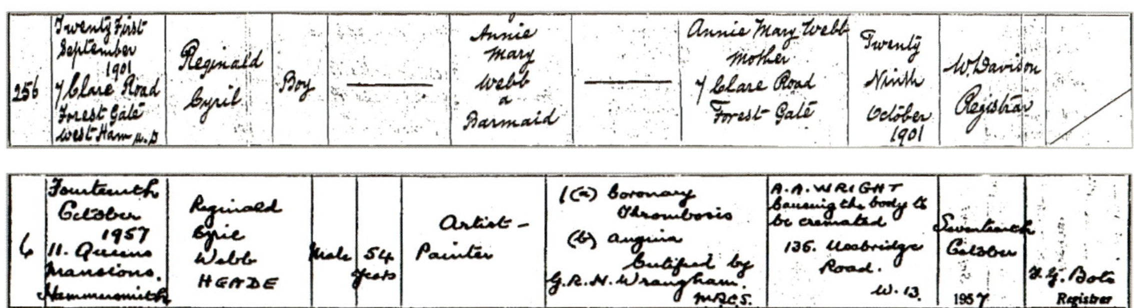

Above: extracts from Heade's birth certificate and death certificate. The death certificate incorrectly records the artist's age as 54 rather than 56. (Images: Crown copyright.)

Below left: a medallion, adapted from a 1915 half-crown coin, presented to Heade with an engraved inscription from the Mercantile Fleet Auxiliary *Peregrine*, a British naval vessel active during World War I. This may well have been the ship on which Heade's uncle Fred served. Below right: a magnifying glass believed to have been Heade's, used by him for fine detail work. (With thanks to Mike Lewis.)

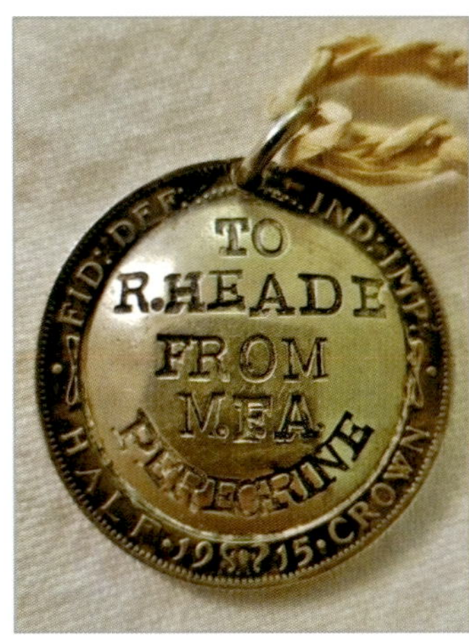

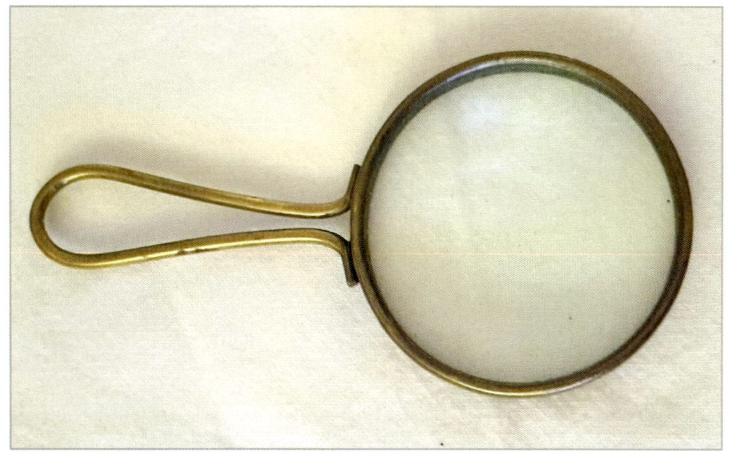

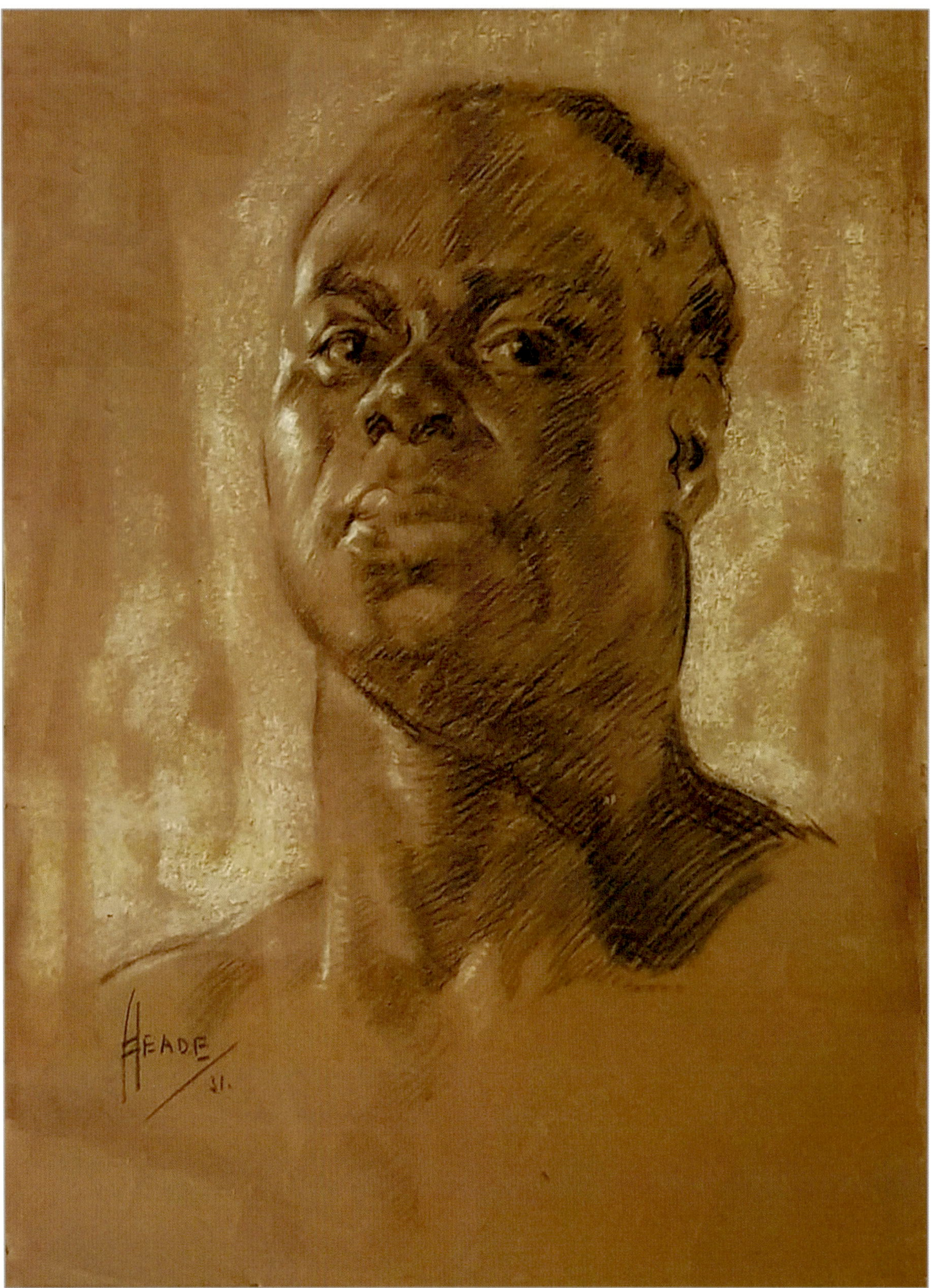

A 1931-dated portrait drawing by Heade. In 1933, two years after its completion, this piece was exhibited at the Royal Academy in London under the title 'Bob'; presumably the name of its otherwise-unknown subject. (With thanks to Mike Lewis.)

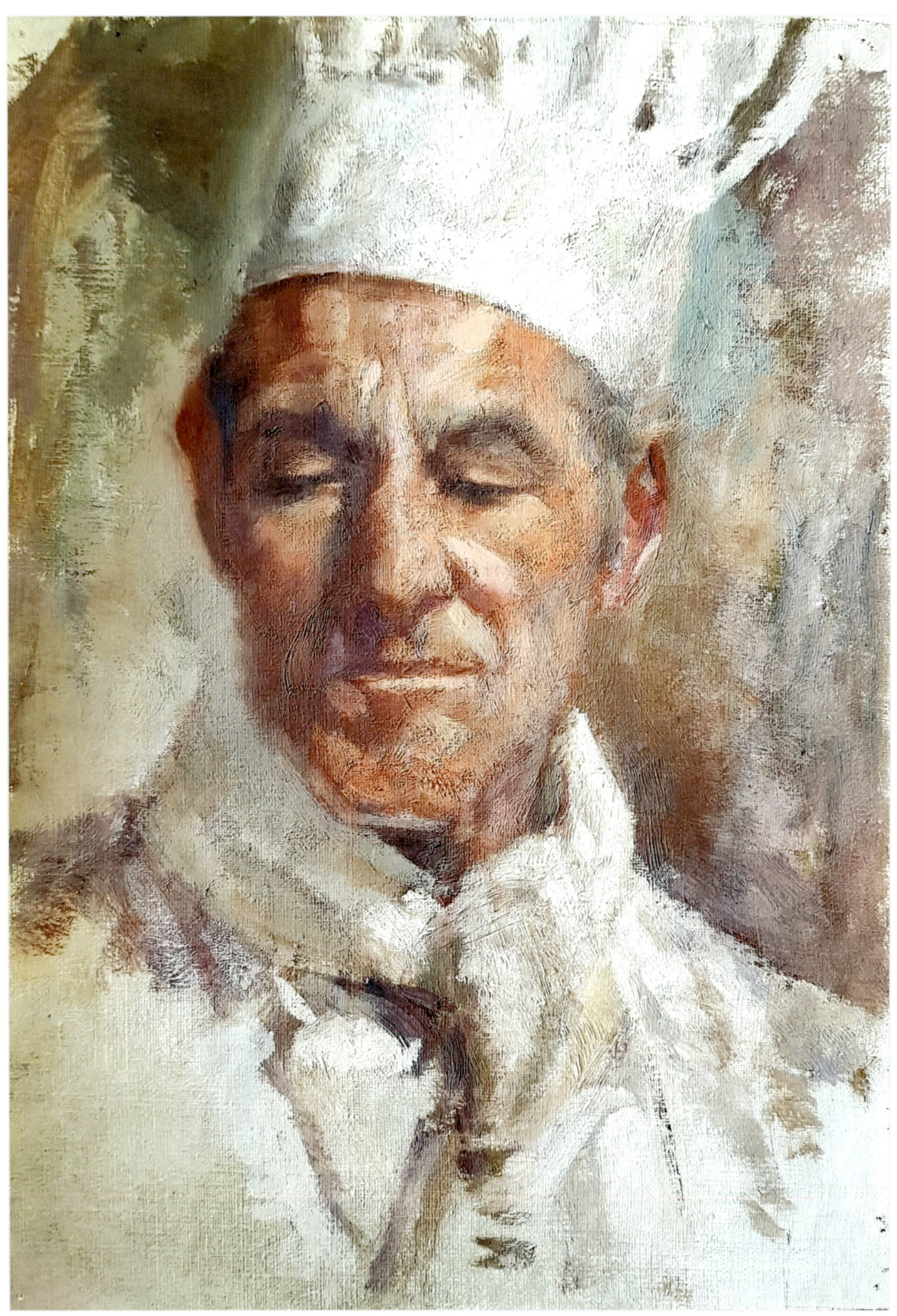

An unsigned and undated oil portrait by Heade.

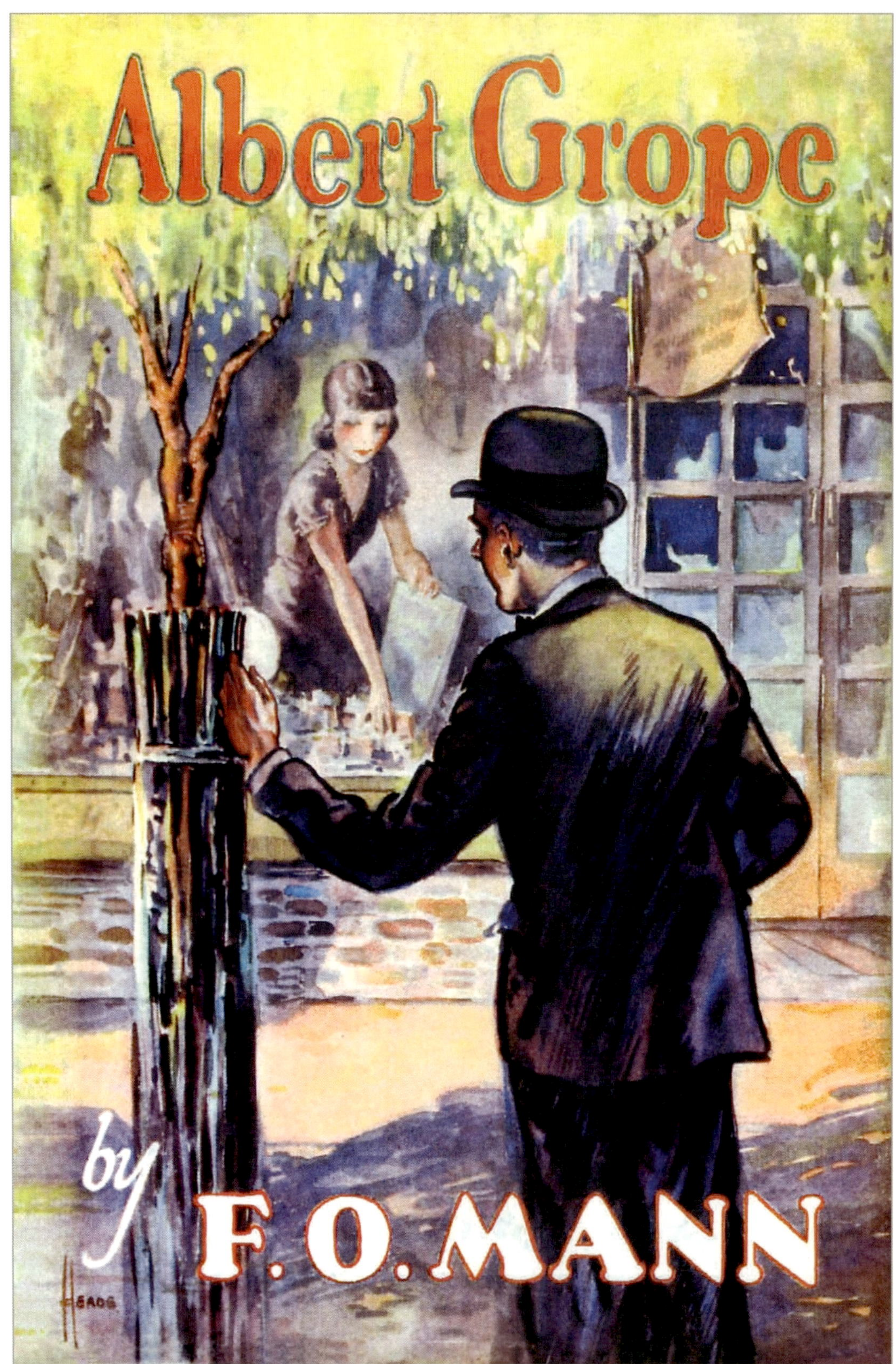

Albert Grope by F O Mann (Faber & Faber, February 1931). Currently the earliest known published work by Heade.

THE 1930s

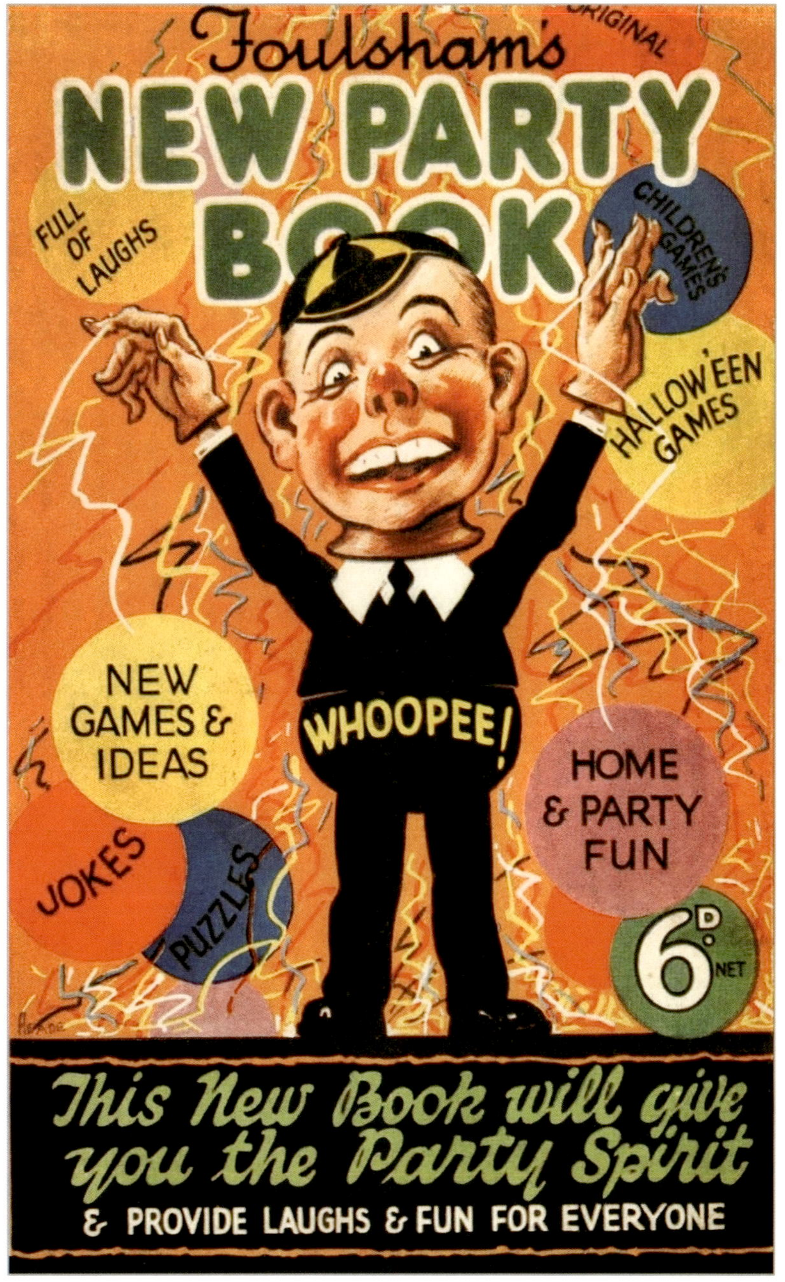

Foulsham's New Party Book (Foulsham's, c1934)

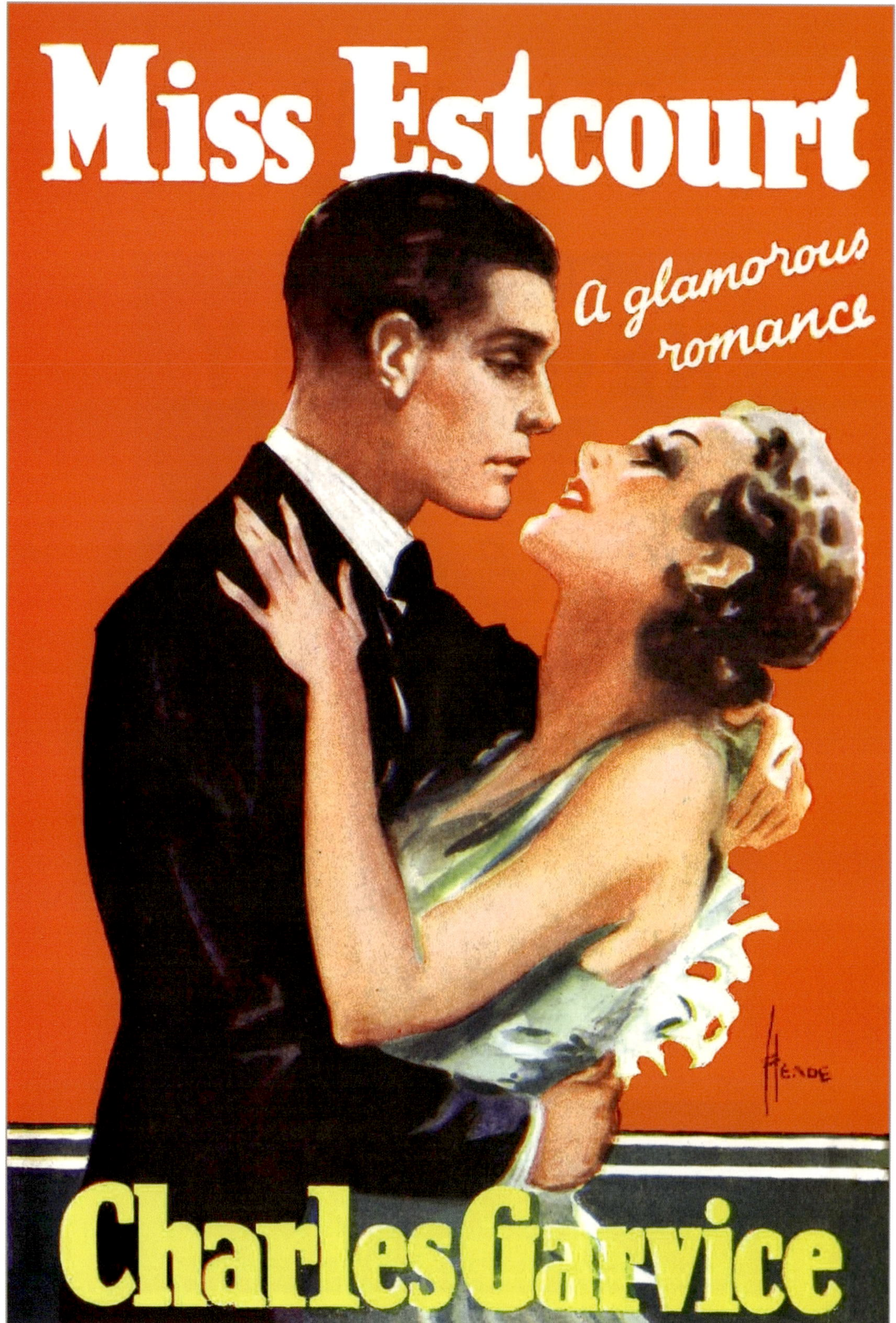

Miss Estcourt by Charles Garvice (Hutchinson, c1932)

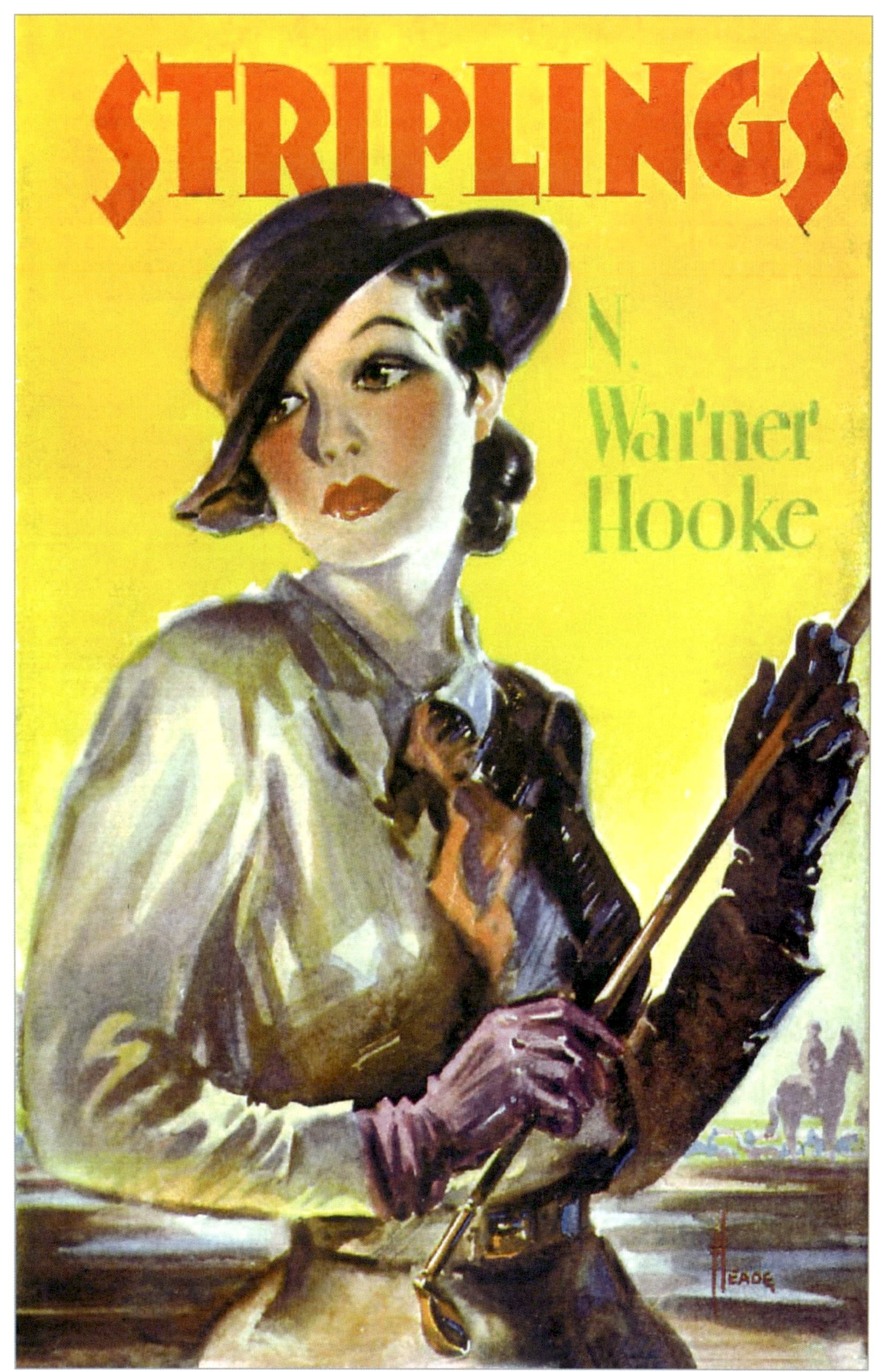

Striplings by N Warner Hooke (Faber & Faber, 1933)

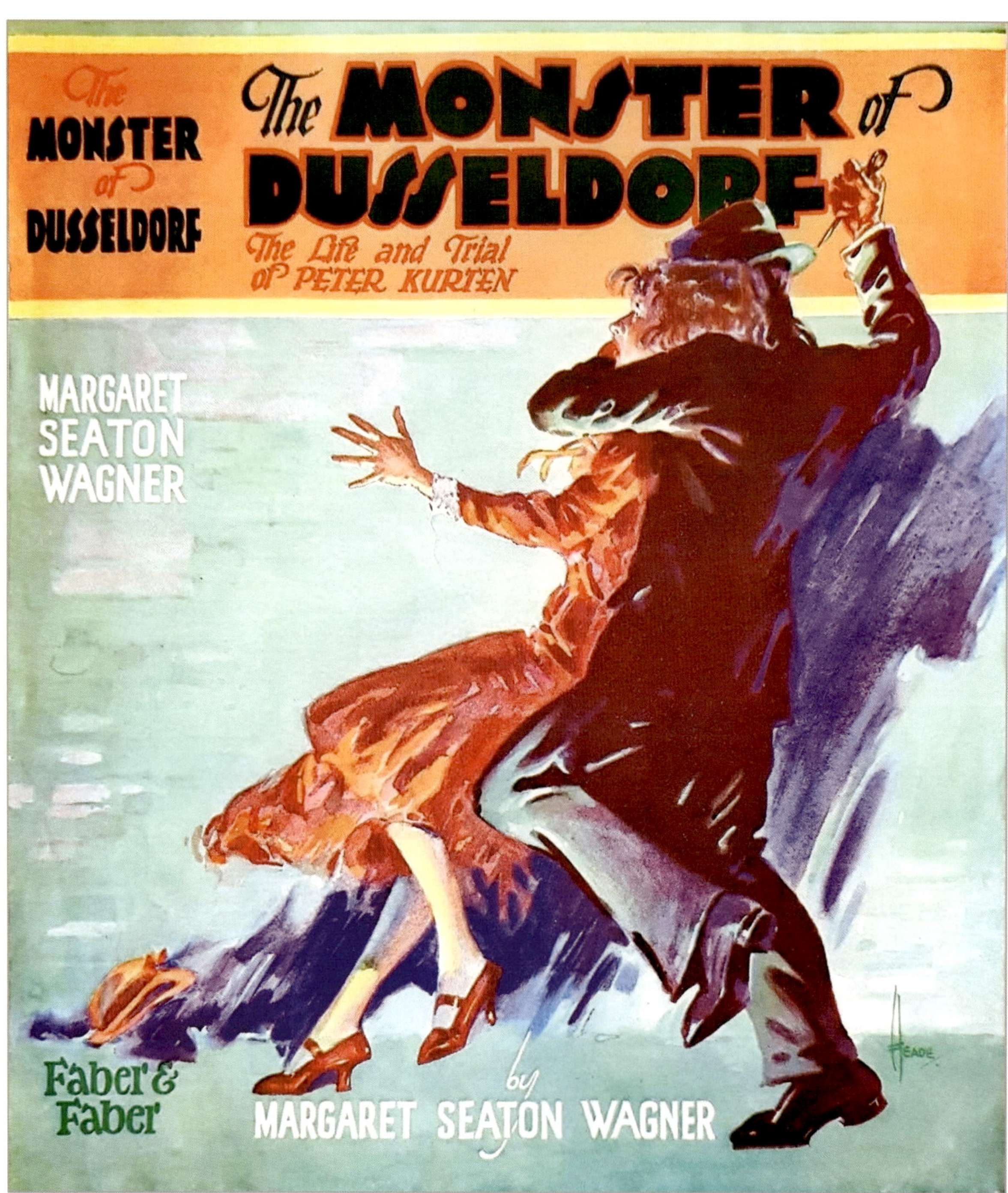

The Monster of Dusseldorf by Margaret Seaton Wagner (Faber & Faber, 1932)

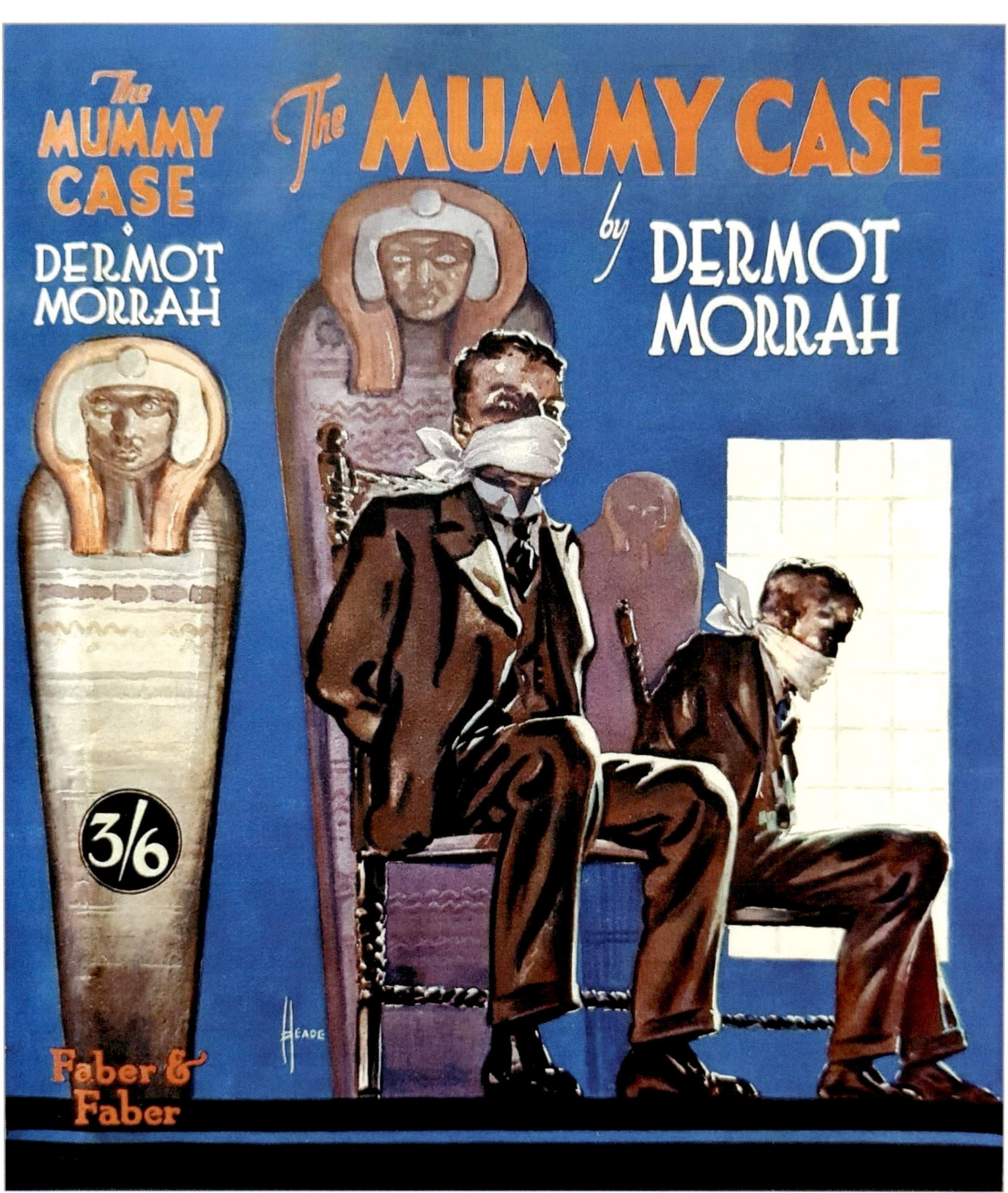

The Mummy Case by Dermot Morrah (Faber & Faber, 1933)

The Charm School by Alice Duer Miller (Hodder & Stoughton, 1936)

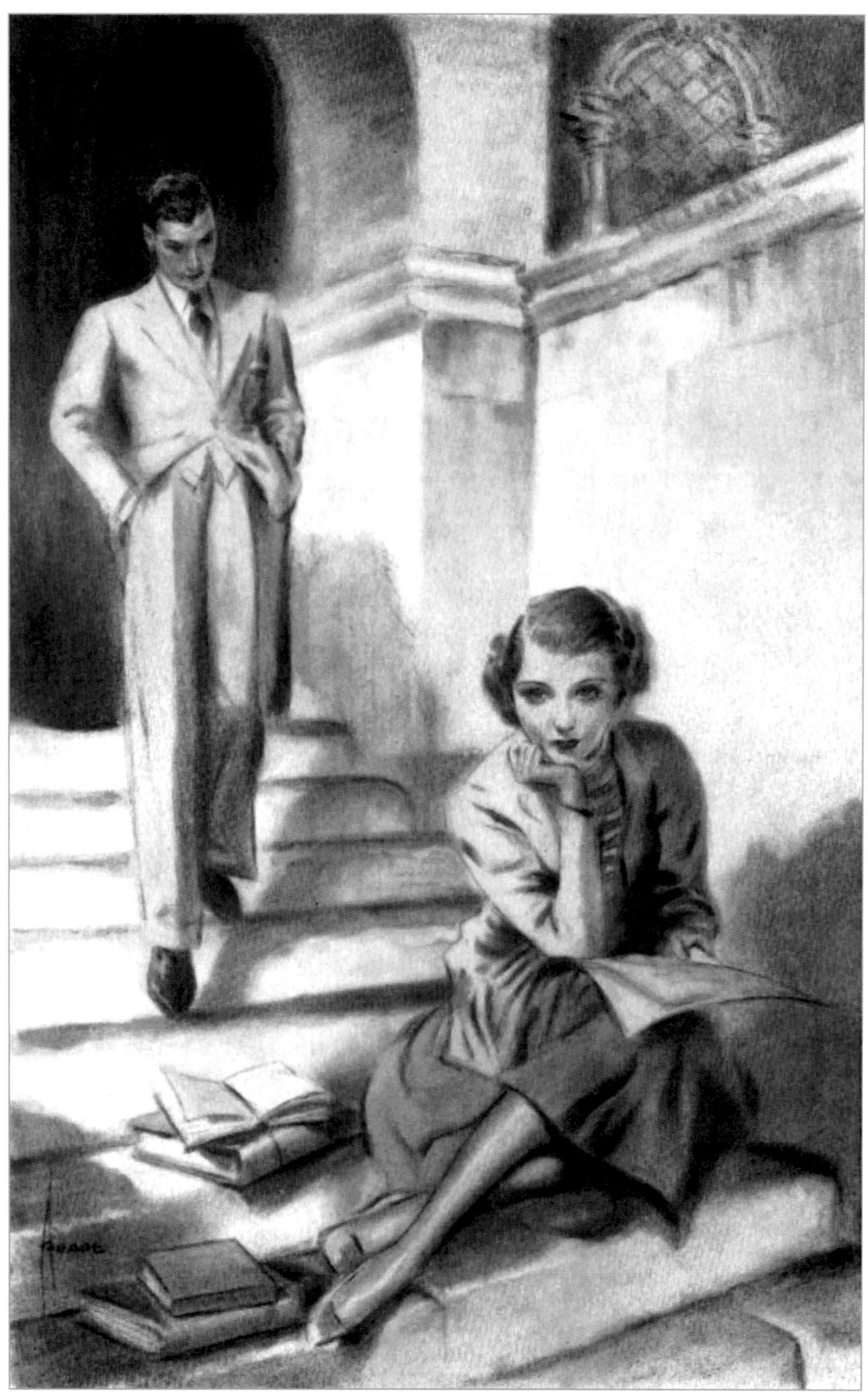

Black and white frontispiece from *The Charm School* by Alice Duer Miller (Hodder & Stoughton, 1936)

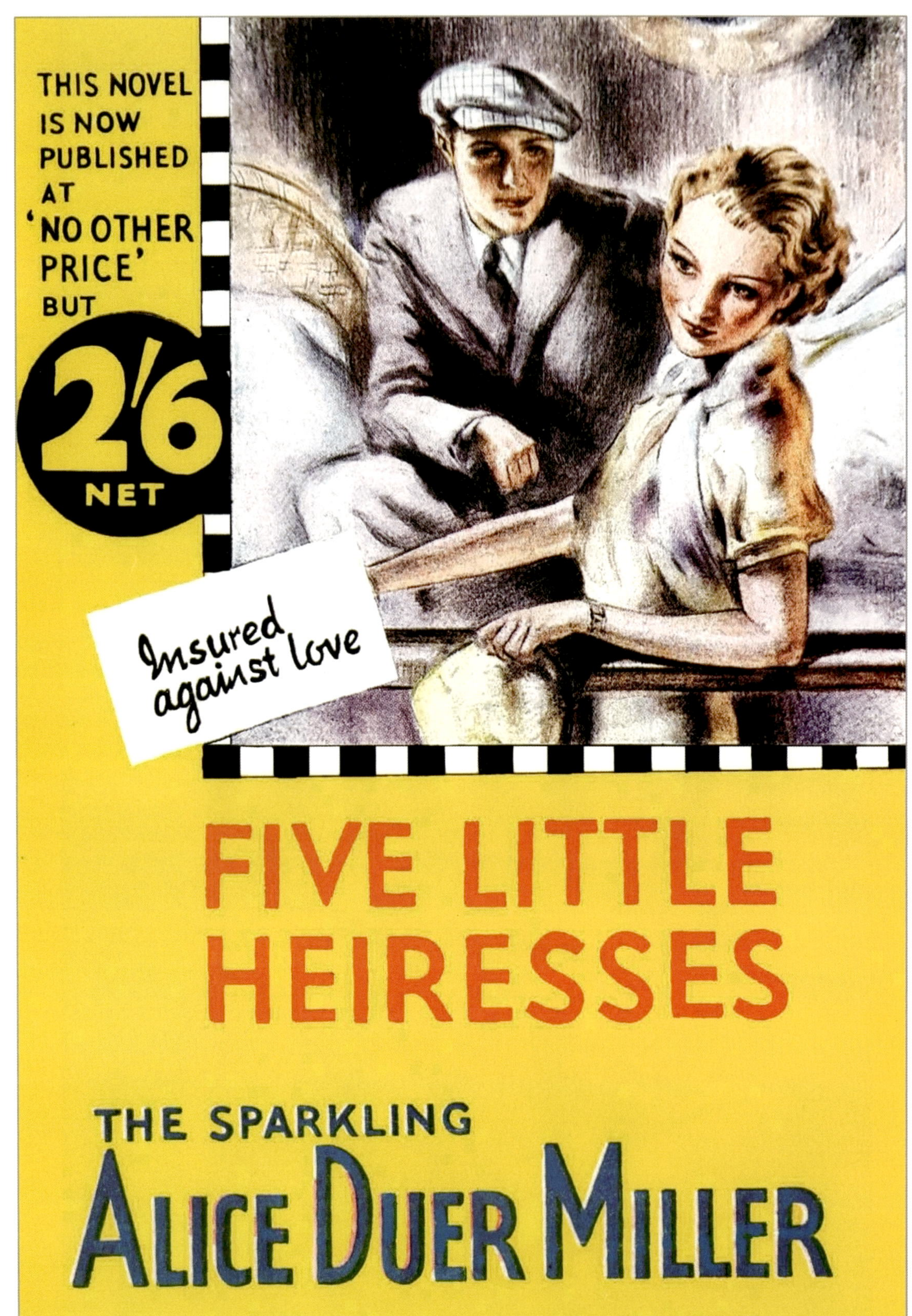

Five Little Heiresses by Alice Duer Miller (Hodder & Stoughton, November 1936)

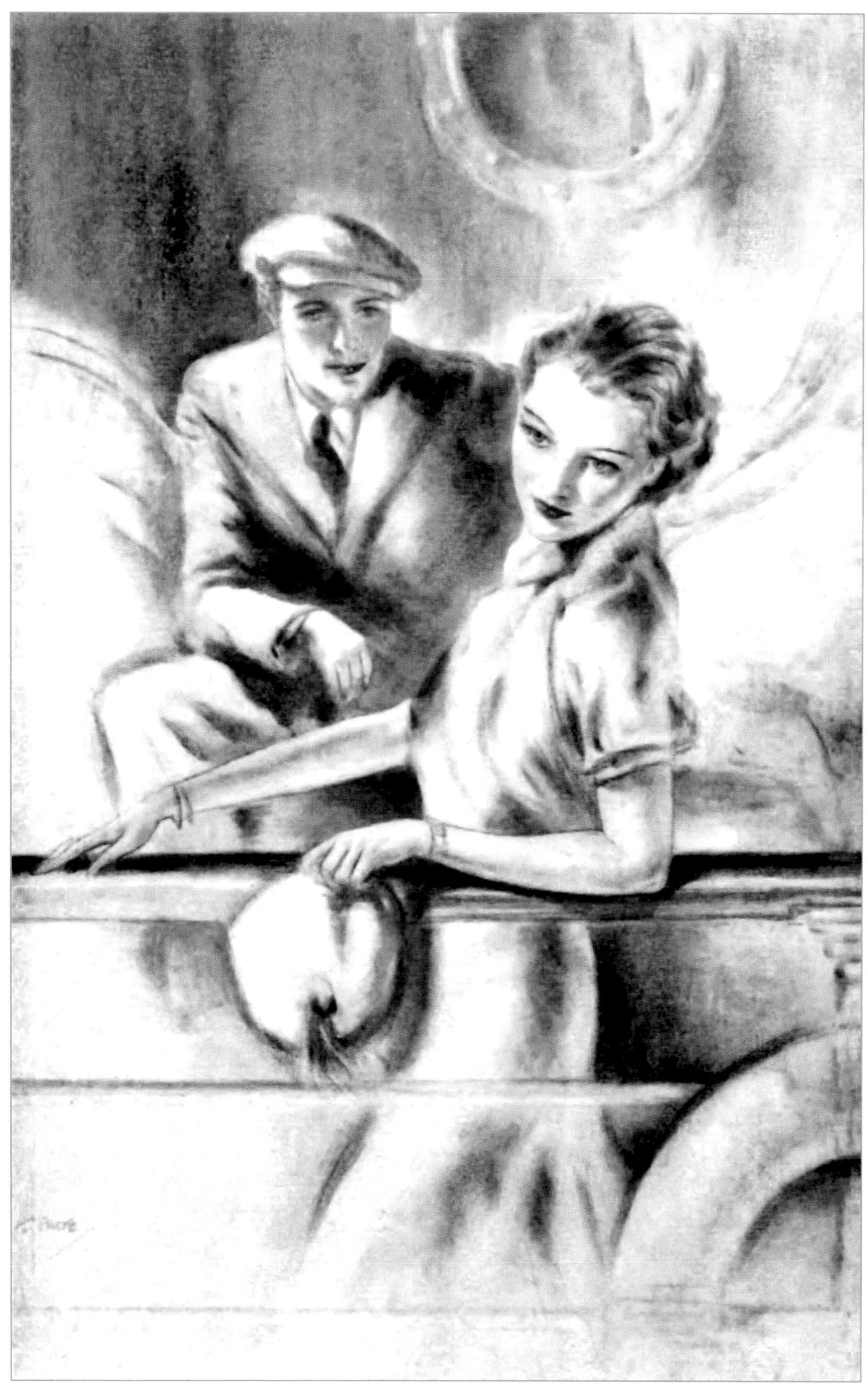

Black and white frontispiece from *Five Little Heiresses* by Alice Duer Miller (Hodder & Stoughton, November 1936)

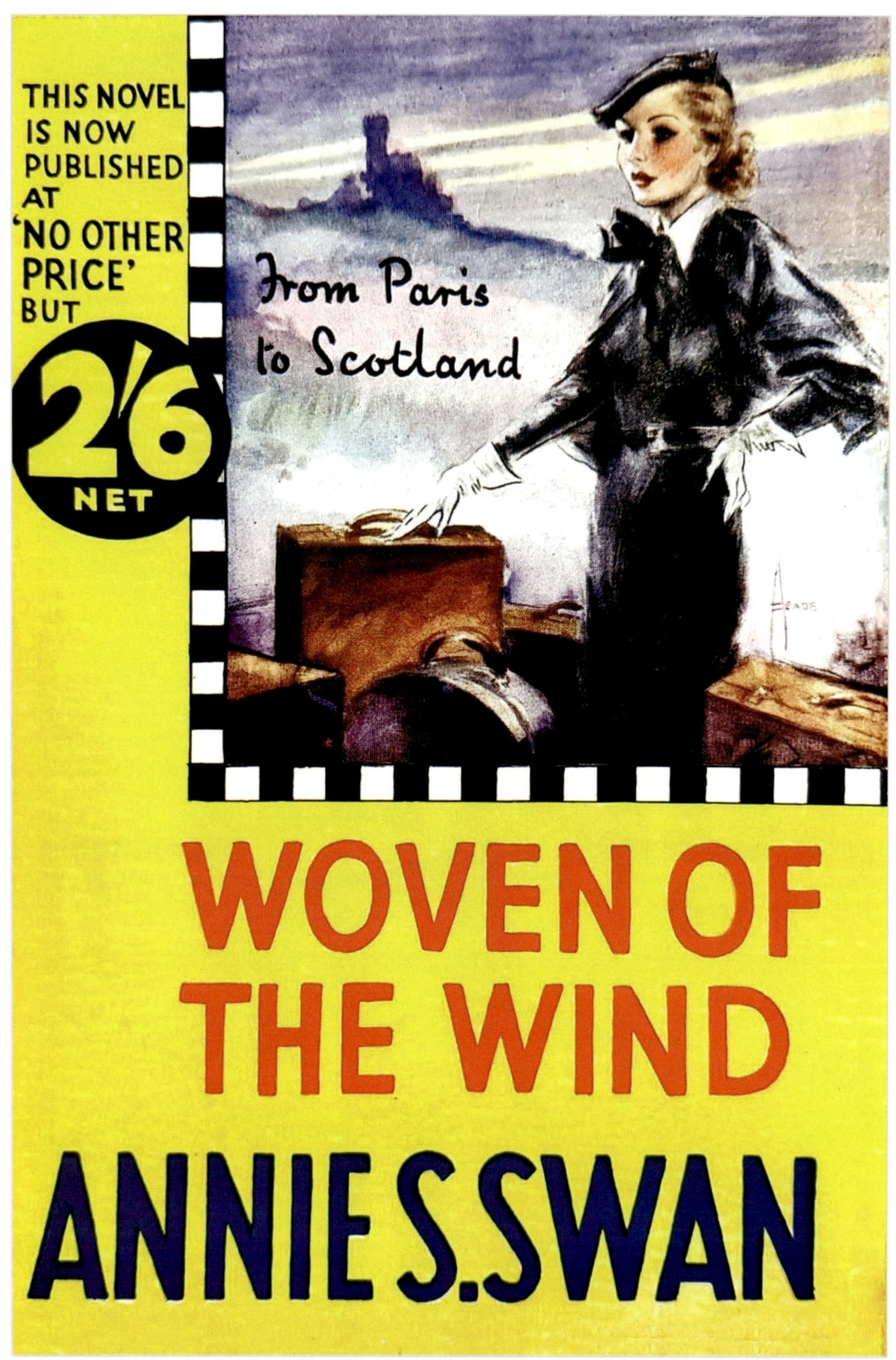

Woven of the Wind by Annie S Swan (Hodder & Stoughton, c1936)

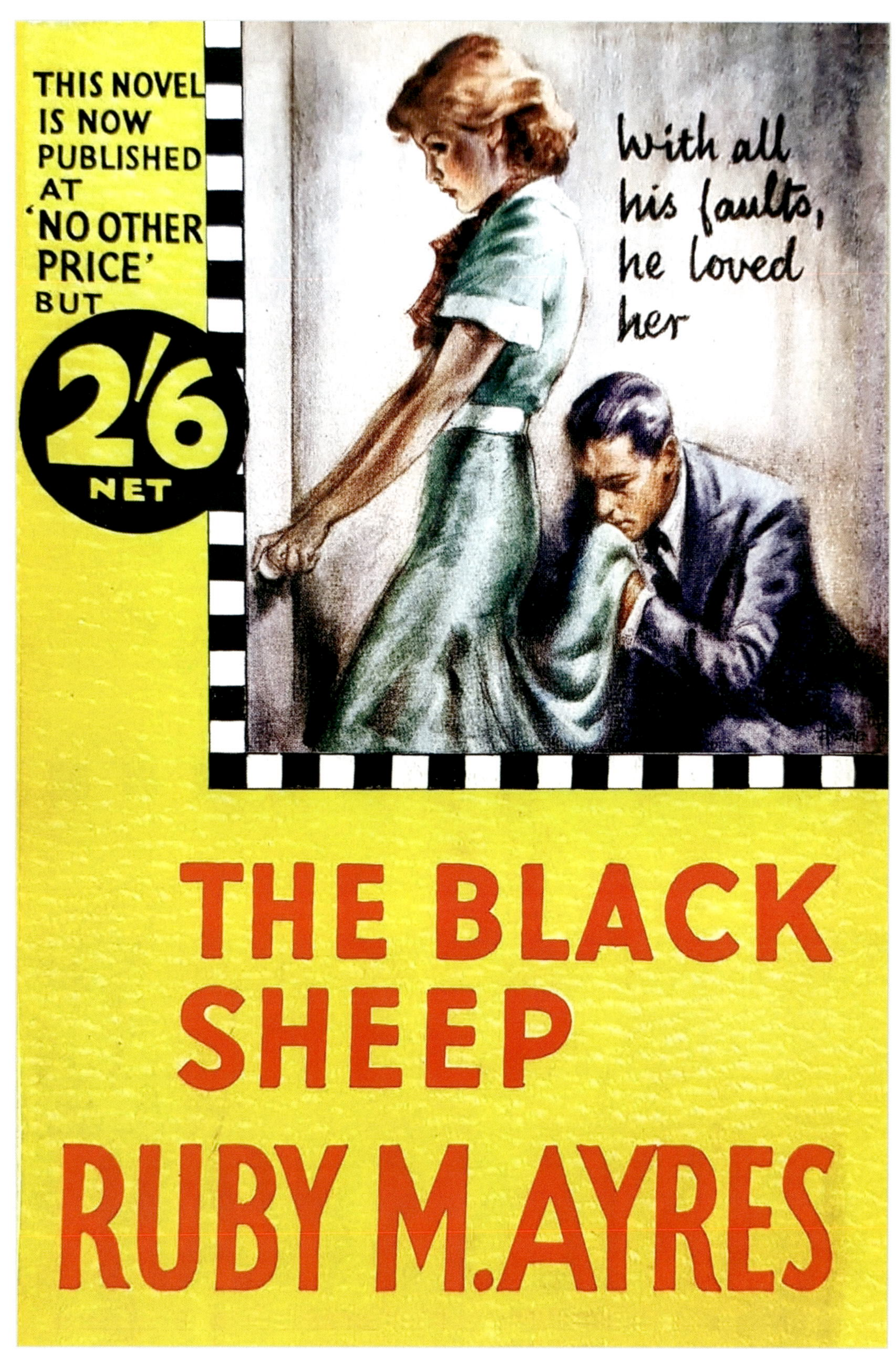

The Black Sheep by Ruby M Ayres (Hodder & Stoughton, c1936)

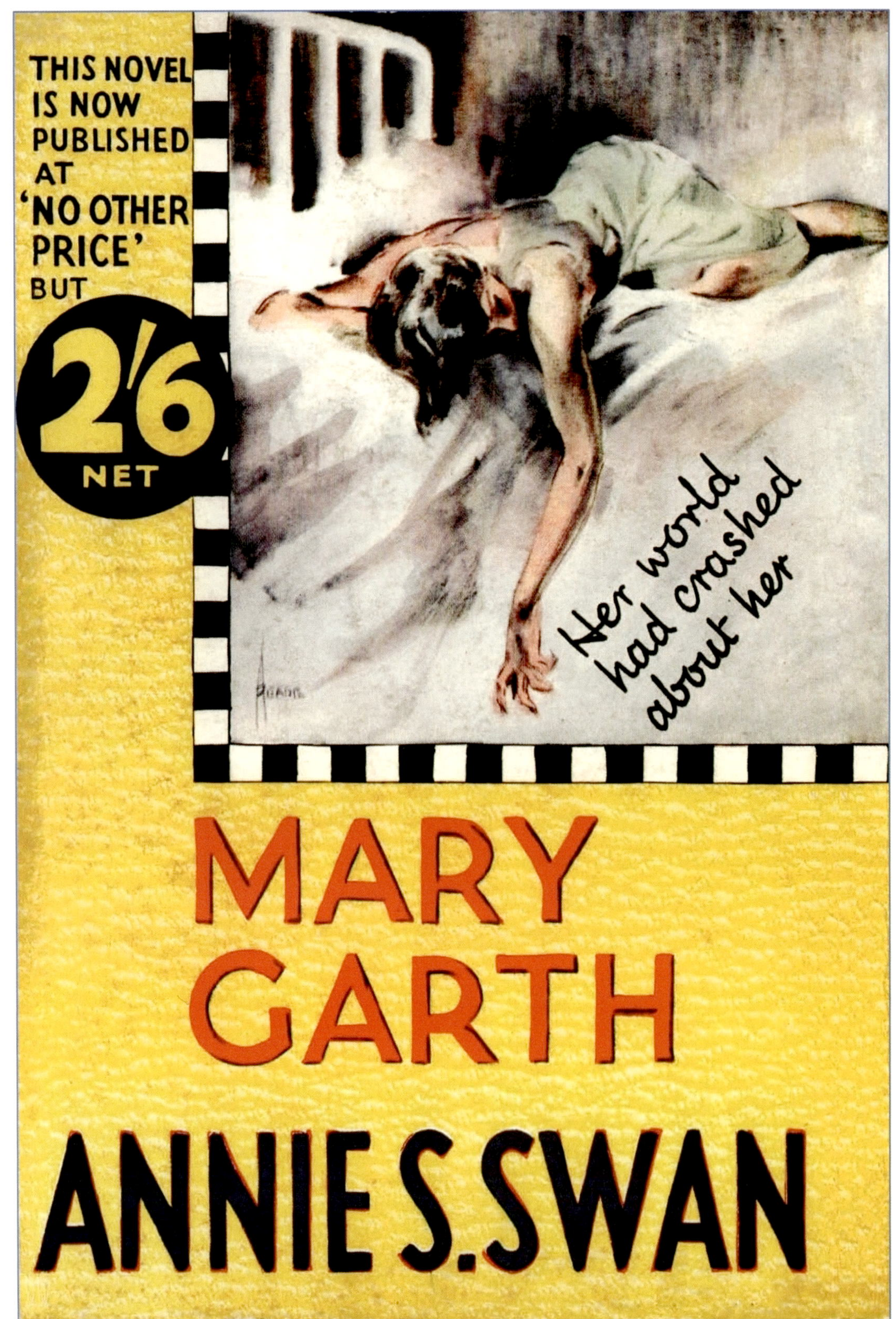

Mary Garth by Annie S Swan (Hodder & Stoughton, c1936)

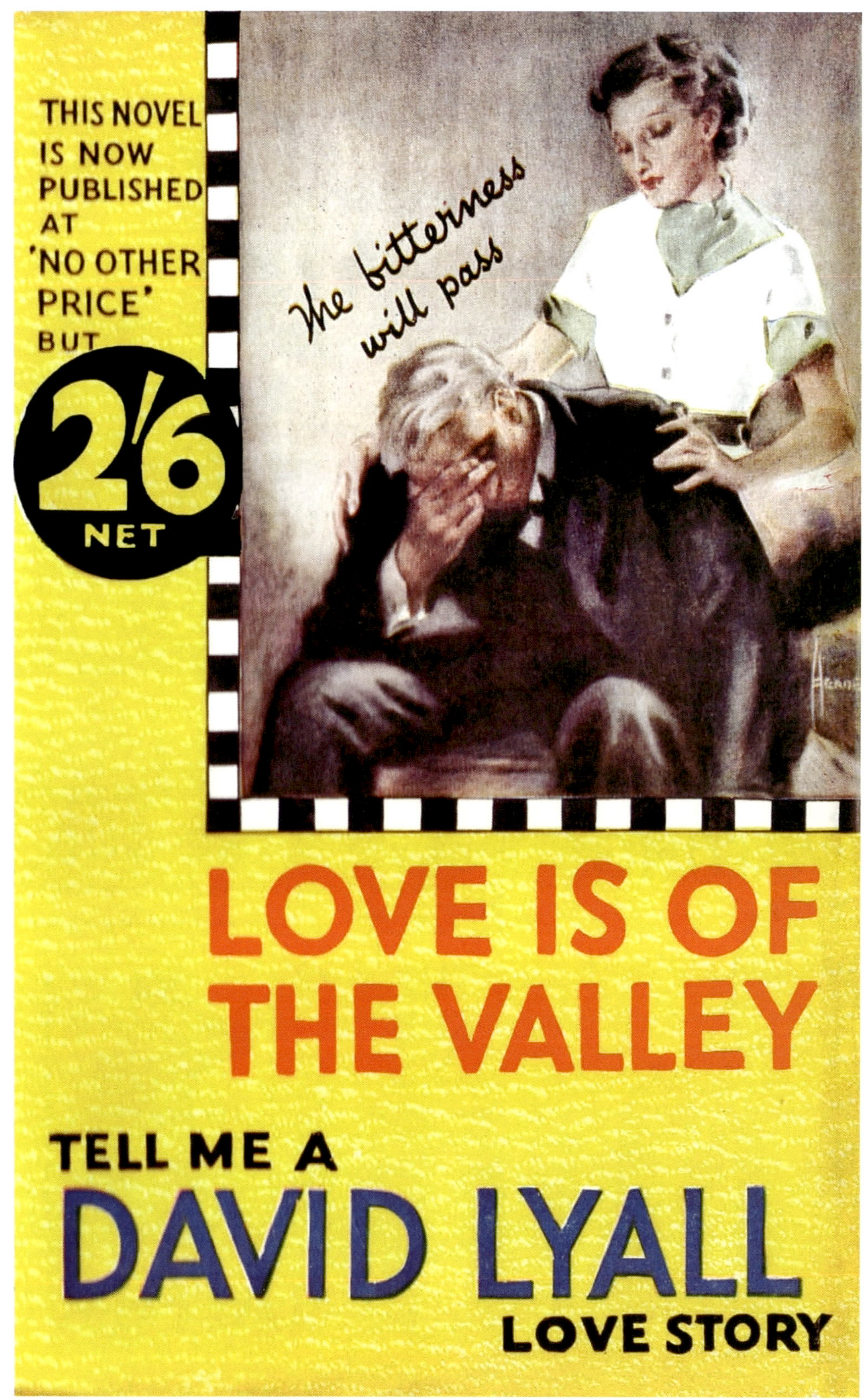

Love is of the Valley by David Lyall (Hodder & Stoughton, 1936). The Lyall name was a pseudonym used by author Annie S Swan.

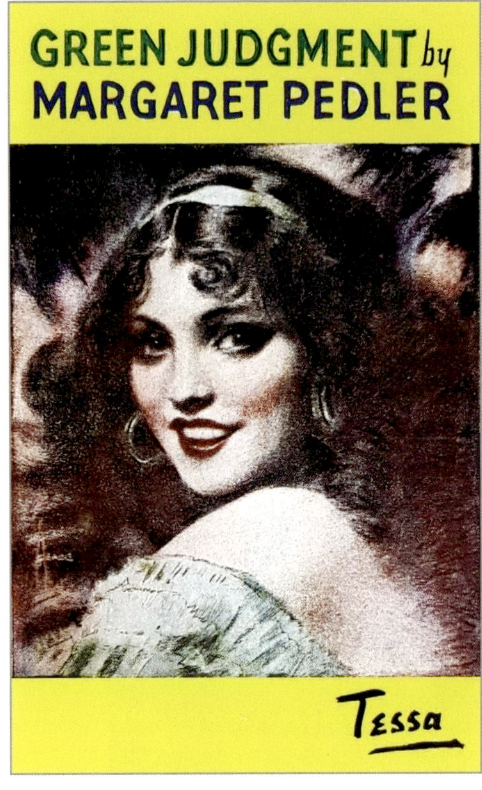

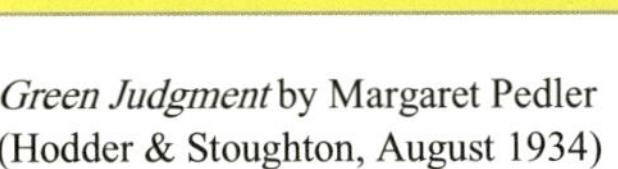

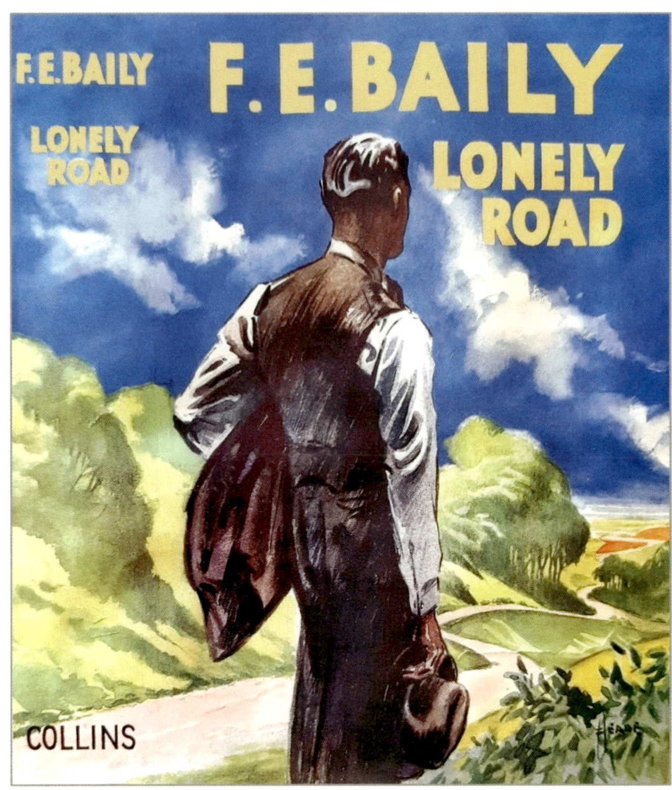

Green Judgment by Margaret Pedler
(Hodder & Stoughton, August 1934)

Lonely Road by F E Baily (Collins, 1936)

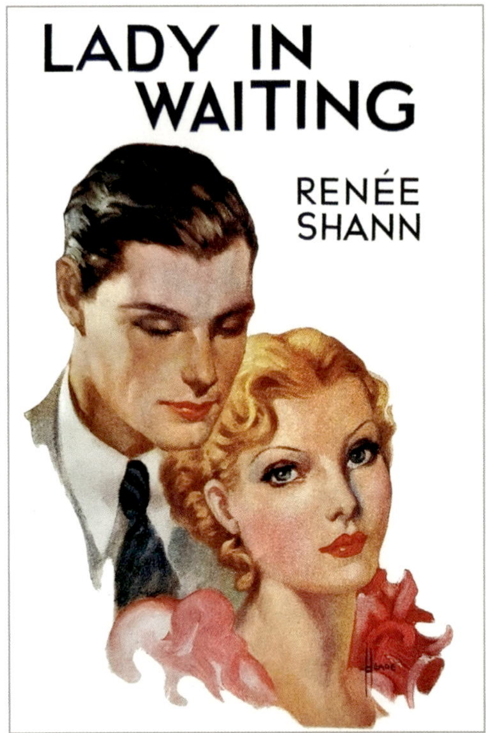

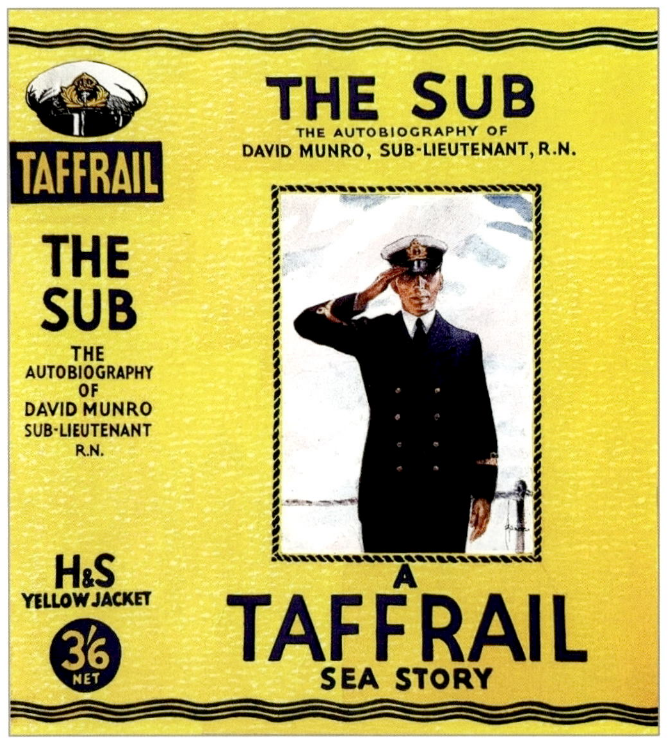

Lady in Waiting by Renée Shann (Collins, 1936)

The Sub by Taffrail (Hodder & Stoughton, 1937)

THE 'PLAY UP …!' SERIES

In the 1910s and 1920s, author Herbert Hayens wrote the 'Play Up …!' series of a dozen novels about the exploits of schoolboy sports teams. Around 1937 (no date is given inside), at least eight of these were reissued by Collins Clear-Type with new dustjacket artwork. (No such editions of the other four have yet been found.) In each case, a section of the artwork was reproduced inside as a colour frontispiece. Although these new dustjacket pieces were all unsigned, the one for *Play Up, Lions!* is now known for sure to have been Heade's work, and it is likely at least some of the others were too. The titles were: *Play Up, Stags!*; *Play Up, Greys!*; *Play Up, Kings!*; *Play Up, Eagles!*; *Play Up, Tigers!*; *Play Up, Jack!*; and *Play Up, Magpies!.*

Right: the confirmed Heade dustjacket for *Play Up, Lions!.*

Below: the probable Heade dustjackets for *Play Up, Kings!* and *Play Up, Tigers!.*

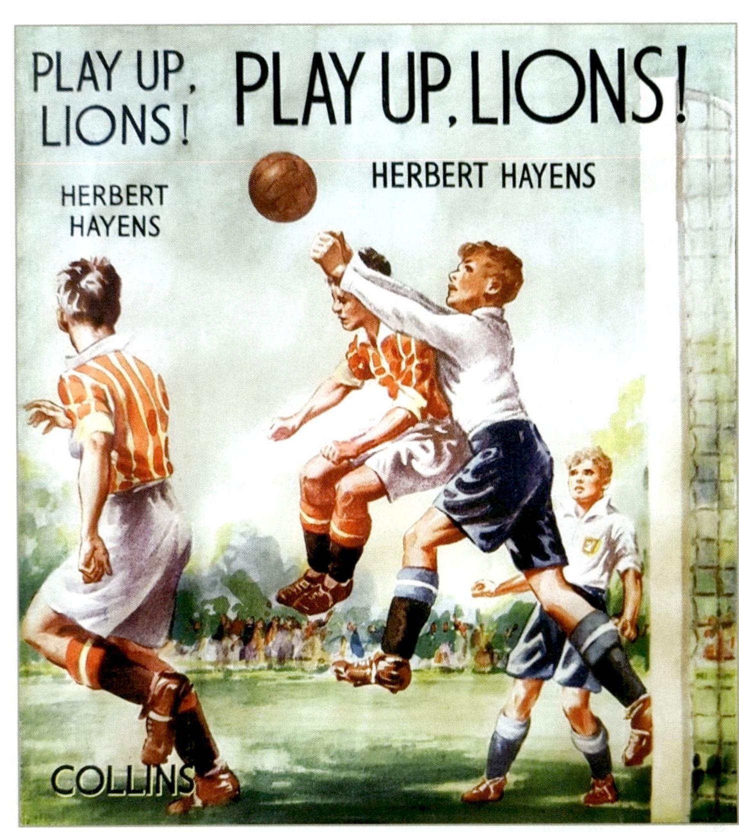

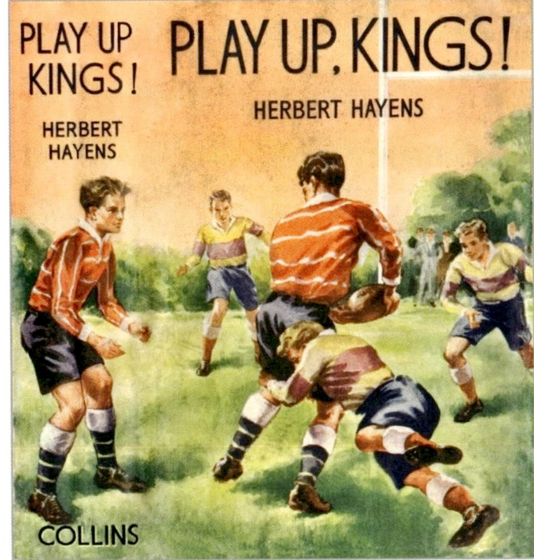

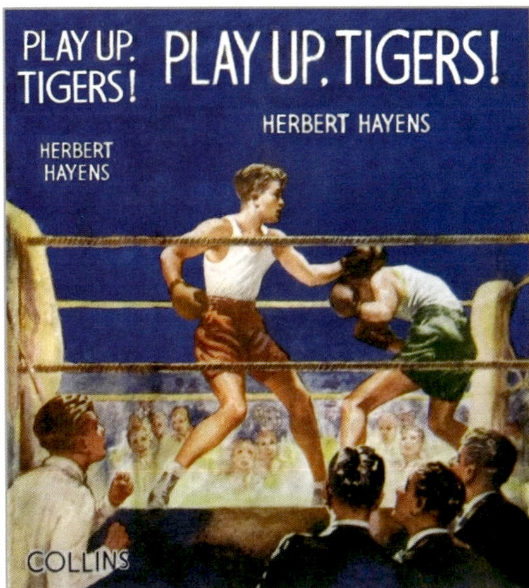

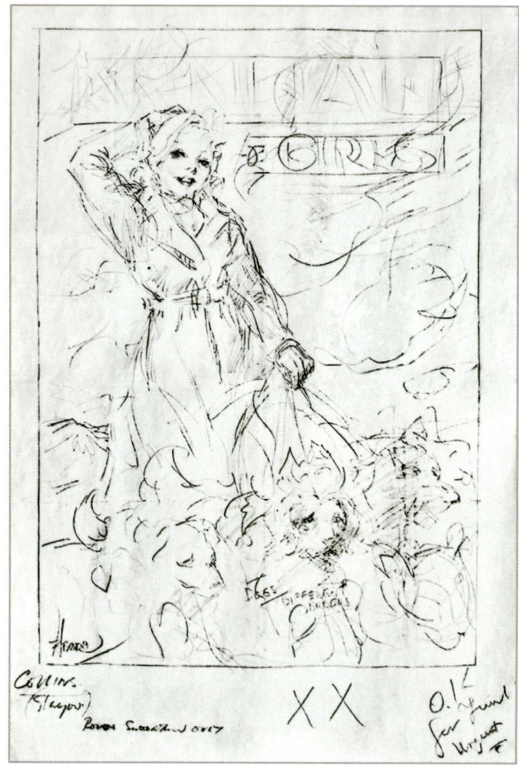

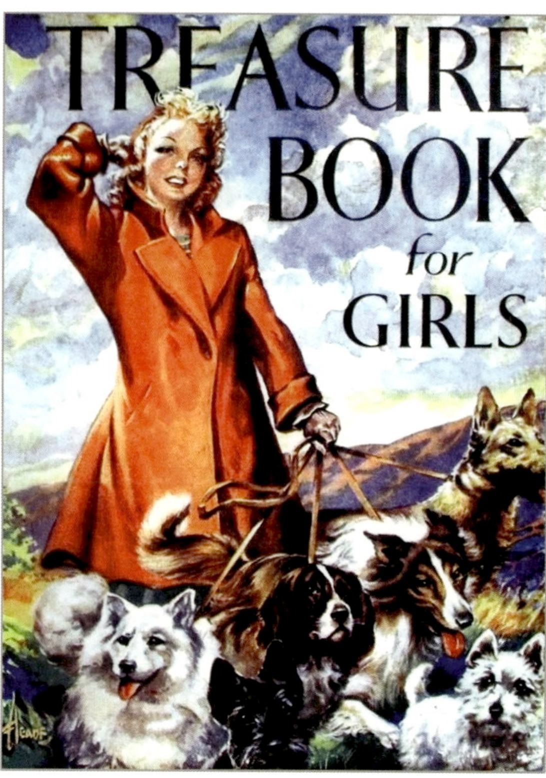

One of two surviving pencil roughs drawn by Heade for the cover of *Treasure Book for Girls* (Collins Clear-Type, c1937), and the as-published version. Annotations on the rough – which bears the working title *Annual for Girls* – brief the artist to include various 'different breeds' of dogs – a requirement he certainly met – and mark the commission as 'urgent.'

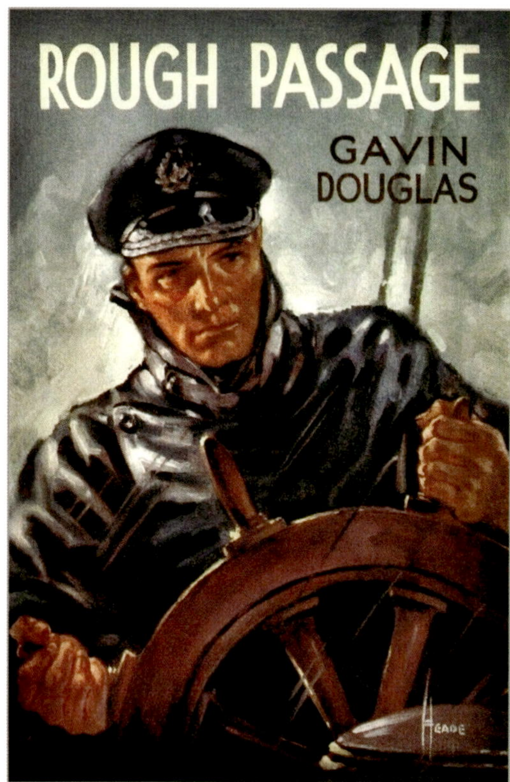

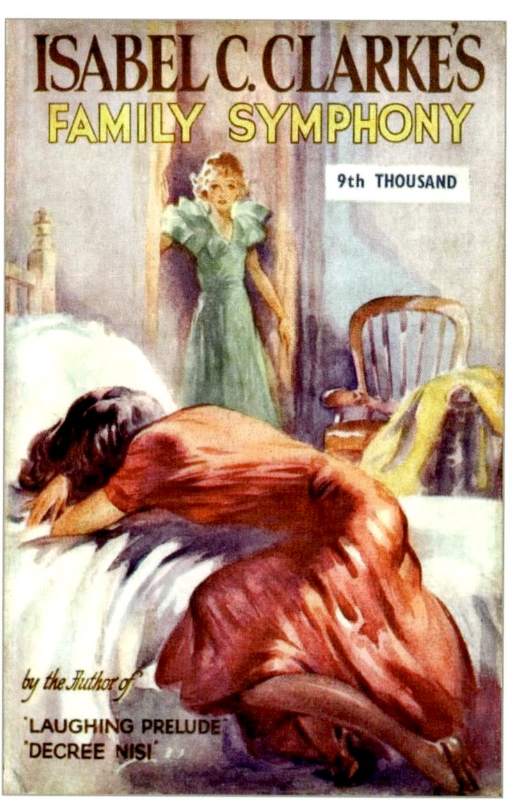

Rough Passage by Gavin Douglas (Collins, 1937)

Family Symphony by Isabel C Clarke (Hutchinson, c1937)

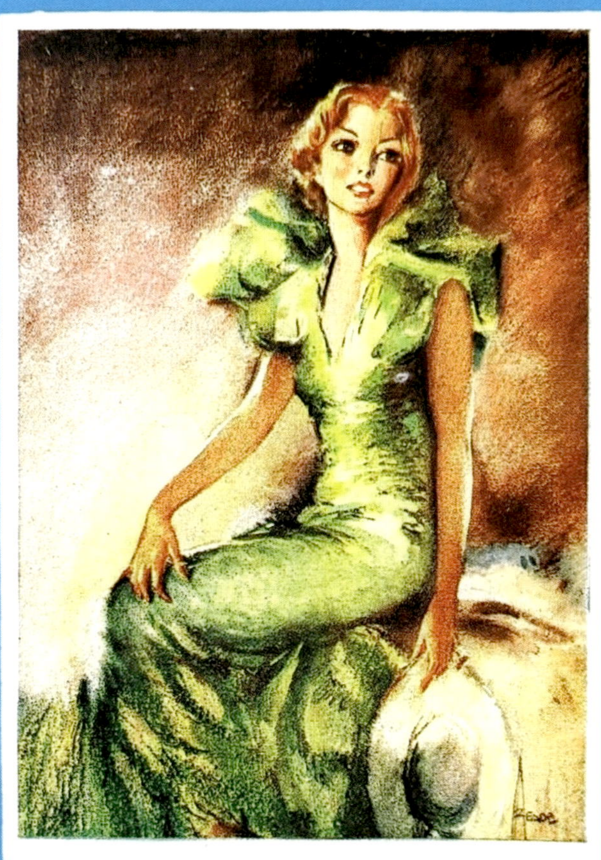

A Year With Juliet by Elizabeth Frayne (Hodder & Stoughton, 1937)

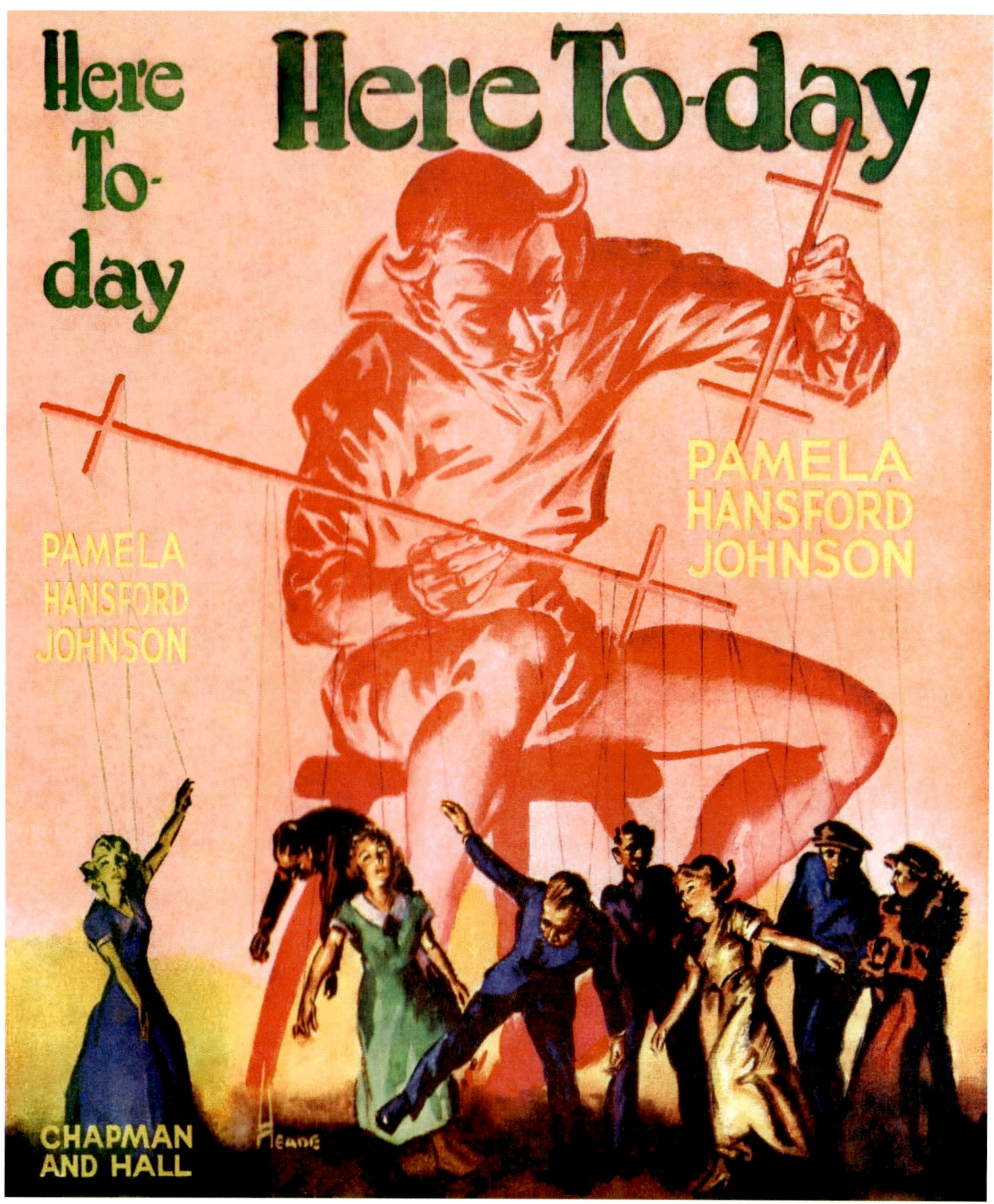

Here To-day by Pamela Hansford Johnson (Chapman & Hall, 1937)

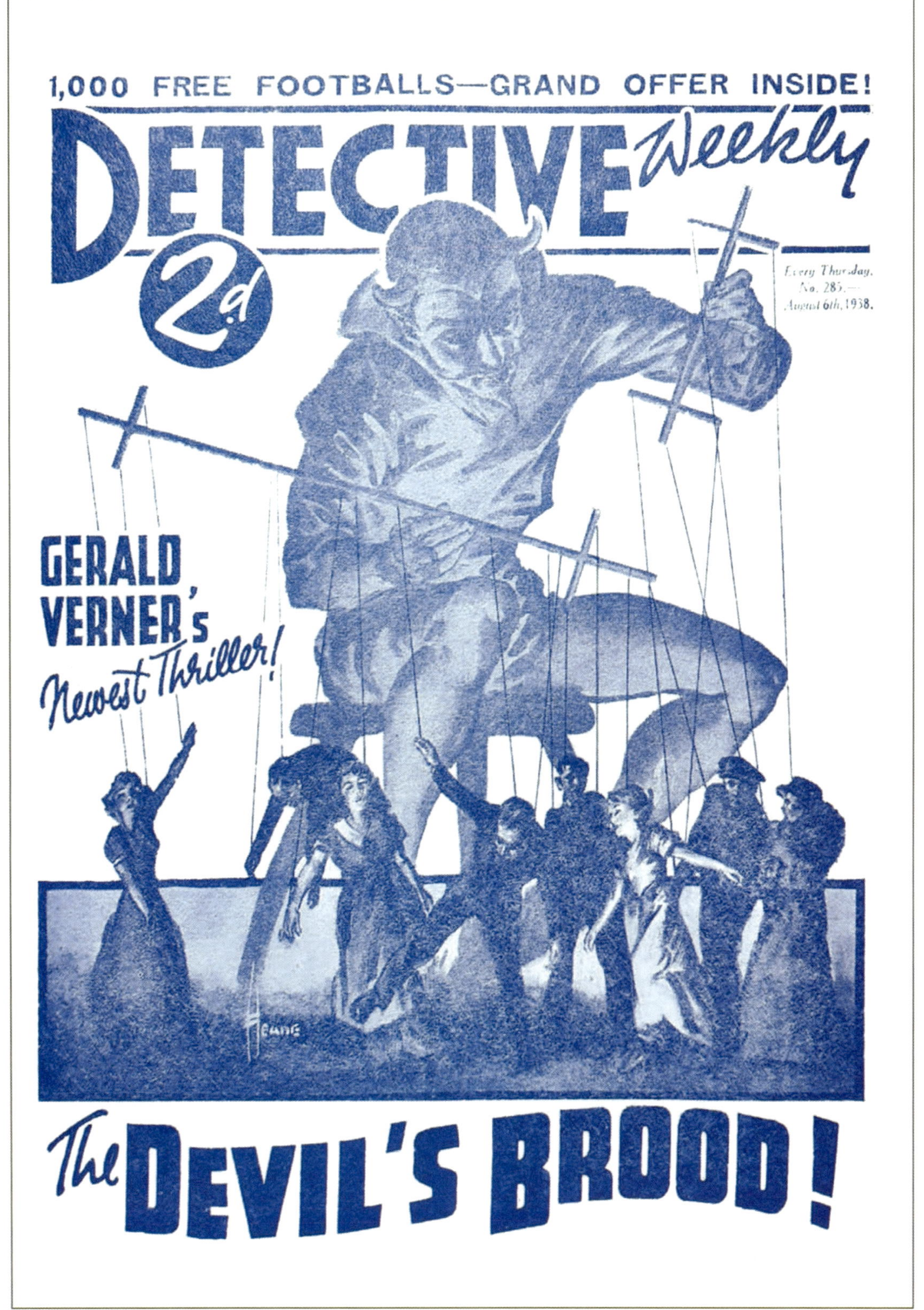

Heade's dustjacket art for *Here To-day* by Pamela Hansford Johnson (see opposite) was repurposed for the cover of # 285 of *Detective Weekly* (Amalgamated, 6 August 1938) (previously presented as only a small image on page 255 of *The Art of Reginald Heade – Special Edition*).

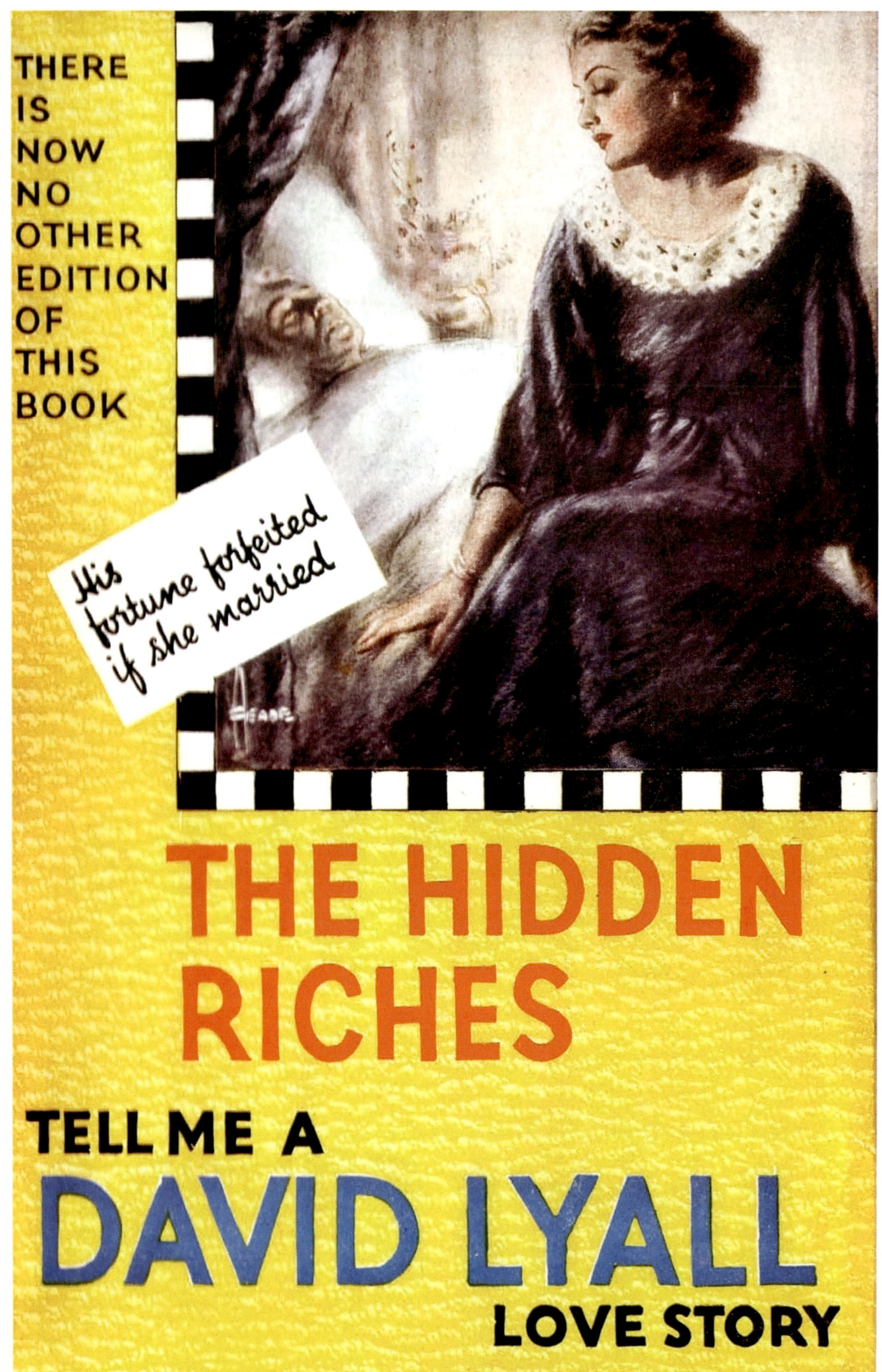

The Hidden Riches by David Lyall (Hodder & Stoughton, 1937)

The Story of an Ugly Man by Ruby M Ayres (Hodder & Stoughton, 1937)

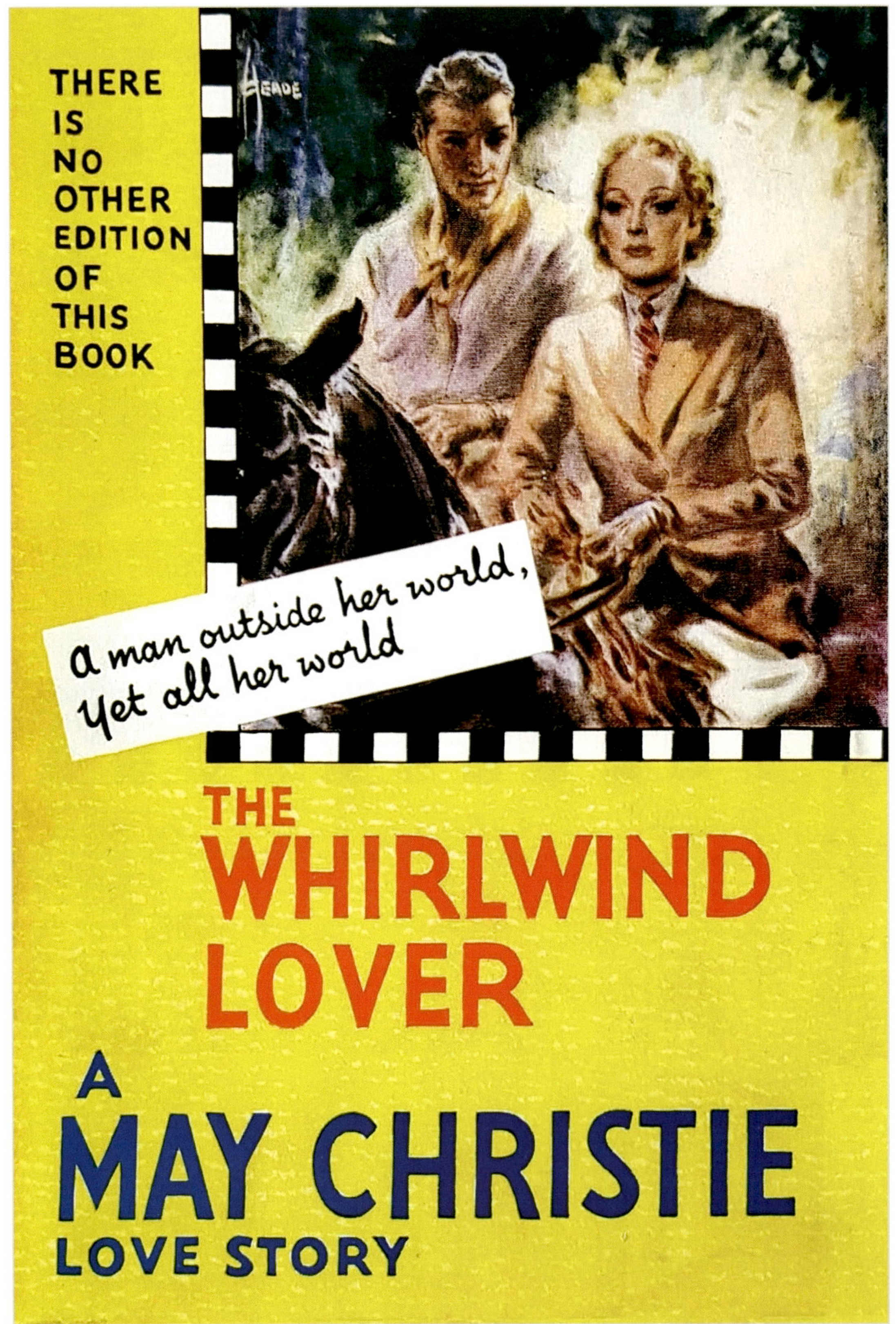

The Whirlwind Lover by May Christie (Hodder & Stoughton, c1937)

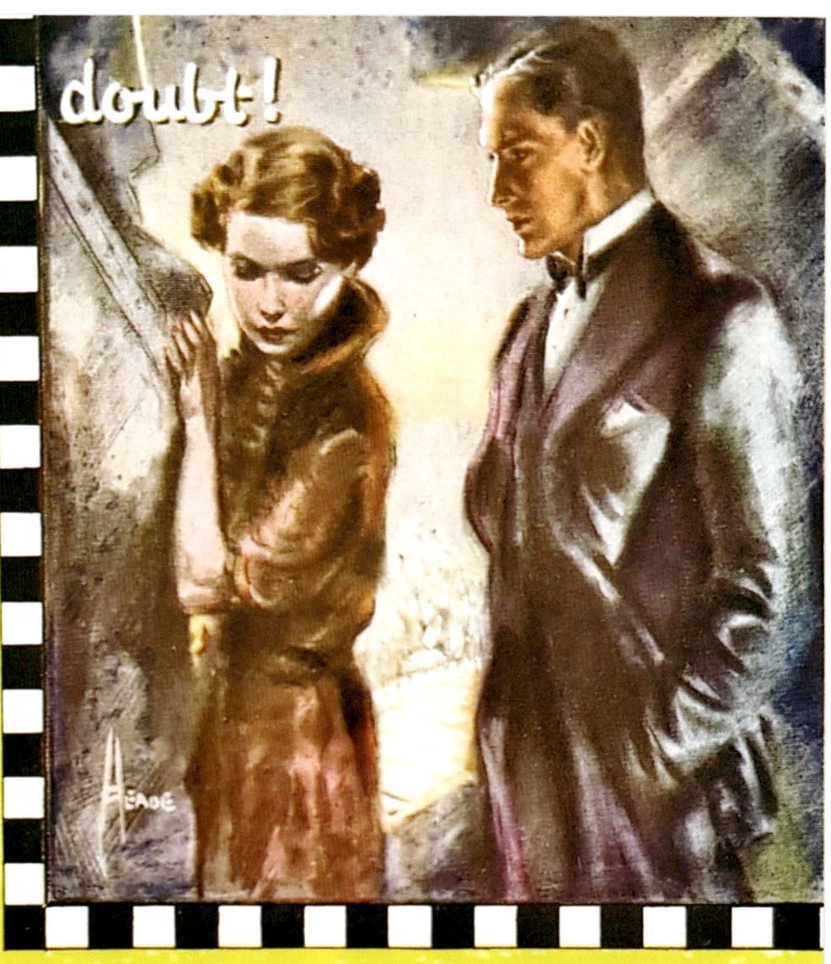

Julia Takes Her Chance by Concordia Merrel (Hodder & Stoughton, c1937)

CIGARETTE ADVERTISEMENTS

Many of Heade's sketches that still survive were executed in pencil on (now somewhat creased) sheets of drafting vellum – a type of flimsy, translucent artists' paper similar to tracing paper. These include the four pieces pictured below, which are believed to have been produced as preparatory drawings for cigarette advertisements, probably in the late 1930s. (A variation on the second one, on standard paper, in which the male figure is without a hat, is also shown at the front of this volume.) They were accompanied by a more finished rough, drawn on a board, as pictured on the facing page. It is unknown what brand of cigarettes these were for, or where they were intended to appear, and no printed copies of the final advertisements have yet been found.

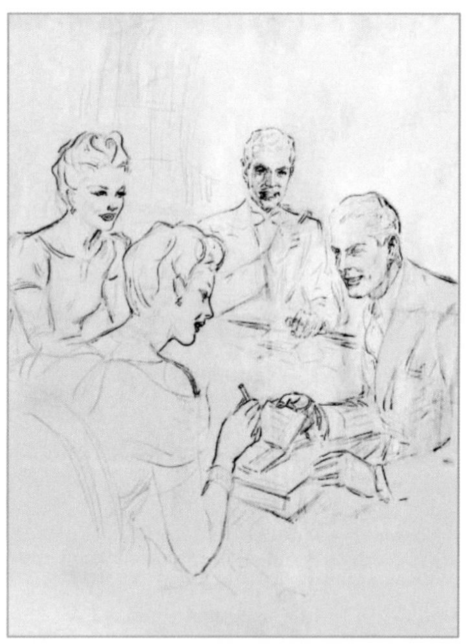
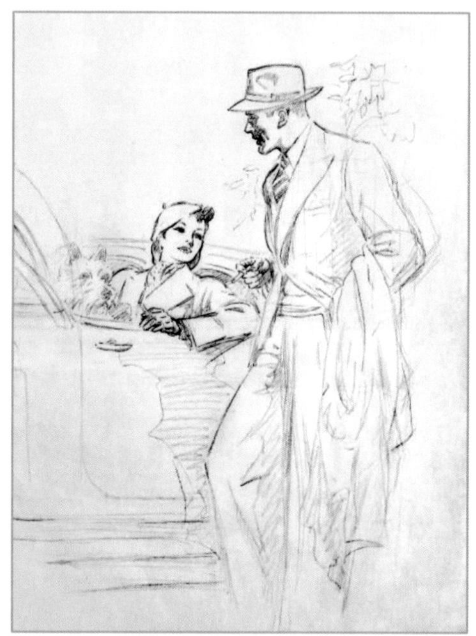
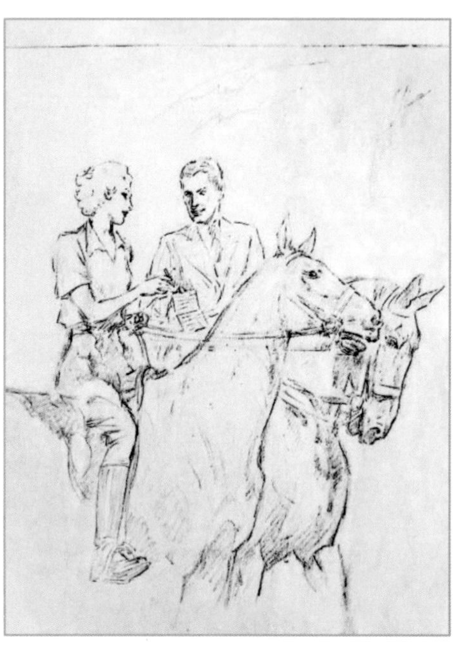
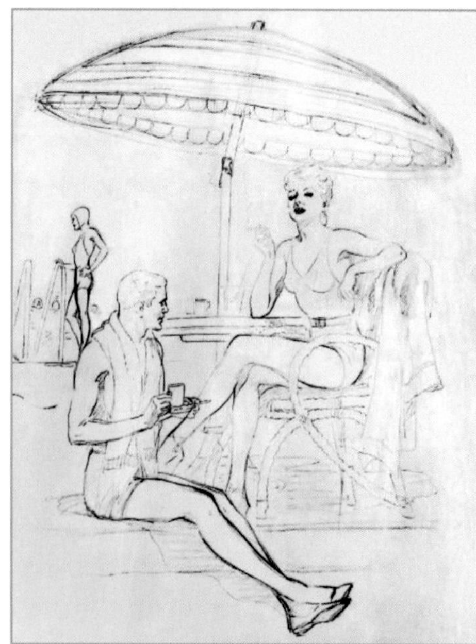

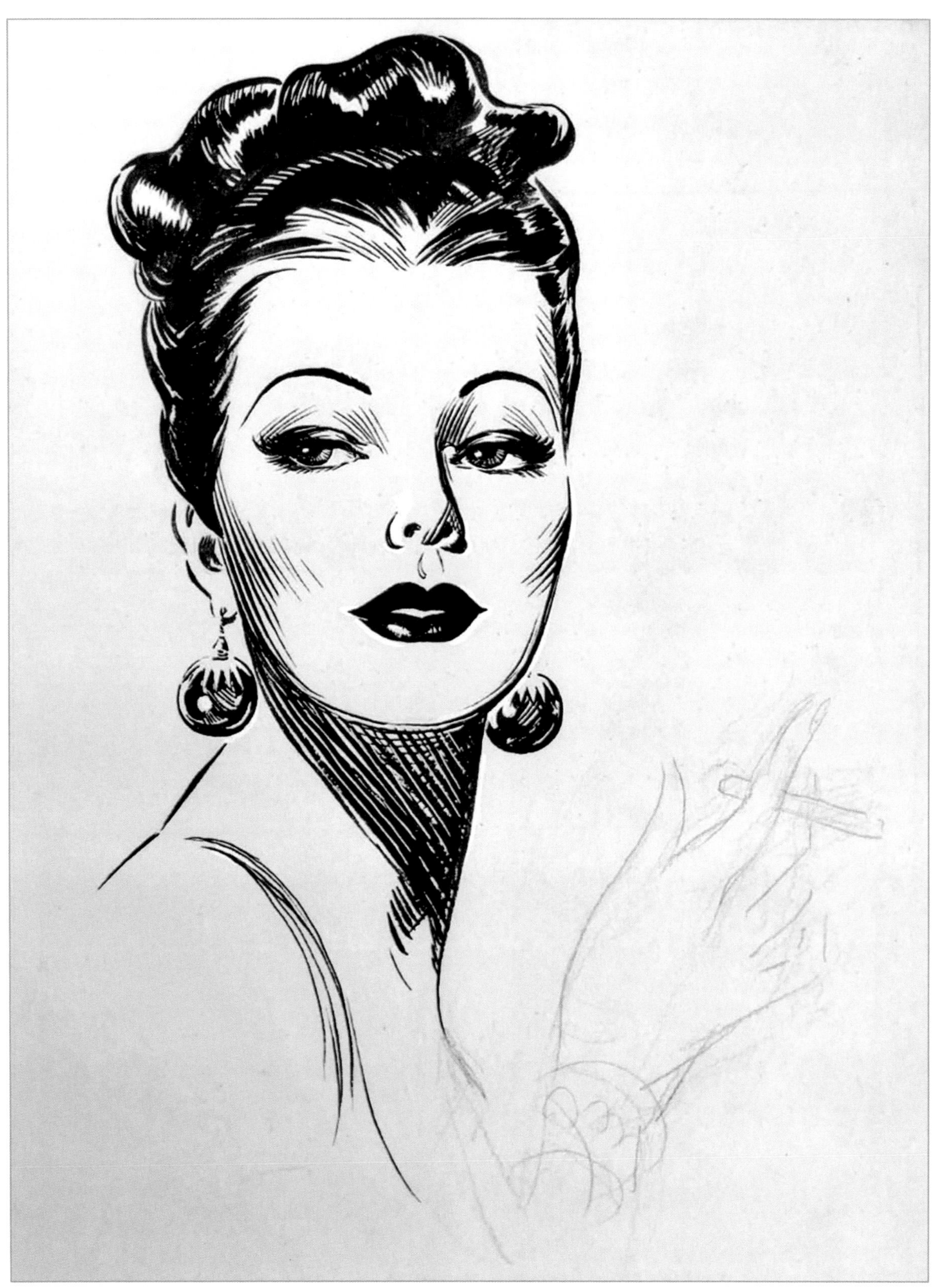

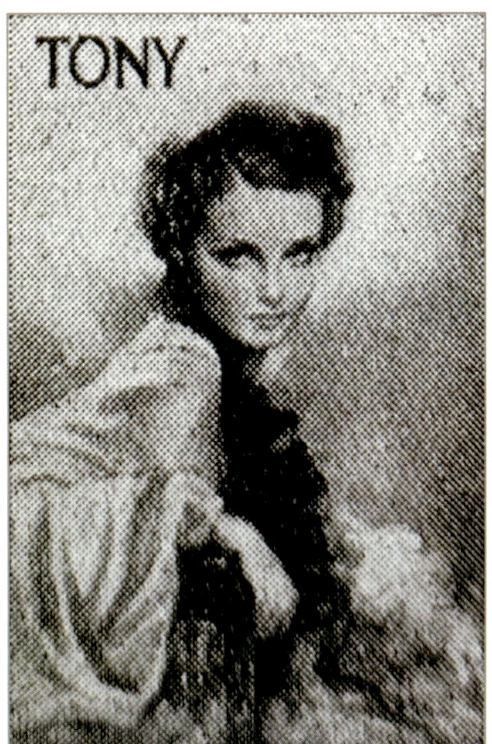

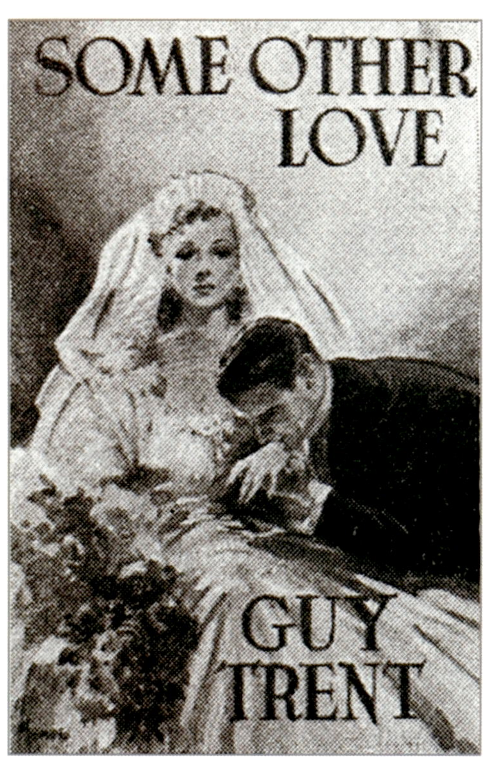

Above: *Tony* by Elizabeth Vernon (Hodder & Stoughton, 12 July 1937) and *Some Other Love* by Guy Trent (Mills & Boon, 1939). Occasionally, pictures of rare Heade dustjacket paintings can be found in contemporary printed items such as publishers' catalogues and magazine advertisements. Both these images derive from such sources. Sadly, no colour copies have yet been found.

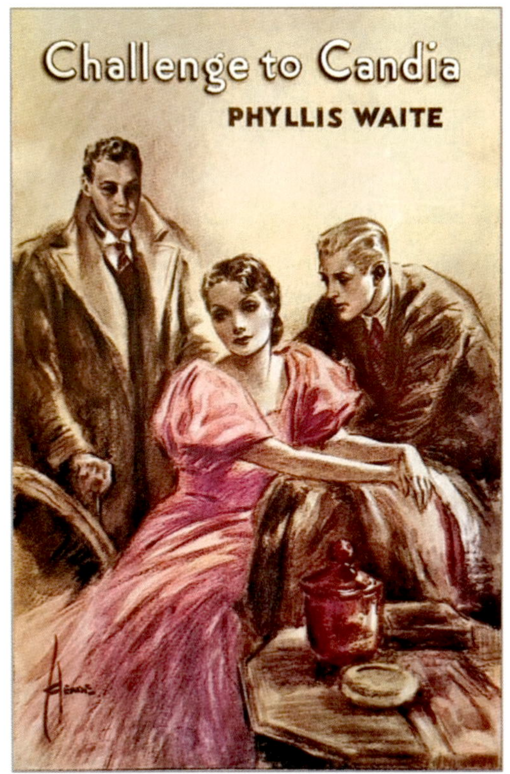

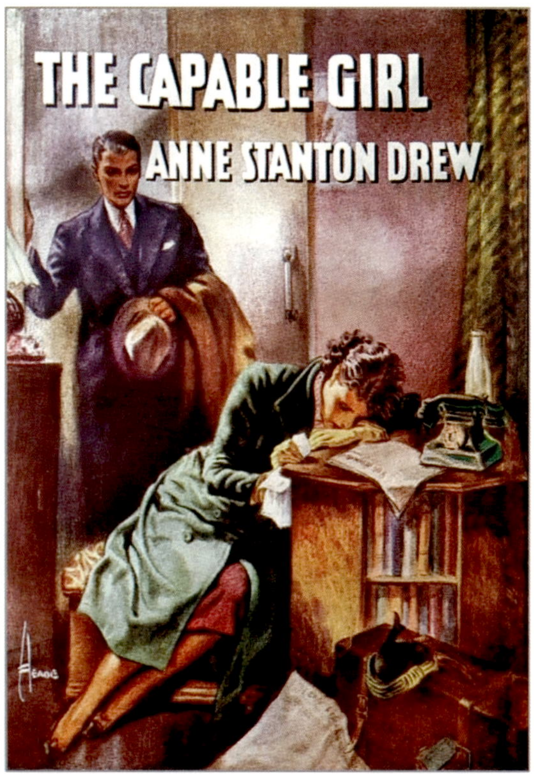

Challenge to Candia by Phyllis Waite and *The Capable Girl* by Anne Stanton Drew (both Hodder & Stoughton 1937)

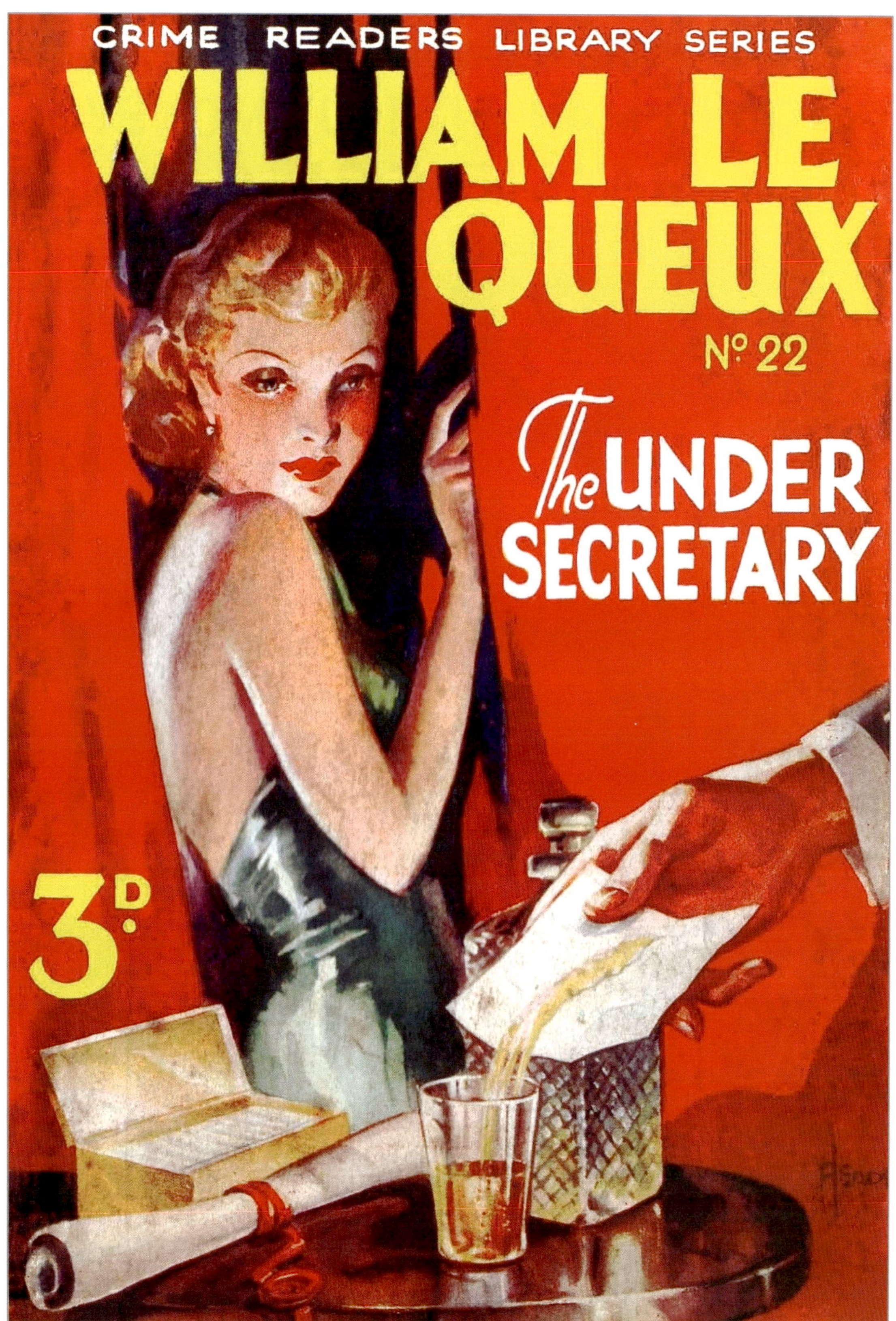

The Under Secretary by William le Queux (Leisure Library Co, 1937)

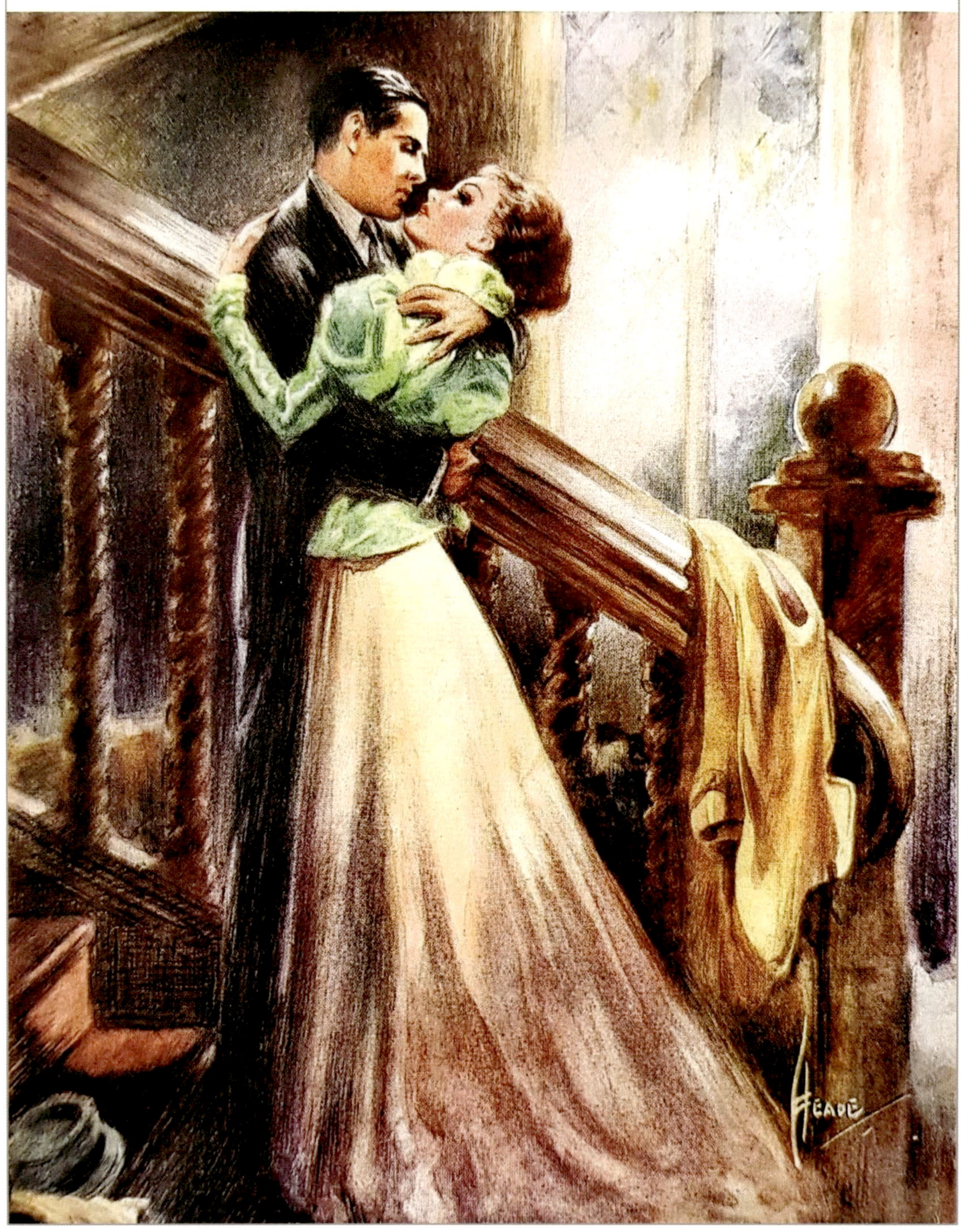

Young Man Without Money by Maysie Greig (Hodder & Stoughton, 1938)

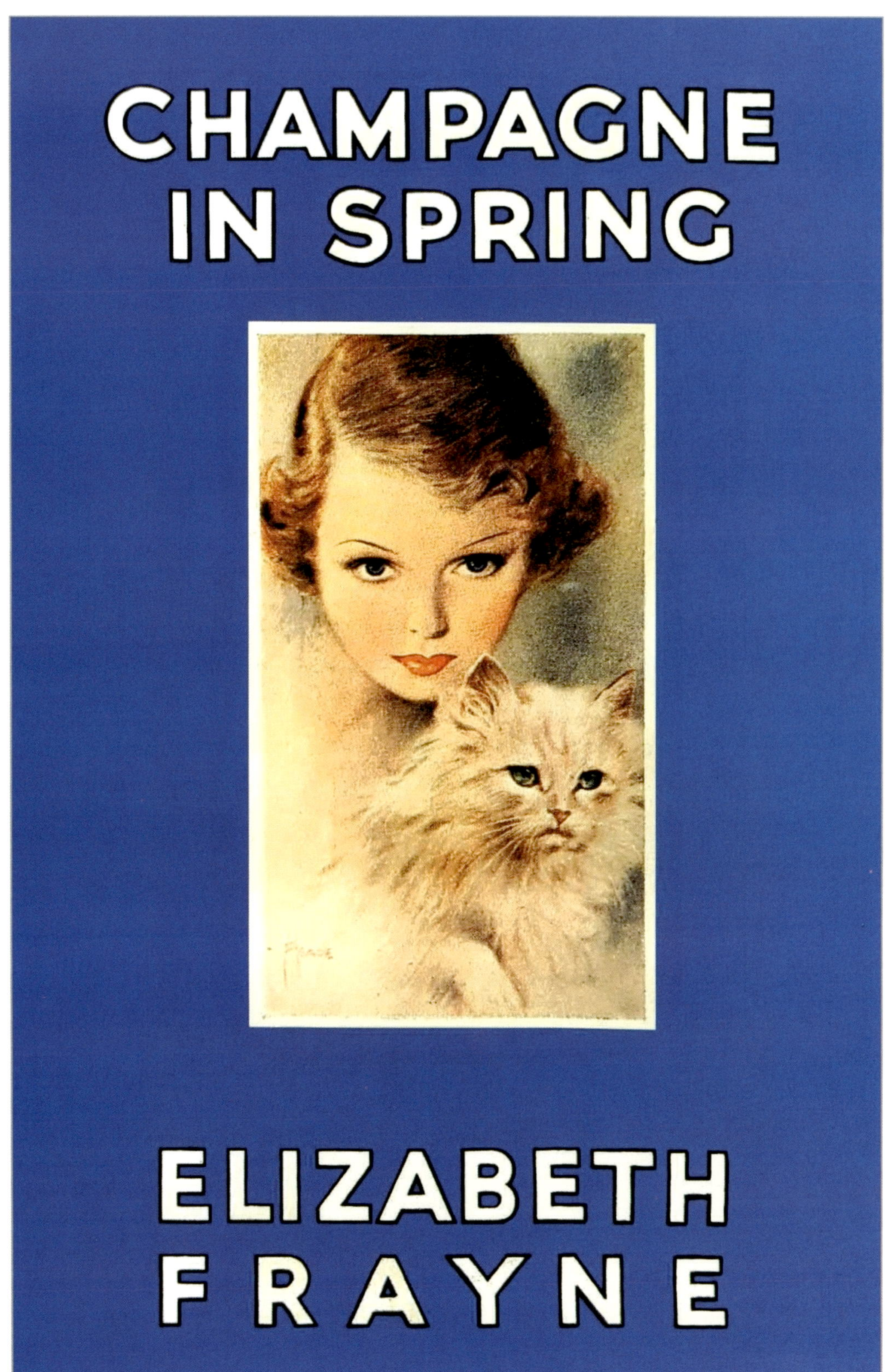

Champagne in Spring by Elizabeth Frayne (Hodder & Stoughton, 1938). The picture of the girl and cat was also used on the book's spine.

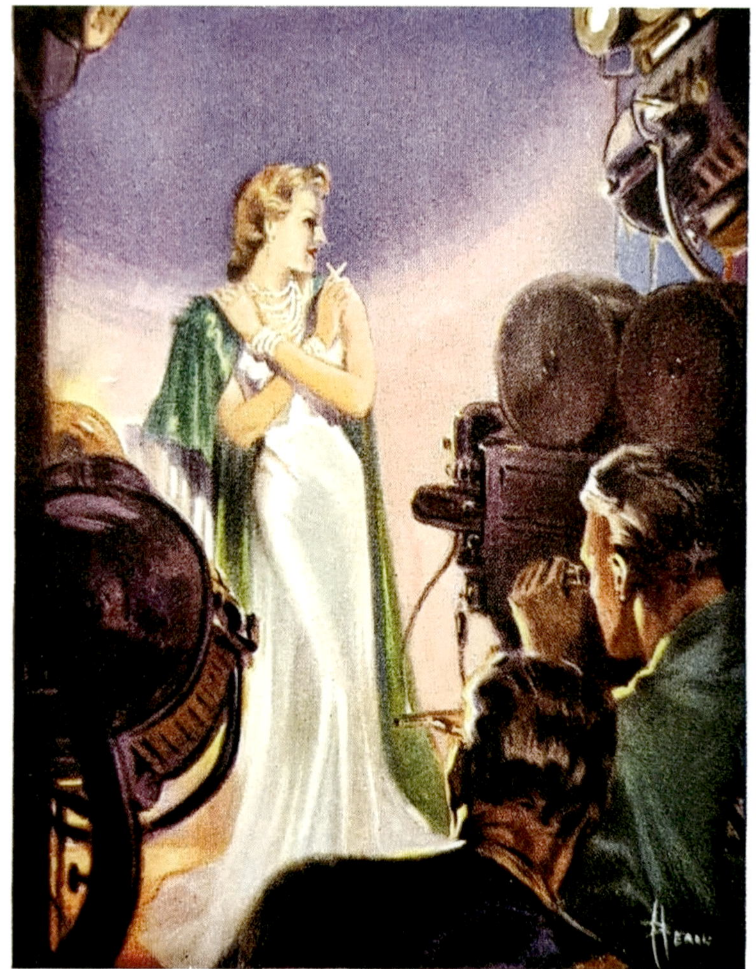

Handmaid to Face by Berta Ruck (Hodder & Stoughton, 1938)

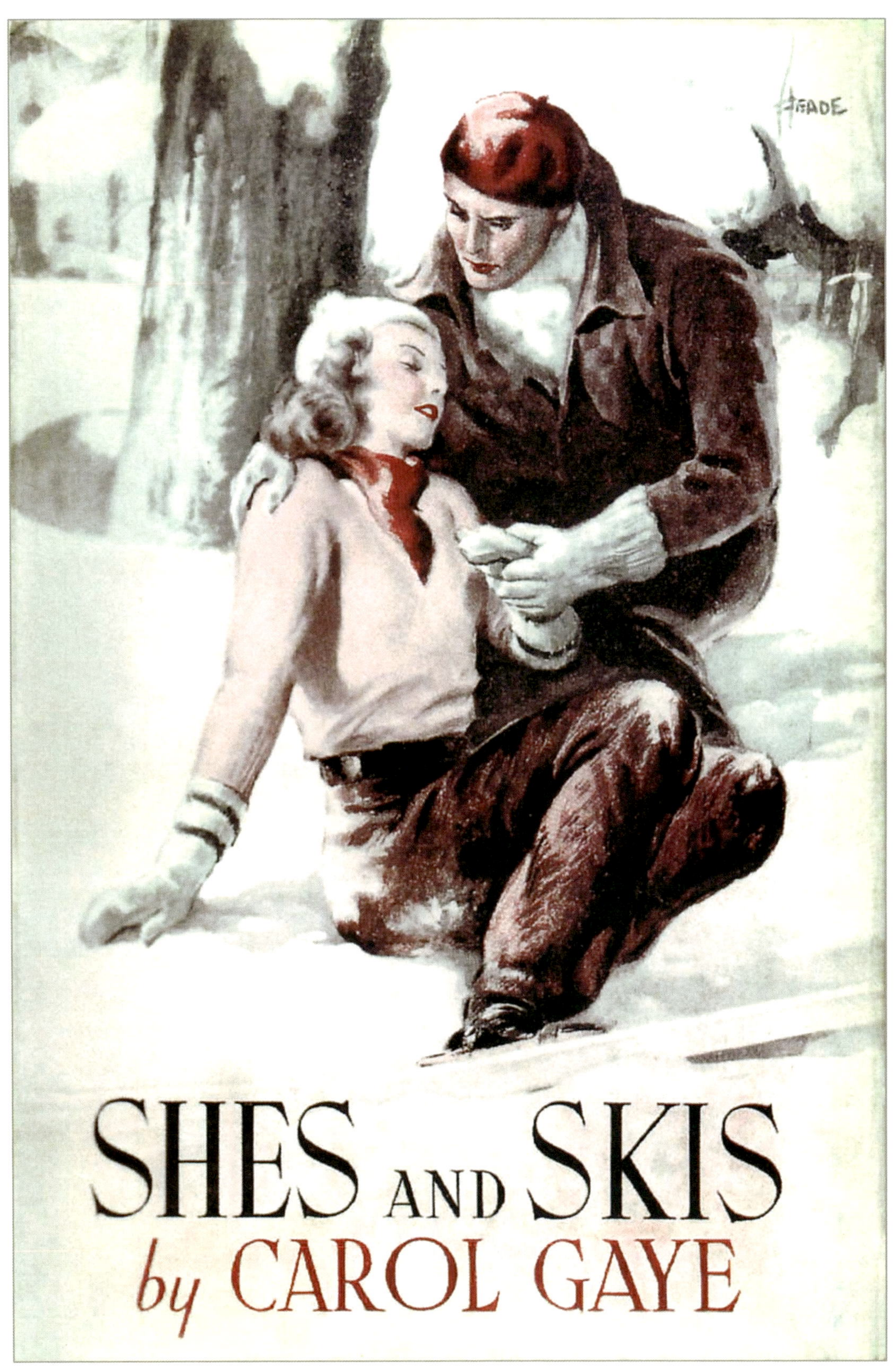

Shes and Skis by Carol Gaye (Collins, 1939)

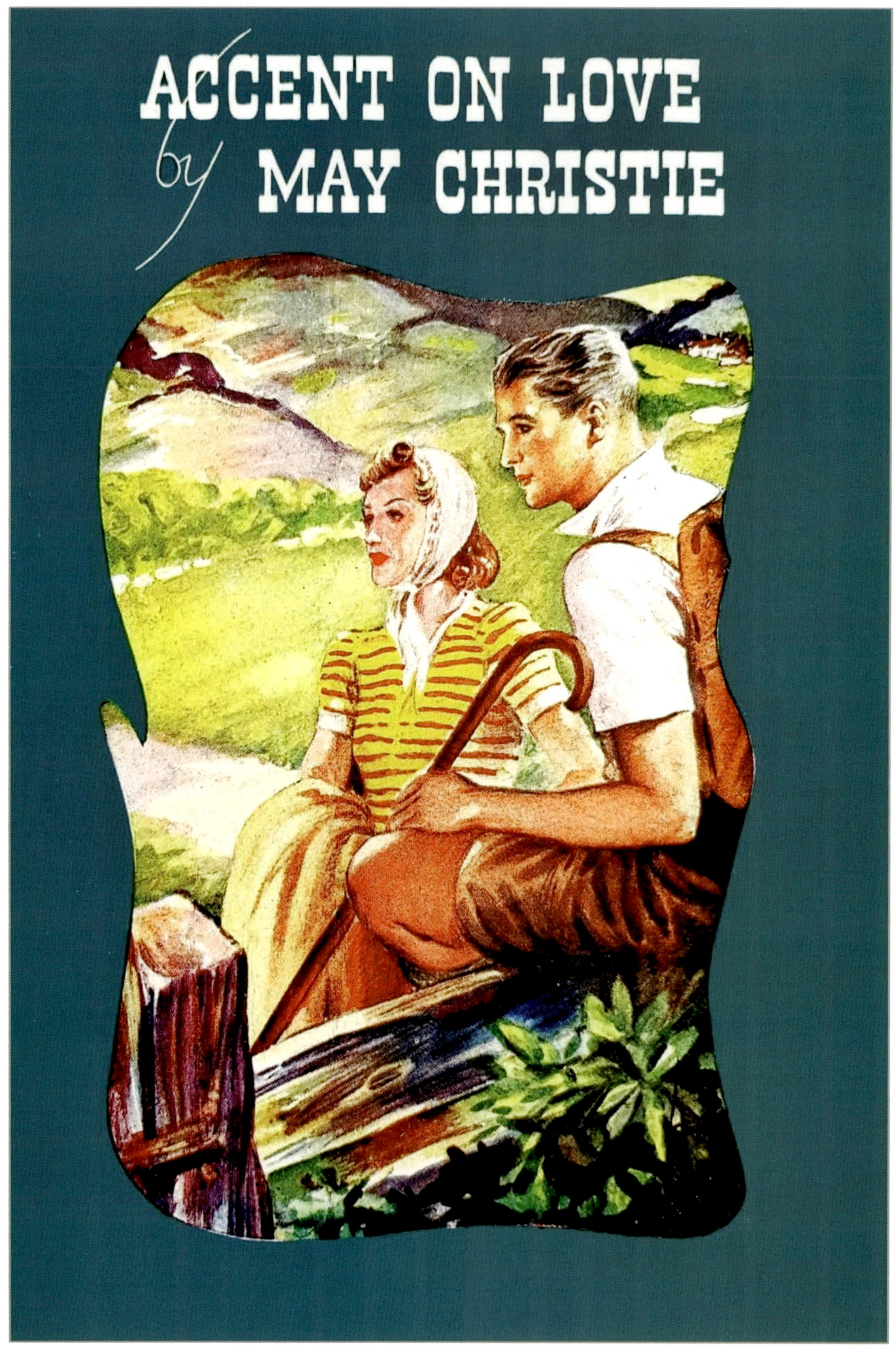

Accent on Love by May Christie (Hodder & Stoughton, 1939)

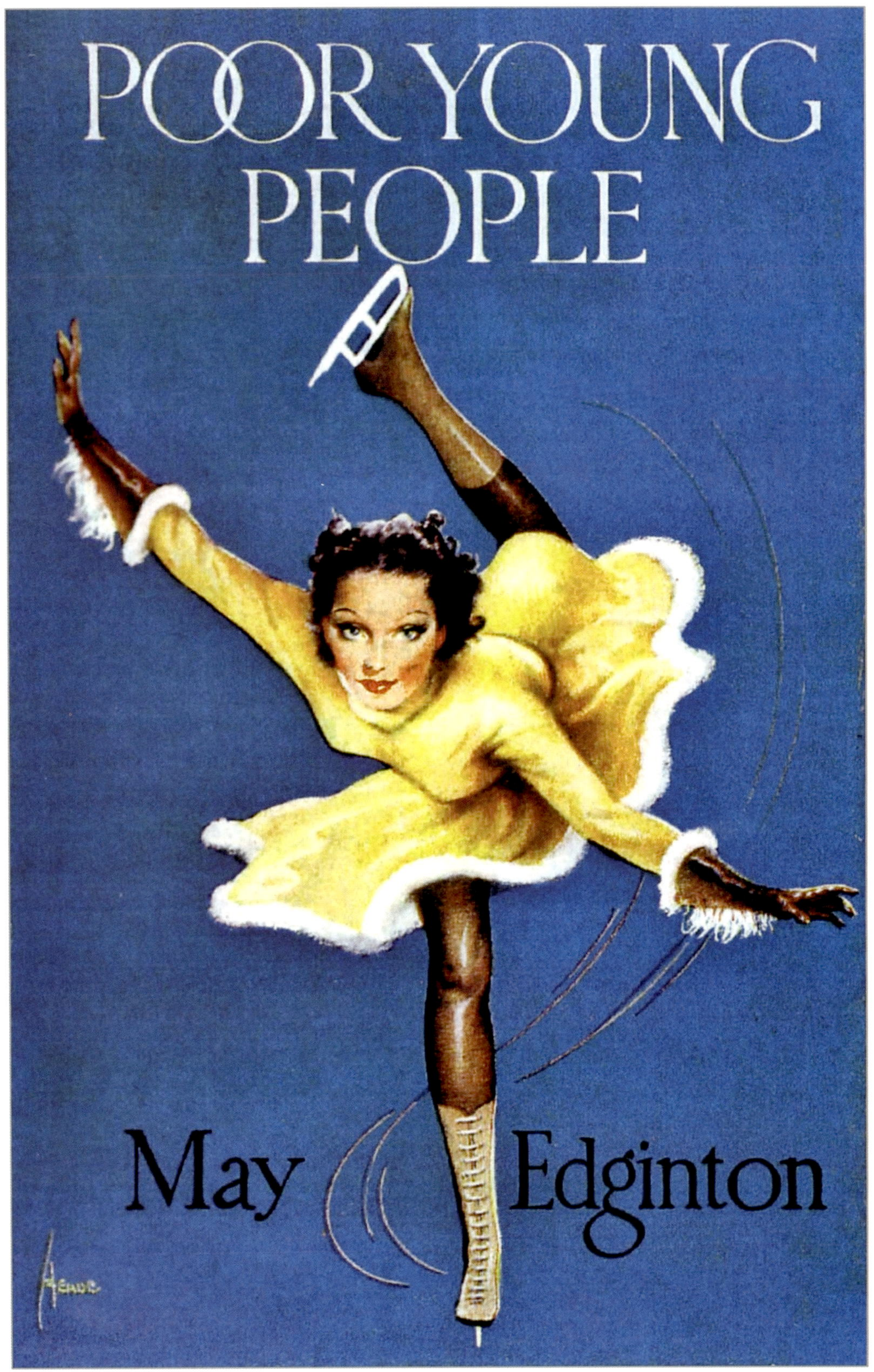

Poor Young People by May Edginton (Collins, 1939)

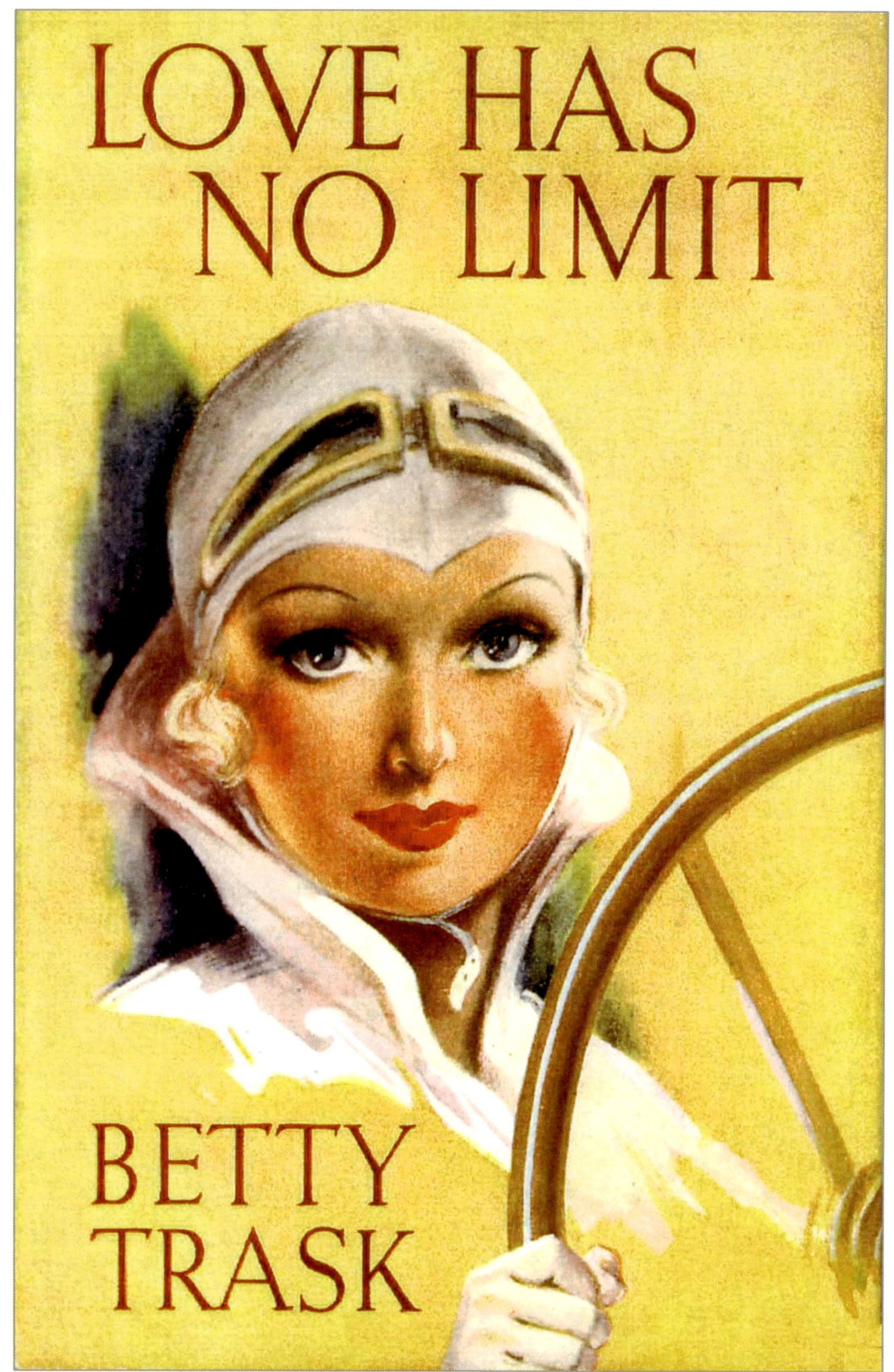

Love Has No Limit by Betty Trask (Collins, 1939)

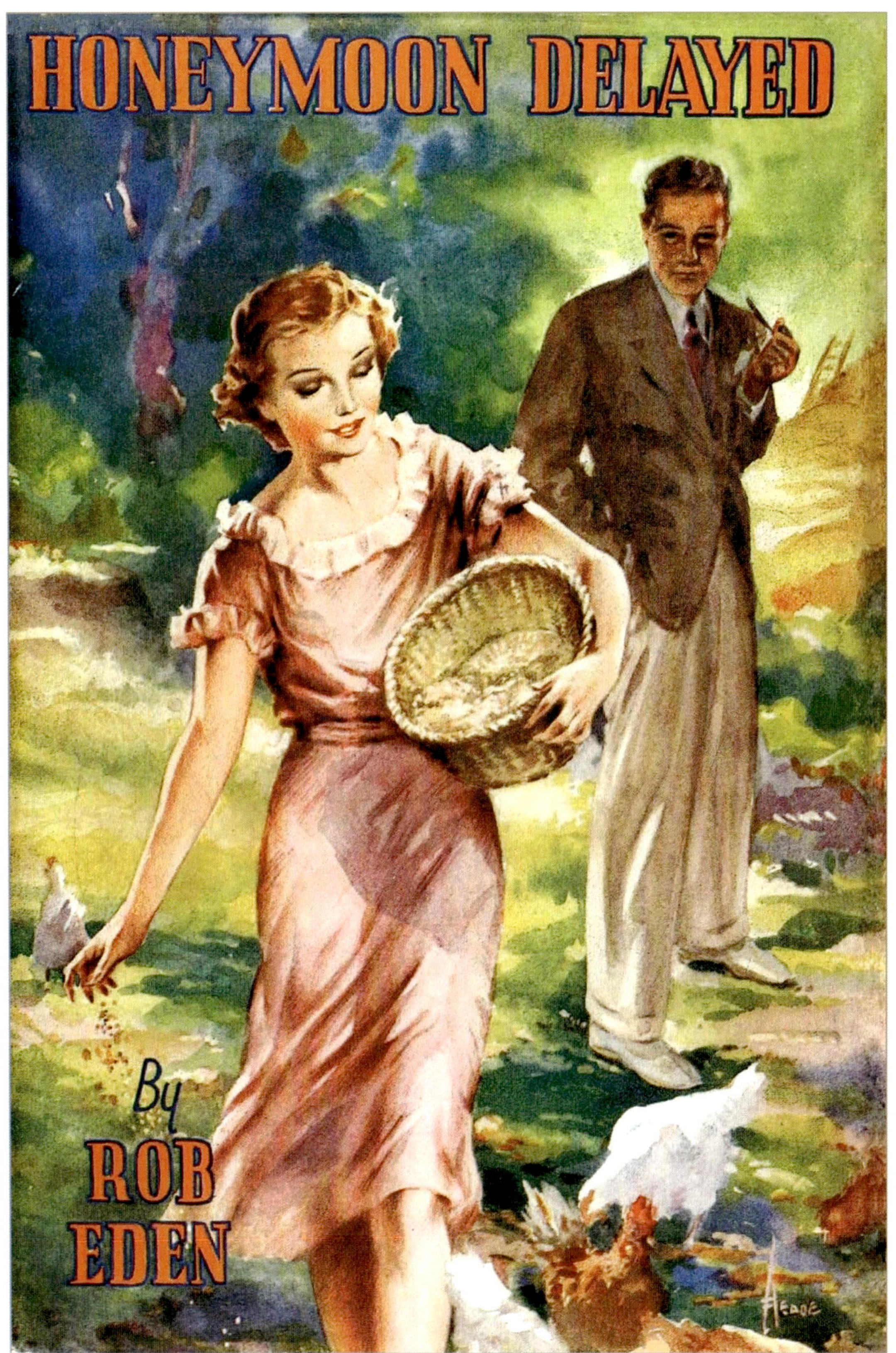

Honeymoon Delayed by Rob Eden (Robert Hale, 1939)

ARTWORK ADAPTATIONS

A number of Heade's cover paintings were used more than once, with either minor or major adaptations – the dustjacket piece for Pamela Hansford Johnson's novel *Here To-day*, for instance, being repurposed for an issue of *Detective Weekly* magazine, as illustrated earlier in this section. Of the main hardback publishers, Hodder & Stoughton were particularly inclined to resort to multiple uses of the same artwork, with their 'Yellow Jacket' and other editions. Three cases in point are shown over this and the facing page. Pictured below left is the original 1937 edition of *Flame in the Wind* by Margaret Pedler, on which Heade's painting was presented in full. Later 'Yellow Jacket' reissues used only sections of the composition. Below right, top: the 1938 edition. Below right, bottom: the 1953 edition. Examples of Heade paintings being reused and repurposed by the hardback publishers Collins and Mills & Boon, and by the pulp paperback publishers, are given in later sections of this volume.

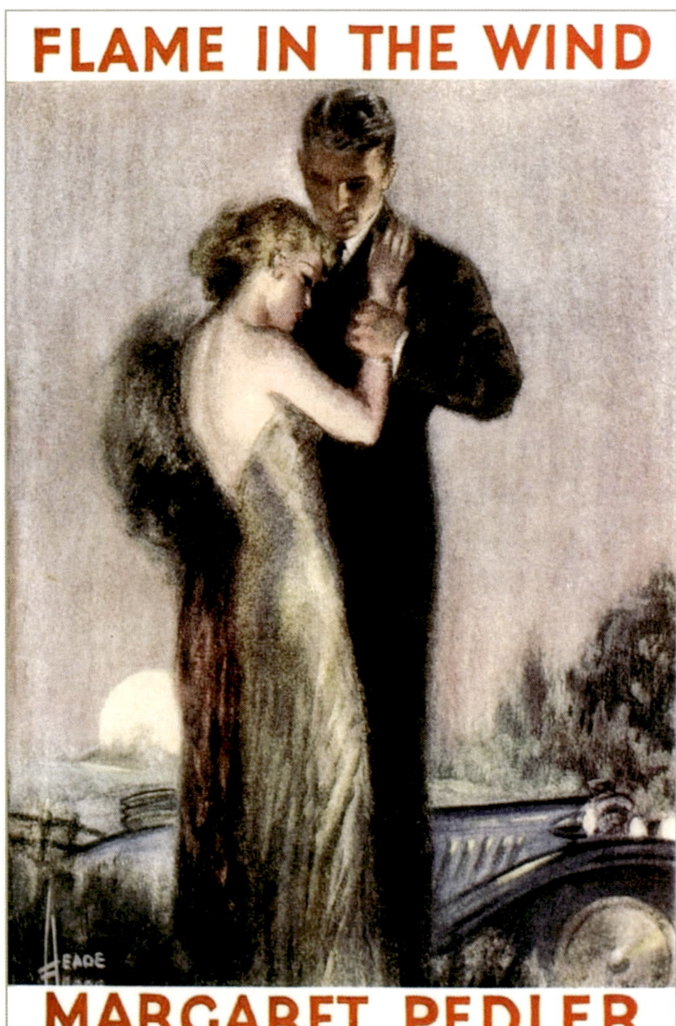

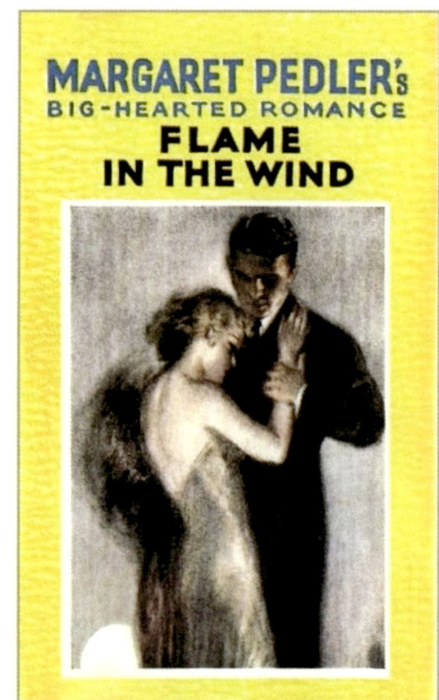

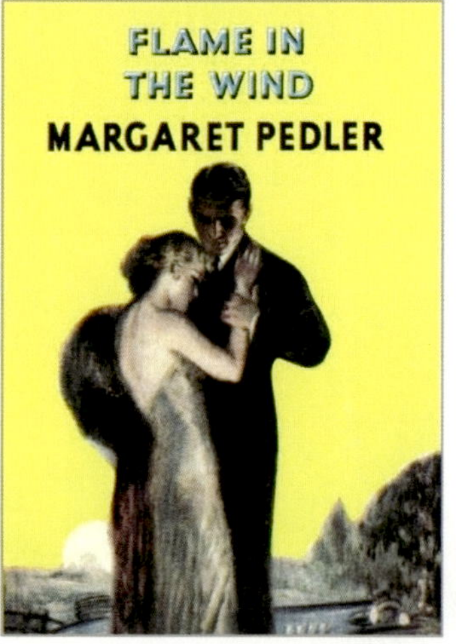

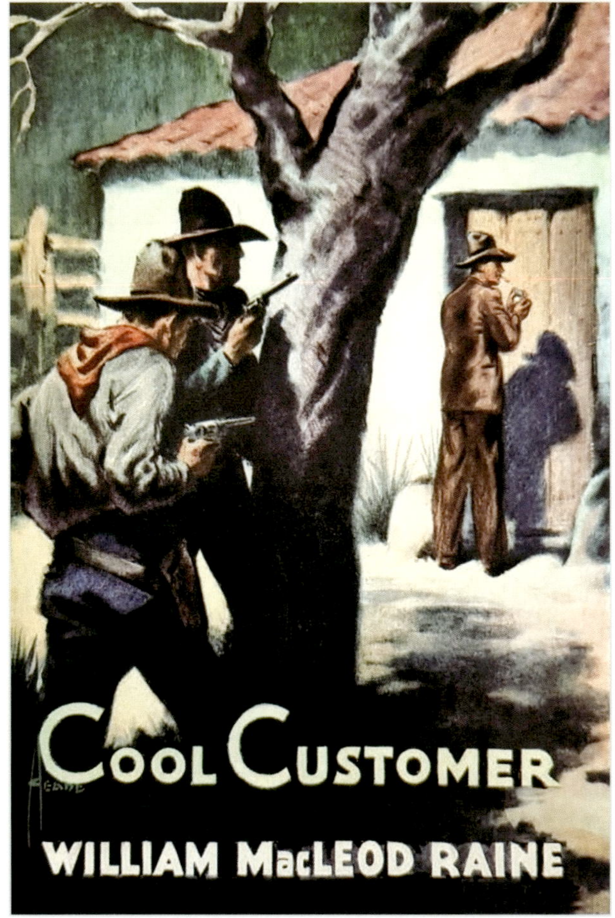
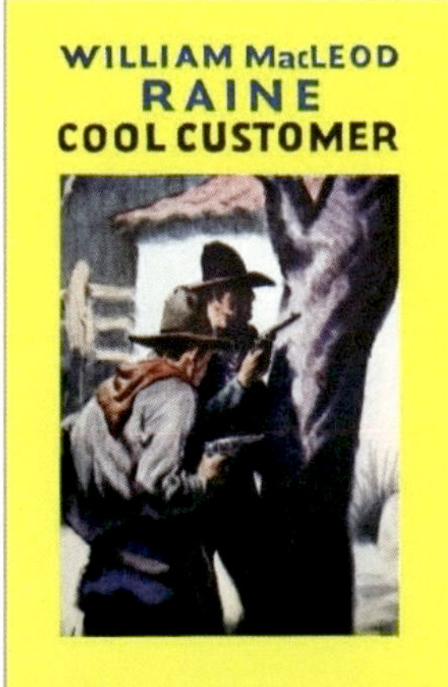
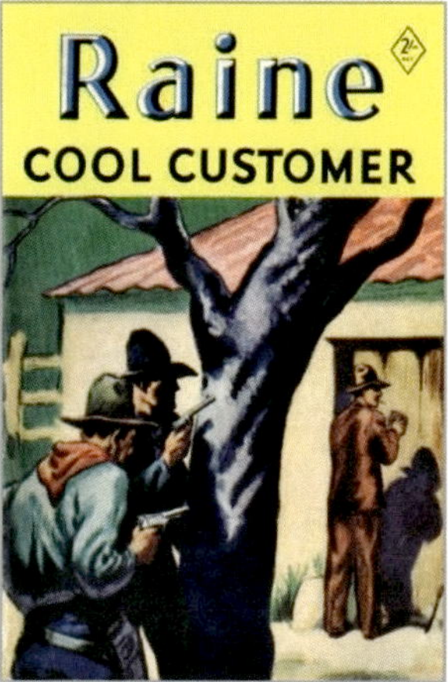

Cool Customer by William MacLeod Raine. Above left, the original 1937 edition; above right, top, a c1940 'Yellow Jacket' reissue; above right, bottom, a 1954 'Yellow Jacket' paperback edition.

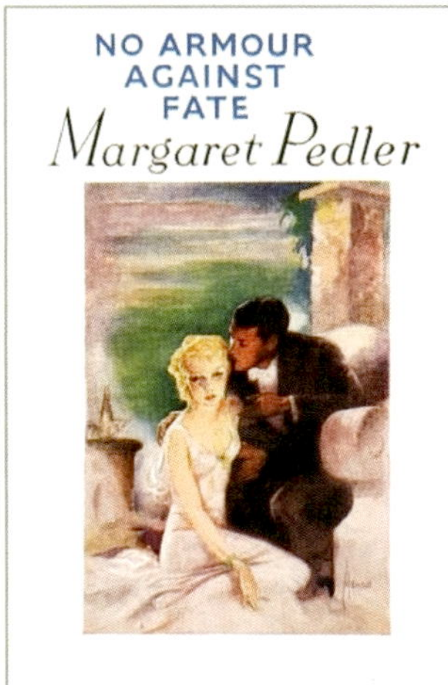
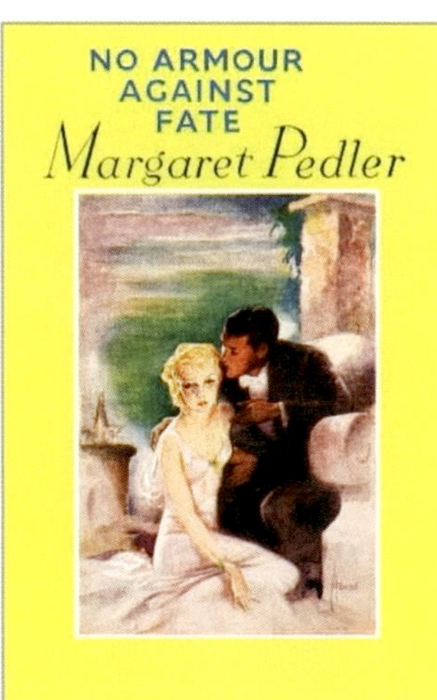
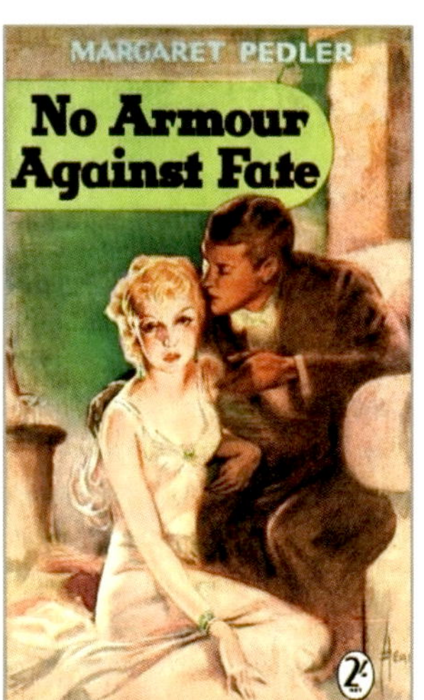

No Armour Against Fate by Margaret Pedler. Above left, the original 1938 edition; above centre, a c1939 'Yellow Jacket' reissue; above right, a 1958 paperback edition. (A further, 1940 'Yellow Jacket' edition was pictured on page 136 of *The Art of Reginald Heade – Special Edition*.)

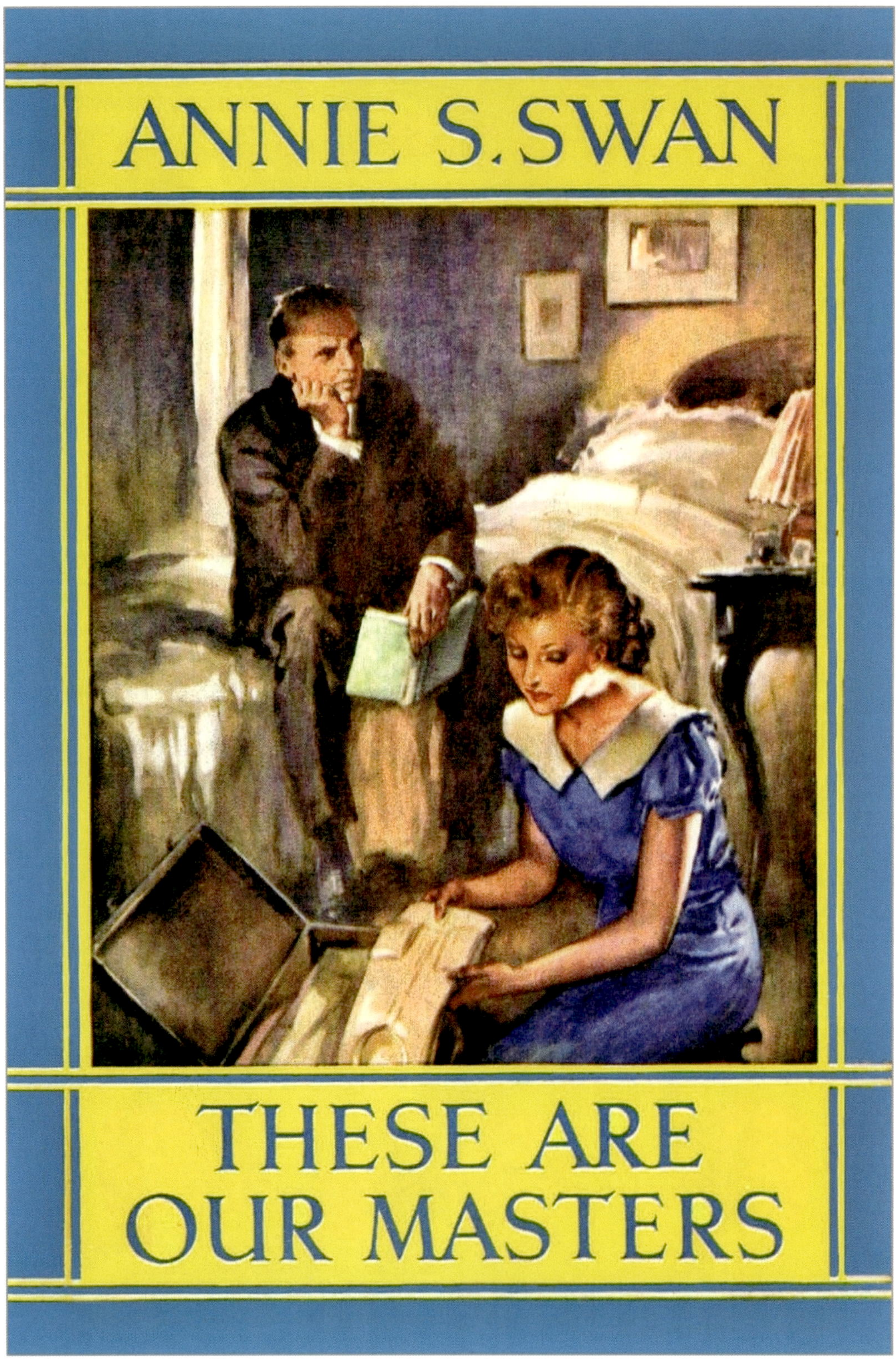

These Are Our Masters by Annie S Swan (Hodder & Stoughton, 1939). Although no signature is visible, the style of this dustjacket piece leaves no room for doubt that it is Heade's work. The book was reissued the following year in a 'Yellow Jacket' edition, with the artwork in more cropped form, as pictured in the Heade checklist at the back of this volume.

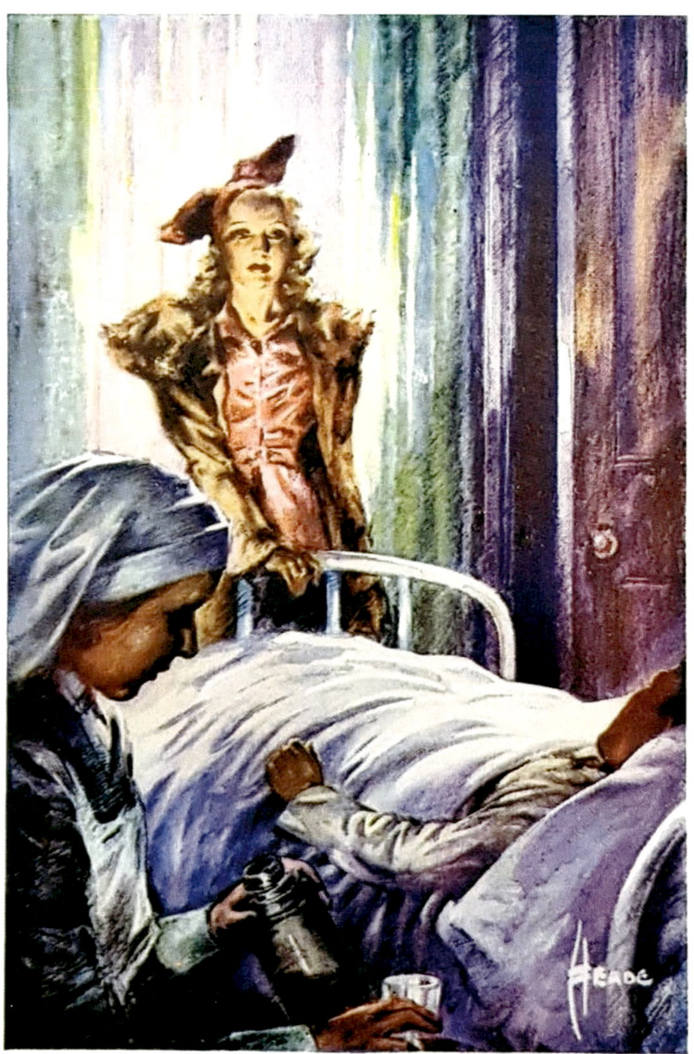

Girl on His Hands by Maysie Greig (Hodder & Stoughton, 1939). This novel was reissued in 'Yellow Jacket' form around a year later, with the artwork rather clumsily adapted by the publisher's art department, as pictured in the Heade checklist at the back of this volume.

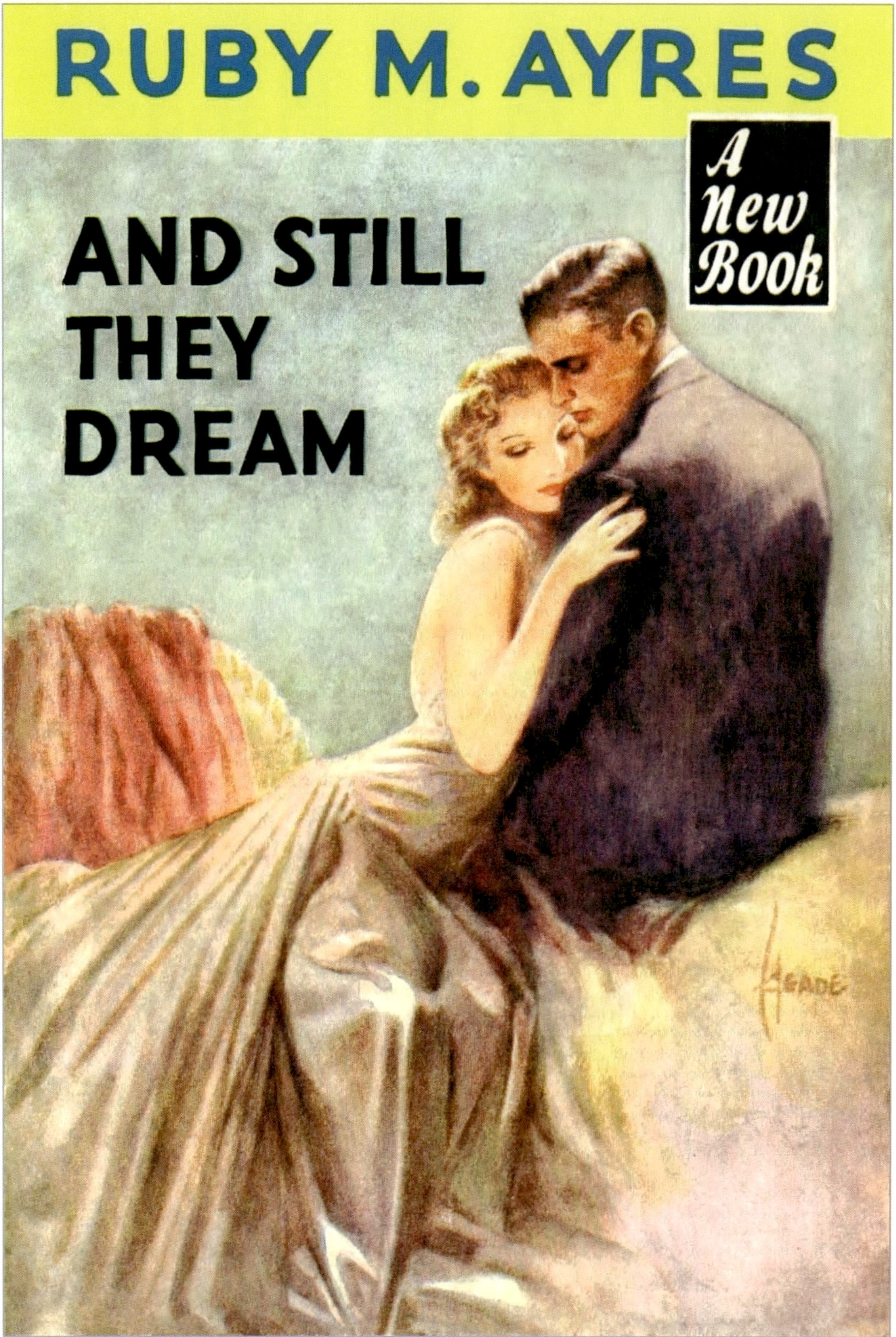

And Still They Dream by Ruby M Ayres (Hodder & Stoughton, 1939). This rare edition was mentioned on page 136 of *The Art of Reginald Heade – Special Edition*, but no image was available at that time.

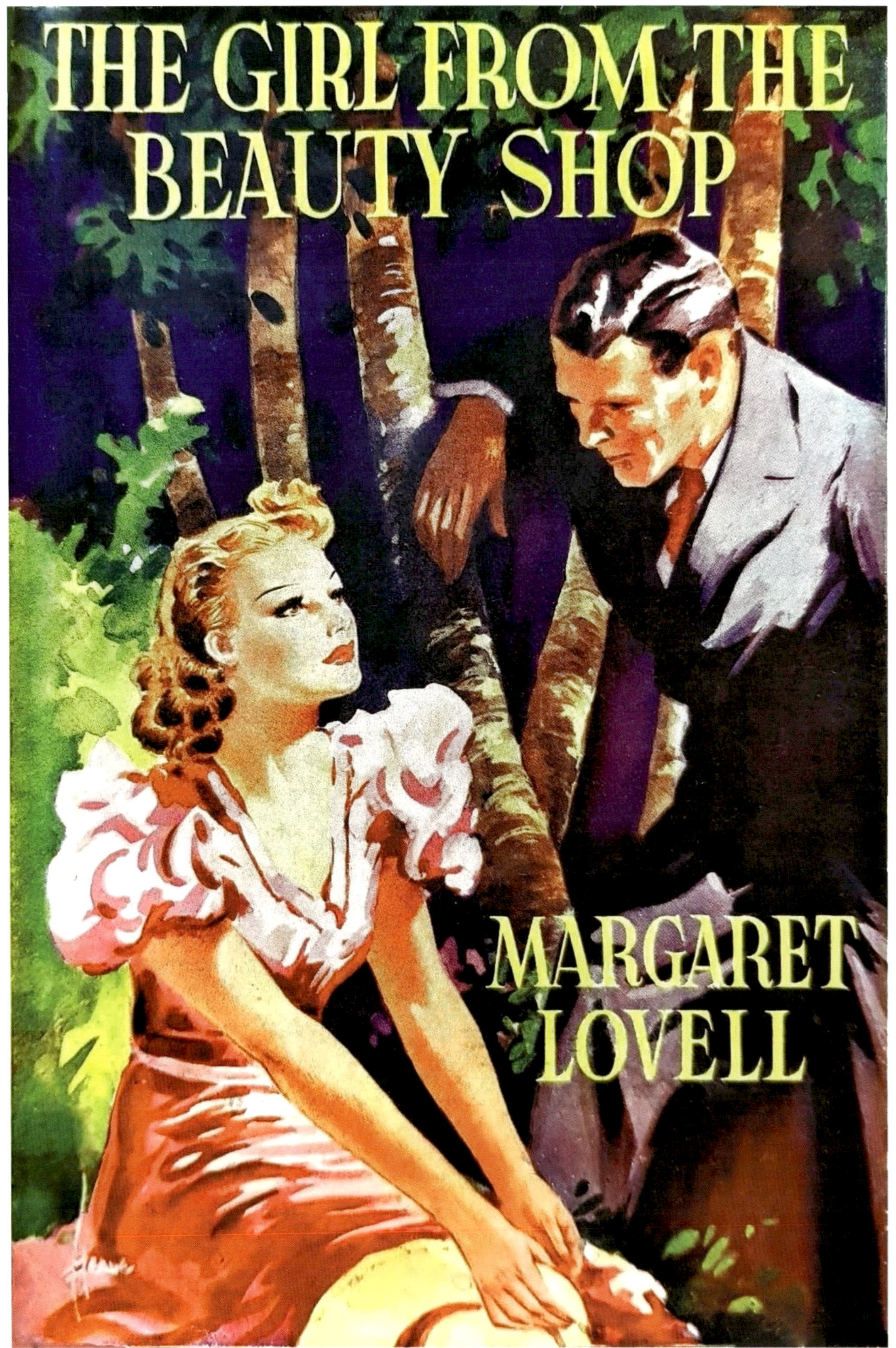

The Girl from the Beauty Shop by Margaret Lovell (Mills & Boon, August 1939)

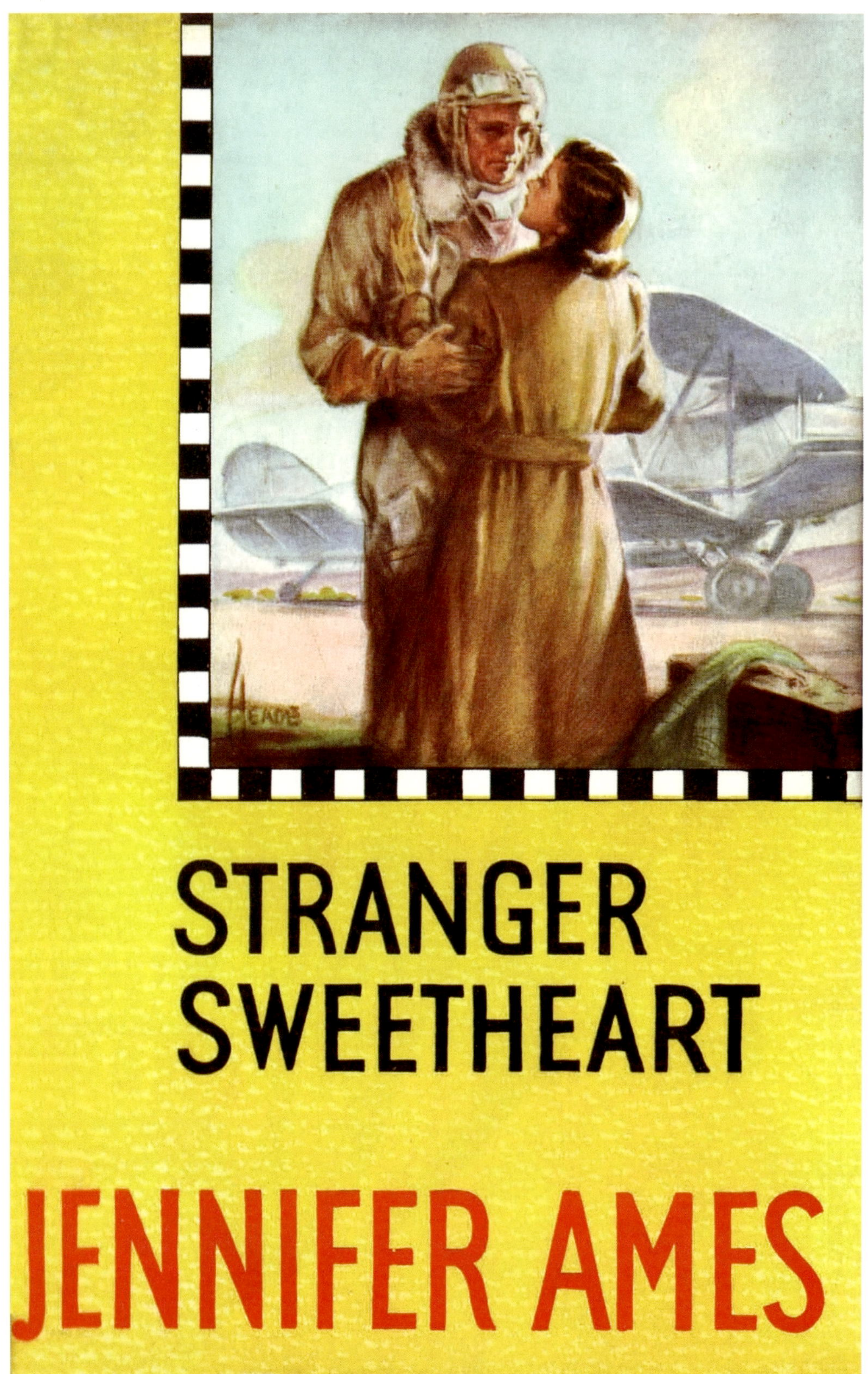

Stranger Sweetheart by Jennifer Ames (Hodder & Stoughton, 1939)

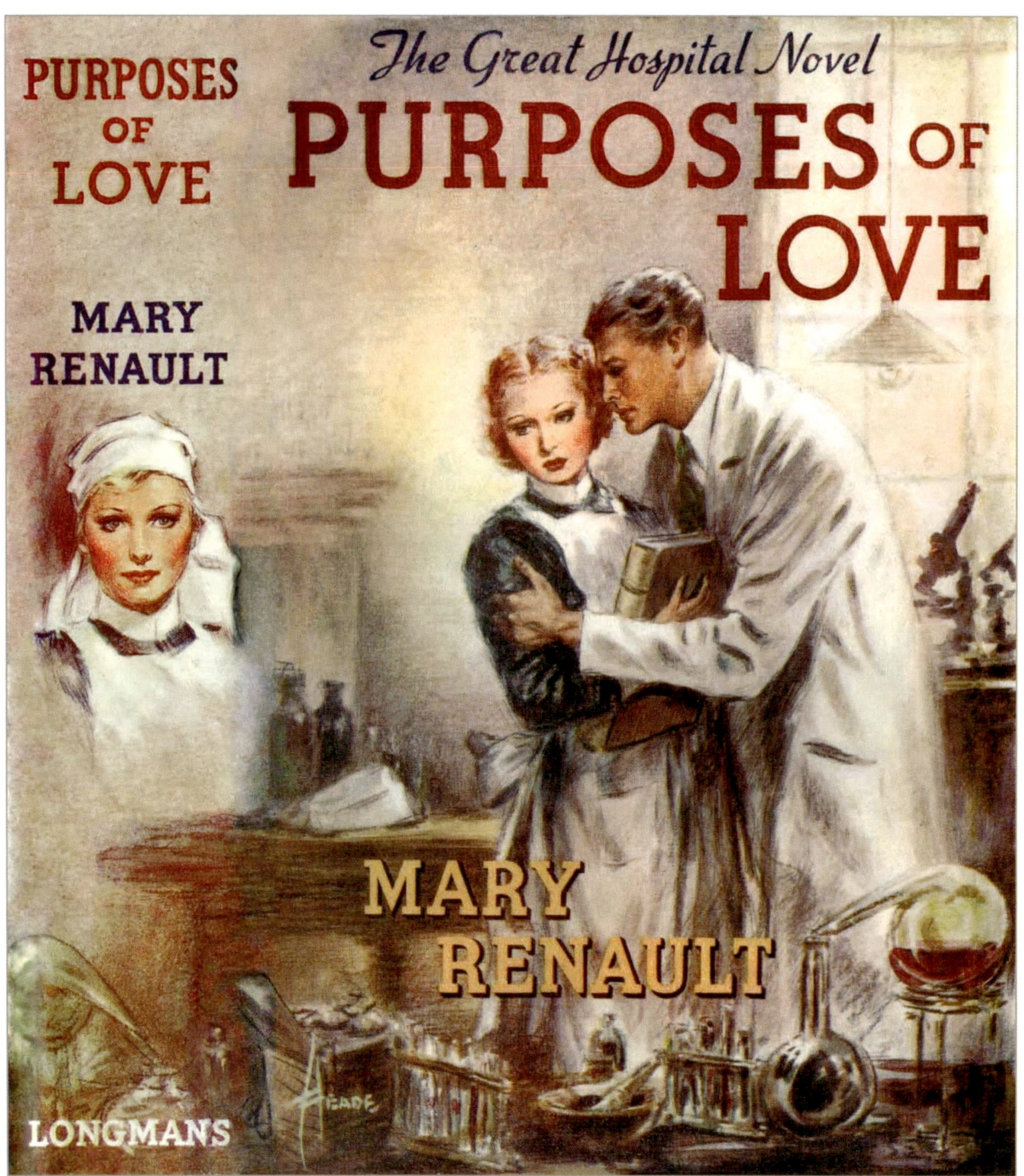

Purposes of Love by Mary Renault (Longmans, January 1939)

The Road to Damascus by Annie S Swan (Hodder & Stoughton, January 1940)

THE 1940s

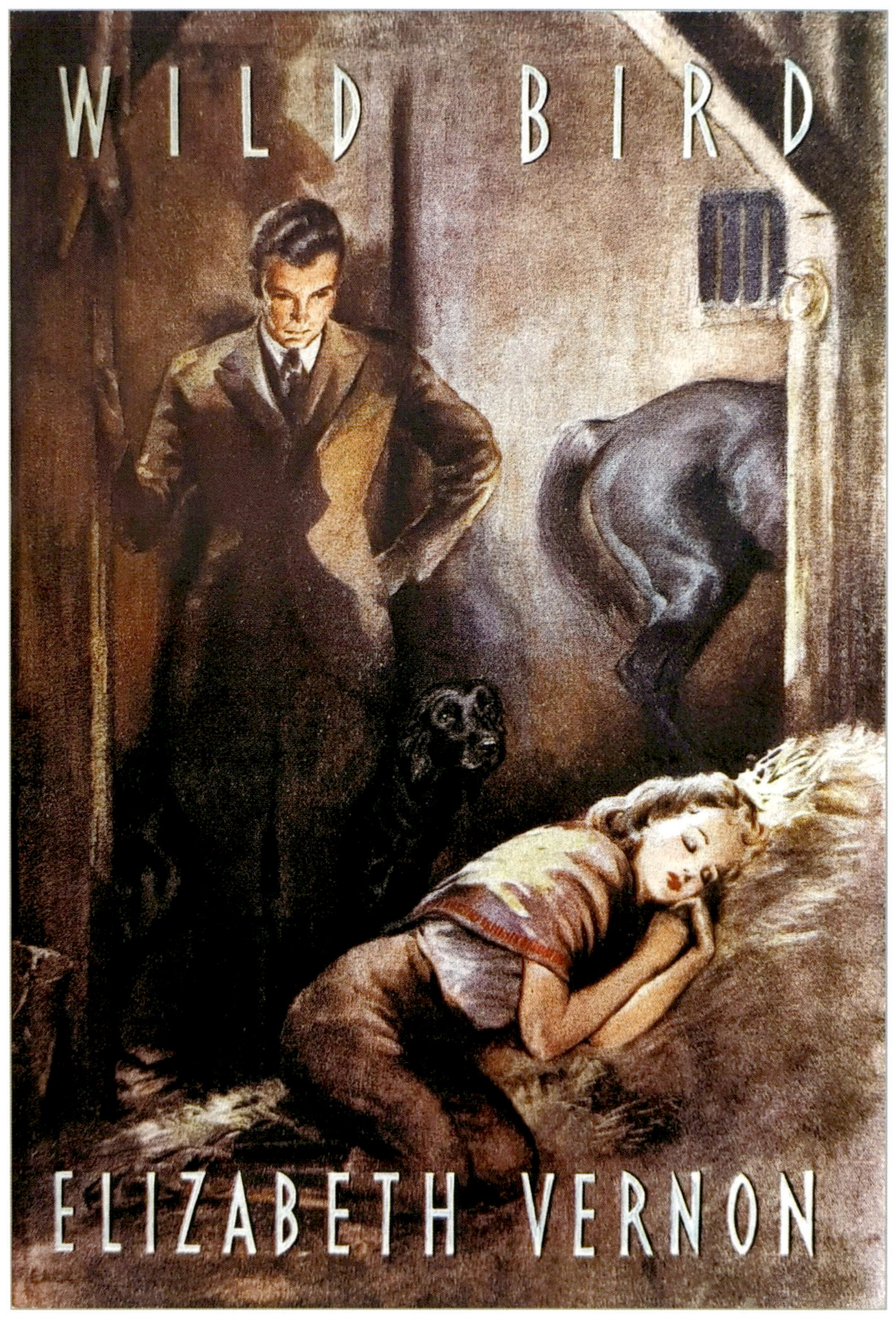

Wild Bird by Elizabeth Vernon (Hodder & Stoughton, 1940)

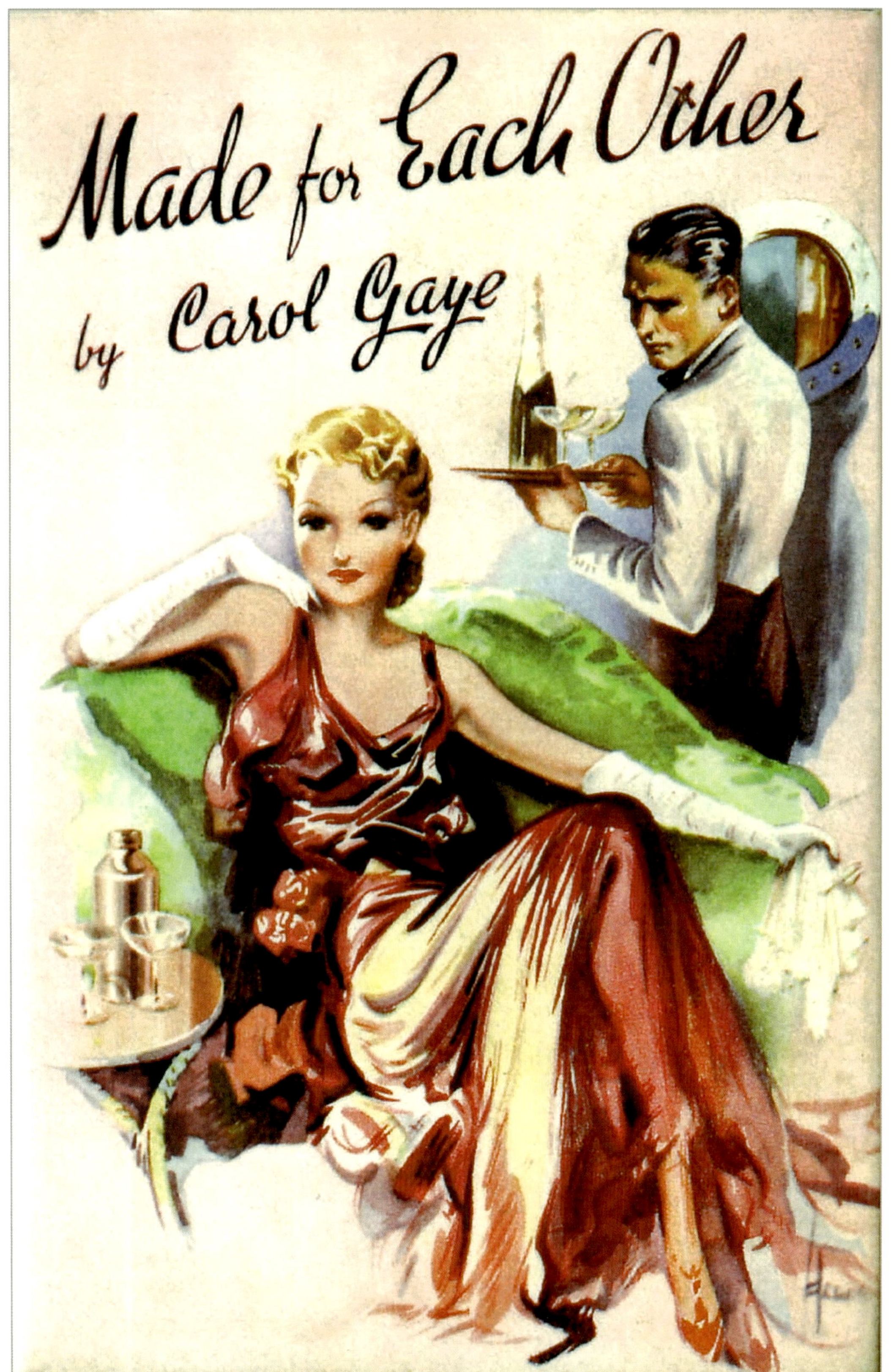

Made for Each Other by Carol Gaye (Collins, 1940)

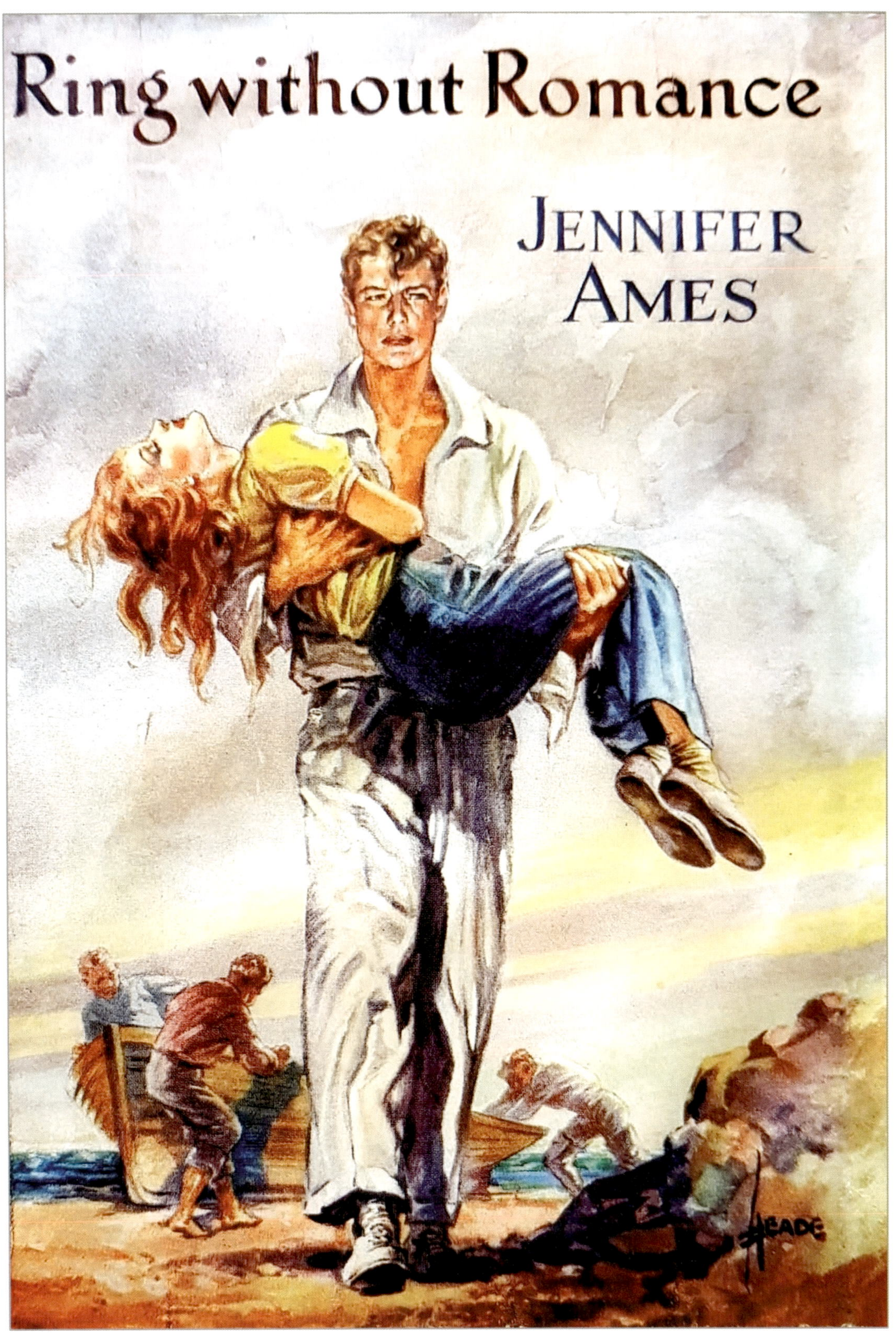

Ring Without Romance by Jennifer Ames (Hodder & Stoughton, 1940)

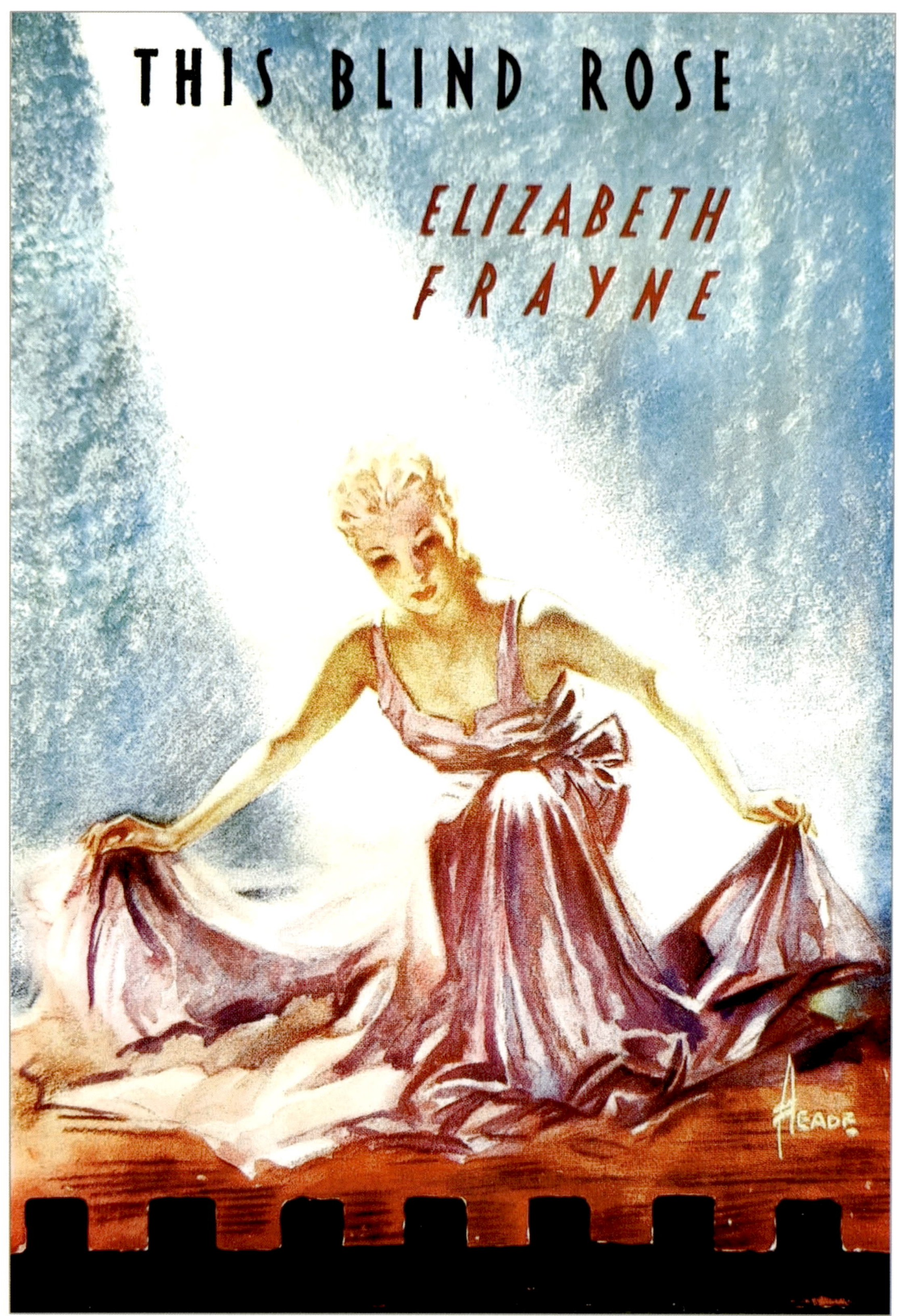

This Blind Rose by Elizabeth Frayne (Hodder & Stoughton, 1940)

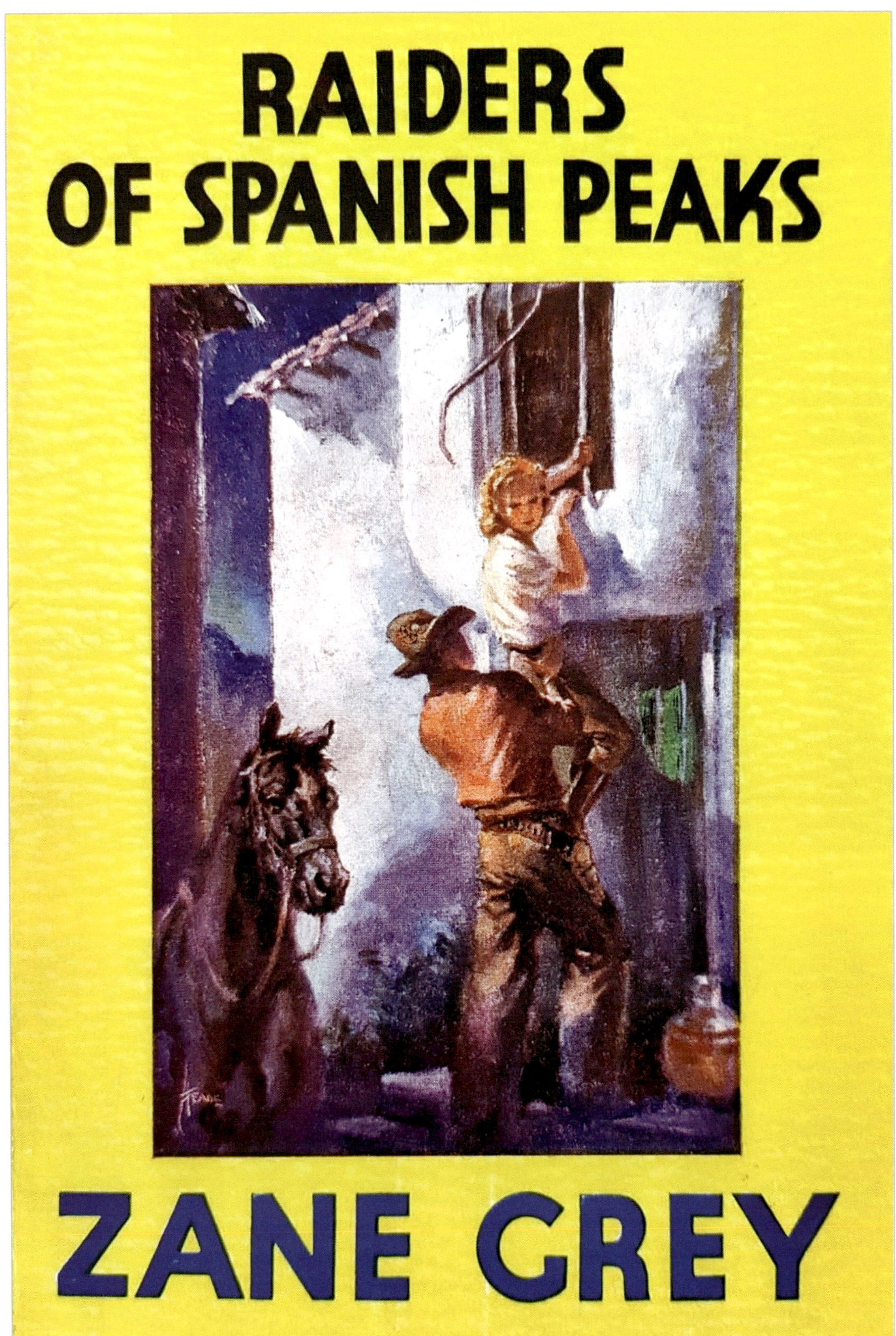

Raiders of Spanish Peaks by Zane Grey (Hodder & Stoughton, 1940)

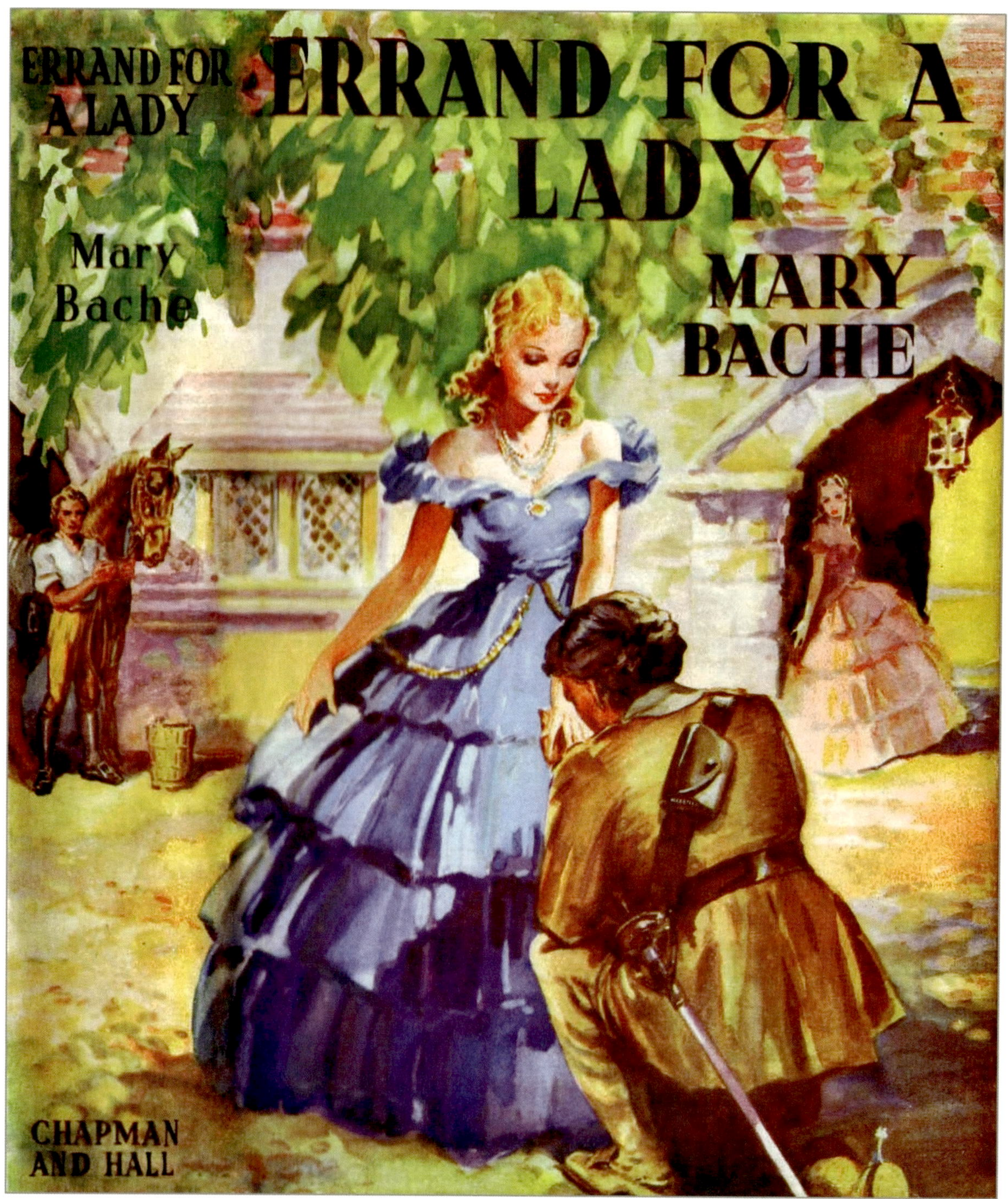

Errand for a Lady by Mary Bache (Chapman & Hall, 1940)

Follow Your Star by Lyndon Snow (Collins, 1941)

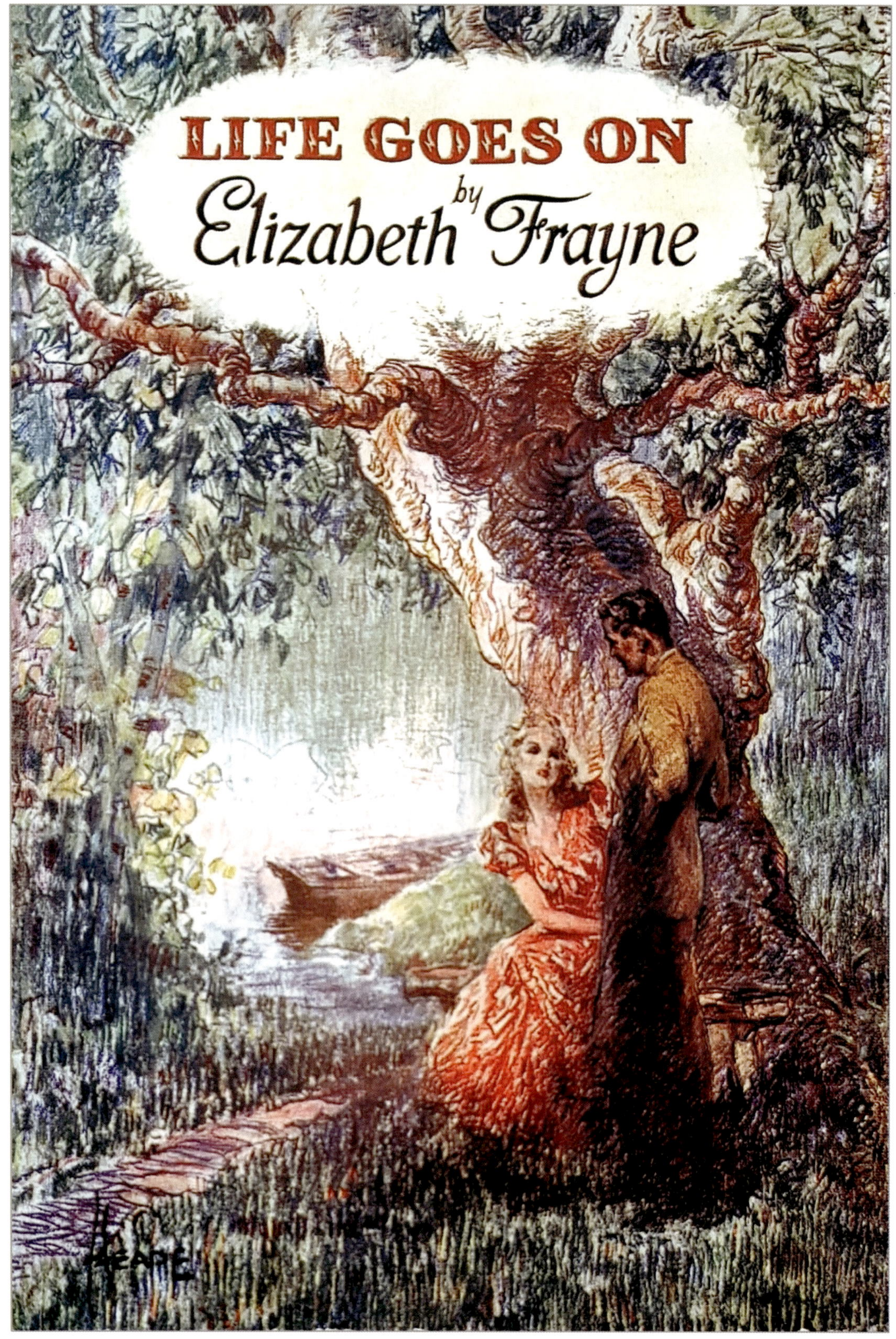

Life Goes On by Elizabeth Frayne (Hodder & Stoughton, 1941)

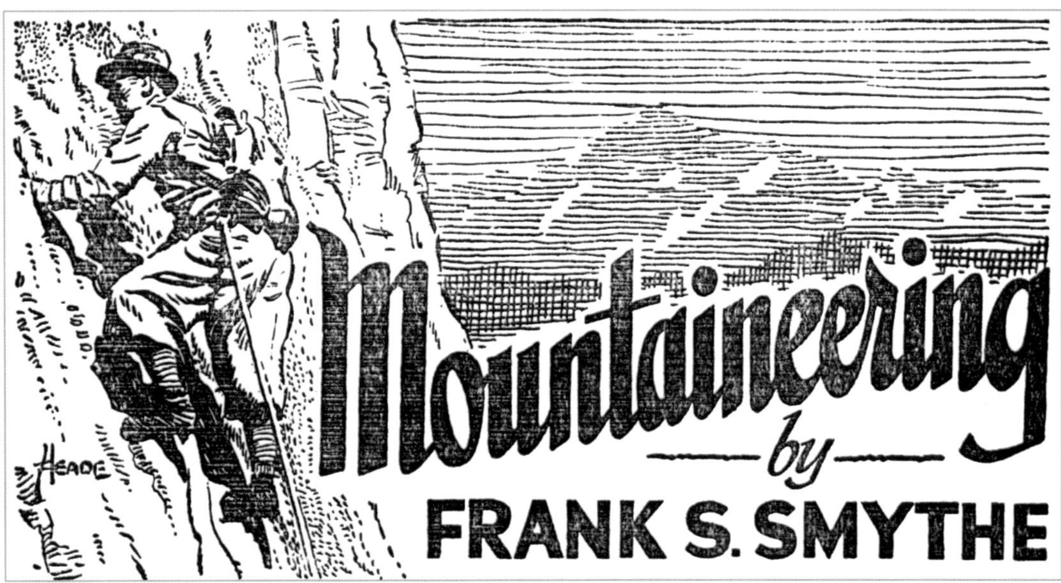

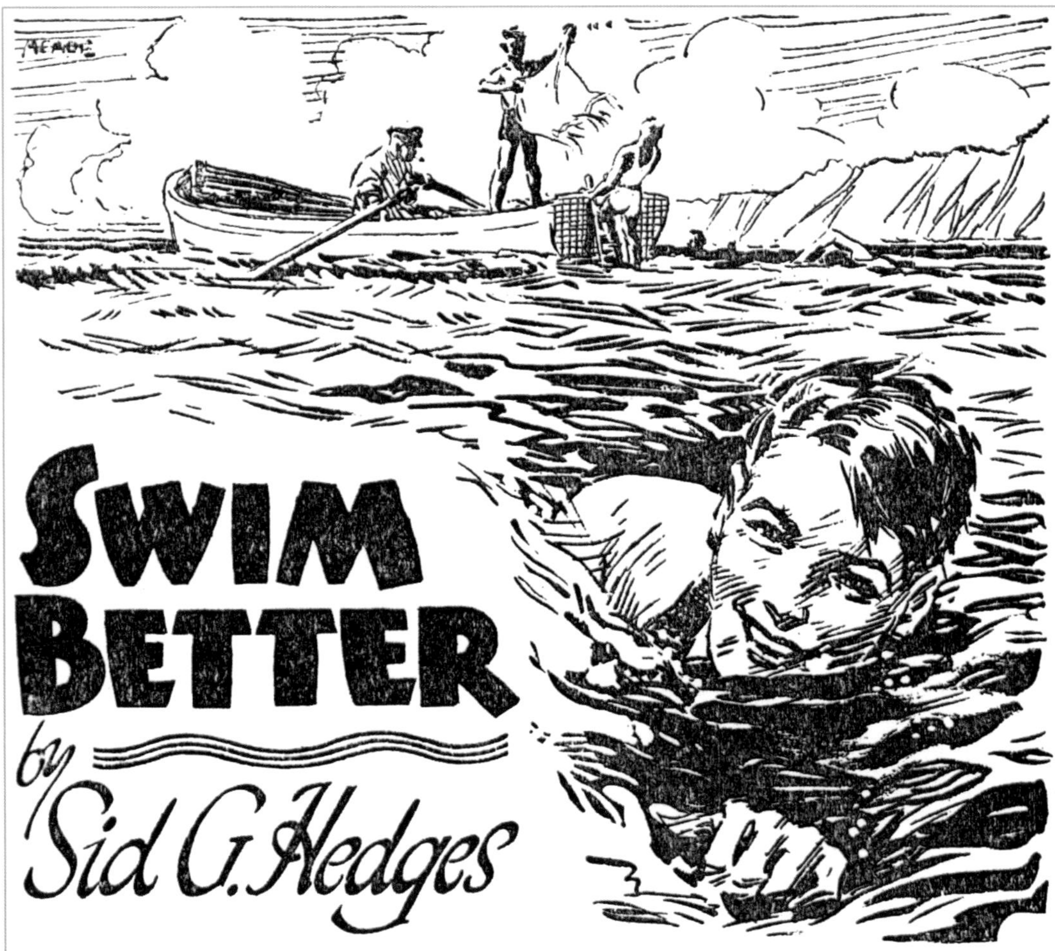

Above: black-and-white illustrations by Heade for two non-fiction articles in *Young Airman's Annual* (Collins, c1941). In addition, this book has now been identified as the original source of the story 'Black-Out Boxing' by Bruce Cooper, later reprinted in *The Bumper Book for Boys* (Collins, 1954), which also had Heade illustrations, as pictured on page 250 of *The Art of Reginald Heade – Special Edition*.

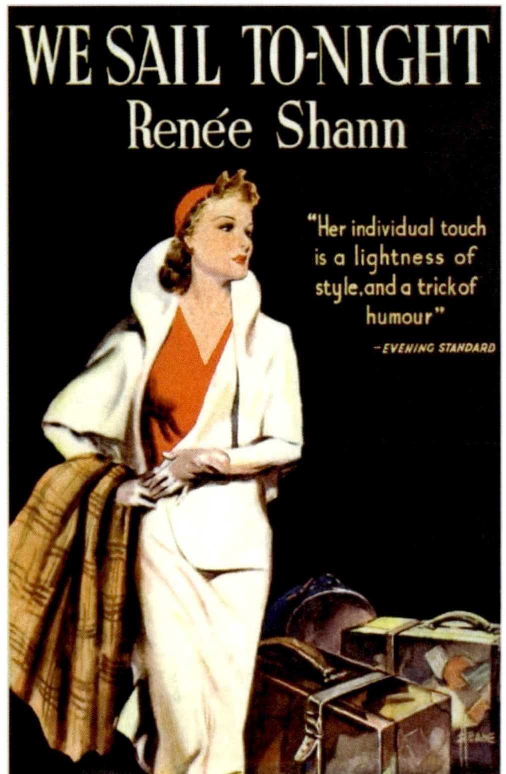

We Sail To-Night by Renée Shann (Collins, 1940)

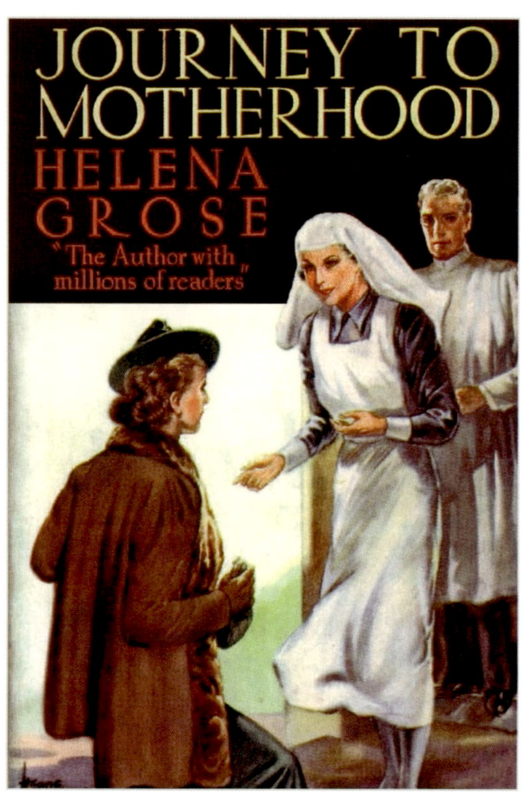

Journey to Motherhood by Helena Grose (Collins, 1940)

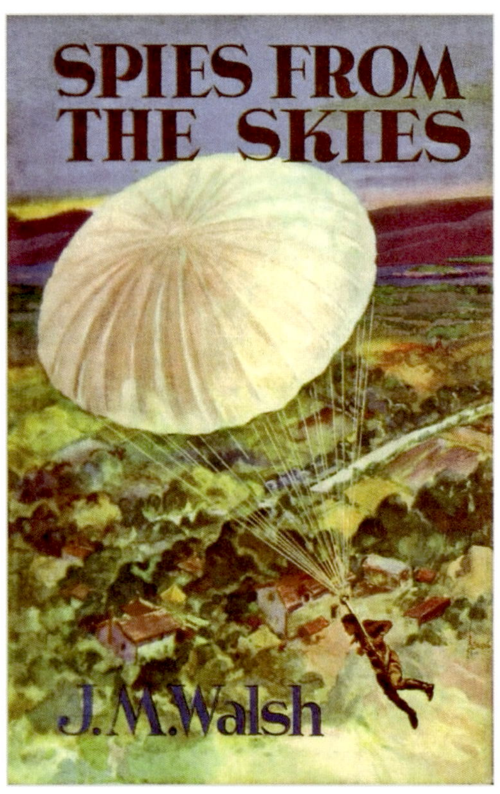

Spies from the Skies by J M Walsh (Collins, 1941)

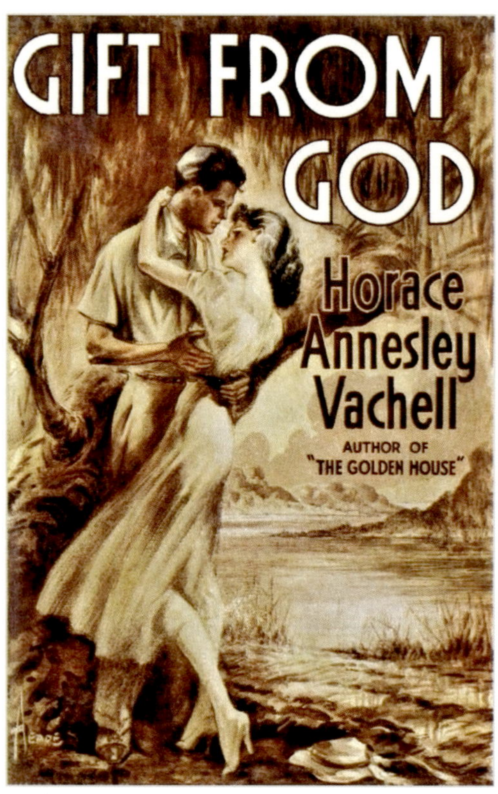

Gift from God by Horace Annesley Vachell (Cassell, 1942)

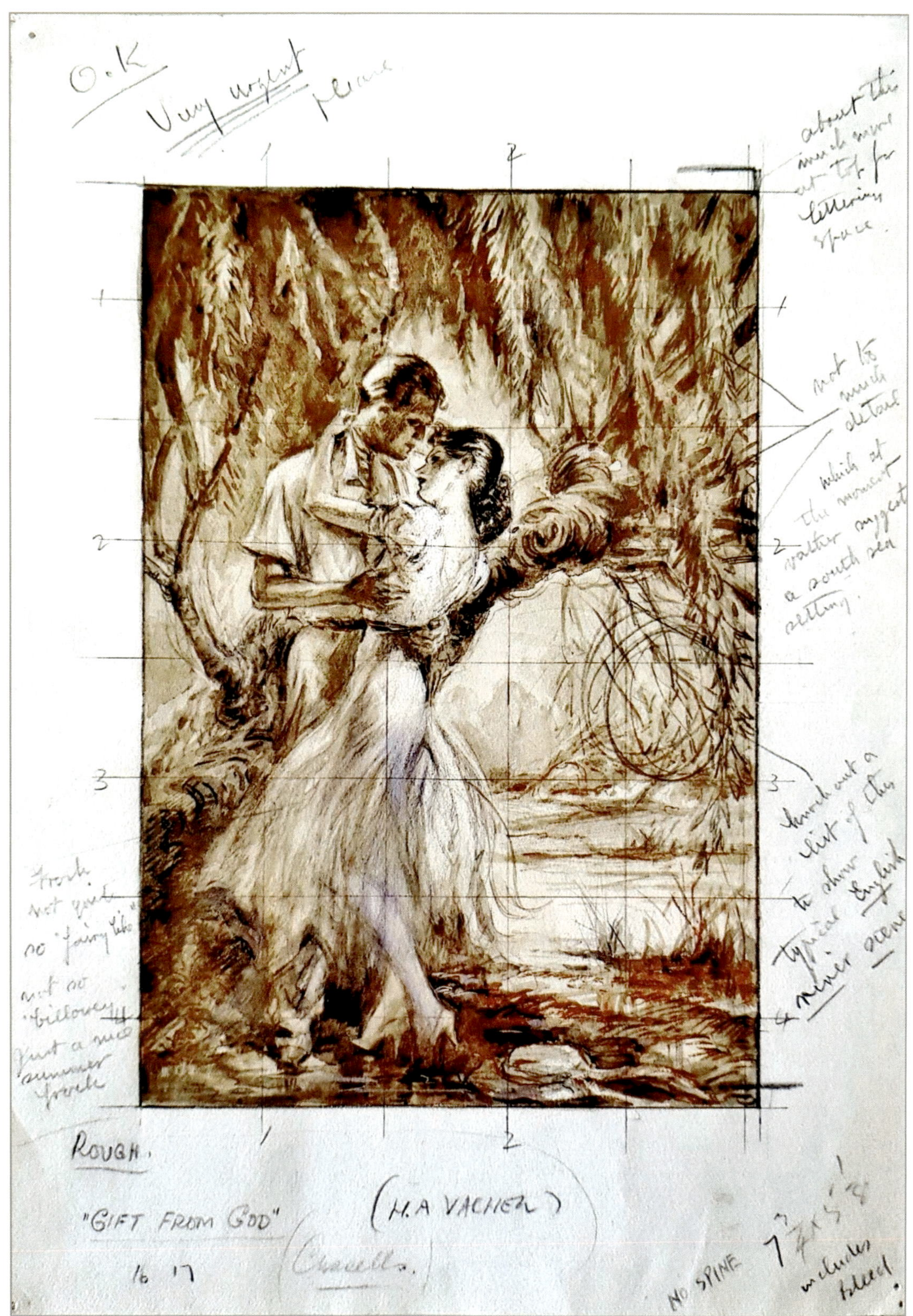

Heade's original rough for *Gift from God* by Horace Annesley Vachell (Cassell, 1942), complete with pencil annotations made by the publisher's art department, including comments to the effect that elements of the composition were too fanciful and exotic for the book's English setting, and in the top left-hand corner a request for the commission to be completed very urgently.

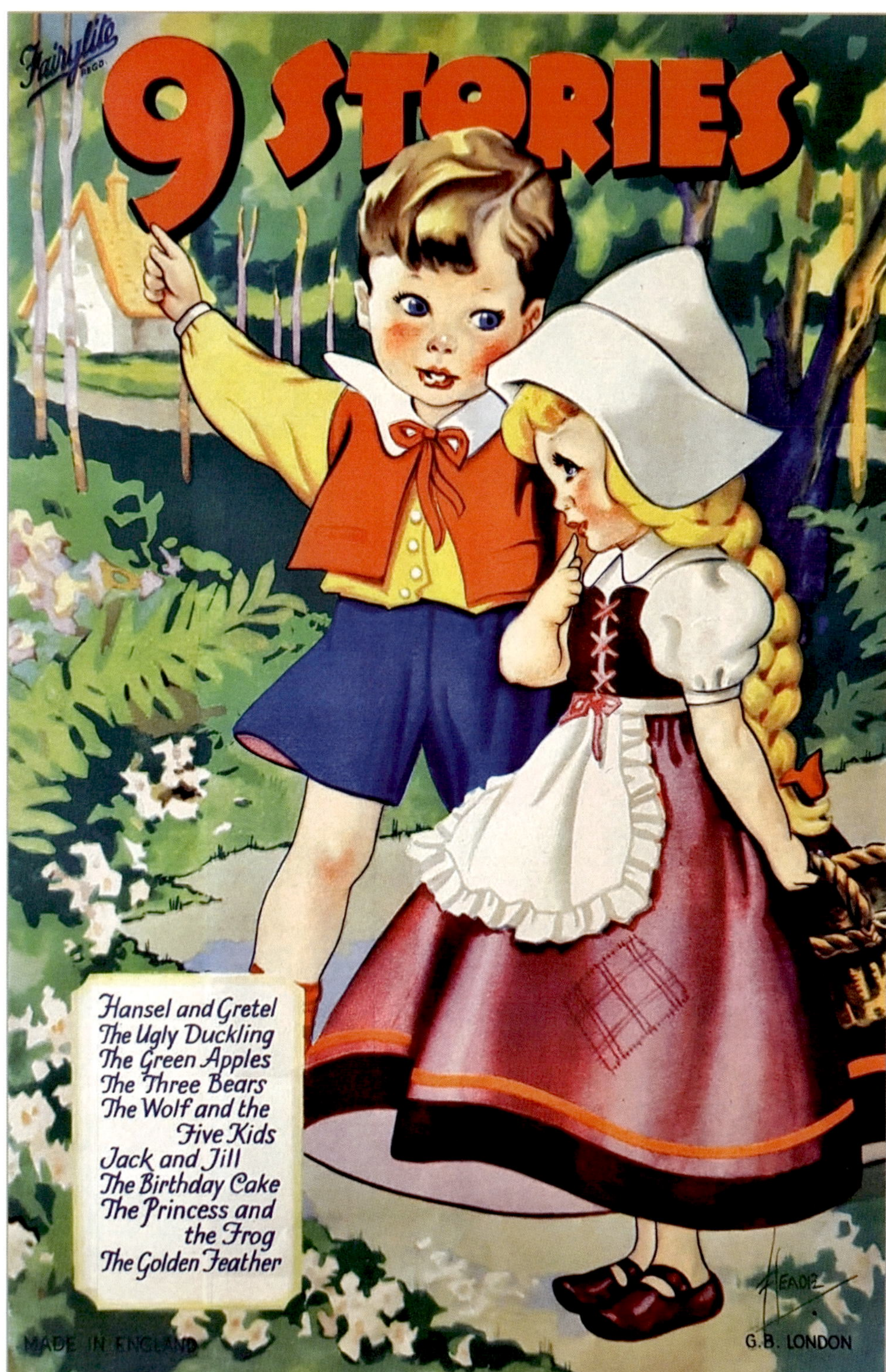

In 1942, publishers G B London issued through their Fairylite children's imprint a large-format, soft-covered book called *9 Stories*, the full-colour artwork for which was all supplied by Heade. The idea was taken from an American book of the same title published in 1938 as the first in a series by Merrill, and some of Heade's compositions likewise drew inspiration from illustrations in that forerunner. The Fairylite book was reissued a number of times, and the later editions were identical to the first, except that all omitted Heade's signature from the front cover, and some of them also the words 'Made in England'. All of Heade's artwork for the book is reproduced over this and the next four pages; the first edition front cover is pictured above.

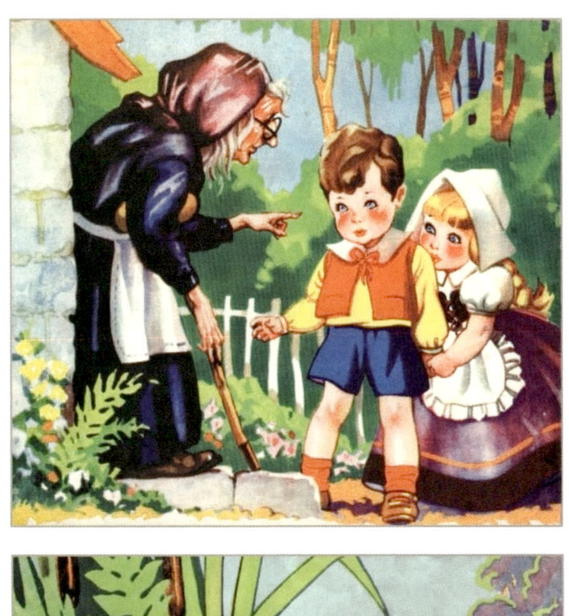 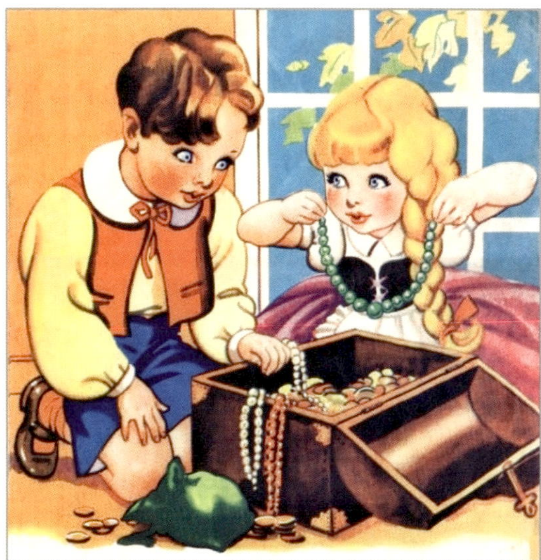

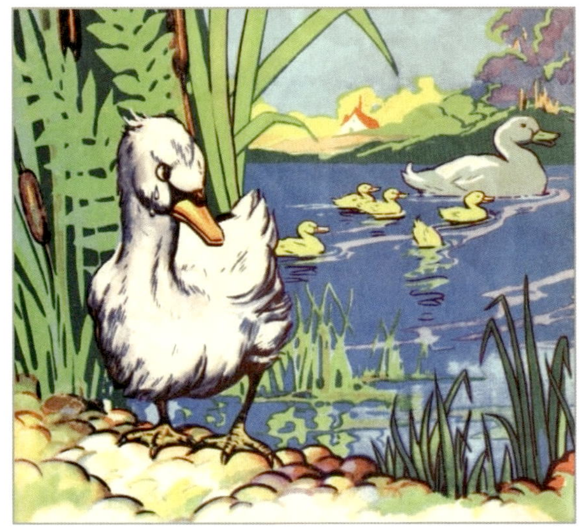 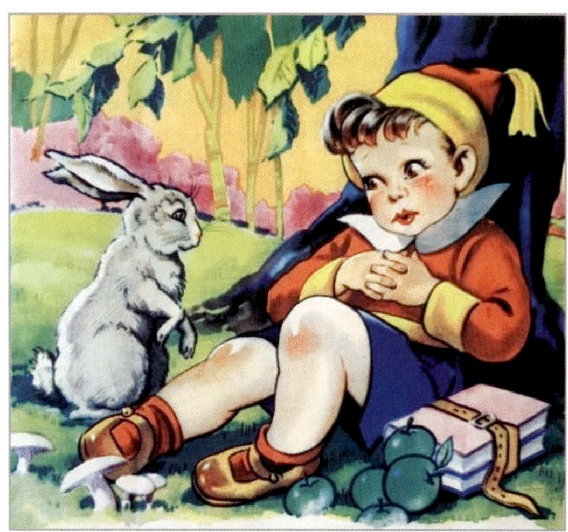

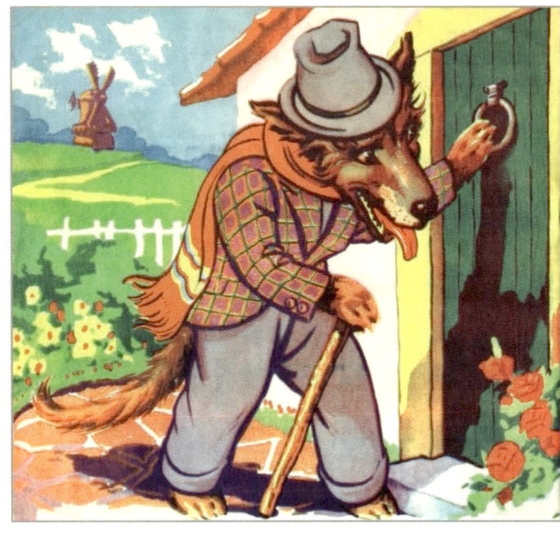 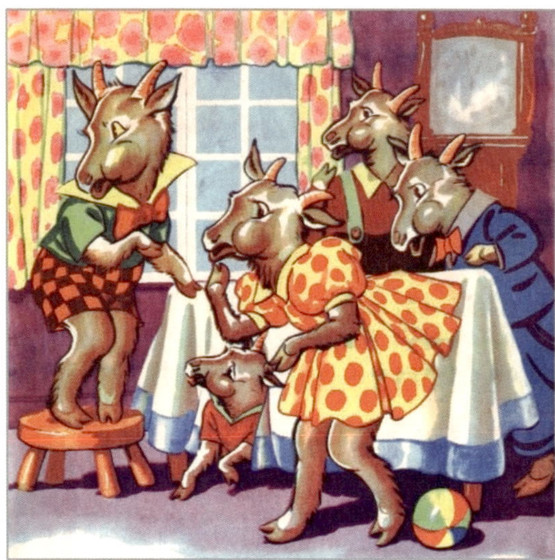

Heade's illustrations for the retold versions of 'Hansel and Gretel' (top row), 'The Ugly Duckling' (middle row left), 'The Green Apples' (middle row right) and 'The Wolf and the Five Kids' (bottom row) in *9 Stories* (Fairylite, 1942).

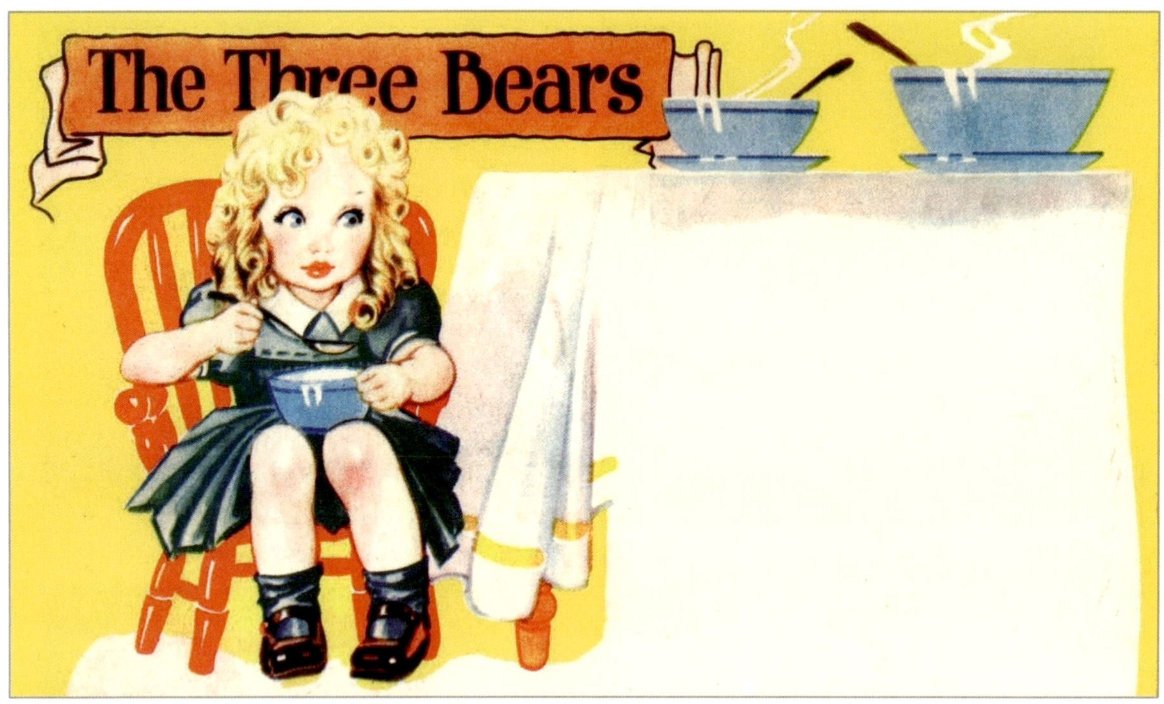

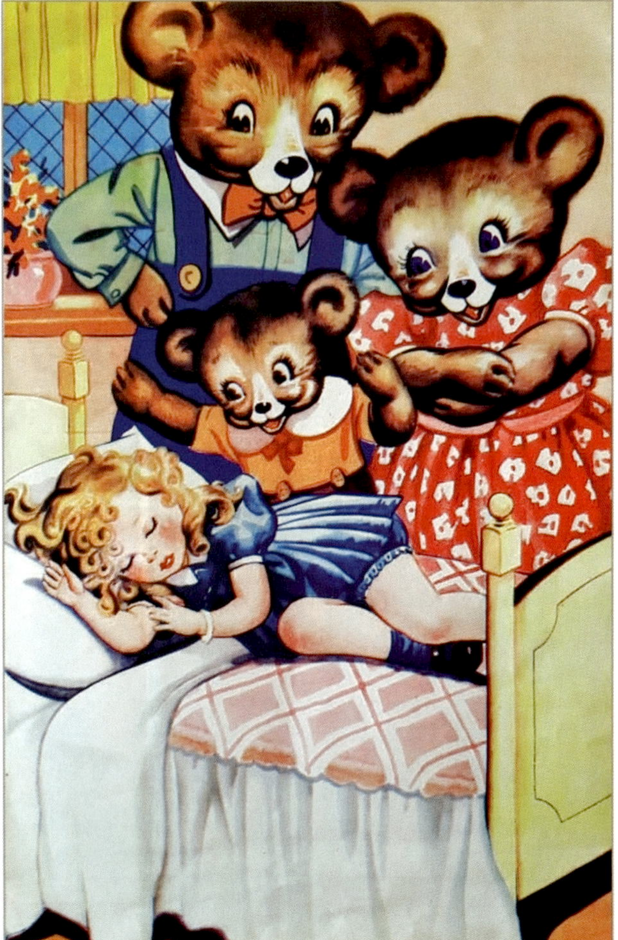

Above and left: Heade's title panel and main illustrations for 'The Three Bears' as retold in *9 Stories* (Fairylite, 1942).

Below: the cover of the American book of the same title, published by the Chicago-based Merrill company in 1938. The somewhat atypical style of art Heade adopted for the Fairylite book was clearly inspired by that of the illustrations in this forerunner. Note, for instance, the similarity between the bears in his main 'The Three Bears' piece on the left, and those on the cover of the American book.

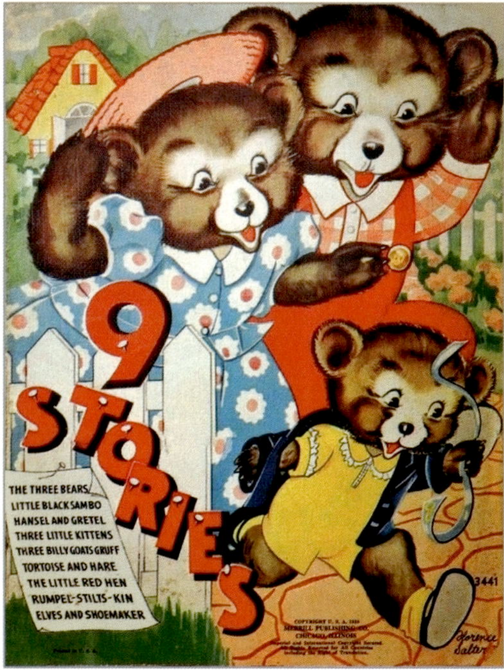

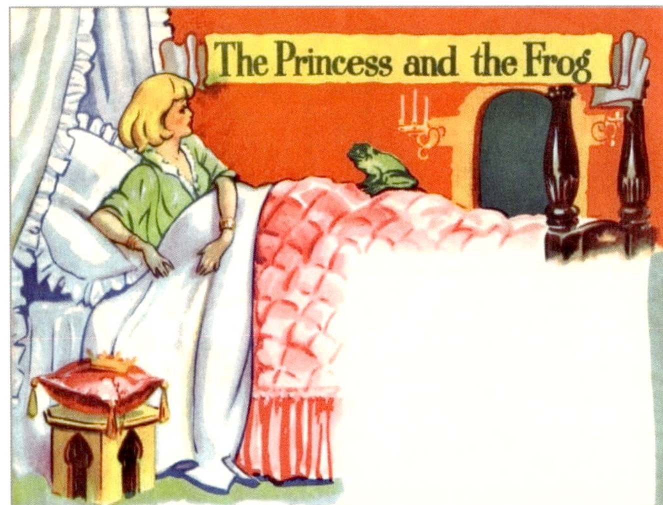

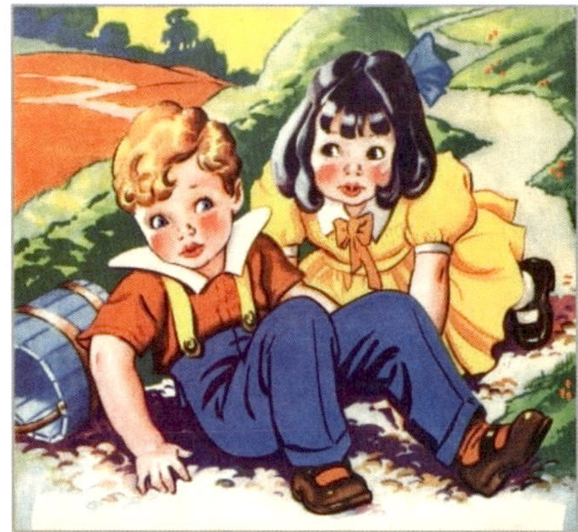

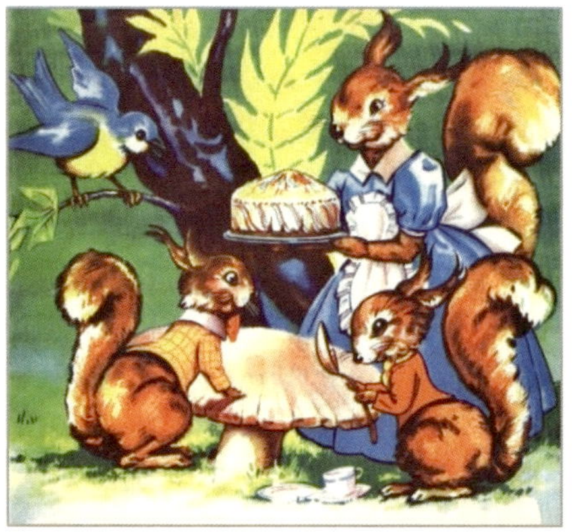

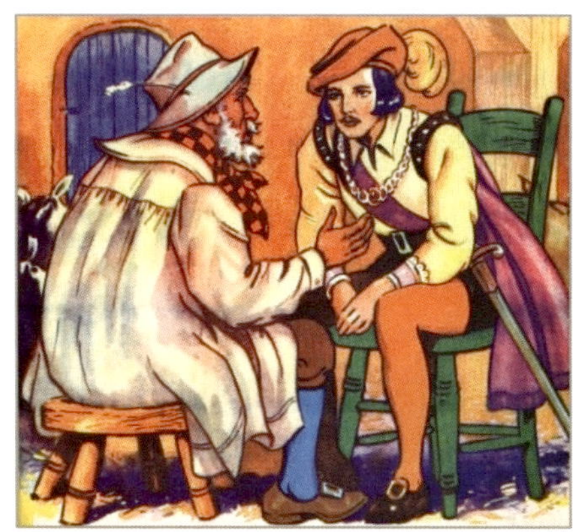

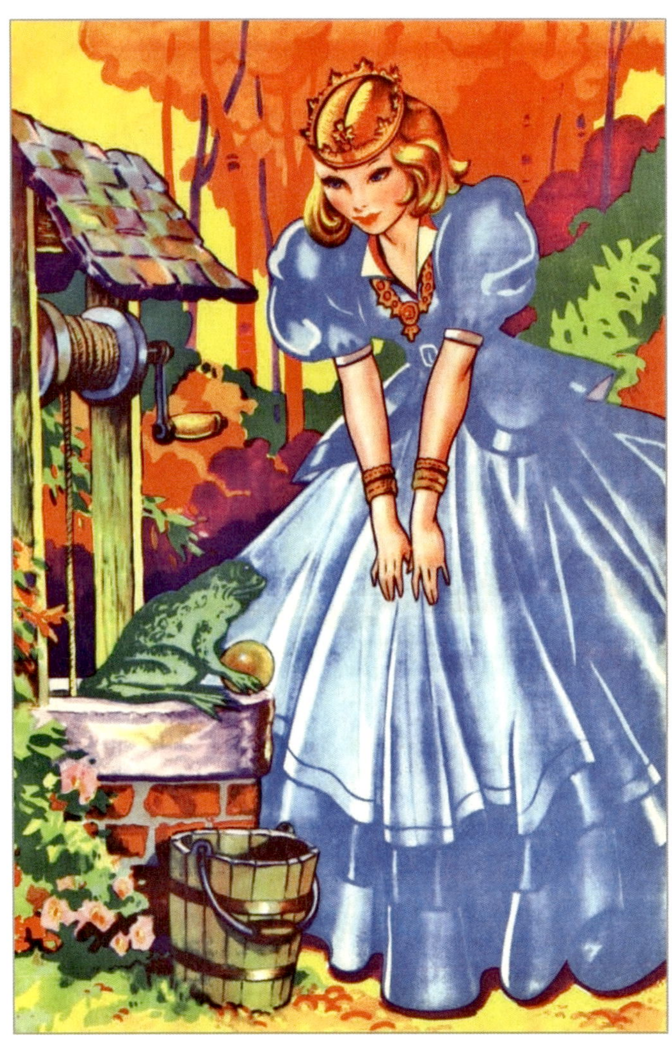

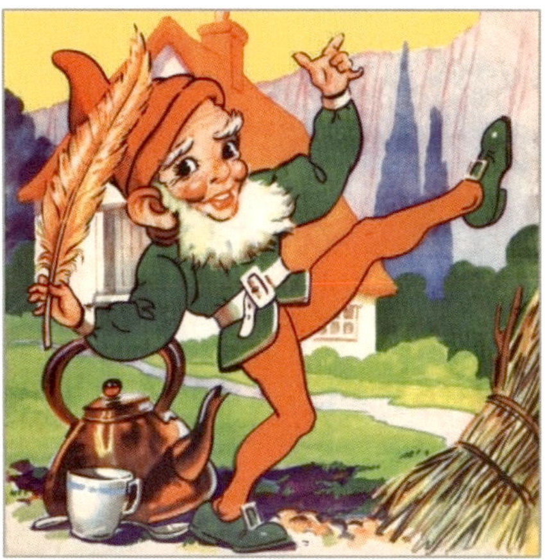

Above: Heade's title panel and main illustrations for 'The Princess and the Frog'. Right: the illustrations for 'Jack and Jill' (top), 'The Birthday Cake' (second down) and 'The Golden Feather' (third down and bottom). All from *9 Stories* (Fairylite, 1942).

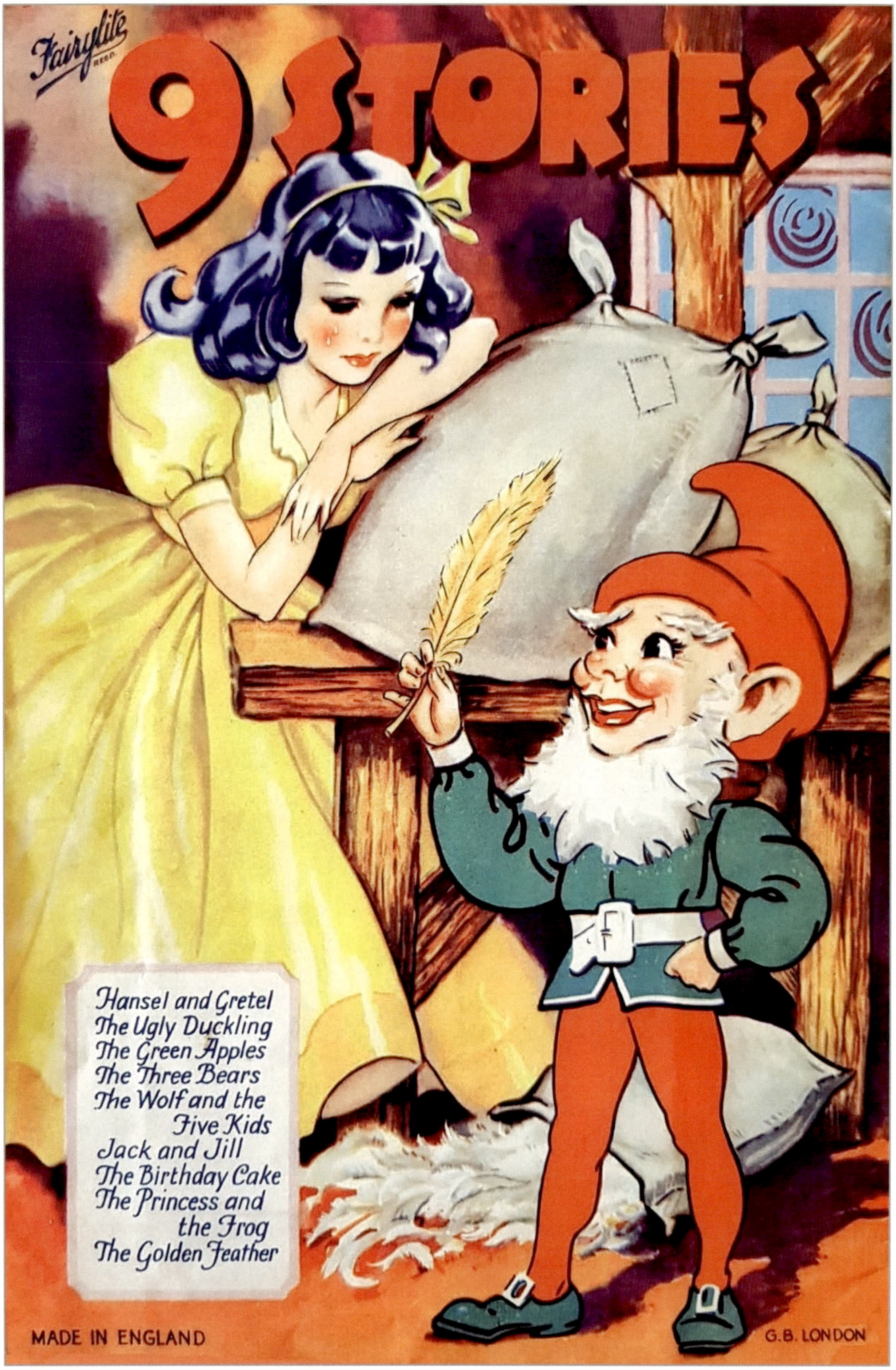

Heade's back cover illustration for *9 Stories* (Fairylite, 1942)

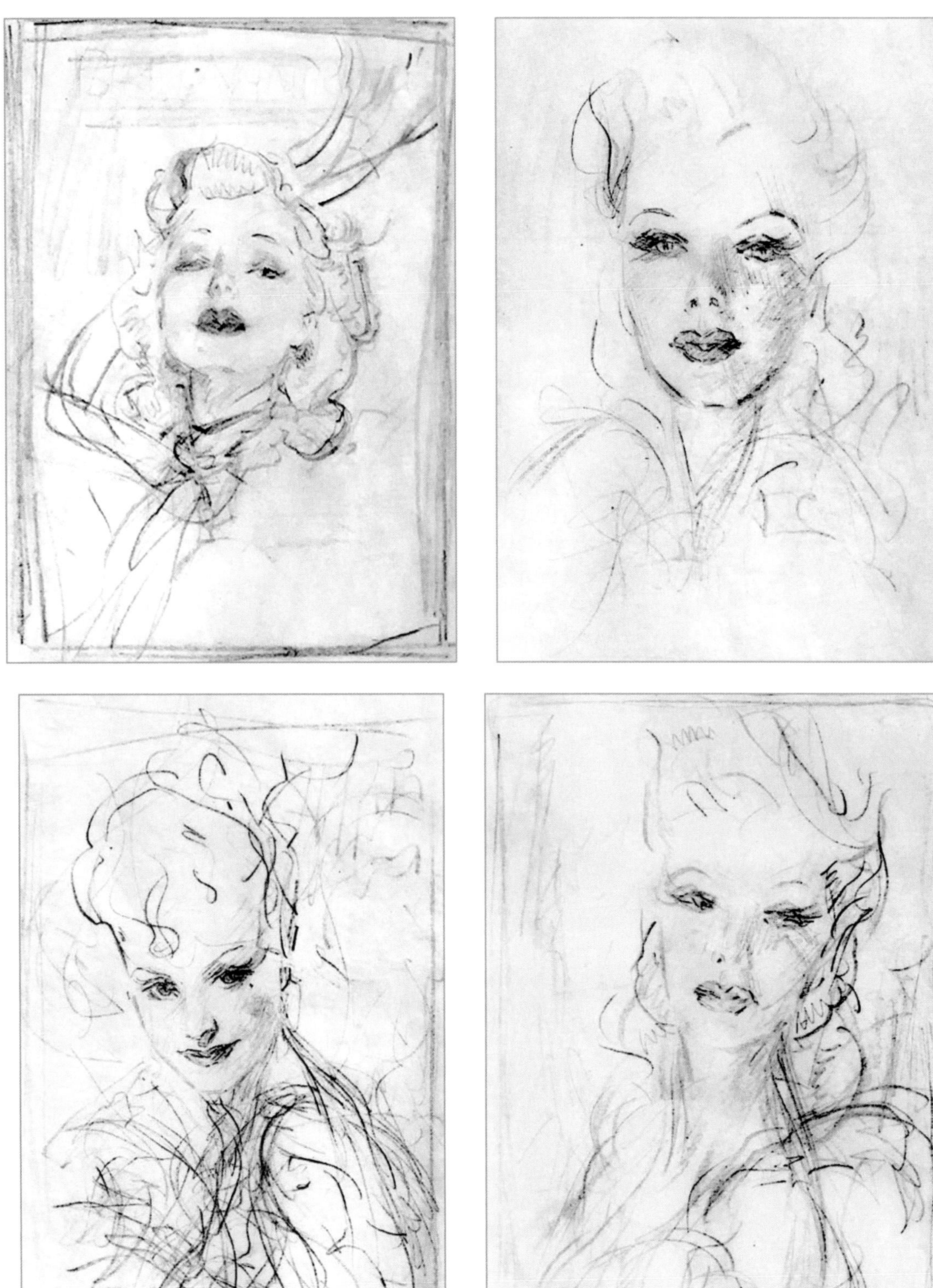

Amongst the surviving original drawings by Heade are a number of head-and-shoulders poses of women. Four are pictured at the very front of this volume, and another four above. In the absence of other information, these are in most cases assumed to have been studies for intended oil portraits, date uncertain. The example at top left is an exception: it can be positively identified as a rough for the cover of the June 1941 issue of *Britannia and Eve* (British National Newspapers); an image of the as-published version is shown in the checklist in the 'Appendix'.

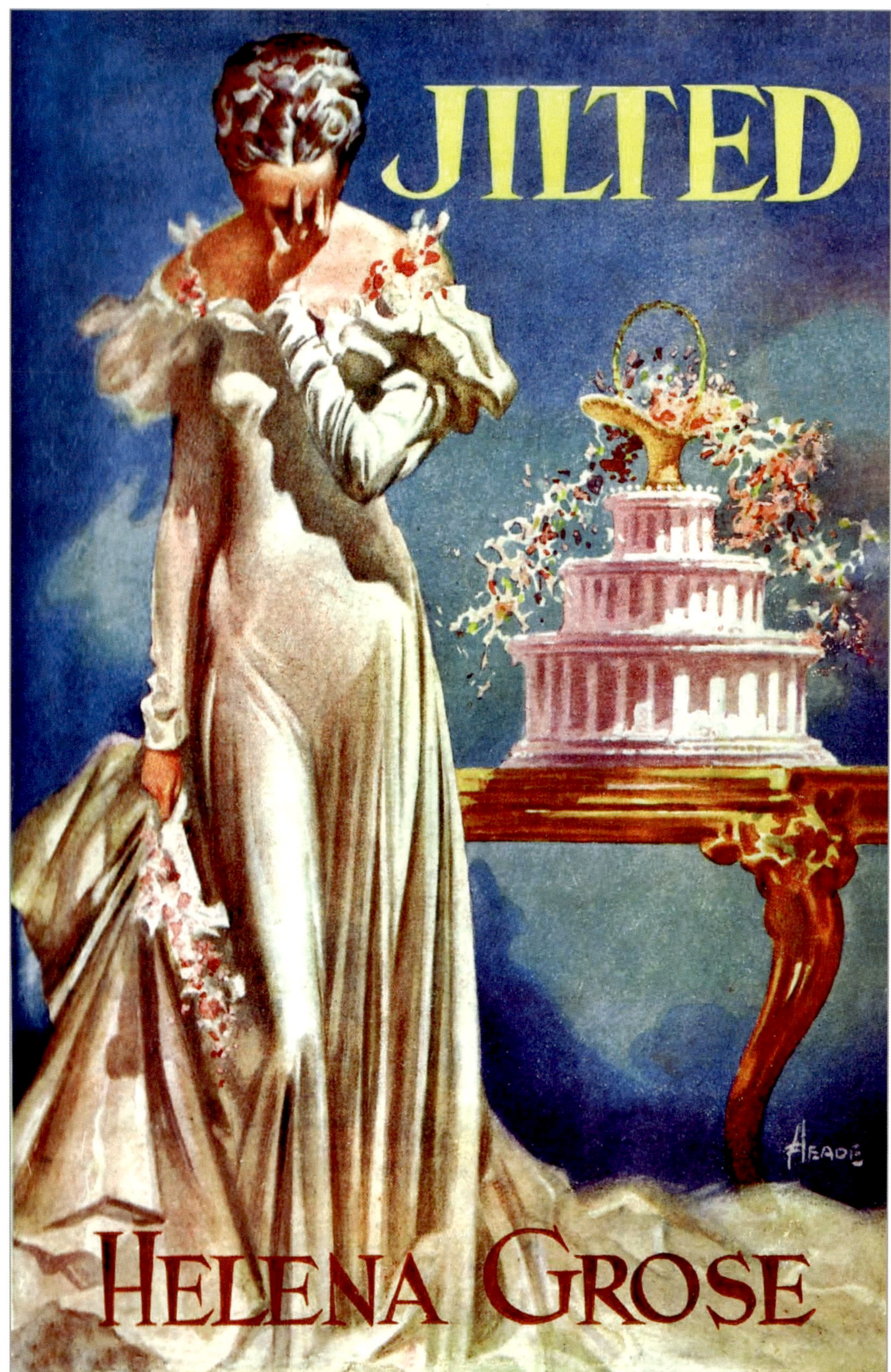

Jilted by Helena Grose (Collins, 1942)

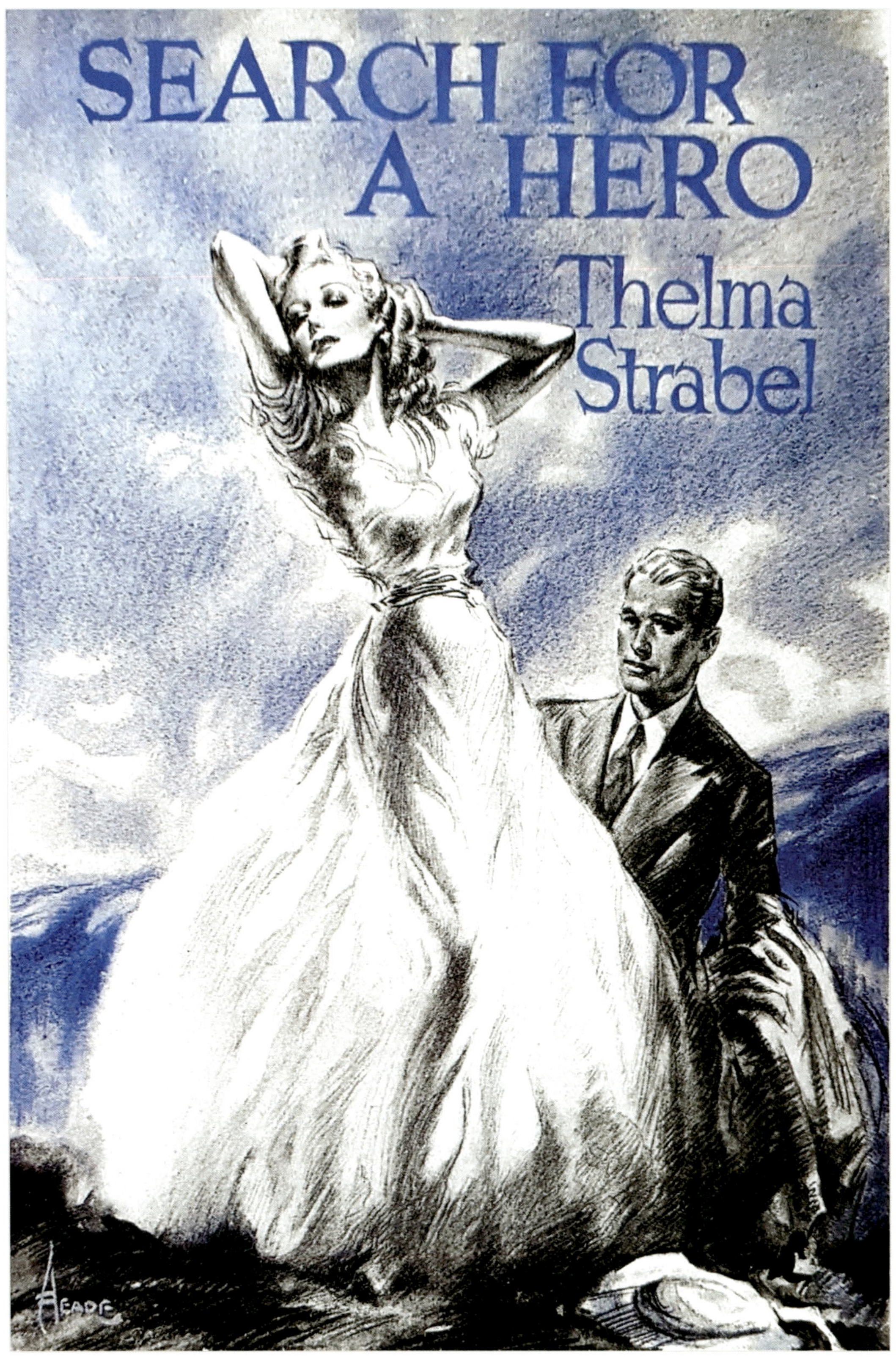

Search for a Hero by Thelma Strabel (Collins, 1942) – a superior quality image to the one previously presented in *The Art of Reginald Heade – Special Edition*. The wide-brimmed ladies' hat in the bottom right-hand corner was a recurring element in Heade's romance dustjacket art.

MR STRAWSTUFF'S PARTY

W PARTRIDGE
ART AGENT

23 BLOOMSBURY SQUARE W C 1

MUSEUM 7181

R.C.W.Heade Esq.   21st.Sept.1942.

Dear Mr.Heade,
            Would you care to do a small book for me,9¾"x7¼"
16 pages (will be printed on art paper) 8 pages 3 colour half
tone and 8 pages(holding story)2 colour half tone. One of these
two colours will have to be fairly dark to print story.

            I have made a rough layout,but change it if you
wish,in other words try and make the book look a bit different if
possible,but try to keep the blocks round about the size I have
suggested.
            All I want for the rough is the cover in colour and one
or two pages inside in colour,the rest in pencil will do.
            Any chance for Friday morning please.

make up as book
actual size please.   Kind regards
                                Yours sincerely,
                                       W.Partridge

P.S.Synopsis enclosed "Mr.Strawstuffs Party" might work up
all right.Please return this synopsis with rough.

At the end of 1942, Strome & Co issued a slim, soft-covered children's story book entitled *Mr Strawstuff's Party*. Heade supplied all of the art for this, having been invited to do so by his agent William Partridge via a letter, reproduced on the left. It is notable that, although the association between agent and artist already stretched back several years by that point, the letter is still expressed in the formal professional terms of the time, with no first names being used. In addition to the finished book, four of Heade's preparatory drawings for the project still survive: the one for the book's title is below left; one for an internal illustration below right; the one for the two-page centrespread bottom left; and the one for the back cover bottom right. The as-published artwork is pictured over the next three pages.

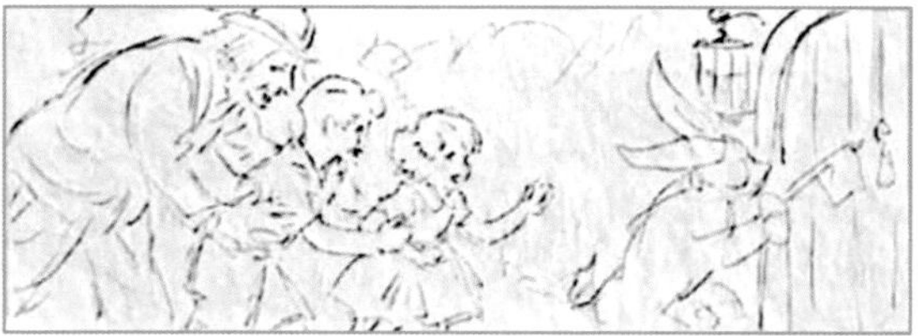

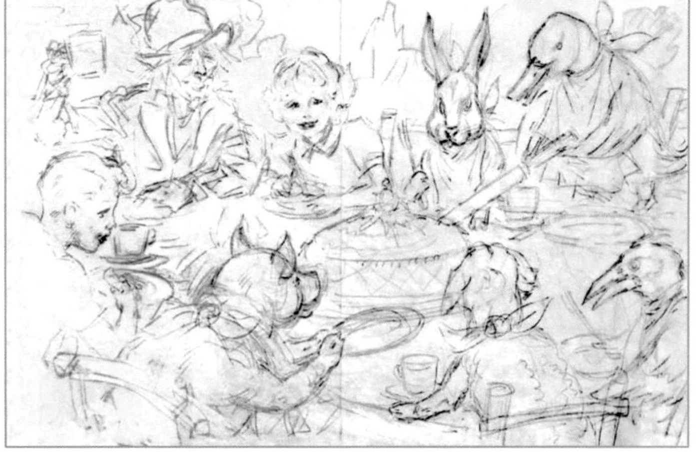

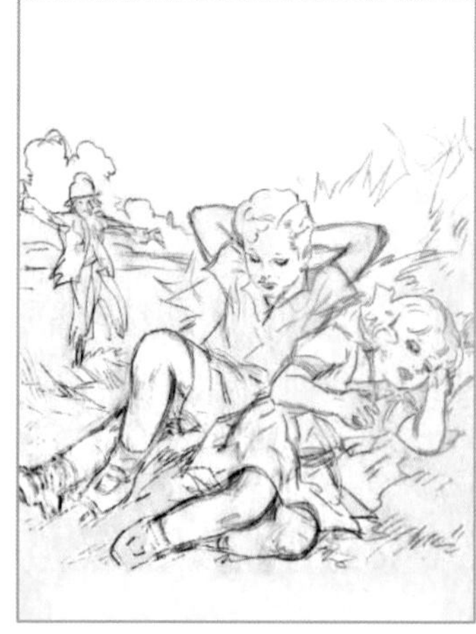

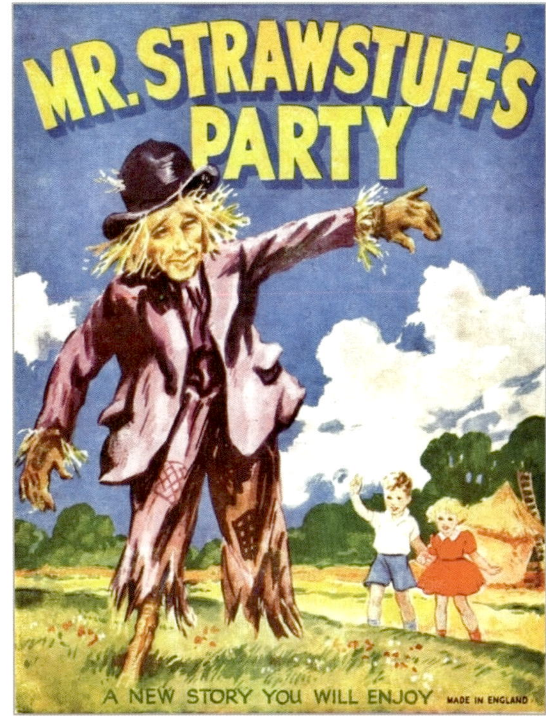

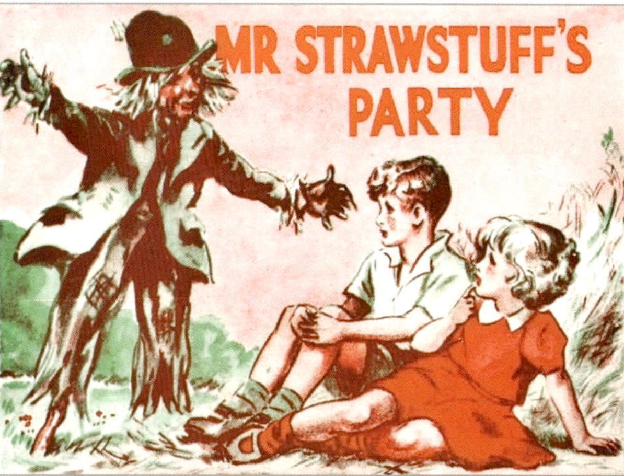

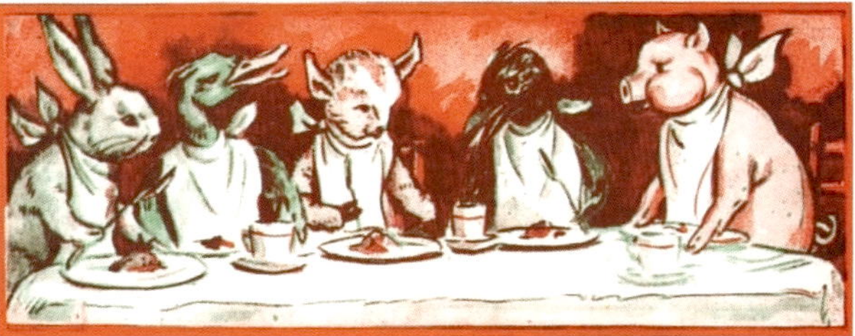

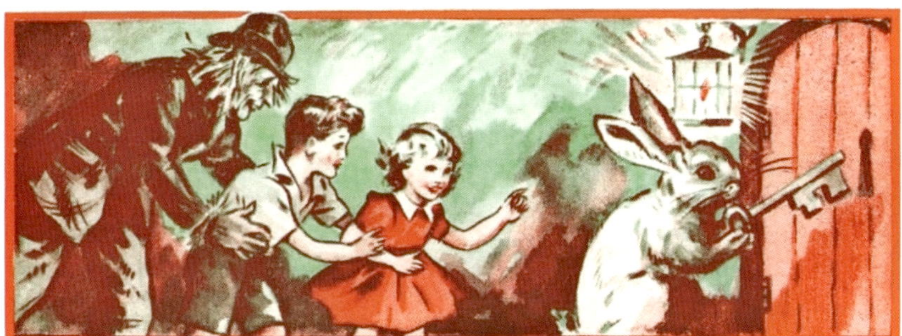

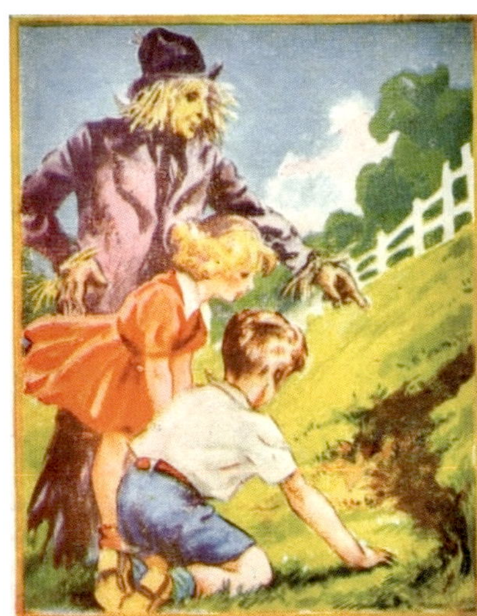

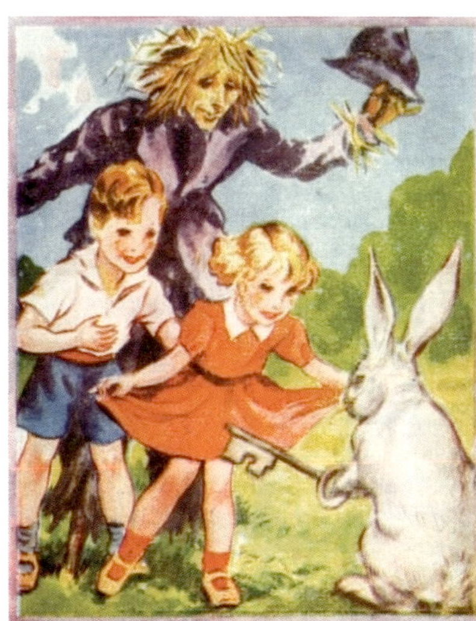

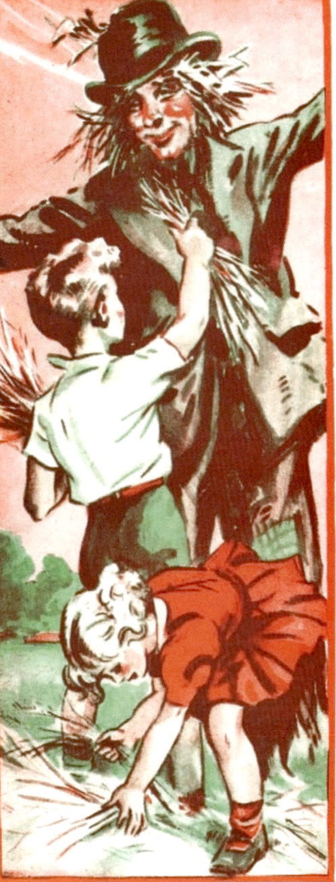

The front cover (top left), title panel (top right) and five further internal illustrations from *Mr Strawstuff's Party* (Strome, 1942)

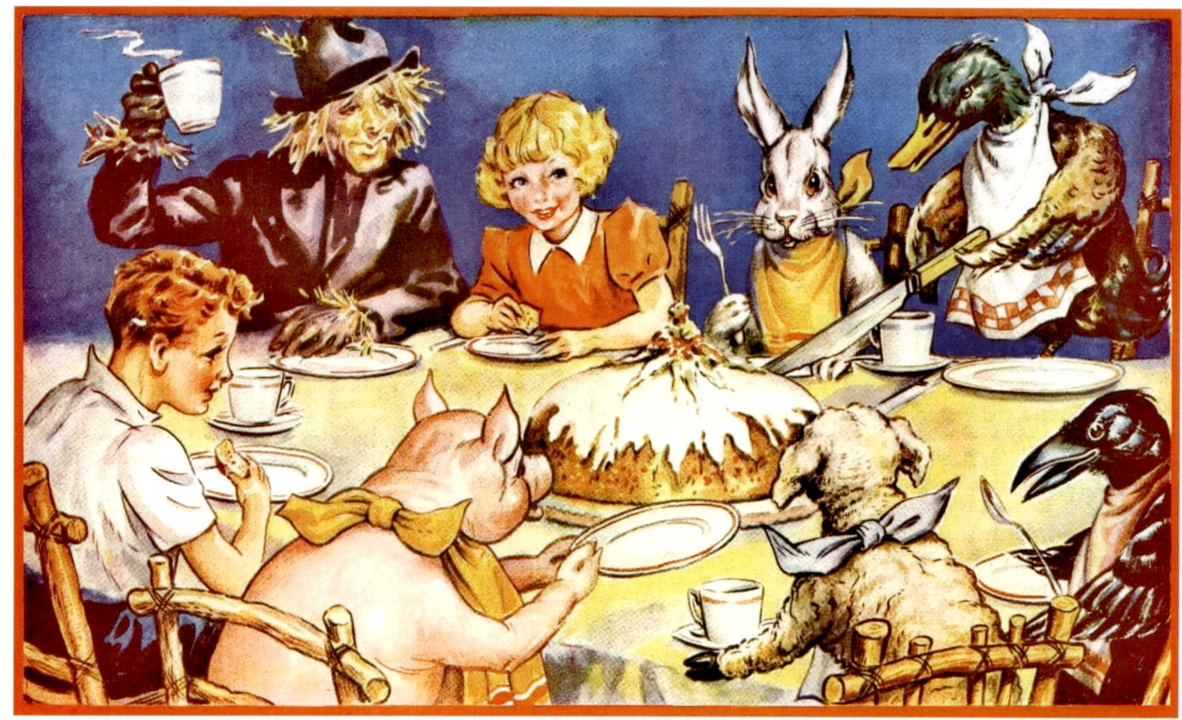

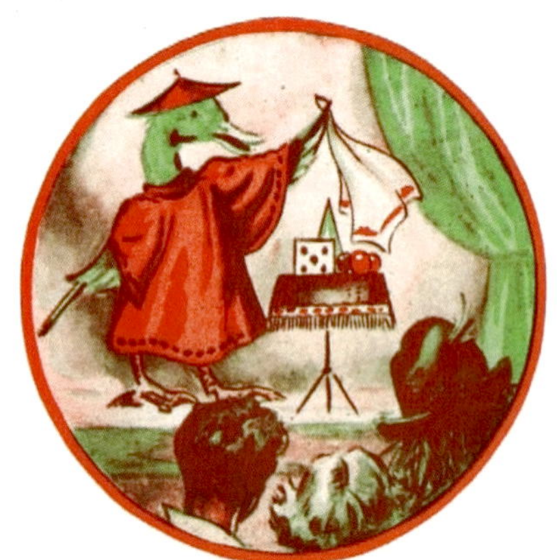

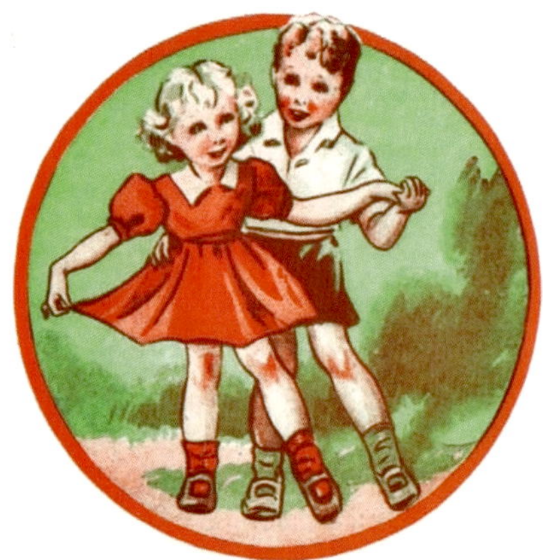

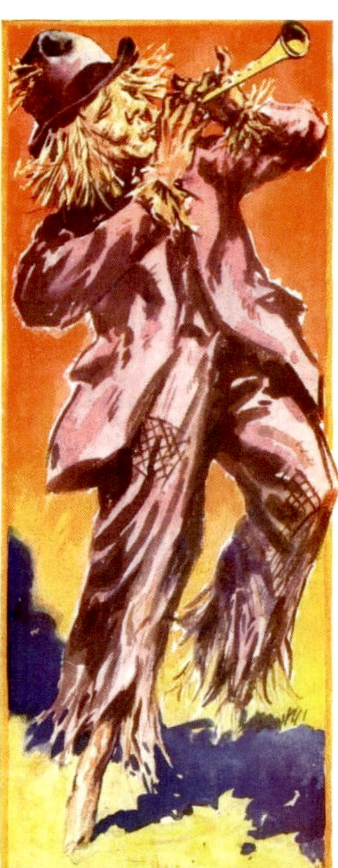

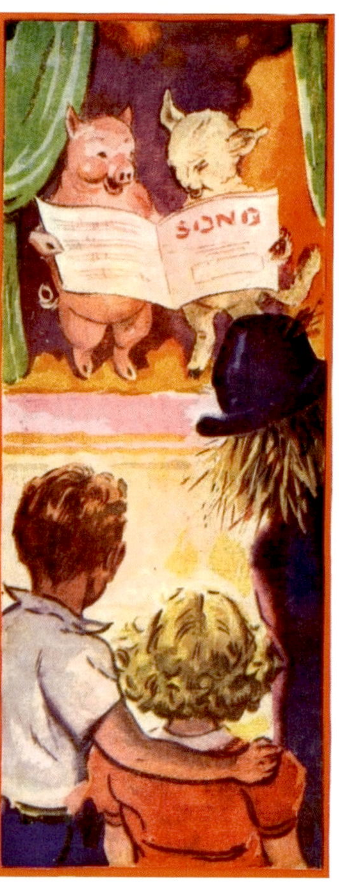

The double-page centrespread (top) and four further illustrations from *Mr Strawstuff's Party* (Strome, 1942)

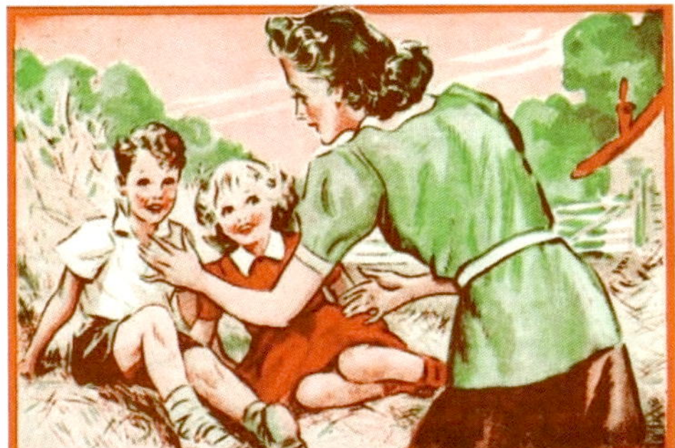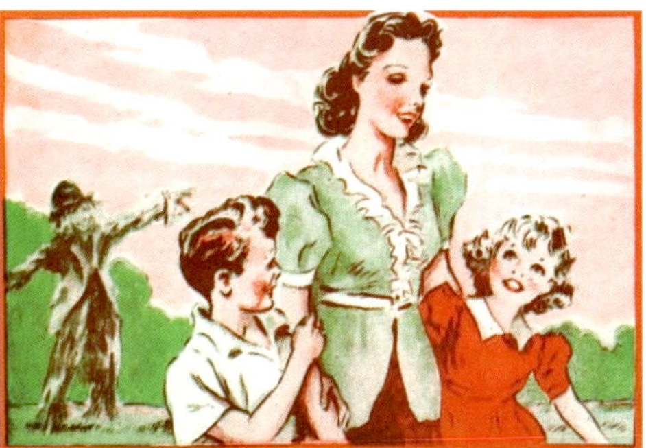

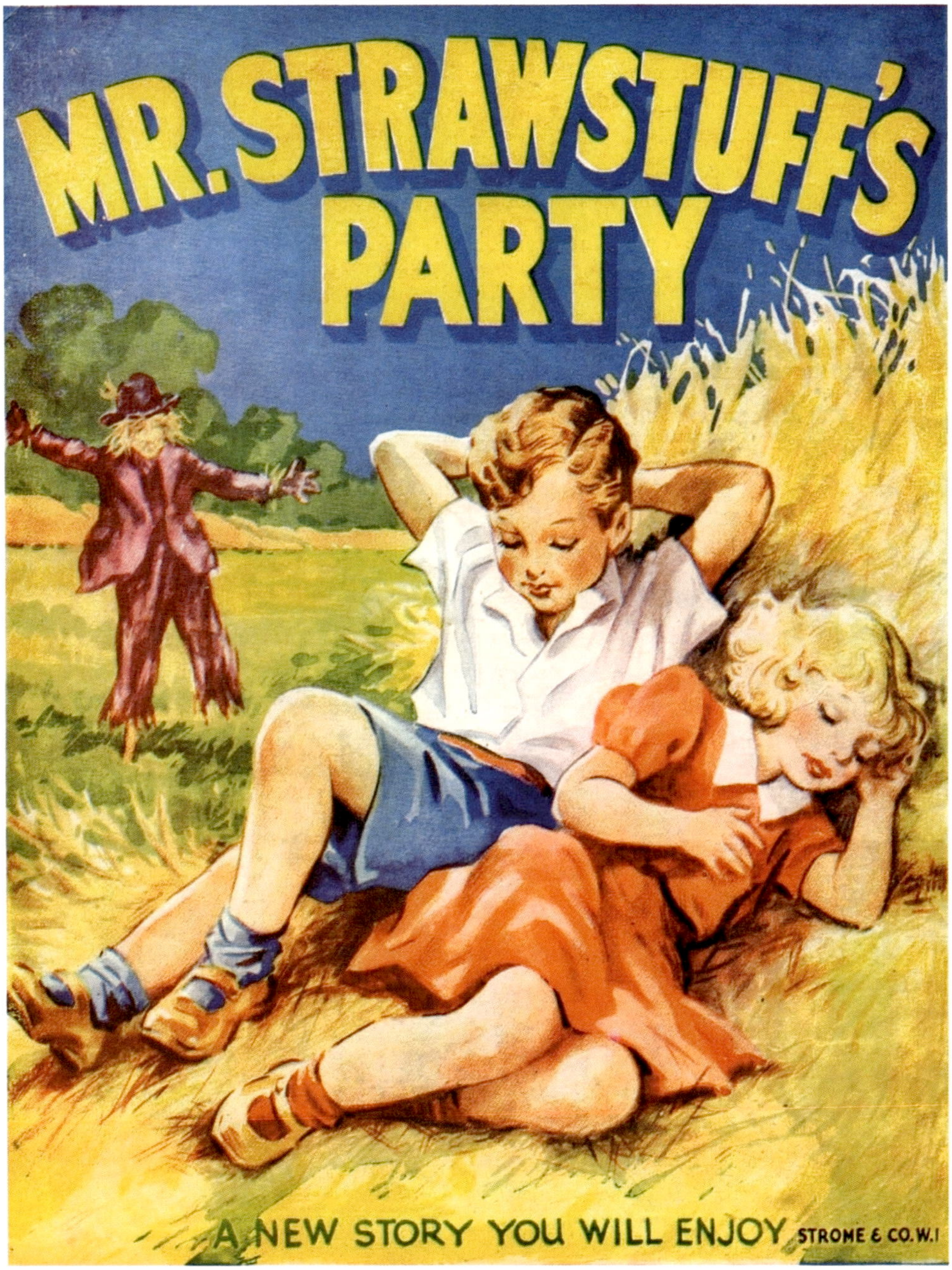

The final two internal illustrations and the back cover from *Mr Strawstuff's Party* (Strome, 1942)

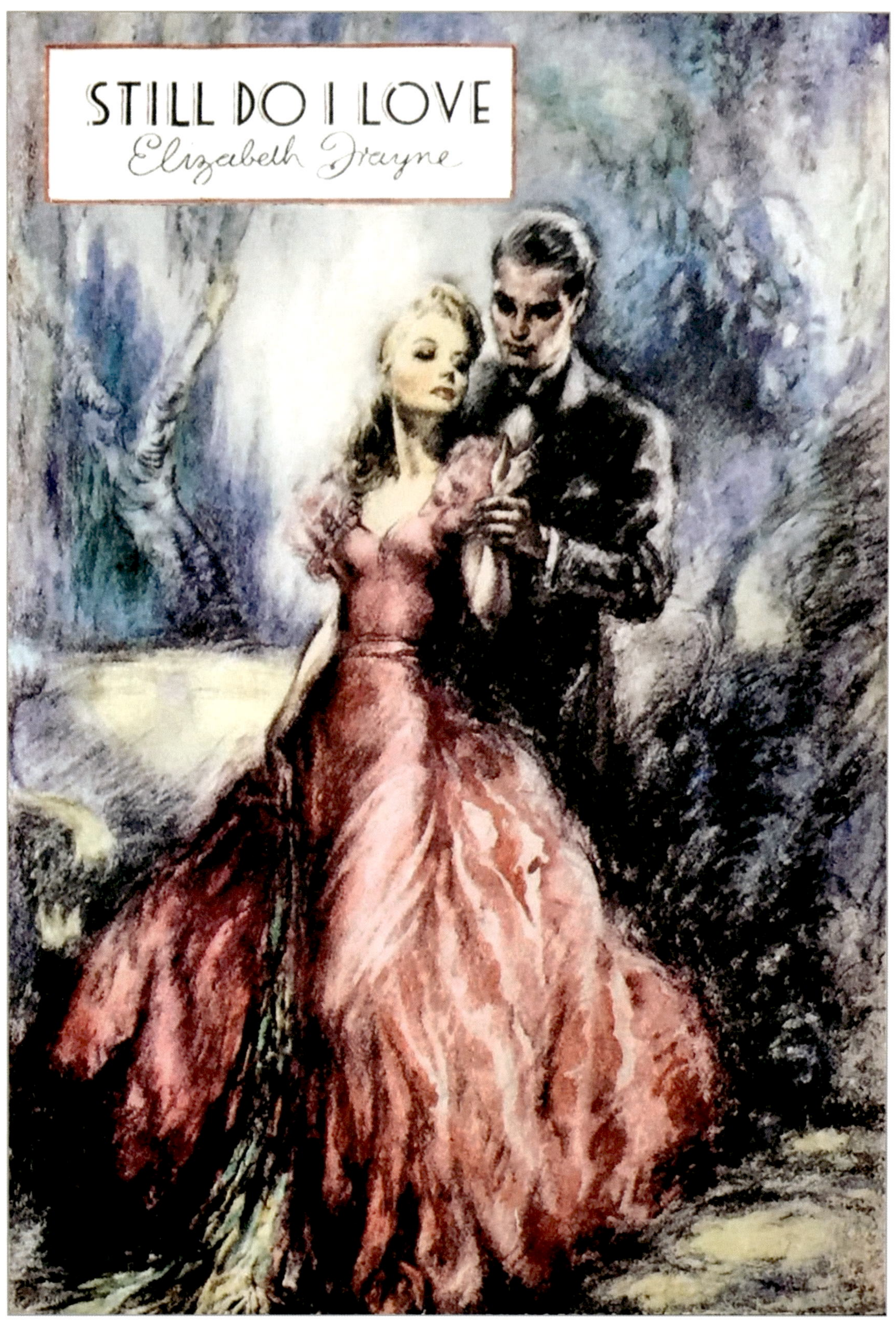

Still Do I Love by Elizabeth Frayne (Hodder & Stoughton, 1942)

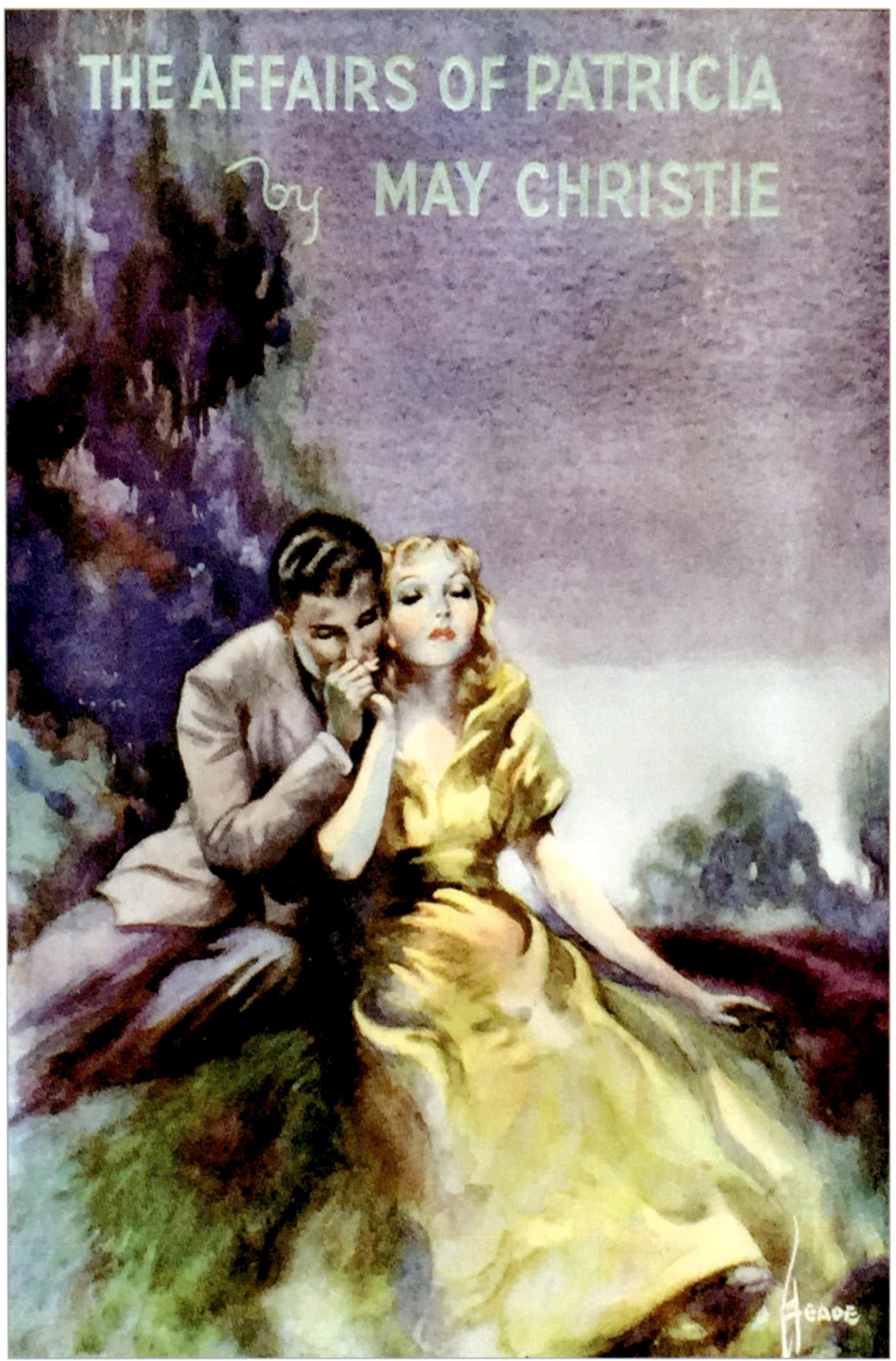

The Affairs of Patricia by May Christie (Hodder & Stoughton, 1942)

MILLS & BOON

It has long been known that Heade provided dustjacket pieces for some of the hardback novels published by romance specialists Mills & Boon, but the full extent of his work for that company has only lately become apparent. The main reason for the previous underestimation of this aspect of the artist's career is the extreme scarcity of surviving copies of early Mills & Boon titles, particularly with their dustjackets intact, which presents a major obstacle for the researcher. However, numerous additional examples have recently been discovered during work on this volume, most of them with the aid of the University of Reading's Special Collections Department, the current repository of Mills & Boon's own archive. Further information about Heade's work for the company has also come to light. For instance, it is now apparent that a number of titles previously thought to have had Heade dustjackets when first published in the late 1930s or early 1940s did not in fact acquire those dustjackets until they were reissued in the 1950s, the artwork in question having been originally painted for earlier editions of entirely different Mills & Boon books. Further complicating matters, in addition to the signed pieces Heade completed for the company, he also supplied a number of unsigned ones, sometimes making definitive identification difficult (hence the inclusion of several possible examples in the 'Is It Heade?' section of this volume). There were hundreds of Mills & Boon novels published between the 1930s and the 1950s – perhaps as many as 2,500 in total – and Heade dustjackets will undoubtedly have featured on many more of them than have so far been tracked down, so the search will go on!

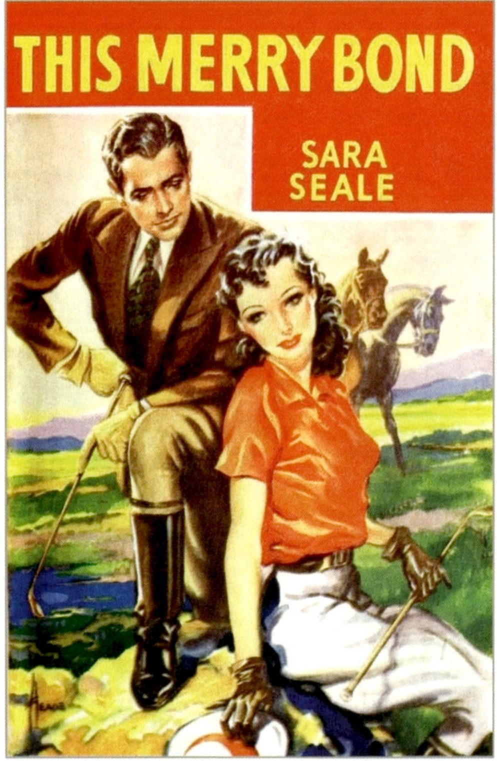

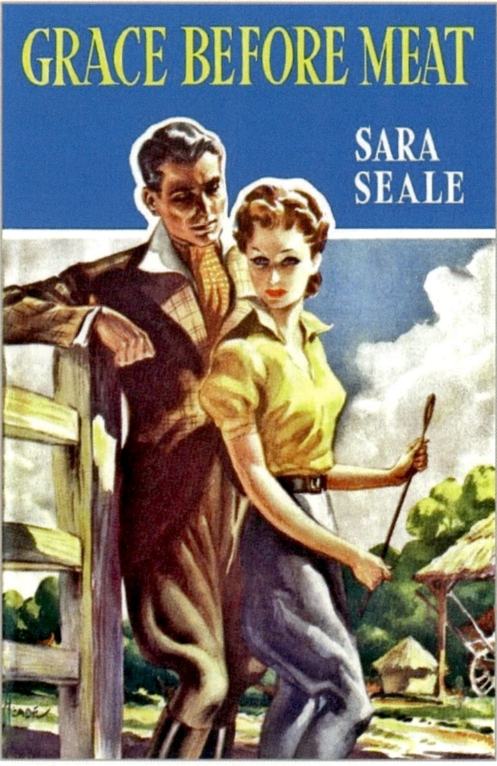

Above left: *This Merry Bond* by Sara Seale. Previously believed to have graced the book's first edition in 1938, and captioned accordingly in *The Art of Reginald Heade – Special Edition*, this dustjacket is now known to have been produced instead for a 1953 reissue. The artwork was reused from a different Mills & Boon title – see facing page.

Above right: *Grace Before Meat* by Sara Seale. Also dated as a 1938 piece in *The Art of Reginald Heade – Special Edition*, this dustjacket actually debuted on a 1952 reissue. (The 1938 first edition had a dustjacket by a different artist.) In this case, the title for which Heade originally painted the artwork is currently unidentified.

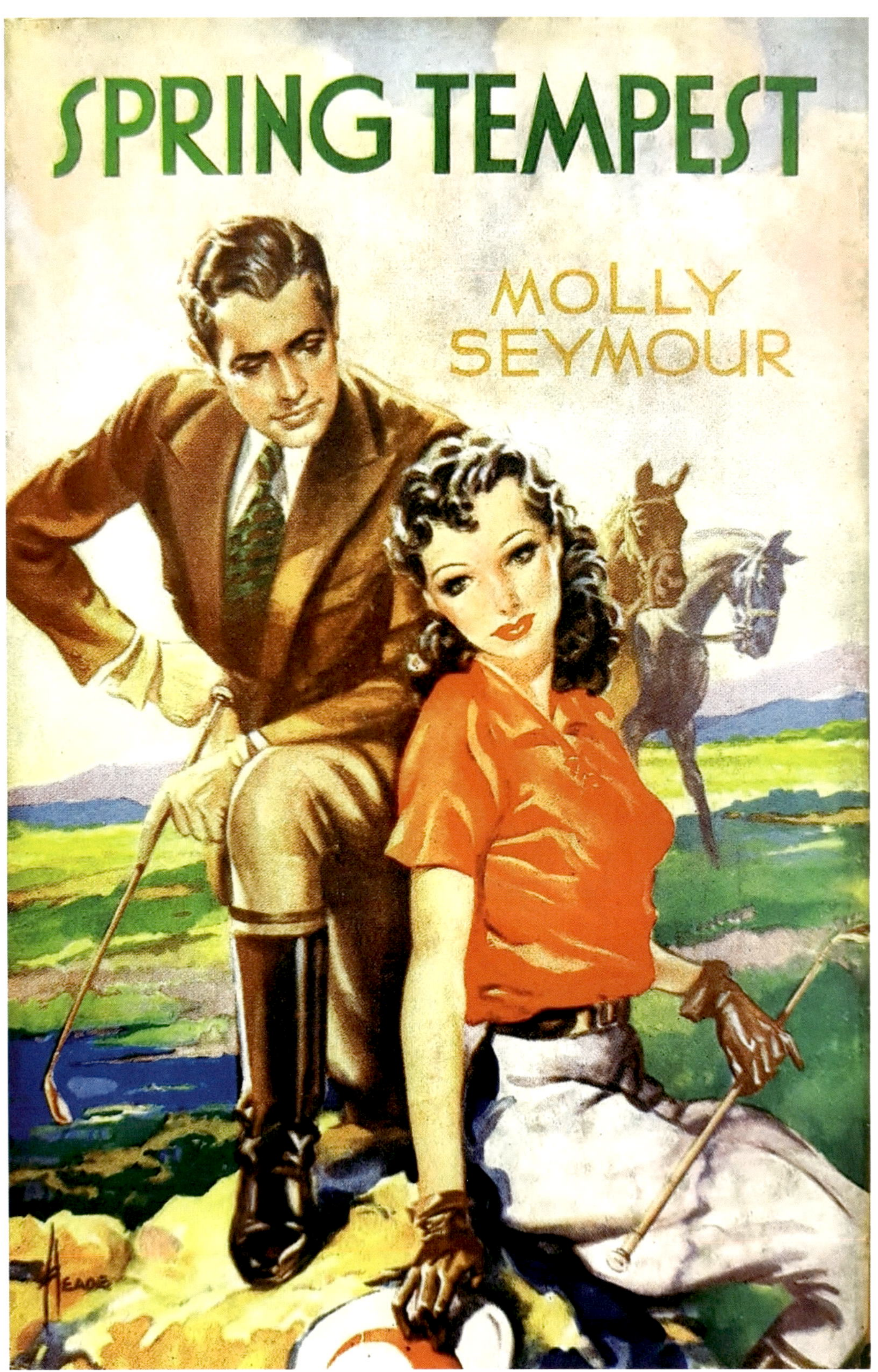

Spring Tempest by Molly Seymour (Mills & Boon, 1941)

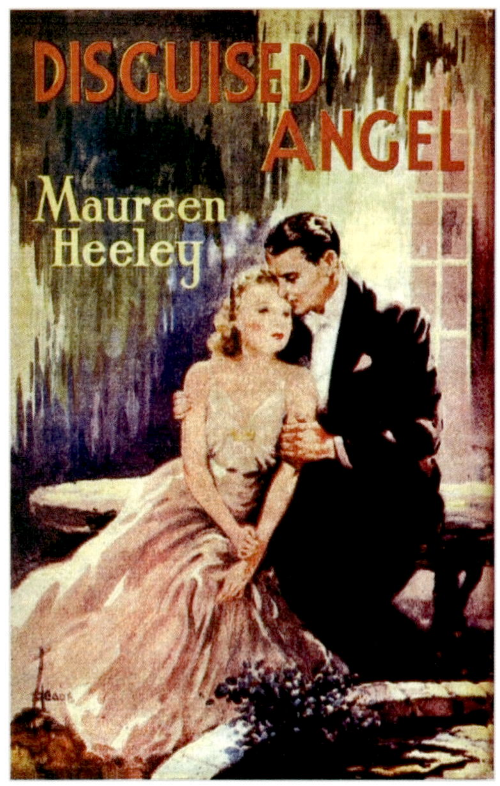

Disguised Angel by Maureen Heeley (Mills & Boon, 1940)

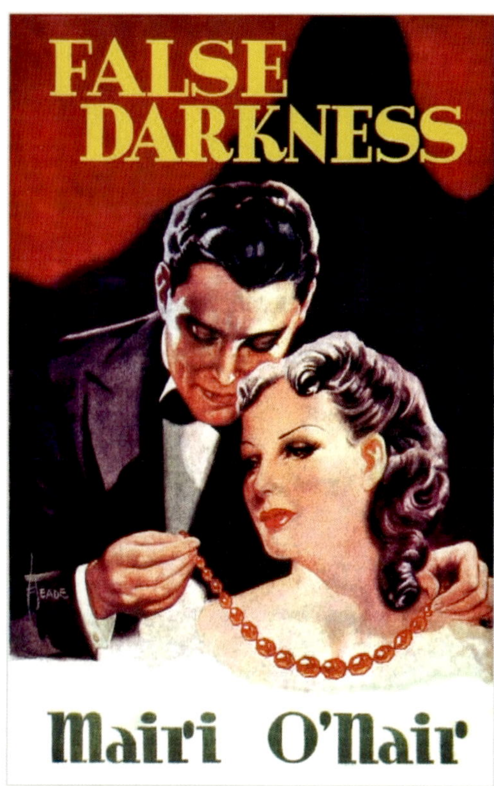

False Darkness by Mairi O'Nair (Mills & Boon, 1940)

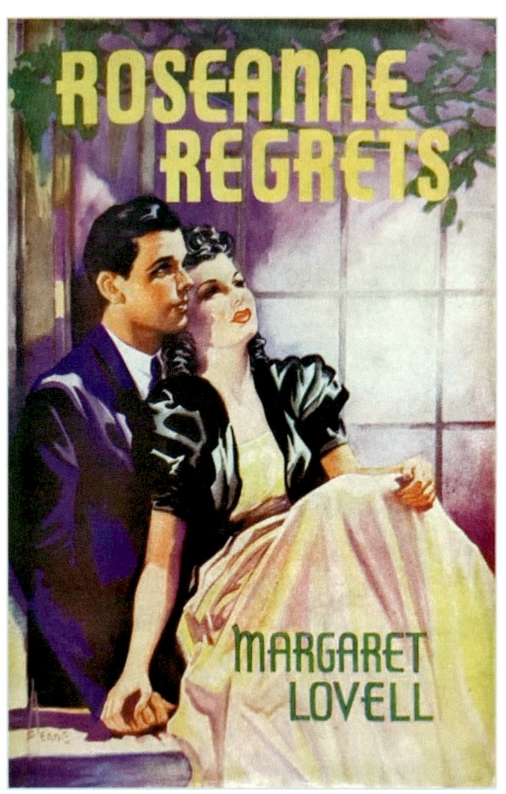

Roseanne Regrets by Margaret Lovell (Mills & Boon, 1940)

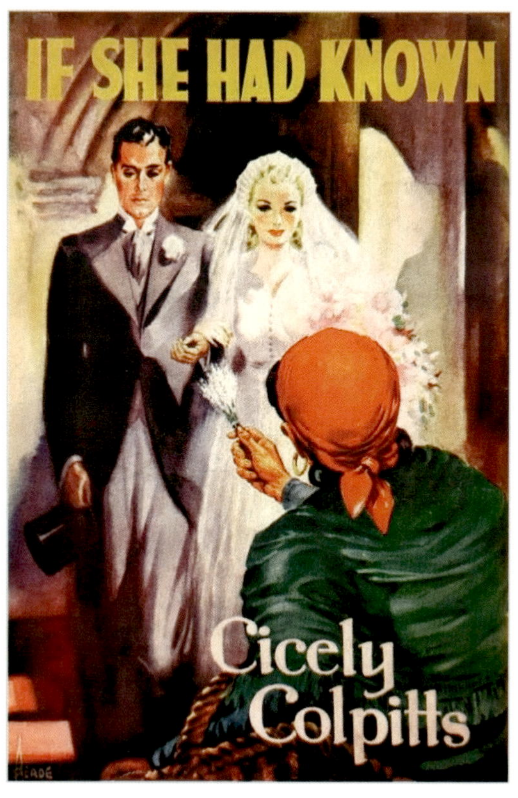

If She Had Known by Cicely Colpitts (Mills & Boon, 1940)

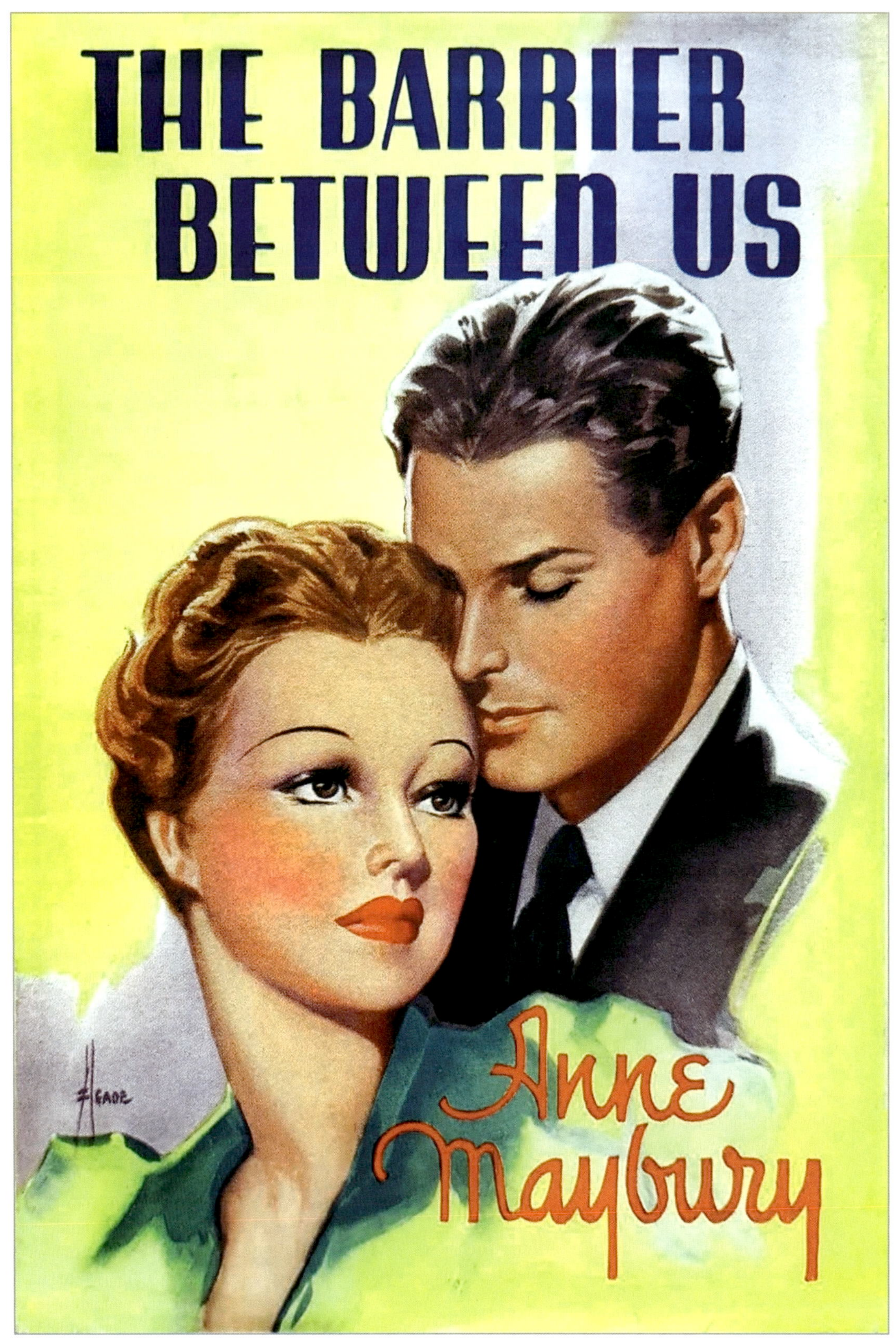

The Barrier Between Us by Anne Maybury (Mills & Boon, May 1940)

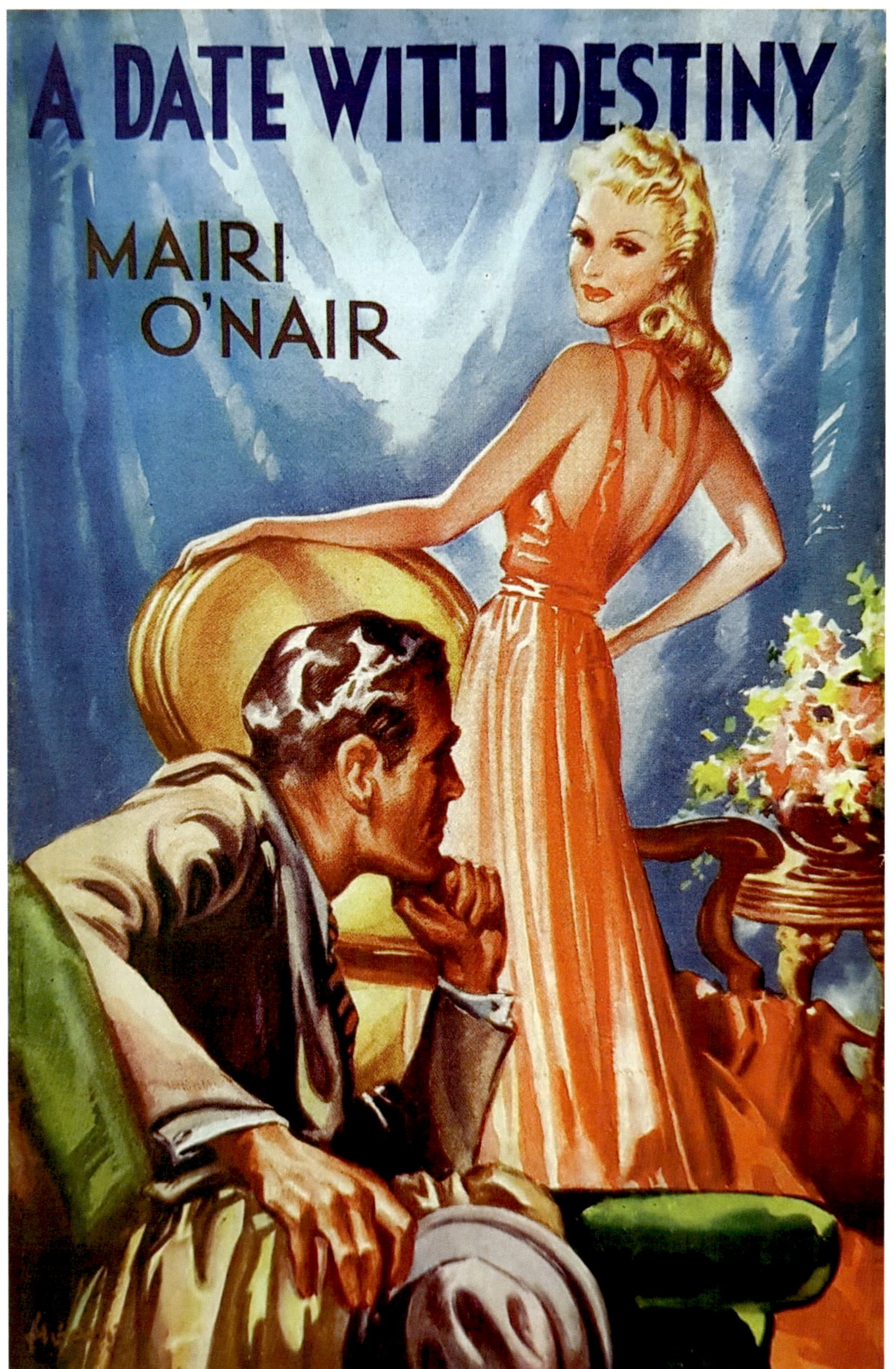

A Date With Destiny by Mairi O'Nair (Mills & Boon, 1940)

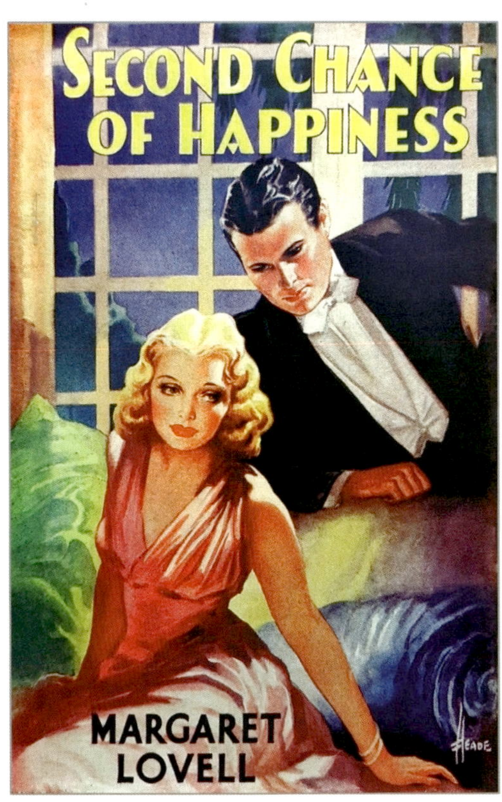

Second Chance of Happiness by Margaret Lovell (Mills & Boon, 1940)

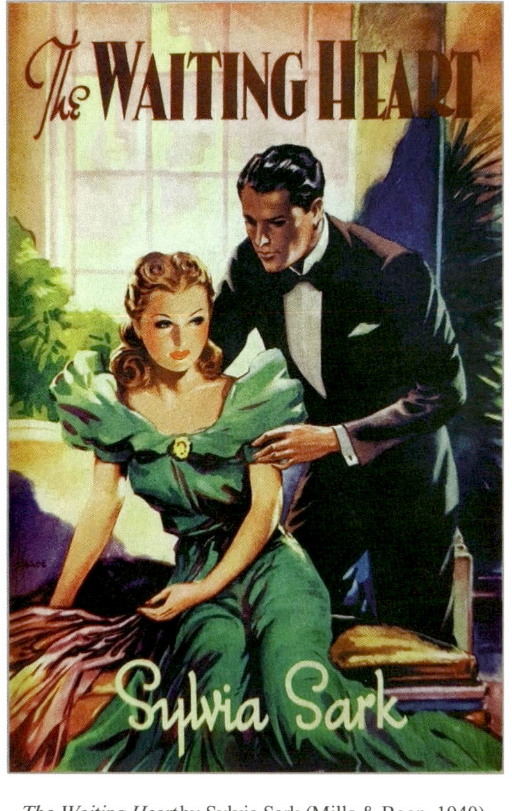

The Waiting Heart by Sylvia Sark (Mills & Boon, 1940)

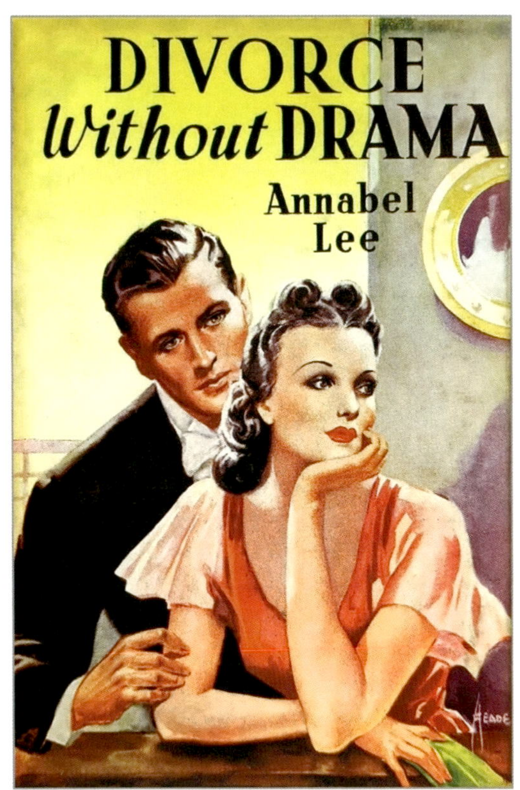

Divorce Without Drama by Annabel Lee (Mills & Boon, 1940)

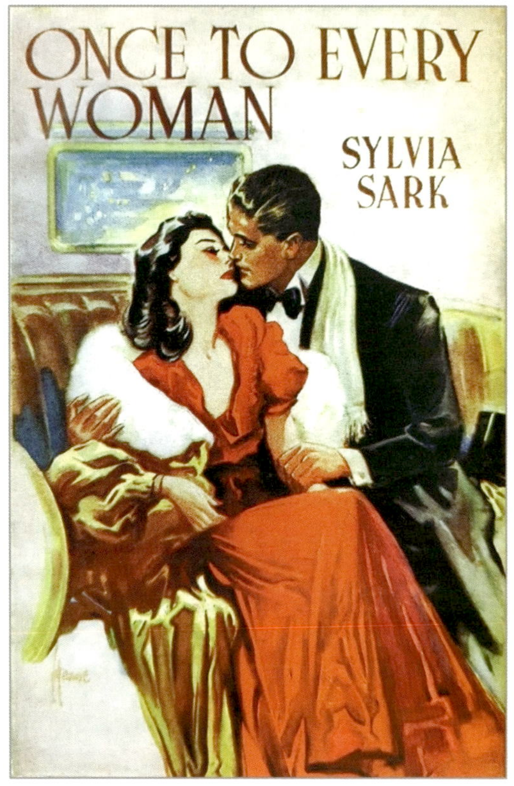

Once to Every Woman by Sylvia Sark (Mills & Boon, 1940)

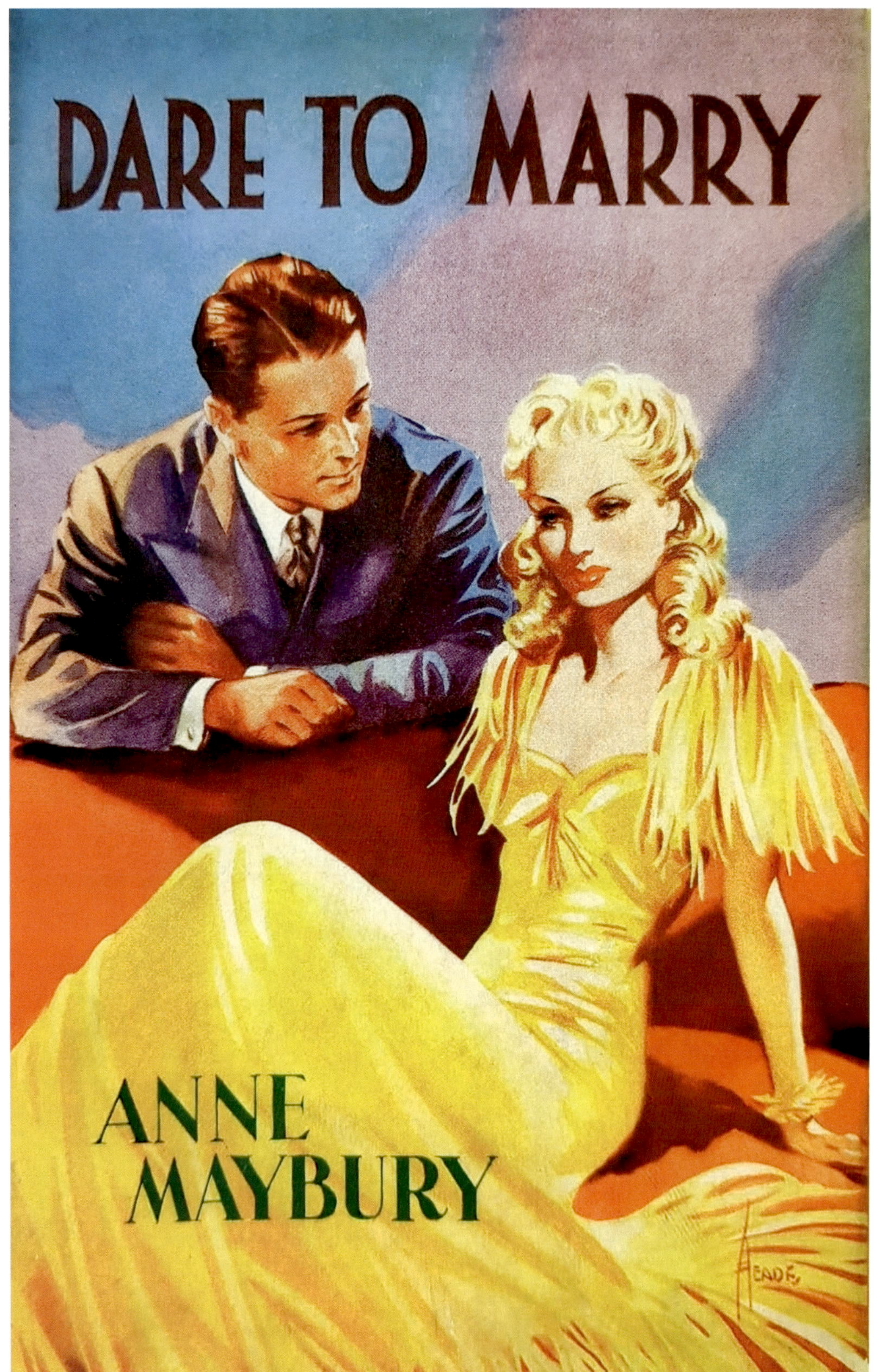

Dare to Marry by Anne Maybury (Mills & Boon, 1940)

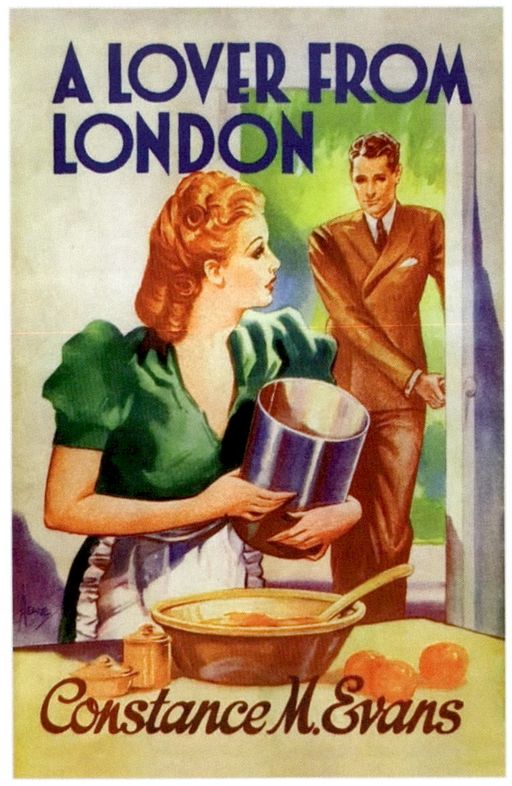

A Lover from London by Constance M Evans (Mills & Boon, 1940)

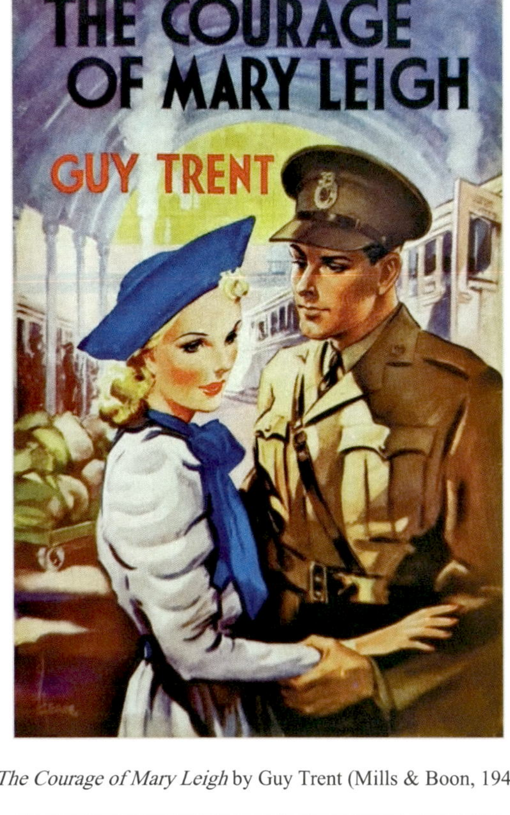

The Courage of Mary Leigh by Guy Trent (Mills & Boon, 1940)

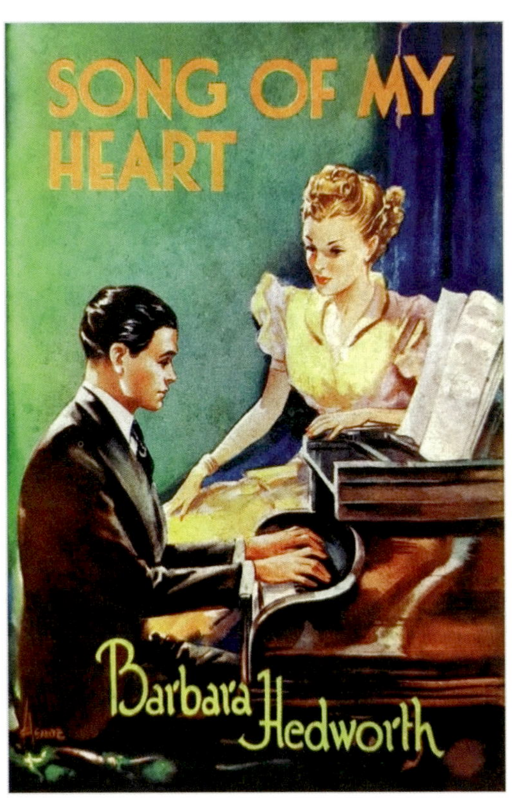

Song of My Heart by Barbara Hedworth (Mills & Boon, 1940)

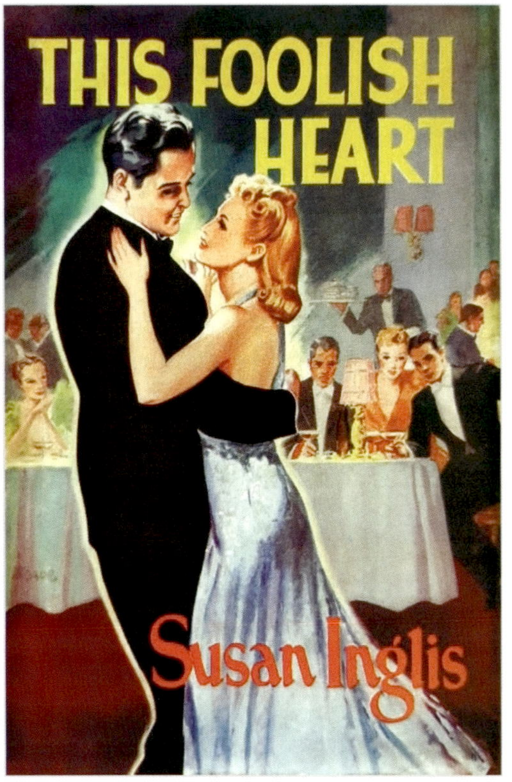

This Foolish Heart by Susan Inglis (Mills & Boon, 1940)

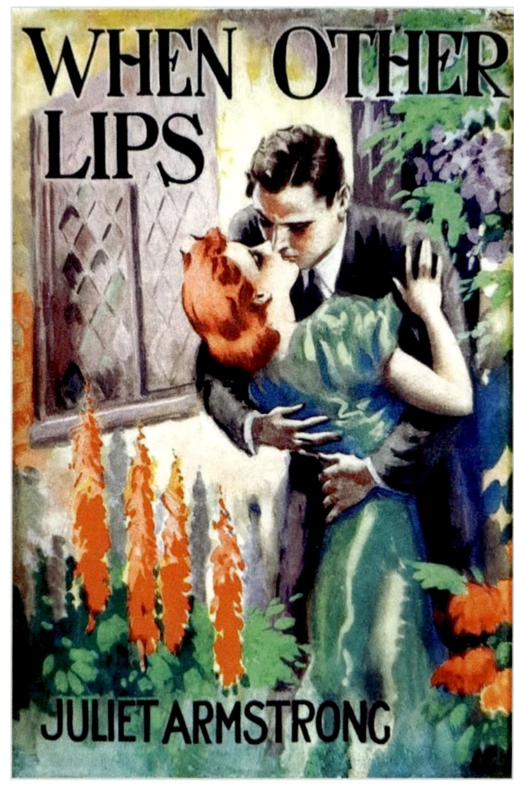

When Other Lips by Juliet Armstrong (Mills & Boon, 1940)

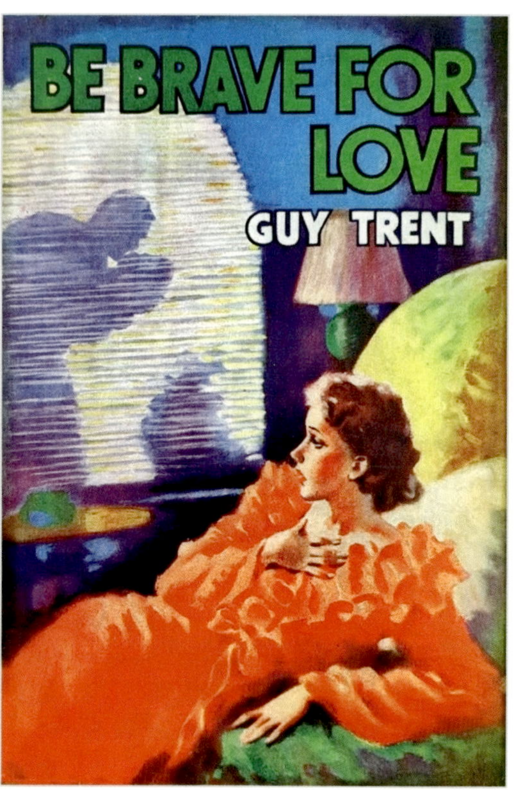

Be Brave for Love by Guy Trent (Mills & Boon, 1940)

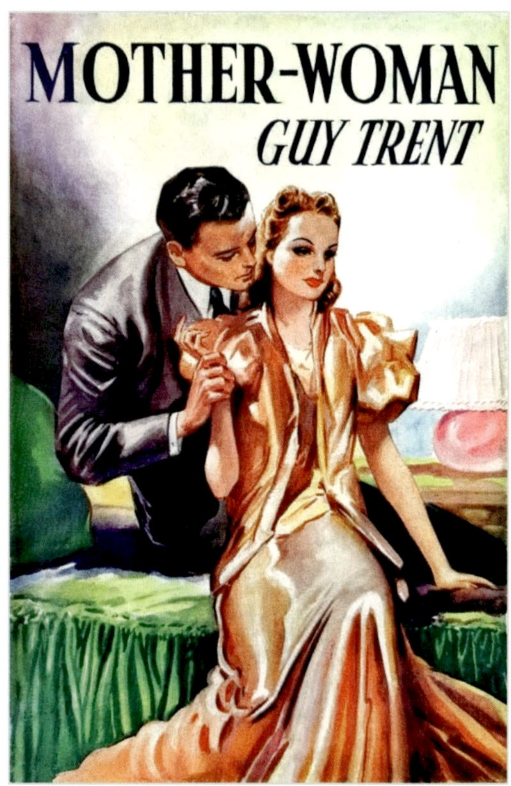

Mother-Woman by Guy Trent (Mills & Boon, 1940)

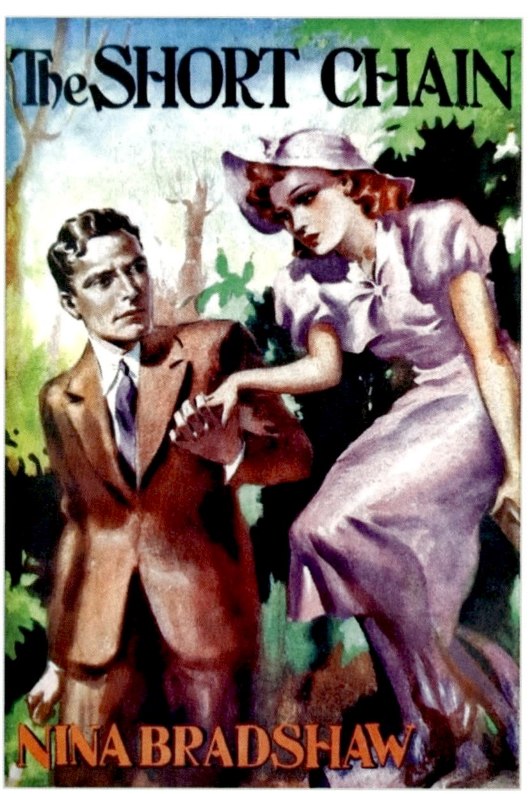

The Short Chain by Nina Bradshaw (Mills & Boon, 1940)

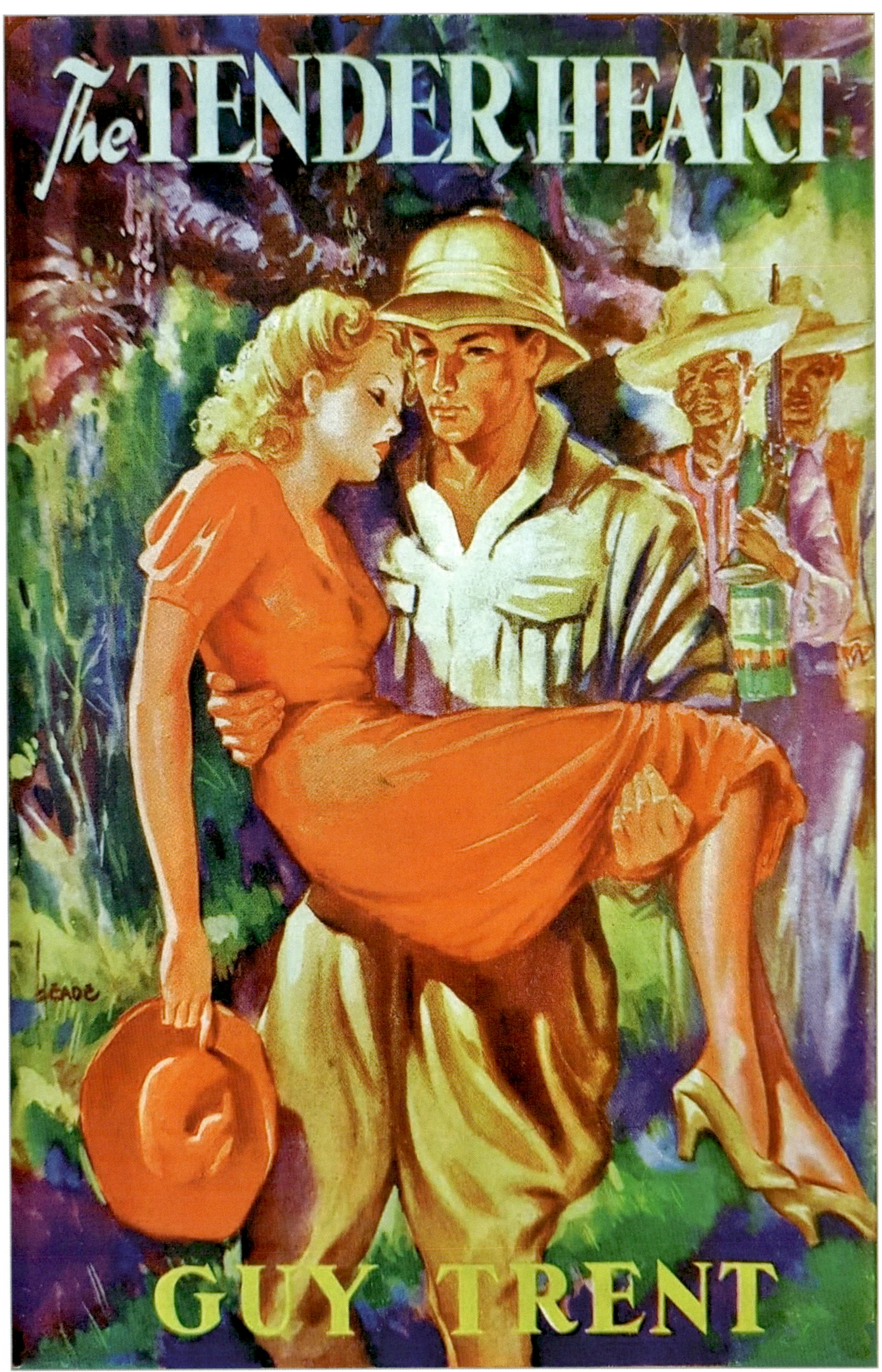

The Tender Heart by Guy Trent (Mills & Boon, 1940)

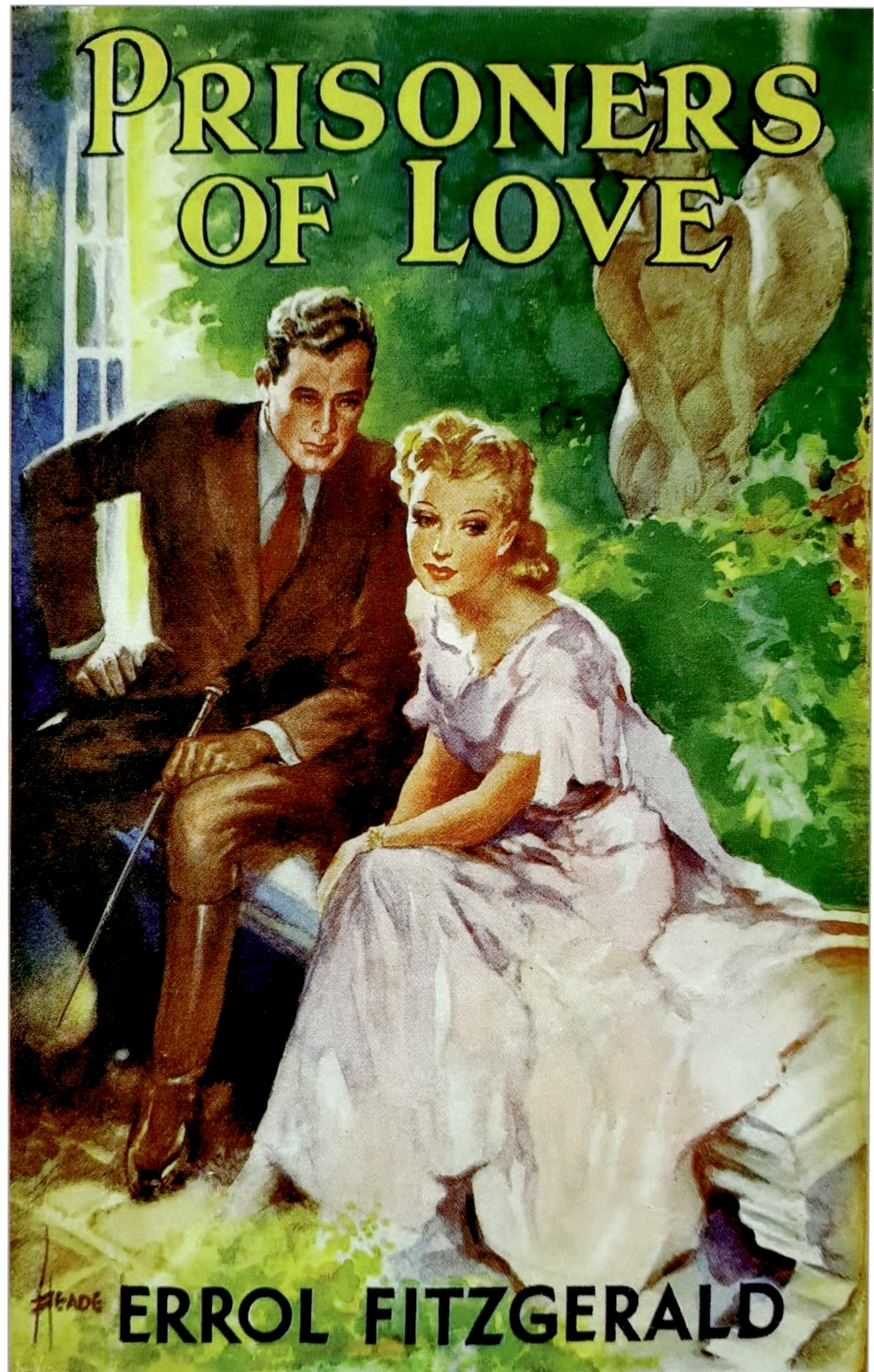

Prisoners of Love by Errol Fitzgerald (Mills & Boon, 1940)

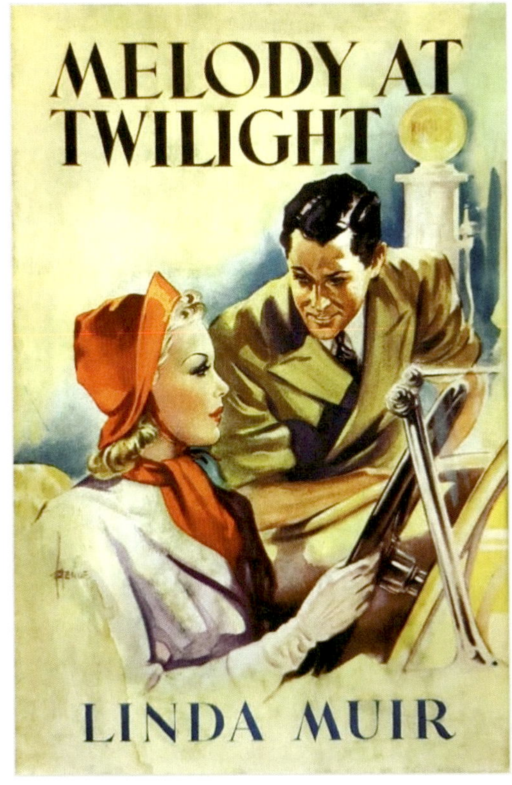

Melody at Twilight by Linda Muir (Mills & Boon, 1940)

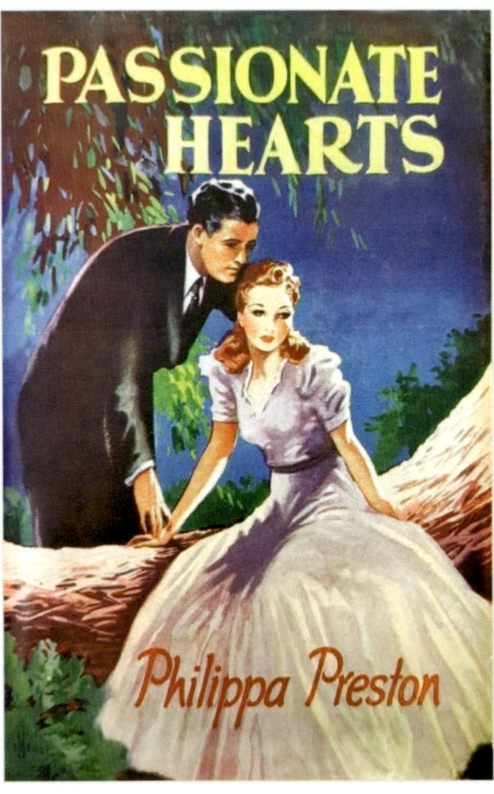

Passionate Hearts by Philippa Preston (Mills & Boon, 1940)

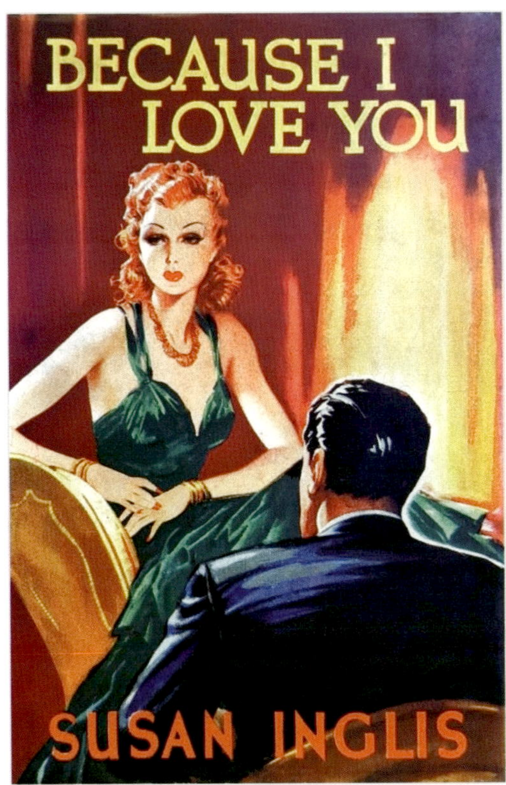

Because I Love You by Susan Inglis (Mills & Boon, 1940)

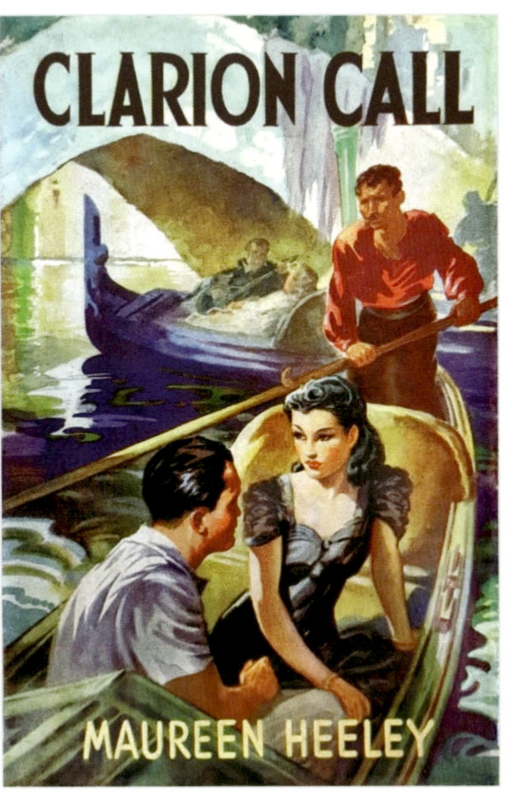

Clarion Call by Maureen Heeley (Mills & Boon, 1940)

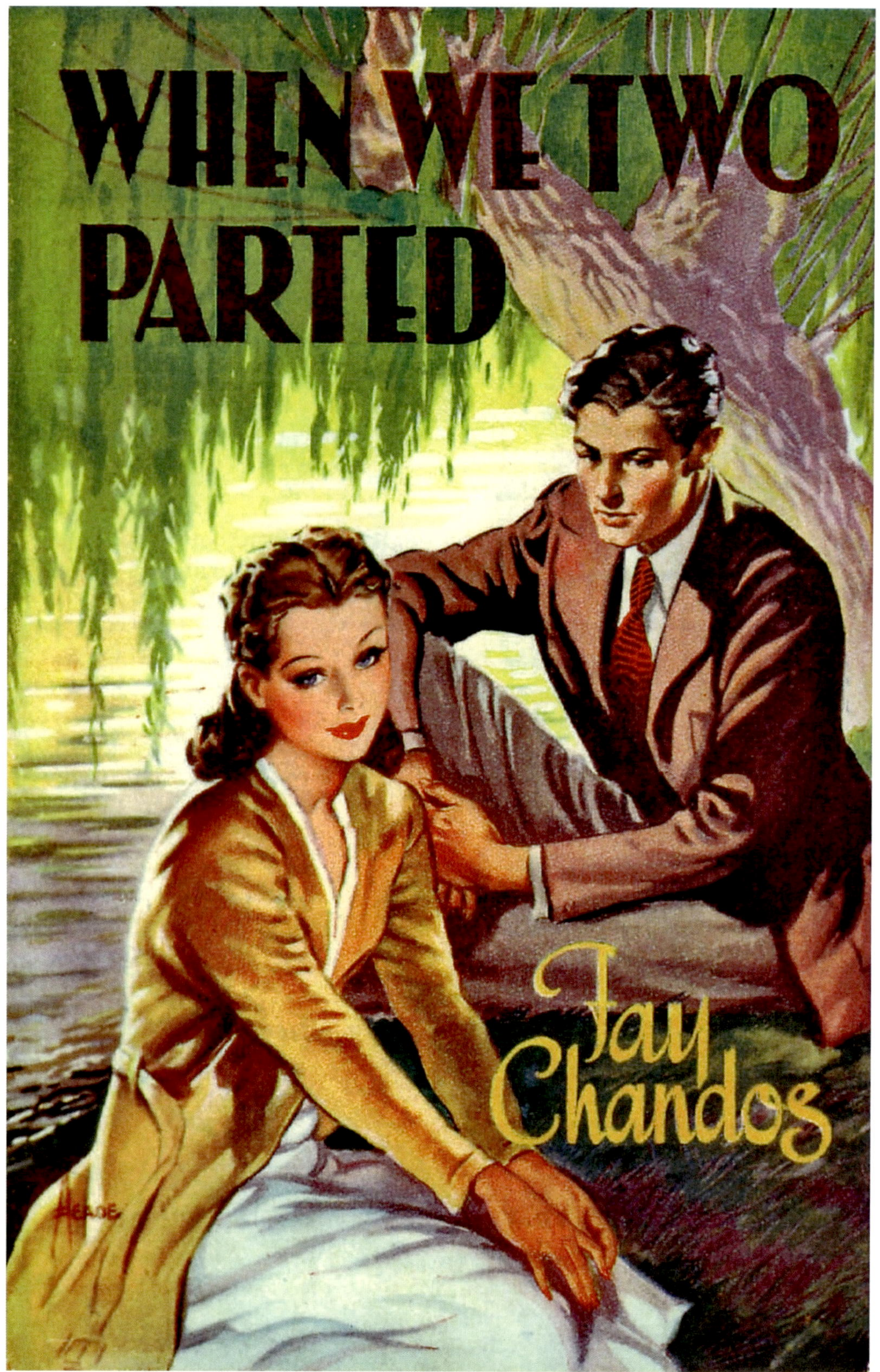

When We Two Parted by Fay Chandos (Mills & Boon, 1940)

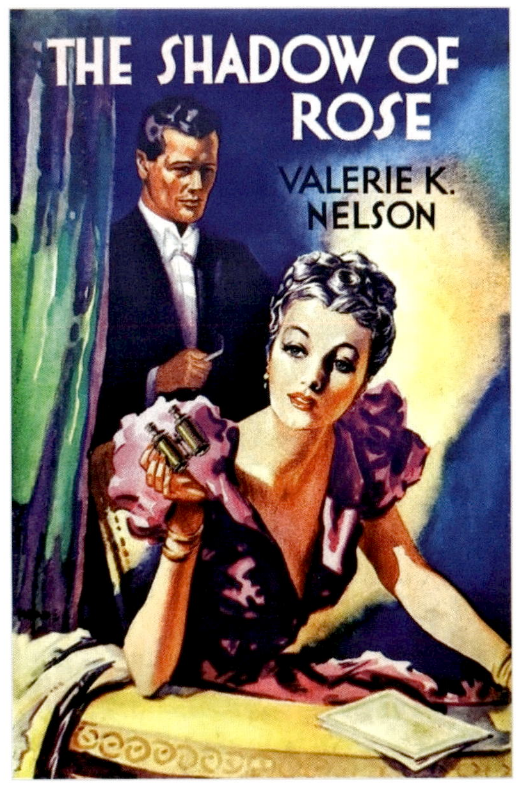

The Shadow of Rose by Valerie K Nelson (Mills & Boon, 1941)

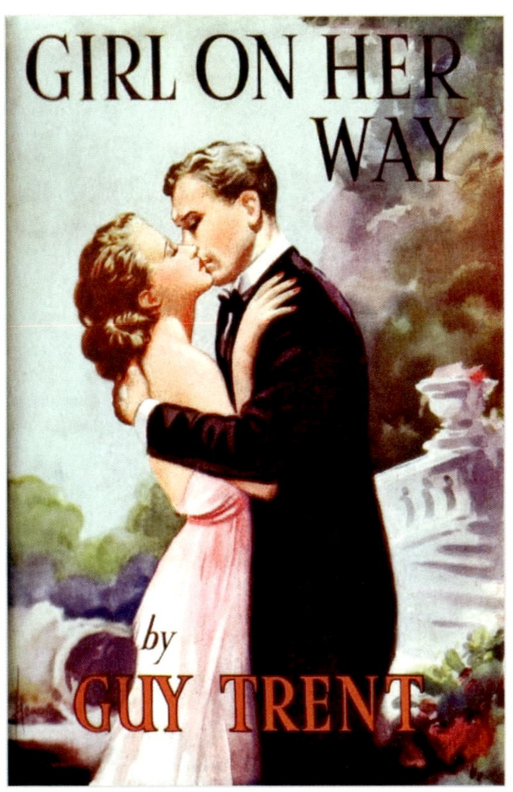

Girl on Her Way by Guy Trent (Mills & Boon, 1940)

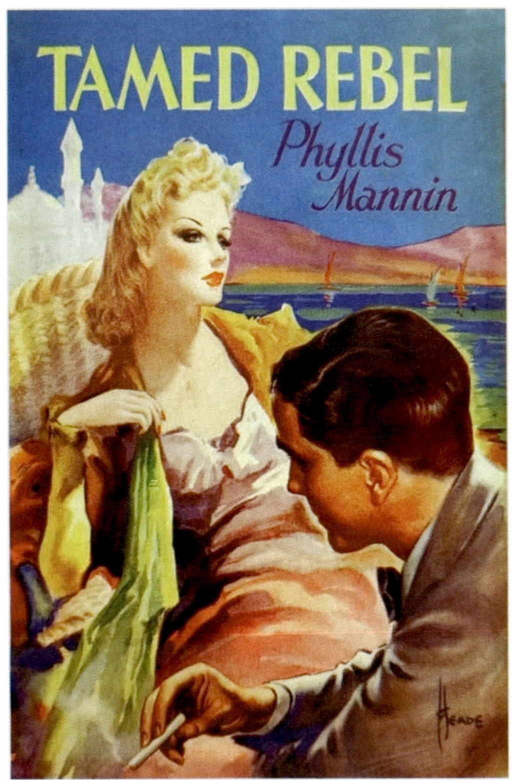

Tamed Rebel by Phyllis Mannin (Mills & Boon, 1941)

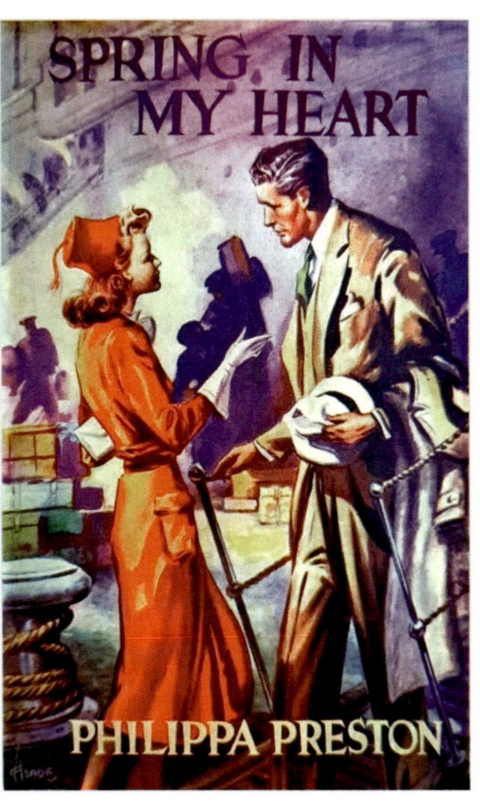

Spring in My Heart by Philippa Preston (Mills & Boon, 1941)

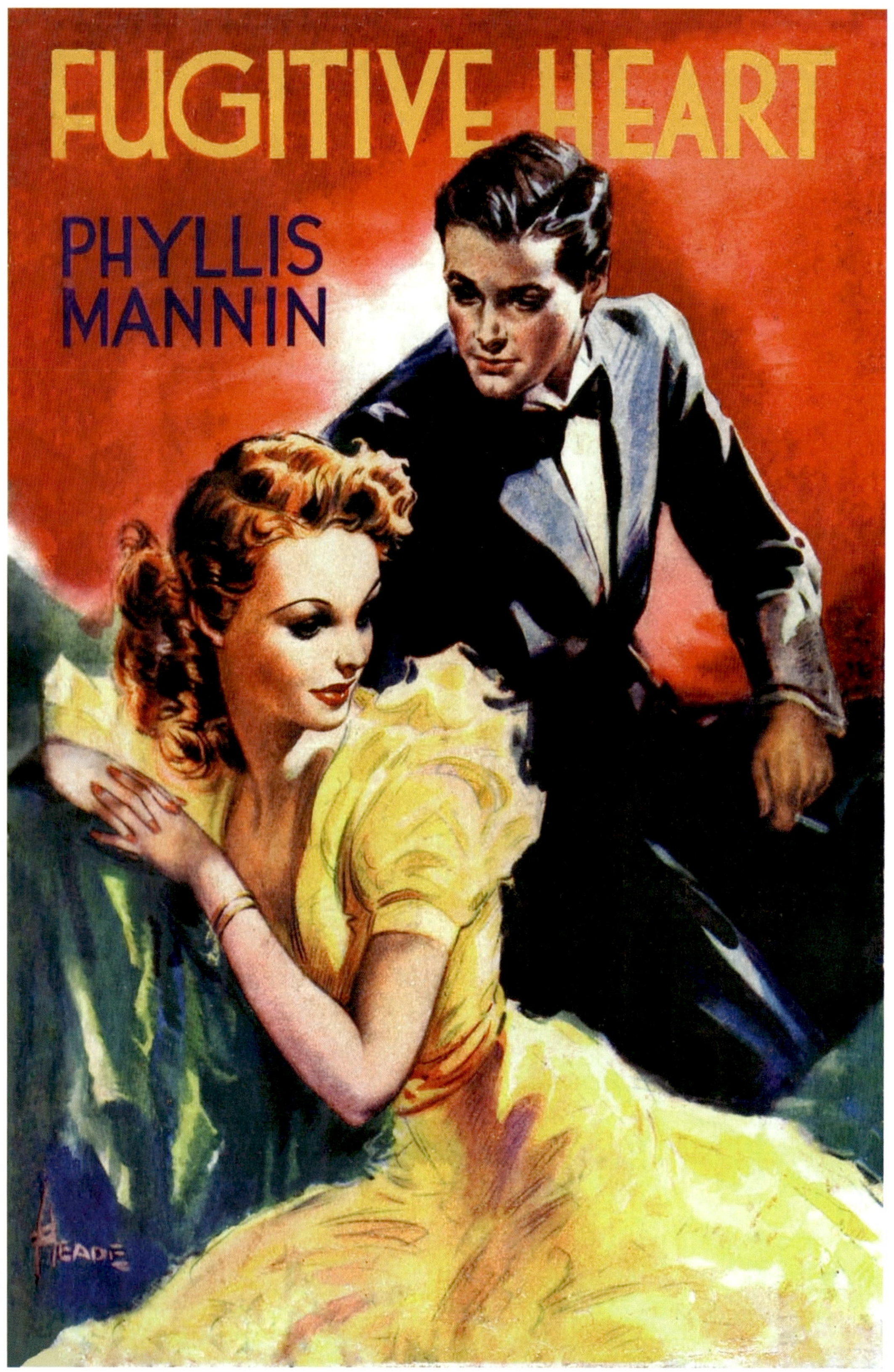

Fugitive Heart by Phyllis Mannin (Mills & Boon, 1941)

Where Fairy Tales End by Margaret Malcolm (Mills & Boon, 1941)

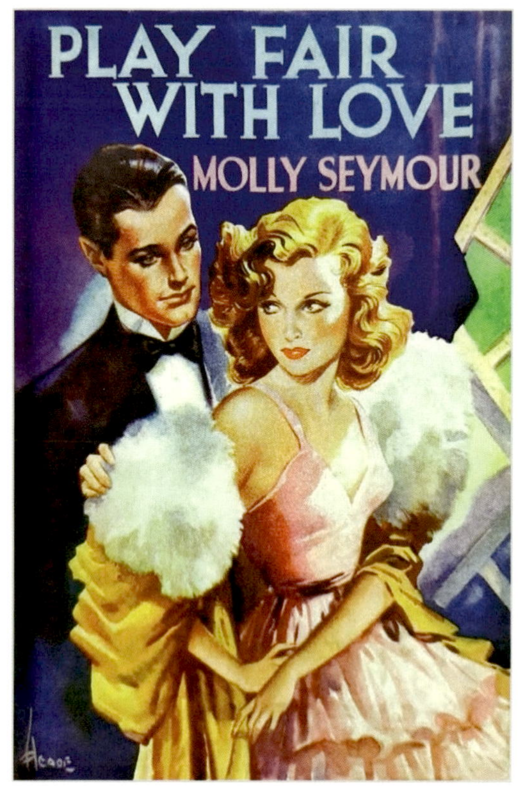

Play Fair With Love by Molly Seymour (Mills & Boon, 1941)

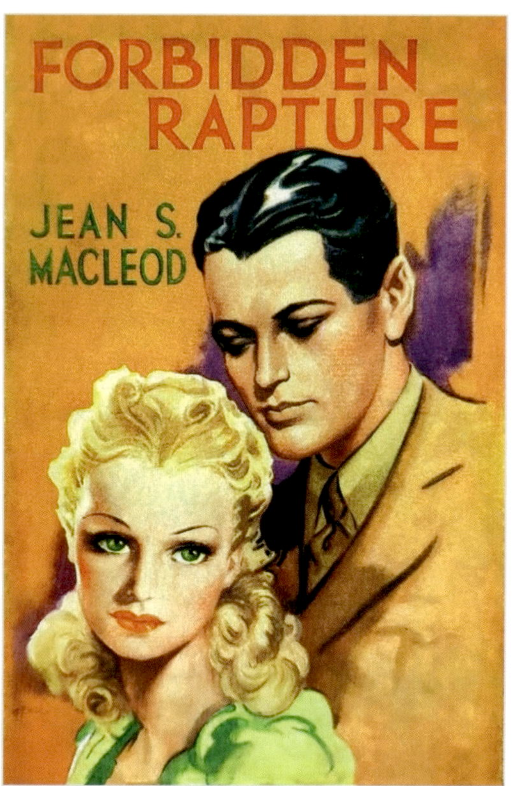

Forbidden Rapture by Jean S MacLeod (Mills & Boon, 1941)

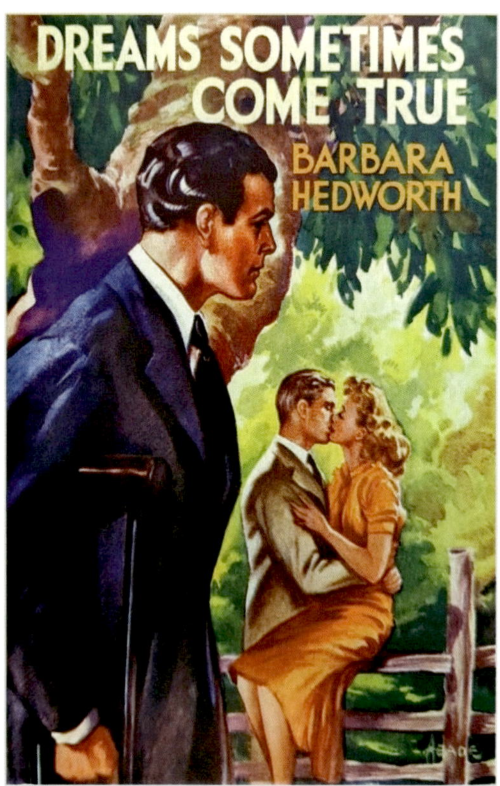

Dreams Sometimes Come True by Barbara Hedworth (Mills & Boon, 1941)

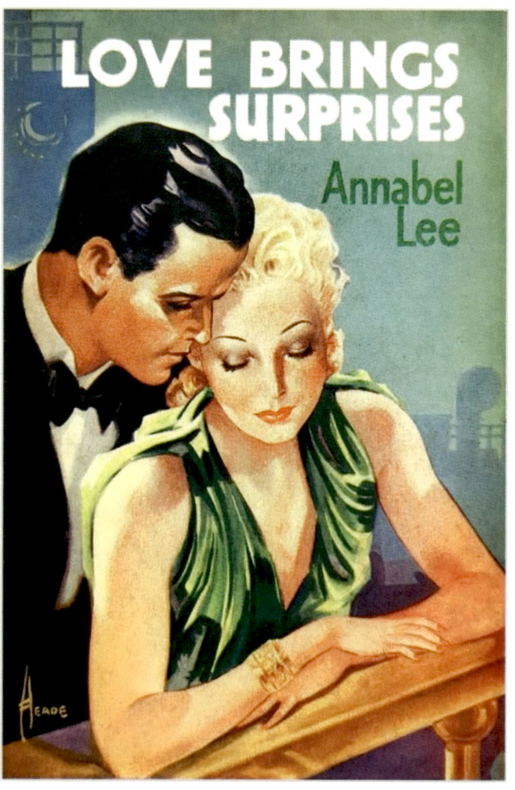

Love Brings Surprises by Annabel Lee (Mills & Boon, 1941)

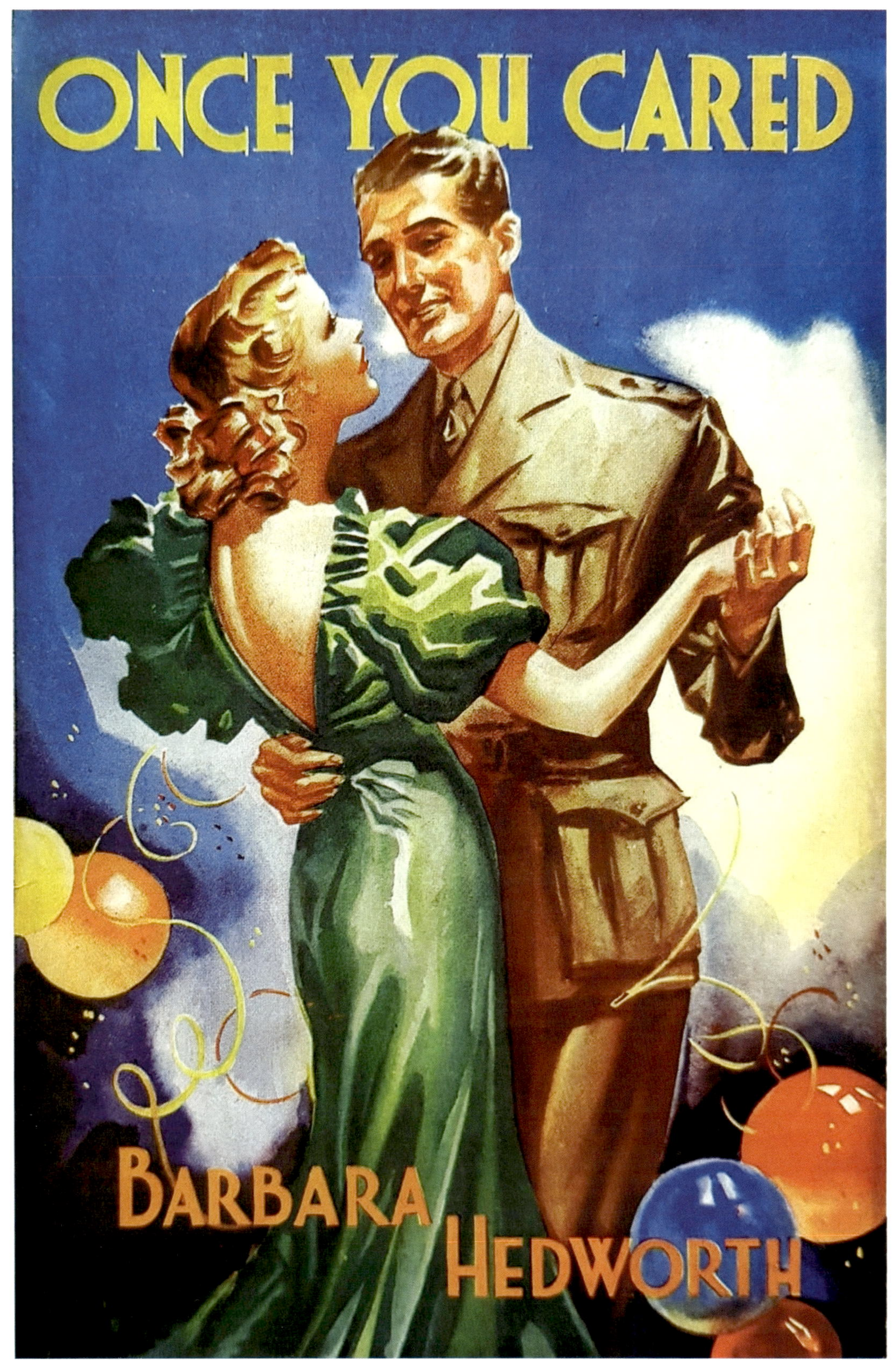

Once You Cared by Barbara Hedworth (Mills & Boon, 1941)

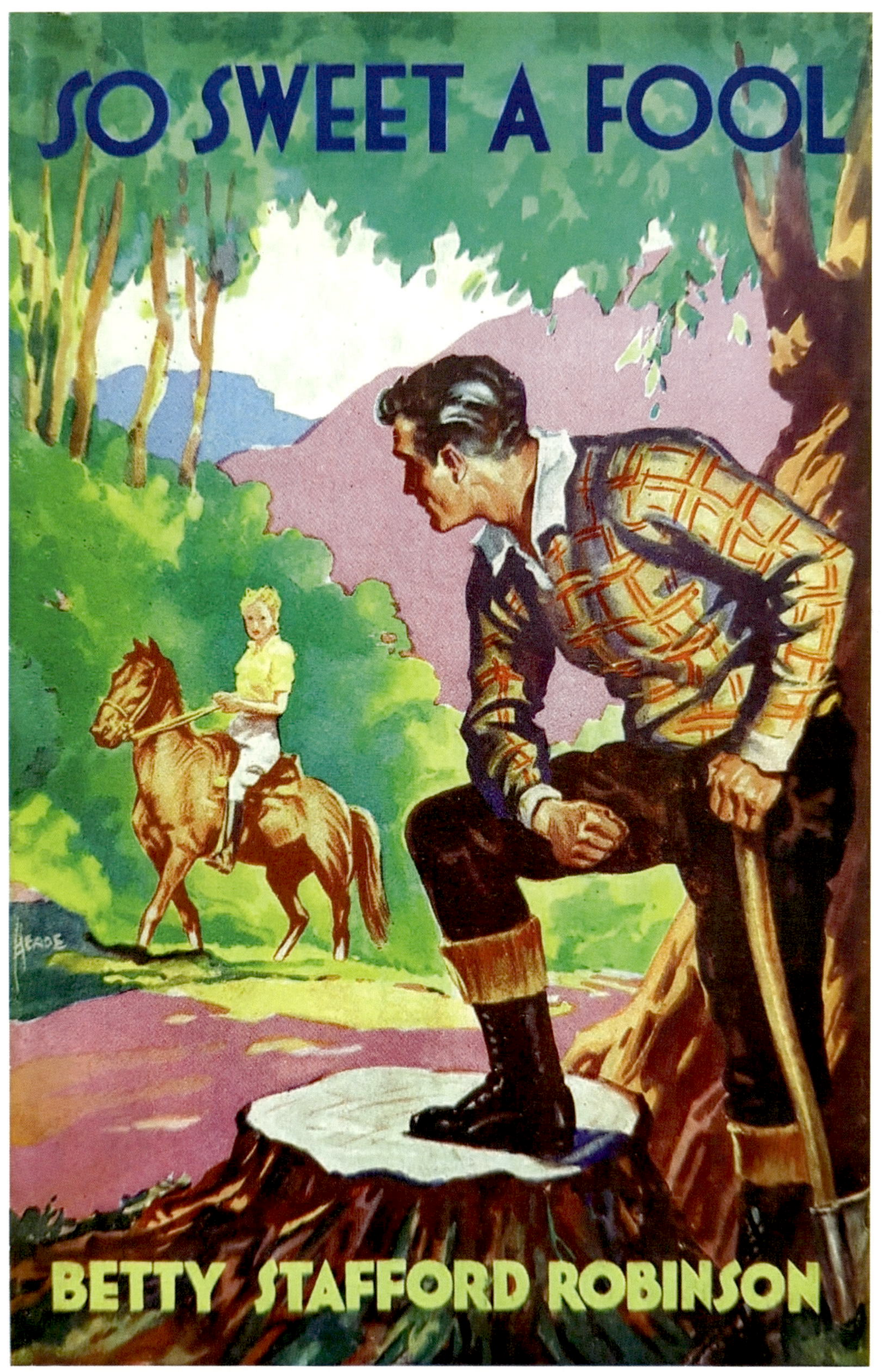

So Sweet a Fool by Betty Stafford Robinson (Mills & Boon, 1941).
A superior-quality image to the one previously presented in *The Art of Reginald Heade – Special Edition*.

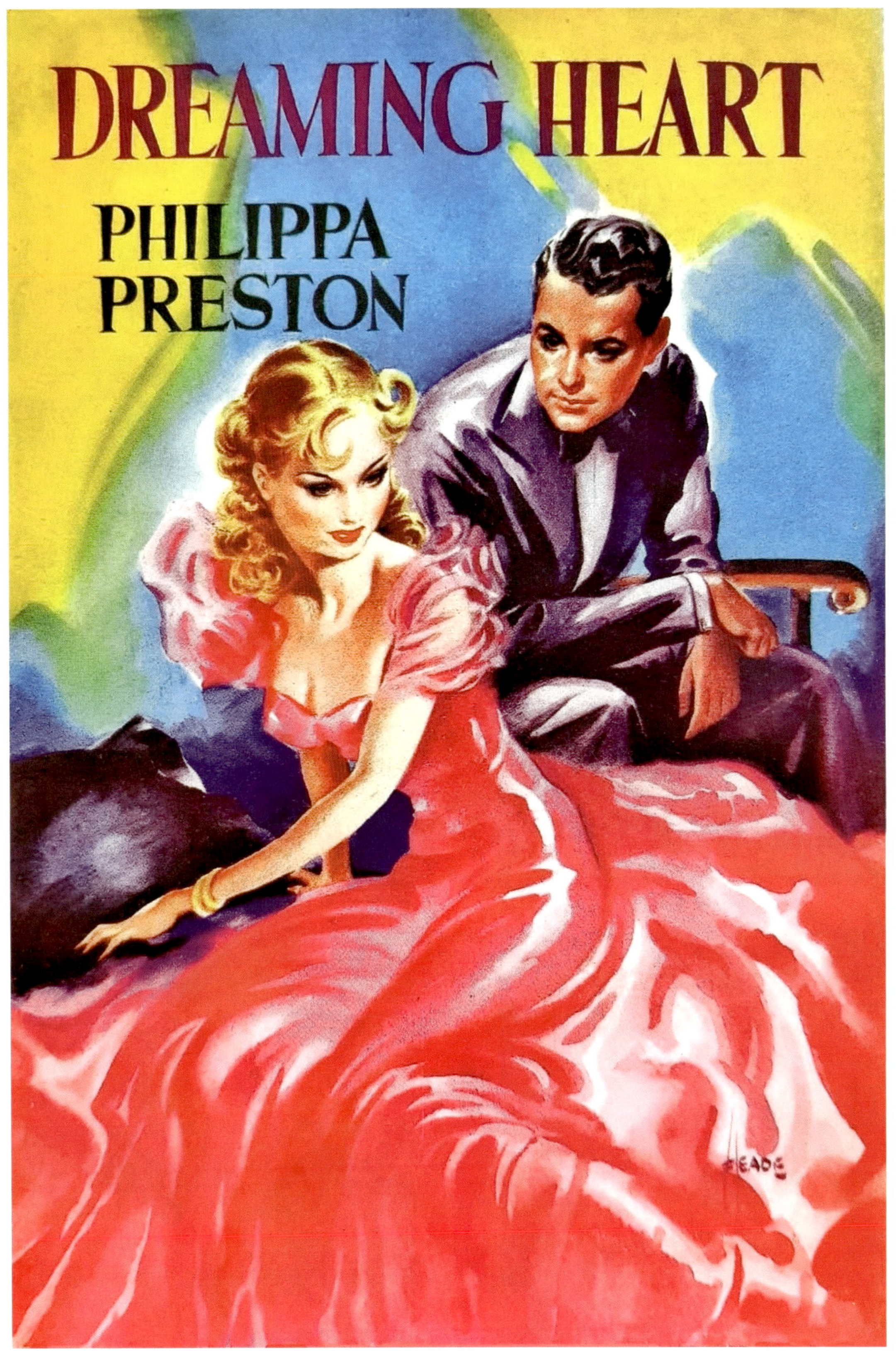

Dreaming Heart by Philippa Preston (Mills & Boon, 1941)

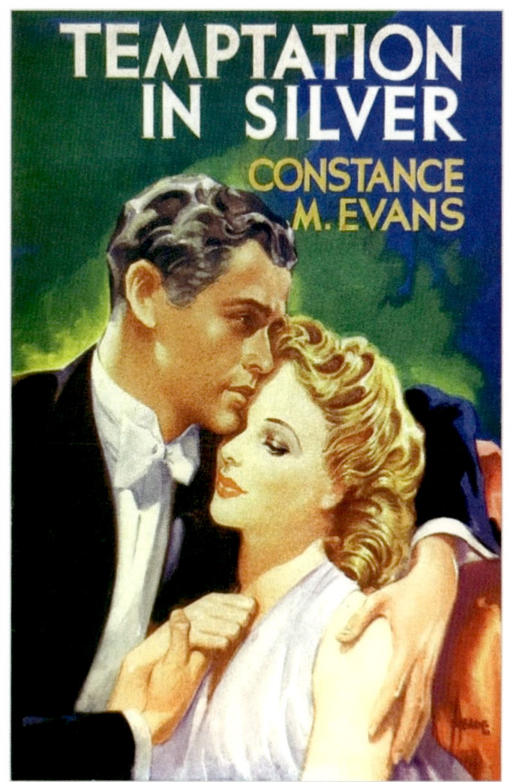

Temptation in Silver by Constance M Evans (Mills & Boon, 1941)

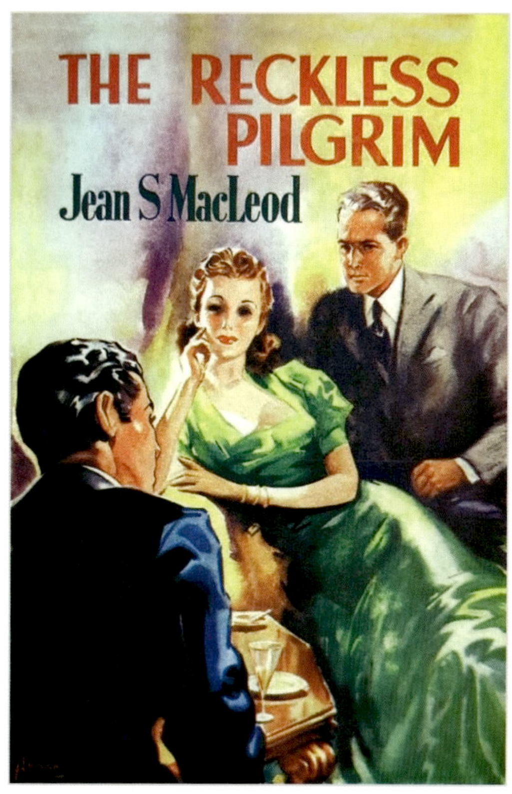

The Reckless Pilgrim by Jean S MacLeod (Mills & Boon, 1941)

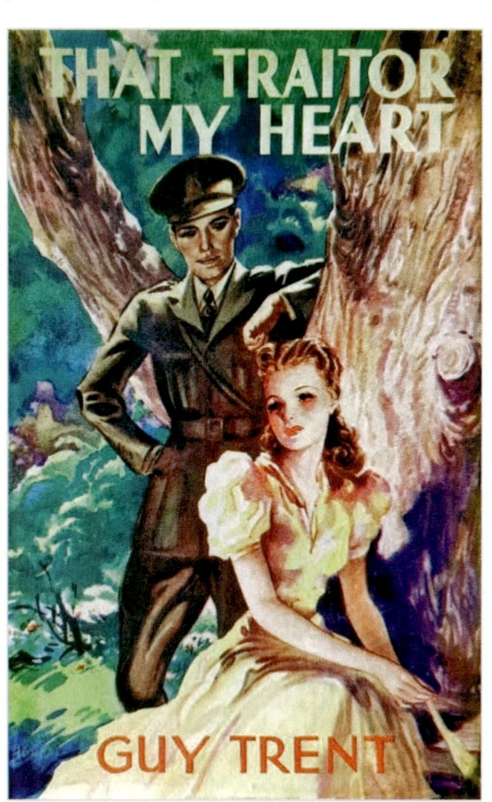

That Traitor My Heart by Guy Trent (Mills & Boon, 1941)

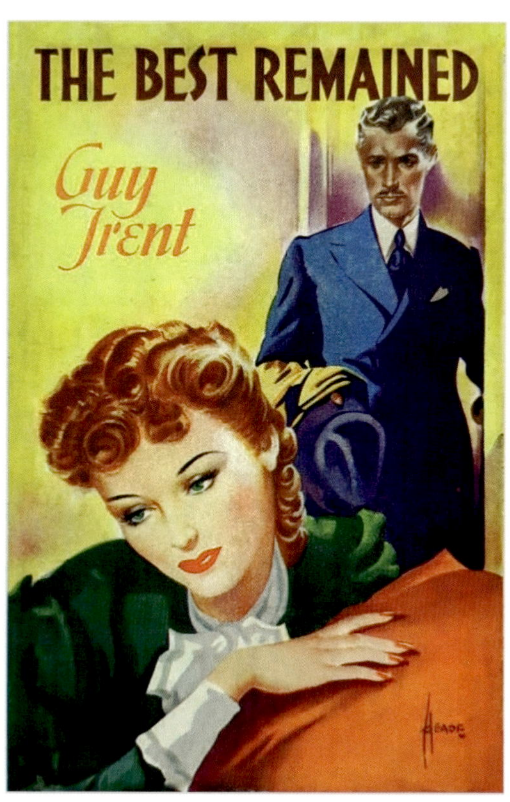

The Best Remained by Guy Trent (Mills & Boon, 1941)

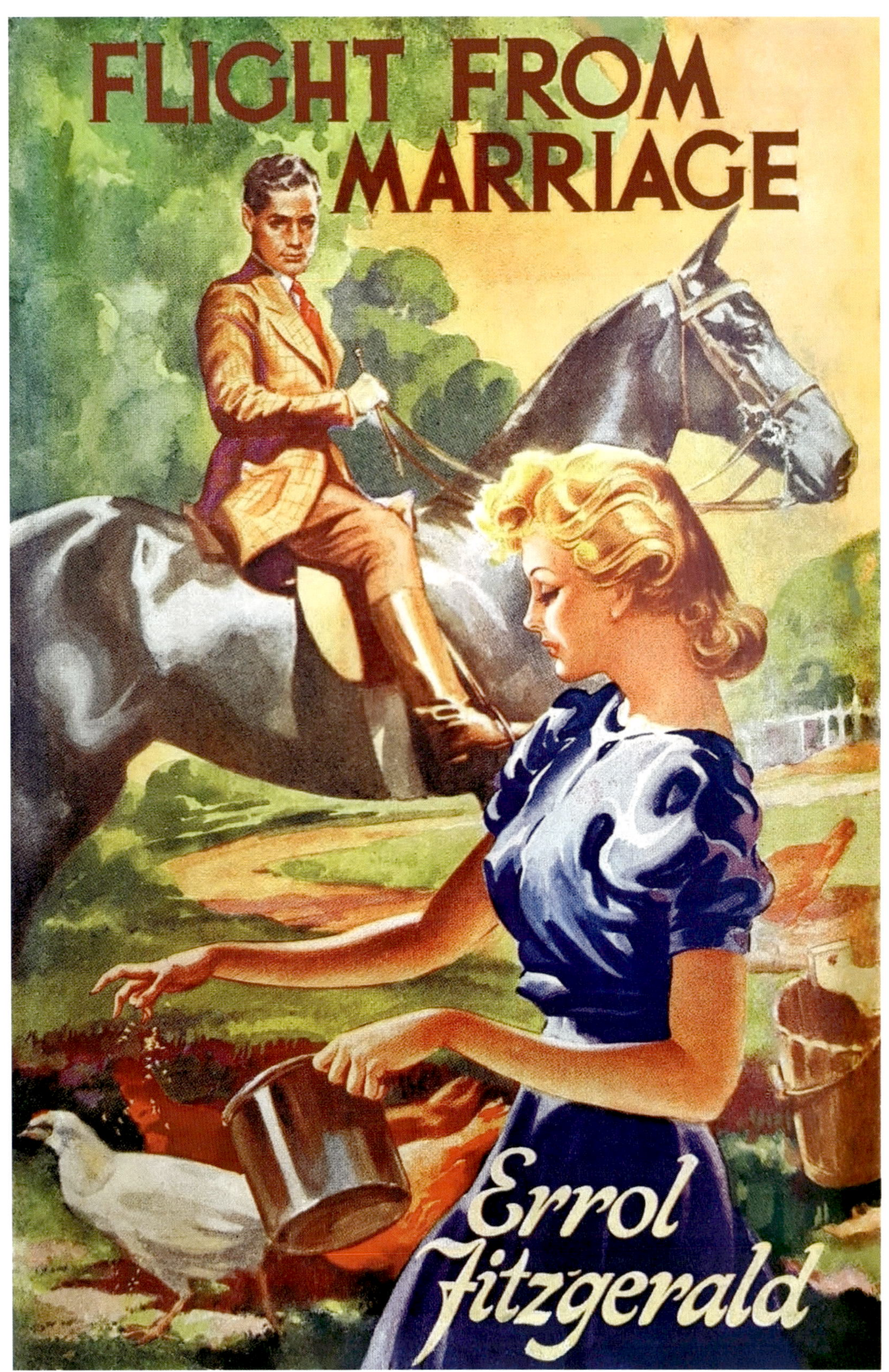

Flight from Marriage by Errol Fitzgerald (Mills & Boon, 1941)

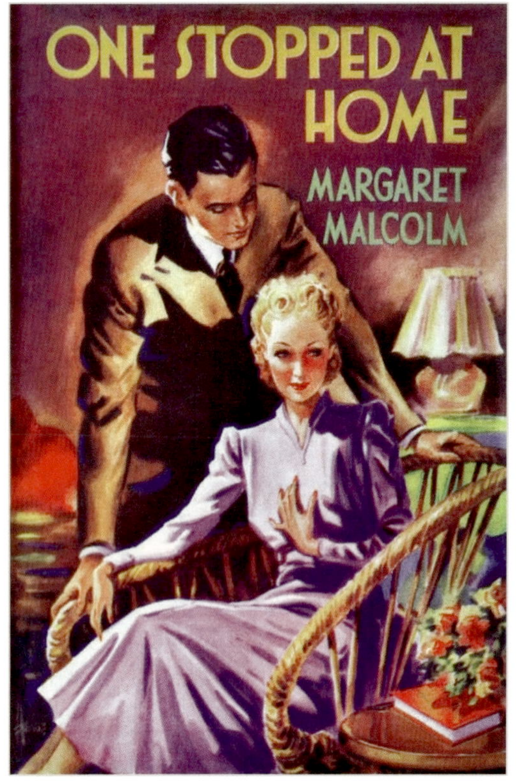

One Stopped at Home by Margaret Malcolm (Mills & Boon, 1941)

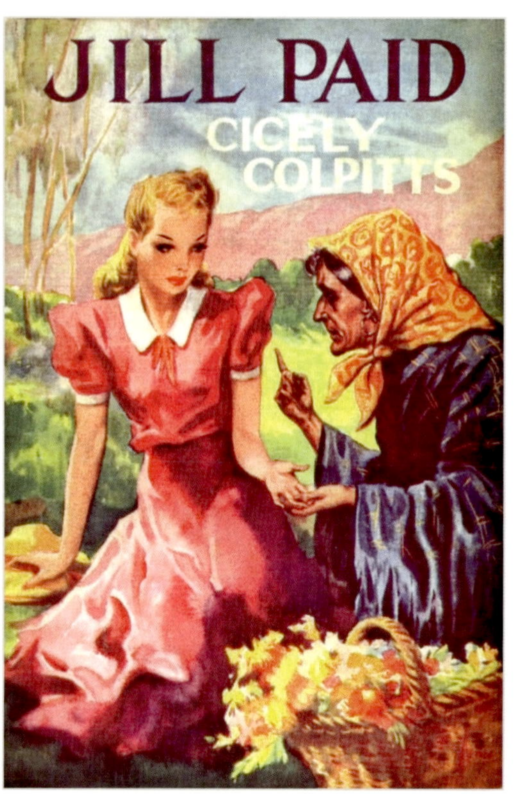

Jill Paid by Cicely Colpitts (Mills & Boon, 1942)

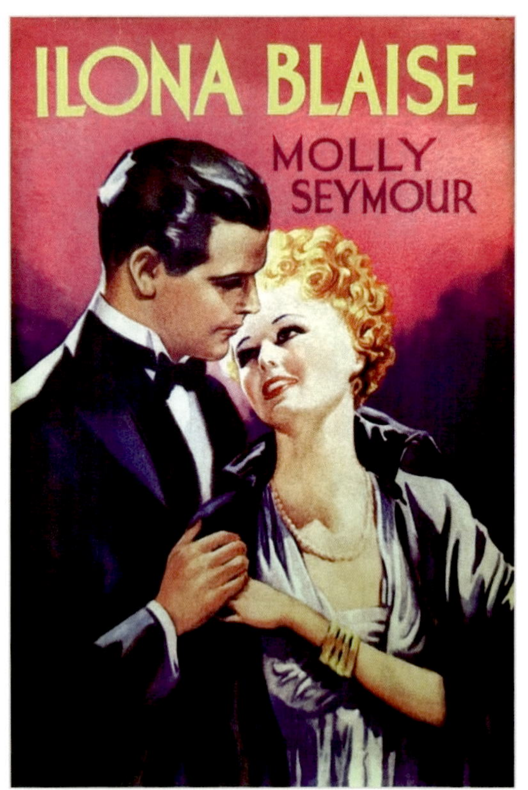

Ilona Blaise by Molly Seymour (Mills & Boon, 1942)

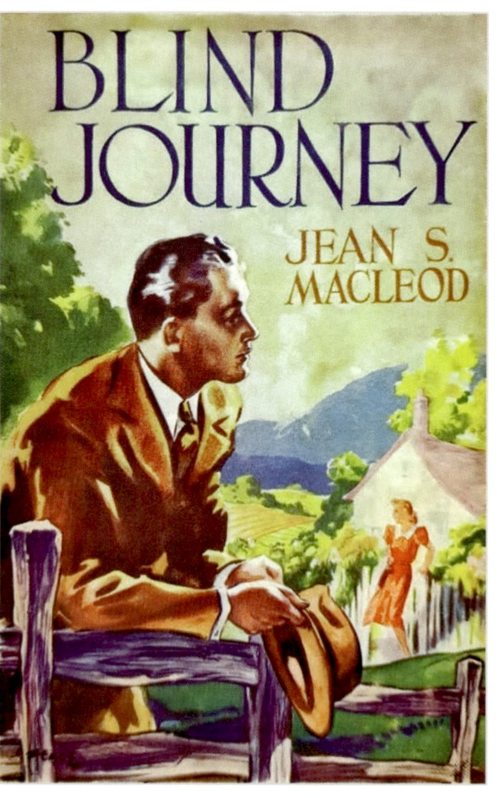

Blind Journey by Jean S MacLeod (Mills & Boon, 1942)

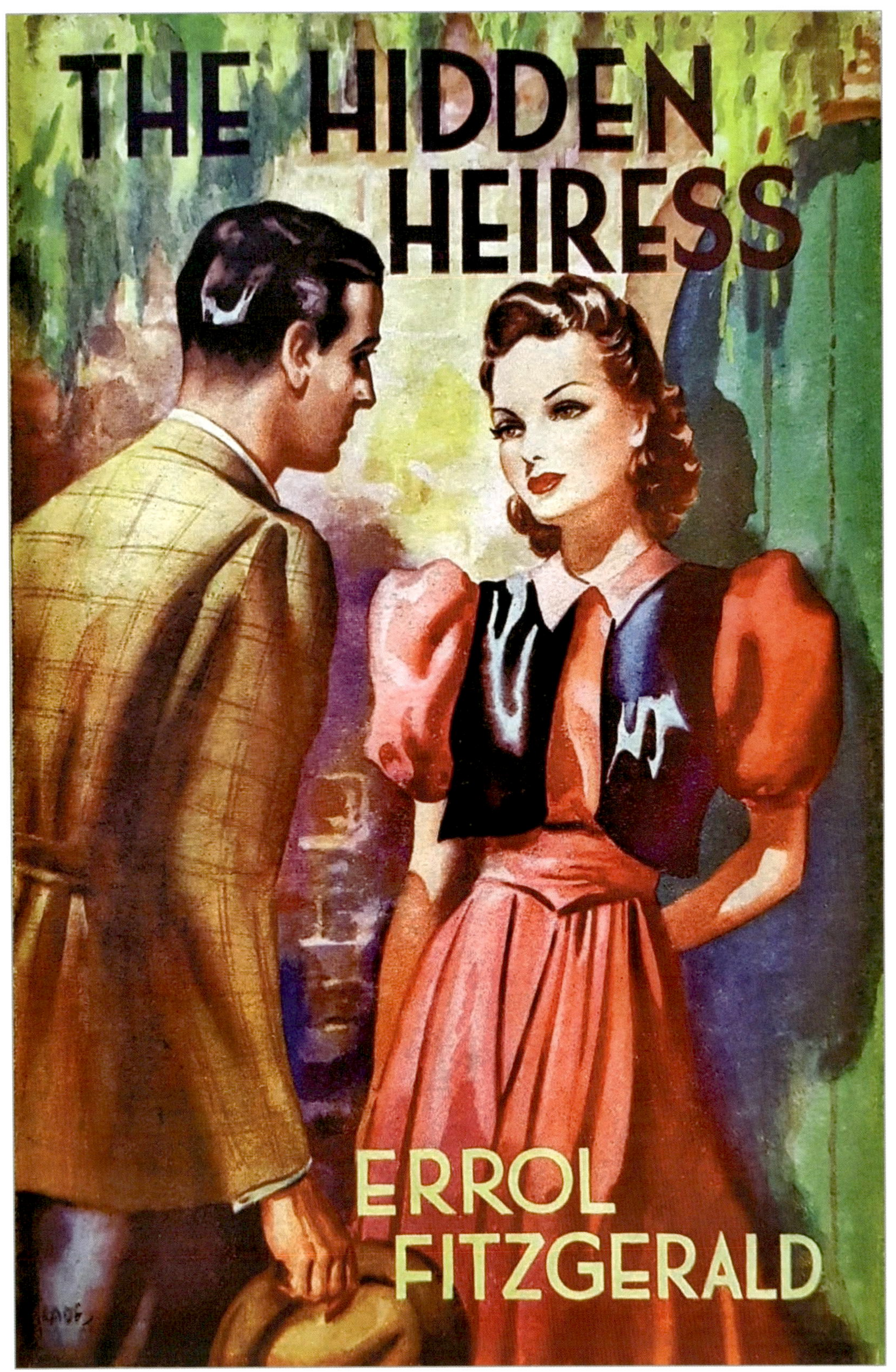

The Hidden Heiress by Errol Fitzgerald (Mills & Boon, 1942)

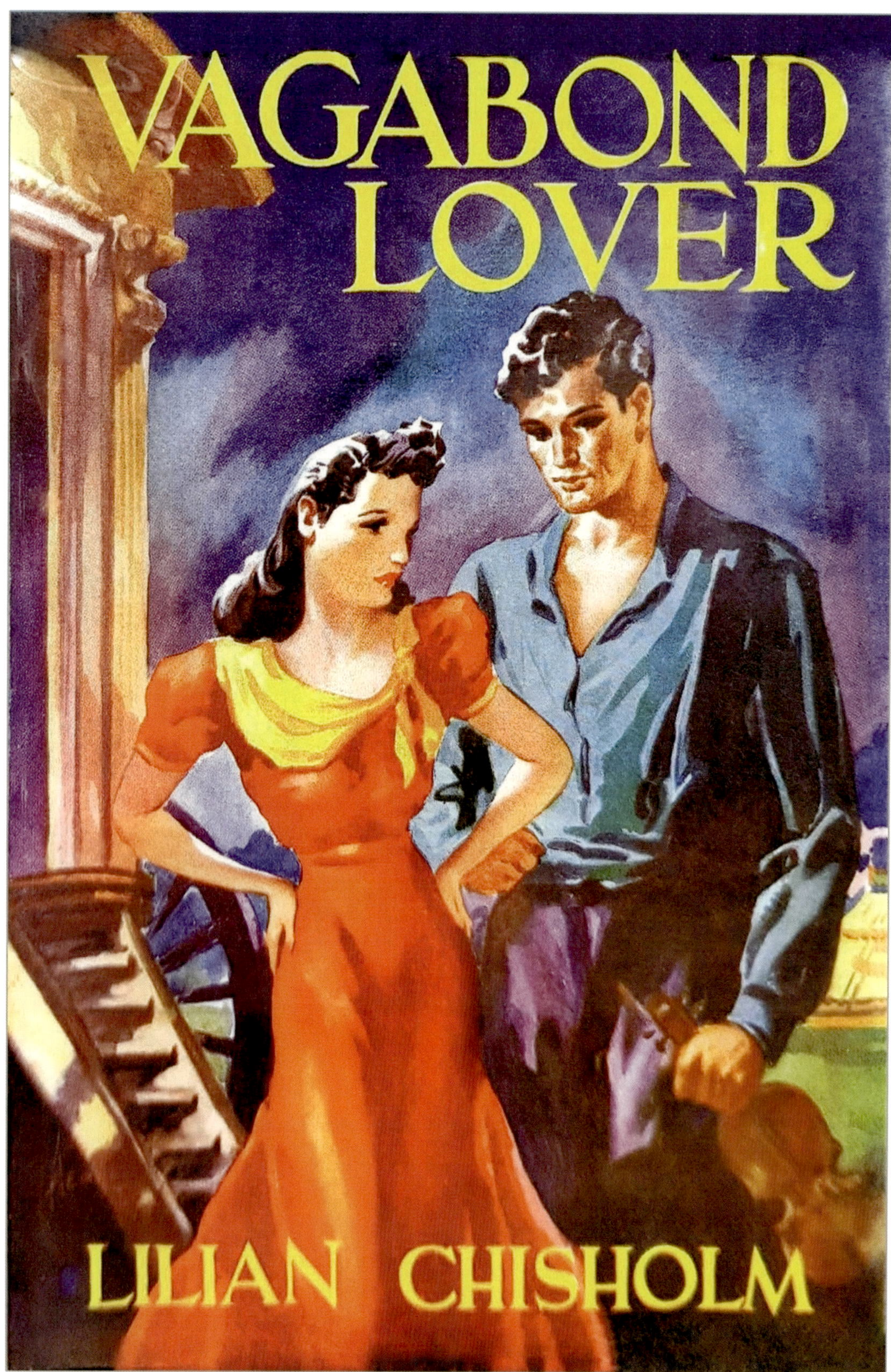

Vagabond Lover by Lilian Chisholm (Mills & Boon, 1942). Reissued in 1956 with the same dustjacket art.

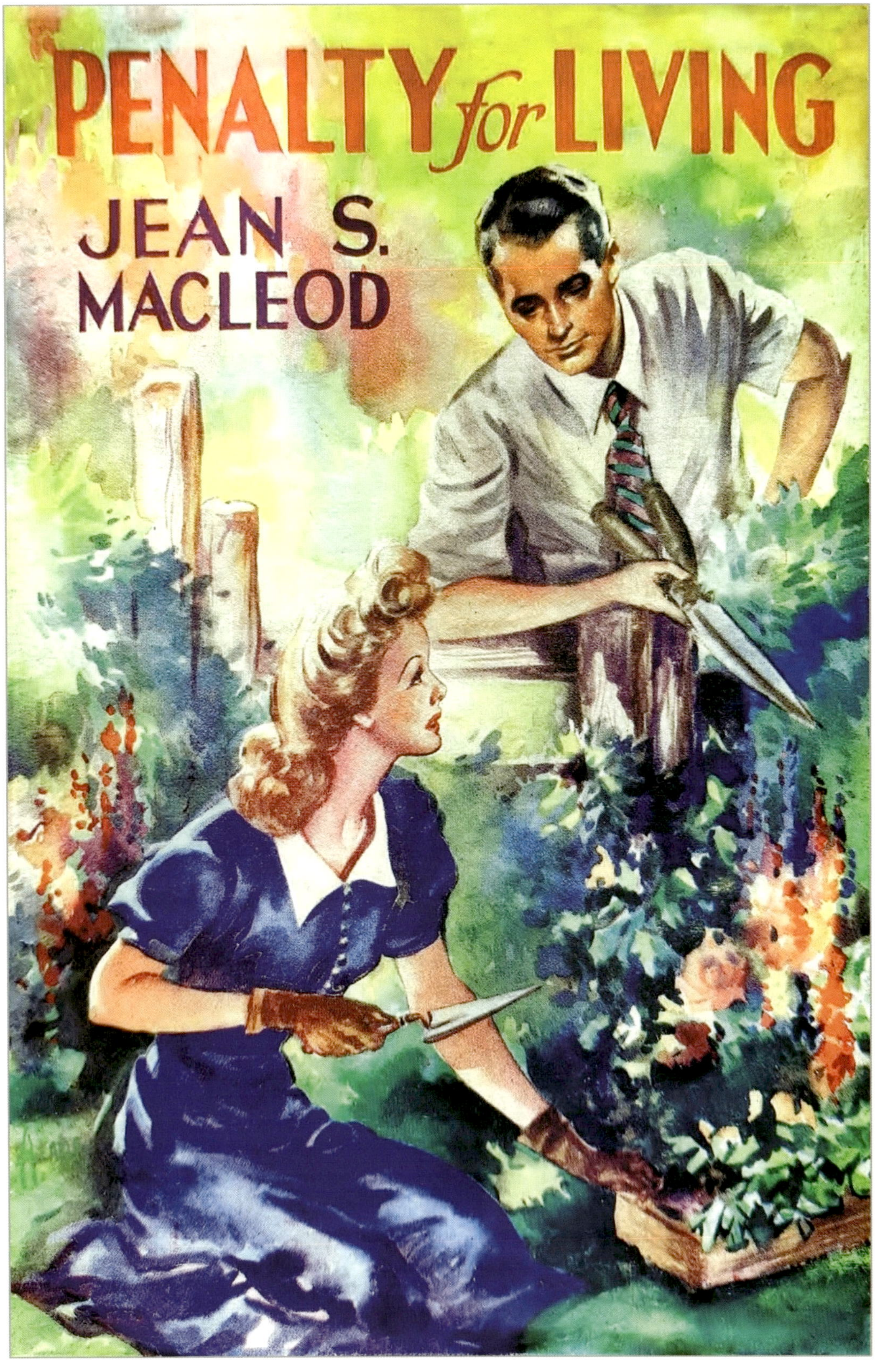

PENALTY *for* LIVING

JEAN S. MACLEOD

Penalty for Living by Jean S MacLeod (Mills & Boon, 1942)

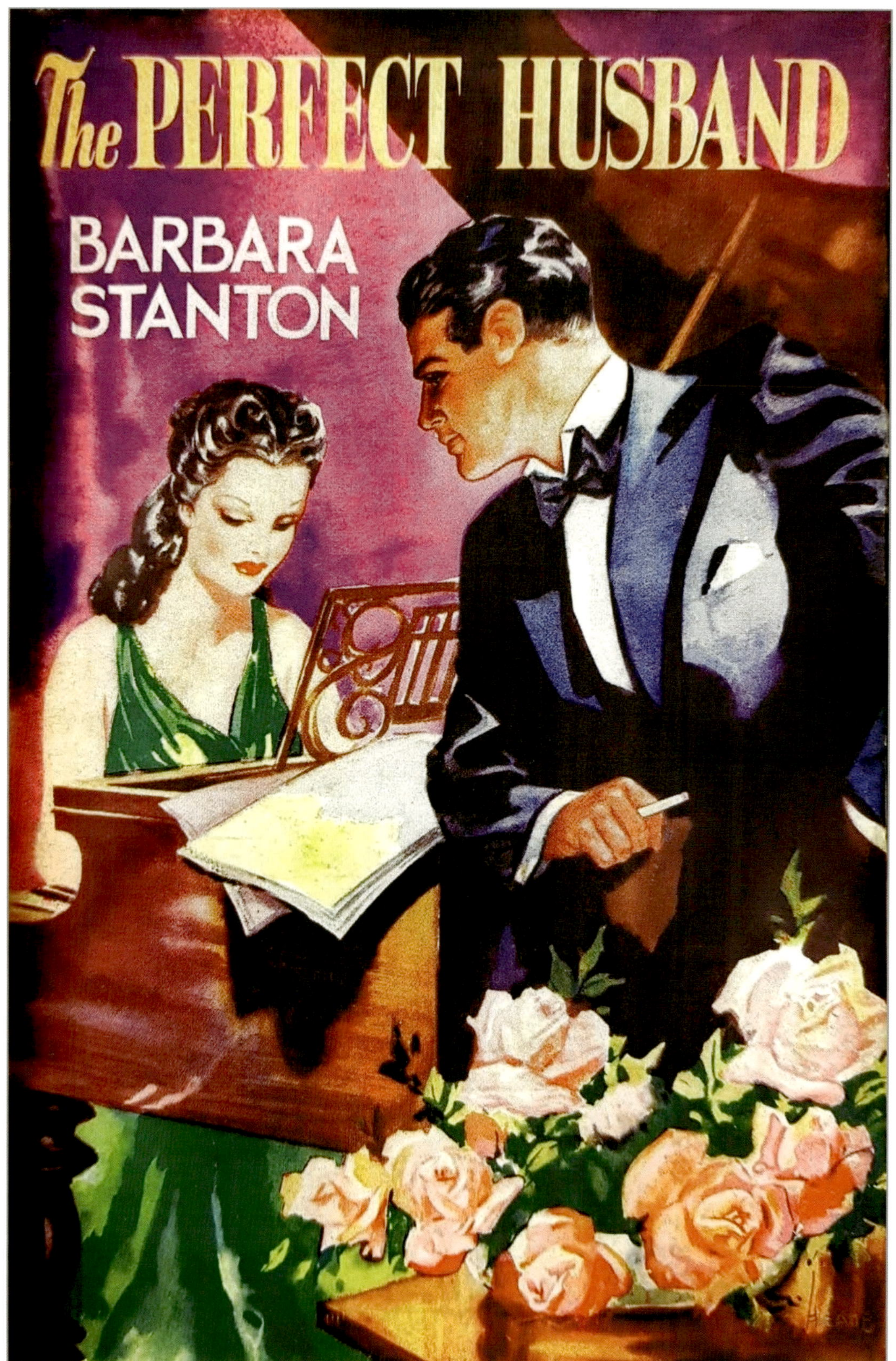

The Perfect Husband by Barbara Stanton (Mills & Boon, 1942)

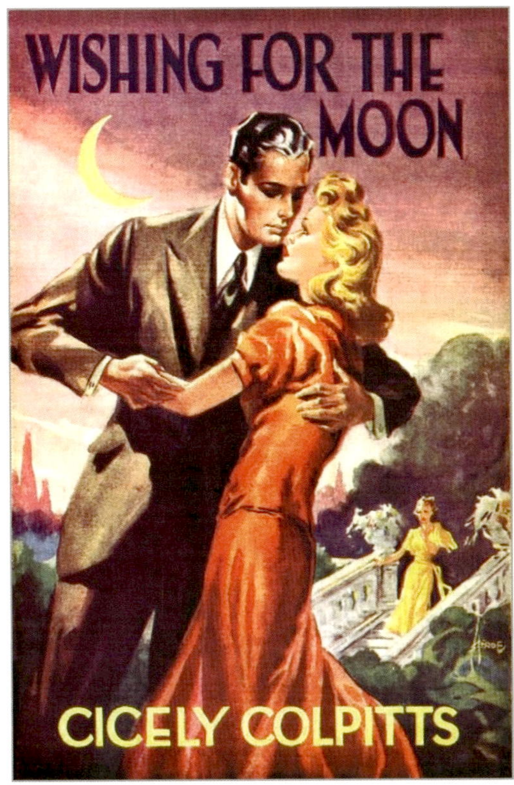

Wishing for the Moon by Cicely Colpitts (Mills & Boon, 1942)

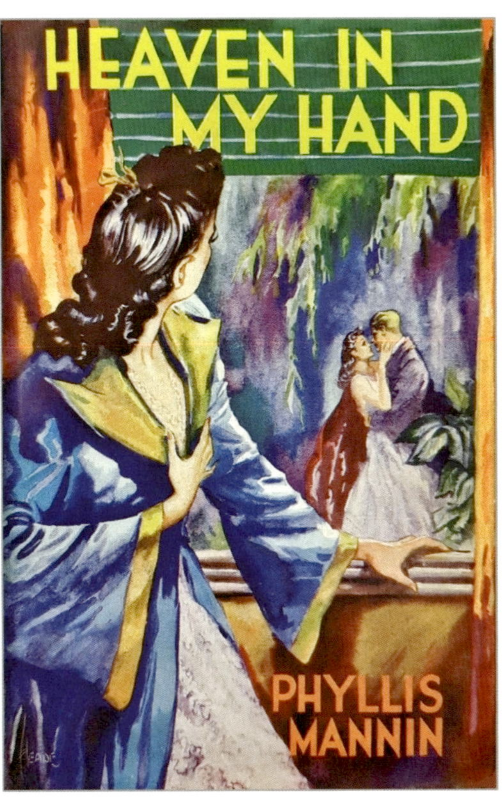

Heaven in My Hand by Phyllis Mannin (Mills & Boon, 1942)

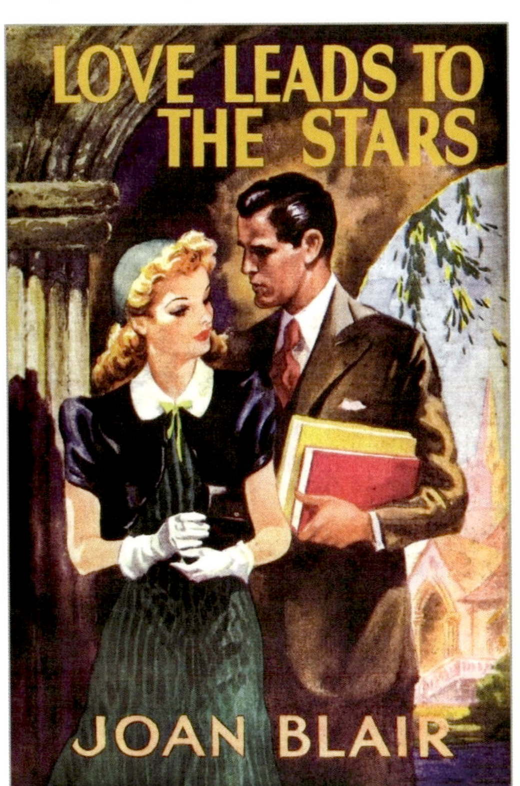

Love Leads to the Stars by Joan Blair (Mills & Boon, 1942)

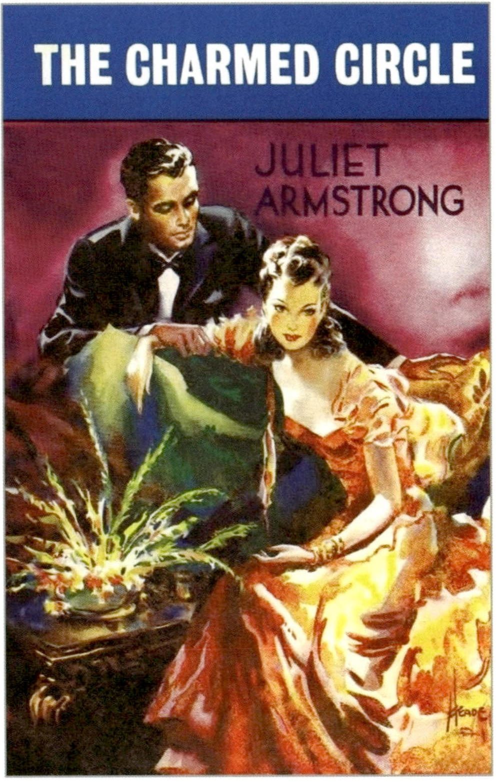

The Charmed Circle by Juliet Armstrong (Mills & Boon, 1957)
– reusing art from a 1940s Mills & Boon title, currently unidentified.

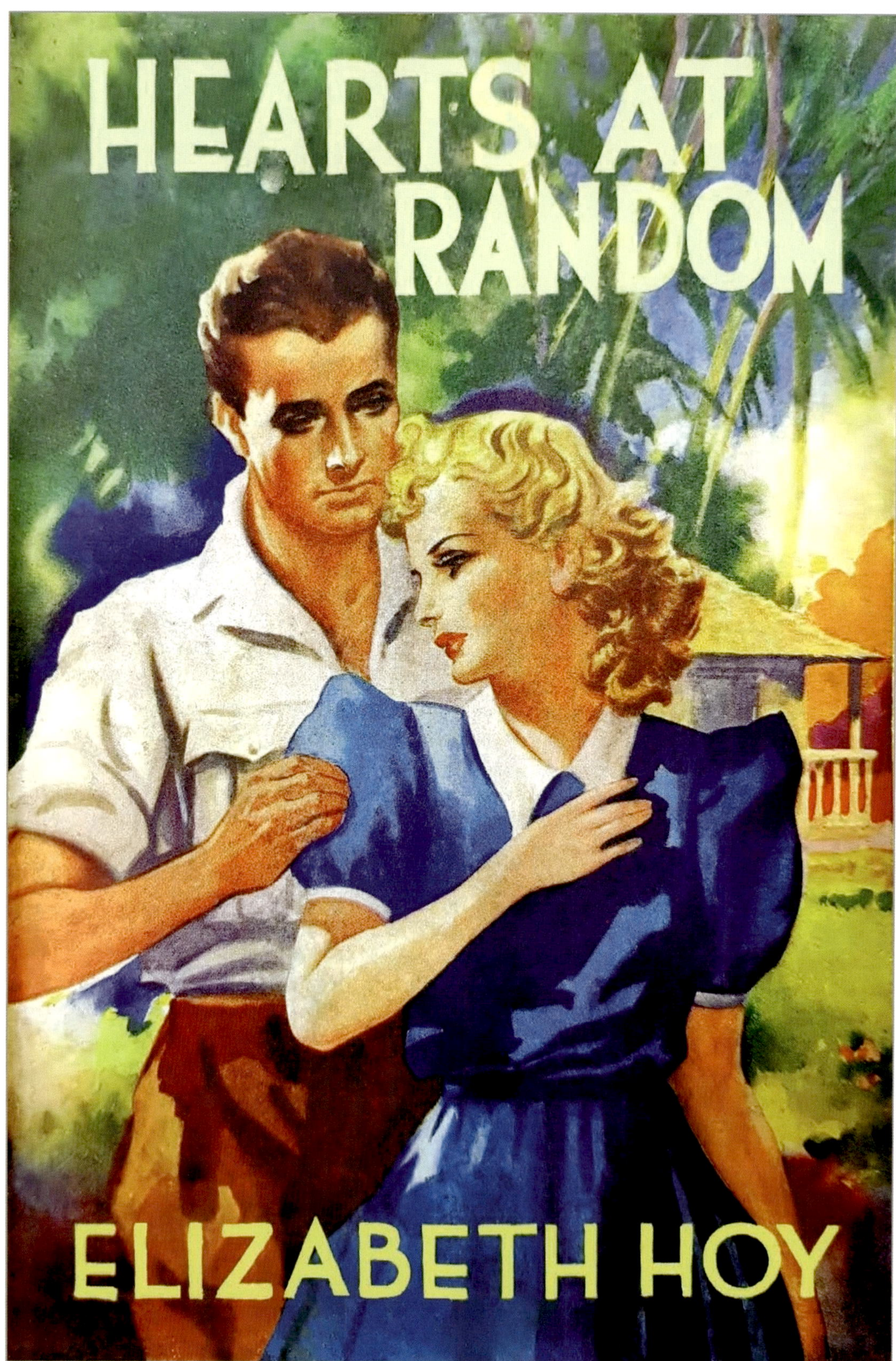

Hearts at Random by Elizabeth Hoy (Mills & Boon, 1942)

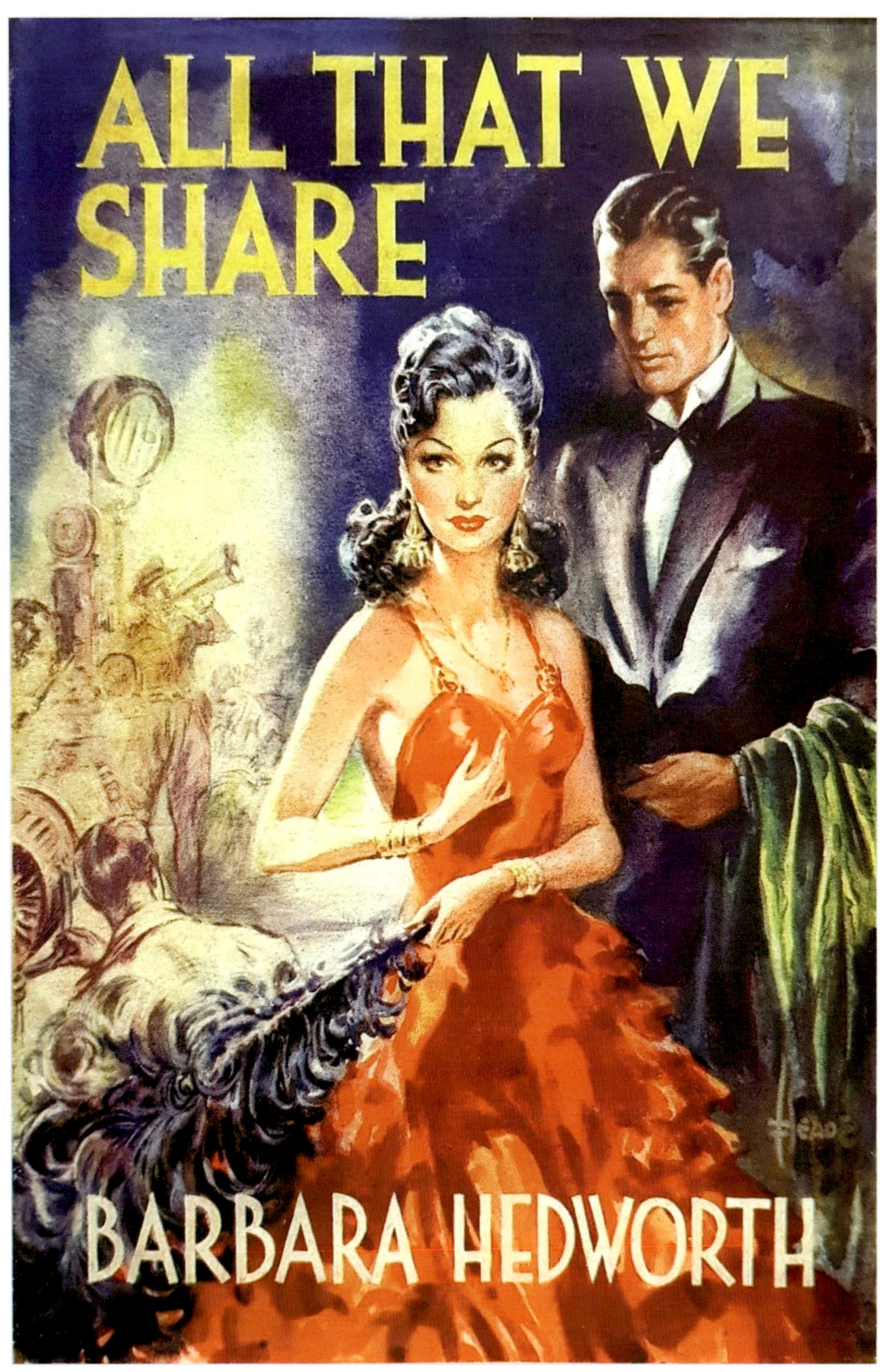

All That We Share by Barbara Hedworth (Mills & Boon, 1942)

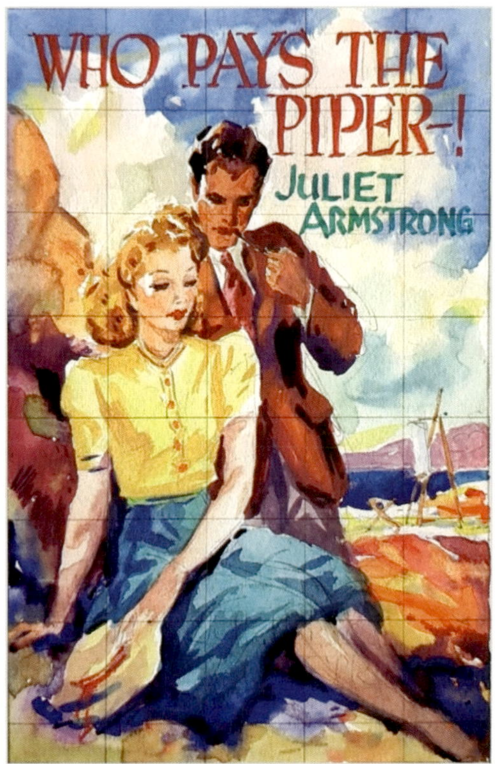

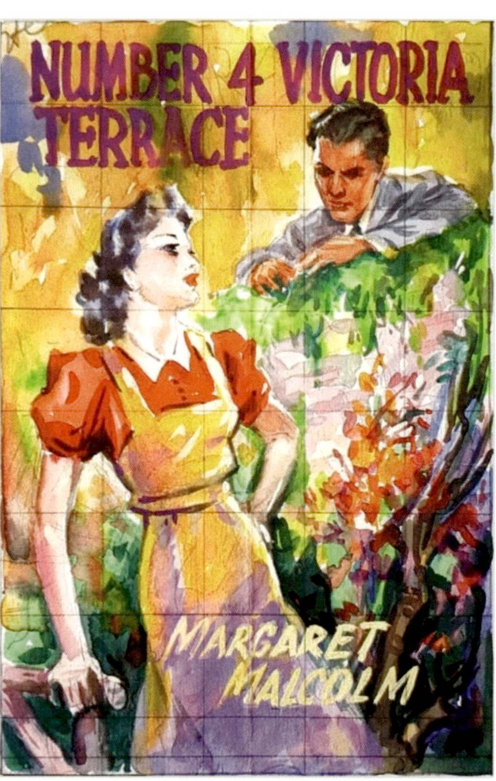

Heade's original roughs for *Who Pays the Piper–!* by Juliet Armstrong (Mills & Boon, 1943) and *Number 4 Victoria Terrace* by Margaret Malcolm (Mills & Boon, 1944). Sadly, no images are currently available of the as-published dustjackets of these two titles.

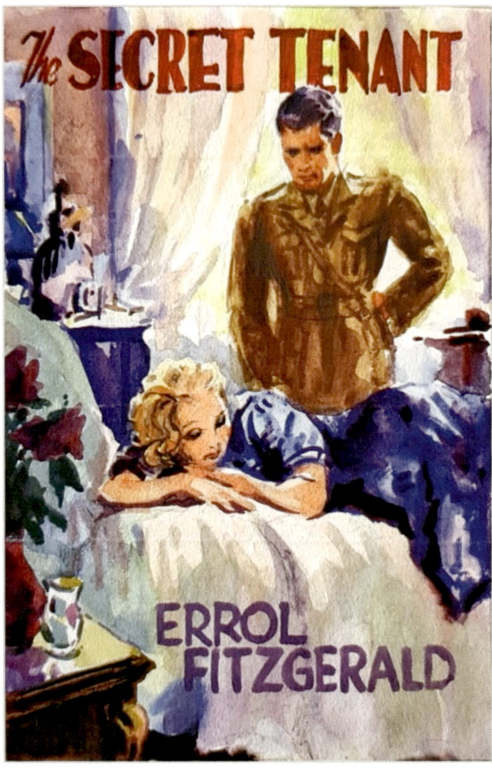

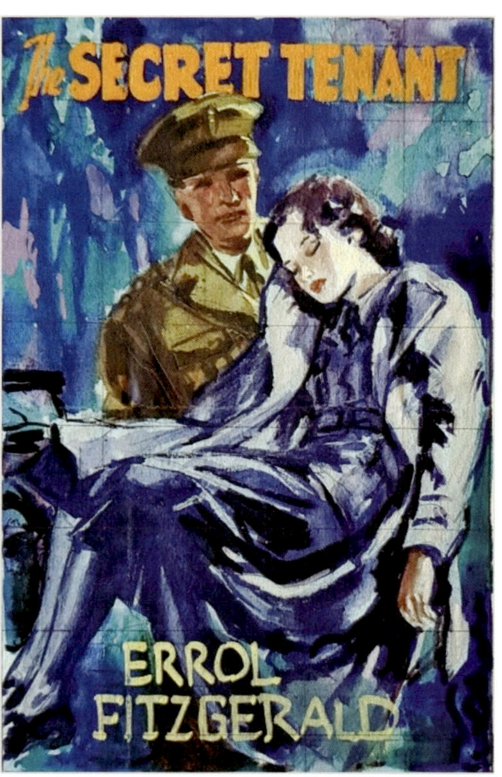

Two different roughs for *The Secret Tenant* by Errol Fitzgerald (Mills & Boon, 1943). The publishers rejected the first as being too suggestive.

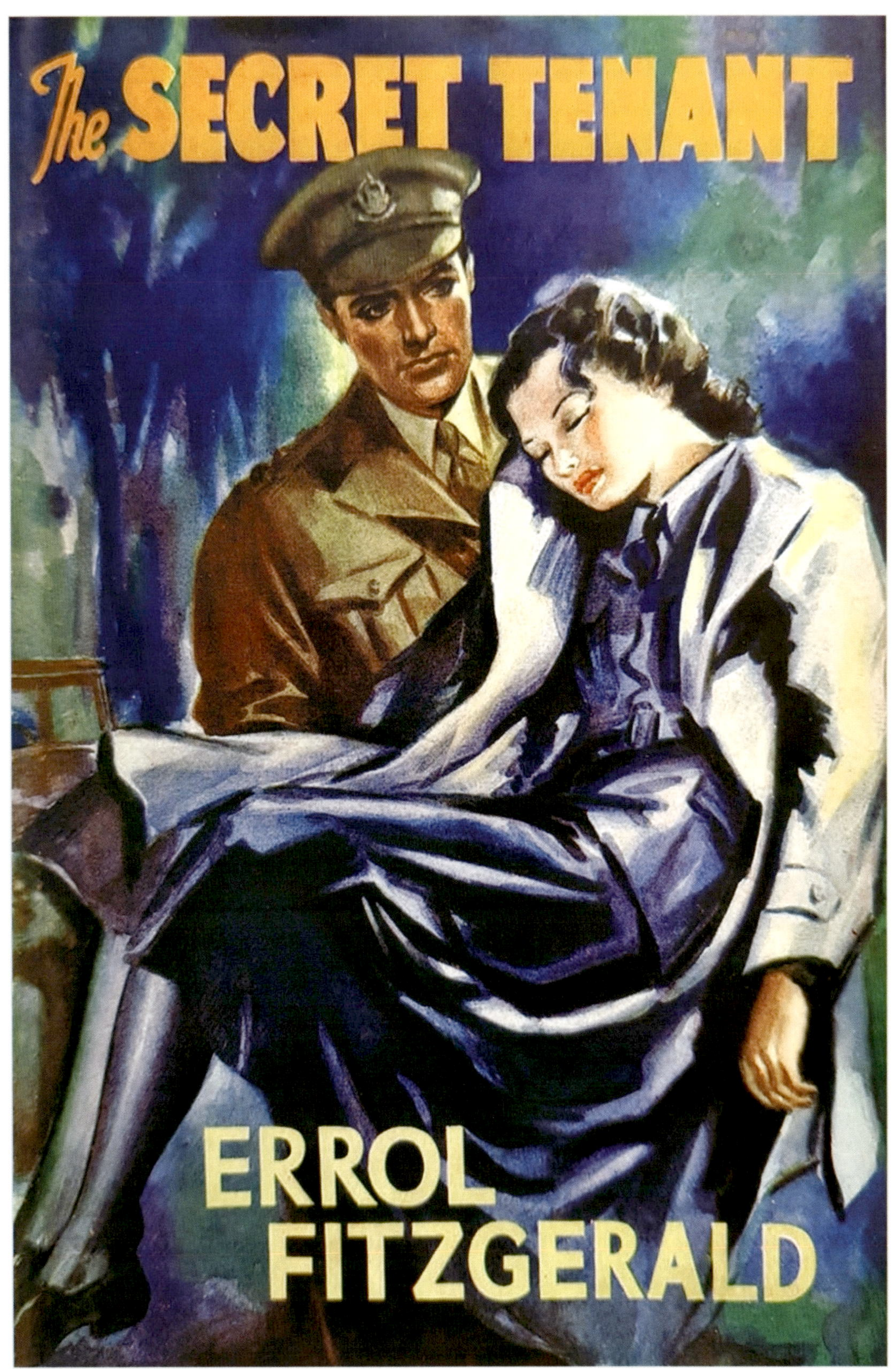

The as-published dustjacket of *The Secret Tenant* by Errol Fitzgerald (Mills & Boon, 1943)

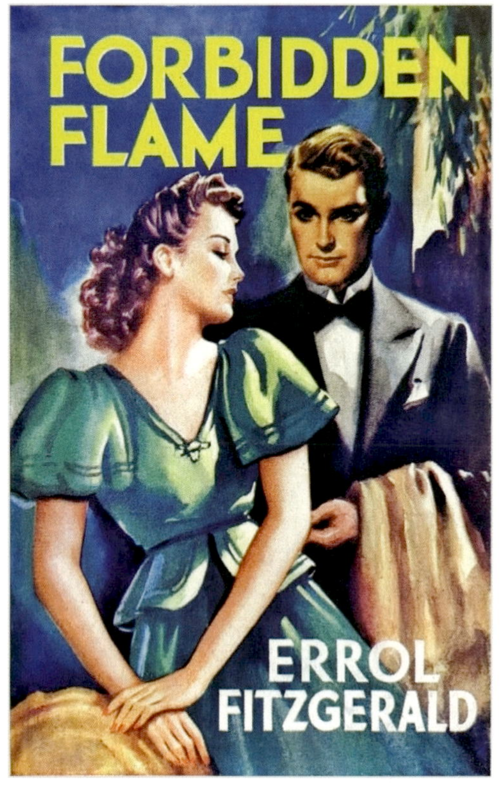

Forbidden Flame by Errol Fitzgerald (Mills & Boon, 1943)

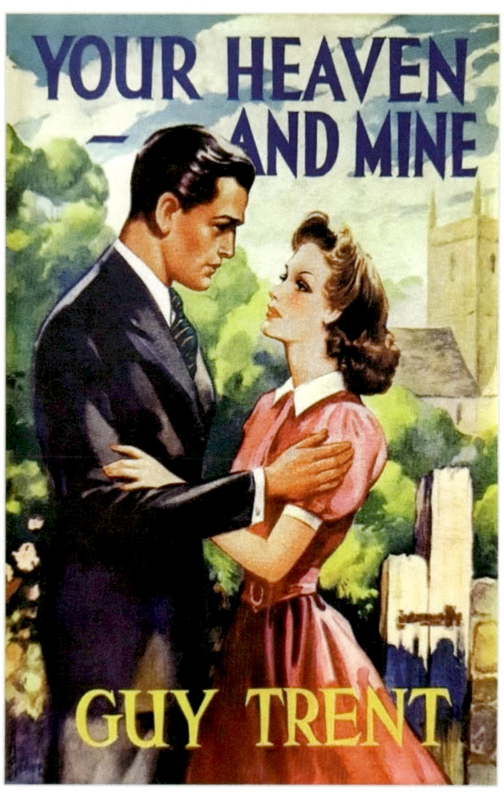

Your Heaven – And Mine by Guy Trent (Mills & Boon, 1943)

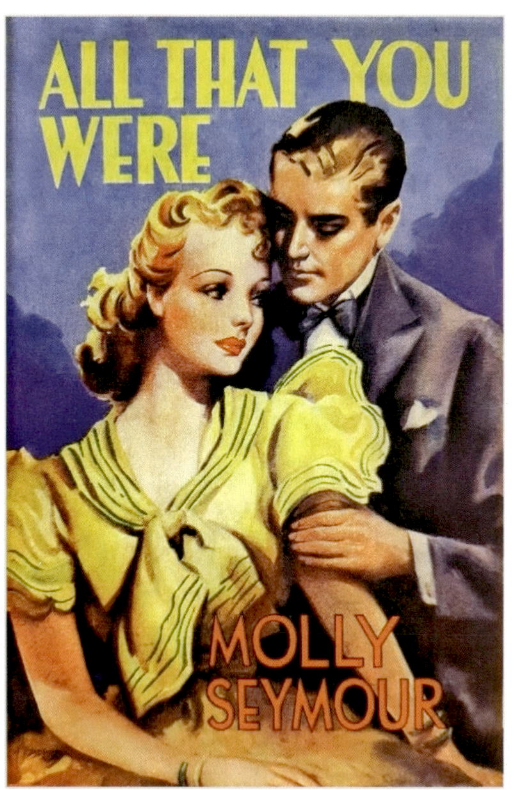

All That You Were by Molly Seymour (Mills & Boon, 1943)

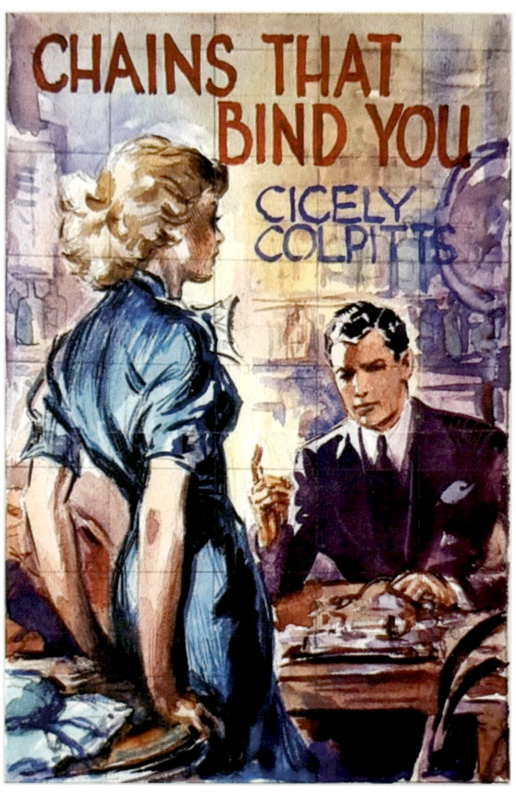

Rough for *Chains That Bind You* by Cicely Colpitts (Mills & Boon, 1943)

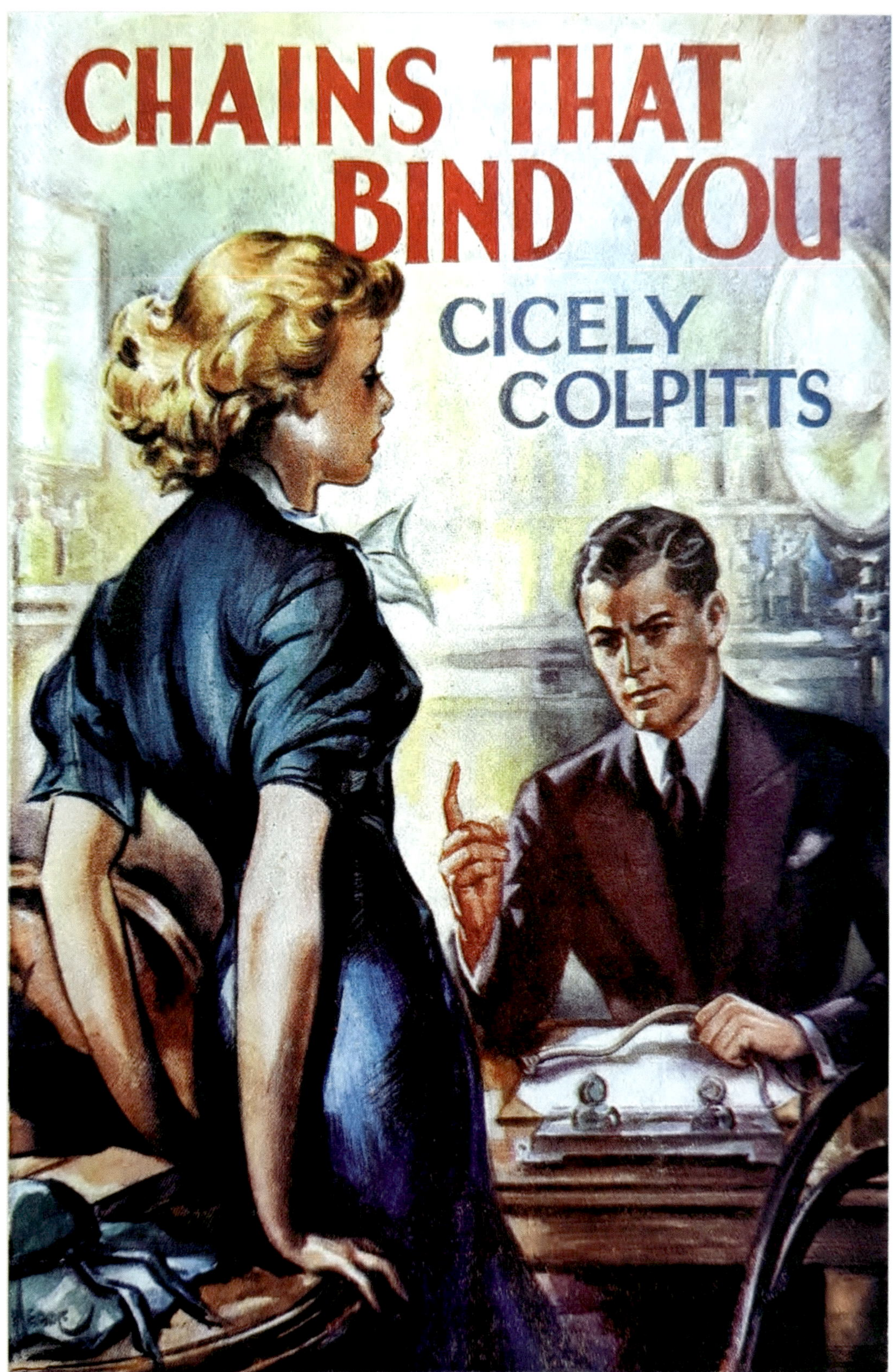

The as-published dustjacket of *Chains That Bind You* by Cicely Colpitts (Mills & Boon, 1943)

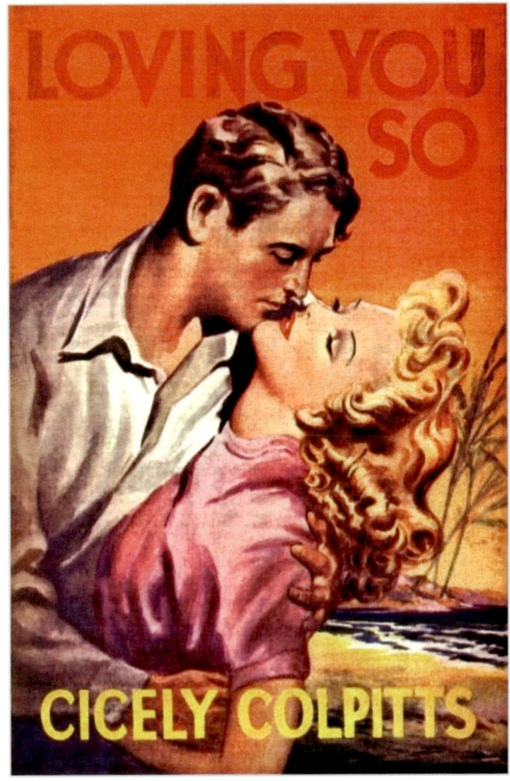

Loving You So by Cicely Colpitts (Mills & Boon, 1943)

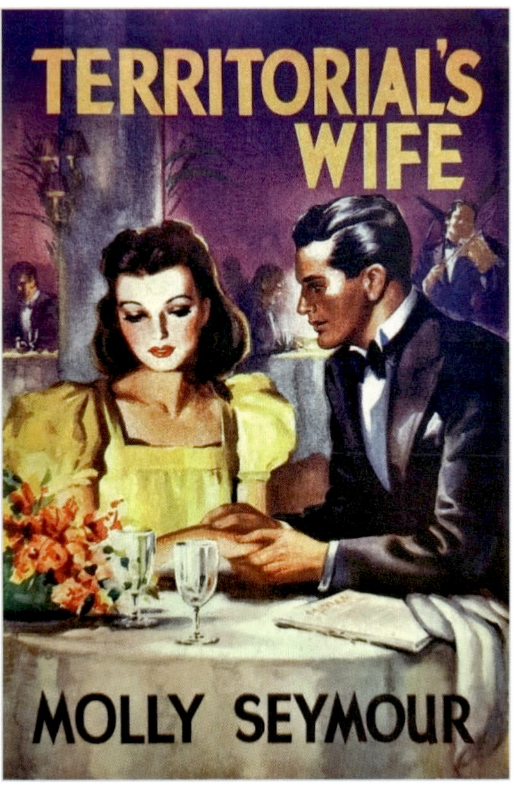

Territorial's Wife by Molly Seymour (Mills & Boon, 1943)

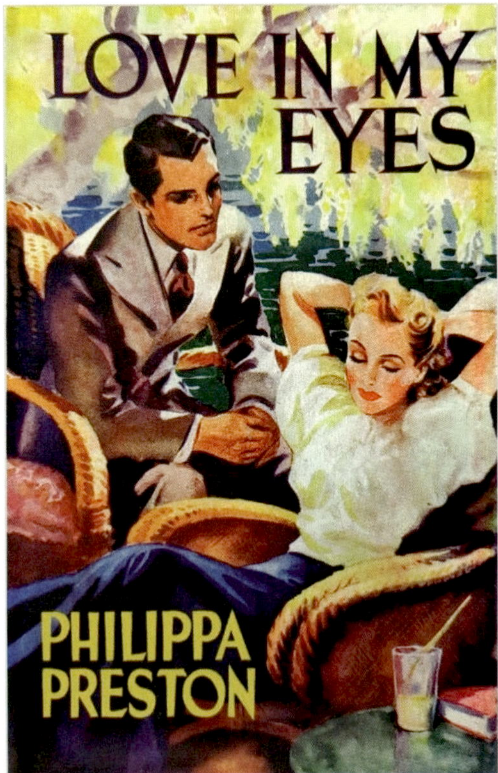

Love in My Eyes by Philippa Preston (Mills & Boon, 1943)

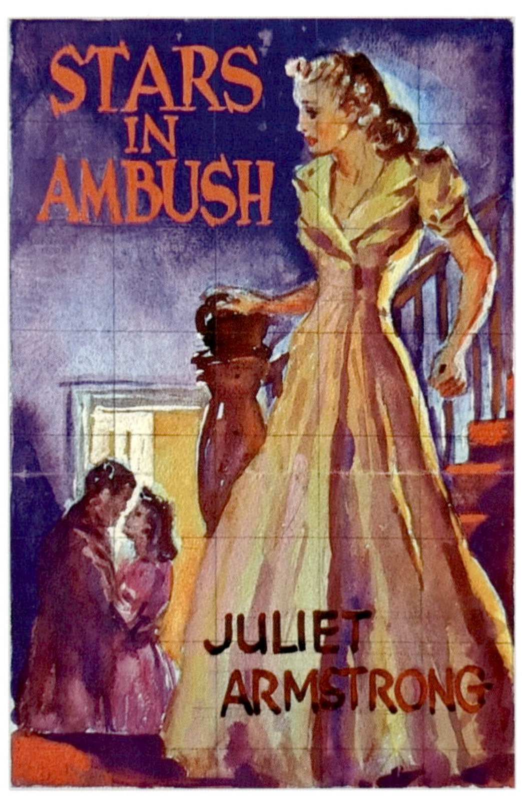

Rough for *Stars in Ambush* by Juliet Armstrong (Mills & Boon, 1943)

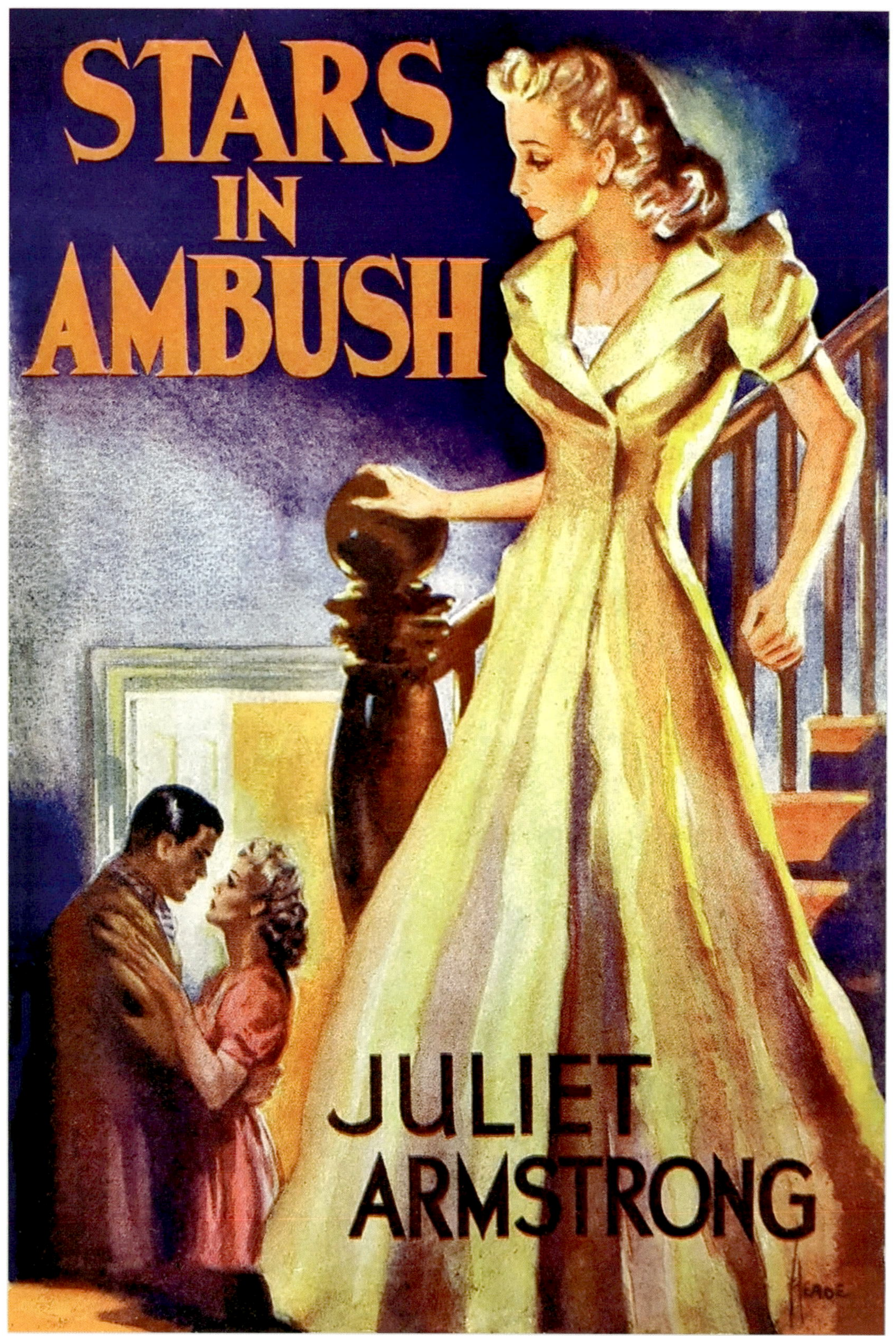

The as-published dustjacket of *Stars in Ambush* by Juliet Armstrong (Mills & Boon, 1943)

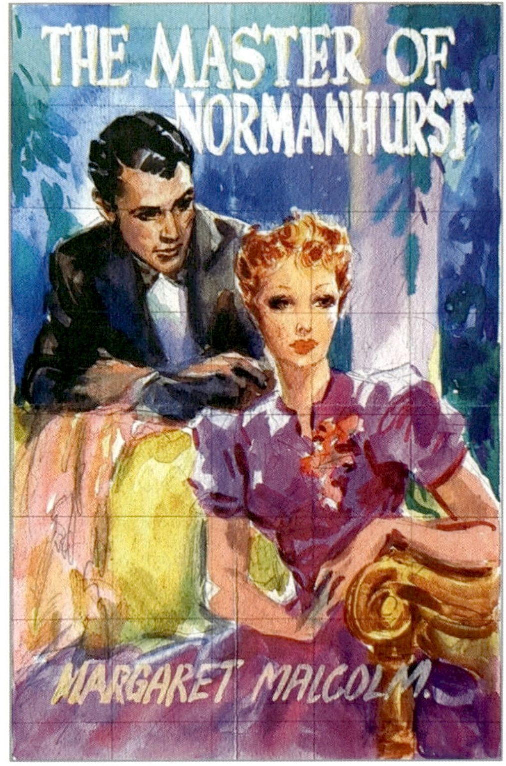

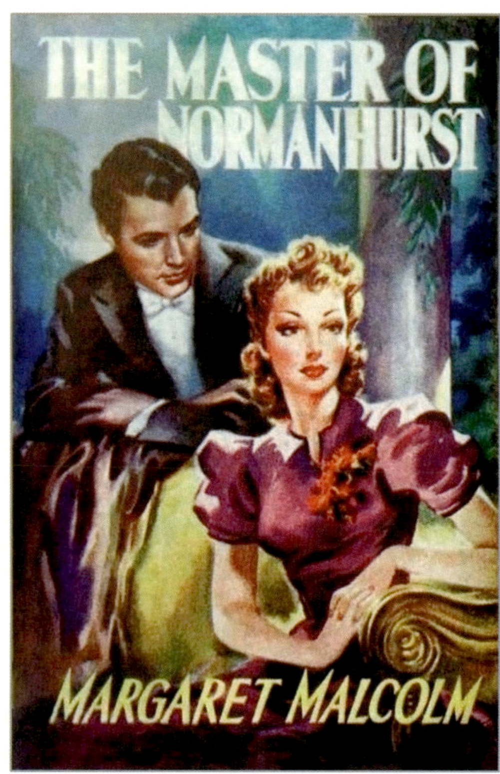

Heade's original rough and the as-published dustjacket for *The Master of Normanhurst* by Margaret Malcolm (Mills & Boon, 1944). The publishers' approval of the rough was subject to the comment that the girl should be made a 'little less sophisticated'. The same artwork was later repurposed by the publishers for a different Margaret Malcolm novel (see below)

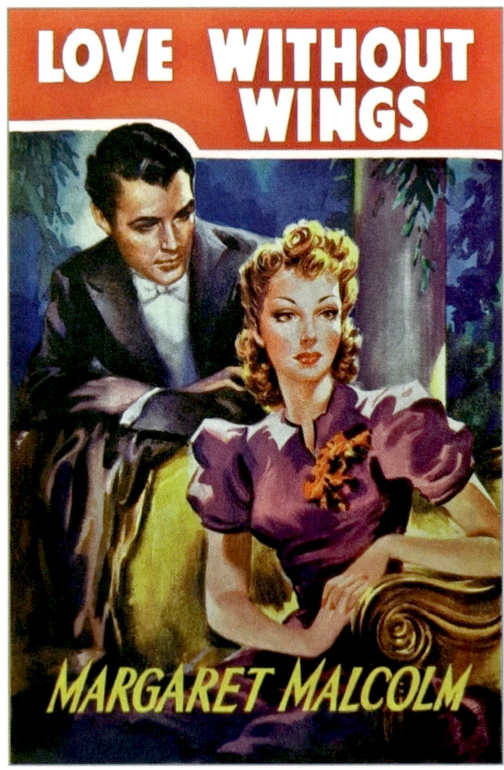

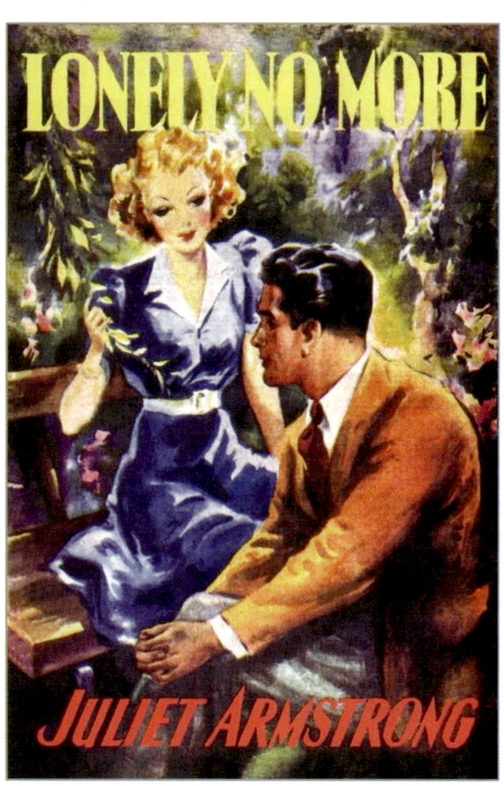

Love Without Wings by Margaret Malcolm (Mills & Boon, 1953)

Lonely No More by Juliet Armstrong (Mills & Boon, 1944)

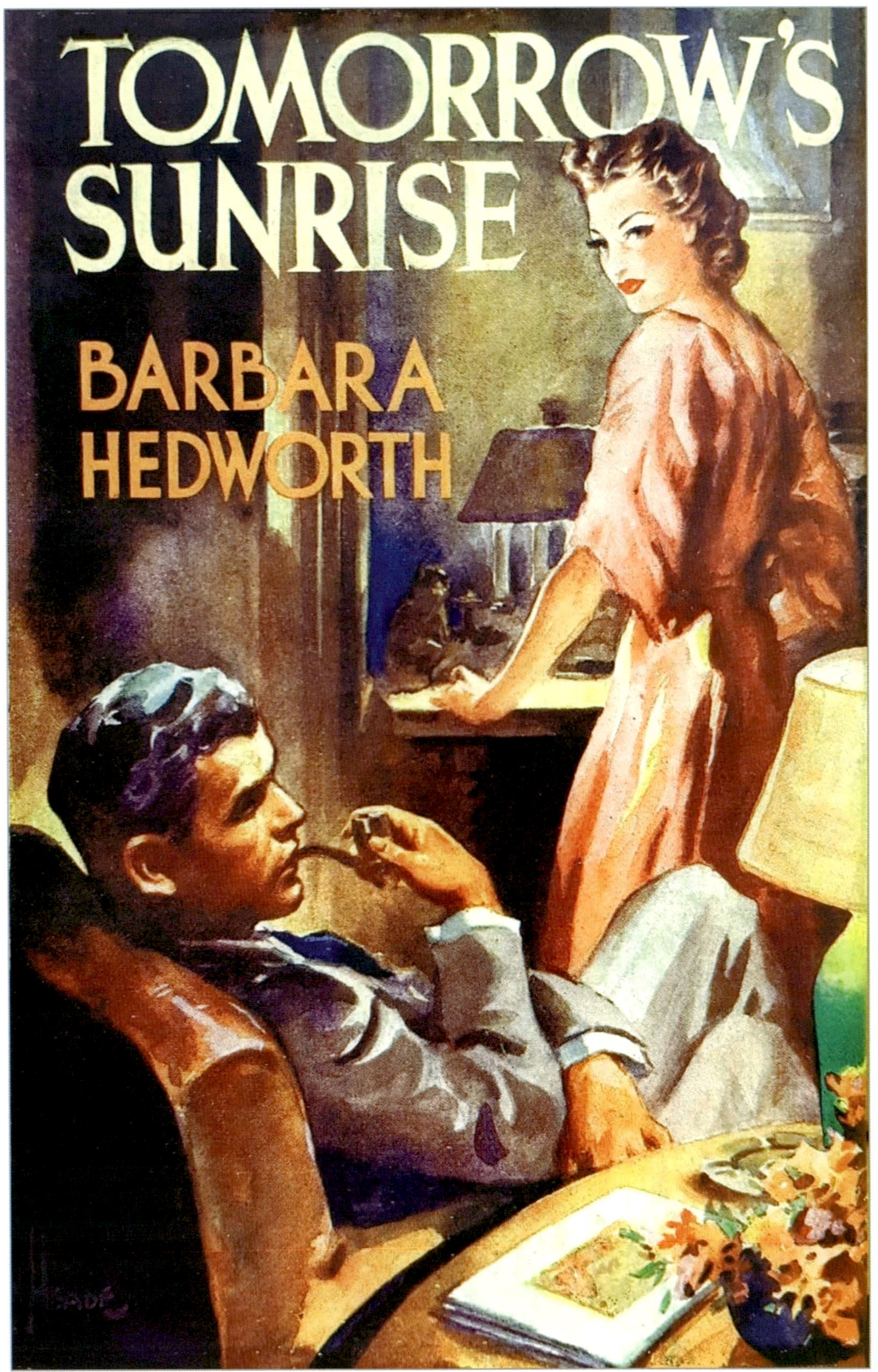

Tomorrow's Sunrise by Barbara Hedworth (Mills & Boon, 1943)

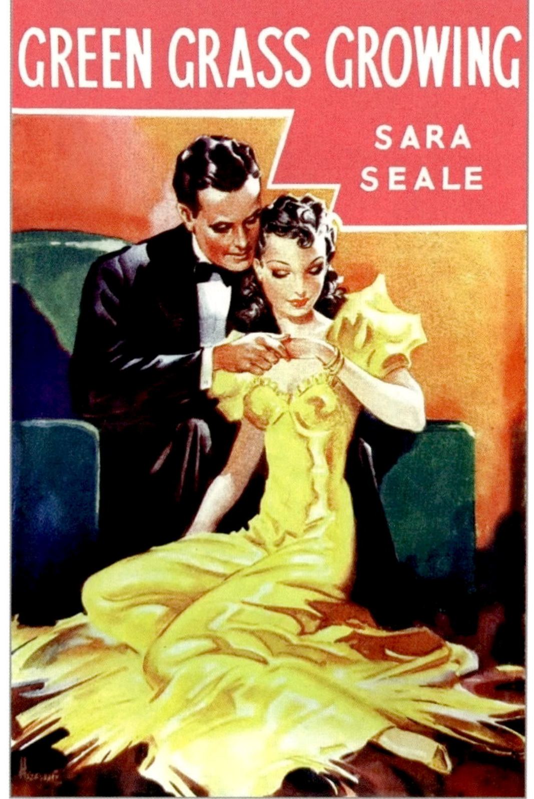

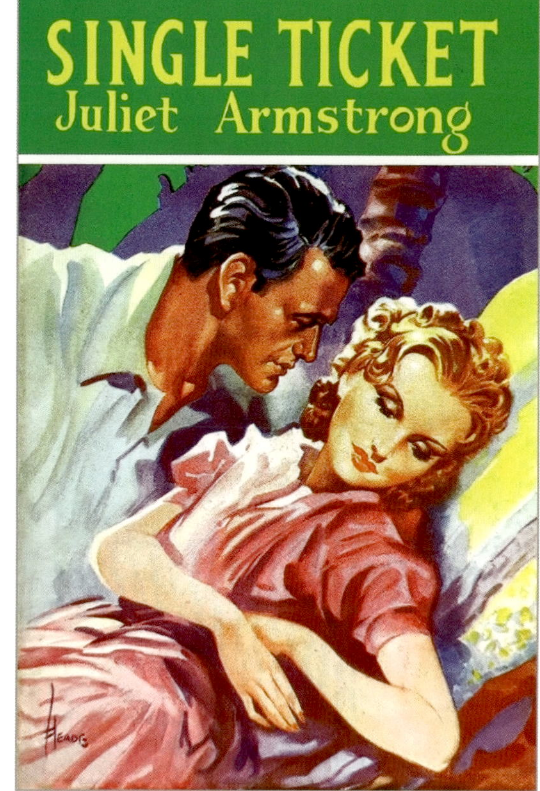

Above, left and right: *Green Grass Growing* by Sara Seale (1954) and *Single Ticket* by Juliet Armstrong (1952), two further 1950s Mills & Boon books reusing 1940s Heade dustjacket art. As usual with reissues of this kind, the publisher's art department placed a coloured band over the upper part of each composition to conceal the original titles and author names – which in these instances are currently unknown. A smaller image of the *Green Grass Growing* piece was included in *The Art of Reginald Heade – Special Edition* but incorrectly captioned as having appeared on that novel's 1940 first edition, which actually had a dustjacket by a different artist.

Right: *Brief Excursion* by Eleanor Farnes (Mills & Boon, 1944). Only a poor-quality image of this dustjacket was available at the time when *The Art of Reginald Heade – Special Edition* was originally published; along with the unusually 'sketchy' style of the art, this led to it being included in the 'Is It Heade?' section on that occasion. However, now that a better-quality image is available, Heade's signature can be clearly seen in the bottom left-hand corner, allowing for the piece to be positively identified as his work. The book was reissued with the same dustjacket in 1957.

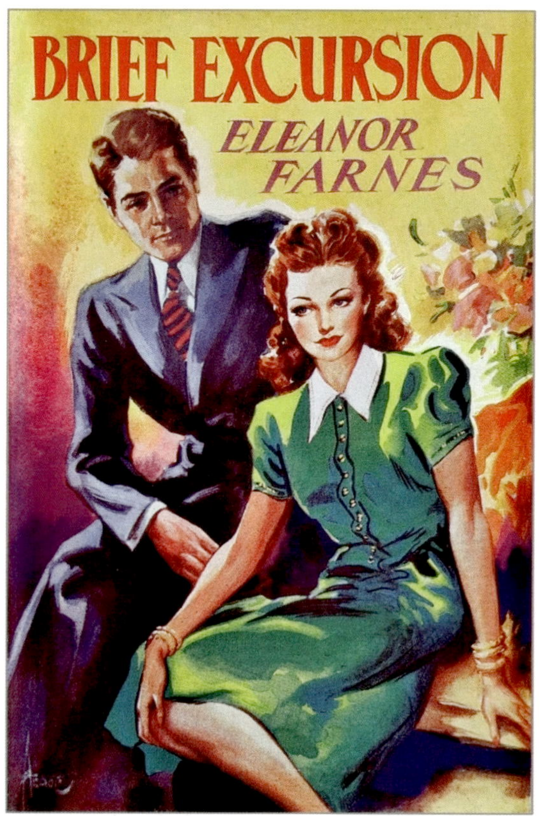

RUSTON ENGINES

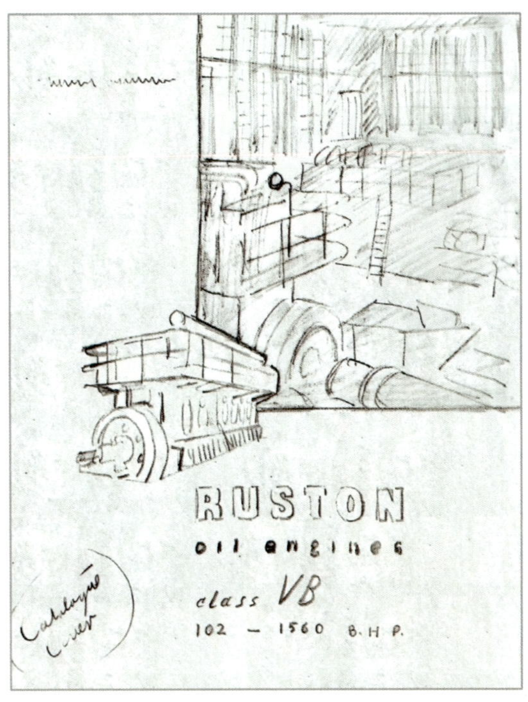

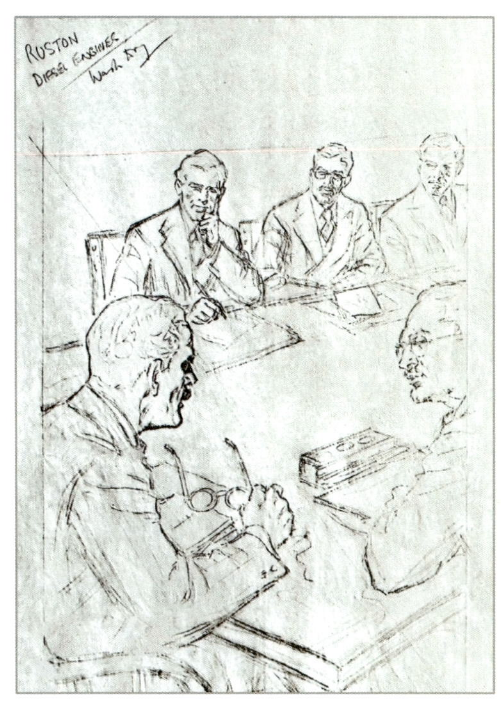

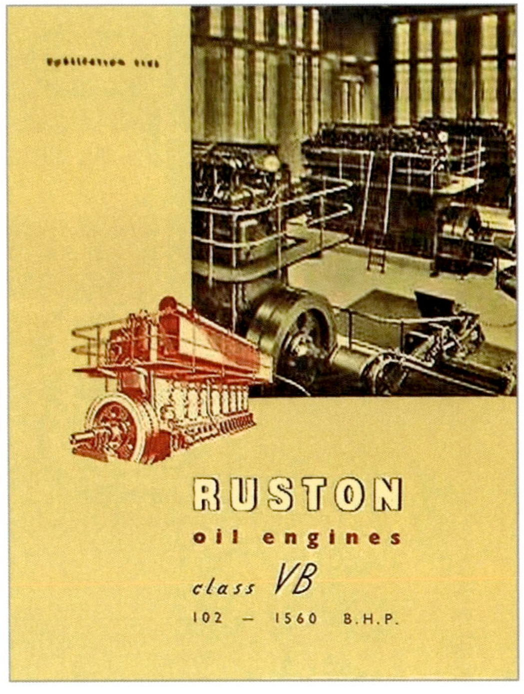

Commercial commissions undertaken by Heade included – probably in the 1940s, although it could possibly have been as early as the previous decade – some work for the long-established Lincolnshire-based Ruston company, renowned for manufacturing oil and diesel engines for industrial and agricultural use. Two of Heade's preparatory sketches for this work still survive: one of them the design for an oil engines catalogue cover (see above left), the other apparently depicting a business meeting or boardroom scene (see above right).

The printed version of the catalogue cover (see left) followed Heade's design very closely. This type of project – known as a lay-out – was an unusual one for the artist to have taken on, but was generally well-paid work, which might explain why he did so on this occasion.

Sadly, no final illustration or printed version of the business meeting piece has yet come to light – although the search continues.

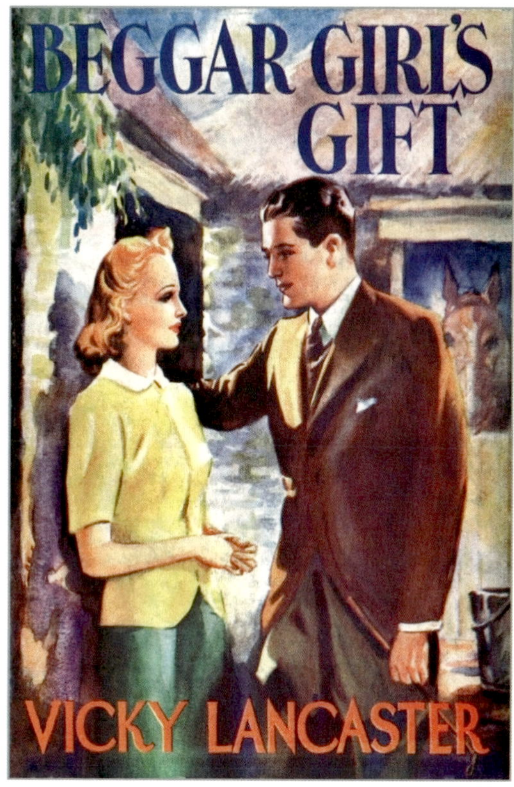

Beggar Girl's Gift by Vicky Lancaster (Robert Hale, 1943)

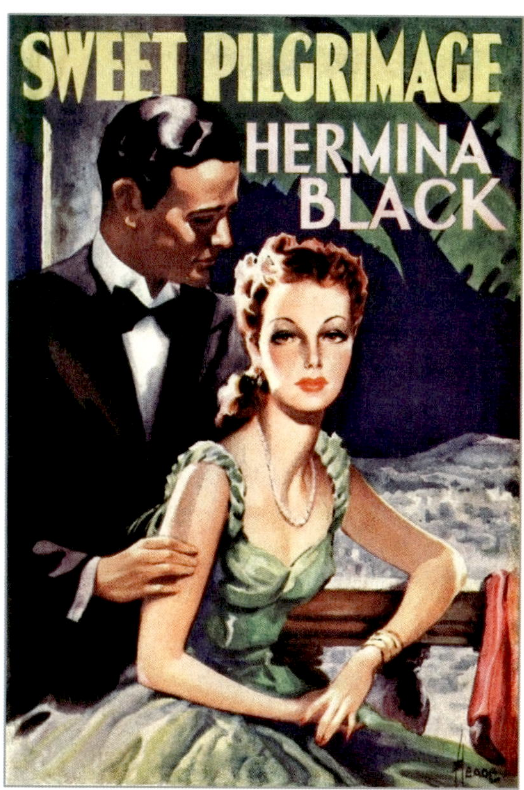

Sweet Pilgrimage by Hermina Black (Robert Hale, 1943)

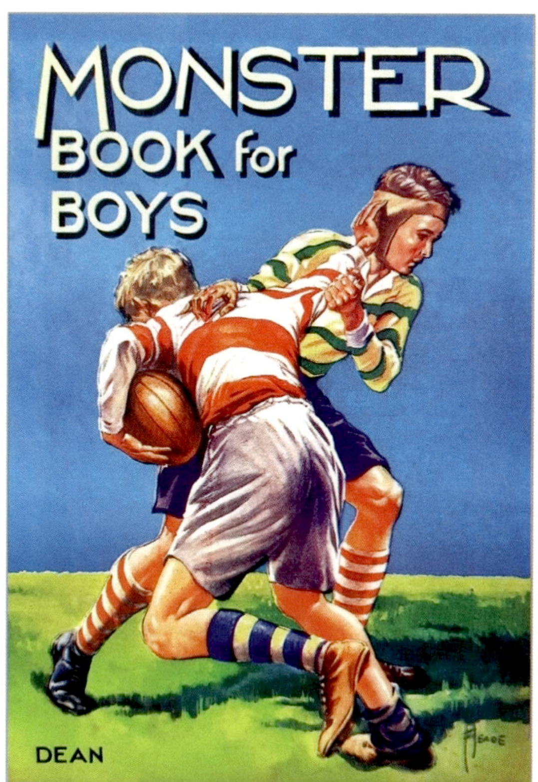

Monster Book for Boys (Dean & Son, 1943)

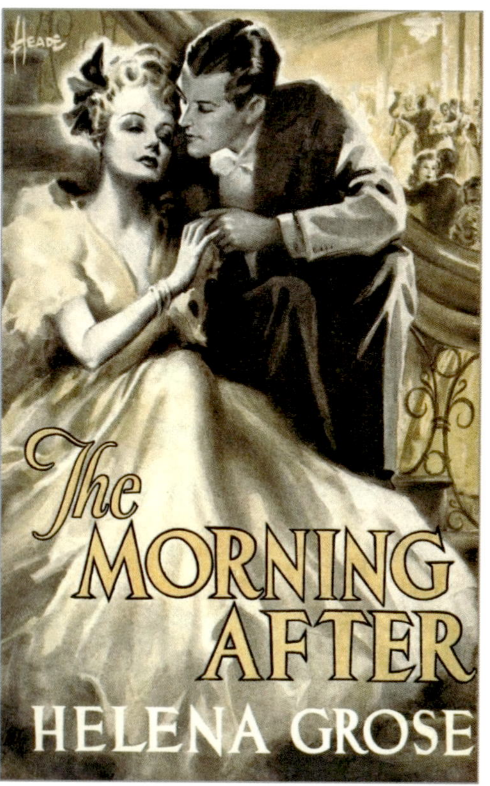

The Morning After by Helena Grose (Collins, 1944)

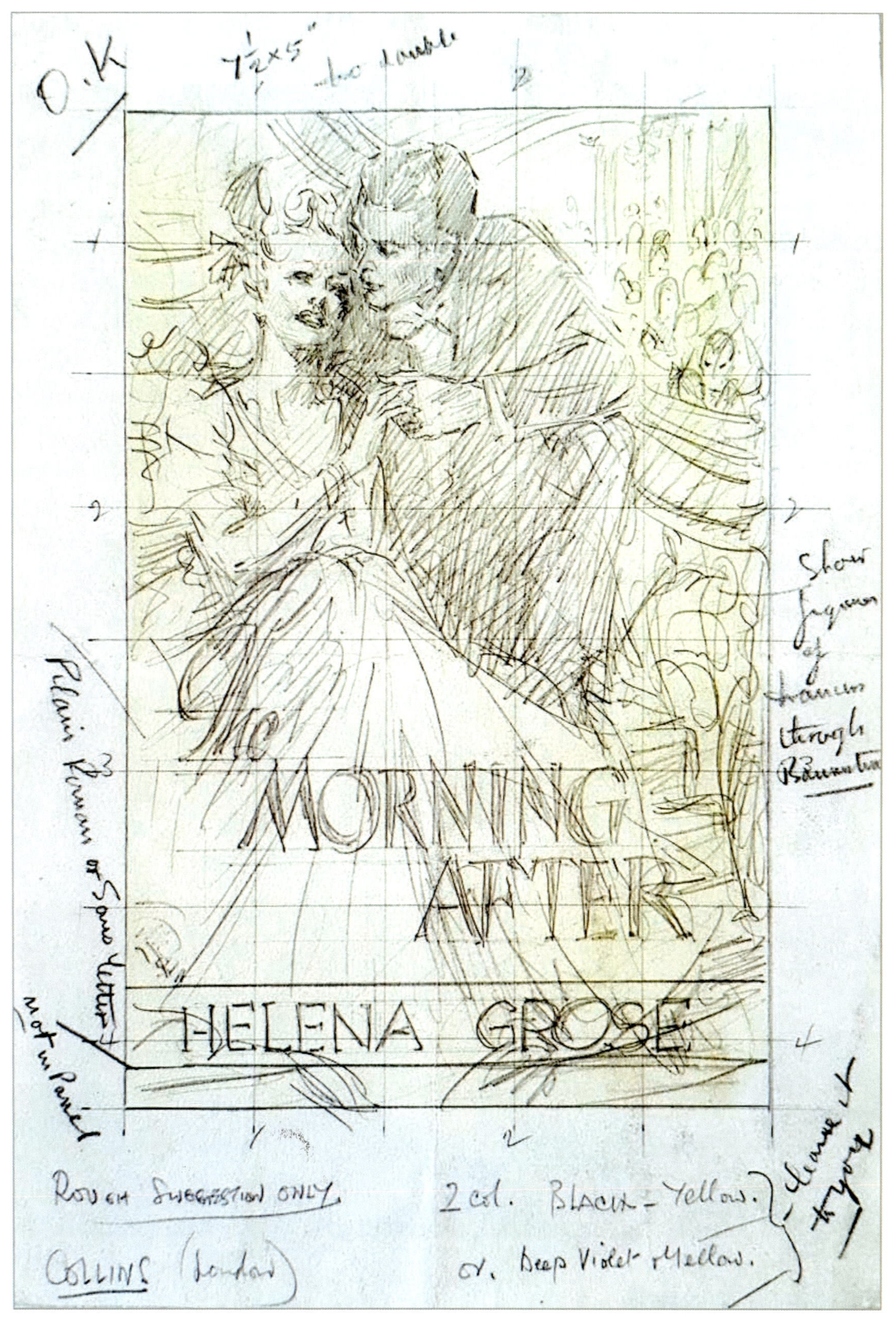

Heade's original rough for *The Morning After* by Helena Grose (Collins, 1944), with annotations by the publisher's art department.

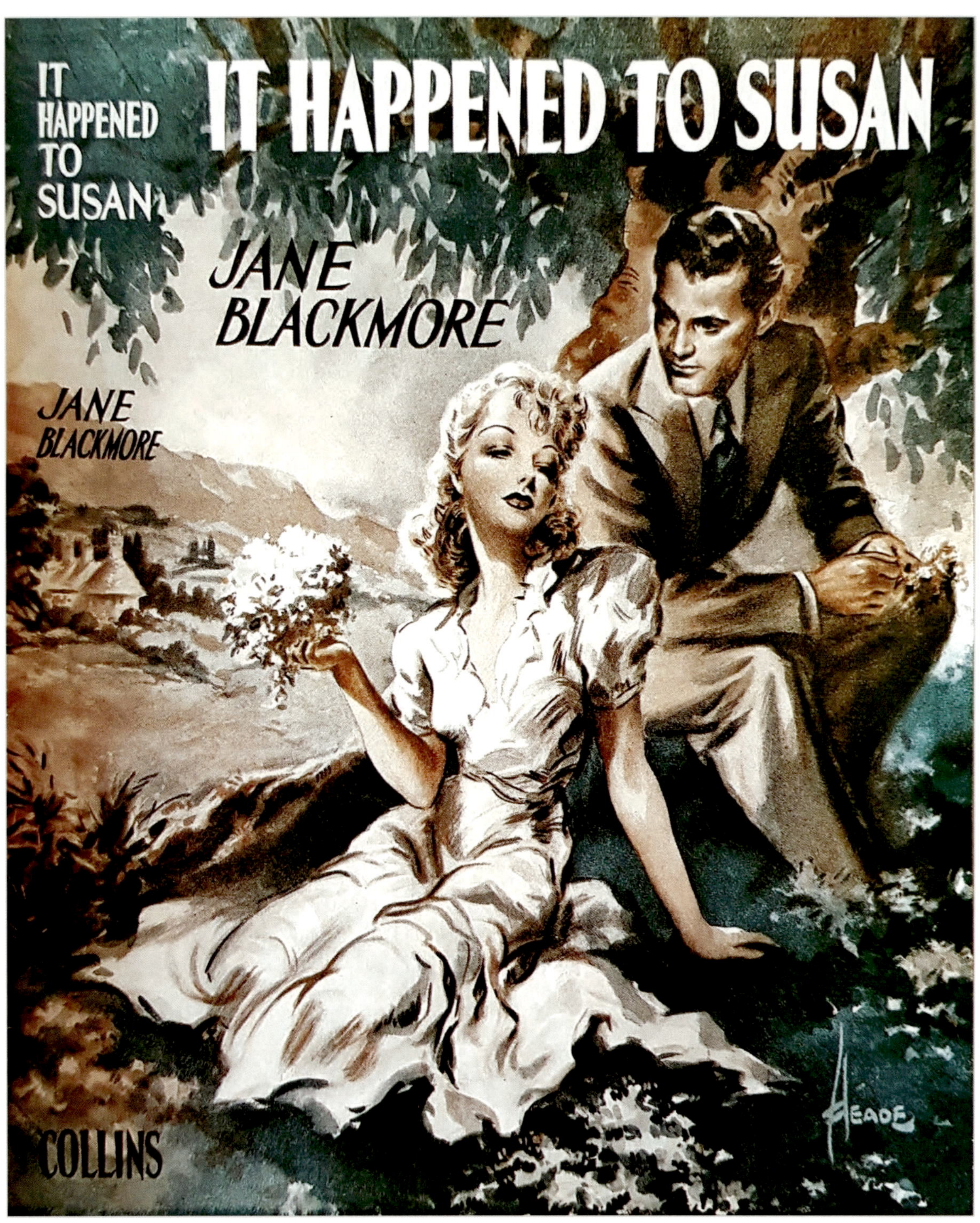

It Happened to Susan by Jane Blackmore (Collins, 1944)

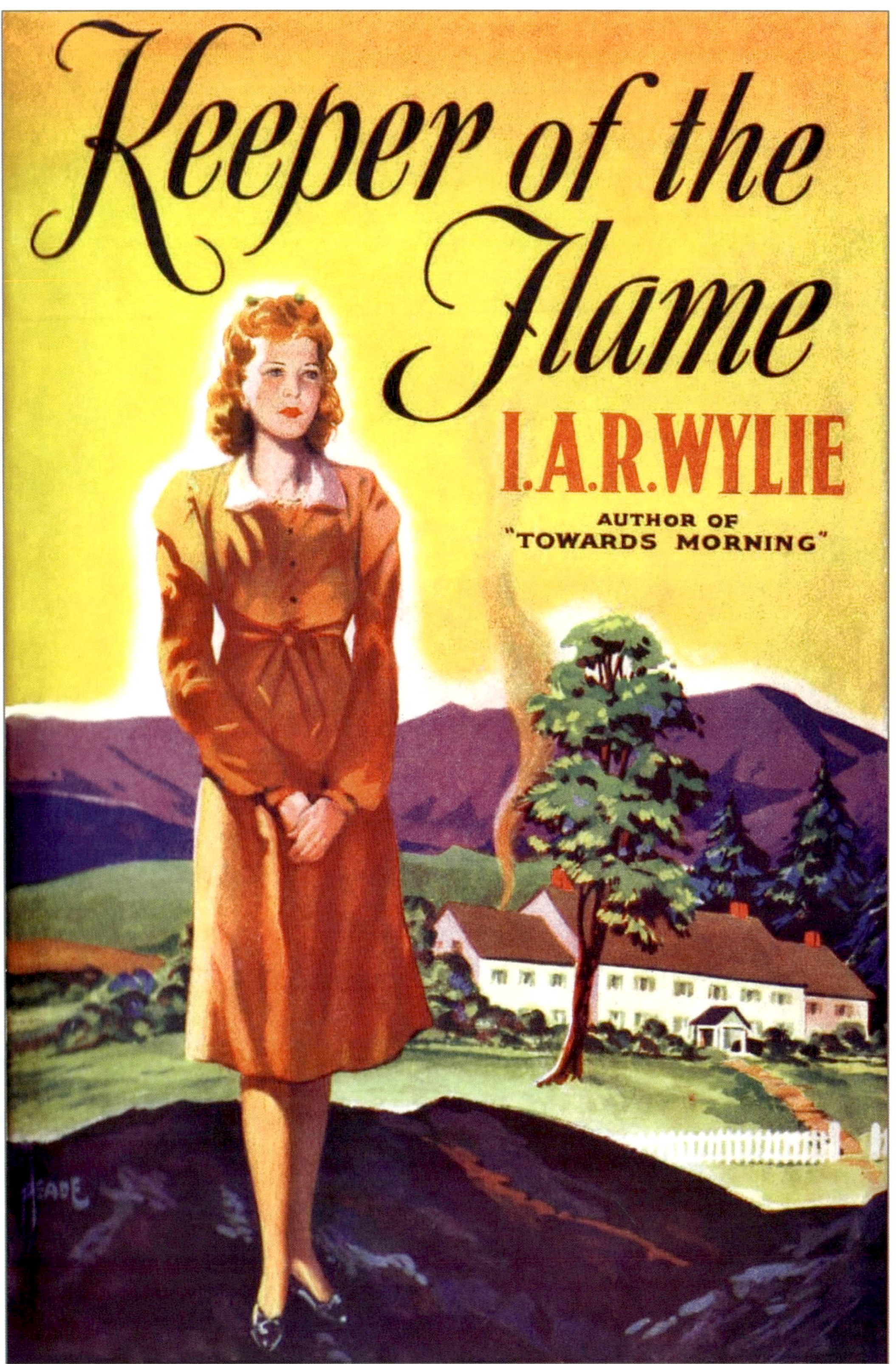

Keeper of the Flame by I A R Wylie (Cassell, May 1943). (Previously presented as only a small image on page 125 of *The Art of Reginald Heade – Special Edition*.)

Around (it is believed) the mid-1940s, Heade painted four signed pieces for a set of monarchy-themed *Costumes Through The Ages* jigsaw puzzles produced by the Good-Win games company. The four titles in the set, which apparently made up the whole of the company's Golden Casket range (so called because of the colour and design of their boxes) – were 1: 'Elizabeth 1558-1603', 2: 'Charles II 1649-1685', 3: 'George III 1760-1820' and 4: 'Victoria 1837-1901'. Sadly, the box lids of these puzzles were rather poorly printed, meaning that they do less than full justice to some fine examples of Heade's work; however, the central pictures are shown over the next two pages.

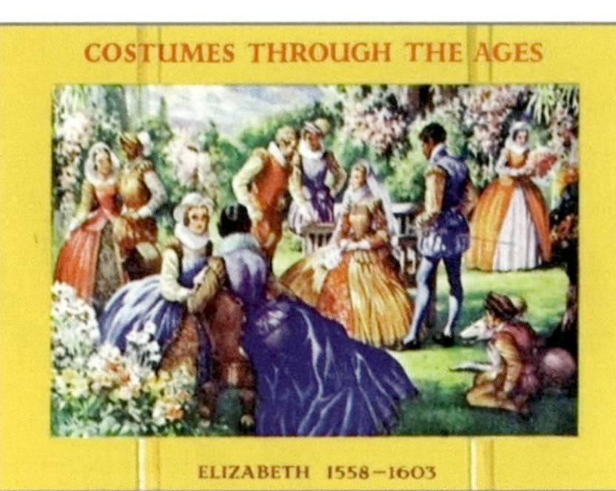

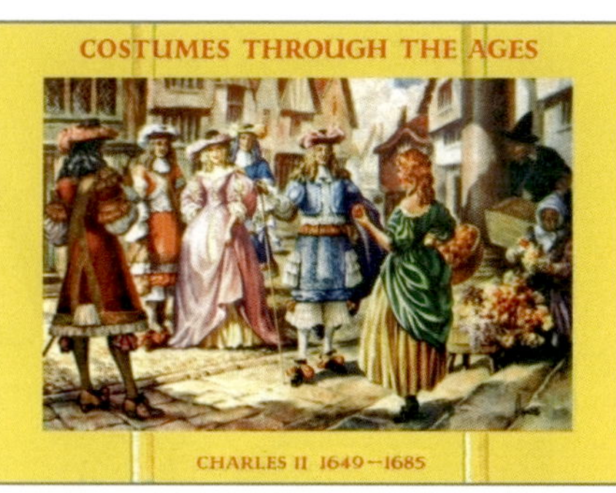

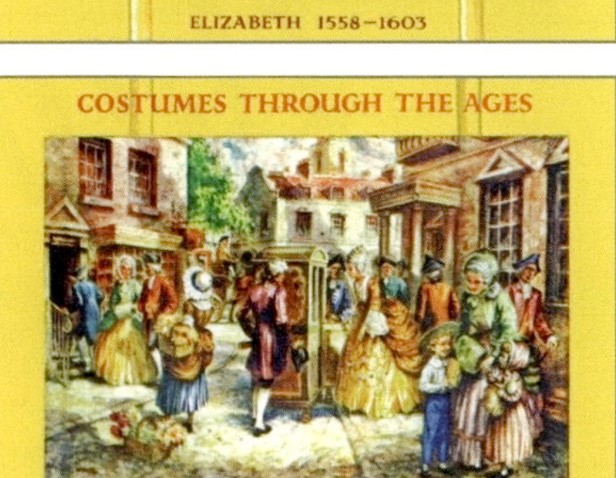

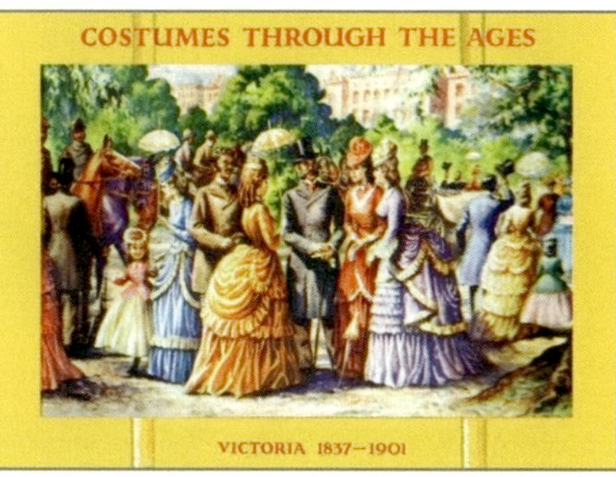

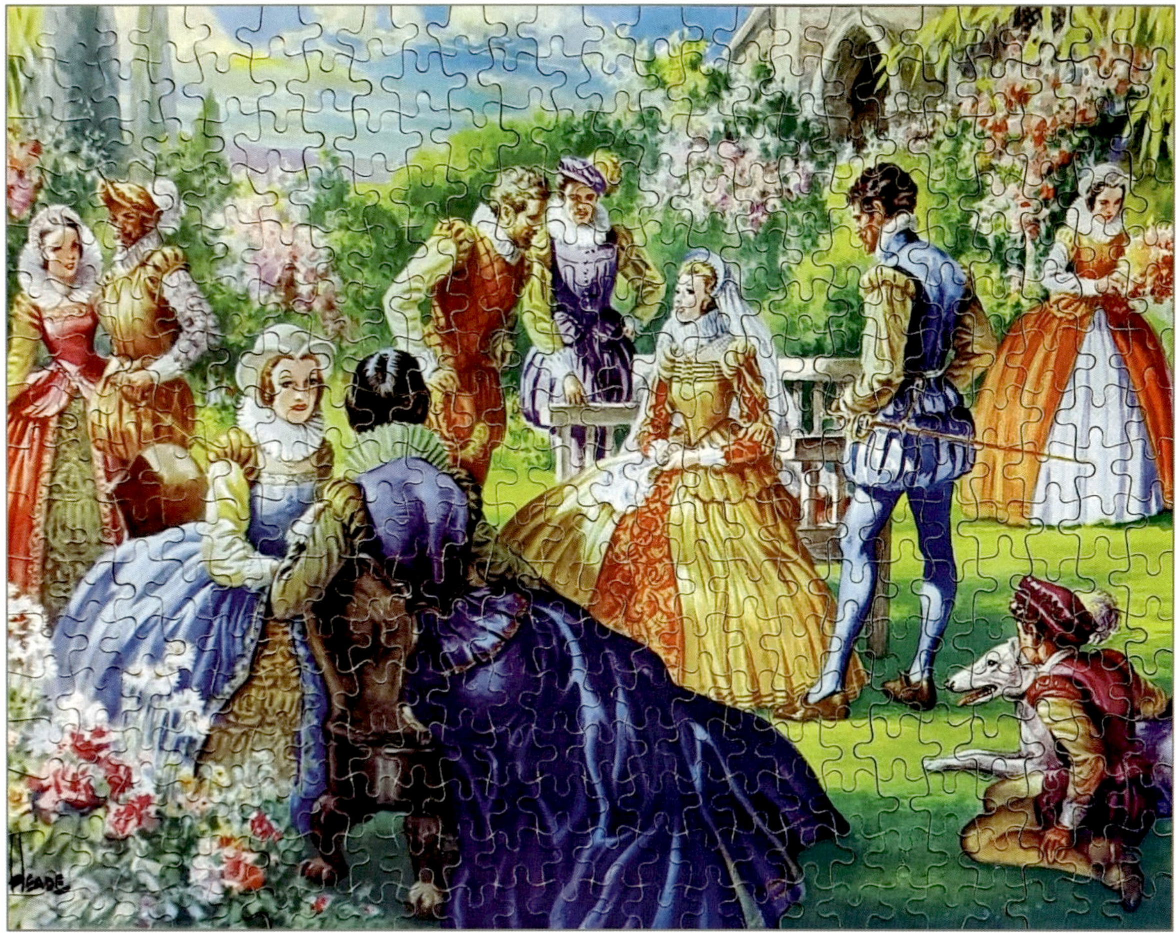

Above: the completed 'Elizabeth 1558-1603' puzzle, showing slightly more picture than the box lid at the top, but slightly less at the sides.

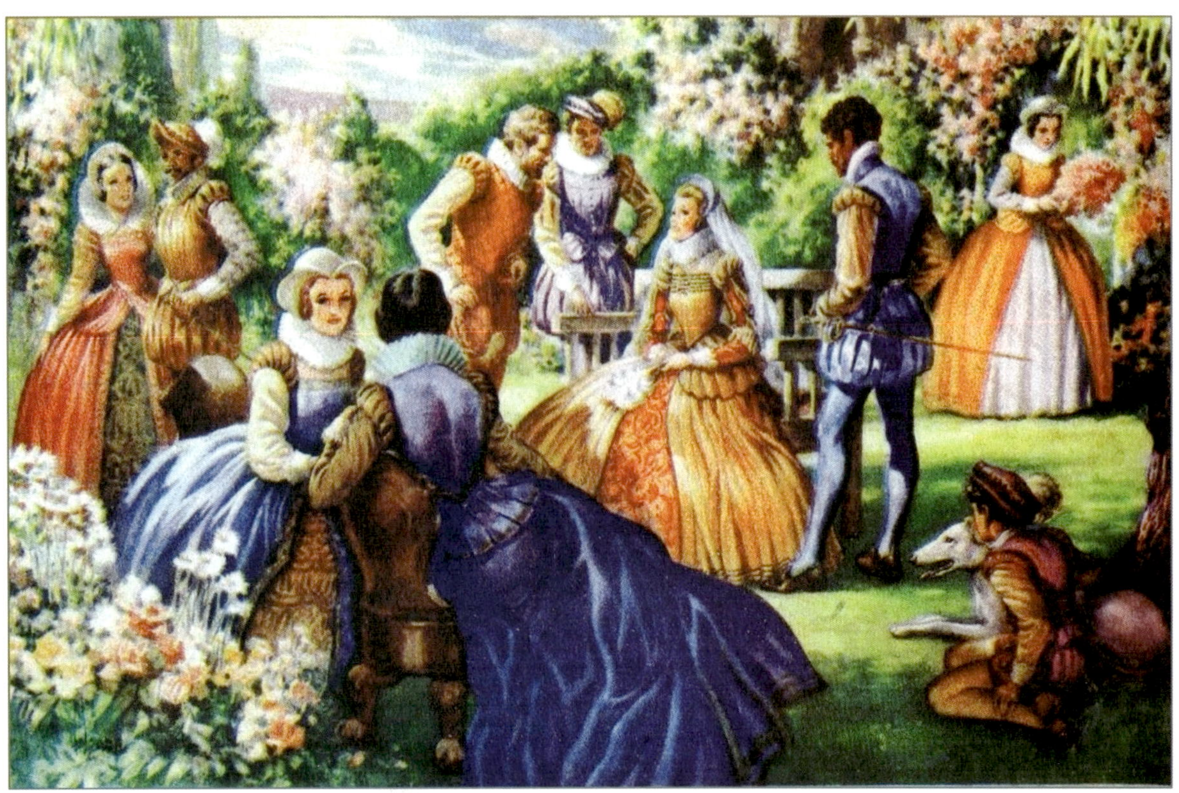

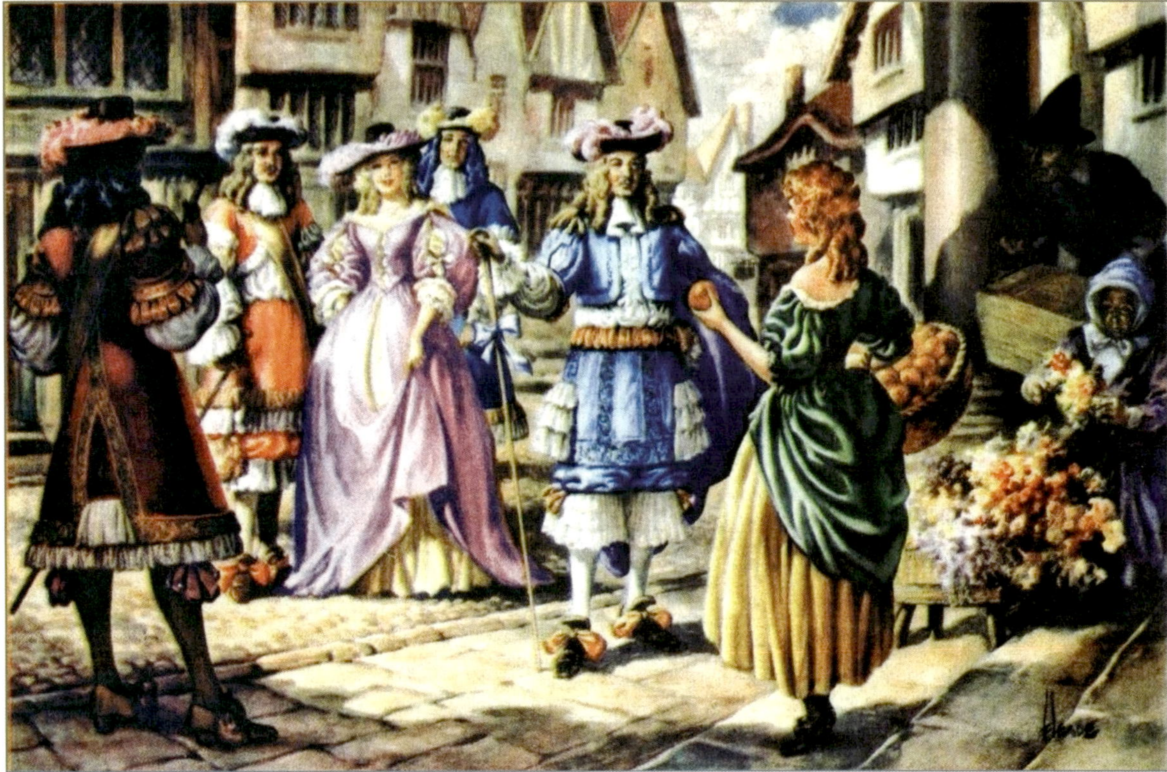

Above: Heade's artwork for the first two puzzles in the Good-Win *Costumes Through the Ages* set: 'Elizabeth 1558-1603' and 'Charles II 1649-1685'.

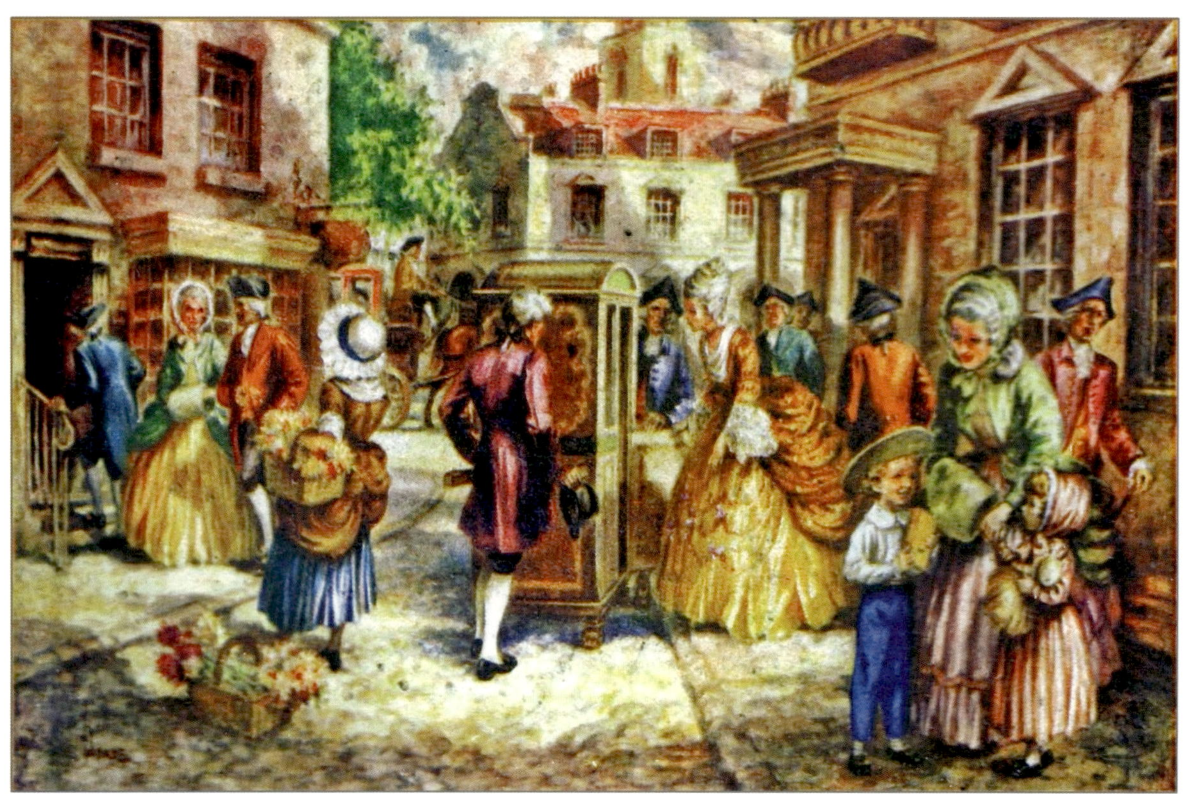

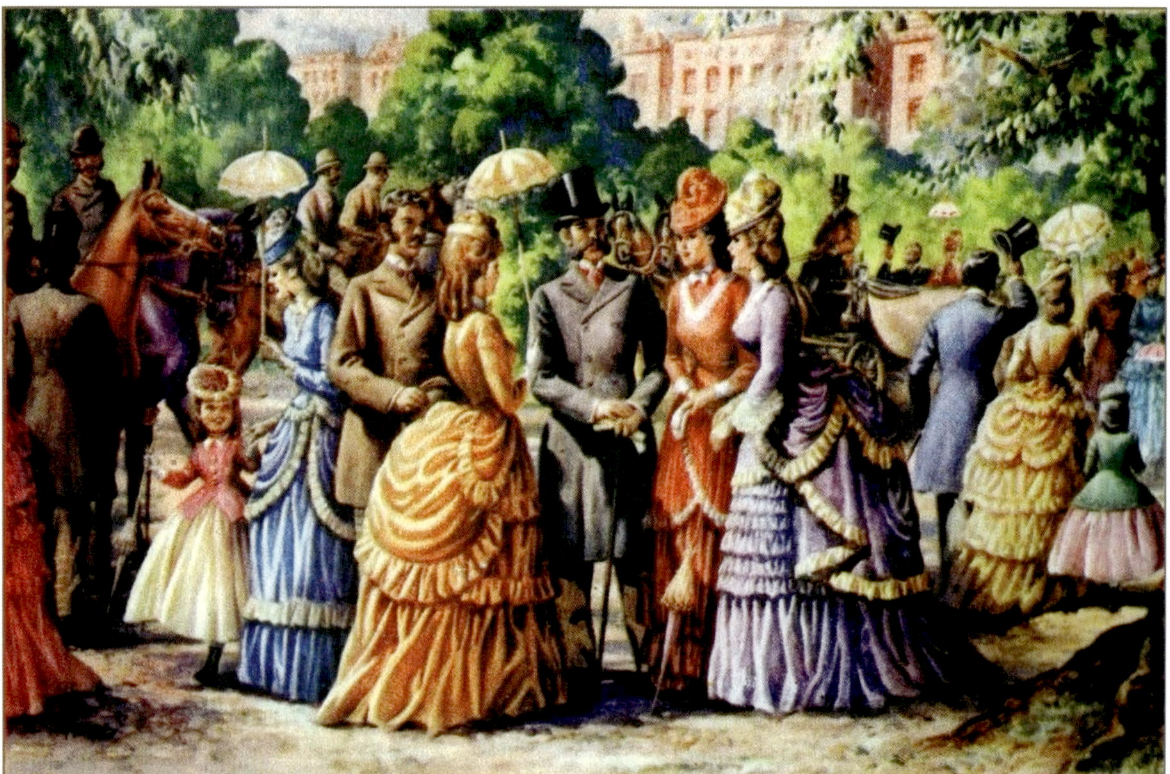

Above: Heade's artwork for the third and fourth puzzles in the Good-Win *Costumes Through the Ages* set: 'George III 1760-1820' and 'Victoria 1837-1901'.

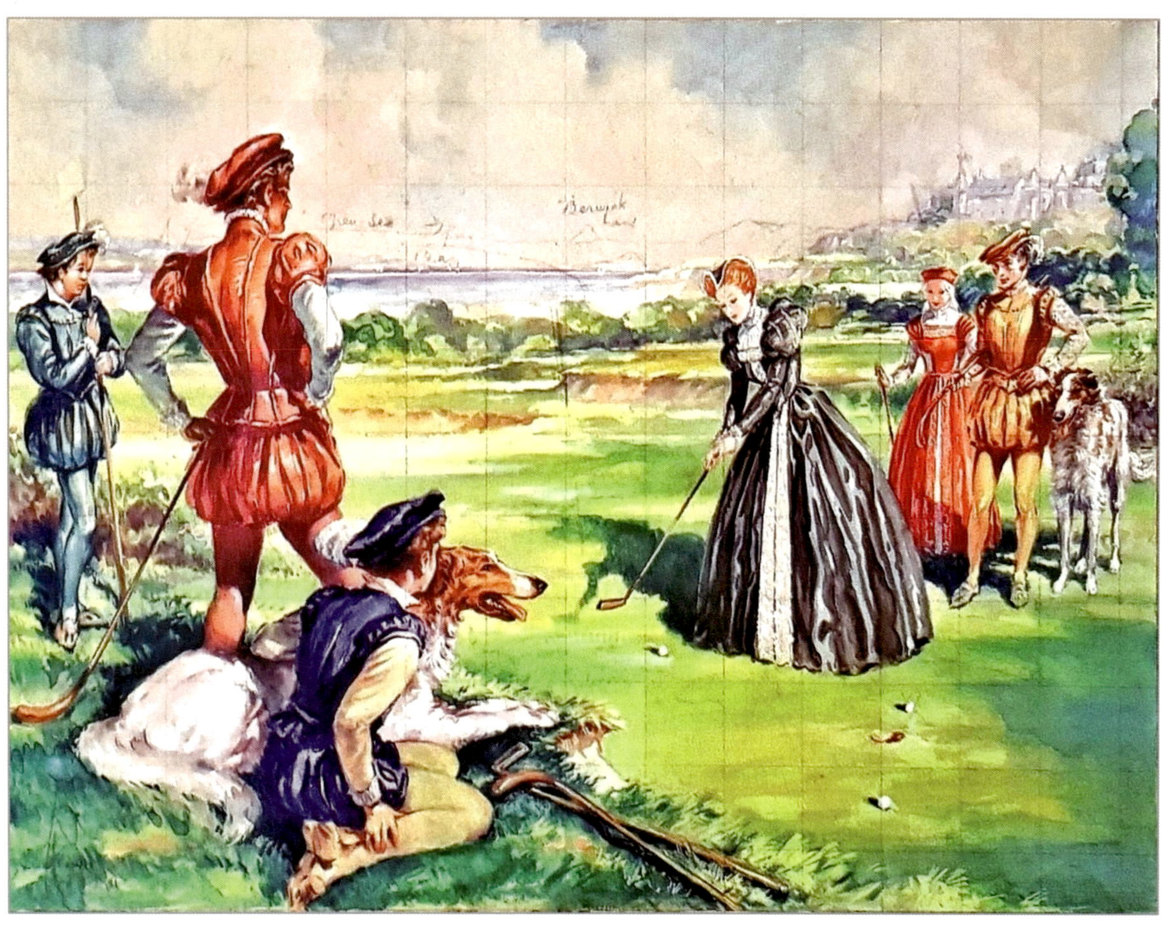

Above: a 1941-dated watercolour rough by Heade for an oil painting entitled 'Mary Queen of Scots Golfing on the Bents Near Seaton Palace – Midlothian'. Possibly an early, unused idea for one of the Good-Win *Costumes Through the Ages* jigsaw puzzles – note that the foreground figure of the boy with the dog is a virtual mirror image of one on the 'Elizabeth 1558-1603' puzzle. (With thanks to Mike Lewis.)

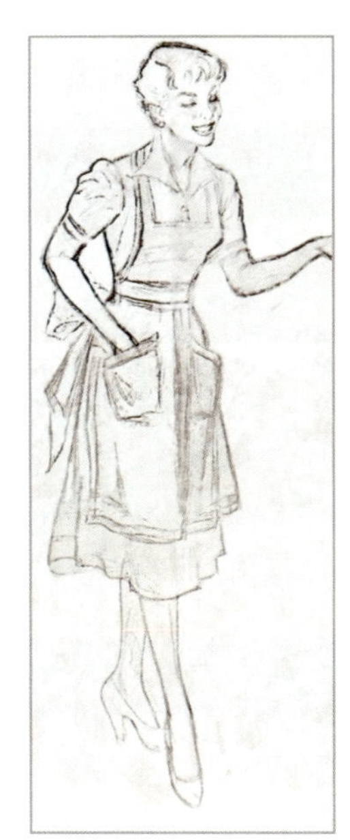
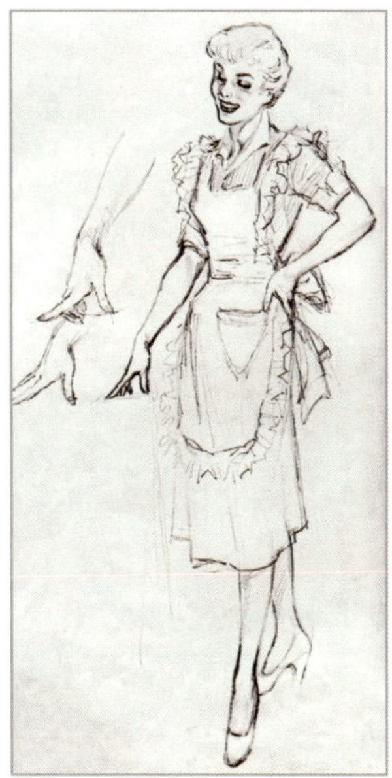

HOUSEWIFE SKETCHES

Surviving Heade drawings include four thumbnail sketches (three shown below) and two larger roughs (left) of an apron-wearing housewife in various poses. These are believed to have been preparatory work for some kind of domestic product advertising, in either the 1940s or the 1950s, but the brand is currently unknown.

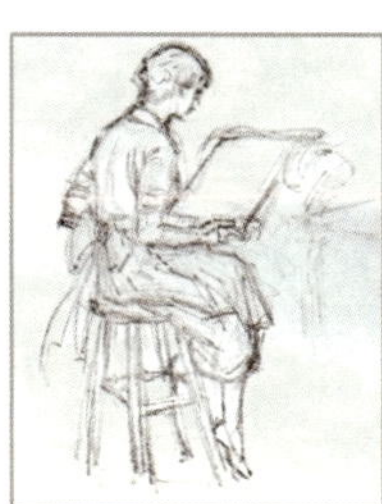
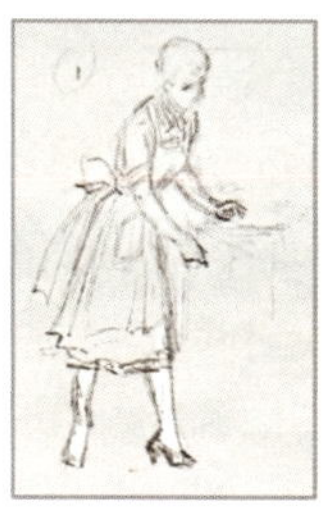
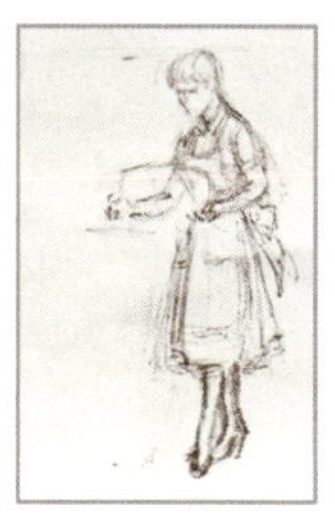

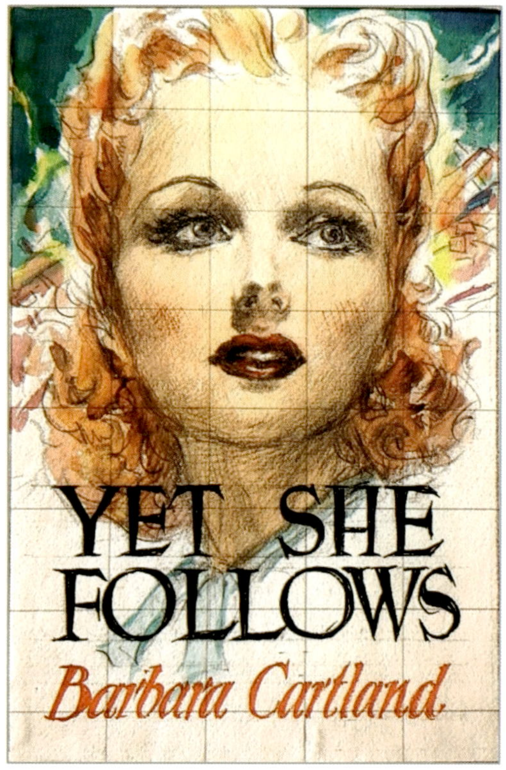
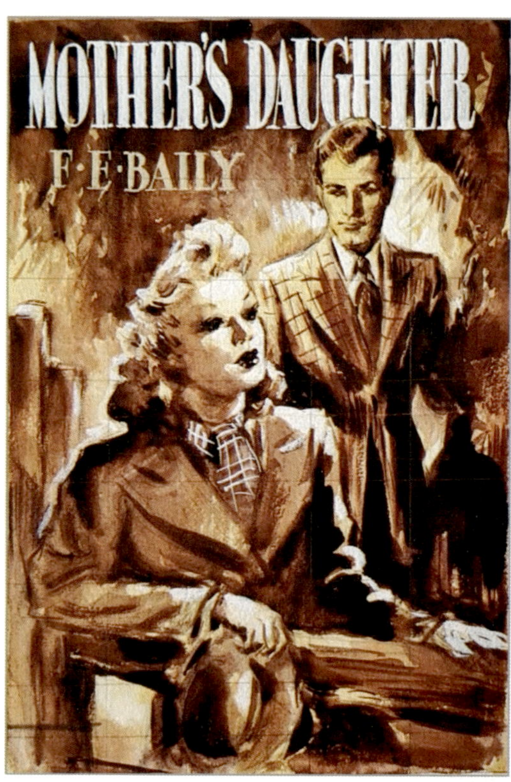

Heade's original roughs for *Yet She Follows* by Barbara Cartland (Robert Hale, 1944) and *Mother's Daughter* by F E Baily (Collins, 1944). No images are currently available of the as-published versions of these two dustjackets.

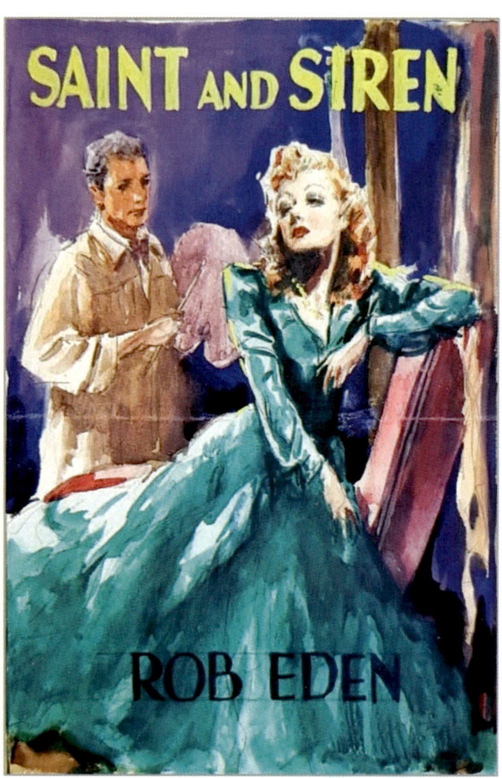
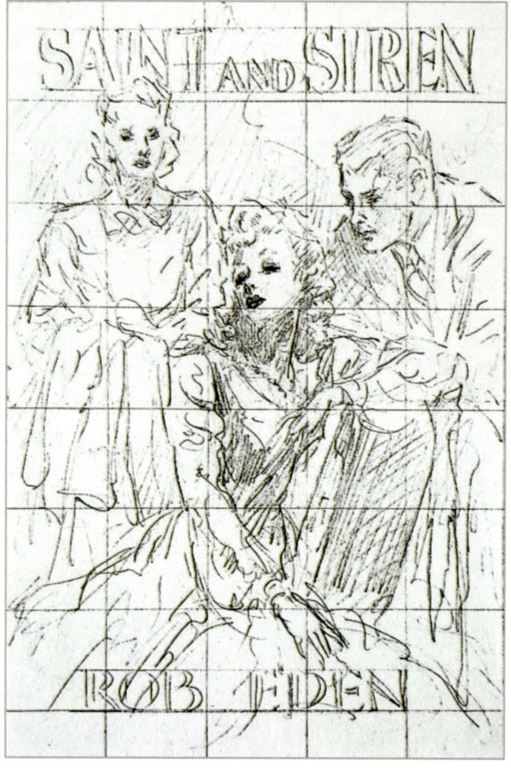

Heade's original painted rough, and revised pencil version, for *Saint and Siren* by Rob Eden (Museum Press, 1943)

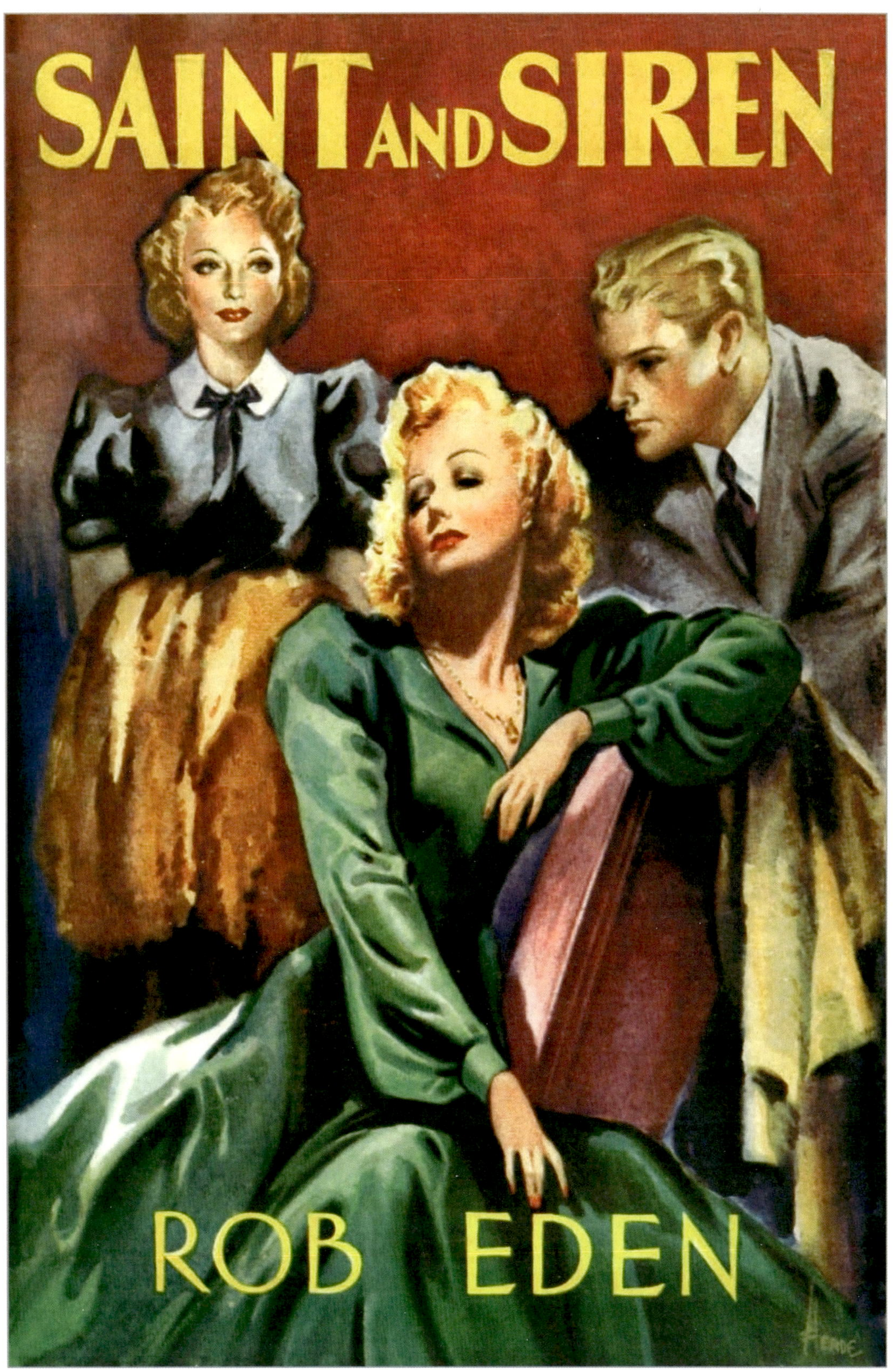

The as-published dustjacket of *Saint and Siren* by Rob Eden (Museum Press, 1943)

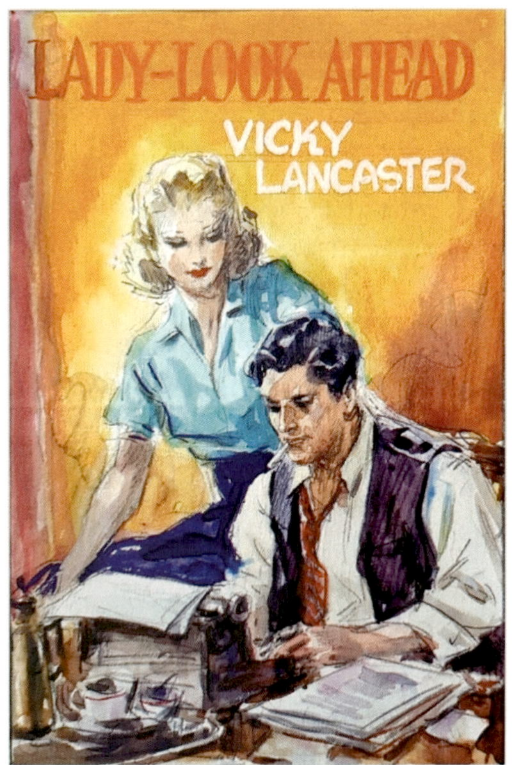

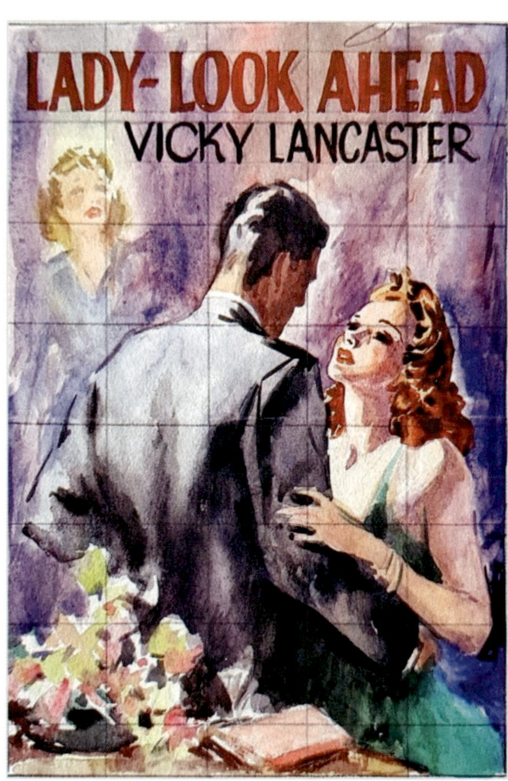

Two original roughs for *Lady – Look Ahead* by Vicky Lancaster (Robert Hale, 1944). The publishers rejected the first as lacking glamour; they disliked the man in shirtsleeves. Heade considered reusing the composition for a later Mills & Boon book, but it is uncertain whether or not he actually did so.

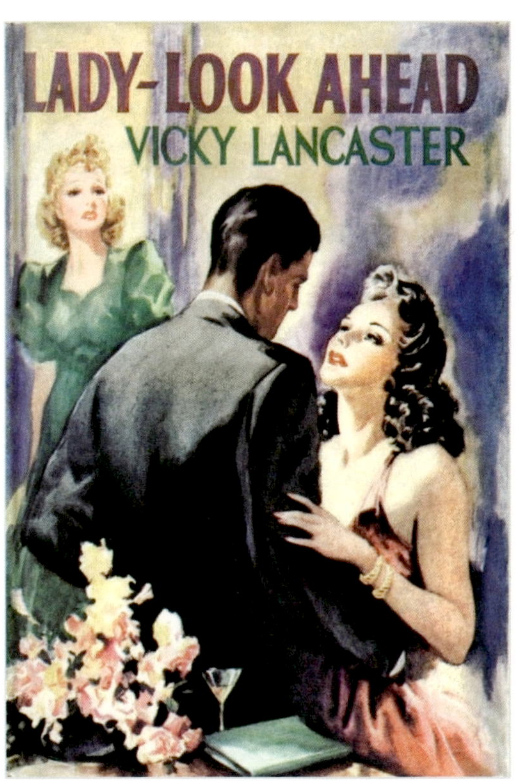

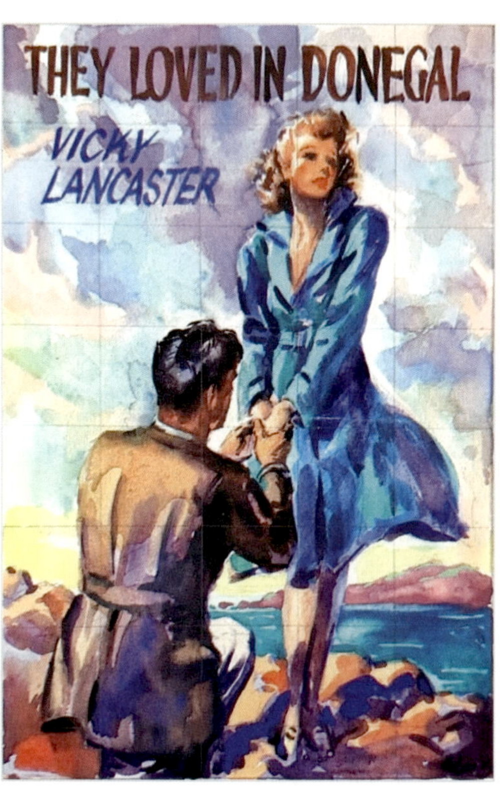

The as-published dustjacket of *Lady – Look Ahead* and Heade's rough for the same author's *They Loved in Donegal* (both Robert Hale, 1944)

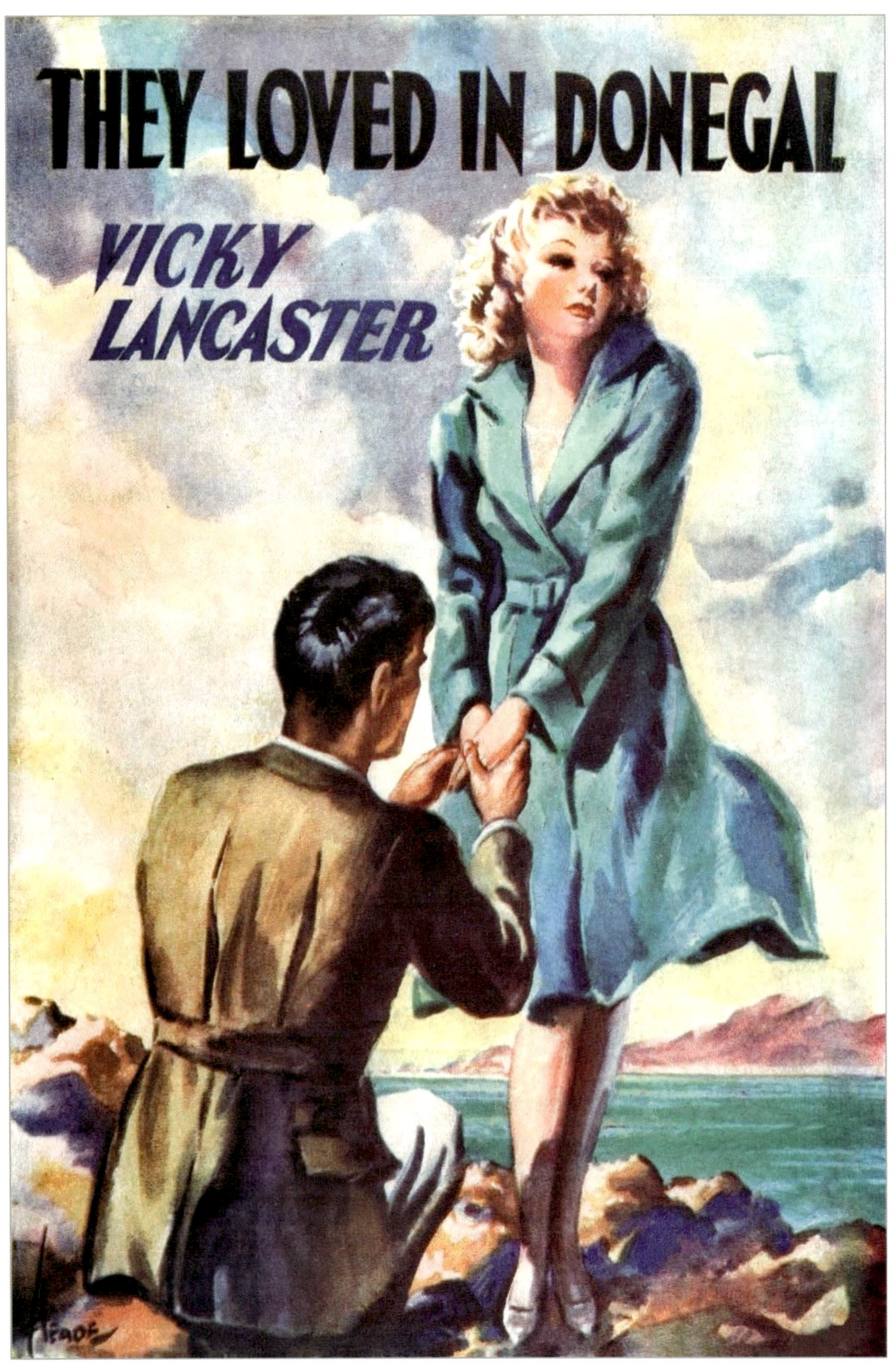

They Loved in Donegal by Vicky Lancaster (Robert Hale, 1944)

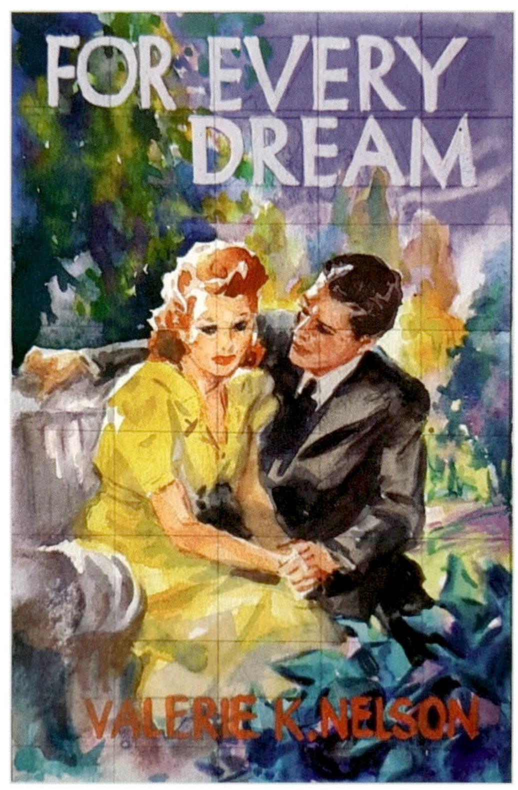 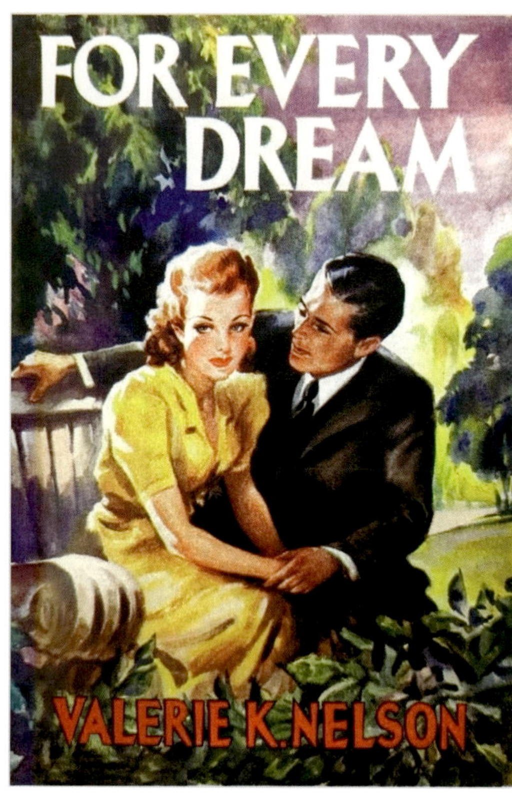

Heade's original rough and the as-published dustjacket of *For Every Dream* by Valerie K Nelson (Mills & Boon, 1944)

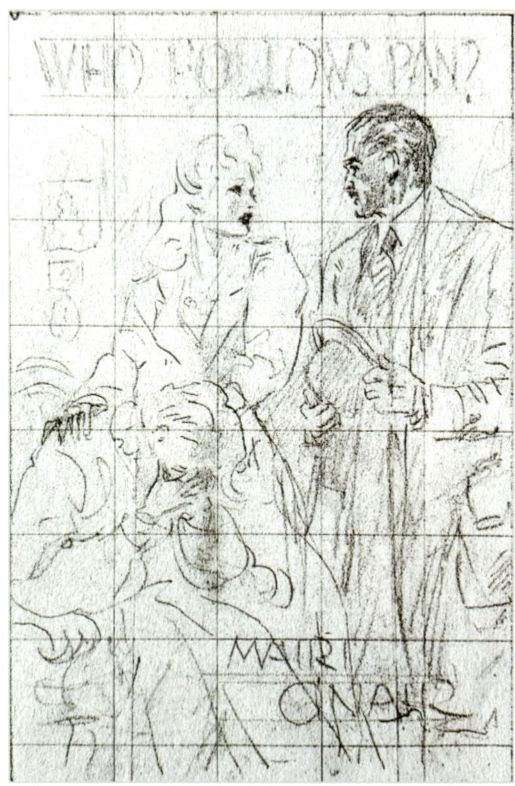 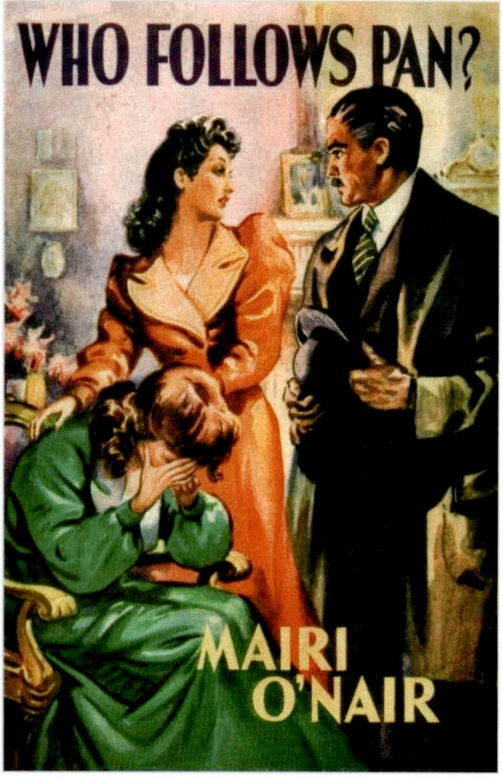

Heade's original rough and the as-published dustjacket of *Who Follows Pan?* by Mairi O'Nair (Mills & Boon, 1944)

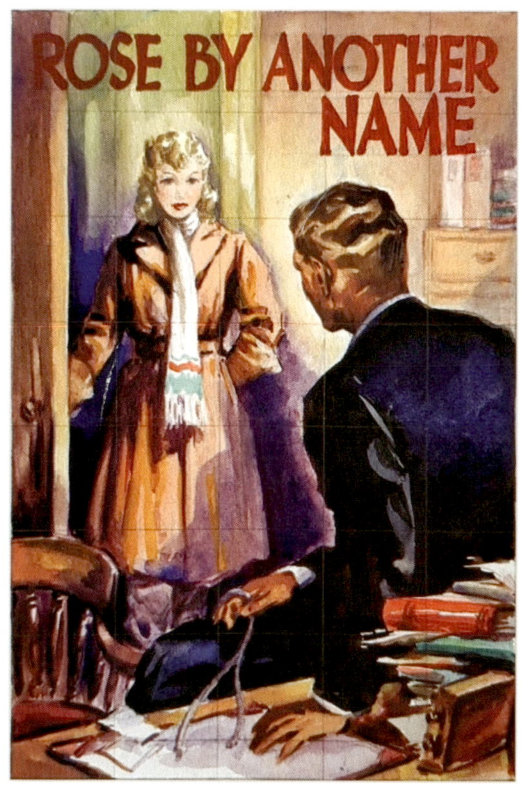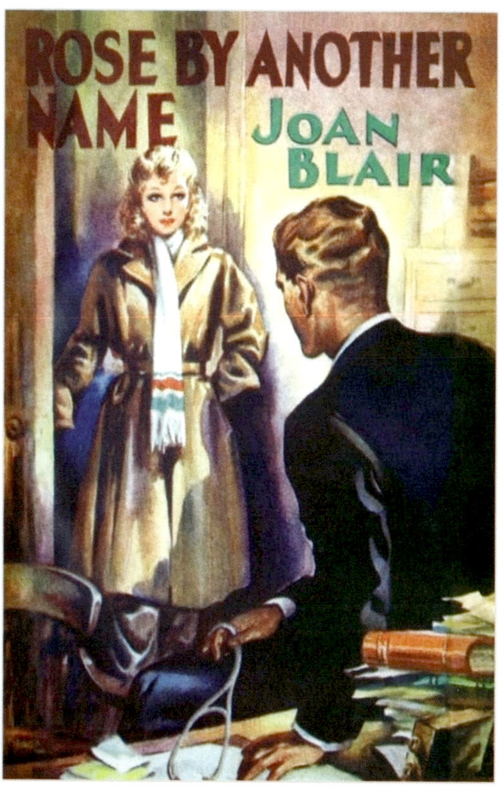

Heade's original rough and the as-published dustjacket of *Rose By Another Name* by Joan Blair (Mills & Boon, 1945)

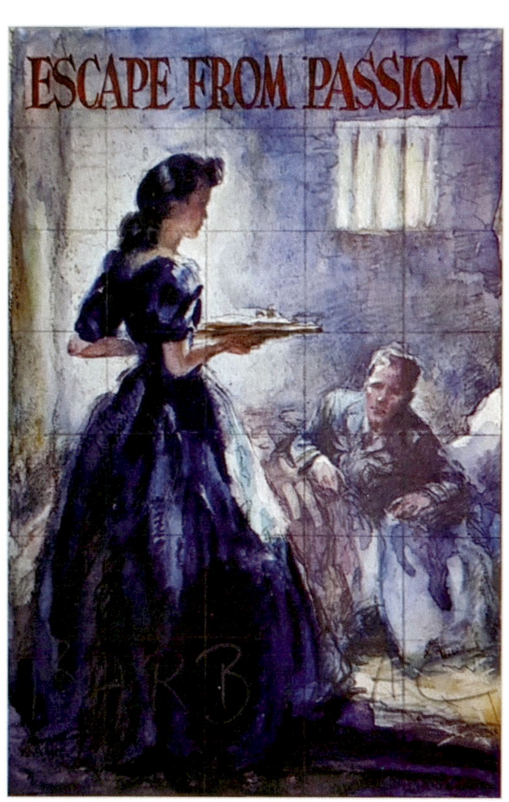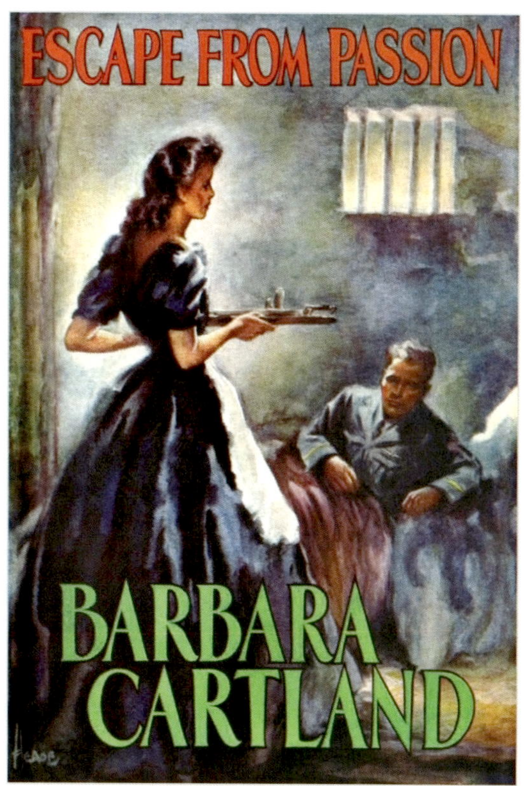

Heade's original rough and the as-published dustjacket of *Escape from Passion* by Barbara Cartland (Robert Hale, 1944)

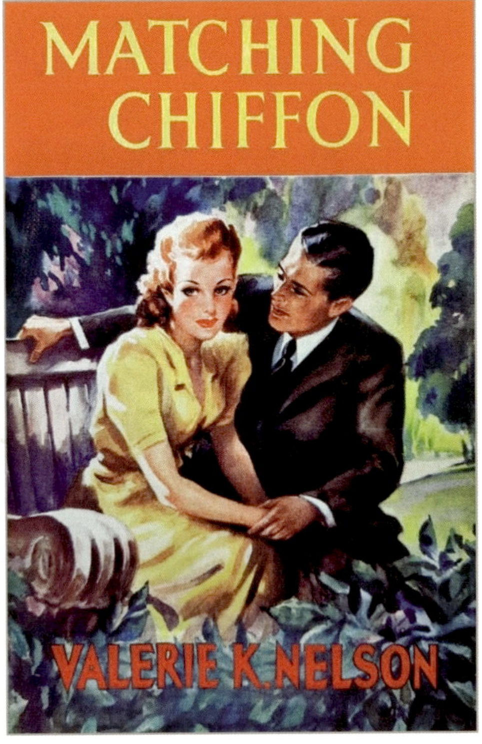

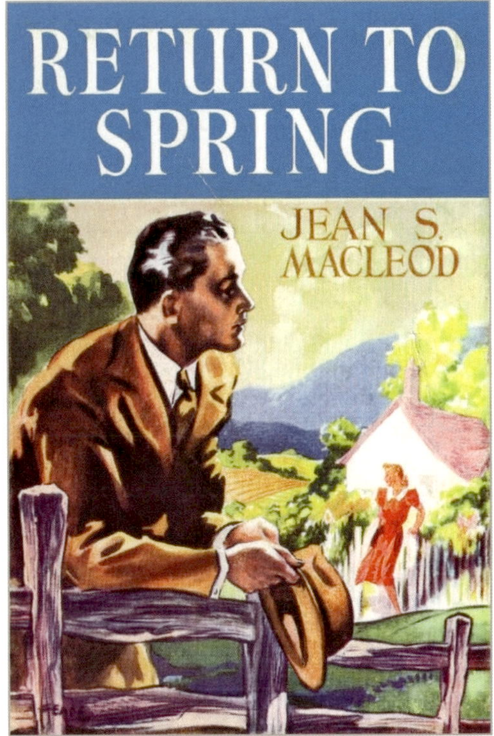

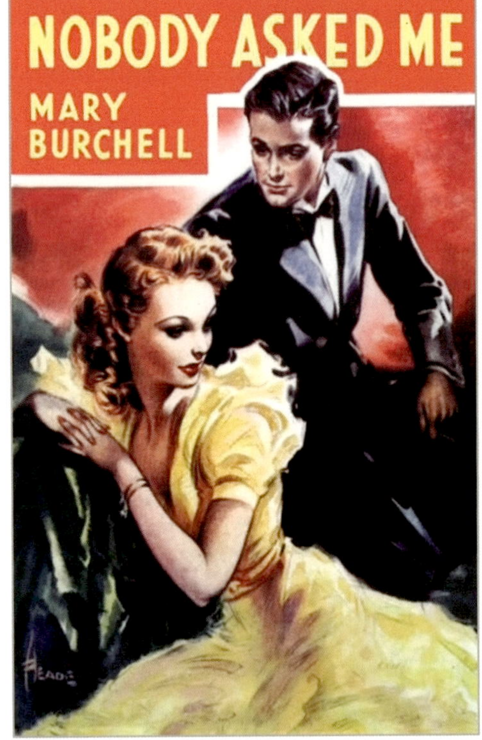

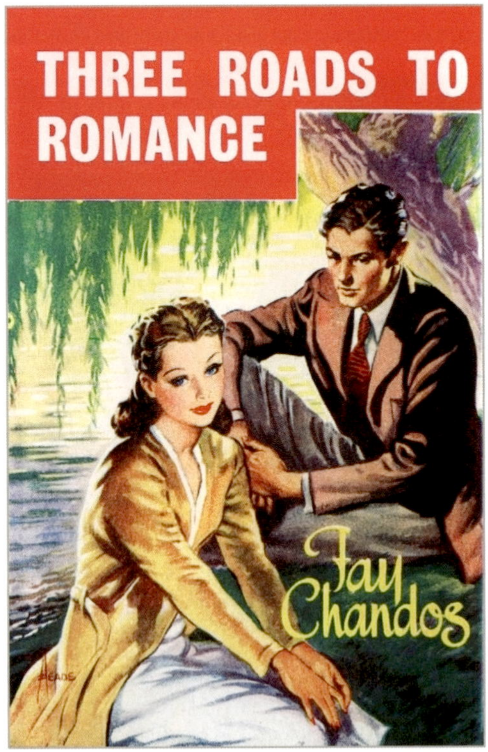

Pictured on this page, another four 1950s Mills & Boon reissues that reused dustjacket art originally painted by Heade for other titles from the same publisher – all four of which are included earlier in this 1940s section: Valerie K Nelson's *Matching Chiffon* (1952), reusing the art from the same author's *For Every Dream* (1944); Jean S MacLeod's *Return to Spring* (1954), reusing the art from the same author's *Blind Journey* (1942); *Nobody Asked Me* by Mary Burchell (1952), reusing the art from Phyllis Mannin's *Fugitive Heart* (1941); and Fay Chandos's *Three Roads to Romance* (1959), reusing the art from the same author's *When We Two Parted* (1940).

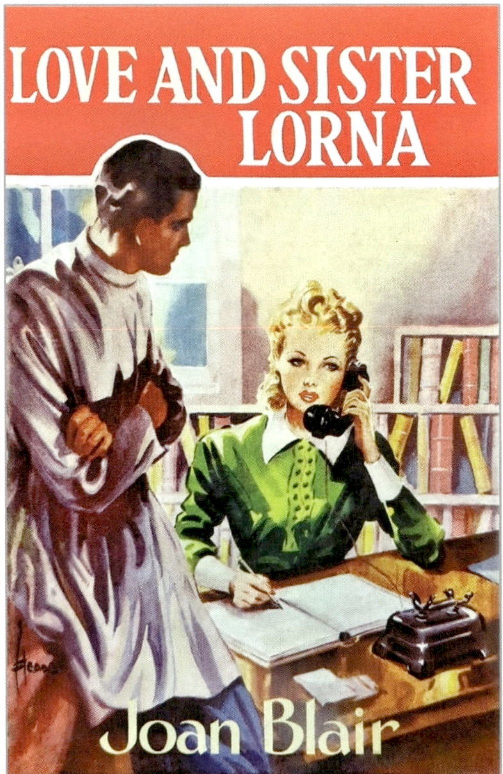

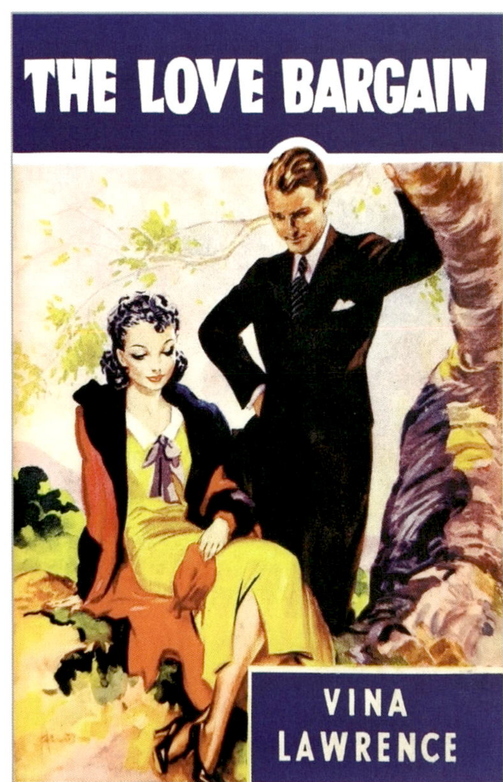

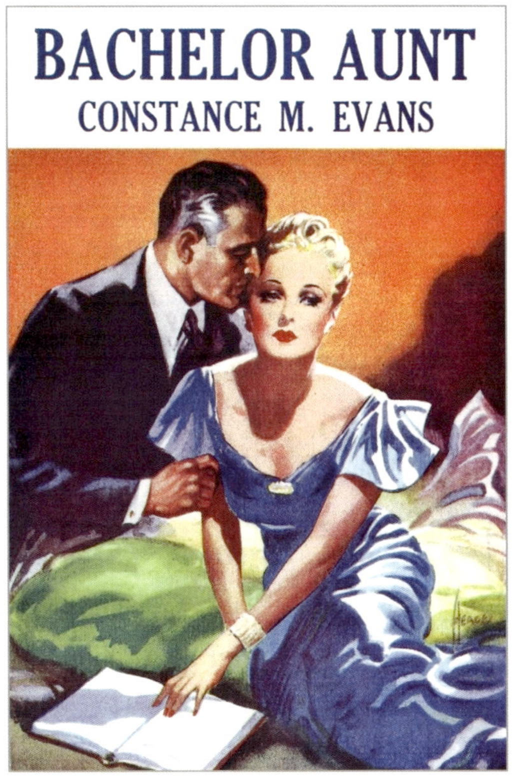

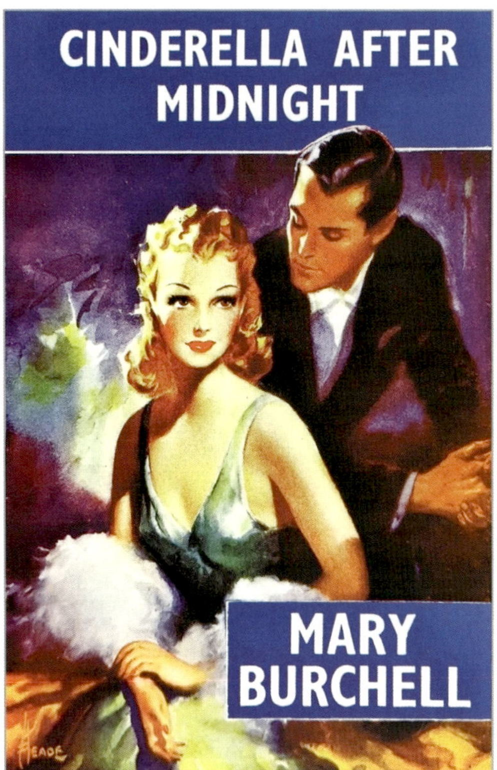

Four further Mills & Boon books reusing Heade dustjacket art originally painted for as-yet-unidentified earlier titles from the same publisher, dating from either the 1940s or perhaps the late 1930s: *Love and Sister Lorna* by Joan Blair (1955), *The Love Bargain* by Vina Lawrence (1956), *Bachelor Aunt* by Constance M Evans (1957) and *Cinderella After Midnight* by Mary Burchell (1959).

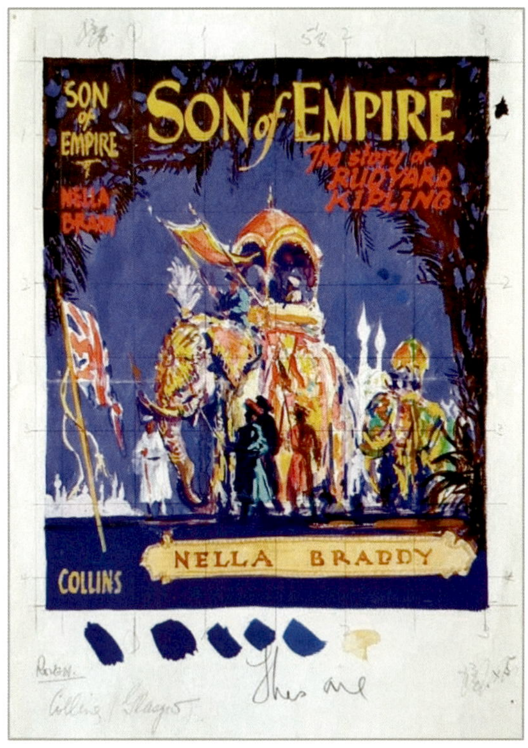

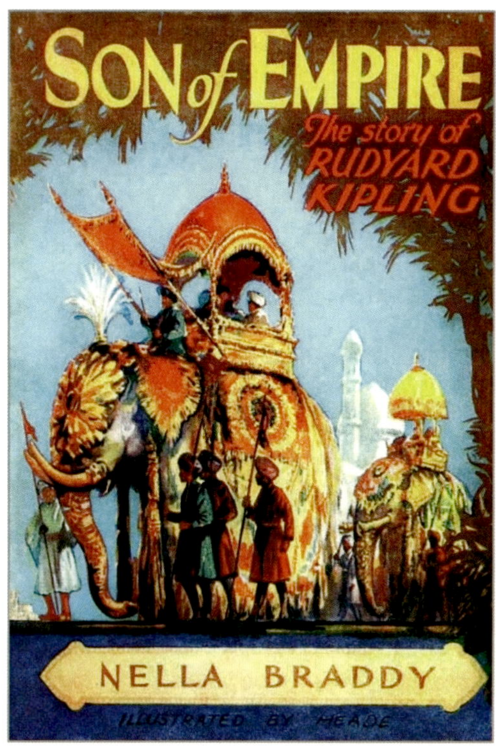

Above: the original rough and the as-published dustjacket of *Son of Empire* by Nella Braddy (Collins, 1945). Note the five different blue tone options offered by Heade, and the publishers' selection of the lightest of these.

THE ARTIST'S AGENT

Heade invariably undertook his commercial work via an agent, and for the greater part of his career this was William Partridge, who himself co-owned and served as a director of three publishing firms, Partridge, Pictorial Art and Regency Publications. Many of Heade's roughs and finished paintings have Partridge's contact details given on the reverse side, either in the form of an affixed business card or in the form of an ink-stamped address and telephone number. At one point, Partridge was based in the Clerkenwell area of London (see business card at top right), but for the majority of the time he conducted his business from addresses in the Bloomsbury area, first an office in Great Russell Street (see ink stamp at bottom right) and secondly one at 23 Bloomsbury Square, both very close to the British Museum.

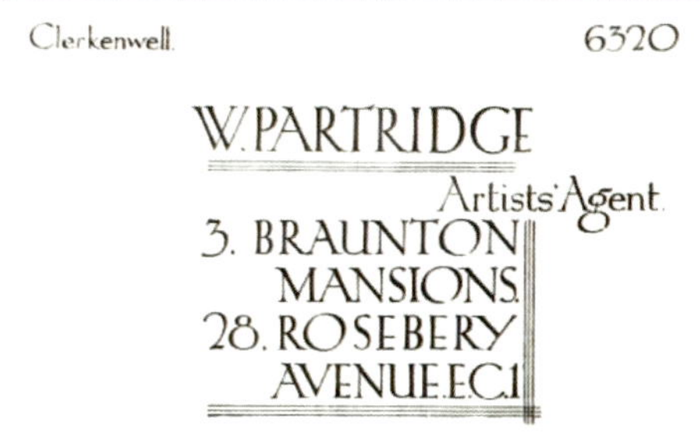

PRETTY POLLY?

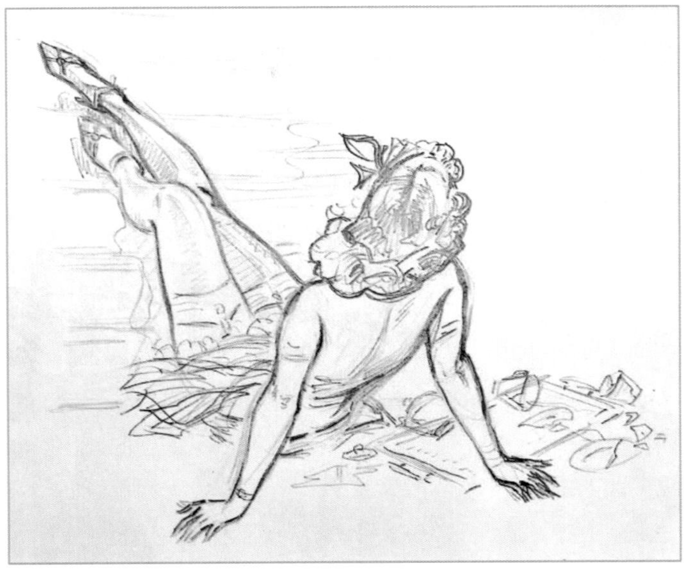

The pencil sketch reproduced on the left was Heade's preparatory drawing for the 'Our Dumb Blonde' cartoon that appeared in the *Sunday Pictorial* newspaper on 7 May 1944 – see overleaf. It is however very similar in composition to a 1943-dated print advertisement for the Pretty Polly stockings range – see below right. This could be simply a coincidence, or an example of Heade taking inspiration from a previously-published source, but on the other hand it could be that the artist was himself responsible for that earlier piece. There is one other still-surviving Heade sketch believed to have been produced for a hosiery advertisement – see below left – perhaps again for Pretty Polly, though this is currently unconfirmed.

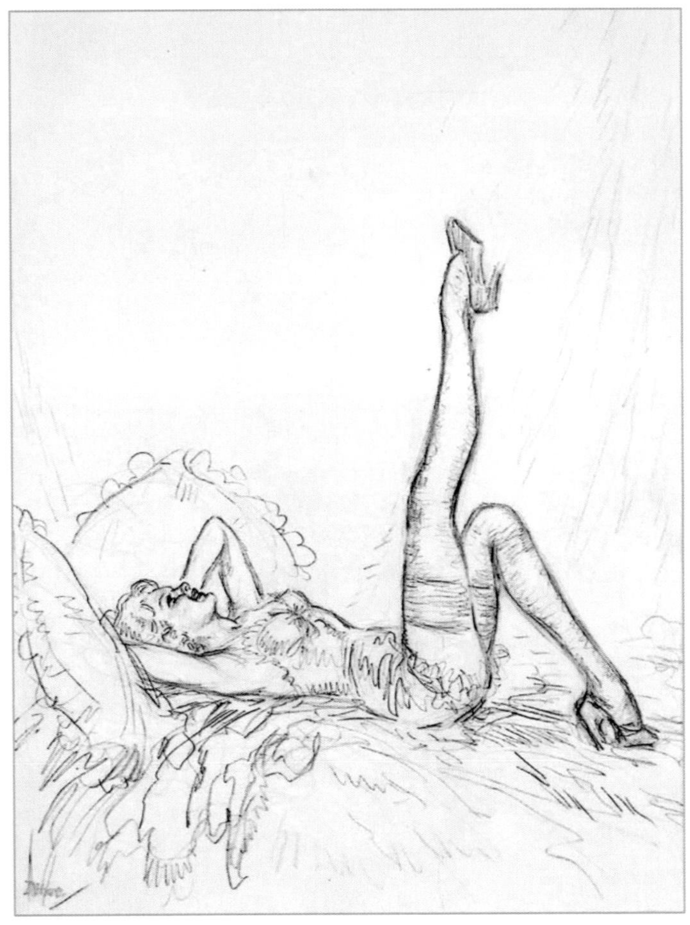

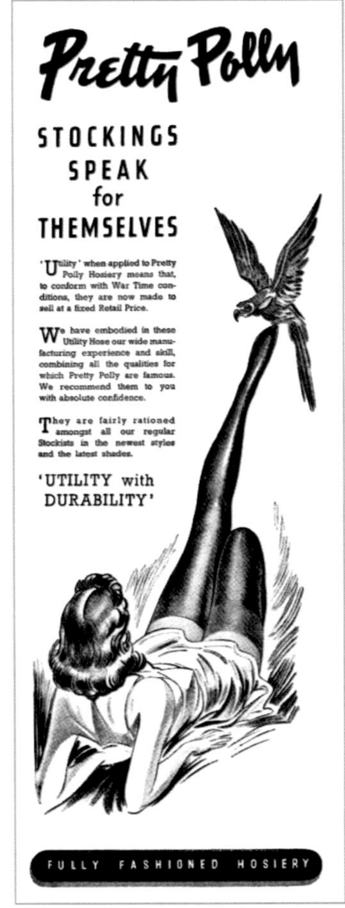

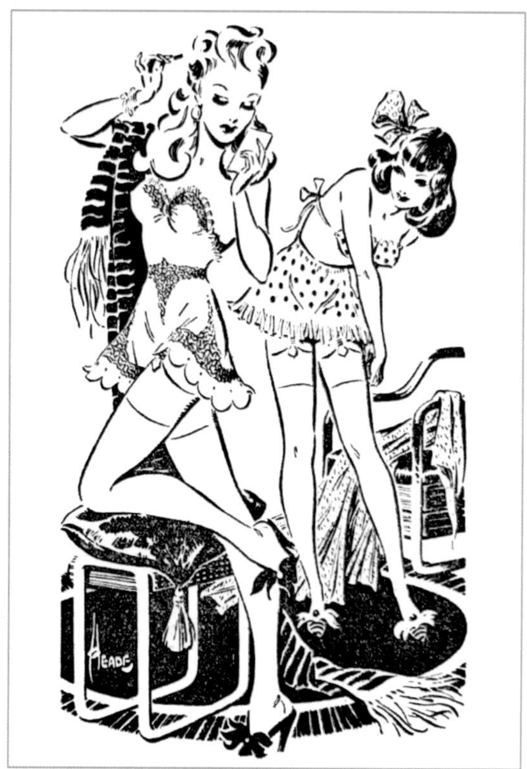 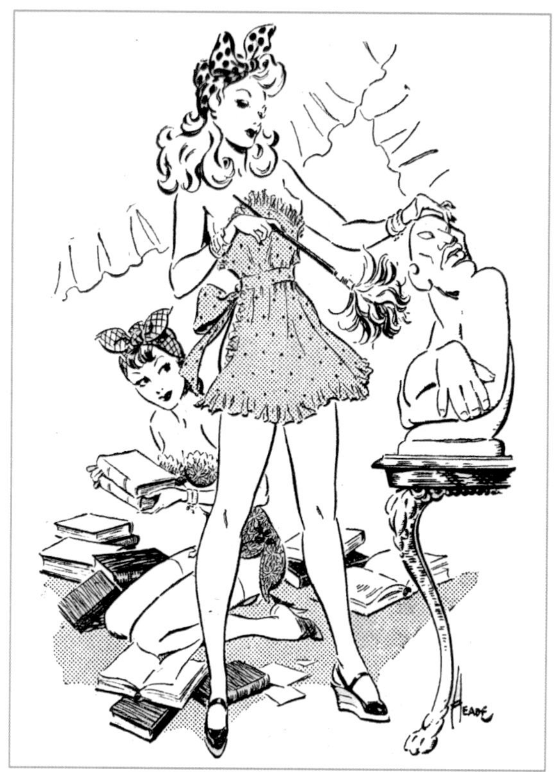

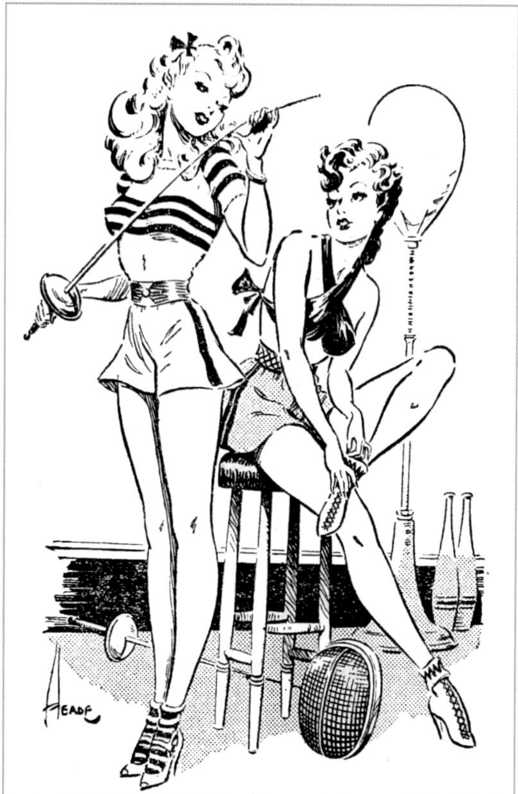 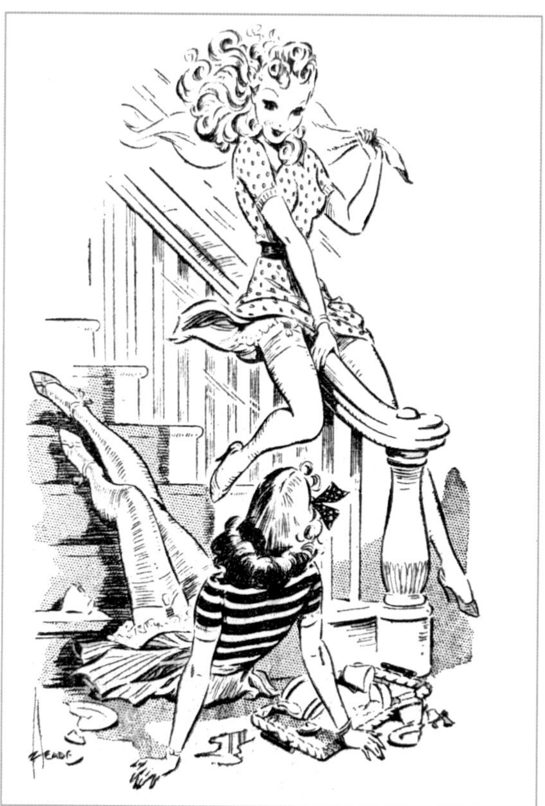

Four of the seven published illustrations Heade contributed to the *Sunday Pictorial* newspaper's long-running 'Our Dumb Blonde' cartoon series (Sunday Pictorial, 2, 9 and 16 April and 7 May 1944). Executed in the style of the series' creator Arthur Ferrier, these cartoons appear to have been the very first pin-up style pieces that the artist completed, and can be seen as forerunners of his pulp paperback cover work.

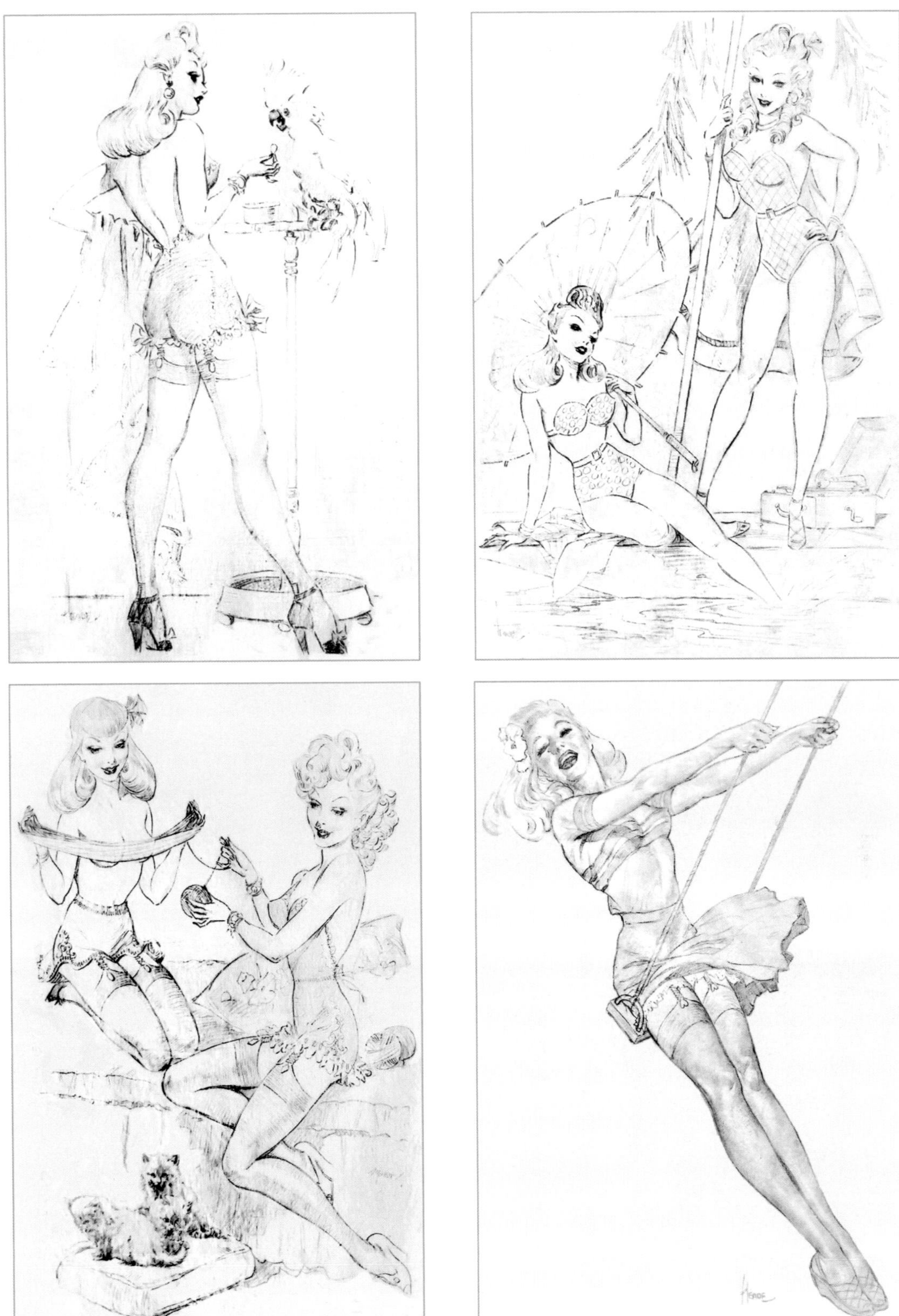

Top left: one of two surving roughs for the seventh and last of Heade's 'Our Dumb Blonde' cartoons (*Sunday Pictorial*, 25 June 1944). Top right and bottom left: roughs for two further proposed 'Our Dumb Blonde' cartoons, both of which went unpublished. Bottom right: a rough for a pin-up-style piece that Heade annotated with the title *Swing Sister*, the intended purpose of this is currently unknown.

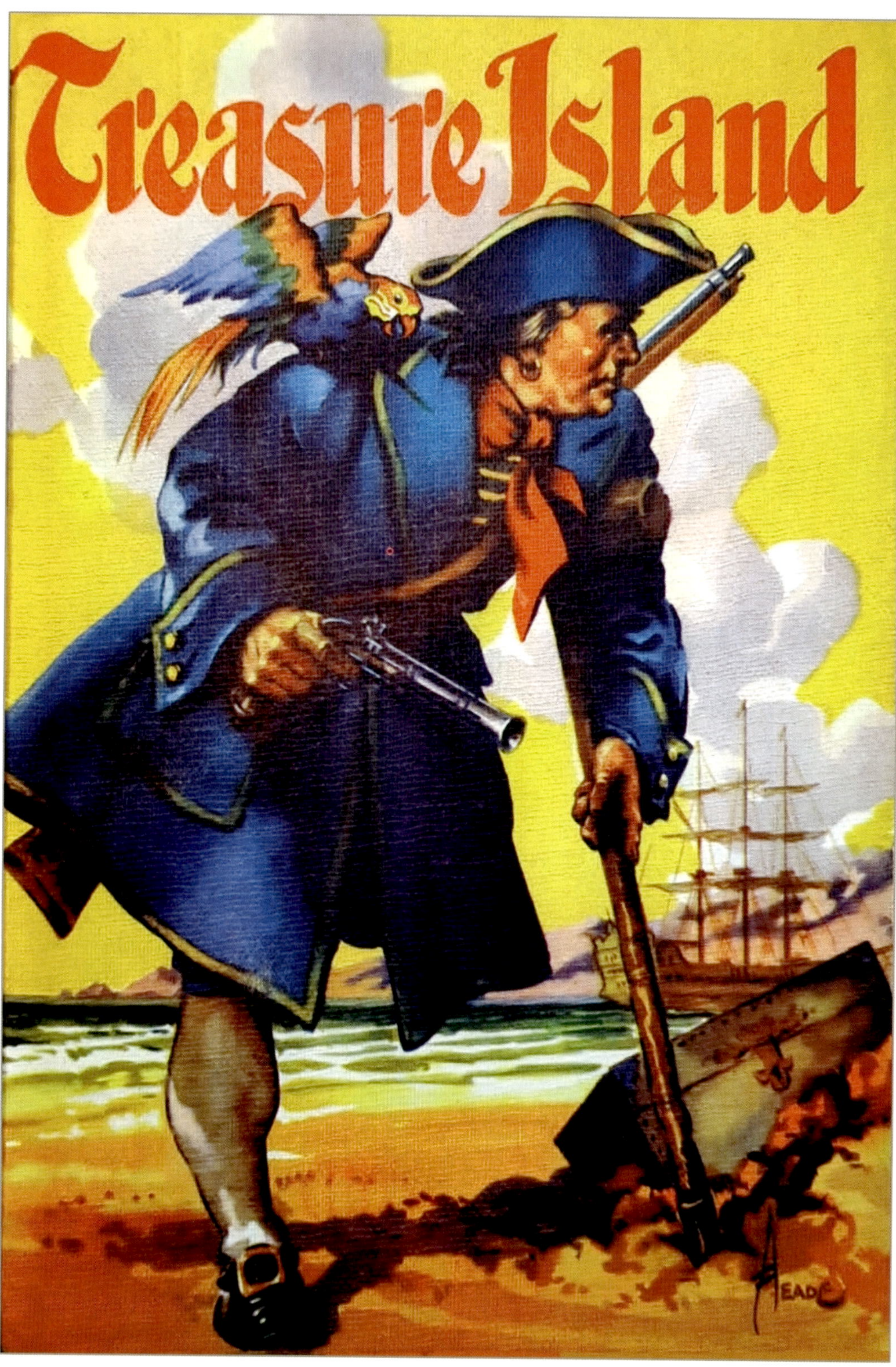

In 1945, some two years before he supplied the artwork for a Partridge edition of Robert Louis Stevenson's *Treasure Island* (as pictured on pages 195 to 202 of *The Art of Reginald Heade – Special Edition*), Heade provided a completely different set of illustrations for an earlier adaptation of the same novel, published by Pocket Editions BCM/Poket and distributed by Atlas Publishing and Distributing. In this instance, the illustrations consisted of full colour front and back covers, five other full colour pieces, including a centrespread, and 11 duotone pieces. All of these are shown across this and the following five pages. Above: the book's front cover.

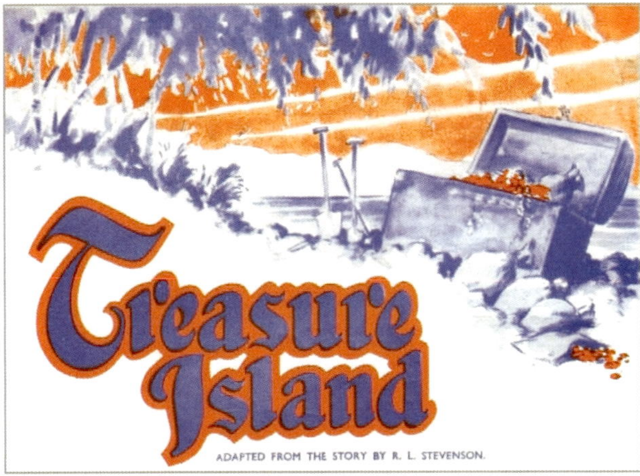

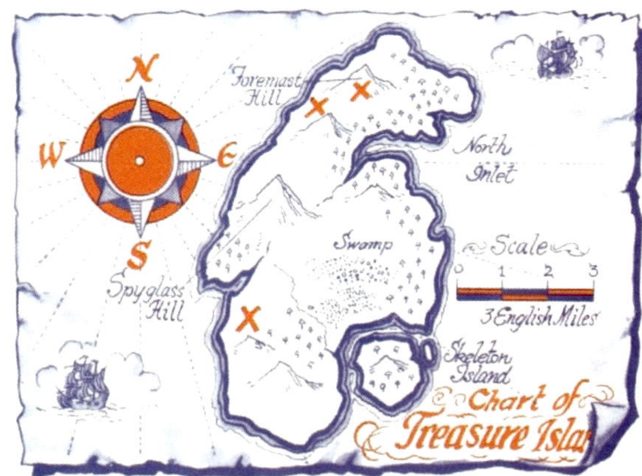

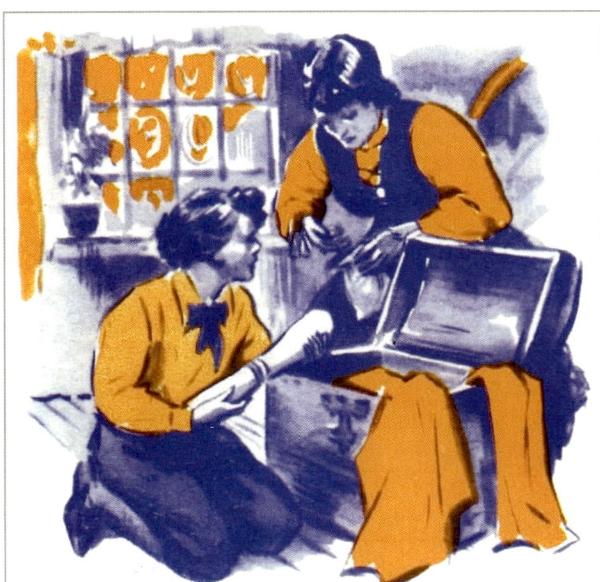

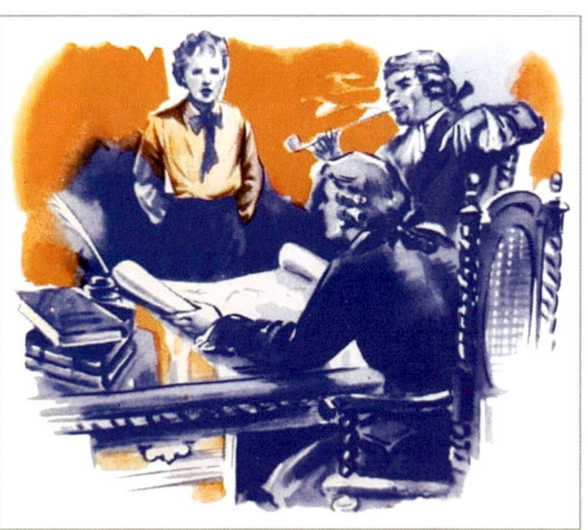

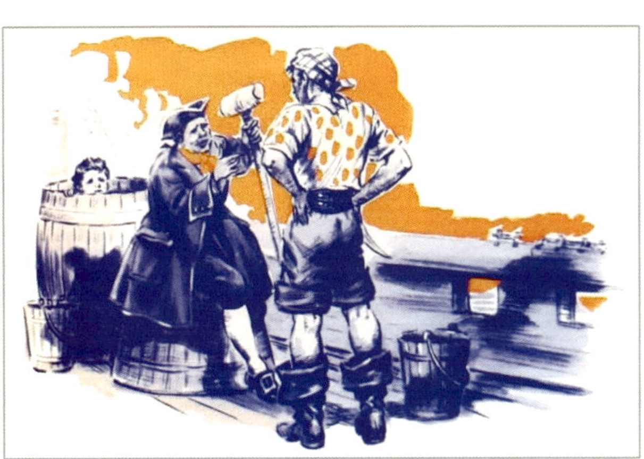

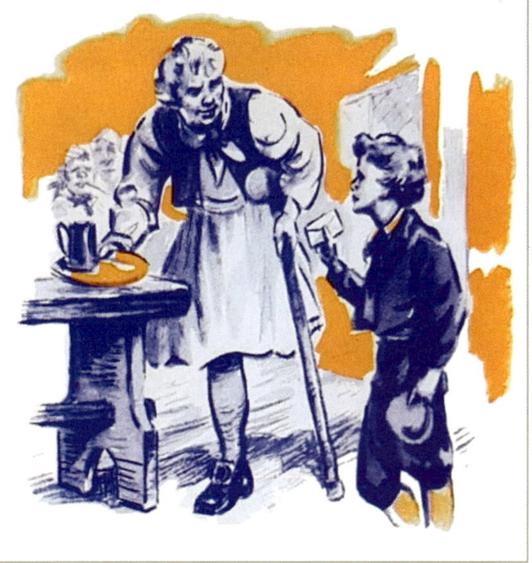

The first six of Heade's duotone illustrations for *Treasure Island* by Robert Louis Stevenson (Pocket Editions BCM/Poket, 1945)

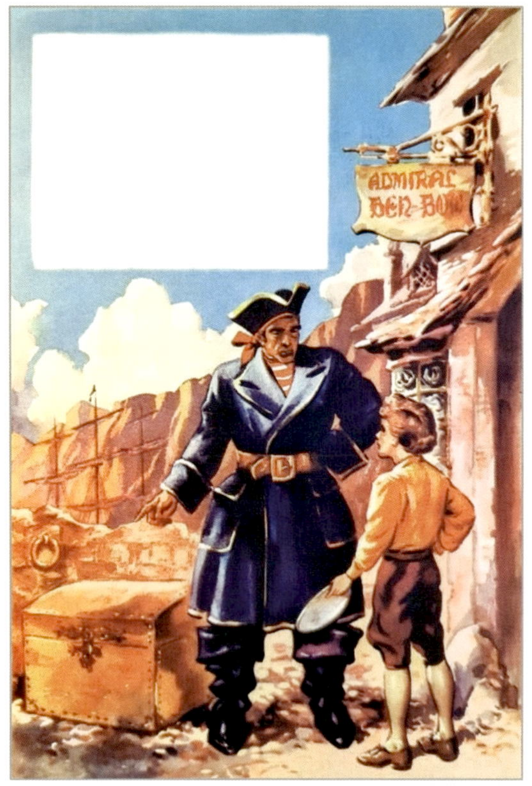

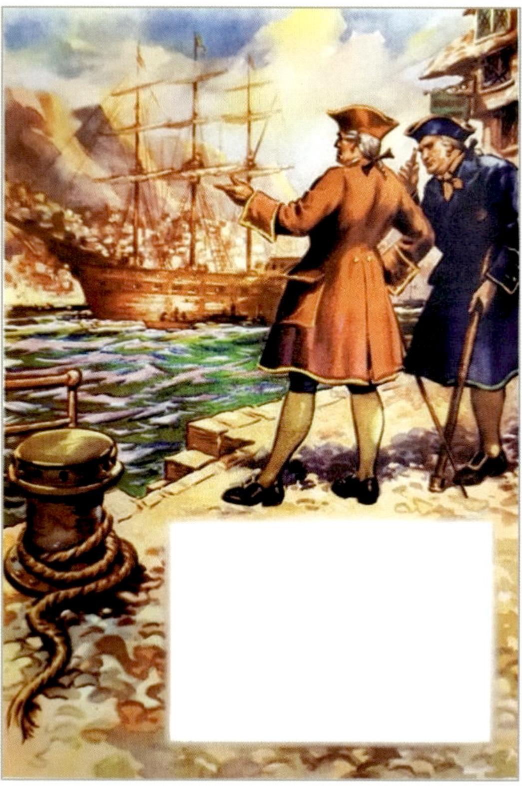

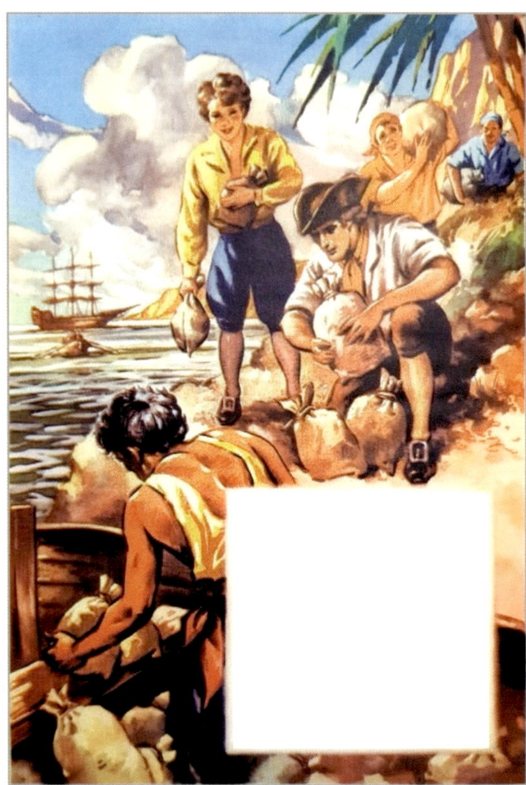

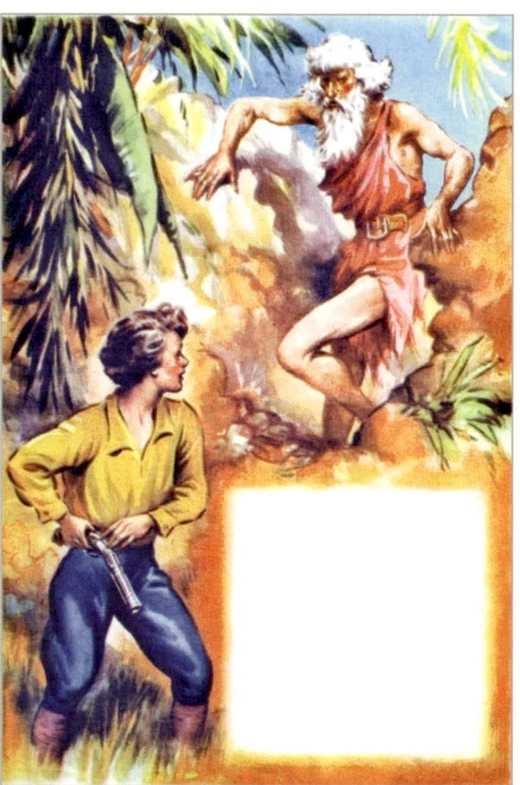

Four full-page colour illustrations for *Treasure Island* by Robert Louis Stevenson (Pocket Editions BCM/Poket, 1945)

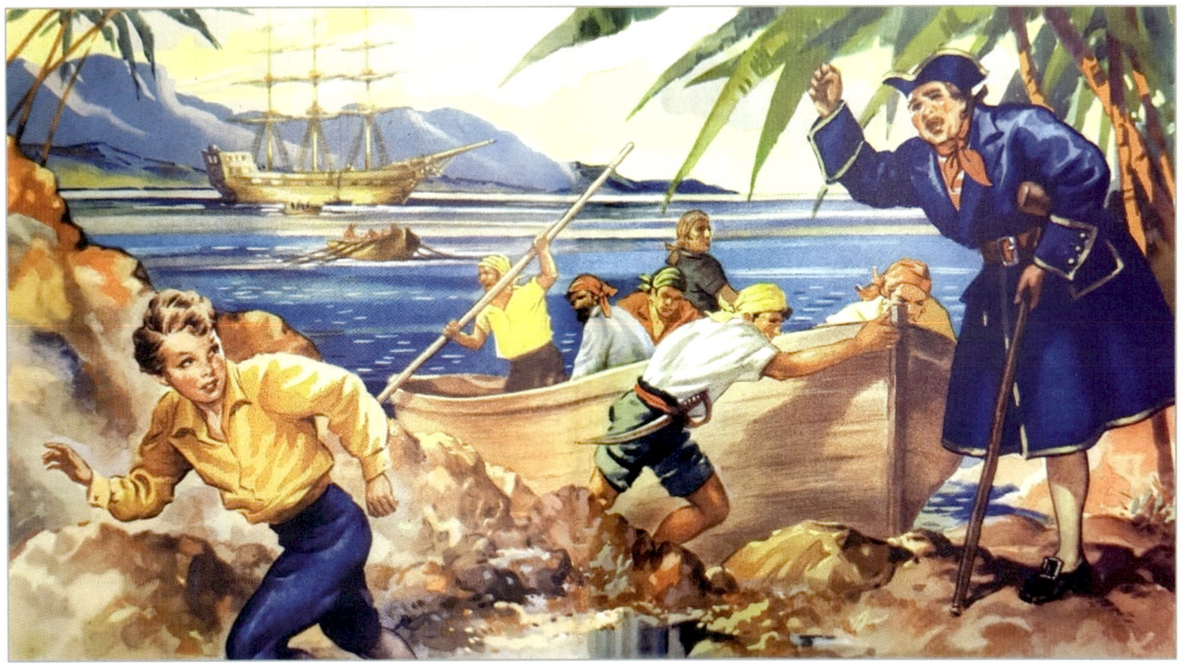

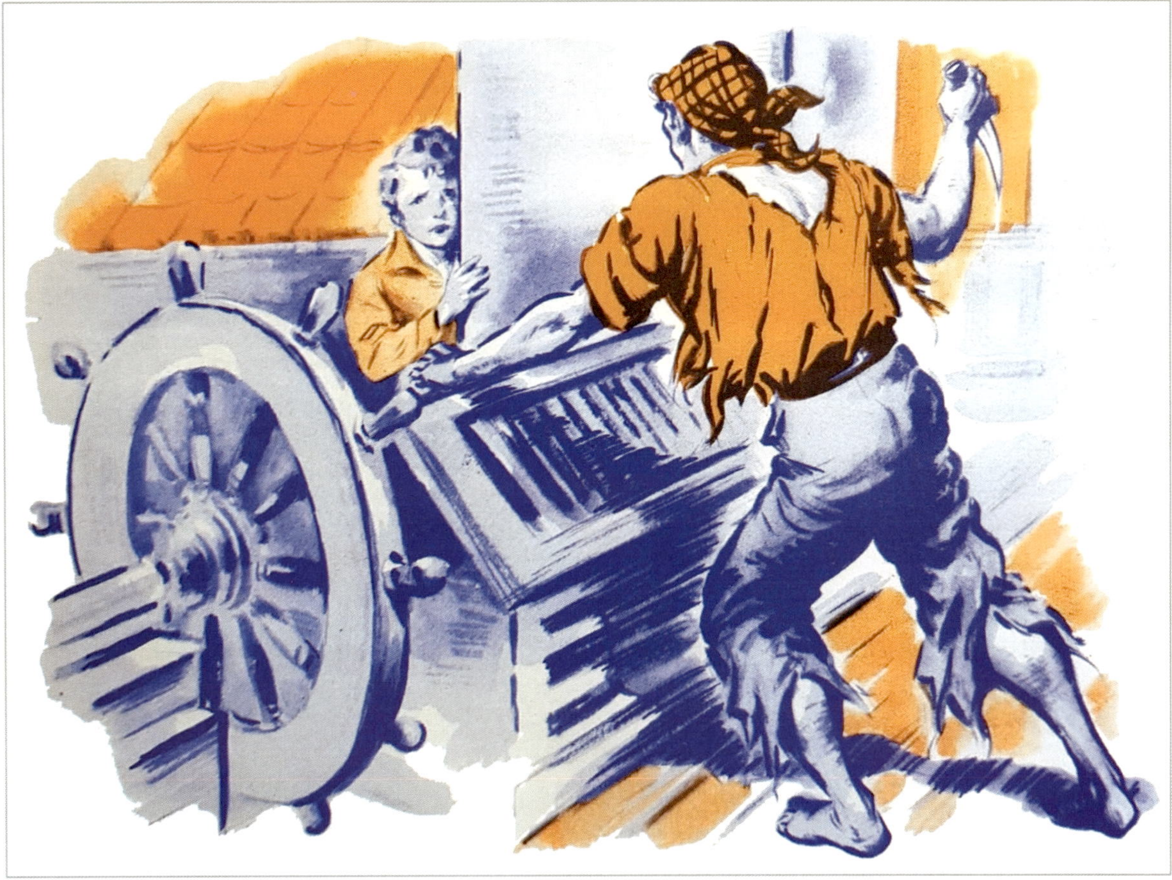

The double-page colour centrespread and another duotone illustration for this adaptation of Robert Louis Stevenson's *Treasure Island* (Pocket Editions BCM/Poket, 1945)

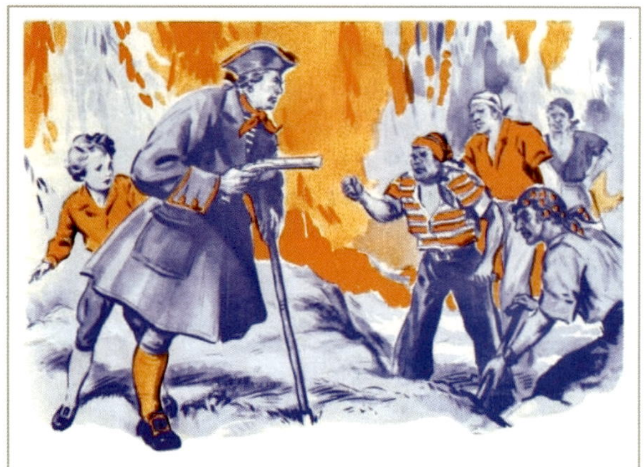

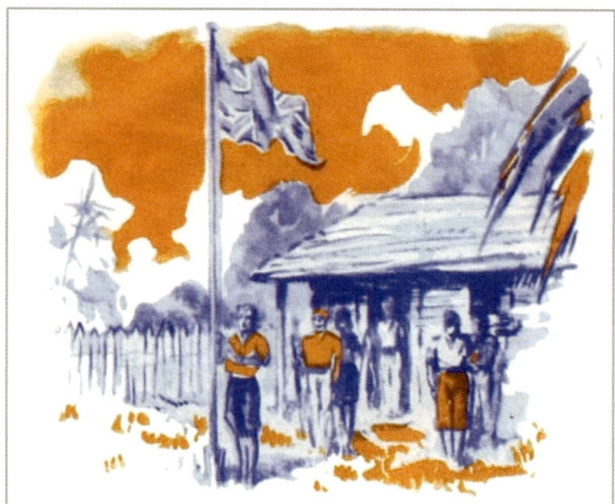

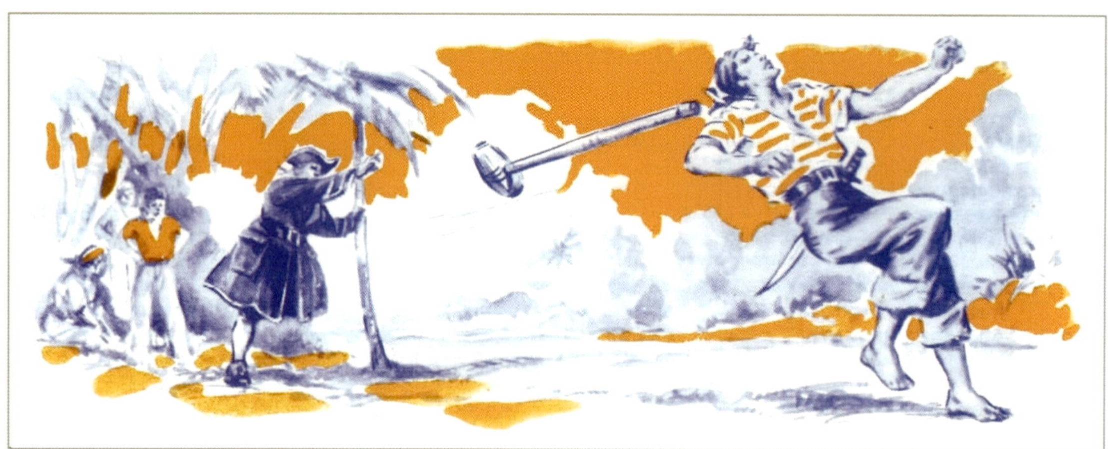

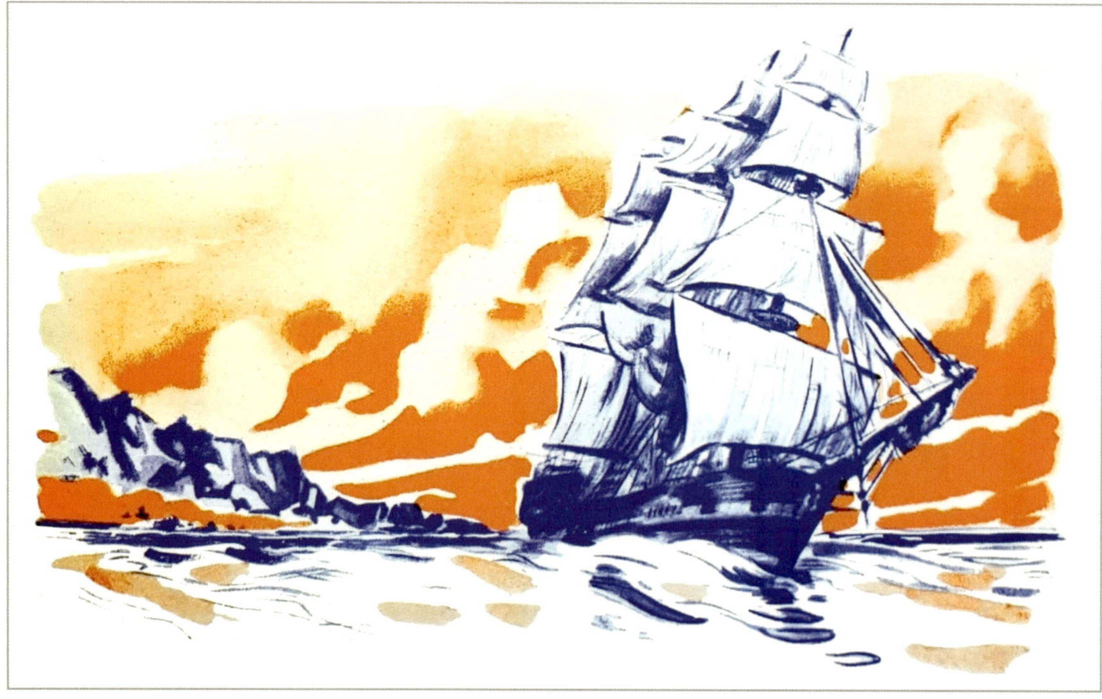

The final four duotone illustrations for *Treasure Island* by Robert Louis Stevenson (Pocket Editions BCM/Poket, 1945)

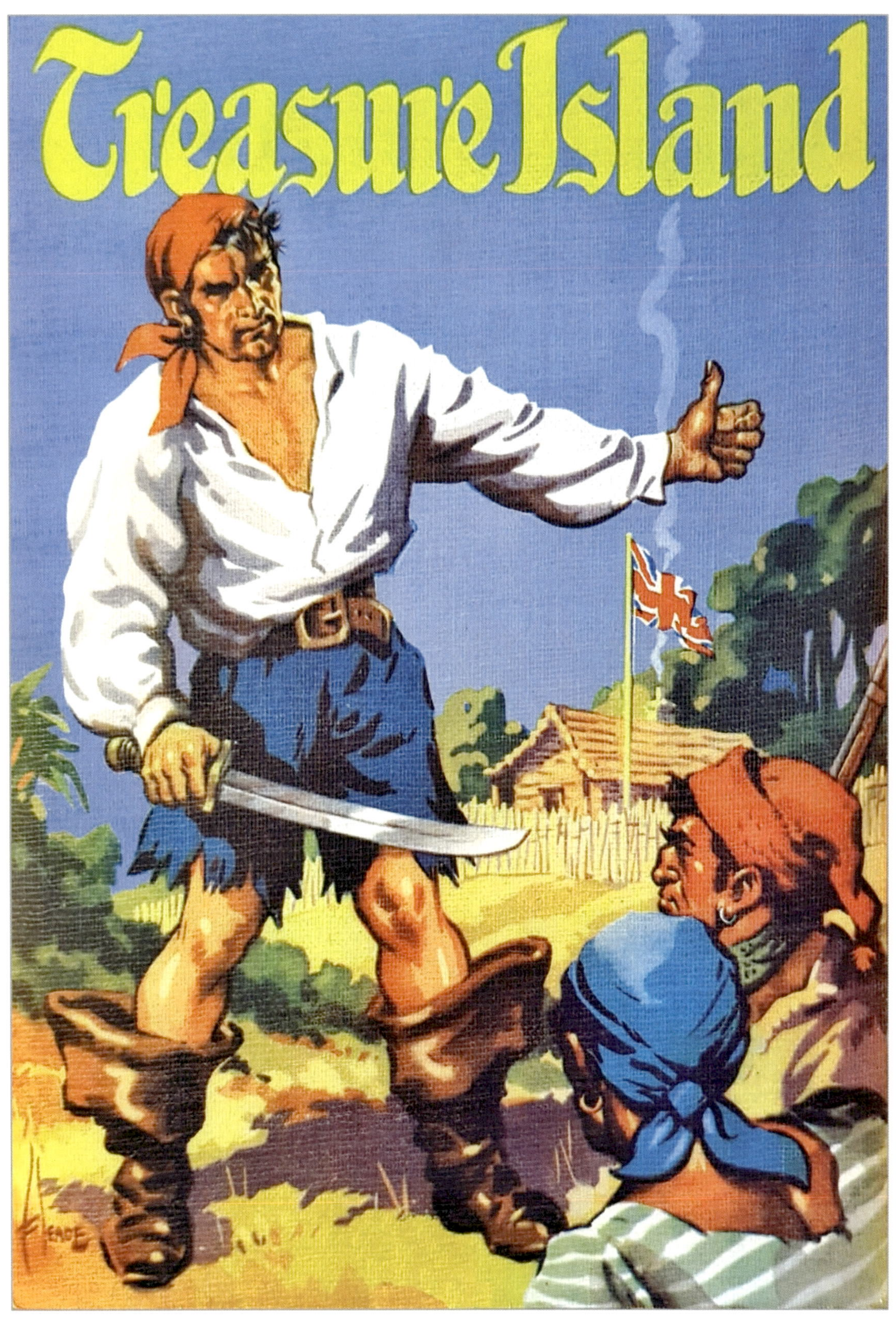

Heade's back cover illustration for Robert Louis Stevenson's *Treasure Island* (Pocket Editions BCM/Poket, 1945)

PANTOMIME POSTERS

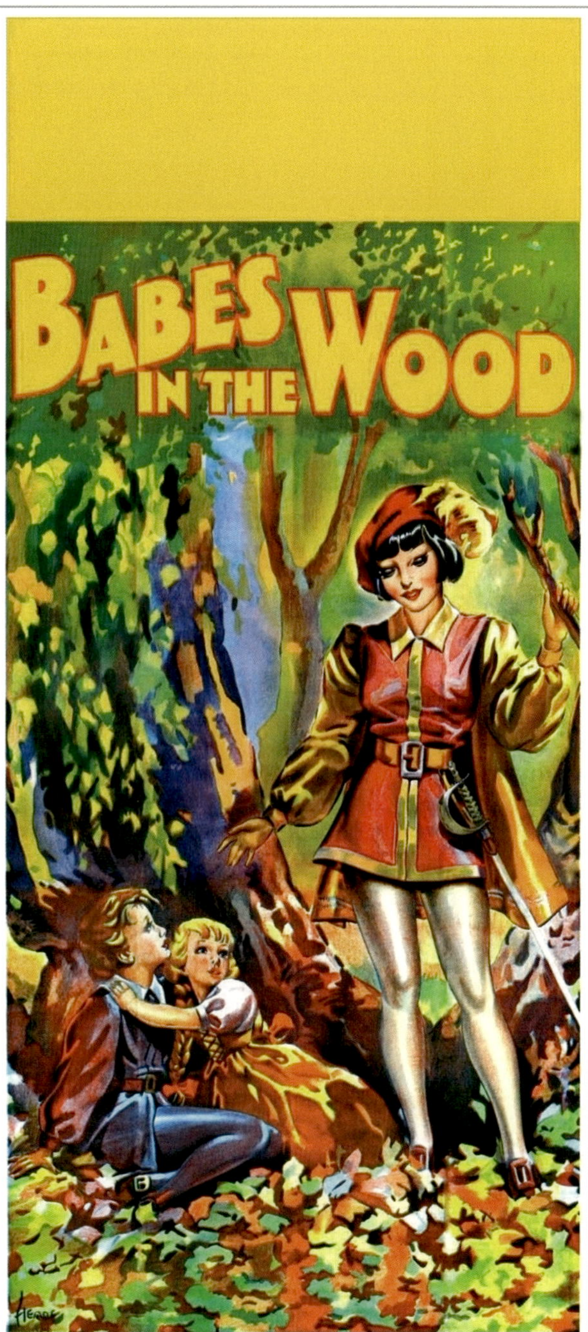

Founded in 1880, Taylors was a firm of printers in Wombwell, South Yorkshire. Amongst the items they produced were a range of posters for popular Christmas pantomimes. Previously thought to date from the late 1930s, but now known to originate from around 1945, these were offered for sale to any regional theatre company that might decide to stage one of the pantomimes. A *Babes in the Wood* example, which came in various sizes including a large, three-sheet version (see left) and a smaller window-card one (see facing page, top left), featured a signed Heade painting (also pictured on page 6 of *The Art of Reginald Heade – Special Edition*). The yellow band at the top was left blank to allow the theatre to add its own details. One production known to have made use of Heade's poster ran from 26 December 1947 to 6 March 1948 at the Grand Theatre in Swansea (see facing page, top right).

A second, landscape-shaped poster, offered in various sizes as part of a set with the first, features art that is probably also by Heade, although in this case the piece is unsigned (see facing page, bottom).

Below: Heade's pencil rough for the small portrait-shaped poster, annotated by Taylors' designer to indicate the need for the blank band at the top.

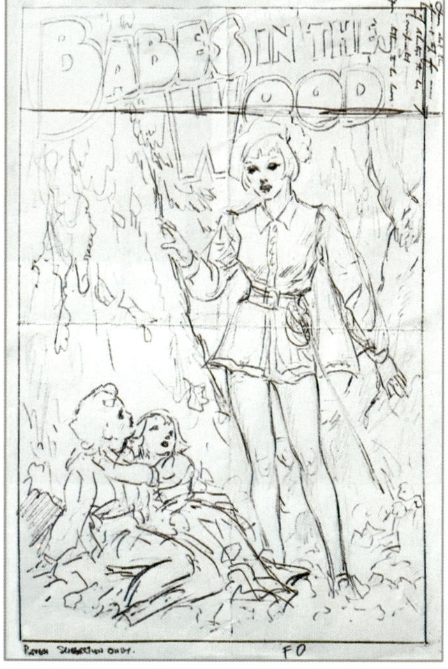

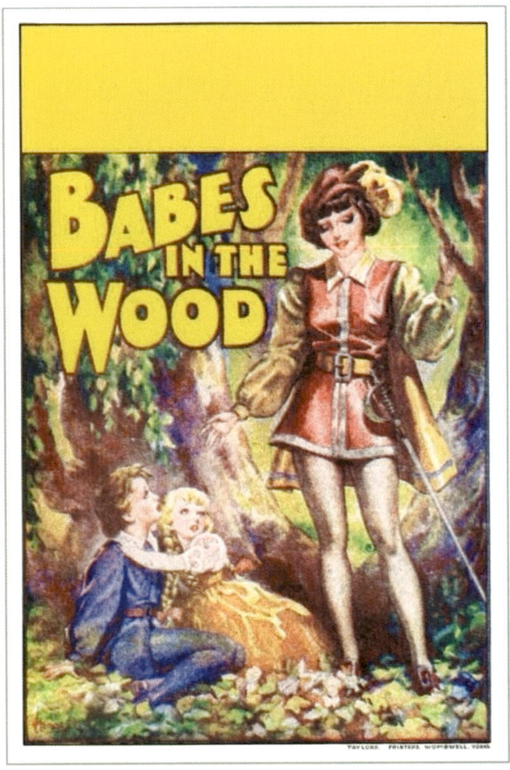

BABES
IN THE
WOOD

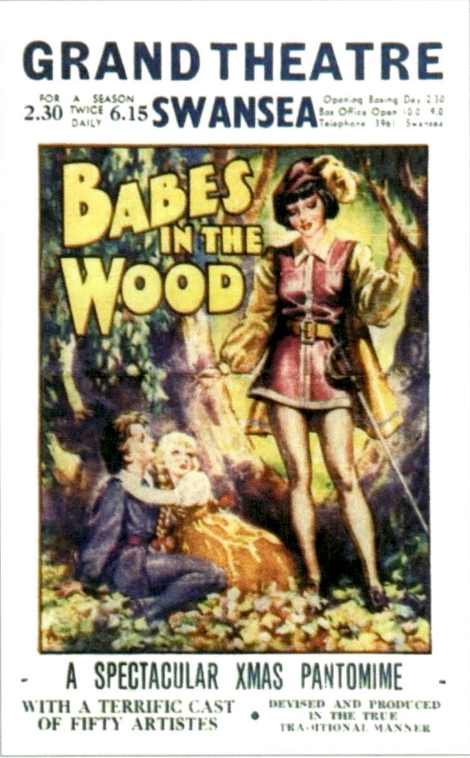

GRAND THEATRE
SWANSEA
FOR A SEASON
2.30 TWICE 6.15
DAILY
Opening Boxing Day 2.30
Box Office Open 10.0 4.0
Telephone 3961 Swansea
BABES
IN THE
WOOD
- A SPECTACULAR XMAS PANTOMIME -
WITH A TERRIFIC CAST
OF FIFTY ARTISTES
DEVISED AND PRODUCED
IN THE TRUE
TRADITIONAL MANNER

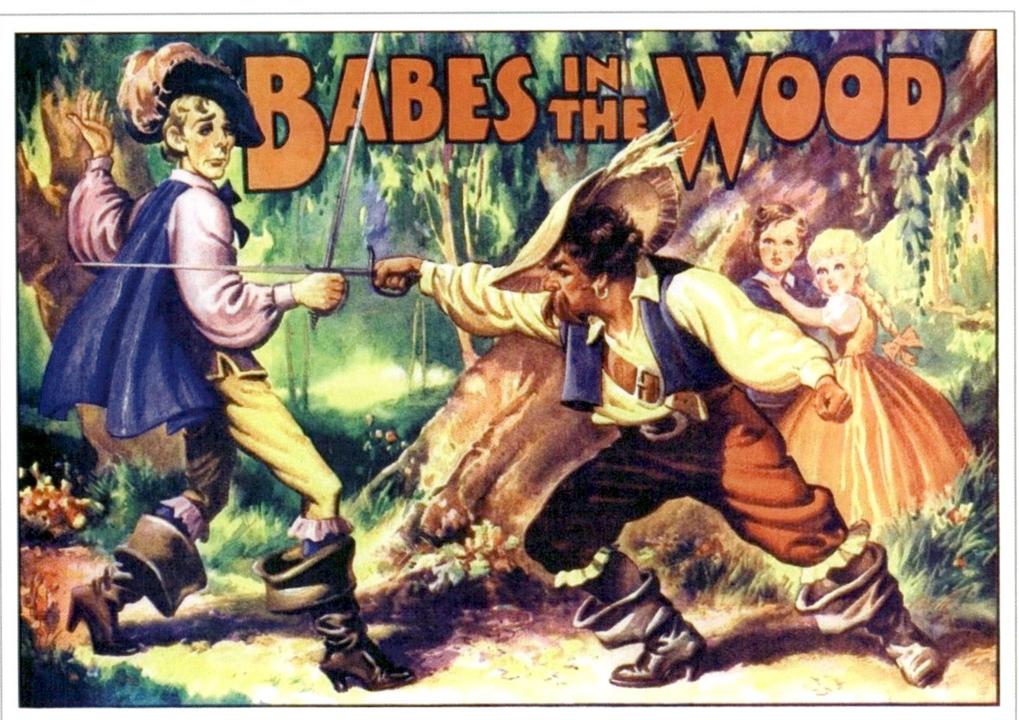

BABES IN THE WOOD

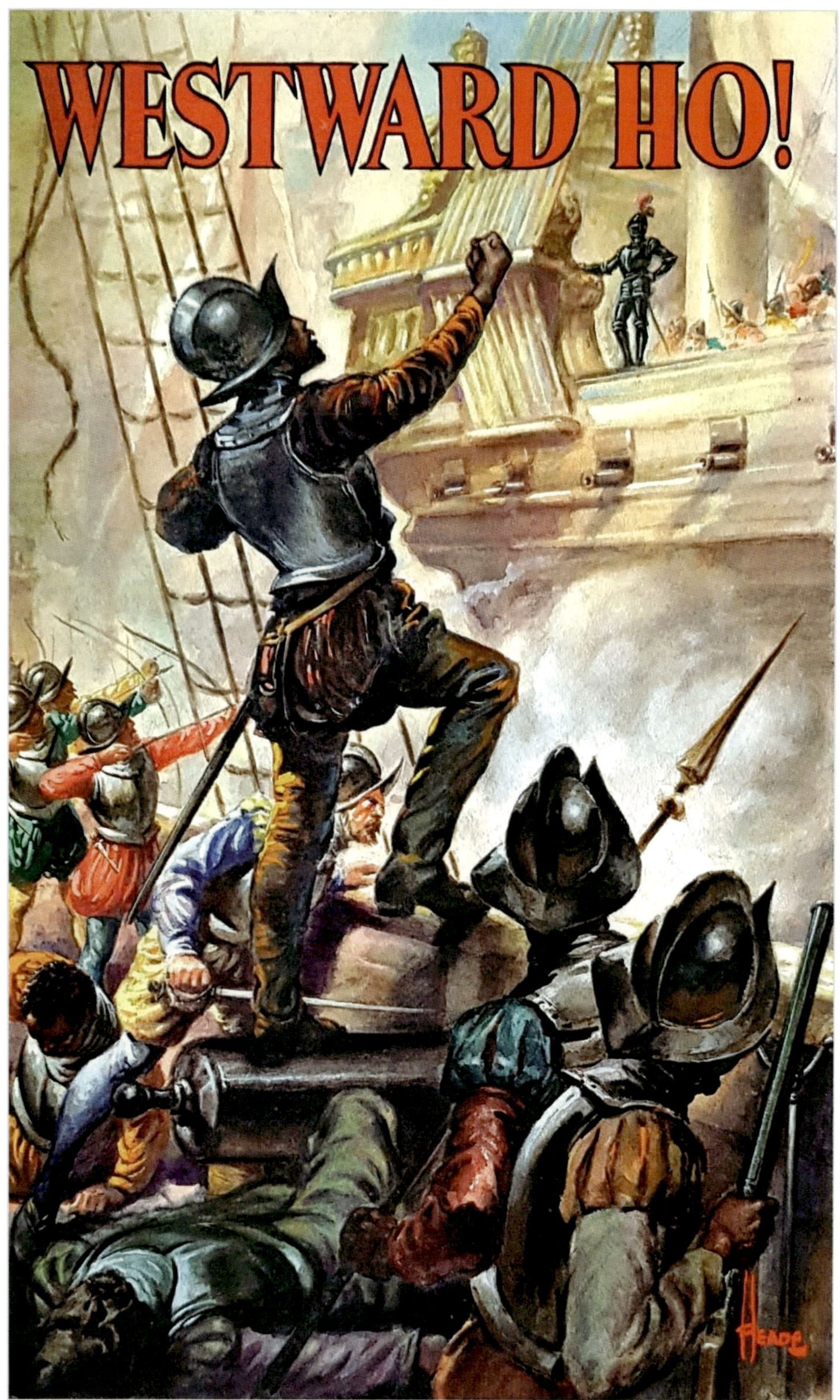

Heade's original painting for *Westward Ho!* by Charles Kingsley (Pictorial Art, 1946). In *The Art of Reginald Heade – Special Edition*, comment was made on the fact that the as-published dustjacket of this book lacked the artist's signature. It can now be seen from the full artwork above that this was simply because the lower part of the composition had been cropped off during the production process – probably due to a late change of mind by the publishers as to the book's dimensions.

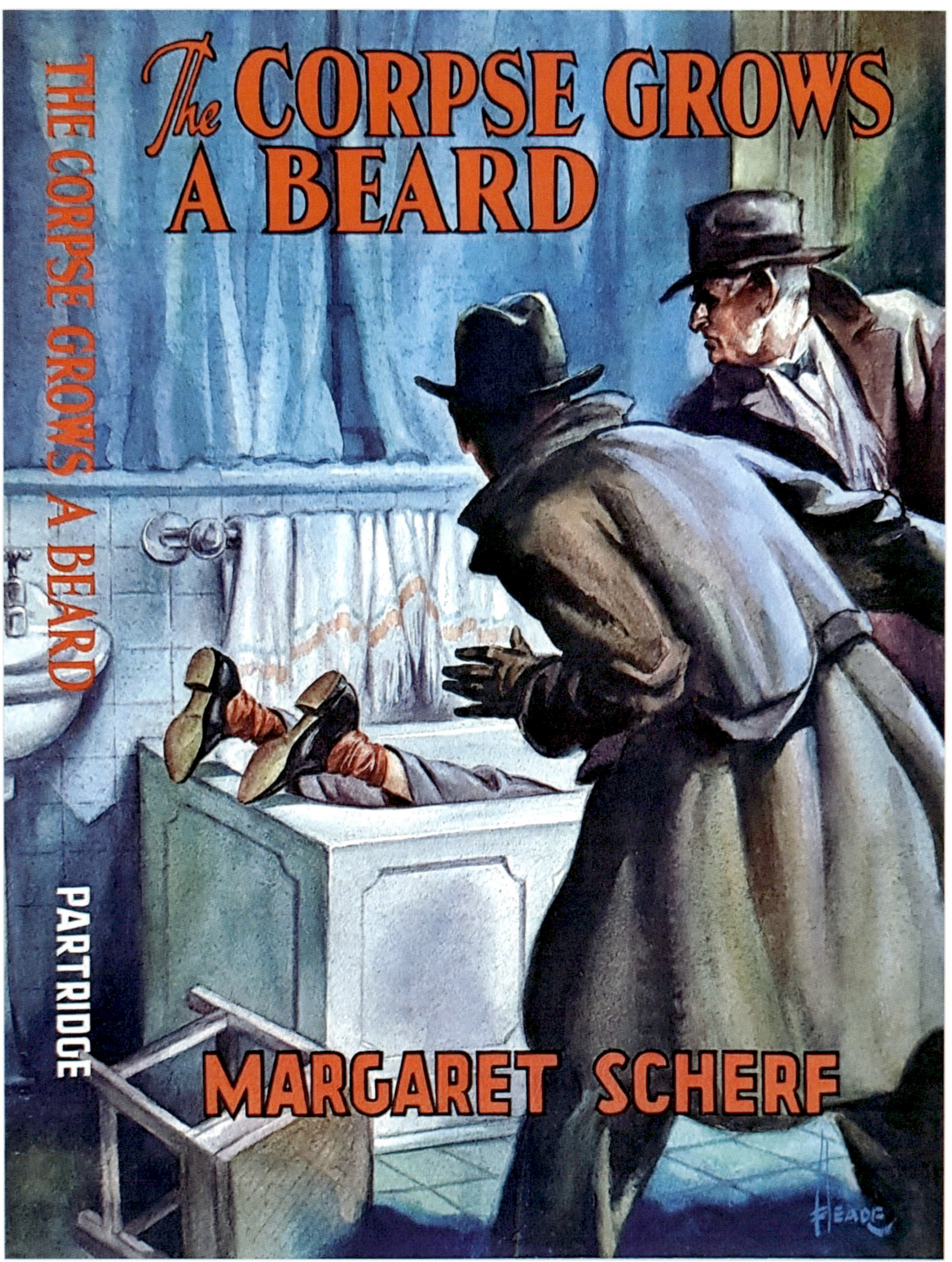

Heade's original painting for *The Corpse Grows a Beard* by Margaret Scherf (Partridge, October 1946)

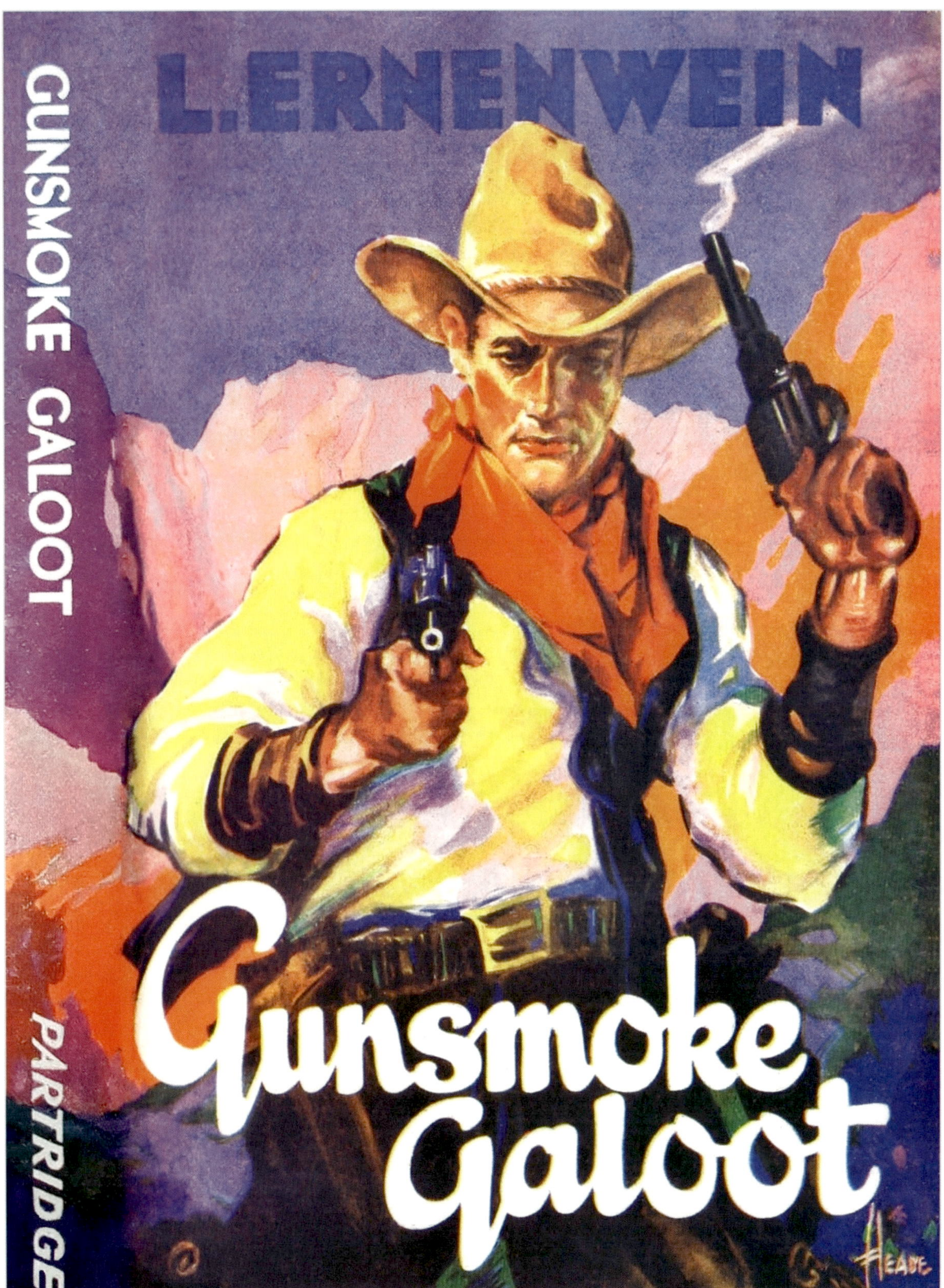

Gunsmoke Galoot by L Ernenwein (Partridge, 1946)

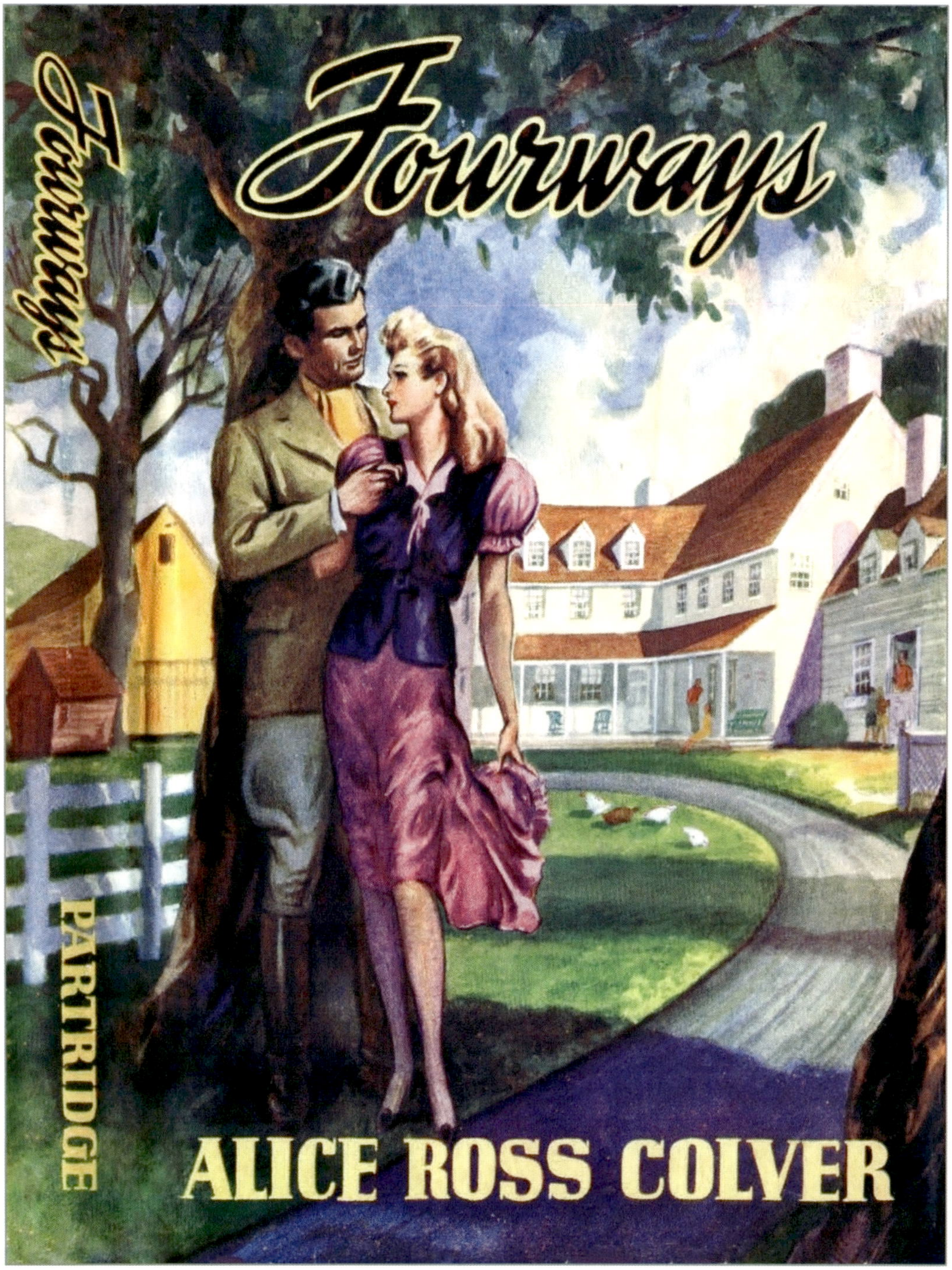

Pictured above is the dustjacket artwork for *Fourways* by Alice Ross Colver (Partridge, 1946), one of a number of pieces that Heade painted in the immediate post-war years for companies co-owned and run by his agent William Partridge. In this case the artist took inspiration from the equivalent American edition, published by Macrae Smith in 1944 – see thumbnail illustration to the right. The setting and even the title lettering of Heade's piece were essentially copied from the American version (which might perhaps be why he left his work unsigned on this occasion); the two foreground figures were his addition.

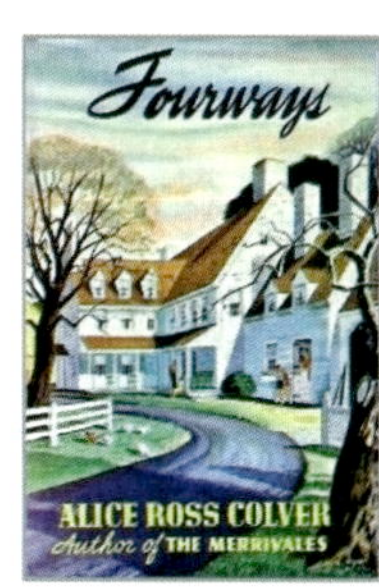

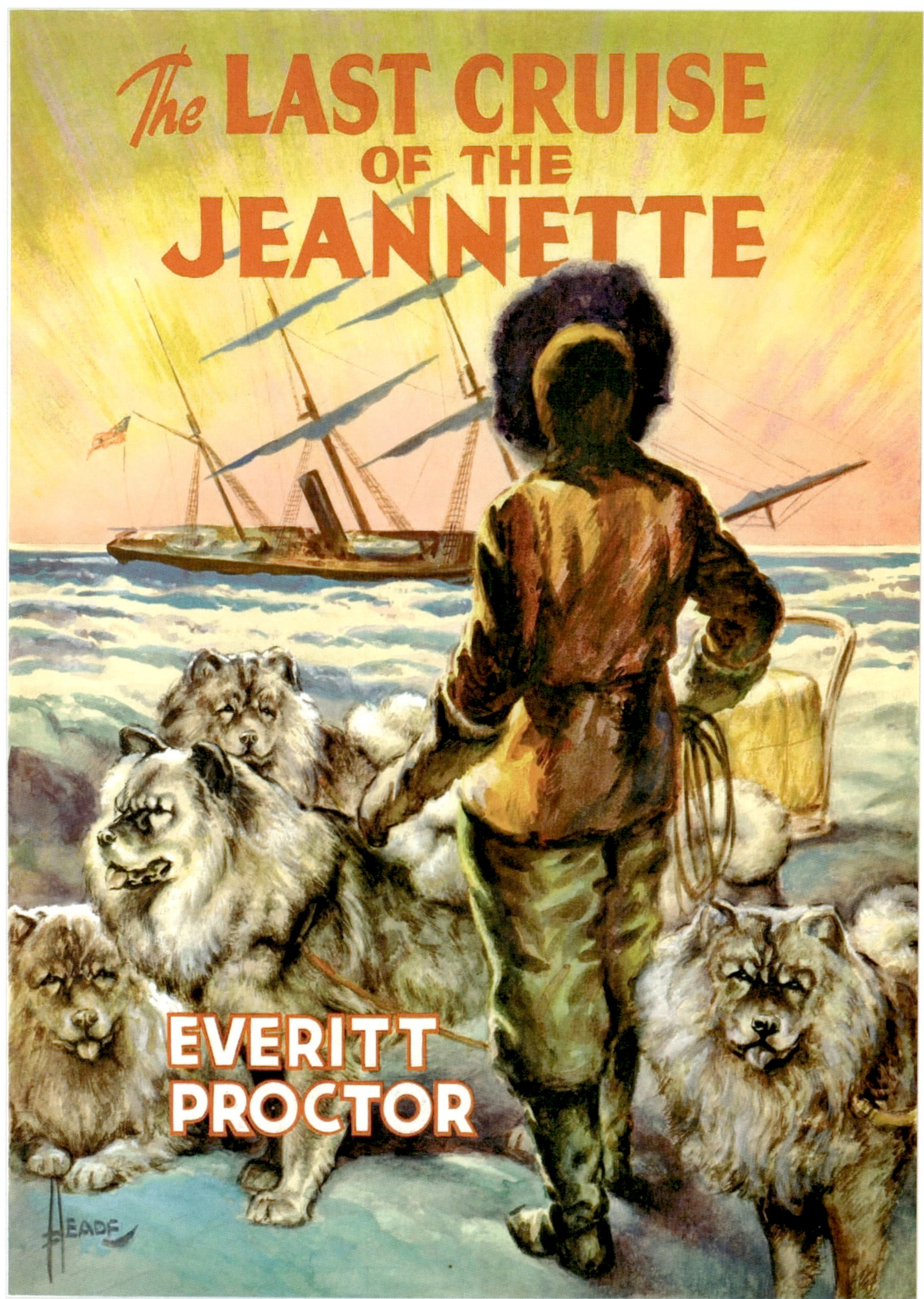

Heade's original painting for *The Last Cruise of the Jeannette* by Everitt Proctor (Pictorial Art, c1946). (Image courtesy the Steve Chibnall Collection.)

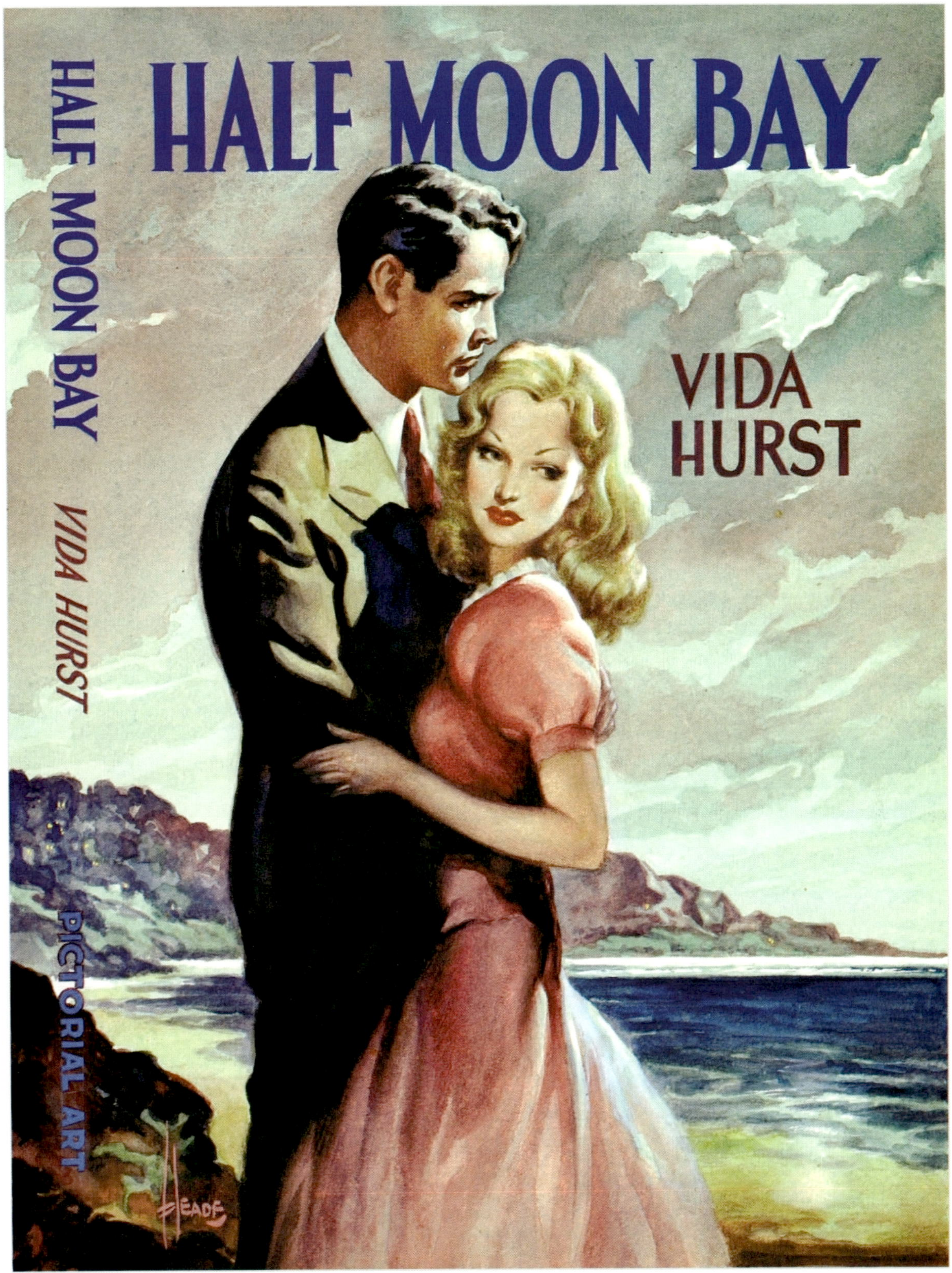

Heade's original painting for *Half Moon Bay* by Vida Hurst (Pictorial Art, 1947). (Image courtesy the Steve Chibnall Collection.)

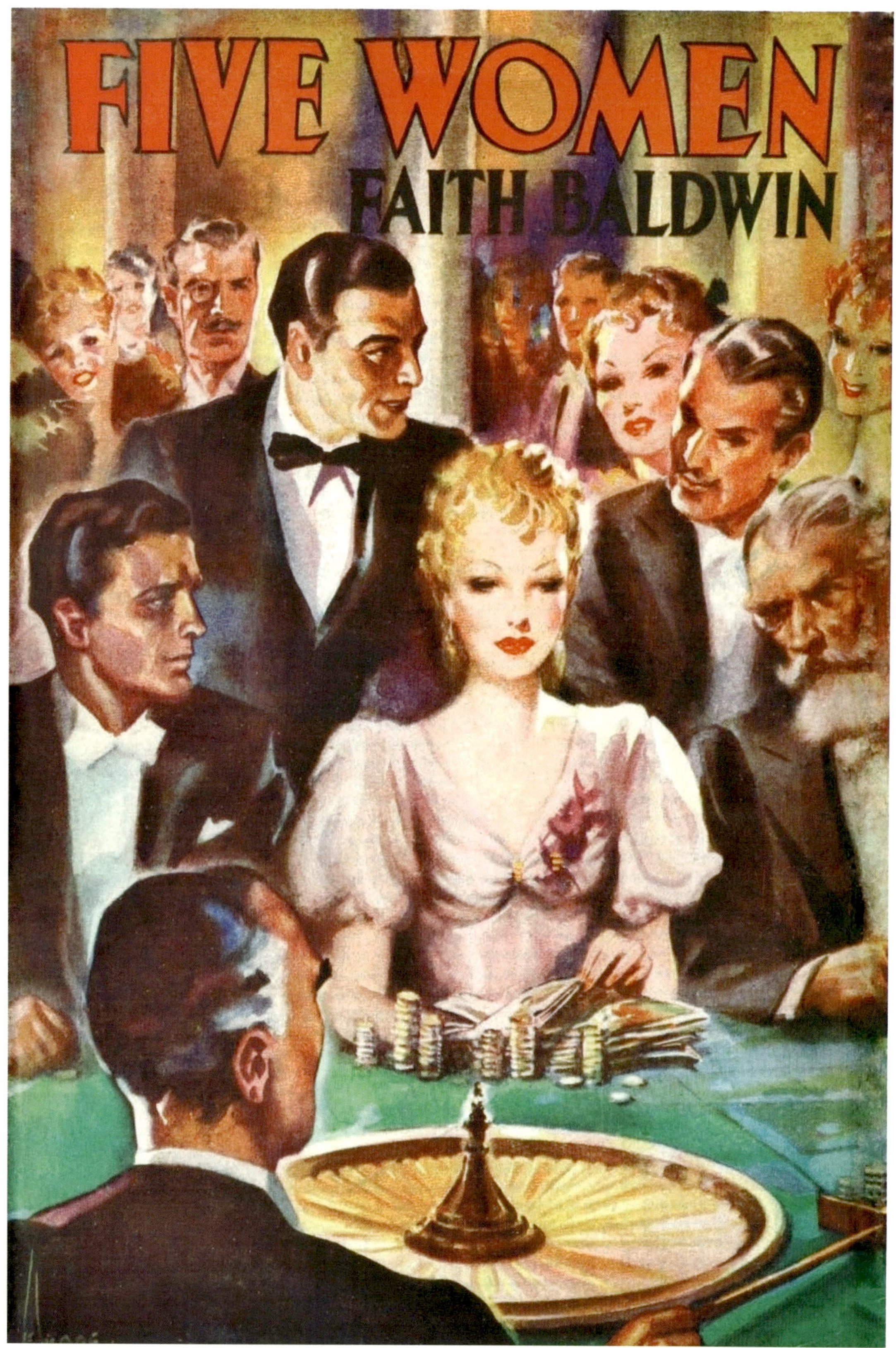

Five Women by Faith Baldwin (Robert Hale, 23 January 1946)

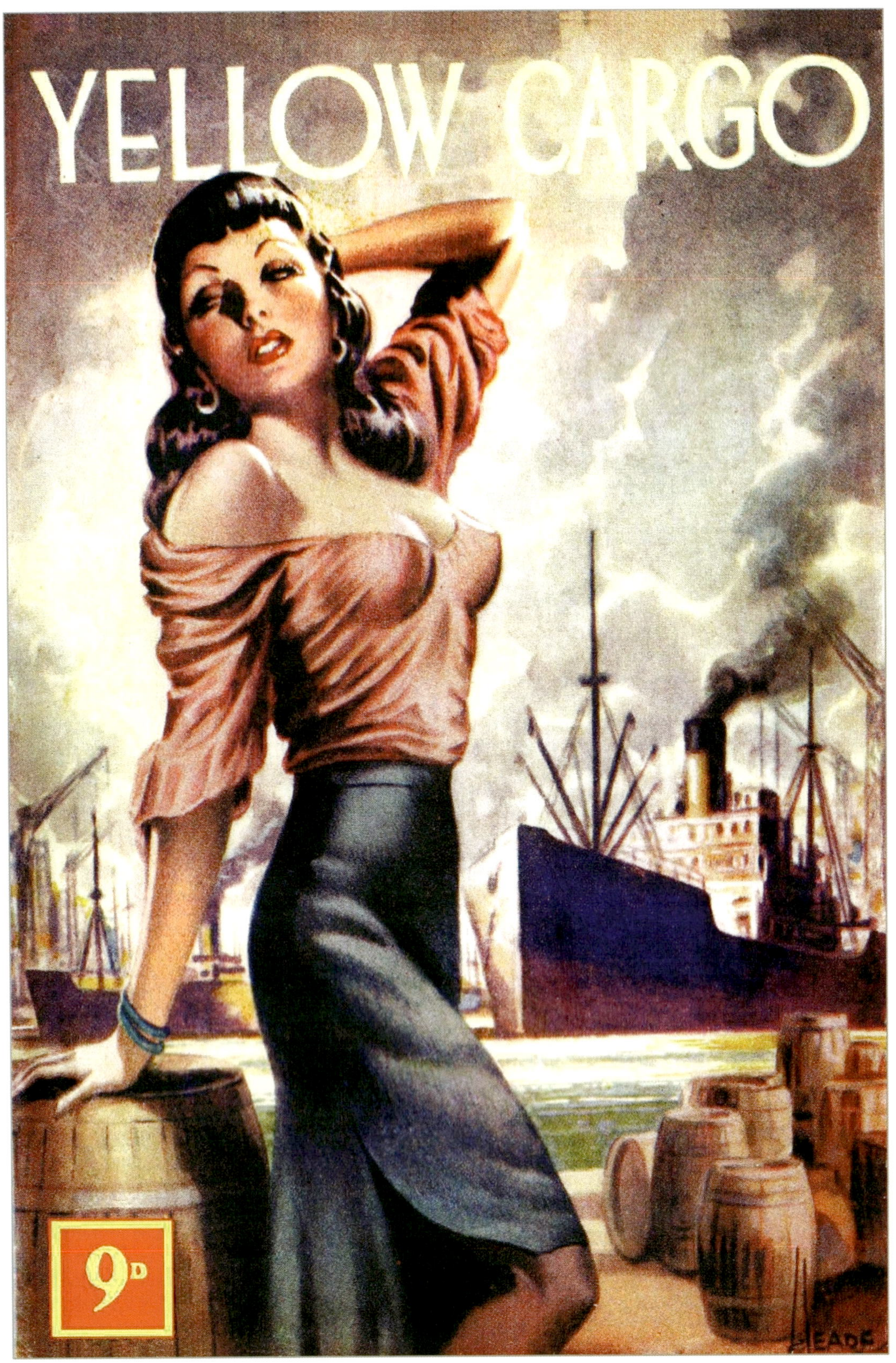

Yellow Cargo by Norman Lazenby (Grant Hughes, 1947)

WHEN JUNGLE DRUMS BEAT!

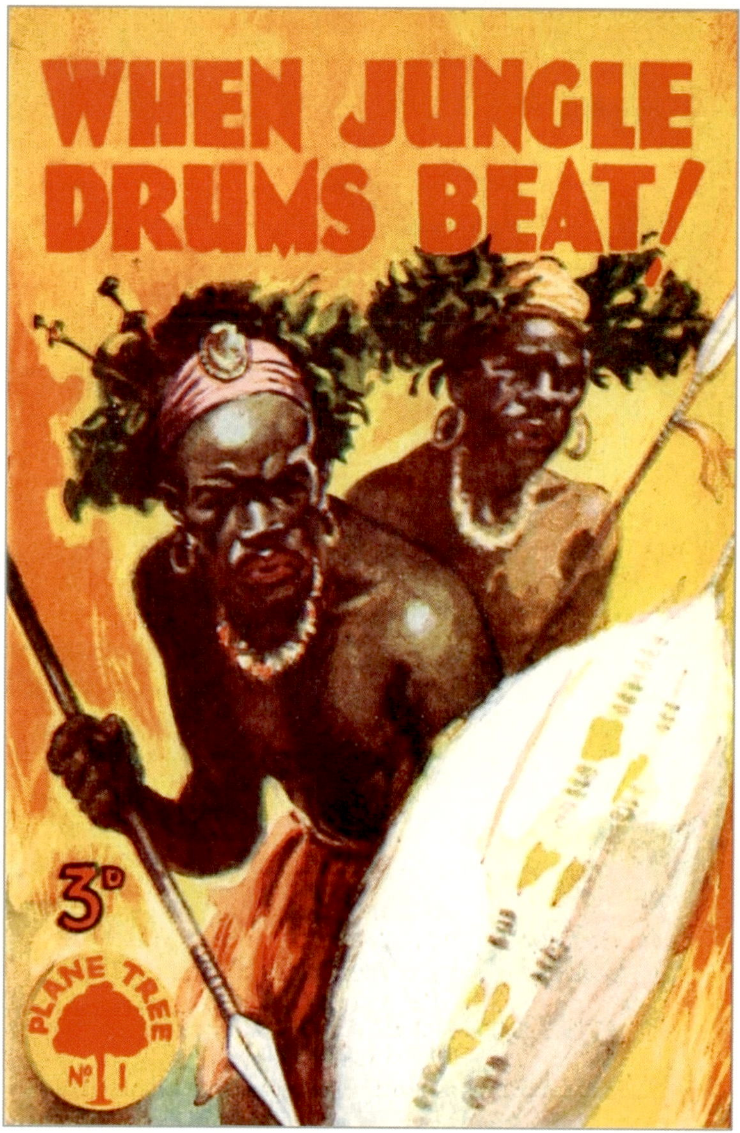

In the 1940s, a number of British publishers issued series of small, flimsy paper booklets – each generally measuring only about five by three inches and containing no more than about thirty stapled-together pages – presenting short, illustrated stories for children. These were sometimes known as 'air raid shelter books' or 'Blitz books', because their compact size made them ideal for children to amuse themselves with while they and their families took refuge from Second World War bombing raids; but they continued to appear for a couple of years after the conflict ended. One company that ventured into this market was Pictorial Art, owned and run by Heade's then agent, William Partridge. It had three such series: 'Adventure Stories', which consisted of twelve titles; 'Little Marvels', which is believed to have run to fifty titles in all, equally divided between 'Fairy Tales' and 'Thrilling Adventures', but seems to have been taken over by a different publisher, W Barton, after the first twenty or so; and 'Plane Tree'. The latter, which is believed to have been published around 1947, consisted of sixteen titles, and the first of them, *When Jungle Drums Beat!* by Leonard Walters, had a colour cover (see above) and six black and white internal illustrations (see facing page) that, although unsigned, are unmistakeably Heade's work. No further 'Blitz books' with Heade art have yet been found, but it is possible that others exist.

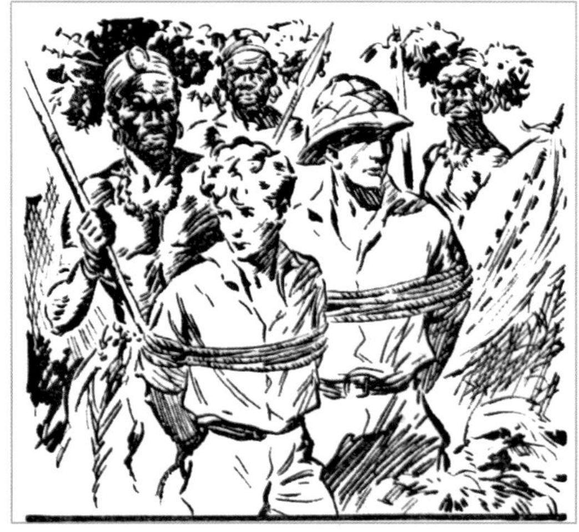 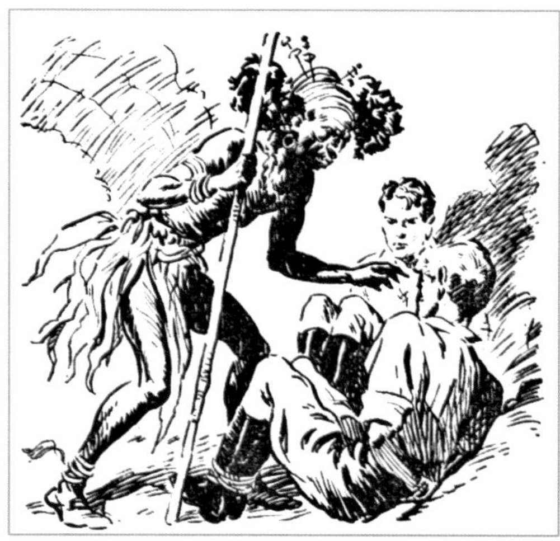

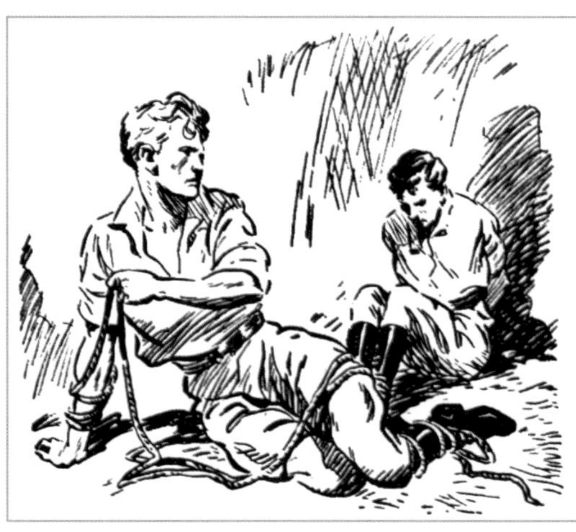 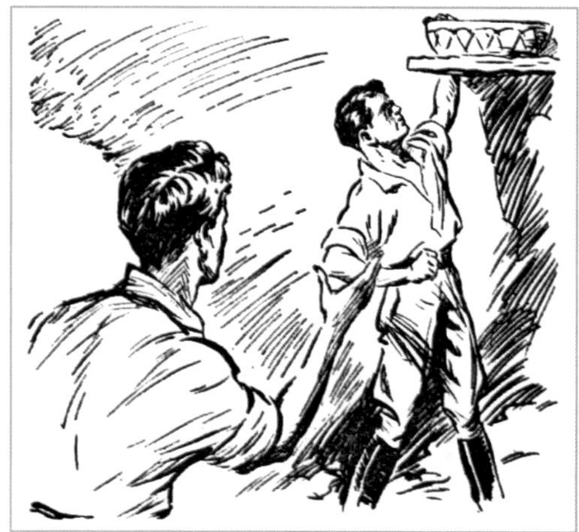

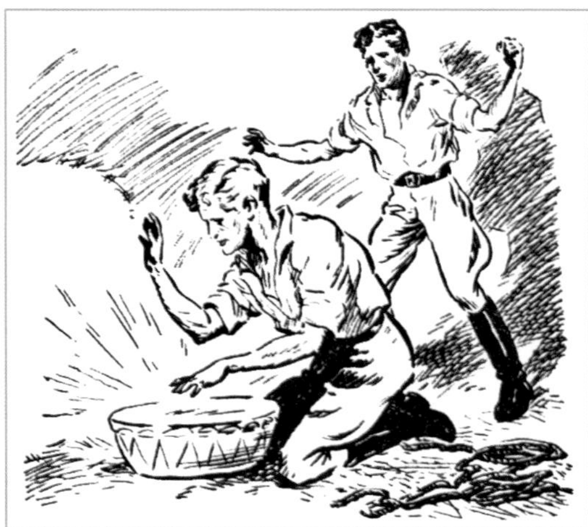 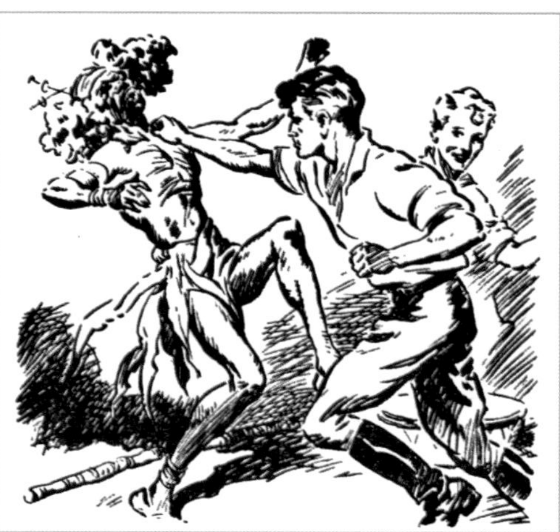

Above: the six black and white internal illustrations from *When Jungle Drums Beat!* by Leonard Walters (Pictorial Art, c1947)

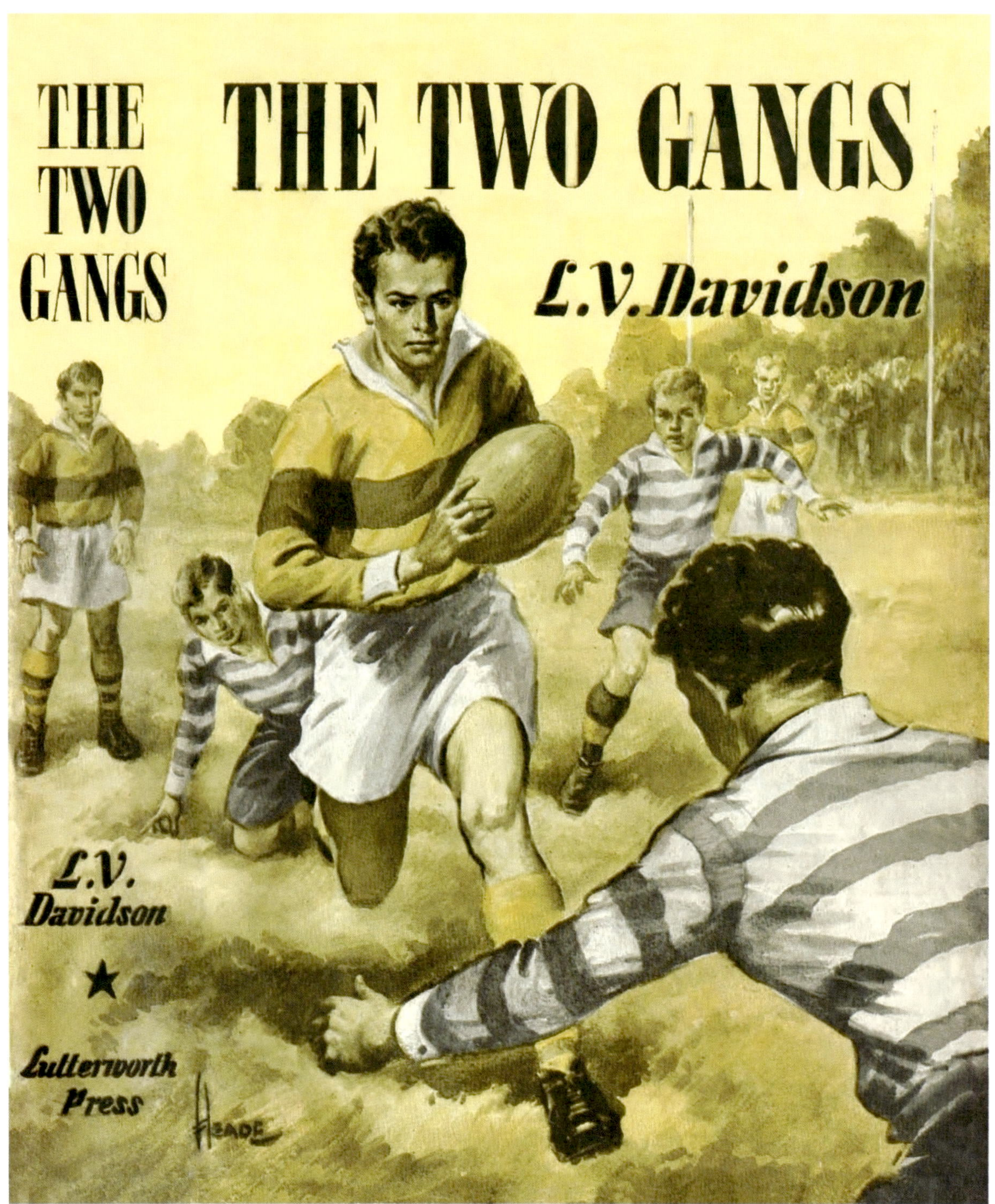

The Two Gangs by L V Davidson (Lutterworth, 1947)

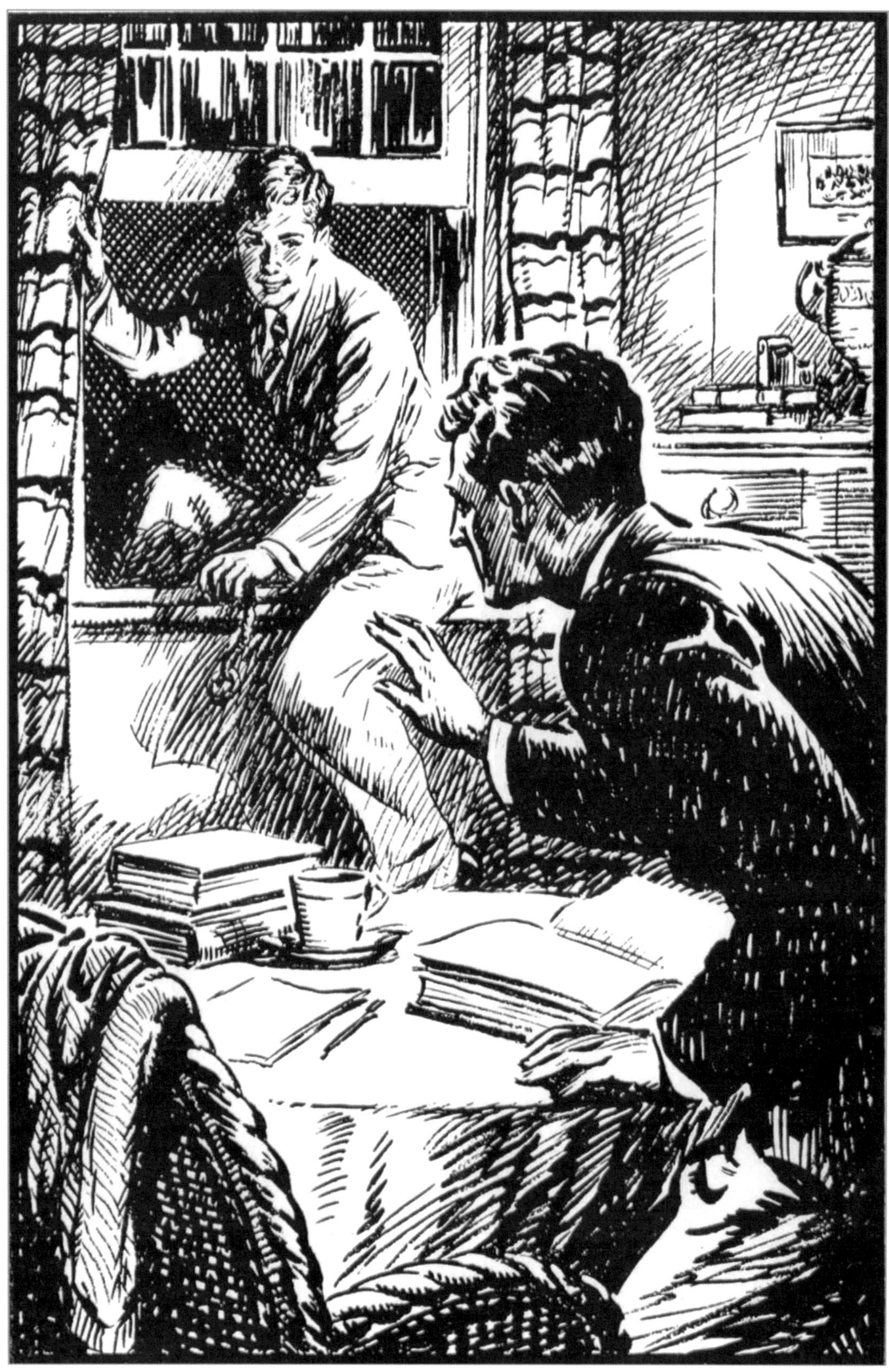

Black-and-white frontispiece from *The Two Gangs* by L V Davidson (Lutterworth, 1947)

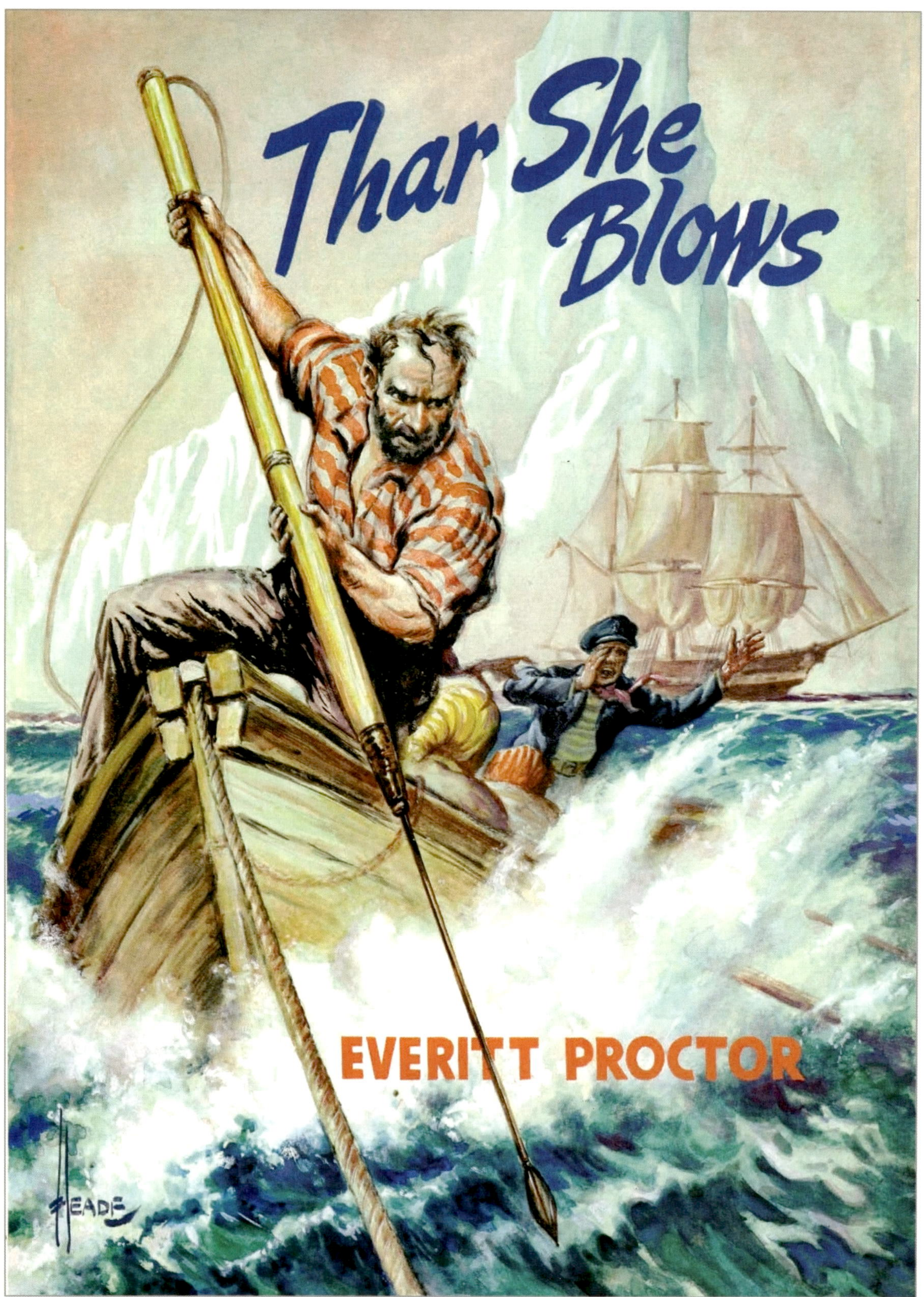

Heade's original painting for *Thar She Blows* by Everitt Proctor (Pictorial Art, April 1947). (Image courtesy the Steve Chibnall Collection.)

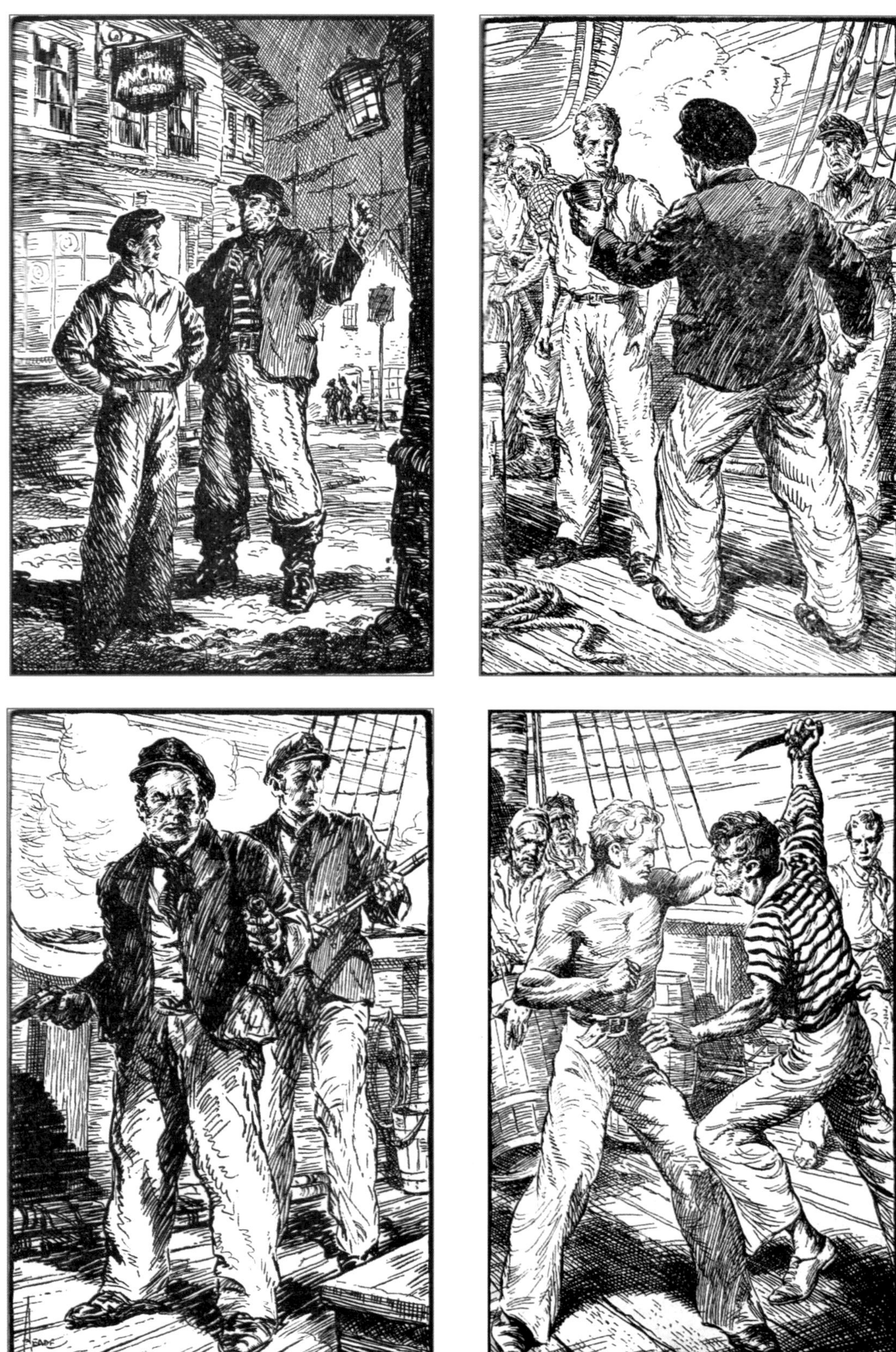

Above: Heade's four internal black and white illustrations for *Thar She Blows* by Everitt Proctor (Pictorial Art, April 1947)

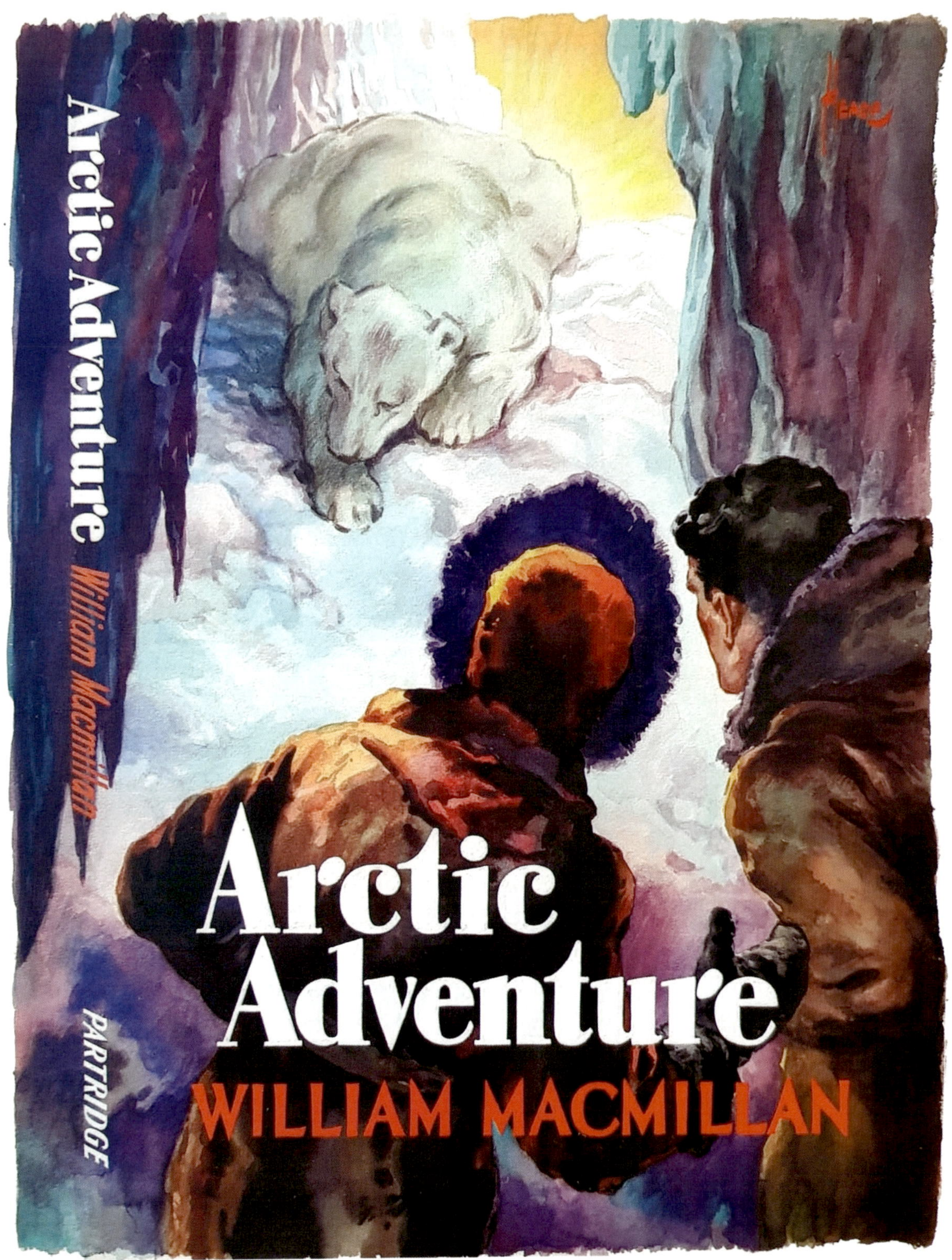

Heade's original painting for the dustjacket of *Arctic Adventure* by William Macmillan (Partridge, c1947). No copy of this book has ever been found, so it uncertain whether or not it actually saw print.

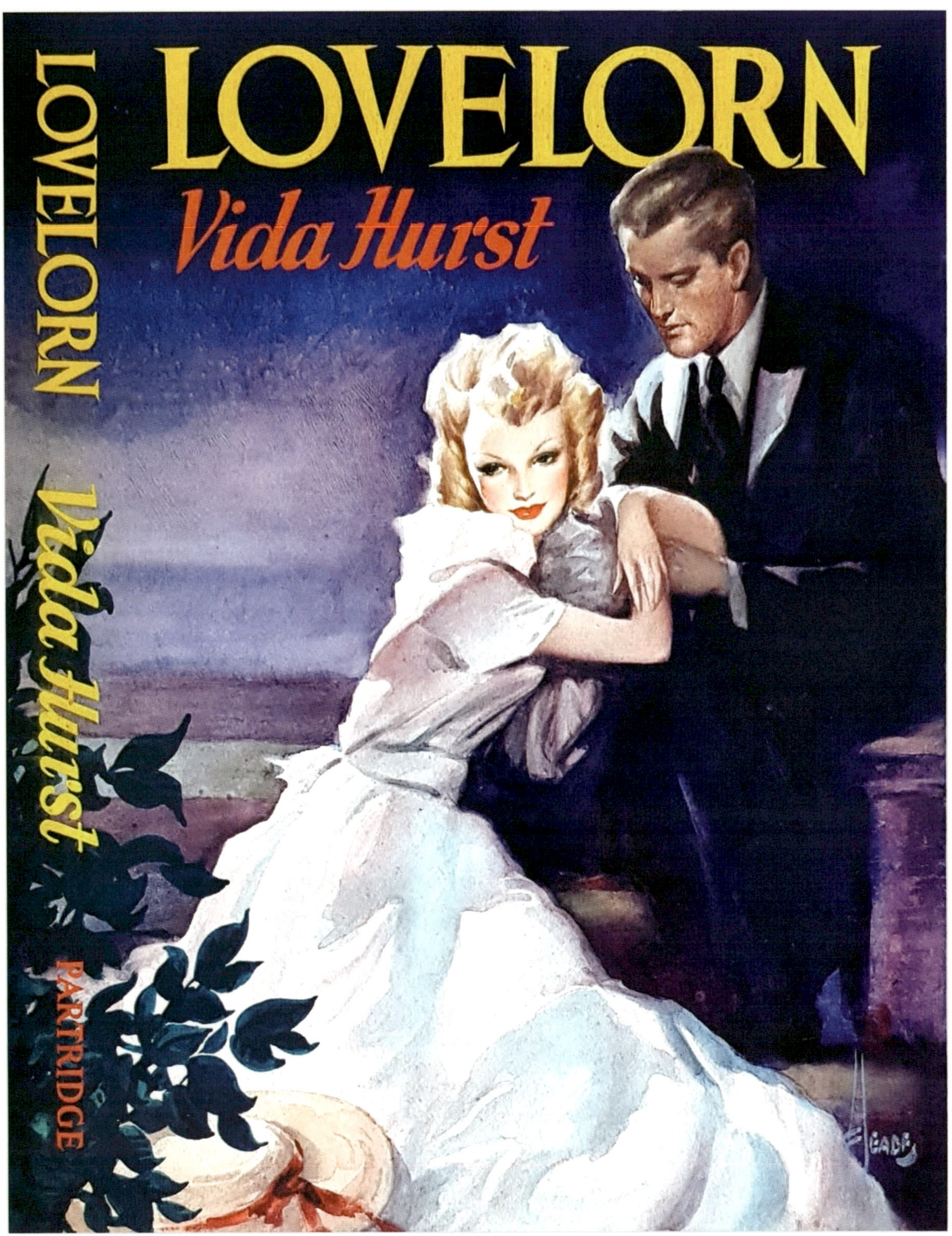

Heade's original painting for *Lovelorn* by Vida Hurst (Partridge, 1947)

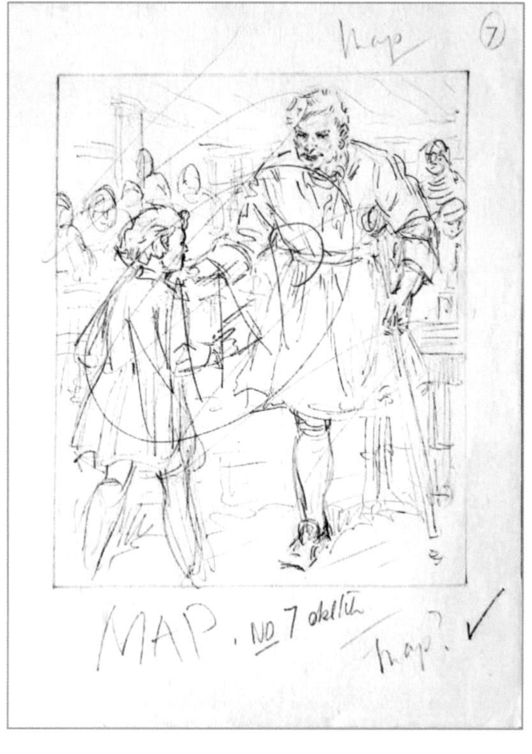

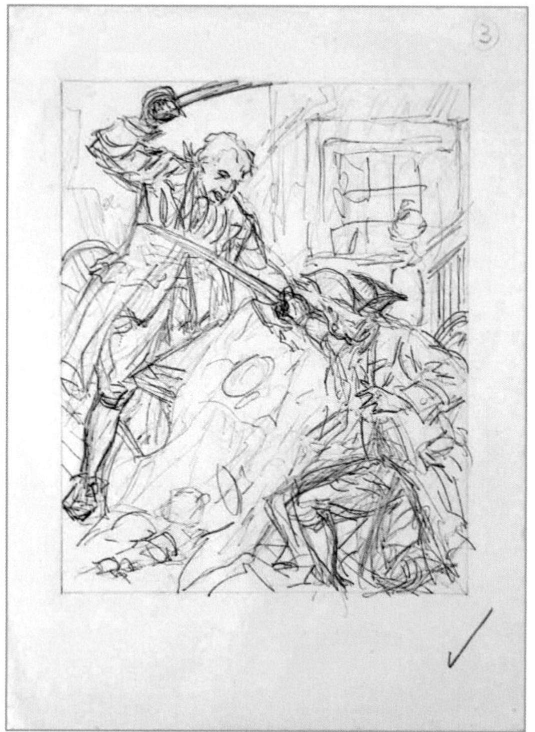

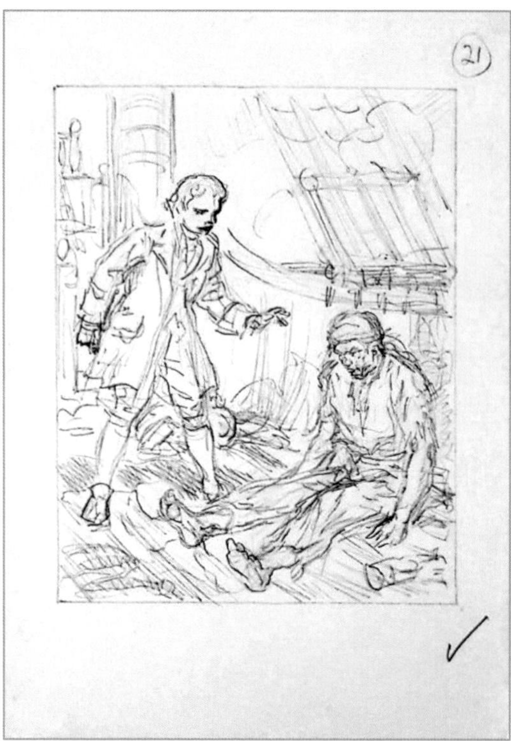

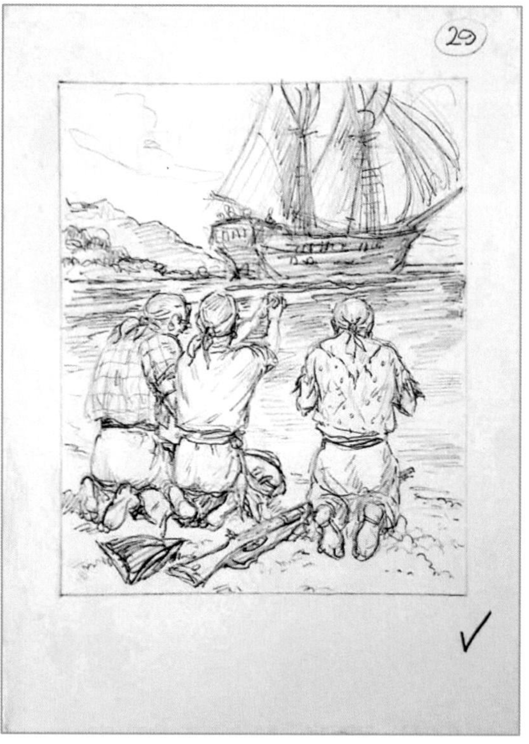

Around 1947, Heade supplied a colour dustjacket piece and 28 other colour illustrations for a Partridge-published adaptation of Robert Louis Stevenson's *Treasure Island* – all reproduced on pages 195 to 202 inclusive of *The Art of Reginald Heade – Special Edition*. Still in existence are pencil-on-paper roughs for 27 of those 29 illustrations., plus one further rough of an ultimately unused piece. Substituted for the latter was a map of the titular island – one of the two published illustrations for which no rough is known to survive. (It is assumed that Heade himself drew the map – no other illustrator is credited – but there is an outside possibility that a different artist was responsible.) Pictured above are the rough of the unused piece (top left), clearly marked as to be dropped in favour of the map, plus those of three of the published illustrations. (With thanks to Mike Lewis.)

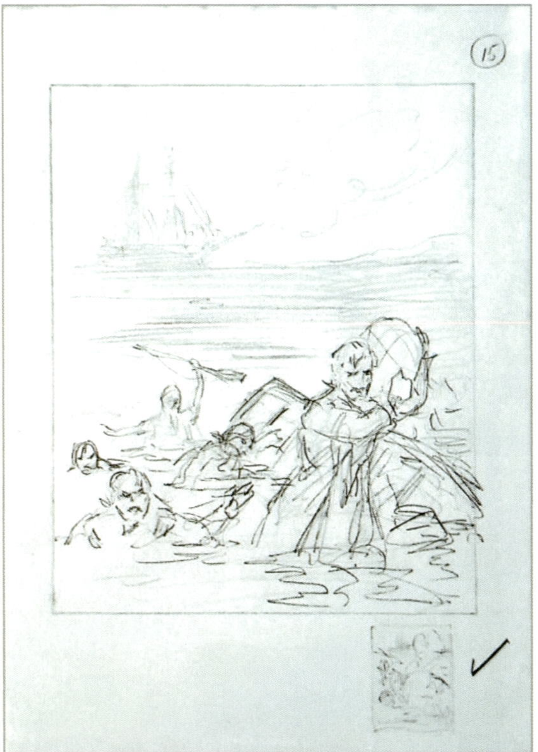 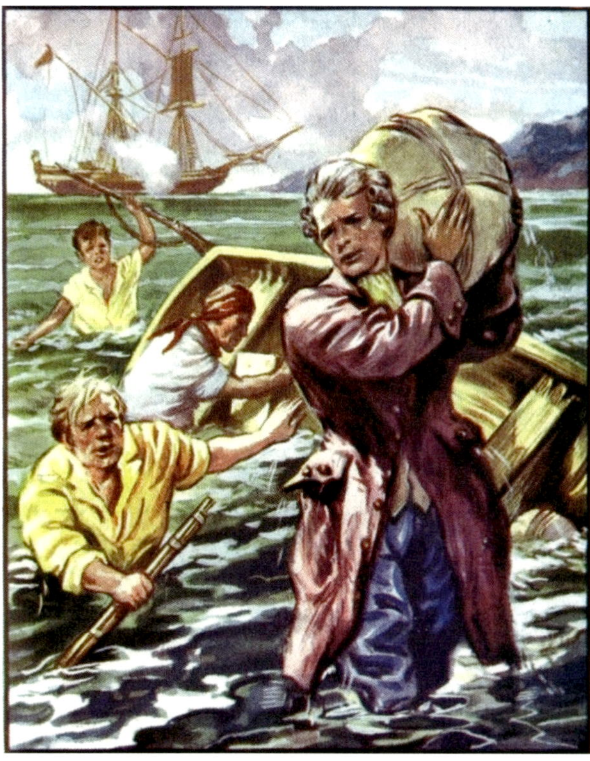

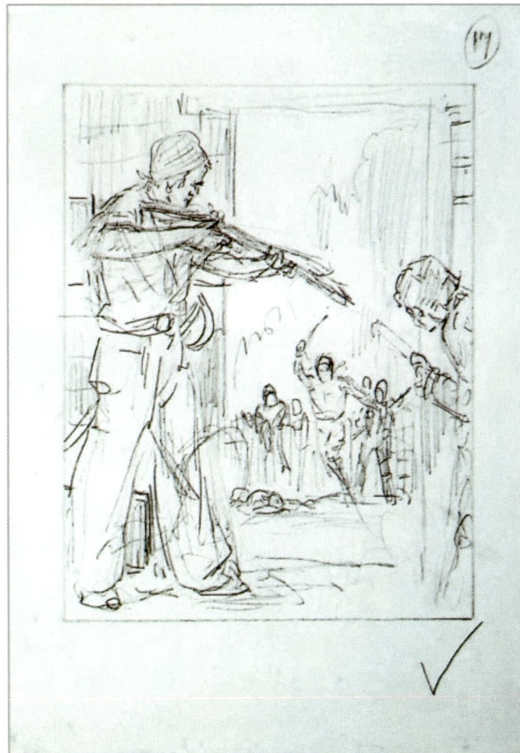 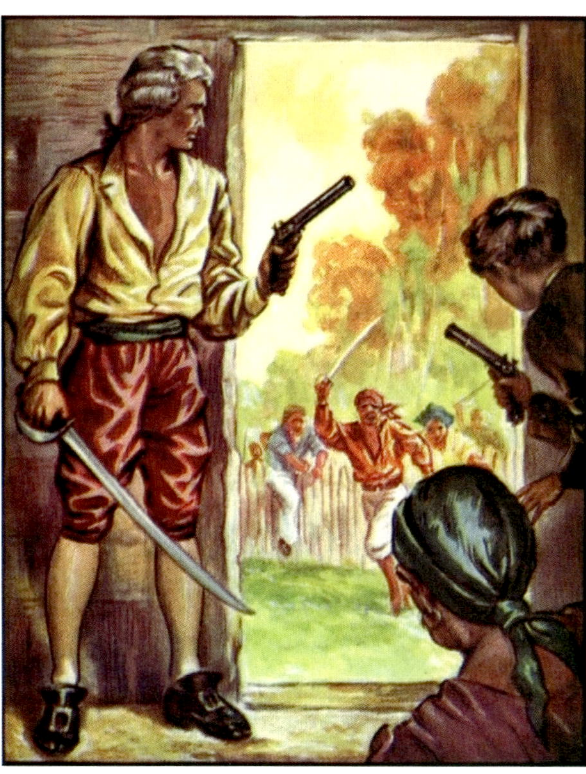

The surviving preparatory roughs for the Partridge adaptation of *Treasure Island* are in most cases very similar in composition to the final published versions. In a few cases, however, Heade made minor modifications. This can be most clearly seen in the two examples above where, for comparison purposes, the roughs are shown alongside the equivalent published pieces. In the first case, a thumbnail sketch of the modified composition is pencilled in the lower margin of the rough. (With thanks to Mike Lewis.)

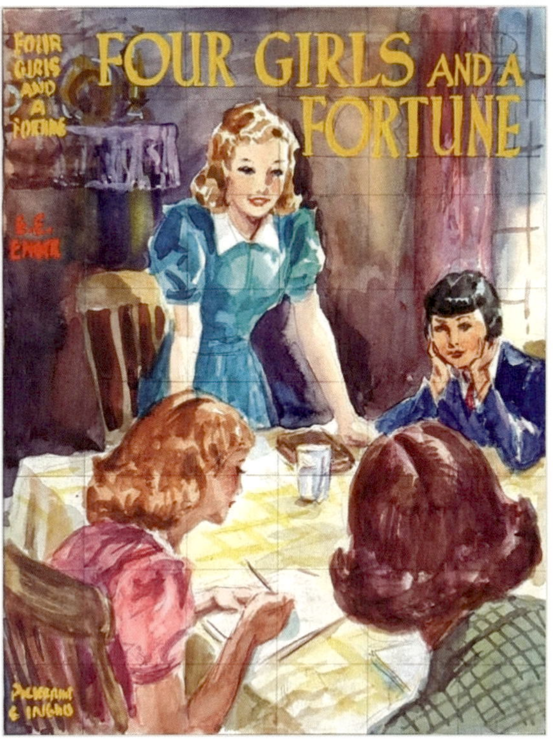 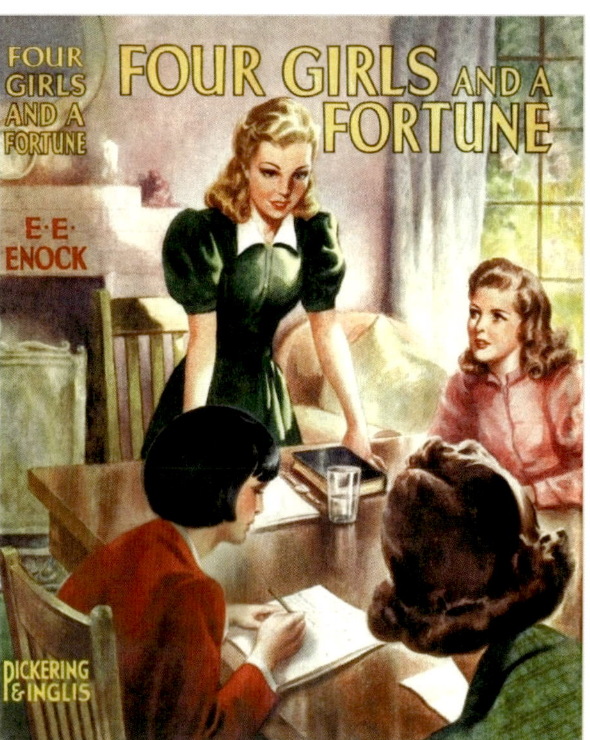

Heade's original rough and the as-published dustjacket of *Four Girls and a Fortune* by E E Enock (Pickering & Inglis, 1948)

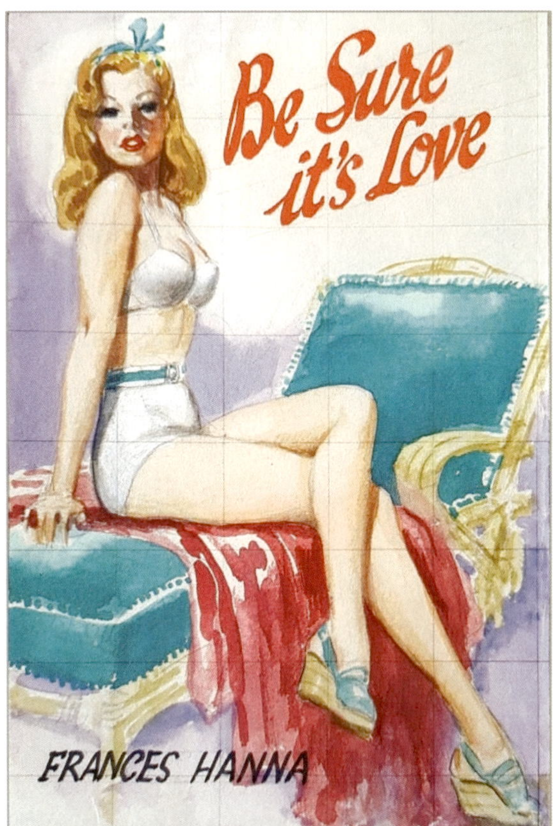 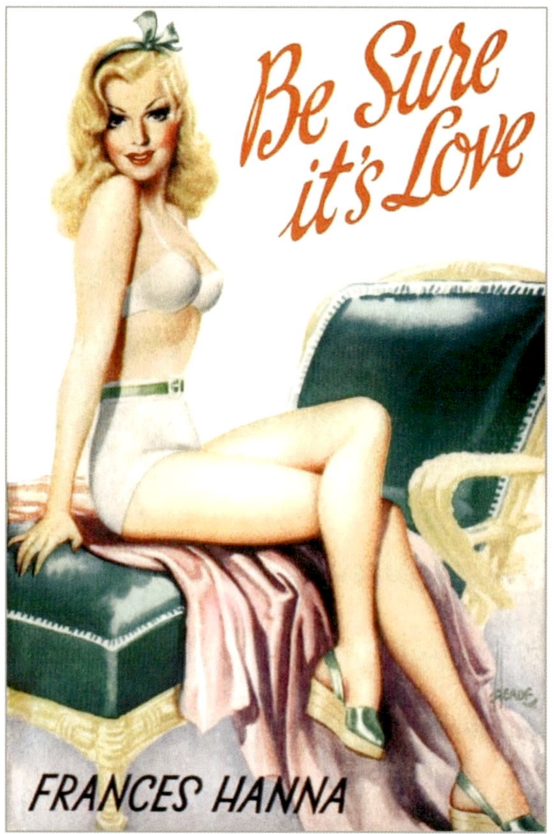

Heade's original rough and the as-published paperback cover of *Be Sure It's Love* by Frances Hanna (Archer, 1948)

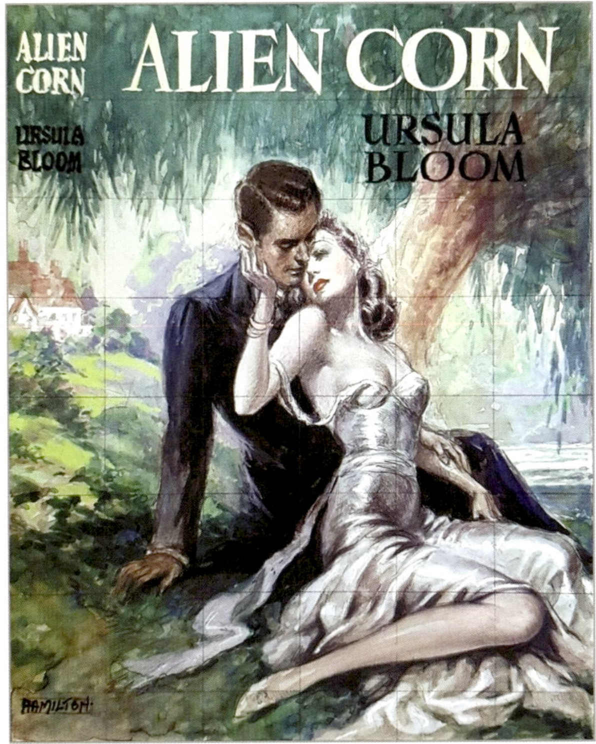
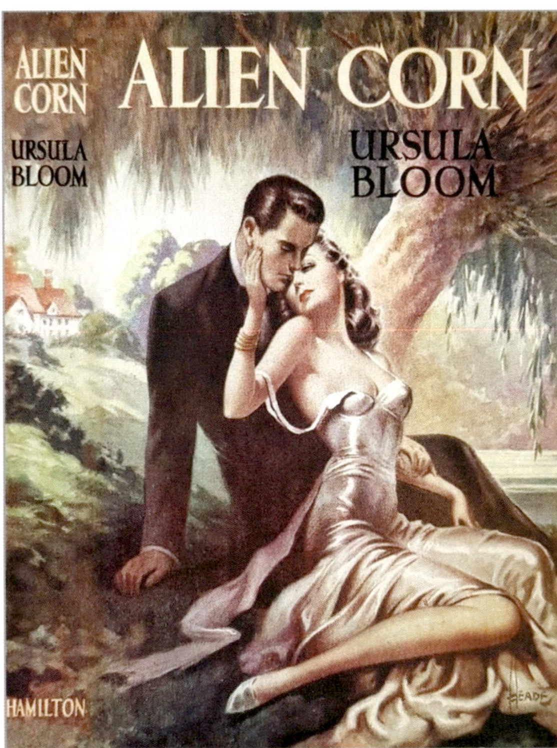

Heade's original rough and the as-published dustjacket of *Alien Corn* by Ursula Bloom (Hamilton & Co, 1947). The precarious state of the woman's décolletage, with her satin dress clinging to her body, is an early example of Heade taking his romantic fiction illustration in a distinctly erotic direction.

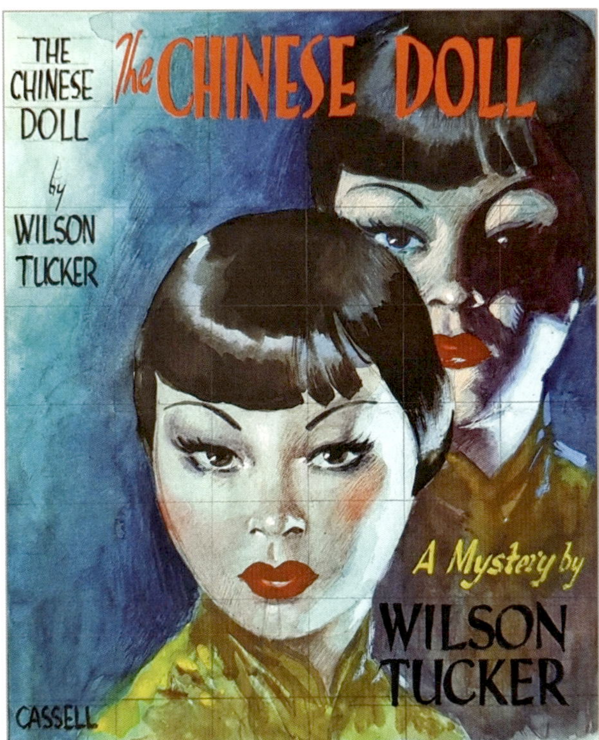
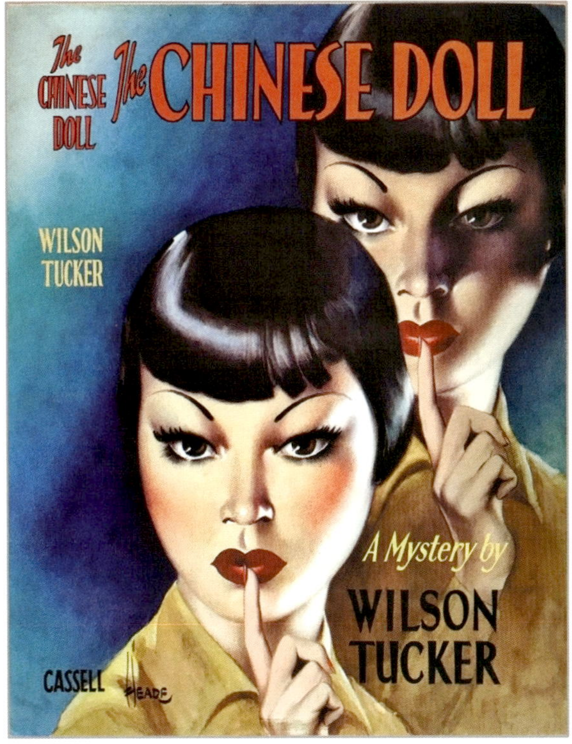

Heade's original rough and the completed original painting for the dustjacket of *The Chinese Doll* by Wilson Tucker (Cassell, 1948)

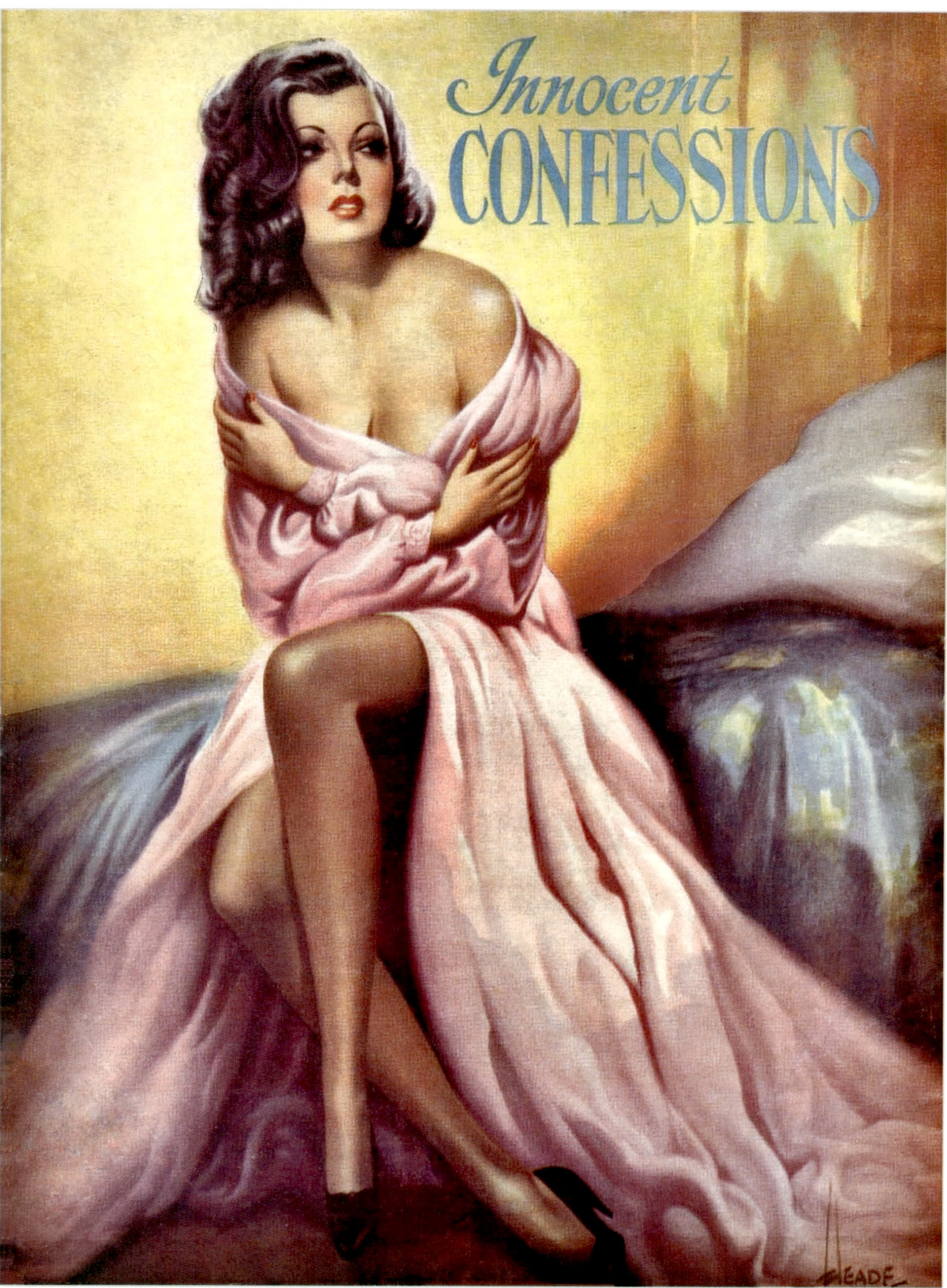

Heade's cover for what is believed to heave been the vonly edition of the intended periodical *Innocent Confessions* (Grant Hughes, c1947). The same art was repurposed for the cover of the paperback book *Blue Smoke for My Lovely!* by Benson Cabot (Hamilton & Co, c1950) (see facing page).

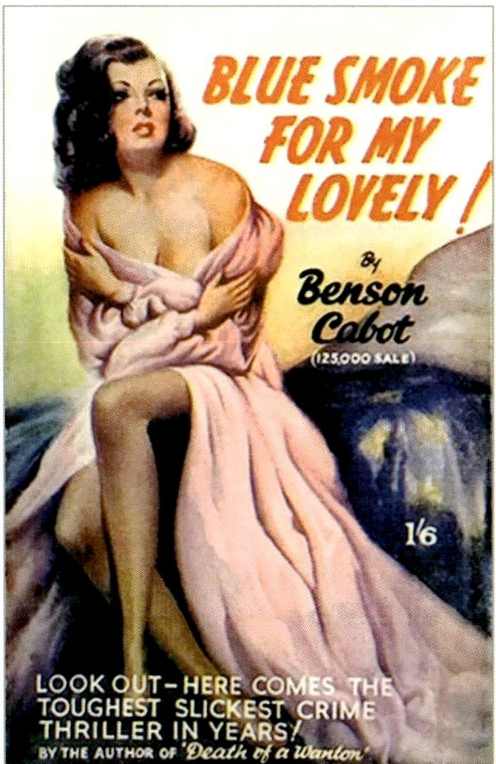

Heade's painted rough for the cover of the sole edition of *Innocent Confessions* (Grant Hughes, c1947), and the finished art as it was reused for the cover of Benson Cabot's *Blue Smoke for My Lovely!* (Hamilton & Co, c1950). Lines marked by the publisher's art department on the rough show how they wanted the woman's breasts to be more fully covered on the finished version.

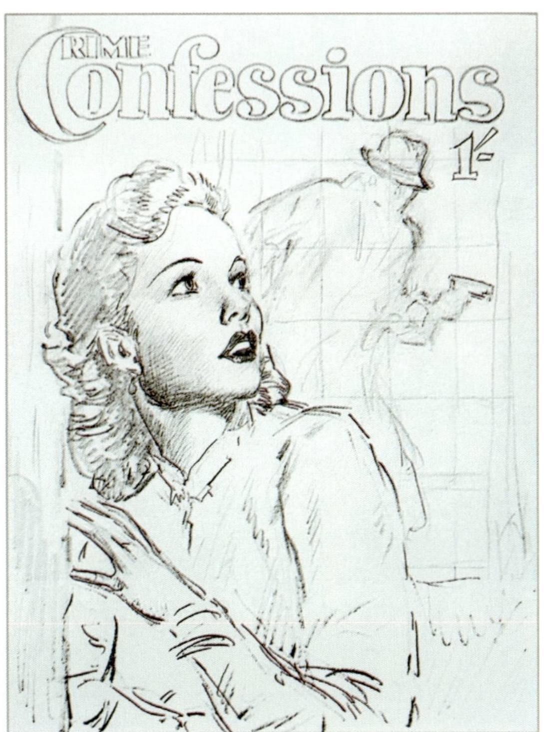

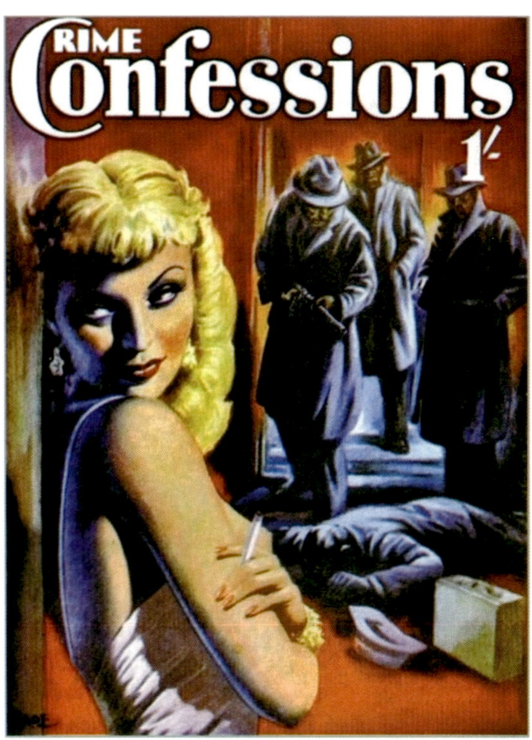

Heade's rough for the cover of another intended periodical, *Crime Confessions* (John Spencer, June 1938), and the as-published version. In this case, the artist was obviously asked to make his female subject less demure.

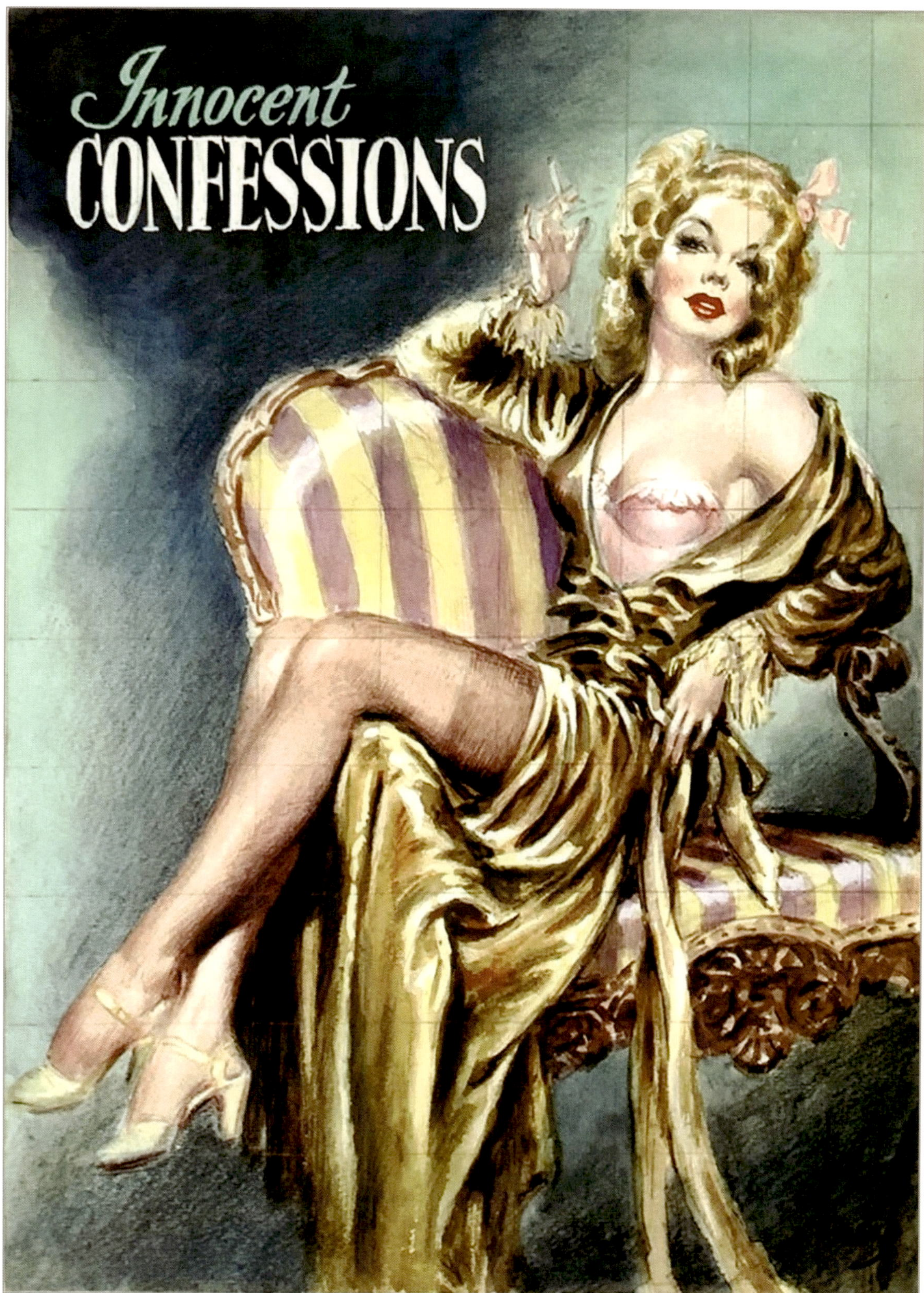

Heade's painted rough for another *Innocent Confessions* cover, marked on the back as having been supplied to Hamilton & Co. As only one issue of *Innocent Confessions* is known to have seen print, this was presumably intended for a proposed second issue that failed to appear.

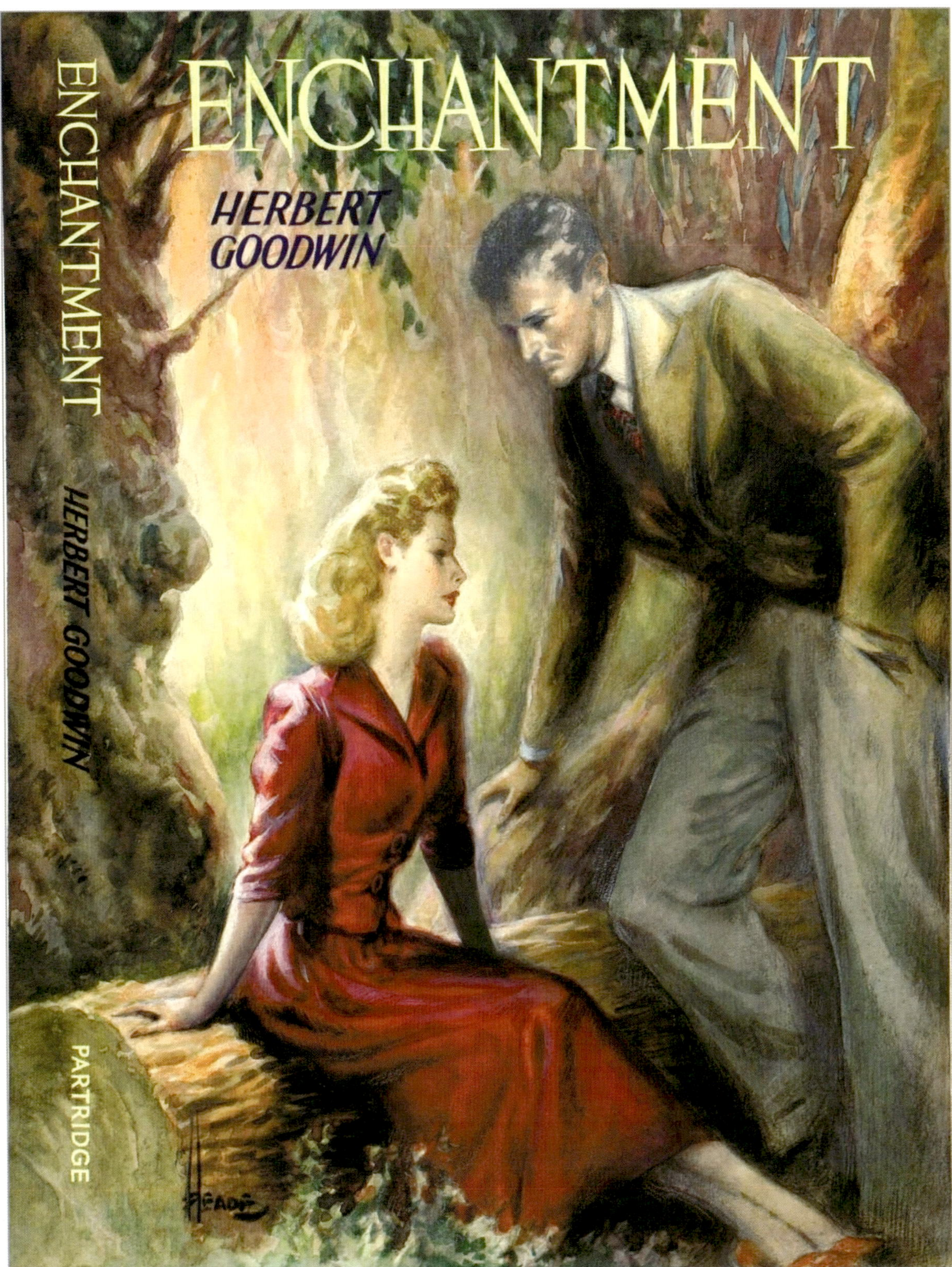

Heade's original painting for *Enchantment* by Herbert Goodwin (Partridge, 1948) (Image courtesy the Steve Chibnall Collection.)

ARTWORK ADAPTATIONS

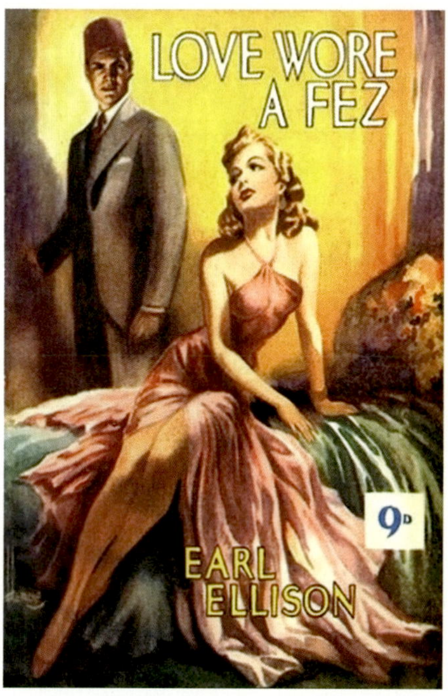

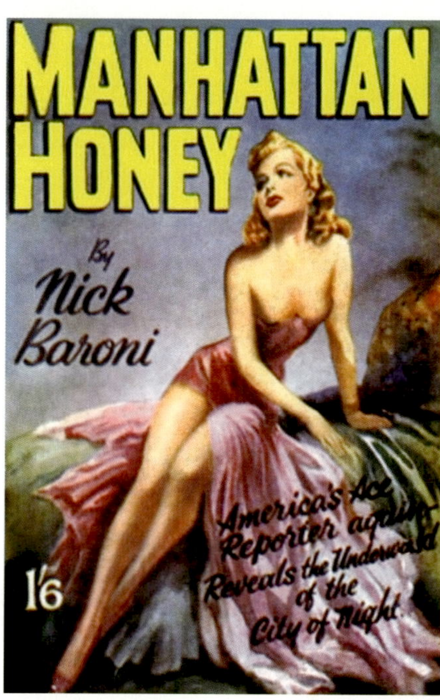

Above left: Heade's cover for *Love Wore a Fez* by Earl Ellison (Grant Hughes, c1947). Above right: the same artwork is adapted for the more revealing *Manhattan Honey* by Nick Baroni (Curtis Warren, c1950).

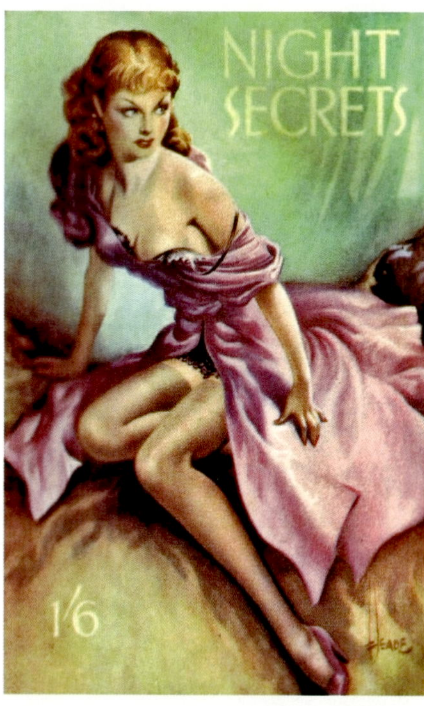

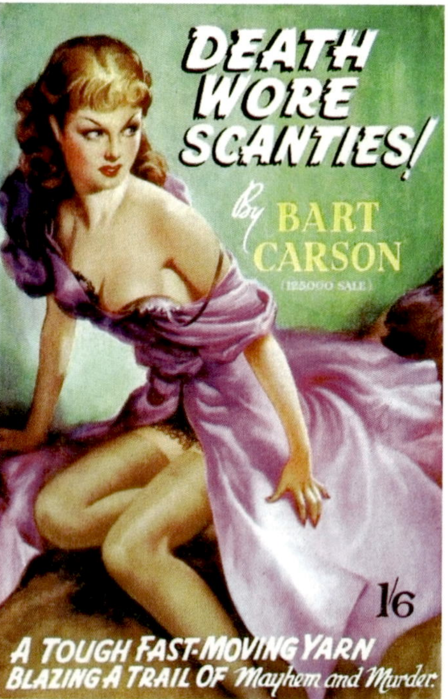

Above left: Heade's cover for *Night Secrets* by N Wesley Firth (Grant Hughes, c1948). Above right: the artwork is repurposed, in slightly cut-down form, for *Death Wore Scanties!* by Bart Carson (Hamilton & Co, c1950).

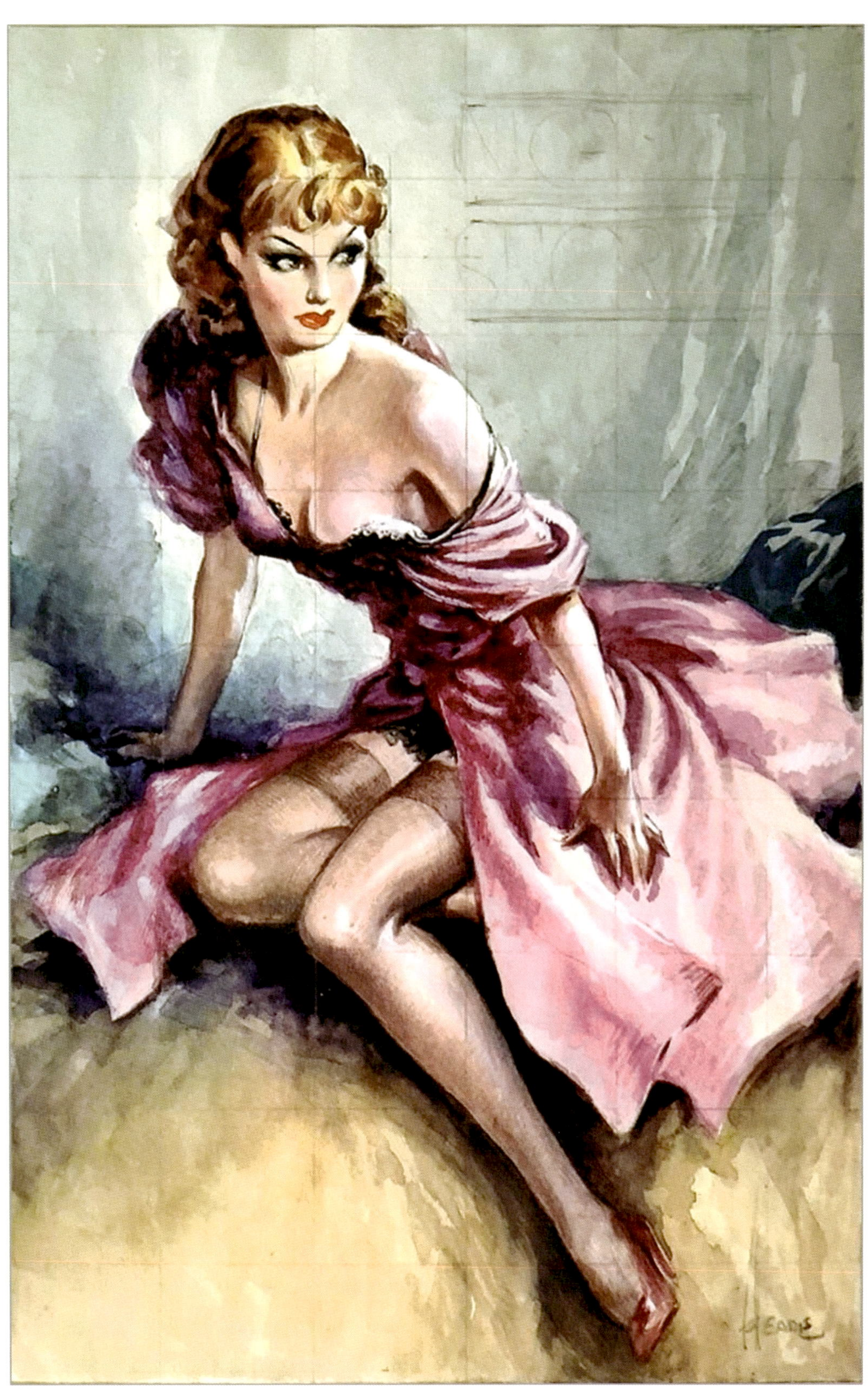

Heade's original rough for *Night Secrets* by N Wesley Firth (Grant Hughes, c1948)

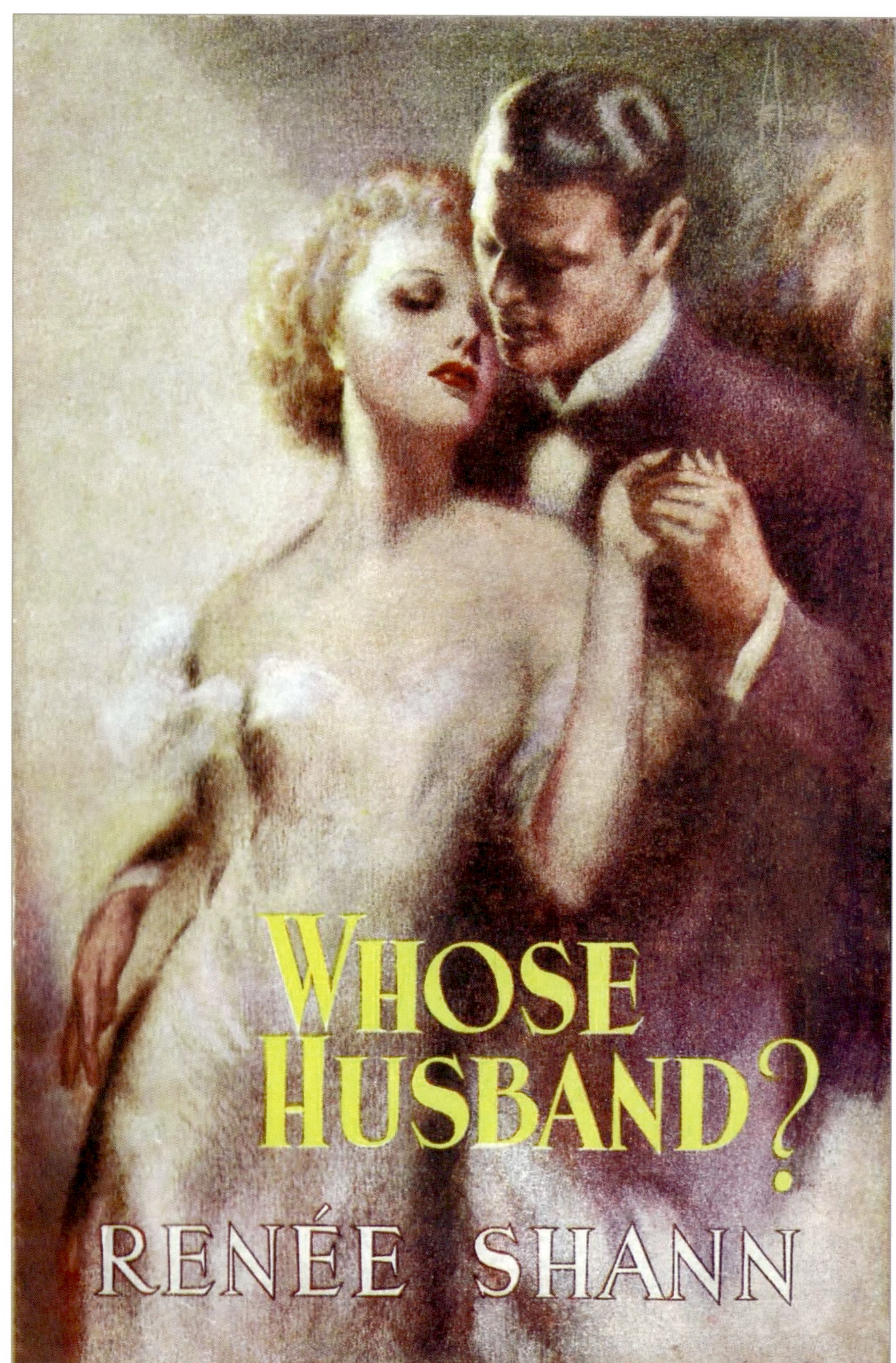

Whose Husband? by Renée Shann (Collins, 1948)

Published by Bear Hudson in 1948, the *Intimate Love Stories* periodical has long been believed to have run for just eight issues, five of which had signed Heade covers and one a possible unsigned example (as pictured on pages 263, 264 and 291 of *The Art of Reginald Heade – Special Edition*). It has now come to light, however, that there was in fact a ninth issue, which also had a signed Heade cover; this is shown above.

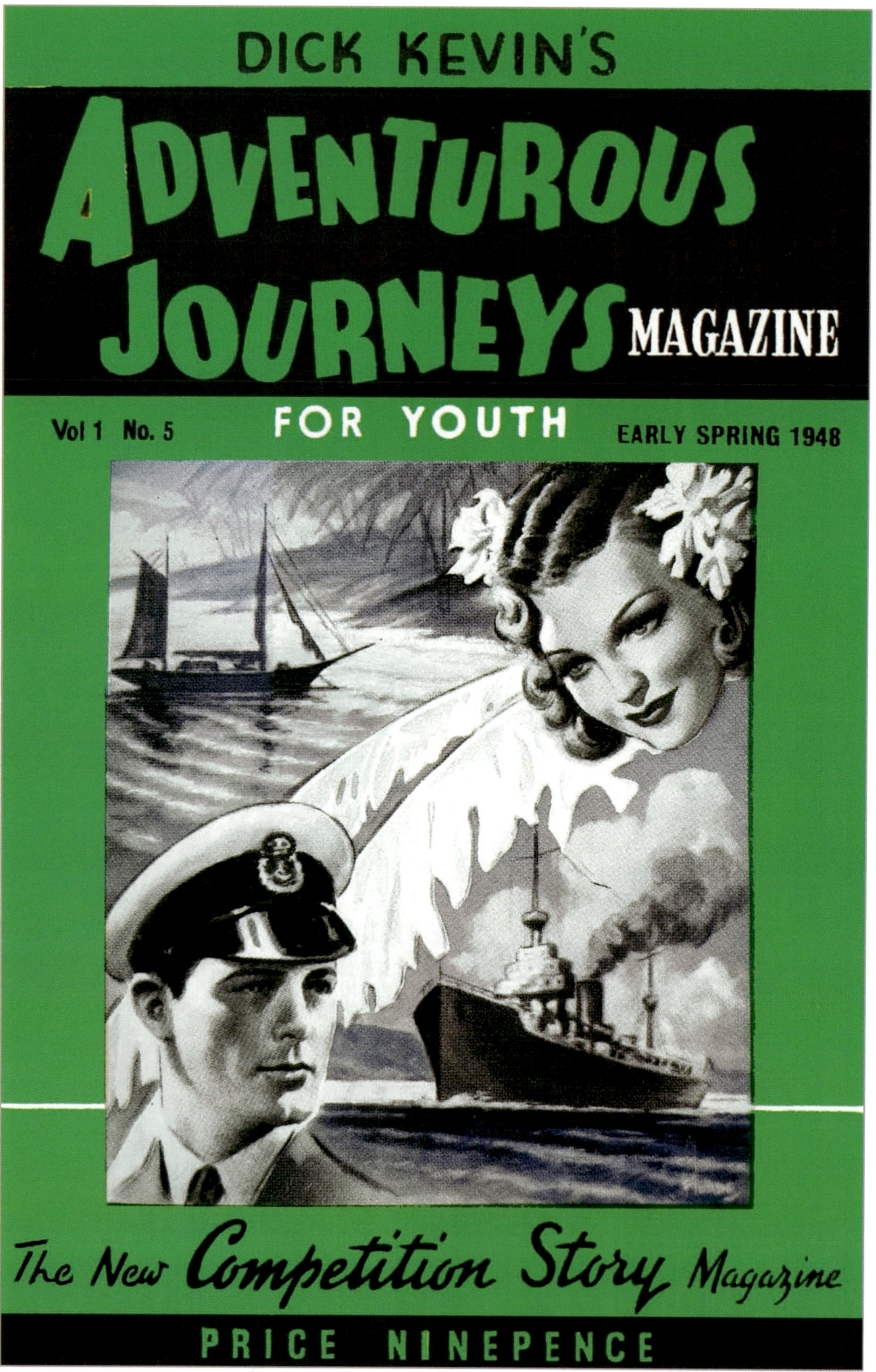

Dick Kevin's Adventurous Journeys Magazine Vol. 1 No. 5 (Devereaux Publications, Early Spring 1948)

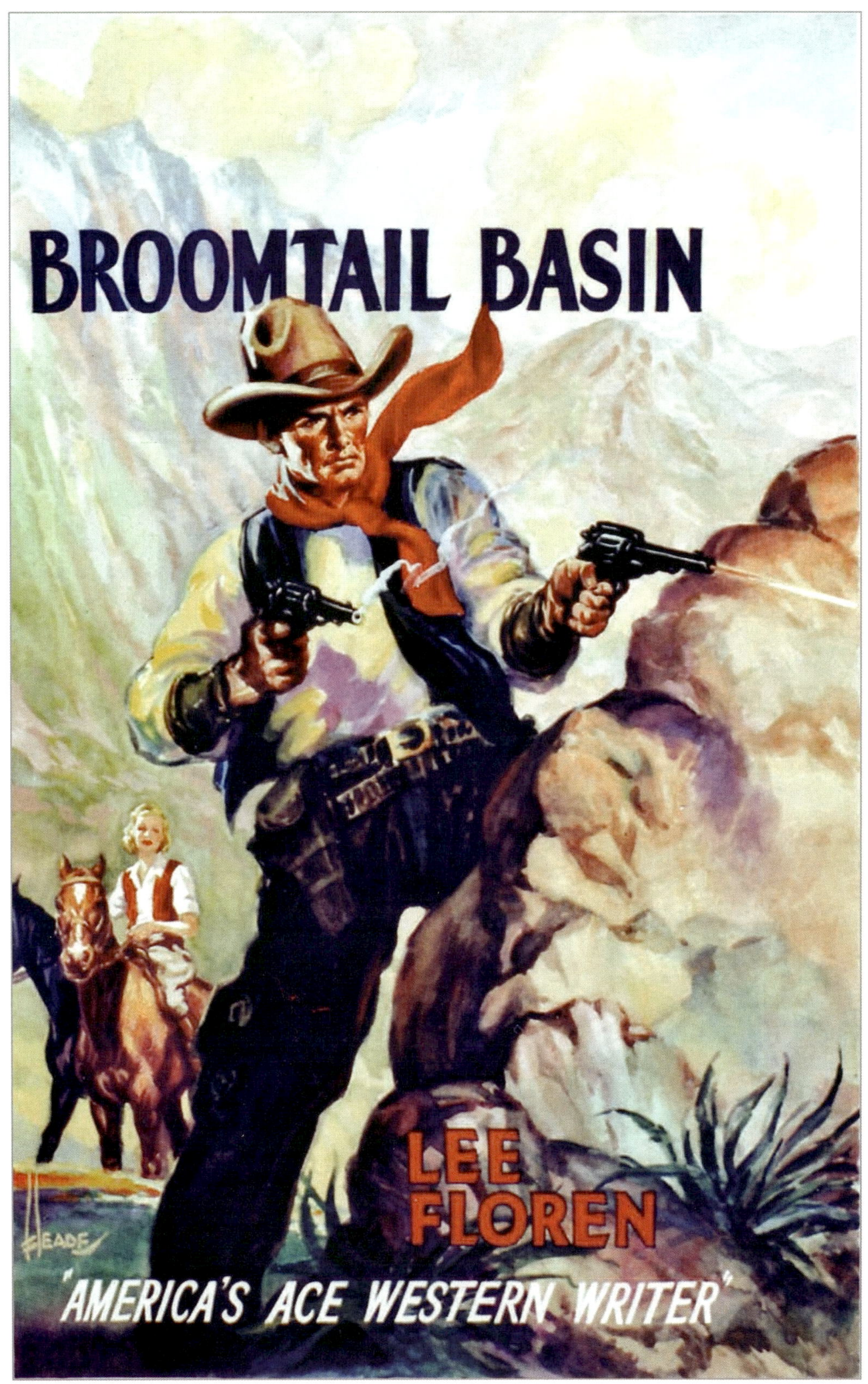

Heade's original painting for *Broomtail Basin* by Lee Floren (Archer, 1947)

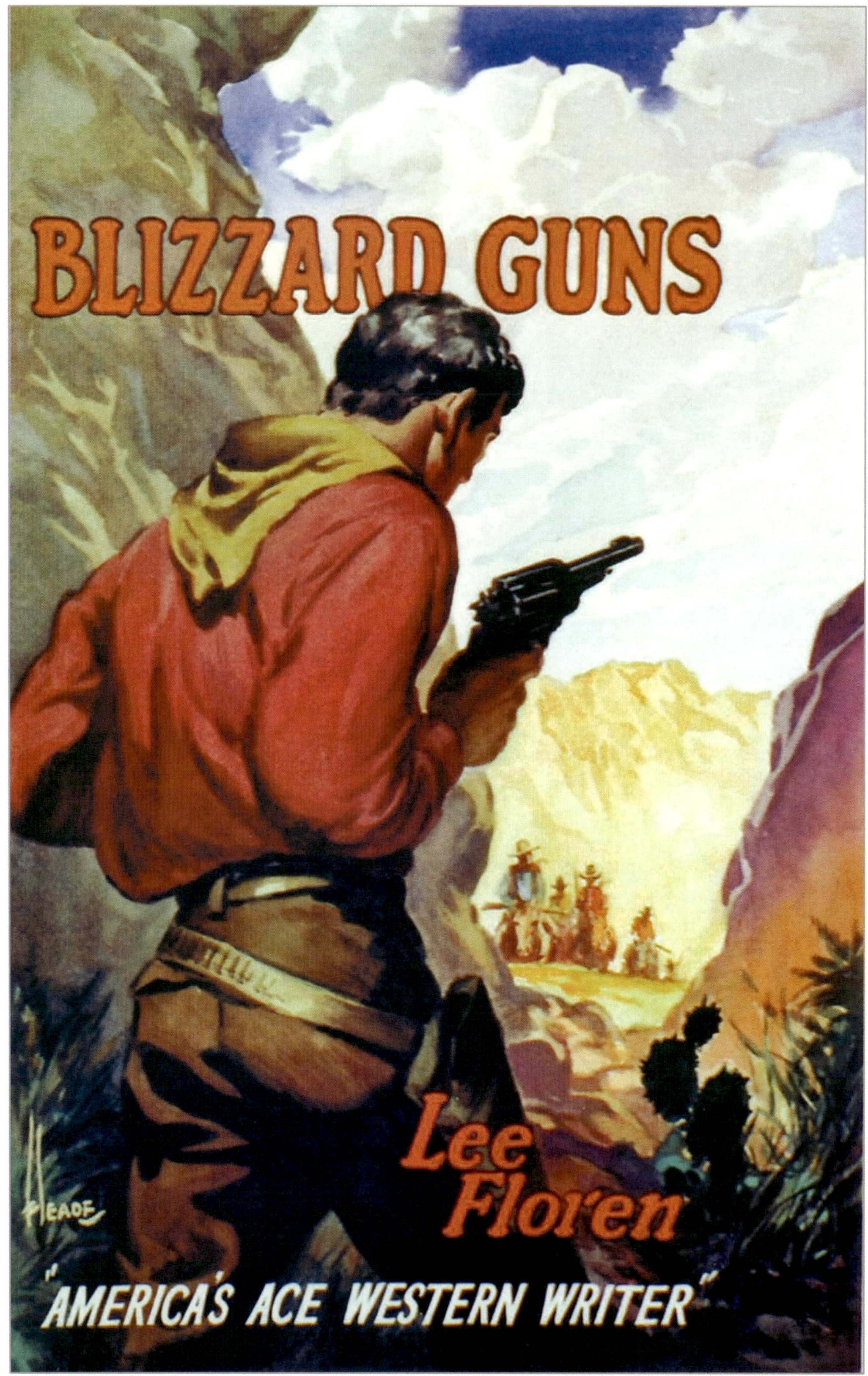

Heade's original painting for *Blizzard Guns* by Lee Floren (Archer, 1948)

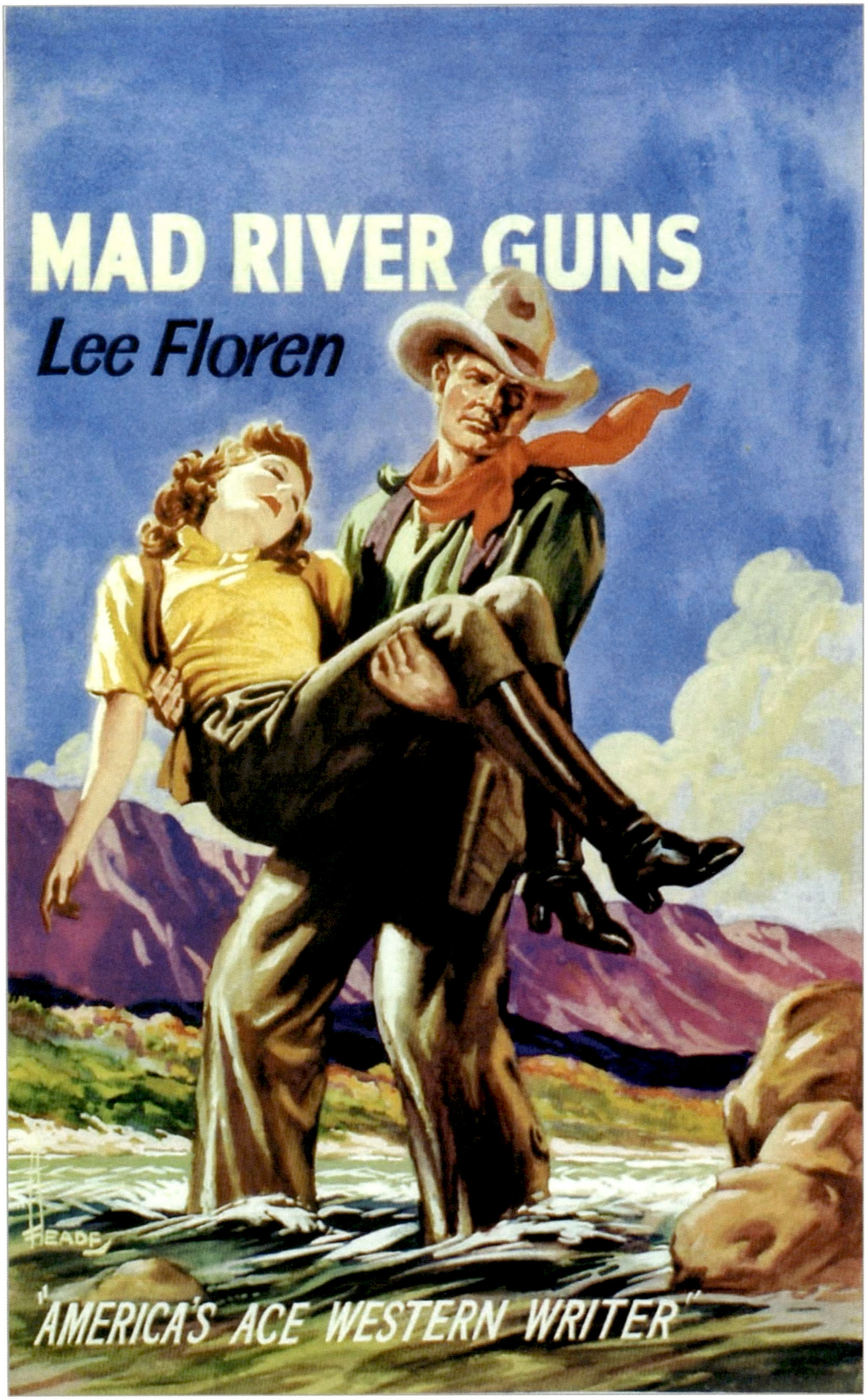

Heade's original painting for *Mad River Guns* by Lee Floren (Archer, 1948)

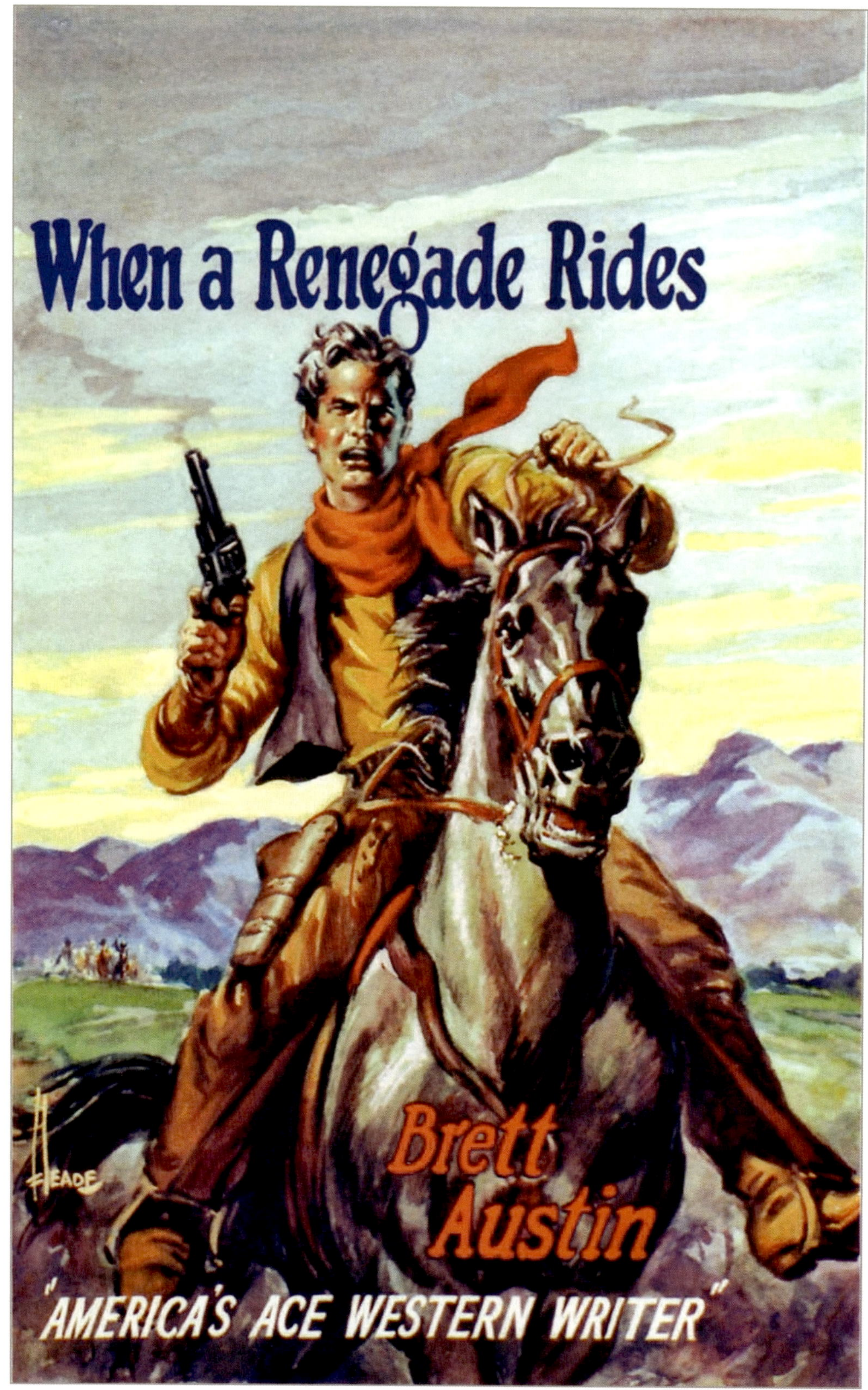

Heade's original painting for *When a Renegade Rides* by Brett Austin (Archer, 1948)

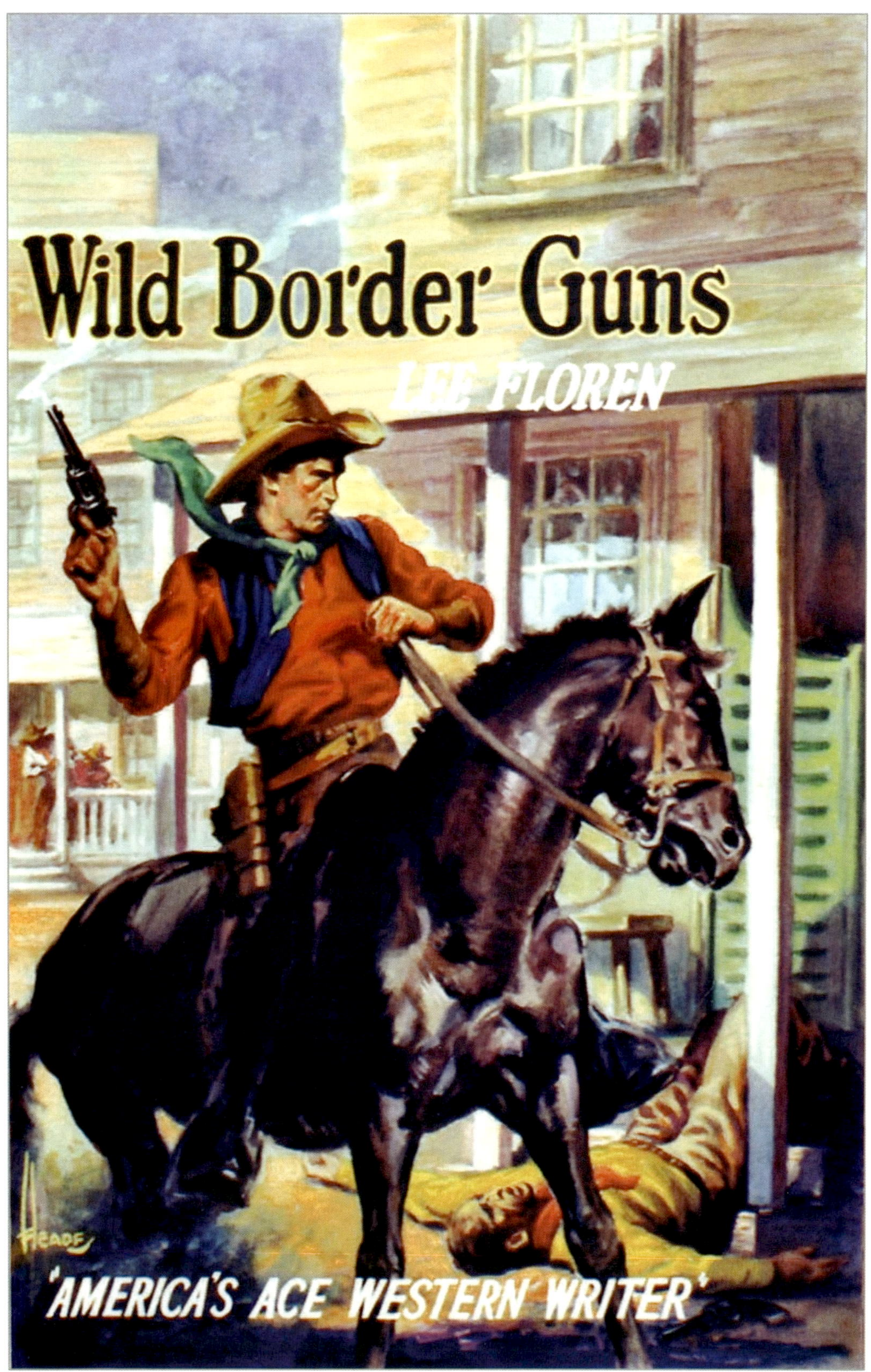

Heade's original painting for *Wild Border Guns* by Lee Floren (Archer, 1948)

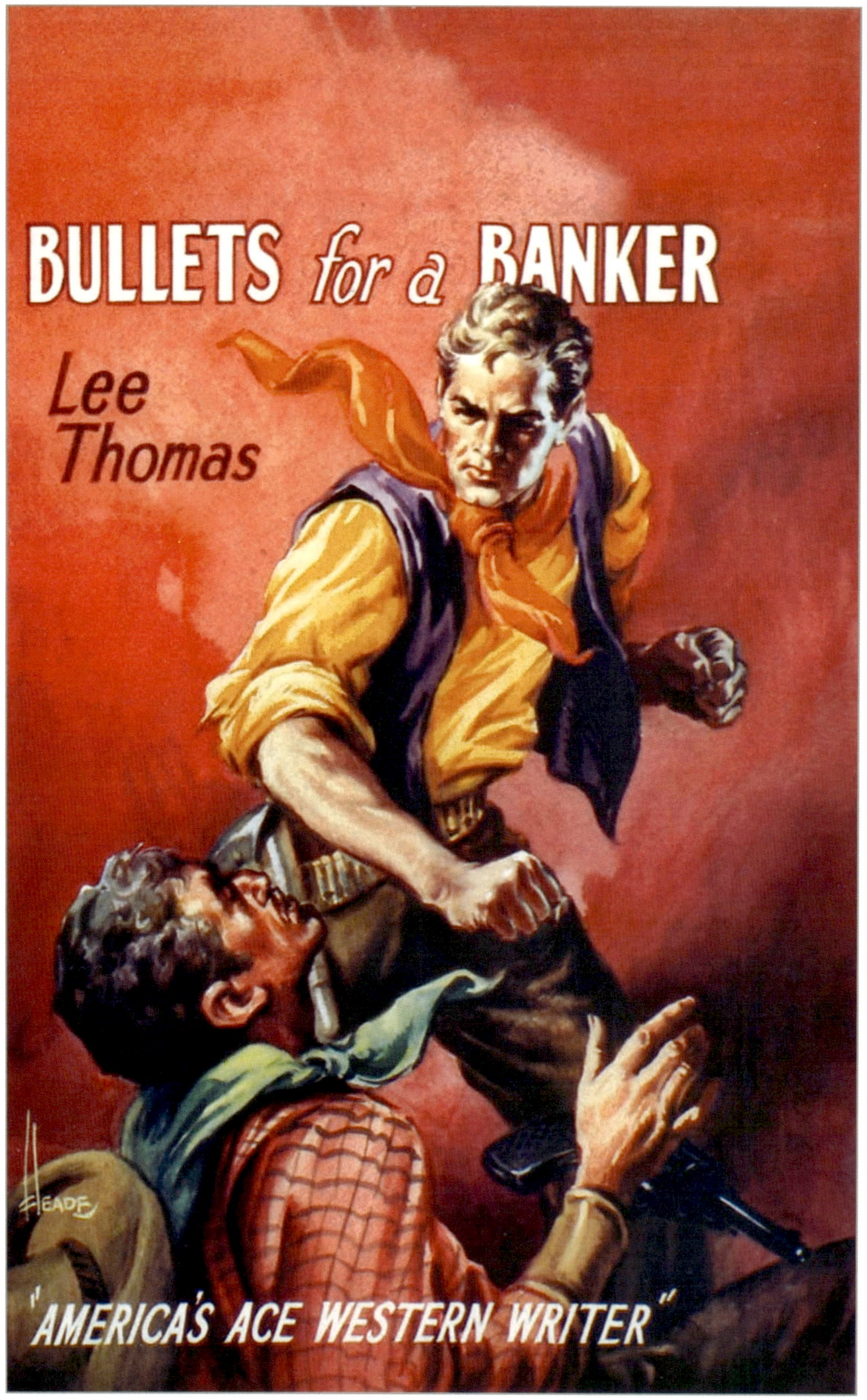

Heade's original painting for *Bullets for a Banker* by Lee Thomas (Archer, October 1948)

CROPPED COVERS

When completing his cover commissions, Heade often made allowance for the fact that the edges of the picture might be cropped off on the as-published book. Particularly good examples of this can be seen in some of the Western pieces he supplied for Raymond and Lilian Locker's Archer Press. Comparing the as-published covers of Brett Austin's *When a Renegade Rides*, Lee Floren's *Blizzard Guns* and *Mad River Guns* and Lee Thomas's *Bullets for a Banker* (see below) with the original paintings (as pictured over the previous few pages), it is obvious that the artist included quite a wide margin, particularly above the book's title, which was largely lost during the production process. Curiously, though, on other, similar books, Lee Floren's *Wild Border Guns* and *Broomtail Basin*, virtually the whole composition, including the margin, was retained on the as-published cover.

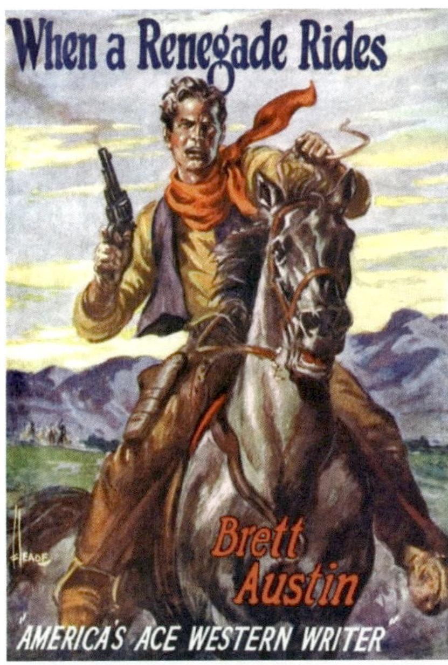

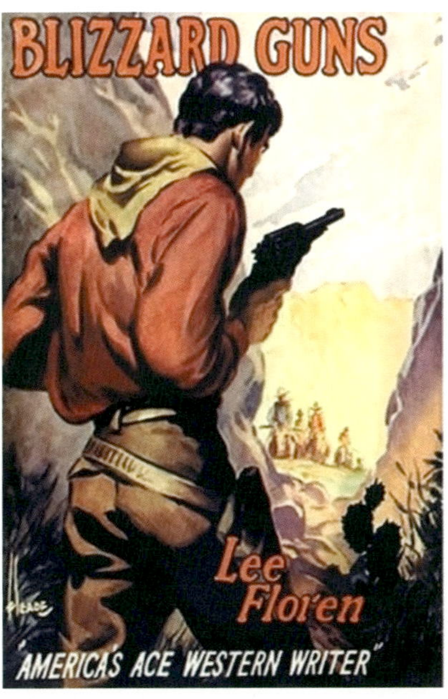

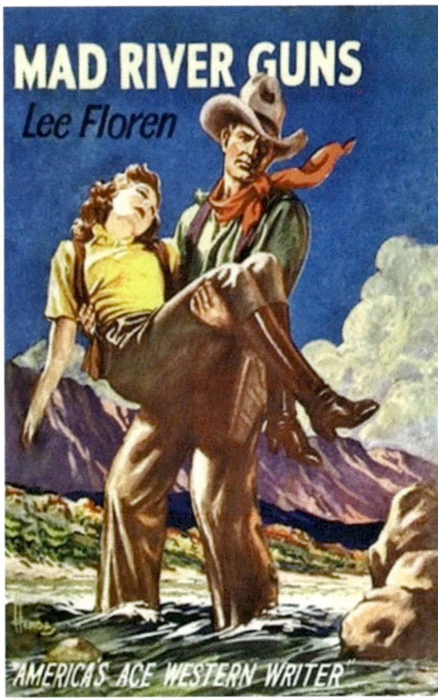

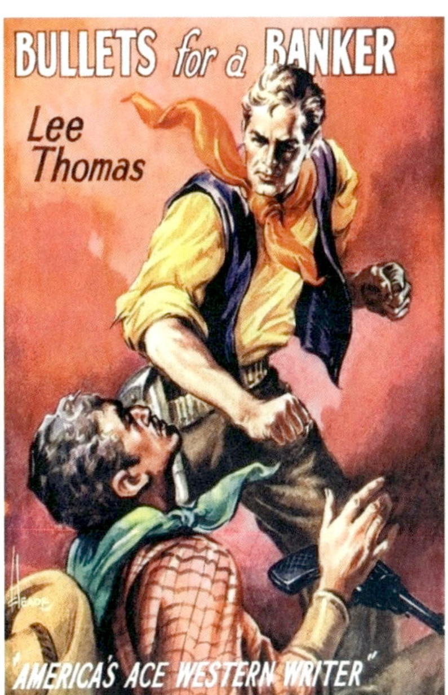

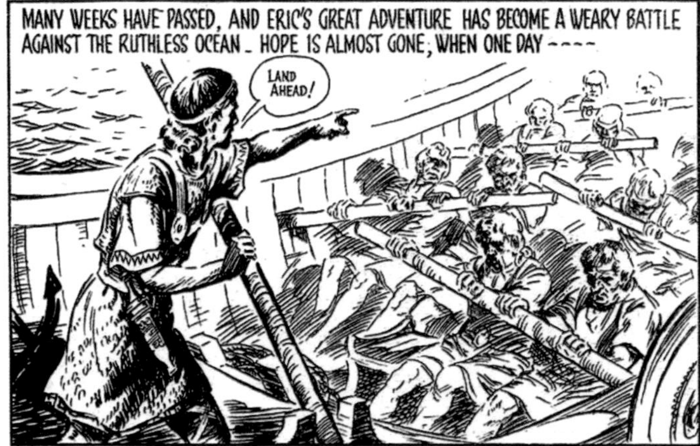

THE SAGA OF ERIC THE RED
By R. C. W. HEADE

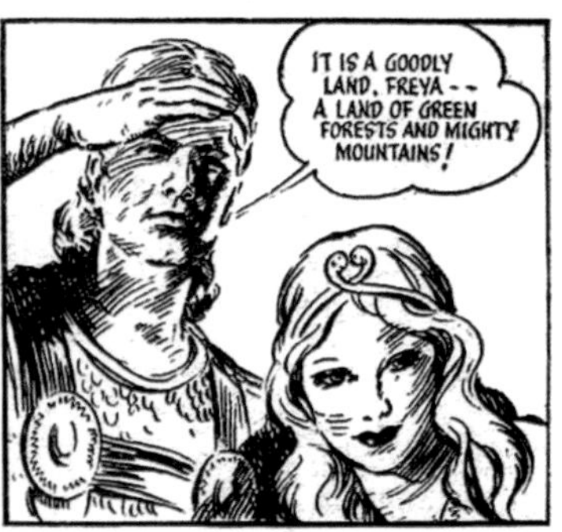

1. The Vikings had been little better than pirates, until Eric the Red rose to lead them to new adventures across the seas. And so, in their longships they had set sail out into the broad Atlantic to find what strange lands lay beyond the mighty waters of the ocean.

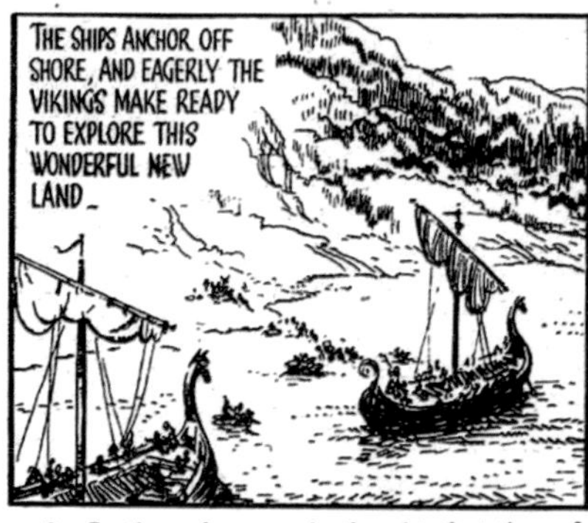

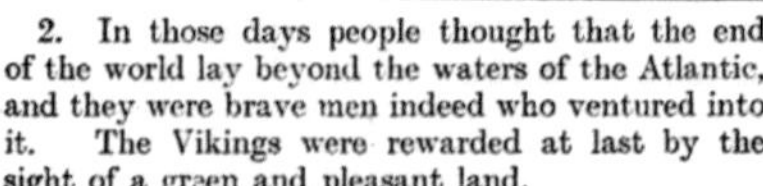

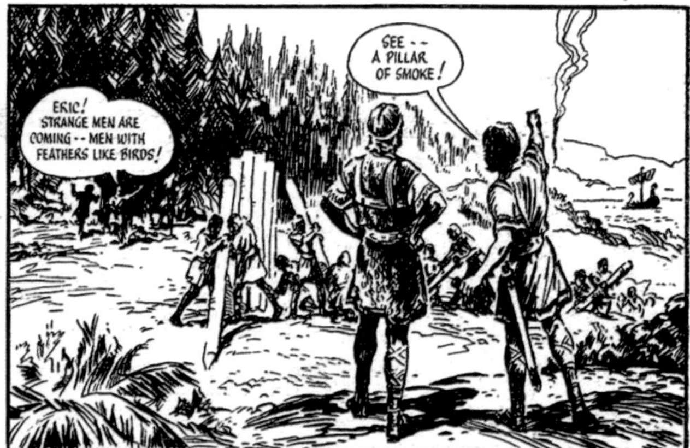

2. In those days people thought that the end of the world lay beyond the waters of the Atlantic, and they were brave men indeed who ventured into it. The Vikings were rewarded at last by the sight of a green and pleasant land.

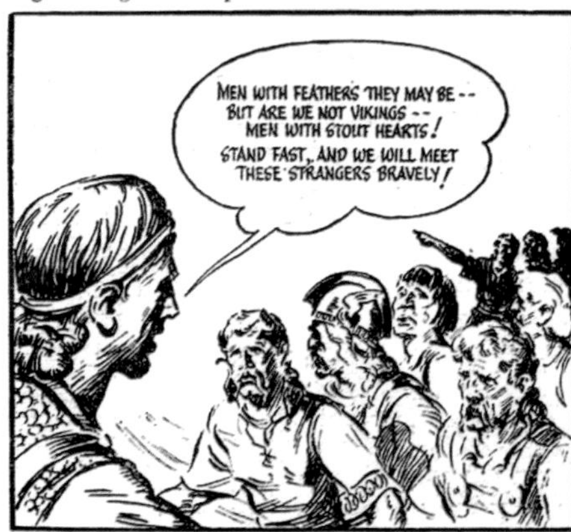

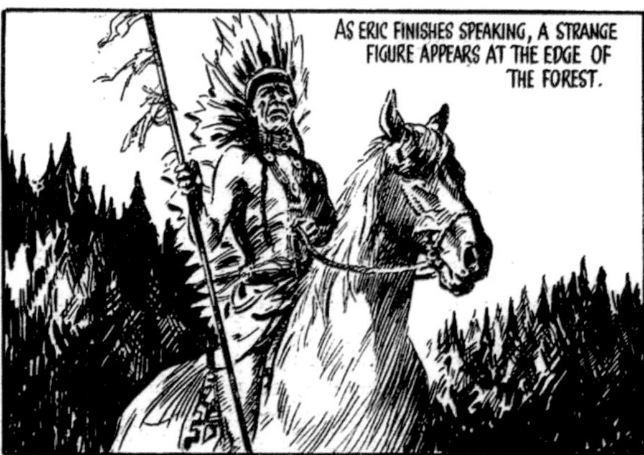

3. Sea Rovers though they were, they were glad enough to set foot on dry land after all those long and weary weeks at sea. Under Eric's direction they went ashore, and started to cut logs to build themselves a shelter. At first they saw no signs of any men in this new land—but they were not left alone for very long. The first sign of danger was a thin column of smoke rising into the clear air from beyond the forest trees. Then came the strange feathered men !

The first volume of *The Art of Reginald Heade* presented a number of examples of Heade's superb comic strip work. This second volume showcases several more, including in this 1940s section two further two-part instalments of *The Saga of Eric the Red*. Above: part 2, page 1, from *Knockout* #525 (Amalgamated, 19 March 1949).

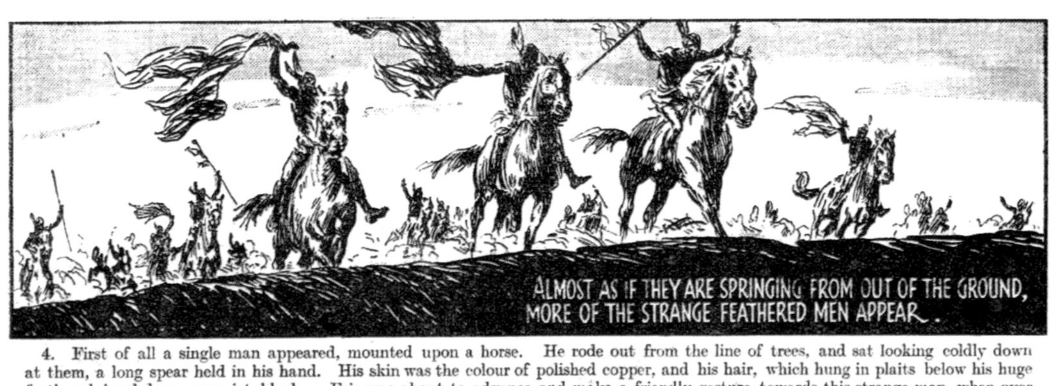

4. First of all a single man appeared, mounted upon a horse. He rode out from the line of trees, and sat looking coldly down at them, a long spear held in his hand. His skin was the colour of polished copper, and his hair, which hung in plaits below his huge feathered head-dress, was jet black. Eric was about to advance and make a friendly gesture towards this strange man, when over a crest of rising ground swept more of the Redmen on horses. The Vikings were outnumbered!

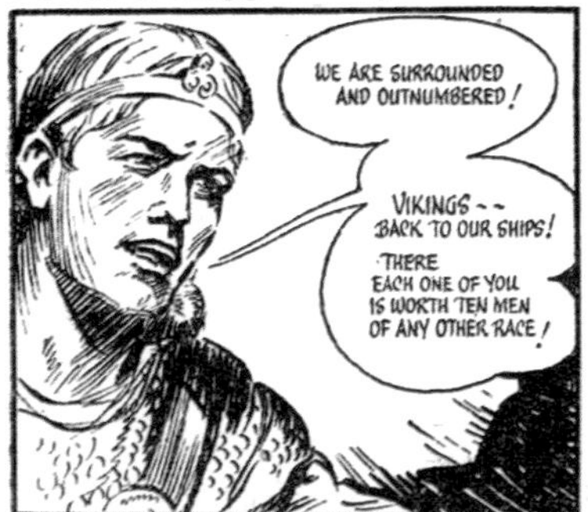

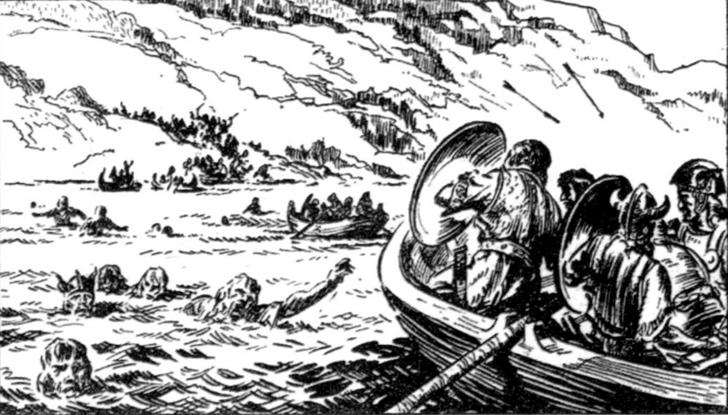

5. With all speed the Vikings beat a retreat back to their longships, while from the mouth of a near-by river more of the Redmen appeared in canoes.

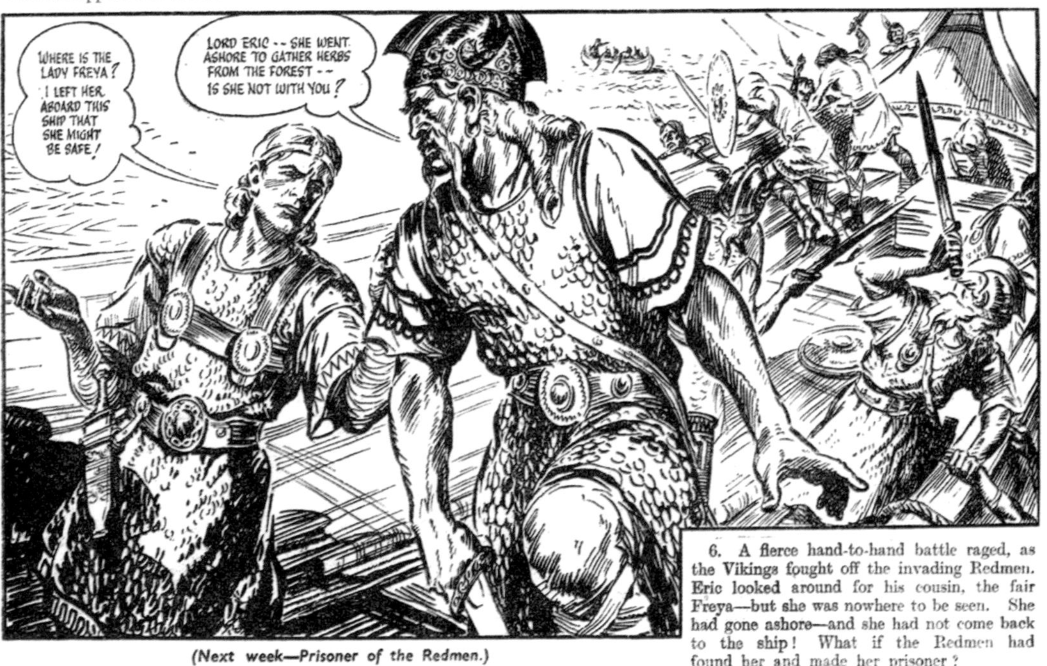

(Next week—Prisoner of the Redmen.)

6. A fierce hand-to-hand battle raged, as the Vikings fought off the invading Redmen. Eric looked around for his cousin, the fair Freya—but she was nowhere to be seen. She had gone ashore—and she had not come back to the ship! What if the Redmen had found her and made her prisoner?

The Saga of Eric the Red part 2, page 2, from *Knockout* #525 (Amalgamated, 19 March 1949). Although Heade provided the art for the story, he did not write the script: that was the responsibility of *Knockout*'s then editor, Leonard Matthews. Matthews also scripted *Sexton Blake and Tinker versus Plague of Crime*, the Sexton Blake story that Heade worked on for the comic that same year.

THE SAGA OF ERIC THE RED

Drawn by R. C. W. Heade

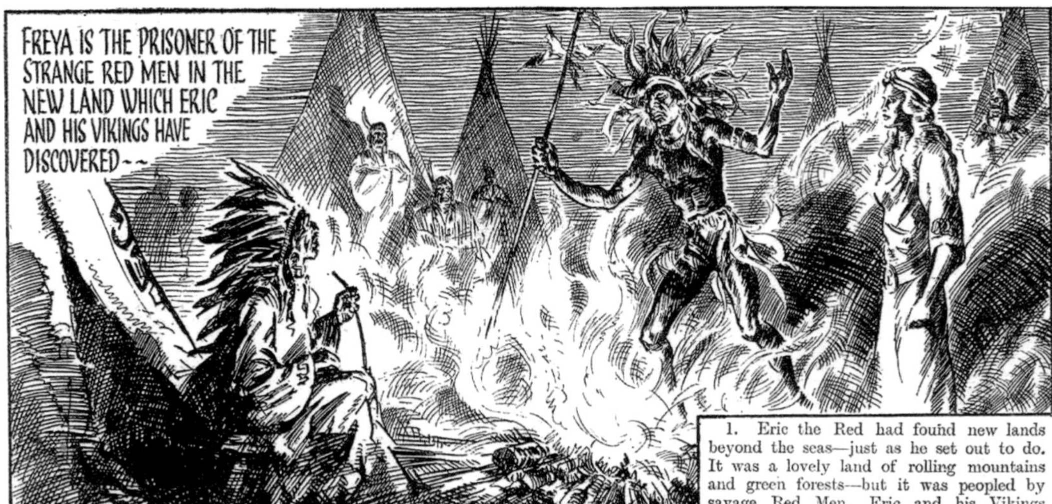

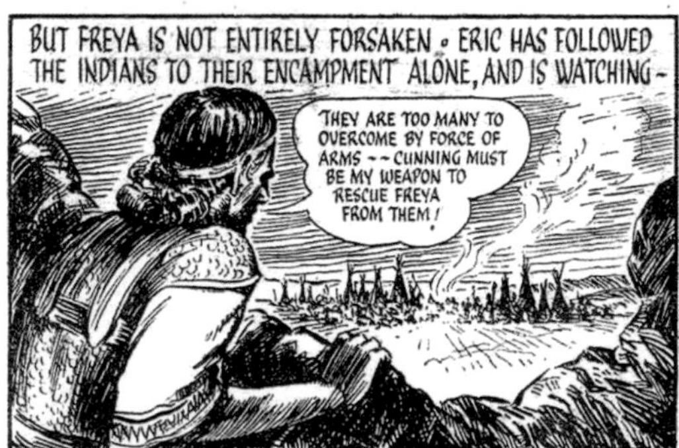

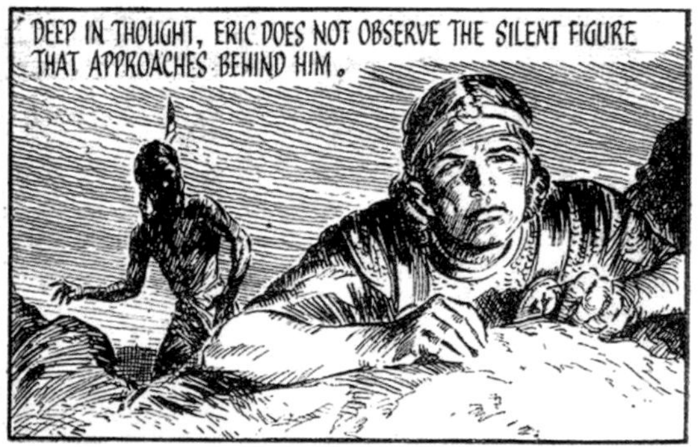

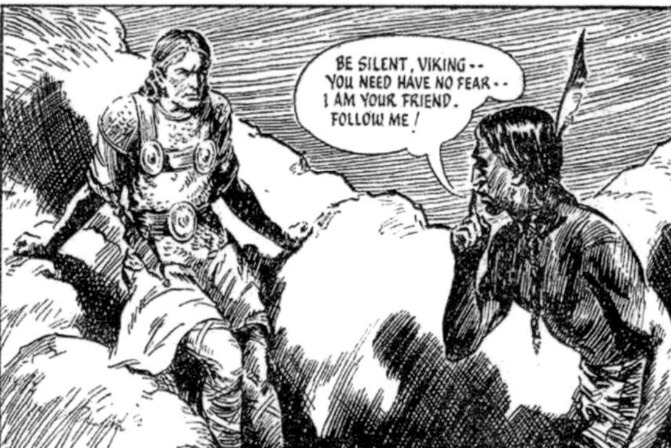

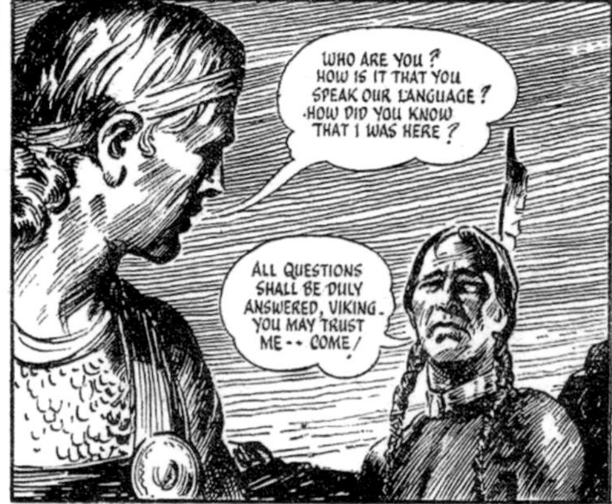

The Saga of Eric the Red, part 4, page 1, from *Knockout* #527 (Amalgamated, 2 April 1949). The story ran for eight instalments in all, and toward the end was retitled simply *Eric the Red*. The whole story was later reprinted, with slight changes to both dialogue and artwork (the latter adaptations possibly made by Heade himself) in *Robin Hood Annual 1958* (Amalgamated, 1957).

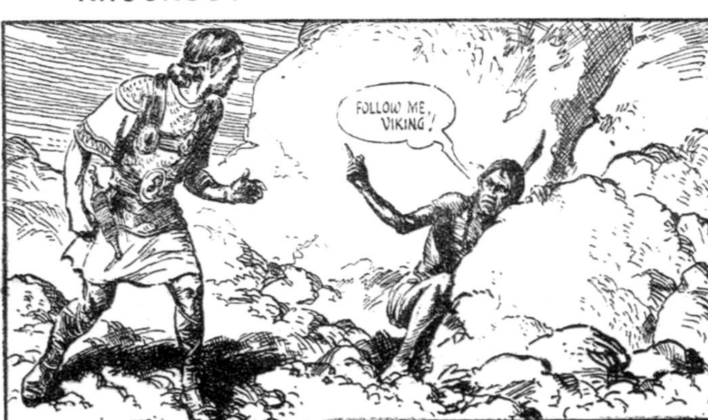

4. For this man was a friend and to Eric's astonishment he spoke the language of the Viking. The Red Man would tell him nothing—all he said was " Follow me."

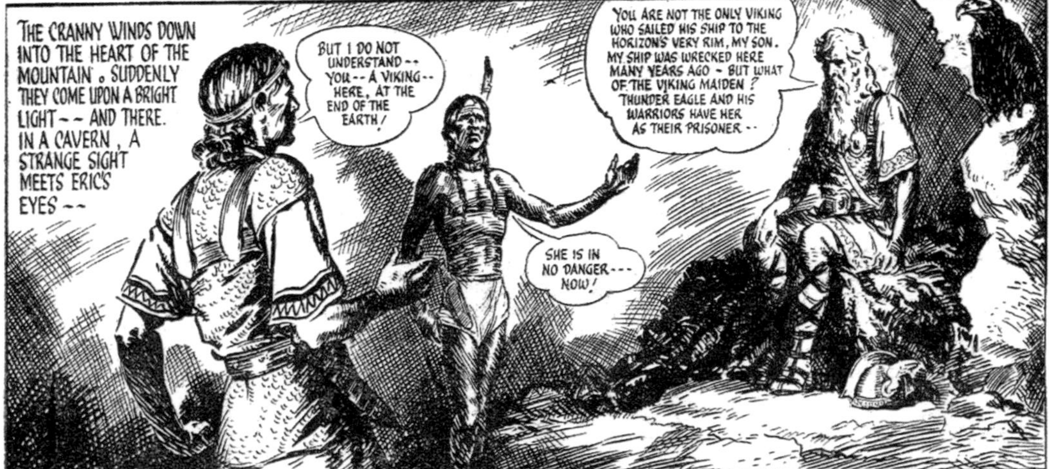

5. He led Eric up the mountain-side and into a tiny cavern, which led down, winding and twisting through the heart of the rock. At last it widened out into a bigger cavern, lit by flaming torches, and there, seated upon a pile of skin rugs, Eric beheld an aged Viking !

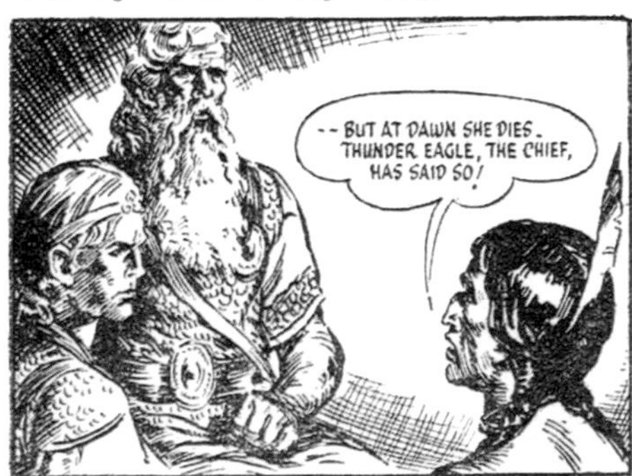

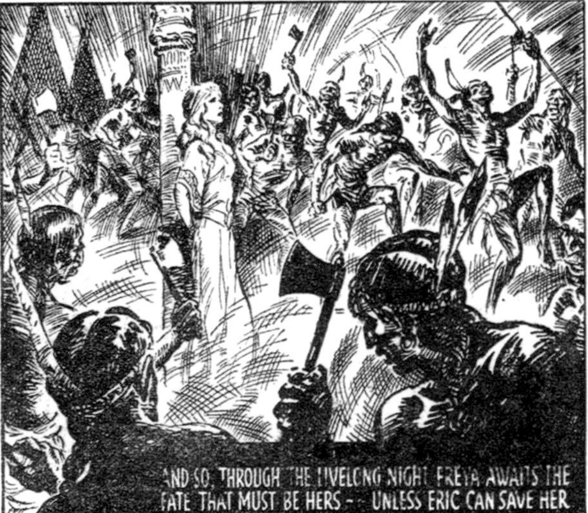

6. So he was not the first Viking to cross the mighty ocean and discover this strange land !   The aged one, whose name was Baldur, promised to aid Eric in rescuing Freya. Meanwhile, poor Freya stood, bound to a post, while the whooping Red Men danced around her !

(Next week—Freya is given to the God of the Mighty River.)

The Saga of Eric the Red, part 4, page 2, from *Knockout* #527 (Amalgamated, 2 April 1949). Heade was credited on all eight instalments of this story – unlike on *Sexton Blake and Tinker versus Plague of Crime*, where (as was common practice at the time) no artwork credit was given.

PRICE VARIANTS

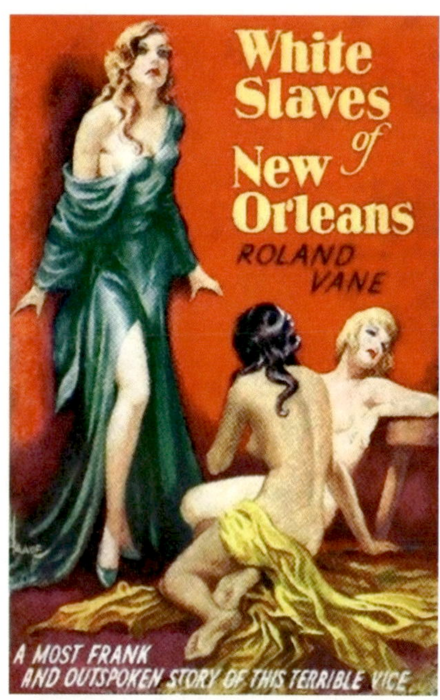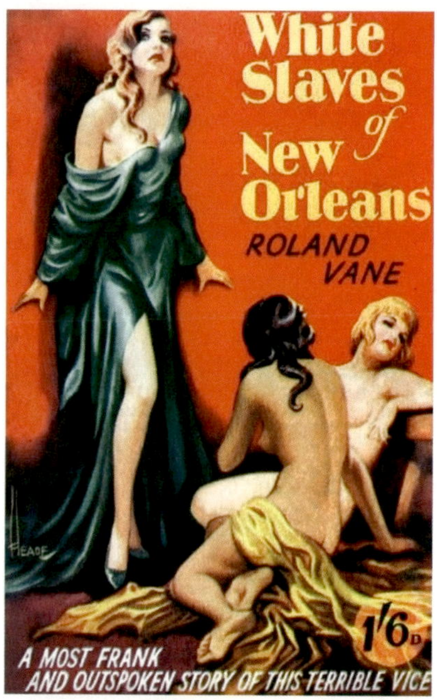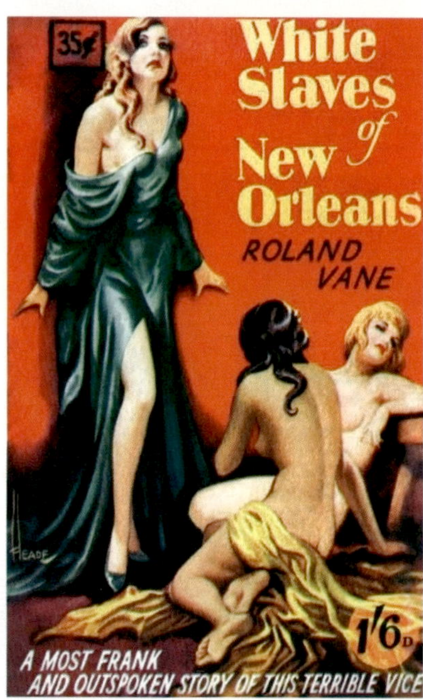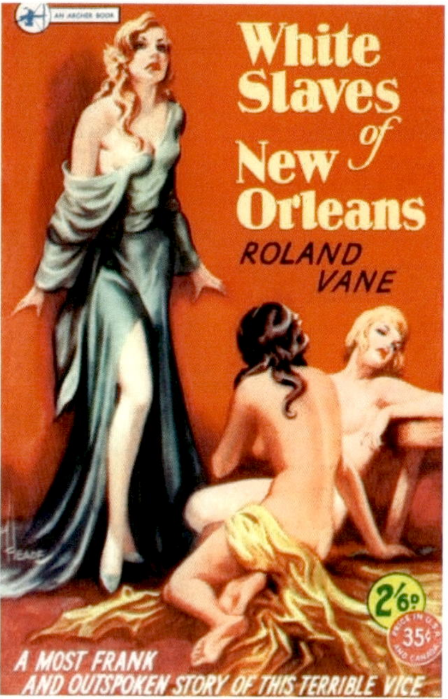

The task of the Heade collector is complicated by the fact that a number of his covers appeared in several different price variants. For example, the first Archer printing of *White Slaves of New Orleans* by Roland Vane, in June 1949, came without a price at all (see top left), but later British printings, in 1949 and 1950, had a 1/6 price overlaid (see top right). Copies used for export to the USA were ink-stamped in one corner with a 35c price (see bottom left), while copies actually published in the USA by Kaywin in 1951 had an Archer logo added and new dual prices overlaid (see bottom right).

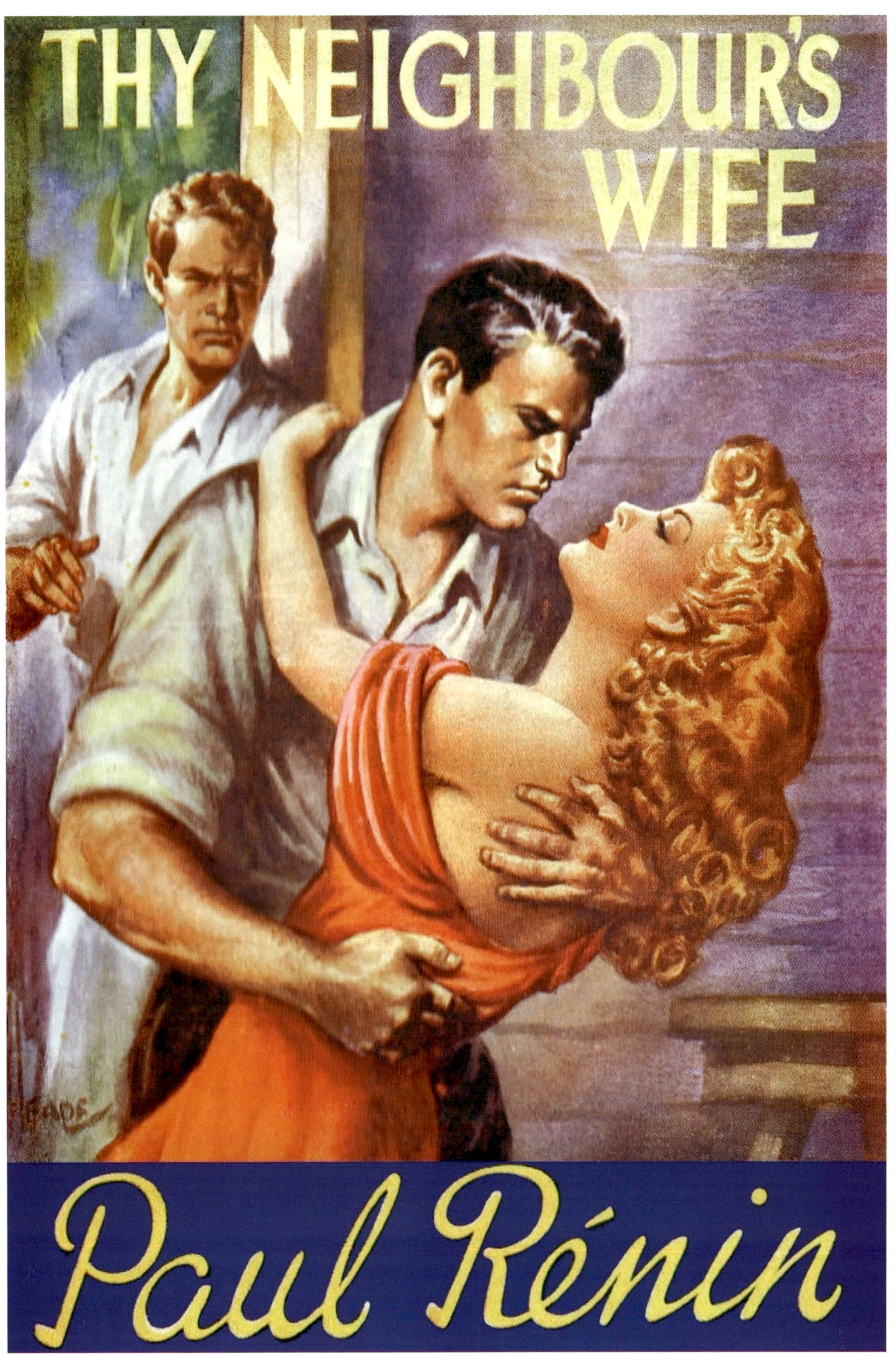

Thy Neighbour's Wife by Paul Rénin (R & L Locker, c1948)

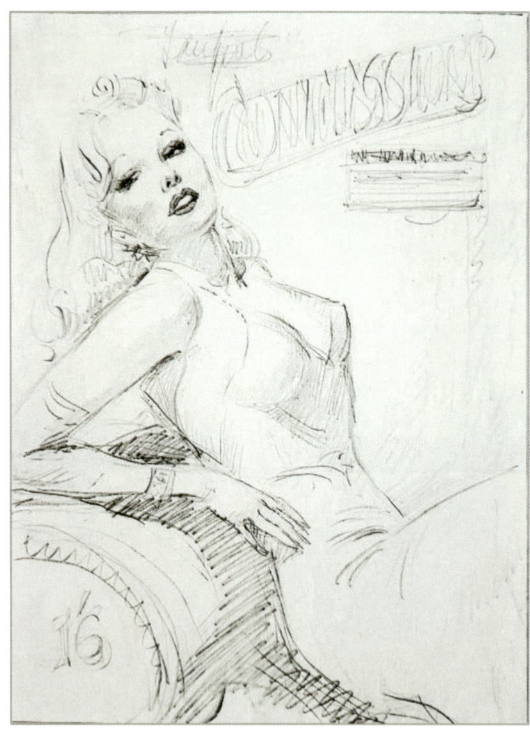

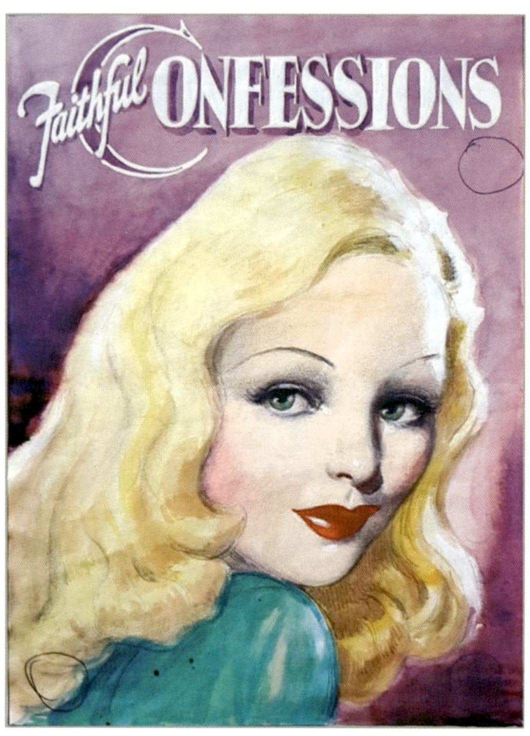

Two roughs prepared by Heade for the cover of the first, and it appears only, edition of the intended periodical *Faithful Confessions* (Martin & Reid, December 1947)

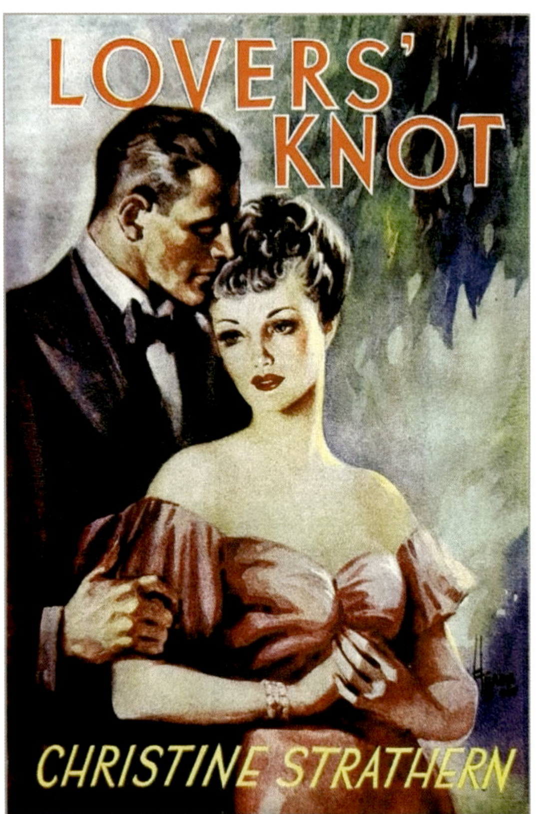

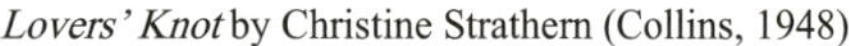

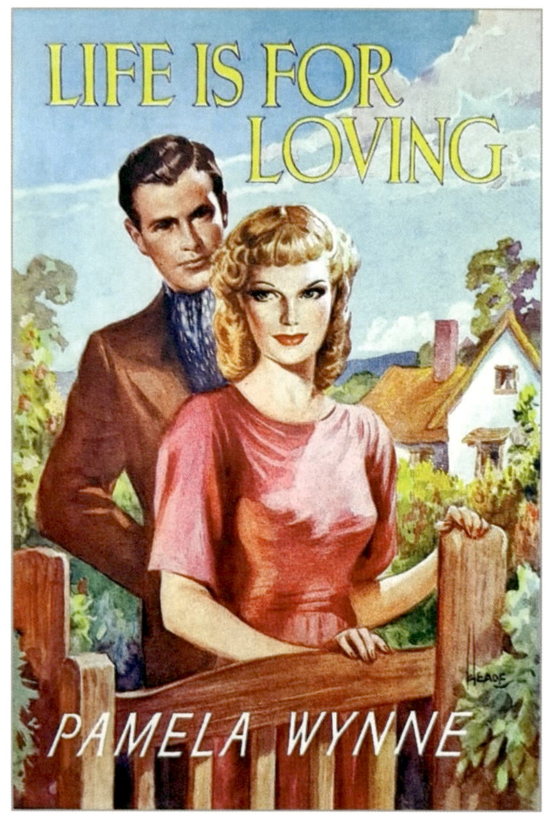

Lovers' Knot by Christine Strathern (Collins, 1948)

Life is for Loving by Pamela Wynne (Collins, 1949)

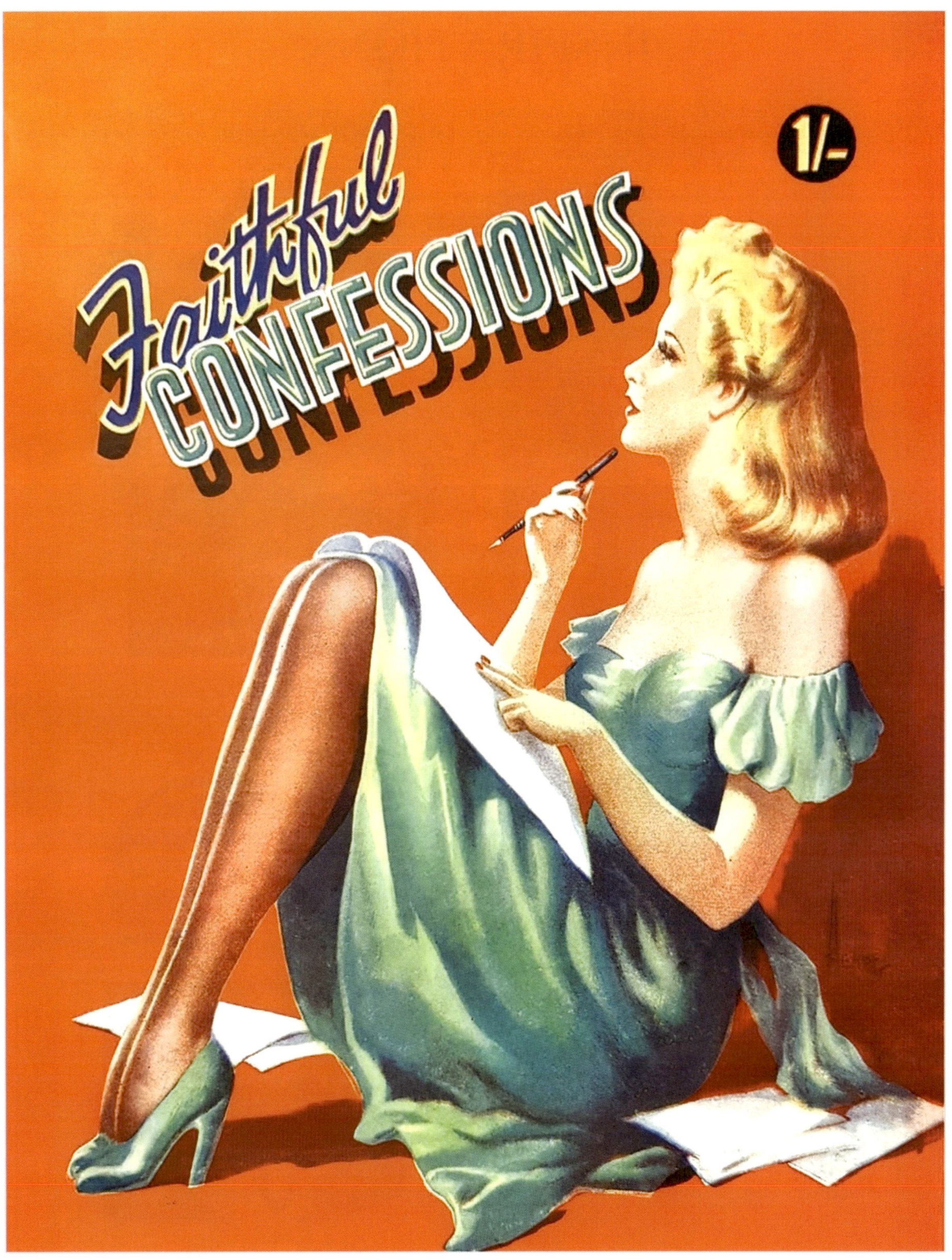

The as-published cover of *Faithful Confessions* #1 (Martin & Reid, December 1947)

INSPIRATIONS

The Art of Reginald Heade – Special Edition described how Heade would often derive inspiration from published sources such as magazines and earlier editions of the books for which he was commissioned to provide covers. Shown below are two further examples from the 1940s.

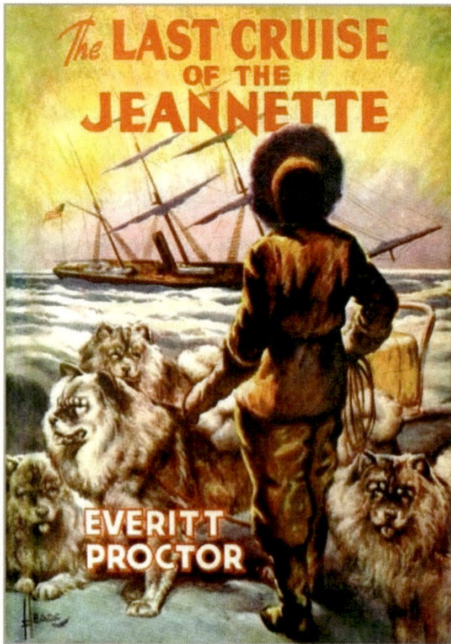
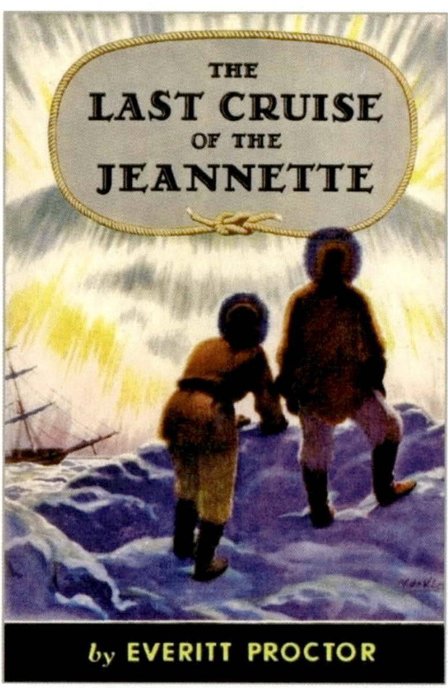

Left: Heade's dustjacket for *The Last Cruise of the Jeannette* by Everitt Proctor (Pictorial Art, 1948). Right: the inspiration: the dustjacket for the American first edition of that title (Westminster Press, 1944).

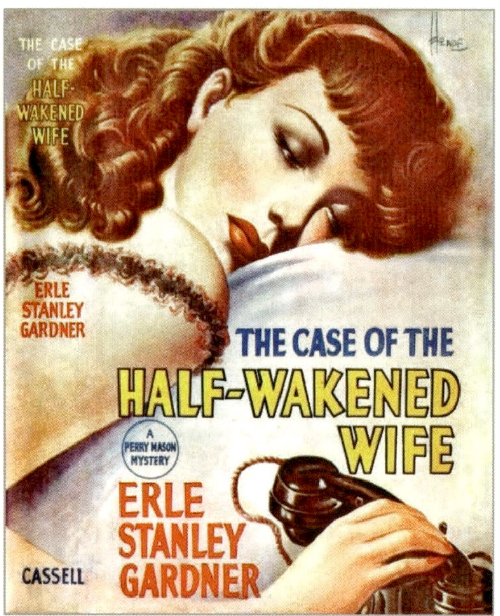
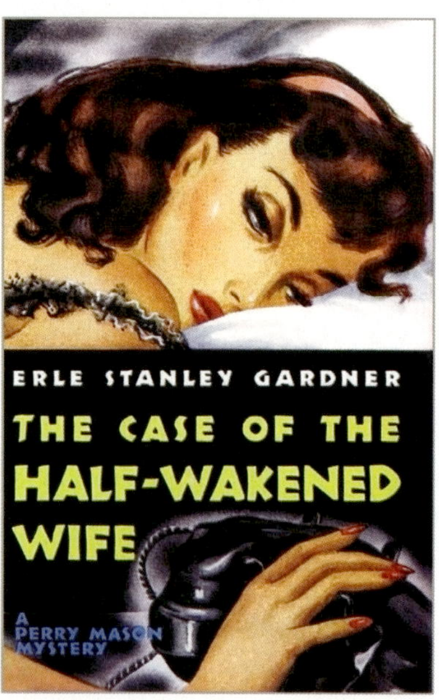

Left: Heade's dustjacket piece for *The Case of the Half-Wakened Wife* by Erle Stanley Gardner (Cassell, 1949). Right: the inspiration: again, the dustjacket for the American first edition (Morrow, 1945).

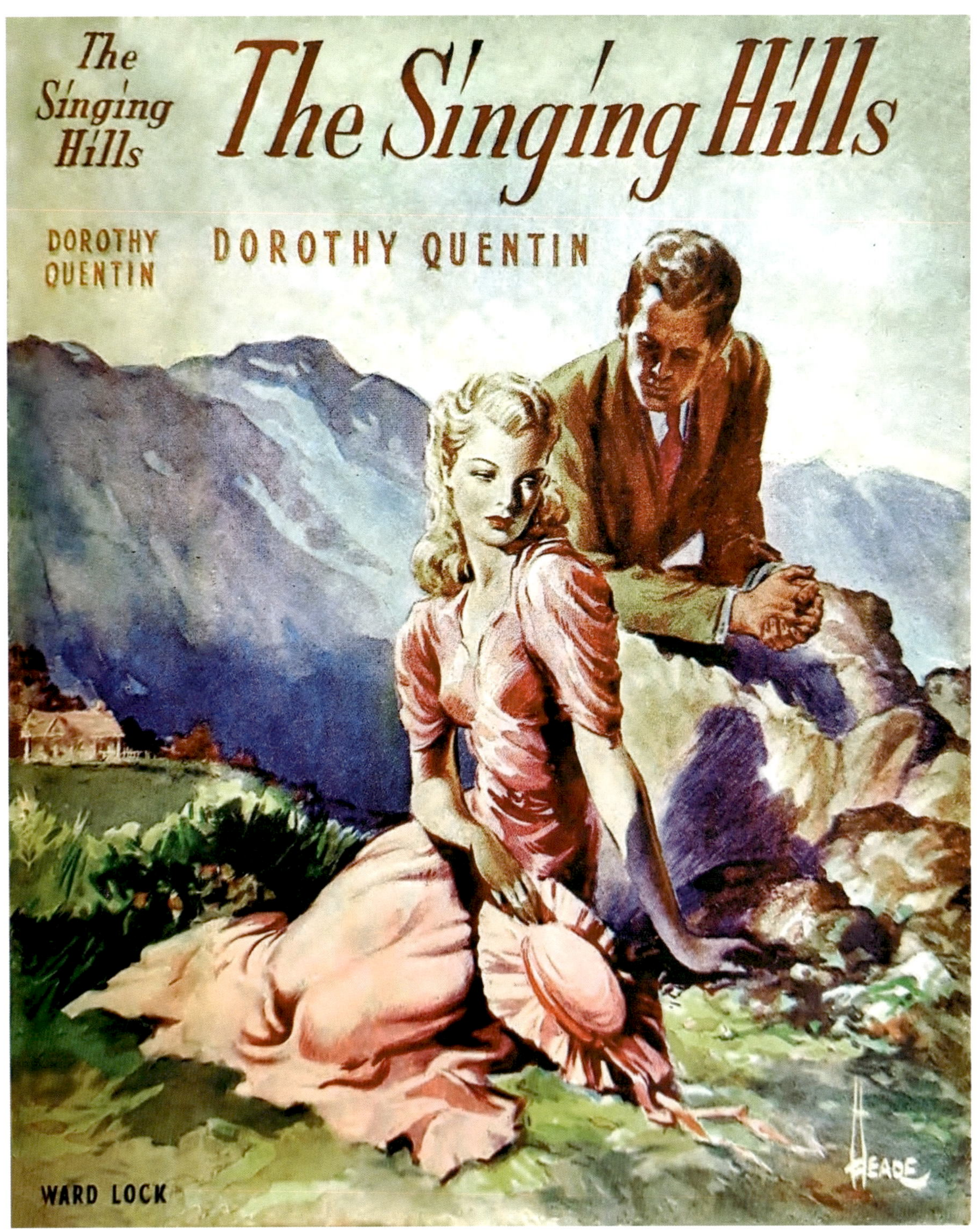

The Singing Hills by Dorothy Quentin (Ward, Lock, 1949)

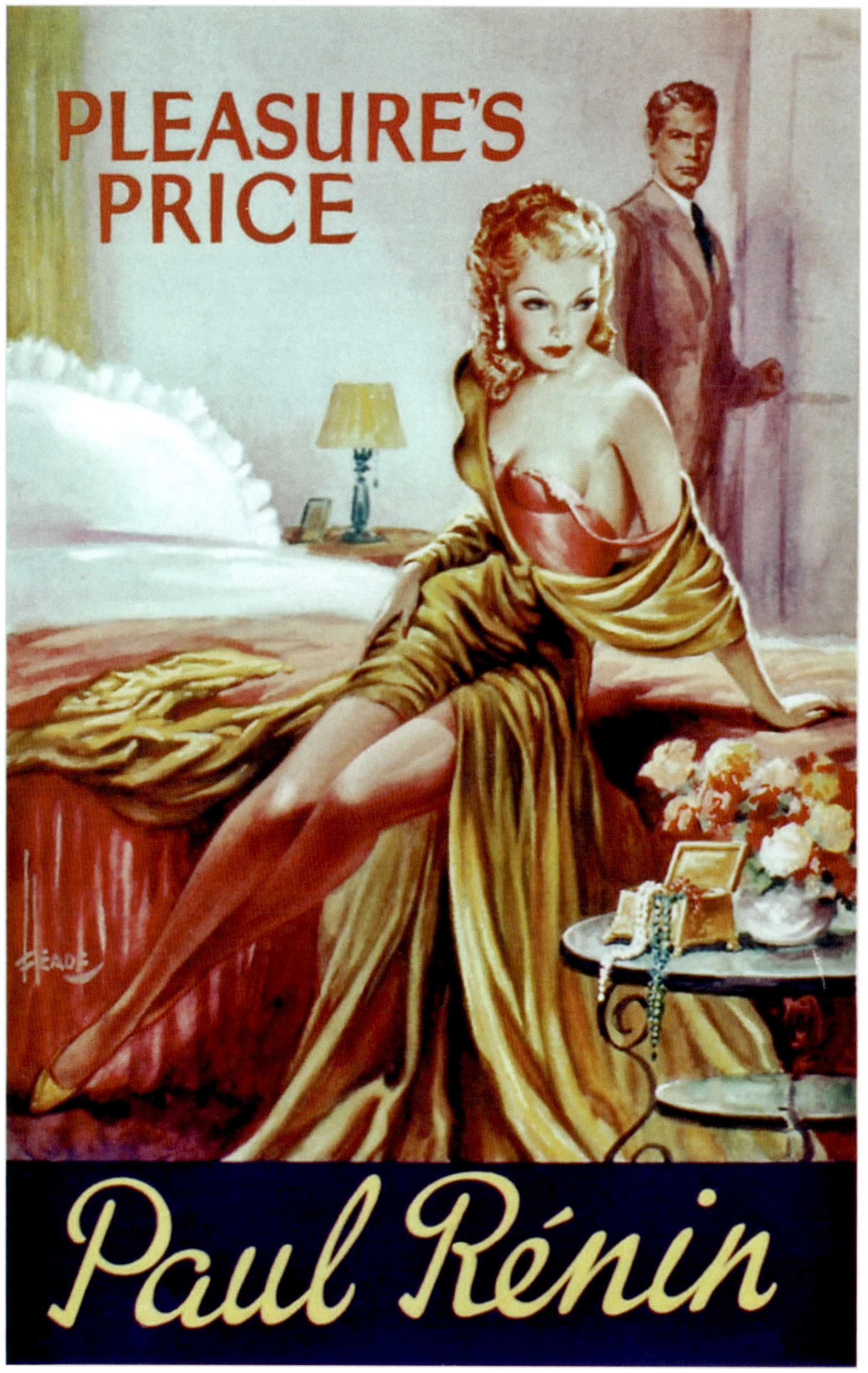

Heade's original painting for *Pleasure's Price* by Paul Rénin (Harborough, 1949). (Image courtesy the Steve Chibnall Collection.)

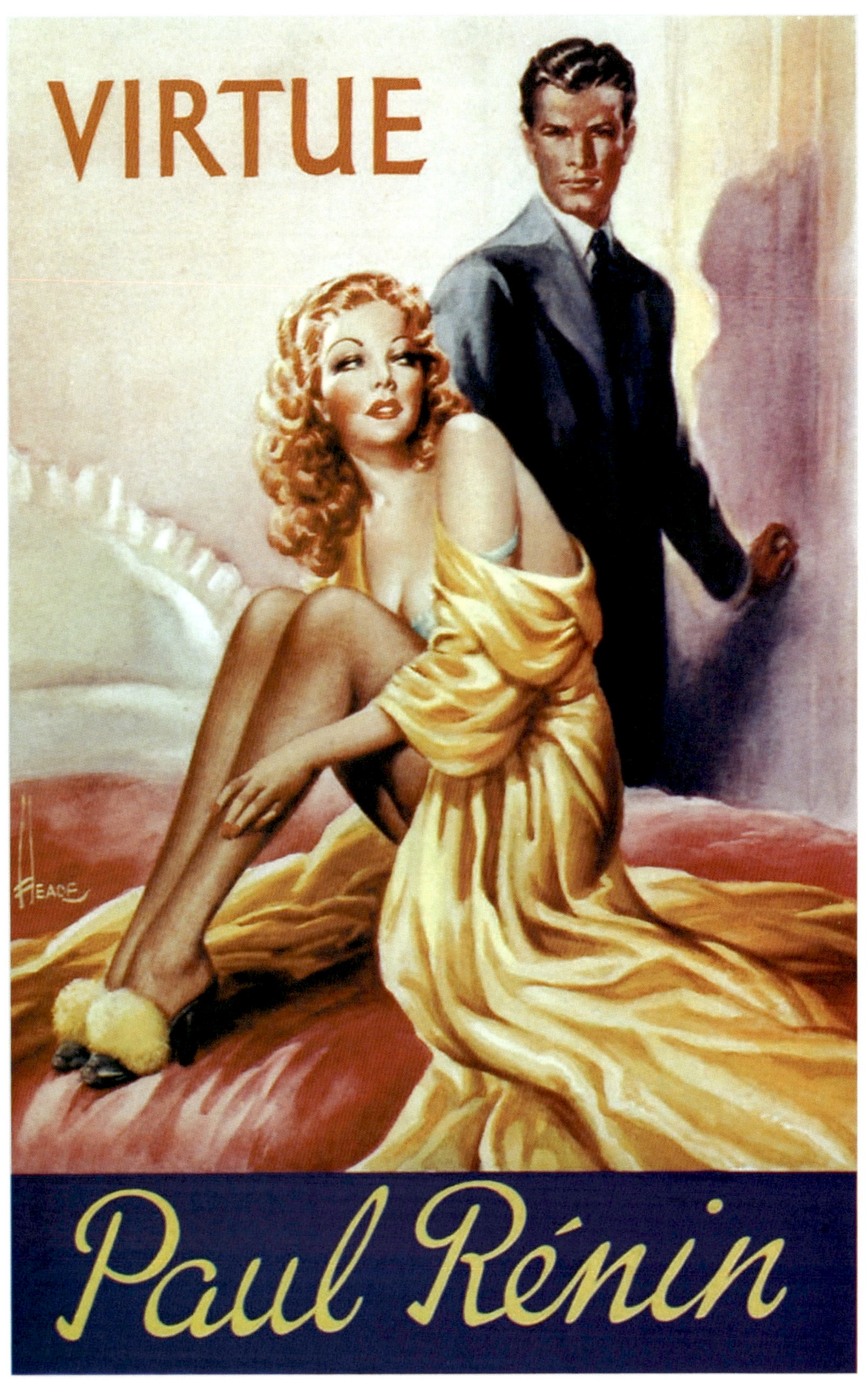

Heade's original painting for *Virtue* by Paul Rénin (Harborough, January 1949). (Image courtesy the Steve Chibnall Collection.)

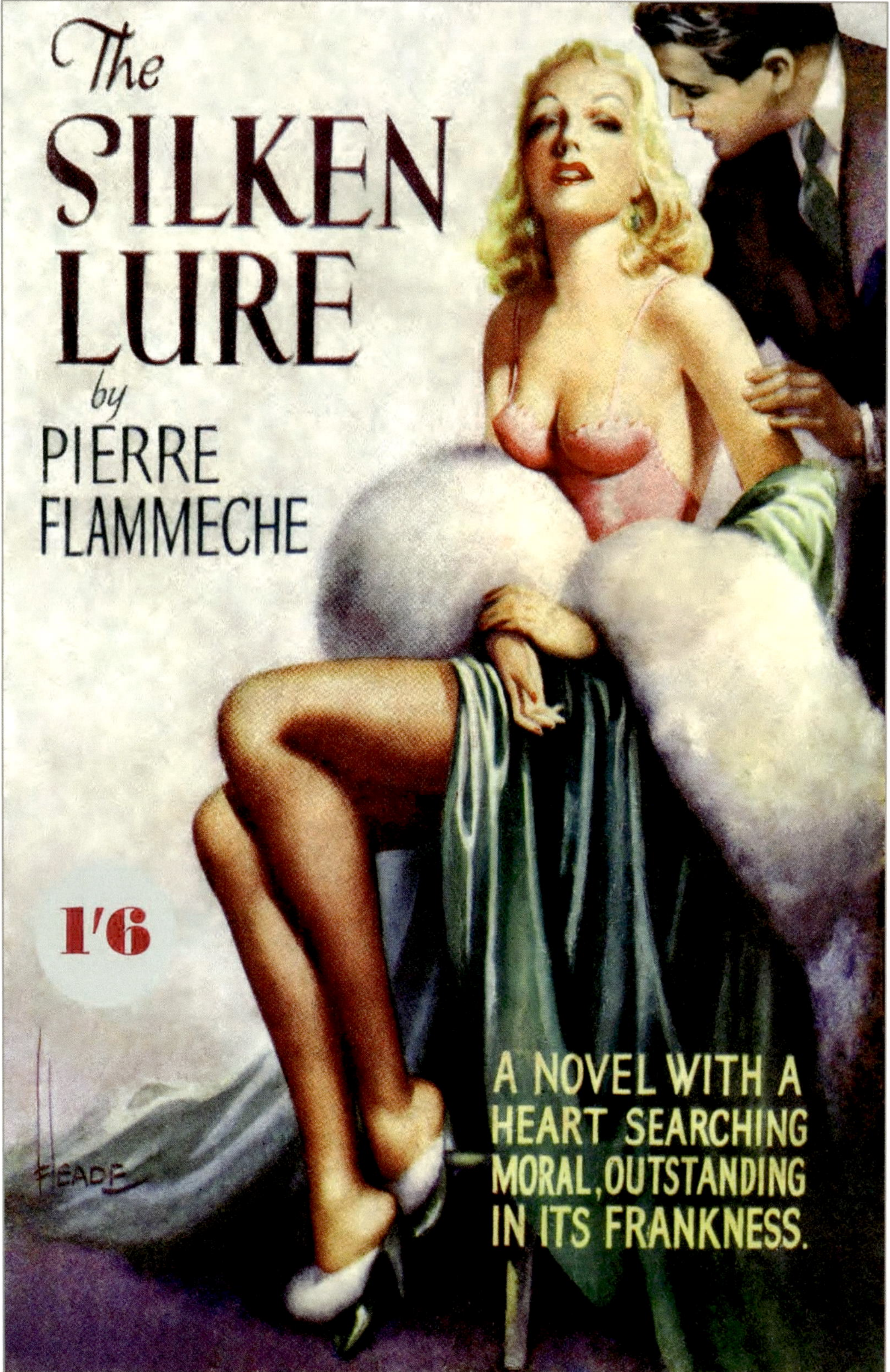

The Silken Lure by Pierre Flammeche (Archer, August 1949). The very rare original British edition of a title – and Heade cover – at one time thought to have appeared only in the US under the Kaywin imprint in 1951. (Image courtesy Steve Holland.)

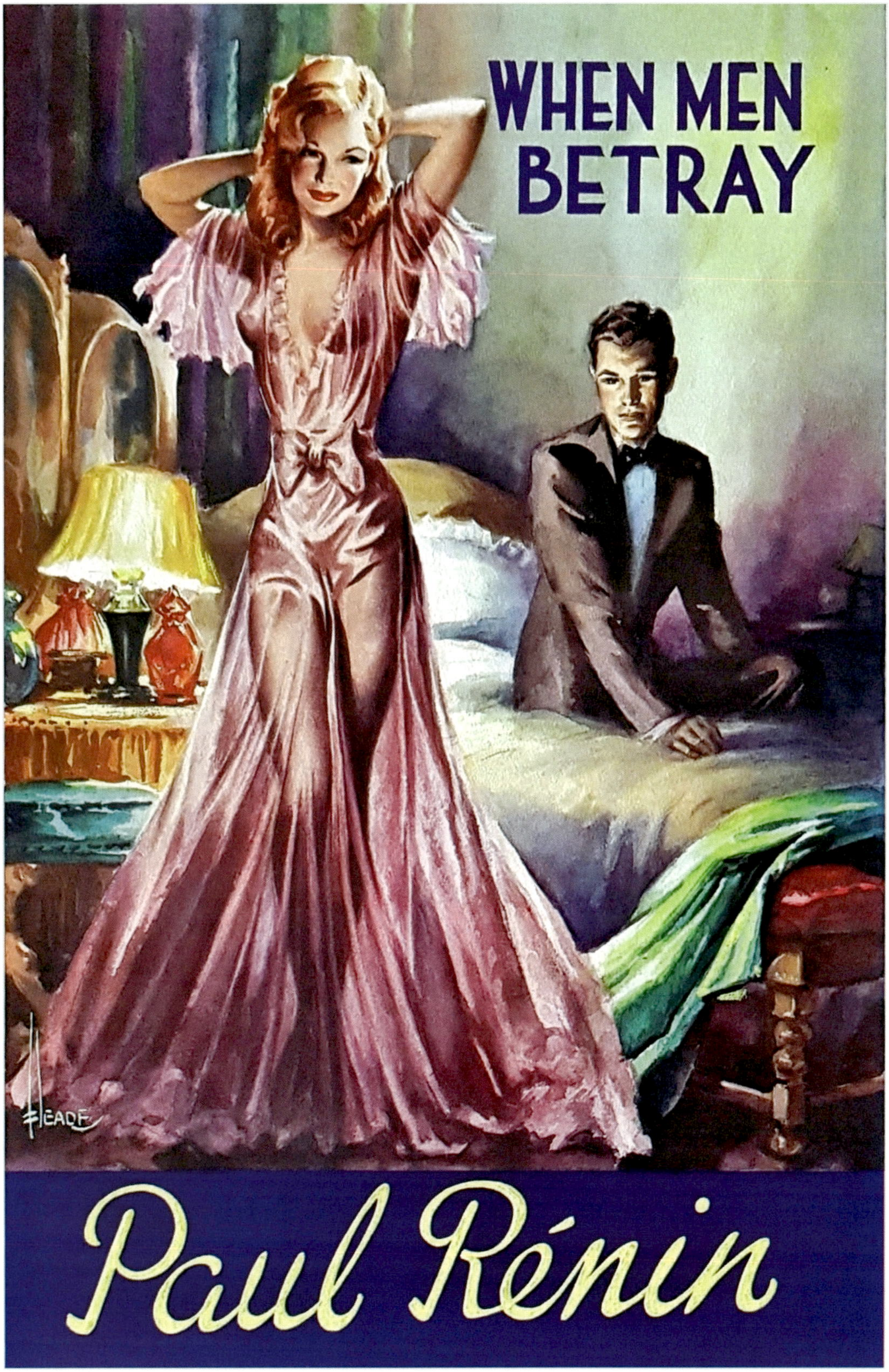

Heade's original painting for *When Men Betray* by Paul Rénin (Harborough, 1949)

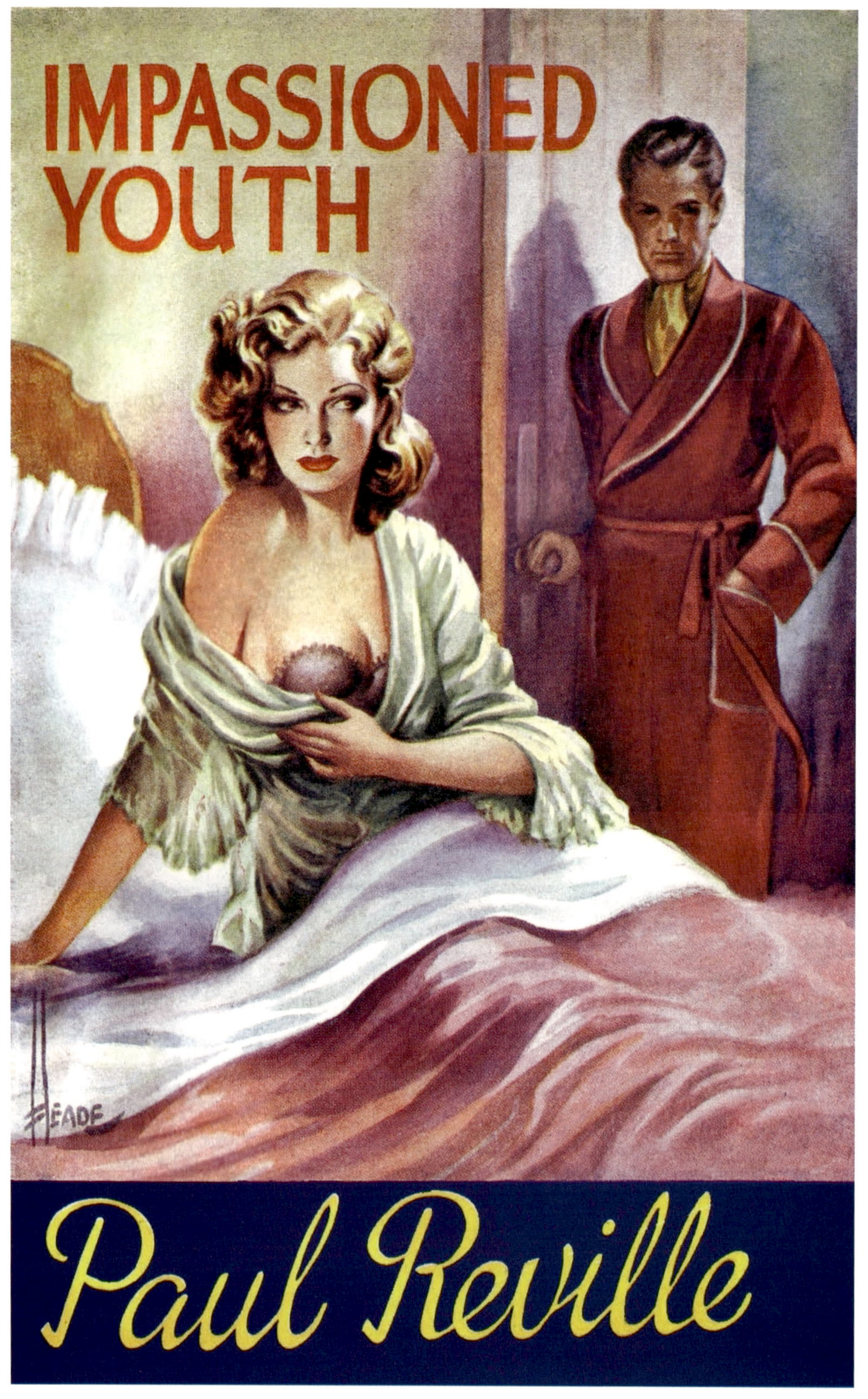

Impassioned Youth by Paul Reville (R & L Locker, c1949)

Make Mine a Shroud by Michael Storme (Harborough, May 1949). The very scarce original British edition of a title more commonly known from its reissue in the US in 1952 under the Leisure Library imprint. This was one of only two Heade-covered Leisure Library books to have made a prior British appearance (the other being the same author's *Hot Dames on Cold Slabs*, first published by Archer in December 1950).

INSPIRATIONS

Below, two examples of Heade pulp paperback covers inspired by 1940s printings of earlier work by other artists.

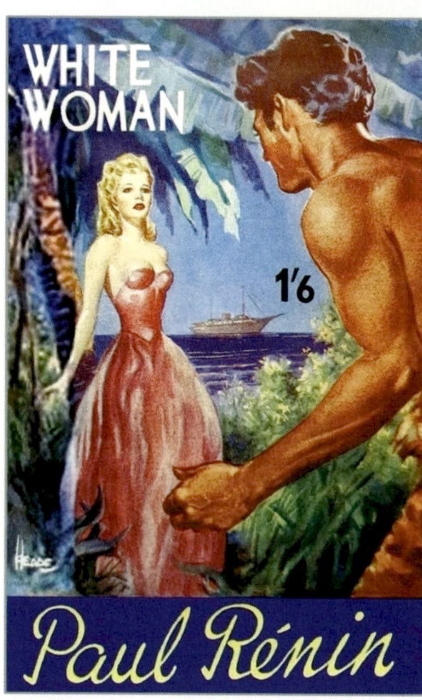
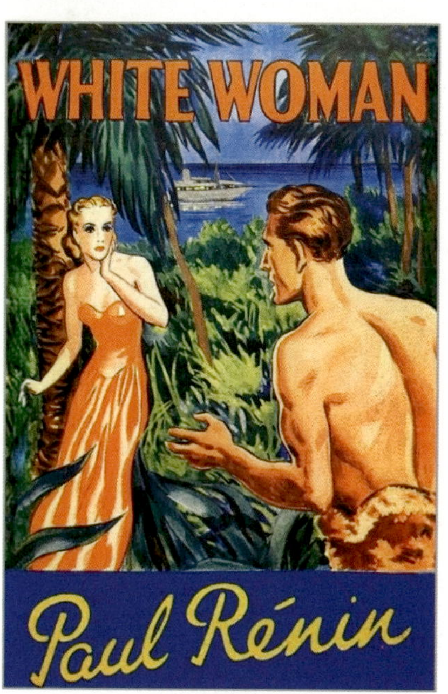

Left: Heade's cover for Paul Rénin's *White Woman* (Harborough, 1949). Right: the inspiration: the cover of a 1940 edition of the same title from publishers Gerald G Swan.

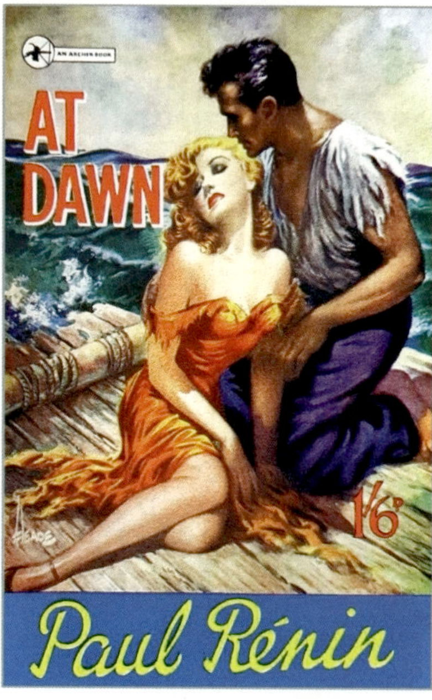
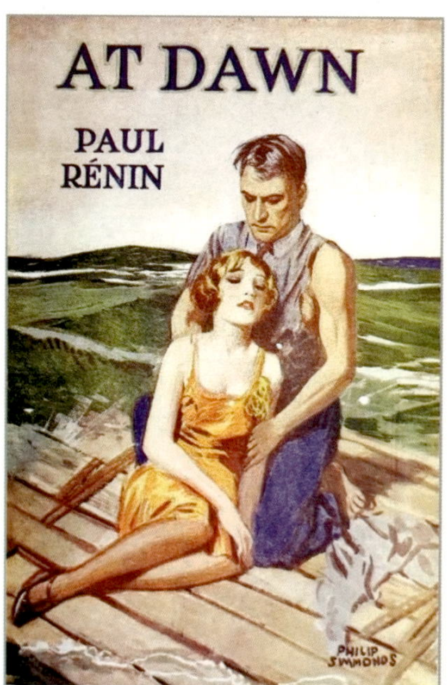

Left: Heade's cover for Paul Rénin's *At Dawn* (Archer, 1953). Right: the inspiration: a 1940 Gerald G Swan edition of the same title, with signed Philip Simmonds cover art originally painted for the c1930 Fiction Features first edition.

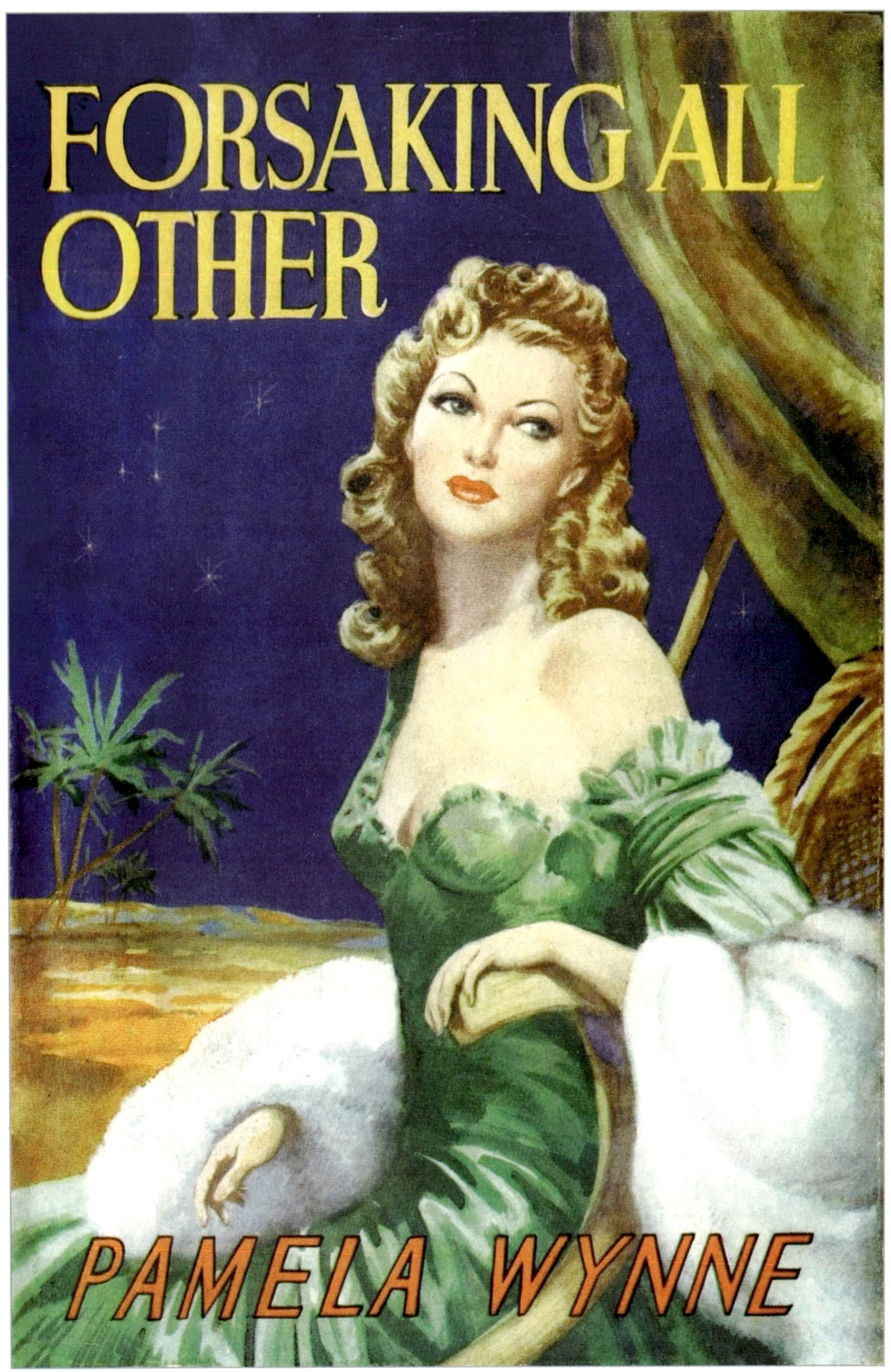

Forsaking All Other by Pamela Wynne (Collins, 1949)

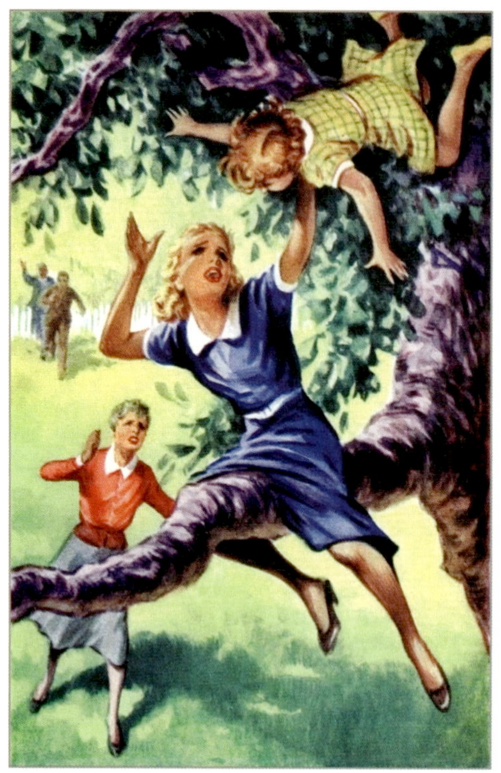

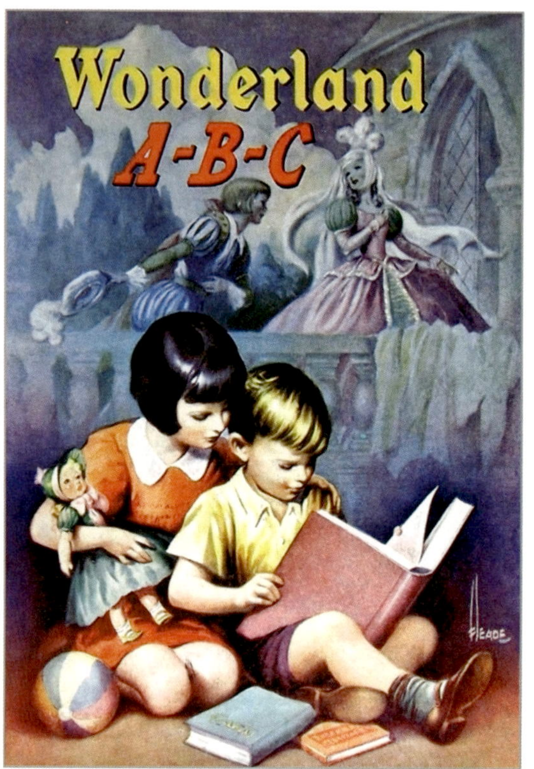

Frontispiece, *Maid of the Abbey* by Elsie J Oxenham (Collins, 1949)

Wonderland A-B-C (Juvenile Productions, c1949)

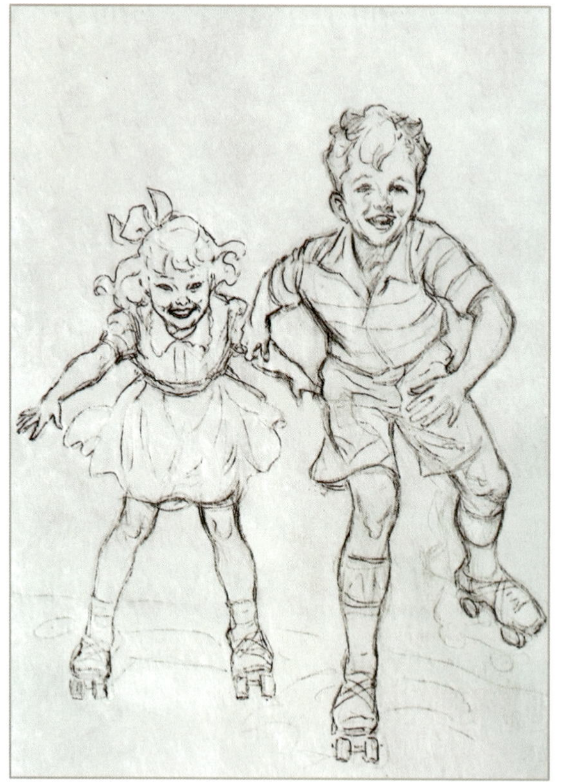

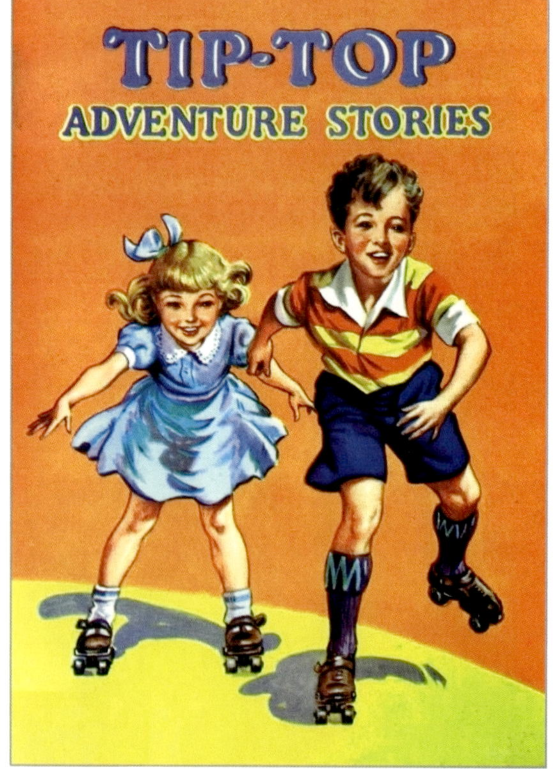

Heade's original rough and the as-published cover of *Tip-Top Adventure Stories* (Amex, c1949). The girl was based by the artist on one of the many photographs that he and his wife took of their daughter Sally.

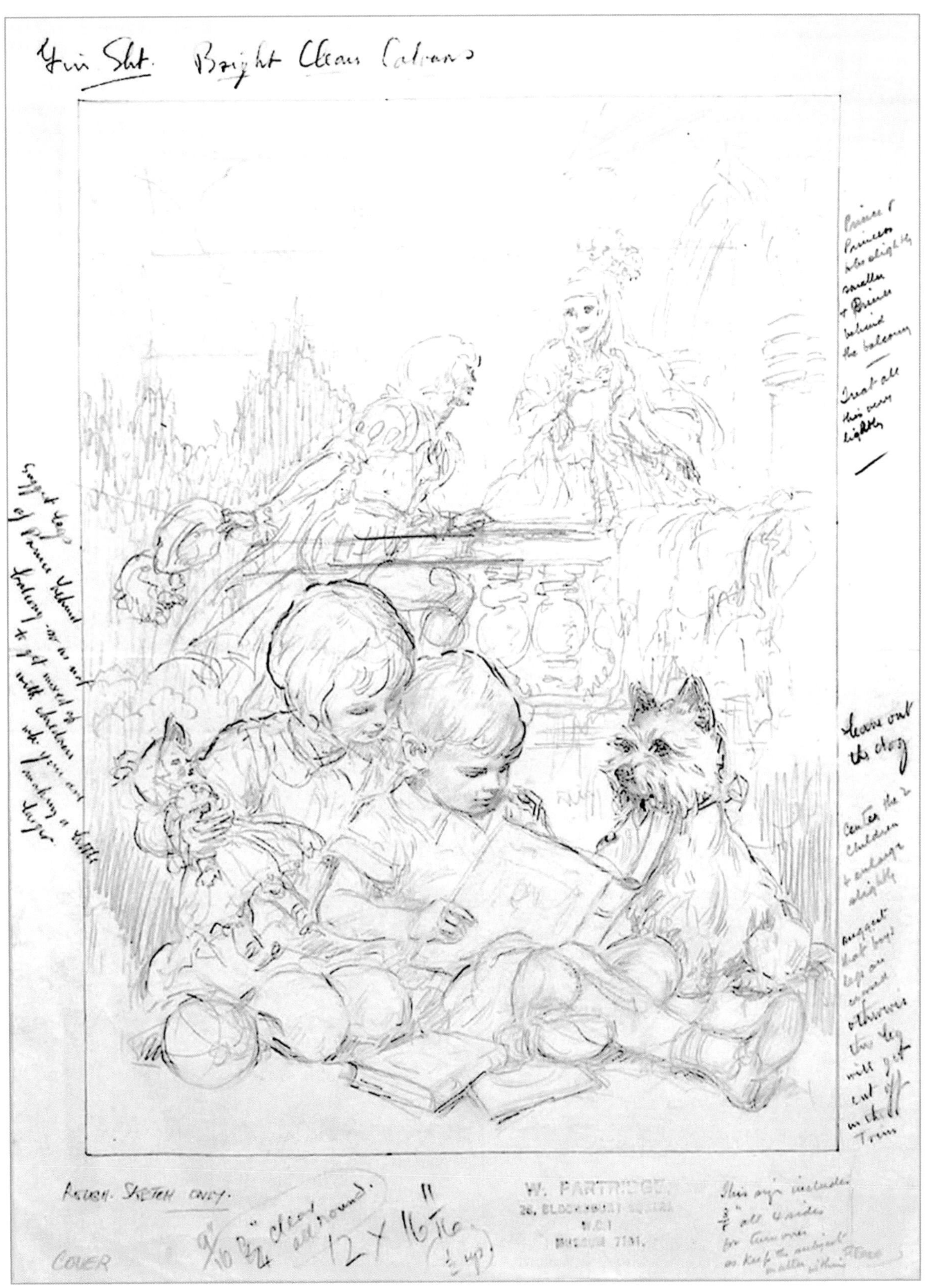

Heade's original rough for *Wonderland A-B-C* (Juvenile Productions, c1949)

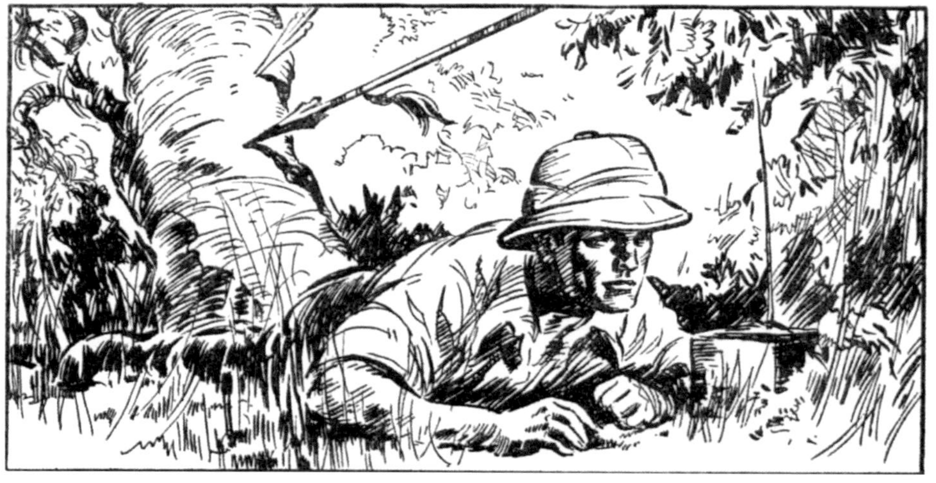

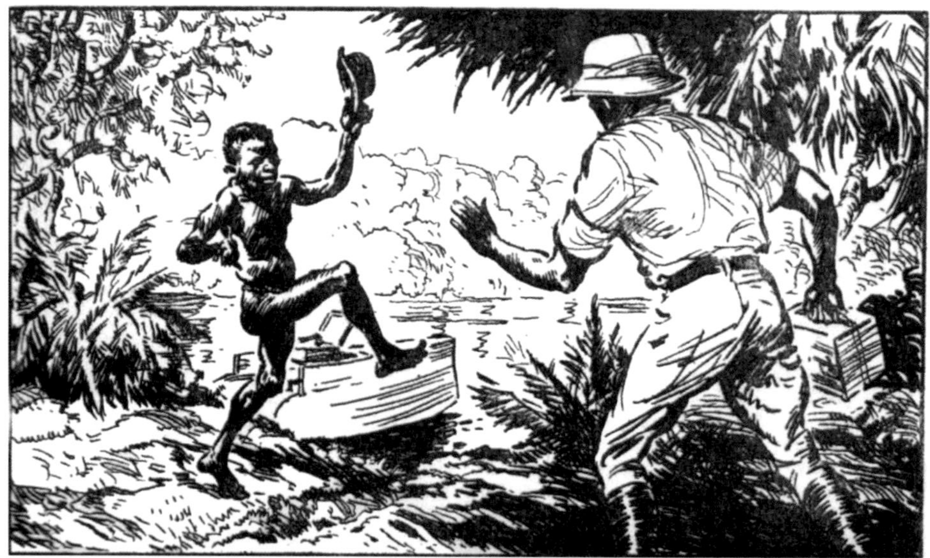

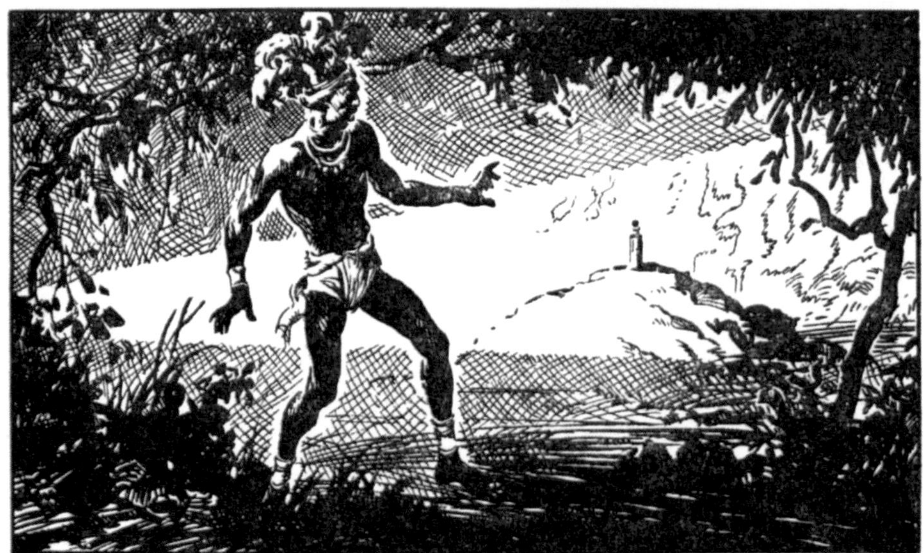

Above: the first three of the five black-and-white illustrations that Heade provided for the short story 'Jungle Joe' by an uncredited author in *Knockout Fun Book 1950* (Amalgamated, 1949).

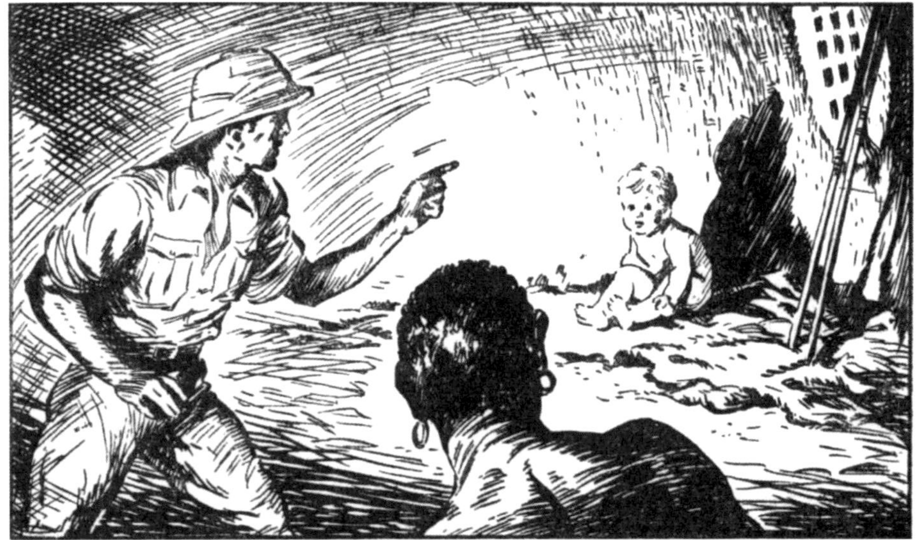

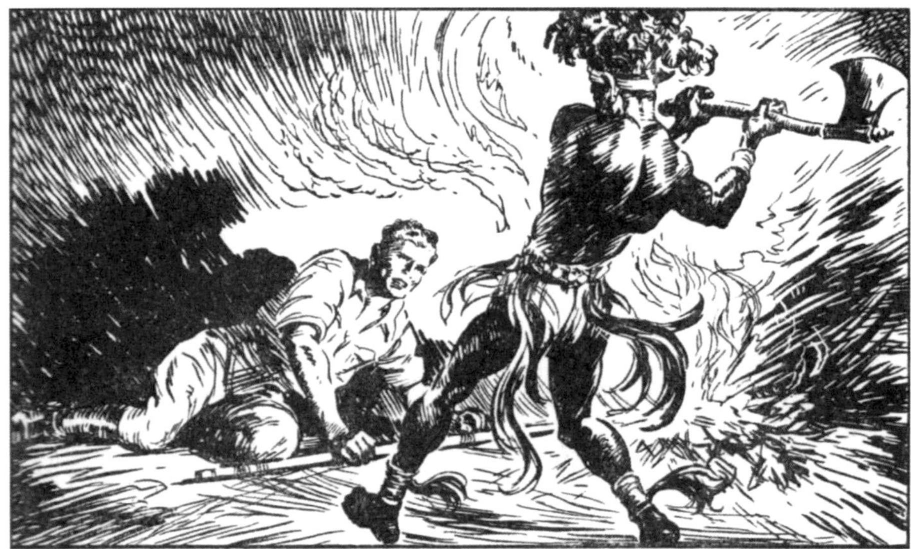

Above: the last two of the five black-and-white illustrations that Heade provided for 'Jungle Joe' in *Knockout Fun Book 1950* (Amalgamated, 1949).

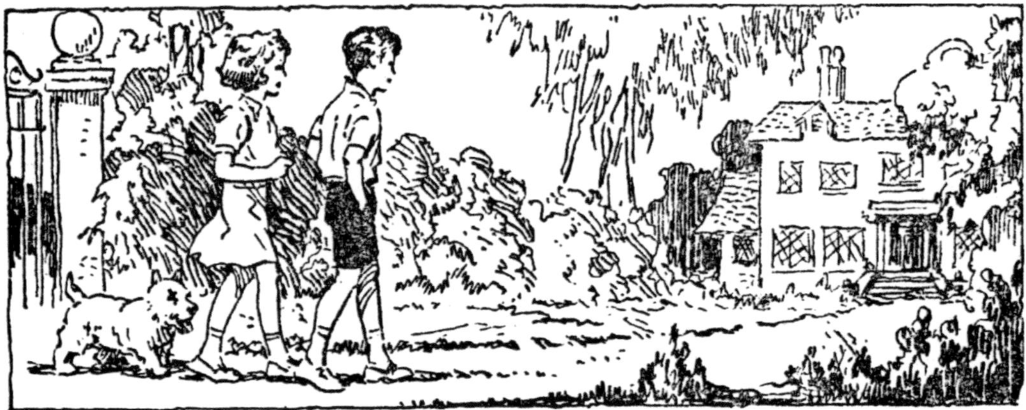

Above: one of Heade's illustrations for 'Patch' by C M Drury, originally published in *The Treasure Box* (The Children's Press, 1947) with red and blue highlight colours probably added by the publisher, then in black-and-white in *The Children's Treasure Book* (Collins, c1950).

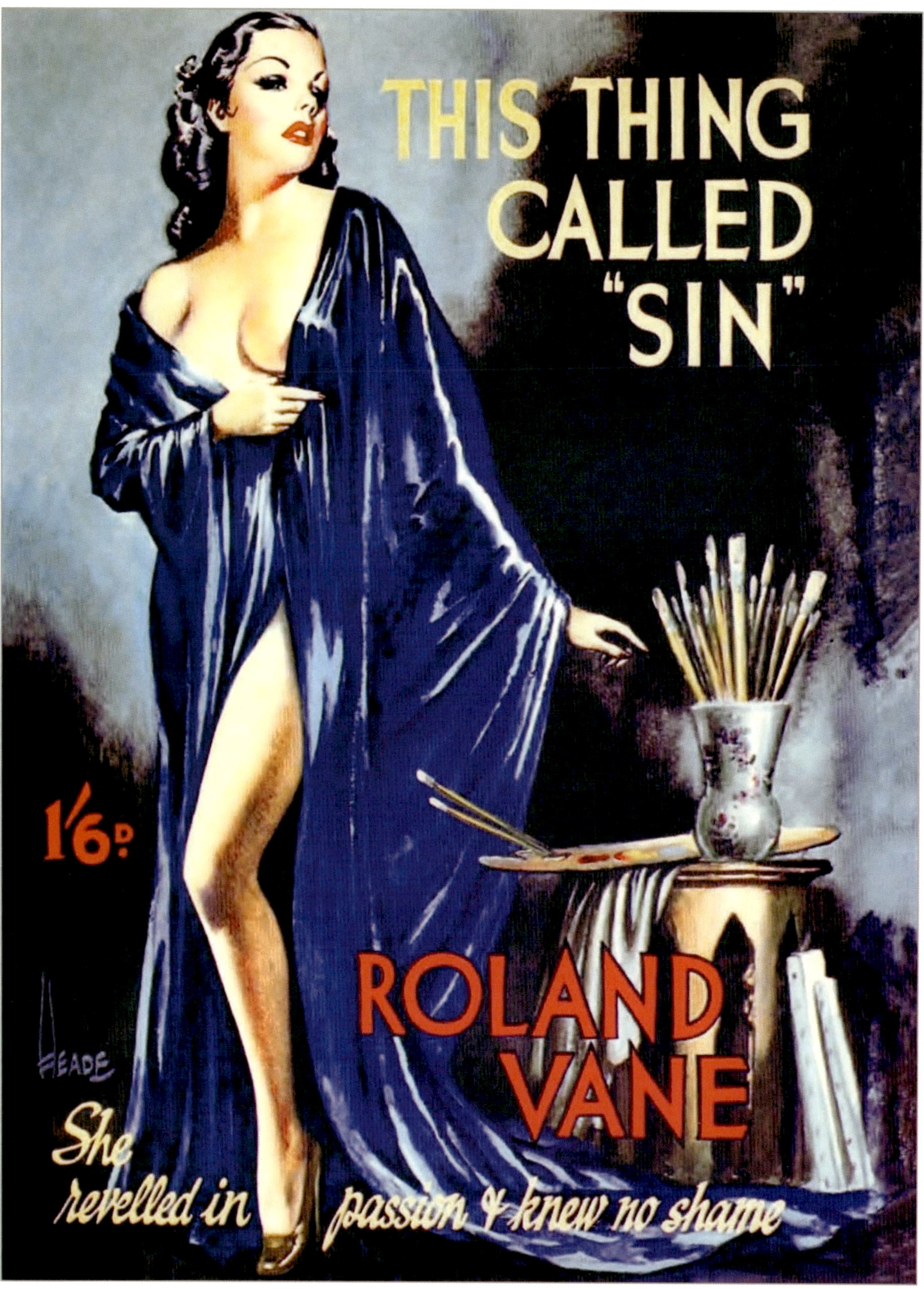

Heade's original painting for *This Thing Called 'Sin'* by Roland Vane (Archer, November 1950)

THE 1950s

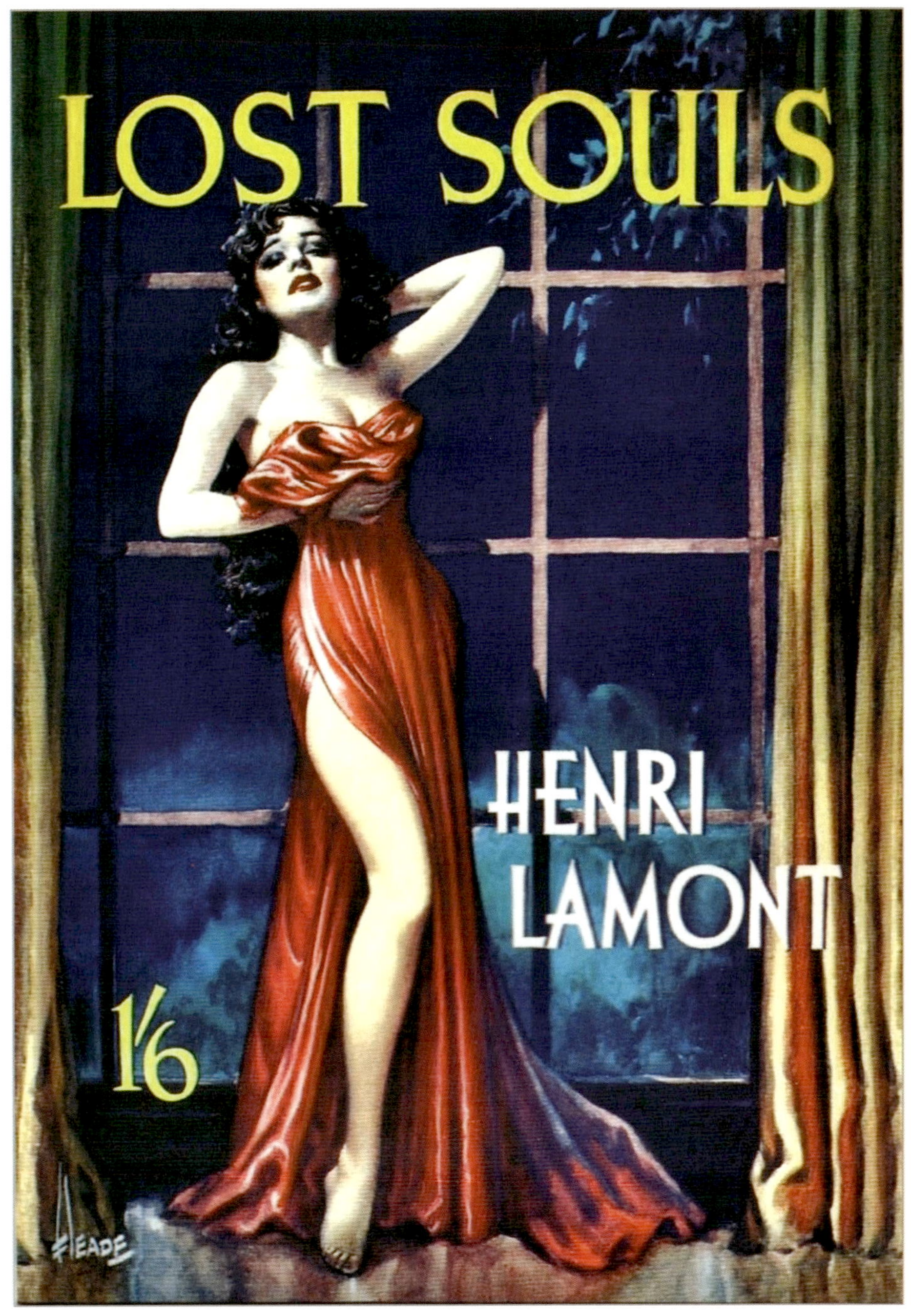

Above: Heade's original painting for *Lost Souls* by Henri Lamont (Archer, May 1953)

WORRALS - THE ILLUSTRATED EDITIONS

At the end of the 1940s, Heade supplied six signed dustjacket paintings for Lutterworth Press's editions of W E Johns' 'Worrals' series of adventure books for girls: specifically, *Worrals of the W.A.A.F.* (1948), *Worrals Carries On* (1948), *Worrals Down Under* (1948), *Worrals in the Wastelands* (1949), *Worrals Goes Afoot* (1949) and *Worrals Investigates* (1950). When these first appeared, a section of Heade's dustjacket art was reproduced inside each as a full colour frontispiece, but some (though not all) printings of *Worrals Investigates* also included four other two-colour illustrations; and in 1950, the same publisher reissued *Worrals of the W.A.A.F.*, *Worrals Carries On*, *Worrals in the Wastelands* and *Worrals Down Under* in 'New Illustrated Edition' form, with four similar two-colour illustrations added to each (though, again, not in all printings, despite the 'New Illustrated Edition' tag). (No such edition of *Worrals Goes Afoot* has yet been identified.) In all cases, these additional two-colour illustrations were unsigned, and while it is possible that they were by a different artist, copying Heade's style and using the character likenesses already established by him in his dustjacket pieces, it is also possible that (as some W E Johns aficionados contend) they were actually by Heade himself. All 20 of these rare illustrations are reproduced over the next five pages.

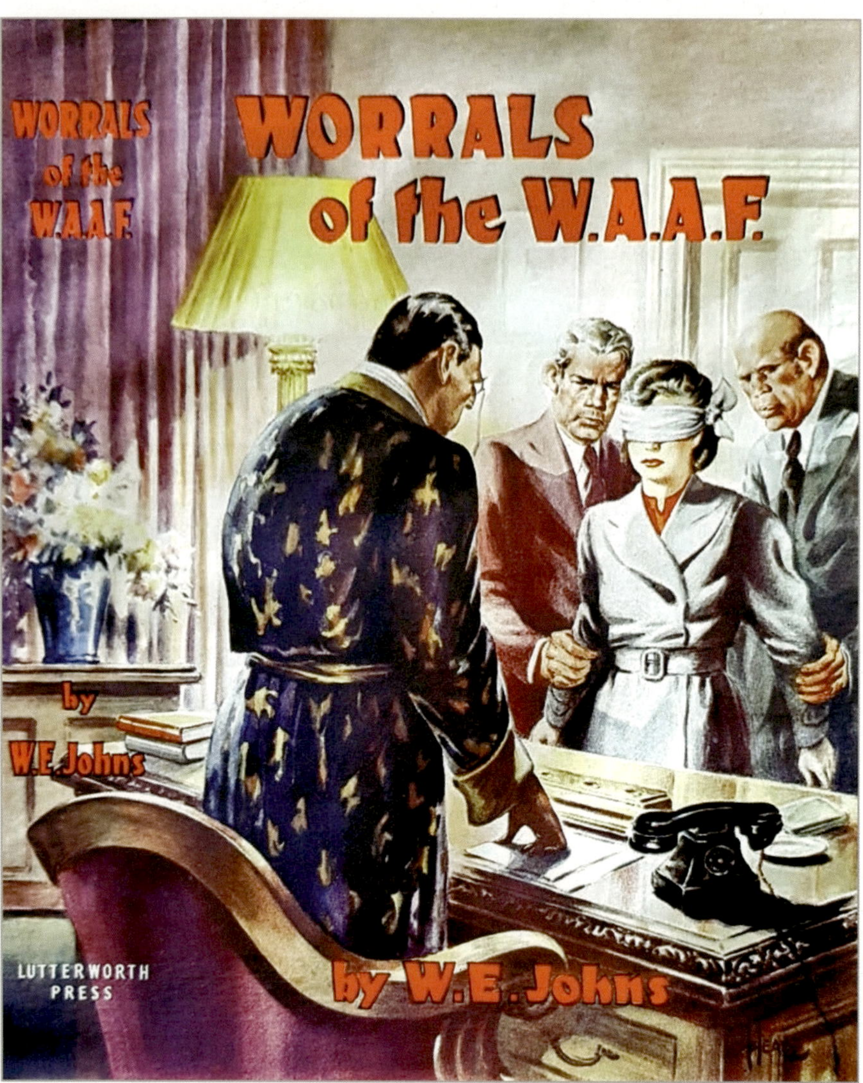

Above: Heade's full dustjacket painting for *Worrals of the W.A.A.F.* The artist's signature (at bottom right corner) is not visible on the as-printed dustjacket; a fact that has previously led to some uncertainty as to the attribution.

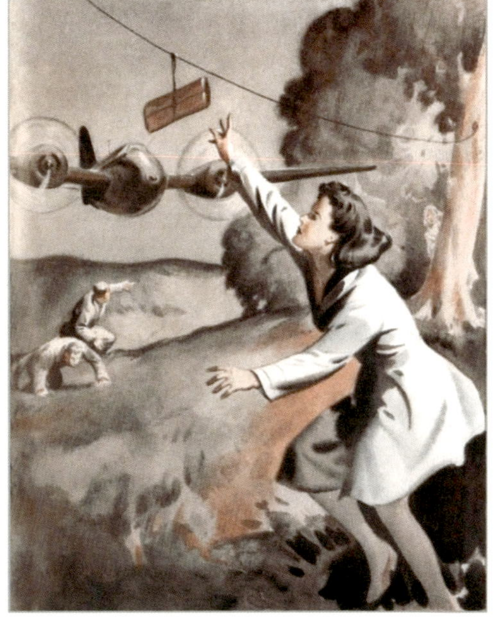
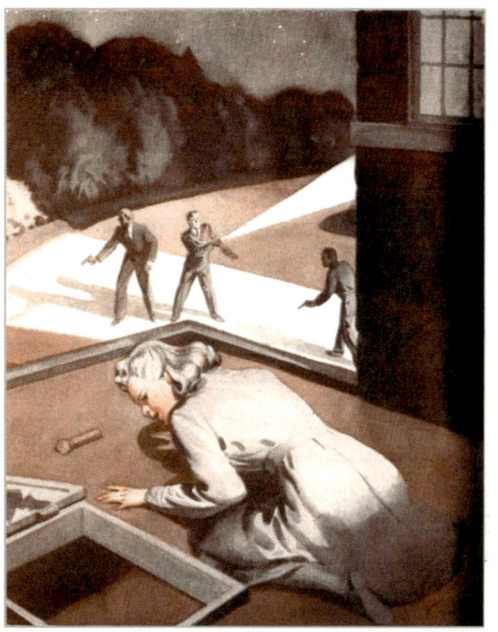
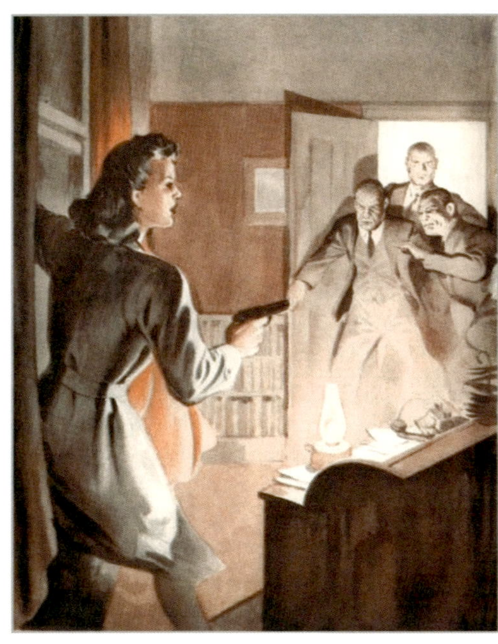
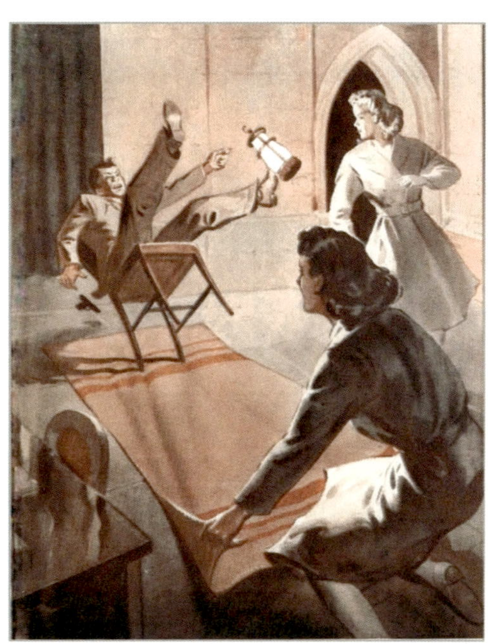

Above: the four internal two-colour illustrations, possibly by Heade, that appeared in some printings of the 'New Illustrated Edition' version of *Worrals of the W.A.A.F.* (Lutterworth, 1950).

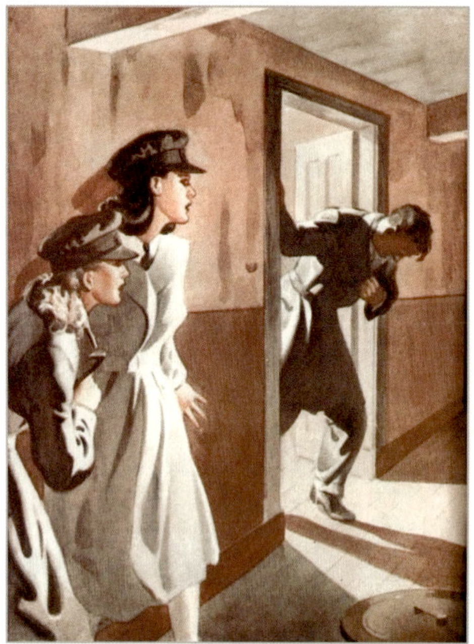
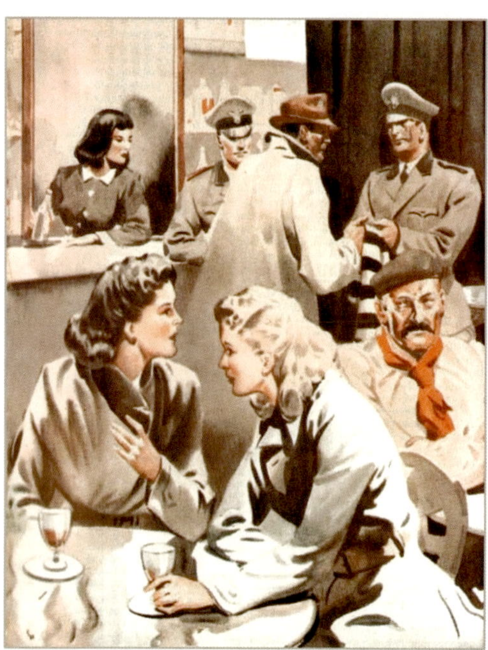
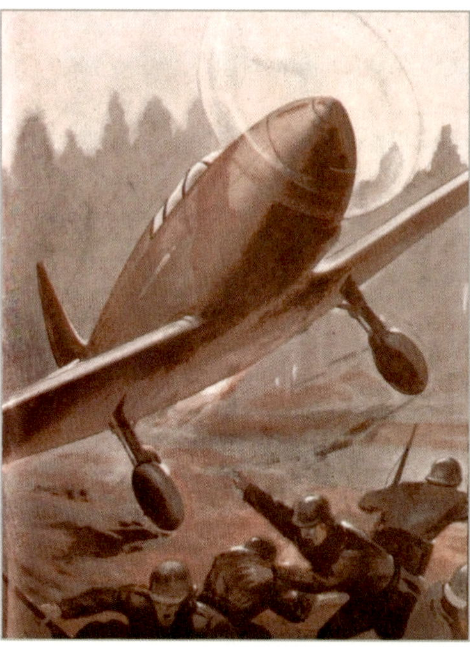
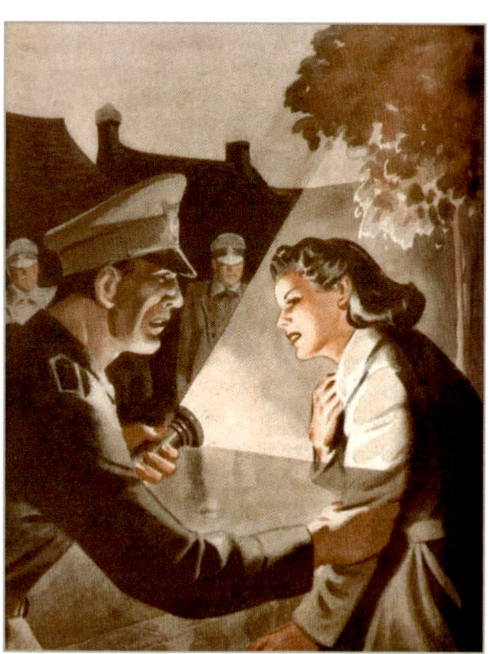

Above: the four internal two-colour illustrations, possibly by Heade, that appeared in some printings of the 'New Illustrated Edition' version of *Worrals Carries On* (Lutterworth, 1950).

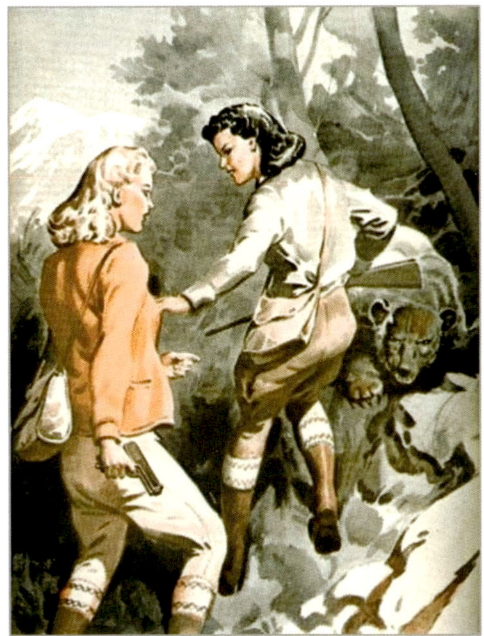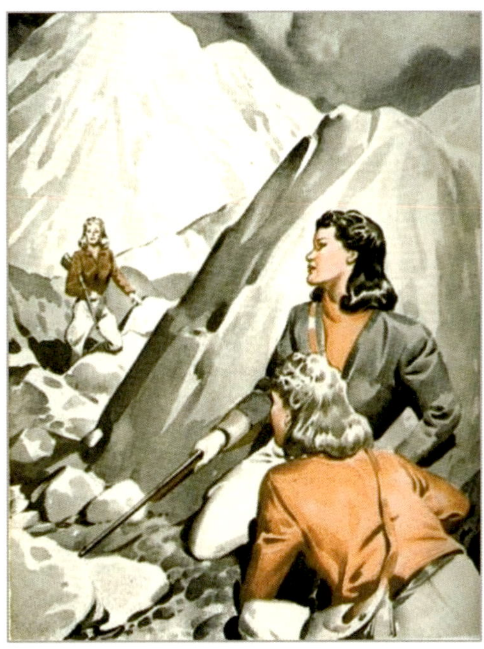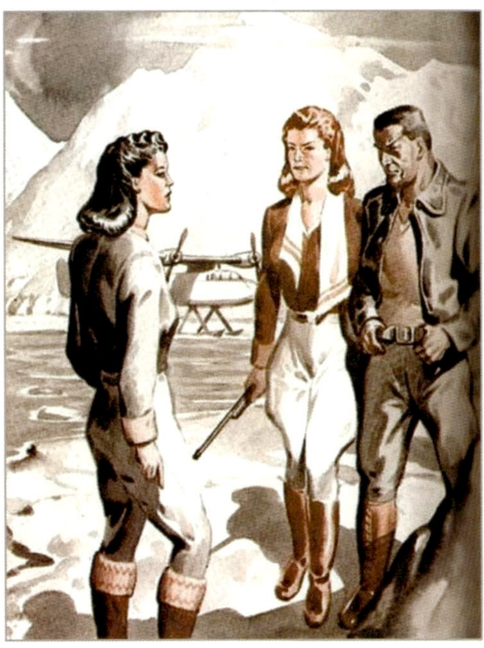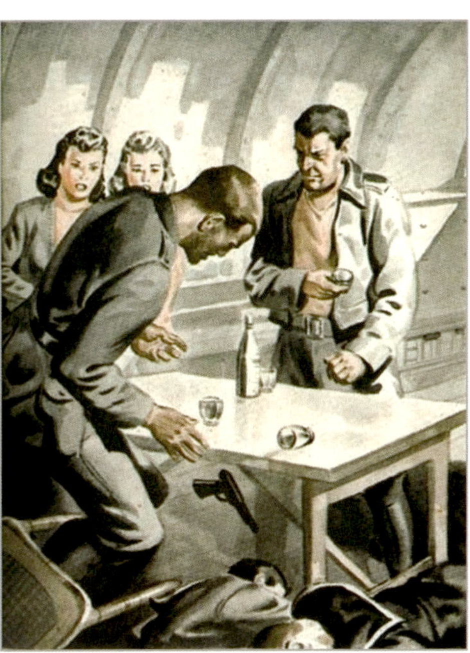

Above: the four internal two-colour illustrations, possibly by Heade, that appeared in some printings of the 'New Illustrated Edition' version of *Worrals in the Wastelands* (Lutterworth, 1950).

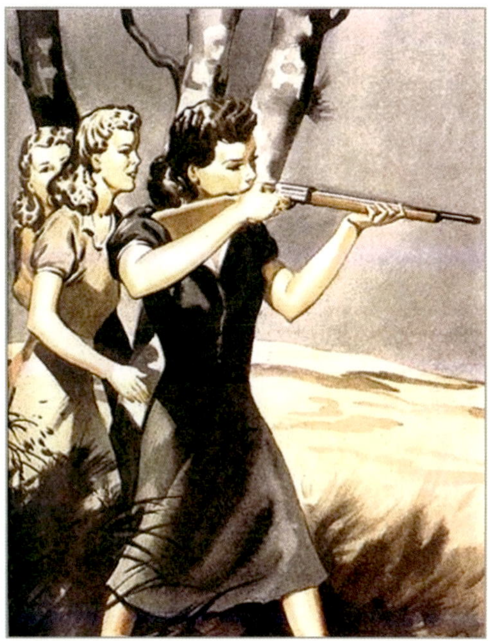
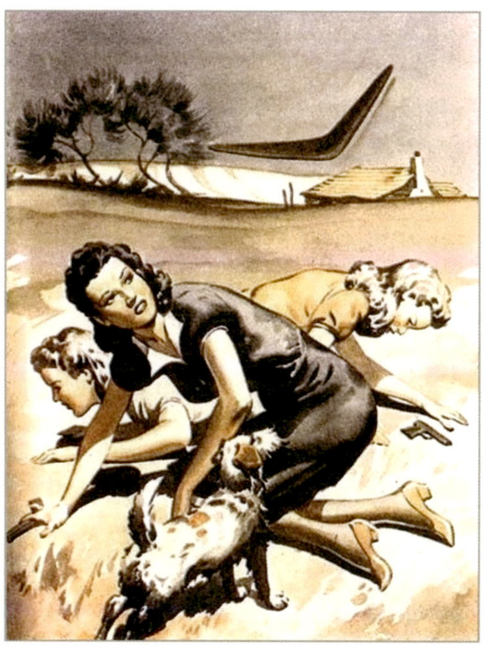
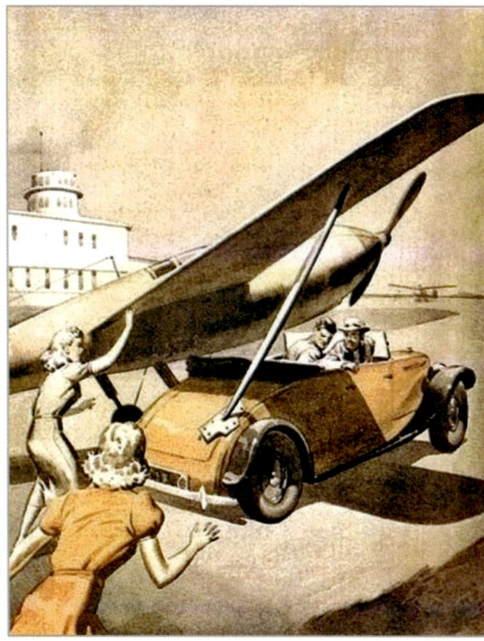
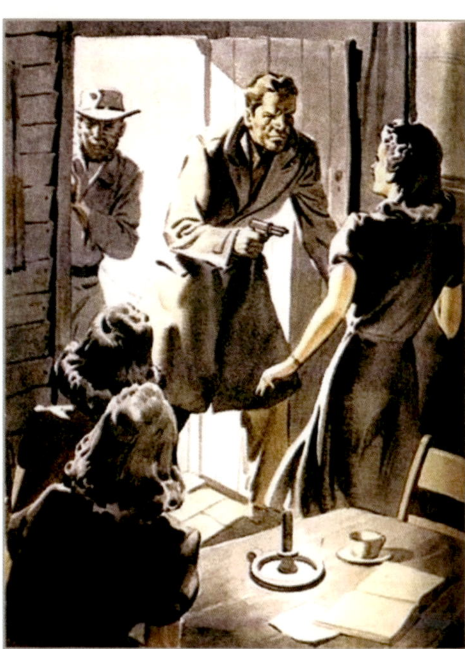

Above: the four internal two-colour illustrations, possibly by Heade, that appeared in some printings of the 'New Illustrated Edition' version of *Worrals Down Under* (Lutterworth, 1950).

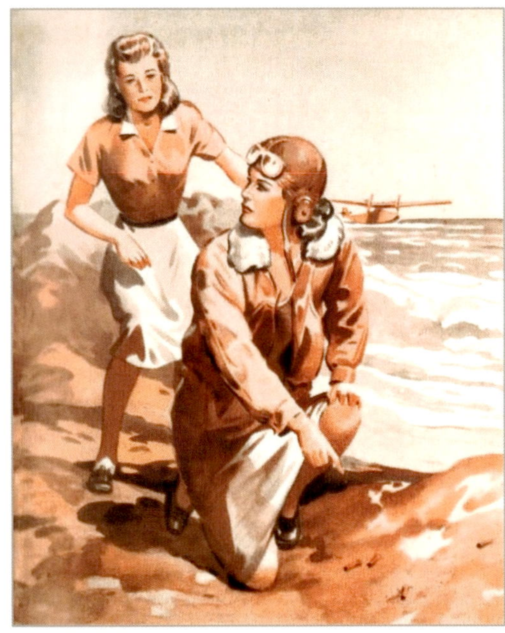 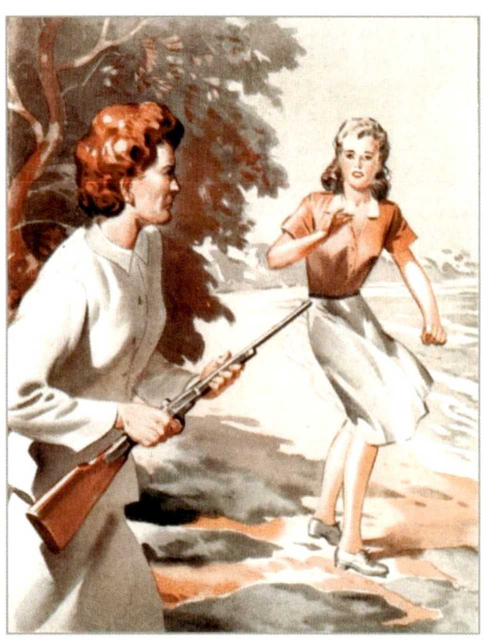

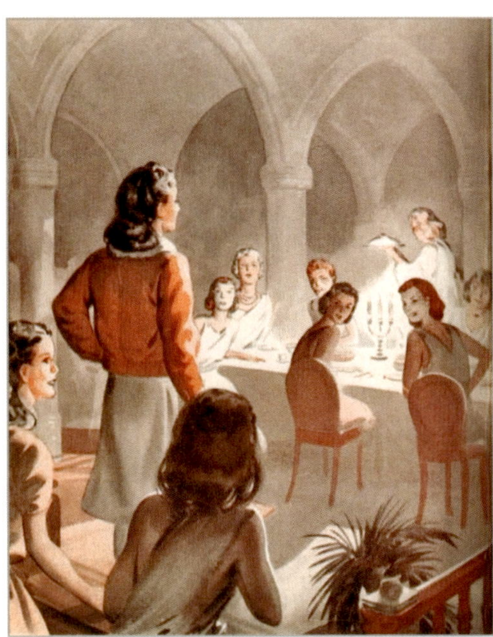 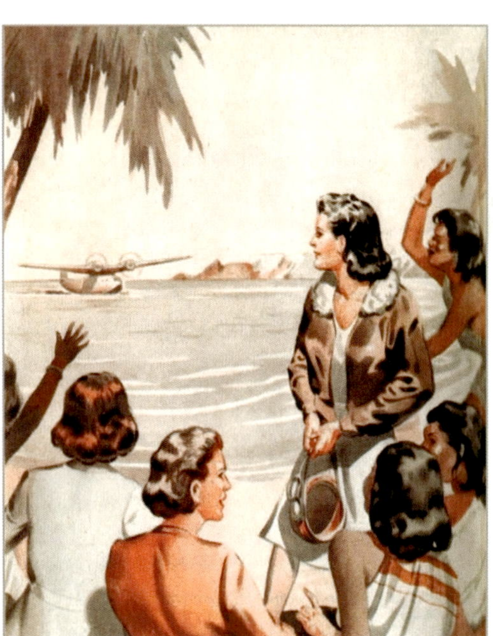

Above: the four internal two-colour illustrations, possibly by Heade, that appeared in some printings of the first edition of *Worrals Investigates* (Lutterworth, 1950).

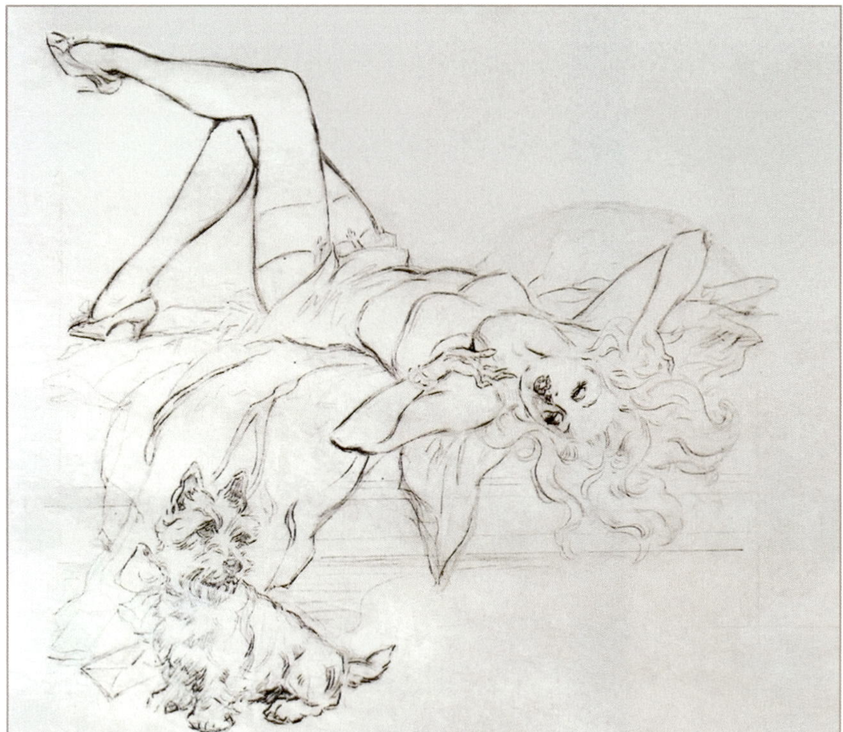

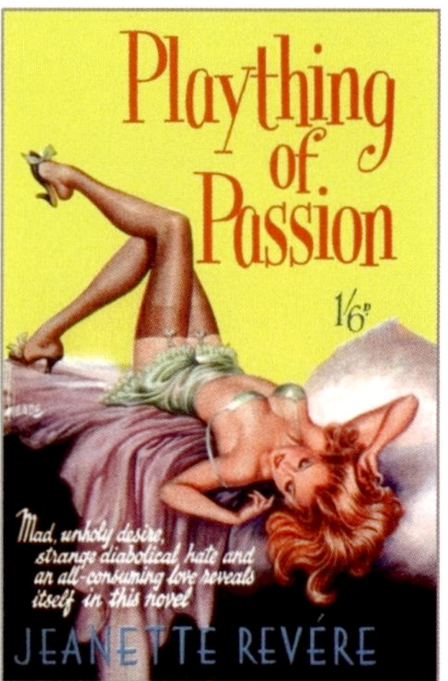

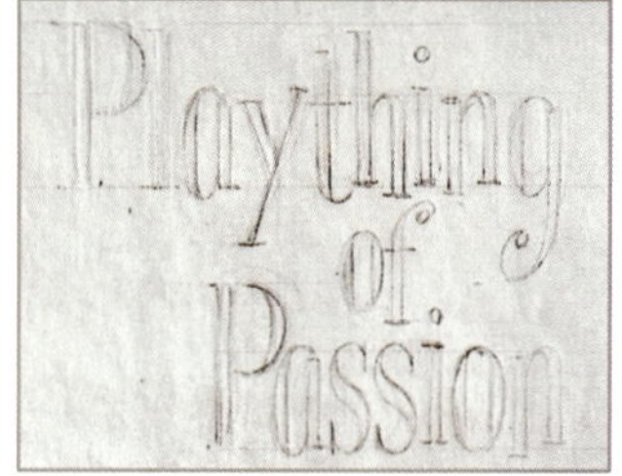

Above left: Heade's original rough for the cover of *Plaything of Passion* by Jeanette Revére (Archer, August 1950). Above right, top: the as-published paperback cover – minus Scottie dog! Above right, bottom: Heade's original rough of the book's title lettering.

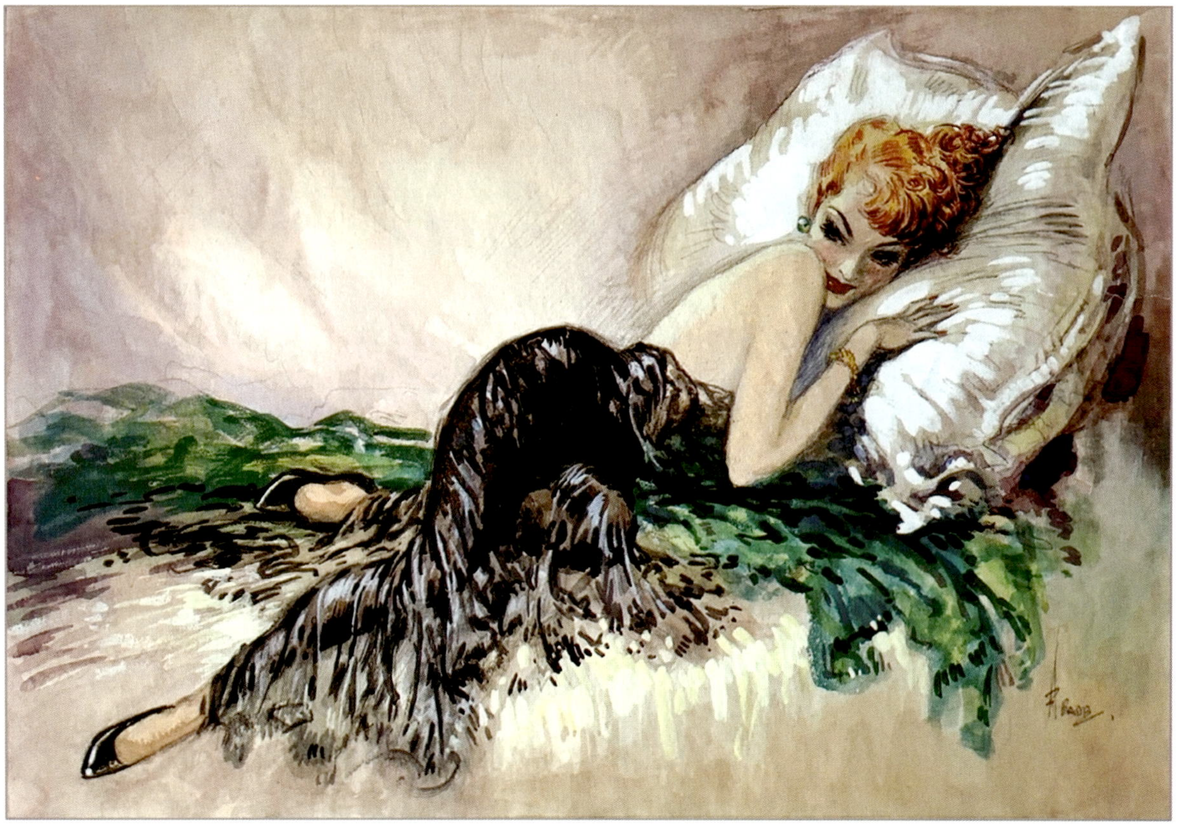

Above: a pin-up style painting by Heade, believed to date from the early 1950s. Its intended purpose is currently unknown.

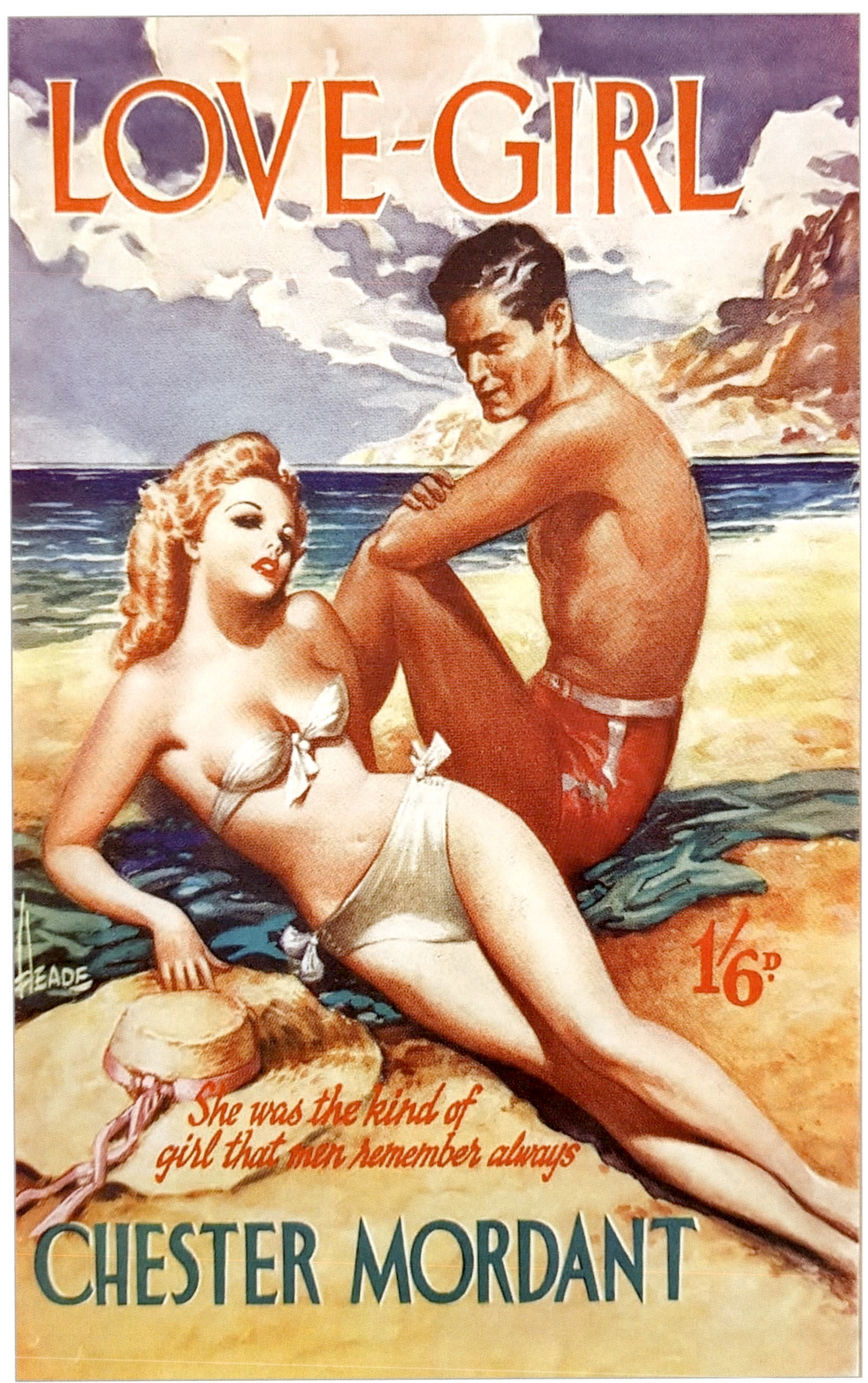

Love-Girl by Chester Mordant (Archer, July 1950)

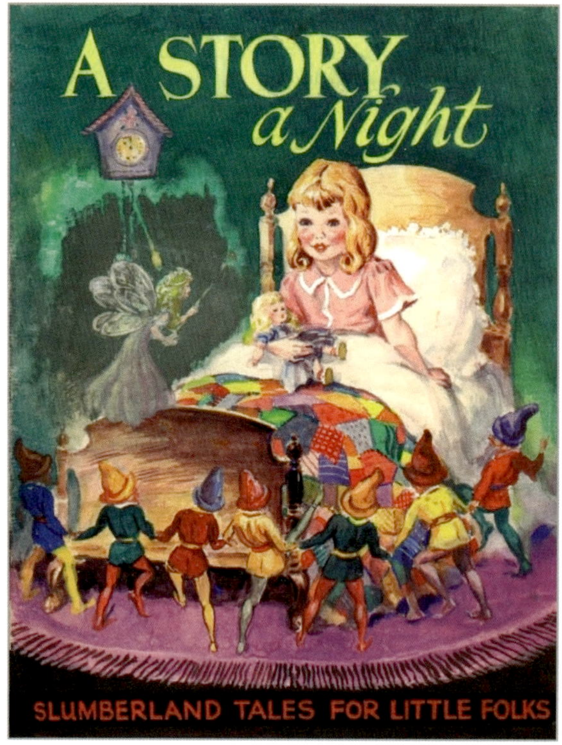

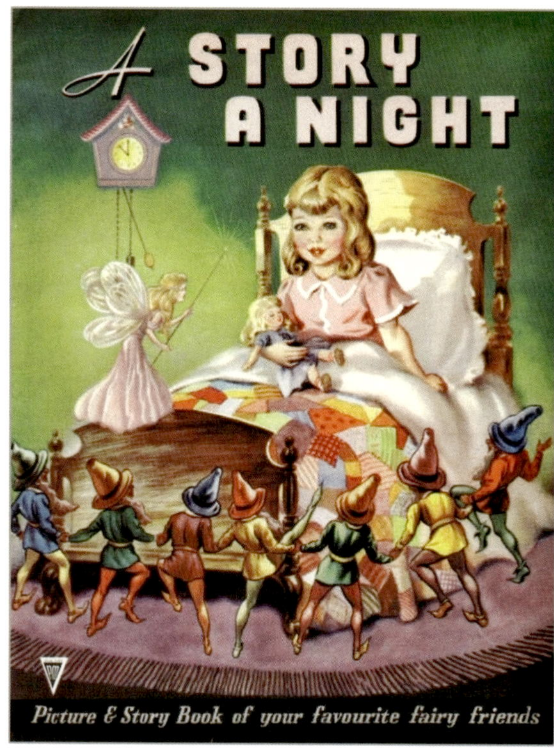

Above: Heade's original rough (left) and the as-published version (right) of the front and back cover of a large-format soft-covered children's nursery rhyme book entitled *A Story a Night*. When *The Art of Reginald Heade – Special Edition* was written, this was believed and stated to have been an unpublished Amex title. A copy of the published book, which actually appeared circa 1950 under the Amex-associated imprint PM (Productions), has only recently been discovered during research for this volume. No other copy is currently known to have survived.

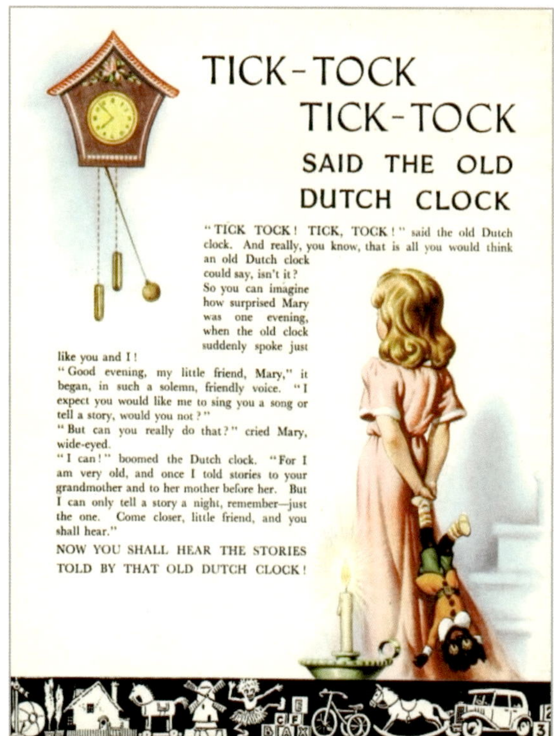

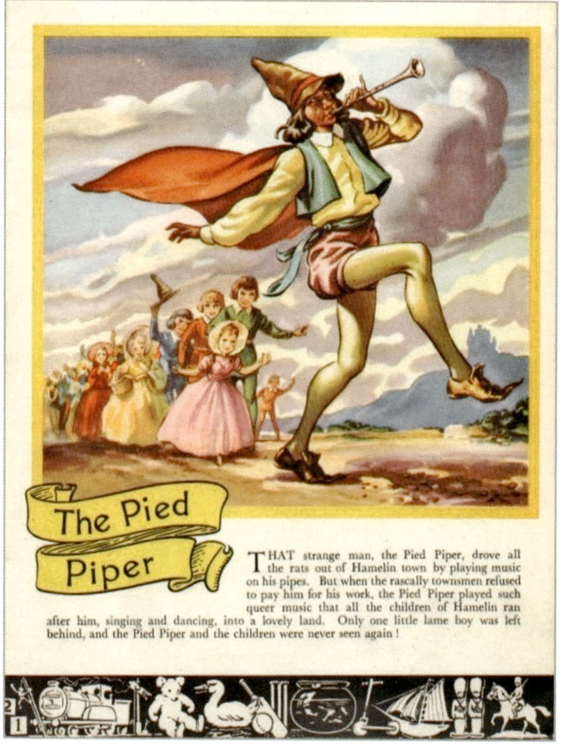

Above: the first two internal pages from *A Story a Night* (PM (Productions), c1950)

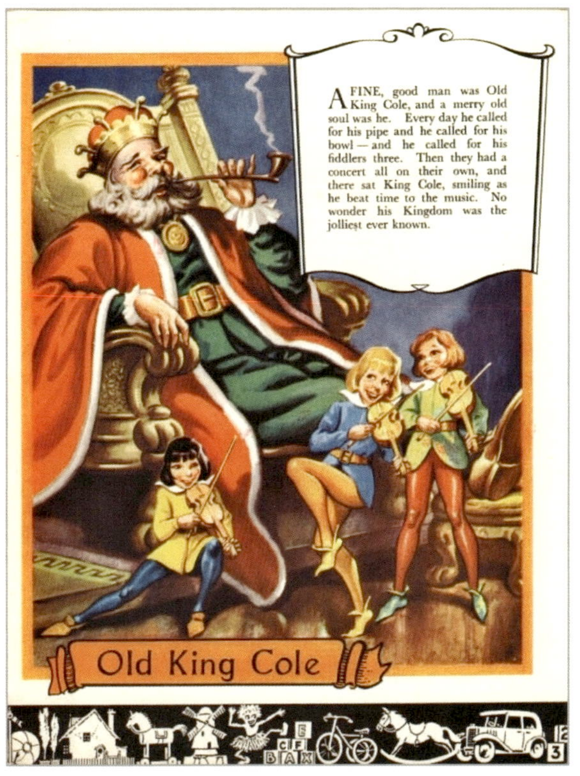

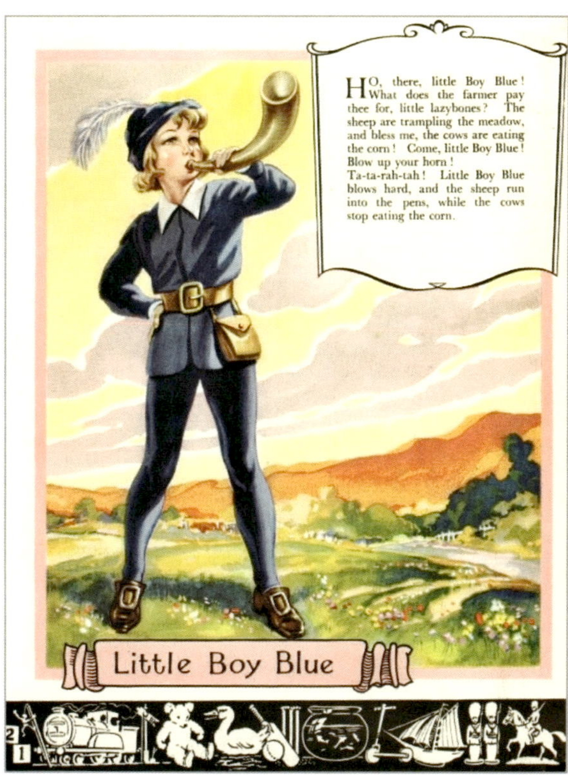

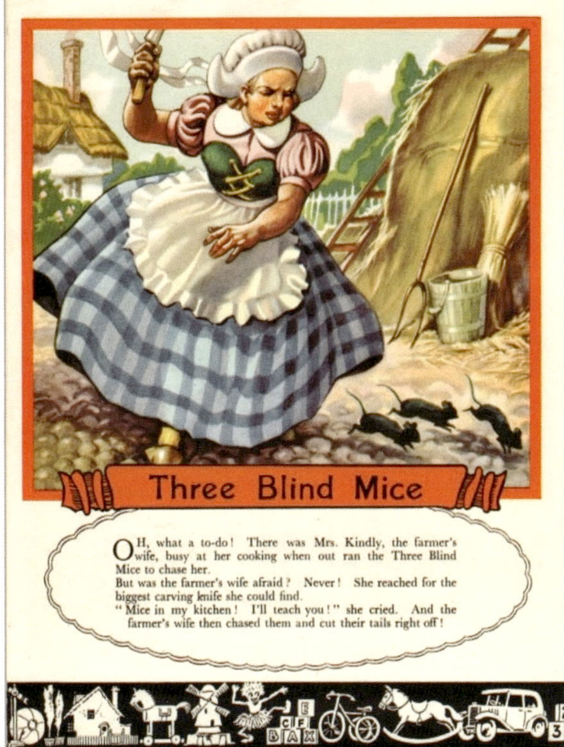

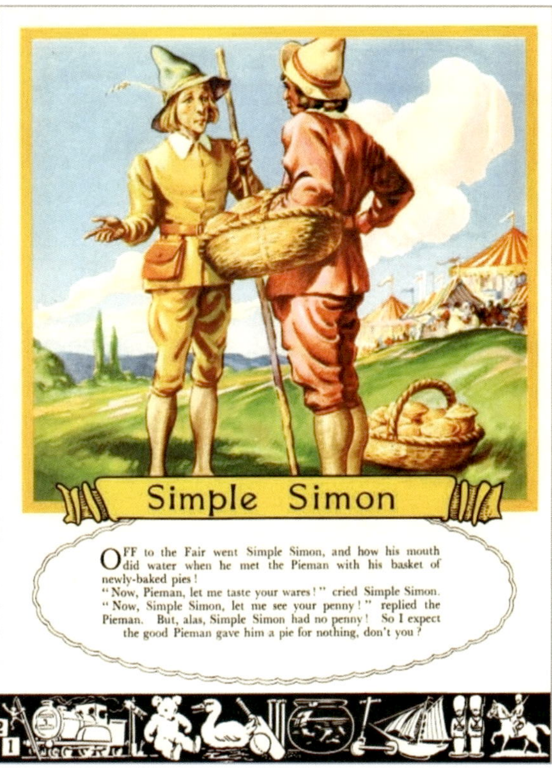

Four further internal pages from *A Story a Night* (PM (Productions), c1950). It is uncertain if Heade was responsible for the small black-and-white illustrations along the bottom page edges, as well as for the main colour illustrations, although it is likely that he was.

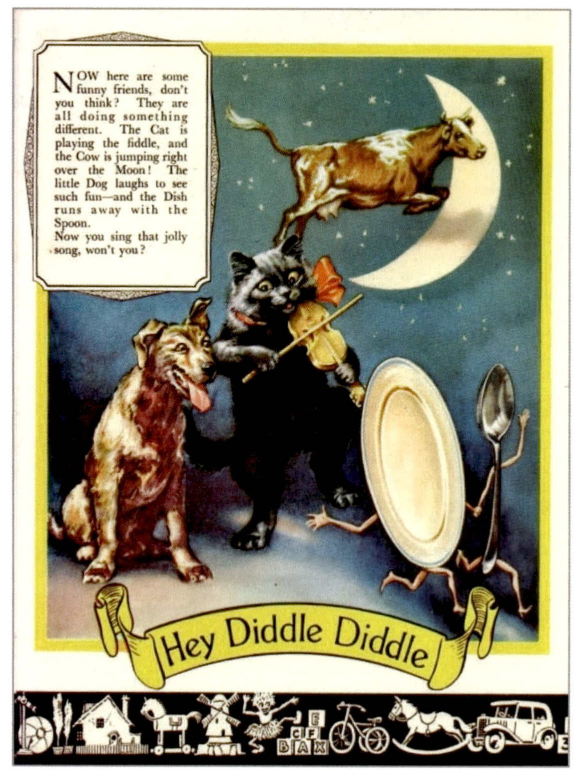

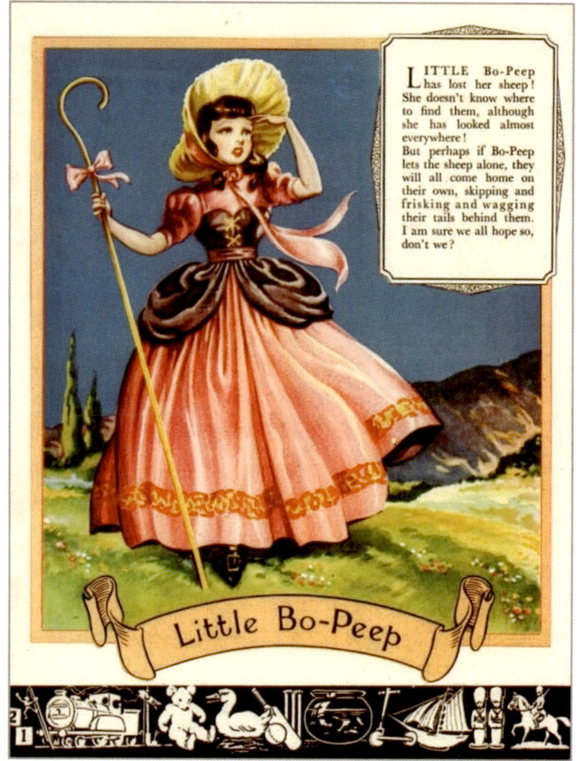

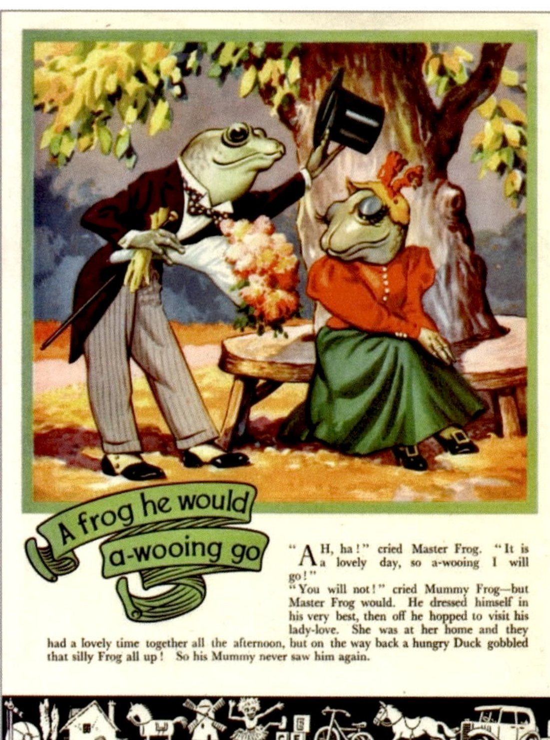

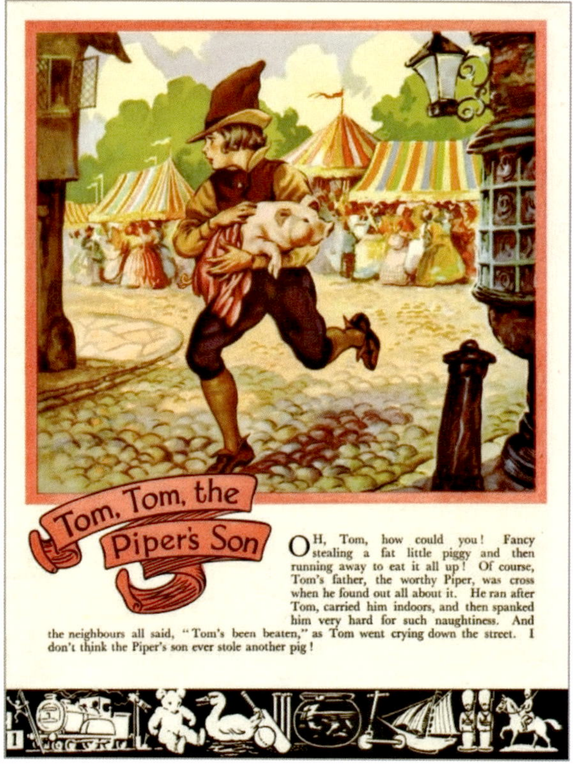

A further four internal pages from *A Story a Night* (PM (Productions), c1950)

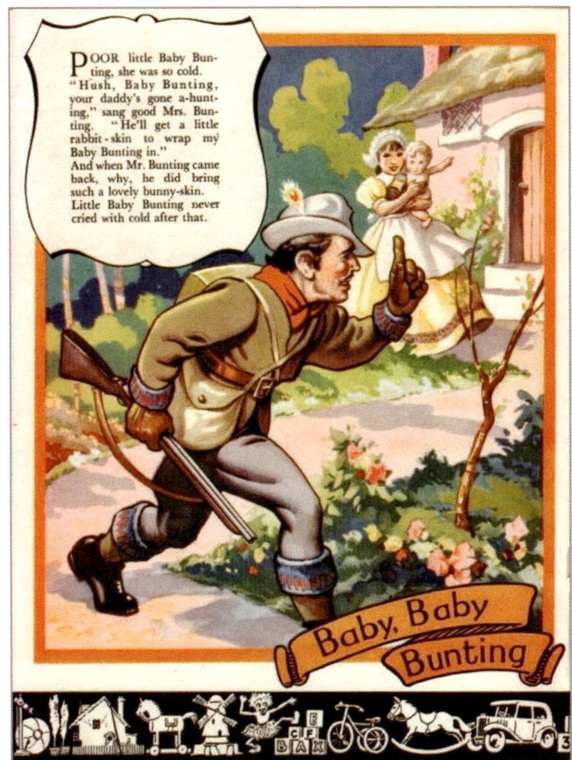

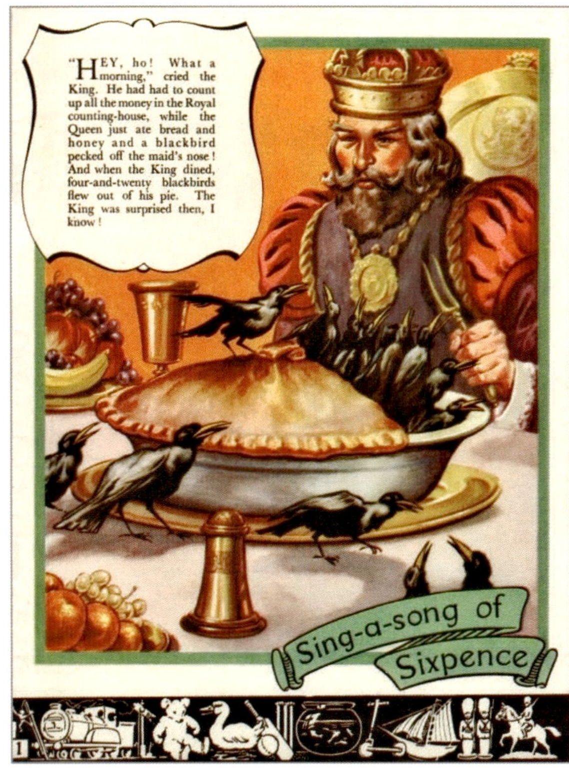

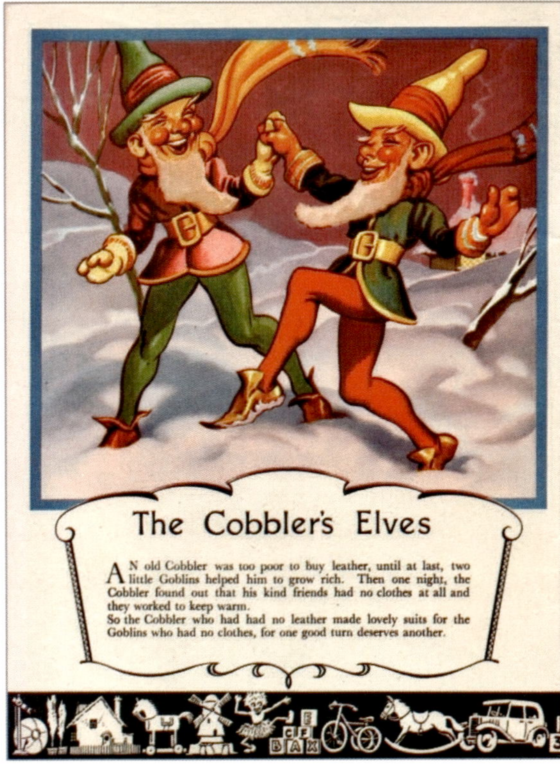

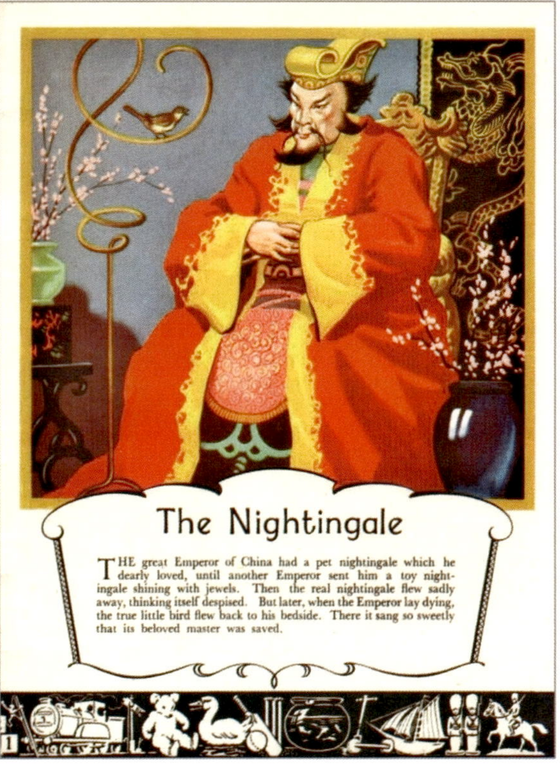

The last four internal pages from *A Story a Night* (PM (Productions), c1950)

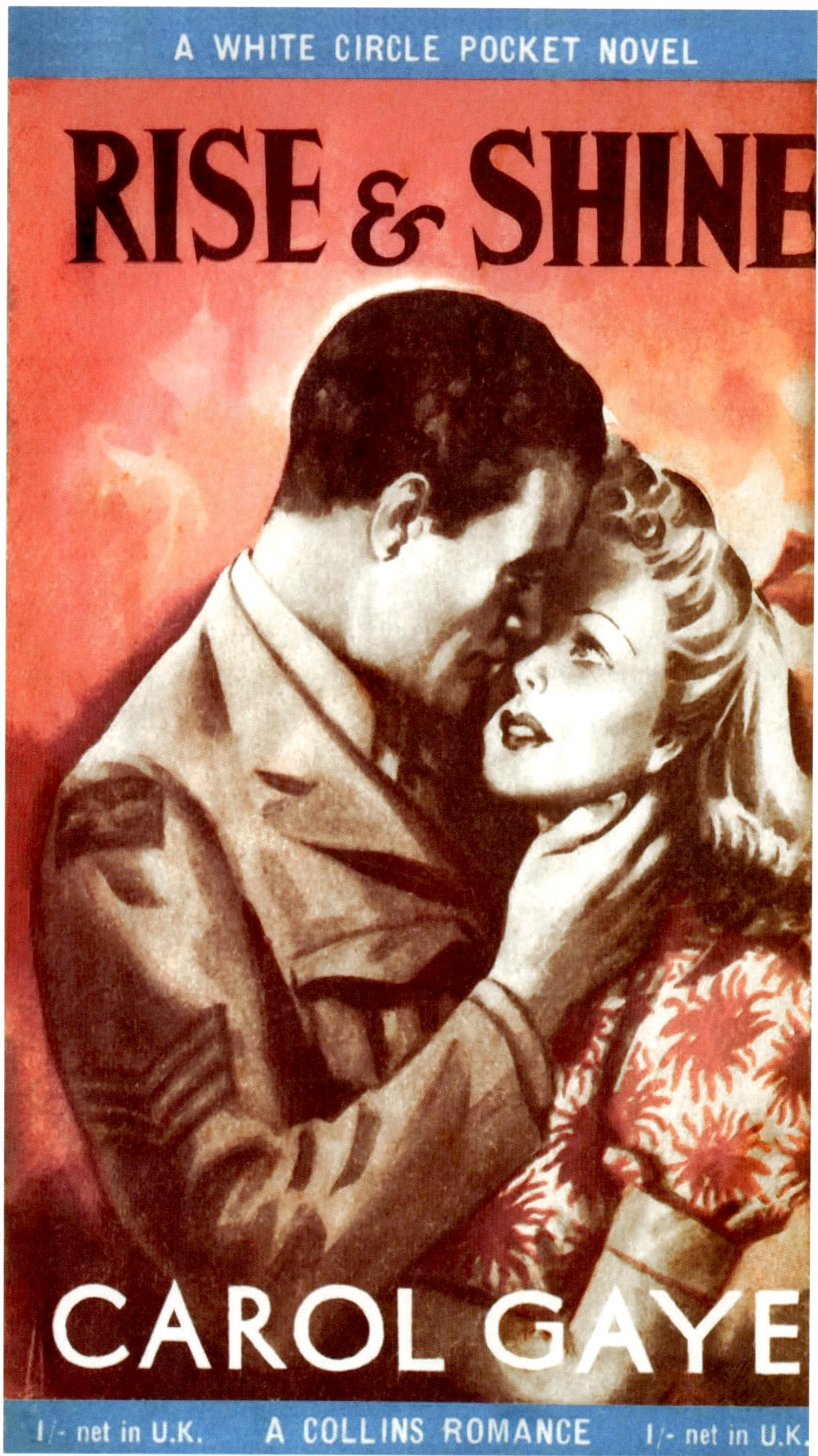

Rise & Shine by Carol Gaye (Collins White Circle, 1950). (Previously presented as only a small image on page 300 of *The Art of Reginald Heade – Special Edition*.) This artwork could have been reused from another book; possibly the same title's 1945 hardback first edition, no image of the dustjacket of which is currently available.

CALENDAR GIRLS

In 1951, Heade created a stapled-together set of roughs for a proposed 1952 calendar, with pin-up style artwork and a cover (see right) with a keyhole-shaped cut-out. It is possible that he produced this in connection with a short-lived, Gaywood-distributed magazine, *Key-hole*, which had a similar cover format – probably inspired by American pulps such as *Whisper*, with its Peter Driben-painted keyhole covers, which had begun to appear in 1949. However, no printed copy of the final calendar has ever come to light, and it may not have been produced. The four inside pages of the rough are shown below.

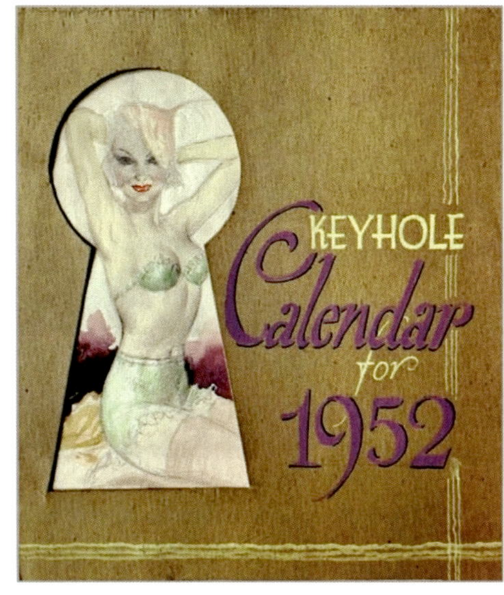

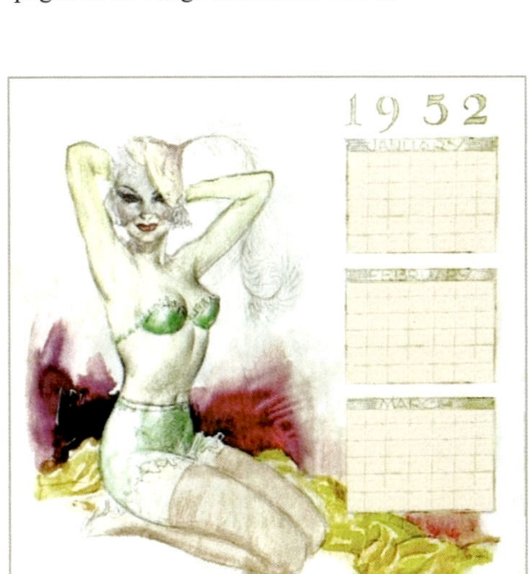

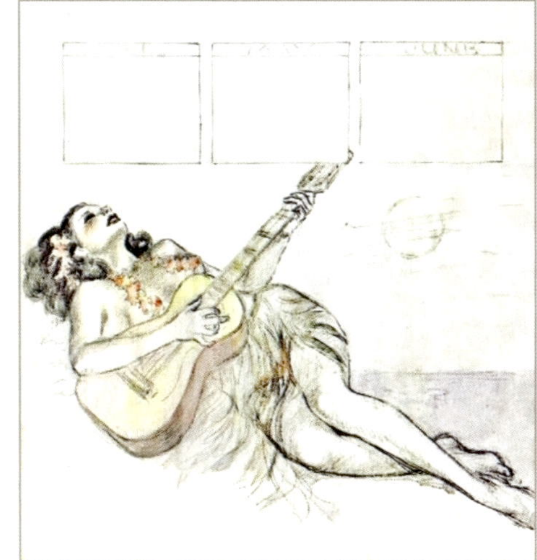

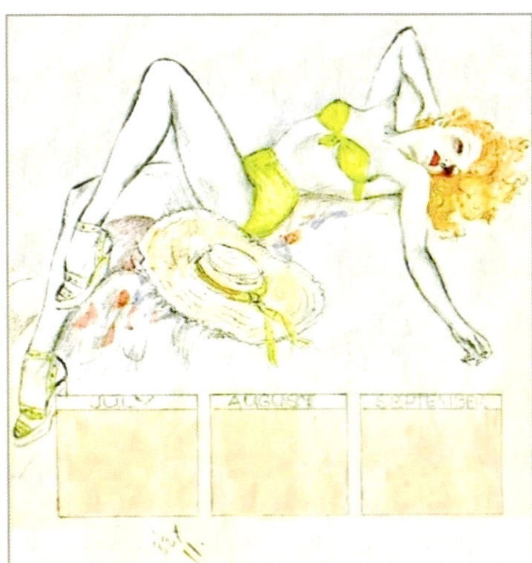

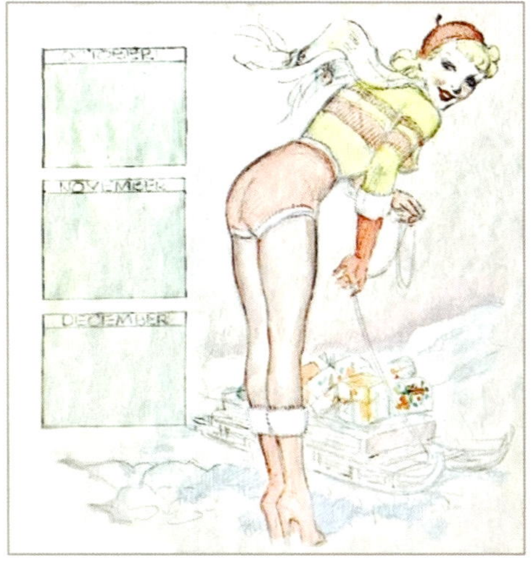

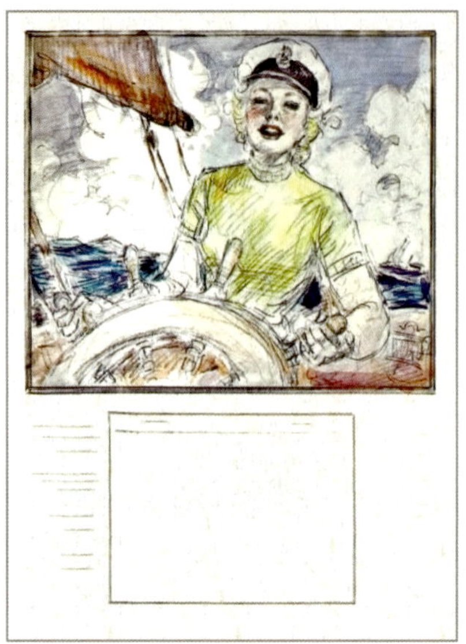 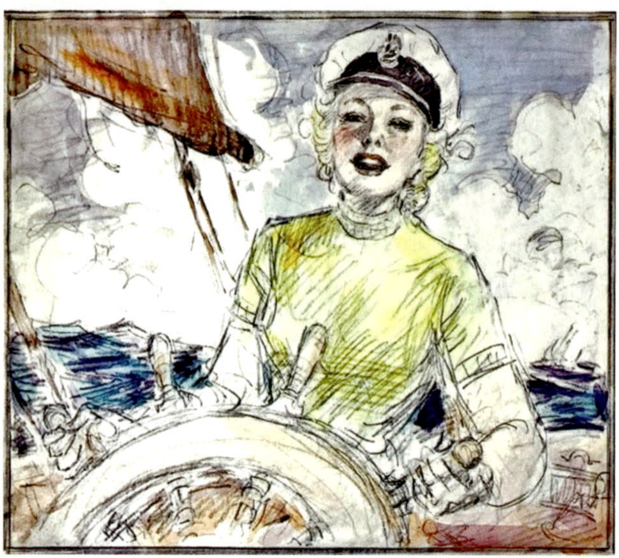

Alongside the keyhole calendar mock-up pictured on the previous page, Heade also produced a rough of an illustrated header card for a smaller calendar. Again, it is uncertain if this item ever saw print. Above left: the full rough of the header card. Above right: a detail of the main illustration.

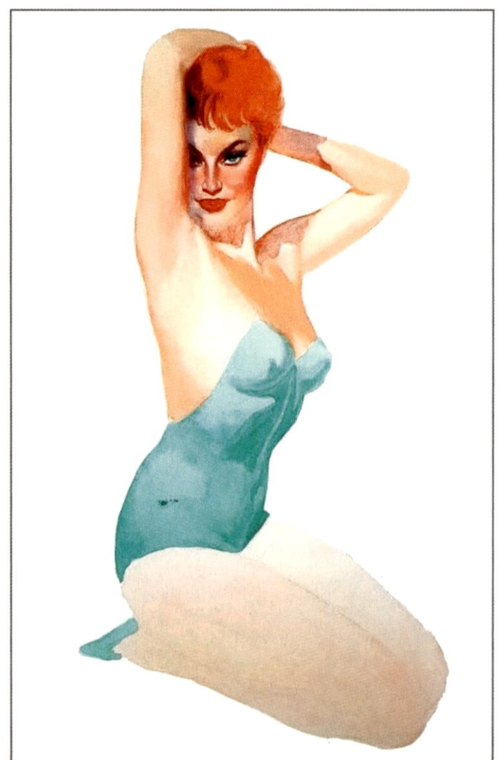 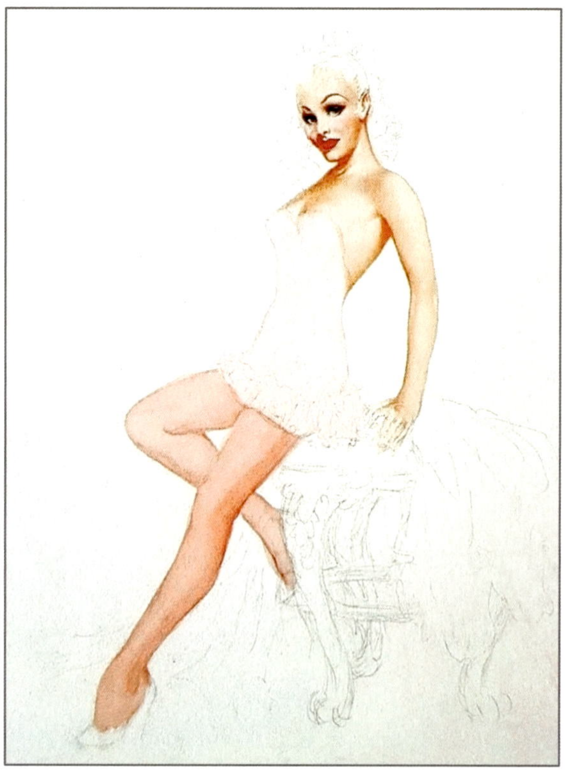

Above: two pin-up-style roughs painted by Heade in the early 1950s. The one on the right is unfinished, and it is unknown for what purpose it was intended. The one on the left is thought to have been produced with a view to being used in an advertisement for Veet depilatory cream, although whether or not this ever came to fruition is uncertain. Note the similarity of composition between this piece and the first of the keyhole calendar roughs on the previous page.

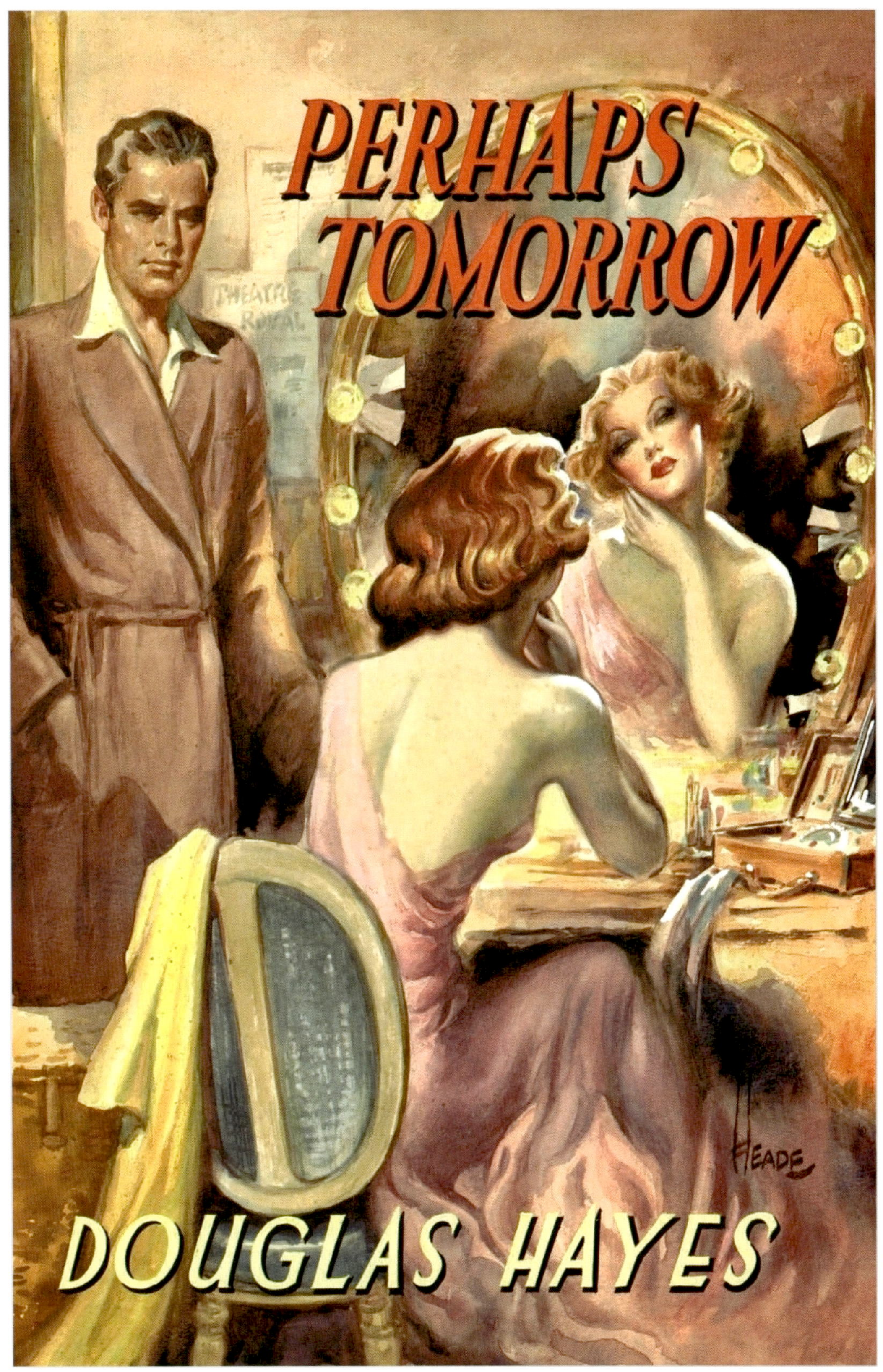

Heade's original painting for *Perhaps Tomorrow* by Douglas Hayes (Partridge, 1951). (Image courtesy the Steve Chibnall Collection.)

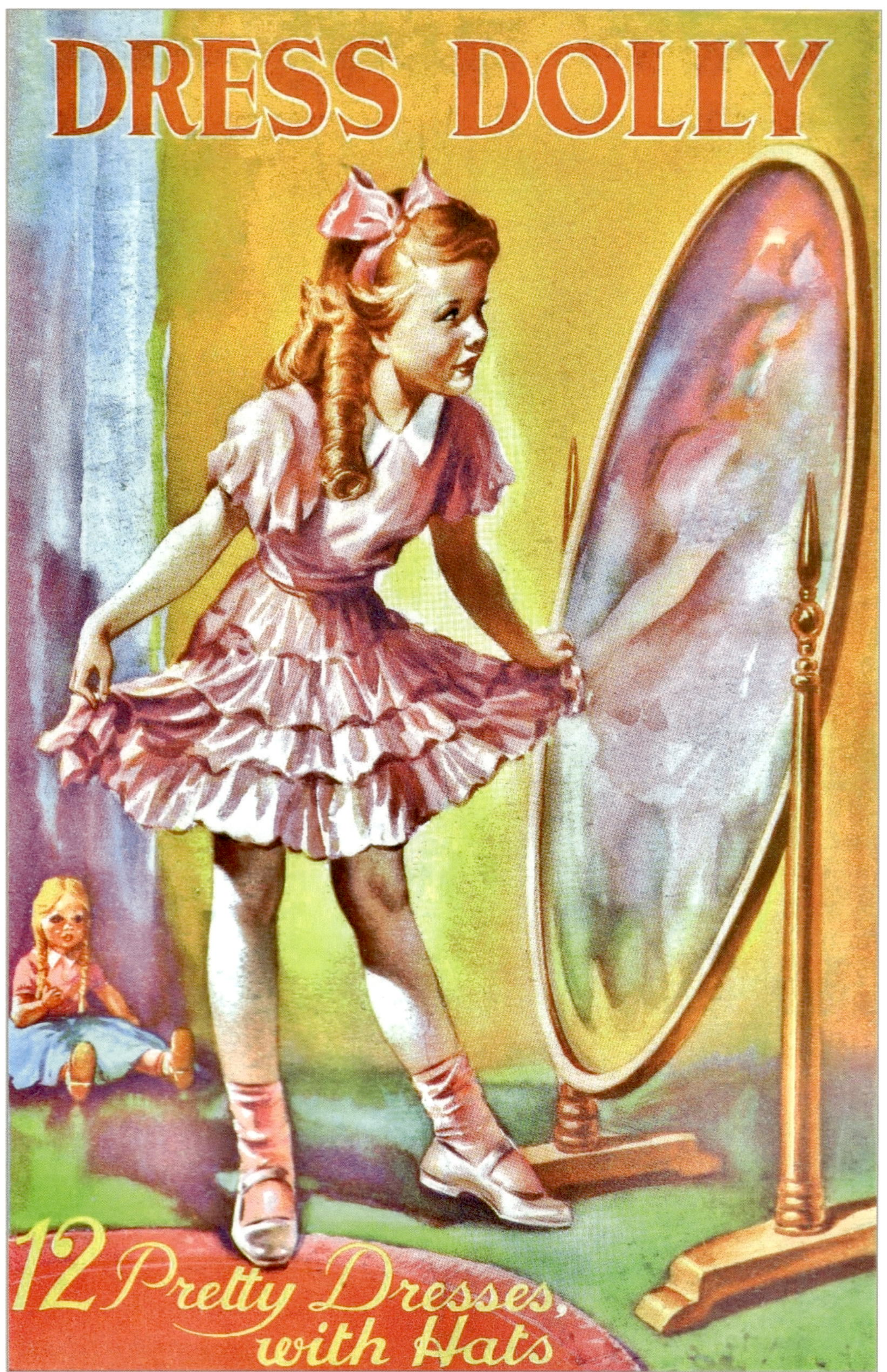

Dress Dolly: 12 Pretty Dresses With Hats (Philmar, c1951) – a portrait of Heade's daughter Sally.

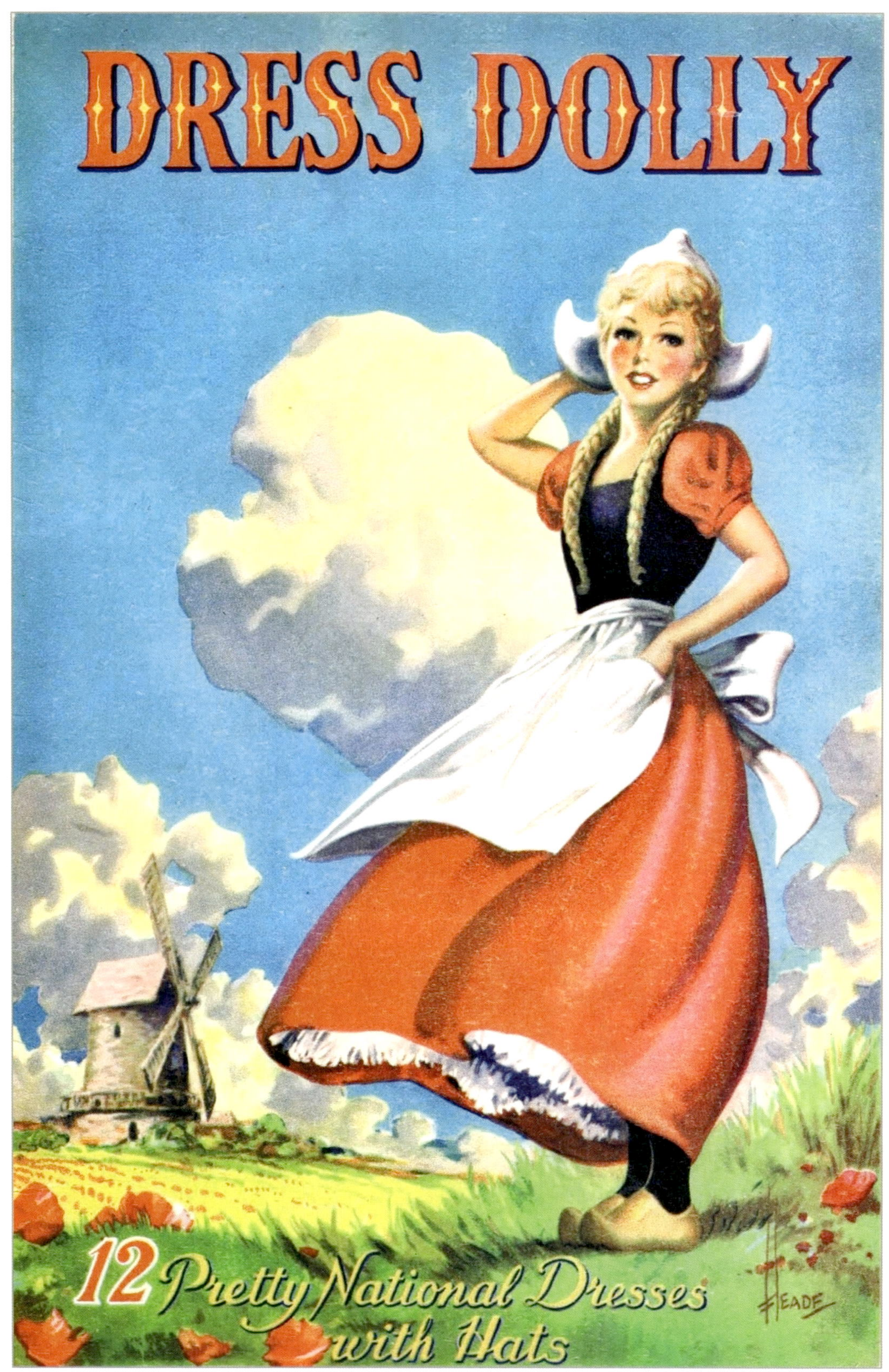

Dress Dolly: 12 Pretty National Dresses With Hats (Philmar, c1951)

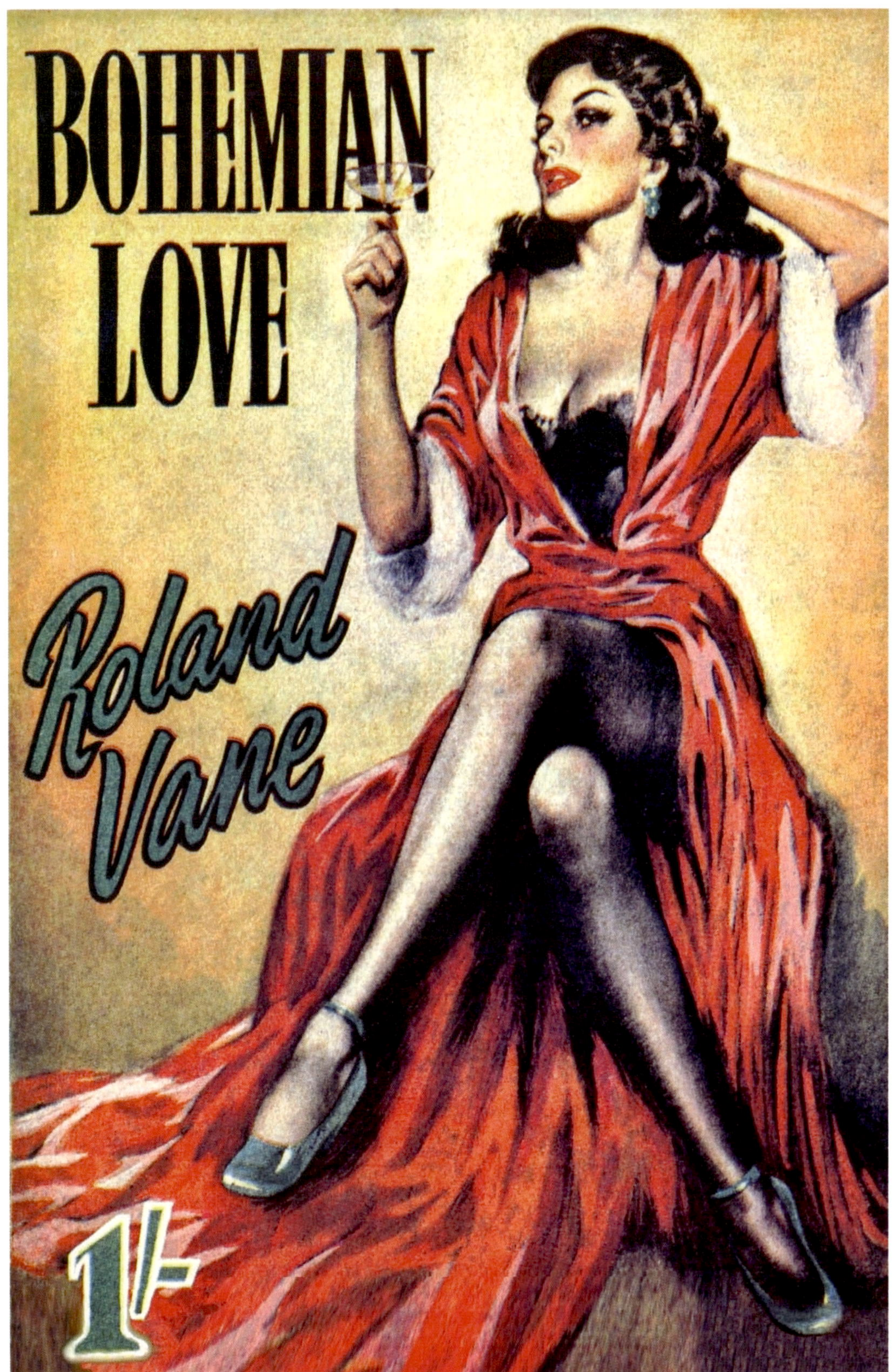

Bohemian Love by Roland Vane (Phoenix, 1952)

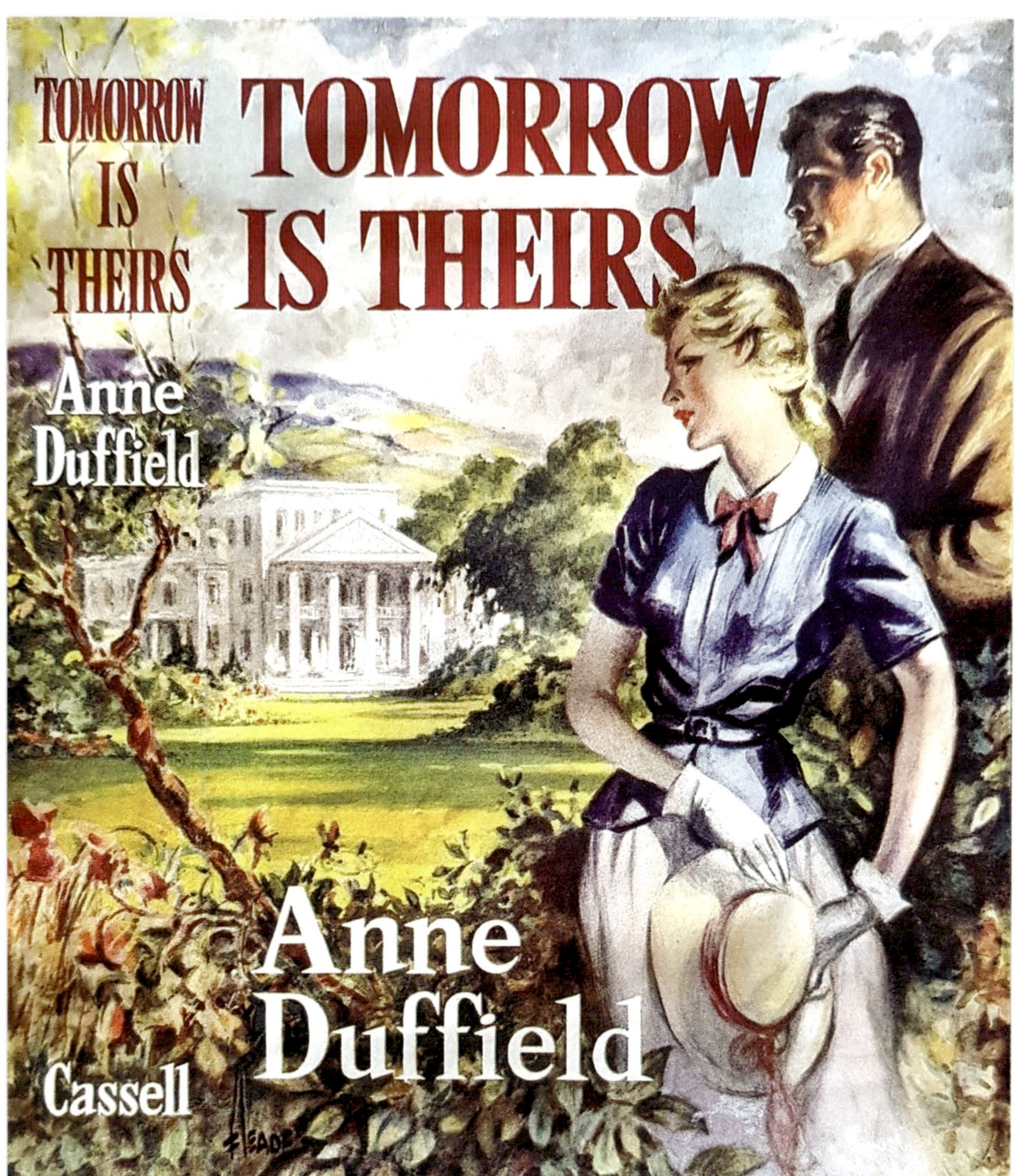

Tomorrow is Theirs by Anne Duffield (Cassell,1951)

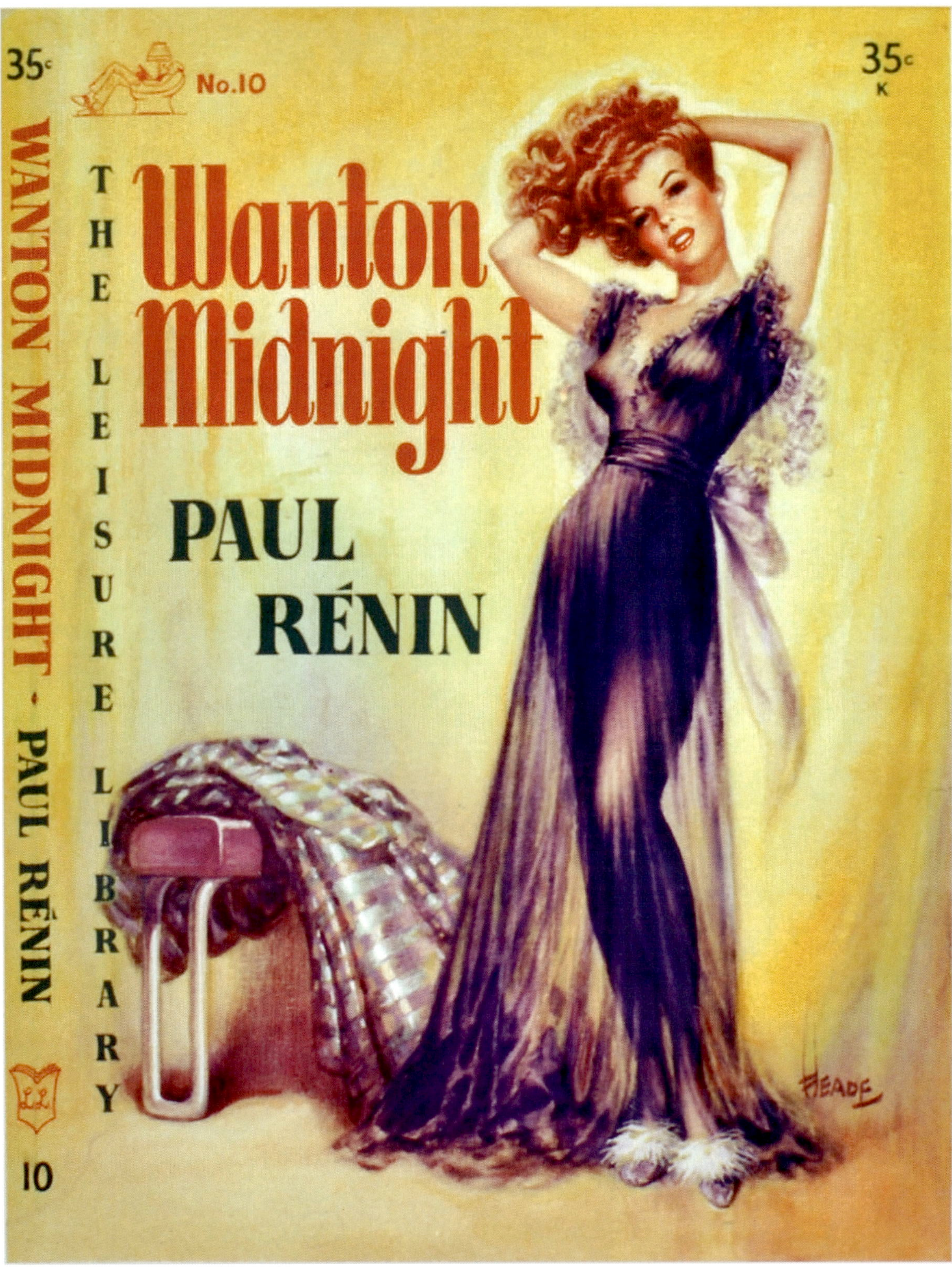

Heade's original painting for the US-published *Wanton Midnight* by Paul Rénin, which was modified before it saw print; the title was amended to *Midnight Sinner* (Leisure Library, 1952). (Image courtesy the Steve Chibnall Collection.)

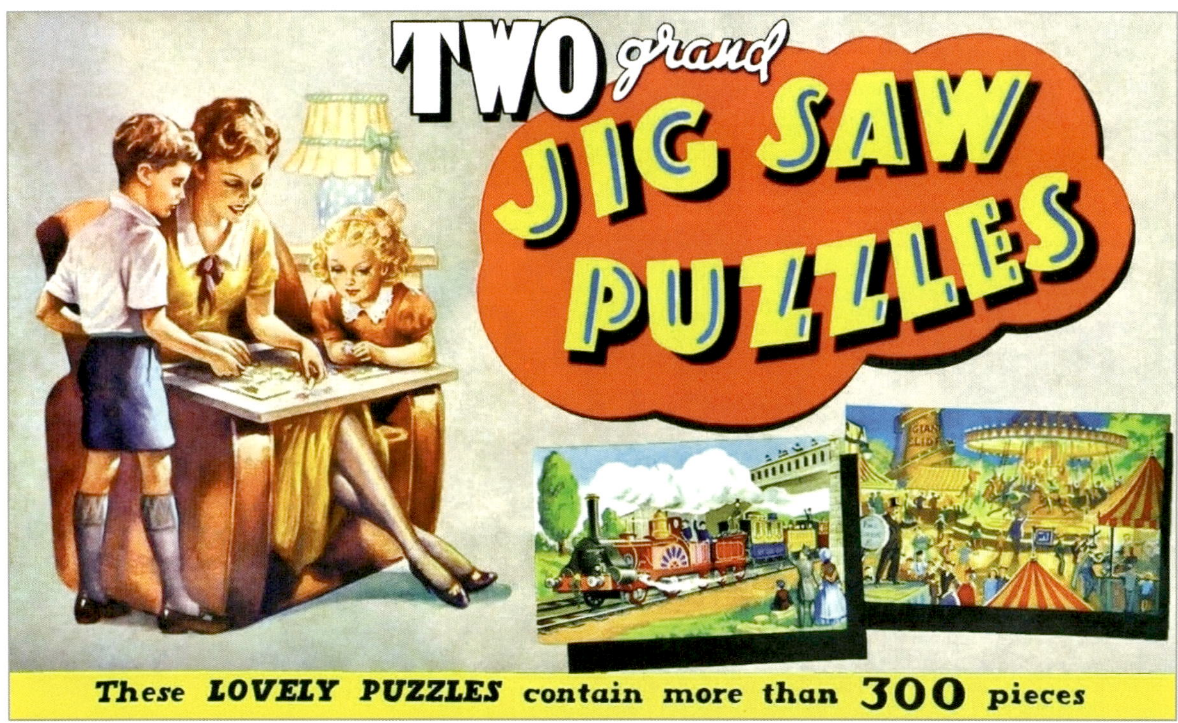

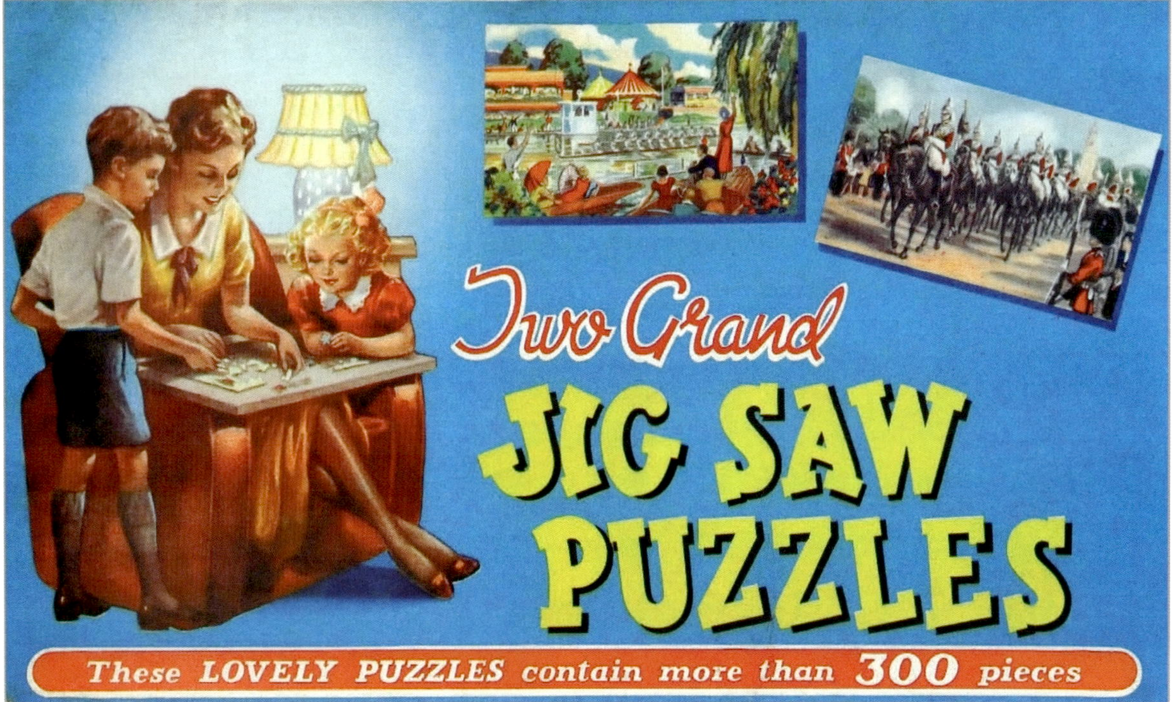

Amongst the commercial products he worked on, Heade supplied artwork of a mother and two children for the box lids of a Philmar range of two-puzzle jigsaw sets. Eight of these have been identified so far – as pictured over this and the next four pages – although there could possibly have been others. The earliest is believed to date from c1950 and the latest from c1955. The jigsaw illustrations themselves were by other artists, except for a 'Cinderella' one included in one of the sets, and a 'Snow White and the Seven Dwarfs' one included in another (the latter being reused from a previously-published Heade piece). (Lower image courtesy the Netherlands Legpuzzel Gilde.)

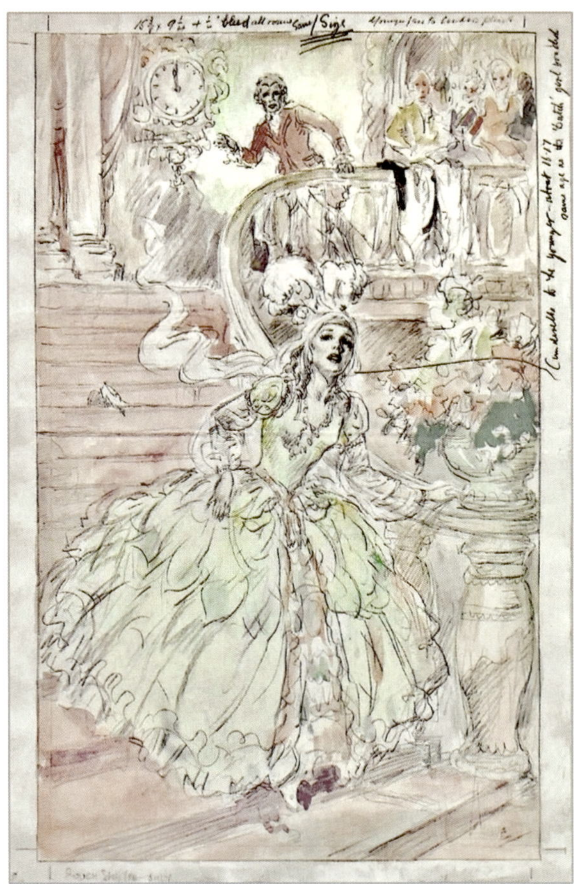

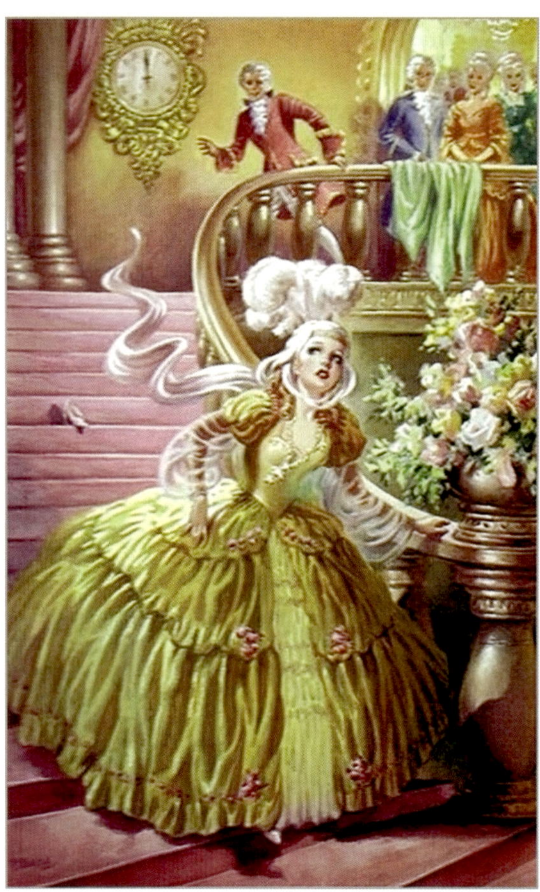

Top: the Philmar two-puzzle jigsaw set including Heade's 'Cinderella' piece. (Image courtesy the Netherlands Legpuzzel Gilde.)
Bottom left: Heade's original rough for the piece. Bottom right: the artist's finished painting. (Finished painting image courtesy Todd Gibson.)

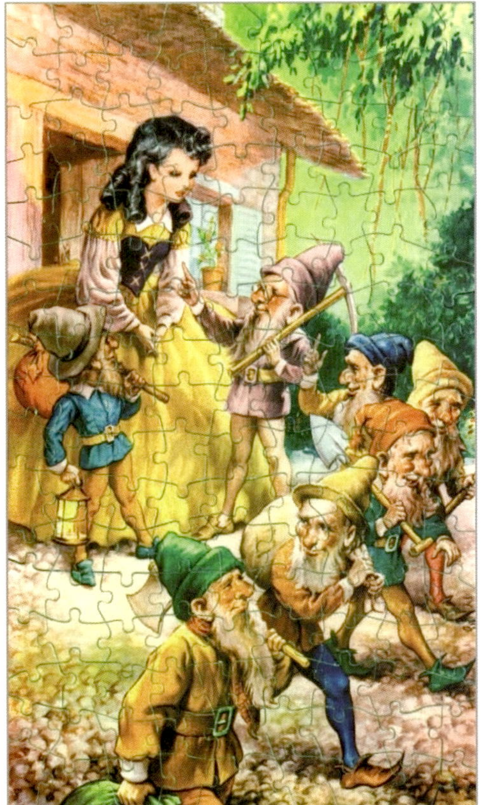

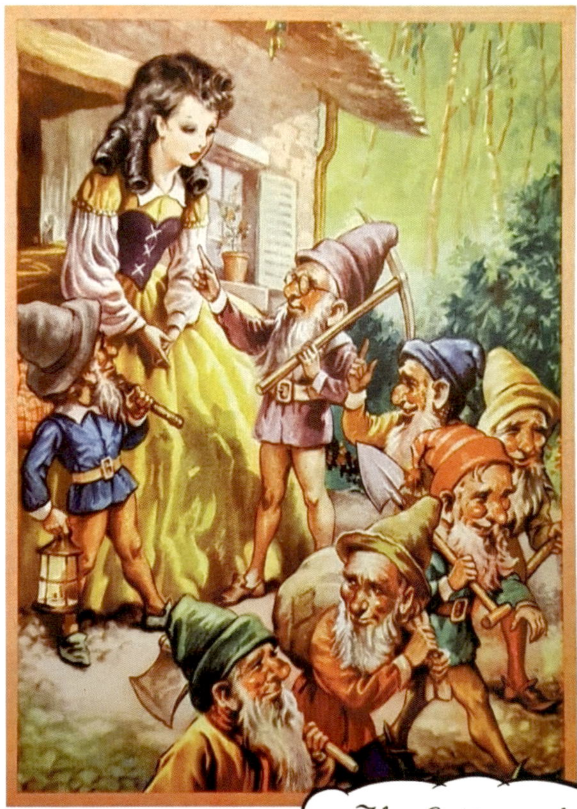

Above left: the completed Snow White puzzle from the Philmar jigsaw puzzle set pictured below.

Above right: the same artwork as it originally appeared, in more cropped form, as one of Heade's full-page illustrations for the children's book *The Fairy Princesses* (Amex, 1952) (as previously pictured on pages 235 to 237 of *The Art of Reginald Heade – Special Edition*).

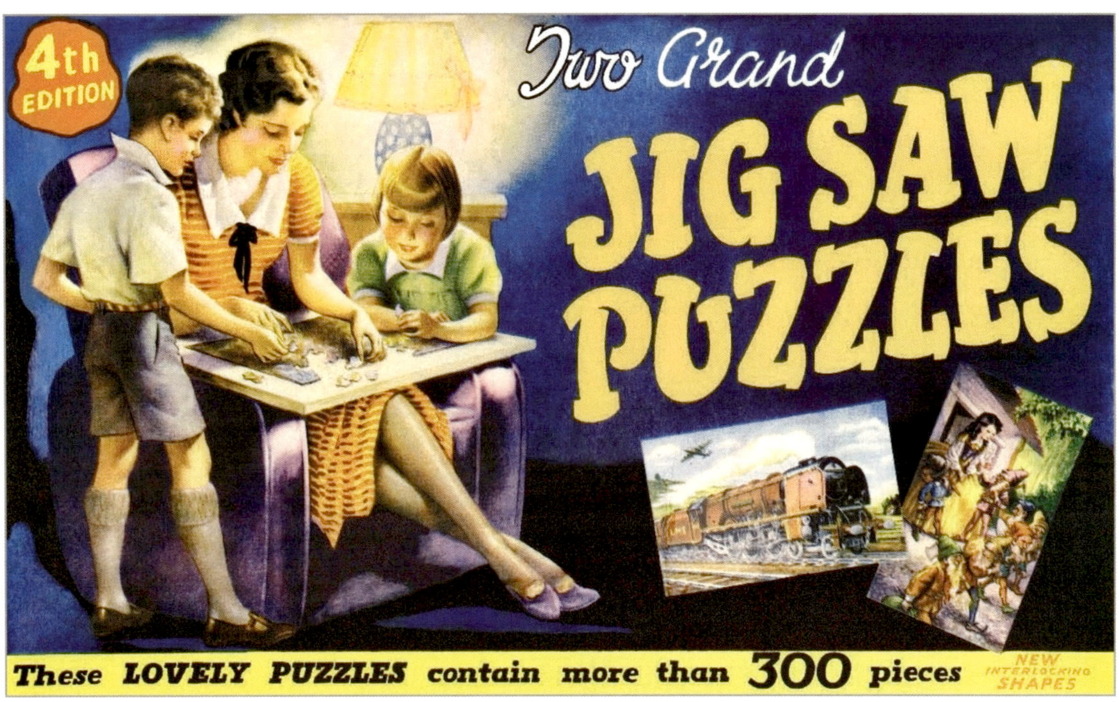

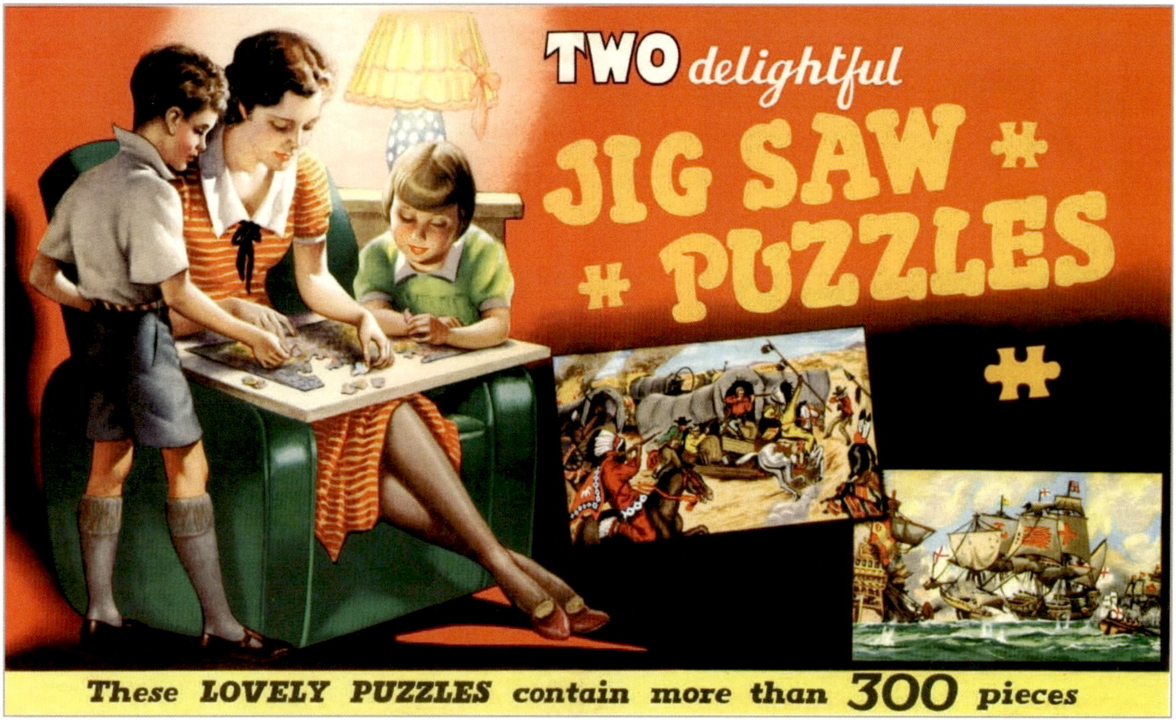

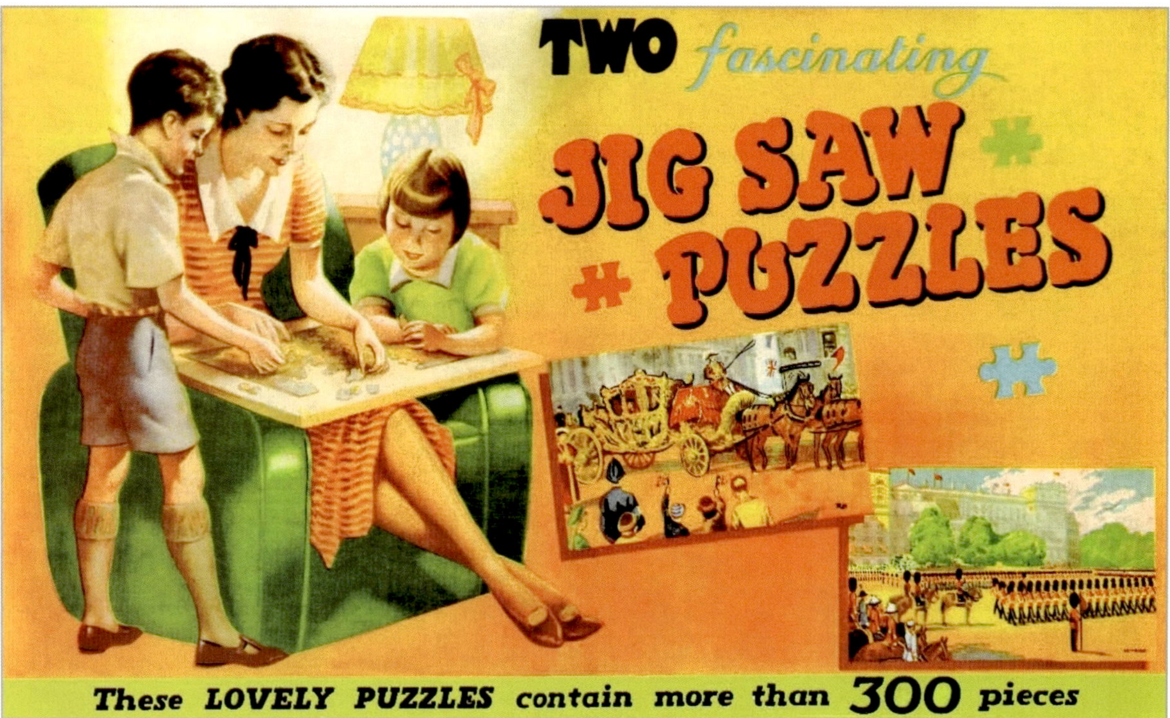

Two further Philmar jigsaw puzzle sets featuring Heade box lid art of a mother and two children.

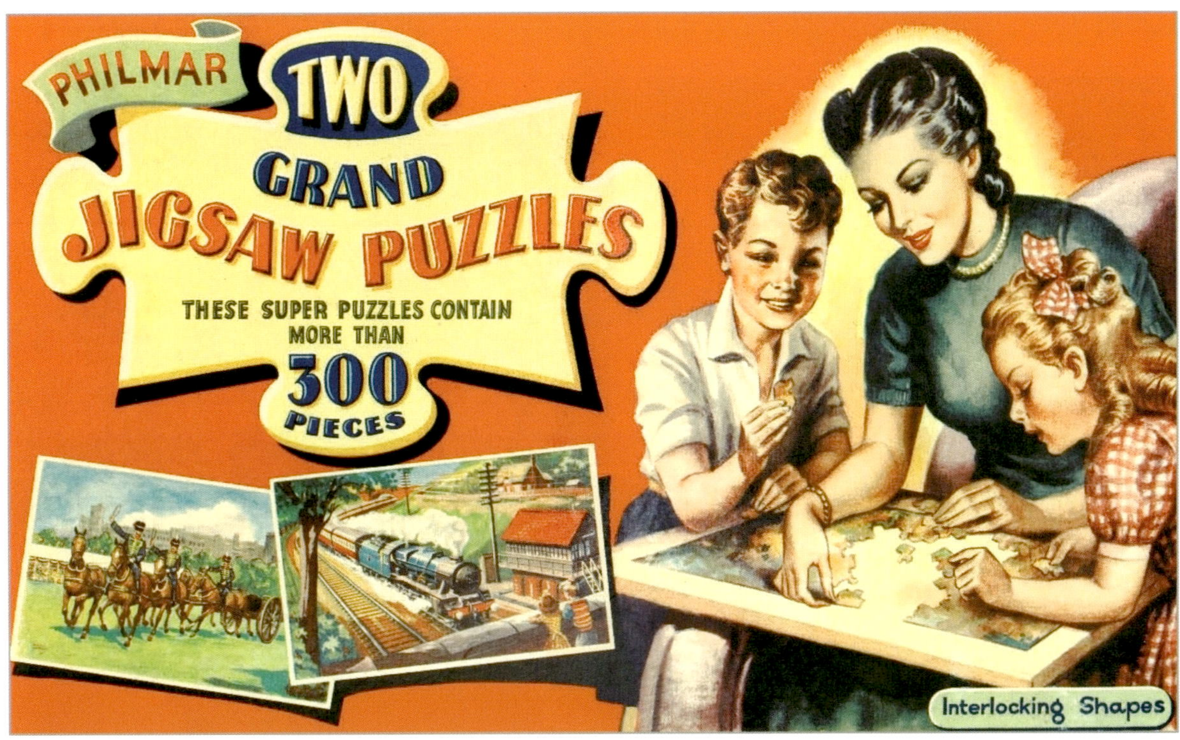

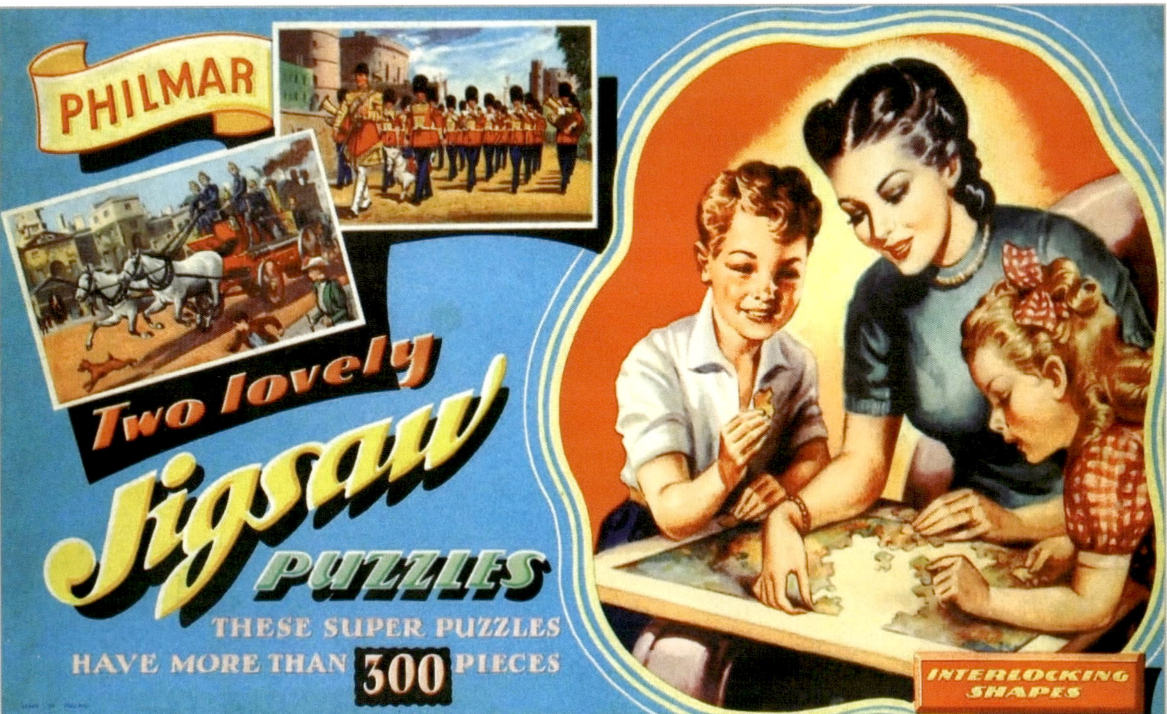

The two Philmar sets shown above, featuring a different Heade box lid illustration of a mother and two children, are believed to have been the last produced in this range, dating from c1955. (Lower image courtesy the Netherlands Legpuzzel Gilde.)

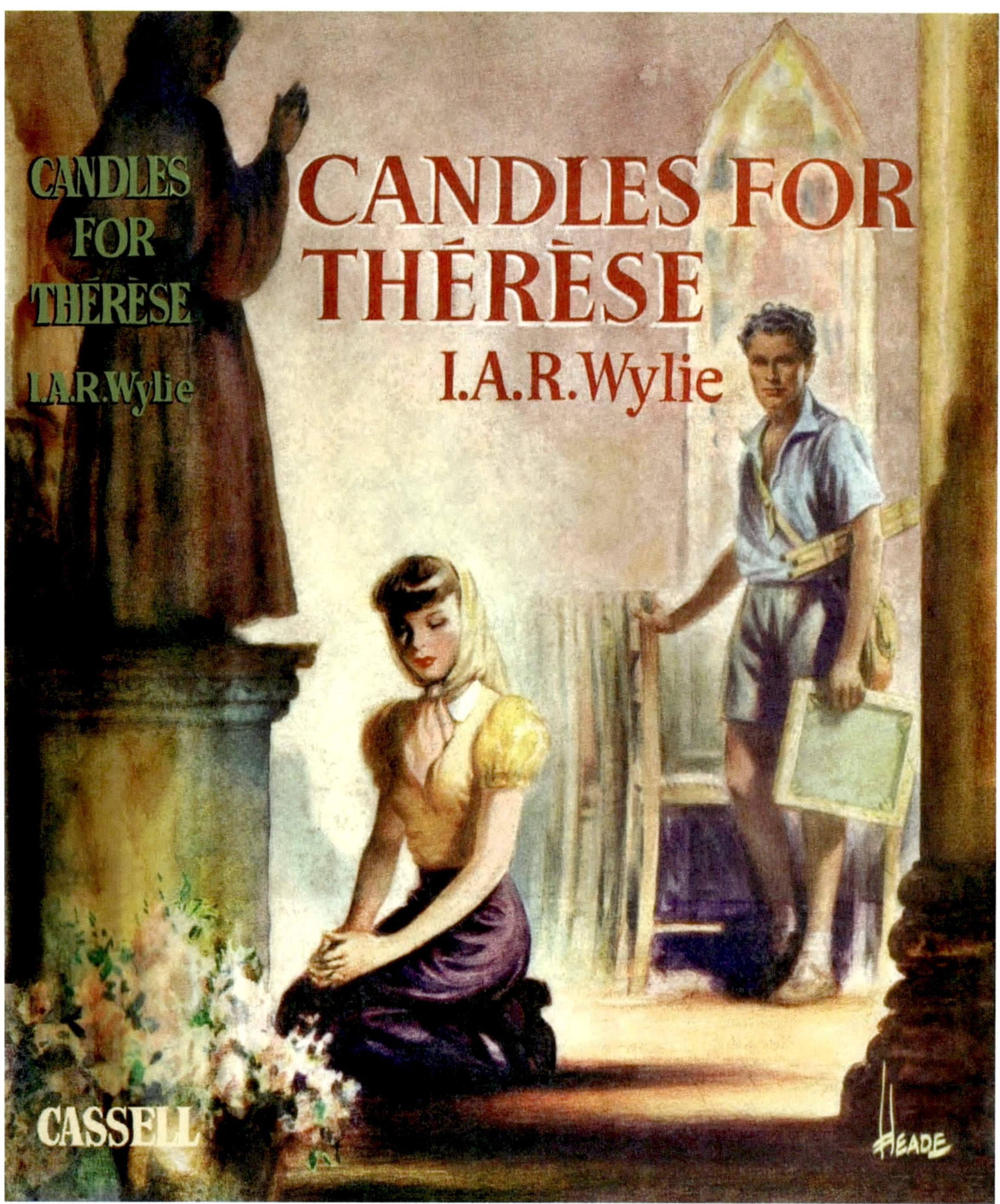

Candles for Thérèse by I A R Wylie (Cassell, 1952)

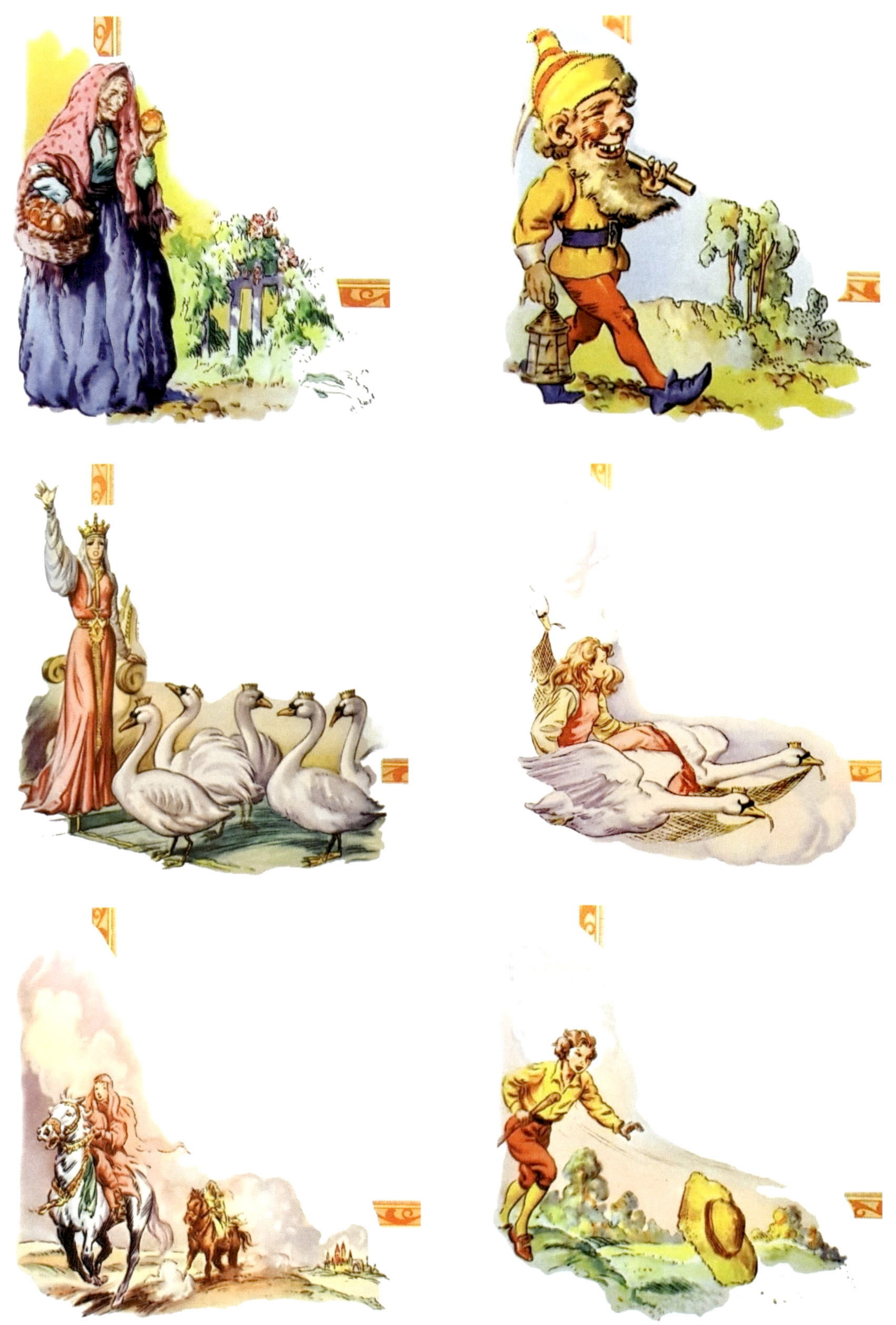

Six of the eight small, page-corner illustrations that Heade provided for *The Fairy Princesses* (Amex, 1952)

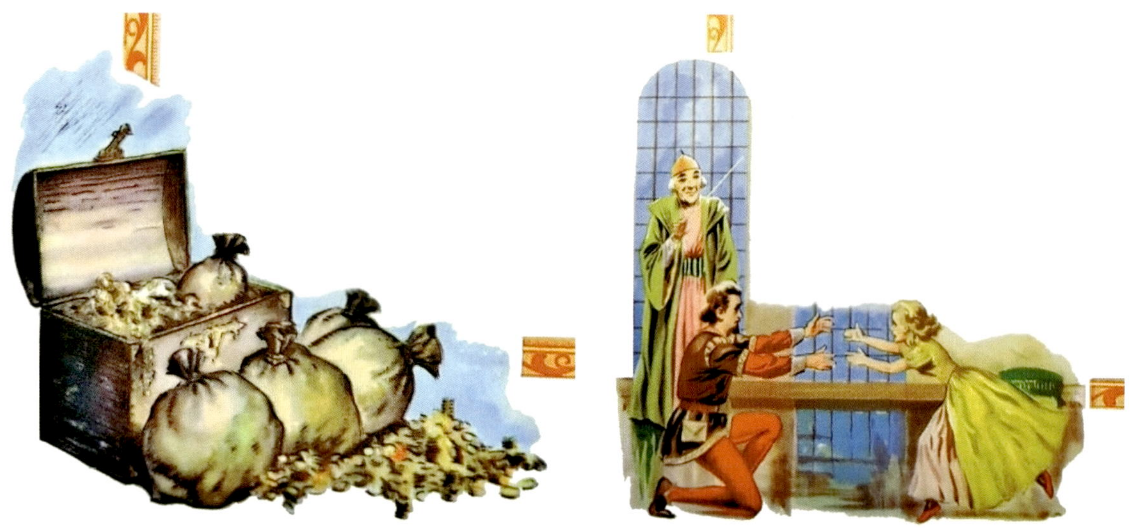

Above: the remaining two small, page-corner illustrations for *The Fairy Princesses* (Amex, 1952)

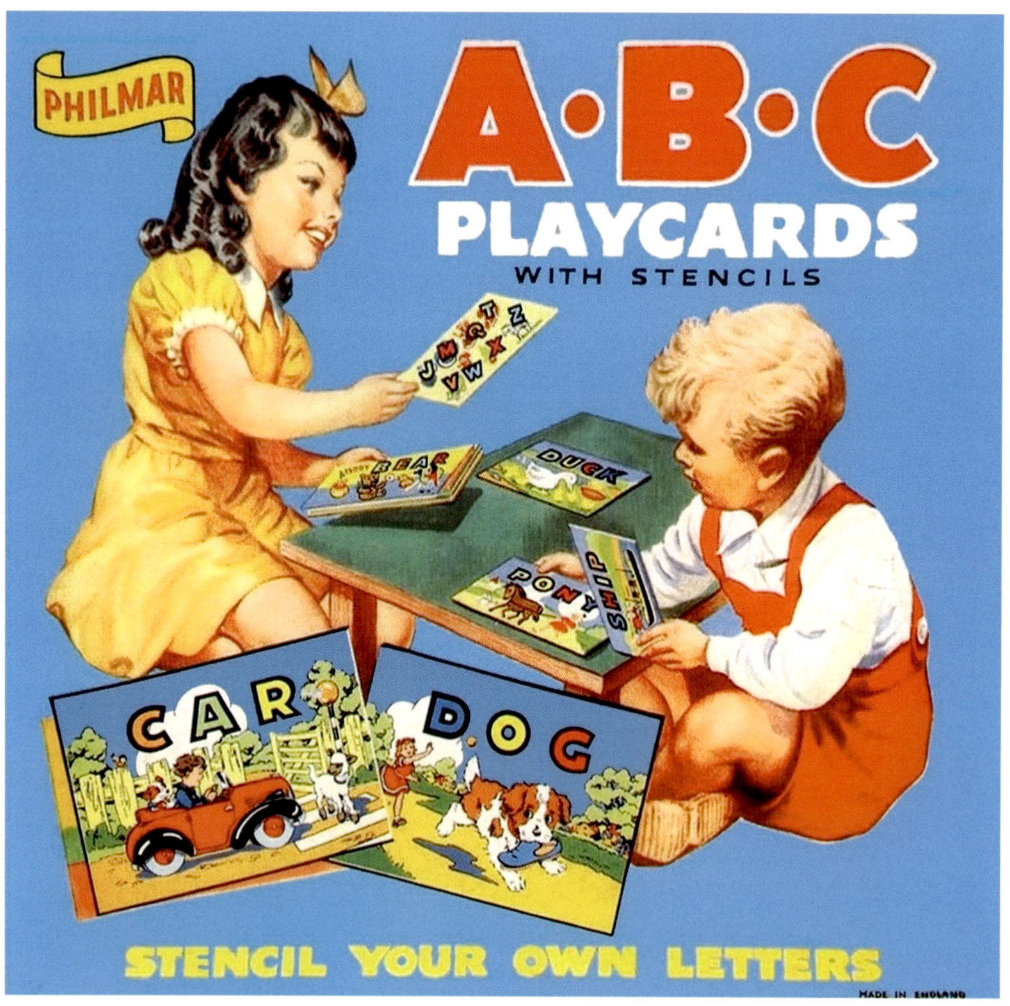

Above: Heade's box lid artwork for a Philmar educational toy, believed to date from the early 1950s.

Right: Heade's original rough for an illustration of three toddlers playing at bath-time. Like those below, and many of the others reproduced elsewhere in this volume, this was drawn in pencil on a sheet of flimsy, translucent drafting vellum, which has since become quite creased over the years, necessitating painstaking digital image restoration to allow for it to be presented here.

The style of this particular rough suggests that the illustration could have been intended for a children's story book, or perhaps for an advertisement for a bath product such as soap or shampoo; the oval in the bottom right-hand corner is clearly intended to indicate where wording such as a story title or a brand name could be placed. However, this is just speculation, as no printed copy of the finished illustration has yet been found. Although it is believed most likely to have been drawn in the early 1950s, the actual date is likewise uncertain at present.

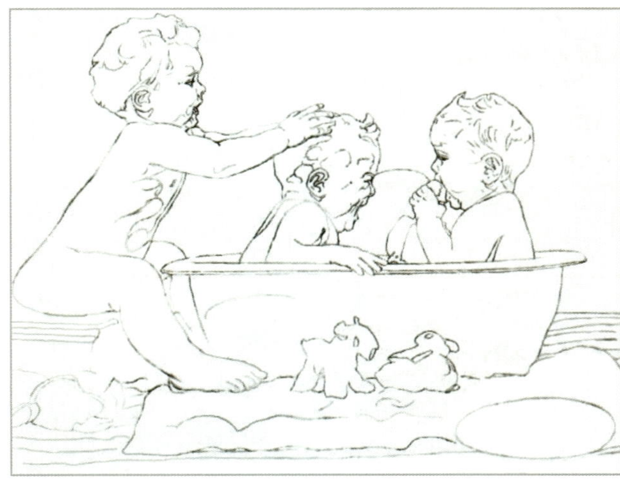

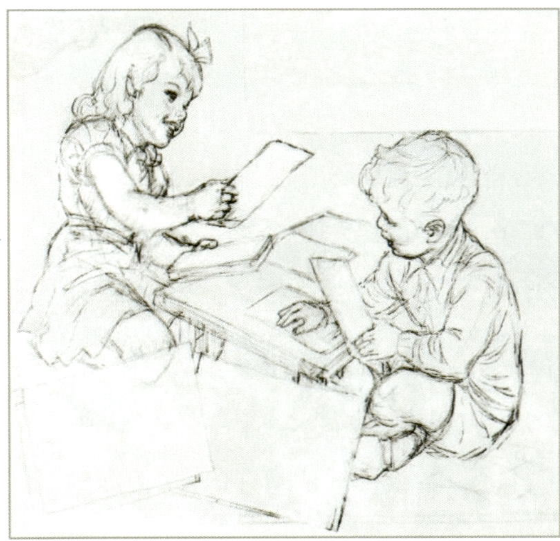

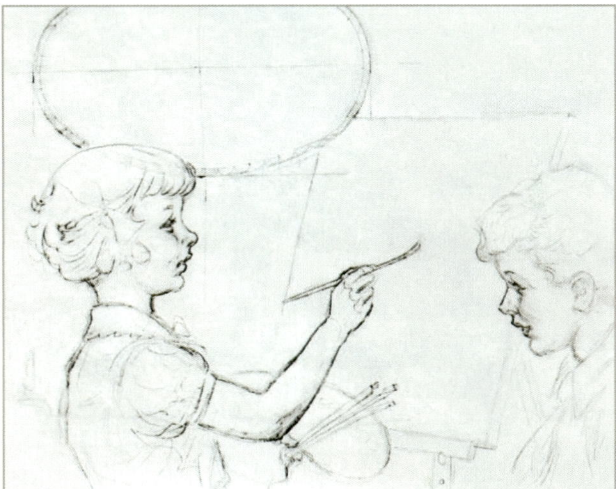

Above left: Heade's original rough for the box lid of the Philmar *A.B.C. Playcards* game pictured on the facing page. Above right: another rough, believed to have been intended for a children's painting activity set or book, although once more a published example has yet to be found. The depiction of the girl painter was again based on a photograph of Heade's daughter Sally.

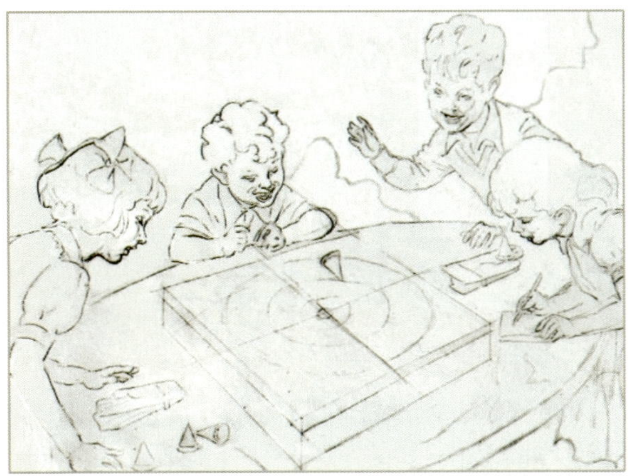

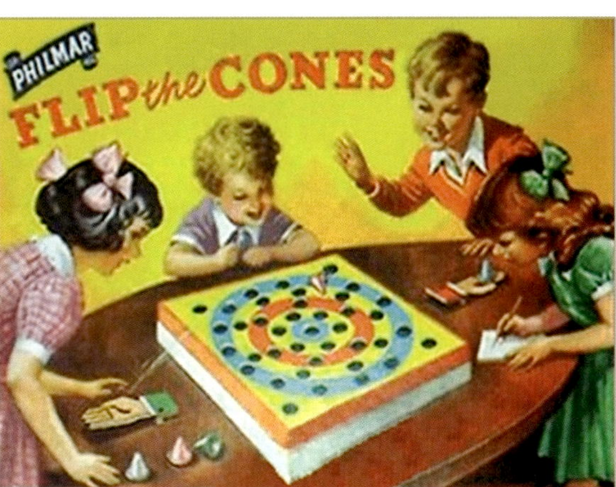

Above left: Heade's original rough for the box lid of another Philmar game, *Flip the Cones*. Above right: the game as it eventually appeared in shops, probably in the early 1950s. This is now a scarce item: although Philmar reissued the game more than once in subsequent years, later editions featured different box lid art, by other artists.

JAMES WALKER

In the early to mid-1950s, Heade supplied some advertisement illustrations for jewellers James Walker, who owned a chain of high-street stores in London and the home counties. These illustrations were generally printed in black and white or duotone, but at least one of them was in colour, and was used by the company for the cover of a free rings catalogue booklet (see opposite), which remained in print until at least 1957. The male figure from this painting was also reused by Heade in his dustjacket piece for the 1954, Hodder & Stoughton-published novel *Merry-Go-Round* by Dorothy Clewes (as pictured in the Bonus Gallery of *The Art of Reginald Heade – Special Edition*).

Below: three Heade-illustrated magazine advertisements for James Walker, the earliest of which (left) appeared in 1952.

Right: a detail from one of these advertisements.

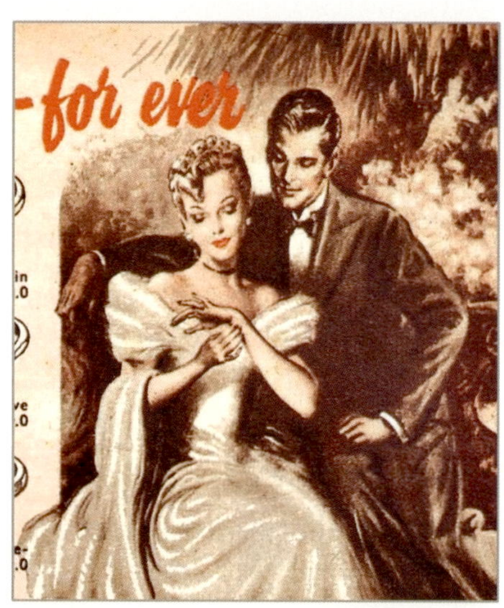

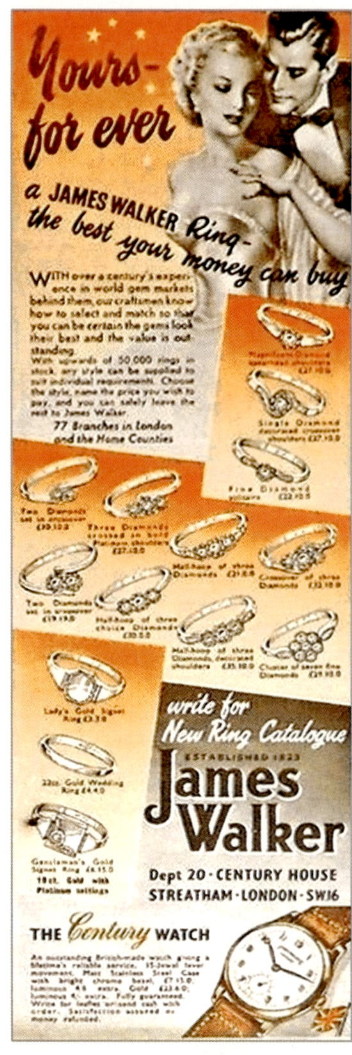

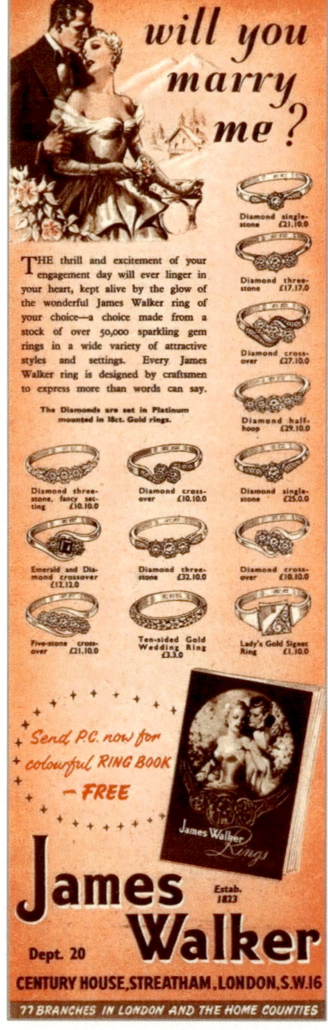

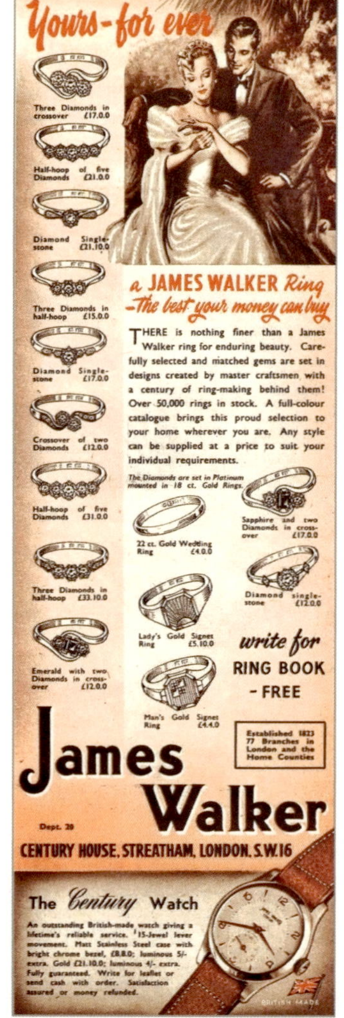

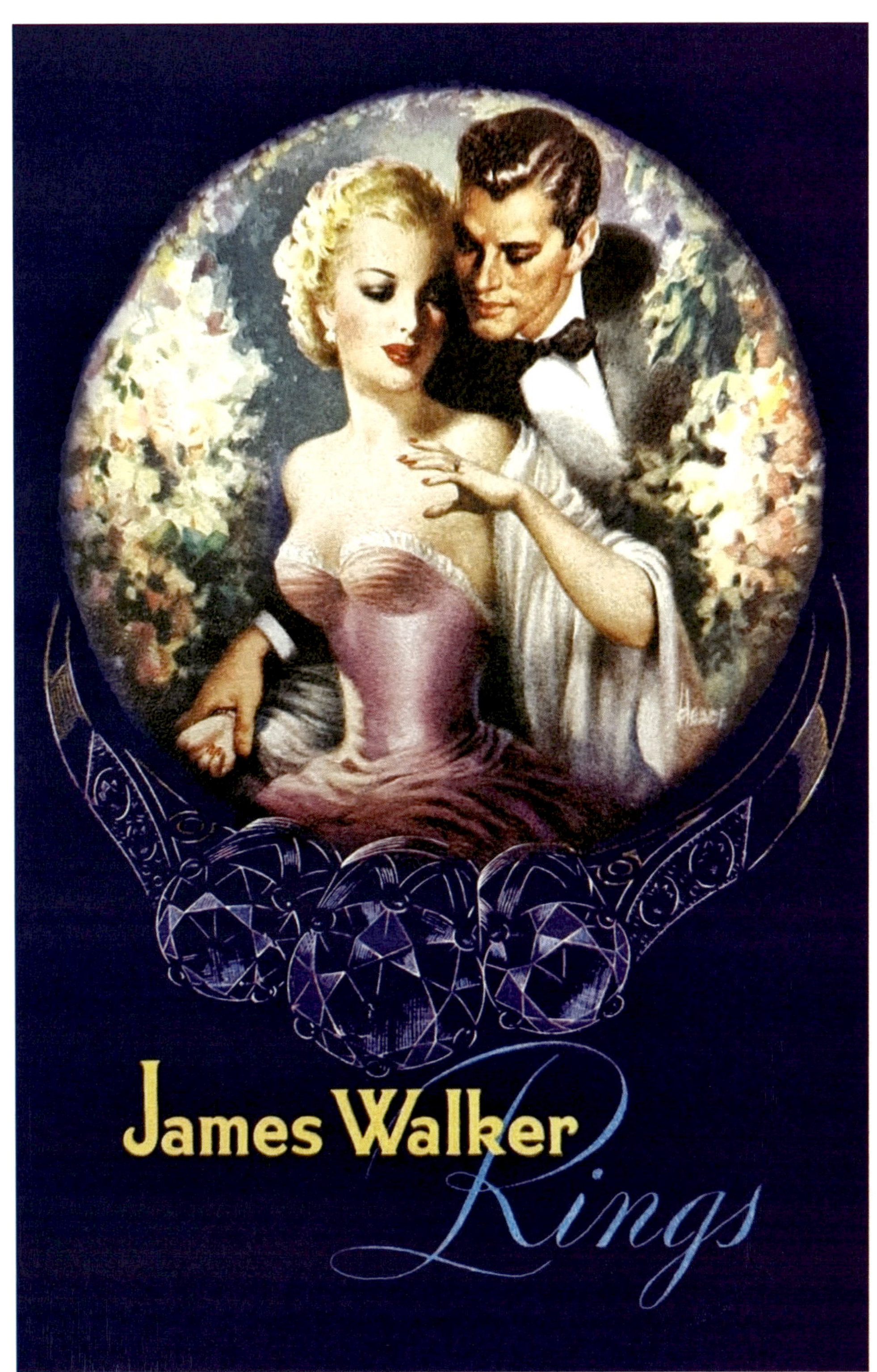

James Walker Rings (James Walker, c1952)

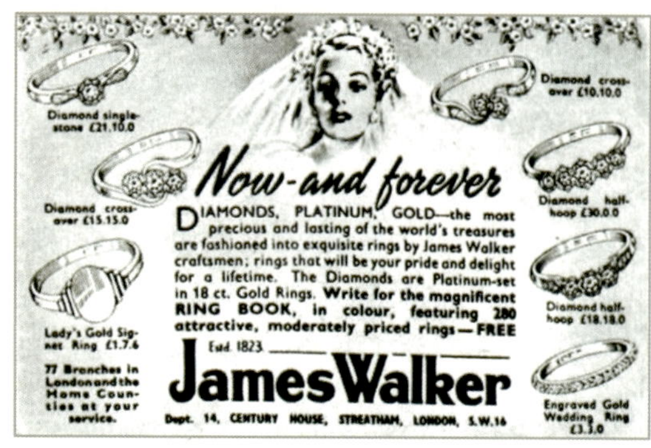

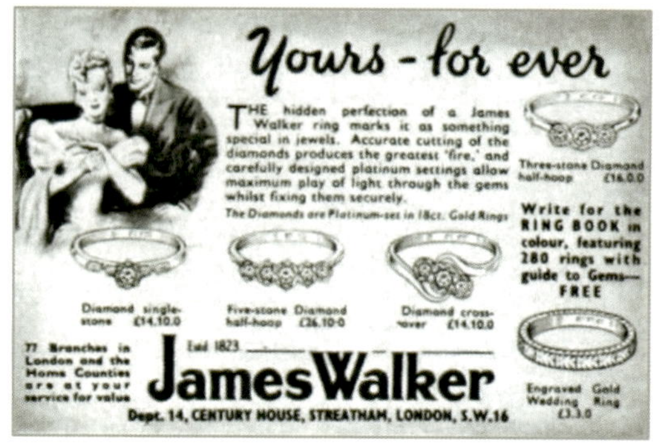

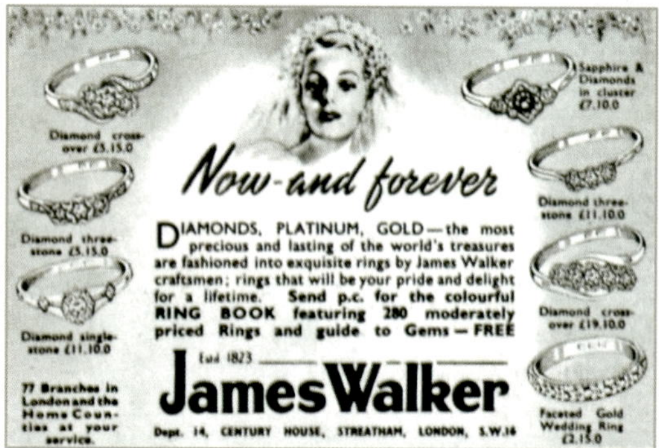

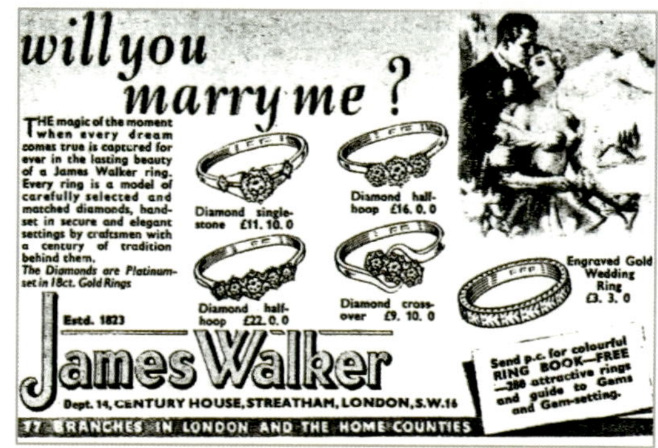

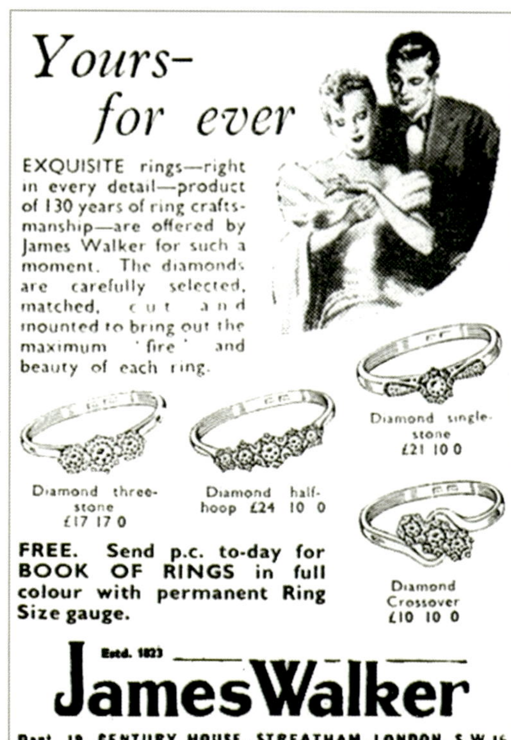

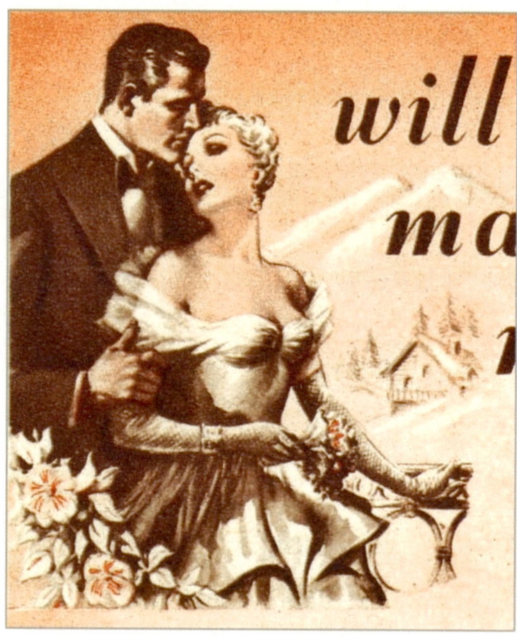

This page: a selection of black and white Heade-illustrated
James Walker press advertisements, ranging in date from 1953
(top left) to 1958 (bottom left), plus a detail from one of the
duotone ones. Publications in which these appeared included
Picture Post and *World Wide Magazine*.

MARX MOCK-UPS

Philip Marx was a highly enterprising businessman, three of whose many companies used Heade artwork: namely Philmar, Amex and PM (Productions). The known published examples are pictured elsewhere in this volume and its predecessor. However, amongst the projects that Heade undertook for Marx, in the late 1940s or early 1950s, were two that it appears may have come to nothing, as no published copies have yet been found. One of these was a Sleeping Beauty-themed book, entitled *Briar Rose*, the artist's still-surviving mock-up for which consisted of 16 stapled-together pages of relatively sketchy black-and-white pencil drawings; the front cover is shown on the right. The other was an Edward L Simmons-authored children's story book called *The Unhappy House*. The mock-up for this, again still-surviving, was more elaborate, with full colour on the front cover, the double-page title spread and some of the internal page illustrations. The book eventually appeared circa 1951 from Bairns Books, another Philip Marx company, under the revised title *The Lonely Little House*, but with art by a different artist. The front cover of Heade's rough, and details of two of the internal pages, are shown below.

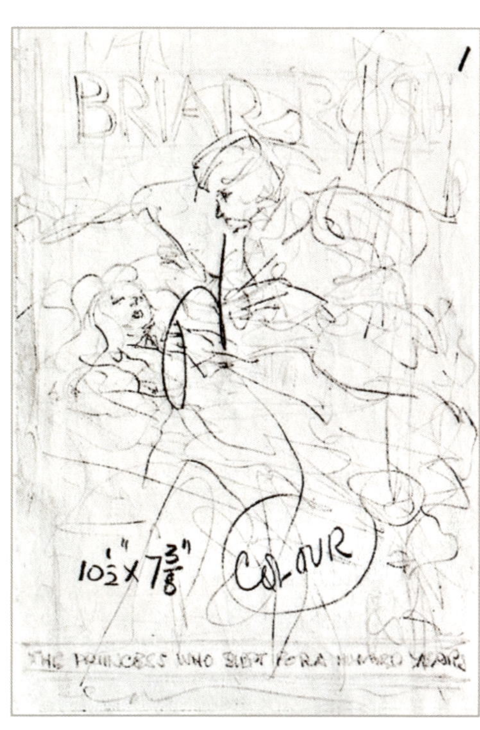

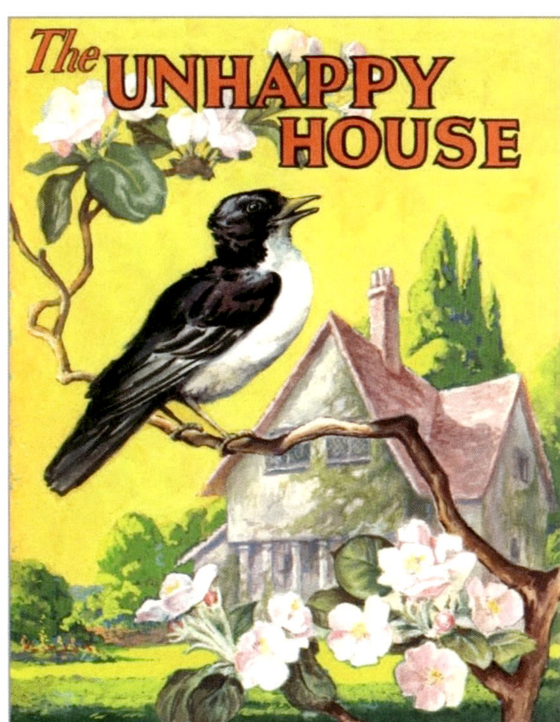

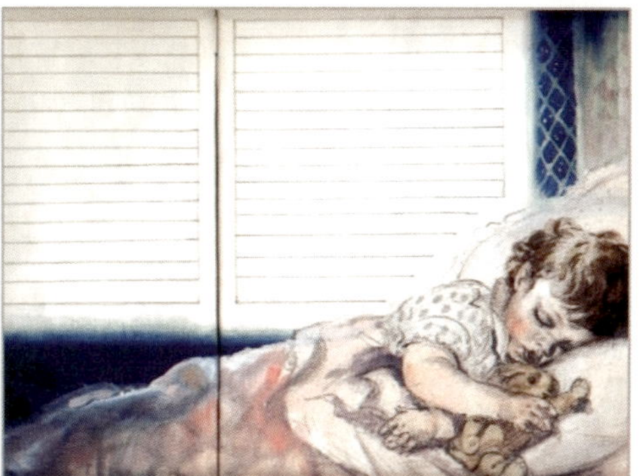

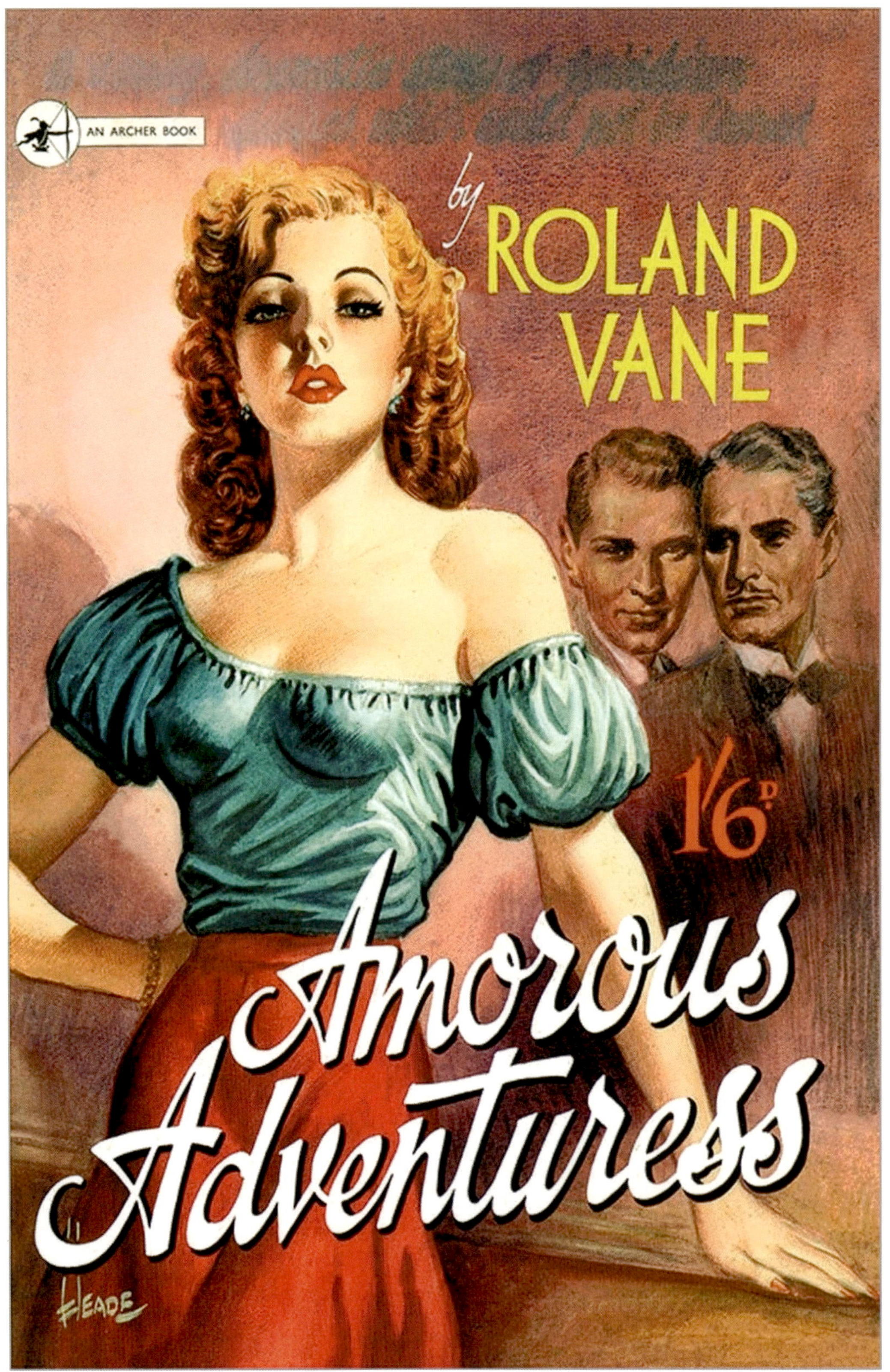

Heade's original painting for *Amorous Adventuress* by Roland Vane (Archer, April 1952). The initial intention was to have some wording appear at the top, and Heade included this in his work, but in the end it was over-painted and did not appear on the as-published cover.

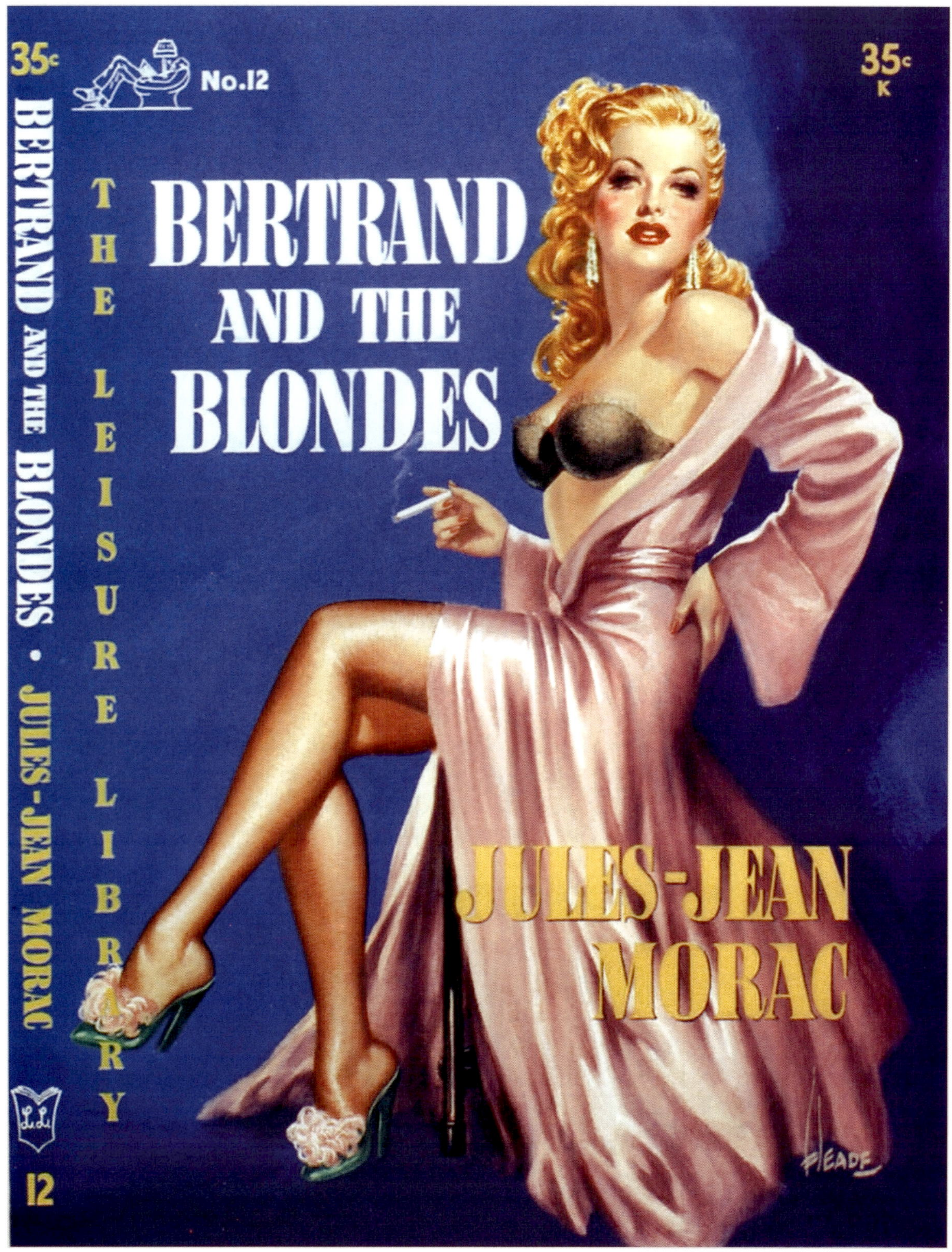

Heade's original painting for the US-published *Bertrand and the Blondes* by Jules-Jean Morac (Leisure Library, 1952).

(Image courtesy the Steve Chibnall Collection.)

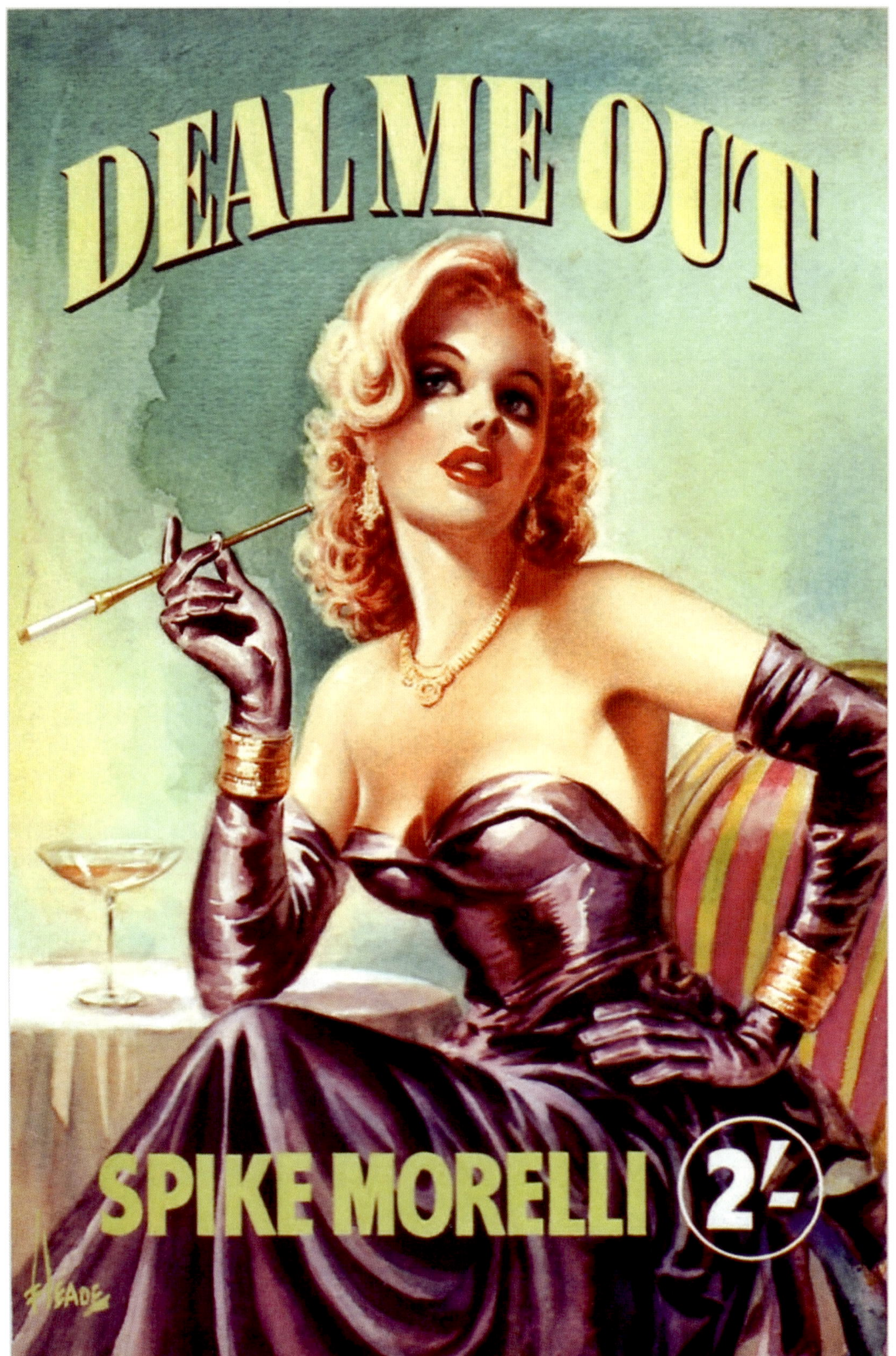

Heade's original painting for *Deal Me Out* by Spike Morelli (Harborough, September 1952). (Image courtesy the Steve Chibnall Collection.)

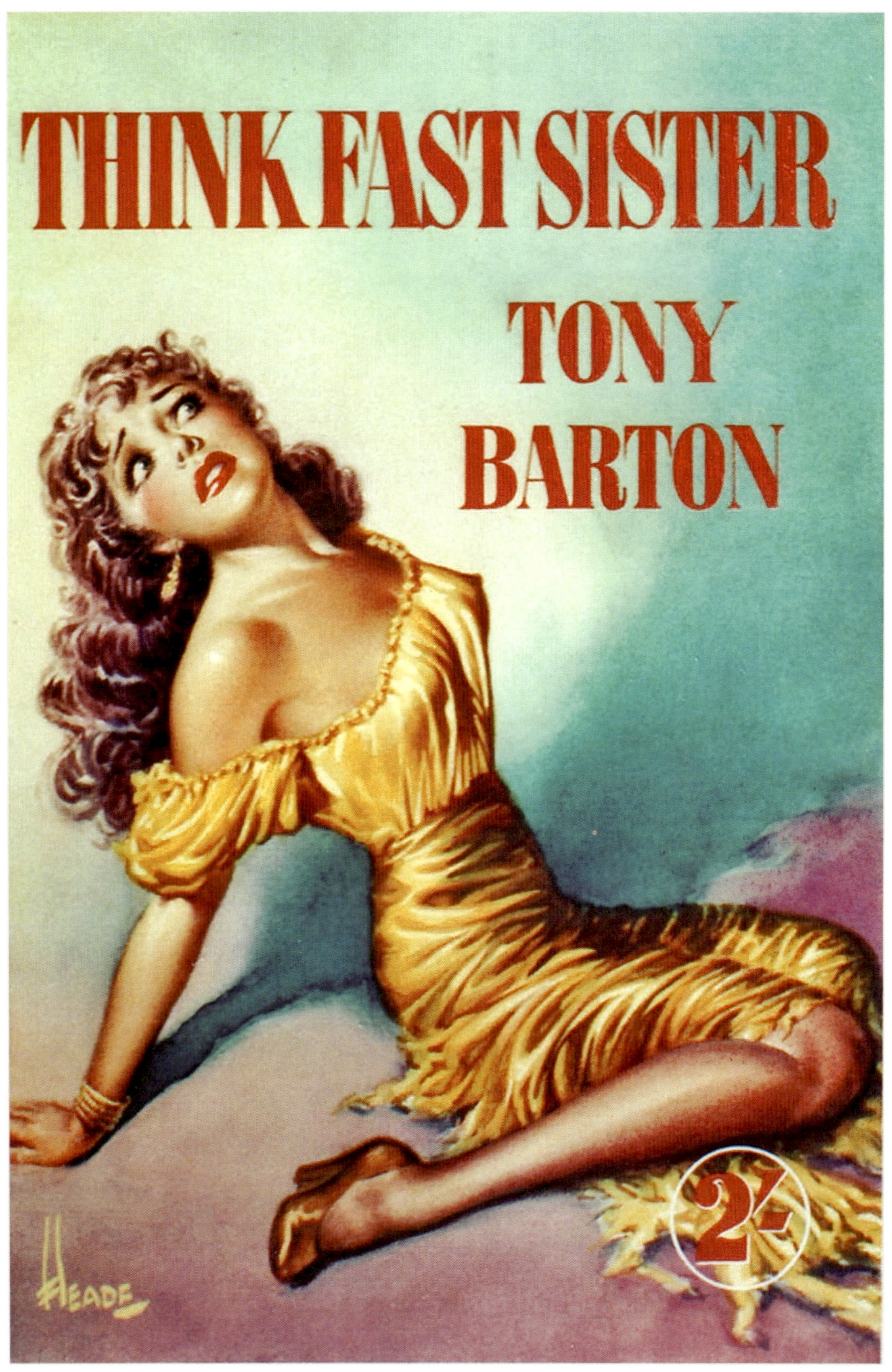

Heade's original painting for *Think Fast Sister* by Tony Barton (Harborough, September 1952). (Image courtesy the Steve Chibnall Collection.)

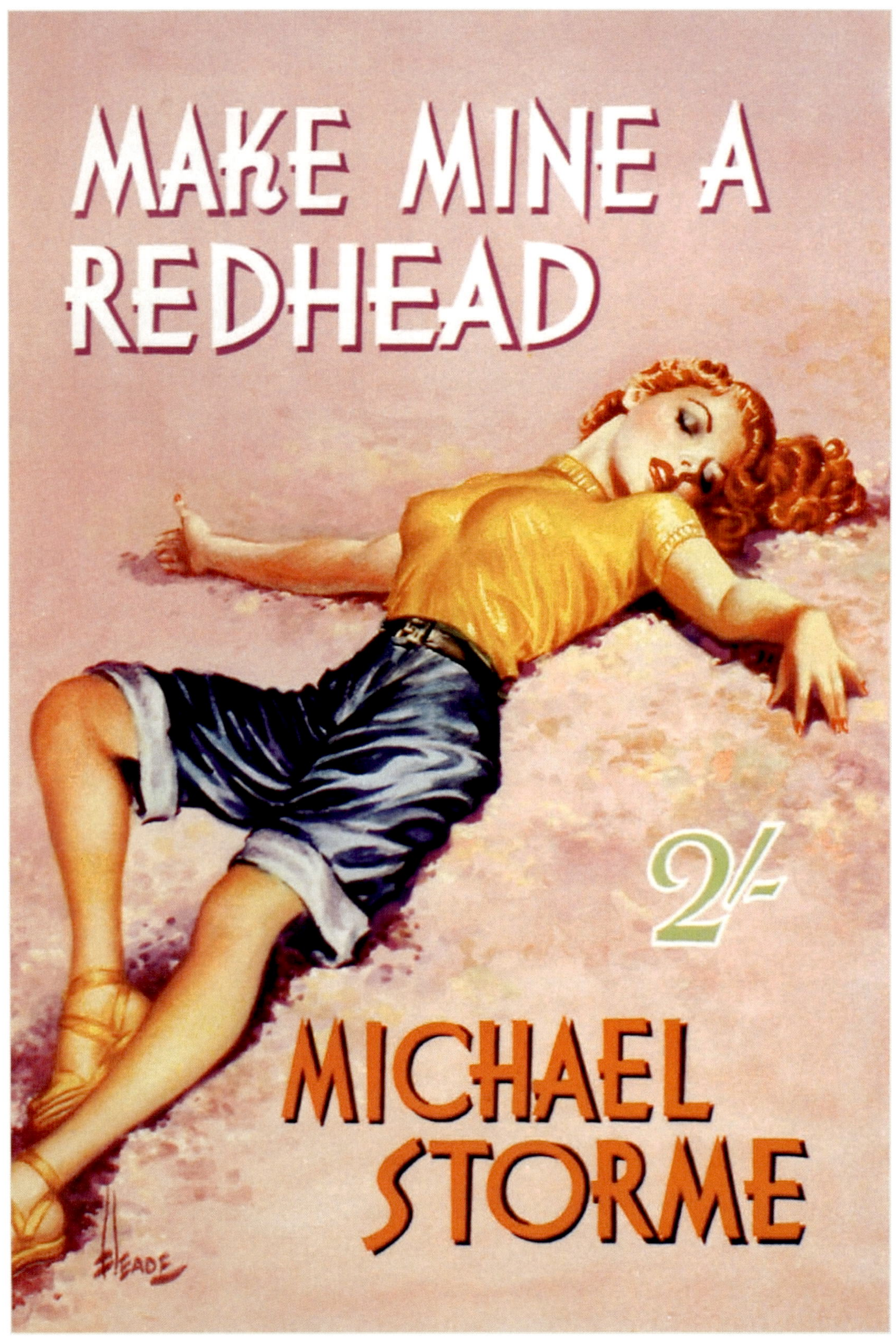

Heade's original painting for *Make Mine a Redhead* by Michael Storme (Harborough, October 1952)

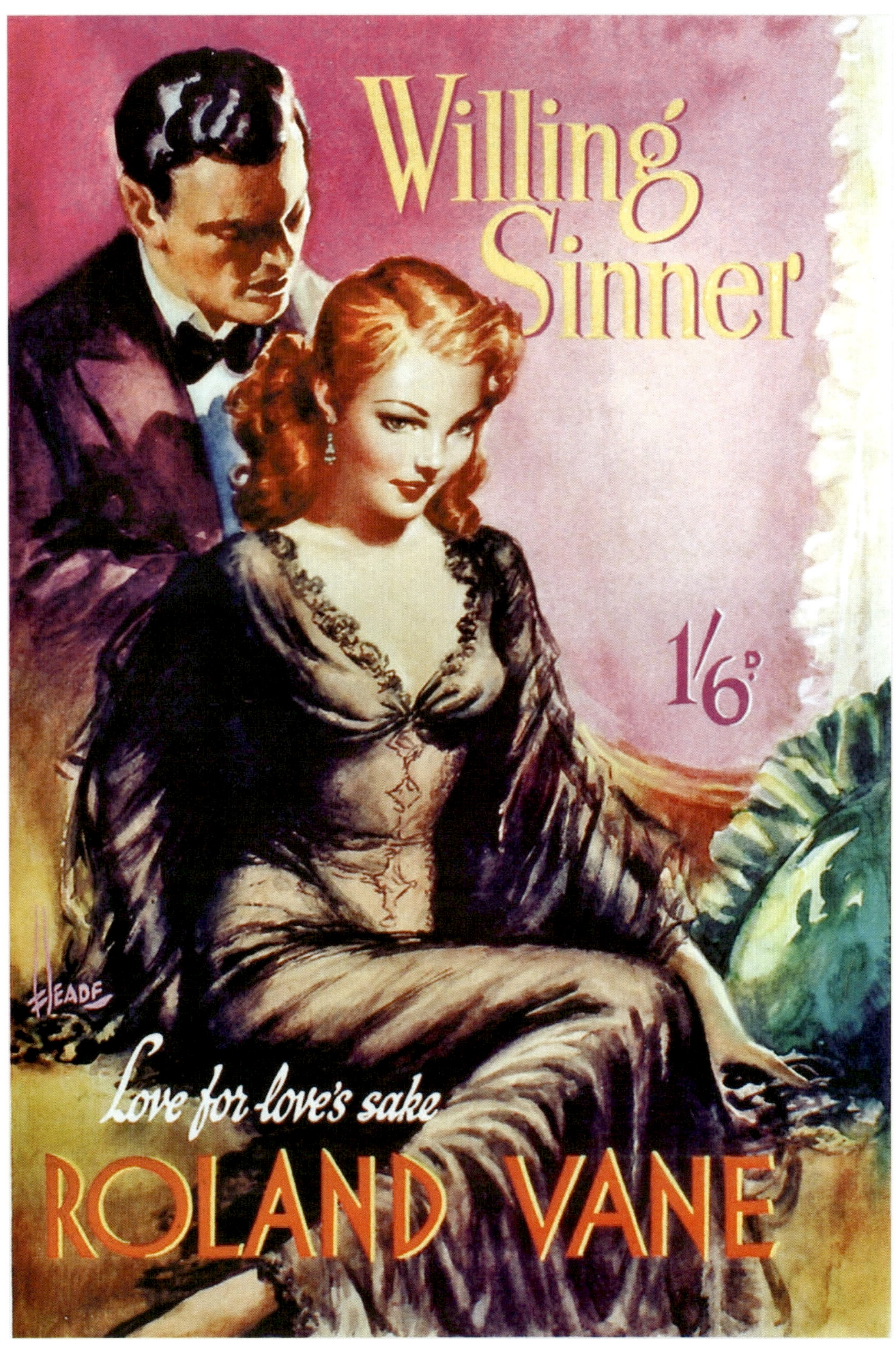

Heade's original painting for *Willing Sinner* by Roland Vane (Archer, November 1952)

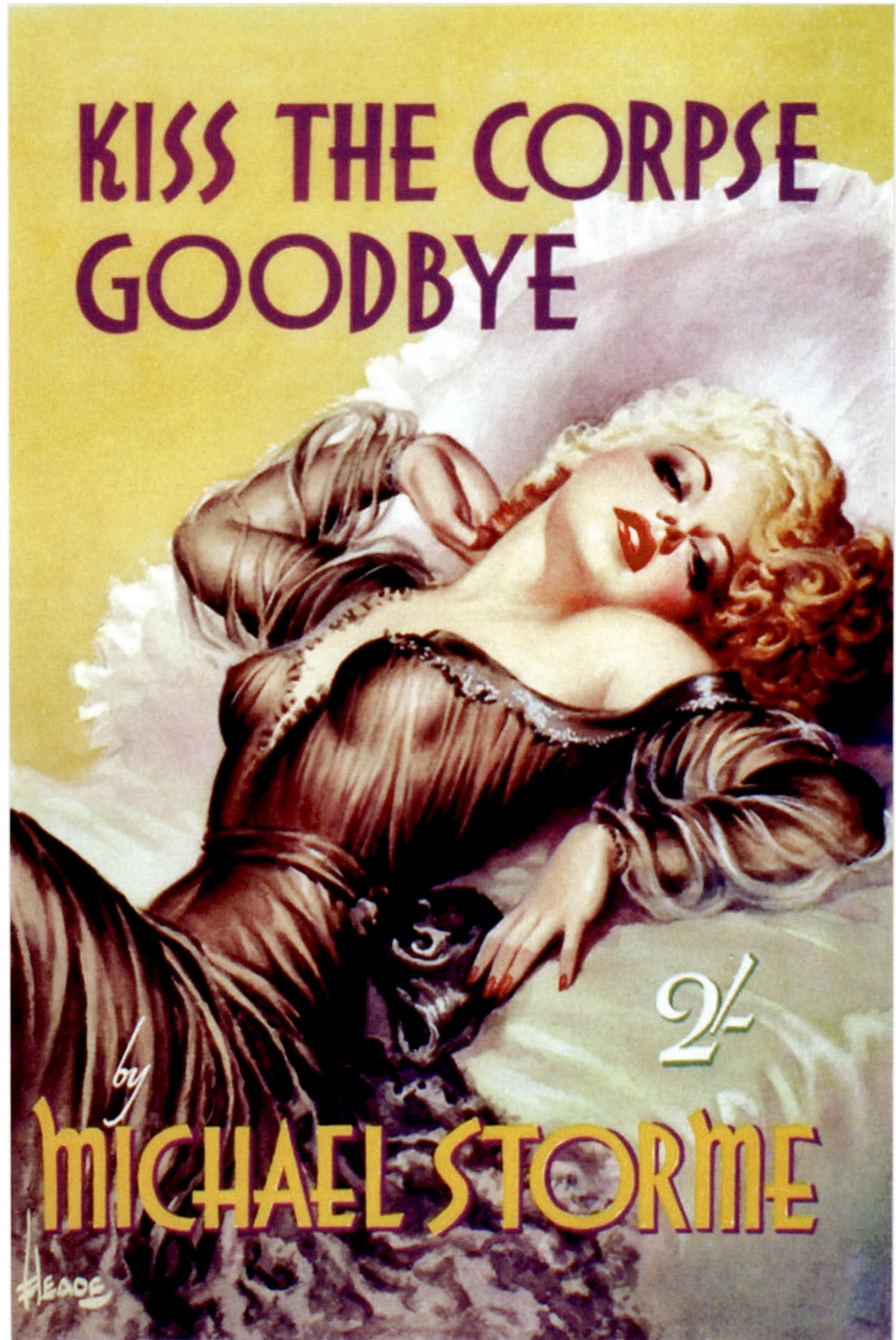

Heade's original painting for *Kiss the Corpse Goodbye* by Michael Storme (Harborough, November 1952). (Image courtesy the Steve Chibnall Collection.)

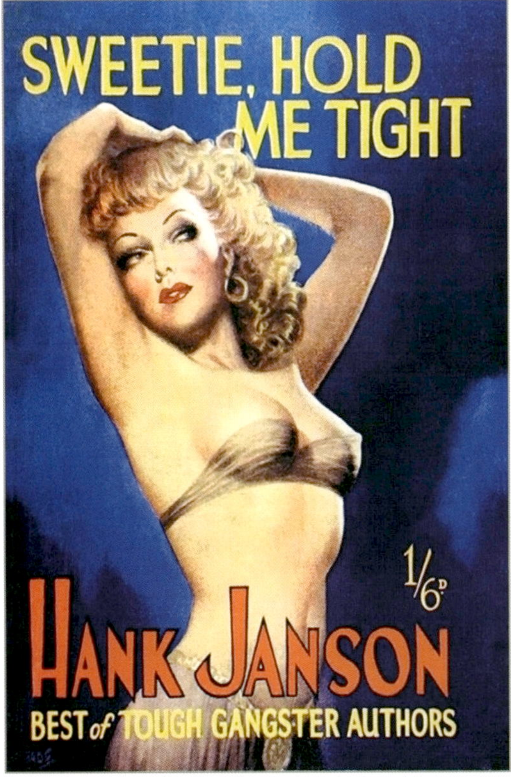

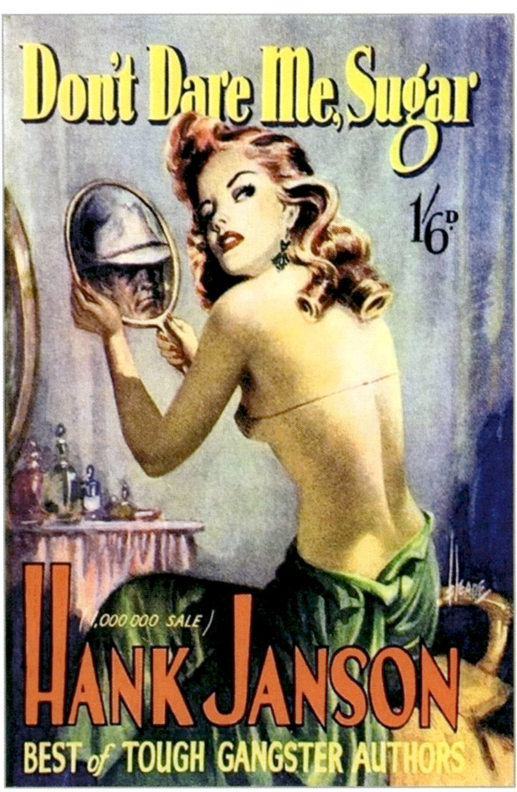

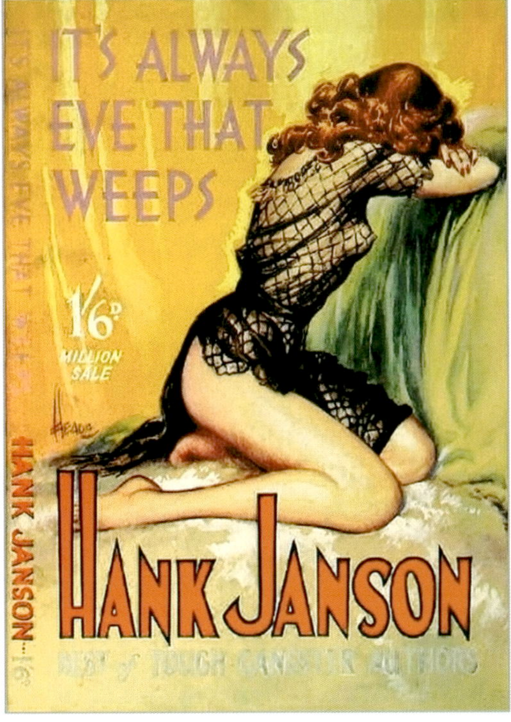

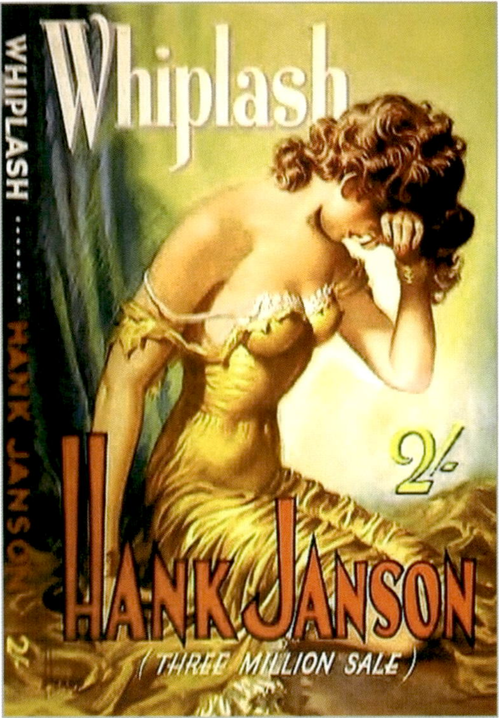

Four of the outstanding Hank Janson pieces for which Heade is perhaps still best known: *Sweetie, Hold Me Tight* (S D Frances, February 1950); *Don't Dare Me, Sugar* (S D Frances, May 1950), the only classic-era Janson cover actually to show Hank's face (reflected in the hand mirror); the original painting for *It's Always Eve That Weeps* (S D Frances, June 1951); and the original painting for *Whiplash* (New Fiction Press, August 1952).

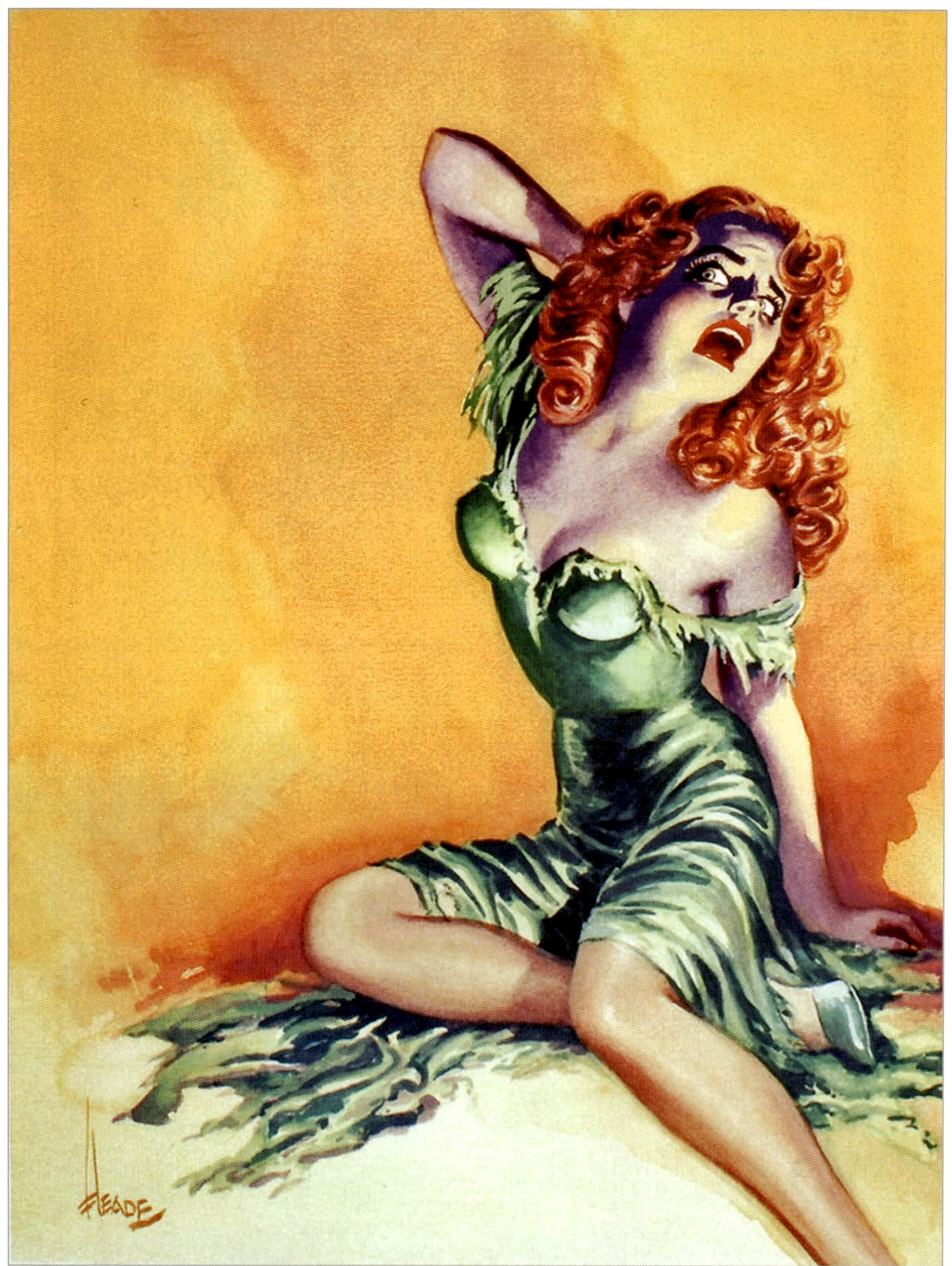

Heade's original painting for the US-published *Honey Hold That Scream* by Tony Angelo (Leisure Library, 1952)

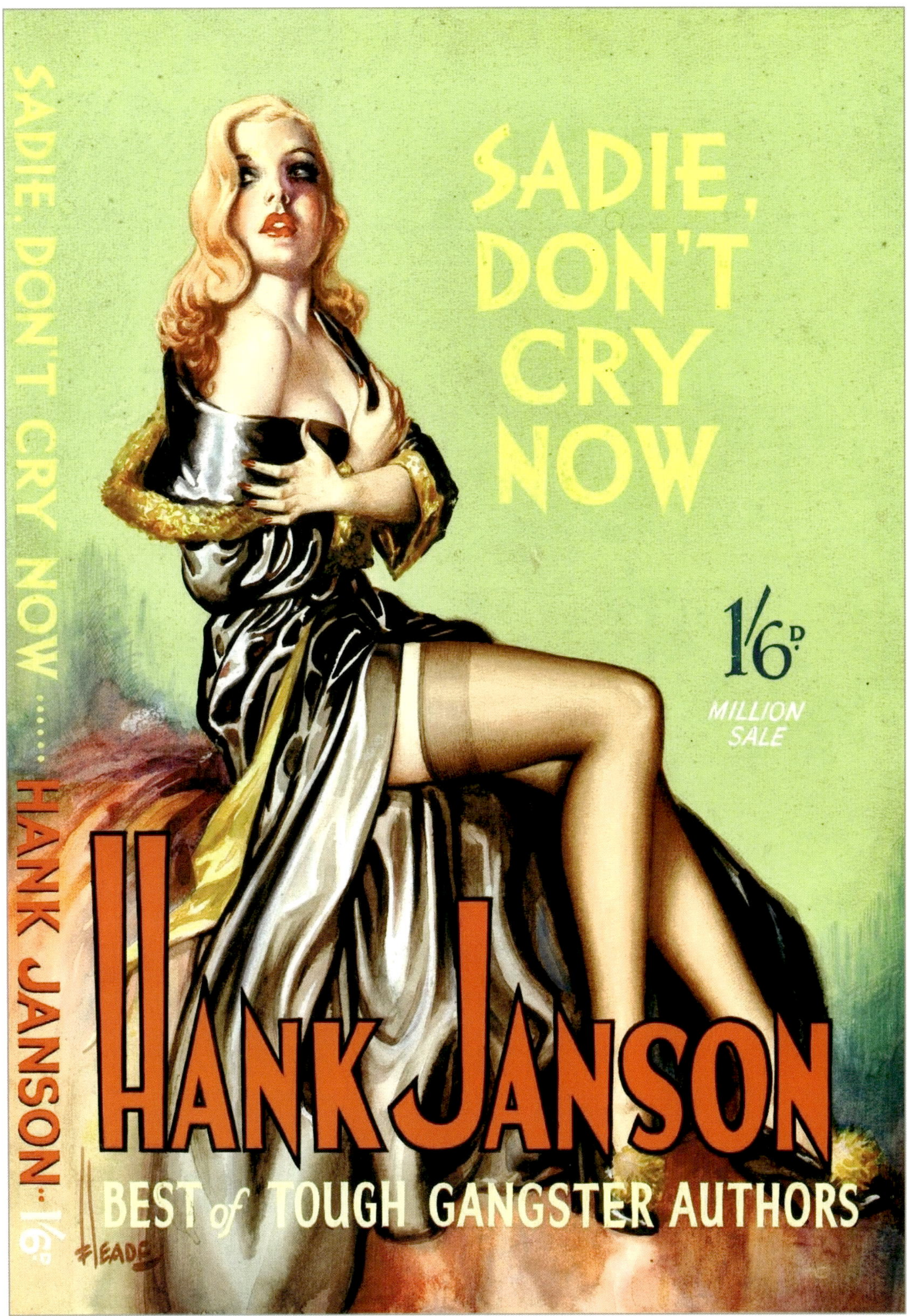

This Heade original was intended to grace the first edition of the Hank Janson novel *Sadie, Don't Cry Now* when it appeared in January 1952, but was dropped prior to publication in favour of a more chaste composition, to try to avoid problems with the authorities. It was reinstated for an ultra-rare 1953 reissue, overprinted with a darker green background and a new 2/- price. (Image courtesy Rian Hughes.)

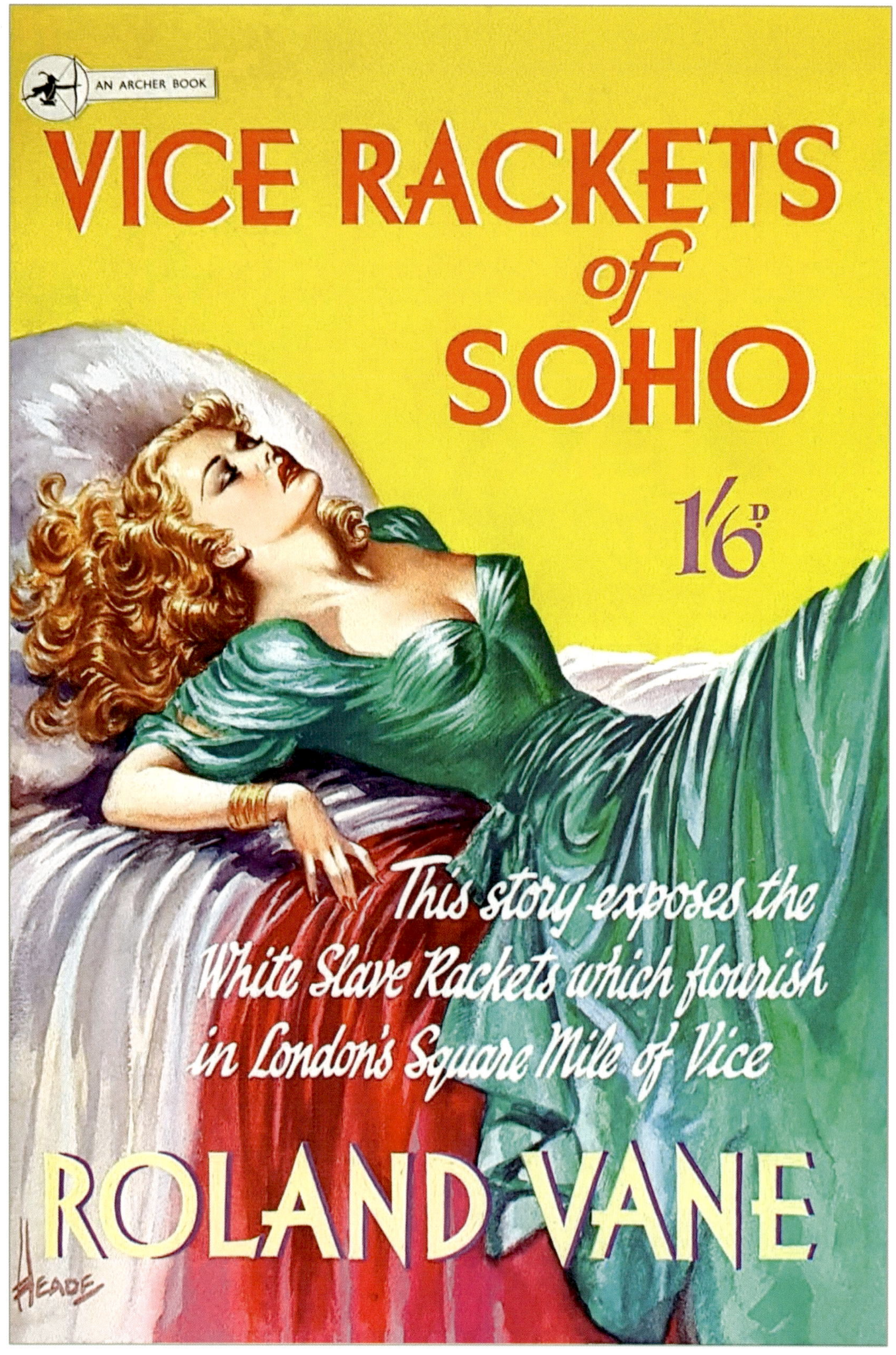

Heade's original painting for the reissue of *Vice Rackets of Soho* by Roland Vane (Archer, August 1953). (Image courtesy a private collector.)

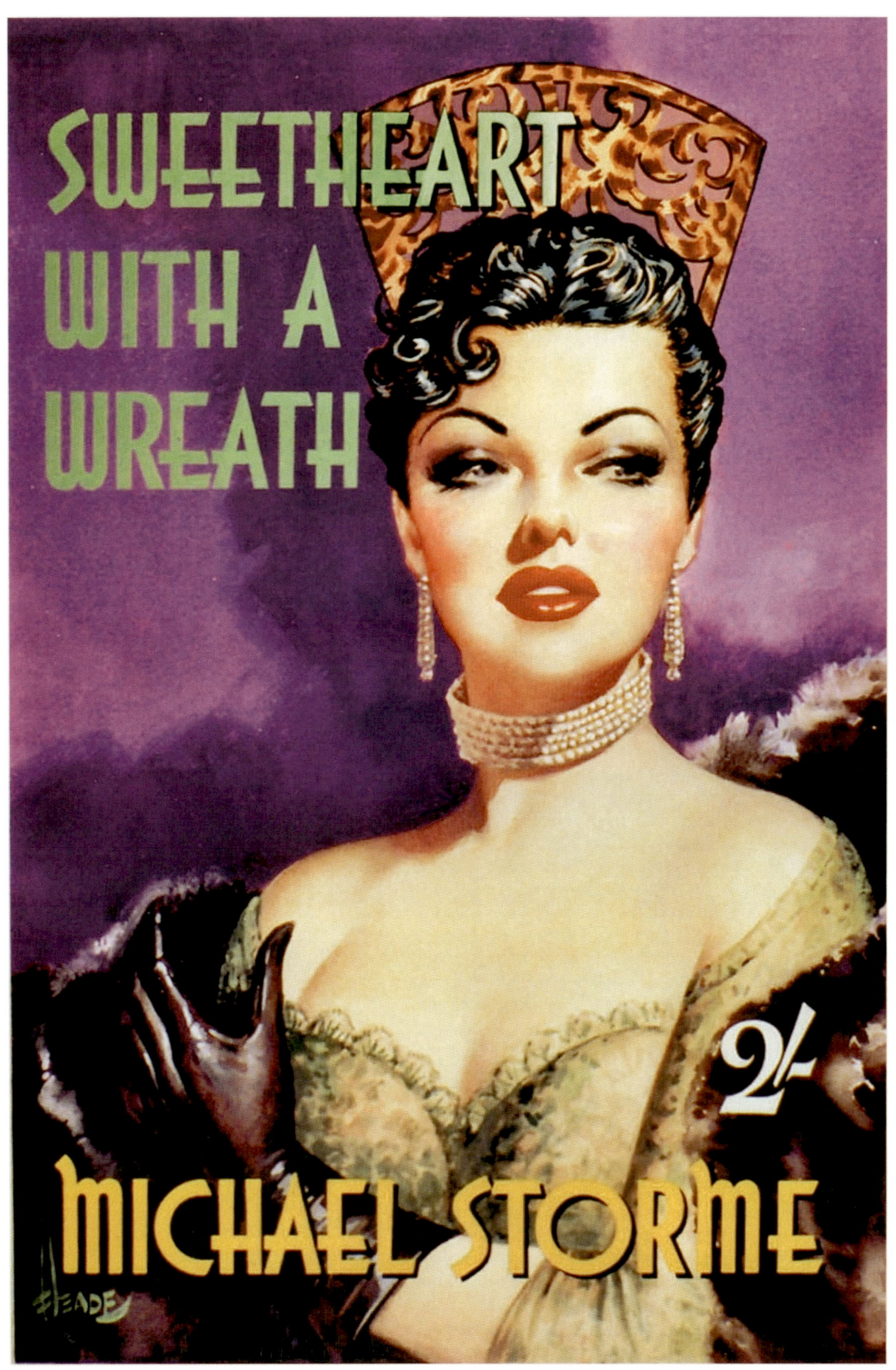

Heade's original painting for *Sweetheart With a Wreath* by Michael Storme (Archer, July 1953). (Image courtesy the Steve Chibnall Collection.)

ARTWORK ADAPTATIONS

As noted in previous sections, a number of Heade's cover paintings were used more than once, sometimes with adaptations. Whereas Hodder & Stoughton often reused artwork for multiple editions of the same books, such as *Flame in the Wind* by Margaret Pedler and *These Are Our Masters* by Annie S Swan, Mills & Boon were more inclined to repurpose 1940s pieces for entirely different 1950s reissues, adding coloured bands to obscure the original title and author's name. Another known example of this is their reuse of the same, currently unidentified earlier Heade painting on two different reissues, *Gone Away* by Marjorie Moore (1954) and *The Bride Goes East* by Romilly Brent (1957) (as both pictured, with date captions now known to be incorrect, in *The Art of Reginald Heade – Special Edition*). Collins meanwhile had Heade's dustjacket painting for the 1948-published Western *The Rider from Yonder* by Norman Fox (see top right) reworked, doubtless by a different artist, for the cover of a 1949-published, Canada-only White Circle Pocket Edition paperback, *Wild Country* by Wade Smith (see bottom right).

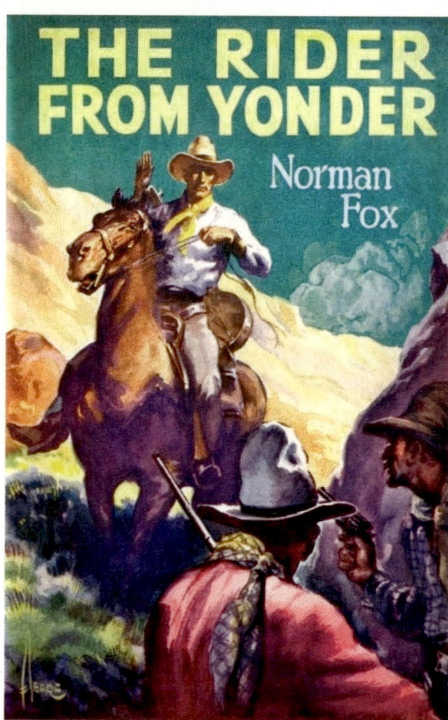

The pulp paperback publishers, too, would sometimes resort to the reuse of artwork. For example, most of Heade's cover paintings for the US-published Leisure Library books also appeared on UK-published titles from Raymond and Lilian Locker's associated companies. Of particular note, in 1953 the painting for the Leisure Library title *Curves Cause Trouble* by Gene Ross was adapted for the Archer book *Sweetheart With a Wreath* by Michael Storme, with the female subject given a different colour and style of hair, plus a tiara. (The adapted painting still survives – see previous page.) Other Leisure Library cover paintings similarly adapted for their UK appearances included those for *This Way for Hell* by Spike Morelli and *Two Smart Dames* by Gene Ross.

One reason for this reuse and adaptation of cover paintings was financial: it saved the publishers the expense of commissioning new pieces. Another, though, was a form of self-censorship by the pulp paperback imprints, to try to avoid incurring the wrath of the authorities, which had already seen numerous books being banned, with copies seized and destroyed, and some of those involved suffering prosecution, conviction and imprisonment under the Obscene Publications Act. The most extreme instance of this self-censorship affecting Heade's work came on two of the 1951 Hank Janson novels, where the artwork was almost completely obscured by being silvered over. In other cases, however, the approach was more subtle. One example discovered subsequent to the publication of *The Art of Reginald Heade – Special Edition* is a 1952 Archer reissue of the Paul Rénin novel *A Fortnight's Folly*. This not only presented Heade's artwork in a print quality notably superior to that of the 1950 Harborough original (albeit with slightly less of the image visible above the title) but also featured one significant change to the composition: the girl bather's towel was extended sideways so that less of her flesh was exposed (see facing page, bottom left and right, for the two different versions).

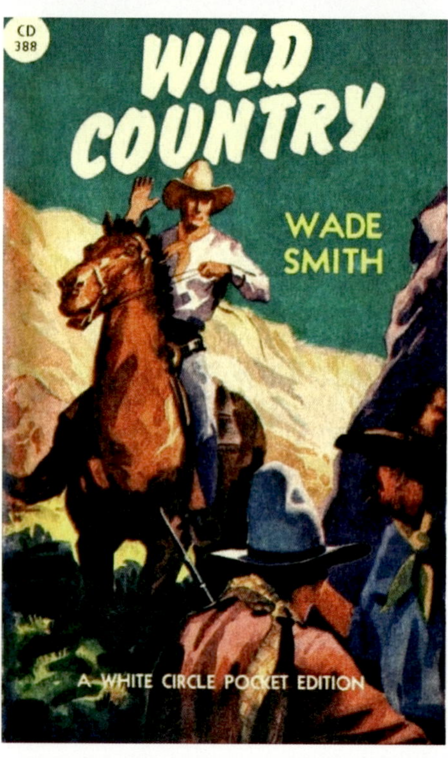

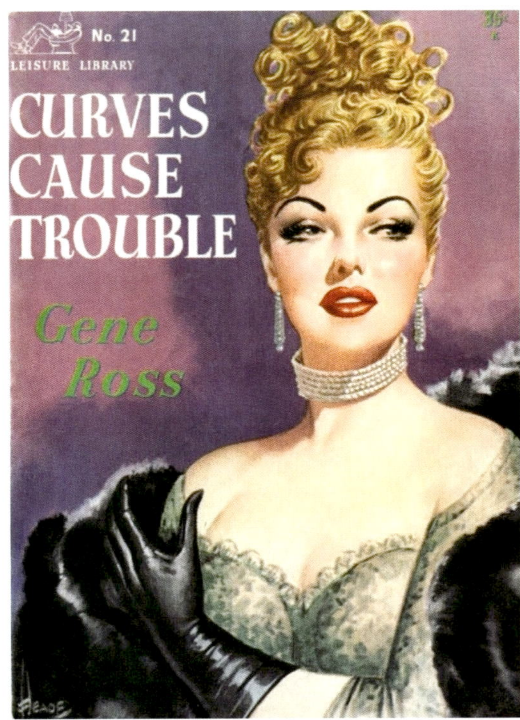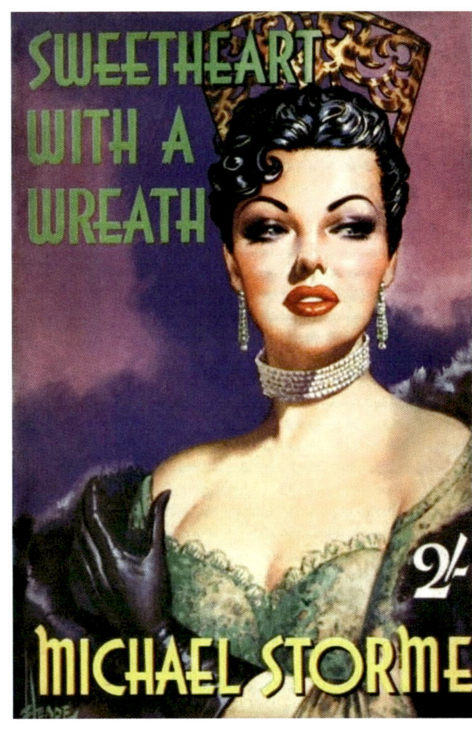

Above: the two 1953-published versions of Heade's original painting for *Sweetheart With a Wreath* by Michael Storme.

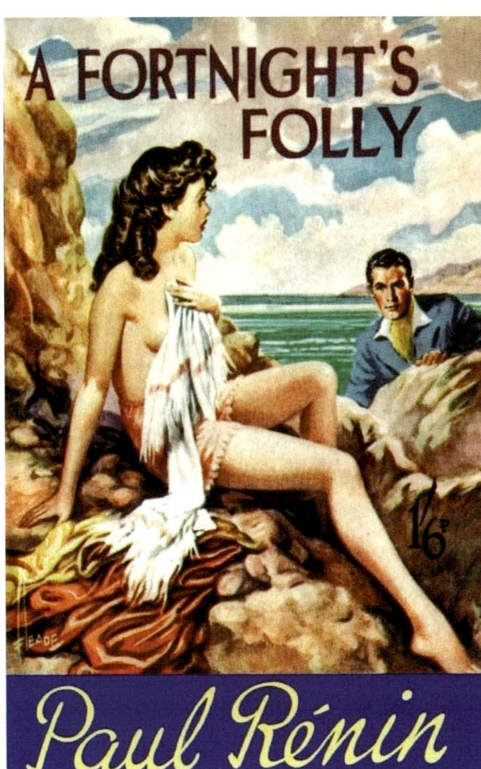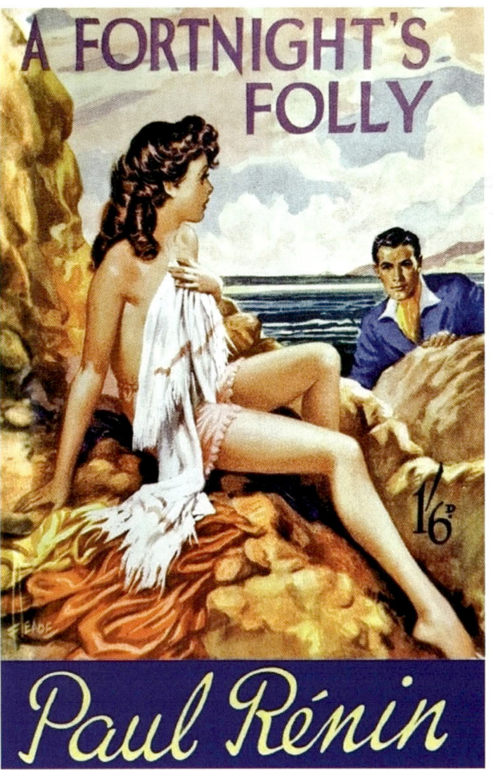

Above: the 1950 original (left) and the self-censored 1952 reissue (right) of Heade's cover for Paul Rénin's *A Fortnight's Folly*.

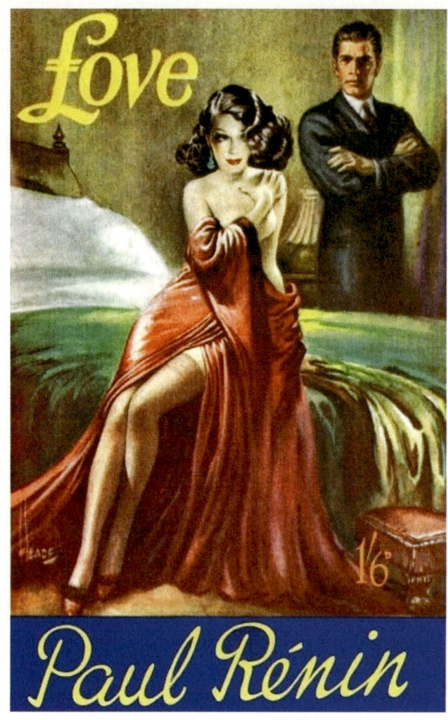

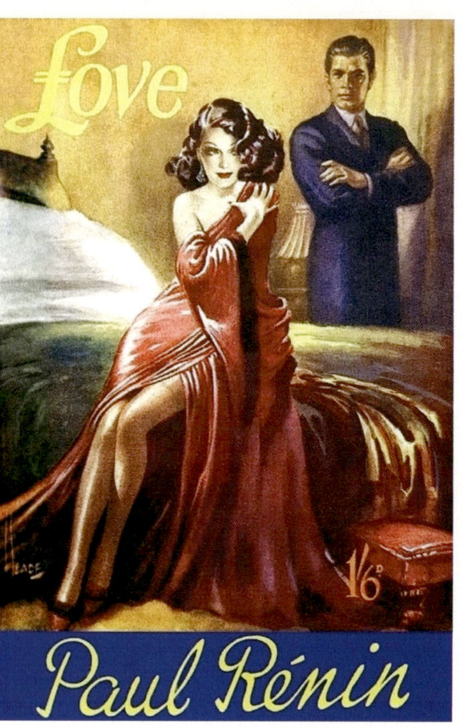

Above: another, previously-identified example of publishers' self-censorship of Heade's work; the c1950 Harborough original (left) and the more chaste 1952 Archer reissue (right) of *Love* by Paul Rénin.

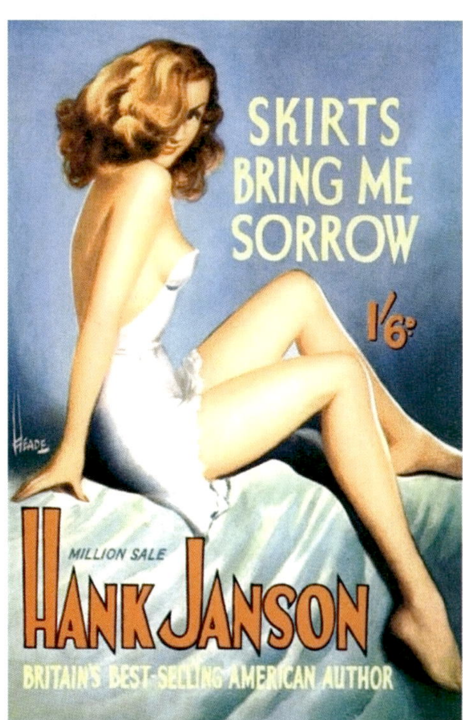

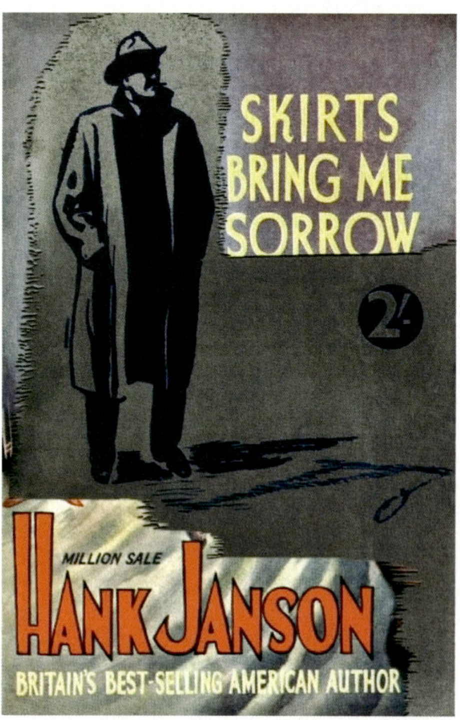

Above: the most extreme form of self-censorship by a pulp publisher: Heade's original art for *Skirts Bring Me Sorrow* by Hank Janson (New Fiction Press, 1951) (left) and the silvered-over, obscured version actually published (right).

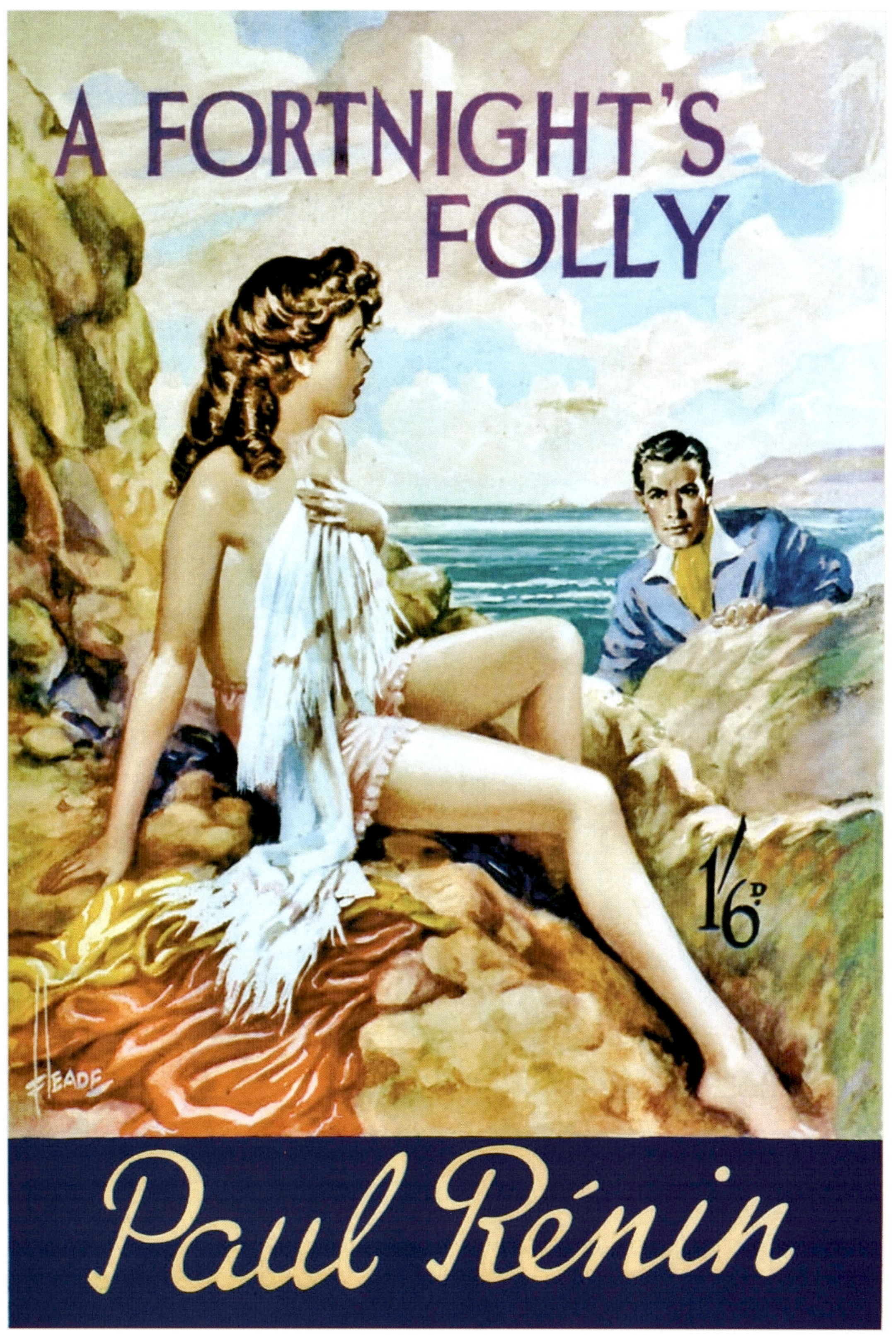

Heade's original painting for *A Fortnight's Folly* by Paul Rénin, as adapted for the self-censored reissue (Archer, 1952).

(Image courtesy the Steve Chibnall Collection.)

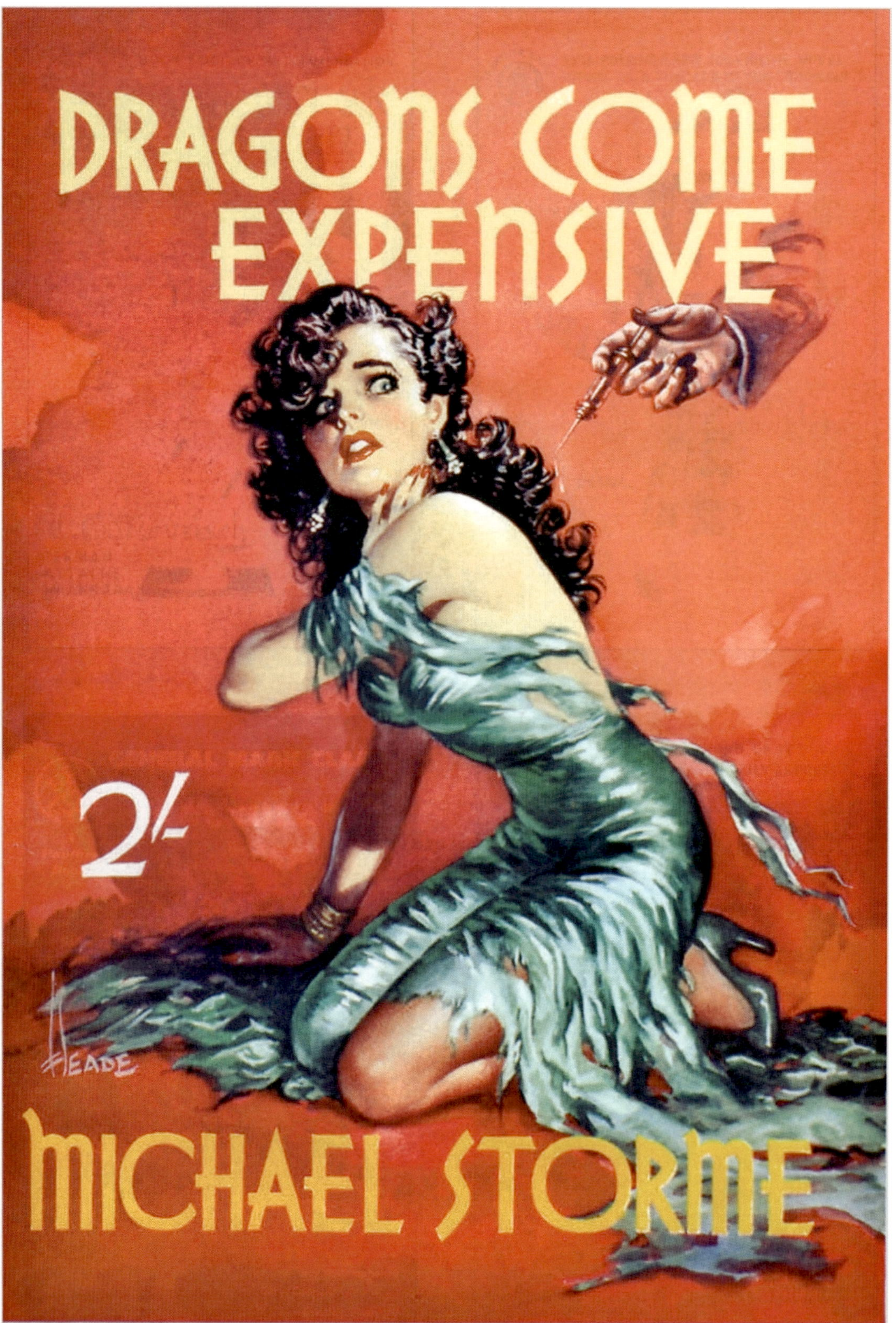

Heade's original painting for *Dragons Come Expensive* by Michael Storme (Harborough, March 1953). The male arm holding the hypodermic did not appear on the printed book cover; presumably it was removed by the publisher's art editor. (Image courtesy the Steve Chibnall Collection.)

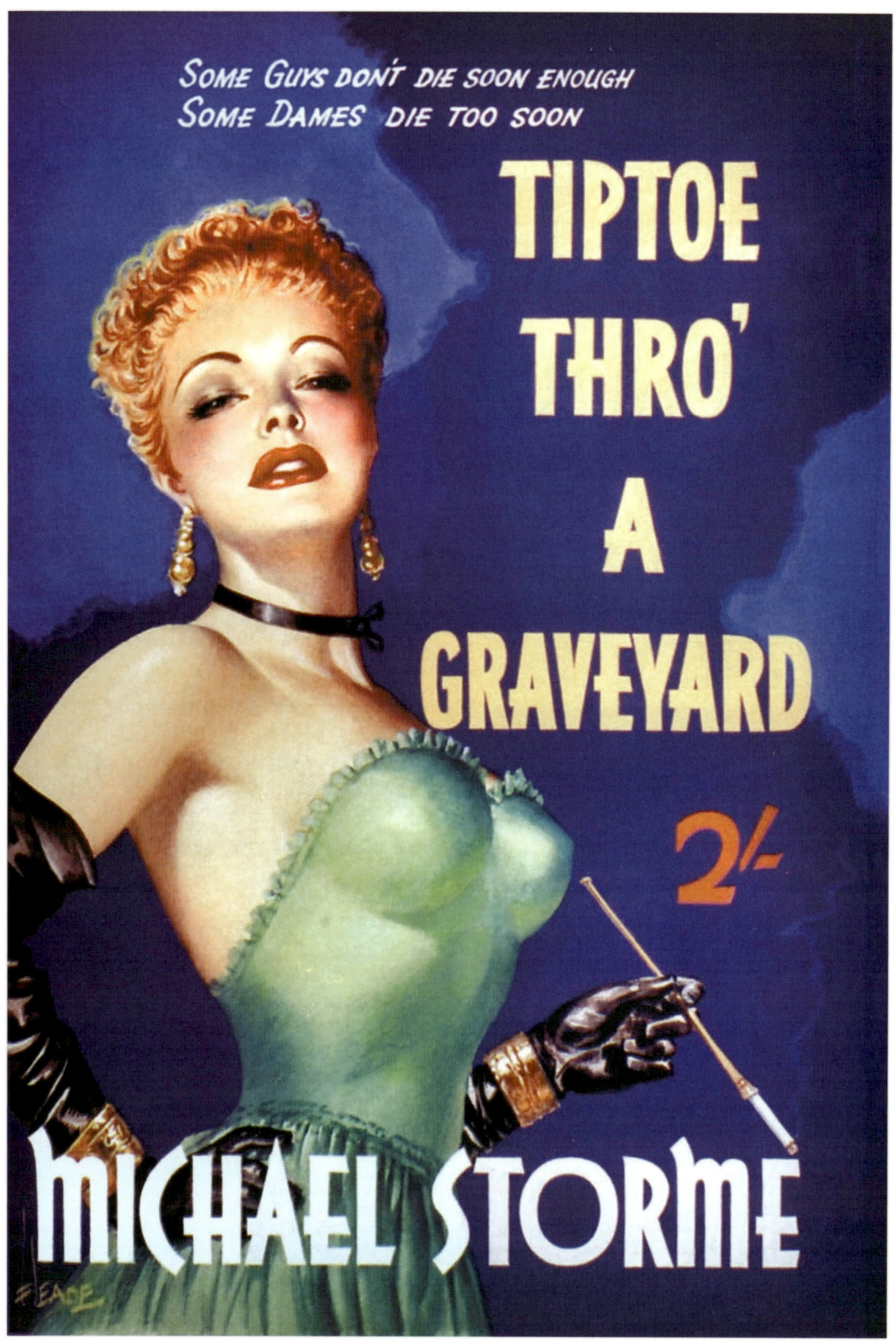

Heade's original painting for *Tiptoe Thro' a Graveyard* by Michael Storme (Harborough, 1953). (Image courtesy the Steve Chibnall Collection.)

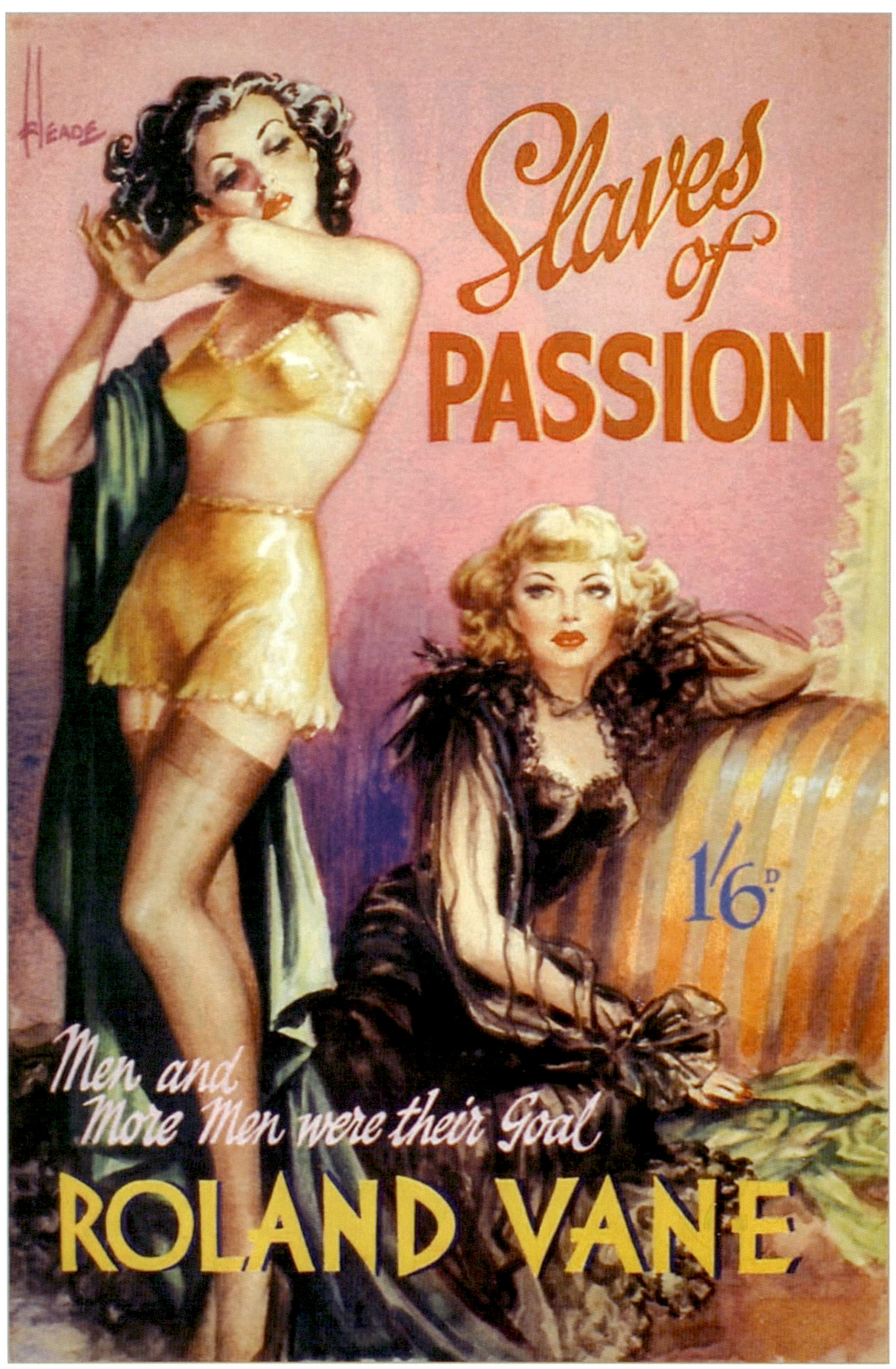

Heade's original painting, unpublished version, for *Slaves of Passion* by Roland Vane (Archer, March 1953). (Image courtesy the Steve Chibnall Collection.)

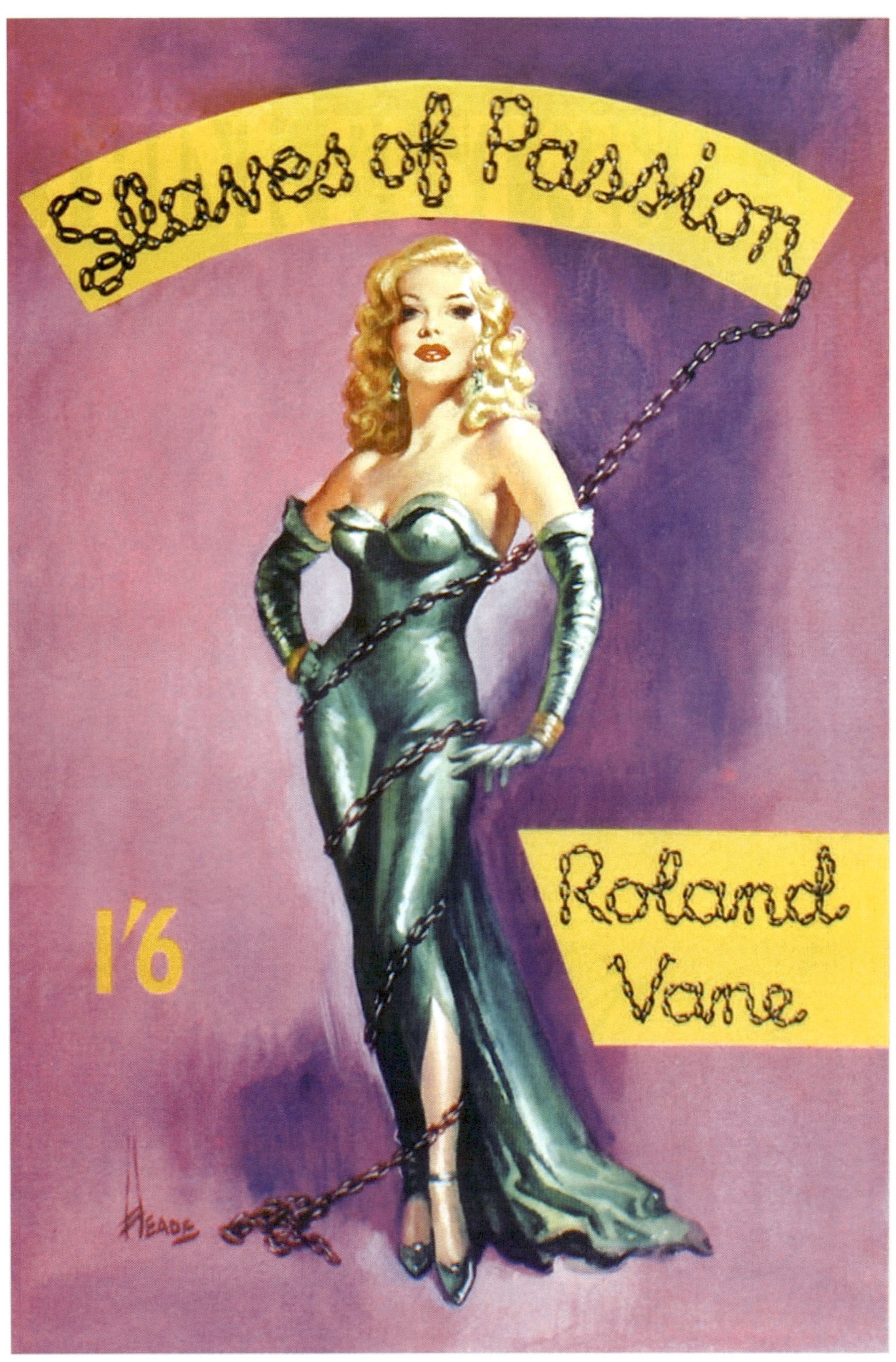

Heade's original painting, published version, for *Slaves of Passion* by Roland Vane (Archer, March 1953). (Image courtesy the Steve Chibnall Collection.)

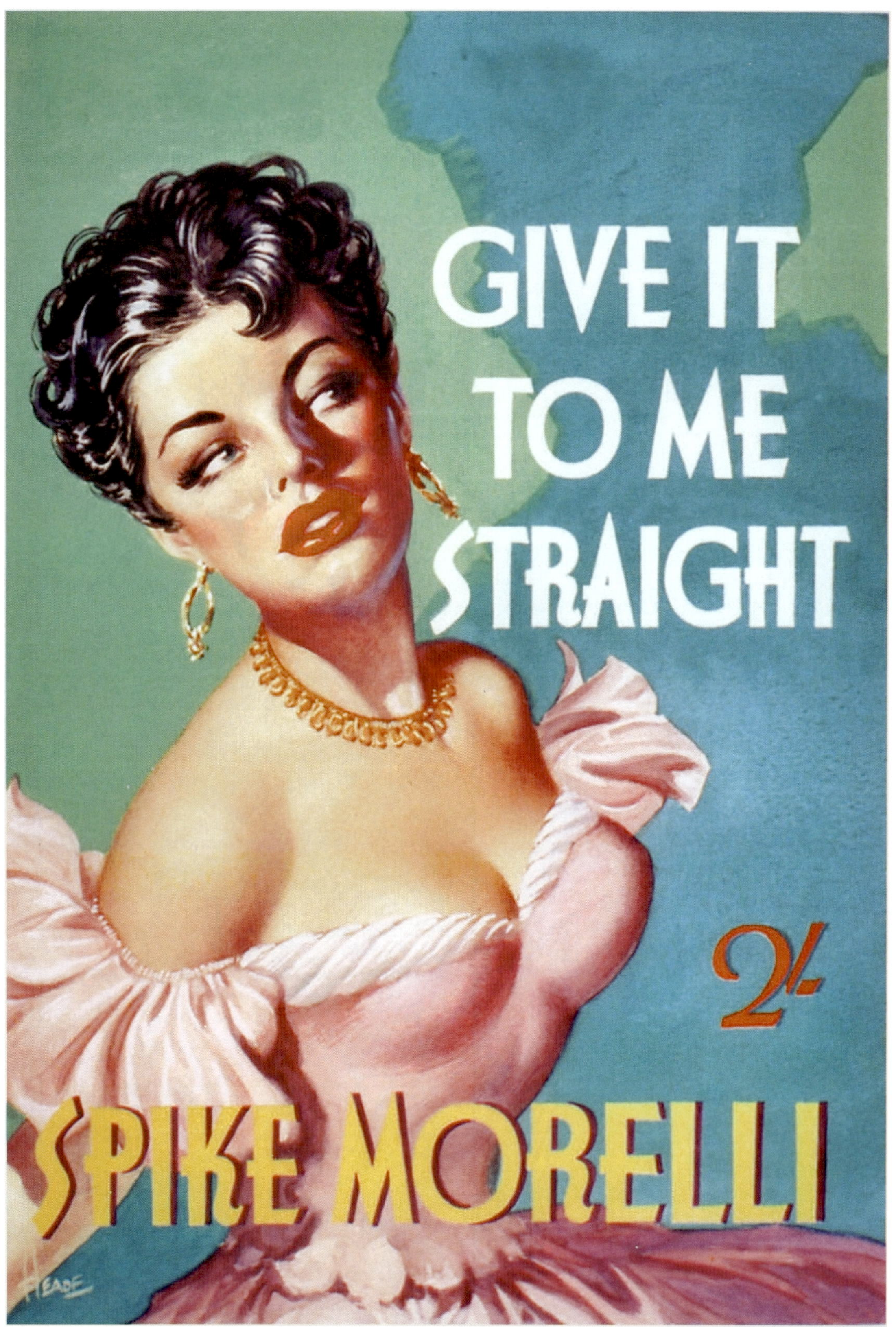

Heade's original painting for *Give It To Me Straight* by Spike Morelli (Harborough, April 1953). (Image courtesy the Steve Chibnall Collection.)

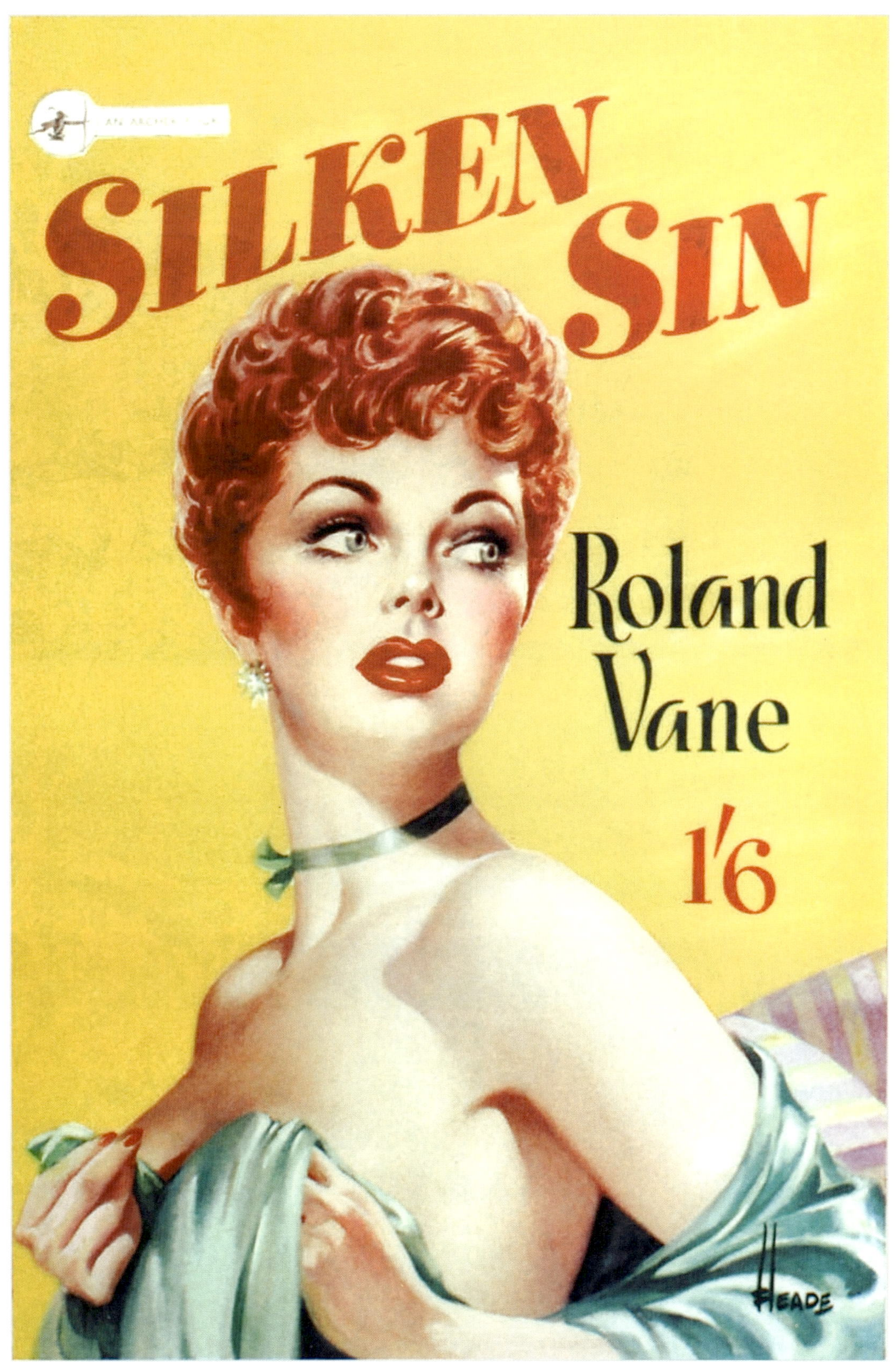

Heade's original painting for *Silken Sin* by Roland Vane (Archer, May 1953). (Image courtesy the Steve Chibnall Collection.)

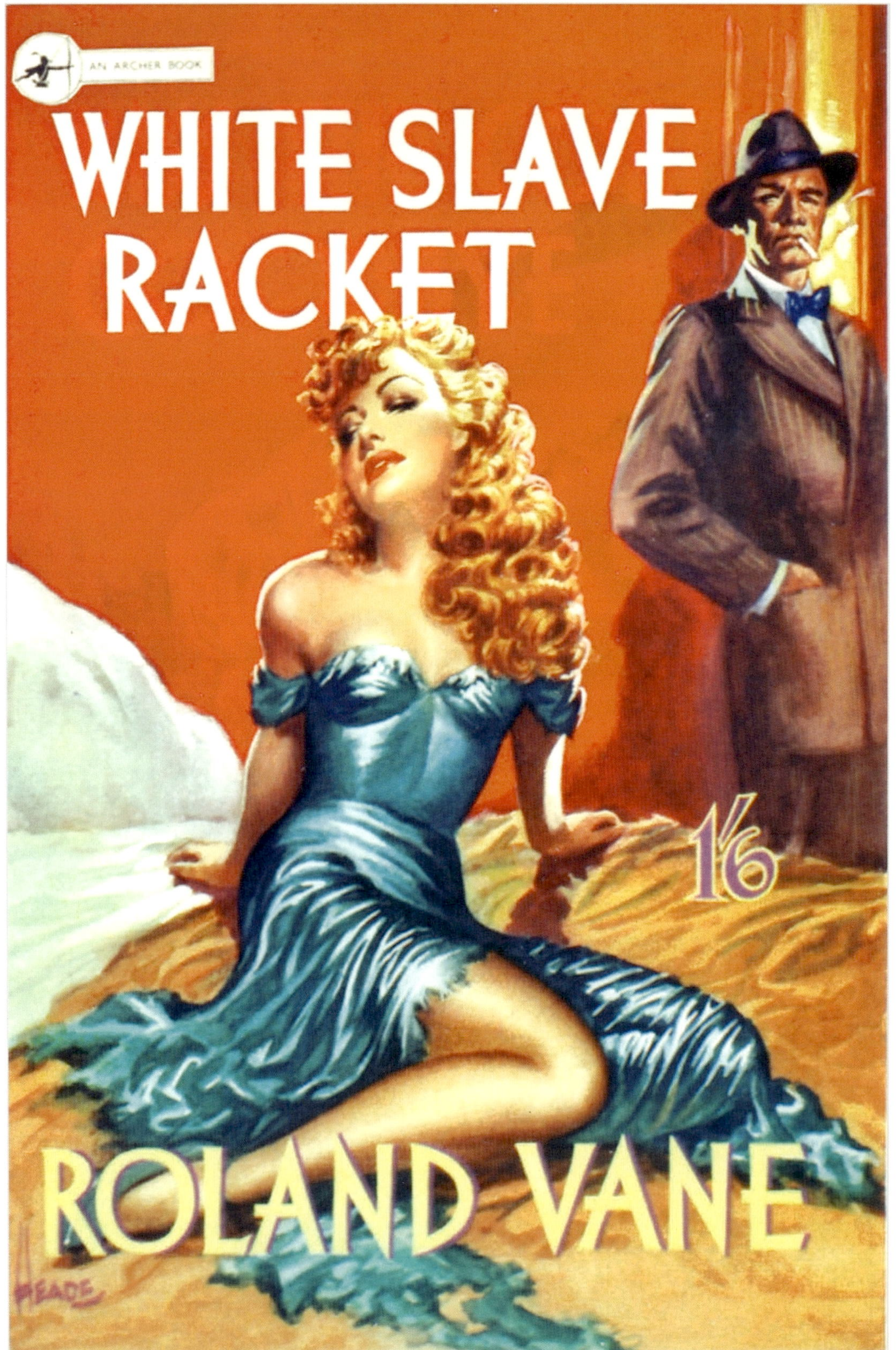

Heade's original painting for *White Slave Racket* by Roland Vane (Archer, July 1953). (Image courtesy the Steve Chibnall Collection.)

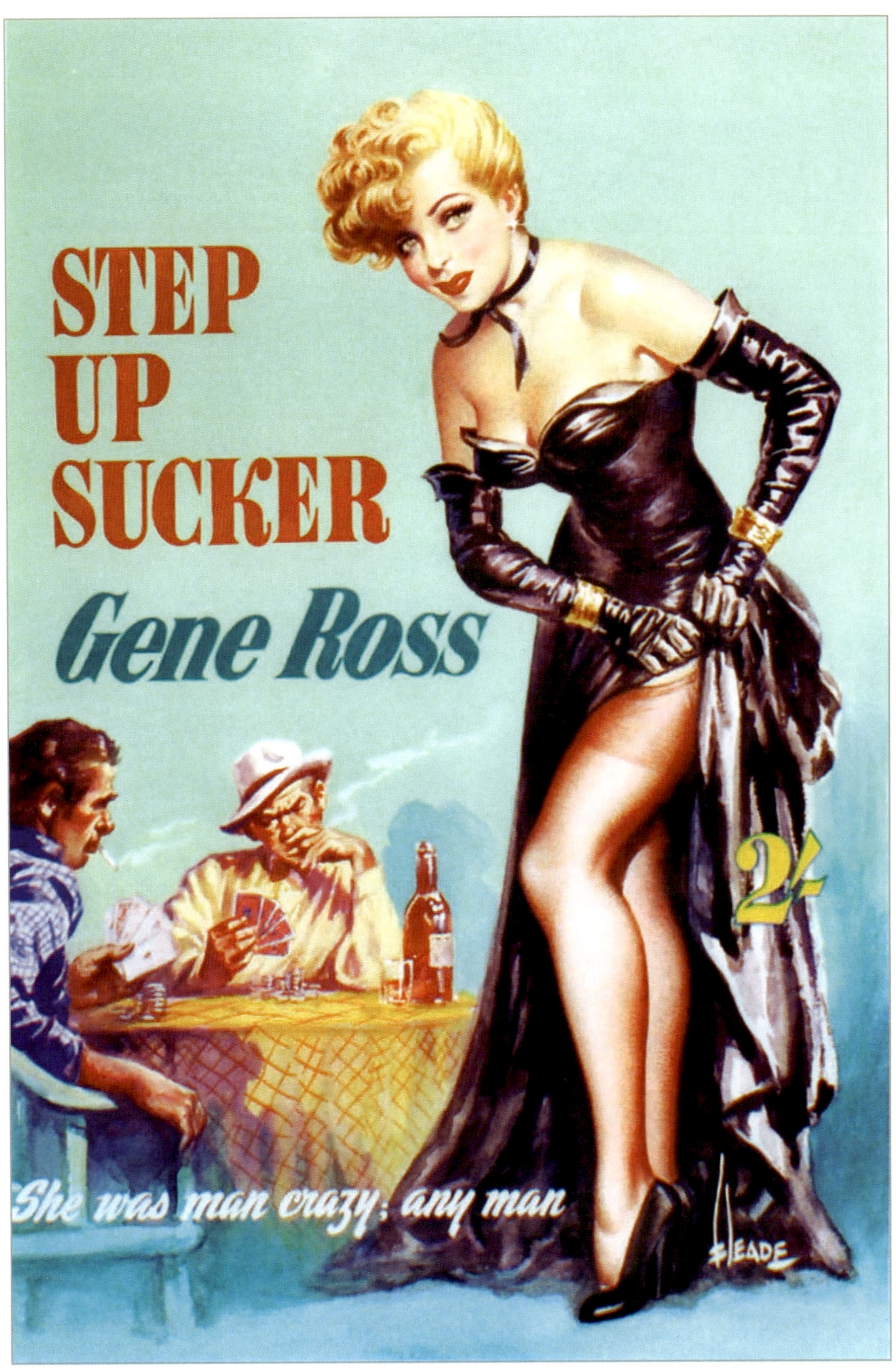

Heade's original painting for *Step Up Sucker* by Gene Ross (Harborough, August 1953). (Image courtesy the Steve Chibnall Collection.)

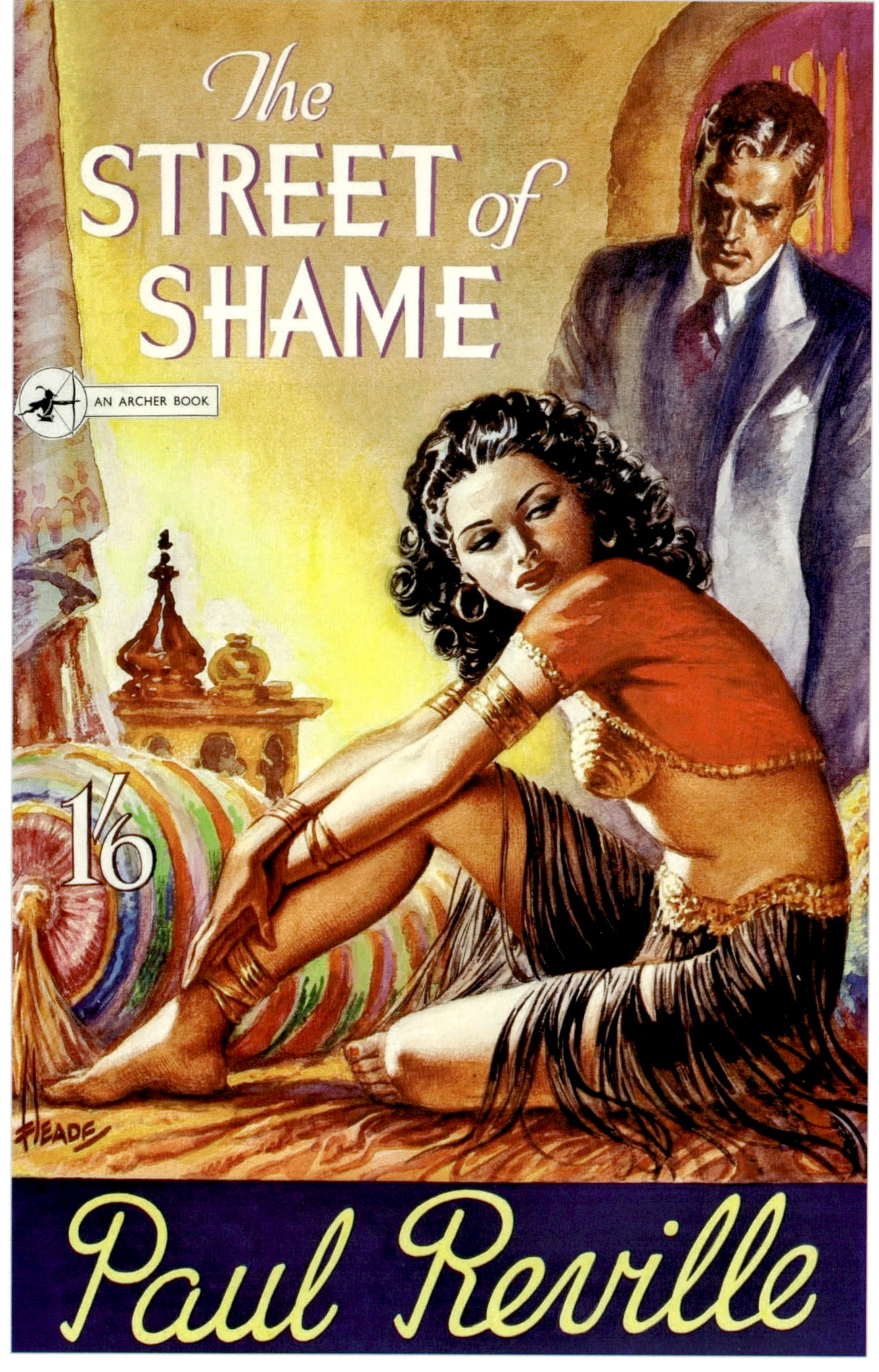

Heade's original painting for *The Street of Shame* by Paul Reville (Archer, August 1953)

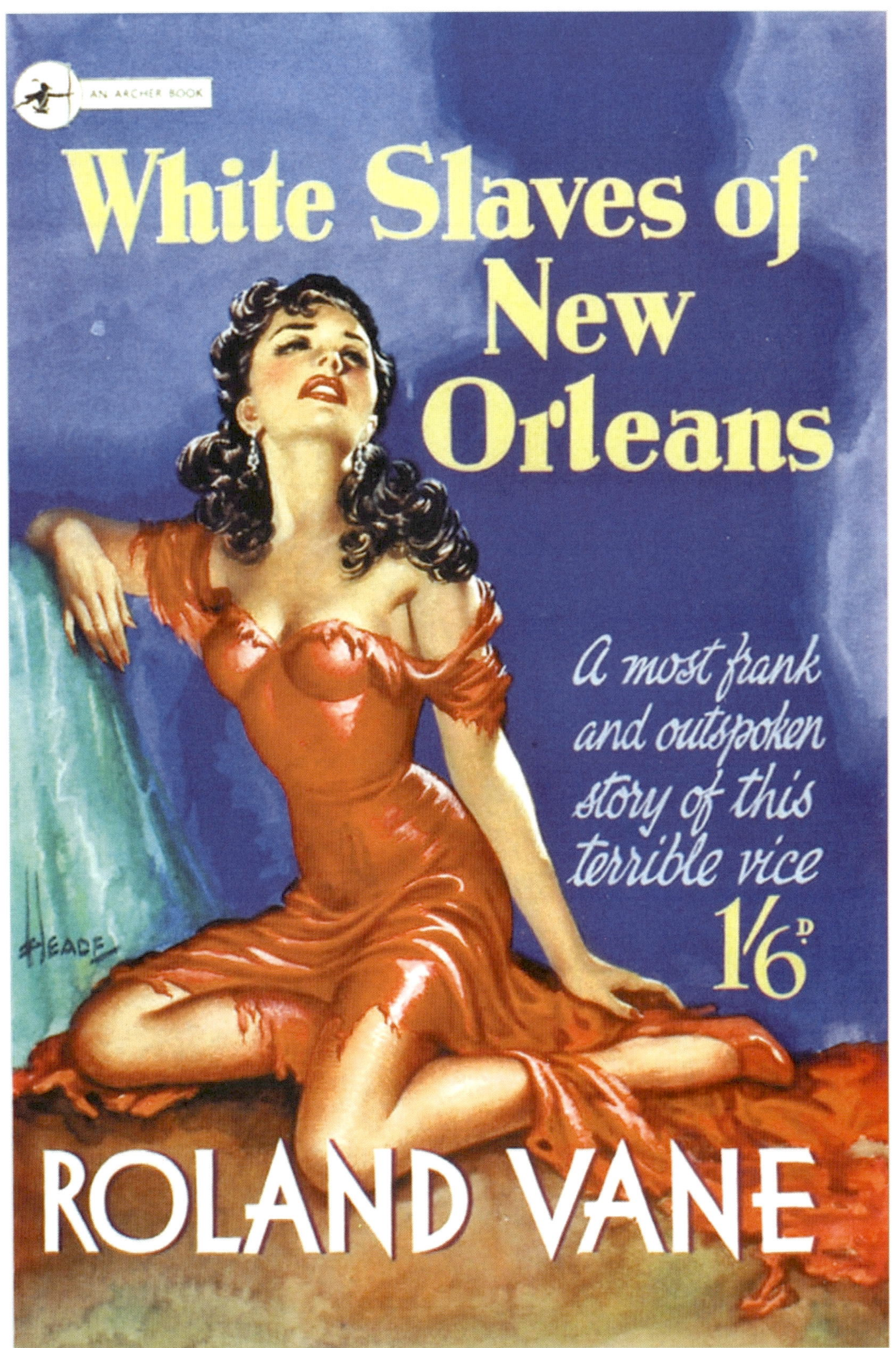

Heade's original painting for *White Slaves of New Orleans* by Roland Vane – reissue (Archer, September 1953)

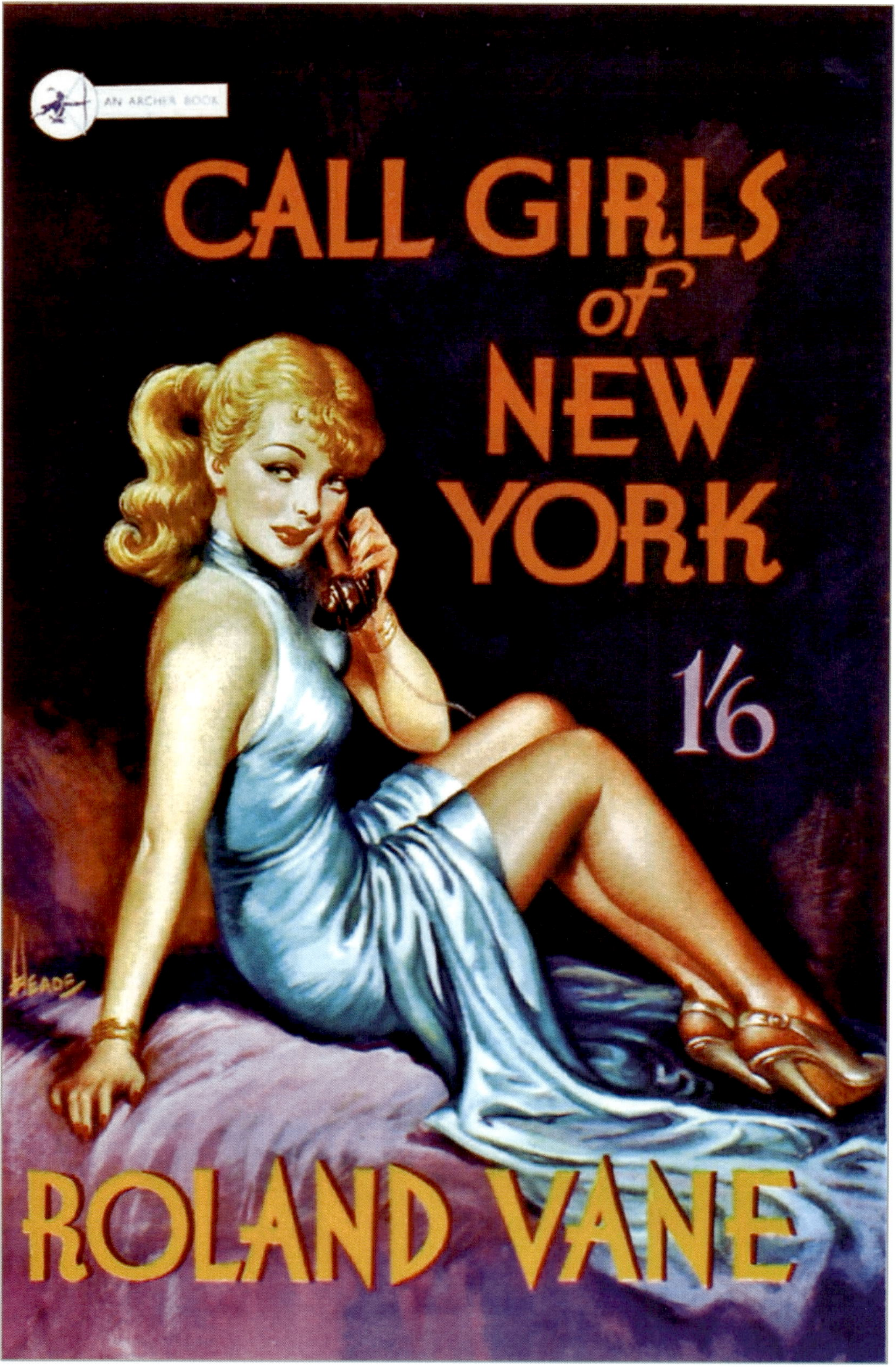

Heade's original painting for *Call Girls of New York* by Roland Vane (Archer, September 1953). (Image courtesy the Steve Chibnall Collection.)

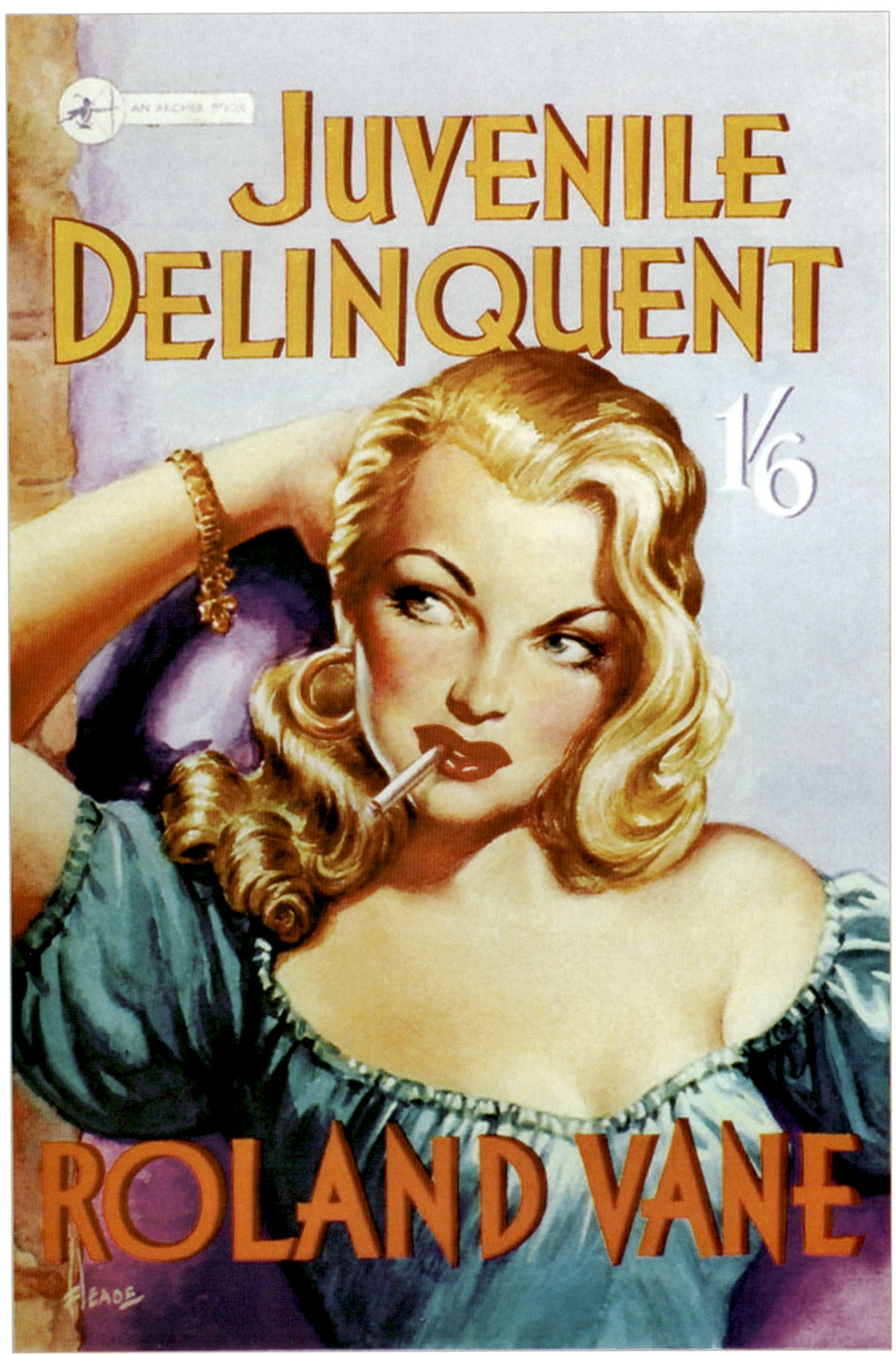

Heade's original painting for *Juvenile Delinquent* by Roland Vane (Archer, October 1953). (Image courtesy the Steve Chibnall Collection.)

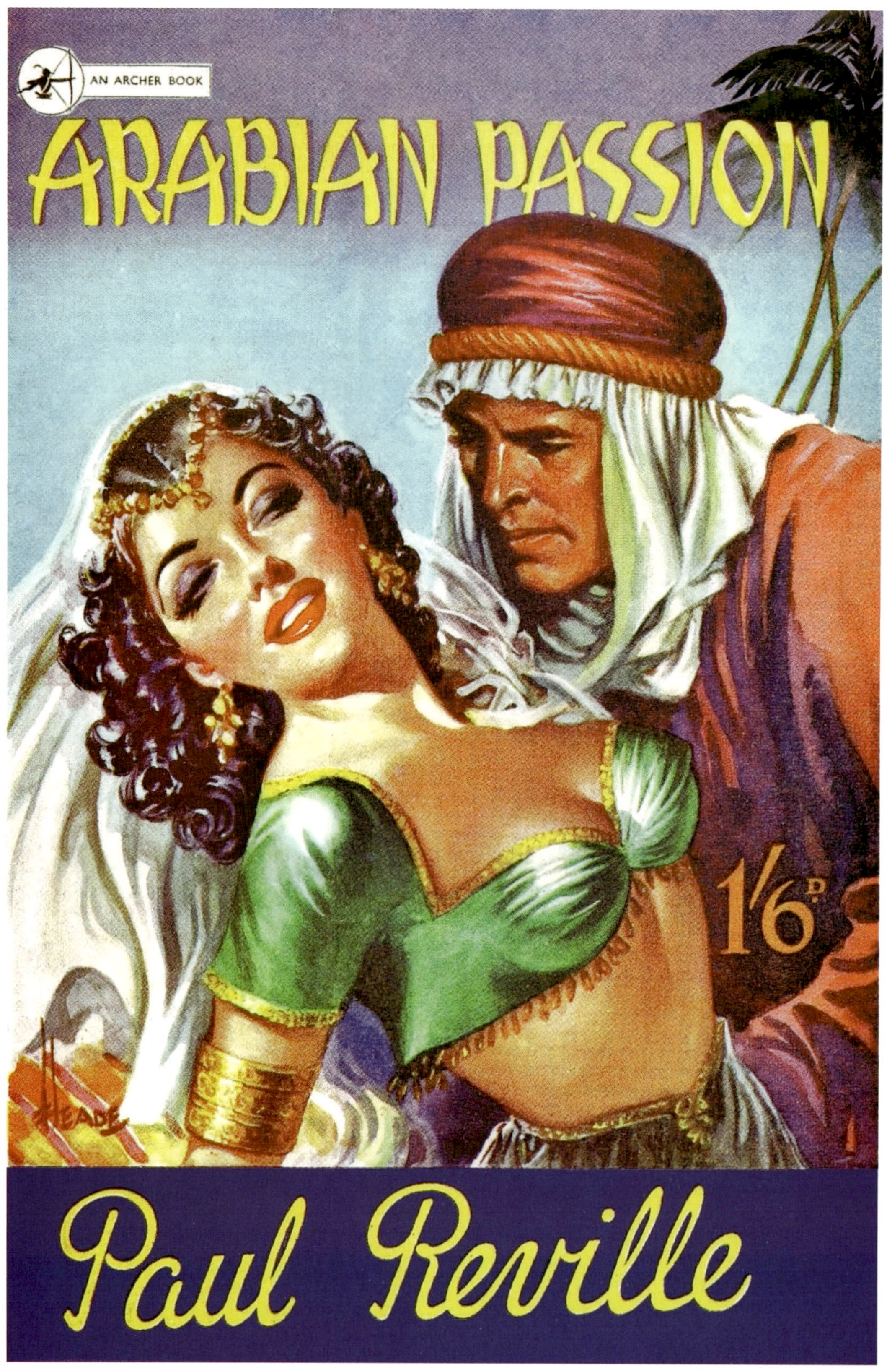

Arabian Passion by Paul Reville (Archer, 1953)

RECURRING MOTIFS

Certain motifs recur multiple times in Heade's cover paintings, doubtless due in part to his reuse of certain favourite reference photographs. This can be clearly seen in the five examples pictured immediately below – *Flame* by Paul Rénin (Harborough, 1950), *The Eternal Conflict* by George Goodchild (Archer, 1950), *When Passion Rules* by Pierre Flammêche (Archer, 1950), *At Dawn* by Paul Rénin (Archer, 1953) and *White Slave Racket* by Roland Vane (Archer, 1953) – where the head and torso of the female figure are in each case positioned almost identically. Likewise, the covers of *Kiss the Corpse Goodbye* by Michael Storme (Harborough, 1952) and *Sin Street* by Paul Reville (Archer, 1953), amongst others, depict women in very similar poses and wearing the same negligee, as shown at bottom left and centre. Certain background items and pieces of furniture also appear numerous times, suggesting that the artist might have kept these as props in his studio. Most notably, variations on a table lamp with a distinctive shade feature in many different paintings. Pictured at bottom right are details from nine examples.

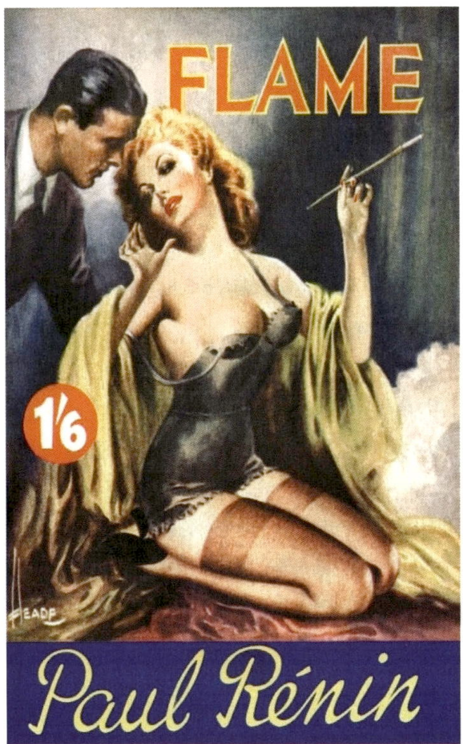

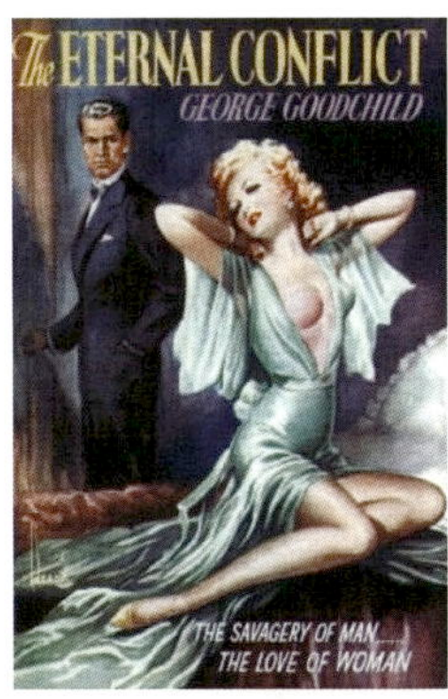

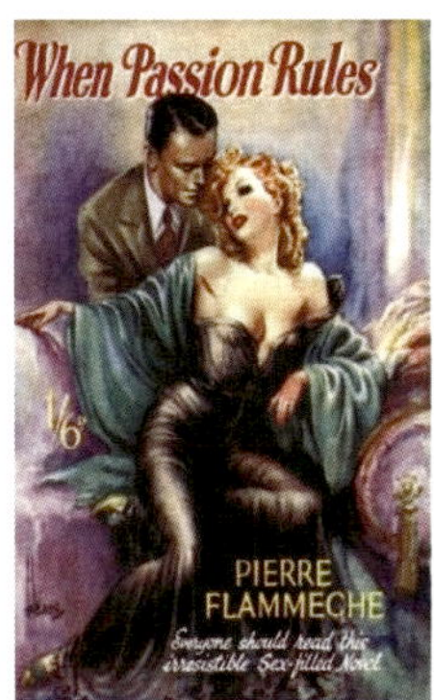

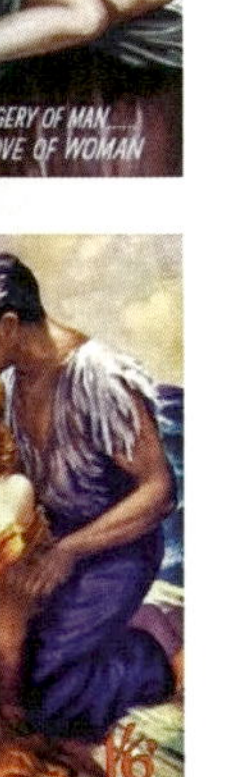

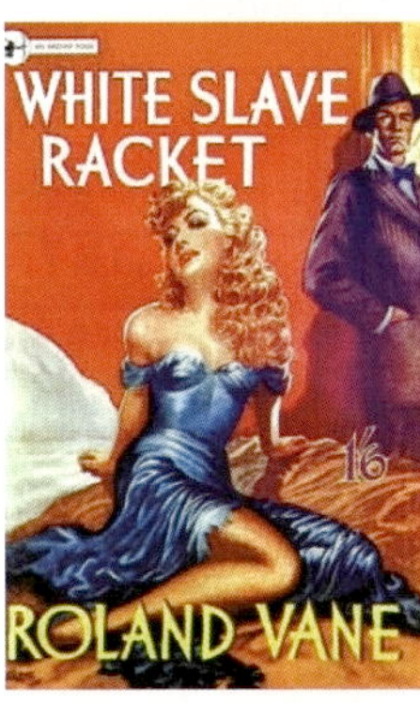

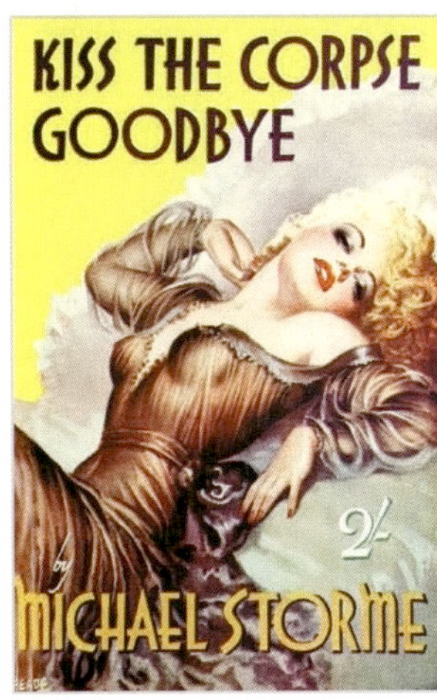

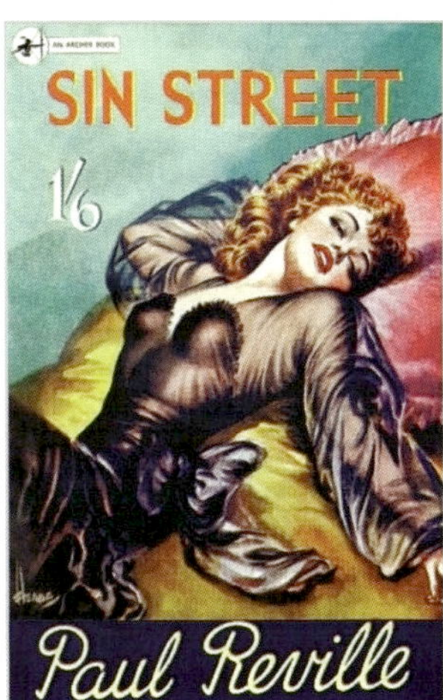

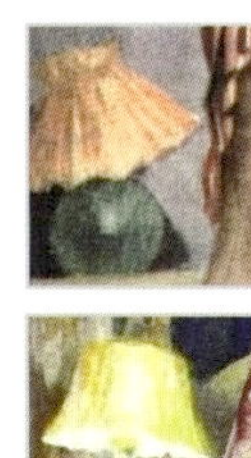
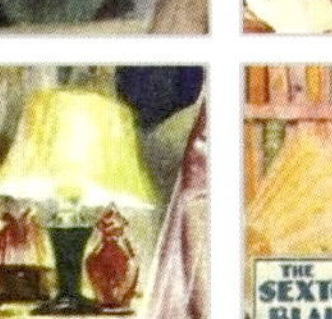
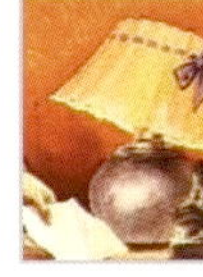
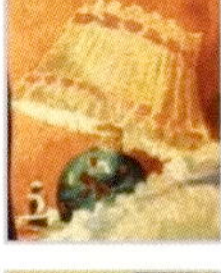
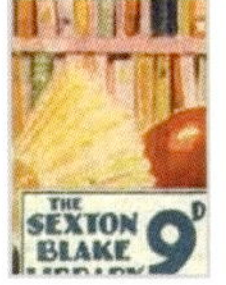
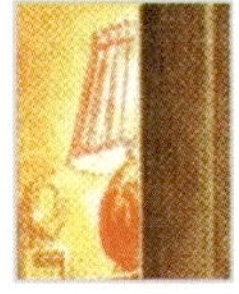

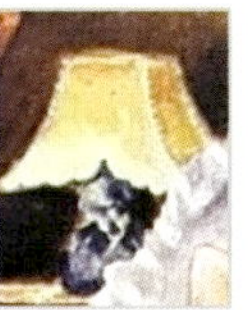
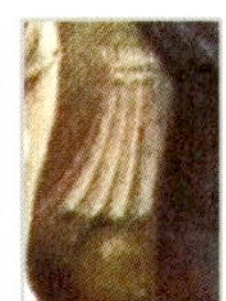
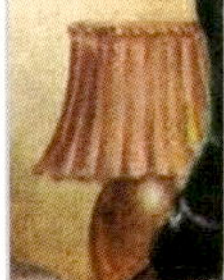

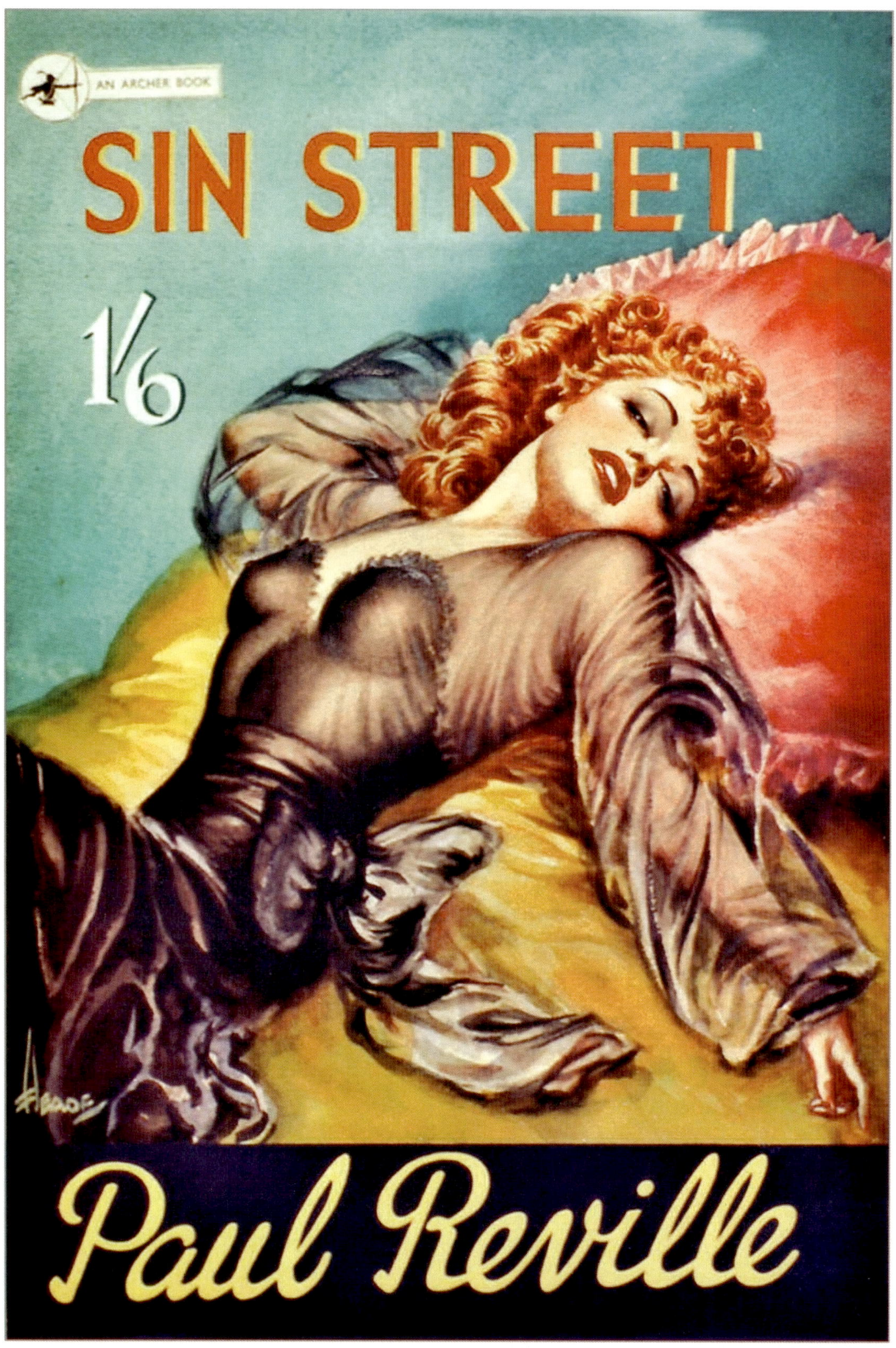

Heade's original painting for *Sin Street* by Paul Reville (Archer, September 1953). (Image courtesy the Steve Chibnall Collection.)

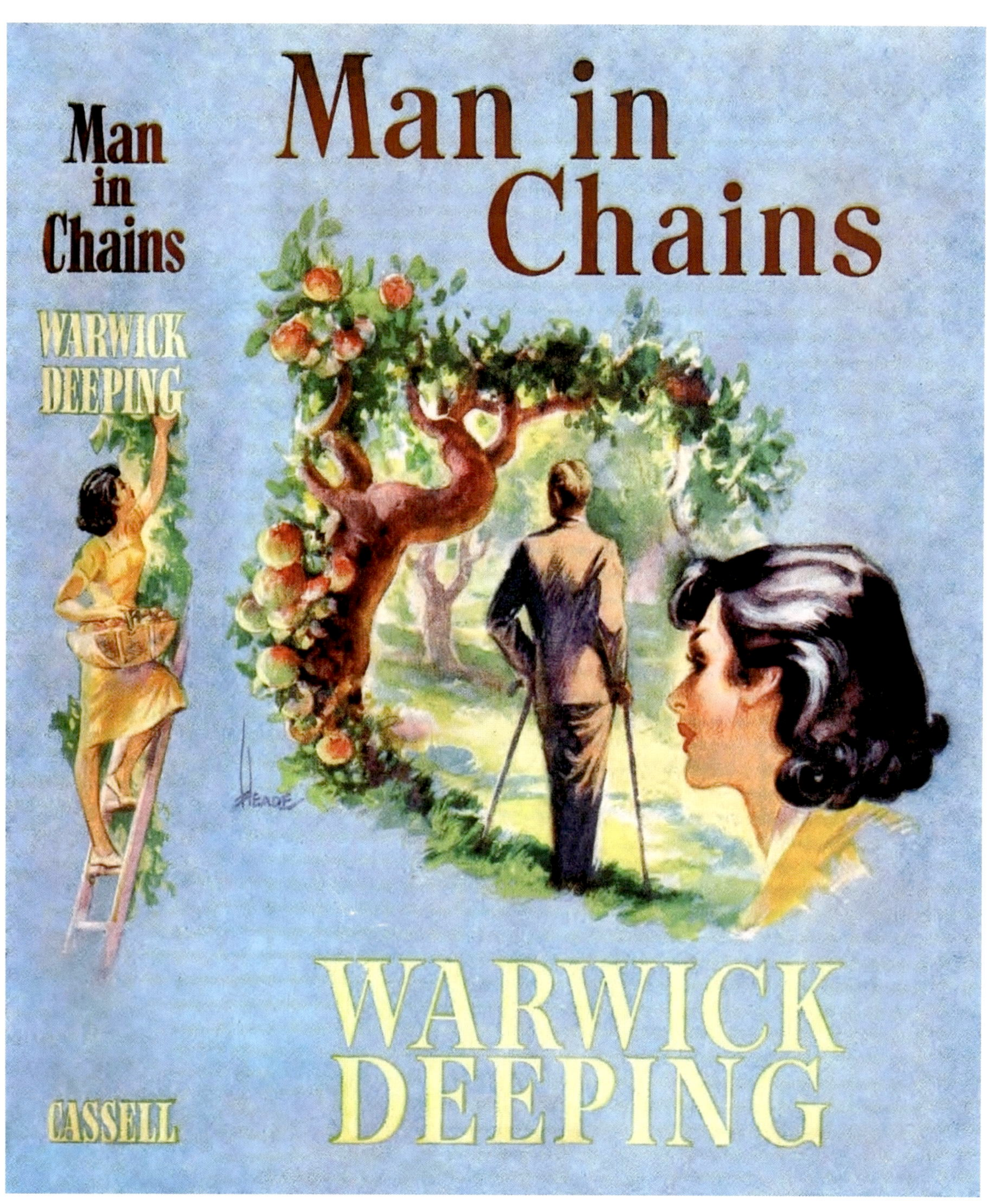

Man in Chains by Warwick Deeping (Cassell, 1953). (Previously pictured in *The Art of Reginald Heade – Special Edition* without the additional spine section illustration, which was not included in all printings of the book.)

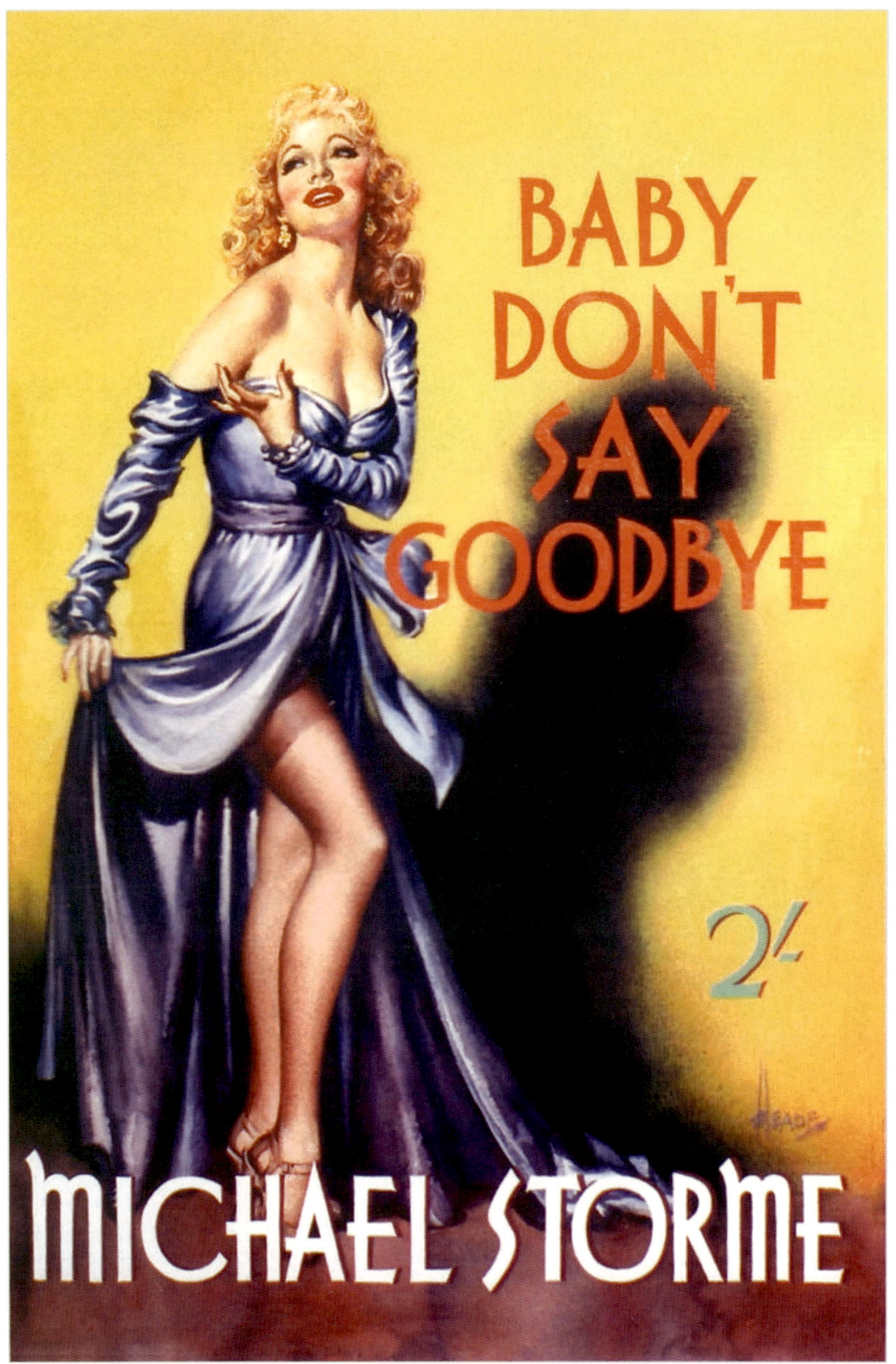

Heade's original painting for *Baby Don't Say Goodbye* by Michael Storme (Harborough, October 1953)

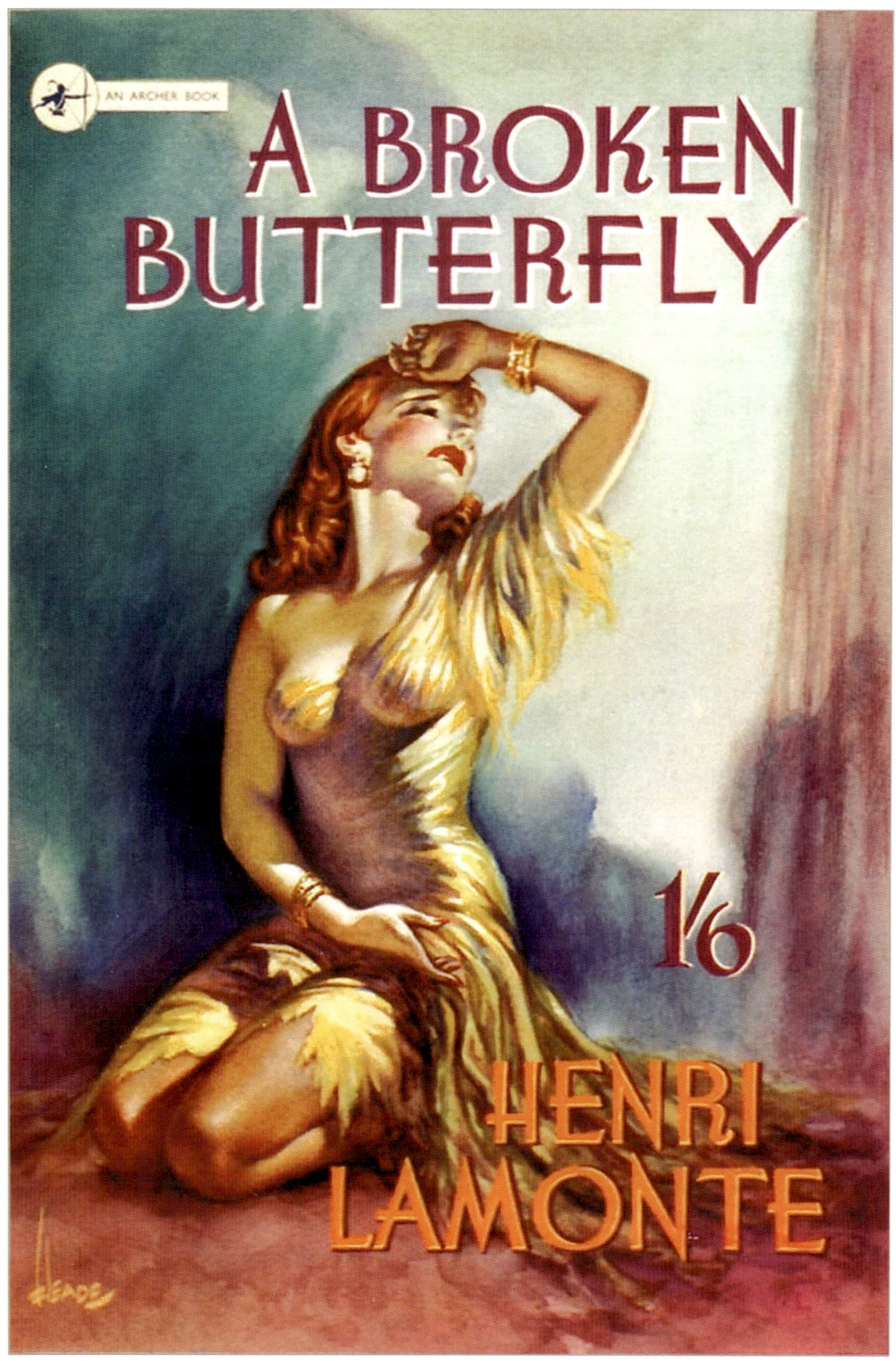

Heade's original painting for *A Broken Butterfly* by Henri Lamonte (Archer, November 1953). (Image courtesy the Steve Chibnall Collection.)

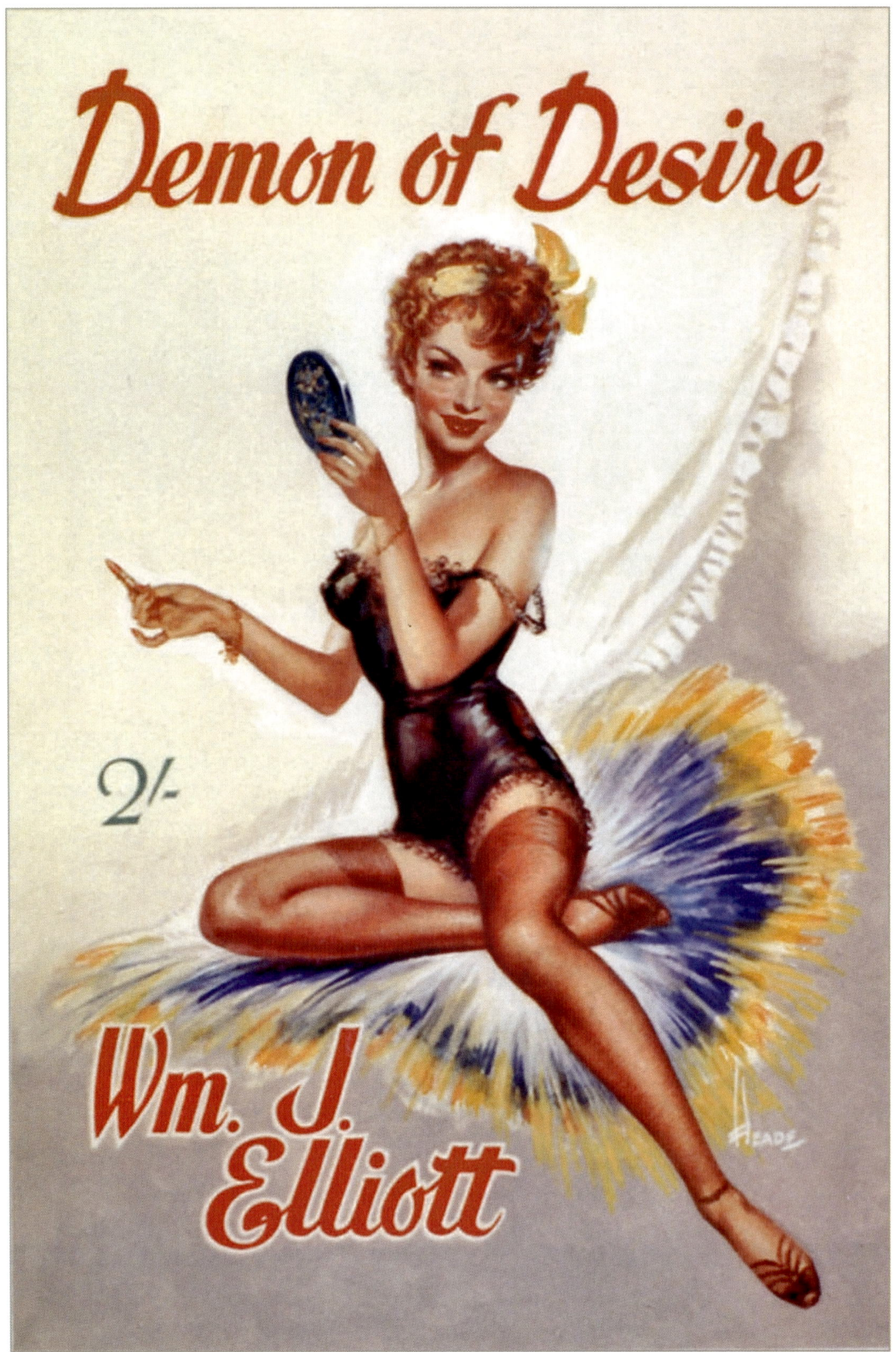

Heade's original painting for *Demon of Desire* by William J Elliott - reissue (Harborough, January 1954). (Image courtesy the Steve Chibnall Collection.)

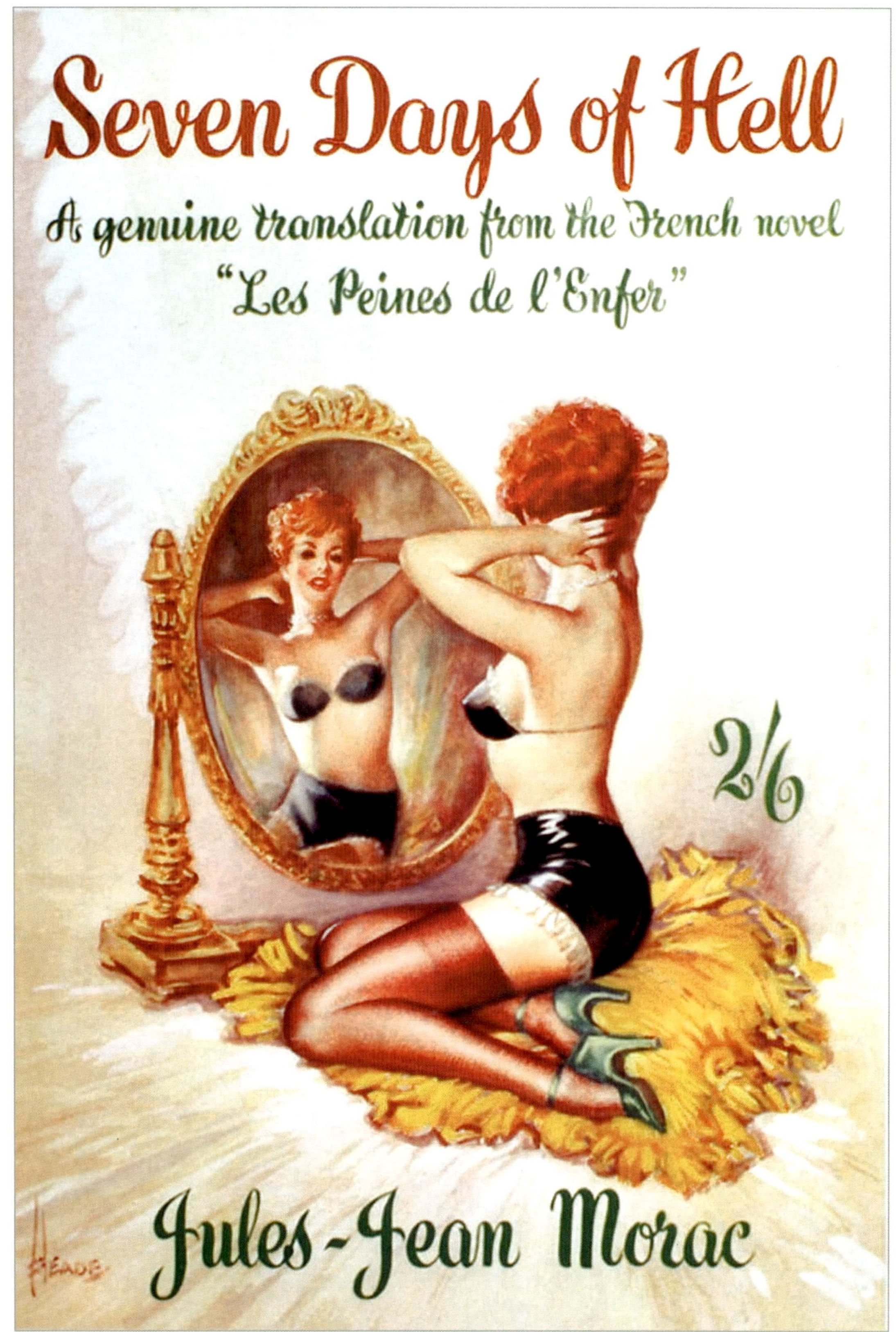

Heade's original painting for the unpublished *Seven Days of Hell* by Jules-Jean Morac (Harborough, c1954). (Image courtesy the Steve Chibnall Collection.)

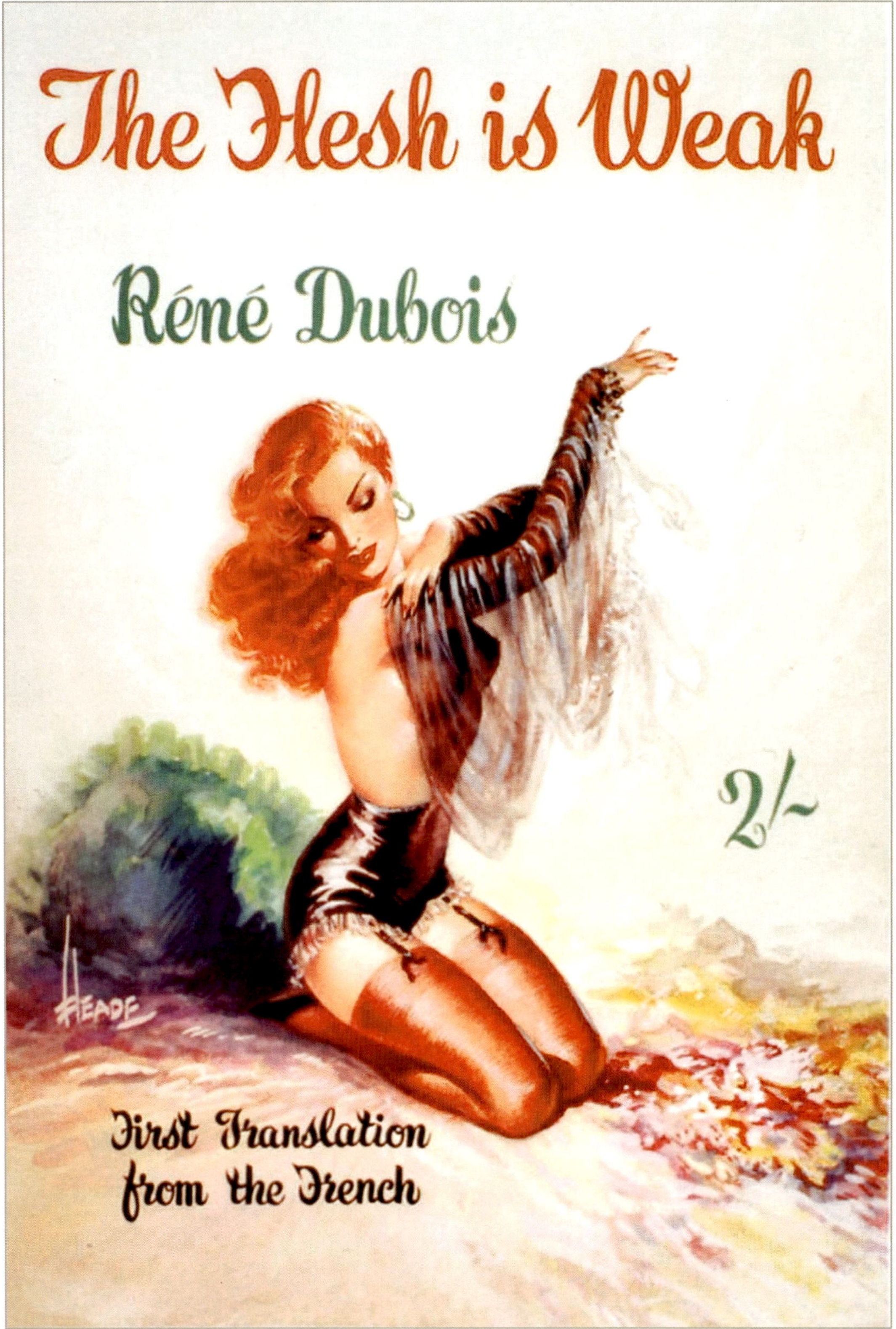

Heade's original painting for the unpublished book *The Flesh is Weak* by Réné Dubois (Harborough, January 1954). For this and the other Harborough books of the same year, Heade drew inspiration from the work of fellow artist David Wright, who was renowned for his covers for novels 'translated from the French'. (Image courtesy the Steve Chibnall Collection.)

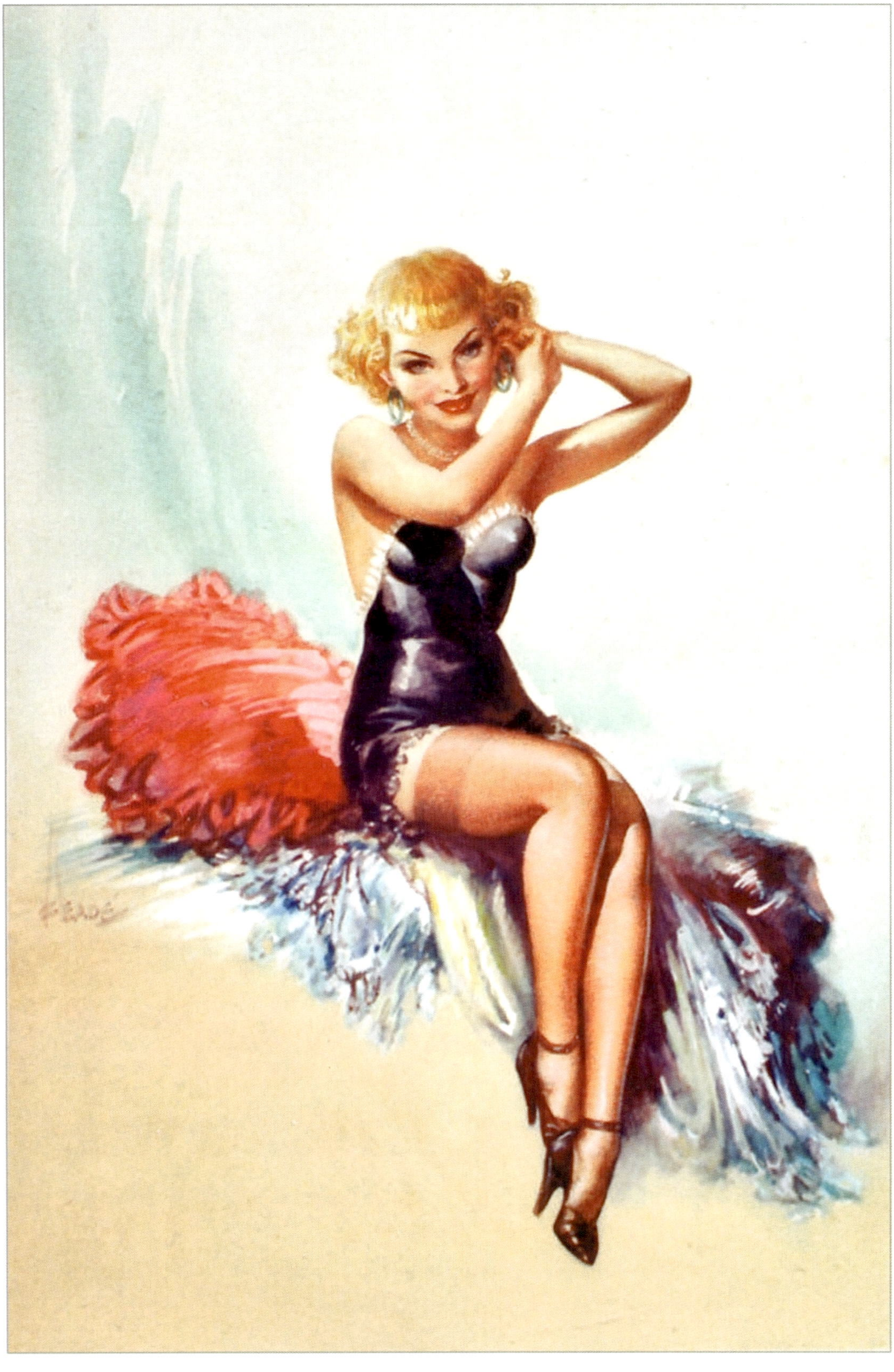

Heade's original painting for an unpublished Harborough or Archer book c1954. Printed here for the first time. (Image courtesy the Steve Chibnall Collection.)

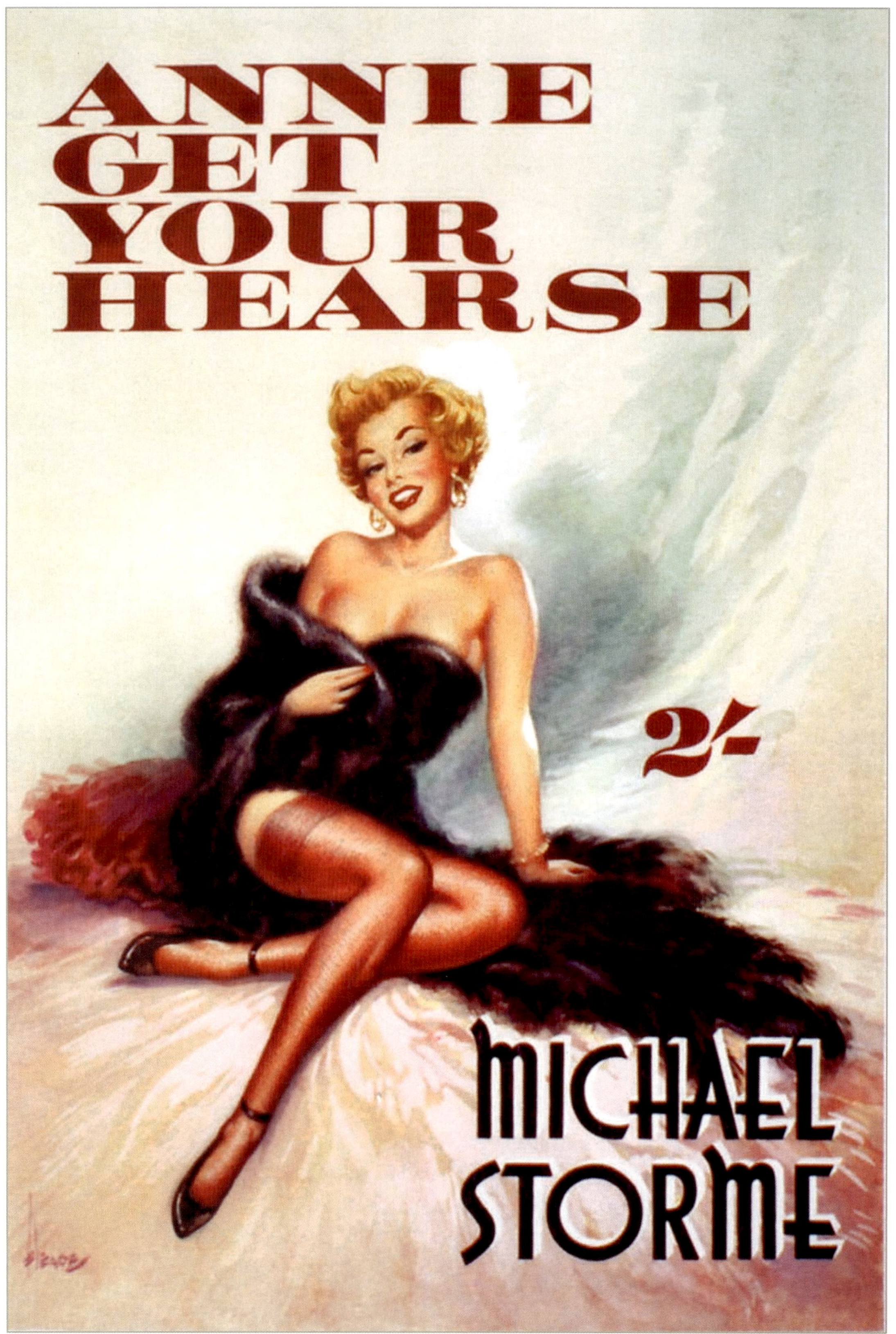

Heade's original painting for the unpublished book *Annie Get Your Hearse* by Michael Storme (Archer, 1954)

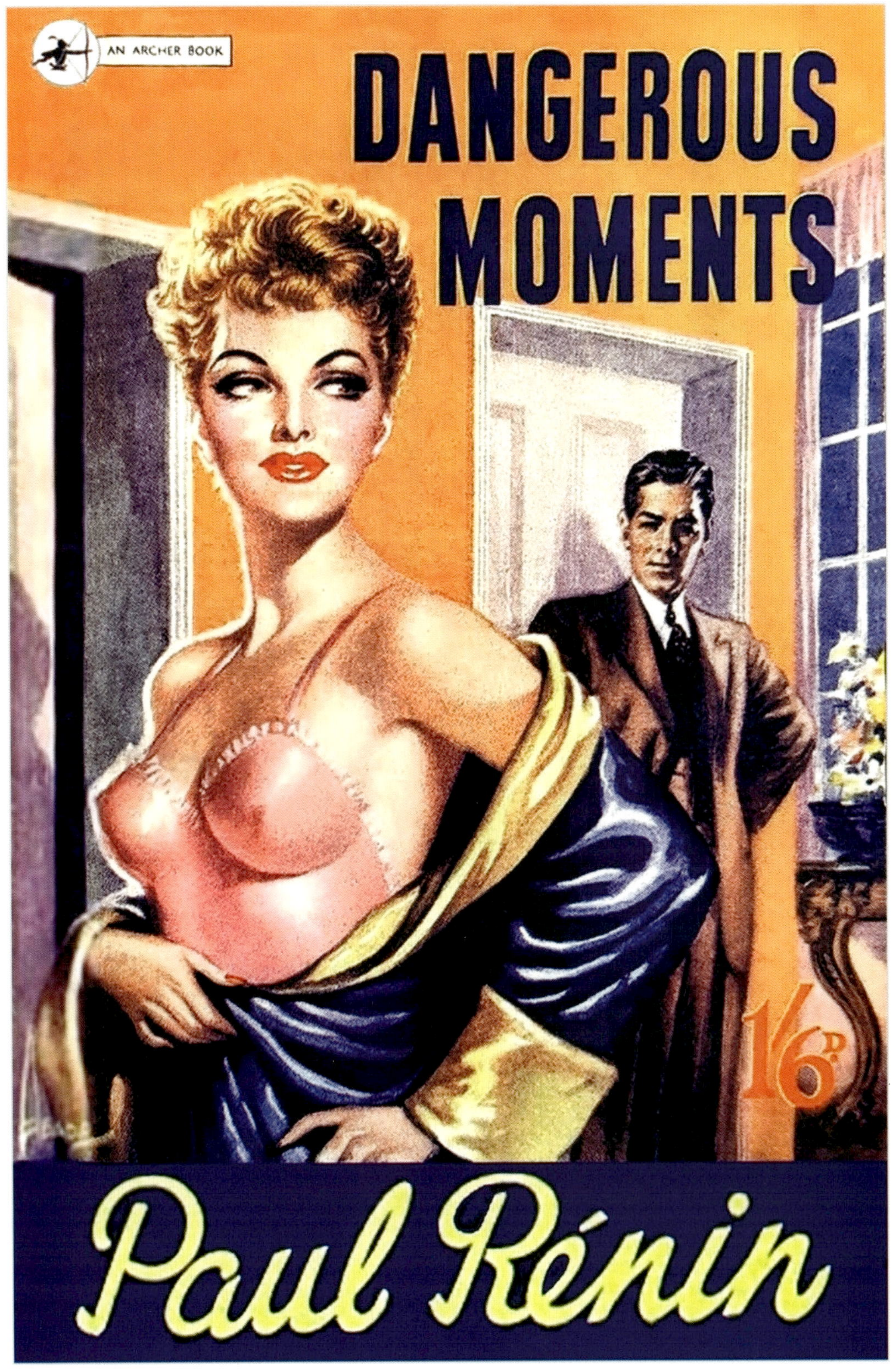

Dangerous Moments by Paul Rénin (Archer, January 1954); one of the last-published Locker company books with Heade cover art. (Previously presented as a smaller, quarter-page image in *The Art of Reginald Heade – Special Edition.*)

SWEDISH BOOKS

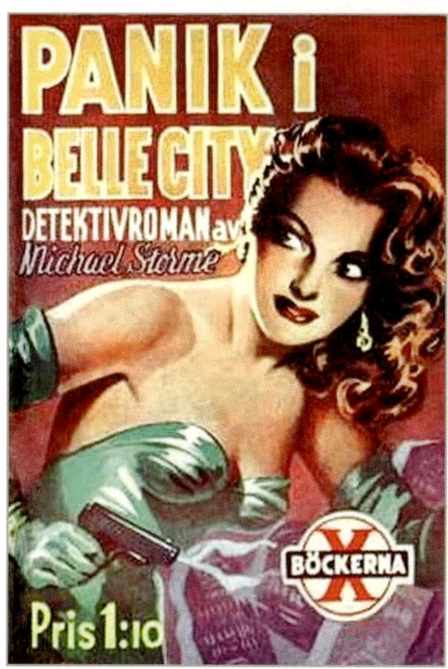

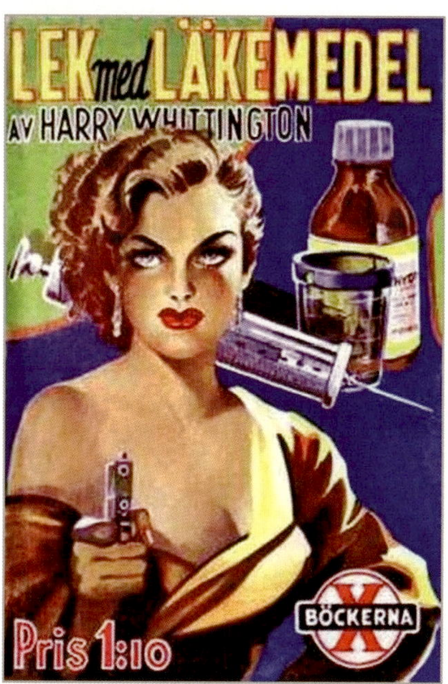

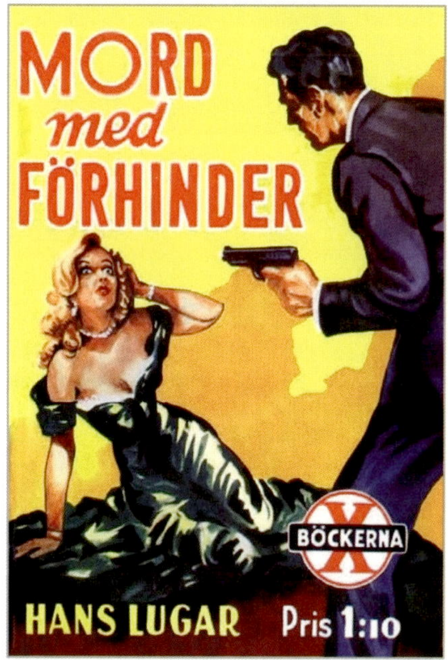

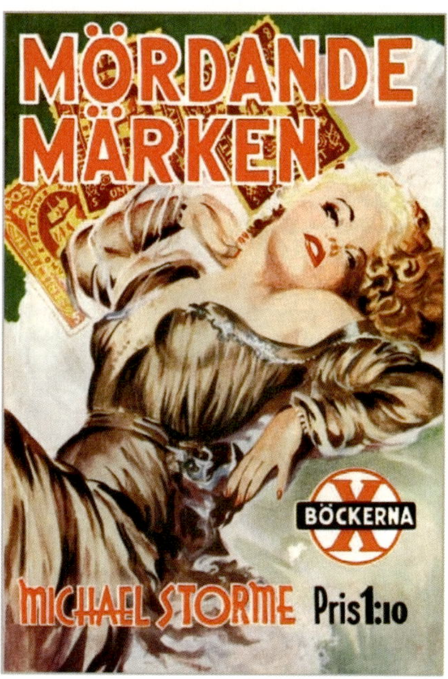

The Art of Reginald Heade – Special Edition included a section on Dutch books that made illicit reuse of Heade cover art. There were also, however, four Swedish books that did likewise. These appeared in a numbered series of pulp paperbacks called X-Böckerna. They were: # 23 *Panik I Belle City* (rough translation: *Panic In Belle City*) by Michael Storme (1954), # 26 *Lek Med Läkemedel* (*Play With Drugs*) by Harry Whittington (1954), # 34 *Mord Med Förhinder* (*Murder With Obstacles*) by Hans Lugar (1955) and # 35 *Mördande Märken* (*Cutthroat Brand*) by Michael Storme (1955). The equivalent Heade originals appeared on: *Me and My Ghoul, Curtains for Carla, You'll Be Better Off Dead* and *Kiss the Corpse Goodbye*, all by Michael Storme (see pages 79, 95, 74 and 70 of *The Art of Reginald Heade – Special Edition*). (First three images courtesy Patrik Myrman.)

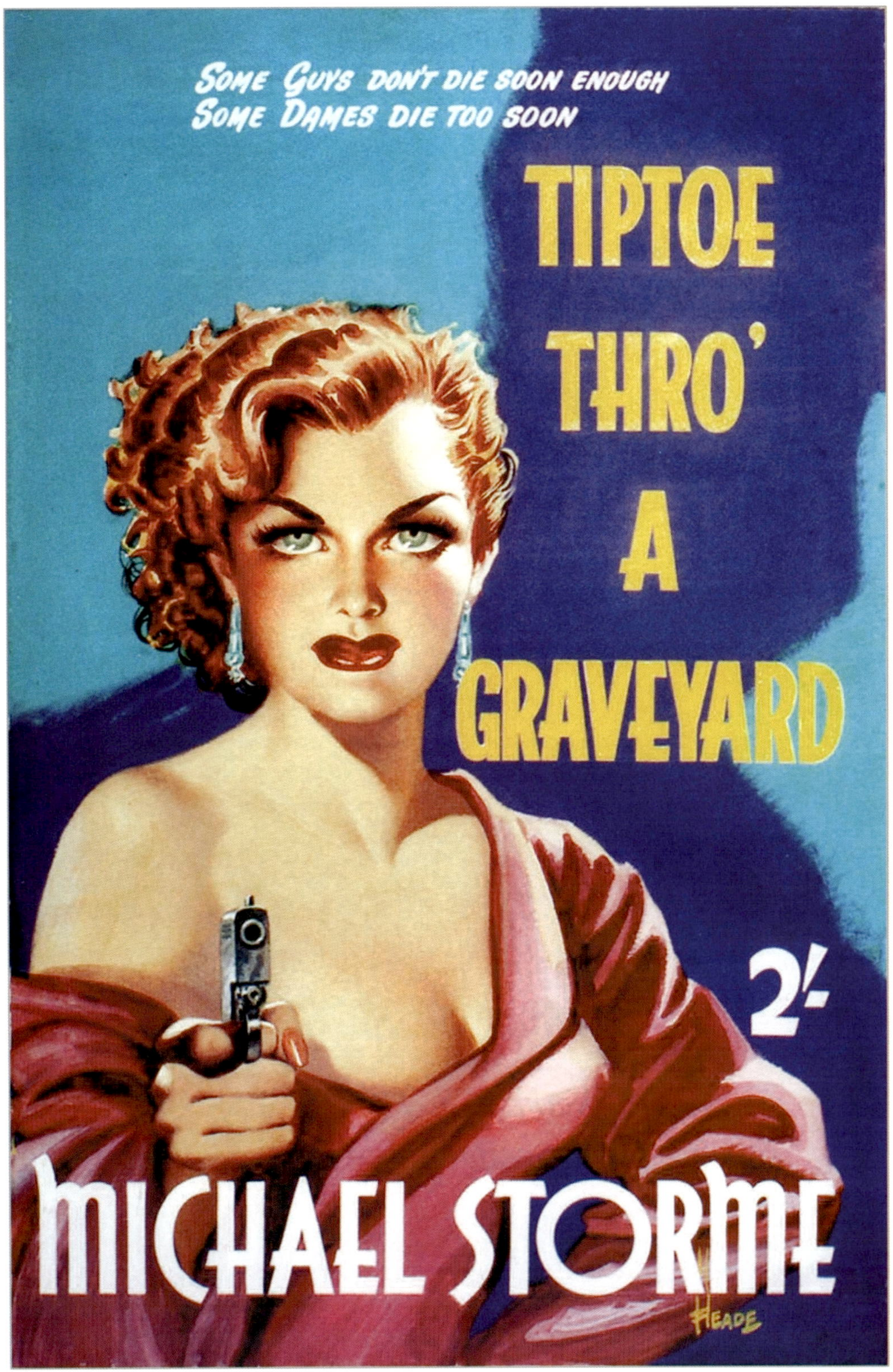

Heade's original painting for *Tiptoe Thro' a Graveyard* by Michael Storme – reissue (Harborough, 1954). No image of this ultra-rarity was available when *The Art of Reginald Heade – Special Edition* was published. It adapts the cover art from the same author's US Leisure Library-published *Curtains for Carla* – the same piece as was also used for the Swedish book *Lek Med Läkemedel* by Harry Whittington (see opposite).

(Image courtesy the Steve Chibnall Collection.)

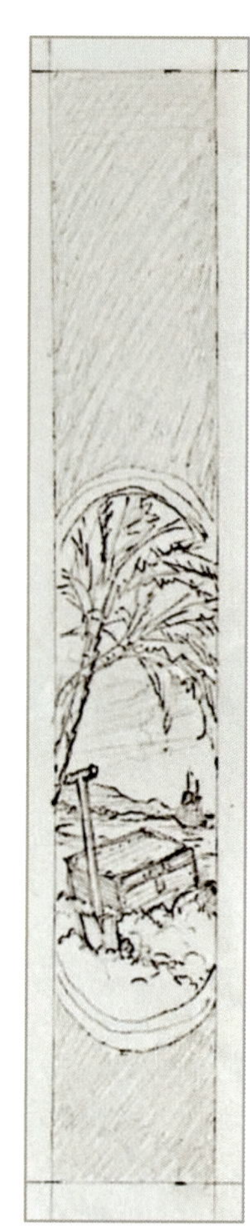

Copy only.

  The rgh for PIECES OF EIGHT has just come to hand, it is of course only a pencil visual, but I think we know Mr Heade's work well enough to agree to his going ahead with the finish.

  Could you ask him to make the background as 'clean' as possible, to allow us to make a decent job when adding the lettering. I expect it willbe a dark background. It will not be necessary to continue design onto the spine as this series has a uniform spine design, which is already in existence. One other small thing, if I remember rightly the chest was packed with gold pieces; I'm not sure if there were trinkets among them. However, you might ask the artist to check on this before drawing the final picture.

  The frontispiece looks most effective and I would be glad if he would go ahead with this subject also.

Have asked Hastings if he wants it shown full or not also age.

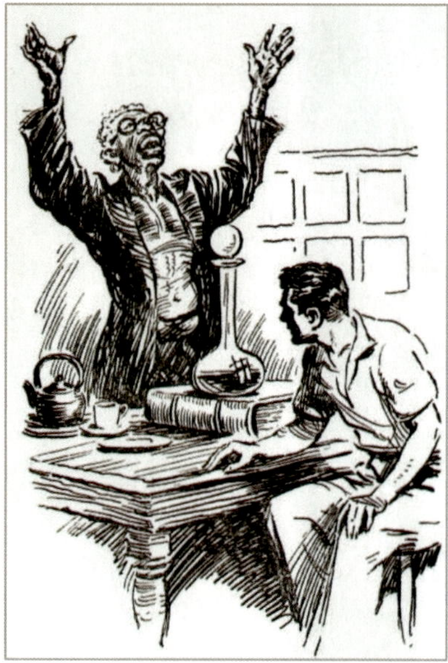

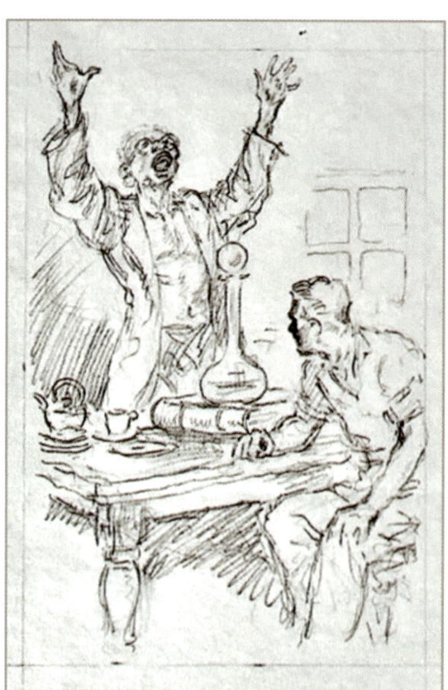

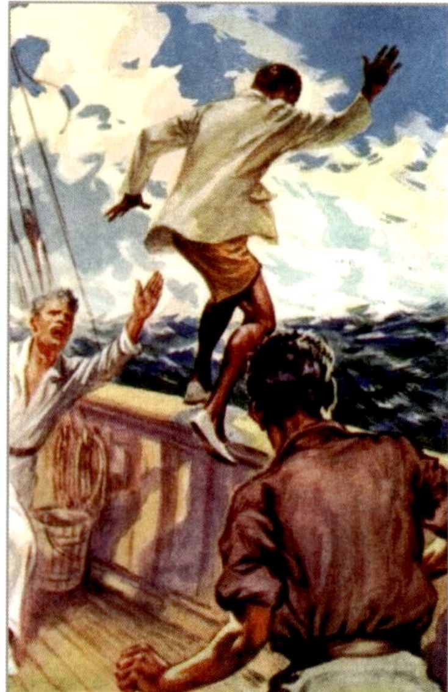

Top left: a note from publishers Collins, with handwritten comment by agent William Partridge, giving Heade the go-ahead to complete the dustjacket and frontispiece for Richard Le Gallienne's *Pieces of Eight*, published in 1954. When the book was reprinted in 1955, a new colour frontispiece, again by Heade, was substituted for the original black-and-white one. In 1957, a reissue from the Collins-associated imprint The Children's Press omitted the frontispiece but added a new spine-section illustration – see facing page. Top right: Heade's original rough for the spine-section illustration. Bottom row: the black-and-white frontispiece, Heade's original rough for this, and the new colour frontispiece.

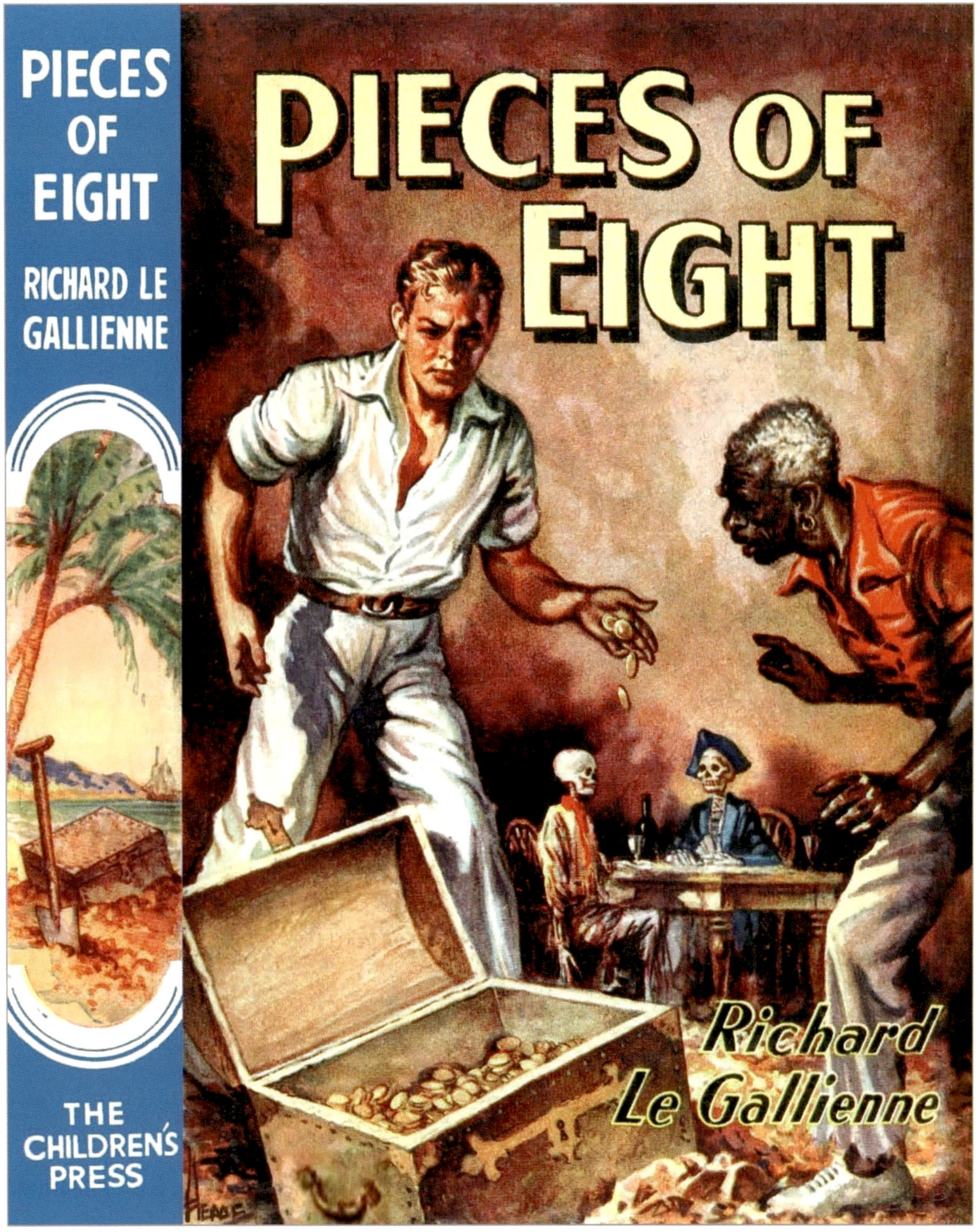

Pieces of Eight by Richard Le Gallienne – reissue (The Children's Press, 1957)

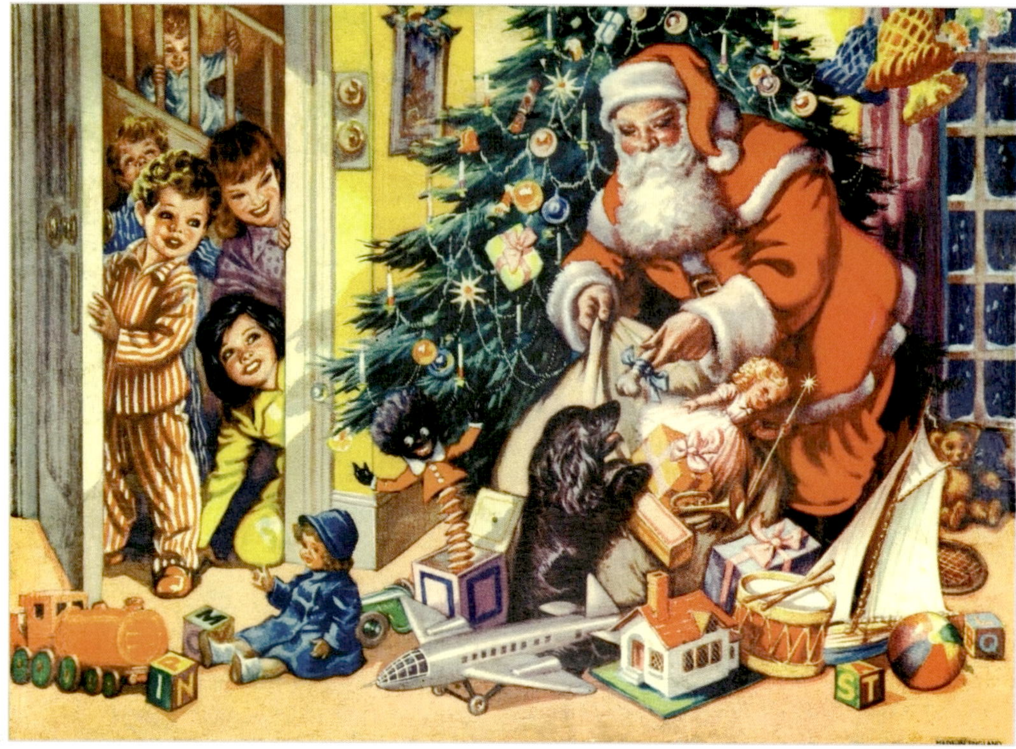

A Christmas-themed jigsaw puzzle with unsigned Heade art. This is believed to have been produced around 1954, but no other details are known; curiously, the box does not even give the name of the manufacturer, although it is thought most likely to have been Philmar.

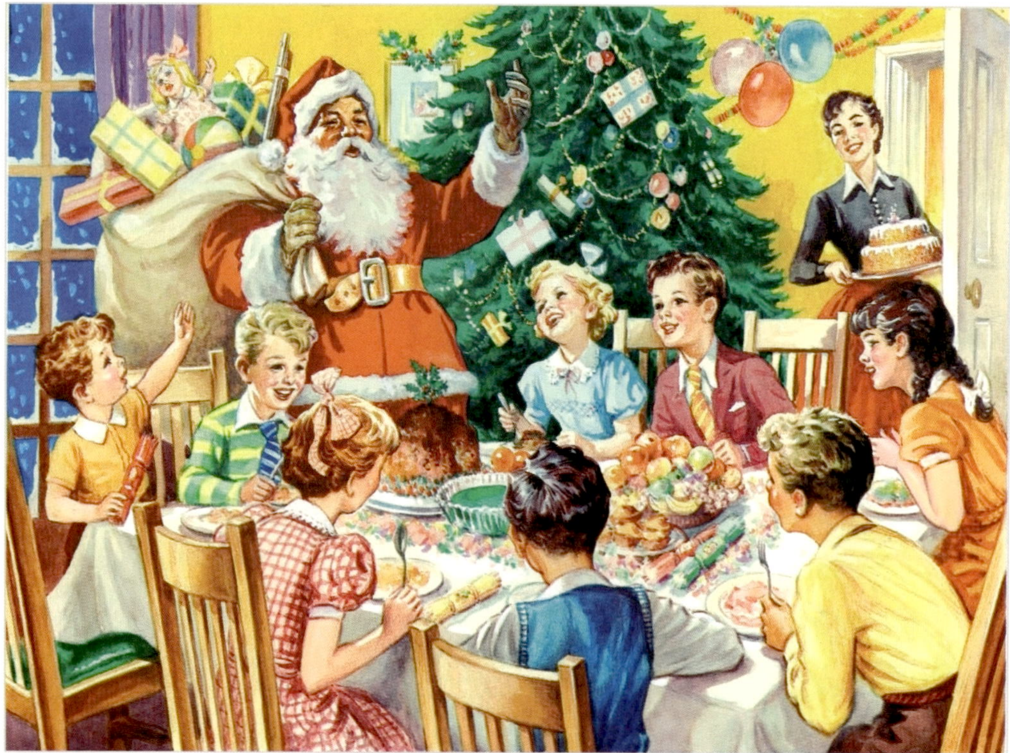

Heade's original, unsigned painting for a *Christmas Party* jigsaw puzzle. This is presumed to have been intended as part of a set with the one above, but again, no further details are known, and it is uncertain if this puzzle even went into production. (Image courtesy the Steve Chibnall Collection.)

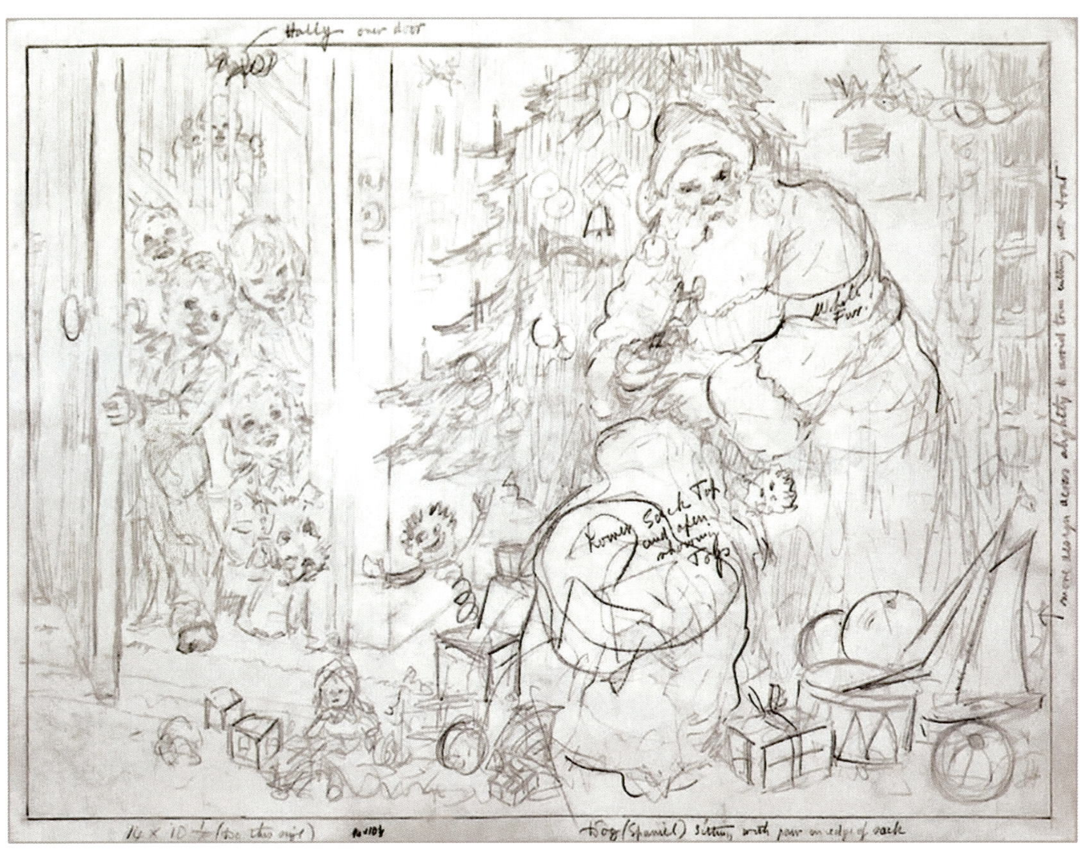

Heade's original rough for the Christmas-themed jigsaw pictured opposite (possibly Philmar, c1954)

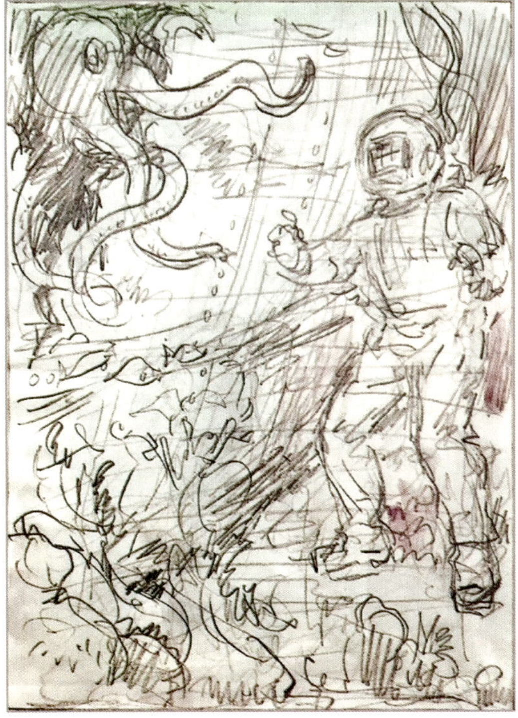

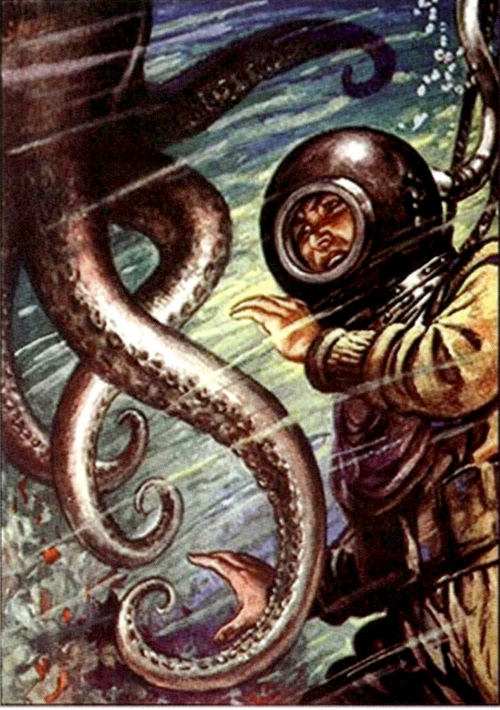

Heade's original rough and the as-published version of the colour plate for the story 'Diver's Son' in *Sea Story Omnibus* (Collins, 1956)

INSPIRATIONS

Below, two further examples, this time from the 1950s, of Heade's work being inspired by images from previously-published sources.

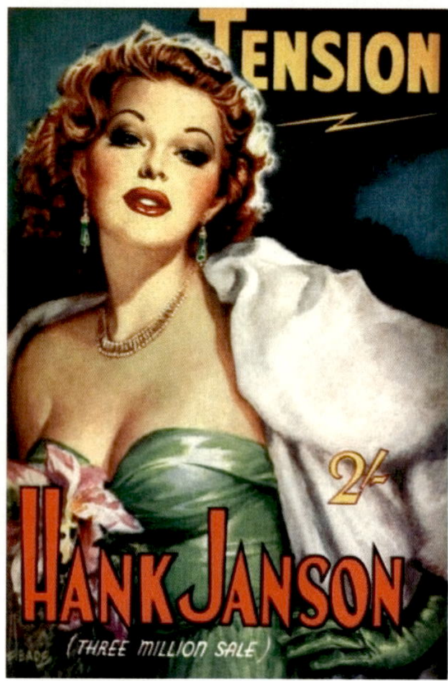
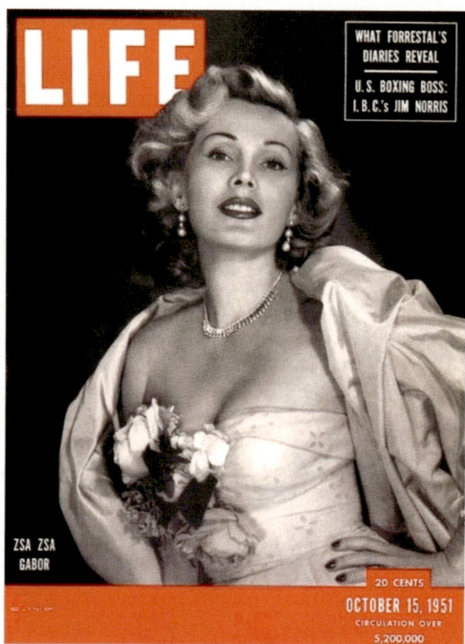

Left: Heade's cover for *Tension* by Hank Janson (New Fiction Press, July 1952). Right: the inspiration: a photograph of actress Zsa Zsa Gabor on the cover of the 15 October 1951 issue of the American magazine *Life*.

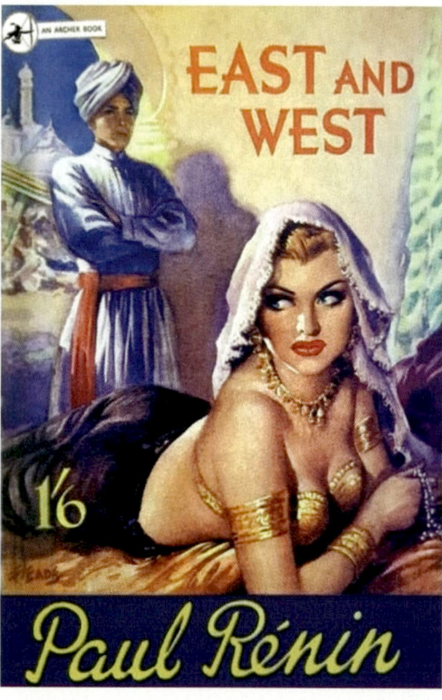
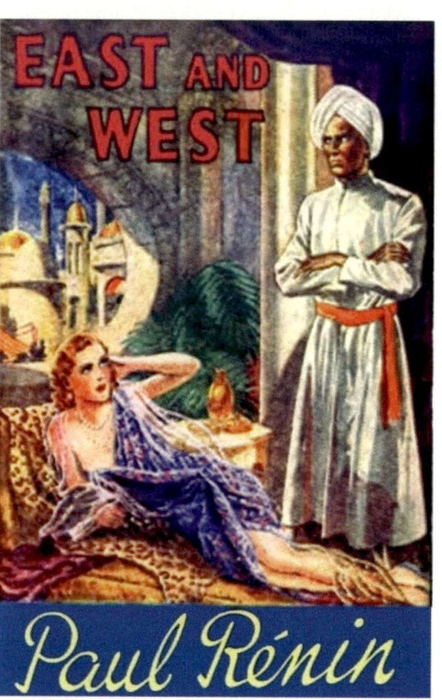

Left: Heade's cover for Paul Rénin's *East and West* (Archer, 1953). Right: the inspiration: an earlier edition of the same title (R & L Locker, c1947). Heade incorporated similar elements, but in a different configuration, to produce a far superior piece.

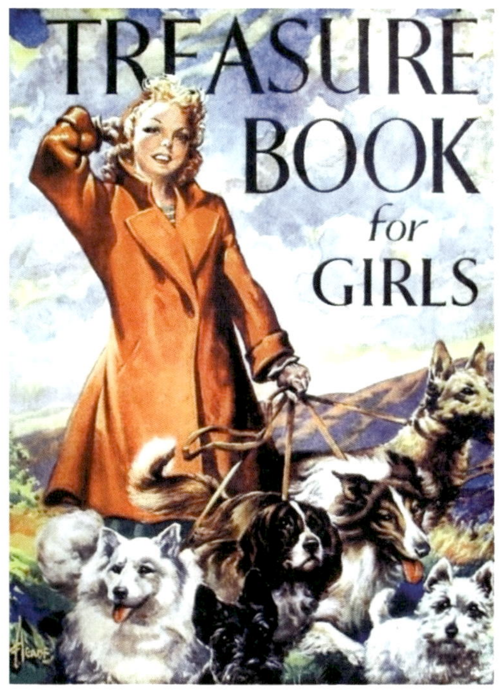

Two unusual examples of Heade compositions apparently being influenced by a celebrated work of fine art are his cover painting for the children's book *Treasure Book for Girls* (Collins, c1937), later reused for two different printings of *The Bumper Book for Girls* (Collins, c1950 and c1954) (as pictured on page 179 of *The Art of Reginald Heade – Special Edition*), and his dustjacket piece for the Scotland-set romantic novel *Because of Sam* by Molly Clavering (Hodder & Stoughton, 1954) – see top left and bottom left respectively. Although not exact copies, these both clearly bear some strong similarities to Charles Wellington Furse's 1903-1904 oil-on-canvas work *Diana of the Uplands* – shown bottom right. The latter painting, for which Furse's wife Katherine (later Director of the Women's Royal Naval Service) posed as a contemporary interpretation of Diana, Roman goddess of the hunt, the moon and nature, was very popular in its day, and used in many early 20th Century advertisements. Given his tendency to rely on printed reference material in his work, it is likely that Heade found a picture of Furse's painting in a magazine or a book – it was included, for instance, in G K Chesterton's two-volume *Famous Paintings* (Funk & Wagnalls, 1912, 1913). It is however possible that he saw it in person, as it was owned and often displayed by the Tate Gallery in London.

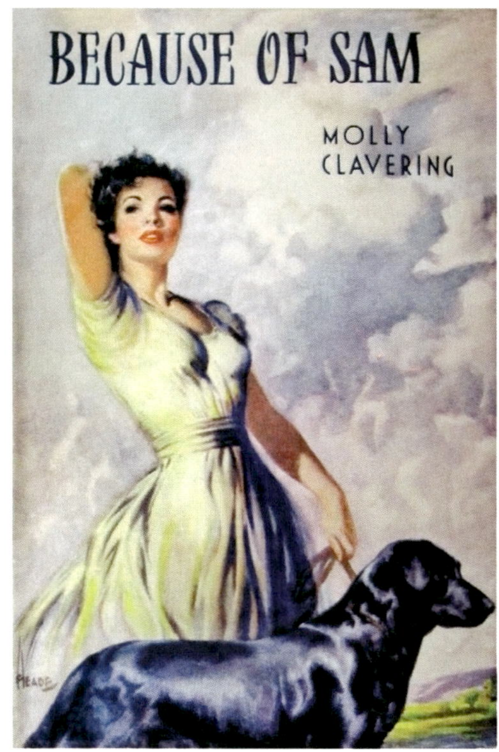

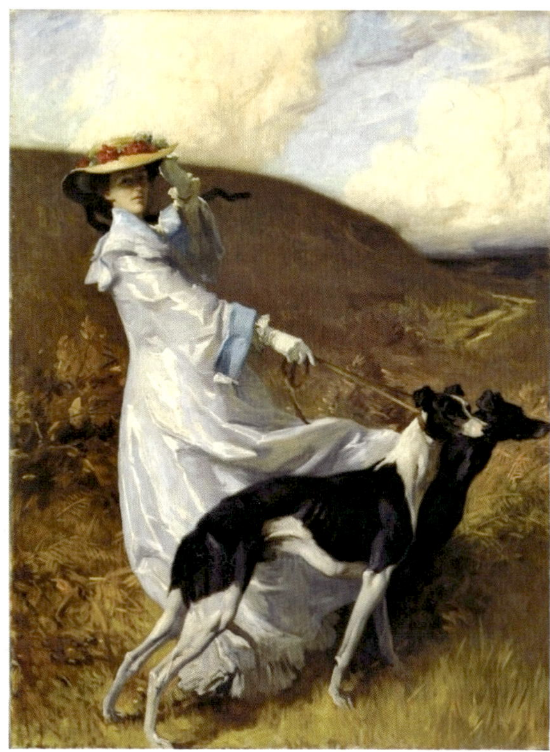

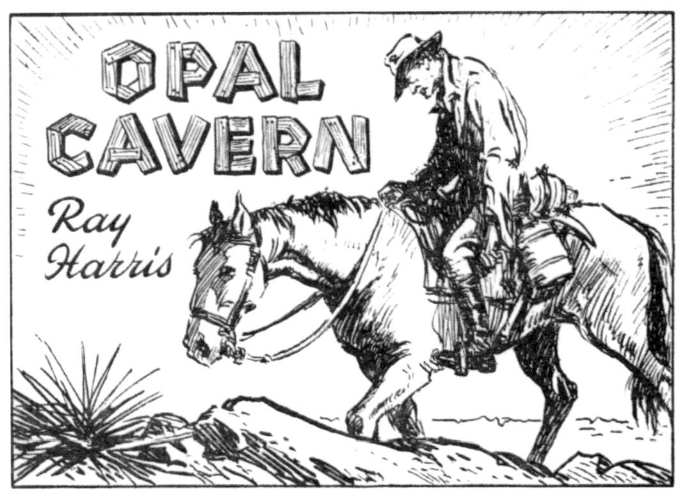

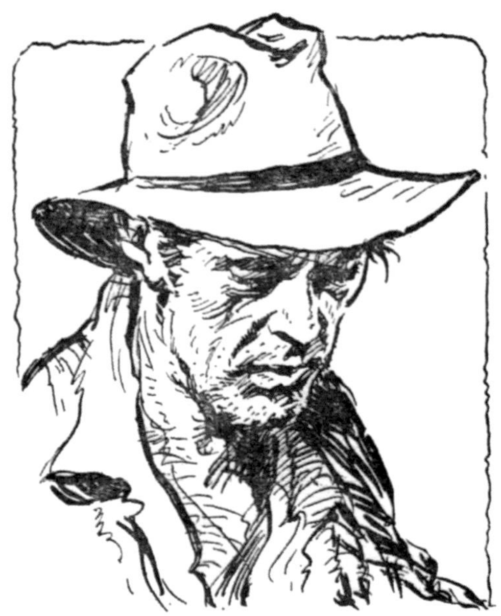

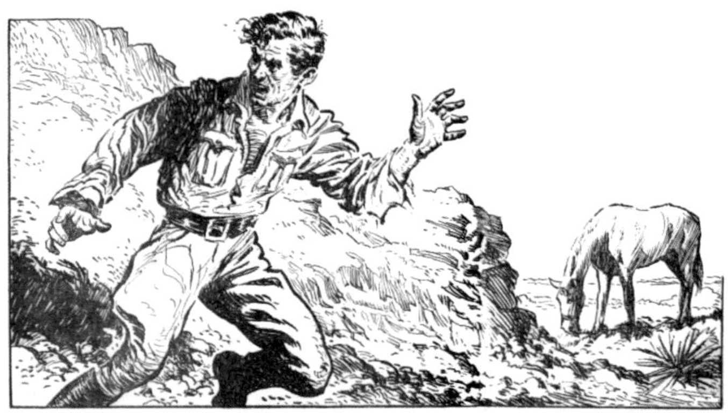

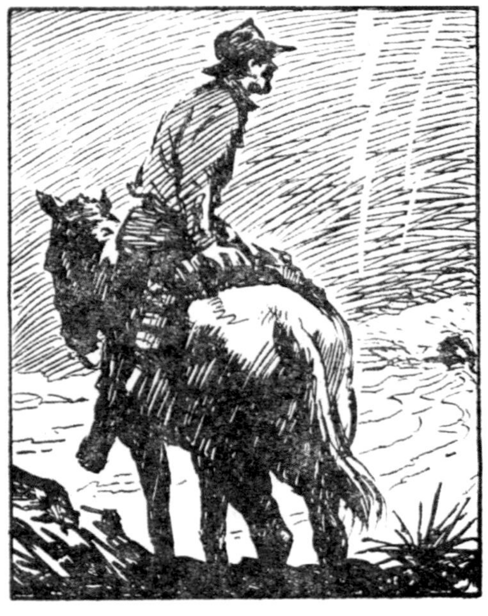

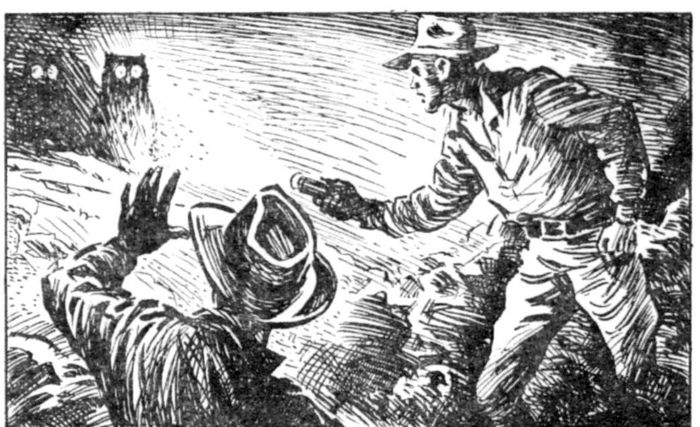

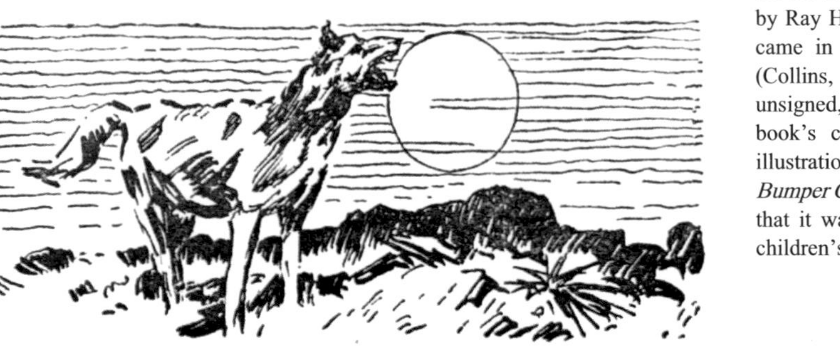

This page: Heade's six black and white illustrations for the short Western adventure story 'Opal Cavern' by Ray Harris, the first known appearance of which came in an edition of the *Collins Boys' Annual* (Collins, c1955). Although the illustrations are unsigned, the artist received a credit for them on the book's contents page. The story, complete with illustrations, was reprinted shortly afterwards in *Bumper Cowboy Book* (Collins, c1956). It is possible that it was originally published in a 1940s Collins children's book, currently unidentified.

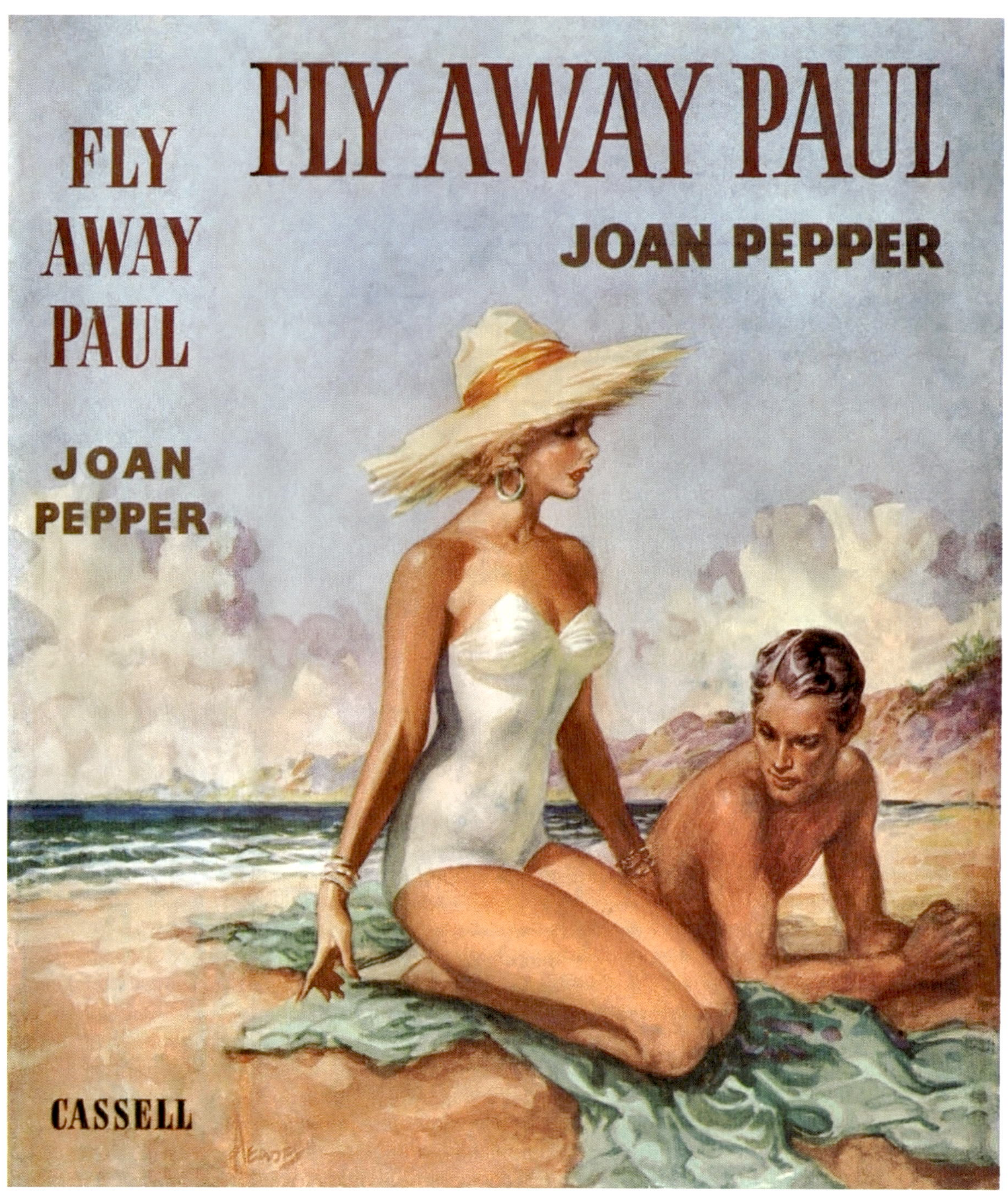

Fly Away Paul by Joan Pepper (Cassell, 1954)

WHEN KNIGHTS WERE BOLD

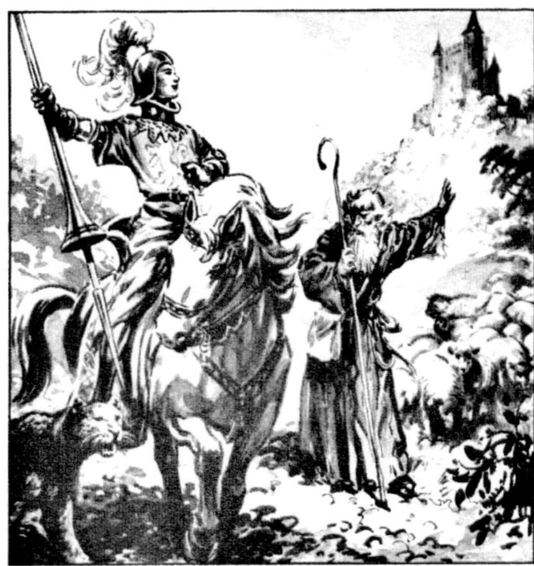

1. Riding in search of adventure, with his loyal friend Fury the leopard, Sir Gareth of the Isles came upon an old shepherd with his flock. "Who lives yonder?" asked the boy knight, pointing to a castle on a hilltop. "It is the home of Sir Bevis, Lord of the Western Hills," replied the greybeard. "At this moment it is a sad place, for the good knight's son Ralph lies very ill in bed."

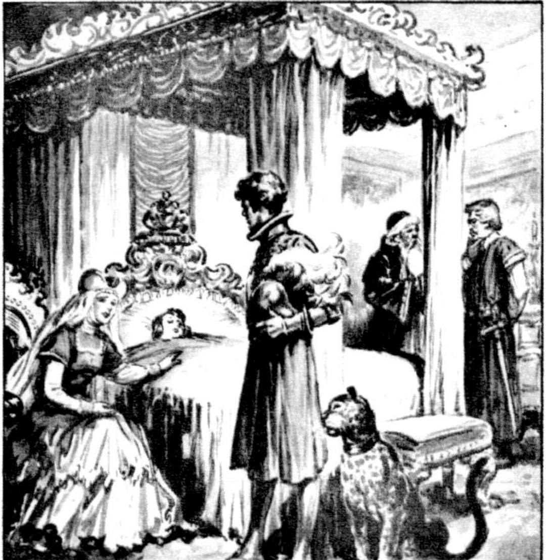

2. Thinking he might be of service to Sir Bevis, the boy knight entered the castle. He was shown into the sick-room where young Ralph lay in bed. Beside him stood his mother and father and the doctor. "He is grieving for his lost horse," the mother told Sir Gareth. "Grey Beauty, his faithful steed, was stolen from him by the bandit knight who dwells in the nearby woods."

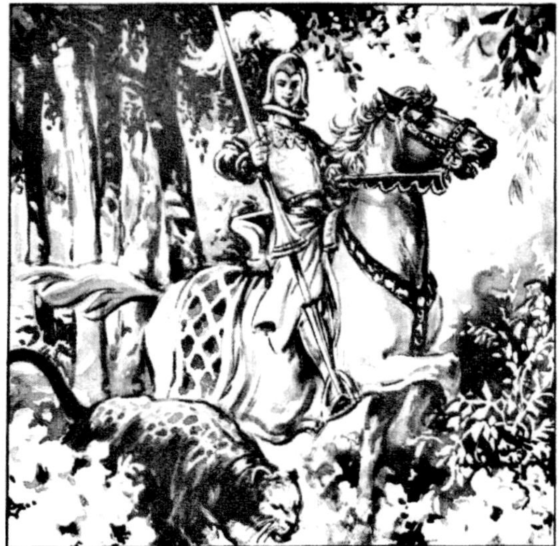

3. Sir Gareth asked what the stolen horse looked like, and then he set off into the woods with Fury sniffing the ground beside him. The leopard had learned Grey Beauty's scent from a spare saddle in the castle stables, and now he hunted high and low for it around the spot where young Ralph had met the bandit knight. At last he gave a low growl of triumph and set off through the trees.

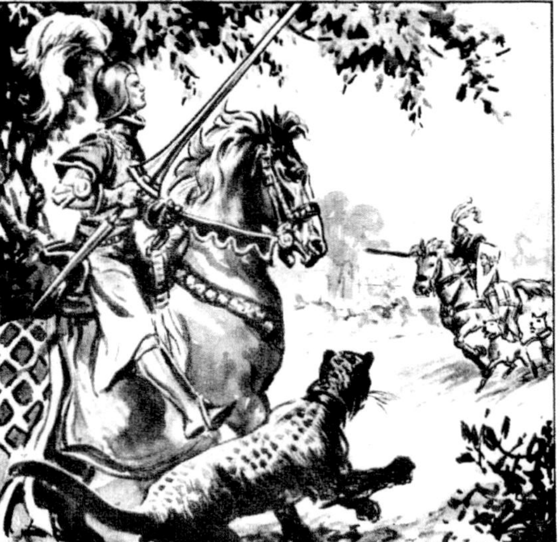

4. The trail was long and Sir Gareth had a hard job keeping up with Fury. At last, they reached the edge of the wood and there ahead of them was a strange knight accompanied by two great dogs. At once, Sir Gareth recognised the stranger's mount from the description that had been given him. It was Grey Beauty! The leopard had found the bandit knight when all others had failed.

The first page of Heade's two-page strip for 'When Knights Were Bold' in *Playhour* # 10 (Amalgamated, 13 December 1954)

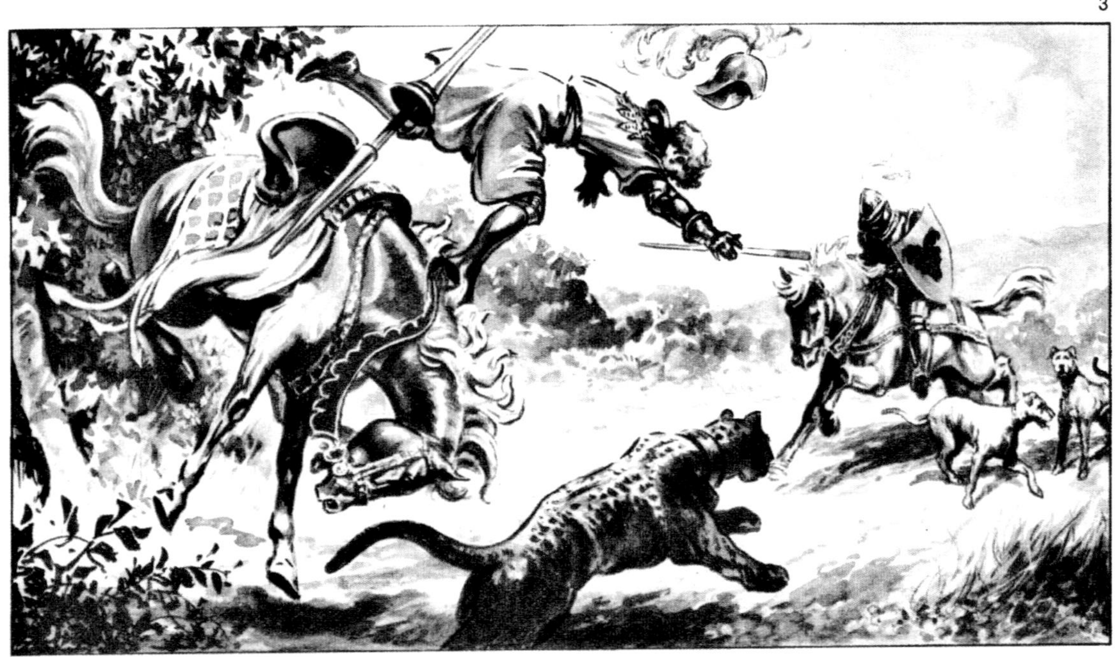

5. The bandit knight did not wait for Sir Gareth to challenge him. He had always avoided defeat and capture in the past by making sure of striking the first blow before his opponent was ready for him. Now he lowered the point of his lance and spurred Grey Beauty into the attack. But Sir Gareth was ready for him, lowering his own lance and urging his mount into a gallop.

6. "Watch those big dogs!" Sir Gareth shouted to Fury as the two knights thundered towards each other. The leopard sprang forward towards the two great hounds trotting by their master's side, and they sheered off, out of reach of his fangs. But at that moment Sir Gareth's horse put his foot in a rabbit hole, and the boy knight was pitched headlong from the saddle.

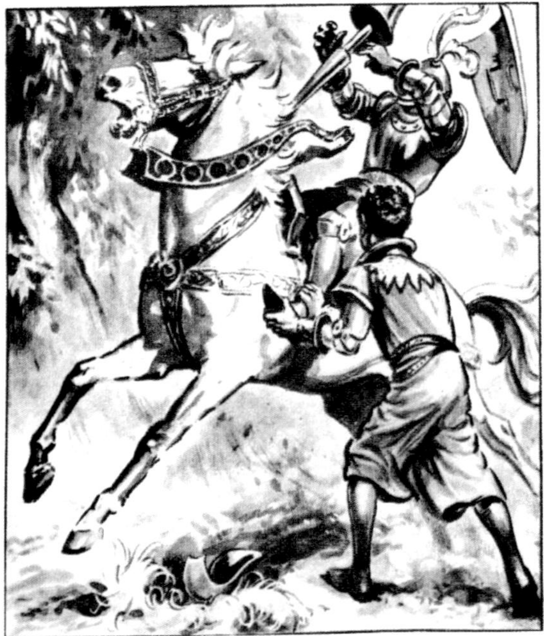

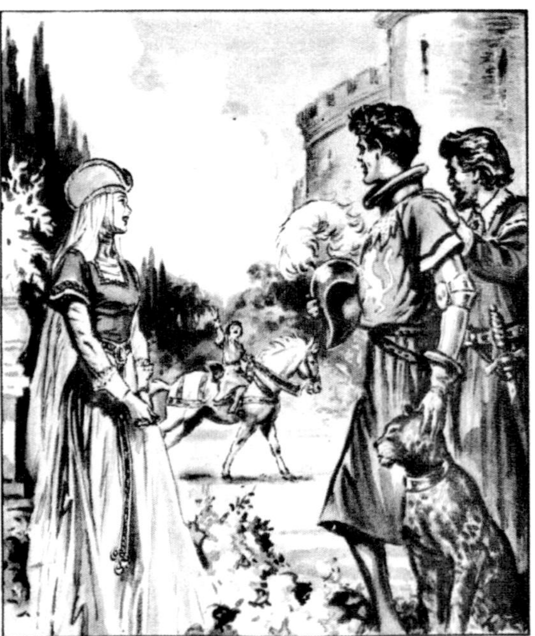

7. With a cry of triumph, the bandit rode at the boy knight. But, nimble as a fox, Sir Gareth scrambled to his feet and seized his enemy by one mailed foot. A swift jerk of the wrists and the bandit was unhorsed. Gareth was upon him in an instant and soon made him his prisoner. Then the boy knight set off back to the castle of Sir Bevis with his prisoner and Grey Beauty.

8. Some days later, Sir Gareth strolled outside the castle walls with Sir Bevis and his lady, watching young Ralph, once again full of health and high spirits, showing off Grey Beauty's paces. "Sir Gareth, we can never thank you enough for what you have done," cried old Sir Bevis. "You must stay with us as long as you please!" But the Boy Knight was eager to set out for fresh adventures.

Look out for another grand adventure of the Boy Knight next week

The second page of Heade's two-page strip for 'When Knights Were Bold' in *Playhour* # 10 (Amalgamated, 13 December 1954)

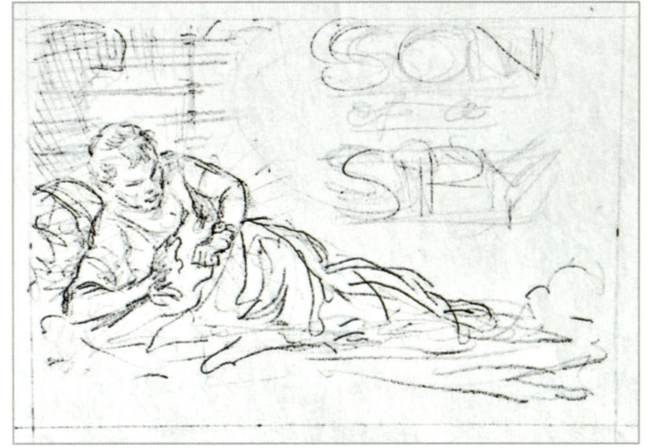

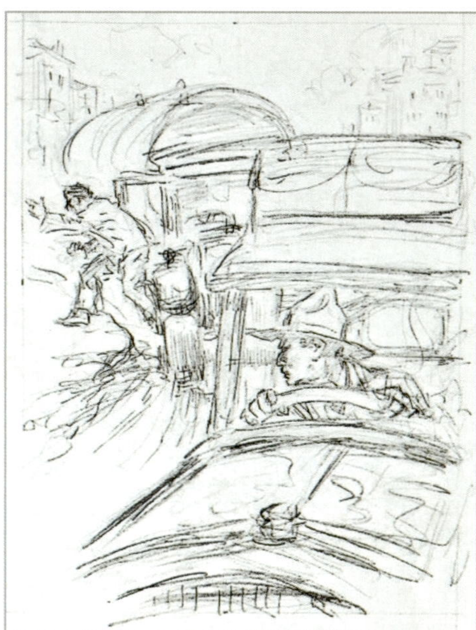

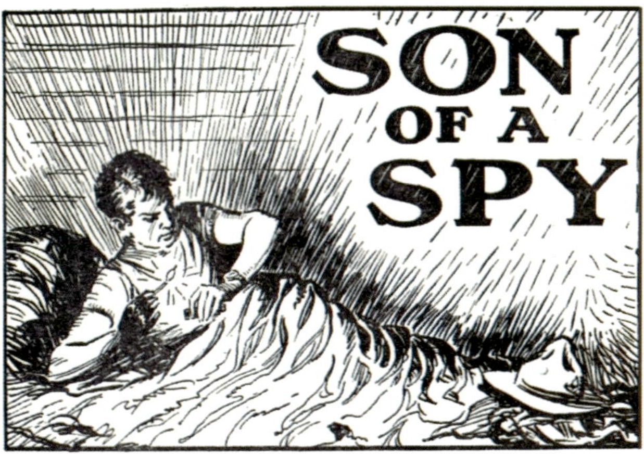

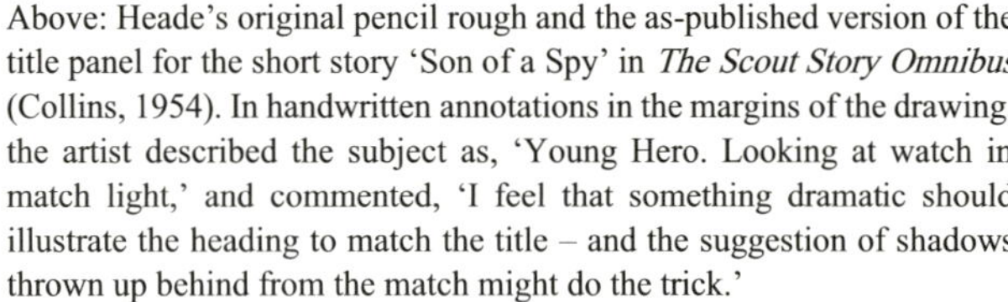

Above: Heade's original pencil rough and the as-published version of the title panel for the short story 'Son of a Spy' in *The Scout Story Omnibus* (Collins, 1954). In handwritten annotations in the margins of the drawing, the artist described the subject as, 'Young Hero. Looking at watch in match light,' and commented, 'I feel that something dramatic should illustrate the heading to match the title – and the suggestion of shadows thrown up behind from the match might do the trick.'

Right: Heade's original pencil rough and the as-published version of the full-page colour illustration for 'Son of a Spy'.

Below: the other two black-and-white illustrations for 'Son of a Spy'.

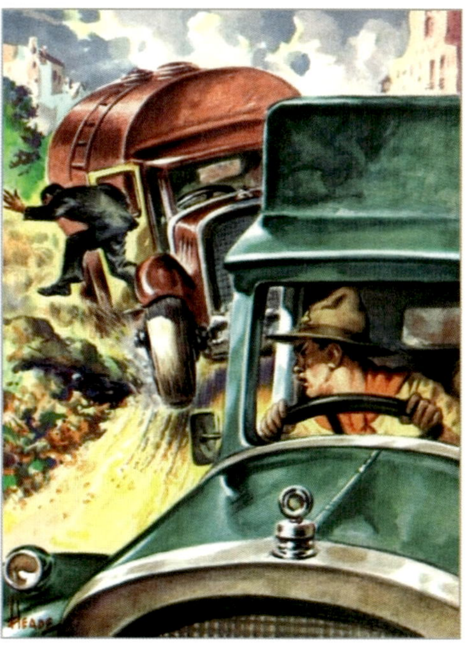

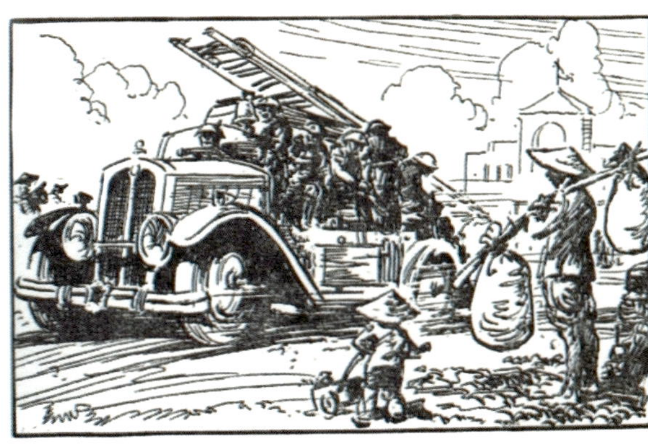

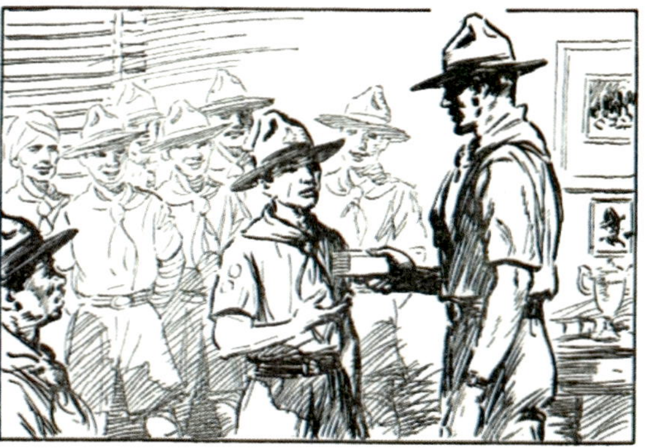

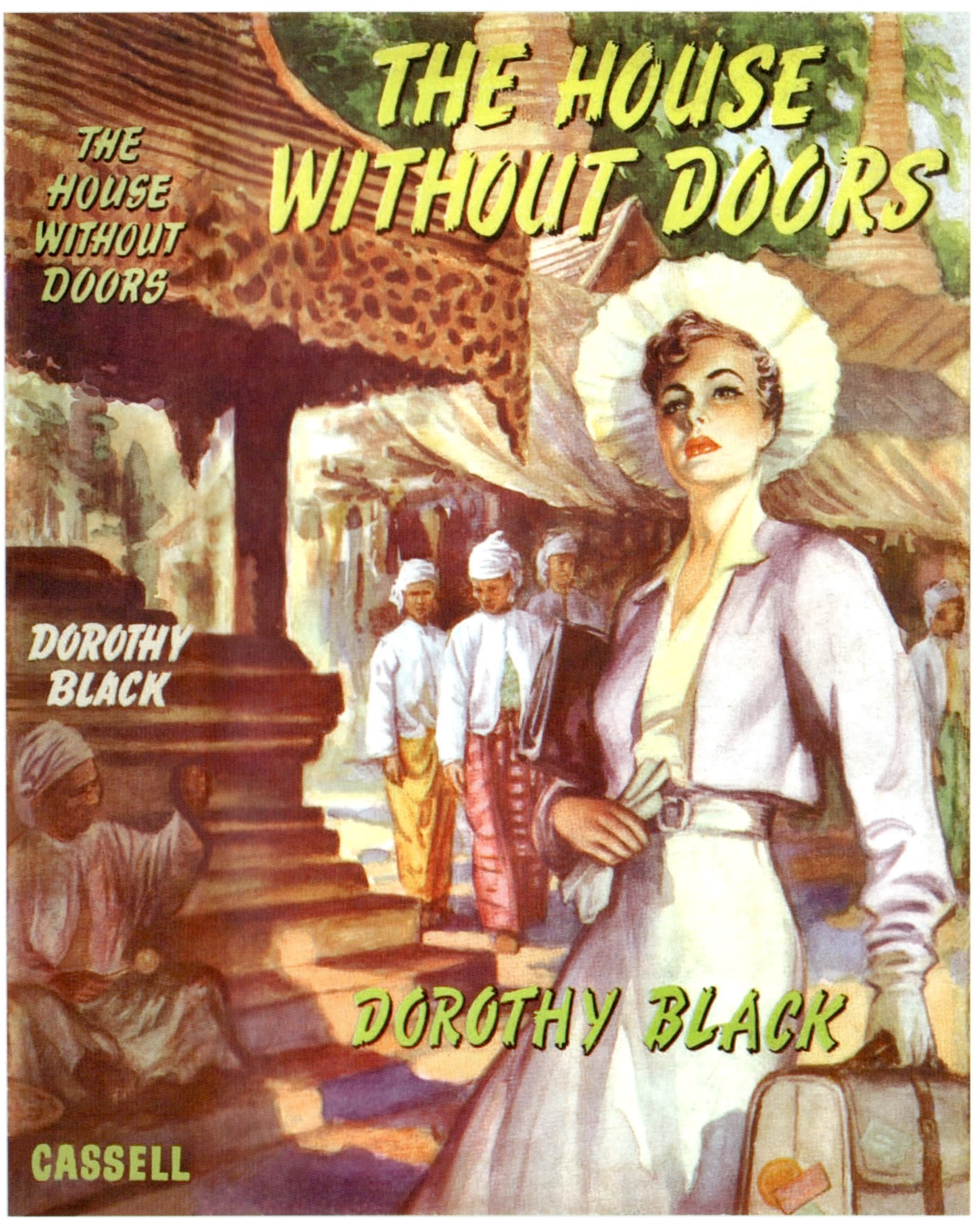

The House Without Doors by Dorothy Black (Cassell, 1955)

LETTERING

By the mid-1950s, it was becoming standard practice for book titles, author credits and any other required lettering to be added to Heade's paintings by the publishers' art departments. Previously, however, the artist typically had to provide the lettering himself. Two examples shown here are his preparatory drawings and the final versions of the lettering for the sheet music of 'Hank Janson Blues' (New Fiction Press, 1953) and a Paul Reville author credit.

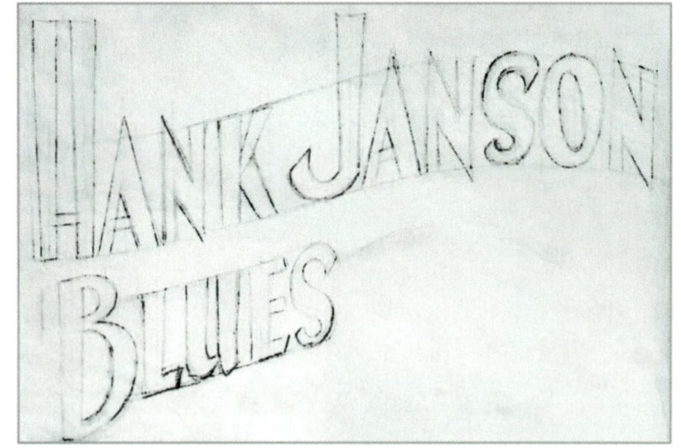

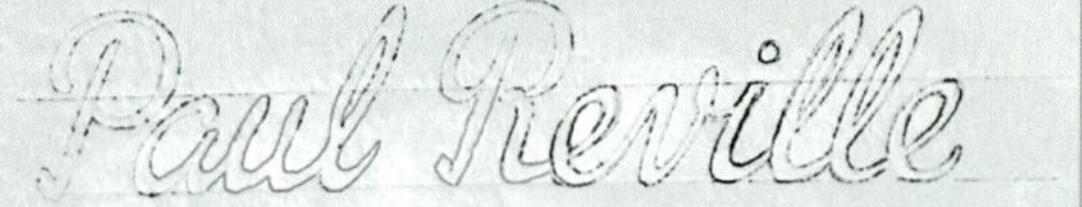

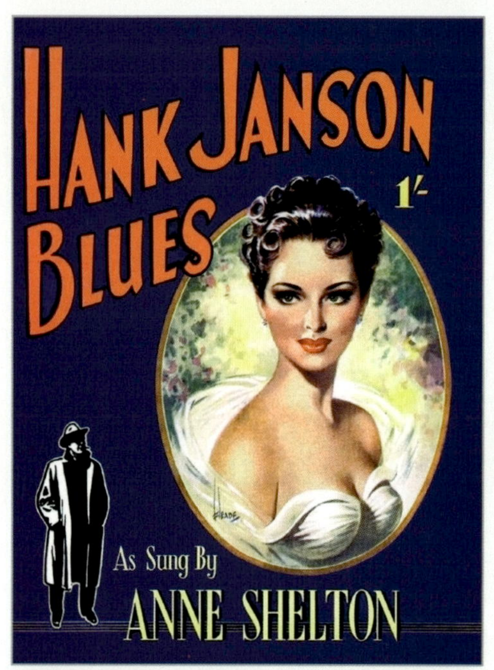

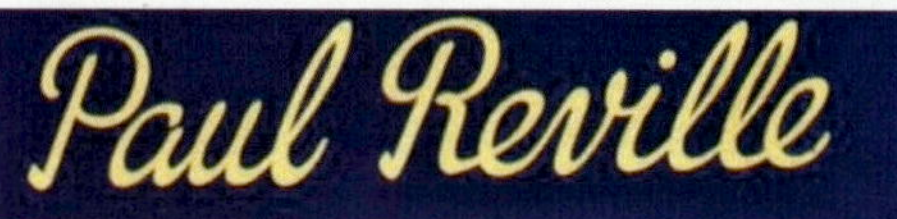

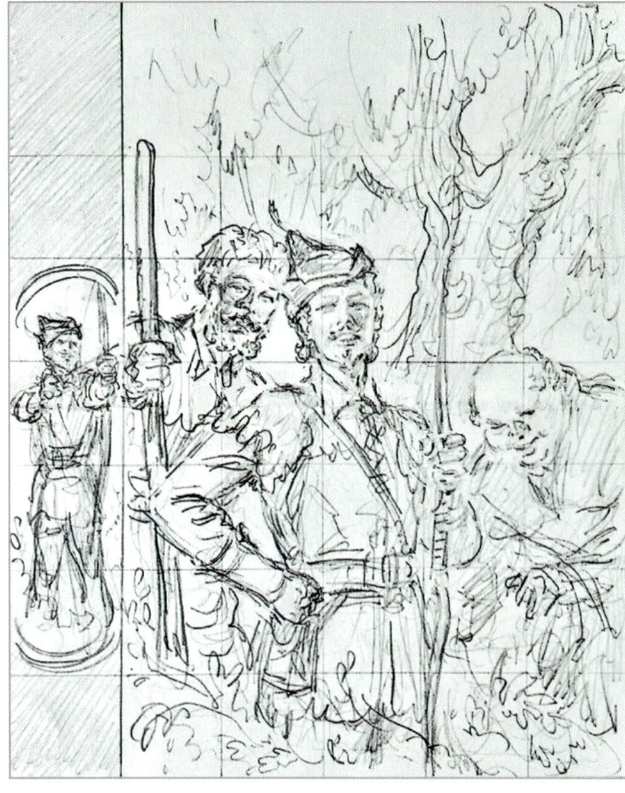

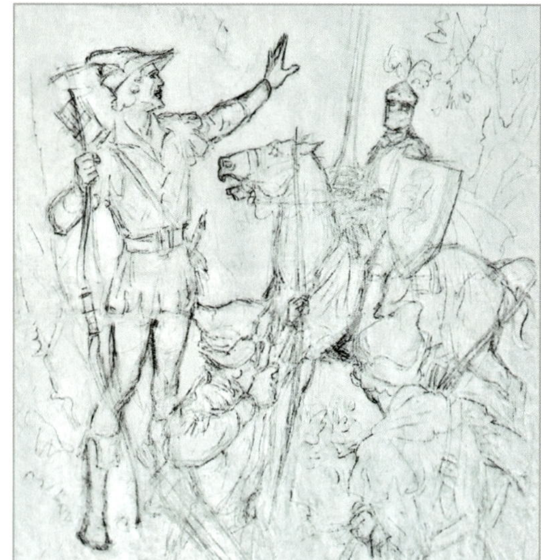

Above: a Robin Hood-themed rough, believed most likely to have been intended for a circa 1954 jigsaw puzzle, though this is currently unconfirmed.

Left: Heade's original rough for the 1956 Children's Press reissue of *Robin of Sherwood* by Major Charles Gilson – see facing page.

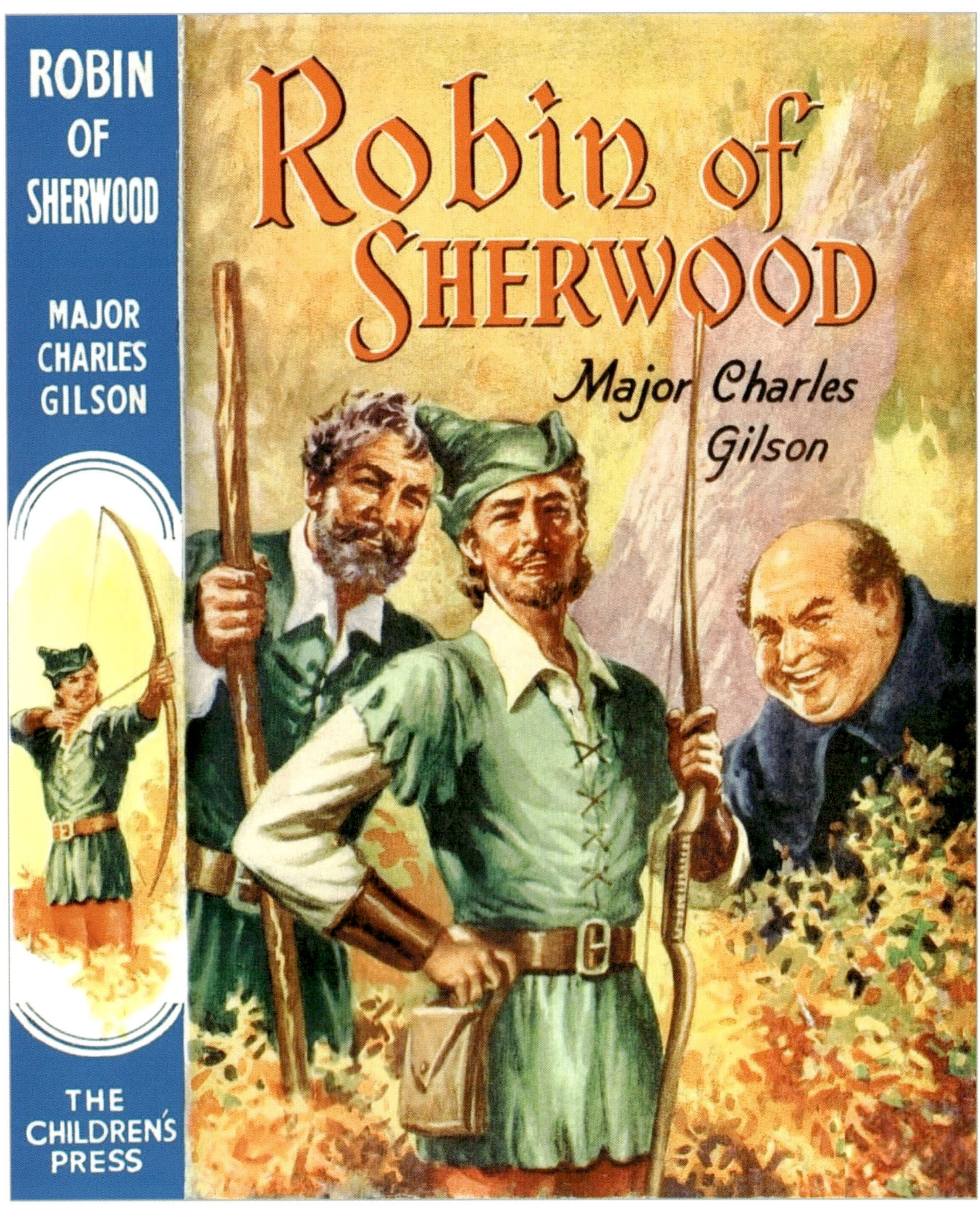

The as-published cover of *Robin of Sherwood* by Major Charles Gilson (The Children's Press, 1956). Previously presented as a smaller image, without the additional spine-section illustration, in the 'Is It Heade?' section of *The Art of Reginald Heade – Special Edition*, but now definitely confirmed as Heade's work.

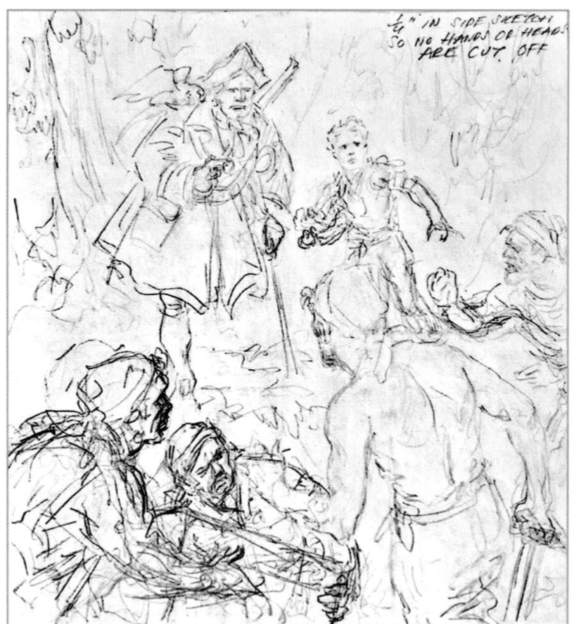
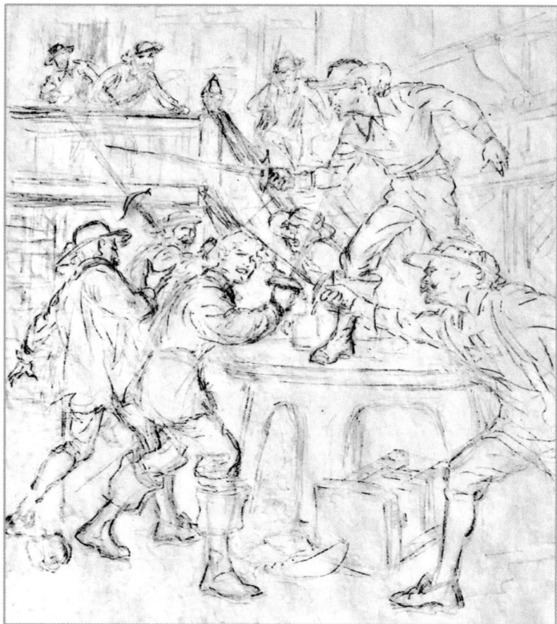

Above left: Heade's original rough for a jigsaw puzzle entitled *Treasure Island*, based on a scene from the Robert Louis Stevenson novel. The artist's deadline for submission of the finished piece was Monday 18 October 1954. Above right: the more developed of two surviving roughs for what appears to be an illustration inspired by Alexandre Dumas's *The Three Musketeers*. Heade was asked to supply the finished piece for this if possible by Wednesday 20 October 1954, just two days after the *Treasure Island* one, and it was doubtless intended for another jigsaw puzzle. However, no actual puzzles corresponding to these drawings have yet been found.

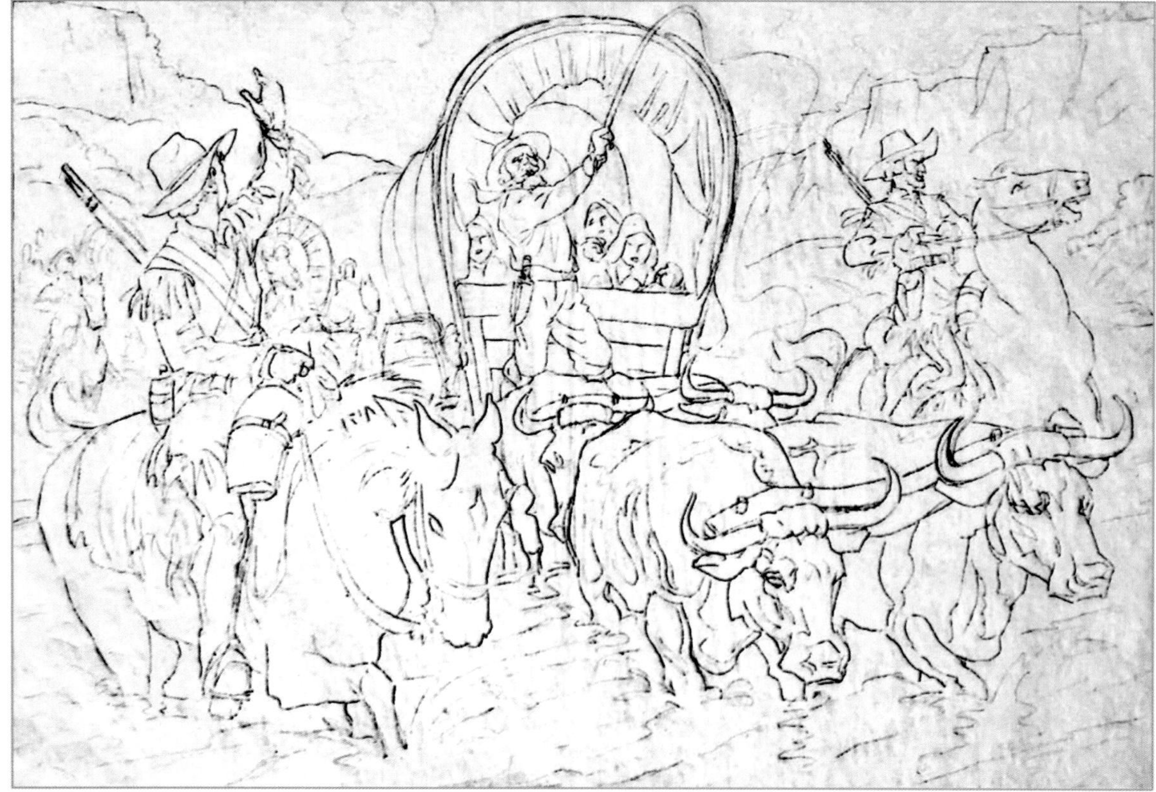

Above: a rough that Heade annotated with the title *Covered Waggon* [sic]. One of a set of four surviving roughs with a Western pioneer theme, probably intended as illustrations for a story in a children's annual type book, as yet unidentified.

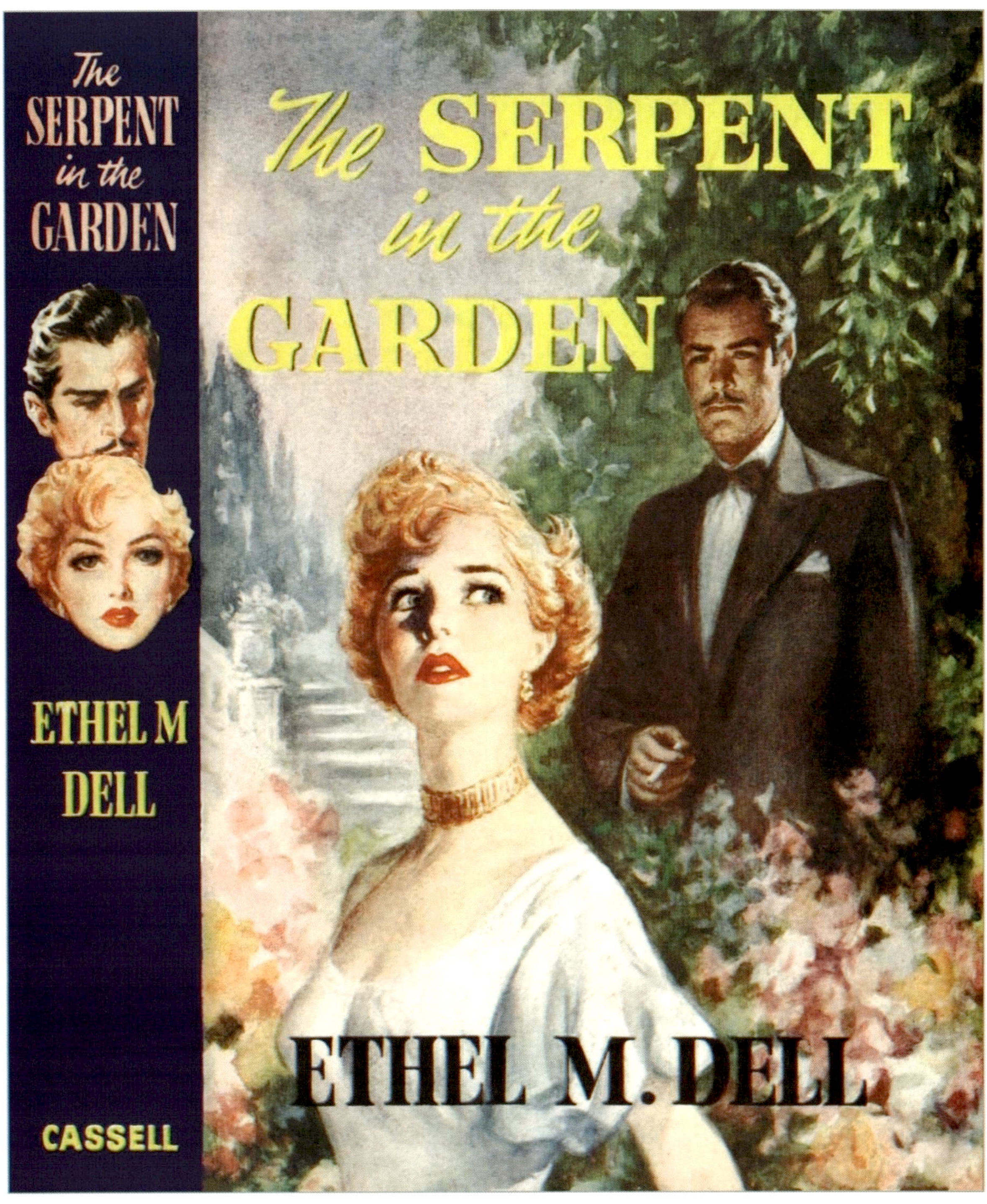

The Serpent in the Garden by Ethel M Dell (Cassell, 1955). Previously presented as a smaller image, without the additional spine-section illustration, in the 'Is It Heade?' section on page 297 of *The Art of Reginald Heade – Special Edition*, but the style of this unsigned piece really leaves no room for doubt that it is Heade's work. In the 1954-1955 transition period from Heade to Cy Webb, few of the artist's paintings were signed.

ALEXANDER MORING

A number of the Hank Janson paperbacks published by Alexander Moring in the mid-1950s had covers that have often been attributed to Heade. It has now been established, however, that only three of those books did in fact feature Heade's work. Of these, only *Menace* (1955) – see facing page – had a piece that had not been previously used by the former Janson publisher Top Fiction Press. *Framed* (1955) – below, top left – reused the Heade artwork from a collection entitled *Deadly Mission*, which is believed to have been unpublished, although a few proof copies were printed. *The Unseen Assassin* (1956) – below, top right – reused the artwork from that title's August 1953 first edition, which placed a Heade-painted female figure and foreground against a Ron Turner-painted background. In this case, the painting was altered slightly to make the figure more fully clothed. The rest of the Alexander Moring Hank Janson books – such as those promoted on the contemporary advertising blotter pictured below, bottom – all had covers by other artists either copying and adapting Heade's earlier work or else attempting to emulate his style.

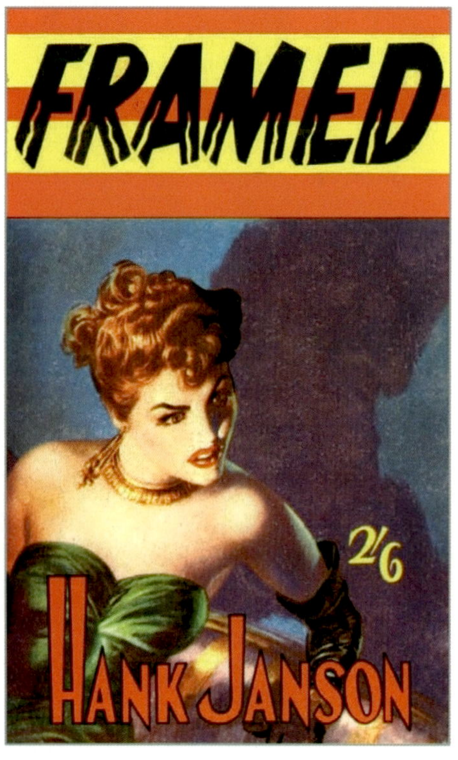

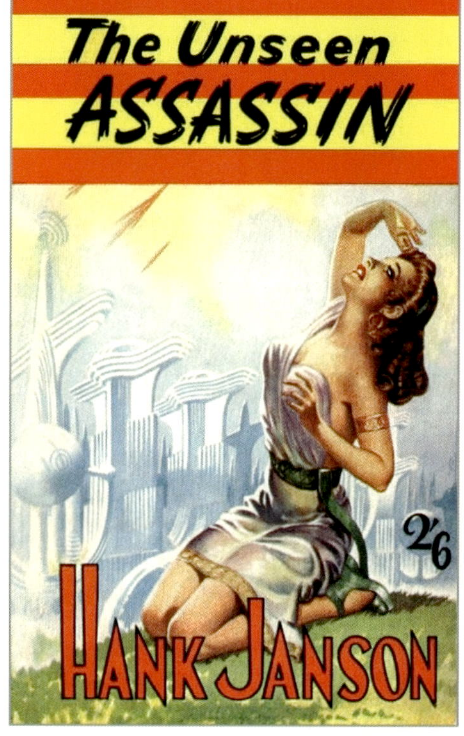

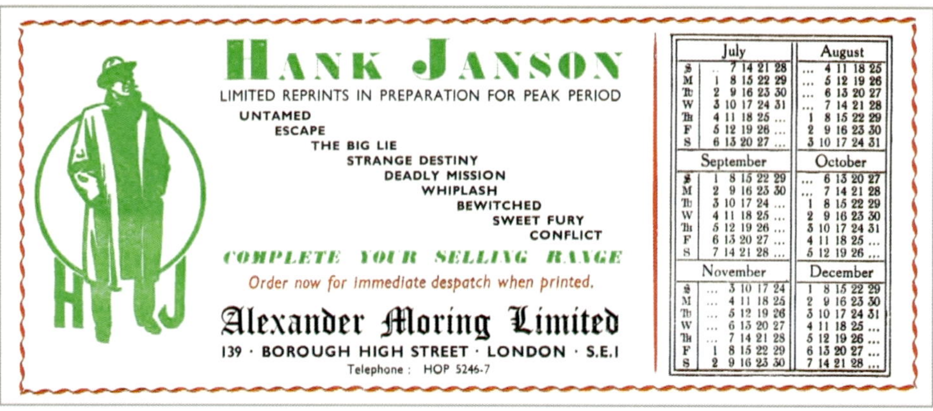

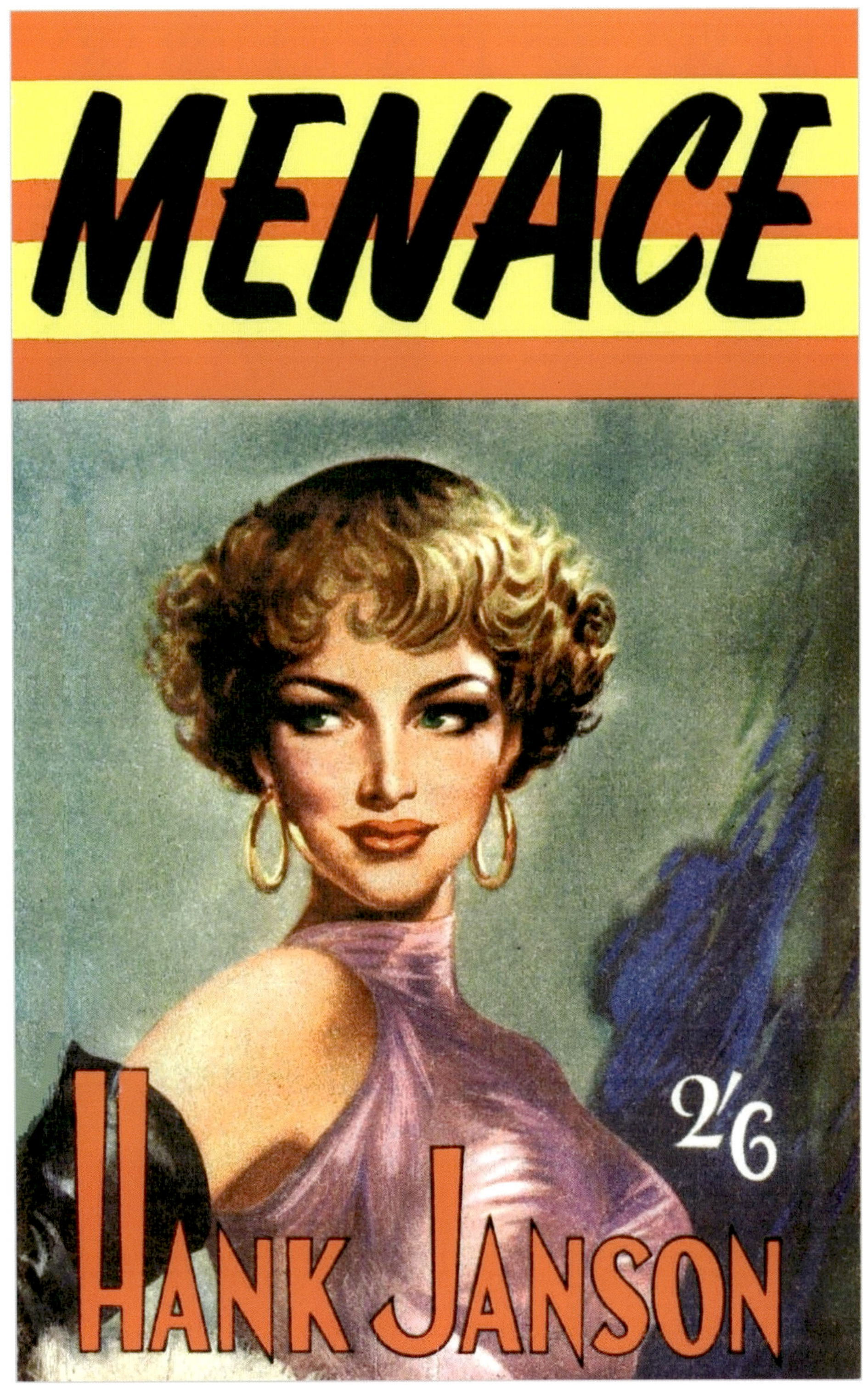

Menace by Hank Janson (Alexander Moring, 1955). The painting appears to be either damaged or uncompleted on the bottom left-hand edge, perhaps explaining why it had not been used previously.

THE SEXTON BLAKE LIBRARY

Heade's cover contributions to Amalgamated's long-running periodicals series The Sexton Blake Library were all unsigned, sometimes making identification difficult. Pictured here are three recently-discovered additional examples that could perhaps be his work. *The Red Stiletto* by Anthony Skene (6 October 1932) appeared some years prior to the others, but the table lamp with a distinctive shade was a recurring motif in Heade's work (as discussed previously). A table lamp appears again on the cover of *Murder in the Air* by John Hunter (January 1955), as does a chair with unusual purple-and-gold-striped upholstery, very similar to that featured in several confirmed Heade paintings, including the cover of the Harborough book *Deal Me Out* by Spike Morelli; this could have been a piece of furniture that the artist kept in his studio. However, if the circular central image of *Murder in the Air* is indeed a Heade piece, it would have to be considered an unusually sketchy one; and in any event the aircraft background certainly looks to have been provided by a different artist. *The Mystery of the Five Guilty Men* by John Drummond (July 1954), although it includes no immediately distinctive elements, is very much in Heade's style, in this instance leaving little room for doubt as to the attribution.

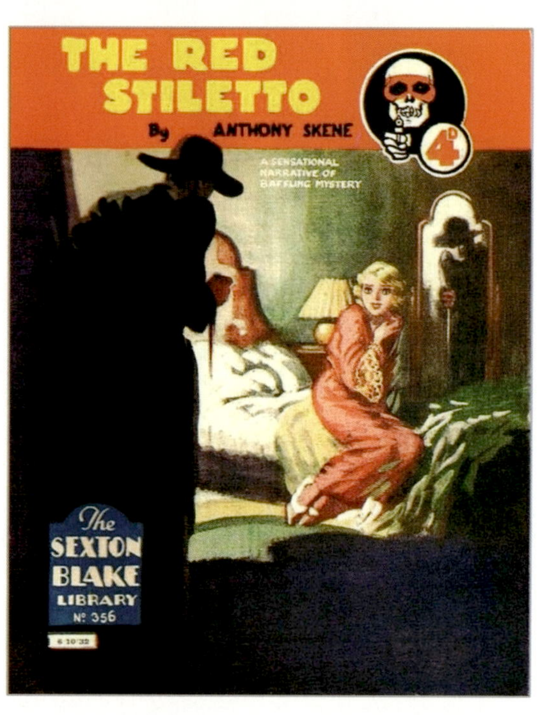

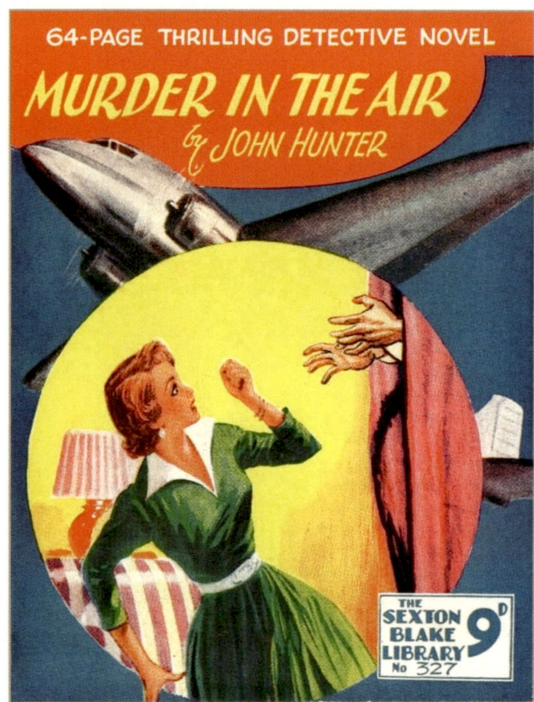

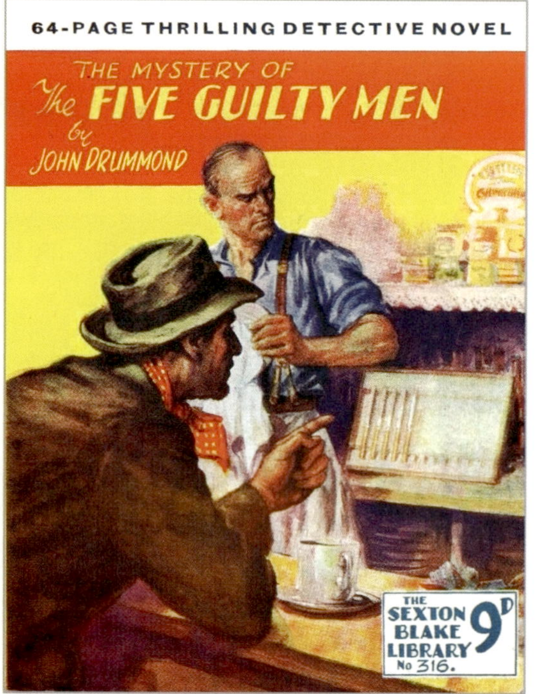

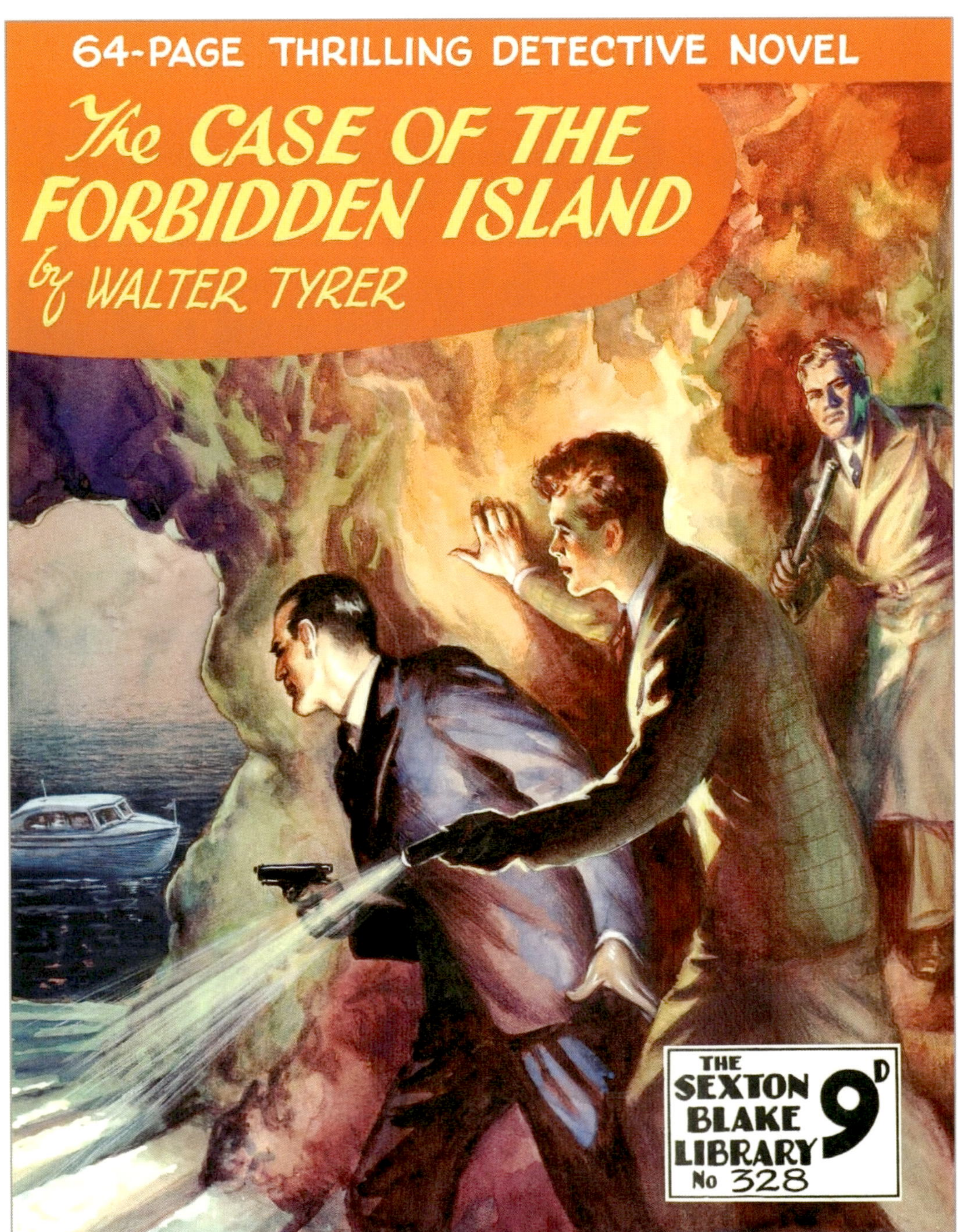

Above: Heade's original painting for Walter Tyrer's *The Case of the Forbidden Island* (Amalgamated, January 1955). This was sold in a Book, Comic and Magazine Art Work auction held at Christie's in London on Thursday 18 March 1993, along with another confirmed Heade cover for The Sexton Blake Library, namely that for Anthony Parsons' *The Man from Maybrick Road* (Amalgamated, December 1954), and one possible one, that for John Hunter's *Murder in the Air* (see opposite). All three were credited only to an anonymous artist. Also included in the auction were four Heade oil paintings for *Britannia and Eve* covers. These were amongst three lots of cover art from that magazine, comprising 14 pieces altogether, all mistakenly described in the auction catalogue as 'calendar girls' and attributed to 'Nar Long', a misspelling of the name of Heade's contemporary Nat Long (who did produce some *Britannia and Eve* covers, at least one of which was included in the auction). (Image courtesy the Steve Chibnall Collection.)

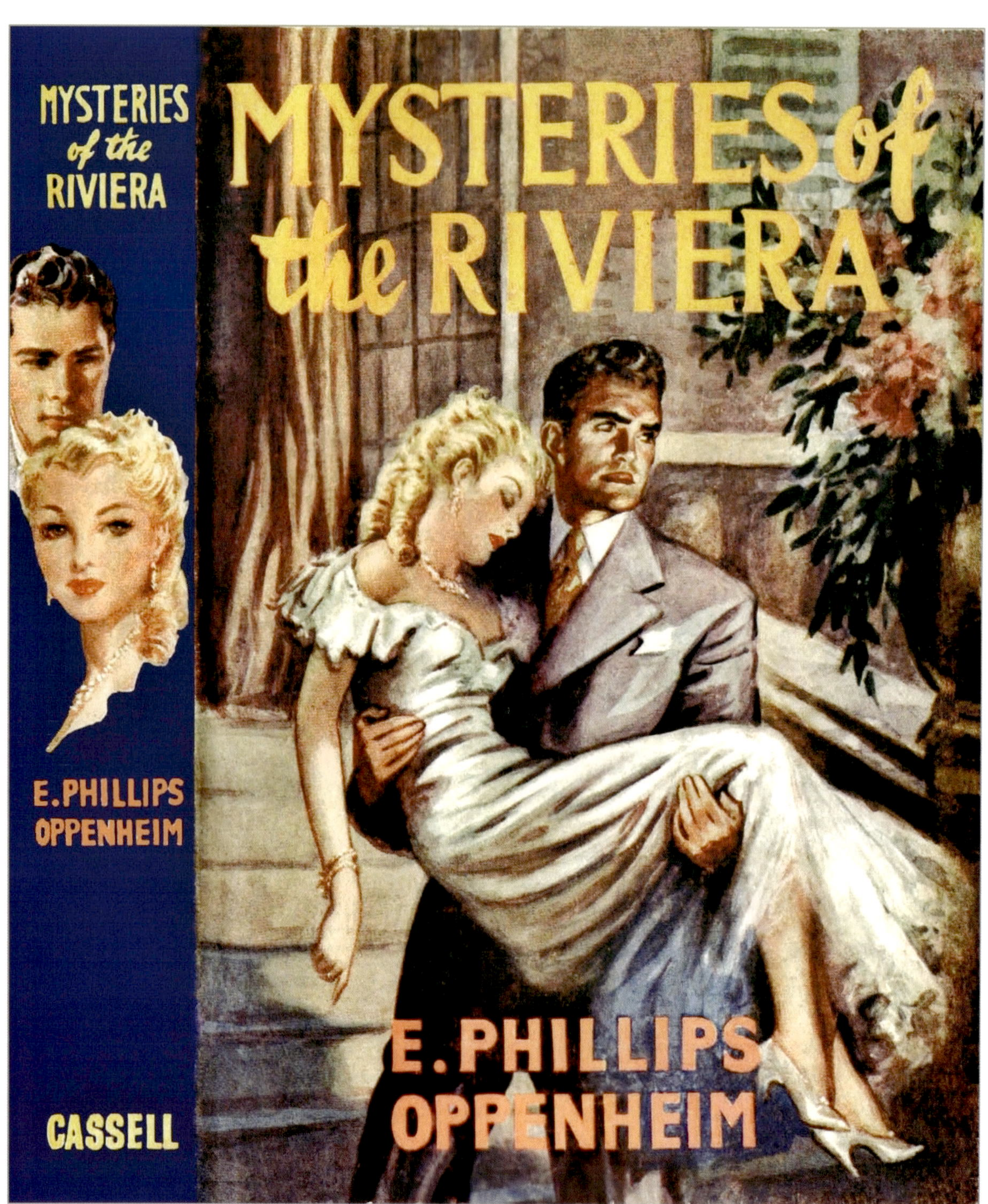

Mysteries of the Riviera by E Phillips Oppenheim (Cassell, 1956)

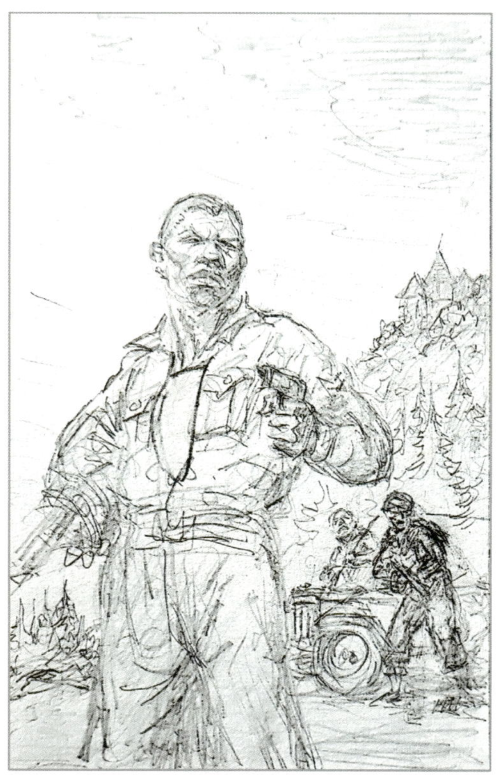 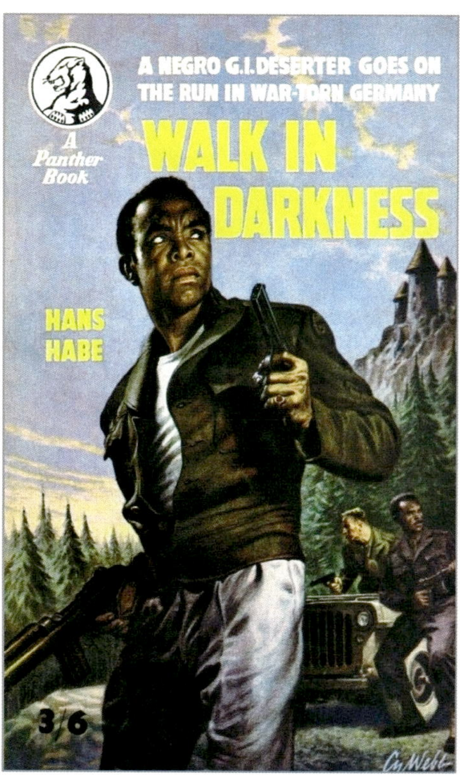

Heade's original rough and the as-published cover of *Walk in Darkness* by Hans Habe (Panther, December 1956)

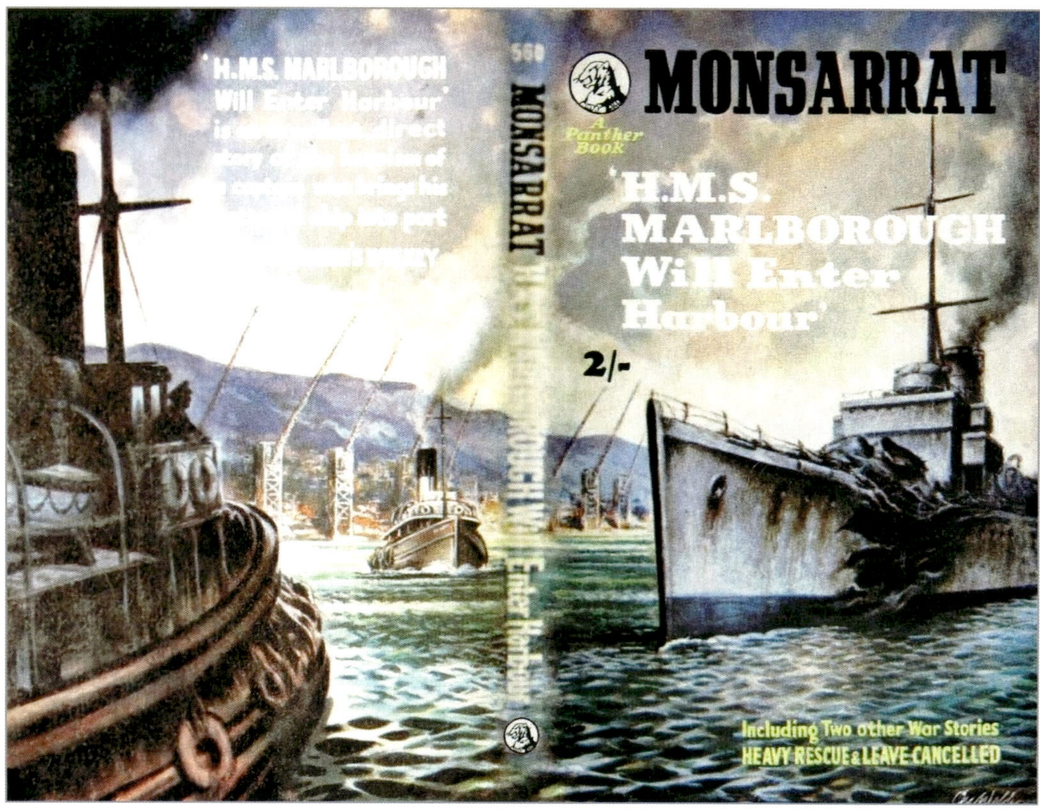

'*H.M.S. Marlborough Will Enter Harbour*' *by Nicholas Monsarrat* (Panther, February 1956)

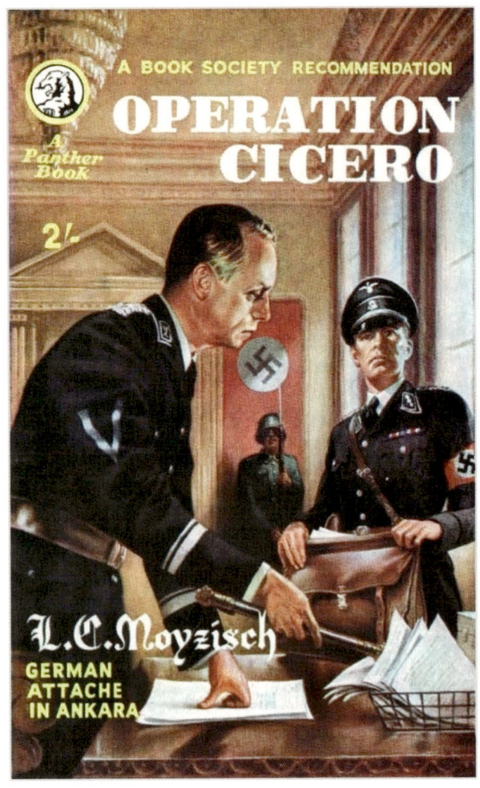

Operation Cicero by L C Moyzisch (Panther, January 1956)

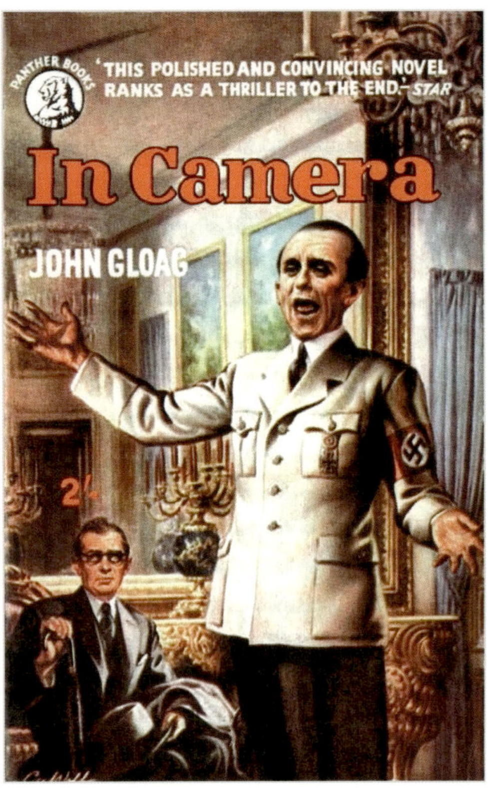

In Camera by John Gloag (Panther, 1956)

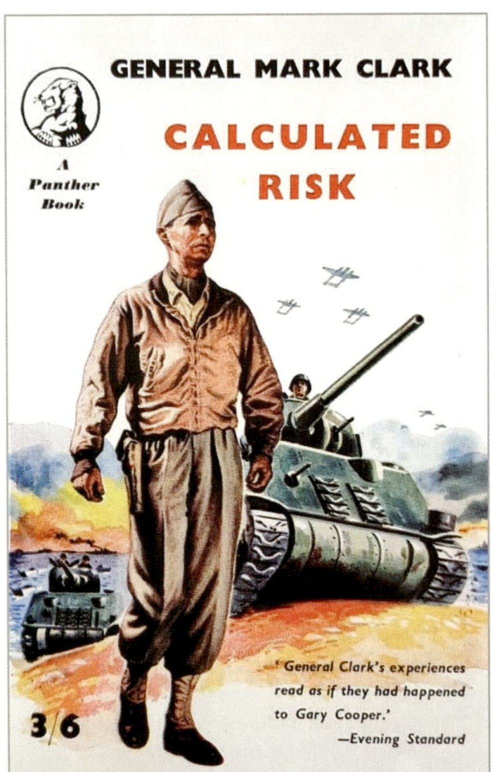

Calculated Risk by General Mark Clark (Panther, 1956)

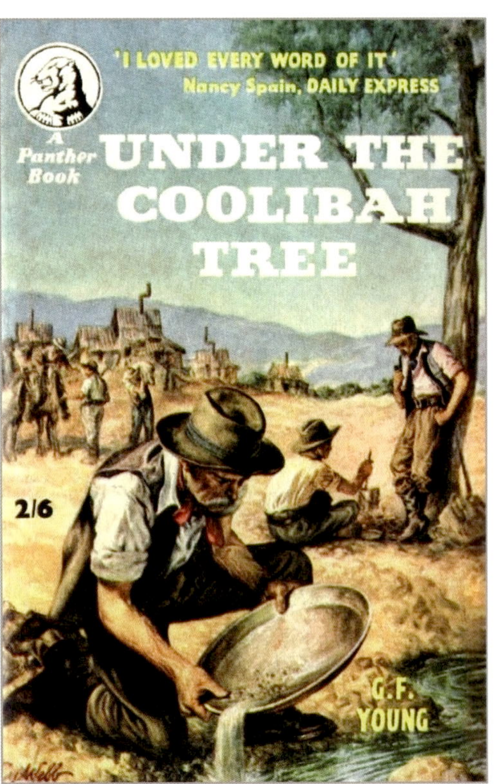

Under the Coolibah Tree by G F Young (Panther, 1956)

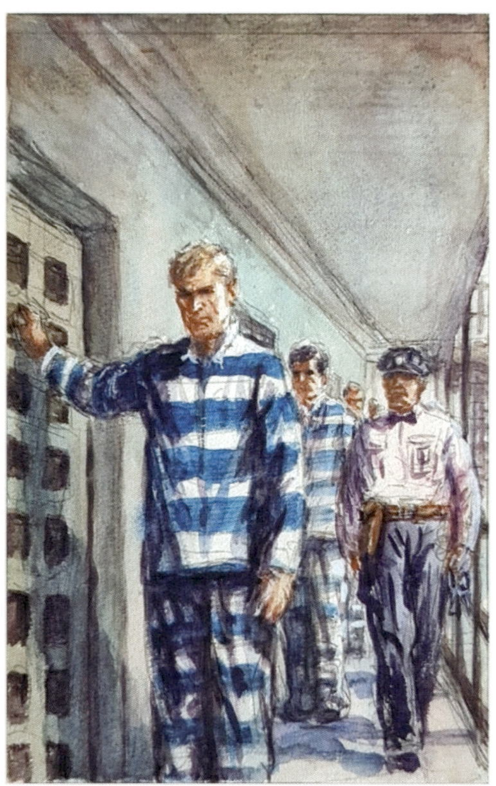 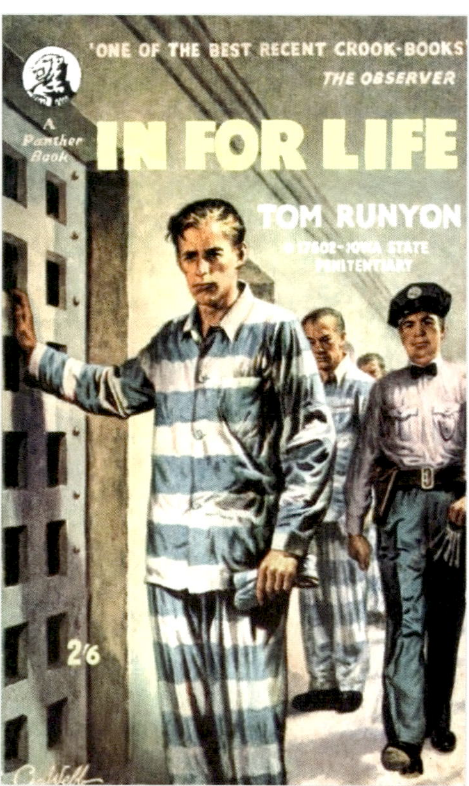

Heade's original rough and the as-published paperback cover of *In For Life* by Tom Runyon (Panther, June 1956)

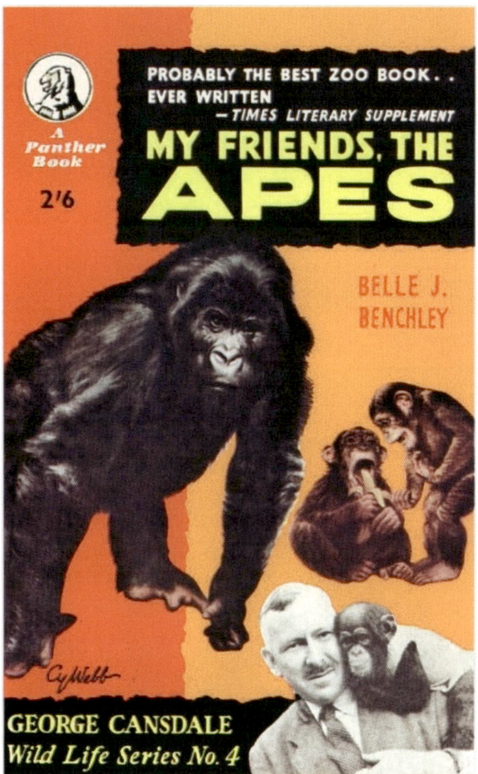

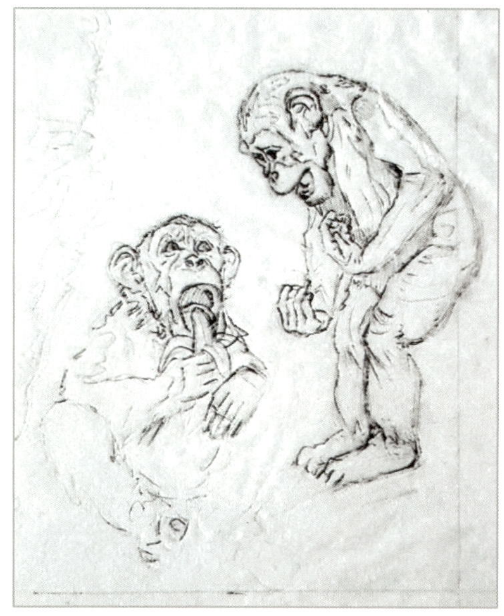

My Friends, the Apes by Belle J Benchley (Panther, July 1956)

Unusually, for *My Friends, the Apes*, Heade was asked to provide not a complete painting but only certain artwork elements for inclusion on the cover. Consequently, in this instance, rather than produce a full rough for approval, he supplied a drawing of just one of these elements, as shown above. It appears that this was in fact traced from a reference photograph, probably found in a magazine.

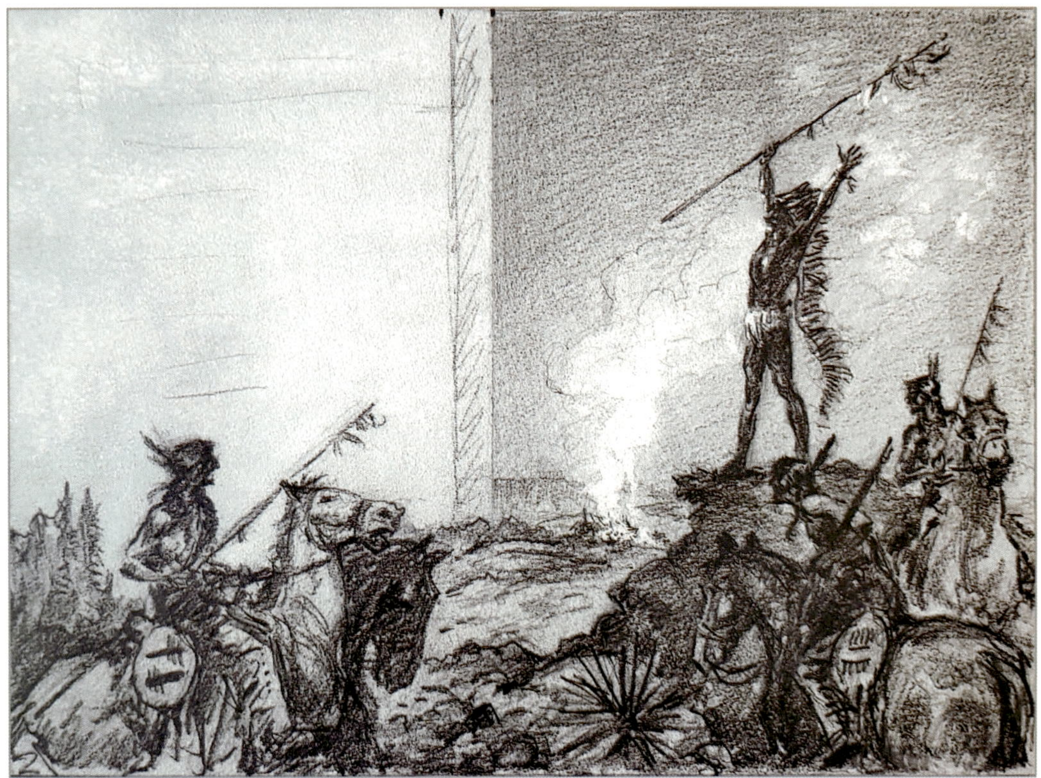

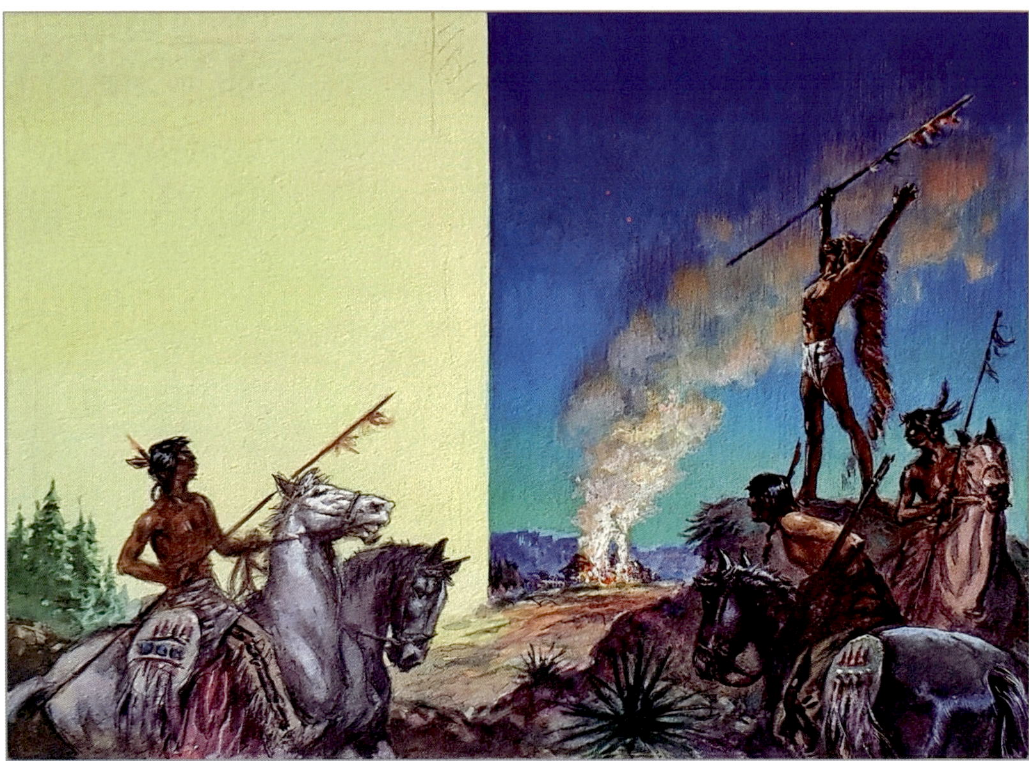

When approaching the Panther and Pan paperback commissions he signed as Cy Webb toward the end of his life, Heade would typically proceed by producing a thumbnail sketch in pencil, then developing this into a full rough in either black-and-white or colour. *Eagle Voice* by John G Neihardt (Panther, June 1956) was unusual, in that the artist prepared both a black-and-white *and* a colour rough, as pictured above.

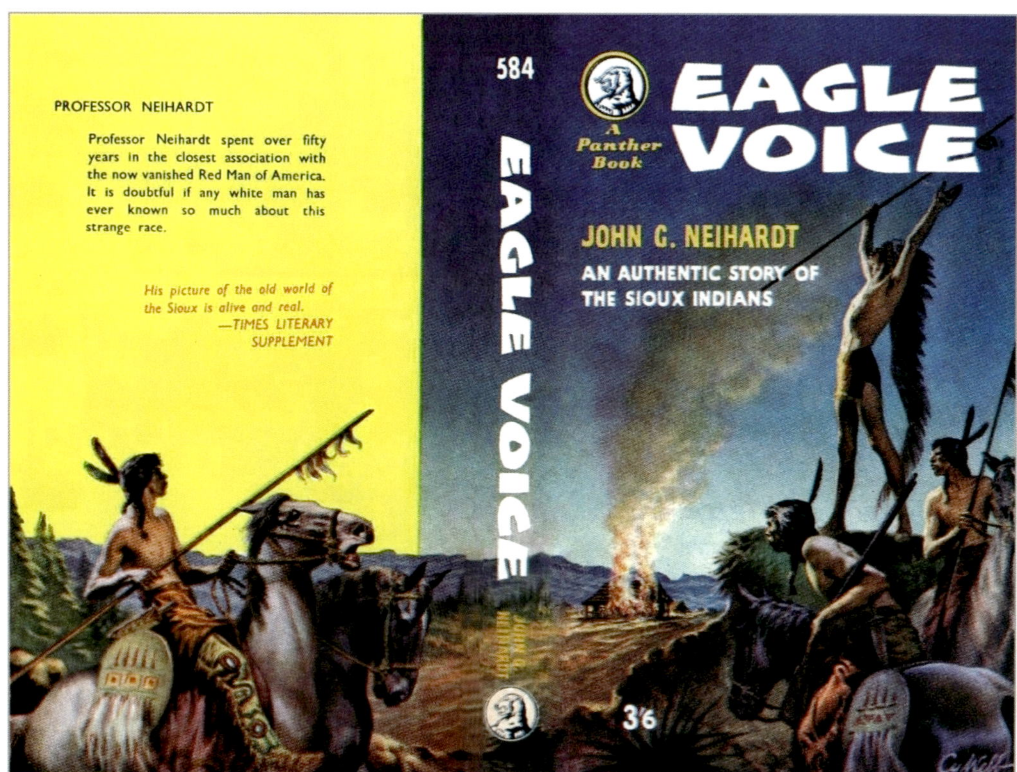

The as-published cover of *Eagle Voice* by John G Neihardt (Panther, June 1956)

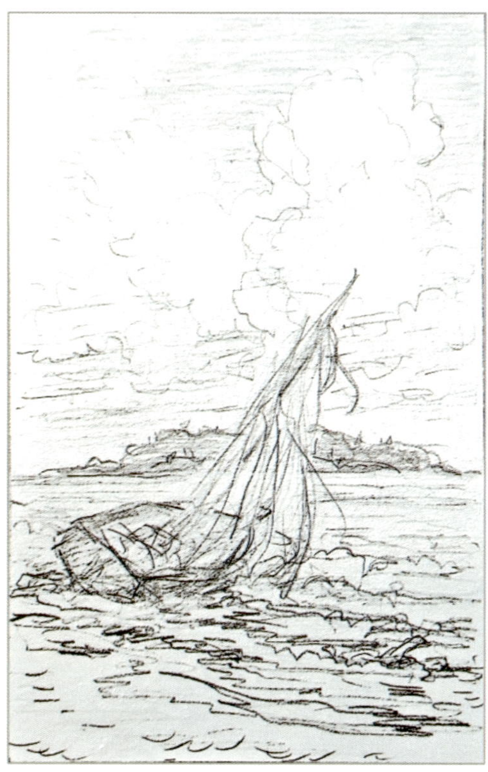

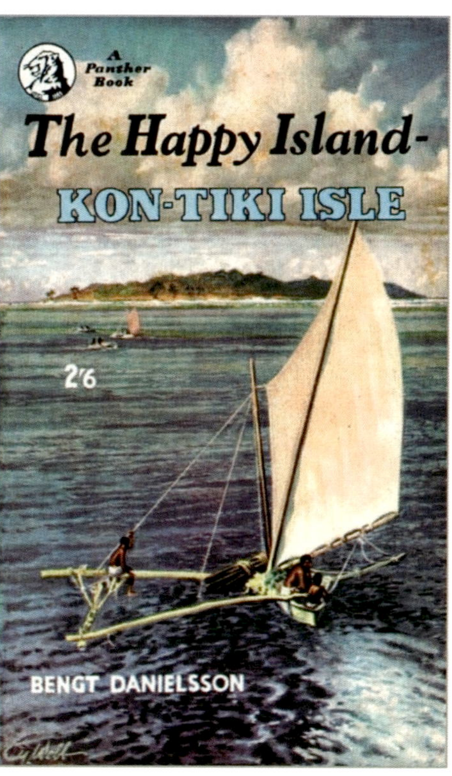

Heade did not always label his roughs, and in a handful of cases this makes identification uncertain. The one pictured above left is thought most likely to have been for *The Happy Island – Kon-Tiki Isle* by Bengt Danielsson (Panther, June 1956), although the boat it depicts is of a type completely different from that seen on the almost photo-realistic as-published cover pictured above right.

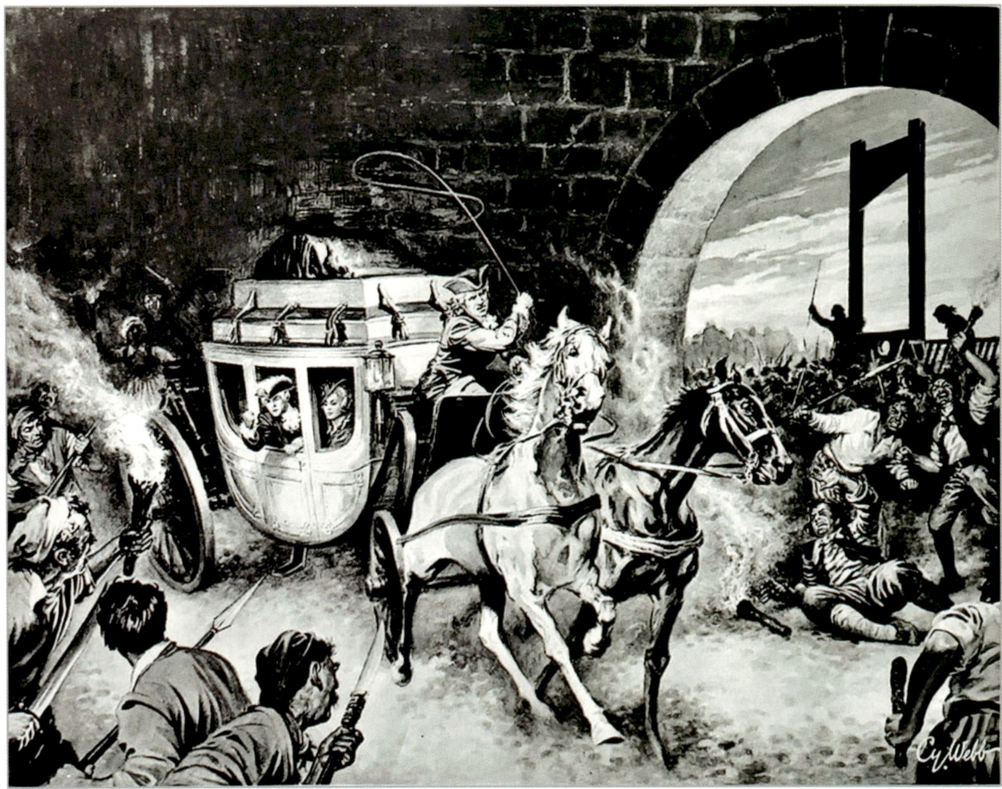

A 'Cy Webb'-signed painting depicting a French Revolution scene. Sadly, no colour image of this is currently available, and it is unknown for what purpose it was commissioned; the shape and composition of the piece make it doubtful it was intended for a book cover.

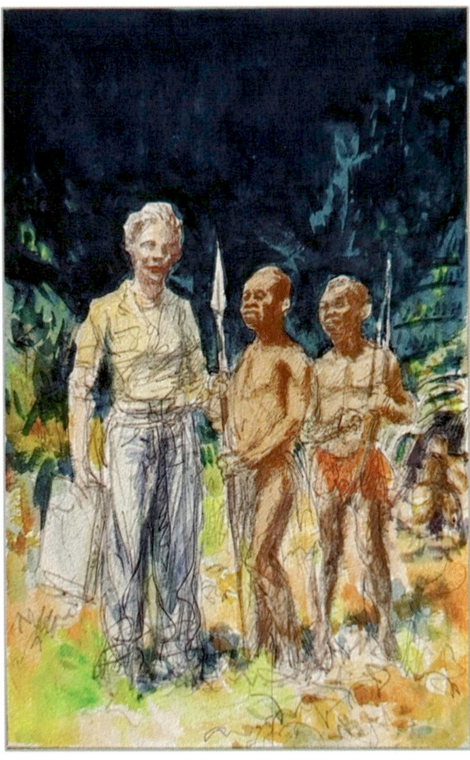

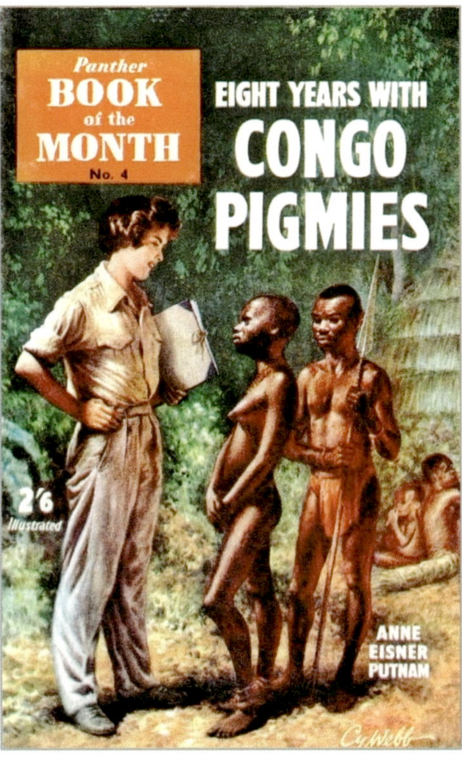

Heade's original rough and the as-published cover of *Eight Years With Congo Pigmies* by Anne Eisner Putnam (Panther, August 1956). At the request of Panther's art department, one figure was changed from male to female for the finished piece, being disarmed in the process.

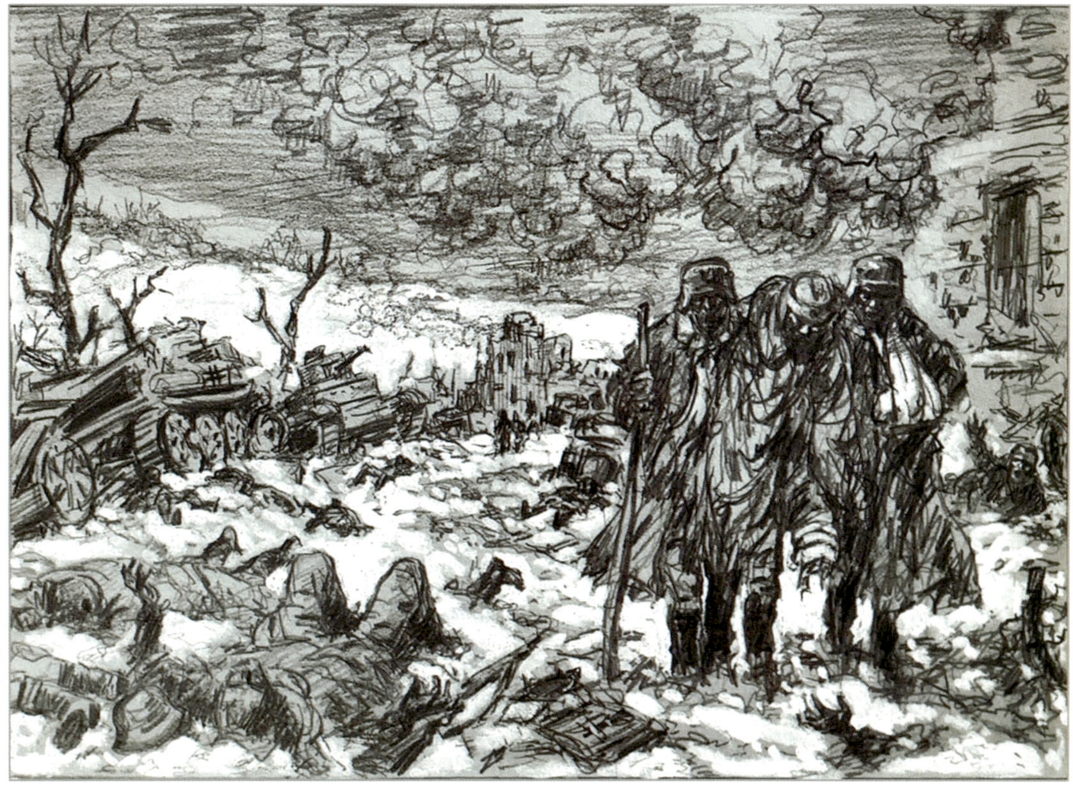

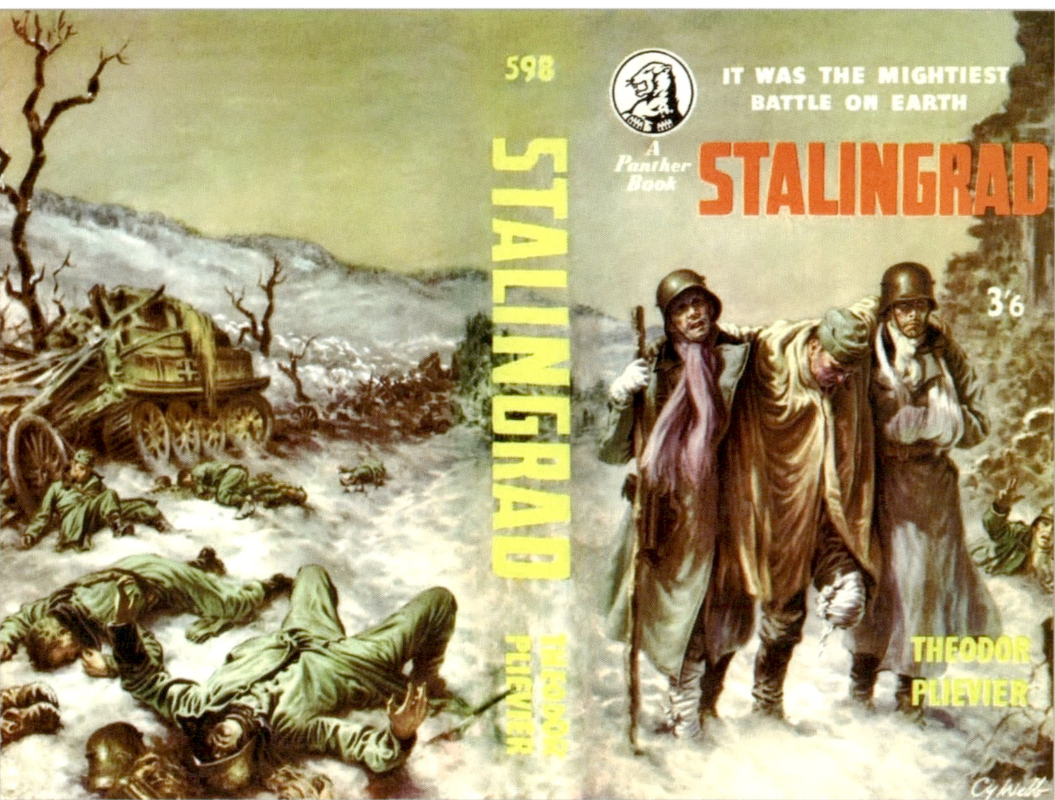

Heade's original rough and the as-published cover of *Stalingrad* by Theodor Plievier (Panther, August 1956)

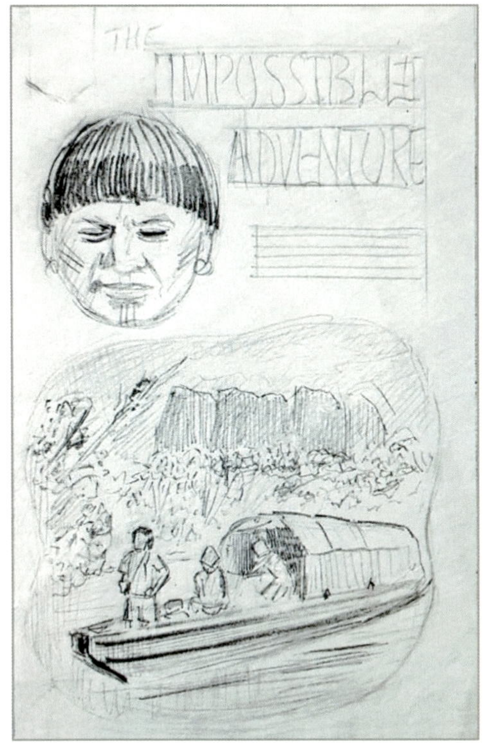
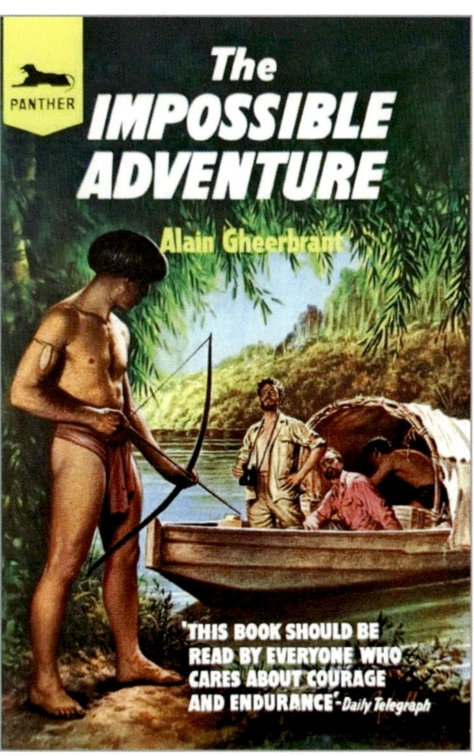

Heade's original rough and the final cover of *The Impossible Adventure* by Alain Gheerbrant (Panther, c1957). It appears that this cover may have been either unused or replaced shortly after publication; copies of the book in general circulation have a cover by a different artist.

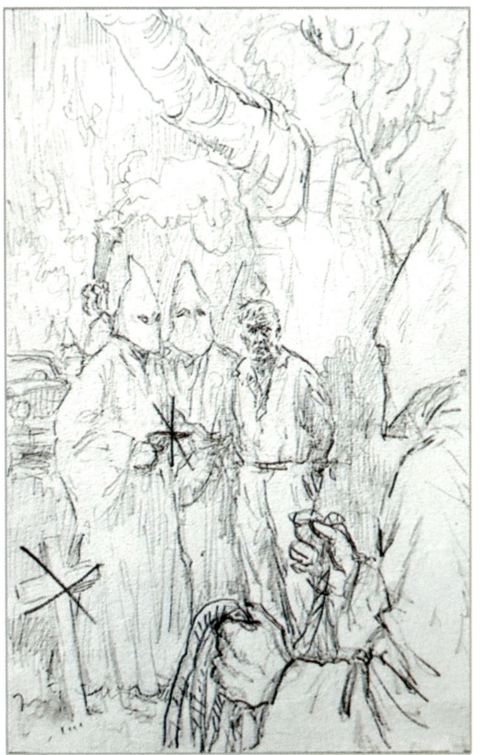
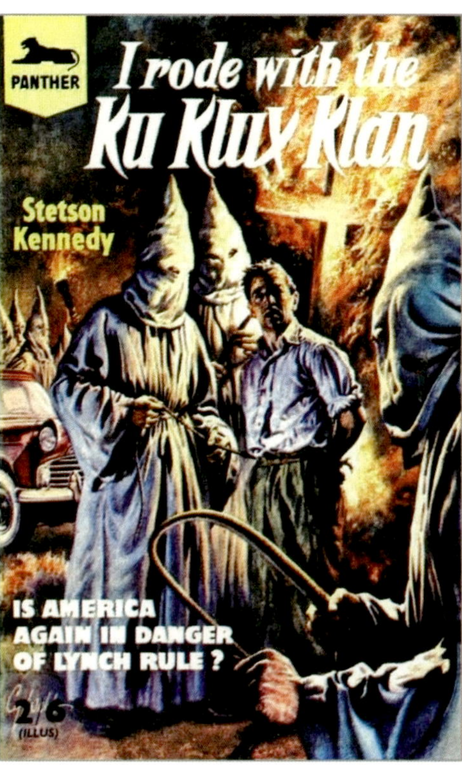

Heade's original rough and the as-published cover for *I Rode With the Ku Klux Klan* by Stetson Kennedy (Panther, May 1957). Heade's plans to include a cross in the left foreground and a gun in the hand of one of the Klansmen were vetoed by the publisher, as indicated by the two instances of crossing-out on the rough, and – further reducing the level of implied violence – the rope noose was changed to a whip.

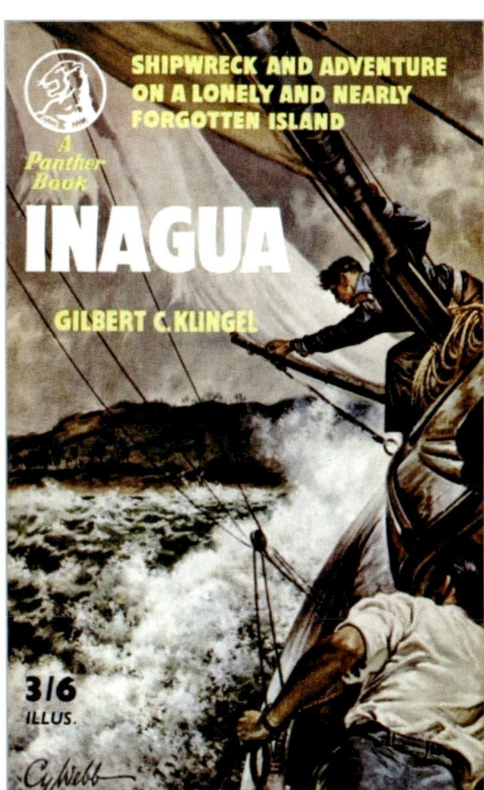

Heade's original rough and the as-published cover of *Inagua* by Gilbert C Klingel (Panther, January 1957)

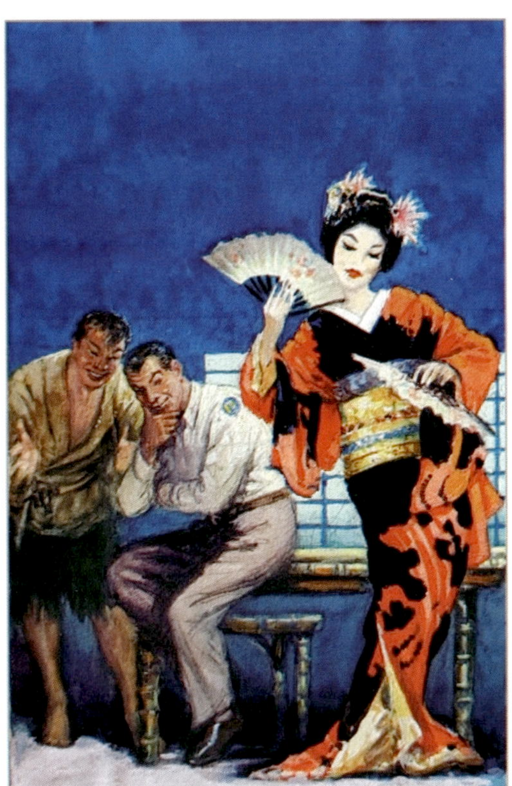

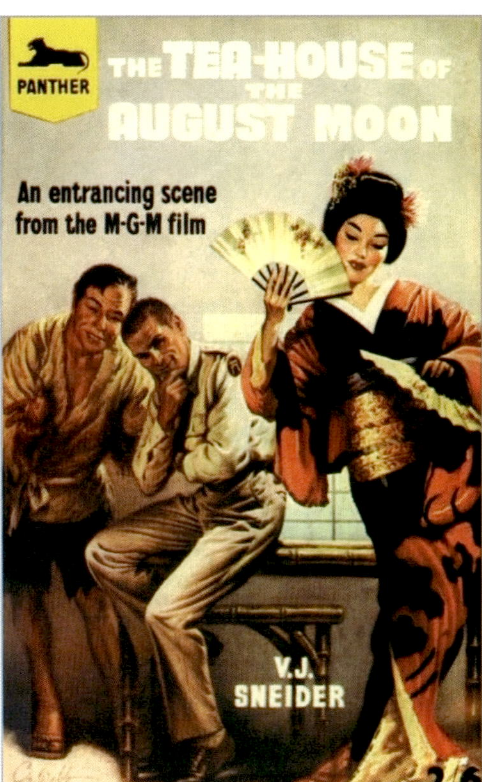

Heade's original rough and the as-published cover of *The Tea-House of the August Moon* by V J Sneider (Panther, 1957)

As noted previously, Heade typically began the process of creating each of his Panther and Pan paperback covers by pencilling a sketch, usually in thumbnail size, in which he worked out the basic details of the composition. Pictured immediately below are two of these sketches, for *Tunnelling to Freedom* by John Fancy (Panther, June 1957) (left) and *Catherine Carter* by Pamela Hansford Johnson (Pan Giant, August 1957) (right). The next stage was to produce a full rough in either black-and-white or colour. Then, if this was approved by the publisher's art department, the artist would complete the actual painting. Finally the art department would add the lettering and logo, and the cover would be sent for printing. Shown on the right and at the bottom of the page are the full rough, the finished painting and the as-published cover for *Tunnelling to Freedom*. The finished painting for *Catherine Carter* is pictured on the facing page.

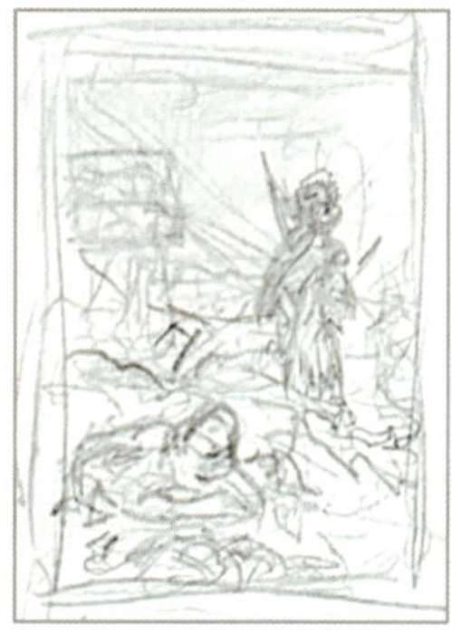
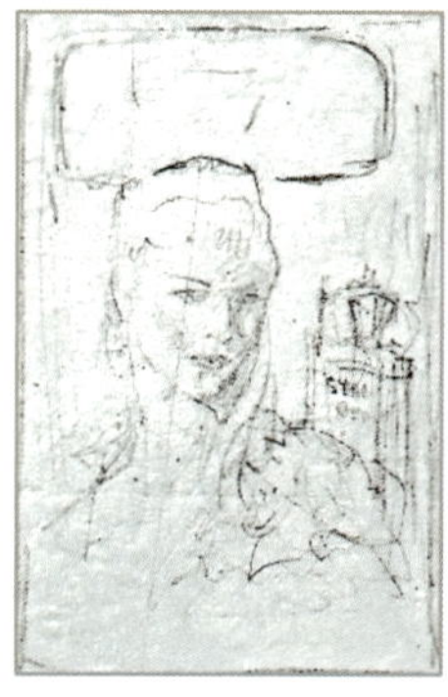
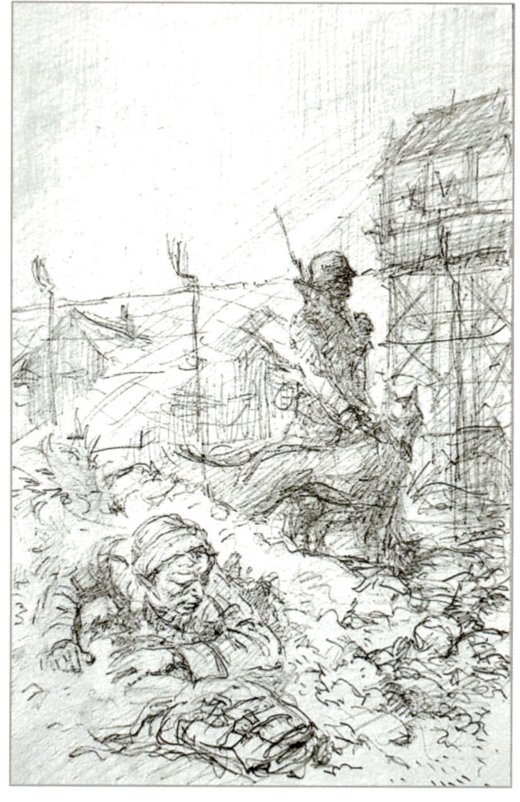
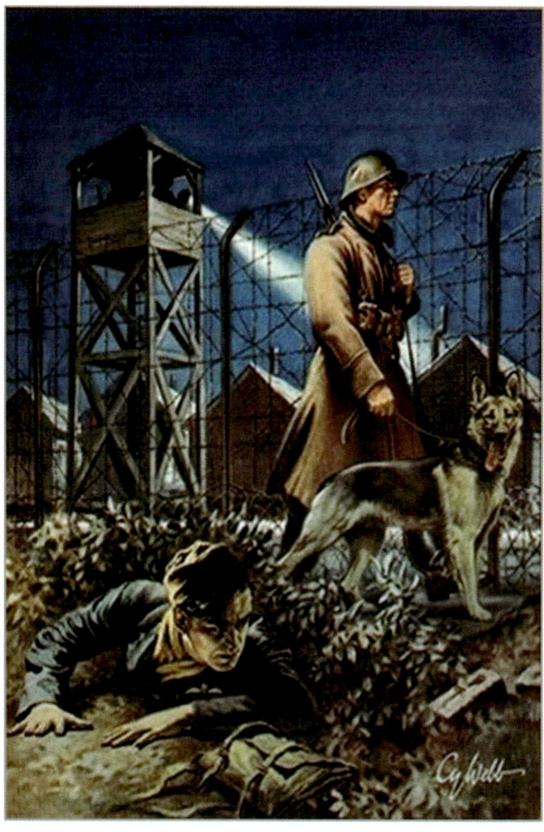
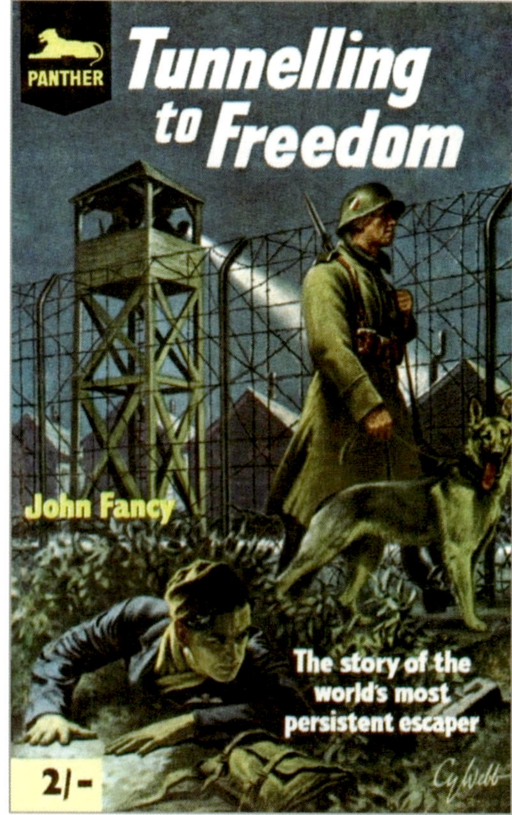

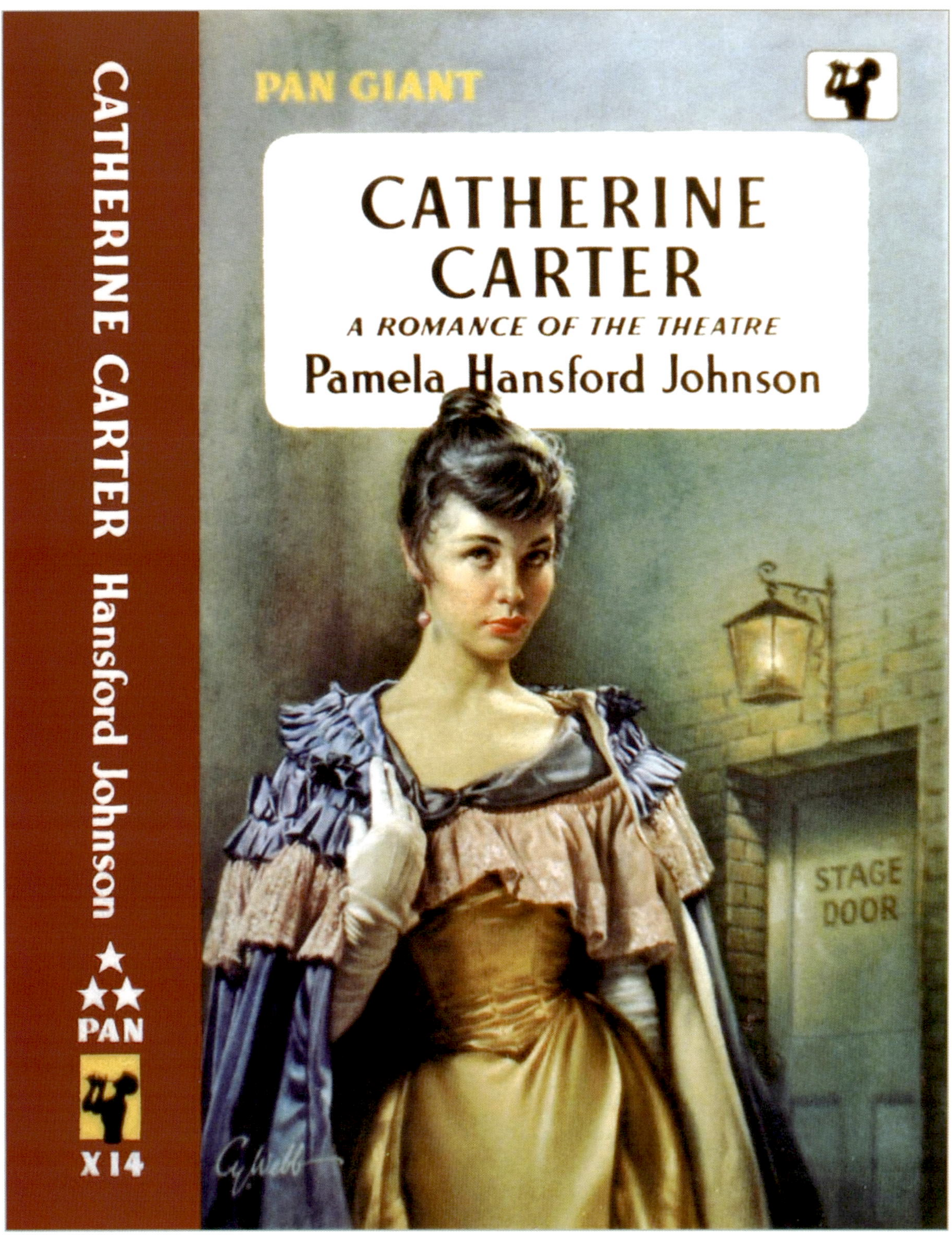

Heade's original painting for *Catherine Carter* by Pamela Hansford Johnson (Pan Giant, August 1957). The title panel was coloured yellow on the printed book. After submitting this piece, in March 1957, Heade received a telegram from Pan, reading: 'Katherine [sic] magnificnet [sic] beyond expectations. Many thanks.' (Image courtesy the Steve Chibnall Collection.)

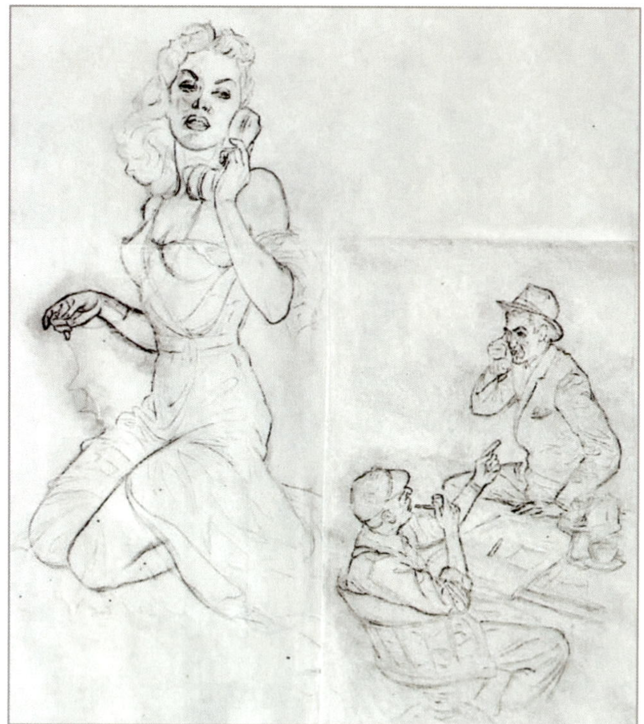

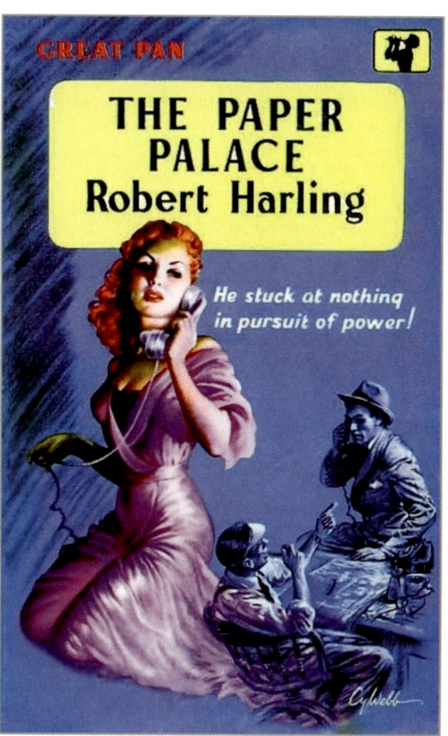

Above left: Heade's original rough for *The Paper Palace* by Robert Harling (Great Pan, April 1958), consisting of two drawings on separate pieces of paper, combined together. Above right: the as-published paperback cover.

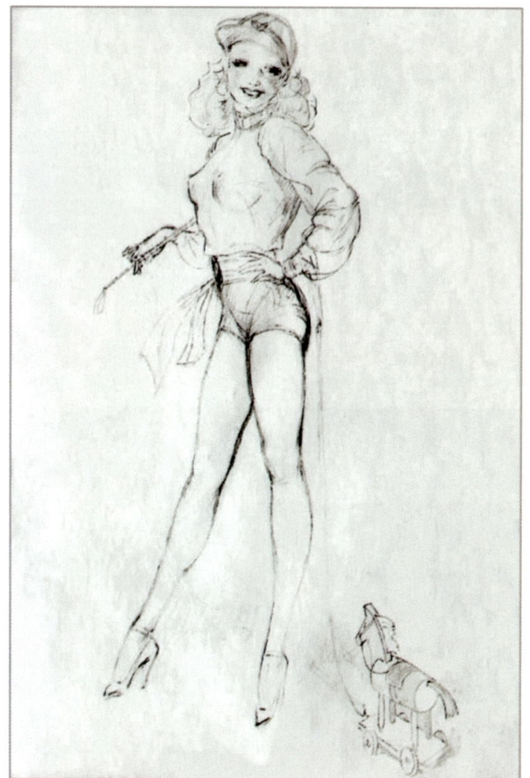

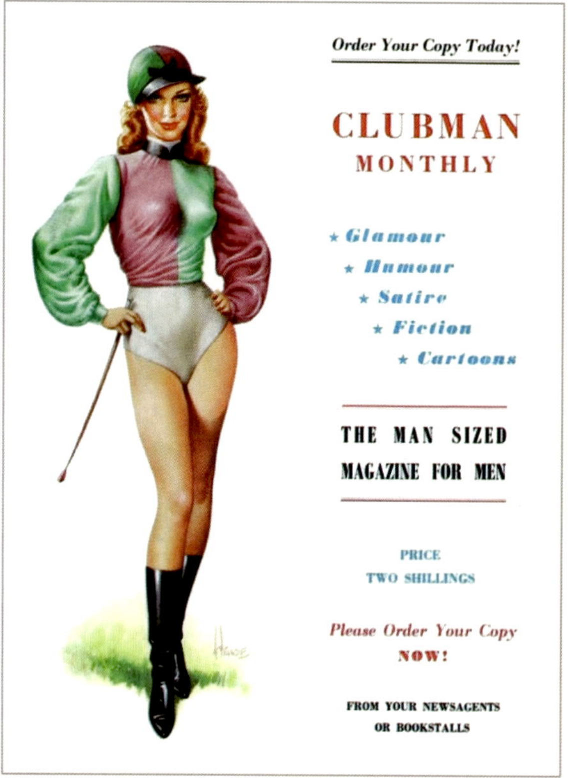

Above left: Heade's rough for a pin-up of a female jockey, probably from the 1950s. Above right: a similar illustration used in an advertisement in two issues of *Bedside Clubman* (Bayard Productions, summer 1953); possibly the rough was an early version of this.

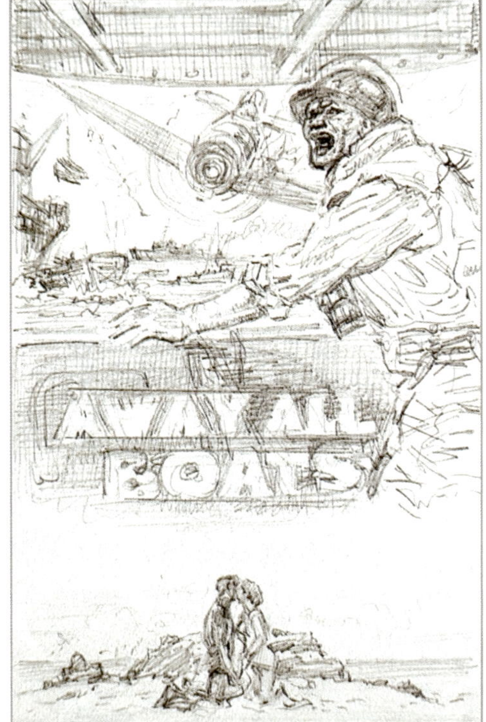 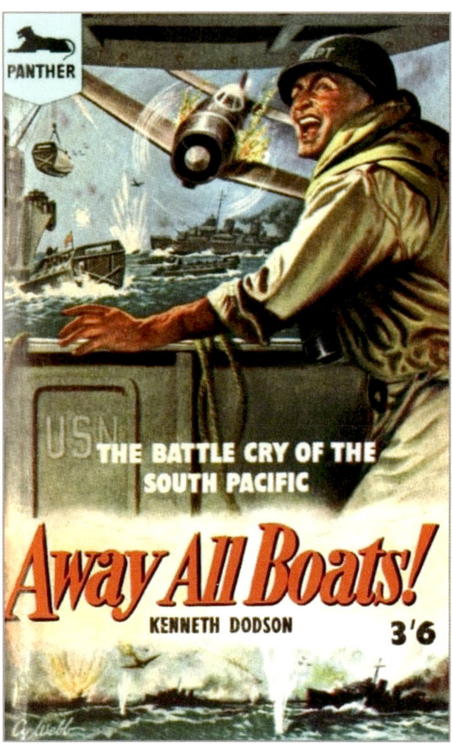

Heade's original rough and the as-published cover of *Away All Boats!* by Kenneth Dodson (Panther, April 1957)

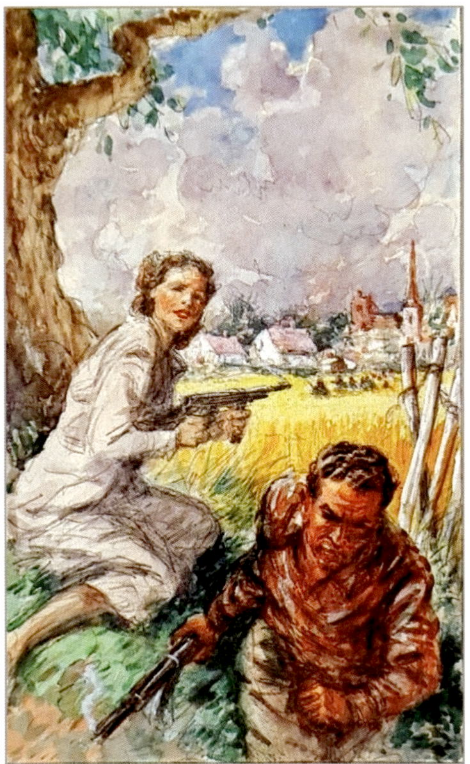 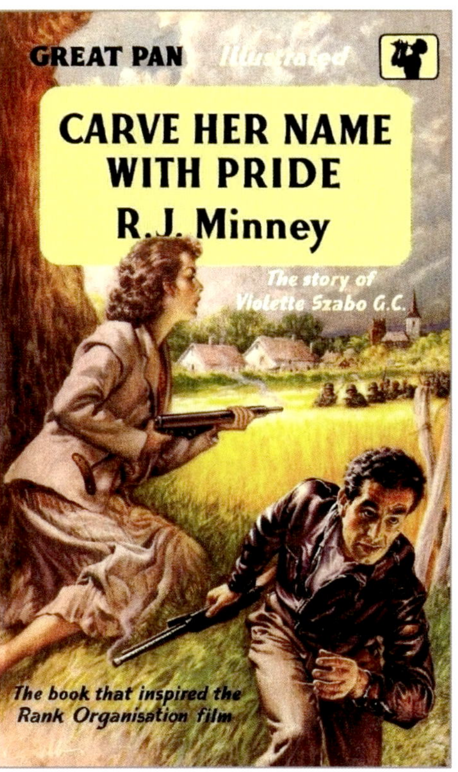

Heade's original rough and the as-published cover of *Carve Her Name With Pride* by R J Minney (Great Pan, January 1958). Note that the face of the female subject, Violette Szabo, was changed to make her appear more resolute. This edition was published to tie in with the Rank-produced movie of the same title, released the following month, but Szabo as depicted in Heade's painting does not resemble the movie's star, Virginia McKenna, suggesting that no reference photo was available to the artist at the time when he undertook his work.

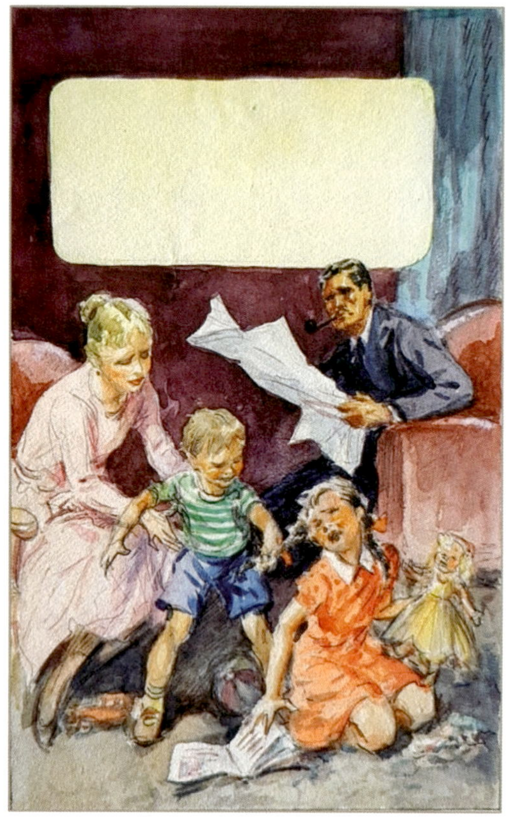 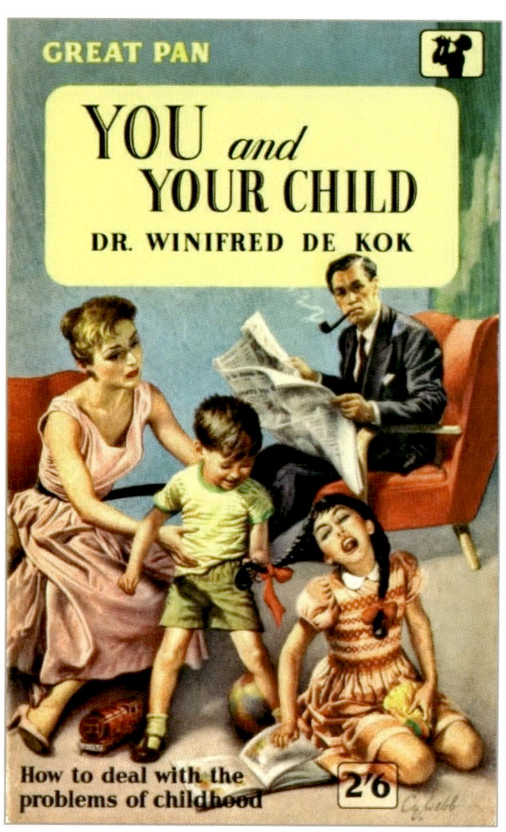

Heade's original rough and the as-published cover of *You and Your Child* by Dr Winifred de Kok (Great Pan, February 1958)

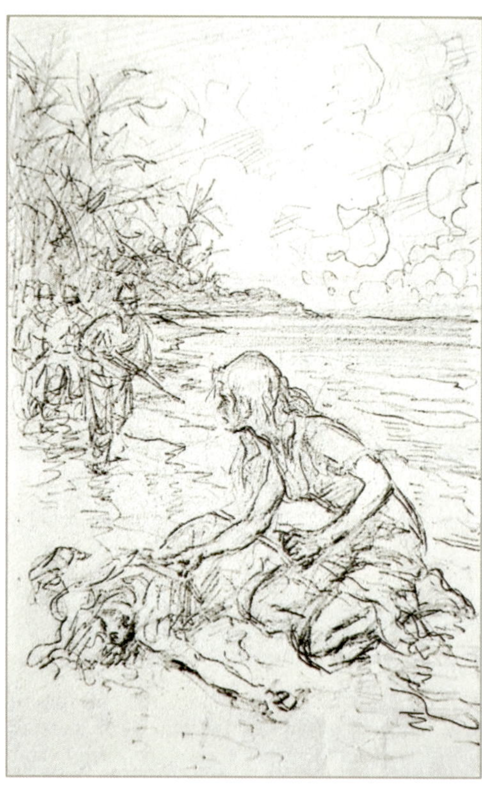

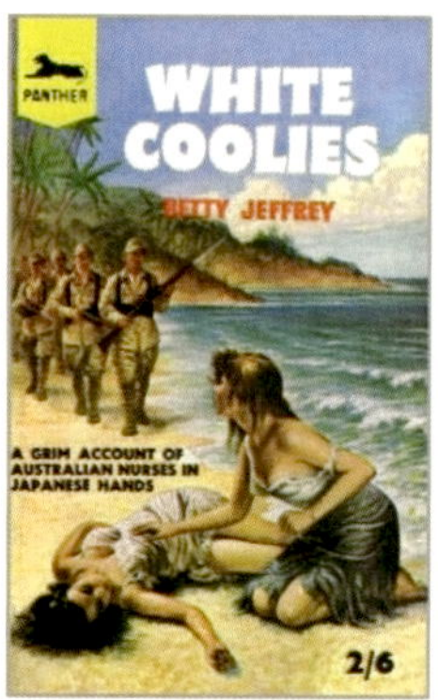

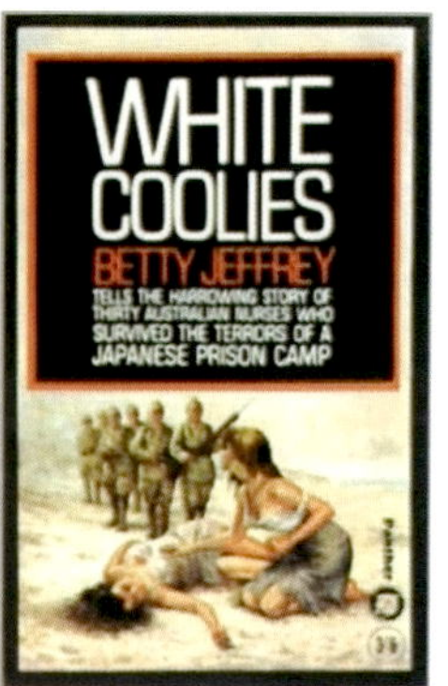

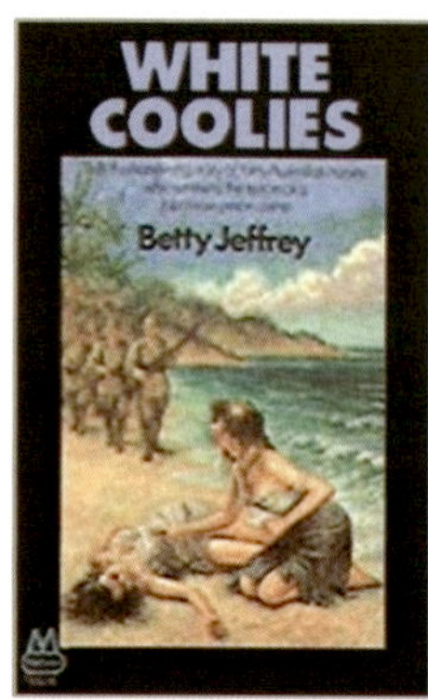

Far left: Heade's original rough for *White Coolies* by Betty Jeffrey, one of the most reprinted of his later covers. Above left: the first Panther edition, published in February 1958. Above right: a reissue from 1967, with elements of Heade's artwork repositioned by Panther's art department. Immediate left: a later edition, this one published by Mayflower in 1969.

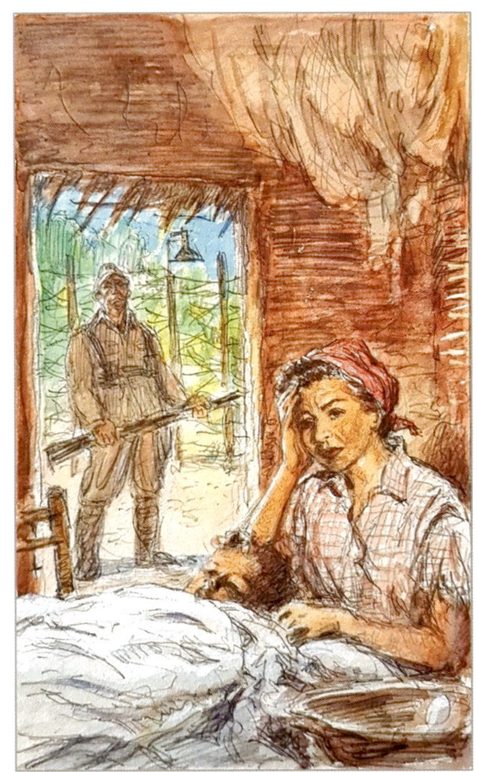 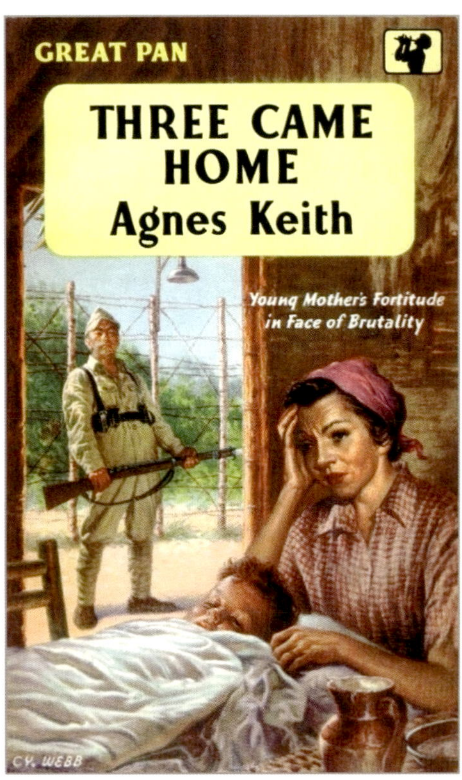

Heade's original rough and the as-published cover of *Three Came Home* by Agnes Keith (Great Pan, April 1958)

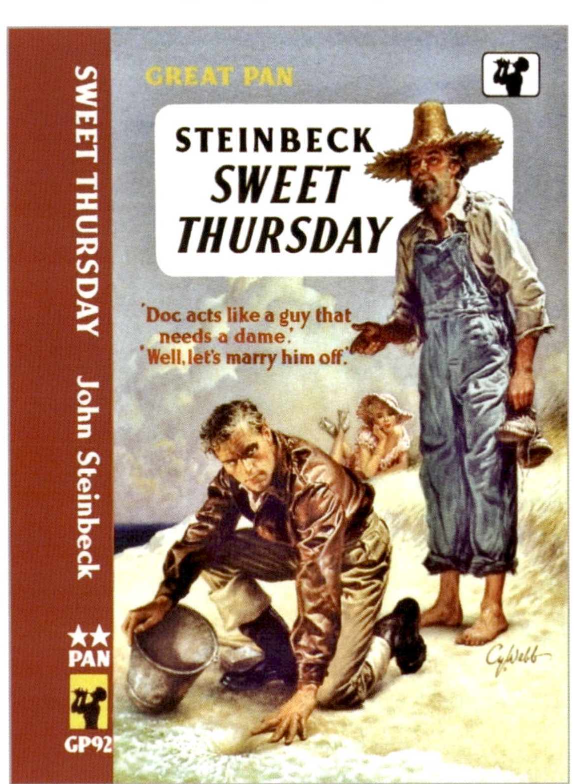 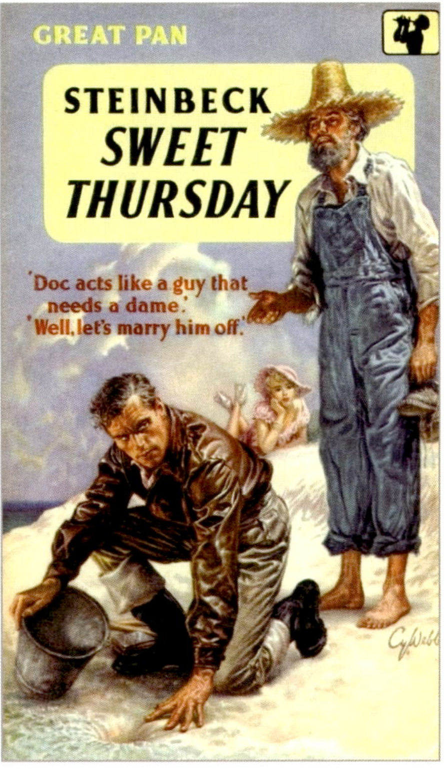

Heade's original painting and the as-published cover of *Sweet Thursday* by John Steinbeck (Great Pan, April 1958).

(Original painting image courtesy the Steve Chibnall Collection.)

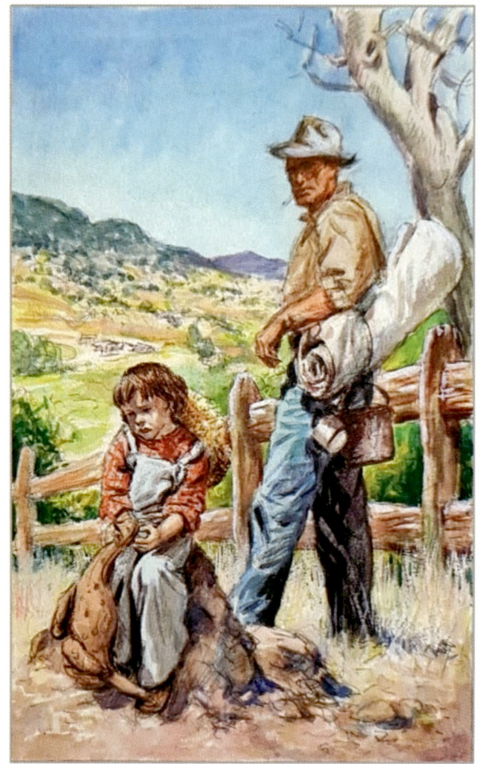
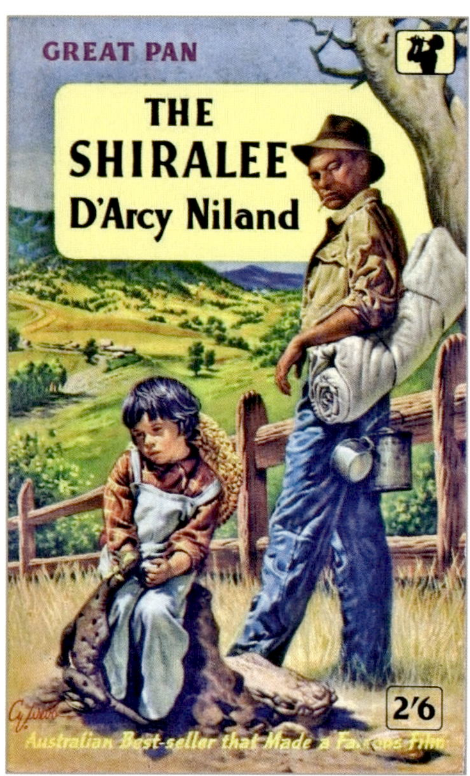

Heade's original rough and the as-published cover of *The Shiralee* by D'Arcy Niland (Great Pan, May 1958)

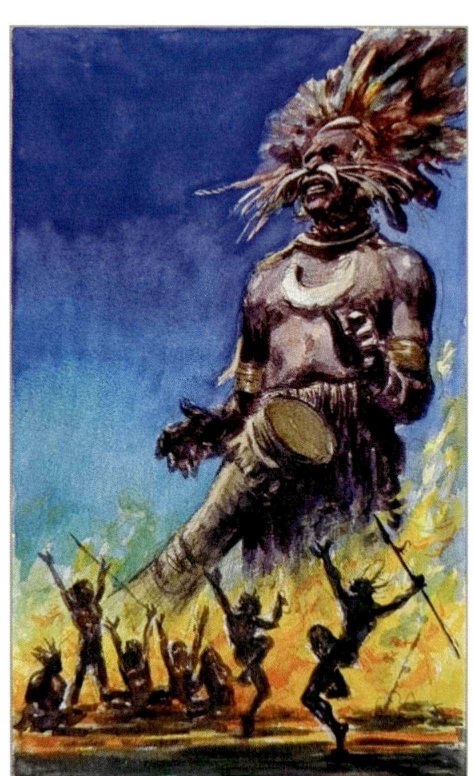
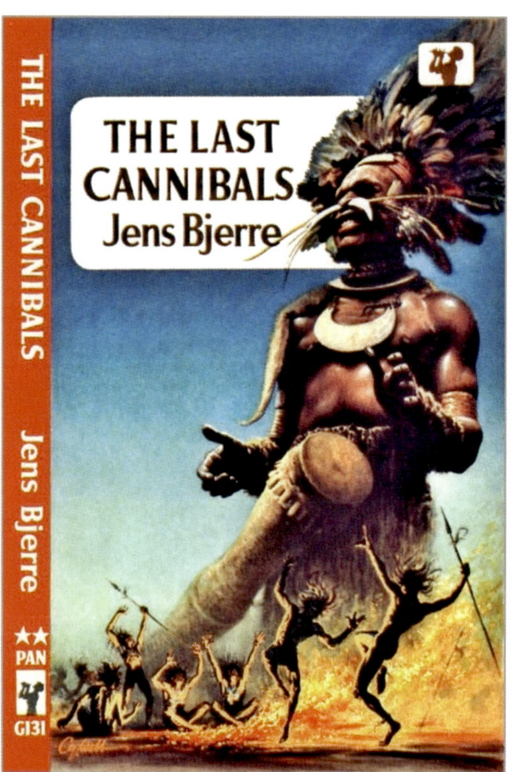

Heade's original rough and original finished painting for *The Last Cannibals* by Jens Bjerre (Pan, June 1958).

(Original finished painting image courtesy the Steve Chibnall Collection.)

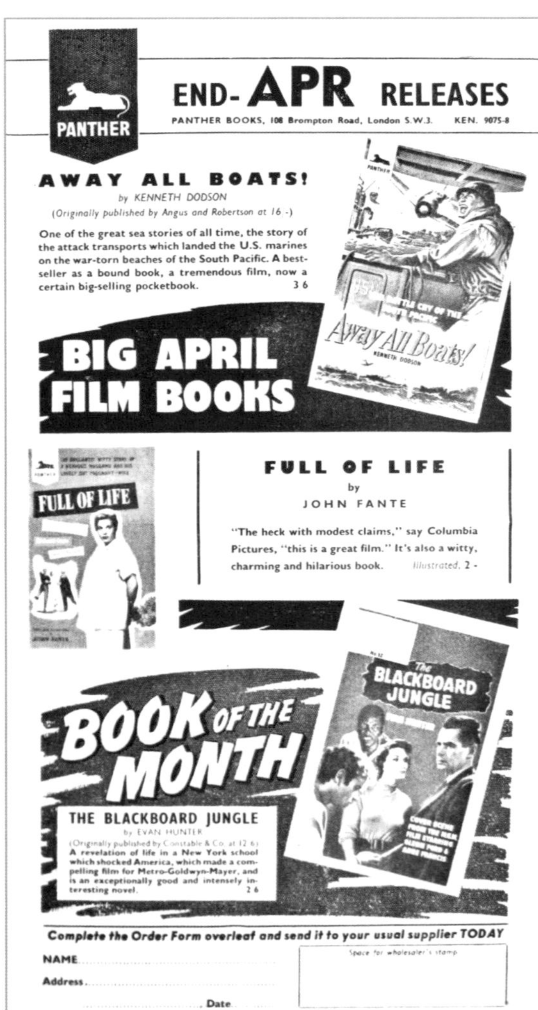

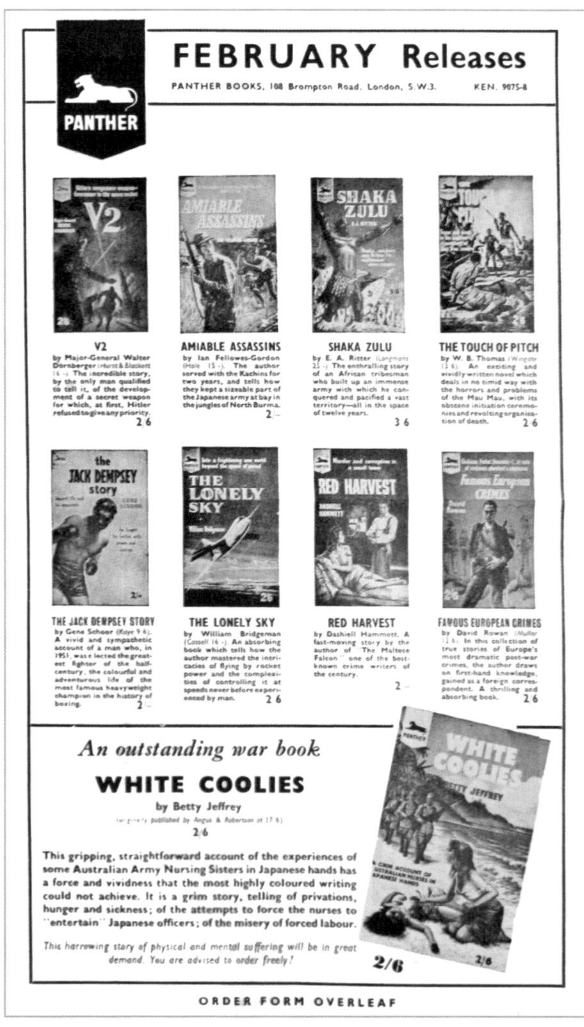

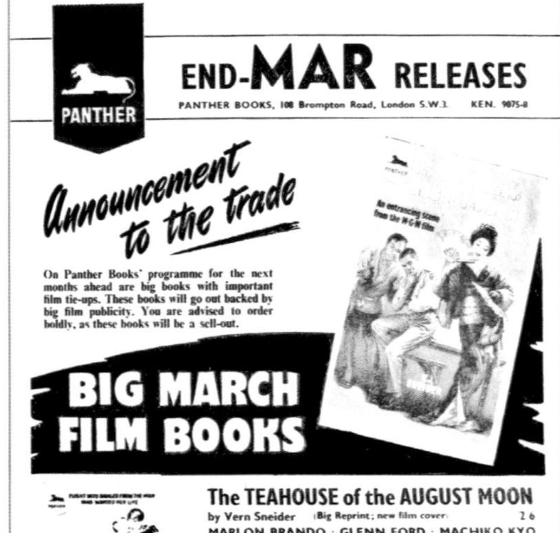

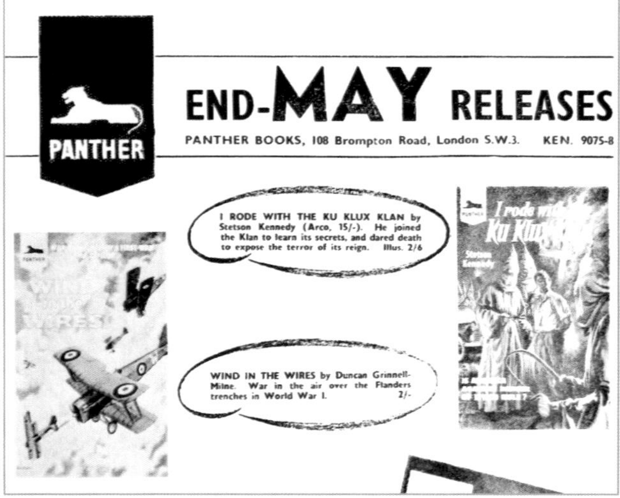

Above: four very rare black-and-white trade advertisements for Panther books published in, respectively, April 1957 (top left), February 1958 (top right), March 1957 (detail, bottom left) and May 1957 (detail, bottom right), including several with Heade cover art signed as 'Cy Webb'.

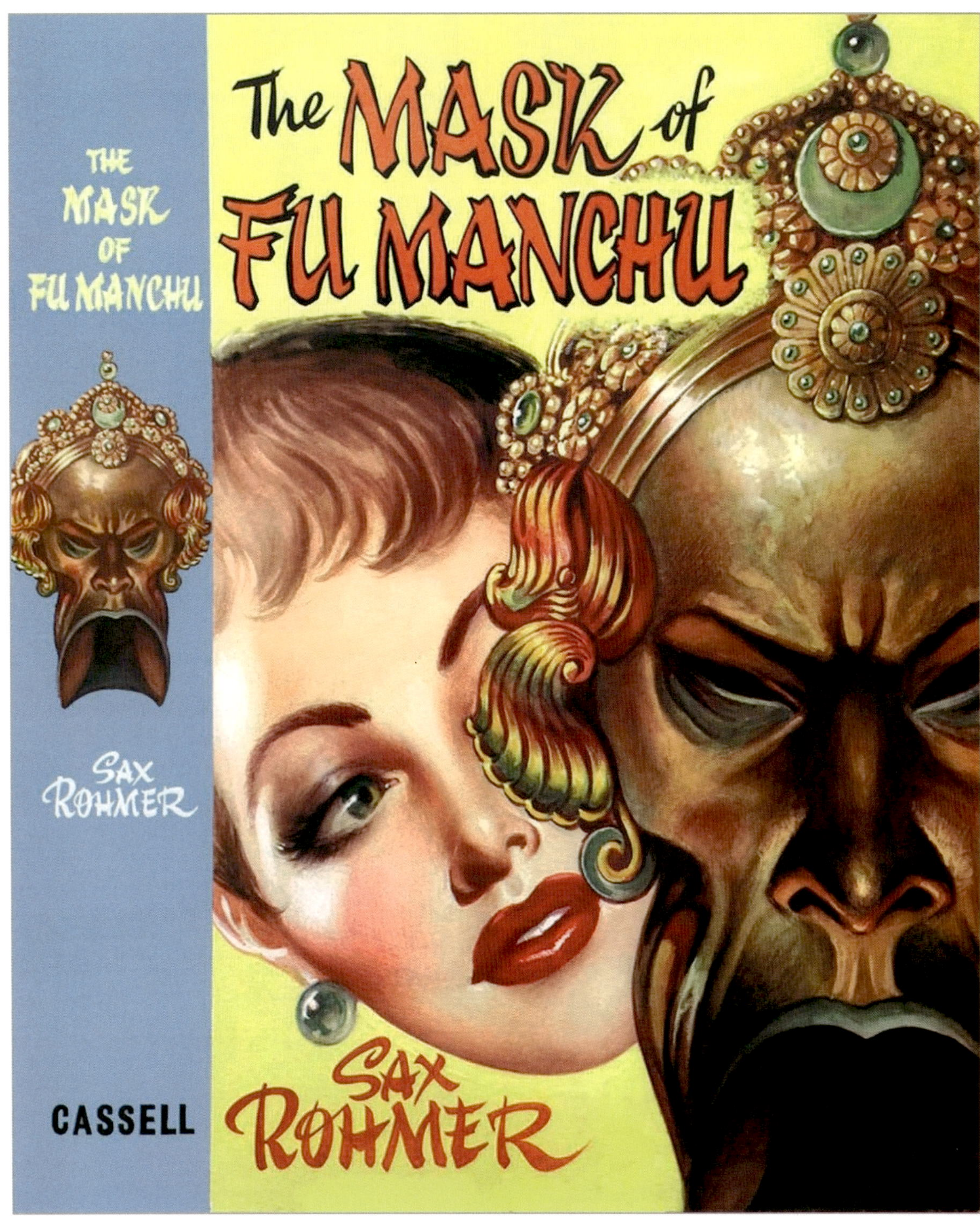

The original dustjacket painting for the hardback novel *The Mask of Fu Manchu* by Sax Rohmer (Cassell, 1955). An unsigned piece, but in this instance the style and quality leave little room for doubt that it is Heade's work – notwithstanding its inclusion in the 'Is It Heade?' section on page 297 of *The Art of Reginald Heade – Special Edition*.

IS IT HEADE?

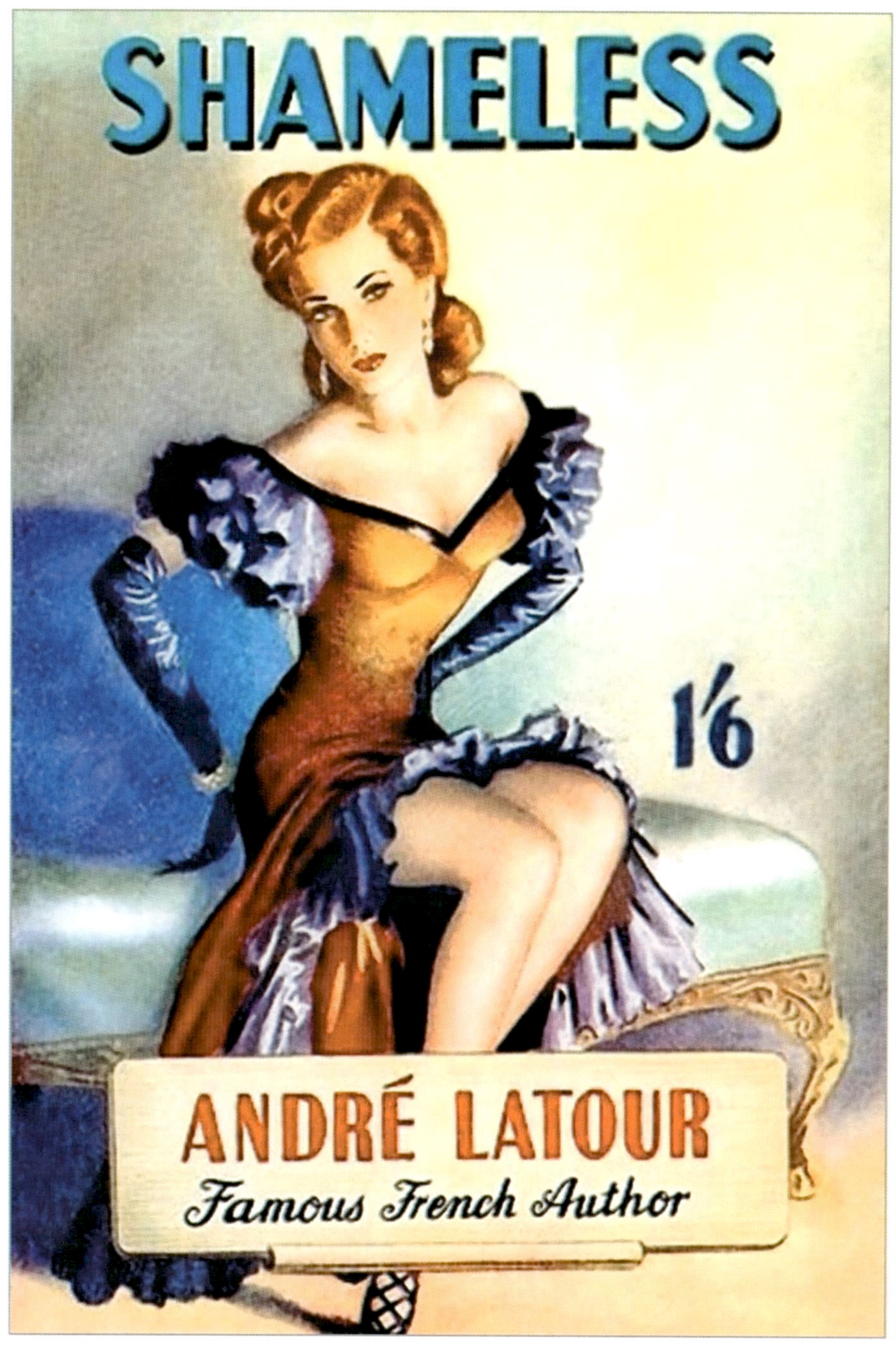

Shameless by André Latour, published by Kaye Publications in 1953 and distributed by Gaywood – a firm with which Heade's name is associated owing to the fact that they also distributed the classic-era Hank Janson novels. Could this piece be by Heade, or is it the work of another artist copying his style …?

As well as newly-discovered items bearing Heade's familiar signature, for which there can be no doubt that he was responsible, there continue to be occasional finds of unsigned art that might possibly be his work but cannot be confirmed as such. One of these is the cover of *Boys' Book of Stories* (Avenue Press, c1937) (see top right), which is similar in composition to signed covers the artist provided for some other mid-1930s children's books, such as *Girls' Book of Stories* (DLMS, 1934), as pictured on page 180 of *The Art of Reginald Heade – Special Edition*. Could this be another Heade piece? Attributions of vintage book cover art are often impossible to make with complete certainty. Two exceptions, however. First, it is now known that the cover piece for the paperback *Opium Venture* by Gerald Sparrow (Great Pan, 1960) (see middle right), included in the 'Is It Heade?' section of *The Art of Reginald Heade – Special Edition*, was in fact painted not by Heade but by James E McConnell. Secondly, it has now come to light that another paperback cover piece previously believed to have been Heade's work as Cy Webb, *Shark Hunter* by William E Young (Panther, 1956) (see bottom right), as pictured on page 285 of *The Art of Reginald Heade – Special Edition*, was regrettably misattributed, and was actually by Harold Johns.

Below: *Pippa* by Mabel Barnes-Grundy (Hutchinson, c1932), a paperback with unsigned cover art that bears some resemblance to Heade's work.

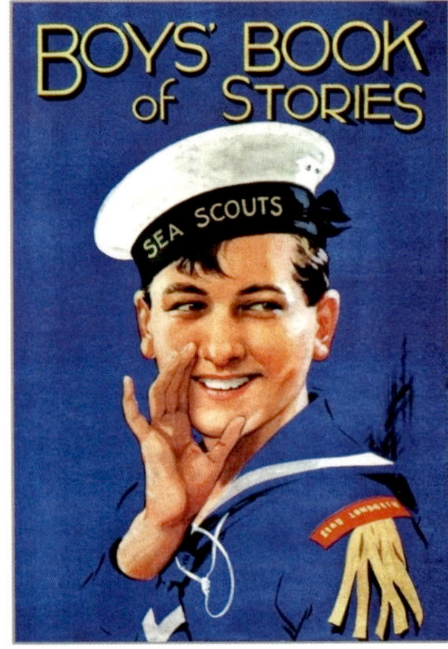

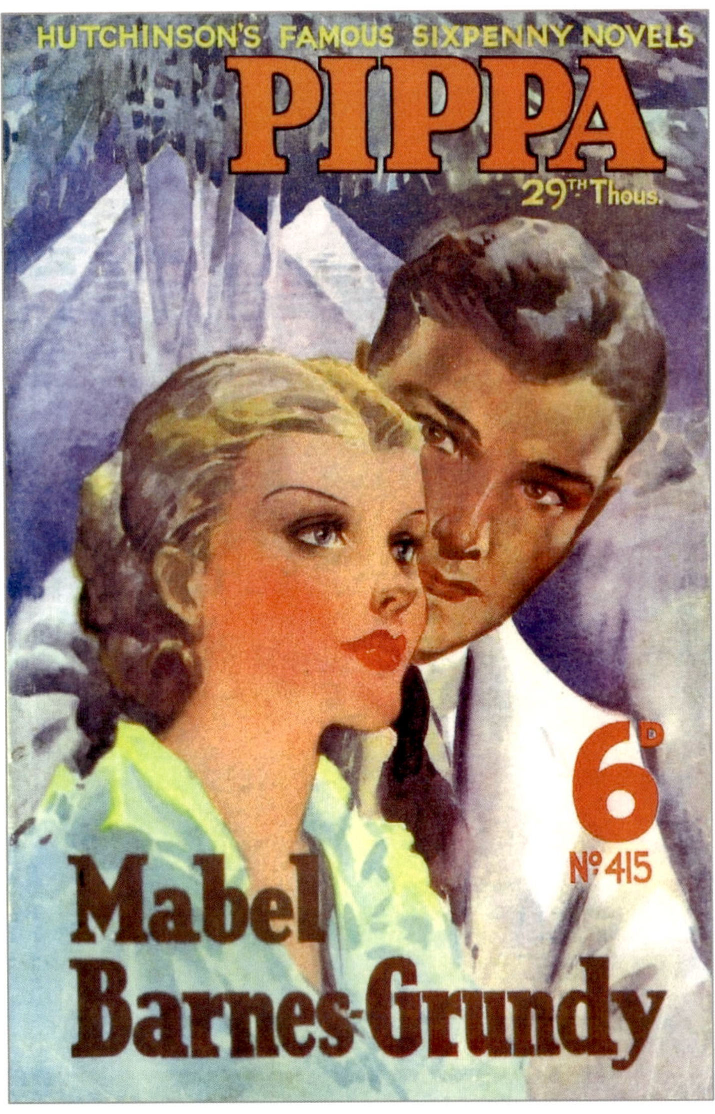

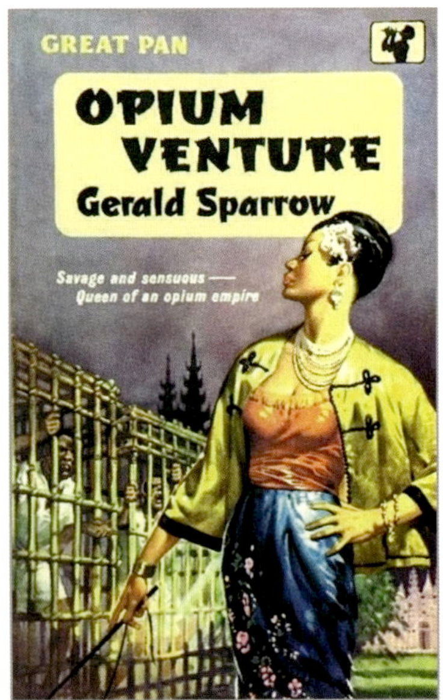

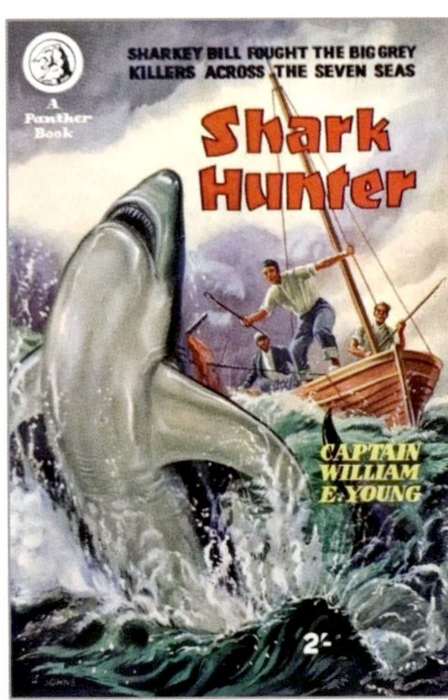

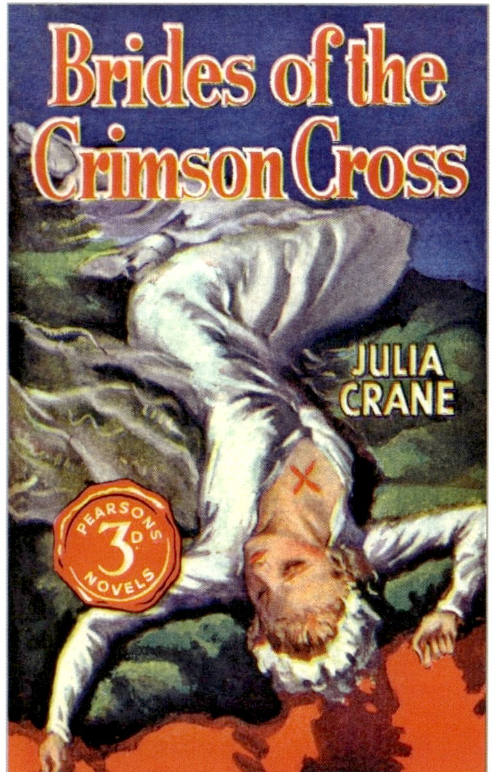

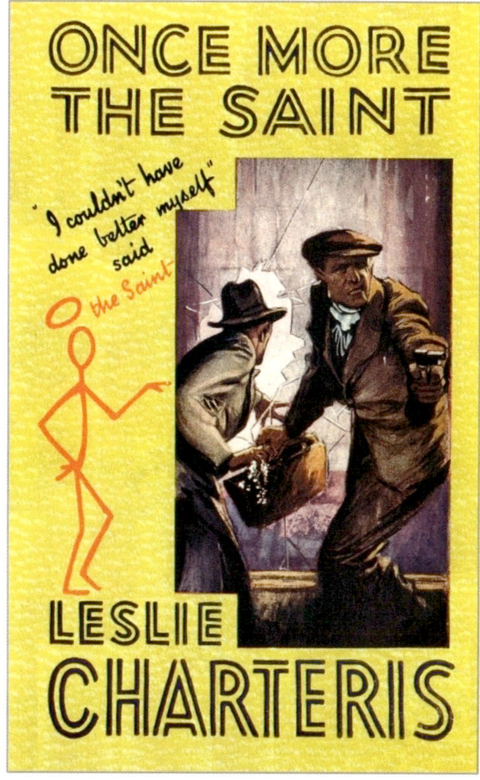

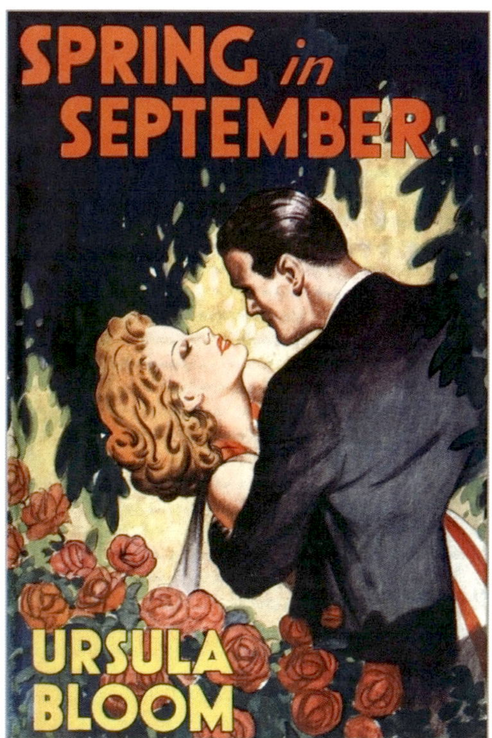

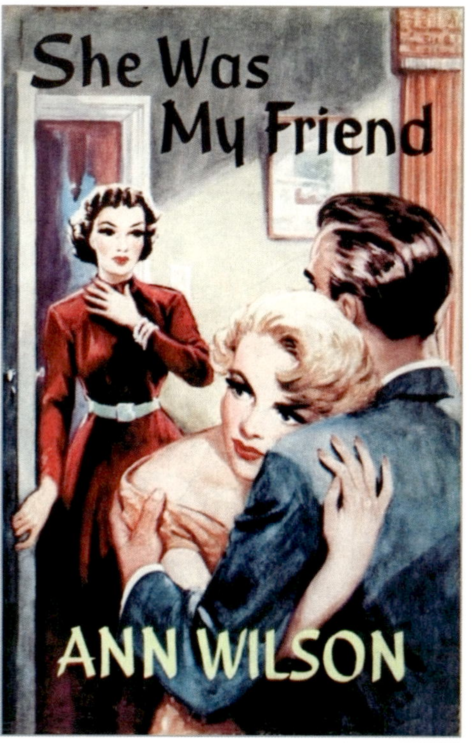

This page, four further pieces of unsigned cover art that could perhaps be Heade's work, although in some cases the execution lacks the level of detail he usually employed. Top left: *Brides of the Crimson Cross* by Julia Crane (Pearsons, c1930s). Top right: *Once More the Saint* by Leslie Charteris (Hodder & Stoughton, 1935). Bottom left: *Spring in September* by Ursula Bloom (Robert Hale, 1941). Bottom right: *She Was My Friend* by Ann Wilson, (Robert Hale, 1956).

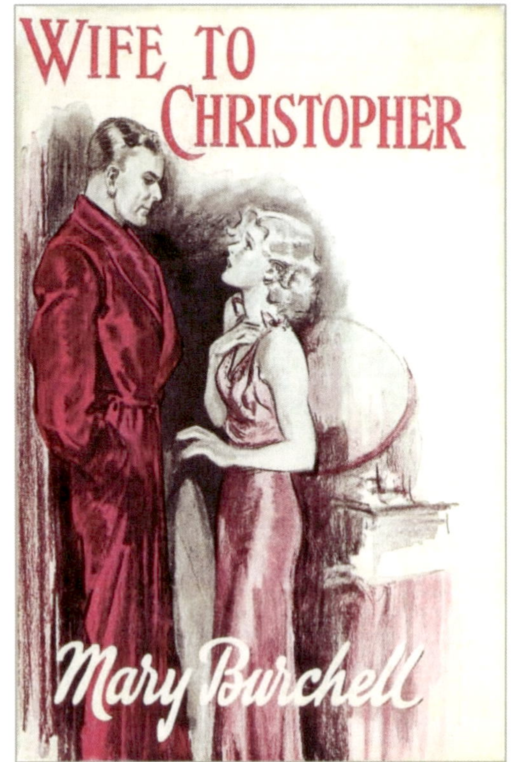

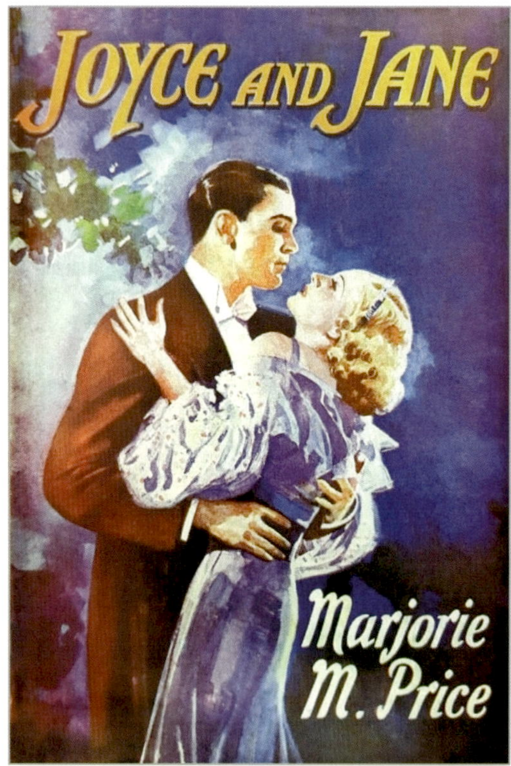

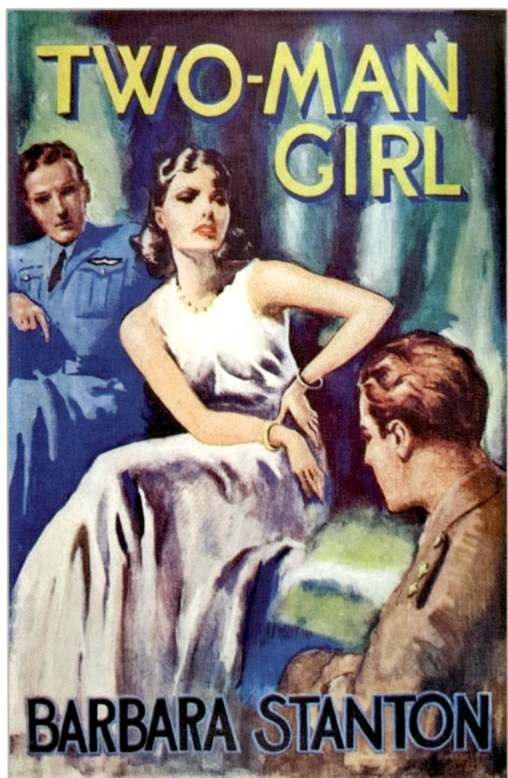

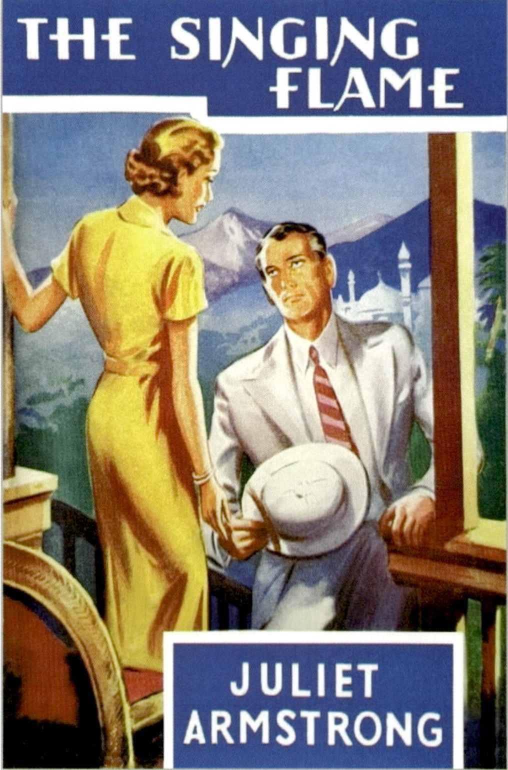

Above, four unsigned Mills & Boon dustjacket pieces that could possibly be further examples of Heade's work for that publisher, but are of uncertain attribution: *Wife to Christopher* by Mary Burchell (1936); *Joyce and Jane* by Marjorie M Price (July 1937); *Two-Man Girl* by Barbara Stanton (1942); and *The Singing Flame* by Juliet Armstrong (1954).

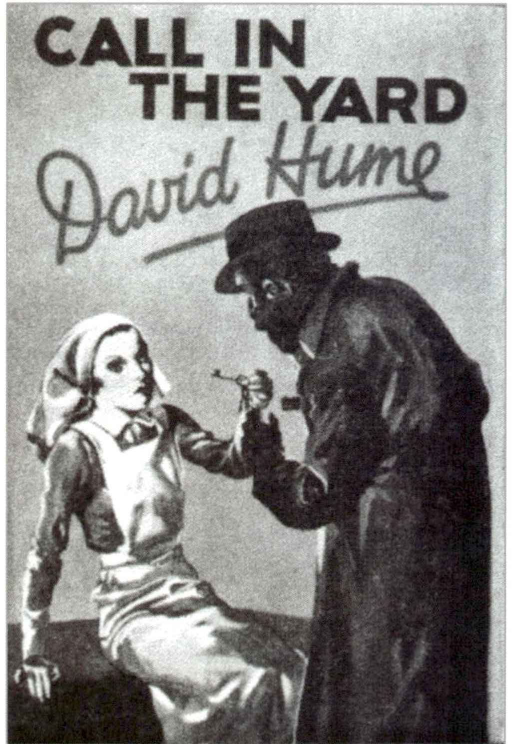

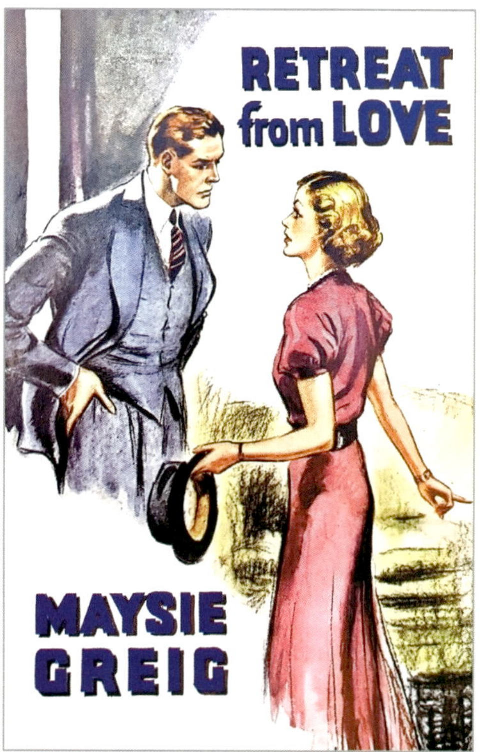

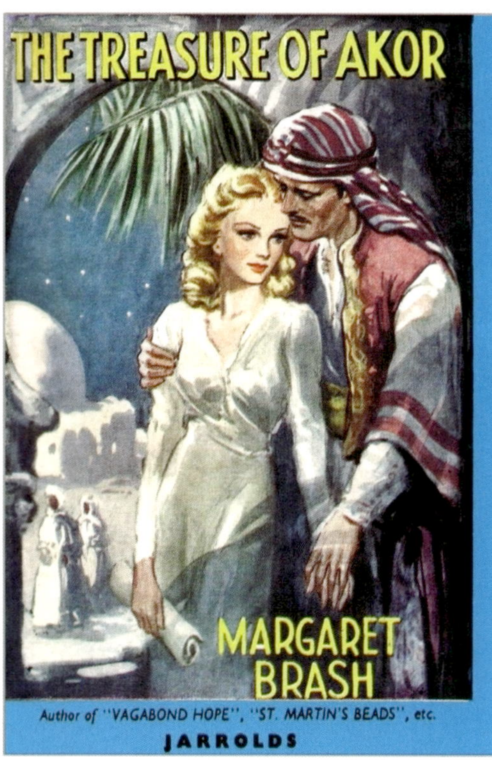

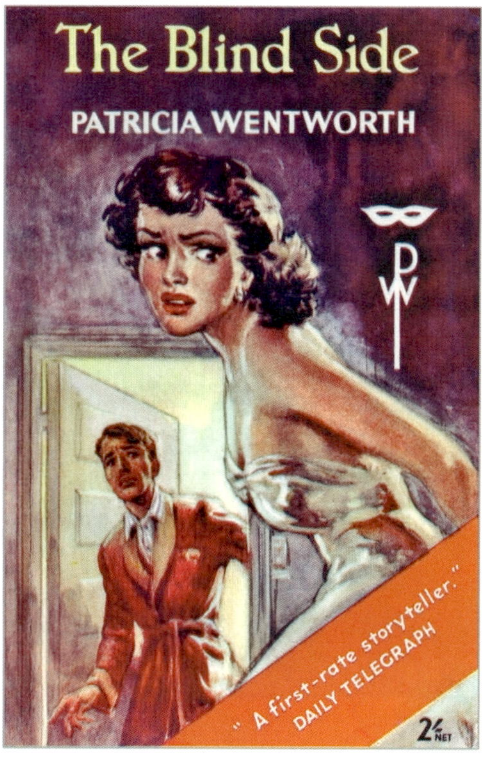

Above: four further unsigned pieces that, while perhaps not immediately recognisable as Heade's work, could well be by him: *Call in the Yard* by David Hume (Collins, 1936); *Retreat from Love* by Maysie Greig (Hodder & Stoughton, 1937); *The Treasure of Akor* by Margaret Brash (Jarrolds, 1946); and the paperback *The Blind Side* by Patricia Wentworth (Hodder & Stoughton, 1955). The Patricia Wentworth cover is believed to have been adapted from the dustjacket of an earlier hardback edition, of which no image is currently available. Likewise, sadly, no colour image of the David Hume dustjacket has yet been located.

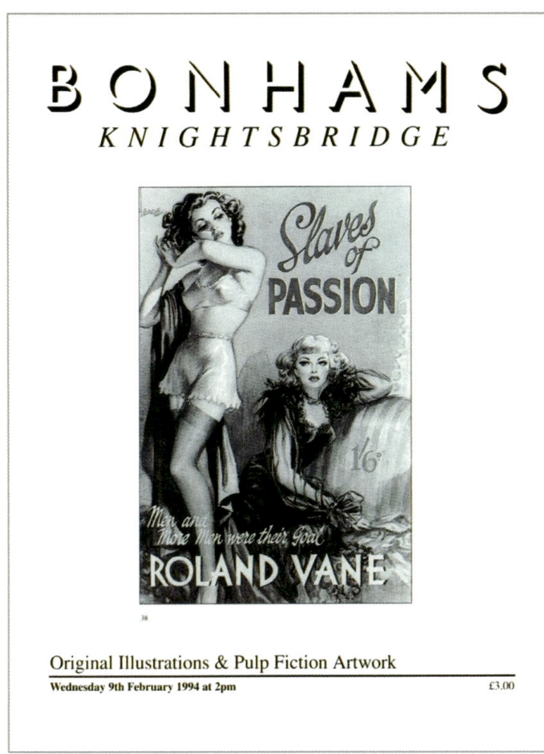

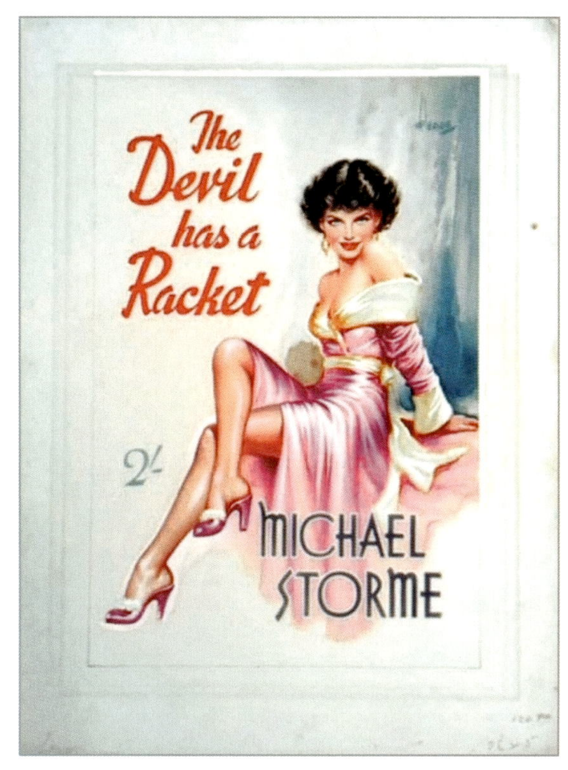

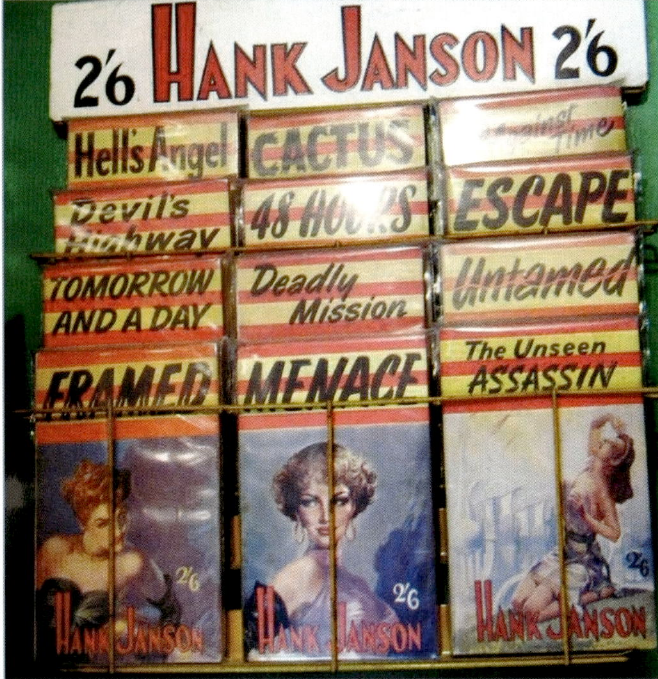

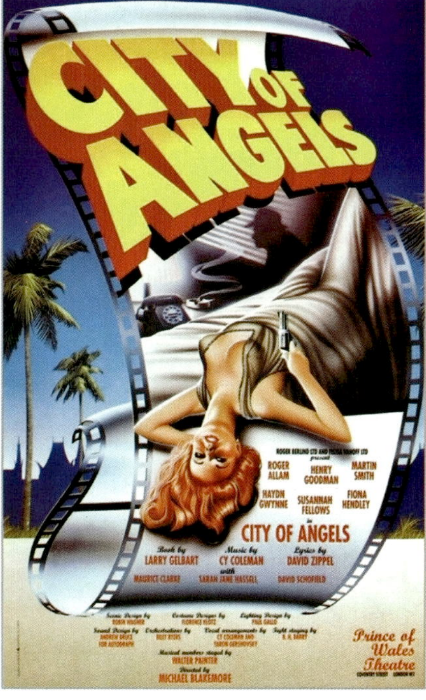

Top left: the catalogue for the sale of numerous examples of Heade's Locker company cover paintings as part of a pulp fiction artwork auction at Bonhams in Knightsbridge, London on 9 February 1994. Top right: Heade's original painting for *The Devil Has a Racket* by Michael Storme (Harborough, January 1954) – one of those included in the Bonhams auction – showing the full art board. Sadly, a number of Heade's surviving paintings have suffered some wear and tear, and in this case water mark damage is visible in the centre of the board. Bottom left: a vintage shop display rack for Alexander Moring's Hank Janson editions, with Heade's three Moring covers to the fore. Bottom right: the poster for a 1993 London stage production of the musical *City of Angels*. The female figure was copied, without credit, from Heade's cover art for the Hank Janson novel *Baby, Don't Dare Squeal* (S D Frances, March 1951). (Moring image courtesy the Steve Chibnall Collection.)

APPENDIX

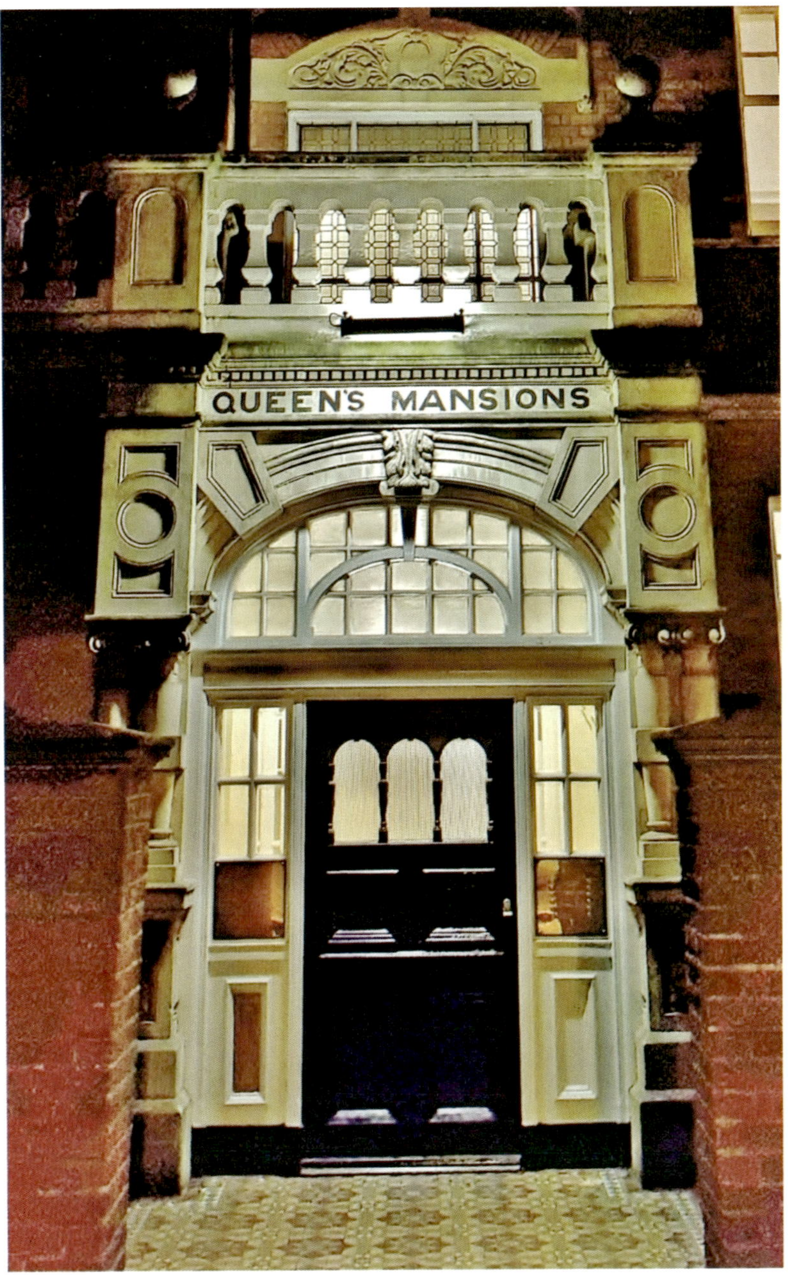

As it appears today, the impressive entrance to the Queen's Mansions building in Brook Green, Hammersmith, London, where Reginald Heade had his last flat and home studio, and undertook much of his work, including all of his celebrated pulp fiction paperback cover paintings.

REMEMBERING HEADE

Presented on this and the next two pages are a selection of quotes, from interviews conducted mainly in the 1990s, in which fellow professionals who knew and worked with Heade remember and pay tribute to the artist.

Pat Owen: Heade is obviously a man of great interest. There was one of his originals hanging on his agent Tony Bowen-Davies's wall for a long time. I don't know what happened to that.

Sam Peffer: It was the cover to Aleister Crowley's [biography] *The Great Beast.*

Pat Owen: That's right. Beautiful thing it was.

Sam Peffer: Beautiful portrait.

John Vernon: He was a very good artist. He was older than we were at the time. I didn't meet him, no; but, you know, the word gets around in the business, people mention it.

James E McConnell: Partridge [agent for both artists] brought Heade along one day. He was very good. He was a better colourist than I was. He looked very young. He looked a fine specimen of a man, really. I probably met him a few years before he died.

Below: Heade's original rough (left) and the as-published cover (right) of John Symonds' *The Great Beast* (Panther, July 1956), a biography of the infamous occultist Aleister Crowley.

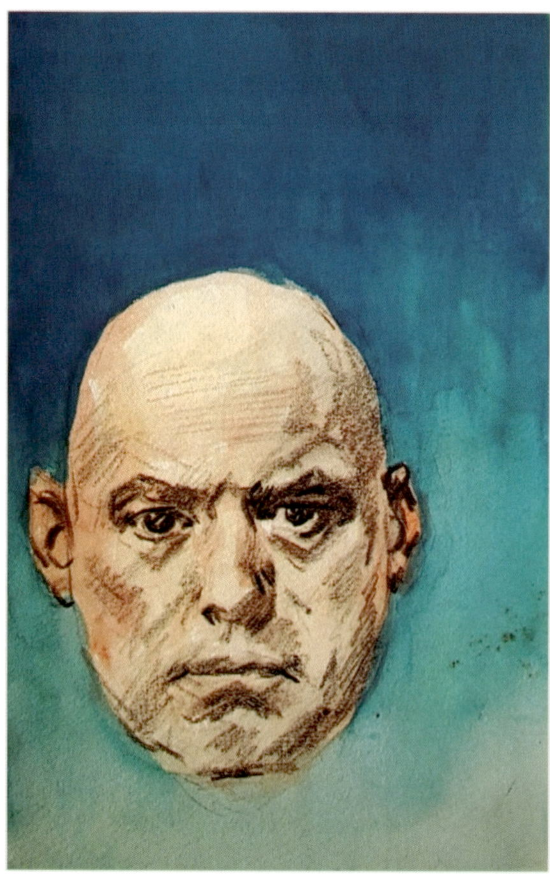

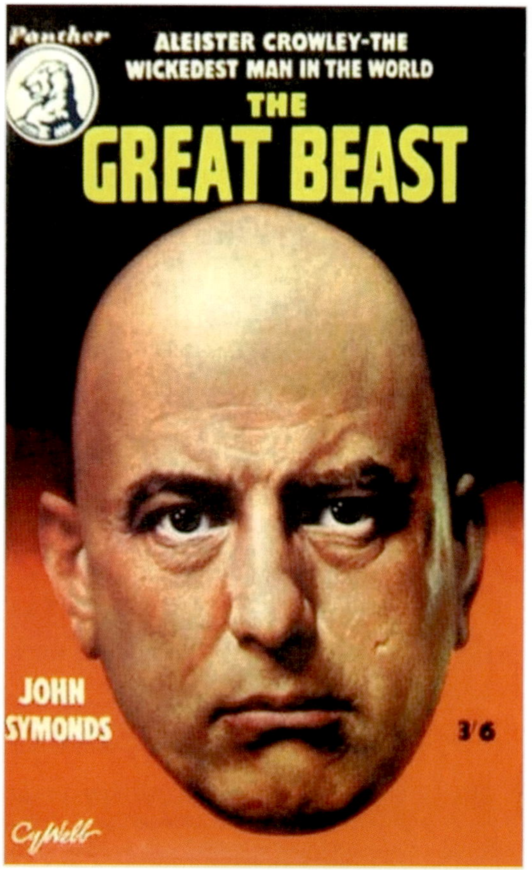

Edward Mortelmans: I met Heade only once, at a meeting to set up Artists Ltd in either 1953 or 1954. The most striking thing about Heade's appearance was the condition of his eyes. He was rather pop-eyed, although I don't think the condition affected his sight. As a painter, he was a great 'stippler', very detailed work. He was almost a pointillist in the way he applied the paint, but actually his first love was pencil drawing. He may have exhibited at the Royal Graphic Society. The person in the covers you have shown me is definitely not him – it wouldn't be, because he would not have used himself. We always used professional models.

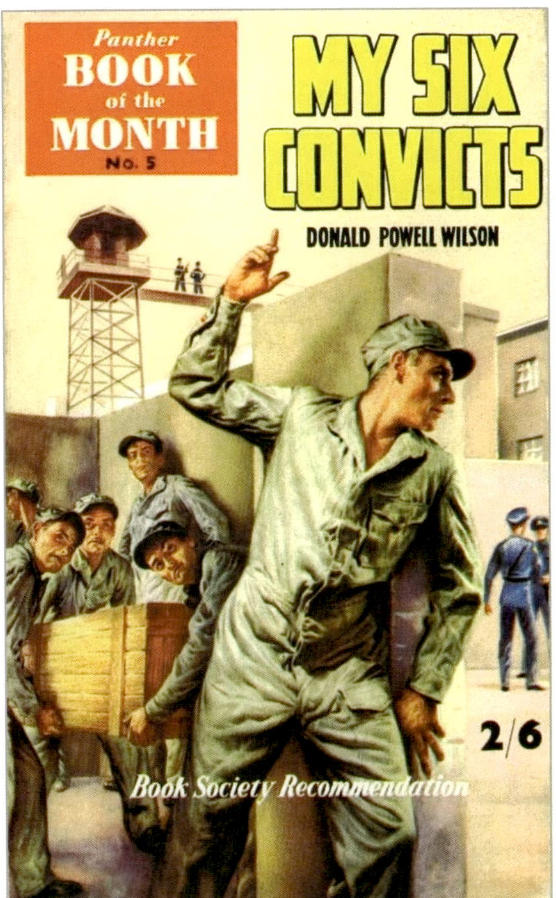

My Six Convicts by Donald Powell Wilson (Panther, 1956)

Stan Boswarva (art director at Pan in the 'Cy Webb' period): I rate Heade the highest of all the artists working for Pan in the 1950s. Second is David Tayler.

Peter Green (assistant art director at Panther Books when Heade was producing covers for the imprint):

Reg Heade was a terrific artist. I suppose he was the highest rated, and he certainly got the highest rates of pay. In fact, I think we dropped him in the end because he wanted to put his rates up even higher. We usually paid 40 guineas a jacket. Like most of the publishing houses, we tried to keep a nucleus of artists whose work we were pleased with. We gave them regular work, otherwise they would drift away. For a lot of artists, I would design the cover, produce the layout and so on, but Reg was more or less allowed to do his own thing – and he always produced suitable covers. Probably no other artist could have come up with the quality of his artwork, and I'm sure his jackets helped to sell the books. But although Reg was a very fine artist, he never did a real bestseller, apart from *Stalingrad*. The contents of the books he worked on weren't particularly popular. They were mundane on the whole.

The artists worked from photos, which we would take for them. We would hire costumes from Fox costumiers in Covent Garden – German uniforms, or whatever might be required – and put them on models we would get from agencies. I forget which agencies we used, but Lucy Clayton was one, I think. Models were pretty cheap at the time, £3 an hour or so. Heade would normally have been by the camera directing the model. Reg Heade used a fellow called Richard Orme as a model quite often. He had a very strong face. I remember we used Burt Kwouk, who later was the Chinese man who used to jump out at Peter Sellers in the Inspector Clouseau films. We used him for lots of oriental characters. It was probably him as the kamikaze pilot on Heade's jacket of *Proud Echo*. I'm pretty sure the main figure in the prison compound in *My Six Convicts* is David Davenport. He was the brother of the actor Nigel Davenport. He was an actor himself. A lot of them used to model. I was actually the model for one of Reg Heade's covers. That's me as a Coldstream guardsman standing to attention on the cover of *They Die With Their Boots Clean*! So Reg Heade worked from photographs, sometimes film stills.

(Continued overleaf.)

Coral and Brass and *Away All Boats*, they would have been film stills probably, but he used his imagination with them.

I'll tell you one odd thing about Reg Heade, though. All the artists would use masking tape on the board around their paintings. The colours would bleed into it, but then they would strip it off and leave a clean line – it didn't matter really, because you would lose an eighth when it was printed. But Reg Heade would religiously go round the painting with a ruling pen and use white paint to give a clean edge all round. No one else bothered

About one painting a week would be an average rate for an illustrator. Many of them must have put in more than a nine-to-five day. When they delivered the painting, it was my job to put on all the type. In the early days, everything was hand-lettered onto film acetate. Even the colophon was hand drawn. The four-colour blocks were done in Holland, and even with customs duties, that was cheaper than producing them in England. The policy in those days was to make jackets as realistic as possible, as much like a photograph as we could get. That had been a successful formula, and it was always said that you shouldn't change a successful formula. We believed that that was what the retailers – people like W H Smith – wanted. But in some ways, I think that was a mistake. Some of the artists got so carried away with detail that the results looked stiff. You must give an artist some freedom, a chance to use his imagination, to put in his own colours. Occasionally paintings would get recycled or over-painted. The Heade example is *The Jack Dempsey Story*, where the figure from *Bare-Knuckle Breed* was taken and reversed – turned him into a southpaw! The shorts were over-painted and the gloves added. If you sent a painting back to an artist for extensive changes, he would charge you, so it would be done in the art department instead. You see, when you bought a painting, it was yours to do with as you liked. The artist would have been paid and couldn't complain.

I met Reg Heade only once or twice. The first time must have been about 1955. Our art editor, Eddie Blandford, would have had more contact with him. There were just the two of us in the art department. It's so long ago – I can't really describe him. All I remember is that he did not look like an artist. In those days, a lot of artists would dress flamboyantly and have long hair, but Reg was a very ordinary-looking sort of man, more like an accountant or an engineer. He wasn't the sort of man you would look twice at.

(Peter Green in conversation with Steve Chibnall, 1991)

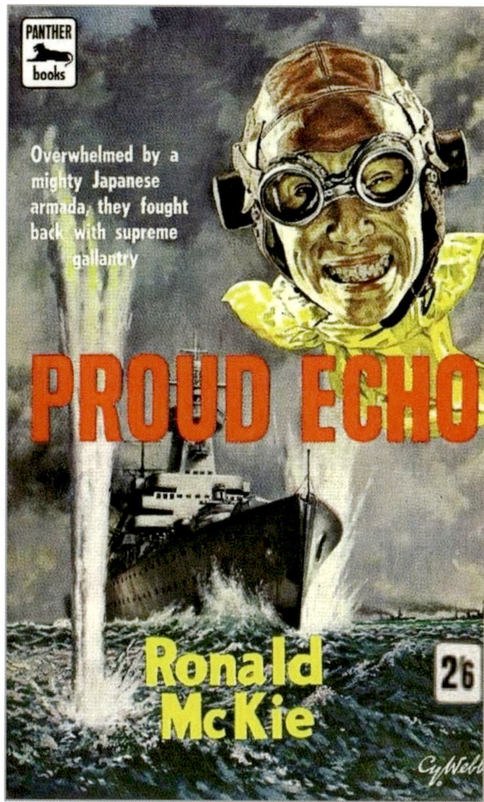

Proud Echo by Ronald McKie (above) and *Coral and Brass* by General Holland M Smith (below), two Panther books published in 1958.

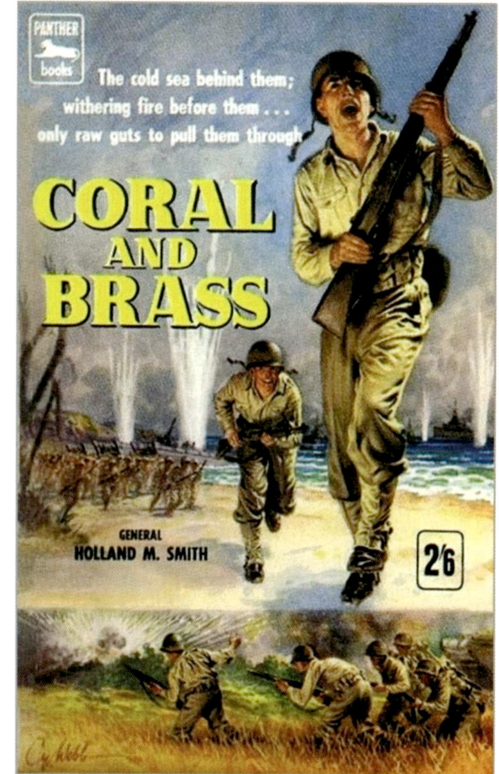

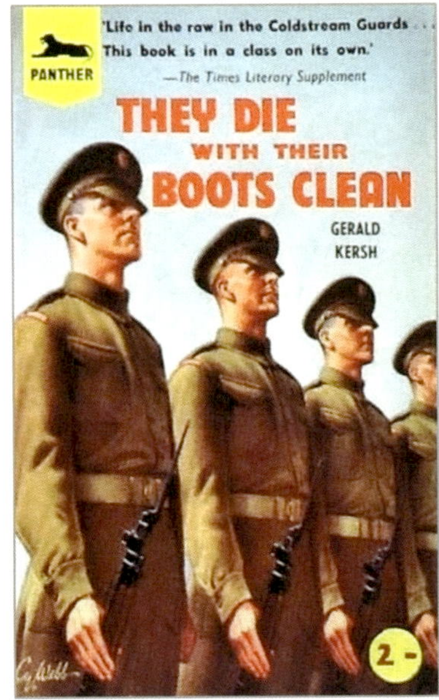

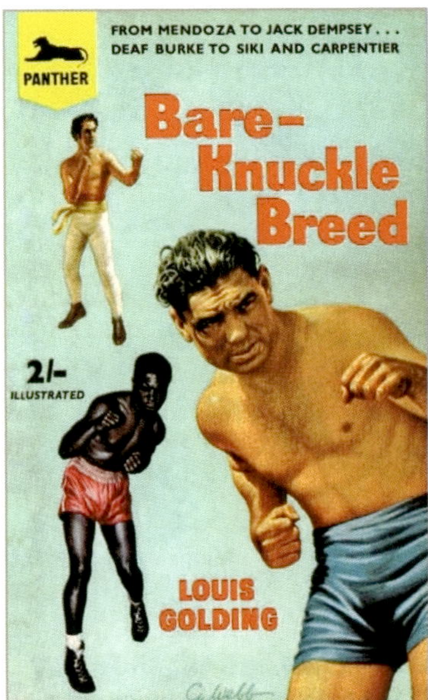

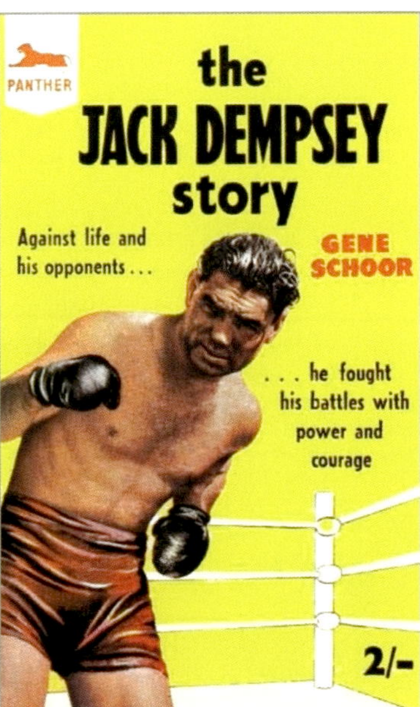

Above left: *They Die With Their Boots Clean* by Gerald Kersh (Panther, June 1957), for which Panther's assistant art director Peter Green was Heade's model.

Above centre: *Bare-Knuckle Breed* by Louis Golding (Panther, April 1957).

Above right: *The Jack Dempsey Story* by Gene Schoor (Panther, January 1958), with the main figure from the *Bare-Knuckle Breed* cover reversed and adapted, without Heade's involvement, by the publisher's art department.

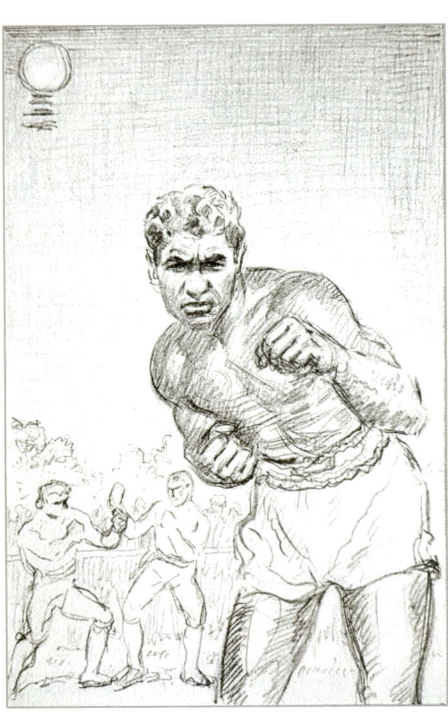
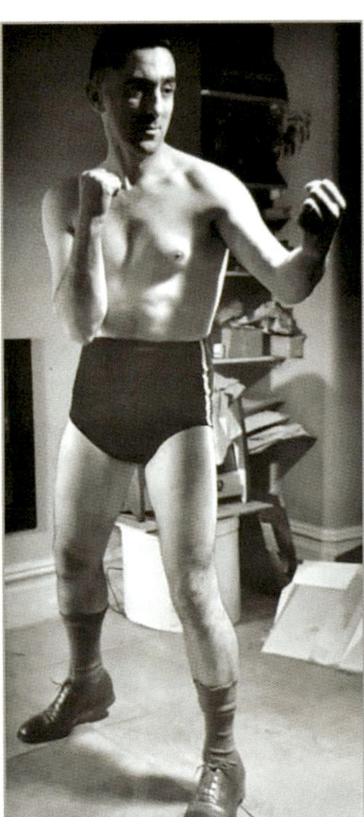
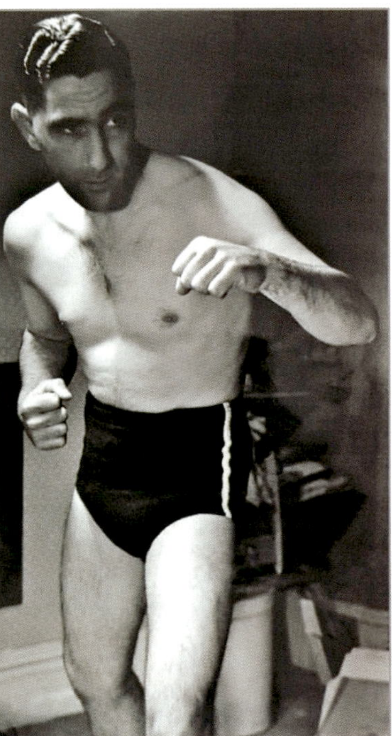

Above left: Heade's original rough for the *Bare-Kunckle Breed* cover.

Above centre and right: two photographs of Heade's downstairs neighbour, Eddie Lewis, taken in the artist's studio at 11 Queen's Mansions for use as reference for *Bare-Knuckle Breed*. (Photographs with thanks to Mike Lewis.)

DANISH E-BOOKS

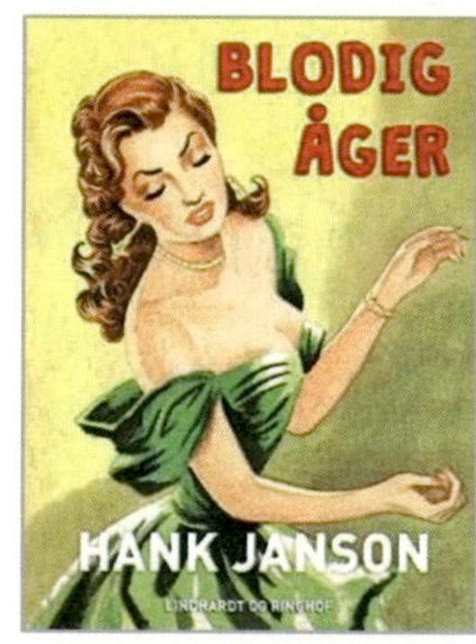

In 2018, by arrangement with Telos Publishing, Danish company Lindhardt Og Ringhof published, in e-book form only, a large number of Danish-language reissues of 1960s and 1970s Hank Janson novels. The covers of sixty of these – all of which are pictured below and over the next three pages – featured adapted versions of Reginald Heade pieces originally painted for the classic-era Janson books of the 1940s and early 1950s, while those of a few others – see right for one example – used similarly adapted versions of different artists' mid-1950s, Alexander Moring-era pastiches of Heade's work.

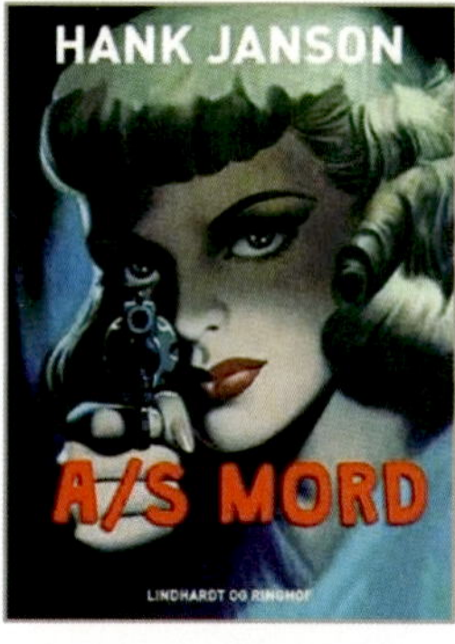
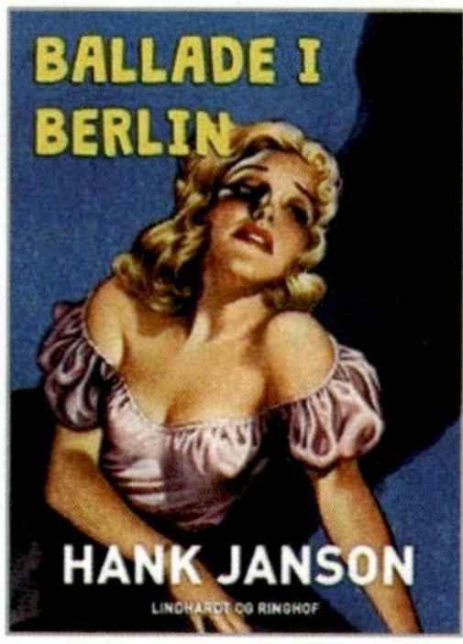
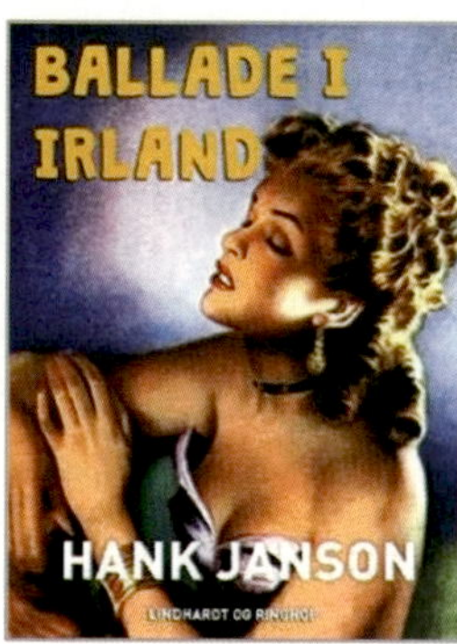
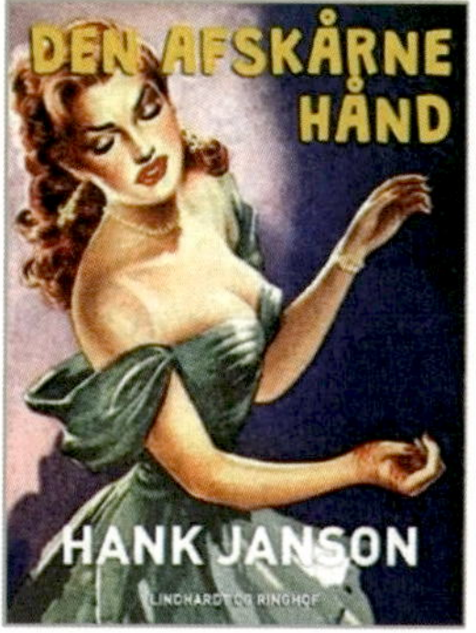

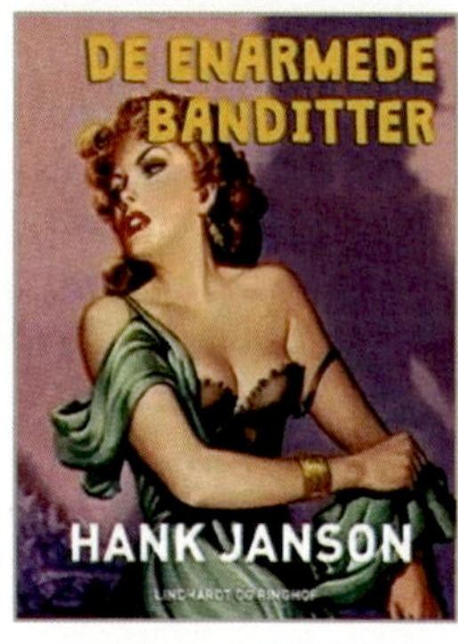
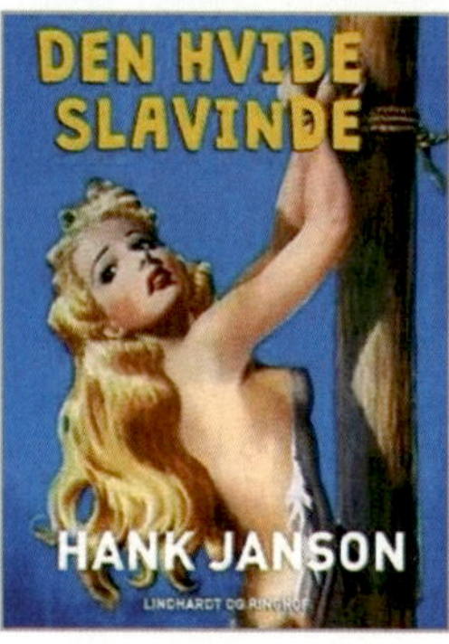
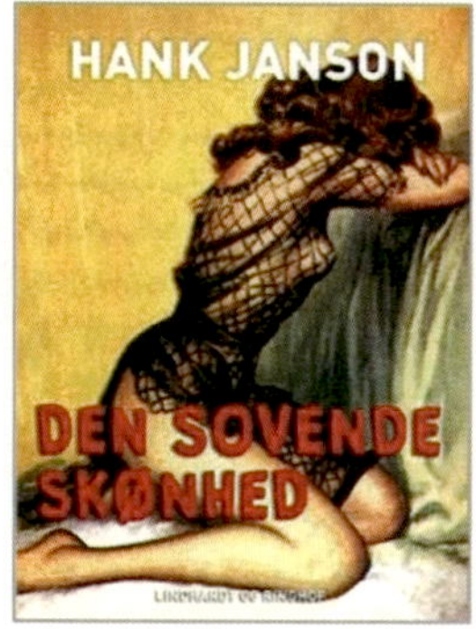
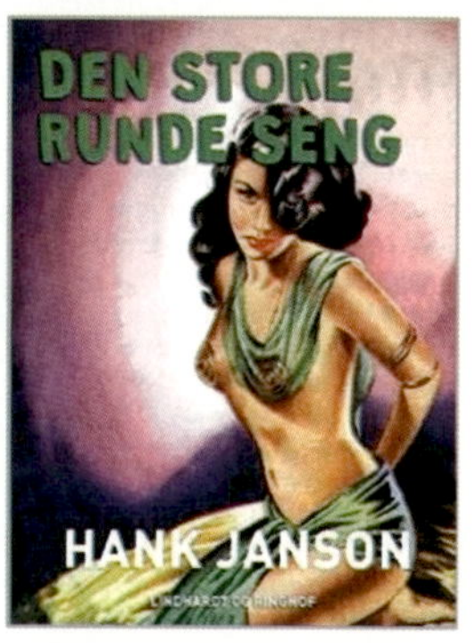

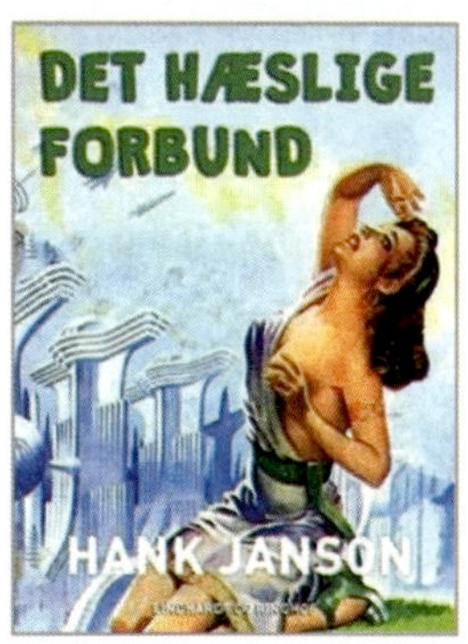
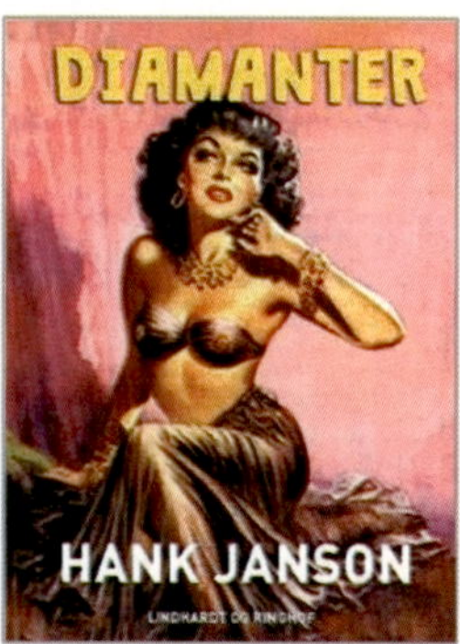
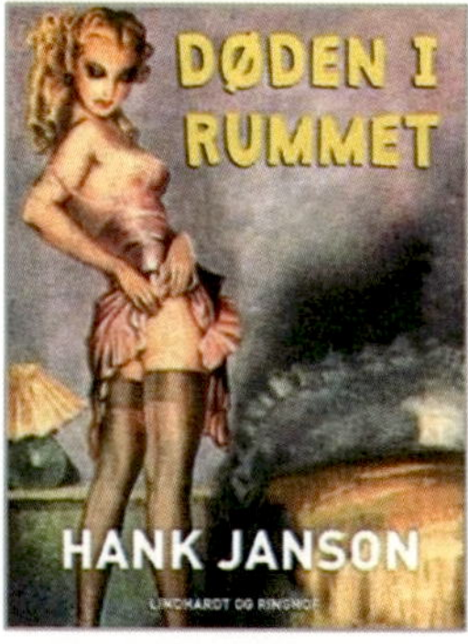
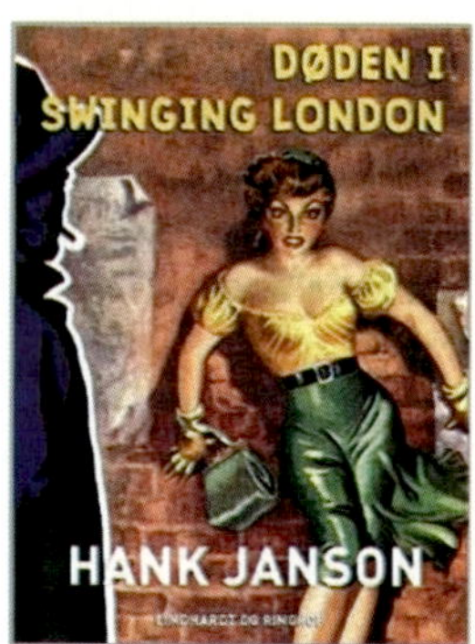

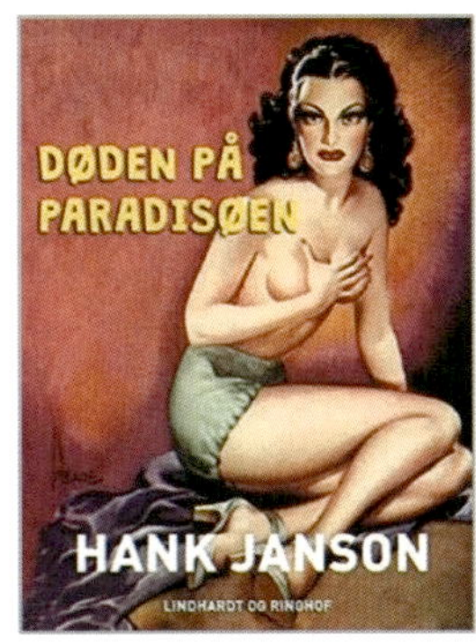
DØDEN PÅ PARADISØEN
HANK JANSON

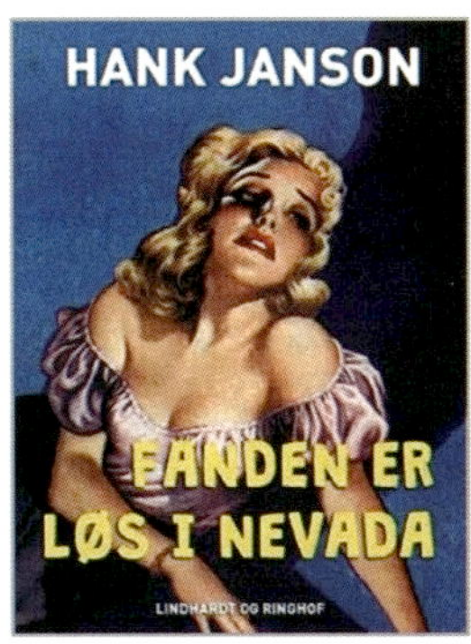
HANK JANSON
FANDEN ER LØS I NEVADA

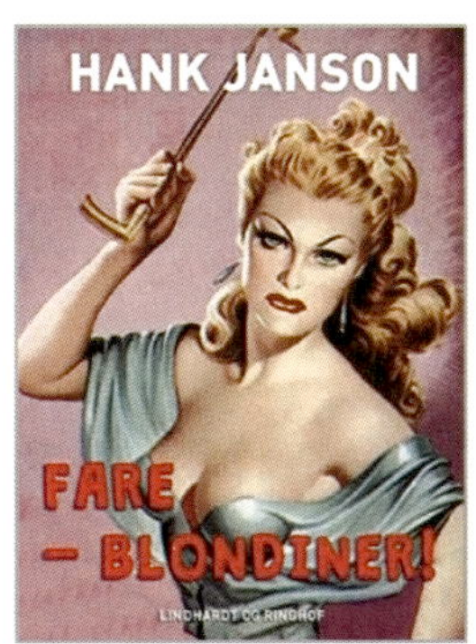
HANK JANSON
FARE, – BLONDINER!

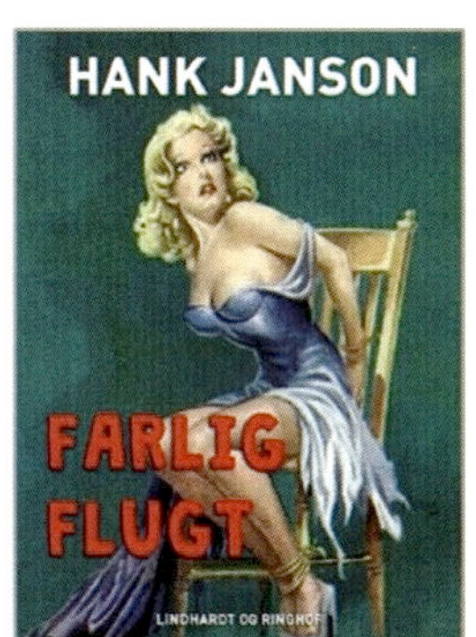
HANK JANSON
FARLIG FLUGT

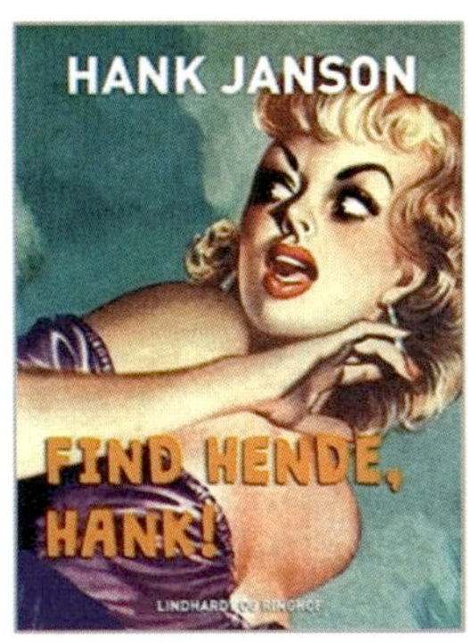
HANK JANSON
FIND HENDE, HANK!

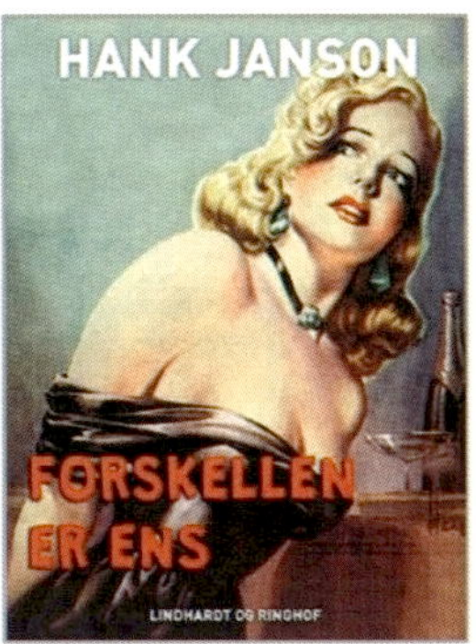
HANK JANSON
FORSKELLEN ER ENS

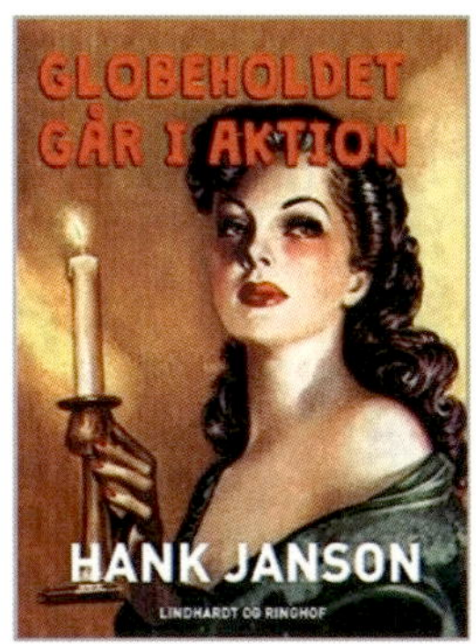
GLOBEHOLDET GÅR I AKTION
HANK JANSON

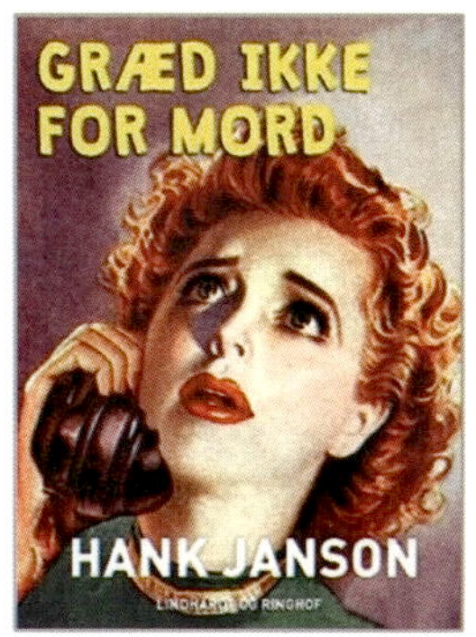
GRÆD IKKE FOR MORD
HANK JANSON

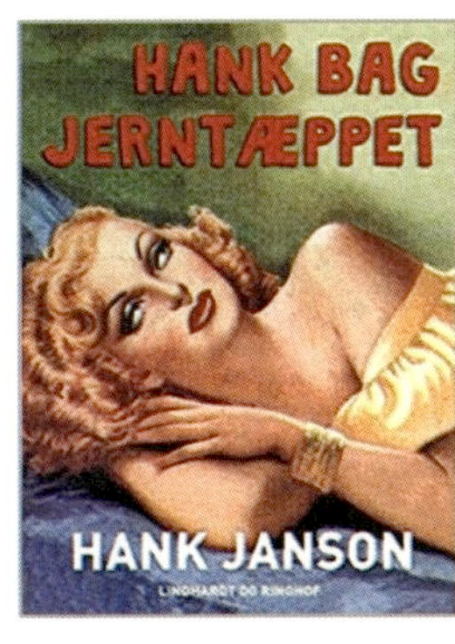
HANK BAG JERNTÆPPET
HANK JANSON

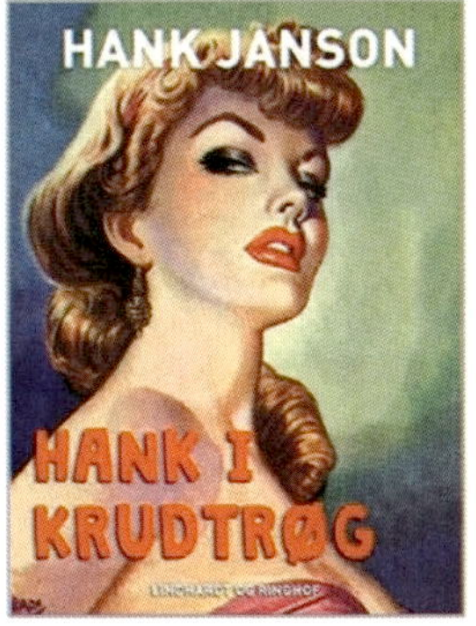
HANK JANSON
HANK I KRUDTRØG

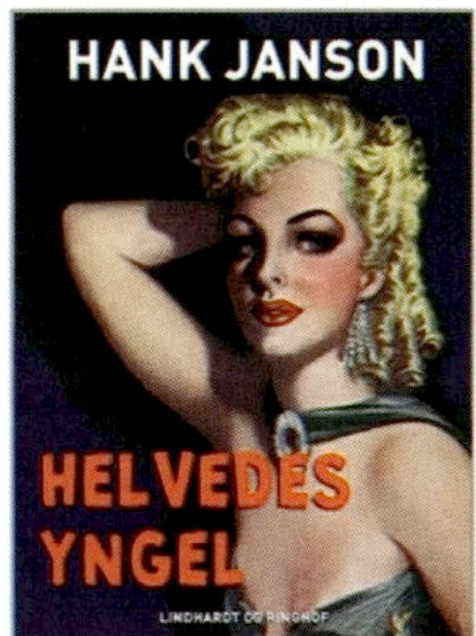
HANK JANSON
HELVEDES YNGEL

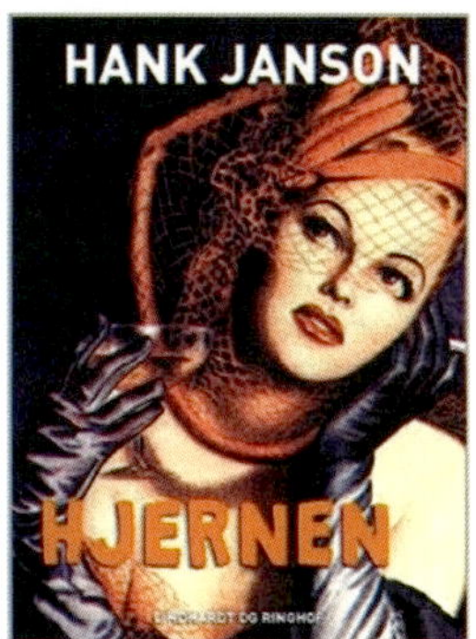
HANK JANSON
HJERNEN

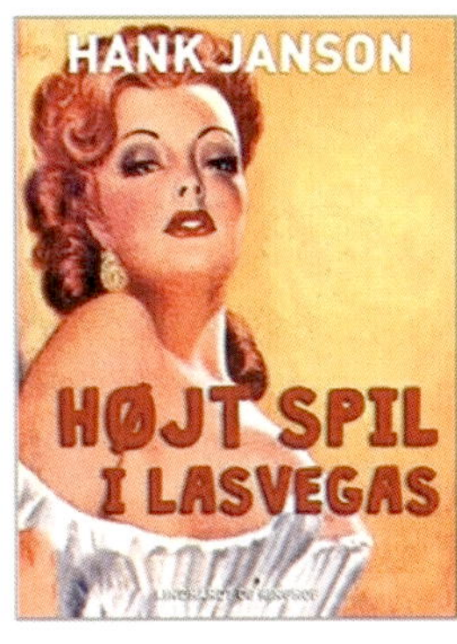
HANK JANSON
HØJT SPIL I LASVEGAS

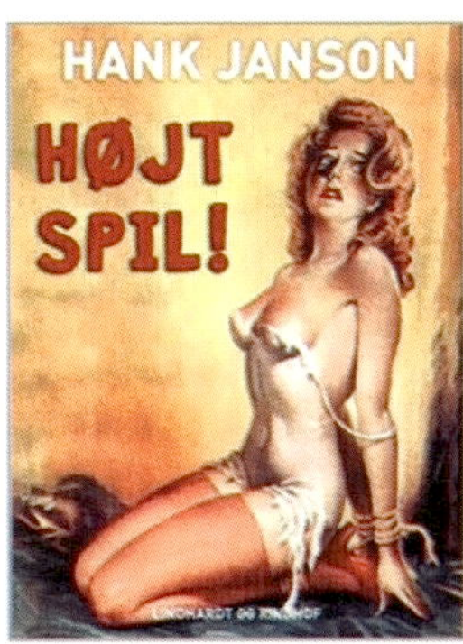
HANK JANSON
HØJT SPIL!

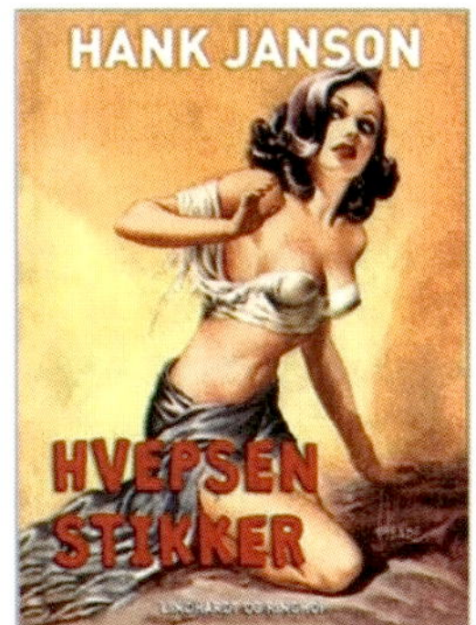
HANK JANSON
HVEPSEN STIKKER

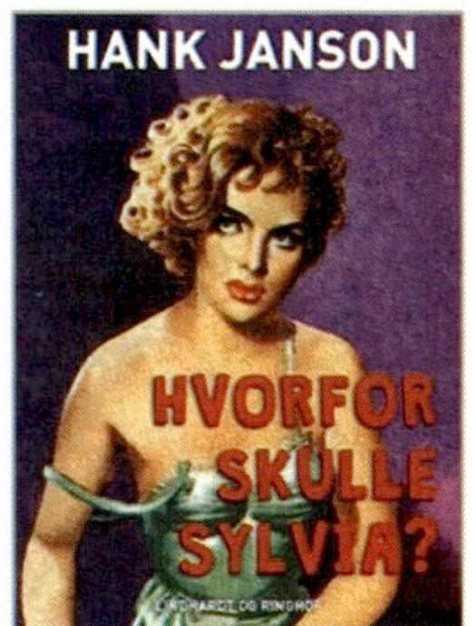
HANK JANSON
HVORFOR SKULLE SYLVIA?

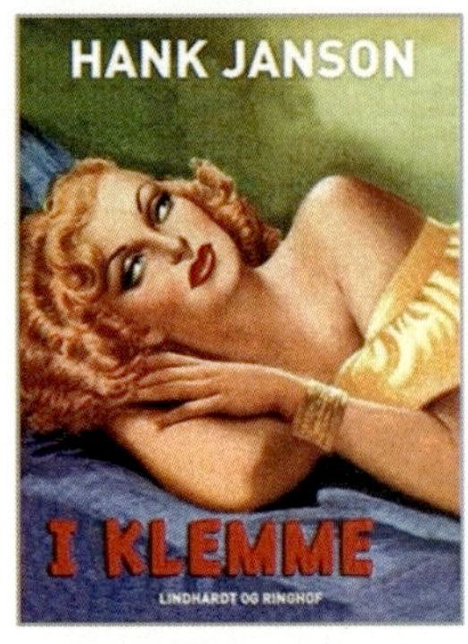
HANK JANSON
I KLEMME
LINDHARDT OG RINGHOF

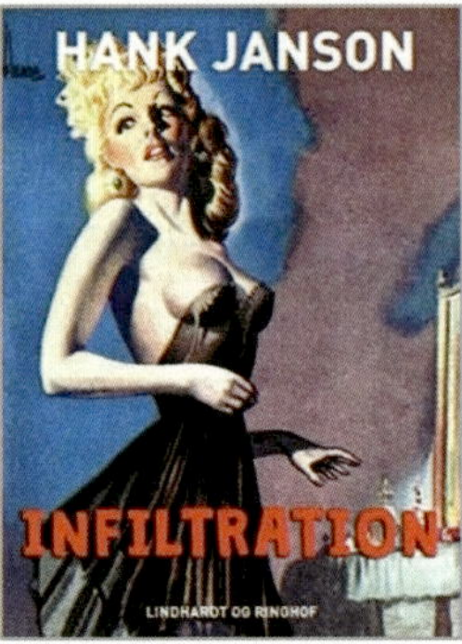
HANK JANSON
INFILTRATION
LINDHARDT OG RINGHOF

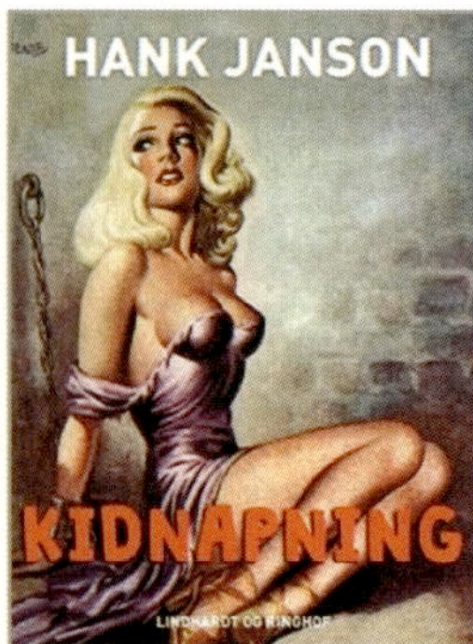
HANK JANSON
KIDNAPNING
LINDHARDT OG RINGHOF

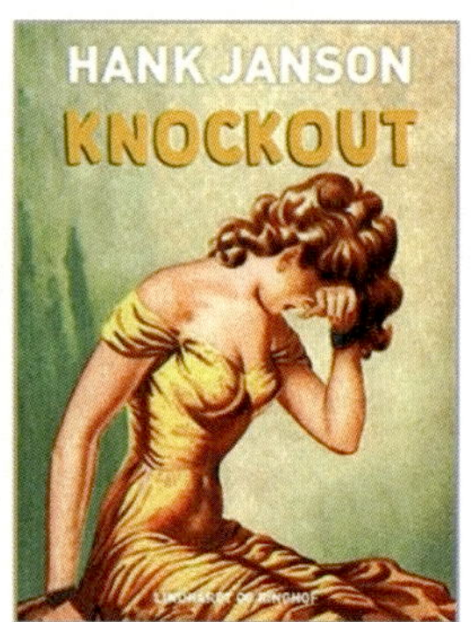
HANK JANSON
KNOCKOUT
LINDHARDT OG RINGHOF

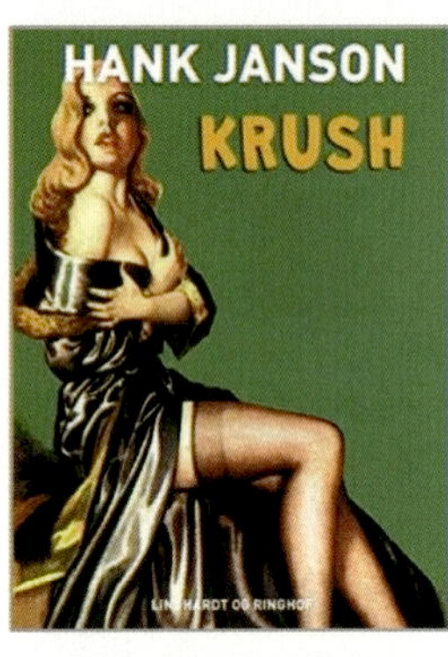
HANK JANSON
KRUSH
LINDHARDT OG RINGHOF

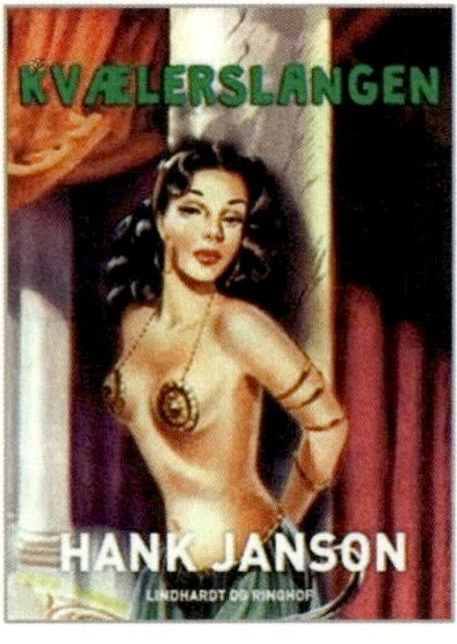
KVÆLERSLANGEN
HANK JANSON
LINDHARDT OG RINGHOF

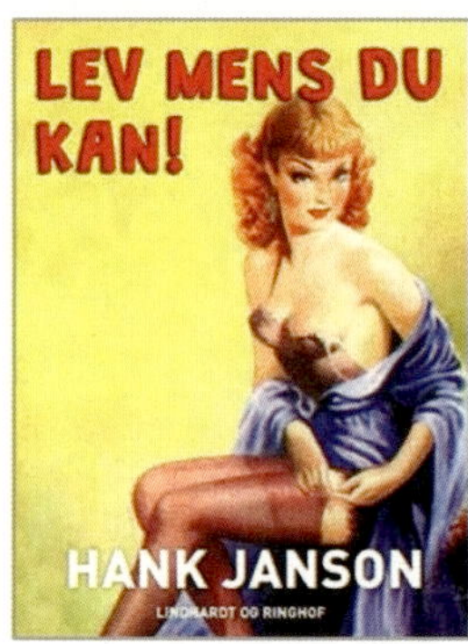
LEV MENS DU KAN!
HANK JANSON
LINDHARDT OG RINGHOF

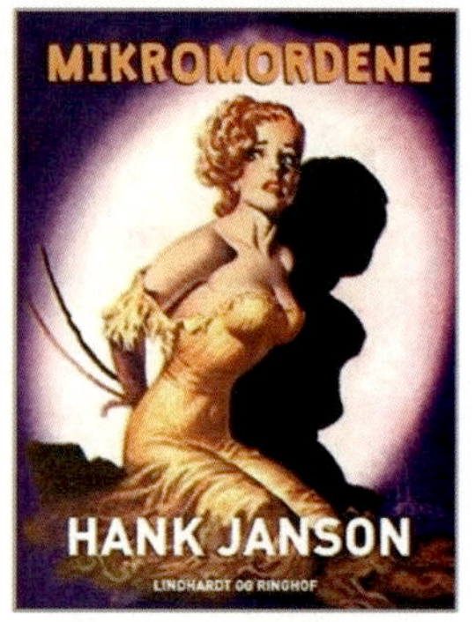
MIKROMORDENE
HANK JANSON
LINDHARDT OG RINGHOF

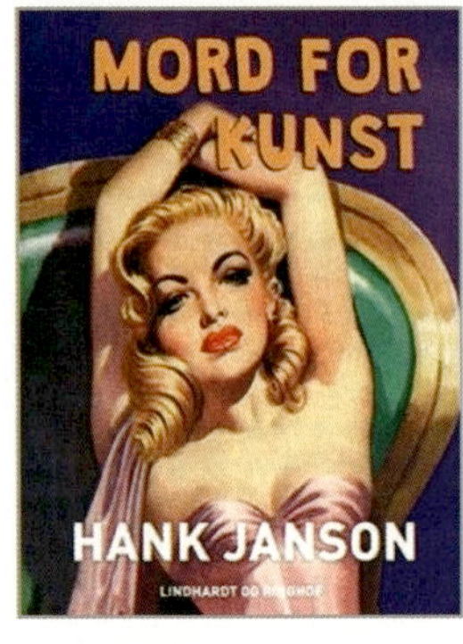
MORD FOR KUNST
HANK JANSON
LINDHARDT OG RINGHOF

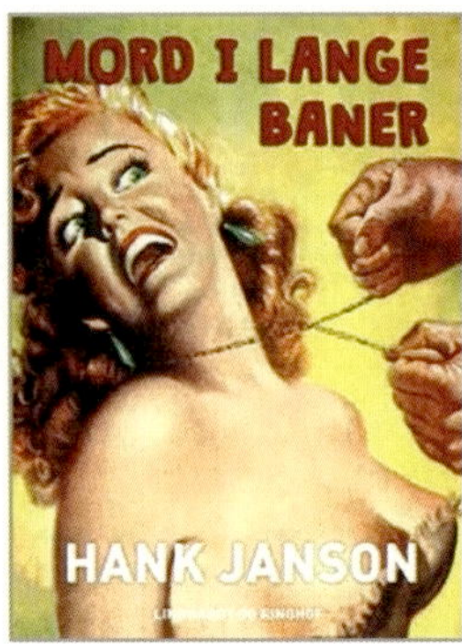
MORD I LANGE BANER
HANK JANSON
LINDHARDT OG RINGHOF

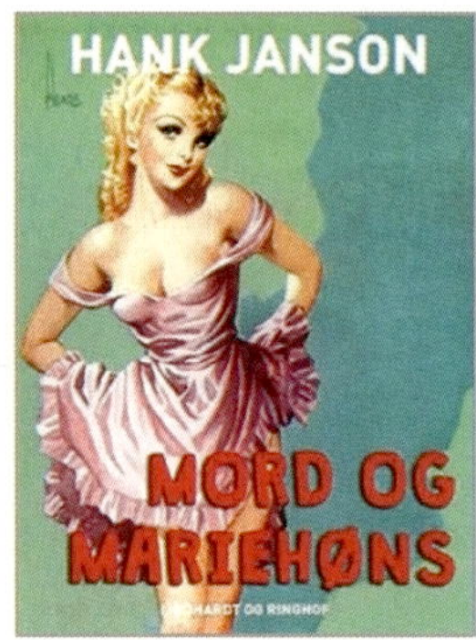
HANK JANSON
MORD OG MARIEHØNS
LINDHARDT OG RINGHOF

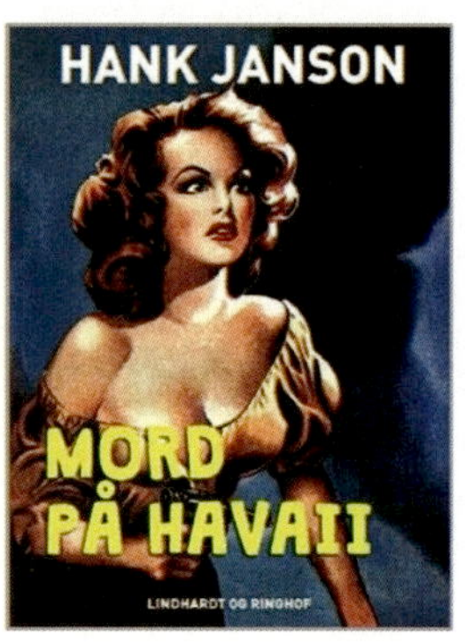
HANK JANSON
MORD PÅ HAVAII
LINDHARDT OG RINGHOF

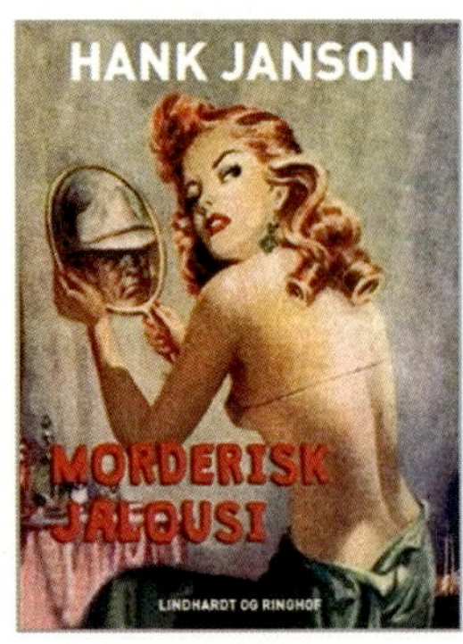
HANK JANSON
MORDERISK JALOUSI
LINDHARDT OG RINGHOF

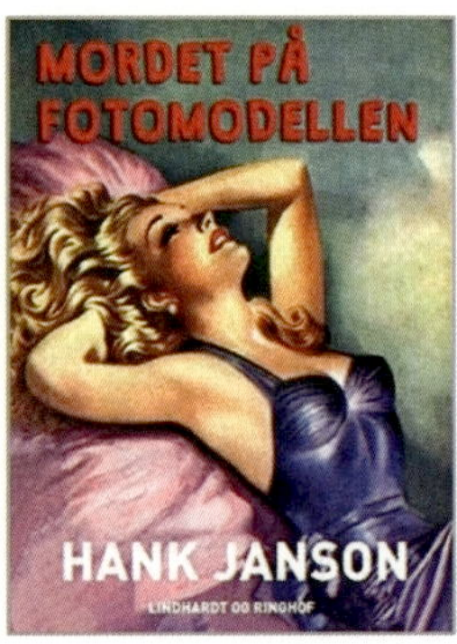
MORDET PÅ FOTOMODELLEN
HANK JANSON
LINDHARDT OG RINGHOF

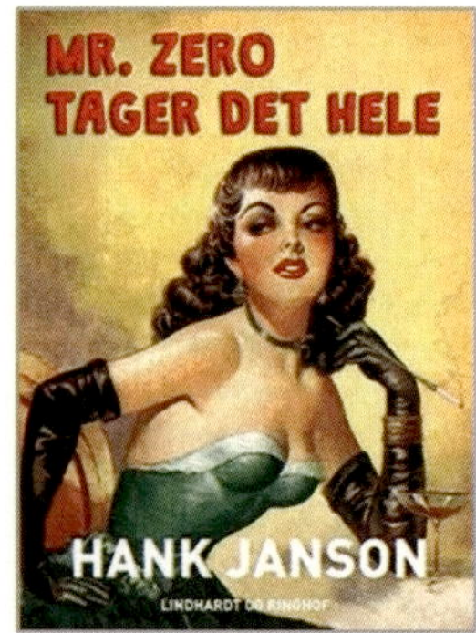
MR. ZERO TAGER DET HELE
HANK JANSON
LINDHARDT OG RINGHOF

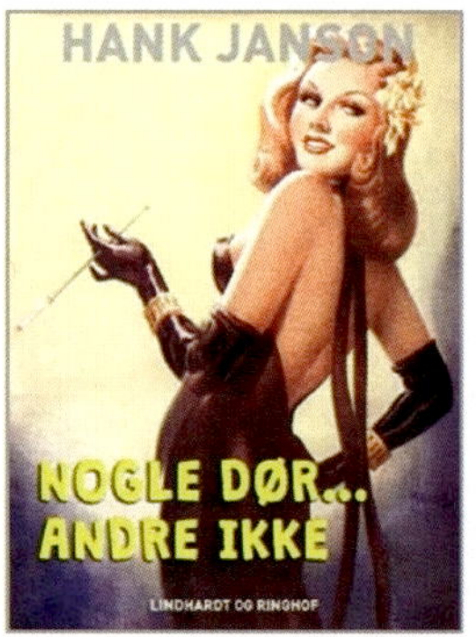
HANK JANSON
NOGLE DØR... ANDRE IKKE
LINDHARDT OG RINGHOF

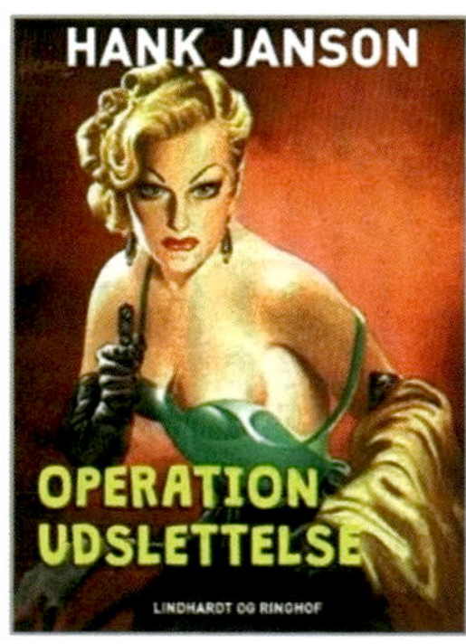
HANK JANSON
OPERATION
UDSLETTELSE
LINDHARDT OG RINGHOF

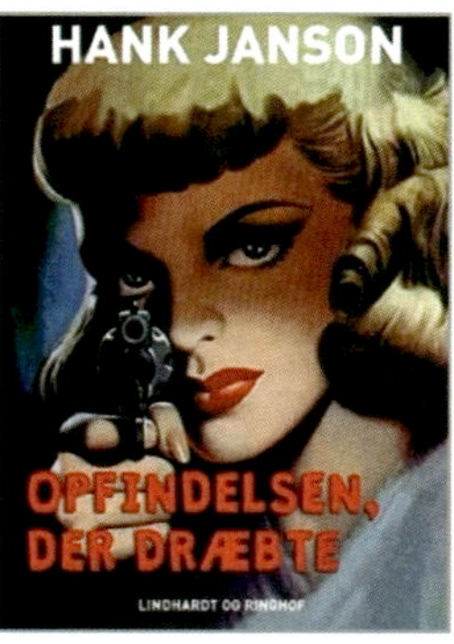
HANK JANSON
OPFINDELSEN,
DER DRÆBTE
LINDHARDT OG RINGHOF

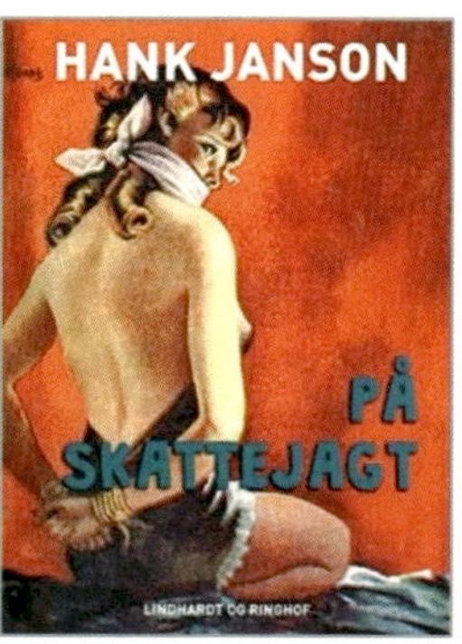
HANK JANSON
PÅ
SKATTEJAGT
LINDHARDT OG RINGHOF

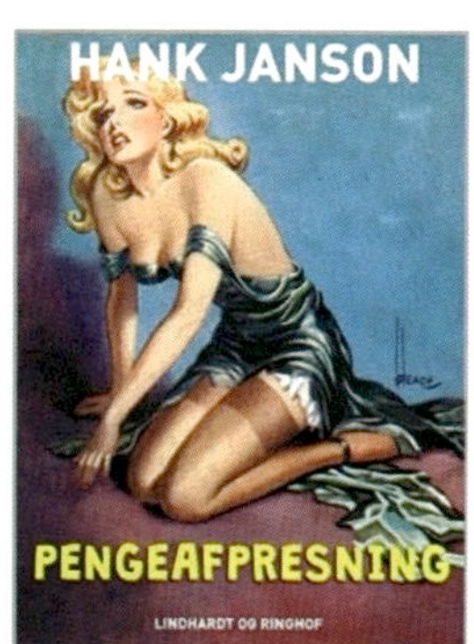
HANK JANSON
PENGEAFPRESNING
LINDHARDT OG RINGHOF

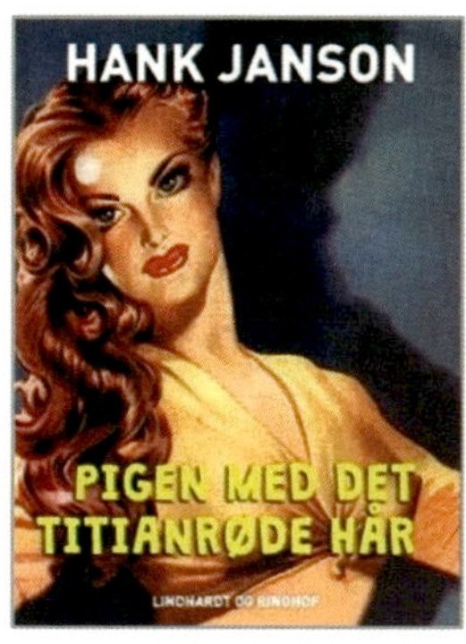
HANK JANSON
PIGEN MED DET
TITIANRØDE HÅR
LINDHARDT OG RINGHOF

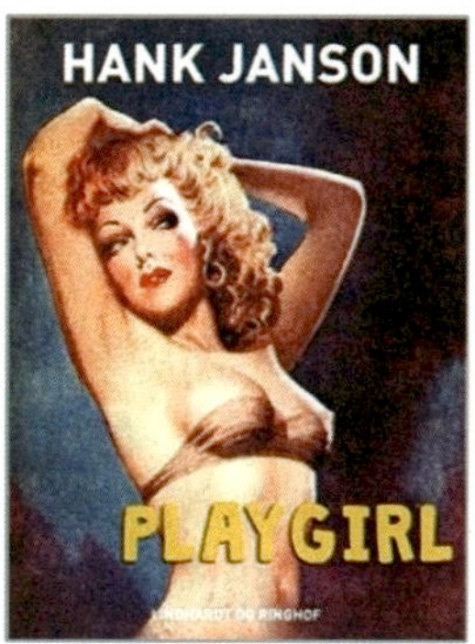
HANK JANSON
PLAYGIRL
LINDHARDT OG RINGHOF

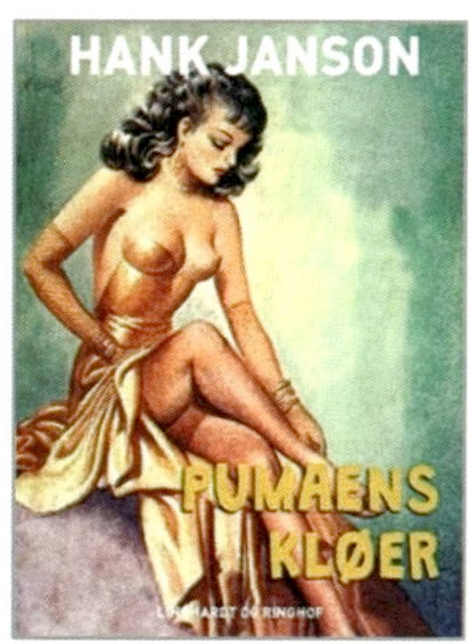
HANK JANSON
PUMAENS
KLØER
LINDHARDT OG RINGHOF

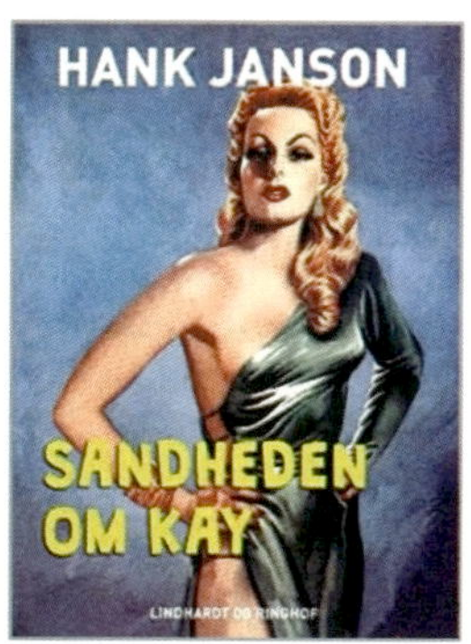
HANK JANSON
SANDHEDEN
OM KAY
LINDHARDT OG RINGHOF

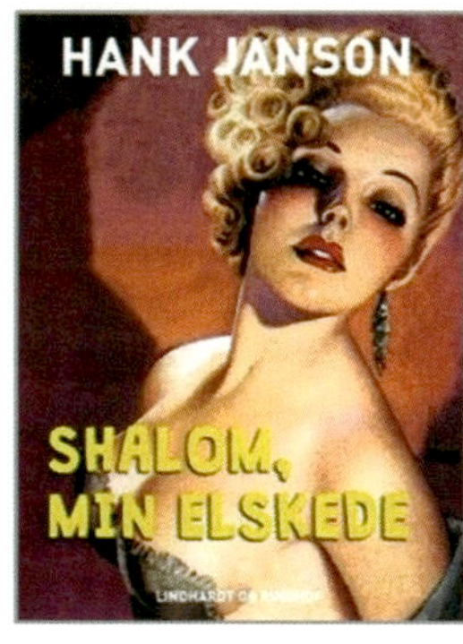
HANK JANSON
SHALOM,
MIN ELSKEDE
LINDHARDT OG RINGHOF

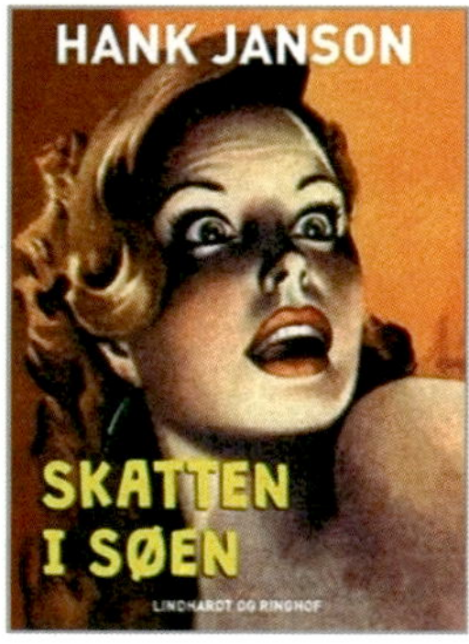
HANK JANSON
SKATTEN
I SØEN
LINDHARDT OG RINGHOF

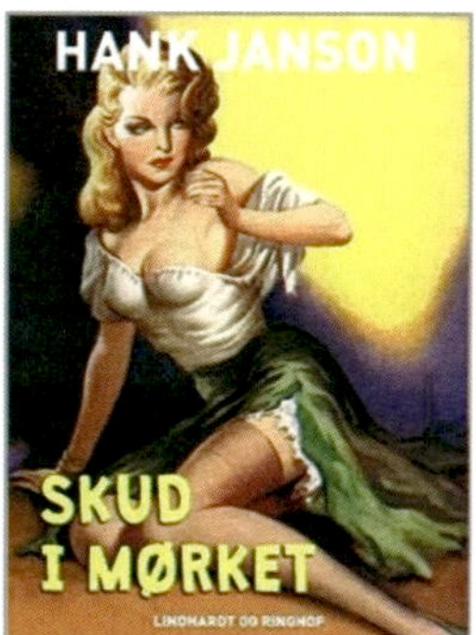
HANK JANSON
SKUD
I MØRKET
LINDHARDT OG RINGHOF

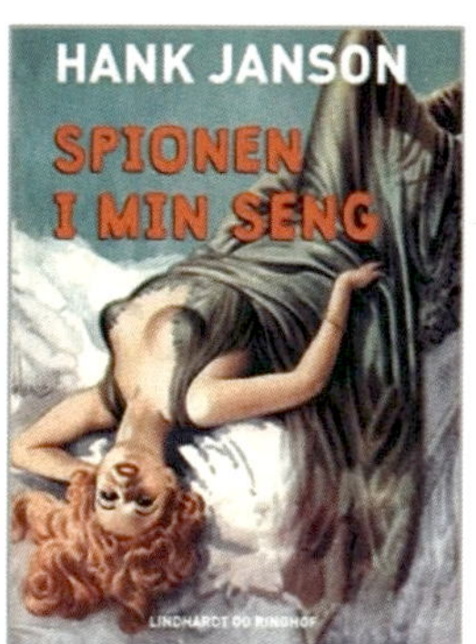
HANK JANSON
SPIONEN
I MIN SENG
LINDHARDT OG RINGHOF

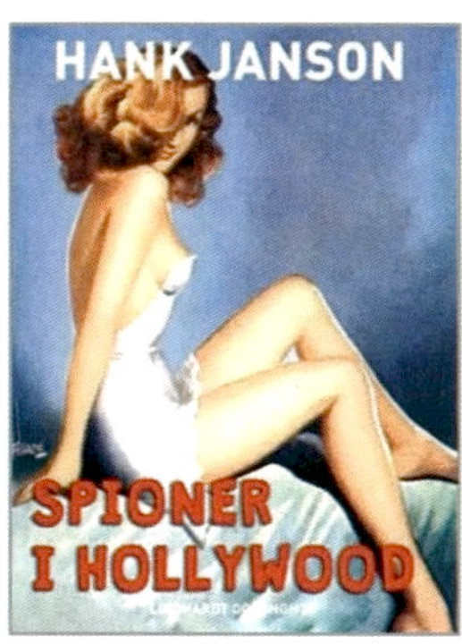
HANK JANSON
SPIONER
I HOLLYWOOD
LINDHARDT OG RINGHOF

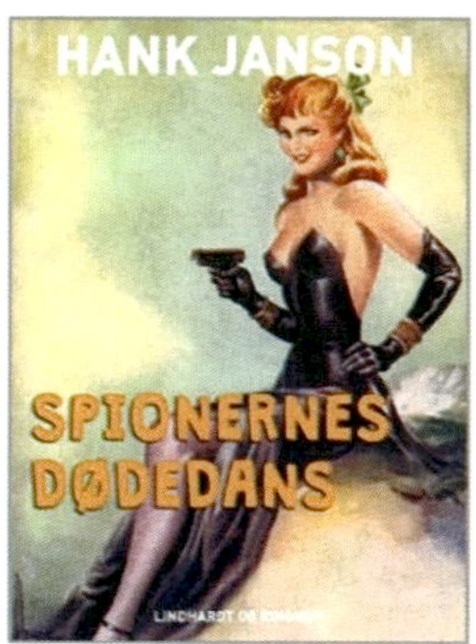
HANK JANSON
SPIONERNES
DØDEDANS
LINDHARDT OG RINGHOF

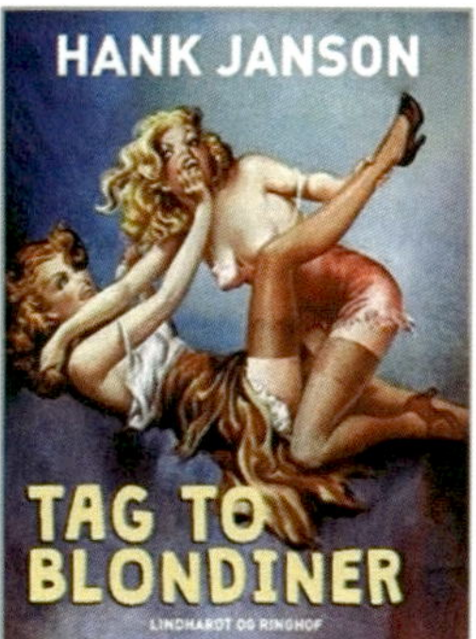
HANK JANSON
TAG TO
BLONDINER
LINDHARDT OG RINGHOF

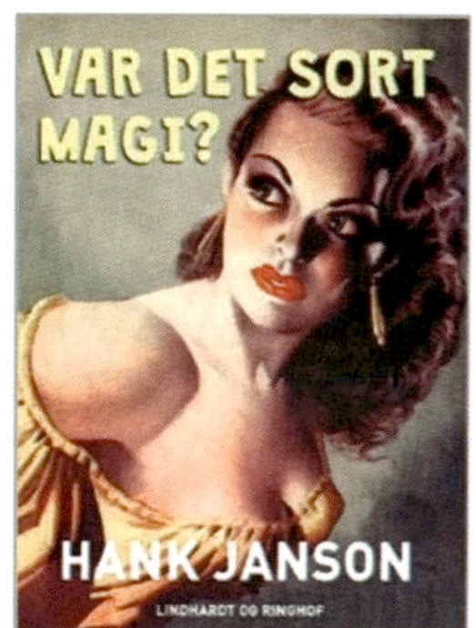
VAR DET SORT
MAGI?
HANK JANSON
LINDHARDT OG RINGHOF

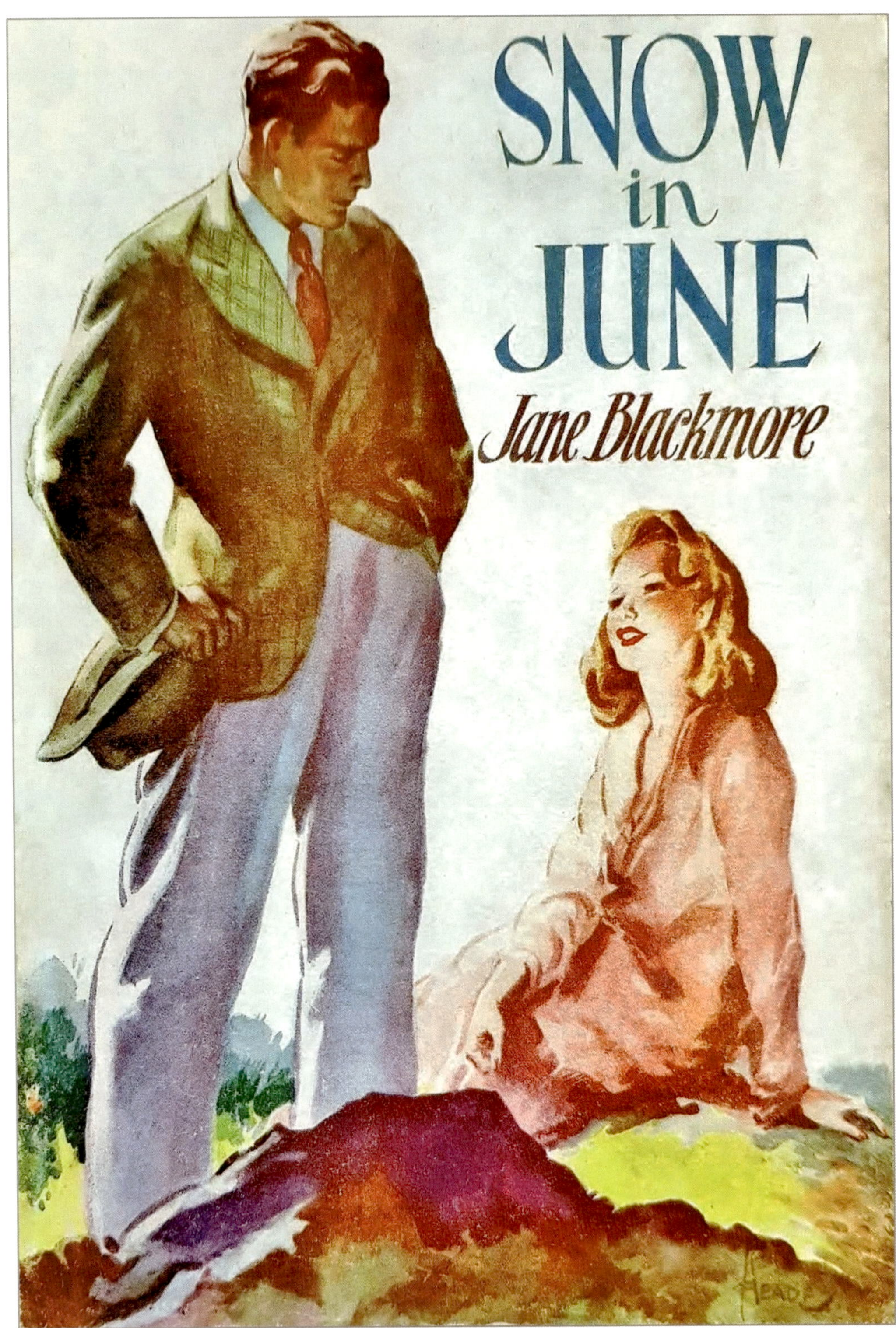

Snow in June by Jane Blackmore (Collins, 1947). According to financial records contained in a work-book kept by Heade's contemporary James E McConnell, Collins paid the lowest fees for cover art of all the London publishers: in 1947 he received (after deduction of agent's commission) seven guineas per painting from Collins as opposed to, for example, nine from Cassell. As publishing recovered with the relaxing of paper rationing over the next few years, rates for artwork increased steadily. By the mid-1950s, artists could expect around £15 for a dustjacket illustration, and more for a mass-market paperback cover.

HEADE CHECKLIST

Set out below is a checklist that aims to include all currently known printed work by Heade – in effect, a *catalogue raisonné*. It is subdivided into four parts: 'Books' (listed alphabetically by publisher and author surname, then by publication date, with associated publishers grouped together); 'Periodicals' (listed alphabetically by publisher and title, then by issue number); 'Commercial Products and Advertising'; and 'Comic Strips Etc'. Where, in the case of unsigned pieces, the authors consider the attribution uncertain, this is indicated by the words 'probably by Heade' or else 'possibly by Heade', depending on the degree of uncertainty. Where items are omitted from the listing despite being pictured in the 'Is It Heade?' section in either this volume or its predecessor, this is because the authors believe, on balance, that they are probably not Heade's work. Where the original finished artwork is either known or believed still to exist, this is denoted by '*'. In the handful of cases where no image of an item is currently available, and the attribution is therefore unconfirmed, this is denoted by '†'. A precise publication date is given in all cases where known, whether by virtue of being printed in or on the item itself or having been determined from other sources; otherwise, an approximate date is suggested, as denoted by 'c'. Hardback dustjackets are indicated by 'd/j' and paperback covers by 'p/b'. Generally, the listing includes only the first edition of each item that featured the Heade artwork; reprints and reissues are mentioned only where considered significant, e.g. due to some particularly noteworthy adaptation. All artwork is in colour unless otherwise stated.

The listing does not include original roughs or preparatory sketches, or any other artwork that was either definitely or possibly not produced with a view to publication. Many still-surviving examples of such items are pictured in earlier sections of this volume; and a few others, of which images are currently unavailable, are known to remain in private collections. As the listing covers only printed items, the Danish e-books detailed in the previous section of this Appendix are also omitted.

Heade was an incredibly prolific artist, undertaking up to as many as a hundred commercial commissions per year, so it is likely that there are many more, currently unknown examples of his work still waiting to be rediscovered – including, research suggests, dozens more ultra-scarce Mills & Boon dustjackets. If any readers are able to help out by supplying additional images or information, we would be enormously grateful if they could get in touch via feedback@telos.co.uk. Who knows? One day, there might even be a *Volume Three* of this book!

Below: this 1945-dated charcoal drawing by Heade, not intended for publication, was at one time speculated to be a self-portrait, but is now known to be of a different sitter, currently unidentified.

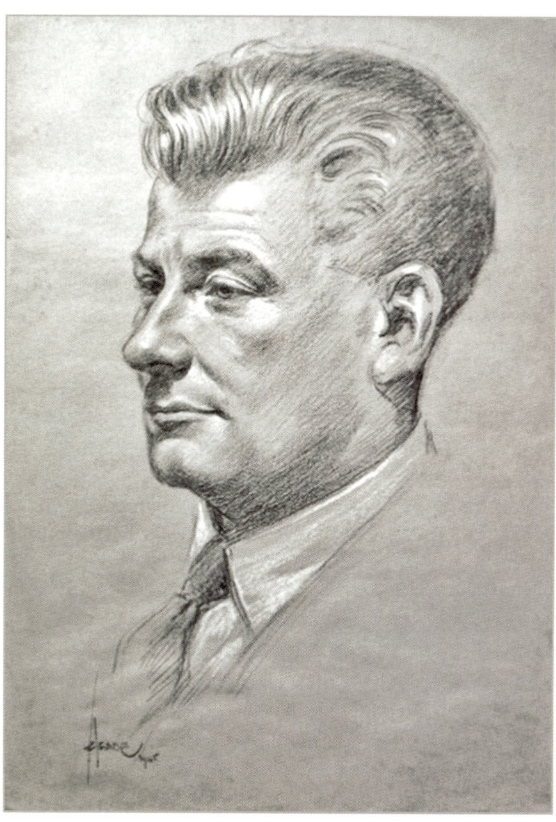

BOOKS

Amalgamated

Anon (ed.), *Knockout Fun Book 1950*, Amalgamated, 1949 (5 b&w illus for short story, Anon, 'Jungle Joe', unsigned)

Amex / PM (Productions)

Anon (ed.), *Mary Goes to Wonderland*, Amex, 1949 (p/b covers and 14 colour illus)
Anon (ed.), *Tip-Top Adventure Stories*, Amex, c1949 (h/b pictorial boards, unsigned)
Anon (ed.), *A Story a Night*, PM (Productions), c1950 (p/b covers and 14 colour illus, unsigned)
Anon (ed.), *The Dancing Princesses*, Amex, 1952 (p/b covers and 17 colour illus, unsigned)
Anon (ed.), *The Fairy Princesses*, Amex, 1952 (p/b cover and 17 colour illus)

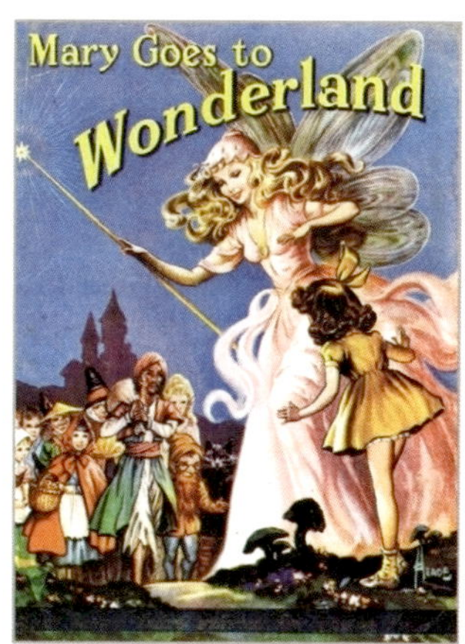

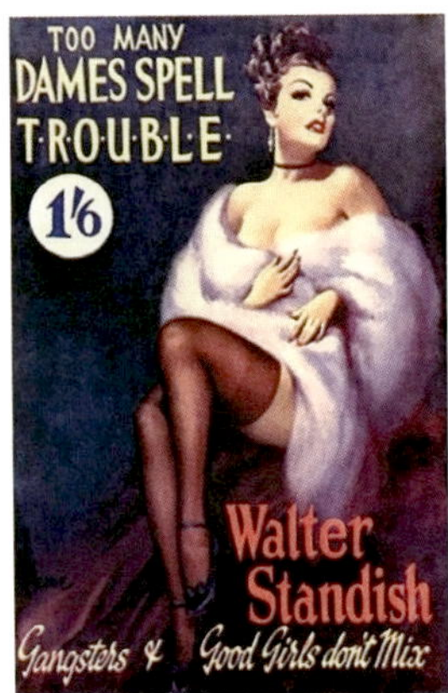

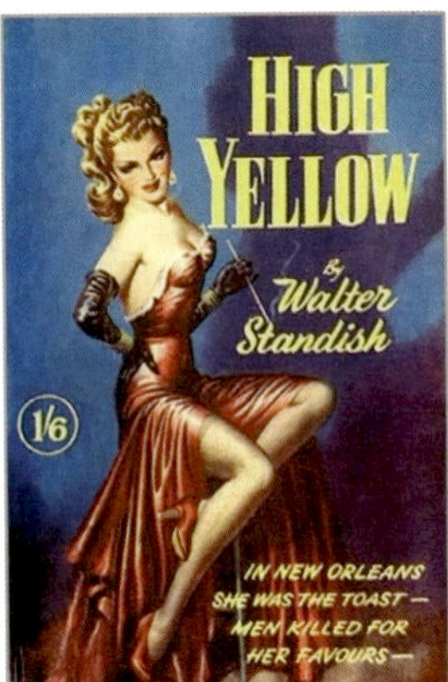

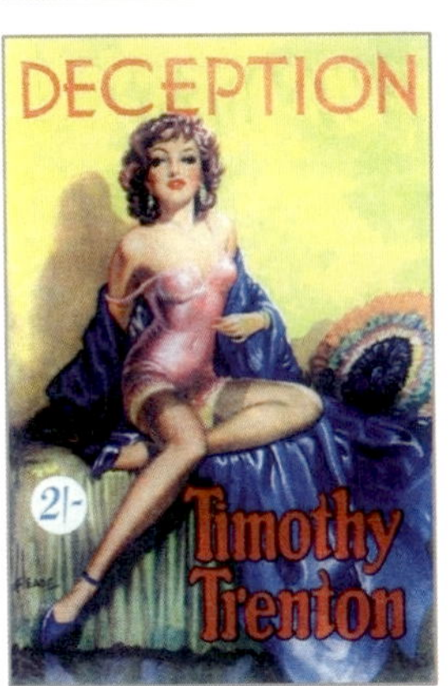

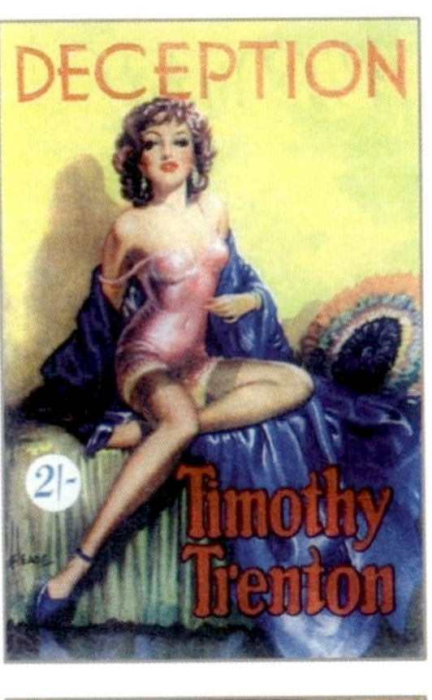

Avenue Press

Anon (ed.), *Happy Time Tales*, Avenue Press, c1935 (pictorial boards)
Anon (ed.), *Boys' Book of Stories*, Avenue Press, c1937 (pictorial boards, possibly by Heade)

Book Club

George R Stewart, *East of the Giants*, Book Club, 1939 (d/j, unsigned, probably by Heade)

Books Are Everything

Steve Chibnall, *Reginald Heade – England's Greatest Artist*, Books Are Everything, 1991 (adapted p/b);
repurposed from John King, *Shuna and the Lost Tribe*, Harborough, 11/1951 (p/b)

Brown Watson

Rex Richards, *Don't Fall, Sucker!*, Brown Watson, 1951 (p/b)
Walter Standish, *Mistress Mine*, Brown Watson, c1952 (p/b)
Walter Standish, *Too Many Dames Spell Trouble*, Brown Watson, c1952 (p/b)
Walter Standish, *High Yellow*, Brown Watson, 1953 (p/b)

Burmont / Sporting World

Timothy Trenton, *Pay-Off for Blondie*, Burmont, 1952 (p/b)
Timothy Trenton, *Some Dames Die Quick*, Burmont, 1952 (p/b)
Timothy Trenton, *Deception*, Burmont, c1952 (p/b)
Timothy Trenton, *Intrigue*, Sporting World, 1953 (p/b)

Cassell

Arnold Bennett, *The Lion's Share*, Cassell's Shilling Novels, 1932 (d/j)
Dorothy Black, *The House Without Doors*, Cassell, 1955 (d/j, unsigned)
Lawrence D Blochman, *Rather Cool for Mayhem*, Cassell, 1953 (d/j, unsigned, possibly by Heade)
Sheila Burns, *Romance of Jenny W.R.E.N.*, Cassell, 1944 (d/j, unsigned, possibly by Heade)
Theresa Charles, *Fairer Than She*, Cassell, 1953 (d/j)
Warwick Deeping, *Man in Chains*, Cassell, 1953 (d/j)
Warwick Deeping, *Sincerity*, Cassell, 1956 (d/j, unsigned)
Ethel M Dell, *The Serpent in the Garden*, Cassell, 1955 (d/j, unsigned)
Anne Duffield, *Repent at Leisure*, Cassell, 1945 (d/j)
Anne Duffield, *Forever Tomorrow*, Cassell, 1946 (d/j)
Anne Duffield, *Tomorrow is Theirs*, Cassell, 1951 (d/j)
Anne Duffield, *Harbour Lights*, Cassell, 1953 (d/j)
Jeanette Eaton, *Betsy's Napoleon*, Cassell, 1953 (d/j; section also used as colour frontis)
Paul Frischauer, *So Great a Queen*, Cassell, 1951 (d/j)
Erle Stanley Gardner, *The Case of the Careless Kitten*, Cassell, 1944 (d/j)
Erle Stanley Gardner, *The Case of the Black-Eyed Blonde*, Cassell, 1948 (d/j)
Erle Stanley Gardner, *The Case of the Gold-Digger's Purse*, Cassell, 1948 (d/j)
Erle Stanley Gardner, *The Case of the Half-Wakened Wife*, Cassell, 1949 (d/j)
Erle Stanley Gardner, *The D.A. Breaks a Seal*, Cassell, 1950 (d/j)
T Rumsey Hamber, *And So Hold On*, Cassell, 1951 (d/j)
William Le Queux, *Mademoiselle of Monte Carlo*, Cassell's Shilling Novels, 1933 (d/j)
D M Locke, *Fatal Fragrance*, Cassell, 1/1950 (d/j)
Lois Montross, *If the Bough Breaks*, Cassell, 1938 (d/j)
Joan Pepper, *Fly Away Paul*, Cassell, 1954 (d/j)
E Phillips Oppenheim, *Mysteries of the Riviera*, Cassell, 1956 (d/j, unsigned)
Baroness Orczy, *Marivosa*, Cassell, 1955 (d/j, unsigned)
Baroness Orczy, *Pimpernel and Rosemary*, Cassell, 1955 (d/j, unsigned)
Sax Rohmer, *Daughter of Fu Manchu*, Cassell, 1955 (d/j, unsigned)
Sax Rohmer, *The Mask of Fu Manchu*, Cassell, 1955 (d/j, unsigned *)
Wilson Tucker, *The Chinese Doll*, Cassell, 1948 (d/j *)
Wilson Tucker, *To Keep or Kill*, Cassell, 1950 (d/j)
Wilson Tucker, *Red Herring*, Cassell, 1953 (d/j)
Horace Annesley Vachell, *Gift from God*, Cassell, 1942 (duotone d/j)

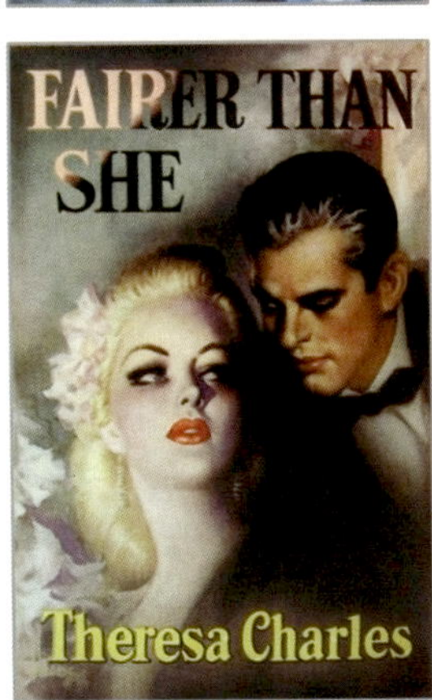

Olive Wadsley, *So Green the Grass*, Cassell, 1952 (d/j)
I A R Wylie, *Keeper of the Flame*, Cassell, 5/1943 (d/j)
I A R Wylie, *Candles for Thérèse*, Cassell, 1952 (d/j)

Chapman & Hall

Pamela Hansford Johnson, *Here To-day*, Chapman & Hall, 1/1937 (d/j); repurposed for *Detective Weekly*, Amalgamated, 6/8/1938, lead story Gerald Verner, *The Devil's Brood* (adapted monochrome cover)
Mary Bache, *Errand for a Lady*, Chapman & Hall, 1940 (d/j, unsigned)

Checker Books

Hank Janson, *Lady, Mind That Corpse*, Checker Books 10 (US), 1949 (adapted p/b); adapted from Hank Janson, *Honey Take My Gun*, S D Frances, 7/1949 (p/b)

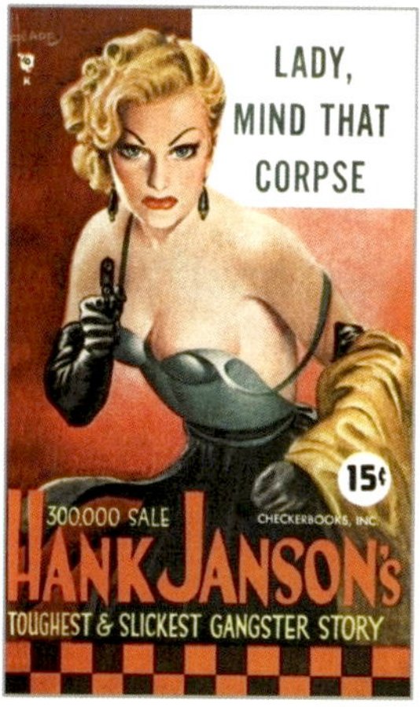

Collins / Collins Clear-Type / Collins White Circle / The Children's Press / Sunshine Press

Jennifer Ames, *I Married Mr. Richardson*, Collins, 1945 (d/j)
Anon (ed.), *Treasure Book for Girls*, Collins Clear-Type, c1937 (pictorial boards); repurposed for *The Bumper Book for Girls*, Collins, c1950 (adapted pictorial boards)
Anon (ed.), *The Triumph Book*, Collins, 1937 (1 colour illus and 4 b&w illus for short story, Victoria Gray, 'Little Miss Detective'); story and accompanying illus reprinted, with colour illus used as frontis, in *Collins Girls' Annual*, Collins, 1941; story and all illus reprinted again, with colour illus used as frontis, in *The Bumper Book for Girls*, Collins, c1950, reissued c1954

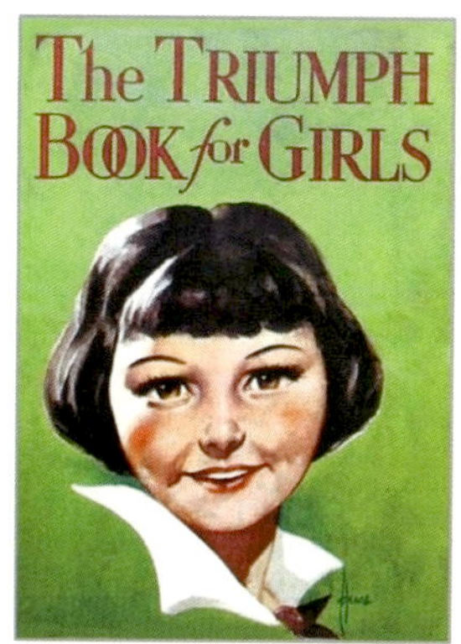

Anon (ed.), *The Triumph Book for Girls*, Collins Clear-Type, 1937 (pictorial boards)
Anon (ed.), *The Triumph Book for Girls*, Collins Clear-Type, 1938 (pictorial boards)
Anon (ed.), *The Young Airman's Annual*, Collins, 1941 (4 b&w illus for short story, Bruce Cooper, 'Black-Out Boxing'; 1 b&w illus for non-fiction article, Frank S Smythe, 'Mountaineering'; and 1 b&w illus for non-fiction article, Sid G Hedges, 'Swim Better'); story and accompanying b&w illus reprinted in Anon (ed.), *The Bumper Book for Boys*, Collins, 1954
Anon (ed.), *The Children's Wonder Book*, Collins, c1941 (1 colour illus); repurposed from Major Charles Gilson, *Robin of Sherwood*, Collins, 1940
Anon (ed.), *Little Stories of Robin Hood*, Collins, 1943 (p/b, 7 other colour illus and 19 b&w illus); repurposed from Major Charles Gilson, *Robin of Sherwood*, Collins, 1940
Anon (ed.), *The Adventures of Robin Hood*, Collins Clear-Type, c1947 (4 colour illus); repurposed from Major Charles Gilson, *Robin of Sherwood*, Collins, 1940
Anon (ed.), *The Treasure Box*, The Children's Press, c1947 (pictorial boards, unsigned; and colour frontis and 6 b&w illus, with red and blue highlight colours probably added by publisher, for short story, 'Patch' by C M Drury, unsigned); story and accompanying illus reprinted, without highlight colours, in Anon (ed.), *The Children's Treasure Book*, Collins, c1950

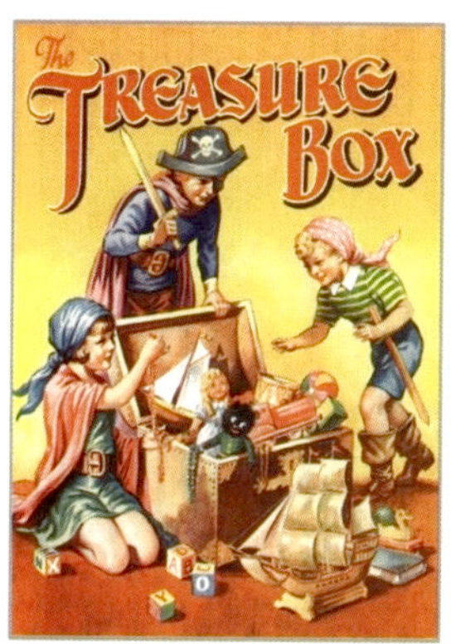

Anon (ed.), *The Bumper Book for Girls*, Collins, c1950 (adapted pictorial boards; plus colour frontis and 4 b&w illus for short story, Victoria Gray, 'Little Miss Detective'); pictorial boards repurposed from Anon (ed.) *Treasure Book for Girls*, Collins Clear-Type, c1937, story and accompanying illus reprinted from *The Triumph Book*, Collins, 1937; reissued, with slightly adapted pictorial boards and the same contents, as Anon (ed.) *The Bumper Book for Girls*, Collins, c1954
Anon (ed.), *The Crackerjack Story Book*, The Children's Press, c1950 (4 b&w illus, with red and blue highlight colours probably added by publisher, for short story, Victoria Stevenson, 'The Puppy That Wouldn't Grow Up')
Anon (ed.), *Favourite Book for Children*, The Children's Press, c1950 (7 b&w illus for short story, 'Breck – The Pony' by Doris Hunter, unsigned but credited); story and accompanying illus reprinted in Anon (ed.), *Collins Bumper Play Book*, Collins, c1954
Anon (ed.), *Uncle Mac's Children's Hour Story Book*, Collins, 1951 (pictorial boards, colour endpapers and two b&w illus, with red highlight colour probably added by publisher); 1 b&w illus reused, without highlight colour, in Anon (ed.) *The Bumper Book for Children*, Collins, 1954

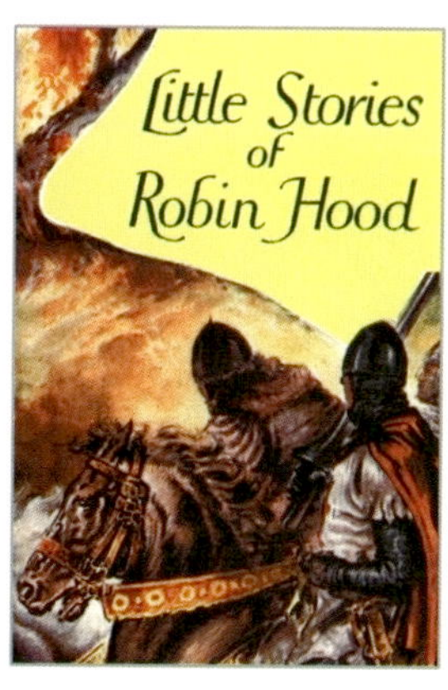

Anon (ed.), *The Scout Story Omnibus*, Collins 1954 (1 colour illus and 3 b&w illus for short story, Anon, 'Son of a Spy')
Anon (ed.), *The Bumper Book for Boys*, Collins, 1954, (5 b&w illus for short story, R Ernest Bailey, 'The Missing Schoolboy'; story and accompanying illus reprinted in Anon (ed.), *The Adventure Book for Boys*, Collins, c1959; probably appeared first in an earlier Collins book, currently unidentified
Anon (ed.), *Collins Boys' Annual*, Collins, c1955 (6 b&w illus for short story, Ray Harris, 'Opal Cavern', unsigned but credited); story and accompanying illus reprinted in Anon (ed.), *Bumper Cowboy Book*, Collins, c1956

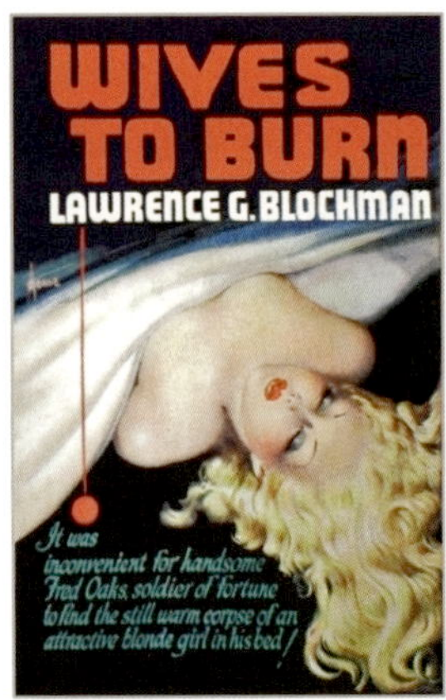

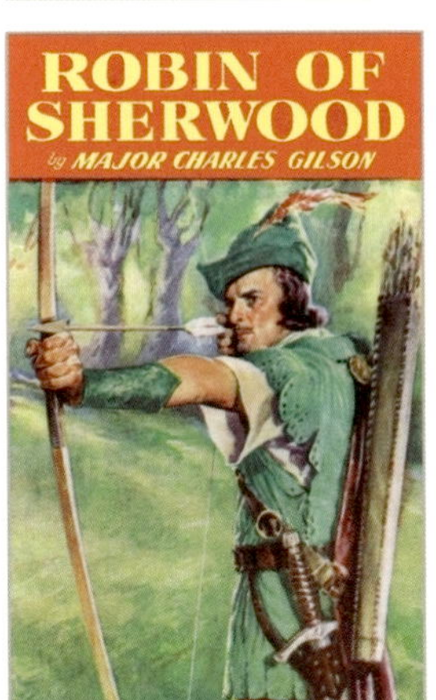

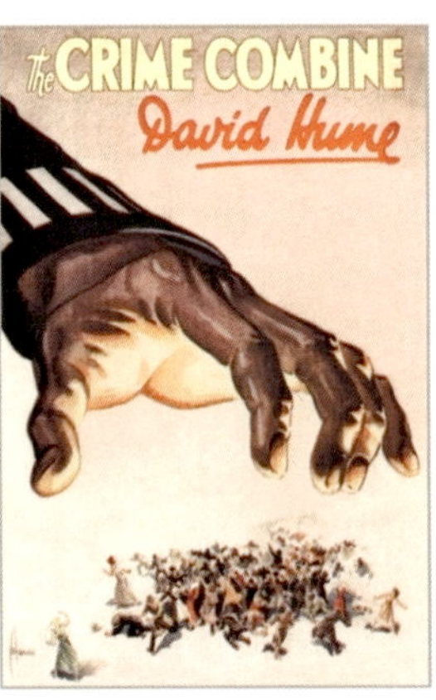

Anon (ed.), *The Sea Story Omnibus*, Collins, 1956 (1 colour illus and 8 b&w illus for short story, Anon, 'Diver's Son')

F E Baily, *The Lonely Road*, Collins, 1936 (d/j)

F E Baily, *Mother's Daughter*, Collins, 1944 (d/j)

Jane Blackmore, *It Happened to Susan*, Collins, 1944 (duotone d/j)

Jane Blackmore, *Snow in June*, Collins, 1947 (d/j)

Lawrence G Blochman, *Wives to Burn*, Collins, 1940 (d/j)

Nella Braddy, *Son of Empire*, Collins, 1945 (d/j, one colour frontis and 38 b&w illus)

Anthony Buckeridge, *Jennings' Little Hut*, Collins, 1954 (d/j and colour frontis)

Hilton Cleaver, *Captain for a Day*, Collins, 1942 (d/j, b&w frontis and 2 b&w illus)

Lavinia R Davis, *Plough Penny Mystery*, Collins, 1944 (d/j)

Lavinia R Davis, *Pony Jungle*, Collins, 1944 (d/j)

Basil C De Guerin, *The Man with Three Eyes*, The Children's Press, 1955 (pictorial boards)

Gavin Douglas, *Rough Passage*, Collins, 1936 (d/j)

James Wedgwood Drawbell, *Love and Forget*, Collins, 1934 (d/j)

May Edginton, *Expensive Lady!*, Collins, 1934 (d/j)

May Edginton, *Favourite Wife*, Collins, 1936 (d/j)

May Edginton, *Poor Young People*, Collins, 1939 (d/j)

May Edginton, *Invitation to Love*, Collins, 1941 (d/j)

Merle Eyles, *Children of the Foam*, Collins, 1939 (d/j)

Hulbert Footner, *The Dark Ships*, Collins Crime Club, 1937 (d/j)

Norman Fox, *The Rider from Yonder*, Collins, 1948 (d/j); repurposed by a different artist for Wade Smith, *Wild Country*, Collins White Circle Pocket Edition CD388 (Canada), 1949 (adapted p/b, unsigned)

Carol Gaye, *Shes and Skis*, Collins, 1939 (d/j)

Carol Gaye, *Made for Each Other*, Collins, 1940 (d/j)

Carol Gaye, *Family Affair*, Collins, 1942 (duotone d/j)

Carol Gaye, *My Heart is Yours*, Collins 1946 (d/j †)

Carol Gaye, *My Love and I*, Collins, 1948 (d/j)

Carol Gaye, *Rise & Shine*, Collins White Circle 363R, 1950 (p/b)

Major Charles Gilson, *Robin of Sherwood*, Collins, 1940 (d/j, colour frontis, 7 colour illus and 28 b&w illus, unsigned but credited); part repurposed for Anon (ed.), *The Children's Wonder Book*, Collins, c1941 (1 colour illus); part repurposed again for Anon (ed.), *Little Stories of Robin Hood*, Collins, 1943 (p/b, 7 colour illus and 19 b&w illus); part repurposed again for Anon (ed.), *The Adventures of Robin Hood*, Collins Clear-Type, c1947 (4 colour illus); reissued as Major Charles Gilson, *Robin of Sherwood*, The Sunshine Press, 1954 (adapted pictorial boards and 28 b&w illus); reissued again as Major Charles Gilson, *Robin of Sherwood*, The Children's Press, 1956 (new d/j, unsigned; 27 b&w illus in initial printings only)

Masie Greig, *Pathway to Paradise*, Collins, 1943 (duotone d/j)

Helena Grose, *Journey to Motherhood*, Collins, 1940 (d/j)

Helena Grose, *Two Were Foolish*, Collins, 1940 (d/j)

Helena Grose, *One Kiss – £1,000!*, Collins, 1941 (d/j)

Helena Grose, *The Morning After*, Collins, 1944 (duotone d/j)

Helena Grose, *Jilted*, Collins, 1942 (d/j)

Helena Grose, *Only You*, Collins, 1/1945 (duotone d/j)

Herbert Hayens, *Play Up, Lions!*, Collins Clear-Type, c1937 (d/j, unsigned; section also used as colour frontis)

Herbert Hayens, *Play Up, Kings!*, Collins Clear-Type, c1937 (d/j, unsigned, probably by Heade; section also used as colour frontis)

Herbert Hayens, *Play Up, Tigers!*, Collins Clear-Type, c1952 (d/j, unsigned, probably by Heade; section also used as colour frontis)

Mary Howard, *There Will I Follow*, Collins, 1948 (d/j); repurposed for Stephen James Walker, *The Art of Reginald Heade*, Telos Publishing, 12/2016 (adapted pictorial boards)

Claude Houghton, *The Riddle of Helena*, Collins, 1934 (d/j)

David Hume, *Call in the Yard*, Collins, 1936 (d/j, unsigned, probably by Heade)

David Hume, *The Crime Combine*, Collins, 1936 (d/j)

David Hume, *You'll Catch Your Death*, Collins, 1940 (d/j)

David Hume, *Stand Up and Fight*, Collins, 1941 (d/j)

David Hume, *Destiny is my Name*, Collins, 1942 (d/j)

David Hume, *Mick Cardby Works Overtime*, Collins, 2/1944 (d/j)

Richard Le Gallienne, *Pieces of Eight*, Collins, 1954 (d/j and b&w frontis, replaced with colour frontis for 1955 reprint); reissued as Richard Le Gallienne, *Pieces of Eight*, The Children's Press, 1957 (d/j)

Stephen Maddock, *Date With a Spy*, Collins, 1941 (d/j)

Elsie J Oxenham, *The Abbey Girls*, Collins, 1937 (d/j, unsigned; section also used as colour frontis)

Elsie J Oxenham, *The Abbey Girls Again*, Collins, 1937 (d/j, unsigned; section also used as colour frontis)

Elsie J Oxenham, *The Girls of the Abbey School*, Collins, 1937 (d/j, unsigned; section also used as colour frontis)

Elsie J Oxenham, *The Abbey Girls go Back to School*, Collins, 1938 (d/j, unsigned; section also used as colour frontis)

Elsie J Oxenham, *Jen of the Abbey School*, Collins, 1938 (d/j, unsigned; section also used as colour frontis)

Elsie J Oxenham, *The New Abbey Girls*, Collins, 1938 (d/j, unsigned; section also used as colour frontis)

Elsie J Oxenham, *The Abbey Girls on Trial*, Collins, 1938 (d/j, unsigned; section also used as colour frontis)

Elsie J Oxenham, *The Abbey Girls Win Through*, Collins, 1938 (d/j, unsigned, probably by Heade; section also used as colour frontis)

Elsie J Oxenham, *The Abbey Girls at Home*, 1938 (d/j, unsigned, possibly by Heade; section also used as colour frontis)

Elsie J Oxenham, *Secrets of the Abbey*, Collins, 1939 (d/j, unsigned but credited, and 3 b&w illus)

Elsie J Oxenham, *Stowaways in the Abbey*, Collins, 1940 (d/j, unsigned but credited, and 3 b&w illus)

Elsie J Oxenham, *Jandy Mac Comes Back*, Collins, 1941 (d/j and 3 b&w illus)

Elsie J Oxenham, *Maid of the Abbey*, Collins, 1943 (d/j, unsigned but credited, and 3 b&w illus); reissued as Elsie J Oxenham, *Maid of the Abbey*, 1949 (d/j, unsigned but credited, with new colour frontis but no b&w illus)

Marjorie M Price, *Jenny Wren*, Collins, 1943 (d/j)

Marjorie Price, *Episode by Moonlight*, Collins, 1947 (d/j)

Mary Raymond, *Paradise is Here*, Collins, 1953 (d/j)

Renée Shann, *Lady in Waiting*, Collins, 1936 (d/j)

Renée Shann, *We Sail To-Night*, Collins, 1940 (d/j)

Renée Shann, *Whose Husband?*, Collins, 1948 (d/j)

Renée Shann, *Off the Main Road*, Collins White Circle 361R, 1950 (p/b)

Wade Smith, *Wild Country*, Collins White Circle Pocket Edition CD388 (Canada), 1949 (adapted p/b, unsigned); repurposed by a different artist from Norman Fox, *The Rider from Yonder*, Collins, 1948 (d/j)

Lyndon Snow, *Follow Your Star*, Collins, 1941 (d/j)

Thelma Strabel, *Search for a Hero*, Collins, 1942 (duotone d/j)

Christine Strathern, *Lovers' Knot*, Collins, 1948 (d/j)

Doreen Swinburne, *Jean Tours a Hospital*, Collins, 1943 (d/j and b&w frontis)

Betty Trask, *Love Has No Limit*, Collins, 1939 (d/j, unsigned)

J M Walsh, *Spies from the Skies*, Collins, 1941 (d/j)

Pamela Wynne, *Life is for Loving*, Collins, 1949 (d/j)

Pamela Wynne, *Forsaking All Other*, Collins, 1949 (d/j, unsigned)

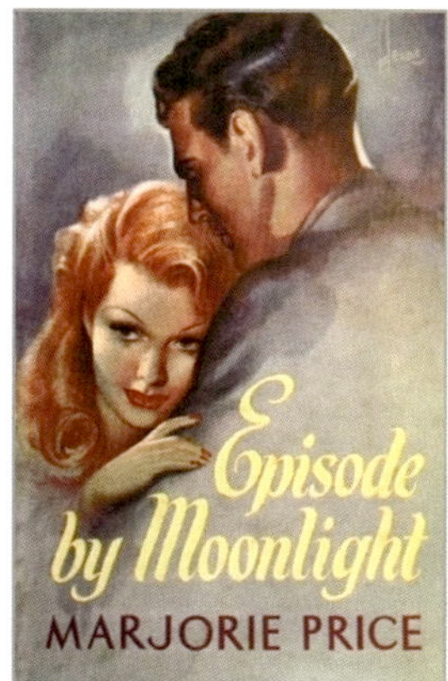

Curtis Warren / Hamilton & Co / Grant Hughes

Nick Baroni, *Manhattan Honey*, Curtis Warren, c1950 (adapted p/b); repurposed from Earl Ellison, *Love Wore a Fez*, Grant Hughes, c1947 (p/b)

Ursula Bloom, *Alien Corn*, Hamilton & Co, 1947 (d/j)

Jeff Bogar, *Lady from Hades*, Hamilton & Co, c1951 (adapted p/b); repurposed from Michael Hervey, *Dark Waterfront*, Hamilton & Co, 1947 (p/b)

Benson Cabot, *Blue Smoke for My Lovely!*, c1950 (adapted p/b); repurposed from Anon (ed.), *Innocent Confessions*, Grant Hughes, c1947 (periodical cover)

Bart Carson, *Death Wore Scanties!*, Hamilton & Co, c1950 (adapted p/b); repurposed from N Wesley Firth, *Night Secrets*, Grant Hughes, c1948 (p/b)

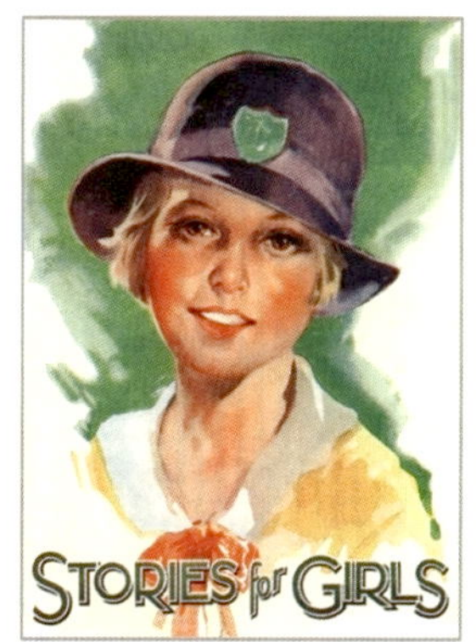

Earl Ellison, *Love Wore a Fez*, Grant Hughes, c1947 (p/b); repurposed for Nick Baroni, *Manhattan Honey*, Curtis Warren, c1949 (adapted p/b)

Earl Ellison, *Desert Intrigue*, Hamilton & Co, 7/1949 (p/b)

N Wesley Firth, *Night Secrets*, Grant Hughes, c1948 (p/b); repurposed for Bart Carson, *Death Wore Scanties*, Hamilton & Co, c1950 (adapted p/b)

Michael Hervey, *Dark Waterfront*, Hamilton & Co, 1947 (p/b); repurposed for Jeff Bogar, *Lady from Hades*, Hamilton & Co, c1951 (adapted p/b)

Norman Lazenby, *Yellow Cargo*, Grant Hughes, 1947 (p/b)

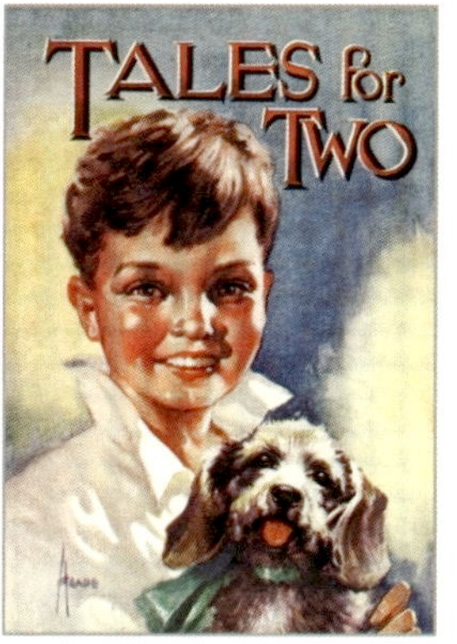

Dean & Son / DLMS

Anon (ed.), *Stories for Girls*, Dean & Son, 1934 (pictorial boards, unsigned)

Anon (ed.), *Tales for Two*, Dean & Son, 1934 (pictorial boards)

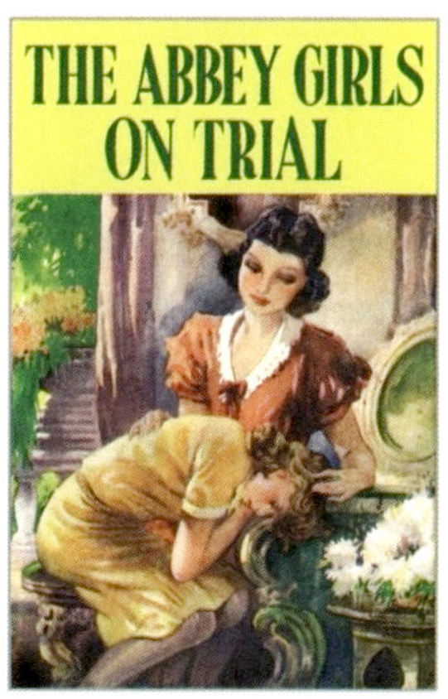

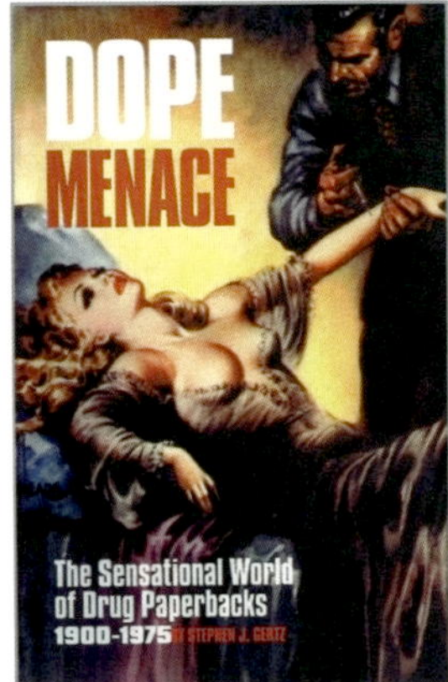

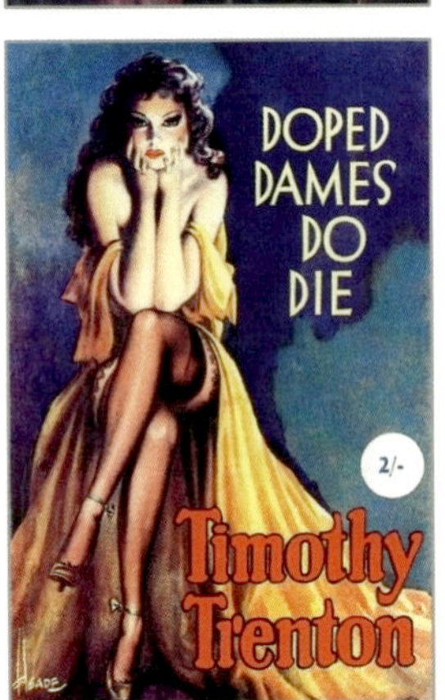

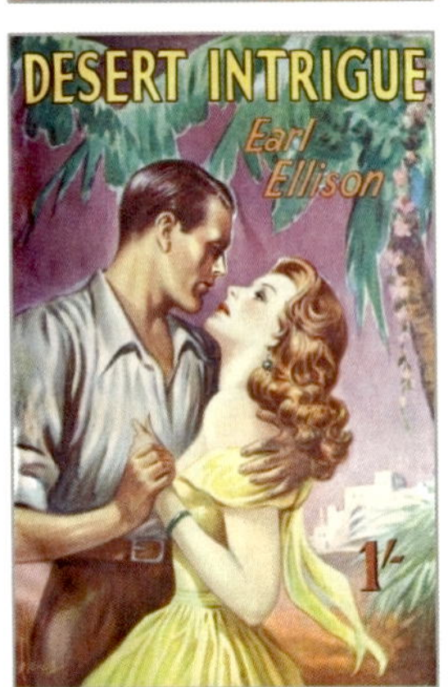

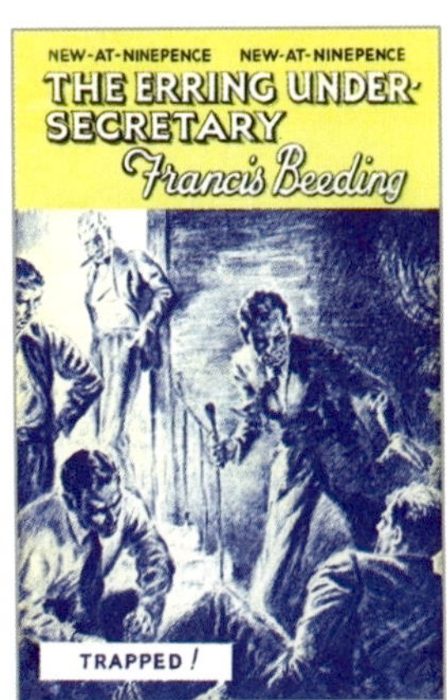

Anon (ed.), *Girls' Book of Stories*, DLMS, 1934 (pictorial boards); repurposed for *Every Girl's Story Book*, Dean & Son, 1937 (adapted pictorial boards)

Anon (ed.), *Every Girl's Story Book*, Dean & Son, 1937 (adapted pictorial boards); repurposed from Anon (ed.), *Girls' Book of Stories*, DLMS, 1934 (pictorial boards)

Anon (ed.), *Monster Book for Boys*, Dean & Son, 1943 (pictorial boards)

Faber & Faber

Anon (ed.), *My Best Adventure Story*, Faber & Faber, 1934 (d/j)
Anon (ed.), *My Best Thriller*, Faber & Faber, c1934 (d/j)
Anon (ed.), *My Best Animal Story*, Faber & Faber, 1935 (d/j)
N Warner Hooke, *Striplings*, Faber & Faber, 1933 (d/j)
F O Mann, *Albert Grope*, Faber & Faber, 2/1931 (d/j)
Dermot Morrah, *The Mummy Case*, Faber & Faber, 1933 (d/j)
Margaret Seaton Wagner, *The Monster of Dusseldorf*, Faber & Faber, 1932 (d/j)

Feral House

Stephen J Gertz, *Dope Menace*, Feral House, 2008 (adapted p/b); repurposed from Roland Vane, *Vice Rackets of Soho*, Archer, 1950 (p/b)

Foulsham

Anon (ed.), *Foulsham's New Party Book*, Foulsham, c1934

Frederick Muller

Harry Sinclair Drago, *Stage Coach Kingdom*, Frederick Muller, 1944 (d/j)
W H B Kent, *The Tenderfoot*, Frederick Muller, 1945 (d/j)

Galliard

Timothy Trenton, *Lady, Your Gun's Showing*, Galliard, c1952 (p/b)
Timothy Trenton, *Doped Dames Do Die*, Galliard, c1952 (p/b)

G B London

Anon (ed.), *9 Stories*, G B London/Fairylite, 1942 (pictorial front and back covers, 14 colour illus)

George G Harrap

Aylmer Hall, *The K.F. Conspiracy*, George G Harrap, 12/1955 (d/j; also reused without lettering as colour frontis)

Hodder & Stoughton

Jennifer Ames, *Stranger Sweetheart*, Hodder & Stoughton, 1939 (d/j)
Jennifer Ames, *Make the Man Notice You*, Hodder & Stoughton, 1940 (d/j)
Jennifer Ames, *Ring Without Romance*, Hodder & Stoughton, 1940 (d/j)
Ruby M Ayres, *Too Much Together*, Hodder & Stoughton Yellow Jacket, 1936 (d/j)
Ruby M Ayres, *The Black Sheep*, Hodder & Stoughton Yellow Jacket, c1936 (d/j)
Ruby M Ayres, *The Story of an Ugly Man*, Hodder & Stoughton, 1937 (d/j)
Ruby M Ayres, *And Still They Dream*, Hodder & Stoughton, 1939 (d/j); reissued as Ruby M Ayres, *And Still They Dream*, Hodder & Stoughton Yellow Jacket, 1953 (adapted p/b); reissued again as Ruby M Ayres, *And Still They Dream*, Hodder & Stoughton, 1962 (adapted p/b)
Francis Beeding, *The Erring Under-Secretary*, Hodder & Stoughton, 1937 (duotone p/b, with two b&w frontis)
Leslie Charteris, *Once More the Saint*, Hodder & Stoughton Yellow Jacket, 1935 (d/j, unsigned, possibly by Heade)
Victor Bridges, *The Gulls Fly Low*, Hodder & Stoughton, 1943 (d/j)
May Christie, *The Whirlwind Lover*, Hodder & Stoughton Yellow Jacket, c1937 (d/j)
May Christie, *Accent on Love*, Hodder & Stoughton, 1939 (d/j)
May Christie, *The Affairs of Patricia*, Hodder & Stoughton, c1942 d/j)
Molly Clavering, *Because of Sam*, Hodder & Stoughton, 1954 (d/j *)
Dorothy Clewes, *Merry-Go-Round*, Hodder & Stoughton, 1954 (d/j, unsigned)
O Douglas, *Jane's Parlour*, Hodder & Stoughton, 1937 (duotone d/j, b&w frontis and 3 b&w illus); reissued as O Douglas, *Jane's Parlour*, Hodder & Stoughton Yellow Jacket, 1940 (adapted d/j)

O Douglas, *The House That is Our Own*, Hodder & Stoughton, 1940 (d/j)

O Douglas, *Penny Plain*, Hodder & Stoughton Yellow Jacket, 1947 (d/j)

Anne Stanton Drew, *The Capable Girl*, Hodder & Stoughton, 1937 (d/j)

Loula Grace Erdman, *The Years of the Locust*, Hodder & Stoughton, 1948 (d/j)

Loula Grace Erdman, *Lonely Passage*, Hodder & Stoughton, 1950 (d/j)

Elizabeth Frayne, *A Year With Juliet*, Hodder & Stoughton, 1937 (d/j)

Elizabeth Frayne, *Champagne in Spring*, Hodder & Stoughton, 1938 (d/j)

Elizabeth Frayne, *This Blind Rose*, Hodder & Stoughton, 1940 (d/j)

Elizabeth Frayne, *Life Goes On,* Hodder & Stoughton, 1941 (d/j)

Elizabeth Frayne, *Still Do I Love*, Hodder & Stoughton, 1942 (d/j, unsigned)

George Goodchild, *McLean Intervenes*, Hodder & Stoughton, 1939 (d/j †)

George Goodchild, *Again McLean*, Hodder & Stoughton Yellow Jacket, 1939 (d/j)

Maysie Greig, *Retreat from Love*, Hodder & Stoughton, 1937 (d/j, unsigned, possibly by Heade)

Maysie Greig, *Young Man Without Money*, Hodder & Stoughton, 1938 (d/j); reissued as Maysie Greig, *Young Man Without Money*, Hodder & Stoughton Yellow Jacket, 1940 (adapted d/j, unsigned)

Maysie Greig, *Girl on His Hands*, Hodder & Stoughton, 1939 (d/j); reissued as Maysie Greig, *Girl on His Hands*, Hodder & Stoughton Yellow Jacket, c1940 (adapted d/j)

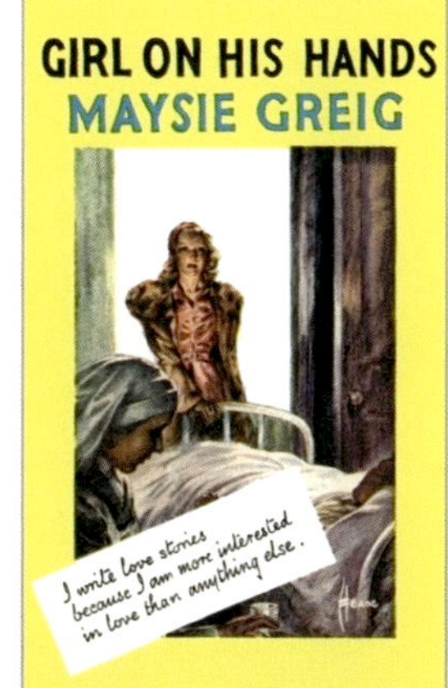

Zane Grey, *West of the Pecos*, Hodder & Stoughton, 1937 (d/j); reissued as Zane Grey, *West of the Pecos*, Hodder & Stoughton Yellow Jacket, 1940 (adapted d/j)

Zane Grey, *Code of the West*, Hodder & Stoughton Yellow Jacket, 1937 (d/j); reissued as Zane Grey, *Code of the West*, Hodder & Stoughton, 1955 (adapted p/b); reissued again as Zane Grey, *Code of the West*, Hodder & Stoughton, 1957 (adapted d/j); reissued again as Zane Grey, *Code of the West*, Hodder & Stoughton, 1962 (adapted p/b)

Zane Grey, *Raiders of Spanish Peaks*, Hodder & Stoughton Yellow Jacket, 1940 (d/j)

Ernest Haycox, *Man in the Saddle*, Hodder & Stoughton, 1939 (d/j)

David Lyall, *Love is of the Valley*, Hodder & Stoughton, 1936 (d/j)

David Lyall, *The Hidden Riches*, Hodder & Stoughton, 1937 (d/j)

Arthur Mee, *Salute the King*, Hodder & Stoughton, 2/1937 (duotone d/j)

Concordia Merrel, *Julia Takes Her Chance*, Hodder & Stoughton Yellow Jacket, c1937 (d/j)

Alice Duer Miller, *Five Little Heiresses*, Hodder & Stoughton, 11/1936 (d/j and b&w frontis)

Alice Duer Miller, *The Charm School*, Hodder & Stoughton, 1936 (d/j and b&w frontis)

Margaret Pedler, *Green Judgment*, Hodder & Stoughton, 8/1934 (d/j)

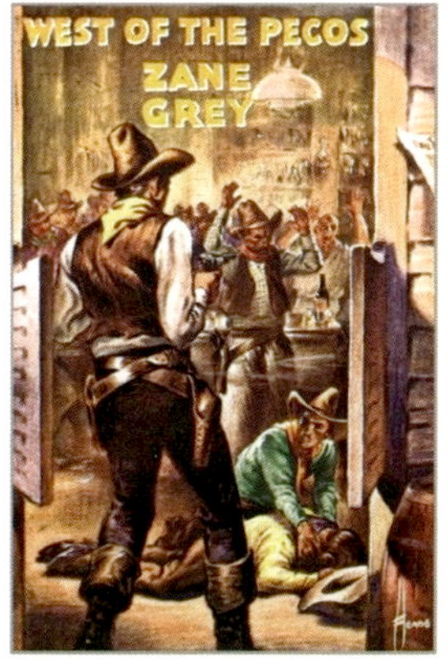

Margaret Pedler, *Flame in the Wind*, Hodder & Stoughton, 1937 (d/j); reissued as Margaret Pedler, *Flame in the Wind*, Hodder & Stoughton Yellow Jacket, 1938 (adapted d/j); reissued again as Margaret Pedler, *Flame in the Wind*, Hodder & Stoughton Yellow Jacket, 1953 (further adapted d/j)

Margaret Pedler, *No Armour Against Fate*, Hodder & Stoughton, 1938 (d/j); reissued as Margaret Pedler, *No Armour Against Fate*, Hodder & Stoughton Yellow Jacket, 1940 (adapted d/j); reissued again as Margaret Pedler, *No Armour Against Fate*, 1958 (adapted p/b)

William MacLeod Raine, *Cool Customer*, Hodder & Stoughton, 1937 (d/j), reissued as William MacLeod Raine, *Cool Customer*, Hodder & Stoughton Yellow Jacket, c1940 (adapted d/j), reissued again as William MacLeod Rain, *Cool Customer*, Hodder & Stoughton, 1954 (adapted p/b)

William MacLeod Raine, *Riders of the Rim Rocks*, Hodder & Stoughton, 1940 (d/j), reissued as William MacLeod Raine, *Riders of the Rim Rocks*, Hodder & Stoughton Yellow Jacket, c1940 (adapted d/j)

Berta Ruck, *Handmaid to Fame*, Hodder & Stoughton, 1938 (d/j)

Annie S Swan, *Woven of the Wind*, Hodder & Stoughton Yellow Jacket, c1936 (d/j)

Annie S Swan, *Mary Garth*, Hodder & Stoughton Yellow Jacket, c1937 (d/j)

Annie S Swan, *Omnibus of Romance*, Hodder & Stoughton, 1937 (d/j)

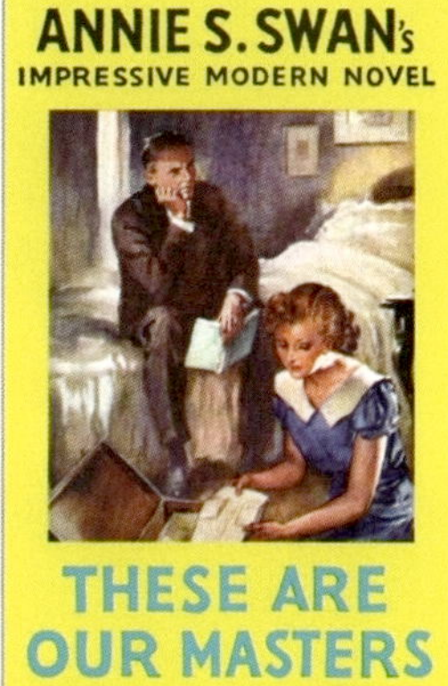

Annie S Swan, *These Are Our Masters*, Hodder & Stoughton, 1939 (d/j, unsigned); reissued as Annie S Swan, *These Are Our Masters*, Hodder & Stoughton Yellow Jacket, 1940 (adapted d/j, unsigned)

Annie S Swan, *The Road to Damascus*, Hodder & Stoughton, 1/1940 (d/j)

Taffrail, *The Sub*, Hodder & Stoughton Yellow Jacket, 1937 (d/j)

Taffrail, *Fred Travis, A.B.*, Hodder & Stoughton, 1939 (d/j), reissued as Taffrail, *Fred Travis, A.B.*, Hodder & Stoughton Yellow Jacket, 1940 (adapted d/j)

Marjorie Hessell Tiltman, *Cock's Nest*, Hodder & Stoughton, 1954 (d/j)

Seldon Truss, *She Could Take Care*, Hodder & Stoughton, (duotone p/b, with two b&w frontis)

Elizabeth Vernon, *Invitation to Stay*, Hodder & Stoughton, 1936 (d/j)

Elizabeth Vernon, *Tony*, Hodder & Stoughton, 12/7/1937 (d/j)

Elizabeth Vernon, *Wild Bird*, Hodder & Stoughton, 1940 (d/j)

Patricia Wentworth, *The Blind Side*, Hodder & Stoughton, 1939 (d/j, unsigned, probably by Heade †); reprinted as Patricia Wentworth, *The Blind Side*, Hodder & Stoughton, 1955 (adapted p/b, unsigned, probably by Heade)

Phyllis Waite, *Challenge to Candia*, Hodder & Stoughton, 26/7/1937 (d/j)

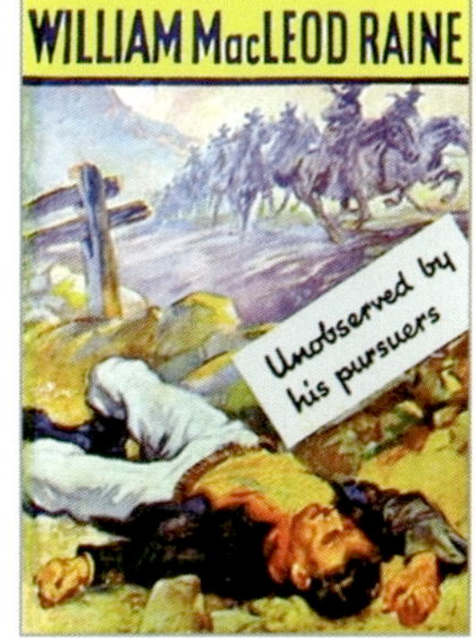

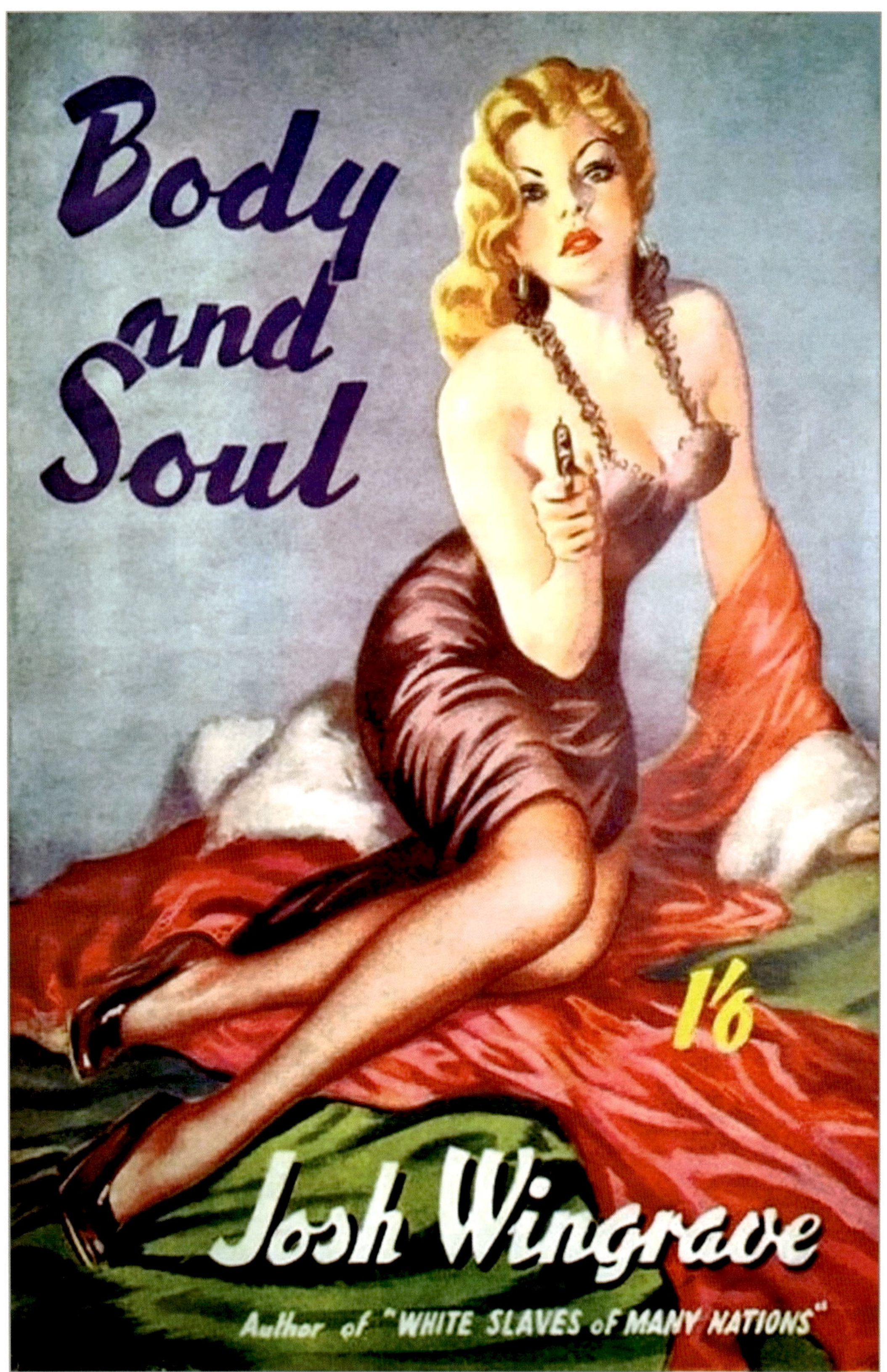

Body and Soul by Josh Wingrave (Kaye Publications, 1952). (Image courtesy David Allsberry.)

F E Mills Young, *Unlucky Farm*, Hodder & Stoughton, 1937 (d/j)

Hurst & Blackett

Janet Gordon, *Just Off Bond Street*, Hurst & Blackett, 1940 (d/j)
Frances Shelley Wees, *Lost House*, Hurst & Blackett, 1939 (d/j)

Hutchinson & Co

Mabel Barnes-Grundy, *Pippa*, Hutchinson's Famous Sixpenny Novels no. 415, c1932 (p/b, unsigned, possibly by Heade); repurposed for Lucas Cleeve, *A Double Marriage*, Jarrolds, c1932 (d/j, unsigned, possibly by Heade †)
Isabel C Clarke, *Family Symphony*, Hutchinson & Co, c1937 (d/j, unsigned)
Charles Garvice, *Miss Estcourt*, Hutchinson Five Star Library, c1932, (p/b)
E W Savi, *The Insolence of Youth*, Hutchinson's Pocket Library no. 22, c1936 (p/b)
Constance M White, *Schoolgirl Reporter*, Hutchinson & Co, 1953 (d/j)

Ivor Nicholson & Watson

Denise Robbins, *Those Who Love*, Ivor Nicholson & Watson, 6/1936 (d/j)
Eve St John-Loe, *Who Feeds the Tiger ...*, Ivor Nicholson & Watson, 1935 (d/j)

Jarrolds

Margaret Brash, *The Treasure of Akor*, Jarrolds, 1946 (d/j, unsigned, probably by Heade)
Lucas Cleeve, *A Double Marriage*, Jarrolds, c1932 (d/j, unsigned, possibly by Heade †); repurposed from Mabel Barnes-Grundy, *Pippa*, Hutchinson's Famous Sixpenny Novels no. 415, c1932 (p/b, unsigned, possibly by Heade)

John Hamilton

David Lindsay, *The Two Red Capsules*, John Hamilton, 1936 (monochrome d/j)

John Gifford

S J Coe, *Crimes of Love, Passion and Poison*, John Gifford, 1952 (d/j)

Juvenile Productions

Anon (ed.), *Wonderland A.B.C.*, Juvenile Productions, c1949 (pictorial boards)
Anon (ed.), *The Children's Picture Dictionary*, Juvenile Productions, 1950 (pictorial boards)

Kaye Publications

André Latour, *Shameless*, Kaye Publications, 1953 (p/b, unsigned, possibly by Heade)
Josh Wingrave, *Body and Soul*, Kaye Publications, 1952 (p/b, unsigned, probably by Heade)

Leisure Library Co.

William Le Queux, *The Under Secretary*, Crime Readers' Library Series no. 22, 1937 (p/b)

Longmans

Mary Renault, *Purposes of Love*, Longmans, 1/1939 (d/j)

Lutterworth

L V Davidson, *The Two Gangs*, Lutterworth, 1947 (duotone d/j and b&w frontis)
Nesta Grant, *On the Run*, Lutterworth, 1948 (duotone d/j and b&w frontis)
Eileen Heming, *Brenda's Home-Coming*, Lutterworth, 1947 (duotone d/j and b&w frontis)
Rupert Jardine, *Lost on Safari*, Lutterworth, 1949 (duotone d/j; also used, without lettering, as b&w frontis)
Captain W E Johns, *Worrals of the W.A.A.F.*, Lutterworth, 1948 (d/j; section also used as colour frontis); reissued by the same publisher in 1950 as 'New Illustrated Edition', some printings of which included four additional duotone illustrations (unsigned, possibly by Heade)
Captain W E Johns, *Worrals Carries On*, Lutterworth, 1948 (d/j; section also used as colour frontis); reissued by the same publisher in 1950 as 'New Illustrated Edition', some printings of which included four additional duotone illustrations (unsigned, possibly by Heade)

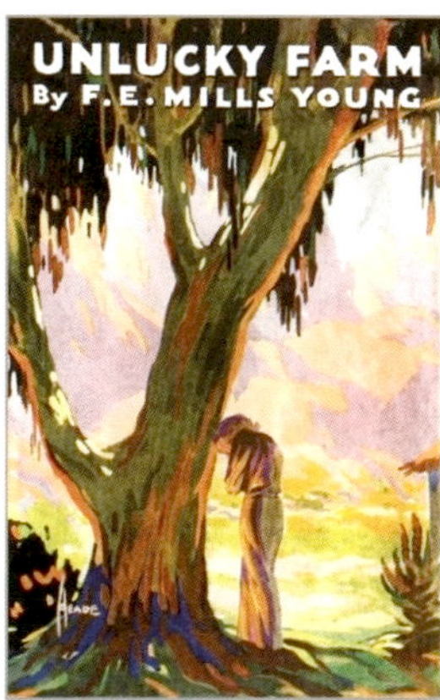
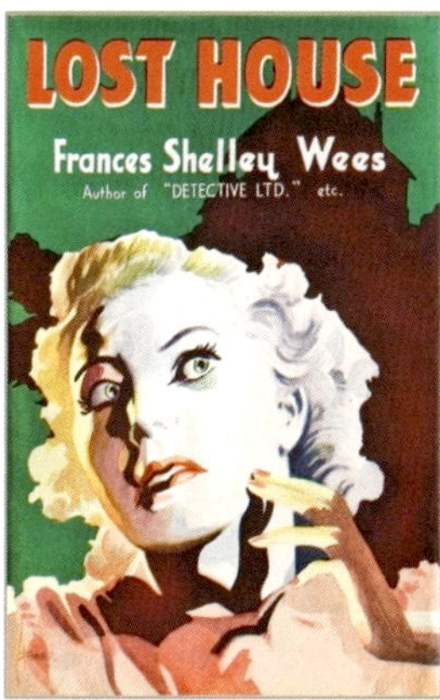
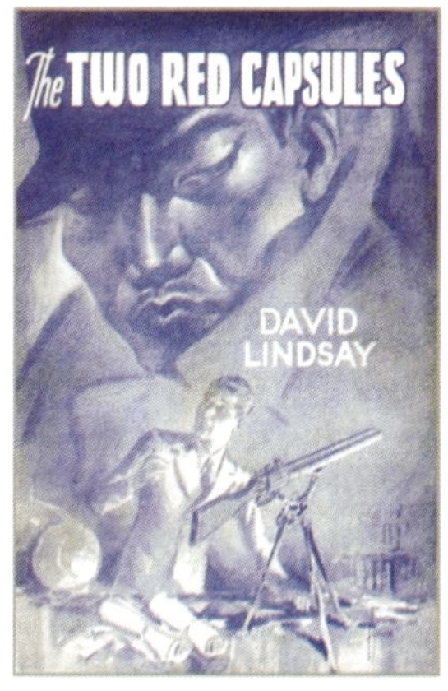
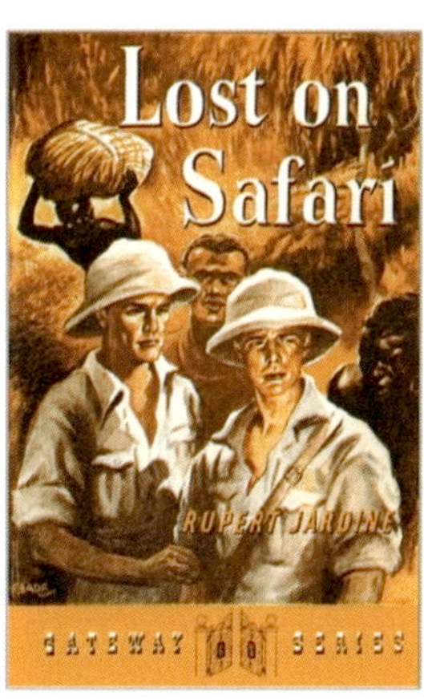

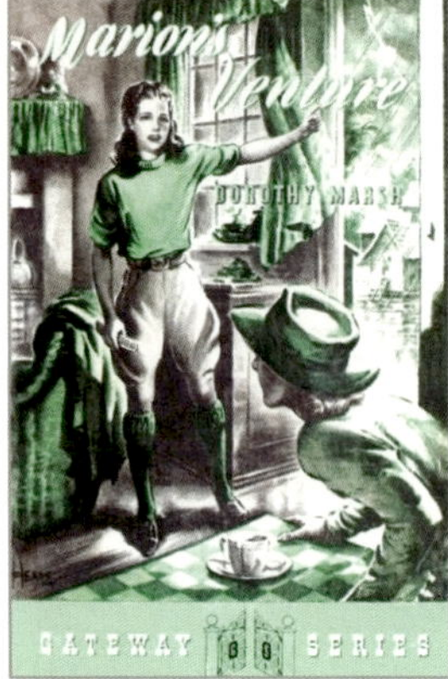

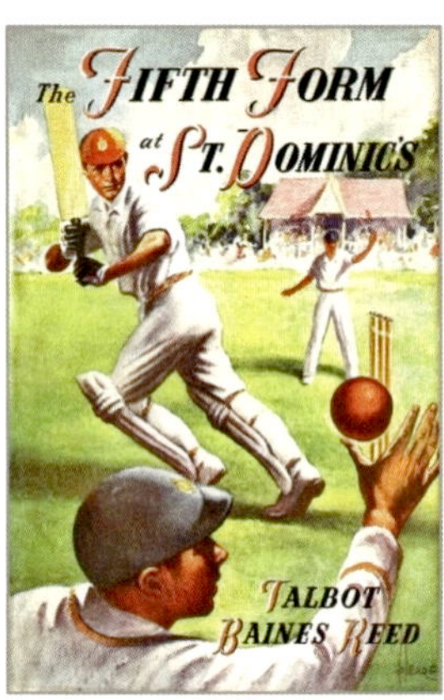

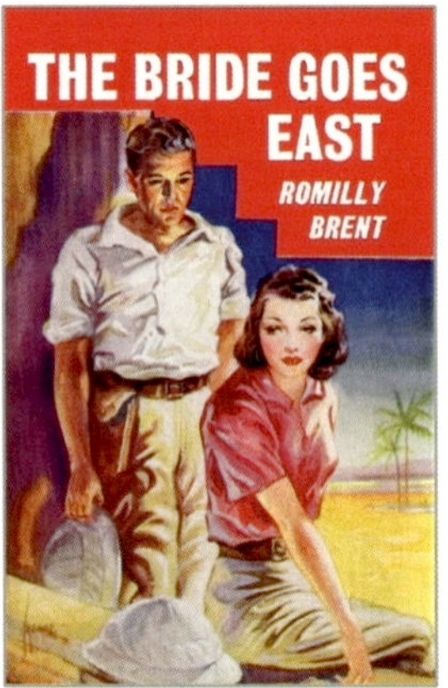

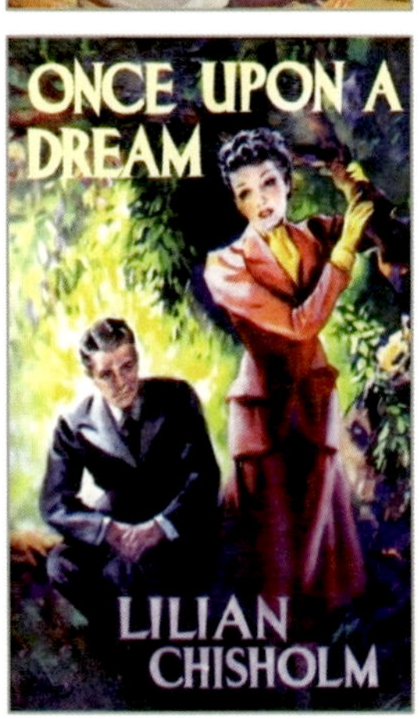

Captain W E Johns, *Worrals Down Under*, Lutterworth, 10/1948 (d/j; section also used as colour frontis); reissued by the same publisher in 1950 as 'New Illustrated Edition', some printings of which included four additional duotone illustrations (unsigned, possibly by Heade)

Captain W E Johns, *Worrals in the Wastelands*, Lutterworth, 1/1949 (d/j; section also used as colour frontis); reissued by the same publisher in 1950 as 'New Illustrated Edition', some printings of which included four additional duotone illustrations (unsigned, possibly by Heade); also reissued as French-language translation, Captain W E Johns, *Le Lac Maudit*, Presses de la Cité (France), 1950 (adapted d/j)

Captain W E Johns, *Worrals Goes Afoot*, Lutterworth, 8/1949 (d/j; section also used as colour frontis); reissued as French-language translation, Captain W E Johns, *Le Démon des Sables*, Presses de la Cité (France), 1950 (adapted d/j)

Captain W E Johns, *Worrals Investigates*, Lutterworth, 7/1950 (d/j; section also used as colour frontis); some printings included four additional duotone illustrations (unsigned, possibly by Heade)

Sylvia Little, *Castle School on Holiday*, Lutterworth, 1948 (d/j; section also used as colour frontis)

Sylvia Little, *Castle School on the Screen*, Lutterworth, 1949 (d/j, unsigned; section also used as colour frontis)

Sylvia Little, *Blood Royal at Castle School*, Lutterworth, 1949 (d/j, unsigned; section also used as colour frontis)

Sylvia Little, *Castle School in the News*, Lutterworth, 1950 (d/j; section also used as colour frontis)

Sylvia Little, *Castle School on the War Path*, Lutterworth, 1950 (d/j; section also used as colour frontis)

Sylvia Little, *Castle School at the Cross-Roads*, Lutterworth, 1950 (d/j; section also used as colour frontis)

Dorothy Marsh, *Marion's Venture*, Lutterworth, 1948 (duotone d/j; also used, without lettering, as b&w frontis)

Talbot Baines Reed, *The Fifth Form at St. Dominic's*, Lutterworth, 1948 (d/j and colour frontis)

Mills & Boon

Juliet Armstrong, *When Other Lips*, Mills & Boon, 1940 (d/j, unsigned)

Juliet Armstrong, *Stars in Ambush*, Mills & Boon, 1943 (d/j)

Juliet Armstrong, *Who Pays the Piper–!*, Mills & Boon, 1943 (d/j)

Juliet Armstrong, *Lonely No More*, Mills & Boon, 1944 (d/j, unsigned)

Juliet Armstrong, *Single Ticket*, Mills & Boon, 1952 (d/j); repurposed from an earlier Mills & Boon book, author and title currently unidentified (d/j)

Juliet Armstrong, *The Singing Flame*, Mills & Boon, 1954 (d/j, unsigned, possibly by Heade); repurposed from an earlier Mills & Boon book, author and title currently unidentified

Juliet Armstrong, *The Charmed Circle*, Mills & Boon, 1957 (adapted d/j); repurposed from an earlier Mills & Boon book by the same author, title currently unidentified (d/j)

Joan Blair, *Love Leads to the Stars*, Mills & Boon, 1942 (d/j, unsigned)

Joan Blair, *Rose by Another Name*, Mills & Boon, 1945 (d/j)

Joan Blair, *Love and Sister Lorna*, Mills & Boon, 1955 (d/j); repurposed from an earlier Mills & Boon book by the same author, title currently unidentified (d/j)

Nina Bradshaw, *The Short Chain*, Mills & Boon, 8/1940 (d/j, unsigned)

Romilly Brent, *The Bride Goes East*, Mills & Boon, 1946 (adapted d/j); repurposed from an earlier Mills & Boon book, author and title currently unidentified (d/j); same artwork also used for Marjorie Moore, *Gone Away*, Mills & Boon, 1954 (adapted d/j)

Mary Burchell, *Wife to Christopher*, Mills & Boon, 1936 (d/j, unsigned, possibly by Heade)

Mary Burchell, *Cinderella After Midnight*, Mills & Boon, 1942 (d/j †)

Mary Burchell, *Nobody Asked Me*, Mills & Boon, 1952 (adapted d/j); repurposed from Phyllis Mannin, *Fugitive Heart*, Mills & Boon, 1941 (d/j)

Mary Burchell, *Cinderella After Midnight*, Mills & Boon, 1959 (new d/j); repurposed from an earlier Mills & Boon book, author and title currently unidentified (d/j)

Fay Chandos, *When We Two Parted*, Mills & Boon, 1940 (d/j); repurposed for Fay Chandos, *Three Roads to Romance*, Mills & Boon, 1959 (adapted d/j)

Fay Chandos, *Three Roads to Romance*, Mills & Boon, 1959 (adapted d/j); repurposed from Fay Chandos, *When We Two Parted*, Mills & Boon, 1940 (d/j)

Lilian Chisholm, *Once Upon a Dream*, Mills & Boon, 1944 (d/j)

Lilian Chisholm, *Vagabond Lover*, Mills & Boon, 1942 (d/j †); reissued as Lilian Chisholm, *Vagabond Lover*, Mills & Boon, 1956 (d/j)

Lilian Chisholm, *Afraid to Dream*, Mills & Boon, 1955 (adapted d/j); repurposed from an earlier Mills & Boon book by the same author, title currently unidentified (d/j)

Cicely Colpitts, *If She Had Known*, Mills & Boon, 9/1940 (d/j)

Cicely Colpitts, *Wishing for the Moon*, Mills & Boon, 1942 (d/j)

Cicely Colpitts, *Jill Paid*, Mills & Boon, 1942 (d/j)

Cicely Colpitts, *Chains That Bind You*, Mills & Boon, 1943 (d/j)

Cicely Colpitts, *Loving You So*, Mills & Boon, 1943 (d/j, unsigned)

Constance M Evans, *A Lover from London*, Mills & Boon, 6/1940 (d/j)

Constance M Evans, *Temptation in Silver*, Mills & Boon, 1941 (d/j)

Constance M Evans, *Bachelor Aunt*, Mills & Boon, 1957 (d/j); repurposed from an earlier Mills & Boon book, author and title currently unidentified (d/j)

Eleanor Farnes, *The Doctor's Wife*, Mills & Boon, 1943 (d/j, unsigned)

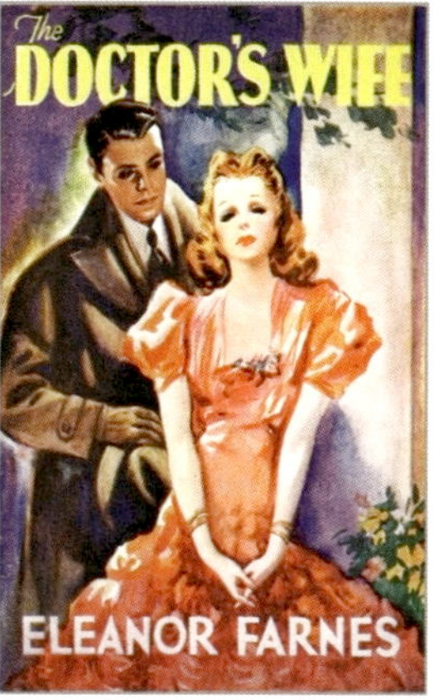

Eleanor Farnes, *Merry Goes the Time*, Mills & Boon, 1953 (adapted d/j, unsigned); repurposed from an earlier Mills & Boon book, author and title currently unidentified (d/j)

Eleanor Farnes, *Brief Excursion*, Mills & Boon, 1944 (d/j)

Errol Fitzgerald, *Prisoners of Love*, Mills & Boon, 1940 (d/j)

Errol Fitzgerald, *Flight from Marriage*, Mills & Boon, 1941 (d/j, unsigned)

Errol Fitzgerald, *The Hidden Heiress*, Mills & Boon, 1942 (d/j)

Errol Fitzgerald, *Forbidden Flame*, Mills & Boon, 1943 (d/j)

Errol Fitzgerald, *The Secret Tenant*, Mills & Boon, 1943 (d/j, unsigned)

Barbara Hedworth, *Song of My Heart*, Mills & Boon, 1940 (d/j)

Barbara Hedworth, *Dreams Sometimes Come True*, Mills & Boon, 1941 (d/j)

Barbara Hedworth, *Once You Cared*, Mills & Boon, 1941 (d/j)

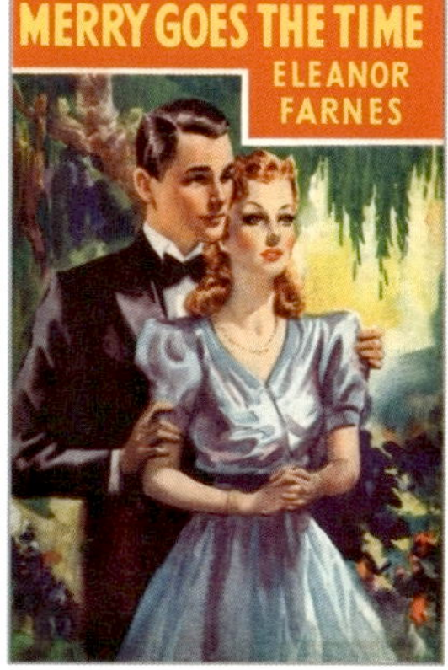

Barbara Hedworth, *All That We Share*, Mills & Boon, 1942 (d/j)

Barbara Hedworth, *Tomorrow's Sunrise*, Mills & Boon, 1943 (d/j)

Maureen Heeley, *Disguised Angel*, Mills & Boon, 1/1940 (d/j)

Maureen Heeley, *Clarion Call*, Mills & Boon, 7/1940 (d/j, unsigned)

Elizabeth Hoy, *Hearts at Random*, Mills & Boon, 1942 (d/j, unsigned)

Susan Inglis, *Because I Love You*, Mills & Boon, 1940 (d/j, unsigned)

Susan Inglis, *This Foolish Heart*, Mills & Boon, 1940 (d/j)

Vina Lawrence, *The Love Bargain*, Mills & Boon, 1956 (d/j); repurposed from an earlier Mills & Boon book, author and title currently unidentified (d/j)

Annabel Lee, *Divorce Without Drama*, Mills & Boon, 1940 (d/j)

Annabel Lee, *Love Brings Surprises*, Mills & Boon, 1941 (d/j)

Margaret Lovell, *The Girl from the Beauty Shop*, Mills & Boon, 8/1939 (d/j)

Margaret Lovell, *Roseanne Regrets*, Mills & Boon, 1940 (d/j)

Margaret Lovell, *Second Chance of Happiness*, Mills & Boon, 1940 (d/j)

Jean S MacLeod, *Forbidden Rapture*, Mills & Boon, 1941 (d/j)

Jean S MacLeod, *The Reckless Pilgrim*, Mills & Boon, 1941 (d/j)

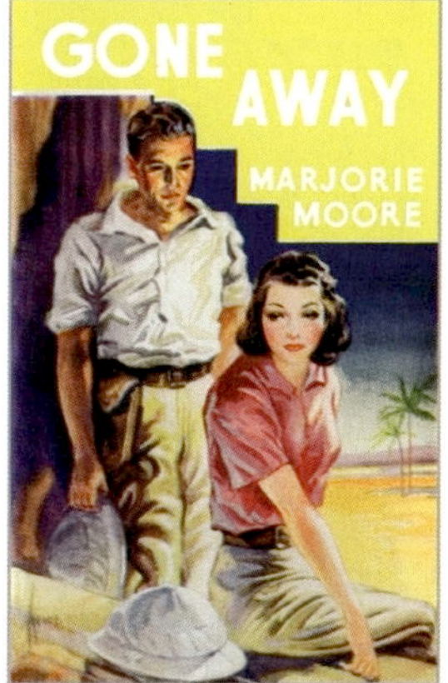

Jean S MacLeod, *Blind Journey*, Mills & Boon, 1942 (d/j); repurposed for Jean S MacLeod, *Return to Spring*, Mills & Boon, 1954 (adapted d/j)

Jean S MacLeod, *Penalty for Living*, Mills & Boon, 1942 (d/j)

Jean S MacLeod, *Reluctant Folly*, Mills & Boon, 1942 (d/j †)

Jean S MacLeod, *Return to Spring*, Mills & Boon, 1954 (adapted d/j); repurposed from Jean S MacLeod, *Blind Journey*, Mills & Boon, 1942 (d/j)

Margaret Malcolm, *One Stopped at Home*, Mills & Boon, 1941 (d/j)

Margaret Malcolm, *Where Fairy Tales End*, Mills & Boon, 1941 (d/j)

Margaret Malcolm, *Number 4 Victoria Terrace*, Mills & Boon, 1944 (d/j)

Margaret Malcolm, *The Master of Normanhurst*, Mills & Boon, 1944 (d/j, unsigned); repurposed for Margaret Malcolm, *Love Without Wings*, Mills & Boon, 1953 (adapted d/j, unsigned)

Margaret Malcolm, *Love Without Wings*, Mills & Boon, 1953 (adapted d/j, unsigned); repurposed from Margaret Malcolm, *The Master of Normanhurst*, Mills & Boon, 1944 (d/j, unsigned)

Phyllis Mannin, *Fugitive Heart*, Mills & Boon, 1941 (d/j), repurposed for Mary Burchell, *Nobody Asked Me*, Mills & Boon, 1952 (adapted d/j)

Phyllis Mannin, *Tamed Rebel*, Mills & Boon, 1941 (d/j)

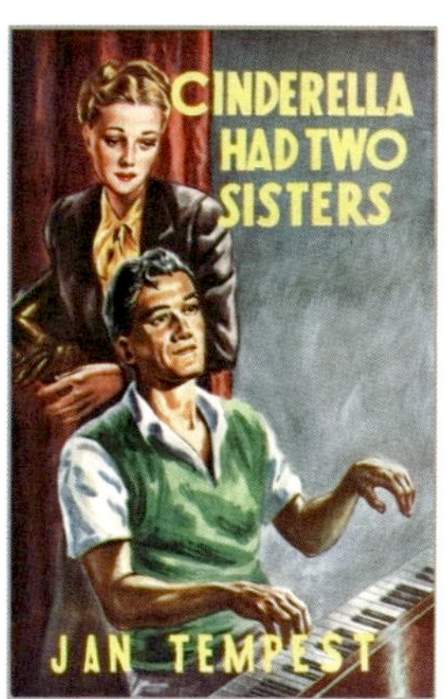

Phyllis Mannin, *Heaven in My Hand*, Mills & Boon, 1942 (d/j)

Anne Maybury, *The Barrier Between Us*, Mills & Boon, 5/1940 (d/j)

Anne Maybury, *Dare to Marry*, Mills & Boon, 1940 (d/j)

Marjorie Moore, *Gone Away*, Mills & Boon, 1954 (adapted d/j); repurposed from an earlier Mills & Boon book, author and title currently unidentified (d/j); same artwork also used for Romilly Brent, *The Bride Goes East*, Mills & Boon, 1946 (adapted d/j)

Linda Muir, *Melody at Twilight*, Mills & Boon, 1940 (d/j)

Valerie K Nelson, *The Shadow of Rose*, Mills & Boon, 1941 (d/j)

Valerie K Nelson, *Love – and Honor*, Mills & Boon, 1942 (d/j †)

Valerie K Nelson, *For Every Dream*, Mills & Boon, 1944 (d/j, unsigned); repurposed for Valerie K Nelson, *Matching Chiffon*, Mills & Boon, 1952 (adapted d/j, unsigned)

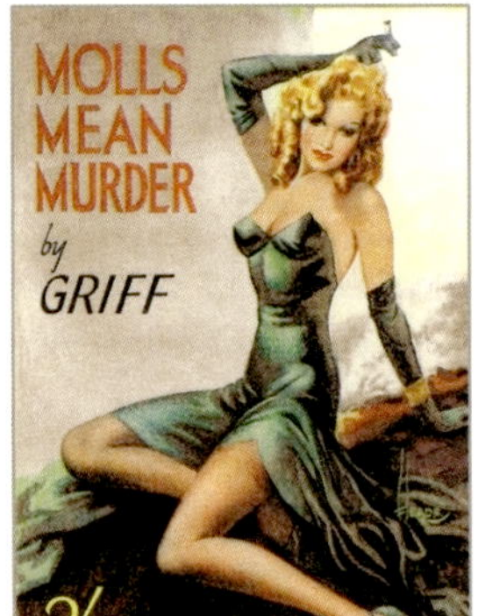

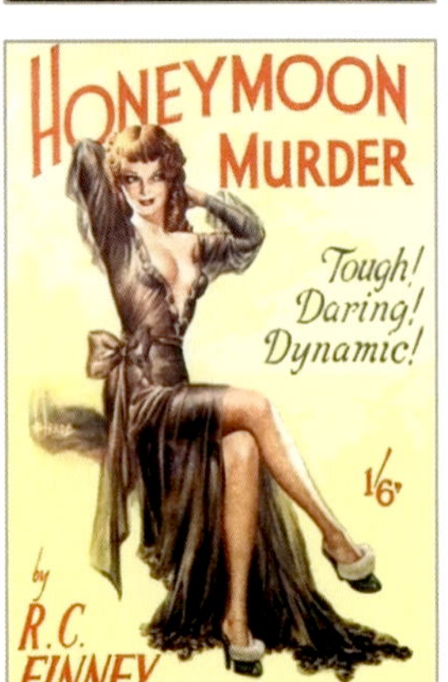

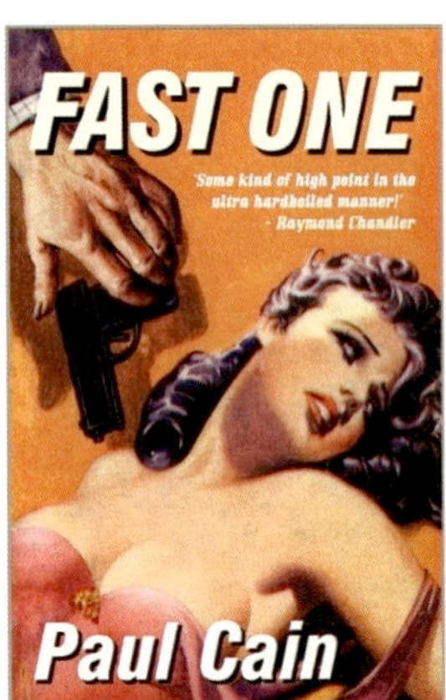

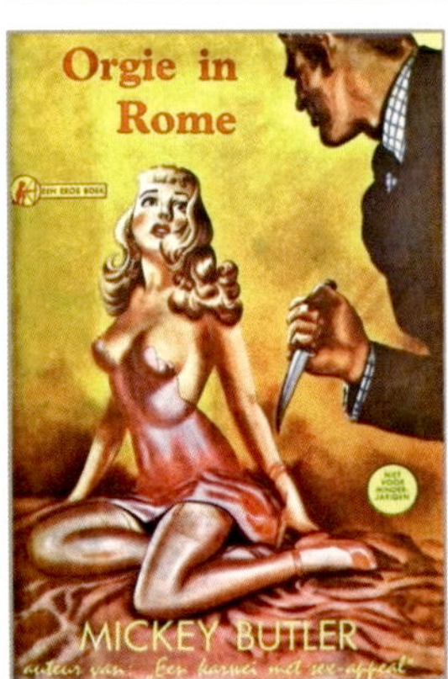

Valerie K Nelson, *Matching Chiffon*, Mills & Boon, 1953 (adapted d/j, unsigned); repurposed from Valerie K Nelson, *For Every Dream*, Mills & Boon, 1944 (d/j, unsigned)
Mairi O'Nair, *False Darkness*, Mills & Boon, 8/1940 (d/j)
Mairi O'Nair, *A Date with Destiny*, Mills & Boon, 1940 (d/j)
Mairi O'Nair, *Who Follows Pan?*, Mills & Boon, 1944 (d/j, unsigned)
Philippa Preston, *Passionate Hearts*, Mills & Boon, 7/1940 (d/j)
Philippa Preston, *Spring in My Heart*, Mills & Boon, 1941 (d/j)
Philippa Preston, *Dreaming Heart*, Mills & Boon, 1941 (d/j)
Philippa Preston, *Love in My Eyes*, Mills & Boon, 1943 (d/j, unsigned)
Marjorie M Price, *Joyce and Jane*, Mills & Boon, 7/1937 (d/j, unsigned, possibly by Heade)
Betty Stafford Robinson, *So Sweet a Fool*, Mills & Boon, 1941 (d/j)
Sylvia Sark, *Once to Every Woman*, Mills & Boon, 1940 (d/j)
Sylvia Sark, *The Waiting Heart*, Mills & Boon, 7/1940 (d/j)
Sara Seale, *Grace Before Meat*, Mills & Boon, 1952 (adapted d/j); repurposed from an earlier Mills & Boon book, author and title currently unidentified (d/j)
Sara Seale, *This Merry Bond*, Mills & Boon, 1953 (adapted d/j); repurposed from Molly Seymour, *Spring Tempest*, Mills & Boon, 1941 (d/j)
Sara Seale, *Green Grass Growing*, Mills & Boon, 1954 (adapted d/j); repurposed from an earlier Mills & Boon book, author and title currently unidentified (d/j)
Molly Seymour, *Play Fair with Love*, Mills & Boon, 1941 (d/j)
Molly Seymour, *Spring Tempest*, Mills & Boon, 1941 (d/j); repurposed for Sara Seal, *This Merry Bond*, Mills & Boon, 1953 (adapted d/j)
Molly Seymour, *Ilona Blaise*, Mills & Boon, 1942 (d/j, unsigned)
Molly Seymour, *Territorial's Wife*, Mills & Boon, 1943 (d/j)
Molly Seymour, *All That You Were*, Mills & Boon, 1943 (d/j)
Barbara Stanton, *The Perfect Husband*, Mills & Boon, 1942 (d/j)
Barbara Stanton, *Two-Man Girl*, Mills & Boon, 1942 (d/j, unsigned, probably by Heade)
Jan Tempest, *Cinderella had Two Sisters*, Mills & Boon, 1948 (d/j, unsigned, probably by Heade)
Guy Trent, *Some Other Love*, Mills & Boon, 1939 (d/j)
Guy Trent, *Be Brave for Love*, Mills & Boon, 1940 (d/j, unsigned)
Guy Trent, *The Courage of Mary Leigh*, Mills & Boon, 1940 (d/j)
Guy Trent, *Girl on Her Way*, Mills & Boon, 11/1940 (d/j)
Guy Trent, *Mother-Woman*, Mills & Boon, 1940 (d/j, unsigned)
Guy Trent, *The Tender Heart*, Mills & Boon, 1940 (d/j)
Guy Trent, *The Best Remained*, Mills & Boon, 1941 (d/j)
Guy Trent, *That Traitor My Heart*, Mills & Boon, 1941 (d/j)
Guy Trent, *Your Heaven – and Mine*, Mills & Boon, 1943 (d/j)

Modern Fiction

Griff, *Dames Don't Forget*, Modern Fiction, c1949 (p/b)
Griff, *Molls Mean Murder*, Modern Fiction, 1949 (p/b)

Moore Publishing

R C Finney, *Honeymoon Murder*, Moore, 5/1947 (p/b)

Museum Press

Rob Eden, *Saint and Siren*, Museum Press, 1943 (d/j)

No Exit Press

Paul Cain, *Fast One*, No Exit Press, 2004 (adapted p/b); repurposed from Michael Storme, *Hot Dames on Cold Slabs*, Archer, 12/1950 (p/b)

P Verbeeck / Eros / P Verbeeck

Mickey Butler, *Orgie in Rome*, P Verbeeck/Eros (Netherlands), 1957 (adapted p/b); repurposed from Spike Morelli, *You'll Never Get Me*, Archer, 10/1950 (p/b)
Kid Maclane, *Zijn Kus Bracht de Dood*, P Verbeeck (Netherlands), 1957 (adapted p/b); repurposed from Paul Rénin, *Flame*, Harborough, 4/1950 (p/b)

Pan

Jens Bjerre, *The Last Cannibals*, Great Pan G131, 6/1958 (p/b, signed as 'Cy Webb' *)
Leslie Charteris, *Alias The Saint*, Pan 254, 8/1954 (p/b)
Dr Winifred De Kok, *You and Your Child*, Great Pan GP99, 2/1958 (p/b, signed as 'Cy Webb' *)
Anne Frank, *The Diary of Anne Frank*, Great Pan G103, 2/1958 (p/b, signed as 'Cy Webb'); repurposed for Anne Frank, *Tales From the House Behind*, Pan G710, 1965 (p/b, unsigned)
Anne Frank, *Tales From the House Behind*, Pan, 1965 (p/b, unsigned); repurposed from Anne Frank, *The Diary of Anne Frank*, Great Pan G103, 2/1958 (p/b, signed as 'Cy Webb')
Peter Freuchen, *Vagrant Viking*, Pan Giant X18, 4/1958 (p/b, signed as 'Cy Webb' *)
Pamela Hansford Johnson, *Catherine Carter*, Pan Giant X14, 8/1957 (p/b, signed as 'Cy Webb' *)
Robert Harling, *The Paper Palace*, Great Pan G114, 4/1958 (p/b, signed as 'Cy Webb' *)
Agnes Keith, *Three Came Home*, Great Pan G113, 4/1958 (p/b, signed as 'Cy Webb')
R J Minney, *Carve Her Name With Pride*, Great Pan G105, 1/1958 (p/b, signed as 'Cy Webb')
D'Arcy Niland, *The Shiralee*, Great Pan G125, 5/1958 (p/b, signed as 'Cy Webb')
John Steinbeck, *Sweet Thursday*, Great Pan GP92, 4/1958 (p/b, signed as 'Cy Webb' *)
E S Turner, *A History of Courting*, Pan Giant X22, 4/1958 (p/b, signed as 'Cy Webb')

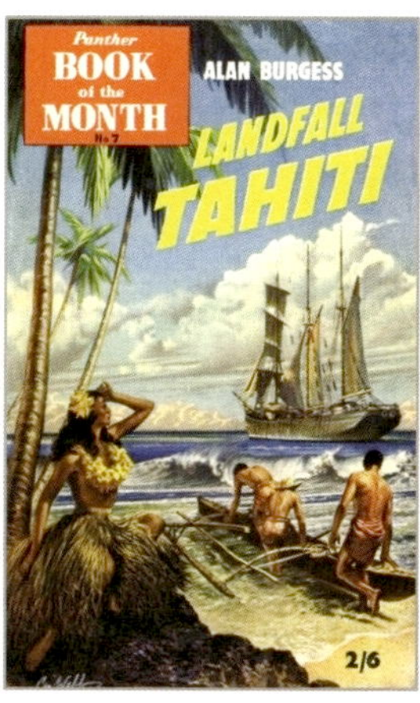

Panther

John T Barnard, *The Endless Years*, Panther 715, 8/1957 (p/b, signed as 'Cy Webb'); reprinted as John T Barnard, *The Endless Years*, Panther, 1958 (adapted p/b, signed as 'Cy Webb')
Belle J Benchley, *My Friends the Apes*, Panther 594, 7/1956 (p/b, signed as 'Cy Webb')
Alan Burgess, *Landfall Tahiti*, Panther 646, 11/1956 (p/b, signed as 'Cy Webb')
Harald Busch, translated by L P R Wilson, *U-Boats at War*, Panther 549 2/1956 (p/b, signed as 'Cy Webb')
Reginald Campbell, *Teak Wallah*, Panther 536, 2/1956 (p/b, signed as 'Cy Webb')
General Mark Clark, *Calculated Risk*, Panther, 1956 (p/b, unsigned; possibly the main figure only, with the background by a different artist)
Roberta Cowell, *Roberta Cowell's Story*, Panther 535, 1/1956 (p/b, signed as 'Cy Webb')
Bengt Danielsson, *The Happy Island – Kon Tiki*, Panther 587, 6/1956 (p/b, signed as 'Cy Webb')
Hugh Oloff De Wet, *The Valley of the Shadow*, Panther 607, 1956 (p/b, signed as 'Cy Webb')
Kenneth Dodson *Away All Boats!*, Panther 677, 4/1957 (p/b, signed as 'Cy Webb')
William Doyle, *Lifer*, Panther 741, 12/1957 (p/b, signed as 'Cy Webb')
Charles Drage, *Two-Gun Cohen*, Panther 583, 5/1956 (p/b, signed as 'Cy Webb')
Charles Duff, *A New Handbook on Hanging*, Panther 577, 4/1956 (p/b, signed as 'Cy Webb')
John Fancy, *Tunnelling to Freedom*, Panther 698, 6/1957 (p/b, signed as 'Cy Webb' *)
Commander F D Fane, *The Naked Warriors*, Panther 806, 12/1958 (p/b, unsigned, probably by Heade)
Nat Fleischer, *John L Sullivan*, Panther 629, 10/1956 (p/b, signed as 'Cy Webb')
Alain Gheerbrant, *The Impossible Adventure*, Panther, c1957 (p/b) (possibly unpublished)
John Gloag, *In Camera*, Panther 555, 2/1956 (p/b, signed as 'Cy Webb')
Louis Golding, *Bare-Knuckle Breed*, Panther 683, 4/1957 (p/b, signed as 'Cy Webb'); repurposed for Gene Schoor, *The Jack Dempsey Story*, Panther 748, 1/1958 (adapted p/b)
Hans Habe, *Walk in Darkness*, Panther 656, 12/1956 (p/b, signed as 'Cy Webb')
Geoffrey Hoare, *The Missing M Macleans*, Panther 561, 2/1956 (p/b, signed as 'Cy Webb')
Evan Hunter, *The Blackboard Jungle*, Panther 685, 4/1957 (p/b, signed as 'Cy Webb')
Betty Jeffrey, *White Coolies*, Panther 738, 2/1958 (p/b, signed as 'Cy Webb'); reissued as Betty Jeffrey, *White Coolies*, Panther, 1967 (adapted p/b, signature removed); reissued again as Betty Jeffrey, *White Coolies,* Mayflower, 1969 (adapted p/b, signature removed)
MacKinlay Kantor, *The Voice of Bugle Ann*, Panther 630, 12/1956 (p/b, signed as 'Cy Webb')
Stetson Kennedy, *I Rode with the Ku Klux Klan*, Panther 695, 5/1957 (p/b, signed as 'Cy Webb')
Gerald Kersh, *They Die With Their Boots Clean*, Panther 702, 6/1957 (p/b, signed as 'Cy Webb')
Gilbert C Klingel, *Inagua*, Panther 662, 1/1957 (p/b, signed as 'Cy Webb')
Martin Lindsay, *Three Got Through*, Panther 633, 12/1956 (p/b, signed as 'Cy Webb')
J P W Mallalieu, *Very Ordinary Seaman*, Panther 570, 3/1956 (p/b, signed as 'Cy Webb')
Jule Mannix, *Married to Adventure*, Panther 710, 8/1957 (p/b, signed as 'Cy Webb')
John P Marquand, *Ming Yellow*, Panther 664, 2/1957 (p/b, signed as 'Cy Webb')
Ronald McKie, *Proud Echo*, Panther 815, 1958 (p/b, signed as 'Cy Webb')
Nicholas Monsarrat, *'H.M.S. Marlborough Will Enter Harbour'*, Panther 560, 2/1956 (p/b, signed as 'Cy Webb')
L C Moyzisch, *Operation Cicero*, Panther 534, 1/1956 (p/b, signed as 'Cy Webb')
John G Neihardt, *Eagle Voice*, Panther 584, 6/1956 (p/b, signed as 'Cy Webb')
R M Patterson, *The Dangerous River*, Panther 660, 2/1957 (p/b, signed as 'Cy Webb')

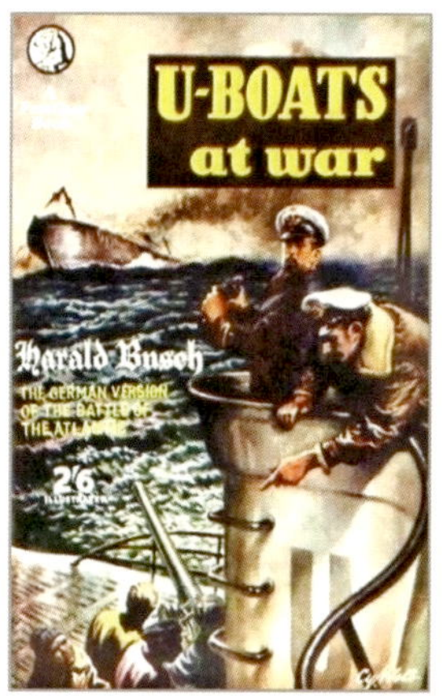

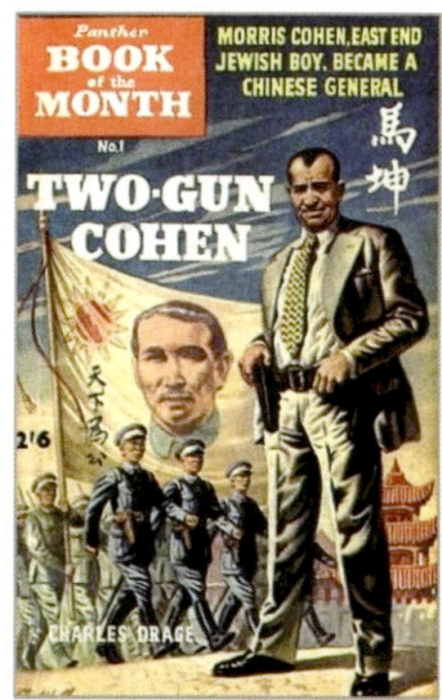

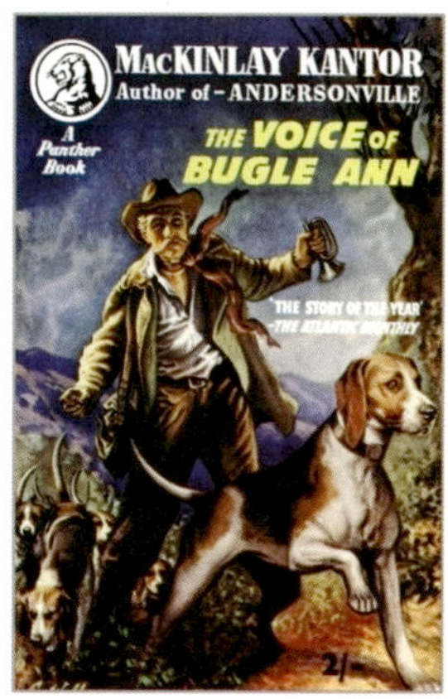

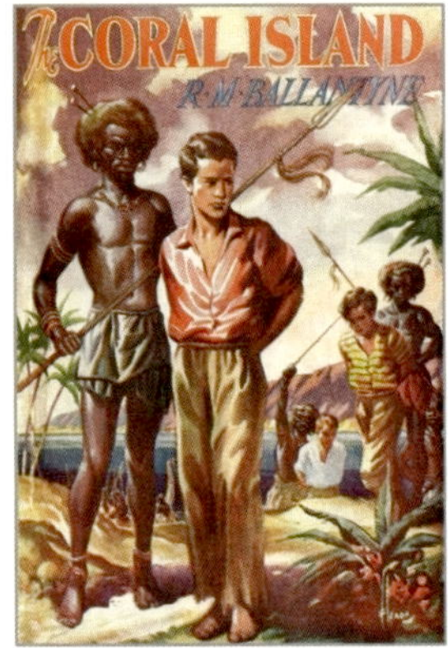

Theodore Plievier, *Stalingrad*, Panther 598, 8/1956 (p/b, signed as 'Cy Webb')
Tom Runyon, *In for Life*, Panther 582, 6/1956 (p/b, signed as 'Cy Webb')
Anne Eisner Putnam, *Eight Years with Congo Pigmies*, Panther 618, 8/1956 (p/b, signed as 'Cy Webb')
Gene Schoor, *The Jack Dempsey Story*, Panther 748, 1/1958 (adapted p/b); repurposed from Louis
    Golding, *Bare-Knuckle Breed*, Panther 683, 4/1957 (p/b, signed as 'Cy Webb')
Holland M Smith, *Coral and Brass*, Panther 847, 12/1958 (p/b, signed as 'Cy Webb')
Vern J Sneider, *The Tea-house of the August Moon*, Panther 527 (film tie-in edition), 1957 (p/b, signed
    as 'Cy Webb')
John Symonds, *The Great Beast*, Panther 612, 7/1956 (p/b, signed as 'Cy Webb')
Tony Van Den Bergh, *The Jack Johnson Story*, Panther 639, 12/1956 (p/b, signed as 'Cy Webb')
Donald Powell Wilson, *My Six Convicts*, Panther 624, ?/1956 (p/b, signed as 'Cy Webb')
G F Young, *Under the Coolibah Tree*, Panther 613, 1956 (p/b, signed as 'Cy Webb')

Partridge / Pictorial Art

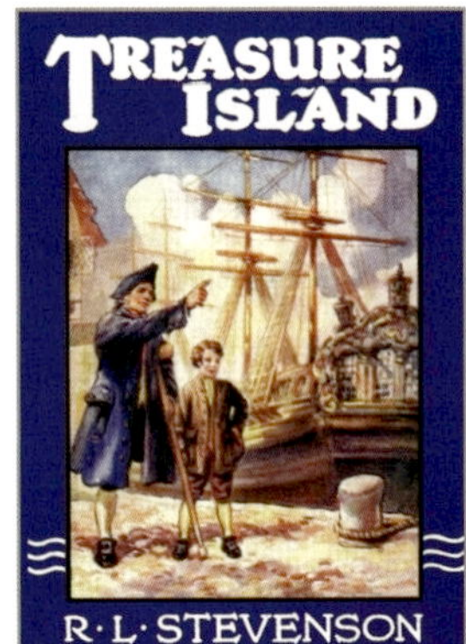

Louisa M Alcott, *Good Wives*, Pictorial Art, c1946 (p/b d/j and ? illus †)
Doug Allen, *Gamblers with Fate*, Partridge, 1947 (d/j)
R M Ballantyne, *The Coral Island*, Pictorial Art, 1946 (p/b d/j and 12 b&w illus)
Hall Bennett, *Make the Man Pay*, Partridge, 1947 (d/j)
Alice Ross Colver, *Fourways*, Partridge, 1946 (d/j, unsigned)
Daniel Defoe, *Robinson Crusoe* (retold), Partridge, 1947 (d/j, 13 colour illus and 15 b&w illus)
L Ernenwein, *Gunsmoke Galoot*, Partridge, 1946 (d/j)
Herbert Goodwin, *Enchantment*, Partridge, 1948 (d/j *)
Douglas Hayes, *Perhaps Tomorrow*, Partridge, 1951 (d/j *)
R Thurston Hopkins and Others, *Corpses Can Walk and Other Stories*, Pictorial Art, c1947 (p/b)
Vida Hurst, *Half Moon Bay*, Pictorial Art, 1947 (d/j *)
Vida Hurst, *Lovelorn*, Partridge, 1947 (d/j *)
Charles Kingsley, *Westward Ho!*, Pictorial Art, 1946 (p/b d/j * and 12 b&w illus, unsigned but credited)
Captain Marryat, *Masterman Ready*, Pictorial Art, c1946 (p/b d/j and 12 b&w illus)
Captain Marryat, *Midshipman Easy*, Pictorial Art, 1946 (p/b d/j * and 12 b&w illus)
William Macmillan, *Arctic Adventure*, Partridge, c1947 (d/j *) (possibly unpublished)
Everitt Proctor, *The Last Cruise of the Jeannette*, Pictorial Art, c1946 (p/b d/j *)
Everitt Proctor, *Thar She Blows*, Pictorial Art, 4/1947 (p/b d/j * and 4 b&w illus)
Margaret Scherf, *The Corpse Grows a Beard*, Partridge, 10/1946 (d/j *)
Rex Spear, *Terror Trail*, Pictorial Art, 1948 (p/b d/j and 3 b&w illus, unsigned but credited)
R L Stevenson, *Treasure Island* (retold), Partridge, c1947 (d/j and 28 colour illus)
Leonard Walters, *When Jungle Drums Beat!*, Pictorial Art, c1947 (p/b and 6 b&w illus, unsigned)

Pearsons

Julia Crane, *Brides of the Crimson Cross*, Pearsons 3d Novels, c1930s (p/b, unsigned, probably by Heade)

People's Friend Library

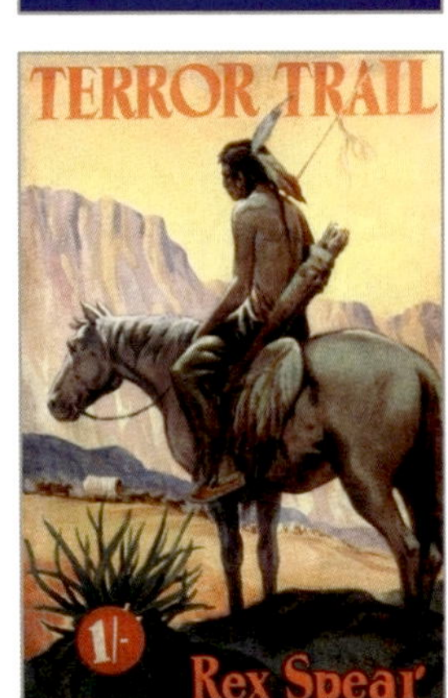

Annie S Swan, *Proud Patricia*, People's Friend Library, 1940 (p/b, unsigned, possibly by Heade)

Phoenix

Roland Vane, *Bohemian Love*, Phoenix, 1952 (p/b)

Pickering & Inglis

Esther E Enock, *Four Girls and a Fortune*, Pickering & Inglis, 1948 (d/j and colour frontis)
Grace Pettman, *Greta's Adventures*, Pickering & Inglis, 1947 (d/j and colour frontis)

Pocket Books (GB)

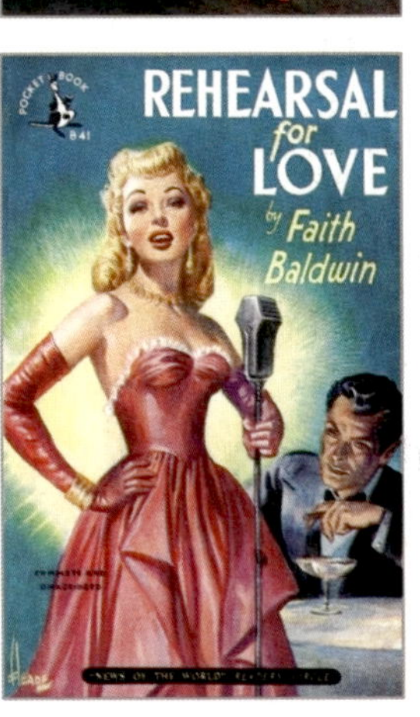

Faith Baldwin, *Rehearsal for Love*, Pocket Books B41, 8/1951 (p/b)

Pocket Editions BCM/Poket (Atlas Distributors)

R L Stevenson, *Treasure Island* (adapted), Pocket Editions BCM/Poket, 1945 (pictorial front and back
    covers, 5 colour and 11 duotone illus)

R & L Locker / Harborough / Archer / Kaywin (US) / Leisure Library (US)

Tony Angelo, *Sinner's Shroud*, Archer, 1/1951 (p/b)
Tony Angelo, *Satan's Sister*, Archer, 4/1951 (p/b)
Tony Angelo, *Honey, Hold That Scream*, Harborough, 4/1952 (p/b)
Tony Angelo, *Honey, Hold That Scream*, Leisure Library no. 17 (US), 1952 (new p/b *)
Mary Archer, *What – No Witnesses?*, R & L Locker, 9/1948 (p/b)
Brett Austin, *When a Renegade Rides*, Archer, 1948 (p/b *)
Tony Barton, *Think Fast Sister*, Harborough, 9/1952 (p/b *)
Muriel Bradley, *The Affair at Ritos Bay*, Harborough, c1953 (p/b)
Rosalind Brett, *Secret Marriage*, R & L Locker, 12/1947 (p/b)
Mary Clare, *White Man's Slave*, Archer, 6/1949 (p/b)
Mary Clare, *White Man's Slave*, Leisure Library no. 24 (US), 1953 (new p/b)
Louis Arthur Cunningham, *Sultry Love*, Archer, 10/1950 (p/b)
Rene Dubois, *The Flesh is Weak*, Harborough, 1/1954 (unpublished p/b *)
Rosamund Du Jardin, *Valley of Desire*, Archer, 10/1950 (p/b)
Rob Eden, *Golden Goddess* (d/j), R & L Locker, 8/1947 (p/b)
William J Elliott, *And Worms Have Eaten Them*, Harborough, 1950 (p/b)
William J Elliott, *The Demon of Desire*, Harborough, 1950 (p/b)
William J Elliott, *Lost Souls in Bohemia*, Harborough, 2/1951 (p/b)
William J Elliott, *Shipwreck Passion*, Harborough, 4/1951 (p/b)
William J Elliott, *Demon of Desire*, Harborough, 1/1954 (new p/b *)
Pierre Flammeche, *The Silken Lure*, Archer, 8/1949 (p/b); reissued as Pierre Flammeche, *The Silken Lure*, Kaywin (US), 1951 (adapted p/b)
Pierre Flammêche, *Spoiled Lives*, Archer, 3/1950 (p/b); reissued as Pierre Flammêche, *Spoiled Lives*, Kaywin (US), 1952 (adapted p/b)
Pierre Flammeche, *When Passion Rules*, Archer, 7/1950 (p/b)
Lee Floren, *Boomtail Basin*, Archer, 1947 (p/b *)
Lee Floren, *Blizzard Guns*, Archer, 1948 (p/b *)
Lee Floren, *Mad River Guns*, Archer, 1948 (p/b *)
Lee Floren, *Wild Border Guns*, Archer, 1948 (p/b *)
Juan Garcia, *Girl of the Bordellos*, Archer 1/1954 (p/b *)
George Goodchild, *The Eternal Conflict*, Archer, 3/1950 (p/b); reissued as Dutch-language translation, George Goodchild, *Het Eeuwige Conflict!*, Uitgevers Masstschappij de Combinatie (Netherlands), 1956 (adapted p/b)
Frances Hanna, *Be Sure it's Love*, Archer, 6/1948 (p/b)
Alan Kennington, *Desirable Alien*, R & L Locker, 12/1947 (p/b)
John King, *Shuna and the Lost Tribe*, Harborough, 11/1951 (p/b); repurposed for Steve Chibnall, *Reginald Heade – England's Greatest Artist*, Books Are Everything, 1991 (adapted p/b)
John King, *Shuna, White Queen of the Jungle*, Harborough, 11/1951 (p/b)
Henri Lamont, *Lost Souls*, Archer, 5/1953 (p/b *)
Henri Lamonte, *A Broken Butterfly*, Archer, 11/1953 (p/b *)
Perry Lindsay, *Overnight Cabin*, Archer, 9/1950 (p/b)
Perry Lindsay, *Brief Pleasure*, Archer, 12/1950 (p/b)
H M Lyttle, *The Tragedies of the White Slaves*, Archer, 1949 (p/b)
Anne Maybury, *Dangerous Living*, R & L Locker, 1944 (p/b)
Jules-Jean Morac, *Seven Days of Hell*, Harborough, c1954 (unpublished p/b *)
Jules-Jean Morac, *Bertrand and the Blondes*, Leisure Library no. 12 (US), 1952 (p/b *)
Chester Mordant, *Love-Girl*, Archer, 7/1950 (p/b)
Spike Morelli, *You'll Never Get Me*, Archer, 10/1950 (p/b); reissued as Spike Morelli, *You'll Never Get Me*, Kaywin (US), 1951 (adapted p/b); repurposed for Dutch-language book, Mickey Butler, *Orgie in Rome*, P Verbeeck/Eros (Netherlands), 1957 (adapted p/b)
Spike Morelli, *Coffin for a Cutie*, Archer, 1950 (p/b); reissued as Spike Morelli, *Coffin for a Cutie*, Harborough, 11/1952 (p/b)
Spike Morelli, *Take It and Like It*, Archer, 1950 (p/b); reissued for Spike Morelli, *Take It and Like It*, Kaywin (US), 1951 (adapted p/b)
Spike Morelli, *Sorry for You, Beautiful*, Harborough, 3/1952 (adapted p/b); repurposed from Spike Morelli, *Death for a Doll*, Leisure Library no. 2 (US), 1952 (p/b)
Spike Morelli, *More Than Kisses, Baby*, Harborough, 4/1952 (p/b *)
Spike Morelli, *Death for a Doll*, Leisure Library no. 2 (US), 1952 (p/b); repurposed for Spike Morelli, *Sorry for You, Beautiful*, Harborough, 3/1952 (adapted p/b)
Spike Morelli, *This Way for Hell*, Leisure Library no. 7 (US), 1952 (p/b); repurposed for Michael Storme, *Me and My Ghoul*, Harborough, 8/1953 (adapted p/b *)

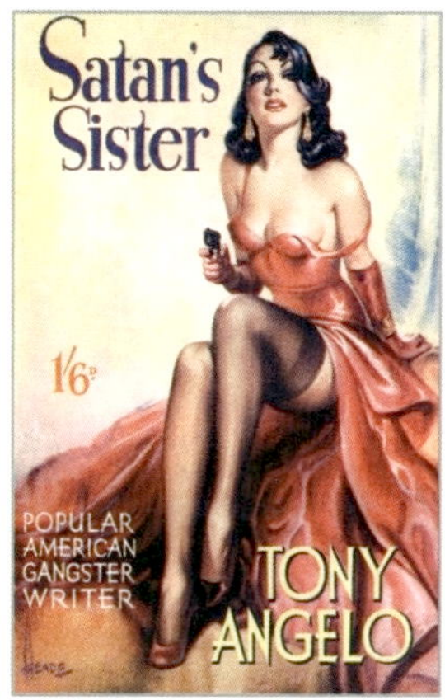
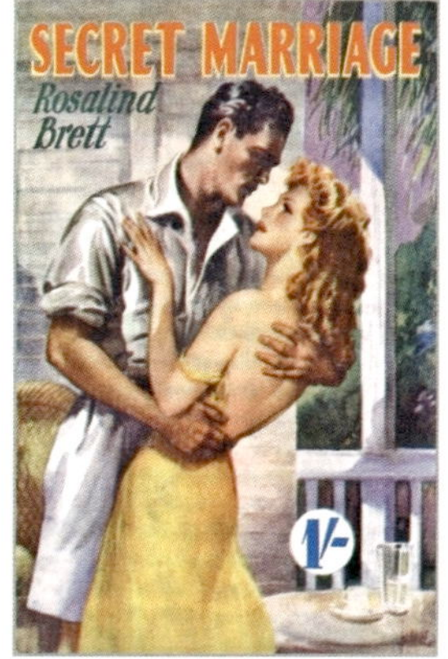
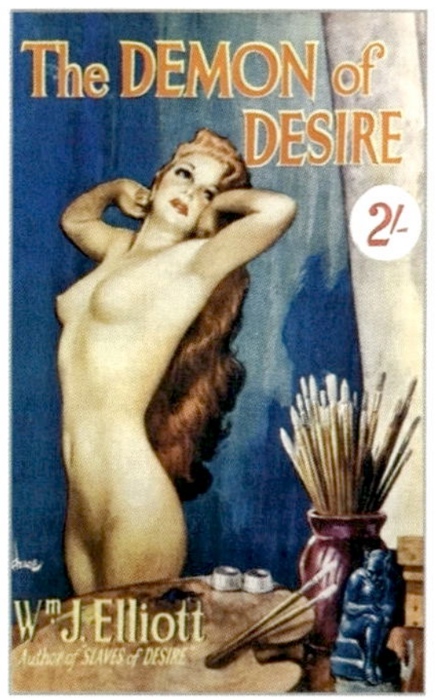
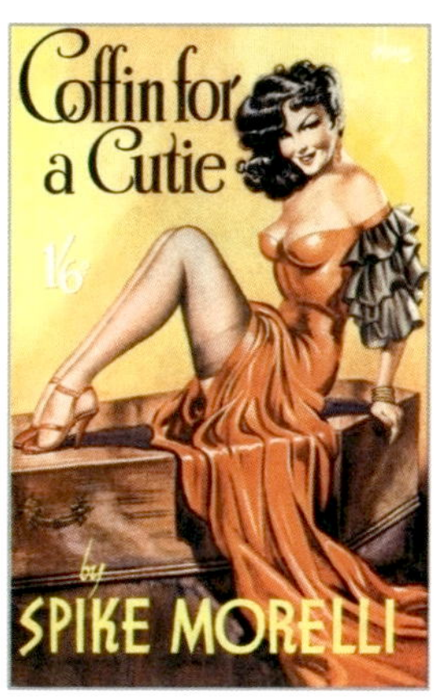

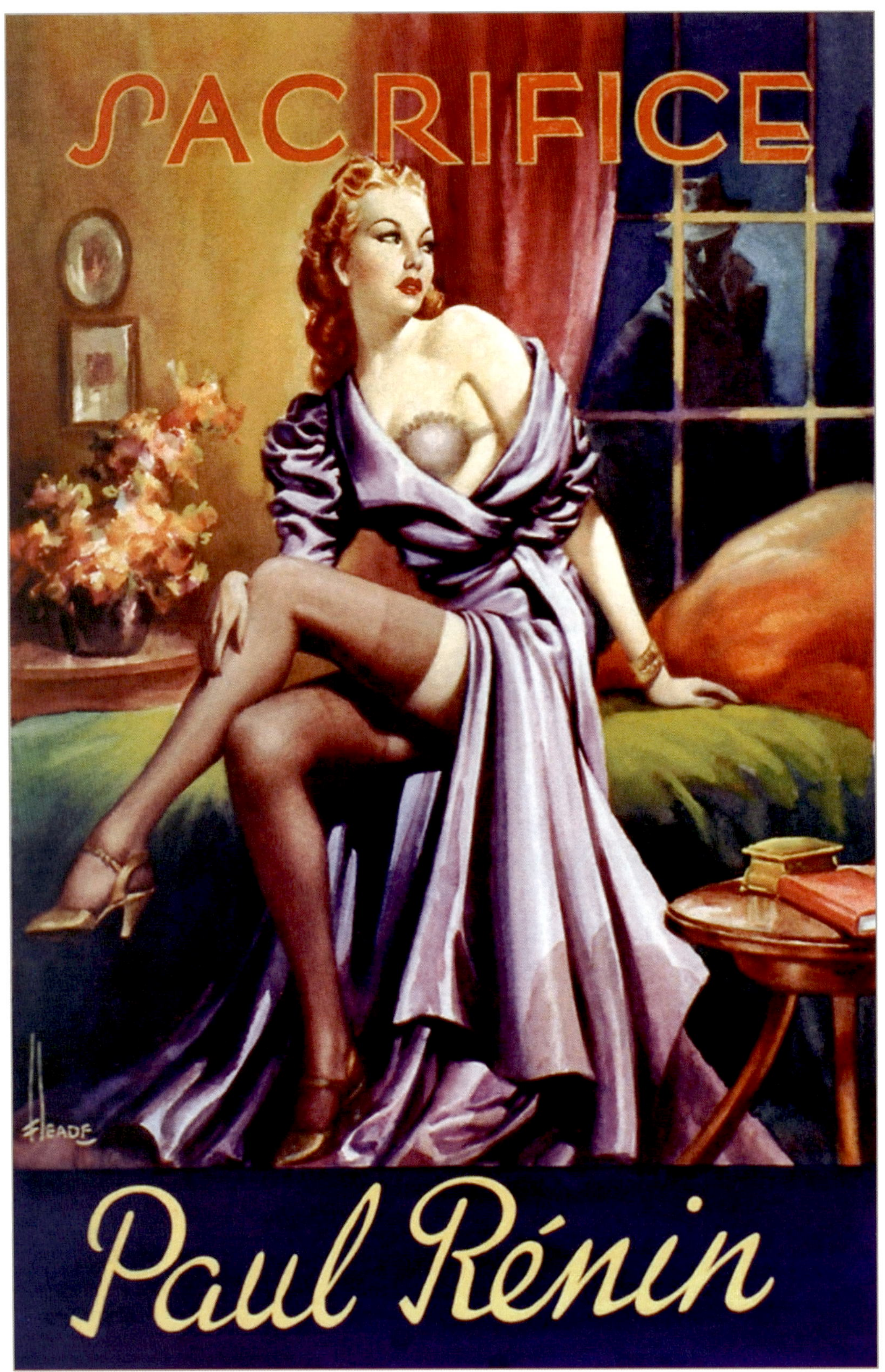

Heade's original painting for *Sacrifice* by Paul Rénin (Archer, 1948). (Image courtesy the Steve Chibnall Collection.)

Spike Morelli, *Deal Me Out*, Harborough, 9/1952 (p/b *)

Spike Morelli, *Give it to Me Straight*, Harborough, 4/1953 (p/b *)

Spike Morelli, *No Place for Me*, Harborough 8/1953 (adapted p/b *); repurposed from Paul Rénin, *She Who Hesitates*, Leisure Library no. 18, US: 1953 (p/b)

Paul Rénin, *Bohemia!*, Harborough, 6/1948 (p/b)

Paul Rénin, *The Kiss of Shame*, Harborough, 11/1948 (p/b)

Paul Rénin, *Foolish Women*, Harborough 12/1948 (p/b)

Paul Rénin, *Sacrifice*, Harborough, 12/1948 (p/b *)

Paul Rénin, *Those Without Shame*, Harborough, c1948 (p/b)

Paul Rénin, *Thy Neighbour's Wife*, R & L Locker, c1948 (p/b)

Paul Rénin, *Virtue*, Harborough, 1/1949 (p/b *)

Paul Rénin, *When Men Betray*, Harborough, 1/1949 (p/b *)

Paul Rénin, *Outrage*, Harborough, 2/1949 (p/b)

Paul Rénin, *Bright Young Things*, Harborough, 2/1949 (p/b)

Paul Rénin, *Dolores*, R & L Locker, 4/1949 (p/b *)

Paul Rénin, *Good Time Girls*, R & L Locker, 4/1949 (p/b)

Paul Rénin, *Atonement*, R & L Locker, 7/1949 (p/b)

Paul Rénin, *Beyond Convention*, R & L Locker, 8/1949 (p/b)

Paul Rénin, *Men Women Love*, R & L Locker, 8/1949 (p/b)

Paul Rénin, *Bitter Sweets*, R & L Locker, 9/1949 (p/b)

Paul Rénin, *Broken Vows*, Harborough, 1949 (p/b)

Paul Rénin, *The Other Woman*, Harborough, 1949 (p/b)

Paul Rénin, *Pleasure's Price*, Harborough 1949 (p/b *)

Paul Rénin, *White Woman*, Harborough, 1949 (p/b)

Paul Rénin, *Afterwards*, R & L Locker, c1949 (p/b)

Paul Rénin, *Flame*, Harborough, 4/1950 (p/b); reissued as Paul Rénin, *Flame*, Kaywin (US), 1951 (adapted p/b); repurposed for Dutch-language book, Kid Maclane, *Zijn Kus Bracht de Dood*, P Verbeeck (Netherlands), 1957 (adapted p/b)

Paul Rénin, *One Night in Paris*, Harborough, 9/1950 (p/b)

Paul Rénin, *Enticed*, R & L Locker, 9/1950 (p/b)

Paul Rénin, *A Fortnight's Folly*, Harborough 1950 (p/b); reissued as Paul Rénin, *A Fortnight's Folly*, Archer 3/1952 (self-censored p/b *)

Paul Rénin, *A Double Life*, Harborough, c1950 (p/b)

Paul Rénin, *£ove*, Harborough, c1950 (p/b); reissued as Paul Rénin, *£ove*, Archer 4/1952 (self-censored p/b)

Paul Rénin, *The Co-Respondent*, Archer, 3/1952 (p/b)

Paul Rénin, *Glamour*, Archer, 9/1952 (p/b)

Paul Rénin, *Week-End Wives*, Archer, 9/1952 (p/b *)

Paul Rénin, *Midnight Sinner*, Leisure Library no. 10 (US), 1952 (adapted p/b); originally intended to be titled *Wanton Midnight* (unpublished p/b *)

Paul Rénin, *Wedding Night*, Leisure Library no. 14 (US), 1952 (p/b); reissued as Paul Rénin, *Wedding Night*, Archer, 10/1953 (adapted p/b)

Paul Rénin, *She Who Hesitates*, Leisure Library no. 18, US: 1953 (p/b); repurposed for Spike Morelli, *No Place For Me*, Harborough, 8/1953 (adapted p/b *)

Paul Rénin, *At Dawn*, Archer, 3/1953 (p/b)

Paul Rénin, *The Brute*, Archer, 3/1953 (p/b)

Paul Rénin, *Carnival Kisses*, Archer, 3/1953 (p/b)

Paul Rénin, *The Return*, Archer, 3/1953 (p/b)

Paul Rénin, *Two A.M.*, Archer, 9/1953 (p/b)

Paul Rénin, *Women I Have Loved*, Archer, 9/1953 (p/b)

Paul Rénin, *Bait*, Archer, 11/1953 (p/b)

Paul Rénin, *East and West*, Archer, 11/1953 (p/b)

Paul Rénin, *Thou Shalt Not*, Leisure Library no. 22 (US), p/b

Paul Rénin, *Dangerous Moments*, Archer, 1/1954 (p/b)

Paul Rénin, *The Seventh Night*, Archer, 1/1954 (p/b)

Jeanette Revére, *Plaything of Passion*, Archer, 8/1950 (p/b); reissued as Jeanette Revére, *Plaything of Passion*, Kaywin (US), 1951 (adapted p/b)

Paul Reville, *Tribulation*, R & L Locker, 2/1948 (p/b)

Paul Reville, *Impassioned Youth*, R & L Locker, c1949 (p/b)

Paul Reville, *Arabian Passion*, Archer, 5/1953 (p/b)

Paul Reville, *A Daughter of Desire*, Archer, 8/1953 (p/b *)

Paul Reville, *The Street of Shame*, Archer, 8/1953 (p/b *)

Paul Reville, *Sin Street*, Archer, 9/1953 (p/b *)

Paul Reville, *Wild Youth*, Archer, 11/1953 (p/b *)

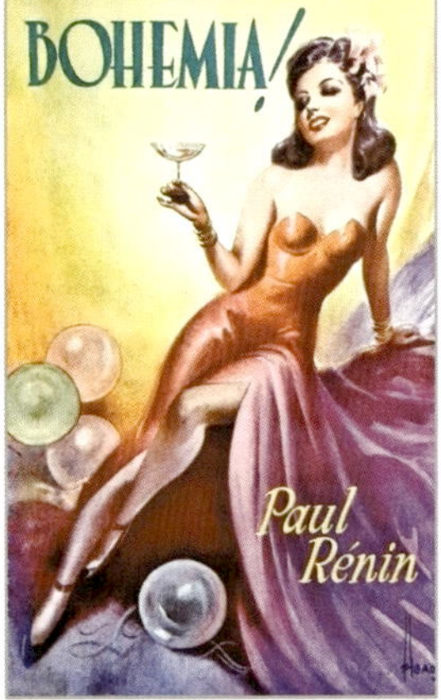

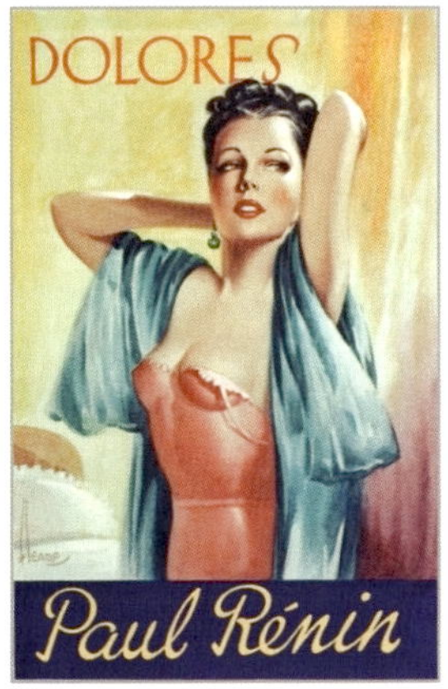

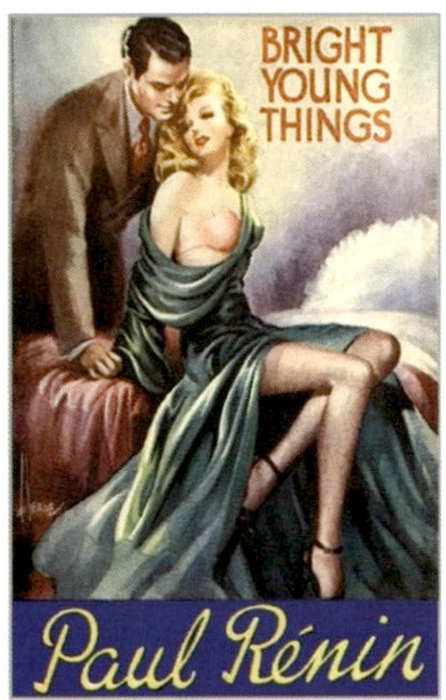

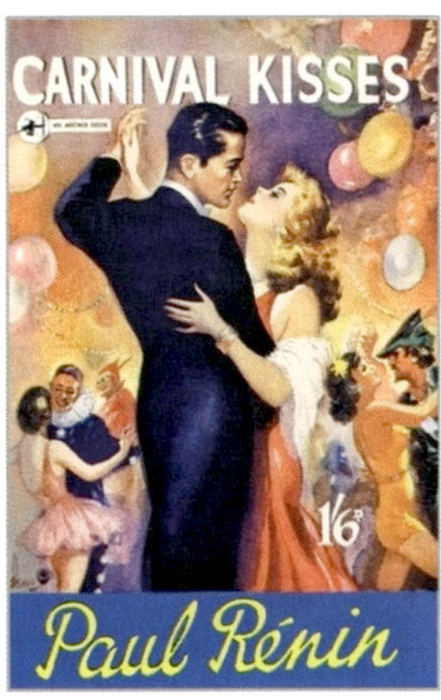

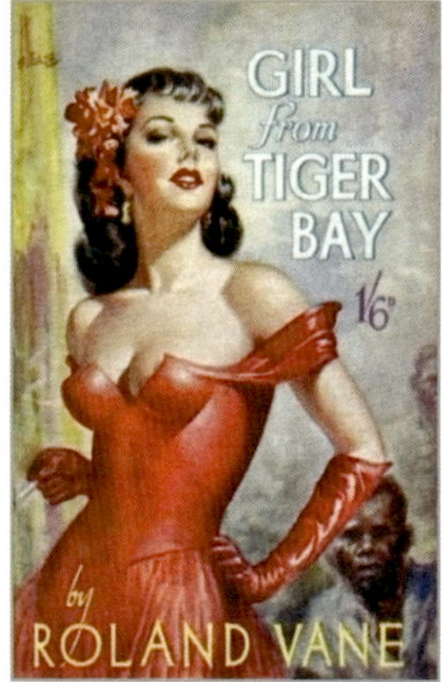

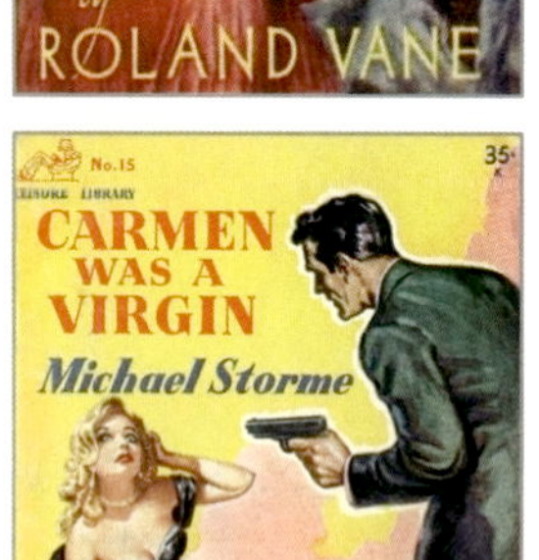

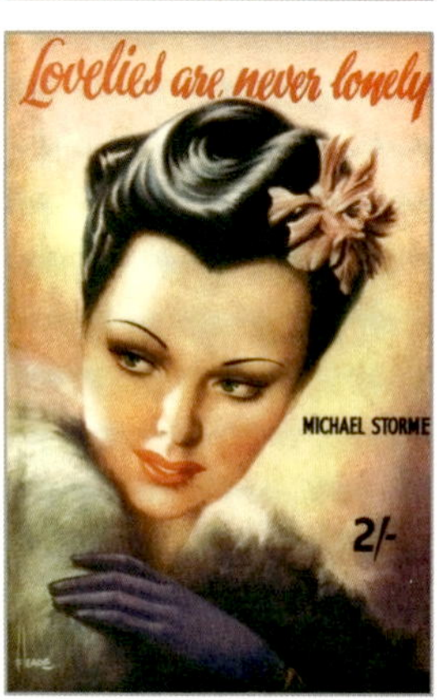

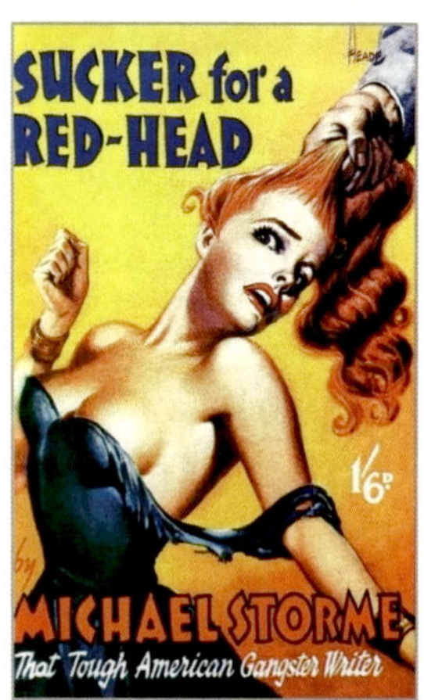

Gene Ross, *This Way for Hell*, Archer, 4/1950 (p/b); repurposed for Stephen James Walker, *The Art of Reginald Heade – Special Edition*, Telos Publishing, 8/2018 (adapted pictorial boards)

Gene Ross, *You're Dead, My Lovely*, Archer, 8/1950 (p/b)

Gene Ross, *Two Smart Dames*, Leisure Library no. 9 (US), 1952 (p/b); repurposed for Roland Vane, *Silken Sin*, Archer, 5/1953 (adapted p/b)

Gene Ross, *Sorry for You, Beautiful*, Leisure Library no. 15 (US), 1952 (p/b); repurposed for Gene Ross, *Step Up Sucker*, Harborough, 8/1953 (adapted p/b *)

Gene Ross, *Curves Cause Trouble*, Leisure Library no. 21 (US), 1953 (p/b); repurposed for Michael Storme, *Sweetheart With a Wreath*, Harborough, 7/1953 (adapted p/b *)

Gene Ross, *Step Up Sucker*, Harborough, 8/1953 (p/b *)

Gene Ross, *Corpse in the Boudoir*, Harborough, 9/1953 (p/b *)

George Ryley Scott, *Gertie Vesser*, Harborough, 1/1954 (p/b)

Virgil Scott, *The Dead Trees Give No Shelter*, Archer, 11/1950 (p/b)

Max Somerset, *Romance ... and Susan*, Archer, 7/1949 (p/b)

Michael Storme, *Make Mine a Shroud*, Harborough, 5/1949 (p/b); reissued as Michael Storme, *Make Mine a Shroud*, Leisure Library no. 4 (US), 1952 (adapted p/b)

Michael Storme, *Sucker for a Redhead*, Archer 8/1950 (p/b *)

Michael Storme, *Dame in My Bed*, Archer, 1950 (p/b); reissued as Michael Storme, *Dame in My Bed*, Kaywin (US), 1951 (adapted p/b)

Michael Storme, *Satan Buys a Wreath*, Archer, 1950 (p/b)

Michael Storme, *Hot Dames on Cold Slabs*, Archer, 12/1950 (p/b); reissued as Michael Storme, *Hot Dames on Cold Slabs*, Leisure Library no. 5 (US), 1952 (adapted p/b); repurposed for Paul Cain, *Fast One*, No Exit Press (2004) (adapted p/b)

Michael Storme, *Elvira Digs a Grave*, Harborough, 3/1952 (p/b)

Michael Storme, *Chicago Terror*, Harborough, 4/1952 (p/b)

Michael Storme, *Stella Buys a Shroud*, Harborough, 4/1952 (p/b)

Michael Storme, *Lovelies Are Never Lonely*, Harborough, 4/1952 (p/b)

Michael Storme, *Make Mine a Redhead*, Harborough, 10/1952 (p/b *)

Michael Storme, *Kiss the Corpse Goodbye*, Harborough, 11/1952 (p/b *); repurposed for Michael Storme, *Mördande Märken*, X-Böckerna No. 35 (Sweden), 1955 (adapted p/b)

Michael Storme, *Curtains for Carla*, Leisure Library no. 11 (US), 1952 (p/b); repurposed for Michael Storme, *Tiptoe Thro' a Graveyard*, Harborough, 1954 (new, adapted p/b *); repurposed again for Swedish-language book Harry Whittington, *Lek Med Läkemedel*, X-Böckerna No. 26 (Sweden), 1954 (adapted p/b)

Michael Storme, *Carmen was a Virgin*, Leisure Library no. 15 (US), 1952 (p/b); repurposed for Michael Storme, *You'll Be Better Off Dead*, Harborough, 3/1953 (adapted p/b)

Michael Storme, *This Woman is Death*, Leisure Library no. 23 (US), 1953 (p/b)

Michael Storme, *Baby Don't Love Hoodlums*, Harborough, 3/1953 (p/b)

Michael Storme, *Dragons Come Expensive*, Harborough, 3/1953 (p/b *)

Michael Storme, *You'll Be Better Off Dead*, Harborough, 3/1953 (adapted p/b); repurposed from Michael Storme, *Carmen was a Virgin*, Leisure Library no. 15 (US), 1952 (p/b); repurposed for Swedish-language book Hans Lugar, *Mord Med Förhinder*, X-Böckerna No. 34 (Sweden), 1955 (adapted p/b)

Michael Storme, *Sweetheart with a Wreath*, Harborough, 7/1953 (adapted p/b *); repurposed from Gene Ross, *Curves Cause Trouble*, Leisure Library no. 21 (US), 1953 (p/b)

Michael Storme, *Me and My Ghoul*, Harborough, 8/1953 (adapted p/b *); repurposed from Spike Morelli, *This Way for Hell*, Leisure Library no. 7 (US), 1952 (p/b); repurposed for Swedish-language book Michael Storme, *Panic I Belle City*, X-Böckerna No. 23 (Sweden), 1954 (adapted p/b)

Michael Storme, *Tiptoe Thro' a Graveyard*, Harborough, 8/1953 (p/b *)

Michael Storme, *Baby Don't Say Goodbye*, Harborough, 10/1953 (p/b *)

Michael Storme, *The Devil Has a Racket*, Archer, 1/1954 (p/b *)

Michael Storme, *Tiptoe Thro' a Graveyard*, Harborough, 1954 (new, adapted p/b *); repurposed from Michael Storme, *Curtains for Carla*, Leisure Library no. 11 (US), 1952 (p/b)

Michael Storme, *Annie Get Your Hearse*, Archer, 1954 (p/b, unpublished *)

Lee Thomas, *Bullets for a Banker*, Archer, 10/1948 (p/b *)

Roland Vane, *White Slaves of New Orleans*, Archer, 6/1949 (p/b); reissued as Roland Vane, *White Slaves of New Orleans*, Kaywin (US), 1951 (adapted p/b)

Roland Vane, *Girl From Tiger Bay*, Archer, 5/1950 (p/b)

Roland Vane, *Sinful Sisters*, Archer, 4/1950 (p/b); reissued as Roland Vane, *Sinful Sisters*, Kaywin (US), 1951 (adapted p/b)

Roland Vane, *Sin-Stained*, Archer, 9/1950 (p/b)

Roland Vane, *This Thing Called 'Sin'*, Archer, 11/1950 (p/b *)

Roland Vane, *Ladies of the Red Lamp*, Archer, 1950 (p/b); reissued as Roland Vane, *Ladies of the Red Lamp*, Kaywin (US), 1951 (adapted p/b)

Roland Vane, *Vice Rackets of Soho*, Archer, 1950 (p/b); reissued as Roland Vane, *Vice Rackets of Soho*, Kaywin (US), 1951 (adapted p/b); repurposed for Stephen J Gertz, *Dope Menace*, Feral House, 2008 (adapted p/b)

Roland Vane, *Pick-Up Girl*, Leisure Library no. 3 (US), 1952 (p/b); reissued as Roland Vane, *Pick-Up Girl*, Archer, 7/1953 (adapted p/b)

Roland Vane, *White Slave Racket*, Leisure Library, no. 8 (US), 1952 (p/b)

Roland Vane, *Amorous Adventuress*, Archer, 4/1952 (p/b *)

Roland Vane, *Woman of Montmartre*, Archer, 9/1952 (p/b *)

Roland Vane, *Willing Sinner*, Archer, 11/1952 (p/b *)

Roland Vane, *Amorous Adventuress*, Leisure Library no. 16 (US), 1952 (new p/b)

Roland Vane, *Slaves of Passion*, Archer, 3/1953 (p/b *)

Roland Vane, *Slaves of Passion* (alternative p/b, unpublished *)

Roland Vane, *Silken Sin*, Archer, 5/1953 (adapted p/b *); repurposed from Gene Ross, *Two Smart Dames*, Leisure Library no. 9 (US), 1952 (p/b)

Roland Vane, *White Slave Racket*, Archer, 7/1953 (new p/b *)

Roland Vane, *Vice Rackets of Soho*, Archer, 8/1953 (new p/b *)

Roland Vane, *Ladies of the Red Lamp*, Archer, 8/1953 (new p/b *)

Roland Vane, *Call Girls of New York*, Archer, 9/1953 (p/b *)

Roland Vane, *White Slaves of New Orleans*, Archer, 9/1953 (new p/b *)

Roland Vane, *Juvenile Delinquent*, Archer, 10/1953 (p/b *)

Slim Vincent, *Dames Are No Dice*, Archer, 1950 (p/b)

Unknown author, untitled painting: seated blonde in black slip and tan stockings, with red pillow, c1954 (p/b, unpublished *)

Robert Hale

Faith Baldwin, *Five Women*, Robert Hale, 23/1/1946 (d/j)

Hermina Black, *Sweet Pilgrimage*, Robert Hale, 1943 (d/j)

Ursula Bloom, *Spring in September*, Robert Hale, 1941 (d/j, unsigned, possibly by Heade)

Barbara Cartland, *Yet She Follows*, Robert Hale, 1944 (d/j)

Barbara Cartland, *Escape From Passion*, Robert Hale, 2/1945 (d/j)

James Hadley Chase, *There's Always a Price Tag*, Robert Hale, 1956 (d/j, unsigned, probably by Heade)

Rob Eden, *Honeymoon Delayed*, Robert Hale, 1939 (d/j)

Vicky Lancaster, *Beggar Girl's Gift*, Robert Hale, 1943 (d/j, unsigned)

Vicky Lancaster, *Lady – Look Ahead*, Robert Hale, 1944 (d/j, unsigned)

Vicky Lancaster, *They Loved in Donegal*, Robert Hale, 1944 (d/j)

Ann Wilson, *She Was My Friend*, Robert Hale, 1956 (d/j, unsigned, possibly by Heade)

Robin Hood Press

Eugene Ascher, *There Were No Asper Ladies*, Robin Hood Press, 1947 (p/b)

Darcy Glinto, *The Hangman is a Woman*, Robin Hood Press, c1953 (p/b *)

Buck Toler, *Tough on the Wops*, Robin Hood Press, 1947 (p/b)

S D Frances / New Fiction Press / Top Fiction Press / Alexander Moring / Comyns

Max Clinten, *No Flowers for the Dead*, S D Frances, 1951 (p/b, unsigned, probably by Heade)

Hank Janson, *This Woman is Death*, S D Frances, 6/1948 (p/b)

Hank Janson, *Lady, Mind That Corpse*, S D Frances, 9/1948 (p/b *)

Hank Janson, *Gun Moll for Hire*, S D Frances, 12/1948 (p/b)

Hank Janson, *No Regrets for Clara*, S D Frances, 3/1949 (p/b)

Hank Janson, *Smart Girls Don't Talk*, S D Frances, 4/1949 (p/b)

Hank Janson, *Lilies for My Lovely*, S D Frances, 5/1949 (p/b)

Hank Janson, *Blonde on the Spot*, S D Frances, 6/1949 (p/b)

Hank Janson, *Honey, Take My Gun*, S D Frances, 7/1949 (p/b); adapted for Hank Janson, *Lady, Mind That Corpse*, Checker Books 10 (US), 1949 (adapted p/b)

Hank Janson, *Angel, Shoot to Kill*, S D Frances, 10/1949 (p/b)

Hank Janson, *Slay-Ride for Cutie*, S D Frances, 11/1949 (p/b)

Hank Janson, *Slay-Ride for Cutie*, S D Frances, (alternative p/b, unpublished); first appeared as thumbnail illustration in Steve Chibnall, *Reginald Heade – England's Greatest Artist*, Books Are Everything, 1991; adapted for Hank Janson, *When Dames Get Tough – With Scarred Faces and Other Rarities*, Telos Publishing, 5/2004 (p/b)

Hank Janson, *Sister, Don't Hate Me*, S D Frances, 12/1949 (p/b)

Hank Janson, *Some Look Better Dead*, S D Frances, 1/1950 (p/b)

Hank Janson, *Sweetie, Hold Me Tight*, S D Frances, 2/1950 (p/b)

Hank Janson, *Torment for Trixy*, S D Frances, 3/1950 (p/b *)

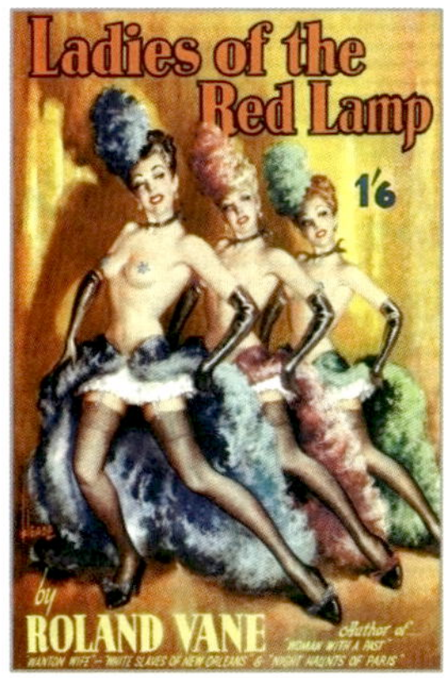

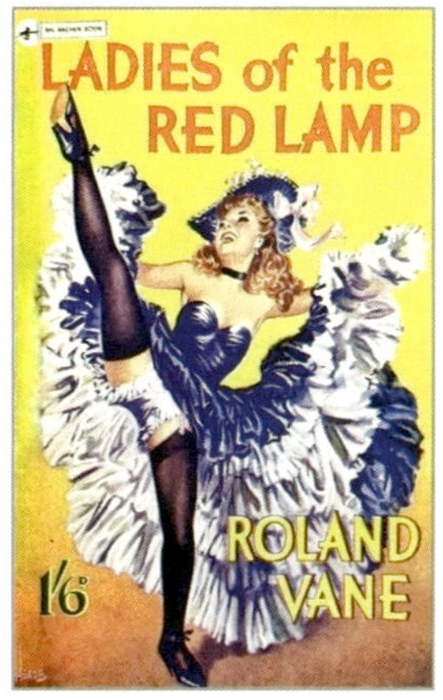

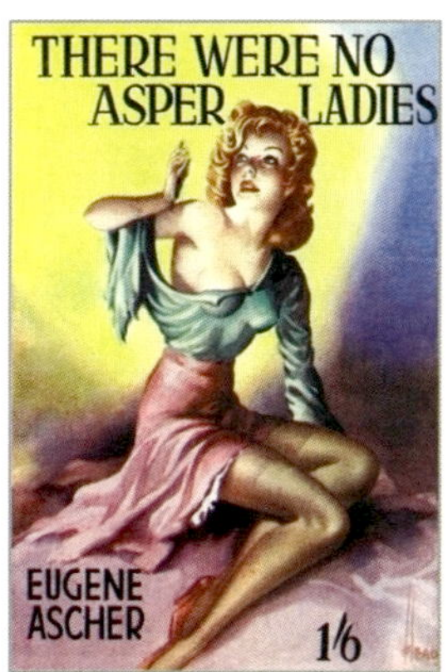

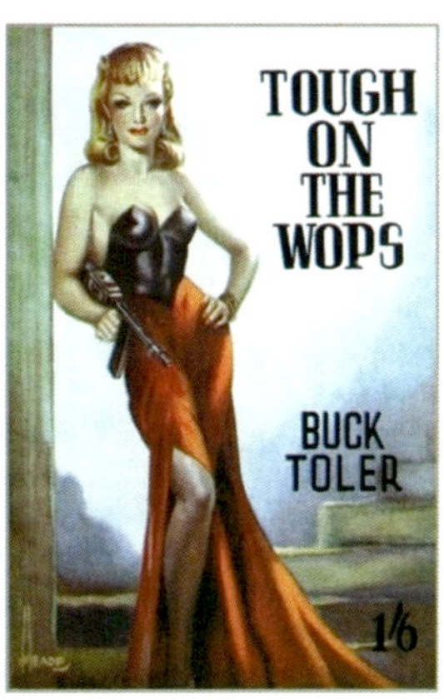

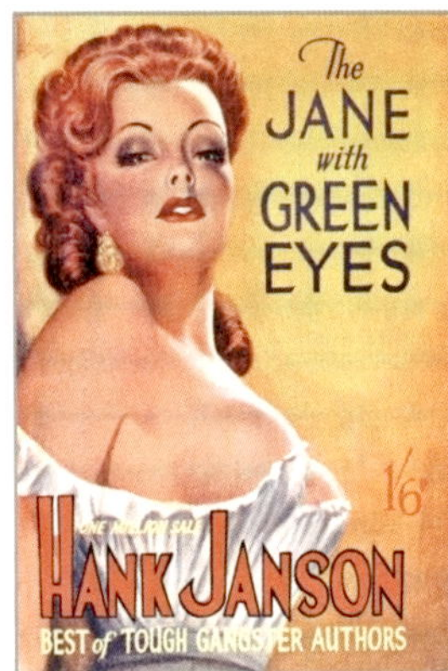

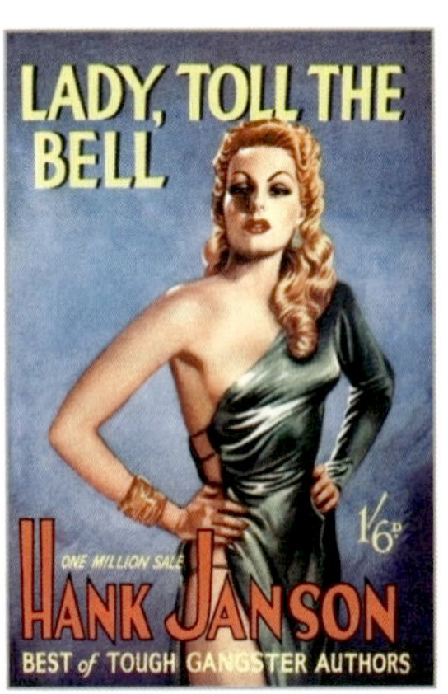

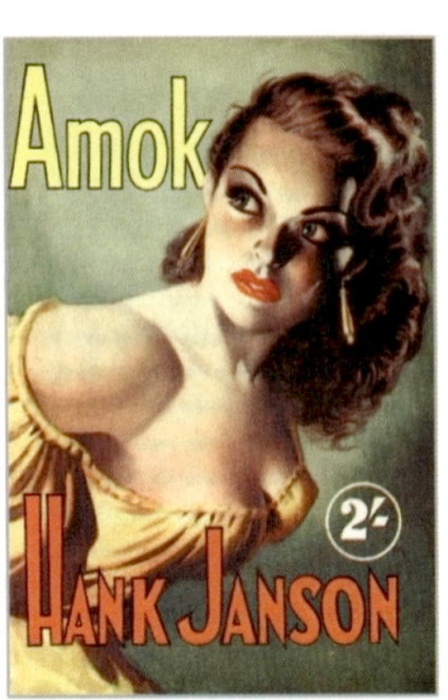

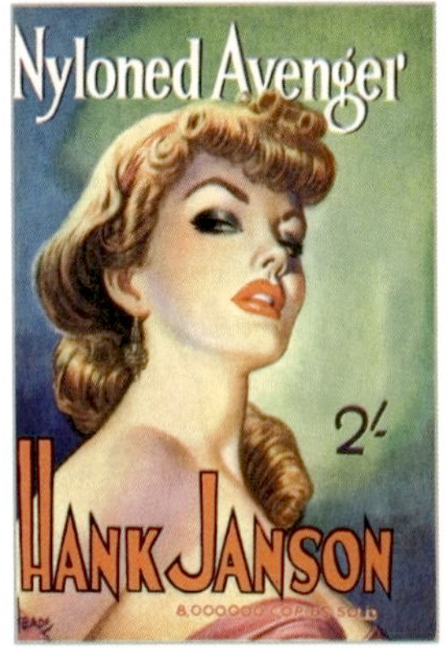

Hank Janson, *Don't Dare Me, Sugar*, S D Frances, 5/1950 (p/b)

Hank Janson, *The Lady Has a Scar*, S D Frances, 6/1950 (p/b)

Hank Janson, *The Jane with Green Eyes*, S D Frances, 7/1950 (p/b *)

Hank Janson, *Lola Brought Her Wreath*, S D Frances, 9/1950 (p/b *)

Hank Janson, *Lady, Toll the Bell*, S D Frances, 10/1950 (p/b *)

Hank Janson, *The Bride Wore Weeds*, S D Frances, 12/1950 (p/b *)

Hank Janson, *Don't Mourn Me, Toots*, S D Frances, 1/1951 (p/b)

Hank Janson, *This Dame Dies Soon*, S D Frances, 2/1951 (p/b *)

Hank Janson, *Baby, Don't Dare Squeal*, S D Frances, 3/1951 (p/b)

Hank Janson, *Death Wore a Petticoat*, S D Frances, 4/1951 (p/b *)

Hank Janson, *Hotsy, You'll Be Chilled*, S D Frances, 5/1951 (p/b)

Hank Janson, *It's Always Eve That Weeps*, S D Frances, 6/1951 (p/b *)

Hank Janson, *Frails Can Be So Tough*, New Fiction Press, 8/1951 (p/b, unpublished); first appeared as thumbnail illustration in Steve Chibnall, *Reginald Heade – England's Greatest Artist*, Books Are Everything, 1991; used for reissue, Hank Janson, *Frails Can Be So Tough*, Telos Publishing, 11/2004 (p/b)

Hank Janson, *Broads Don't Scare Easy*, New Fiction Press, 11/1951 (p/b, copies recalled for self-censorship by silvering); used for reissue, Hank Janson, *Broads Don't Scare Easy*, New Fiction Press, 12/1952 (p/b)

Hank Janson, *Skirts Bring Me Sorrow*, New Fiction Press, 8/1951 (p/b, copies recalled for self-censorship by silvering); first appeared as thumbnail illustration in Steve Chibnall, *Reginald Heade – England's Greatest Artist*, Books Are Everything, 1991; used for reissue, Hank Janson, *Skirts Bring Me Sorrow*, Telos Publishing, 11/2003 (p/b)

Hank Janson, *Sadie, Don't Cry Now*, New Fiction Press, 1/1952 (p/b)

Hank Janson, *The Filly Wore a Rod*, New Fiction Press, 2/1952 (p/b)

Hank Janson, *The Filly Wore a Rod*, New Fiction Press (alternative p/b, unpublished); first appeared as thumbnail illustration in Steve Chibnall, *Reginald Heade – England's Greatest Artist*, Books Are Everything, 1991

Hank Janson, *Kill Her if You Can*, New Fiction Press, 3/1952 (p/b *)

Hank Janson, *Murder*, New Fiction Press, 4/1952 (p/b)

Hank Janson, *Conflict*, New Fiction Press, 6/1952 (p/b)

Hank Janson, *Auctioned*, New Fiction Press, 6/1952 (p/b, unsigned)

Hank Janson, *Tension*, New Fiction Press, 7/1952 (p/b)

Hank Janson, *Whiplash*, New Fiction Press, 8/1952 (p/b *)

Hank Janson, *Accused*, New Fiction Press, 10/1952 (p/b)

Hank Janson, *Killer*, New Fiction Press, 11/1952 (p/b)

Hank Janson, *Persian Pride*, New Fiction Press, 11/1952 (p/b, unsigned, possibly by Heade)

Hank Janson, *Suspense*, New Fiction Press, 12/1952 (p/b)

Hank Janson, *Pursuit*, New Fiction Press, 1/1953 (p/b)

Hank Janson, *Vengeance*, New Fiction Press, 2/1953 (p/b)

Hank Janson, *Torment*, New Fiction Press, 4/1953 (p/b)

Hank Janson, *Amok*, New Fiction Press, 5/1953 (p/b *)

Hank Janson, *Corruption*, Top Fiction Press, 6/1953 (p/b)

Hank Janson, *Desert Fury*, New Fiction Press, 7/1953 (p/b, unsigned)

Hank Janson, 'Hank Janson Blues', New Fiction Press, 1953 (sheet music)

Hank Janson, *Lilies for My Lovely*, New Fiction Press, 1953 (new p/b); originally intended for Hank Janson, *Milady Took the Rap*, New Fiction Press, 10/51 (p/b)

Hank Janson, *Sadie, Don't Cry Now*, New Fiction Press, 1953 (new p/b *); reissue, originally intended for 1/1952 first edition

Hank Janson, *Silken Menace*, Top Fiction Press, 7/1953 (p/b *)

Hank Janson, *Nyloned Avenger*, Top Fiction Press, 8/1953 (p/b)

Hank Janson, *One Man in His Time*, Top Fiction Press, 8/1953 (p/b)

Hank Janson, *The Unseen Assassin*, Top Fiction Press, 8/1953 (p/b, unsigned, figure and foreground by Heade, background by Ron Turner); adapted for Hank Janson, *The Unseen Assassin*, Alexander Moring, 4/1956 (p/b)

Hank Janson, *Deadly Mission*, Top Fiction Press, 9/1953 (p/b, probably unpublished); painting modified for Hank Janson, *Framed*, Alexander Moring, 9/1955 (p/b)

Hank Janson, *Framed*, Top Fiction Press, 1953 (unpublished, possibly intended for d/j of abandoned hardback *); copied by a different artist for Hank Janson, *Untamed*, Alexander Moring, 1955 (p/b)

Hank Janson, *Woman Trap* (p/b, unsigned, advertised but unpublished *); adapted for Hank Janson, *Women Hate Till Death*, Telos Publishing, 7/2003

Hank Janson, *Perfumed Nemesis* (p/b, unsigned, advertised but unpublished)

Hank Janson, *Blonde Dupe* (p/b, unsigned, advertised but unpublished); adapted for Steve Holland, *The Trials of Hank Janson*, Telos Publishing, 5/2005

Hank Janson, *Dainty Dynamite* (p/b, unsigned, advertised but unpublished)

Hank Janson, *Menace*, Alexander Moring, 1955 (p/b, unsigned, possibly a previously-unused rough)

Hank Janson, *Framed*, Alexander Moring, 1955 (p/b); adapted from Hank Janson, *Deadly Mission*, Top Fiction Press, 9/1953 (p/b, probably unpublished)

Hank Janson, *The Unseen Assassin*, Alexander Moring, 4/1956 (p/b, unsigned, figure and foreground by Heade, background by Ron Turner); adapted from Hank Janson, *The Unseen Assassin*, Top Fiction Press, 8/1953 (p/b)

Link Shelton, *Dead Men Don't Love*, S D Frances, 1948 (p/b); repurposed for Stephen James Walker and Steve Chibnall, *The Art of Reginald Heade – Volume Two*, Telos Publishing, 8/2020 (adapted pictorial boards)

Mark Shane, *The Lady Bites the Dust*, Comyns, 11/1952 (p/b, unsigned, probably by Heade)

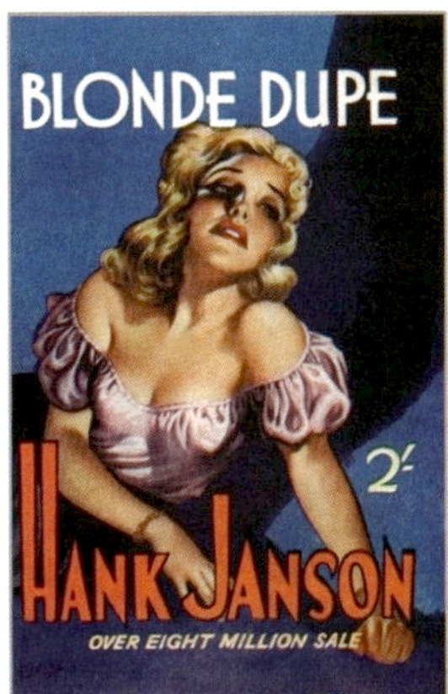

Strome

Anon (ed.), *Mr Strawstuff's Party*, Strome, 1942 (p/b, pictorial front and back covers, 5 colour and 8 duotone illus, all unsigned)

Telos Publishing

Hank Janson, *Women Hate Till Death*, Telos Publishing, 7/2003 (p/b, unsigned); adapted from Hank Janson, *Woman Trap* (p/b, unsigned, advertised but unpublished)

Hank Janson, *When Dames Get Tough – With Scarred Faces and Other Rarities*, Telos Publishing, 5/2004 (p/b); adapted from Hank Janson, *Slay-Ride for Cutie*, S D Frances, (alternative p/b, unpublished)

Steve Holland, *The Trials of Hank Janson*, Telos Publishing, 5/2005 (p/b, unsigned); adapted from Hank Janson, *Blonde Dupe* (p/b, unsigned, advertised but unpublished)

Stephen James Walker, *The Art of Reginald Heade*, Telos Publishing, 12/2016 (adapted pictorial boards); repurposed from Mary Howard, *There Will I Follow*, Collins, 1948 (d/j)

Stephen James Walker, *The Art of Reginald Heade – Special Edition*, Telos Publishing, 8/2018 (adapted pictorial boards); repurposed from Gene Ross, *This Way for Hell*, Archer, 4/1950 (p/b)

Stephen James Walker and Steve Chibnall, *The Art of Reginald Heade – Volume Two*, Telos Publishing, 8/2020 (adapted pictorial boards); repurposed from Link Shelton, *Dead Men Don't Love*, S D Frances, 1948 (p/b)

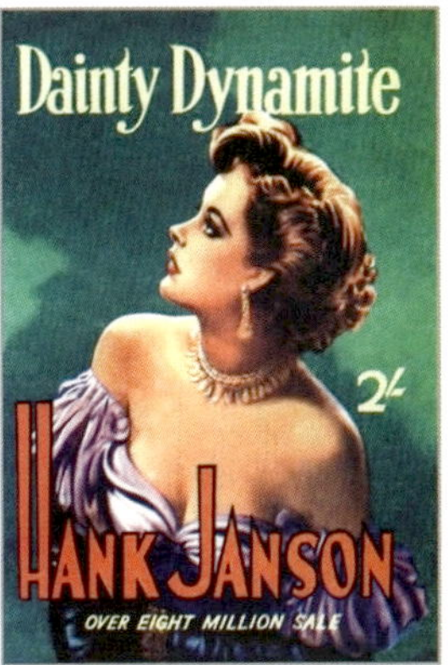

Thomas Nelson

Philip Beaufoy Barry, *The Mystery of the Blue Diamond*, Thomas Nelson, 1954 (d/j and b&w frontis)

Michael Poole, *The Duffer of Danby*, Thomas Nelson, 1953 (d/j and b&w frontis)

G H Tempany, *The Eight Days' Feud*, Thomas Nelson, 1953 (d/j and b&w frontis)

Reid Whitly, *The Boy Chief*, Thomas Nelson, 1954 (d/j and b&w frontis)

Thriller Book Club

Manning O'Brine, *Killers Must Eat*, Thriller Book Club, 1952 (d/j)

Ward, Lock

Margaret Cameron, *Nicolette Detects*, Ward, Lock, 1949 (d/j and b&w frontis, unsigned, probably by Heade)

Bessie Marchant, *The Fortunes of Prue*, Ward, Lock, 1949 (d/j, unsigned, possibly by Heade)

Dorothy Quentin, *The Singing Hills*, Ward, Lock, 1949 (d/j)

Ethel Turner, *Three Little Maids*, Ward, Lock, c1945 (d/j)

Valentine, *Passing By*, Ward Lock, 1949 (d/j)

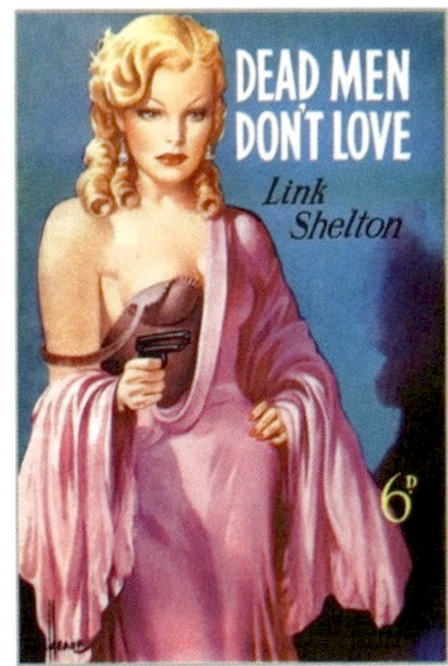

X-Böckerna

Michael Storme, *Panic I Belle City*, X-Böckerna No. 23 (Sweden), 1954 (adapted p/b); repurposed from Michael Storme, *Me and My Ghoul*, Harborough, 8/1953 (adapted p/b *)

Harry Whittington, *Lek Med Läkemedel*, X-Böckerna No. 26 (Sweden), 1954 (adapted p/b); repurposed from Michael Storme, *Curtains for Carla*, Leisure Library no. 11 (US), 1952 (p/b)

Hans Lugar, *Mord Med Förhinder*, X-Böckerna No. 34 (Sweden), 1955 (adapted p/b); repurposed from Michael Storme, *You'll Be Better Off Dead*, Harborough, 3/1953 (adapted p/b)

Michael Storme, *Mördande Märken*, X-Böckerna No. 35 (Sweden), 1955 (adapted p/b); repurposed from Michael Storme, *Kiss the Corpse Goodbye*, Harborough, 11/1952 (p/b)

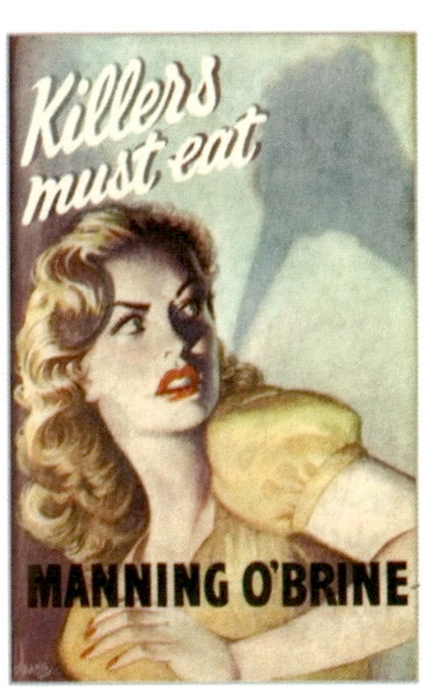

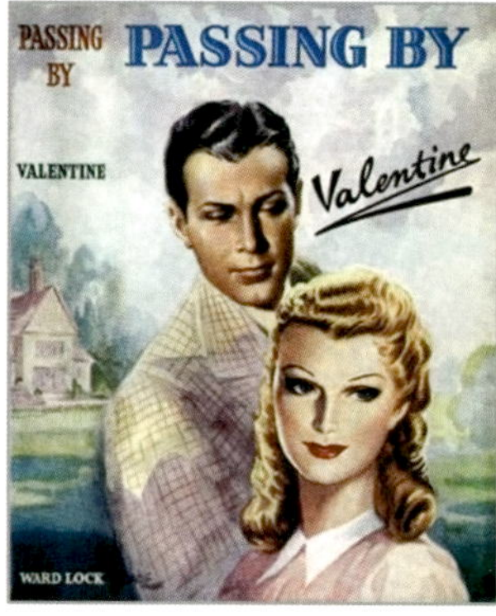

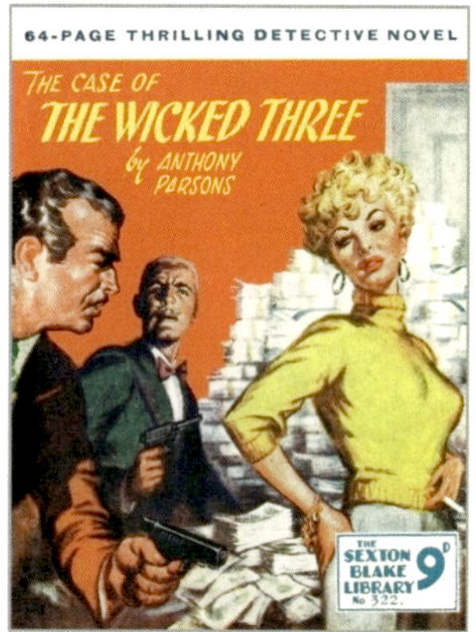

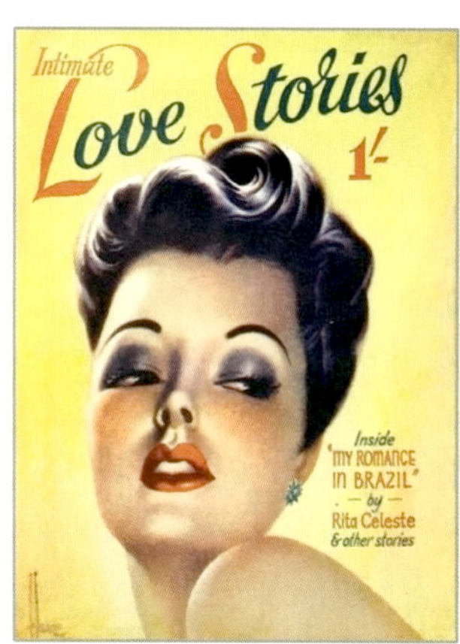

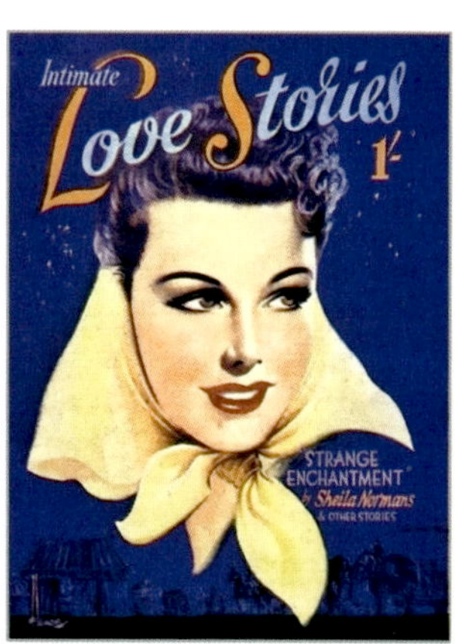

PERIODICALS

Amalgamated

Detective Weekly, Amalgamated, 6/8/1938, lead story Gerald Verner, *The Devil's Brood* (adapted monochrome cover); repurposed from Pamela Hansford Johnson, *Here To-day*, Chapman & Hall, 1/1937 (d/j)

The Sexton Blake Library

Anthony Skene, *The Red Stiletto*, The Sexton Blake Library, no 356, Amalgamated, 6/10/1932 (cover, unsigned, probably by Heade)
Rex Hardinge, *The Riddle of the Invisible Menace*, The Sexton Blake Library, no. 315, Amalgamated, 7/1954 (cover, unsigned)
John Drummond, *The Mystery of the Five Guilty Men*, The Sexton Blake Library, no. 316, Amalgamated, 7/1954 (cover, unsigned)
Walter Tyrer, *The Crime in Room 37*, The Sexton Blake Library, no. 321, Amalgamated, 10/1954 (cover, unsigned)
Anthony Parsons, *The Case of the Wicked Three*, The Sexton Blake Library, no. 322, Amalgamated, 10/1954 (cover, unsigned)
Hugh Clevely, *The Case of the Criminal's Daughter*, The Sexton Blake Library, no. 323, Amalgamated, 11/1954 (cover, unsigned)
George Rees, *The Secret of the Suez Canal*, The Sexton Blake Library, no. 324, Amalgamated, 11/1954 (cover, unsigned)
Rex Hardinge, *The Victim of the Devil's Bowl*, The Sexton Blake Library, no. 325, Amalgamated, 12/1954 (cover, unsigned)
Anthony Parsons, *The Man from Maybrick Road*, The Sexton Blake Library, no. 326, Amalgamated, 12/1954 (cover, unsigned *)
John Hunter, *Murder in the Air*, The Sexton Blake Library, no. 327, Amalgamated, 1/1955 (cover, unsigned, possibly partly by Heade *)
Walter Tyrer, *The Case of the Forbidden Island*, The Sexton Blake Library, no. 328, Amalgamated 1/1955 (cover, unsigned *)
Anthony Parsons, *The Secret of the Roman Temple*, The Sexton Blake Library, no. 337, Amalgamated, 6/1955 (cover, unsigned)

Thriller Comics Library

Edgar Wallace, *Again the Ringer*, Thriller Comics Library, no. 18, Amalgamated, 6/1952 (cover, unsigned, possibly by Heade)
Rafael Sabatini, *The Black Swan*, Thriller Comics Library, no. 61, Amalgamated, 5/1954 (cover)
Anon (ed.), *Captain Kidd – Buccaneer*, Thriller Comics Library, no. 96, Amalgamated, 8/1955 (cover, unsigned); repurposed for Anon (ed.), 'The Bold Buccaneer', *Comet* (comic), Amalgamated, 3/5/1958 (no. 511) (adapted colour back cover illus)
Anon (ed.)*, Musketeers at Bay*, Thriller Comics Library, no. 104, Amalgamated, 11/1955 (cover, unsigned, probably by Heade)
Anon (ed.), *Captain Kidd of the Spanish Main*, Thriller Comics Library, no. 105, Amalgamated, 11/1955 (cover)

Bayard Productions

Anon (ed.), *Bedside Clubman*, Bayard Productions 1/1953 (colour illus of female jockey in advertisement for *Clubman*); reprinted in Anon (ed.) *Bedside Clubman*, Bayard Productions, 6/1953

Bear Hudson

Anon (ed.), *Intimate Love Stories*, Bear Hudson, 2/1948, lead story Rita Celeste, 'My Romance in Brazil' (cover)
Anon (ed.), *Intimate Love Stories*, Bear Hudson, 3/1948, lead story Sheila Normans, 'Strange Enchantment' (cover)
Anon (ed.), *Intimate Love Stories*, Bear Hudson, 4/1948, lead story Gaspard Latouche, 'The Marriage That Wasn't' (cover)
Anon (ed.), *Intimate Love Stories*, Bear Hudson, c6/1948 lead story, May Rains, 'My Prisoner Lover' (cover)

Anon (ed.), *Intimate Love Stories*, Bear Hudson, c7/1948, lead story, John F Watt, 'Night-Club Girl' (cover, unsigned, probably by Heade)

Anon (ed.), *Intimate Love Stories*, Bear Hudson, 7/1948, lead story, Sheila Hayes, 'Mayfair Mannequin' (cover)

Anon (ed.), *Intimate Love Stories*, Bear Hudson ?/1948, lead story Terry Hindley, 'Glamour Girl Number One' (cover)

Anon (ed.), *Thrilling Romances*, Bear Hudson, no. 2, 1948 (cover)

Anon (ed.), *Thrilling Romances*, Bear Hudson, no. 3, 1948 (cover)

British National Newspapers

Britannia and Eve, vol. 6 no. 4, 4/1933 (cover, unsigned but credited)
Britannia and Eve, vol. 7 no. 1, 7/1933 (cover, unsigned but credited)
Britannia and Eve, vol. 7 no. 2, 8/1933 (cover, unsigned but credited)
Britannia and Eve, vol. 7 no. 3, 9/1933 (cover, unsigned but credited)
Britannia and Eve, vol. 7 no. 4, 10/1933 (cover, unsigned but credited)
Britannia and Eve, vol. 7 no. 5, 11/1933 (cover, unsigned but credited)
Britannia and Eve, vol. 7 no. 6, 12/1933 (cover, unsigned but credited)
Britannia and Eve, vol. 8 no. 1, 1/1934 (cover, unsigned but credited)
Britannia and Eve, vol. 8 no. 3, 3/1934 (cover, unsigned but credited)
Britannia and Eve, vol. 9 no. 1, 7/1934 (cover, unsigned but credited)
Britannia and Eve, vol. 9 no. 6, 12/1934 (cover, unsigned but credited)
Britannia and Eve, vol. 11 no. 3, 9/1935 (cover, unsigned but credited)
Britannia and Eve, vol. 13 no. 5, 11/1936 (cover, unsigned but credited)
Britannia and Eve, vol. 14 no. 4, 4/1937 (cover, unsigned but credited)
Britannia and Eve, vol. 14 no. 6, 6/1937 (cover, unsigned but credited)
Britannia and Eve, vol. 15 no. 1, 7/1937 (cover, unsigned but credited)
Britannia and Eve, vol. 15 no. 2, 8/1937 (cover, unsigned but credited)
Britannia and Eve, vol. 15 no. 3 9/1937 (cover, unsigned but credited)
Britannia and Eve, vol. 15 no. 5, 11/1937 (cover, unsigned but credited)
Britannia and Eve, vol. 21 no. 6, 12/1940 (cover, unsigned but credited)
Britannia and Eve, vol. 22 no. 3, 3/1941 (cover, unsigned but credited)
Britannia and Eve, vol. 22 no. 6, 6/1941 (cover, unsigned but credited)
Britannia and Eve, vol. 23 no. 4, 10/1941 (cover, unsigned but credited)
Britannia and Eve, vol. 24 no. 4, 4/1942 (cover, unsigned but credited *)
Britannia and Eve, vol. 25 no. 4, 10/1942 (cover, unsigned but credited)
Britannia and Eve, vol. 25 no. 6, 12/1942 (cover, unsigned but credited *)
Britannia and Eve, vol. 26 no. 1, 1/1943 (cover, unsigned but credited)
Britannia and Eve, vol. 26 no. 3, 3/1943 (cover, unsigned but credited *)
Britannia and Eve, vol. 27 no. 1, 7/1943 (cover, unsigned but credited)
Britannia and Eve, vol. 27 no. 2, 8/1943 (cover, unsigned but credited *)
Britannia and Eve, vol. 27 no. 3, 9/1943 (cover, unsigned but credited)
Britannia and Eve, vol. 27 no. 4 10/1943 (cover, unsigned but credited)
Britannia and Eve, vol. 28 no. 1, 1/1944 (cover, unsigned but credited)
Britannia and Eve, vol. 28 no. 4, 4/1944 (cover, unsigned but credited)
Britannia and Eve, vol. 28 no. 6, 6/1944 (cover, unsigned but credited)
Britannia and Eve, vol. 29 no. 1, 7/1944 (cover, unsigned but credited)
Britannia and Eve, vol. 29 no. 4, 10/1944 (cover, unsigned but credited)
Britannia and Eve, vol. 35 no. 5, 11/1947 (cover, unsigned but credited)

Devereaux Publications

Anon (ed.), *Dick Kevin's Adventurous Journeys Magazine*, vol. 1 no. 5, Devereaux Publications, 1948 (duotone cover)

Grant Hughes

Anon (ed.), *Innocent Confessions*, Grant Hughes, c1947 (cover); repurposed for Benson Cabot, *Blue Smoke for My Lovely!*, Hamilton & Co, c1950 (adapted p/b)

John Spencer

Anon (ed.), *Crime Confessions*, John Spencer, 6/1948 (cover)

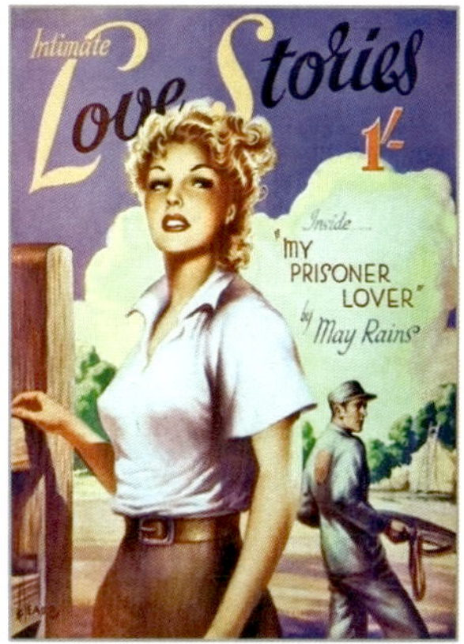

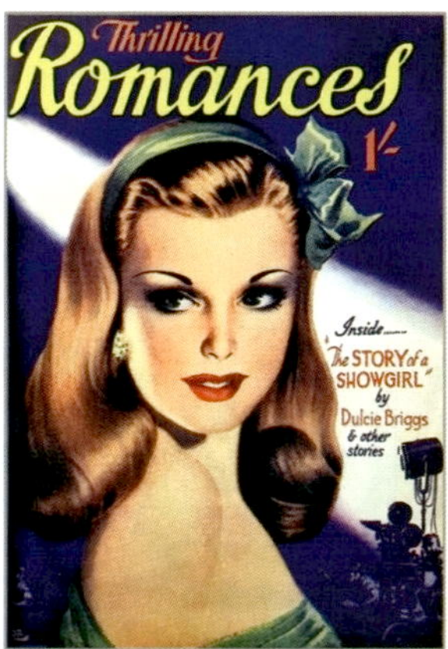

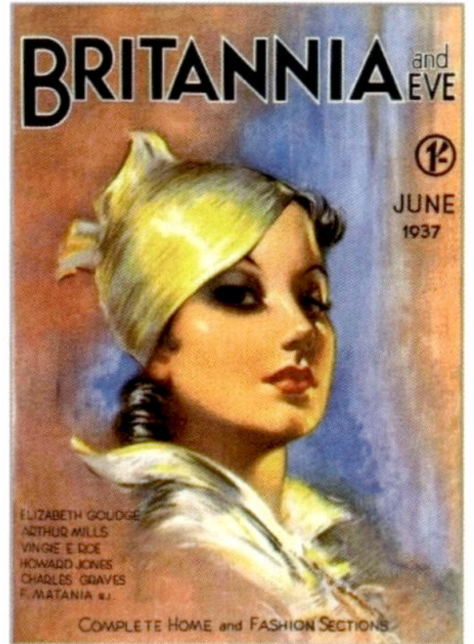

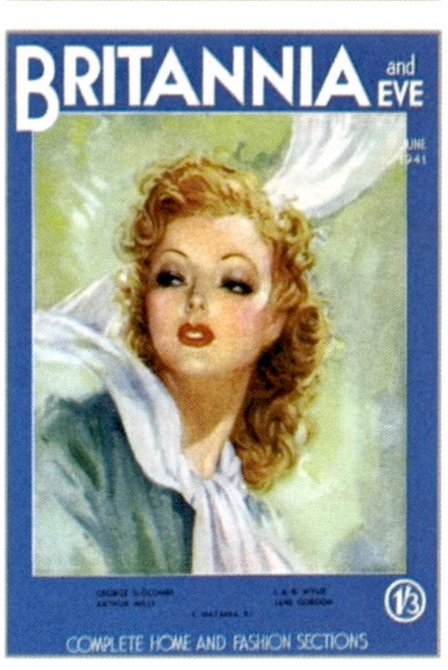

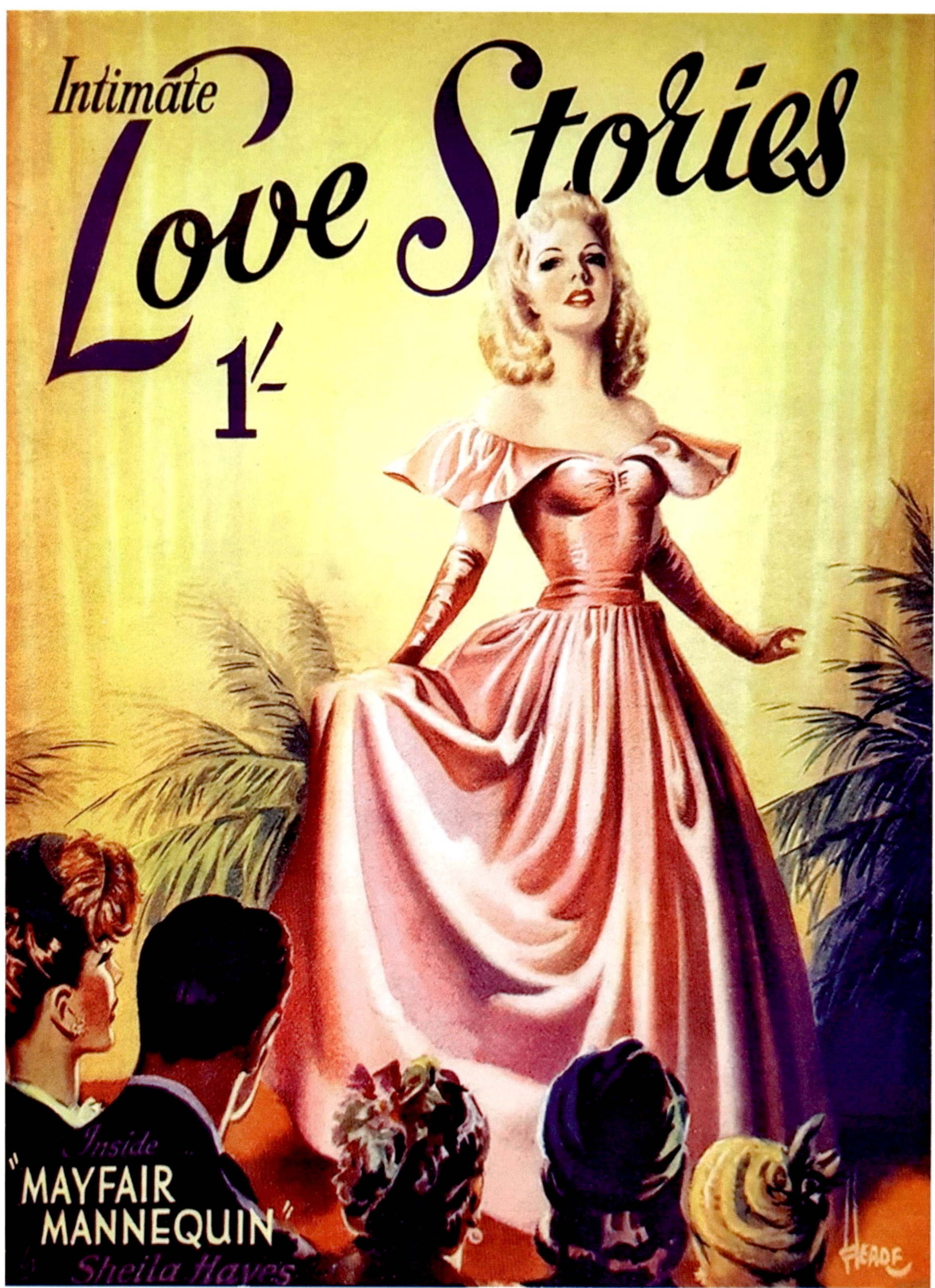

Heade's cover for a July 1948 edition of *Intimate Love Stories* (Bear Hudson)

Martin & Reid

Anon (ed.), *Faithful Confessions*, no. 1, Martin & Reid, 12/1947 (cover)

Rayburn Productions

Anon (ed.), *Personal Confessions*, no. 1, Rayburn Productions, c1947 (cover)

Western Press

Anon (ed.), *Revealing Confessions*, Western Press, 3/1948 (cover)
Anon (ed.), *Revealing Confessions*, Western Press, 4/1948 (cover)

COMMERCIAL PRODUCTS AND ADVERTISING

<u>Jigsaws and Games</u>

Good-Win

Costumes Through the Ages, no. 1: 'Elizabeth 1558-1603', Good-Win Golden Casket, c1944 (jigsaw
    illus)
Costumes Through the Ages, no. 2: Charles II '1649-1685', Good-Win Golden Casket, c1944 (jigsaw
    illus)
Costumes Through the Ages, no. 3: 'George III 1760-1820', Good-Win Golden Casket, c1944 (jigsaw
    illus)
Costumes Through the Ages, no. 4: 'Victoria 1837-1901', Good-Win Golden Casket, c1944 (jigsaw
    illus)

Philmar

Dress Dolly: 12 Pretty Dresses with Hats, Philmar, c1940s (cover illus, unsigned)
Dress Dolly: 12 Pretty National Dresses with Hats, Philmar, c1940s (cover illus)
The Steeplechase, Philmar, c1947 (jigsaw illus, unsigned but credited); reissued as *The Steeplechase*,
    Philmar Focus, c1950s (jigsaw illus, unsigned)
A.B.C. Playcards, Philmar, early 1950s (box lid illus, unsigned)
Flip the Cones, Philmar, early 1950s (box lid illus, unsigned)
Two Grand Jig Saw Puzzles: 'Express Train' by Arthur Neal and 'The Fun 'o the Fair' by C A Mold
    RI, Philmar, c1950 (box lid illus, unsigned)
Two Grand Jig Saw Puzzles: 'Mail Coach' by R Mills and 'Cinderella' by R C W Heade, Philmar,
    c1950 (box lid illus, unsigned; and jigsaw illus *)
Two Grand Jig Saw Puzzles: 'The Household Cavalry' by R Mills and 'The Regatta' by C A Mold,
    Philmar, c1950 (box lid illus, unsigned)
Two Grand Jig Saw Puzzles, 4th Edition: 'The *L.M.S. City of Hereford*' by L G Goodwin and 'Snow
    White and the Seven Dwarfs' by R C W Heade, Philmar, c1953 (box lid illus, unsigned; and jigsaw
    illus, unsigned but credited, reusing colour illus from *The Fairy Princesses*, Amex, c1952)
Two Fascinating Jig Saw Puzzles: 'Trooping the Colour' by A E Vincent and 'The Lord Mayor's
    Coach' by Reginald Mills, Philmar, c1954 (box lid illus, unsigned)
Two Delightful Jig Saw Puzzles: 'July, 1588' by William McDowell and 'Surrounded' by Edwin
    Phillips, Philmar, c1954 (box lid illus, unsigned)
Two Lovely Jigsaw Puzzles: 'Clear the Way' by R Mills and 'Welsh Guards on Parade' by B Long,
    Philmar, c1955 (box lid illus, unsigned)
Two Grand Jigssaw Puzzles: 'Full Speed Ahead' by T E North and 'The Musical Ride' by S Lumley,
    Philmar, c1955 (box lid illus, unsigned)
Father Christmas jigsaw puzzle, Philmar (unconfirmed), c1954 (jigsaw illus, unsigned)
Christmas Party jigsaw puzzle, Philmar (unconfirmed), c1954 (jigsaw illus, unsigned *)

<u>Calendars</u>

Keyhole Calendar for 1952, unknown manufacturer, 1951 (cover plus 4 illus) (possibly unproduced)
Calendar header card, unknown manufacturer, 1951 (illus) (possibly unproduced)

<u>Posters</u>

Babes in the Wood, Taylors of Wombwell, Printers, c1945 (pantomime poster illus, portrait orientation,
    two versions, various sizes)

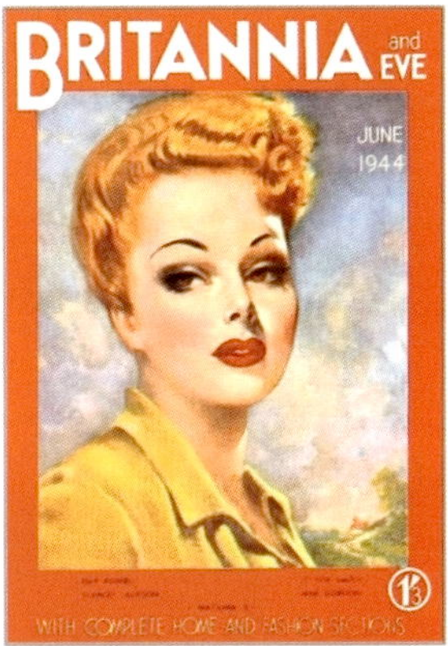

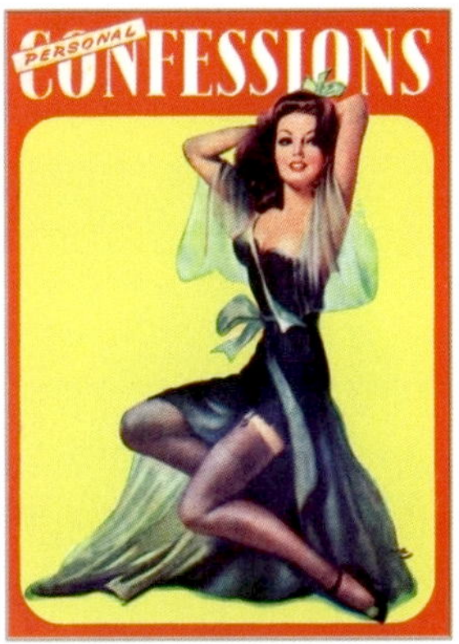

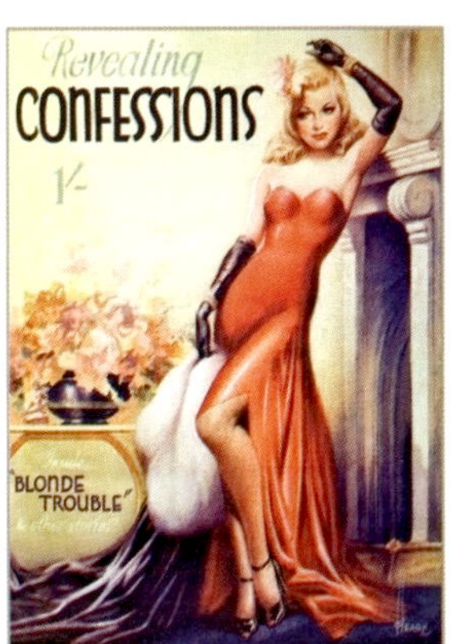

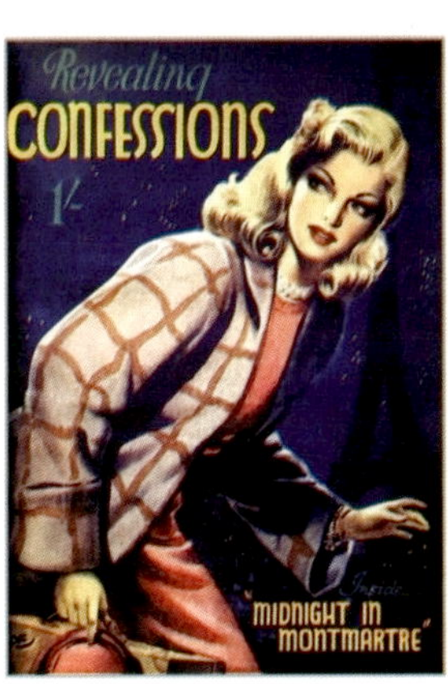

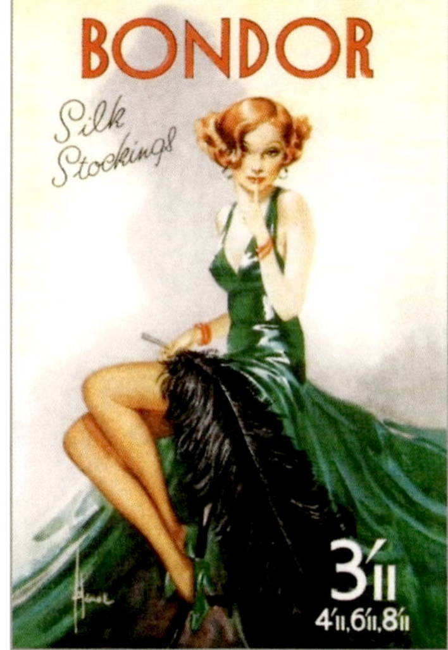

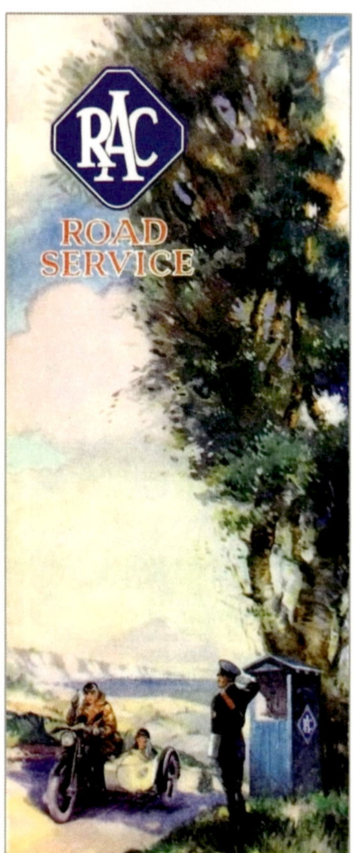

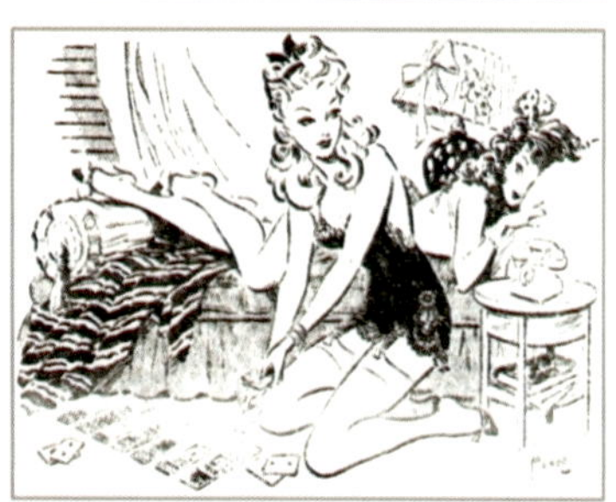

Babes in the Wood, Taylors of Wombwell, Printers, c1945 (pantomime poster illus, landscape orientation, various sizes, unsigned, probably by Heade)

<u>Product Advertising</u>

Bondor Silk Stockings, Bondor, c1939 (advertising showcard)
Cigarette advertisements, unknown brand, c1930s (illus) (possibly unpublished)
RAC Road Service, RAC, c1945 (brochure cover)
Ruston Engines, product catalogue cover and illus, c1940s (illus)
James Walker, advertisements, c1952 to c1954 (b&w and duotone illus, unsigned)
James Walker Rings, product catalogue, c1952 (cover)
Veet, advertisement, c1950s (illus) (possibly unpublished)

COMIC STRIPS ETC

Collins / The Children's Press

Anon (ed.), *Collins Children's Annual*, Collins, 1952 (three-page comic strip, 'Robin Hood: The Outlaw of Sherwood Forest', b&w with red highlight colour probably added by publisher, unsigned but credited); reprinted, without highlight colour, in Anon (ed.), *The Bumper Book for Children,* Collins, 1954; reprinted again, with red and orange highlight colours probably added by publisher, in Anon (ed.), *The Crackerjack Book for Children,* The Children's Press, c1955

Amalgamated

Leonard Matthews (uncredited), 'The Saga of Eric the Red' / 'Eric the Red', *Knockout* (comic), Amalgamated, weekly editions of 12/3/1949 to 30/4/1949 inclusive (no. 524 to no. 531 inclusive) (two-page b&w comic strip instalments (8), unsigned but credited) (title changed part-way through); reprinted, with amended dialogue and artwork, in Anon (ed.) *Robin Hood Annual 1958* (book), Amalgamated, 1957
Leonard Matthews (uncredited), 'Sexton Blake versus Plague of Crime' / 'Sexton Blake and Tinker versus the Astounding John Plague', *Knockout* (comic), Amalgamated, weekly editions of 16/4/1949 to 7/5/1949 inclusive (no. 529 to no. 536 inclusive) (two-page b&w comic strip instalments (8), unsigned) (title changed after first instalment); reprinted in Anon (ed.) *Knockout Fun Book 1956* (book), Amalgamated, 1955, with the surname 'Plague' changed to 'League' throughout.
Anon (ed.), 'The Captain from Castile', *Knockout* (comic), Amalgamated, weekly editions of 9/7/1949 July to 23/7/1949 inclusive (no. 541 to no. 543 inclusive) (two-page b&w comic strip instalments (3), unsigned, possibly by Heade)
Anon (ed.), 'Robin Hood', *Sun* (comic), Amalgamated, weekly editions of 18/9/1954 to 6/11/1954 inclusive (no. 293 to no. 300 inclusive) (two-page b&w comic strip instalments (8), unsigned); reprinted as 'Robin Hood and the Crusader's Castle' in Anon (ed.) *Robin Hood Annual 1958* (book), Amalgamated, 1957, with added highlight colour and amended dialogue and artwork; latter version reprinted again, without colour and with dialogue translated into Finnish, in Anon (ed.) *Nastasarjat* No.3 (comic book), Valiolehdet Oy, 1964
Anon (ed.), 'When Knights Were Bold', *Playhour* no. 10 (comic), Amalgamated, 13/12/1954 (two-page b&w comic strip instalment (1), unsigned)
Anon (ed.), 'The Bold Buccaneer', *Comet* (comic), Amalgamated, 3/5/1958 (no. 511) (adapted back cover illus); repurposed from Anon (ed.), *Captain Kidd – Buccaneer,* Thriller Comics Library, no. 96, Amalgamated, 8/1955 (cover, unsigned)

Associated Press

Anon (ed.) 'Mary Read – Soldier and Pirate', *Answers* (magazine), Associated Press, weekly editions of 15/3/1952 to 31/5/1952 inclusive (one-page b&w comic strip instalments (12), unsigned but credited)

Sunday Pictorial Newspapers

'Our Dumb Blonde', *Sunday Pictorial* (newspaper), Sunday Pictorial Newspapers, weekly editions of 2/4/1944, 9/4/1944, 16/4/1944, 23/4/1944, 7/5/1944, 21/5/1944 and 25/6/1944 (b&w single-panel cartoons)

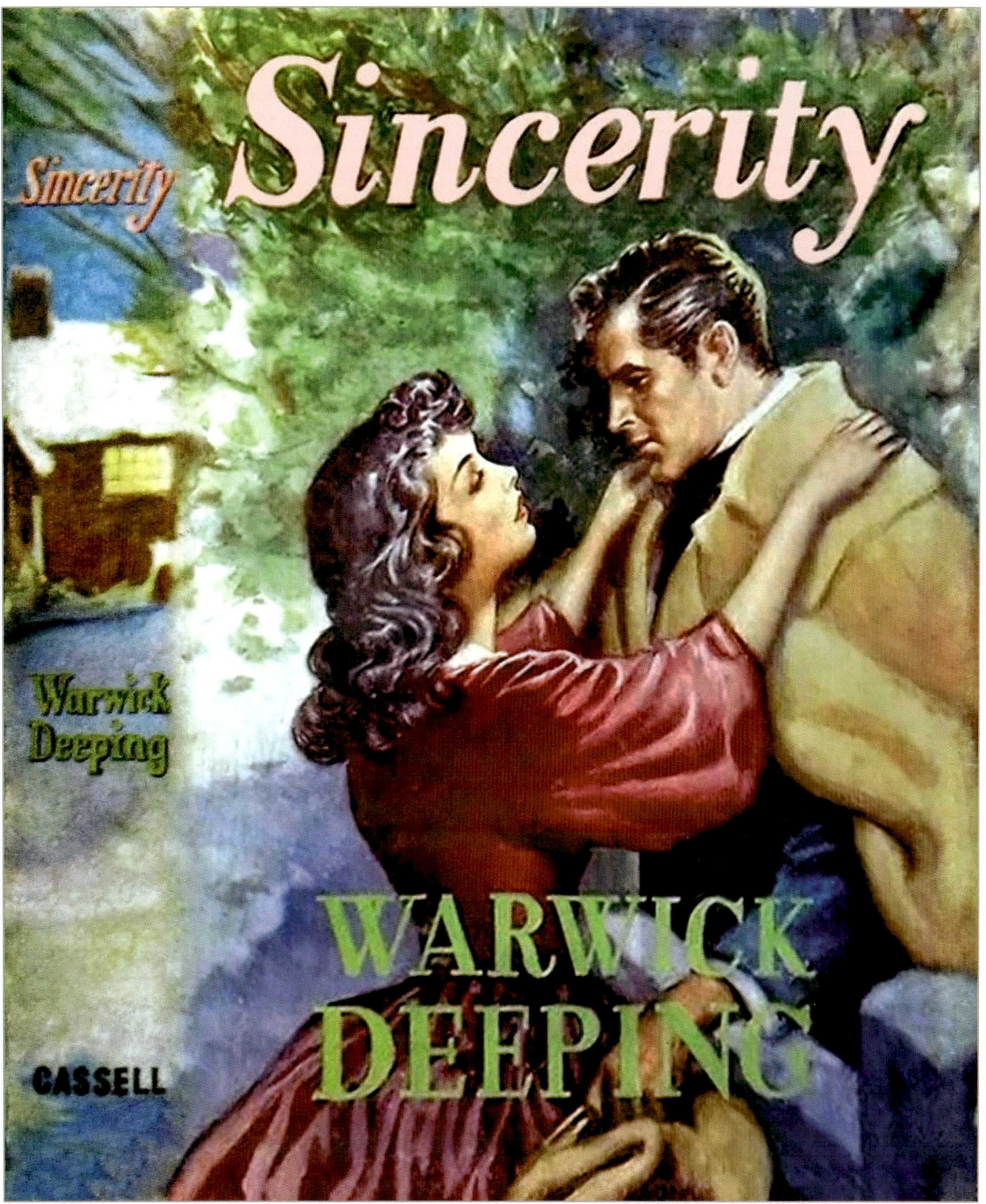

Sincerity by Warwick Deeping (Cassell, 1956)

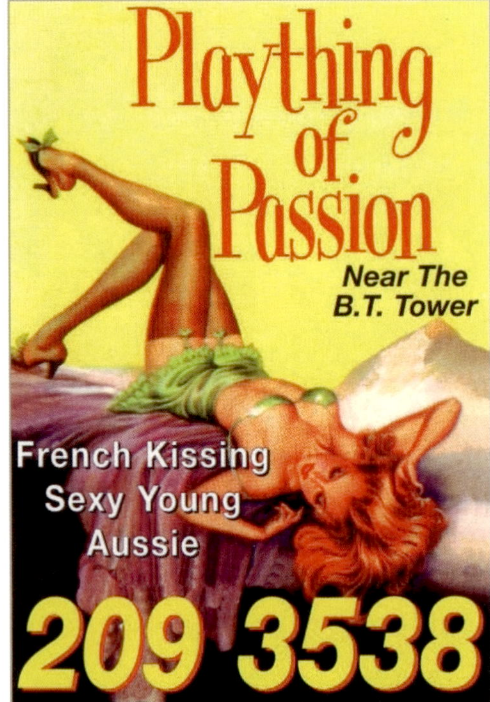

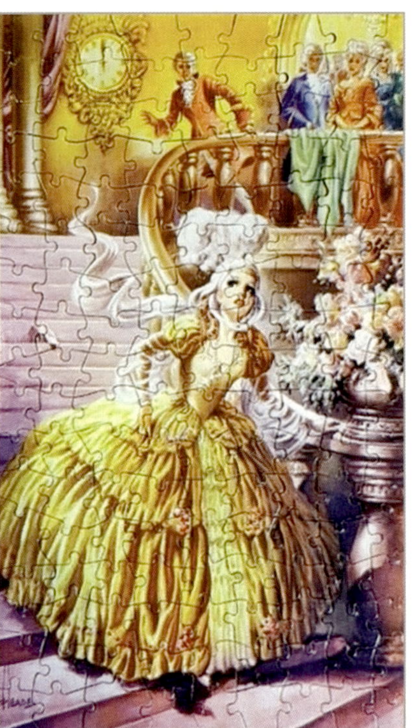

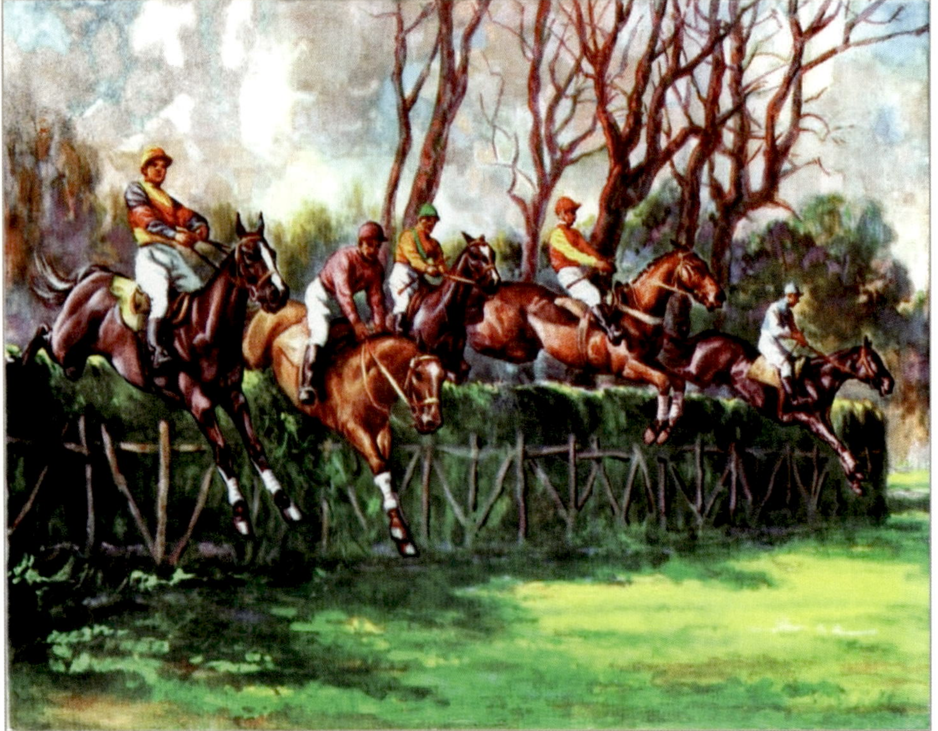

Top left: in the years since his death, Heade's work has sometimes been reused by enterprising designers for various unintended purposes. Some of his book cover and advertising pieces have appeared in postcard form; one of his *Babes in the Wood* pantomime posters has adorned a Christmas card; and, in the unusual example pictured here, his cover for *Plaything of Passion* by Jeanette Revére (Archer, August 1950) was adapted by a London-based sex worker for her phone-box business card. Top right: the completed 'Cinderella' puzzle included in one of Philmar's *Two Grand Jig Saw Puzzles* sets, c1950. Bottom: Heade's full artwork for Philmar's *The Steeplechase* jigsaw puzzle, previously believed to be a 1930s item – and captioned as such in *The Art of Reginald Heade – Special Edition* – but now thought to date from c1947.

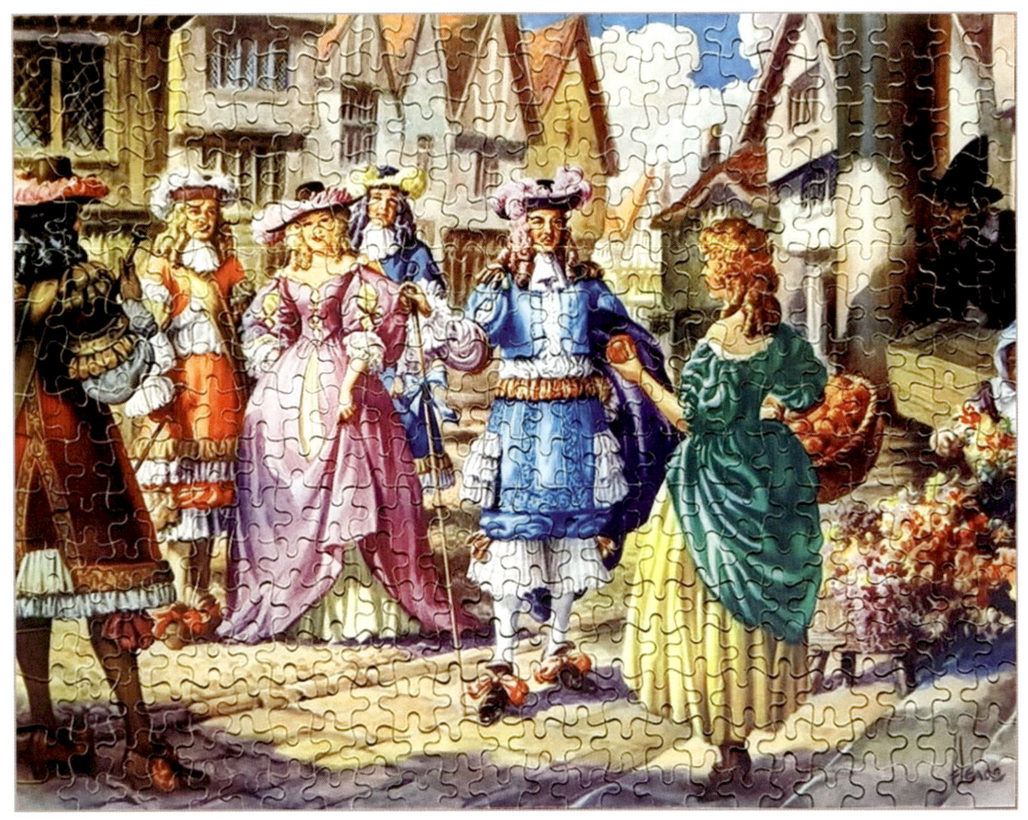

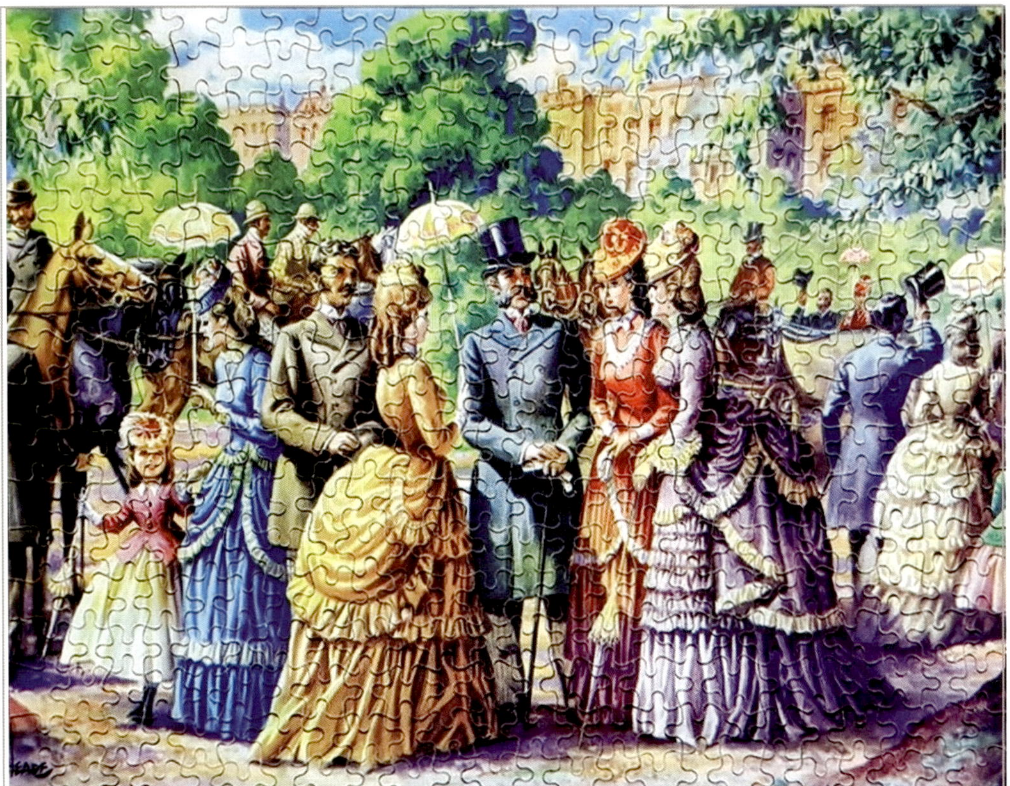

The completed Good-Win *Costumes Through the Ages* jigsaws entitled 'Charles II 1649-1685' (top) and 'Victoria 1837-1901' (bottom).

ALSO AVAILABLE
FROM TELOS PUBLISHING

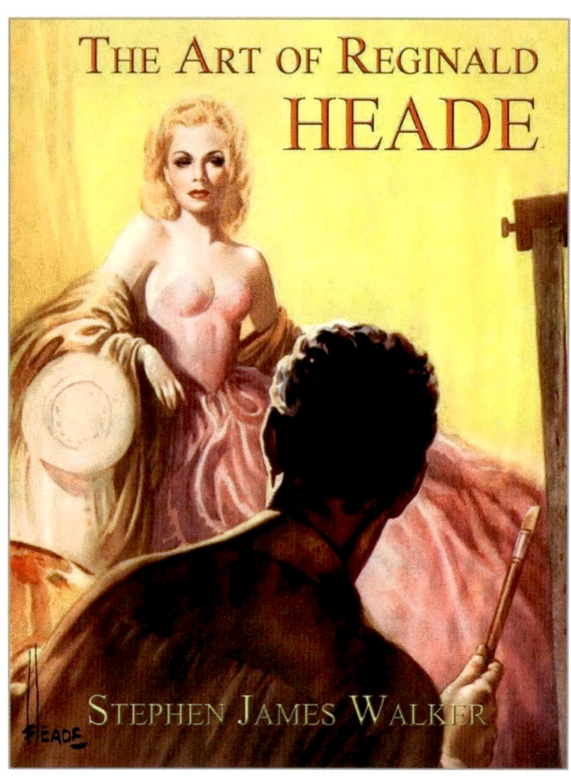

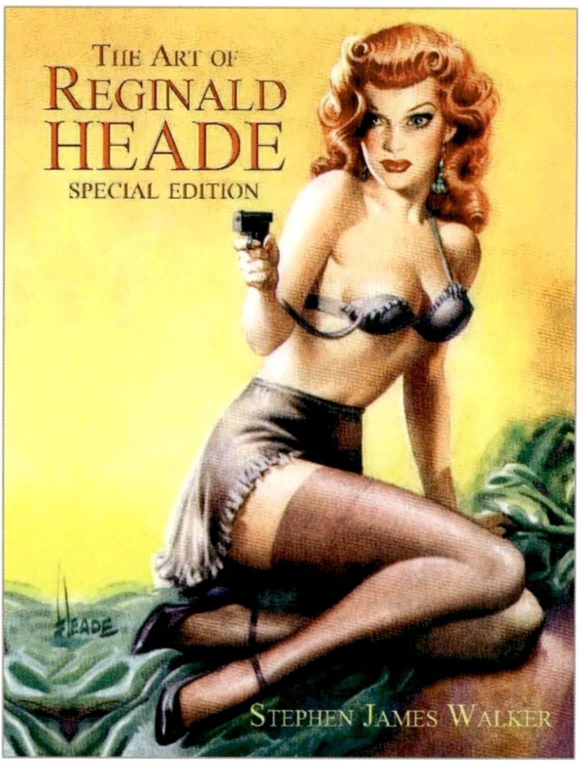

THE ART OF REGINALD HEADE

168pp. Large format 22cm x 28cm hardback.
Fully illustrated in full colour throughout.
ISBN 978-1-84583-115-8
Published 31 December 2016

The first volume of author Stephen James Walker's
acclaimed presentation of the work of Reginald Heade.

THE ART OF REGINALD HEADE – SPECIAL EDITION

318pp. Large format 22cm x 28cm hardback.
Fully illustrated in full colour throughout.
ISBN 978-1-84583-116-5
Published 24 August 2018

The extensively expanded and revised Special Edition of the
first volume, featuring even more of Heade's classic artwork.

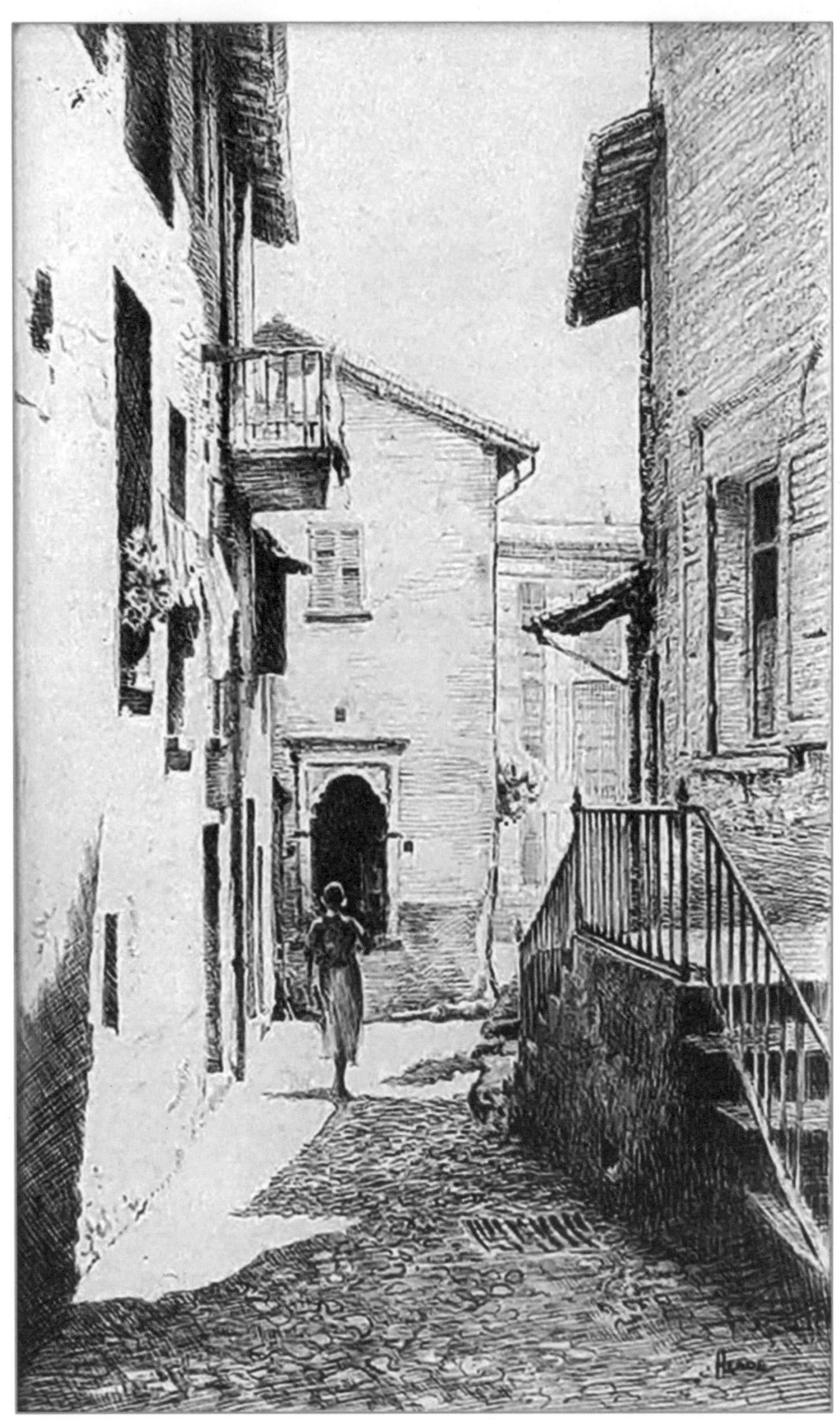

An undated drawing of a street in Castagnola, Switzerland. This piece was framed for exhibition, possibly in one of the Royal Academy's annual summer shows.